Blood and Sacrifice

What the Experts Are Saying About *Blood and Sacrifice*

"Blood and Sacrifice, the history of the 16th Infantry Regiment, is a soldier's perspective of peace and war from Boston Harbor in 1861 to Saudi Arabia in 1991. The victories and sacrifices of the soldiers, NCOs, and officers of this proud regiment give us the bayonet edge of our army from the American Civil War to today.

"The unique and enduring relationship of America's army with the American people comes alive as you read this well-researched and documented history. This account of the selfless and courageous journey of the soldiers of the 16th Infantry clearly will be an important book for members of the regiment but perhaps more significant will be its role in expanding the knowledge base regarding the contributions of young American soldiers."

General Gordon R. Sullivan, U. S. Army (Retired)
President of the Society of the First Infantry Division
Former United States Army Chief of Staff, June 1991-June 1995
Author, *Hope Is Not a Method: What Business Leaders Can Learn from America's Army* (with Michael V. Harper)

"Many of us believe that the United States Army would be a still better army than it is if it made better use of its regimental histories and traditions. This book makes a major contribution in that direction. It is a finely detailed account of a famous infantry regiment, incorporating also much of the history of the division of which the 16th Infantry has been a part since the First World War, the Big Red One."

Russell F. Weigley
Author, *A Great Civil War: A Military and Political History, 1861-1865; The Age of Battles: The Quest for Decisive Warfare from Breitenfeld to Waterloo; The American Way of War: A History of United States Military Strategy and Policy*

"Blood and Sacrifice transcends the history of the 16th Infantry to reveal the broader tale of the American army since the Civil War. Rich in character portraits and fine brush strokes of detail, the book is authoritative, comprehensive, and compelling. Steven Clay's narrative is reminiscent of the best of the British regimental histories, and that is very good indeed."

Rick Atkinson
Pulitzer Prize winning *Washington Post* correspondent, author of *Crusade: The Untold Story of the Persian Gulf War*

"This detailed, descriptive history of the 16th Infantry is a fitting tribute to one of the army's greatest regiments."

Edward M. Coffman
Author, *The War to End All Wars: The American Military Experience in World War I; The Old Army: A Portrait of the American Army in Peacetime, 1784-1898*

"Colonel Steven Clay's collective biography of the U.S. 16th Infantry does complete justice to all the soldiers who have made the regiment an elite unit in the U.S. Army since the Civil War. This book shows the importance of tradition in molding a regiment that can face Omaha Beach and the rubber plantations of Vietnam and their stubborn defenders. The 16th Infantry's story is the history of the U.S. Army."

Allan R. Millett
Author, *A War to Be Won: Fighting the Second World War*
(with Williamson Murray); editor, *Military Effectiveness*
(3 vols., with Williamson Murray); author, *Military Innovation
in the Interwar Period*

"Steven Clay's stirring tribute to the 16th Infantry Regiment is well researched and clearly written. The battle scenes are moving. The regiment's proud heritage comes alive."

Martin Blumenson
Author, *Heroes Never Die: Warriors and Warfare in World War II,
Breakout and Pursuit* (U.S. Army official history), *The Battle of the
Generals: The Untold Story of the Falaise Pocket;* editor, *The Patton
Papers* (2 vols.)

"Lieutenant Colonel Clay deserves praise for producing the best unit history I have ever seen. *Blood and Sacrifice* is everything a unit history should be and more. The scope and depth of Clay's research are unprecedented. The author brought to life the experiences of soldiers and leaders in this great regiment. Clay captures the human dimension of close combat in compelling accounts of the most momentous battles in American military history. The accounts of the 16th Infantry Regiment in battle are balanced with an examination of the Regiment's service and training in peacetime. This book is more than a comprehensive history of one regiment; *Blood and Sacrifice* permits a deep understanding of the challenges, rewards, sacrifices, and social dynamics of service in the U.S. Army from the Civil War to the present. Clay should be commended for his efforts."

Lieutenant Colonel H. R. McMaster
Commander, 1st Squadron, 4th Cavalry
Author, *Dereliction of Duty: Lyndon Johnson, Robert McNamara,
The Joint Chiefs of Staff, and the Lies that Led to Vietnam*

Cantigny Military History Series

John F. Votaw, General Editor
Steven Weingartner, Editor

The Cantigny Military History Series is sponsored by the Cantigny First Division Foundation. The series presents conferences and related publications that address issues consonant with the foundation's mission to preserve and promote the history of the 1st Infantry Division of the U.S. Army within the context of America's military history.

The conferences are hosted by the First Division Museum at Cantigny, the estate of the late Colonel Robert R. McCormick. Cantigny is located in Wheaton, Illinois, approximately thirty-five miles from Chicago.

Other Cantigny Military History Series Books

Cantigny at Seventy-Five
A Professional Discussion
May 28-29, 1993

No Mission Too Difficult
Old Buddies of the 1st Infantry Division
Tell All About World War II
By Blythe Foote Finke

Blue Spaders
The 26th Infantry Regiment, 1917-1967

A Weekend With the Great War
Proceedings of the Fourth Annual Great War
Interconference Seminar
September 16-18, 1995

The Greatest Thing We Have Ever Attempted
Historical Perspectives on the Normandy Campaign

In the Wake of the Storm:
Gulf War Commanders Discuss Desert Storm

Cantigny Military History Series

Blood and Sacrifice
The History of the 16th Infantry Regiment
From the Civil War Through the Gulf War

Steven E. Clay
Lieutenant Colonel, USA

Foreword by Colonel Gerald K. Griffin, USA (Ret.)
Honorary Colonel of the 16th Infantry Regiment

Cantigny First Division Foundation
16th Infantry Regiment Association
Chicago and Maryland
2001

Printed in the United States of America

First Edition

ISBN: 1-890093-11-4
Library of Congress Catalog Card Number: 00-133400

Cover illustration by Ann Marie Clay

Published by
The Cantigny First Division Foundation
1 South 151 Winfield Road
Wheaton, IL 60187
630/668-5185

Cantigny Military History Series
Series General Editor: John F. Votaw
Editor: Steven Weingartner
Design and Production: Wildenradt Design Associates

In accordance with official policy guiding the writing and publication of works by United States government employees, including members of the armed forces, the author affirms that the writing of this book was not undertaken as part of the author's official duties; that the invitation to write the book was extended to the author because of his expertise in the field covered by the book and not because of his official position as a serving officer in the United States Army; that the 16th Infantry Association has no direct or indirect interest that may be substantially affected by the performance or nonperformance of the author as a serving officer in the United States Army; that the information contained in the book does not draw substantially on ideas and/or data that constitute nonpublic information; that the subject of the book does not deal in significant part with any matter to which the author has been assigned over the past year in his capacity as a United States Army officer, or to any ongoing army policy or program.

Views and opinions of the author are his alone. The Robert R. McCormick Tribune Foundation, Cantigny Foundation, and Cantigny First Division Foundation, and their respective directors and officers, disclaim responsibility for statements, of fact or opinion, made by the author.

Contents

Maps

Chapter 7: The Sidewalks of New York

Chapter 8: "The Big One"

Foreword

This book is dedicated to all soldiers who ever served in the l6th Infantry Regiment and to their families. They are special men with special families. I know this because I was fortunate enough to have served with Company A and Headquarters & Headquarters Company of the 2nd Battalion in Vietnam in 1965-66. It was an experience I will never forget. Although some may question the professionalism of the Vietnam-era soldier, those with whom I served were every bit as professional as any I encountered in my time in the army. Those men were the best damn soldiers in the army, and I am still proud of every one of them.

As one of the founders of the 16th Infantry Regiment Association and its Honorary Colonel, I have gained far more from the regiment than I have given. My long association with so many great soldiers and their families has led me to appreciate just how great this regiment really is and how important it is to trumpet the heroic exploits of this outfit.

Much has been written about the regiment and its wartime exploits from World War I onward, but little attention has been given to its peacetime history or its wartime record from before 1917. It is to correct those omissions that the regimental association has endeavored to ensure the publication of this book. The battle legacy of the regiment was fashioned by its soldiers on many a bloody field—Gaines' Mill, Gettysburg, the Wilderness, San Juan Hill, Soissons, Meuse-Argonne, Sicily, Omaha Beach, Vietnam, and the Middle East. But its history was also shaped by those who served proudly during peacetime in places like the desolate plains of Kansas and Texas, Mexico, the Philippines, and Germany. These men kept the traditions and history of the regiment alive even during periods when it was not popular to be a soldier. Their contributions and sacrifices are often overlooked. Through this book, the 16th Infantry Regiment Association will ensure that those soldiers are remembered too.

We could not have succeeded in this publication if it had not been for all those who made contributions to our efforts to produce this history. One gentleman, however, requires special recognition. He is Jim Lipinski, our regimental archivist, who has devoted so much time and effort to getting us off on the right foot and assisting with the editing of this work. We also owe a special thanks to our author, researcher, and resident historian, Lieutenant Colonel Steven E. Clay, and John Votaw of the First Division Museum in Wheaton, Illinois, who supervised the final editing and preparation for publication. Without their efforts, there would be no book. It was truly a team effort.

I hope everyone enjoys reading this history of the 16th Infantry Regiment. This book stands as a tribute to all those 16th Infantrymen who have gone before and to those who will follow and serve their country in the best damn infantry regiment in the army. Semper Paratus!

Colonel (Ret.) Gerald K. Griffin
Honorary Colonel of the Regiment
Fort Washington, Maryland
July 2001

Preface

General Dwight D. Eisenhower called them his "praetorians." A German military attaché, after witnessing their charge at San Juan Hill during the Spanish American War, remarked that he "never saw troops fight better." A Union soldier, watching their actions from Little Round Top during the Battle of Gettysburg, was profoundly moved by the "determined skill and bravery" they exhibited in hard combat with the Confederates.

The men referred to were, in each instance, soldiers of the 16th Infantry Regiment. Since the First World War a component unit of the 1st Infantry Division—the famed "Big Red One"—the 16th Infantry is one of the United States Army's most praised and decorated regiments. In a period spanning over 140 years, from the Civil War to the present, it has participated in nearly all of America's major conflicts, and in many of the U.S. Army's most fiercely fought battles.

The story of the 16th Regiment is the subject of this impressive new volume by Steven Clay, the official historian of the 16th Infantry Regiment Association. Drawing on a wealth of archival sources, including official histories as well as personal accounts, and illustrated with more than two hundred photographs and maps, Clay fully chronicles the proud history of the regiment from its beginnings in the opening months of the Civil War to the present day. The regiment's combat actions and achievements are detailed in chapters on the Civil War; the Indian Wars; the Spanish-American War and the Philippine Insurrection; the Mexican Punitive Expedition; the First World War; the Second World War; the Vietnam War; and the Gulf War.

In particular, the author presents exhaustive treatments of three of the regiment's most difficult battles: Soissons in the First World War; Omaha Beach in the Second World War; and Courtenay Plantation in the Vietnam War.

The 16th's peacetime postings are also described, in sections dealing with the post-Civil War Reconstruction; service during the early years of the twentieth century in the continental United States, and in the Philippines and Alaska; the interwar years between world wars; and duty in Germany after World War II.

Blood and Sacrifice, which is part in the Cantigny Military History Series, represents a joint publishing effort uniting the Cantigny First Division Foundation with the 16th Infantry Regiment Association. Our thanks go out to all those involved with the association, with a special word of appreciation to Colonel Gerald K. Griffin, USA (Ret.), the honorary colonel of the regiment. Colonel Griffin's supportive role and many contributions to the project ensured that the partnership between Cantigny and the association would be a successful one.

Veterans of the 16th Infantry and historians alike are sure to find *Blood and Sacrifice* a compelling narrative of an outstanding regiment—one that has served with honor and distinction in the past, and which stands ready to continue in that tradition in future conflicts and assignments.

John F. Votaw
General Editor, Cantigny Military History Series
Executive Director, First Division Museum at Cantigny
June 2001

Acknowledgments

A book of this sort is not written in a vacuum. Numerous people have assisted with this one in so many ways, some knowingly, others unknowingly. Unfortunately, space does not permit acknowledging all of them, so I will recognize those who have contributed the most.

First, I would like to thank Colonel Gerald Griffin (Ret.) and the members of the 16th Infantry Regiment Association for their patience and assistance with the creation of this history. Jerry and the board of directors took a chance on "hiring" me for this task and I appreciate their trust in my ability and encouragement in getting this job done.

I also want to thank Colonel Scott Knoebel. This book had its genesis in 1994 when I was still working for Colonel Knoebel as his battalion S3 in the 1st Battalion, 16th Infantry, at Fort Riley. It was his interest in the regiment's history and encouragement that started me on the path to writing the history of this great outfit.

Thanks are in order also for my two superiors at the Combat Studies Institute, Colonel Jerry Morelock and Colonel Clay Edwards. Both of these men gave me the precious time I needed (often at critical moments in the academic year) to take time off from my executive officer duties and travel to the National Archives and other locations to do the research necessary for this story.

There are so many people who assisted me with information for this book that I am not sure I remember them all. But those who were most helpful include: John Votaw, executive director of the Cantigny First Division Museum in Wheaton, Illinois, and general editor of the Cantigny Military History Series; Andrew Woods of the Colonel Robert R. McCormick Research Center at the Cantigny First Division Museum; Terry Van Meter, Bill McHale, and Tom Metsala from the U.S. Cavalry/1st Infantry Division Museum at Fort Riley, Kansas; John Slonaker at the U.S. Army Military History Institute, Carlisle Barracks, Pennsylvania; Romana Danysh at the U.S. Army Center of Military History, Fort McNair, D.C.; and Pam Kontowicz at the Combined Arms Research Library, Fort Leavenworth, Kansas.

Many veterans of the 16th Infantry contributed their time for oral interviews to add flavor to this monograph, and others also contributed personal papers, audio tapes, photographs, and other personal items. Some of the most helpful in this regard were Eston White, Karl Wolf, Y. Y. Phillips, Sidney "Skip" Baker, Jack Teegarden, Phil Hall, John Libs, Ken Alderson, Henry Orton, Martin "Paddy" Roughn, Ronald Watts, Art Fuentes, John Copeland, Charlie Silk, Harley Reynolds, Willard Latham, Edmund Daley, Bob Humphries, Charlie Hangsterfer, Ed Coates, and Kenneth Cassels.

Two others who provided me a great deal of support in various ways in the process of putting this work together are Major Drew Sullins, public affairs officer for the Maryland National Guard, and Ival Lawhon, photographer for the *St. Joseph News-Press* (Missouri). Drew was instrumental in getting me over to Normandy for a visit to Omaha Beach in September 1999. As I have found on numerous occasions, having an opportunity to walk the actual terrain where events occurred makes a significant difference in how you relate the written story. My time on Omaha Beach that day was critical to my understanding of the fighting that occurred on June 6, 1944.

Ival provided me with a great deal of assistance with the book's photography. Many of the photos had to be reshot from books and albums and Ival was kind enough to open his home and provide me with his equipment and expertise in this effort.

A critical step in relating any story in writing is the editing process. In my case, I have had the luck of engaging the services of four gentlemen who are among the best in the trade. The first of these was Jim Lipinski, of Alexandria, Virginia, who also happened to spend the entire World War II period as a member of the 16th Infantry. Jim gave me a lot of information about his personal experiences, and also performed the initial edit of the book. Don Gilmore, from Fort Leavenworth, performed the detailed mechanical edit of the work and did a superb job. Don gave me a lot of good ideas on how to tell the story with just the right words. Steven Weingartner, editor of the Cantigny Military Series, did the buffing and polishing of the final product; he was ably assisted by John Lindley. I am grateful to the fine work that these four men performed.

A special word of thanks goes out to the incomparable Dr. Russell F. Weigley, who graciously took time from his busy schedule to read my manuscript, and whose comments and suggestions made the finished product a far better book than it might otherwise have been.

I would like to thank God and my family for their help in seeing this effort through. There were times when it seemed that I would never be done with this book, especially because I had several other irons in the fire at the same time I was writing it. The good Lord and my family helped me maintain my patience and good spirits when things got busy.

It is to my father, Lieutenant Colonel (Ret.) Raymond Clay, that I give all my thanks for my interest in history. When I was small, he was always relating to my siblings and me some historical fact or other as we traveled through the United States on summer vacation or between duty assignments. I was fascinated by his stories and was eager to learn more. That eagerness transformed into a happy habit of reading history books, earning a master's degree in history, and eventually teaching history at the Command and General Staff College at Fort Leavenworth. So far, it has been a lifetime of learning and enjoyment. Thanks, dad.

Finally, I want to express my gratitude to my wife, Elizabeth, and my two daughters, Ann and Virginia. I spent six years working on this book and the last two have been particularly time consuming. Though I spent countless hours away from home on research trips, or sitting in front of the computer when I was at home, the three of them have been patient through it all. Ann even did a great deal of the artwork and illustrations for the book. Now that it is done, I will try to make up for it by spending a little more time being a husband and father.

Steven E. Clay
Leavenworth, Kansas
June 2001

Introduction

"To the Regiment!" a toast that has been used in countless messes in many armies, demonstrates the closeness of the men who identify with a regiment and its history. But what is a regiment? It is not the colors, or the coat of arms, nor the special accoutrements worn on the uniform that identify the wearer as a member of the organization, though these symbols are the regiment's most tangible continuity. It is the soldiers themselves who constitute the regiment, and it is their service and exploits that ultimately build the history and myths with which their successors identify themselves as members of the regiment. This monograph records the story of one such unit for the purpose of sharing its history with those people who enjoy and appreciate the tale of the United States Army, for the 16th Infantry played an important role in almost every war and expedition of the Army since the War of the Rebellion. It is especially intended to help members of the 16th Infantry—past, present, and future—to know and understand what their predecessors accomplished in the service of the United States.

Since 1798, several units have borne the designation "16th Infantry Regiment," the first of which was activated on July 16 of that year under the command of Lieutenant Colonel Rufus Graves. The regiment was one of forty authorized by Congress to be raised in response to the threat of war with France over press gangs and American sovereignty at sea. The war never materialized, however, and the unit was disbanded June 15, 1800. The second regiment to bear the name was activated on January 11, 1812, Lieutenant Colonel Cromwell Pearce, commanding. This time, the 16th Infantry was activated for service in the War of 1812 and participated in the assault on Fort George (May 27, 1813), the Battle of Stoney Creek (June 6, 1813), and the Battle of Williamsburg (November 11, 1813). Two years later, after the war was over and the American people's prevailing distrust of a standing army once again took hold, the 16th Infantry was consolidated with the 2nd Infantry on May 17, 1815, and disappeared from the rolls. The next 16th Infantry Regiment was authorized on February 11, 1847, and formed under the leadership of Lieutenant Colonel Tibbetts for service in the War with Mexico. Battles such as the one at Papgayos (August 27, 1847), and Chapultepec-Mexico City (September 12-14, 1847) distinguished this unit's reputation until it went the way of its predecessors on August 10, 1848. The fourth regiment to be so designated was constituted on May 3, 1861, and served in the western theaters during the Civil War, but it too vanished in the consolidation of infantry regiments that occurred in April 1869.

Though all of the organizations described above bore the appellation "Sixteenth Regiment, United States Infantry," their relationship to the grand outfit that now bears the designation is one of name only. Through its lineal accounting system, the Center of Military History (and CMH's predecessors) has determined that there is no connection between the previous regiments and today's 16th Infantry. The story that follows is that of the men who have served our great nation for over 140 continuous years in the current 16th United States Infantry Regiment.

Fort Independence, Missouri, birthplace of the 16th Infantry Regiment

Chapter One
The Civil War

The conduct of both officers and men in this severe contest was deserving of all praise, and was all I could wish.

Colonel Sidney Burbank, July 21, 1863

Early on the sultry morning of August 1, 1861, a small group of officers and sergeants stepped off a ferry boat onto the docks of Castle Island, a small, sandy spit of land situated within cannon shot of the city of Boston, Massachusetts. Looming before them was Fort Independence, an imposing, gray edifice that had been, and still was, an integral part of the coast defenses of Boston Harbor. Only the day before the post had been the home of the 13th Massachusetts Volunteer Infantry, but that unit had departed to bolster the defenses of Washington, D.C. After the defeat at the First Battle of Bull Run, the War Department had called frantically for reinforcements to protect the city from Confederate invasion, and the 13th had responded to the call, leaving Fort Independence largely vacant. With the departure of the Massachusetts men, the post now became home to another unit, the 11th U.S. Infantry, which was the first of the new three-battalion regiments authorized by the president to reinforce the Regular Army.

The contingent of officers and NCOs arriving at Fort Independence that August morning was led by Lieutenant Colonel Edmund L. Schriver, a New York businessman who was an 1829 graduate of West Point. Schriver had spent seventeen years in the 2nd Artillery, rising to the rank of captain, before resigning in 1846 to pursue a civilian career. Offered the lieutenant colonelcy of the 11th Infantry in May 1861, Schriver accepted and was one of the first officers to arrive in Boston to begin forming the new regiment.[1] Now, as second-in-command of the 11th Infantry, he led his subordinates into the fort to begin the difficult process of building a regiment of U.S. Regulars. Little did these men know that they would be the founding members of a regiment that has become one of the most decorated, blooded, and storied in the United States Army. Today, the organization is known as the 16th Infantry Regiment.

The current 16th Infantry traces its roots to the 1st Battalion, 11th Infantry, which was constituted in the United States Army by order of President Lincoln on May 3, 1861, and organized at Fort Independence during the month of August. For the most part, the Civil War history of the 11th U.S. Infantry revolves around the activities of the 1st Battalion. The 2nd and 3rd Battalions were organized piecemeal between 1862 and 1865, but only the 1st participated in the regiment's

Civil War actions as an organized unit. The 2nd Battalion spent the war activating its companies one at a time at Fort Independence, though five of those companies were able to get into the field to serve with the 1st Battalion before the war was over. Beyond that, the only other action 2nd Battalion elements saw was at the Boston draft riot of July 1863. Additionally, the 3rd Battalion, which did not begin organizing until August 1863, was designated the regimental depot battalion. As such, it was responsible for training replacements for the units involved in the fighting in Virginia (the same duties the 2nd Battalion performed until August 1863).[2] Only A Company was organized before the end of the war, and it served as the regiment's basic training company for new recruits.

The first colonel of the regiment was Colonel Montgomery C. Meigs, a West Point graduate and an engineer officer. His early career was spent building and improving coastal fortifications. In 1852, he was summoned to take charge of the construction of the Washington, D.C. aqueduct which, when completed, was the largest masonry arch in the world. In April 1861, along with Lieutenant Colonel Erasmus D. Keyes and Lieutenant David Porter, U.S. Navy, Meigs led a secret relief expedition to the beleaguered garrison of Fort Pickens, Florida. For his success in this undertaking, Meigs was promoted to colonel and was awarded command of the 11th Infantry on May 14, 1861. However, his tenure was short-lived. The following day he was appointed quartermaster general and promoted to brigadier general, in which capacity he performed superbly, directing the massive logistical efforts of the Union armies throughout the war.[3]

The command next fell to Keyes (also promoted to full colonel) on May 15. Though Keyes remained the official commander of the regiment until May 3, 1864, after July 1861 he was so in name only. He spent a total of nine days in command of the regiment at Fort Independence before being summoned to assist in the defense of Washington. Later that month he was assigned to command a brigade (which he led during First Manassas), having been promoted to brigadier general of volunteers retroactively to May 14. He was later directly appointed by President Abraham Lincoln to command the newly formed IV Corps in August 1862.[4] Therefore, the task of actually organizing the regiment's elements, and commanding them in the field, fell initially to Lieutenant Colonel Schriver, and later to other capable officers at the regimental command level.

On May 14, 1861, the officers for the 1st Battalion headquarters, staff, and companies were officially assigned to the regiment, but only a handful were immediately available for duty. Most of those appointed came from volunteer regiments, civilian life, or were recalled from retirement; only a few were West Point men. The battalion commander was Major Delancey Floyd-Jones, an 1846 graduate of West Point. Upon commissioning, Floyd-Jones was first assigned to the 7th Infantry, but was transferred shortly thereafter to the 4th Infantry. He served in the latter during the Mexican War, participating in the siege of Vera Cruz, the Battles of Cerro Gordo and Molino Del Rey, and the capture of Mexico City. After short tours in Mississippi and Michigan, he spent most of his career in the West serving in California and at numerous posts in Oregon. In May 1856, he participated in the Rogue River expedition and was involved in the engagement at the Mackanoslany Villages. He was at Fort Hoskins, Oregon, when he was notified of his promotion to major in May 1861 and summoned to Fort Independence, where he arrived about August 30 to assume command of the 1st Battalion.[5]

Upon his arrival, Floyd-Jones was the senior professional officer assigned to the regiment, and it fell primarily to him to tutor, train, and otherwise prepare the regiment's officers to assume the responsibility of leading soldiers in combat. A young lieutenant by the name of John H. Patterson, who later won fame in the Battle of the Wilderness, wrote of the training:

Professional work began at once, Colonel Schriver's first order directing recitations in tactics and the Army regulations. There was not an enlisted man present at this time. The officers were drilled in the school of the squad with and without arms. Captain [Henry L.] Chipman was our drill master. Major Floyd-Jones joined soon after we went down to the fort and partially relieved Colonel Schriver of what must have been the irksome task of hearing our every weekday recitations. I remember that the War Department issued to each officer the Ordnance Manual, Wayne's Sword Exercise, the Army Regulations, and Scott's Tactics. Scott was soon changed for Hardie [sic, Hardee], the latter for U.S. Infantry Tactics, a change of title only, Hardie having gone over to the Confederacy.[6]

In spite of Floyd-Jones's steady efforts, the effect of having few other professional officers to help him perform this training produced limited success. One officer later wrote of these novice leaders, noting that, with the exception of Schriver and Floyd-Jones, "all the line officers were civilian appointments, several of whom proved to be unworthy selections and were ultimately separated from the service."[7] Even after almost two years of wartime duty, one soldier, writing about the regiment's lieutenants, would complain how they

invariably show that they were appointed green from civil life by those who have authority. They don't understand the tactics so well as 1/4 of the privates! although highly educated otherwise. The idea of many that none but graduates from West Point get commissions is a mistake. Few are promoted from the ranks as they should be. No, I will rise on my own merits if at all. I can say, and not boast, that I know more about the drill than half the lieutenants.[8]

To make up the shortfall in experienced officers, the regiment was fortunate to receive some exceptionally fine non-commissioned officers from the recruiting depot at Governors Island, New York. Sergeants Charles Bentzoni, Oscar Hagan, James Kennington, and Patrick Fitzmorris arrived in August to assume duties as the company first sergeants and rapidly began to whip the new recruits into shape. They were merciless in their labors to impose so-called Old Army ideals of discipline, drill, and dress on the 11th Infantry. They set the standard for recruits to live up to, and their efforts helped ensure that the regiment would weather the bloody battles of the next four years. All of these men, save Fitzmorris, were later commissioned in the regiment due to their meritorious service. The practice of commissioning NCOs who proved themselves worthy leaders became somewhat of a tradition in the 11th Infantry during the war, and no less than nineteen were so appointed.[9]

One of the regiment's lieutenants appointed from a volunteer unit was the celebrated Francis E. Brownell. He was originally a private in the 11th New York Volunteer Infantry, aptly nicknamed the "Fire Zouaves" because the regiment had been recruited from New York City fire companies, and also because they had put out a fire that threatened to burn down the famous (or was it the infamous?) Willard's Hotel in Washington, D.C. The commander of the 11th was the colorful Colonel Elmer Ephraim Ellsworth. After leading his regiment into Alexandria, Virginia (a town that had enthusiastically supported secession), on May 24, 1861, Ellsworth spotted a Confederate flag flying over the well-known Marshall Boarding House. The colonel assembled a few men as guards and rushed off to the hotel to remove the symbol of defiance. Among the guards was Private Brownell. Entering the hotel, Ellsworth went to the top of the building and tore down the flag, but upon coming down the stairs, he was shot and mortally wounded by the hotel owner, James T. Jackson. Reacting swiftly, Brownell leveled his rifle and, in turn, killed Jackson on the spot. As a reward, Brownell was appointed to second lieutenant in the Regular Army and assigned to the 11th Infantry.[10]

Their initial training completed, the regimental officers' next challenge was the formidable task of recruiting to bring their units to full strength. Some eight to twelve officers were at all times engaged in this duty, but even so recruitment proceeded at a frustratingly slow pace. Most Northerners were not interested in joining the Regular Army, known for its strict discipline, but preferred the company of their hometown friends and the more lax atmosphere of the local militia or state volunteer regiments. This continued to be a problem for the regulars throughout the war, although unlike the volunteer units, the regulars' replacement system did replenish, albeit slowly, their combat losses. That 11th Infantry recruiters apparently recruited heavily in the state of Indiana is evidenced by Governor Oliver P. Morton's claim that by January 1864 over four hundred Hoosiers had been enlisted in the regiment (though this is doubtful).[11] Also, a number of the 11th's officers were from Indiana, though the regiment appears to have had a healthy cross-section of officers from all over the Northern states. Governor Morton's claims notwithstanding, heavy recruiting of the regiment's enlisted men appears to have been conducted in Massachusetts, Illinois, Iowa, and New York as well.

Despite difficulties, recruiting efforts began to pay off and the regiment steadily grew. At the end of August, the enlisted strength had grown to ninety-six. By the end of September, the regiment had 179 men, and by mid-October, regimental enlisted strength stood at 210. This recruiting push, however, enabled the 11th Infantry to organize only Companies A, B, D, and G before the regiment's departure from Fort Independence for the field in October.[12]

Fort Independence was the regiment's home station and recruit training depot. It was a typical star-shaped fortress not dissimilar to the shape of the red V Corps badge on the current 16th Infantry unit insignia. Originally designed to provide coastal defense for Boston Harbor, the fort mounted fifty cannon, manned by elements of the 4th U.S. Artillery. It also served as a temporary prison for soldiers, primarily from state volunteer regiments, who had been sentenced for desertion and a wide variety of mostly minor offenses. The fortress was an impressive structure which, along with the prison guards, security, and strict military discipline, no doubt gave many a raw recruit a sense of foreboding upon arrival. But for some recruits, especially those fresh off the farm, service at Fort Independence could be a positive experience. Private Ira S. Pettit from Slash Road, Wilson, New York, recalled that

After examination, we were marched to the clothing room and fully equipped. I got another pair of pants, blue like the overcoat, a nice dress coat, and a pair of shoes. When we drill a while longer we shall be supplied with guns, cartridge boxes, and a pair of white gloves. We drill five hours each day (Saturdays and Sundays excepted) in the fatigue suit; after supper at seven o'clock, every man puts on his blue pants and dress coat, buttons are to be kept bright and the shoes well polished, and ready to "fall in" at the command for dress parade. Then you may believe we show up. Uncle Sam takes good care of his boys as any parents can of their children; we dress up every day in much better style than most people do when they go to church. There is perfect order here; every man is to keep himself clean and take good care of his clothes; if he makes his

appearance in the ranks without his buttons well brightened and shoes well polished, he gets severely chastised; no spitting even, is allowed upon the floor nor upon the stone walks within the fort; the squad rooms are to be swept several times per day…I have not slept in as good a place since I left home….This indeed is a delightful place.[13]

In addition to the requirement of recruiting for the regiment's line companies, Lieutenant Colonel Schriver was also assigned the task of assembling the regimental band. To satisfy this requirement, he dispatched an officer to New York City to enlist the needed musicians. In relatively short order, the recruiter assembled eight each of the finest buglers, fifers, and drummers to be found anywhere. Under the tutelage of Band Leader Jason N. Gardner and Drum Major W. E. Giddings, the band evolved into what apparently was a superb musical organization and one that would carry on a tradition of high standards until its separation from the regiment on the eve of World War II. Private Pettit wrote home on several occasions concerning the skill of the band, stating: "There is a fine brass band here and we have splendid music. There are eight snare drummers, some of whom I can beat: but there is one who leads [Drum Major Giddings], no man I ever heard play can approach." Upon departure of the band from Fort Independence, Pettit wrote: "The band started for the regiment last night, which is near Washington….Dress parade went off rather dull to night without the band music. I tell you they are accomplished, and they have splendid instruments." During the regiment's riot duty in New York City, Pettit recorded: "O we cut a swell in New York. Dress-parade and guard mount was worth seeing! The Band of the 11th Infantry is the most accomplished of any in the service."[14]

During this period the men were drilled; instructed in the use of the .58 caliber Springfield rifle, bayonet, and other accoutrements; and otherwise prepared for combat. One of the marksmanship training techniques used by the 11th Infantry at Fort Independence had the soldiers just coming off of guard duty firing their weapons at a "mark" or target to clear their pieces. If the soldier failed to hit the mark, he was required to reload and given another chance.[15]

The companies were required to undergo tactical training as well. Private Pettit wrote:

We had sport not long ago on a battallion [sic] drill: the two companies united, and each soldier had 12 rounds of blank cartridges in his box; we would load and fire by battallion, fire by company, fire by rank, by platoon and by file; also at will. We would charge upon the enemy and retreat, loading and firing on the run; practice skirmishing, and many other manavers.[sic] It was the sound of battle, but no dead were carried off the field.[16]

Such training, while not especially intensive, nevertheless

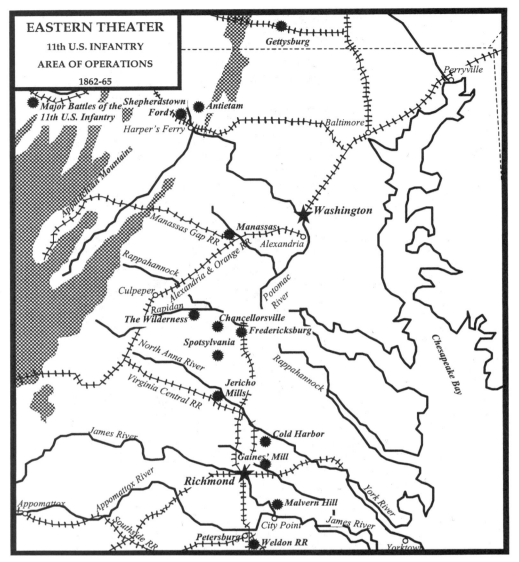

EASTERN THEATER
11th U.S. INFANTRY
AREA OF OPERATIONS
1862-65

Major Battles of the
11th U.S. Infantry

Gettysburg

Perryville

Shepherdstown
Ford

Antietam

Baltimore

Harper's Ferry

Appalachian Mountains

Manassas Gap RR

Washington

Manassas

Alexandria

Rappahannock

Culpeper

Alexandria & Orange RR

Potomac River

Rapidan

The Wilderness

Chancellorsville

Fredericksburg

Spotsylvania

North Anna River

Rappahannock

Chesapeake Bay

Virginia Central RR

Jericho Mills

Cold Harbor

James River

Gaines' Mill

Appomattox River

Richmond

York River

Appomattox

Southside RR

Malvern Hill

James River

City Point

Petersburg

Weldon RR

Yorktown

Map 1-1.

ensured that the soldiers of the 11th Infantry had, at the very least, practiced aimed shots with their rifles and practiced standard maneuvers before departing for the battlefields of Virginia.

By October, the situation in Virginia dictated that more troops be sent to reinforce the areas around Washington, D.C. Therefore, on October 14, 1861, the four companies of the 1st Battalion (referred to as the "11th Infantry Regiment" through the rest of this chapter, as it was in most official histories detailing combat actions of the 11th, even though it was really the 1st Battalion) only partially organized, yet deemed ready for field service, boarded trains and was transferred to Perryville, Maryland, to pull guard duties around installations north of Washington.

At Perryville, the 11th Infantry was joined by another so-called New Army regiment, the 14th U.S., which had also just arrived from its home post of Fort Trumbull, Connecticut.

Both regiments were encamped in tents along the banks of the Susquehanna River, opposite Havre-de-Grace near the ferry, and remained there until January. By then, the men had built the crude but comfortable "Shebang" shelters (temporary log huts) that they would come to know well and even grow fond of during the war.[17]

While building and improving their encampment, the regiment was tasked to guard the railroad crossings of the Susquehanna River at Havre de Grace. Concurrently, they pulled myriad other duties including guarding the ferry, providing boat guards for some of the river traffic, guarding cattle, and providing camp pickets. They also furnished guards for a huge group of mules and wagons that was assembling in the area. This wagon park was that of the Army of the Potomac, which was forming up for transport to Fort Monroe in the spring.[18]

At Perryville, recruit detachments continued to arrive from Fort Independence, and with them, Companies C and E were able to organize on February 15, 1862 in accordance with Regimental Order Number 5. All but two companies of the 11th Infantry were organized by this time (not including the other two battalions), and the regiment consisted of fifty-six officers and 373 enlisted men.[19] These numbers are somewhat deceiving, because they include all personnel assigned to the regiment. At Perryville, however, only 270 men were present for duty. This large disparity between "assigned" and "present for duty" would continue throughout the war, and was mainly caused by personnel being absent without leave (AWOL) or absent because of illness or detached duty assignments such as recruiting.

Though still drastically understrength in assigned enlisted personnel for a battalion of its size (which should number some one hundred men per company), the regiment itself was at full strength for assigned officers. Of the fifty-six officers assigned to the 11th, only twenty-two were in the field with the 1st Battalion. The remainder were still employed in recruiting duties throughout the Northeast and Midwest, at Fort Independence training the incoming recruits, or detached for service on the staffs of major commands. Despite the diminutive size of the regiment, by March it had received orders to join the Army of the Potomac.

The Peninsula Campaign
March 28–July 1, 1862

On March 7, the 11th Infantry left Perryville, joining Brigadier General George Sykes's Infantry Reserve Brigade, Army of the Potomac, at Arlington Heights, Virginia, on the 9th. Sykes's brigade now consisted of the Regular Army's 2nd, 3rd, 6th, 10th, 11th, 12th, and 17th Regiments, and the 5th New York Volunteers, known as the "Duryee Zouaves."[20]

Many of the Old Army regiments of Sykes's Brigade had already distinguished themselves by their coolness under fire at First Bull Run. There, they had prevented the Confederates from handing the Union Army an even severer defeat by their determined stand at Stone Bridge, which allowed the army to escape. Now, the green troops of the New Army regiments joined up with their unimpressed veteran brethren in what had now become known as "Sykes's regulars."[21]

Much excitement was engendered in the troops by their arrival in Washington. Here were thousands of soldiers, all preparing for the next big campaign, and it was soon in coming. Within a few days of arrival, Sykes's Infantry Reserve Brigade was sent on a reconnaissance toward Manassas after Major General Joseph Johnston's evacuation of the formidable Confederate line there. After a brief, uneventful, scouring of the terrain in that direction, Sykes was ordered to move his brigade to Alexandria where it arrived on April 15, and set up accommodations at the Theological Seminary. At Alexandria, Lieutenant Colonel Schriver was notified that he had been appointed chief of staff to Brigadier General Irvin McDowell. He soon departed. That evening, Major Floyd-Jones assumed command of the field elements of the 11th Infantry.[22]

On March 26, the 11th Infantry, along with the other regiments of Sykes's Brigade, broke camp and marched to the waterfront. As the citizens of Alexandria gathered to watch, the brigade of regulars marched smartly down the cobblestone streets of the city. It was an impromptu parade of sorts: colors snapping in the breeze, soldiers' brogans tramping in step, row upon row of burnished steel barrels against the shoulders of the men. All combined to provide the rebellious citizenry of Alexandria a picture of what a disciplined fighting force ought to at least look like; how they would fight remained to be determined. On to the wharves they marched, where dozens of steamers and transports prepared to move the Army of the Potomac to Fort Monroe to join Major General George B. McClellan's forces for the Peninsula Campaign.[23]

Boarding a transport with the 4th Infantry, the regiment sailed down the Potomac River to Chesapeake Bay and debarked at Old Point Comfort on March 28. The brigade camp was briefly established at Hampton until April 5 when it was moved to a location farther north. On April 12, the regulars moved again to Camp Winfield Scott near Yorktown and set up their cantonment next to General McClellan's headquarters. Repairing roads, guard duty, and preparation of trenchworks kept the 11th busy during the actions around Yorktown, but the regiment saw no significant action as the Confederates abandoned the city the day before the final assault was to take place.[24]

During May, the recruits of F and H Companies departed Fort Independence under the control of their NCOs and bivouacked at Camp Sturgis upon their arrival at Washington, D.C. They were too late to link up with the rest of the regiment before it departed for the peninsula, so the companies were temporarily assigned to the Military District of Washington, where they were to conduct security duties for the city's defenses. In a letter to the secretary of war, the commander of the district, Brigadier General Samuel D. Sturgis, wrote that he considered the units under his command "raw and undisciplined" and that all, except the 59th New York Volunteers, needed significant amounts of training before they could be used to mount a viable defense of Washington. His assessment probably included the two companies of the 11th Infantry which, apparently, had not been trained as rigorously as the other companies during the regiment's stay at Fort Independence.[25] It was just as well that those two companies were held at Washington for the time being. The regiment was about to receive its baptism of fire, and their presence may well have been more hindrance than help.

In mid-May 1862, Sykes's brigade was assigned to the newly activated V Corps under Major General Fitz John Porter. Ready or not, the 11th Infantry joined the corps in its movement towards Richmond and what would be its first engagement of the Civil War. On May 20, the Infantry Reserve Brigade was dissolved, and the regiment, along with the 2nd, 6th, 10th, and 17th U.S. Infantry Regiments, was organized into the 2nd Brigade, 2nd Division, V Corps. The 1st Brigade was composed of the 3rd, 4th, 12th and 14th U.S. regulars. These two brigades with the 3rd Brigade (5th and 10th New York Volunteers) became known as the "Regular Division" of the Army of the Potomac—the famous "Sykes's regulars."[26]

After the evacuation of Yorktown, the 11th Infantry moved with the V Corps northwest up the peninsula through Williamsburg, Cumberland, White House, and Tunstall's Station, finally arriving at New Bridge on the Chickahominy. There, near Gaines' Mill, the regulars established Camp Lovell, named after the 2nd Brigade commander, Major Charles S. Lovell, 10th Infantry. All in all, life at Camp Lovell was more like being at a summer camp than on active campaign. Though they were in the field, the men of the 11th Infantry slept under canvas and enjoyed the generally good weather. On May 27, however, the V Corps was ordered north in a driving rainstorm toward Hanover Court House to conduct a reconnaissance in force and burn bridges over the Pamunkey River to secure the right flank of the Union Army. Though a sharp fight developed near Hanover Court House, the regulars were not engaged in this action because Porter held them in reserve. On May 31, the Army of the Potomac engaged units of Major General James Longstreet's command at Fair Oaks, but again the regulars remained inactive, along with the rest of the V Corps, north of the Chickahominy.

The only other event of note came on June 13, when J. E. B. Stuart was making his famous ride around the Army of the Potomac. Up to that point, life at Camp Lovell had been relatively serene. When it appeared that Stuart might attack into the corps flank, Porter called the entire command to arms. About sundown, the entire V Corps was formed up and marched out to intercept the rebel cavalry, but after some futile casting about in the dark, Major Floyd-Jones countermarched the regiment and headed back to Camp Lovell empty-handed. Musing on the event, Lieutenant James H. Patterson wondered what the whole thing was all about and came to the humorous conclusion that it must have been "strategy, my boy."[27]

Mechanicsville
June 26, 1862

The minor sparring in which the Army of the Potomac and the Army of Northern Virginia had engaged thus far was about to erupt into a full-blown fight. In late June, General Robert E. Lee commenced his efforts to seize the initiative from the federal army that threatened Richmond. Late on June 26, in a severe rainstorm, the V Corps' right flank was attacked from the west by A. P. Hill's Division. The Confederate attack was poorly executed, however, and was driven back after reinforcements were moved to that flank by Major General Porter. At Mechanicsville, Sykes's men were, as usual, held in reserve for the purpose of plugging holes or conducting counterattacks. The 11th Infantry, although on the field and close to the fighting, was not engaged.[28] As darkness closed on the battlefield, the fighting stopped and Porter was directed to take up new positions farther south. The night's march took the regiment right back to the vicinity of old Camp Lovell near Gaines' Mill.

Gaines' Mill
June 27, 1862

Before dawn on June 27, the V Corps was ordered to pull back to a new line with its left flank along the Chickahominy River and Sykes's regulars on the right flank near the village of Cold Harbor. The 2nd Brigade was initially centered behind the rest of the 2nd Division as a reserve. About 10:00 a.m. that morning, however, the 11th and 3rd Regiments were detailed to protect and support Captain Augustus P. Martin's 3rd Battery, Massachusetts Light Artillery, on the line.[29] Martin's battery was located between Sykes's division and Brigadier General George W. Morell's 1st Division. Before them lay four to eight hundred yards of open ground backed by a thick wood that concealed the rebels' approach.

As the men of the 11th Infantry wheeled into line, the booming cannon and the rattle of muskets along other parts of the line told them that their first test was imminent. Throughout the ranks, anxiety ran high in anticipation of their baptism of fire. After almost a year of service for many of them, the waiting to see if they could stand the strain of battle was about to end. As perspiration dripped from their foreheads in the hot June sun, they reached with trembling fingers into cartridge boxes to load the Springfield rifles with which they would do their bloody work. Once loaded, they stood nervously but determinedly in two blue lines of battle. At the fore, the red, white, and blue national and regimental banners fluttered in the breeze, contrasting sharply with the rich green hues of the Virginia countryside. The soldiers of the New Army regiments had something to prove to the Old Army, and today they would demonstrate that they had the mettle to be as good as the best.

After a pause in the fighting, the Confederates resumed their attack about noon. The initial assault came from Longstreet and A. P. Hill's divisions against the corps' left flank, followed by the divisions of Major General D. H. Hill and Major General Thomas J. "Stonewall" Jackson against Sykes's division. The 11th Infantry, though partially protected by a slight rise in the ground, was subjected to a heavy cannonade for almost six hours. The Confederates charged again and again but were repeatedly repulsed. A total of twenty-six rebel regiments flayed against Sykes's division, but to no avail. About 5:30 p.m., however, a fierce assault by John Bell Hood's Texas Brigade broke the federal center near General Porter's headquarters and the enemy soon threatened to surround the regulars. At that time, Major Floyd-Jones moved the regiment farther forward to provide covering fire for Martin's Battery as the artillerymen pummeled Hood's forces. Later General Sykes wrote:

> [T]he 10th, 11th, and 17th U.S. Infantry (which, though always under fire, had been my principal reserve) were brought forward in the handsomest manner, winning the admiration of their brigade commander, Major Lovell, by their wonderful coolness and steadiness; but the tide was too strong for them. Few in numbers, they could not stem it.[30]

Martin's 3rd Massachusetts continued to fire, supported by the riflemen of the 11th Infantry, until ordered to finally withdraw before they were overrun. When the rebels were only 150 yards away, Martin fired thirty-six rounds of double-shot canister to slow their advance. That, coupled with the riflemen's fire, allowed the battery time to limber up and get away.[31]

Continuing to fire several volleys, the 11th, 10th, and 17th were soon in danger of being surrounded and captured as other Union regiments fled past them. The rebel fire was now directed at the cluster of regulars that dared to stand their ground in the face of this charge. Most of the 11th's casualties

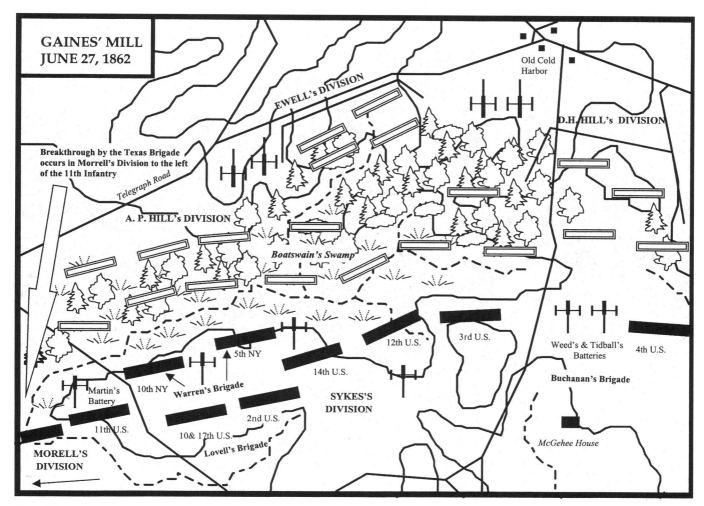

**GAINES' MILL
JUNE 27, 1862**

EWELL's DIVISION

Old Cold Harbor

D.H. HILL's DIVISION

Breakthrough by the Texas Brigade occurs in Morrell's Division to the left of the 11th Infantry

Telegraph Road

A. P. HILL's DIVISION

Boatswain's Swamp

5th NY

10th NY

Warren's Brigade

12th U.S.

3rd U.S.

Weed's & Tidball's Batteries

4th U.S.

Martin's Battery

14th U.S.

Buchanan's Brigade

SYKES'S DIVISION

11th U.S.

2nd U.S.

10 & 17th U.S.

Lovell's Brigade

McGehee House

MORELL'S DIVISION

Map 1-2.

during the Peninsula Campaign occurred in the next few minutes. Men began to fall all along the line, including Sergeant Fitzmorris, now the regimental color sergeant, who was killed as he steadied the command by boldly bearing the colors at the center of the line. Colonel Gouverneur K. Warren, commanding the 3rd Brigade of Sykes's division, credited the 11th and 2nd regulars with holding the Confederate onslaught:

> To our left was the 11th U.S. Infantry, also supporting batteries. Toward the evening the enemy succeeded in forcing back the division to our left, when the batteries we were supporting were withdrawn, we throwing in all the fire our diminished numbers would permit. We here witnessed the firm stand of the 11th U.S. Infantry on our left, and the charge of the 2nd U.S. Infantry on our right. The advance of the enemy on our front was thus effectually checked.[32]

The successful stand further endangered the regiment, however. Remaining cool in this desperate situation, Floyd-

Jones ordered the line to fall back in fighting order. In his report of the action, he later wrote, "Being thus left entirely alone with a handful of men, and in danger of being cut off, the regiment was in good order withdrawn to the second position occupied by our forces."[33] That second position was around the McGehee House, where the regiment, along with the rest of the regulars, fought a stubborn rear-guard action. Fighting desperately until sundown, the regulars held on as the rest of the V Corps escaped across the Grapevine Bridge.

Porter's V Corps streamed over the Grapevine Bridge all that night and moved south while covering the rear of the army. The 11th Infantry, covering the corps move, crossed the Chickahominy about 4:00 a.m. on the 28th, and continued to move south that day and the next. After crossing White Oak Swamp in the early morning of June 29, the regiment was deployed in skirmish lines as a rear guard and to protect the corps wagon train as they continued on to the next battle position. After the trains were safely away, the regulars again took up a line of march south on the 30th.

Turkey Bridge
June 30, 1862

The regiment reached the vicinity of Malvern Hill about 11:00 a.m. that morning. There, Floyd-Jones received orders to reinforce Warren's much-depleted 3rd Brigade. The 5th and 10th New York Regiments, which made up that brigade, had been badly used up at Gaines' Mill and now numbered only six hundred muskets, so the 11th was attached to bolster their line. Given the weakened condition of the 3rd Brigade, Sykes positioned the 11th to defend the River Road at Turkey Bridge where it was not expected to be seriously engaged in the next fight. There, the regiment took up new positions about noon, once again supporting Martin's battery of Napoleons. Each regiment pushed out skirmishers and pickets beyond a wood to their front. The rest of the men threw up light works constructed from fence rails and prepared to meet any attack coming their way. Meanwhile, on the hill, the V Corps also prepared for an onslaught as the remainder of the army continued to straggle into position.

On Malvern Hill, the 2nd Division held the federals' vital left flank with Warren's 3rd Brigade (11th Infantry attached) anchored on Turkey Run in the valley southwest of the hill. The 1st Brigade of regulars was on the right of the V Corps line and the regulars of the 2nd Brigade in the center. An additional thirty-six guns of the V Corps' batteries were positioned above on Malvern Hill, and could easily throw their firepower at any Confederates foolish enough to advance down the River Road. Of his positions on Malvern Hill Sykes later remarked, "Nothing could be more commanding than the line I held."[34]

The Confederate force that eventually did venture down the River Road was commanded by Brigadier General Theophilus H. Holmes. Holmes's division consisted of seven thousand men, mostly from North Carolina and Virginia, and six batteries of artillery. Riding with Holmes, General Robert E. Lee observed Union troops moving onto the hill; he believed

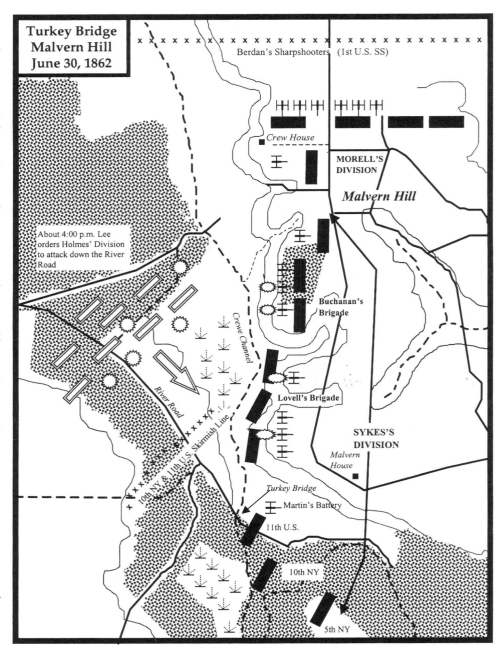

Map 1-3.

they were a demoralized, disorganized mob. Wanting to take advantage of their condition, he directed Holmes to flank the Union position by attacking southeast along the River Road. Holmes began his movements about 4:00 p.m. The 3rd Brigade pickets northwest of Turkey Bridge soon detected the Confederate units moving into position, and runners were sent to the main line to give the alert. All three regiments immediately stood to their works to receive the attack.

As Holmes moved his artillery forward to support the assault down the road, he was astonished to find, not the demoralized rabble of a defeated army, but the well-prepared 3rd Brigade to his front, supported by the 2nd Division and thirty-six cannon on the bluffs overlooking his assembly areas along the road. The federals began pouring fire on his units from their well-selected positions. Supported by four gunboats on the James River, the Union artillery destroyed or drove off Holmes's batteries in short order. The added small arms fire from the riflemen of the 3rd Brigade and the 11th Infantry prevented Holmes's troops from massing and the attack on Turkey Bridge fell apart. A cavalry charge drove the remainder of the rebel troops from the field by about 6:00 p.m.[35]

The 3rd Brigade's actions at Turkey Bridge bought time for the Union corps commanders to complete their defenses on Malvern Hill.

Malvern Hill
July 1, 1862
The following day, McClellan's Army of the Potomac was arrayed on the hill in the shape of a large horseshoe. After the previous day's fight, Morell's 1st Division assumed the positions on the army's left previously held by the 2nd Division. Warren's 3rd Brigade, still reinforced by the 11th Infantry and Martin's Battery, maintained the watch on the River Road in the valley between the hill and the James, while the 1st and 2nd Brigades were drawn up behind in a position from where they could support Warren or Morell.[36]

Just after noon, Warren advanced the 3rd Brigade through the wood to the north where the pickets had been the day before. There, the regiments threw up another line of barricades using rails, stones, logs and any other available material. The position faced a large cornfield which could be easily swept by Martin's Battery and small arms fire. About 1:00 p.m. the Confederates appeared to be forming for another attack down the road, but fire from Martin's Napoleons and the gunboats drove them off in short order.[37]

After a series of confused maneuvers, the Confederates finally assaulted the main Union positions about mid-afternoon on 1 July, but the massed effects of Union infantry small-arms and artillery fires thwarted Lee's rebels. Morell's brigades were able to defeat the first attacks, but had to be relieved by Sykes's troops after running out of ammunition.[38] Resuming their positions of the previous day, the regulars also handily repulsed the waves of attacking Confederates. After losing fifty-five hundred men on the slopes of Malvern Hill, Lee called off the assaults at 9:00 p.m. and the two armies parted, Lee to Richmond, and McClellan to Harrison's Landing. In spite of his comments to the contrary, McClellan's Peninsula Campaign was over, but not before the 11th Infantry had suffered seven soldiers killed and twenty-eight wounded during the fighting.[39]

Soon after Malvern Hill, the 11th Infantry moved to Harrison's Landing where F and H Companies finally joined the regiment, less company officers, on July 5. There, the two companies were formally organized by the assignment of officers. At Harrison's Landing, the regiment prepared defenses and guarded federal supply dumps and supply barges coming up the James River until mid-August, when the Army of the Potomac was directed to return to the defenses of Washington. The V Corps was detached, however, and ordered to reinforce the new Army of Virginia then organizing under the command of Major General John Pope. Departing Harrison's Landing the evening of August 14, the corps marched all night toward a crossing site over the Chickahominy River, and arrived there the next morning. The corps then went into positions along the river to protect the remainder of the army as it crossed over on a sixteen-hundred-foot pontoon bridge built by the 50th New York Engineers. The next day, Porter's command reached Williamsburg, where Porter received word that the bulk of Lee's army was heading for Washington. Time became of the essence.

Departing Williamsburg, the V Corps traveled to Newport News, where they boarded transports on the 19th, and steamed up the Potomac to disembark at Aquia Creek Landing, twenty miles southwest of Washington, D.C. The regiment then began the race west to Warrenton Junction, Virginia, where it would join the Army of Virginia.[40]

Second Manassas Campaign
August 27-31, 1862
The march to join the Army of Virginia was not a pleasant one. First, by some misfortune, the regiment's personal baggage was misdirected when they arrived at Aquia Creek Landing. Next, starting out at a breakneck pace, the V Corps marched across east-central Virginia in the blazing summer heat. The men's discomfort was increased by the choking clouds of dust raised by thousands of men moving on the clogged roads. After a brief stop near Fredericksburg, the corps turned north for Warrenton Junction, where it arrived on August 27.

At Warrenton Junction, the regiment was initially detailed to guard the supply trains of Pope's Army. To the northeast, Major General Joseph Hooker's Division was defending the federal line of communication at Bristoe Station and was attacked by elements of Jackson's wing that had just captured and looted the huge supply depot at Manassas Junction in the federal rear. Departing Warrenton Junction at 4:00 a.m. on August 28, the 11th Infantry was dispatched to Bristoe Station with Sykes's division to reinforce Hooker. Coming out of a wood near the station, the regiment was briefly surprised by a rebel force that opened fire, then melted away before the regulars could get on line to engage.[41]

On the 29th, the Army of Virginia was engaged in heavy fighting against Lee's army on the old Bull Run battlefield. As Pope's troops slugged it out with Jackson's wing, the regiment marched and countermarched all day but never engaged the enemy, even though the V Corps was summoned forward repeatedly by Pope for employment that afternoon. The column finally marched up the Manassas-Gainesville Road, passed

Bethlehem Church, and halted in place. As the fighting built to a crescendo to the north of the V Corps, the regiment at last moved to a position in a wood near the Nealon House where it might engage the enemy. Captain John W. Ames, commanding C Company, described the preparations:

When we came to an open plain, where we could see the edge of the fight, we went into a long line of battle and posted several batteries of artillery. Here we shook out our flags and loaded our muskets; the aides and officers rode up and down our lines, and we really looked and felt like soldiers once more, seeing how martial an array we could get up.[42]

Presently, the artillery began blasting away as Ames's C Company deployed. Skirmishers moved out ahead of the regiment to spar with the Confederate line. About halfway to the far woodline, the skirmishers were stopped and ordered to begin firing into the trees. Then, inexplicably, the men were ordered to return to the regiment. Upon arrival, the men were formed up and marched away from the fight! Though the regulars were not especially anxious to get into scrapes, there was a distinct deflation of morale when they were withdrawn from battle without doing their part. Ames recalled, "It was shameful! We all felt the sting of reproach, though the fault was not ours, when the wounded came struggling wearily by us....I know we asked each other why we were skedaddling, and we all felt indignant...."[43]

Porter's failure to get his corps into the battle subsequently prompted Pope to accuse him of treachery. Pope, a Republican, believed that Porter, a Democrat who also happened to be one of McClellan's favorites, had purposefully avoided battle so that the Army of Virginia might fail, thereby forcing Lincoln to reappoint McClellan to overall field command of the Union armies in the east. Having swayed others to his view, Pope ensured that Porter was court-martialed and cashiered from the service—despite the fact that it was the V Corps that had ultimately saved the Army of Virginia from destruction. At any rate, without having contributed much to the fight that day, Porter's corps bivouacked that night near Bethlehem Church, two miles south of the scene of the day's fighting.[44]

Well before dawn, the regiment made another long and tiring march in the dark. The V Corps started back toward Manassas, then headed north toward the Warrenton Turnpike on the Sudley Road. By 8:30 a.m. May 30, Sykes's division arrived at the site of the first battle of Bull Run. Sykes positioned his troops in a plowed field near the Dogan House, facing west and drawn up in a column of brigades. The 2nd Brigade's left was on the Warrenton Turnpike, just behind the 1st Brigade, and the 3rd Brigade, in reserve, was drawn up behind the 2nd. The 11th Infantry, at this time, was located in the right center of the 2nd Brigade. Through most of the day the regiment lounged in a position where the ground lay open before them, sloping down, then slightly upward, with a country fence-line off in the distance near a wood. The men were perceptibly nervous about the coming fight as they listened to the sounds of battle gradually approaching.

The fighting to the front came noticeably closer; and soon, the officers assembled their troops for battle. As the men stood in the battle line with "blanched cheeks and ashy faces," the waiting was almost unbearable. Suddenly, the battle arrived, bursting through the woods to their front. Confederate artillerists wheeled up their guns through the woods and began to bang away at the regulars. Soon the 11th Infantry took its first casualties. A solid shot bounded along the ground, smashing through the A Company line and cutting a corporal in two before burying itself in the body of the man behind.[45] The regiment would suffer galling artillery fire most of the day.

About 4:00 p.m., Sykes was ordered forward to support an attack by Brigadier General Dan Butterfield's division. Butterfield attacked on the right, across Lewis Lane, and into Starke's Division of Jackson's wing, defending along an unfinished railroad cut. As the fighting to the right front grew hotter, wounded men from Butterfield's units straggled back through the regulars' line in high spirits and were "very jolly and full of enthusiasm." One man claimed, "Whaled [sic] 'em like hell, boys; no show for you to-day." But before long, the frivolity stopped. The number of retiring troops multiplied; many seemed unwounded, a sign that men were deserting the ranks. The appearance of unorganized groups stoutly fighting their way to the rear indicated the remnants of broken regiments.[46]

The 2nd Brigade was moved forward to support Butterfield's men. As it approached the edge of Groveton Wood, the brigade ran into a previously unseen, but nonetheless very real, foe. This Confederate force consisted of four Alabama regiments under Brigadier General Cadmus Wilcox. A heavy volume of small arms fire broke out and lasted for about forty-five minutes. Wilcox's Alabamians had been advancing east through the wood after attacking into Butterfield's flank, but were unable to break through the regulars at this position. Behind Wilcox, Hood's Texas Brigade began to drift to the right of the Alabama troops. The Texans crashed into the 5th New York Volunteers positioned on Chinn Ridge, wrecking that regiment and thus exposing the 2nd Division's left flank.[47] Captain Ames described the action:

Finally, we halted, while our Major [Floyd-Jones] got some orders from an Aid[e]; and then we formed for the first time, a line of battle, facing the enemy. How snappishly the officers swore out their orders, in bringing us out of column into line! But it was done as prettily as on parade. As soon as the line was formed, we were faced to the left. "Right shoulder shift, arms! Forward, double quick, march!" And off we went—not at a double quick, but at a run. Evidently the danger was now on our left [in

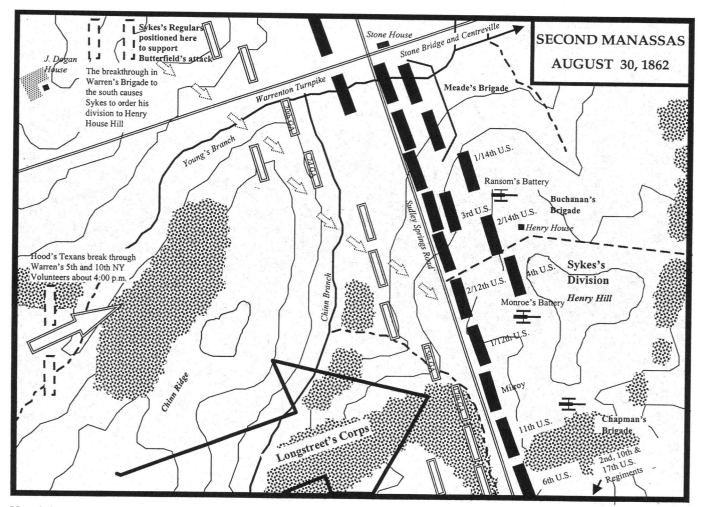

Map 1-4.

the vicinity of the 5th New York]. Fierce as the attack had been in front, all that seemed secondary now; and the opening roar on our left told of a movement there, portentous of further defeat.[48]

Suddenly, Sykes's position was untenable. He gave orders to retire the division back to the vicinity of the Henry House. In the meantime, Pope and McDowell hailed Lieutenant Colonel William Chapman, commanding the 2nd Brigade, and directed his command to move to positions along the Manassas-Sudley Road to protect the army's left flank. Chapman barked the orders and off the brigade went "at the double-quick." Captain Ames described the retrograde to Henry House Hill:

On we went over hill and hollow, running till we panted like dogs, and I thought we should all fall from sheer exhaustion. Stumbling over the remnants of a fence, we found ourselves, finally, in a country lane, and almost as soon as we struck it we came to a halt. There was partial lull in the firing just then. For a few minutes, we seemed

to have found a quiet retreat in that lane. Good luck or skill had taken us into a first rate position for defense; and the lull gave us time to dress our rank back to the roadside. Somehow too, the run had cheered us up; in spite of the look of utter defeat the field had worn, we all seemed to feel the contagion of confidence. Our fear had all gone; we examined our musket-locks; shoved our cartridge boxes round to the front of our belts, and picked out such slim shelter as the shallow little road-side ditch could afford.[49]

Chapman's entire brigade stood waiting and peering toward the distant wood for the coming assault. An eerie silence fell upon the field that lasted for only a few minutes but which seemed much longer. Suddenly, the crash of musketry broke the calm and waves of gray-clad men advanced out of the trees bellowing the familiar "rebel yell." The Union artillery posted on Henry House Hill behind Chapman's line began blasting holes in the advancing Confederate lines. The 11th Infantry had been detailed to support one of the batteries, and since their position in the little country lane was directly forward of the guns, they had to stand and fire as the guns were reloaded. Then, the men would be ordered to lie flat as the cannon were fired over their heads. Each blast of the battery would shower the men with unburned powder grains and bits of burning flannel, and smother them with "great puffs of hot smoke." After the battery volley, the troops would again be ordered back on their feet to fire into their attackers.[50]

After forty-five minutes of holding off troops of Longstreet's wing, the rest of the Regular Division formed on the 2nd Brigade's right. The 1st Brigade was a welcome addition to the fight. Longstreet's men kept up the pressure and made at least three distinct charges against the regulars' line.

The battle culminated on Henry House Hill, and the final fighting of the day centered on the gallant stand of the V Corps line, anchored on the regulars. Porter had been directed by Pope to cover the army's retreat to Centreville and, as it had at Gaines' Mill, the Regular Division formed the army's rear guard and fought desperately as the rest of the Army of Virginia streamed across the Stone Bridge. By late evening, the army was across, and Sykes's division began its withdrawal, even as a last Confederate skirmish line was repulsed. In his history of the V Corps, Captain William H. Powell, 4th U.S. Infantry, described the high command's assessment of the regulars' contribution to the day's battle:

> The last volley had been fired, and as night fell upon us the division of regulars of Porter's corps was ordered to retire to Centreville. It had fought hard on the extreme left to preserve the line of retreat by the turnpike and the stone bridge. We were gloomy, despondent, and about "tired out"; we had not had a change of clothing from the 14th to the 31st of August, and had been living, in the words of the men, on "salt horse, hard tack, and chicory juice." As we filed from the battle-field into the turnpike leading over the stone bridge, we came upon a group of mounted officers, one of whom....called out in a loud voice:
> "What troops are these?"
> "The Regulars," answered somebody.
> "Second Division, Fifth Corps," replied another.
> "God bless them! They saved the army," added the officer solemnly. We learned that he was General Irvin McDowell.[51]

Shortly after they crossed the bridge, a steady summer rain began to soak the tired men. Through the night of August 30-31, the regulars marched in the dark, drizzly gloom to Centreville, where the troops finally went into camp.

In his report of the battle, Major Floyd-Jones stated, "Throughout the day both officers and men behaved well." He went on to praise the actions of two sergeants, a corporal, and the color bearer, Corporal Edmund Burgoyne, who would eventually work his way up to become the regimental sergeant

major in 1864. Speaking of Major Floyd-Jones and his other regimental commanders, General Sykes stated that they were "zealous, energetic, and active" in executing their duties. In his after-action report, Chapman wrote: "It is with greatest pleasure I bear testimony to the splendid conduct of my command. It challenged unqualified admiration."[52]

Though the army had once again been driven from the field, the 11th Infantry, along with the rest of the regulars, had fought with distinction and had every reason to be proud. Remembering General McDowell's fervent praise, one soldier later reminisced that, "we had not before seen our own merit in so strong a light, nor realized the value of the work we had done in that country lane."[53] In short, they had saved the army, and possibly the Union. Had the Army of Virginia been destroyed, the fate of the Union would truly have been in doubt. This would not be the last time that the 11th Infantry and the regulars would be responsible for protecting the army from disaster.

The 11th Infantry, having started the campaign with an effective force of 270 muskets, suffered four killed and twenty wounded during the fighting. For several days, details under Captain James K. Lawrence, commanding G Company, and Lieutenant William Fletcher, were dispatched to the field to police the wounded and bury the dead of Sykes's division. That work concluded, the V Corps marched away to rejoin the Army of the Potomac.

The regiment marched north on September 2 to Tennallytown near Washington where the V Corps rejoined McClellan's army that evening. Leaving Tennallytown on September 7, 1862, the massive army (which now included much of what had been the Army of Virginia) marched north to find and destroy Lee's Army of Northern Virginia. Lee, in the meantime, was on the march. He had convinced President Jefferson Davis that an invasion of Maryland might bring that state into the Confederacy. Lee decided to test his theory to see whether he could wrest Maryland away from the Union, and, while there, sustain his army on that state's rich agricultural resources.

For a week, most of McClellan's troops moved north on a route that resulted in a clash with the rebels at South Mountain. The V Corps, however, moved north on a route farther to the east, taking the 11th Infantry through Rockville, Frederick, and Middletown, Maryland. The corps arrived near Sharpsburg on September 15, where it consolidated with the army for the next big battle.[54]

Antietam Campaign
September 15-30, 1862

Only light skirmishing occurred on the 16th as McClellan slowly moved his troops into position and developed his plan. This delay was a serious mistake, for Lee had fewer than twenty thousand troops facing McClellan's seventy thousand that day. Nevertheless, by dawn of the 17th, the Army of the Potomac was finally deployed for the fight. The V Corps formed the

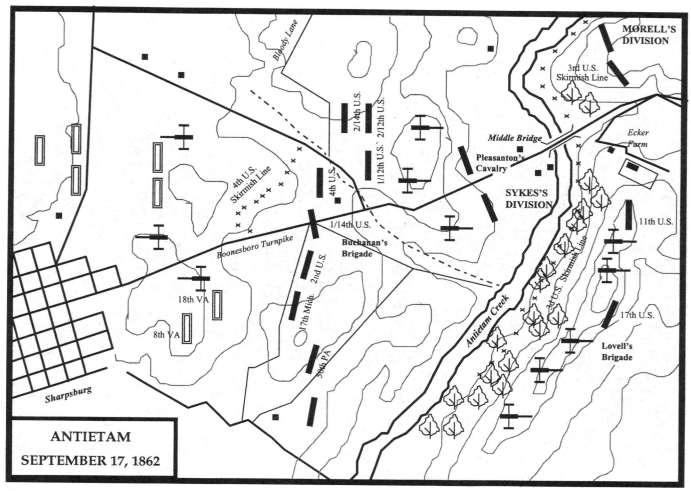

Map 1-5.

center of the Union line at Antietam with Morell's division extending from the Boonesborough Turnpike north, and Sykes's division from the pike south. Initially near the center of the division, the 11th Infantry moved to positions on high bluffs just southeast of the Middle Bridge where it guarded Captain Stephen H. Weed's Battery I, 5th U.S. Artillery, and several other batteries firing on rebel positions in the town of Sharpsburg. Throughout most of the 17th, the regiment remained in position east of Antietam Creek waiting for orders to advance.

The fighting that day for the most part occurred on the flanks of the V Corps, but by late afternoon, Sykes's infantry (less the 11th and 17th Regiments, held in reserve) and Alfred Pleasonton's cavalry had advanced across the Middle Bridge. The 2nd Brigade, once again under the command of Major Lovell, pushed forward to within a thousand yards of Sharpsburg and discovered that the rebel lines were very weak just east of the town along Cemetery Hill. From their positions on the bluffs, the men of the 11th U.S. could see directly into the eastern fringes of the town and noted very little enemy

activity. In fact, Lee had stripped his center of troops to reinforce his crumbling flanks so that only a mere shell held the line in front of Sharpsburg.

After getting Lovell's report, Sykes was so convinced of his ability to break through that he ordered the regulars to prepare to attack. In the meantime, the intelligence about the Confederate center had filtered back to Porter, who then reported the situation to McClellan. But as usual, the timid commanding general refused to push his advantage, fearing that he would need the V Corps as a last reserve. The regulars were ordered to stay put and guard the batteries, and a rare opportunity was lost to win a decisive victory against Lee that probably would have ended the war.[55]

Though the September 17 fighting at Antietam is billed as the bloodiest day in American history, for the men of the 11th Infantry the fighting was light and they suffered only one casualty. That casualty was Private Patrick Clark, G Company, who was dazed by a spent grape shot that struck him in the head.[56] On the 18th, only light skirmishing took place, but a welcome addition to the regiment was happily received. The band arrived from Fort Independence, having left the post a week before. The following day, the V Corps moved through Sharpsburg after McClellan allowed Lee to withdraw virtually unmolested across the Potomac.

Shepherdstown Ford
September 20, 1862

On the evening of the 19th, Porter ordered Sykes to send a reconnaissance force across the Potomac on the morrow to pursue the retreating rebels. Sykes selected Lovell's 2nd Brigade to lead. On the morning of the 20th, it crossed the river at Boeteler's Ford about 7:00 a.m. Once across, Lovell directed the 11th Infantry to lead the brigade and Floyd-Jones ordered D Company, under Lieutenant George A. Head, thrown out as skirmishers. The brigade, accompanied by General Sykes, advanced down the Charlestown Road to their initial objective, a line of woods about one mile south of the Potomac. Approaching to within thirty or forty feet of the wood, the 11th's skirmishers discovered three thousand of "Stonewall" Jackson's Confederates, supported by artillery, advancing

toward them. A brisk round of fire broke out as the forces met. Quickly deducing that the rebel force was too strong to take on with only the 2nd Brigade, Sykes ordered Lovell to return to positions nearer the river and sent word back to Warren's 3rd Brigade to cross the river to provide support on Lovell's right. As the regiment fell back "in good order," Union artillery massed on the Maryland side of the river began to pound the rebels, and soon the Union line began to put up a fierce resistance.[57]

The 11th Infantry, with the rest of 2nd Brigade, slowly fell back, firing as they went. Upon reaching the Potomac, Major Floyd-Jones assembled the regiment on a small hill near the bluffs of the river and began to volley into the Confederates with good effect.[58] Brigadier General William D. Pender's North Carolina brigade and Brigadier General James J. Archer's Tennessee brigade assaulted the federal line but were driven back by the combined volleys of the Union infantry and artillery. The resistance from the little brigade of regulars was such that Jackson thought he was facing a much larger part of the Army of the Potomac. The strength of the Confederate

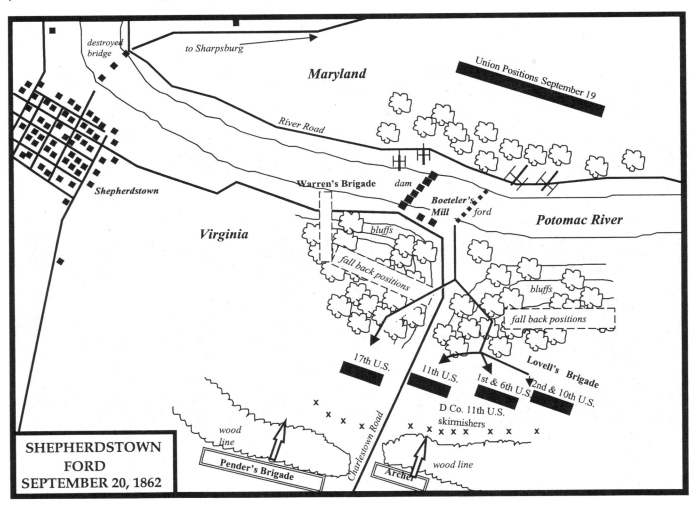

Map 1-6.

attack, however, also prompted General Porter to order the Union troops to withdraw. The regiment recrossed the river having suffered only three wounded, two of whom subsequently died. When it was determined that the enemy did not appear to be in retreat, the regulars returned to their camp near Sharpsburg and conducted picket duty for the next month.[59]

On October 13, A Company, 2nd Battalion joined the regiment having left Fort Independence on September 25. The company was a welcome addition to the depleted ranks of the regiment. Under the command of Captain Francis M. Cooley, ably assisted by 2nd Lieutenant Wright Staples, the company consisted of almost seventy men, or nearly twice the size of the other companies. Cooley and his men arrived just in time to participate in their first combat action.[60]

Leetown Reconnaissance
October 16-17, 1862

Still encamped near Sharpsburg, the 11th was again detailed, on October 16, to reconnoiter south of the Potomac River as part of a force commanded by Brigadier General Adolphus A. Humphries. Crossing the Potomac under the command of Captain Henry Chipman, the regiment encountered enemy pickets just beyond Shepherdstown. Chipman formed the regiment into skirmish lines and advanced, pushing the Confederates back about eight miles before heavy rains forced a halt to the attack. During the skirmishing, E Company lost two men killed. The following morning, the skirmishers redeployed and moved south for eight to ten miles, advancing as far as Leetown, but encountered no resistance. Around mid-afternoon, the regiment was ordered to halt and received orders to return to Sharpsburg, where they remained until October 30.[61]

During the Antietam Campaign, the 11th Infantry marched more than 115 miles, participated in several major actions or skirmishes, but only suffered four killed and three wounded.

On October 31, the 11th Infantry began a slow march back to central Virginia to find Lee's army. The following day found the regiment at Harpers Ferry, where it crossed back into Virginia. Through early November, the men of the 11th Infantry tramped the roads on a route that took them through Snickersville, Middleburg, and New Baltimore. They arrived at Warrenton on the 9th. There the Army of the Potomac went into camp for a rest; the troops looking forward to finally going into winter quarters. Morale was high and everybody went about the work of setting up camps with enthusiasm. But then, the news hit that McClellan had been relieved from command of the army, and the esprit of the rank and file dropped precipitously. Orders came down to turn out the V Corps along the Warrenton Pike on November 10 to bid farewell to the popular general.

That morning, the entire V Corps, as well as other corps, was drawn up along the pike by brigades to pay a last tribute to their beloved leader. McClellan, mounted on a large black stallion, looked every bit the picture of a great captain as he rode down the road between thousands of soldiers, most cheering, some weeping. Once again, the regulars demonstrated the discipline that separated them from the volunteer regiments. One participant described the scene:

[McClellan] rode along the wildly cheering lines of soldiers drawn up in review order until he reached the right of the line of the regular division. Here, with one simultaneous crash of wood and polished steel the long blue line came to the "present" and the battle torn standards bowed gracefully forward in salute....Who could have believed that these men, with their bronzed visages, their battle-scarred bodies and their proud, soldierly bearing, could weep? Yet some of them did. But their habits of discipline, their military pride and trained stoicism held the same stern sway over them in this moment as at all other times. Not a murmur, not a cheer broke out from the serried front. "Silent as the grave" this war-torn soldiery stood motionless in martial salute to their beloved chief passing along their lines for the last time.[62]

After resting and refitting for ten days at Warrenton, the army moved again. On November 18, the regiment arrived at Hartwood Church, Virginia, where the men camped for five wretched days in cold rain and snow, with little food to eat, nor dry wood with which to cook even if they had had food. The men aptly nicknamed the place "Camp Misery." On November 23, the regiment marched to still another camp on the Henry Farm near Potomac Creek, northeast of Falmouth, Virginia. The regiment's new camp had at one time been the property of the Virginia firebrand, Patrick Henry, and was now owned by one of his descendants.[63]

The camp on Potomac Creek was intended to be a permanent winter camp; so, upon occupation, the regulars reinstituted evening parade, guard mount, and inspections. As the only regulars in the Army of the Potomac, Sykes's division was openly derided by the volunteers for their attention to detail and soldierly habits. But many volunteers secretly admired these professional soldiers for their iron discipline and high standards. One soldier from the 22nd Massachusetts, after visiting his brother who was a regular, wrote home:

Oh Father, how splendidly the regulars drill; it is perfectly sickening and disgusting to get back here and see our regiment and officers maneuver, after seeing those West Pointers and those veterans of eighteen years service go through guard mounting. I need not go into detail, nor mention any of the differences; you know it all. I am only glad I saw for now I know I am a better soldier after seeing them perform.[64]

Another wrote:

> On one of our visits we witnessed a parade of the regulars, which we had never seen before, and we watched with envious eye the sharp, simultaneous click of their guns, as they executed the manual of arms, and wondered if our regiment would ever approach such perfection of dress, equipment, drill and absolute discipline, or if we would ever command a company of regulars.[65]

Like all soldiers, the men of the regular regiments did their share of grumbling. Even so, they were proud of their discipline and professionalism. They knew they were the Army of the Potomac's fire brigade for desperate situations. They had already saved the army from disaster on several occasions. Their pride showed through not only in their drill but in their words as well. They wanted people to know they were the professionals and feared being mistaken for state troops. For example, Private Pettit wanted his sister to ensure that she directed her letters "to the 11th U.S. Infantry or 'twill be thought I'm a volunteer."[66]

At the "Camp Near Potomac Creek, VA" as the Henry Farm became officially labeled, the regiment went into winter quarters in early December. The entire Army of the Potomac, now commanded by Major General Ambrose E. Burnside, was encamped in and around Falmouth opposite of Fredericksburg, Virginia, where the Army of Northern Virginia was ensconced. On December 11, the regiment broke camp and marched the short distance to a camp on Stafford Heights opposite Fredericksburg. The next engagement would severely test the mettle of the units of the Army of the Potomac, volunteer and regular alike.

Fredericksburg
December 13-16, 1862

From their camp on Stafford Heights on the east side of the Rappahannock River, the men of the 11th Infantry could see the Confederates entrenched on Marye's Heights beyond the town and wondered how difficult it would be to take that high ground. They would soon find out. Covered by Union batteries and a brigade of the II Corps that had seized the town after an assault landing, the 50th New York Engineers built pontoon bridges at three locations across the Rappahannock over the next two days. Fighting opened the morning of December 13 on the federal left, as elements of Major General William B. Franklin's Left Grand Division (I and XI Corps) attacked Jackson's divisions near Hamilton's Crossing. That effort repulsed, Major General Ambrose Burnside ordered the Right Grand Division to seize Marye's Heights. About 11:00 a.m., the II and IX Corps began a series of attacks against the heights, but each wave was repulsed in succession.

About 1:00 p.m., the V Corps, now under the command of Major General Daniel Butterfield after Porter's relief, began crossing the Rappahannock. The 1st and 3rd Divisions moved into a line west of the town, positioned behind the disorganized fragments of the II and IX Corps still huddled at the foot of Marye's Heights. The 11th Infantry advanced over the upper pontoon crossing site at about 4:00 p.m. and moved through the center of Fredericksburg on George and Hanover streets, taking up positions on the left of Sykes's 2nd division which was held in reserve behind the two lead divisions.

Surveying the fields before them, the regulars could see the futile results of the attack that had gone in before them. After watching the 3rd Division getting severely mauled while making its assault against the low stone wall held by the Georgians of Brigadier General Thomas Cobb, the regulars received their orders to move forward and prepare to make an attack. Their orders directed them to take the position with bayonets and to not discharge their weapons until they had reached Cobb's entrenchments.[67] Huddled together for warmth, their frosty breath floating in the cold December air, the men listened to the heavy fire and cries of the wounded as they tensely waited for the command that would send them into the cauldron. Finally it came.

As darkness fell, Captain Charles S. Russell, temporarily commanding the 11th Infantry, advanced the regiment from the western edge of town and moved through heavy, but ineffective, rebel fire. The regiment, moving on line with the 2nd Brigade, advanced along the north side of Hazel Run to a position about three hundred yards beyond the town and tumbled into a ditch. Miraculously, there were no casualties yet. Perhaps the rebels were too focused on picking off the other Union troops lying prone before the wall.

As the regulars crouched in the muddy ditch, poised to make their assault, orders came postponing the attack until the poor wretches stranded forward of the ditch could be evacuated. Remaining in the ditch until near midnight, the brigade was ordered forward to a linear depression only seventy-five yards from, and paralleling, the stone wall that hid Cobb's Georgians. Creeping into this shallow furrow, the regulars lay among the hundreds of dead and wounded men who had previously attempted to seize the wall before them. There, the men of the 11th Infantry prepared to make a night assault, certain that the losses would still be frightful against such a formidable position. Mercifully, additional orders came to hold in place.[68]

As they lay on the cold, damp ground during the night of December 13-14, the men of the 11th Infantry were surprised to observe men of the units previously thrashed by the rebels spring up in ones and twos, some wounded and some not, to make their way to the rear. They had lain in the open, sometimes for hours, not daring to twitch for fear of being shot, until an opportune time arrived to make good their escape. Apparently, the arrival of the regulars made the time seem right.

The night was bitterly cold, but fortunately Major George L. Andrews, now commanding the 2nd Brigade, had the foresight to have the men retain their packs for the assault. Unlike their comrades in the 1st Brigade, the men of the 11th at least

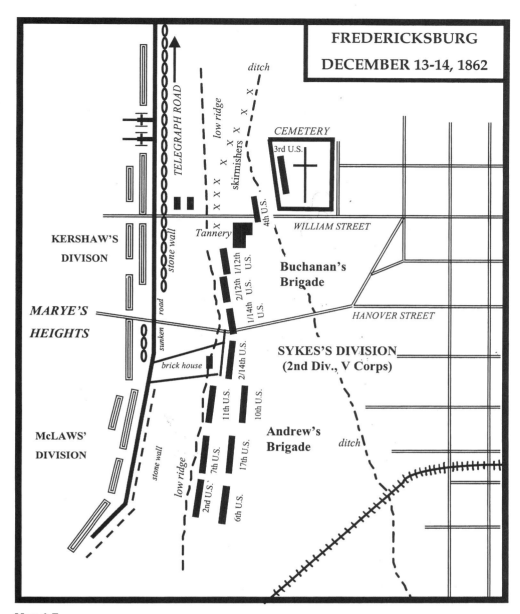

FREDERICKSBURG
DECEMBER 13-14, 1862

CEMETERY

3rd U.S.

ditch

low ridge

TELEGRAPH ROAD

skirmishers

4th U.S.

stone wall

Tannery

WILLIAM STREET

KERSHAW'S
DIVISON

sunken road

2/12th 1/12th U.S.

1/14th U.S.

**Buchanan's
Brigade**

*MARYE'S
HEIGHTS*

HANOVER STREET

brick house

2/14th U.S.

SYKES'S DIVISION
(2nd Div., V Corps)

McLAWS'
DIVISION

stone wall

low ridge

11th U.S.

10th U.S.

7th U.S.

17th U.S.

2nd U.S.

6th U.S.

**Andrew's
Brigade**

ditch

Map 1-7.

had their blankets and greatcoats with them to keep warm that frosty winter night.

As morning broke, the Confederates again delivered small arms fire, attempting to hit the Union troops now dug in or laying near the base of the hill. For the regulars out front, the position was maddening, for one could not even roll over for danger of being hit. The soldiers of the 11th found cover by lying on the ground behind the shallow rise that gave them their only protection. They lay there all that day, bullets whizzing inches over their heads, waiting for the dreaded orders that would launch their assault. But no orders came, so they lay there, occasionally trading shots with the rebel soldiers behind the wall. Anxiously, the day wore on and finally turned to night

when orders came to return to the cover of the town.

Slowly making their way back in the dark, Sykes's regulars gained the relative safety of the city streets, where they promptly stoked fires and ate their first hot meal in several days. The regiment remained in Fredericksburg trading long-range fire with the rebel troops on Marye's Heights until the 16th, when it was ordered to return to its camp at Falmouth.[69] As before, the regulars performed as the covering force while the army retreated under cover of darkness across the pontoon bridges. Amazingly, the Confederates allowed the withdrawal to proceed unmolested, and the regiment made its way back to the camp on Potomac Creek.

At Fredericksburg, the regiment was able to escape severe casualties even though it was in an extremely perilous situation. The toll was only one killed, two officers and eighteen men wounded. It undoubtedly would have been much greater had the assault been made. The resistance of the enemy behind the wall was such that in his report to the corps commander, Major Andrews remarked, "The position proved to be the most trying of any I have ever known troops to assume, and eventually put to the severest test the nerve and endurance of the oldest and most courageous of our officers and men." Attesting to the soldierly abilities of his regiment below Marye's Heights, Captain Russell reported to the brigade commander that "both officers and men of my command showed the tenacity and disciplined courage characteristic of regular troops."[70]

The "Mud March"
January 19-25, 1863

Embarrassed by the Fredericksburg debacle, Burnside planned a new campaign to dislodge the Confederates from the city by attacking it from the west. This misadventure proved to be a disaster, and soon became known as the "Mud March." On

January 19, the Army of the Potomac headed northwest along the Rappahannock toward Banks' Ford in an attempt to attack Marye's Heights from the rear. That afternoon, torrential winter rains began and continued throughout the following day, turning the roads into quagmires. The 11th Infantry went as far as two miles west of their winter quarters before stopping the first day. On the second day they made it to Stafford Court House and went no further. The rains had brought the army to a halt, with wagons and artillery sinking in the mud. With only ten miles to move to Banks' Ford, the army could not even make it that far, much to the delight of the gleeful Confederates who watched the fiasco. After three days of this agony, Burnside realized the futility of the effort and ended the campaign. Thoroughly soaked and demoralized, the army struggled its way back to camps near Falmouth. Burnside was relieved of command on the 25th and "Fighting Joe" Hooker installed as the new commander of the Army of the Potomac.[71]

The regiment wintered in and near their camp at the Henry Farm, where it pulled guard and picket duties and built breastworks for defense. In February, it became apparent that the army was going to remain in place for a while, so the 11th Infantry was detailed to build additional fortifications to protect the railroad bridge across Potomac Creek. To protect themselves against the cold of winter, the troops constructed log huts and used their shelter halves, or other materials, for roofing. The soldiers' ingenuity inspired them to build what, for them, were luxurious abodes, complete with bunk beds, chairs, and fireplaces. They then settled into camp routine for the next three months.

By this time, the Regular Army regiments of Sykes's division had suffered numerous casualties in almost every battle since the Peninsula Campaign. The loss of troops through casualties, illness, and desertion, combined with the inadequate flow of replacements from the respective regimental recruit training depots, had severely reduced the Regular Army formations. Desertion was by far the biggest problem for all units, regular or volunteer. For example, the casualties for the 11th Infantry in 1862 were eighteen killed or mortally wounded, forty-six wounded, and twenty-four missing, for a total of eighty-eight combat-related losses. However, the regiment suffered 118 desertions over the same period.[72] The "Mud March" increased the flow of desertions from the Army of the Potomac, further bleeding the already minuscule regular regiments. As a result, Major General George G. Meade, the V Corps commander after Butterfield, requested and received approval from the War Department to inactivate certain companies in the regiments to bring the remaining companies to something closer to full strength.[73]

For the 11th Infantry, some help was on the way. On January 6, 1863, Company B, 2nd Battalion, left Fort Independence by train to join the 1st Battalion in the field. After a short stopover in Washington, D.C., the company arrived at the camp at Potomac Creek in time to participate in

the "Mud March." However, on March 10, 1863, by order of Meade's directives, both Companies A and B of the 2nd Battalion were reduced to minimum manning (one officer and four enlisted) and the remaining troops were transferred to companies of the 1st Battalion.[74]

Almost a month later, on March 29, Companies C and D of the 2nd Battalion arrived at Potomac Creek from Fort Independence to join the regiment. Company C was an interesting organization, as about half of the men were enlistees from volunteer regiments who had been prisoners at Fort Independence. They had become disgusted with their own outfits and had deserted, been caught, and convicted. The men were talked into enlisting in the 11th Infantry by Captain Henry G. Thomas, the commander of C Company. After experiencing orderly military life at Fort Independence under the stern but fair discipline of the Regular Army, these men agreed with Captain Thomas that it was better to become regulars once their sentence was up, rather than be returned to the volunteer regiments from which they had deserted.[75]

The field existence of Companies C and D was short-lived as they too were directed to be reduced to minimum manning on April 1. The distribution of 2nd Battalion men among the companies of the 1st Battalion allowed the 11th Infantry to retain all eight companies on active duty. It was to be the only regular regiment in Sykes's division to remain so organized after the March-April 1863 reorganization.[76]

On the chilly spring morning of April 7, the regiment formed up with the rest of the 2nd Brigade at their camp at Potomac Creek. As their breath hung frosty in the air, the troops stood by for preinspection by NCOs checking for shined buttons and blackened boots. The occasion was a brigade review for President Lincoln, which for the vast majority of the soldiers was the first time they had seen their commander in chief, and they wanted to look their best. The next morning, the entire V Corps was marched five miles to a large open field to be reviewed by the president. From the field, the troops had a full view of Fredericksburg, which meant that the Confederates, who still held the town could also see them as they paraded.[77]

About this time, Major Floyd-Jones returned to resume command after another leave of absence and after commanding the 2nd Brigade for a short time. The troops spent most of April chopping wood, pulling guard and picket duties, and refitting for the coming spring campaigns. The weather that spring was cold and rainy; nonetheless, the regiment departed Potomac Creek on April 27, 1863, and headed northwest for Kelly's Ford in a feint devised by Hooker to draw the Confederates out of Fredericksburg.[78]

Chancellorsville
May 1-4, 1863

The V Corps began crossing Kelly's Ford on April 28, then turned and headed back southeast. The column, consisting of the V, XI, and XII Corps, had circled north around the

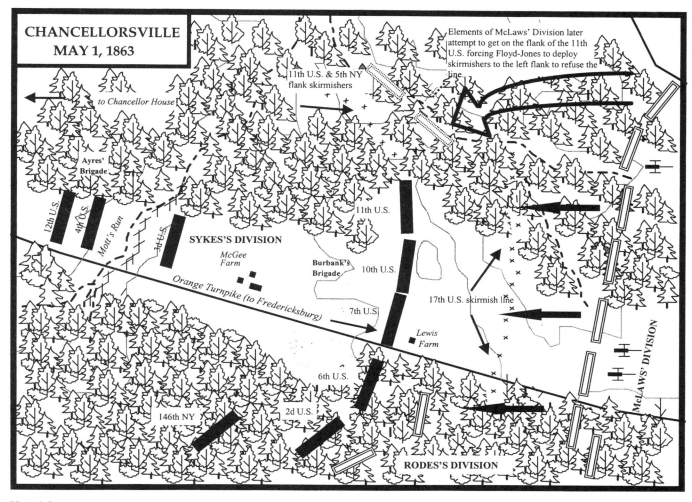

Map 1-8.

Confederate position at Fredericksburg to come into positions in Lee's rear at Chancellorsville. After crossing Kelly's Ford, the V Corps headed for Ely's Ford, moving on a separate axis from the other two corps. The 11th Infantry crossed Ely's Ford on the night of April 29-30. Wading in the swirling, icy-cold, and chest-deep Rapidan, the men struggled up the muddy bank on the far side in a pouring rain and huddled around fires to wait for morning. Moving slowly after first light, the 11th Infantry passed through Chancellorsville crossroads about 4:00 p.m. on the 30th and took up positions southeast of the Chancellor House. Initial contact occurred near the house with troops of Anderson's Division, who beat a hasty retreat after discovering the V Corps' presence. Later that day, the 2nd Division was detached from V Corps and Meade started the rest of his command on a march to encircle the Confederate right flank. Meanwhile, the 2nd Division remained on the Plank Road and encamped just east of the Chancellor House preparing for its advance on the morrow.[79]

Early on the morning of May 1, the 11th Infantry relieved the 10th Infantry of division provost duties, which primarily consisted of netting stragglers and guarding the supply trains. Company F, totaling some fifty-seven men, was assigned the detail.[80] The remainder of the regiment fell in with 2nd Brigade, forming up for a push down the Old Orange Turnpike towards Fredericksburg. The first fighting of the battle took place between the 2nd Division and Major General Lafayette McLaws' Mississippians about noon one and a half miles to the east of the crossroads. The 2nd Brigade, now commanded by Colonel Sidney Burbank of the 2nd Infantry, was deployed across the turnpike with the 2nd and 6th Infantry Regiments on the south side, and the 11th, with the 7th and 10th Infantry Regiments, on the north. Sykes deployed Brigadier General Romeyn B. Ayres' 1st Brigade on Burbank's left and the 146th New York on the right.

Driving the rebel skirmishers back on their regiments, the regulars led Sykes's advance down the road, moving across a small stream called Mott's Run. At Mott's Run, the regiment clambered over a rail fence, reformed on the colors carried by

Color Sergeant Edmund Burgoyne, and advanced to a small cluster of farm outbuildings, all the while moving in the parade ground style only the regulars could perform in the face of the enemy. During the advance, the Virginians of Brigadier General William Mahone's brigade "stubbornly opposed" the march, but the "movement of the regulars was irresistible." Upon reaching the outbuildings, Sykes then ordered the units forward to seize a small hill still farther east.[81]

The 2nd Brigade again moved forward, straddling the road, with the 11th Infantry still on the far left. The advance was made so quickly that the regiment, with help from the 10th Infantry, captured some thirty rebel prisoners as they swept over the hill. The soldiers of the 2nd Brigade, justifiably proud of their textbook assault, then hastily prepared defenses, and waited for the units of Slocum's XII Corps to move up to cover Sykes's flanks. It was not to be. The troops of General Richard H. Anderson's Division had advanced westward through the Wilderness and slammed into Slocum's federals as they struggled through the thick foliage attempting to reach Sykes's right flank. The XII Corps never would link up with Sykes.

In front of the 2nd Brigade, McLaws' Confederates began pressing forward and feeling around for the brigade's left flank, held by the 11th Infantry. The rebels found it and wheeled up an artillery piece to begin blasting at the regiment with cannon fire as well as rifle fire. The regiment, determined not to allow its flank to be turned, returned volley for volley. Floyd-Jones directed the regiment to partially refuse to the left to face the Confederates there, but it was becoming apparent that the 2nd Brigade was in danger of being flanked on both sides and cut off from the rest of Sykes's division.[82] It was a delicate position, to say the least.

After initially being pushed back, rebel reinforcements arrived, allowing McLaws to heavily counterattack the Union line. These attacks went on for over an hour, but the regulars stood firm. Unable to gain contact with the units on his flanks, Sykes still feared that he might be flanked by Anderson's troops to the south, but he was also confident that he could still hold the dearly bought ground if Slocum's corps could be brought up on line. Hooker, however, having learned of Sykes's situation, ordered the Regular Division back to McGee's House near the Chancellorsville crossroads. Grudgingly complying with Hooker's order, Sykes met the Division of Major General Winfield S. Hancock coming up behind him. The combined forces of Sykes and Hancock, in turn, stopped McLaws cold. After observing the steadiness of the regulars in their advance and retrograde, Brigadier General Gouverneur Warren, now the chief engineer of the Army of the Potomac, reported, "I have never seen the steadiness of our troops more tried and proved."[83]

Later that day, Hooker, in what appeared to be a loss of confidence, ordered his entire army back to positions around Chancellorsville, turning the initiative over to Lee. The 11th Infantry returned to the position of its campsite of that morn-

ing, where it remained until later that night. At 1:00 a.m. on May 2, it moved with the entire V Corps north of Chancellorsville into positions along the Mineral Springs Road to provide protection for the line of communication to United States Ford. Just after their arrival, the regulars repulsed a feeble sortie of Confederate infantry groping in the dark for the army's left flank. At first light, the regiment went to work felling trees to build breastworks for protection from the onslaughts of Jackson's men that they were sure were coming. But, inexplicably, the attack did not materialize. It remained quiet to their front all day.[84]

It was quiet for good reason. Jackson was not coming their way. Instead he marched his columns of butternut-clad "foot cavalry" south and west of the entire Army of the Potomac to attack Hooker's rear. About 5:00 p.m., Jackson's troops crashed into the flank of the XI Corps, setting that hapless formation to flight. Then an incident occurred reminiscent of the regulars' actions at First Bull Run when they stopped the stampede of troops to the rear.

The XI Corps was a relatively new corps made up of mostly green German and Scandinavian immigrant soldiers, and the aggressive attack by Jackson's hard-boiled veterans so unnerved them that they quickly broke, fleeing for Ely's and United States Fords. Hearing of the disaster, Meade ordered the Regular division to arrest the flow of refugees bolting for the north side of the Rapidan. Upon receiving the alarm, the 11th Infantry fell in with the rest of the 2nd Brigade, formed into columns and was soon pounding down the road at the double-quick to stem the retreating mob.

The regulars headed for the junction where the road from Chancellorsville split off in the direction of the two crossings. What they found there was chaos. Panicked soldiers, many without weapons, hats, or equipment, were clogging the road, fleeing for their lives. The regulars quickly deployed across the road, where their officers sternly ordered the retreating troops to stop and reform. Failing to completely halt the mob, Major Floyd-Jones directed the regimental band to begin playing. The bandmaster wisely chose "Hail Columbia!" and "The Star-Spangled Banner." The songs appealed to the patriotism of many of these demoralized men, most of whom turned around with a new resolve and began organizing a new defensive line to protect the rear of the Army of the Potomac.[85]

That night the regiment, having helped diffuse the problem with the XI Corps, once again went to work building extensive breastworks on the new V Corps line, which now ran along the road leading to Ely's Ford facing southwest. At 7:00 p.m., several companies of the 11th Infantry went forward to relieve the 6th Infantry as the picket line in front of the 2nd Brigade, while the rest continued to work on the defenses. They feverishly continued their efforts through the night and all day of May 3, but no further attacks were made against them.

The 4th of May was also quiet for the 11th Infantry, but the regiment did have a bit of a scare from a Confederate force outfitted as Union troops. Private Pettit described this episode:

> During the night [of May 3] a rebel battery riged in our style and costume and supported by some of Stewart's Cavalry succeeded in geting around and obtained a favorable position to shell one of our hospitals across the river where we lay. Monday morning at early dawn they opened fire on us a dozen or so shots. A shell burst directly over the hospital tent killing several wounded, a few came hobbling along through the woods where we were, panic stricken! A shell came whizing along striking in a hollow some 20 rods before reaching us another directly over us striking as far beyond us and mortally wounded a man while packing a mule. That was the closest. The teamsters flew into excitement trying to hitch up and get off! [W]e slung on our knapsacks and got in readiness in short order. The Rebels yelled tremendously and all was confusion, we could not see how many there were for the extensive forrests. I supposed that by some cunning plan during the night [they] got in our rear and that we were goners [for] sure: but however we were soon pacified by the intelligence that a force of our cavalry took a dash on them and took every one prisoners: they have been or will probably will be all shot for thus coming out in disguise and commiting so cowardly an act which is contrary to all rules of civil warfare.[86]

After five days of fighting around Chancellorsville, Fredericksburg, and Salem Church, Hooker decided that the Army of the Potomac had had enough. He directed Meade's V Corps to hold Lee in check while the army slipped across the rain-swollen Rappahannock at United States Ford. As usual, and as they had done so many times in the past, Sykes's regulars were given the task of holding the rebels at bay as the rest of the army beat a retreat over the pontoon bridges at the ford. They held a thin line of defense that was in great peril of attack during the entire crossing operation, but Lee was content to leave the regulars alone. The V Corps crossed the night of May 5-6, Sykes's division crossing last, and the field was left to Lee.

At Chancellorsville, the regiment lost seven men killed, sixteen wounded, and five missing, most casualties having occurred during the spectacular advance on the 1st. The performance of Major Floyd-Jones's regiment did not go unnoticed. Colonel Burbank wrote: "Where all did so well it is difficult to discriminate but I desire to name...Major DeLancey Floyd-Jones for the coolness with which he commanded his regiment...." Floyd-Jones in his own report praised his men and wrote: "The success attained on the 1st instant was due to the coolness and bravery exhibited by the officers and men, all of whom behaved well." He went on to single out several first sergeants and men, noting that "Sergeant Edmund Burgoyne, Company G (color-bearer), was particularly distinguished."[87]

Arriving on May 6, the regiment returned to its old camp at the Henry Farm near Falmouth, where it remained to perform provost duties and camp improvements until June. On June 4, they marched to Benson's Mill and performed picket duty there until the 13th. For the remainder of the month, the regiment moved north with the Army of the Potomac, shadowing Lee's army as it moved through Pennsylvania, and performing a wide variety of duties at numerous locations. The days were hot, the roads dusty, and the army pushed on at a rapid pace. Many of the soldiers began falling out from the grueling march, and several men in the 11th reportedly died from sunstroke.[88] On June 13, they marched to Watwood Church, and continued on through Warrenton Junction to Catlett's Station the next day. The 15th found them digging in at Manassas Junction, preparing to fight a battle that failed to materialize. Two days later, the regiment moved to Gum Springs and from there to Aldie Gap on the 18th to perform picket duty. On the 25th, they left Aldie Gap, crossed the Potomac at Edwards Ferry, and spent the night near the mouth of the Monocacy River. The next few days were spent pulling provost duty near Frederick, Maryland, and on the 30th, the 11th Infantry moved through Liberty, Union Town, and Frizzleburg and camped at Pipe Creek, Maryland near Middleburg that night. On the 1st of July, the regiment crossed into Pennsylvania about 10:00 a.m. and moved north toward the little town of Gettysburg.[89]

Gettysburg
July 1-3, 1863

As the initial shots were exchanged between Brigadier General John Buford's Union cavalrymen and Major General Henry Heth's Confederate infantry at Seminary Ridge on July 1, the men of the 11th Infantry were still on the road marching with a purpose; but to where, and for what purpose, they had no idea. The regiment moved through Taneytown and Hanover, and, just past Hanover, they went into camp in the early afternoon for a rest. It being the first of the month, Major Floyd-Jones apparently thought this break would be a good opportunity to prepare the muster and pay rolls, and so the regiment held the monthly muster. About sunset, word was received that the V Corps must march for Gettysburg immediately. The tired men unstacked their arms, fell in to the road, and turned west to the sound of the guns. The purpose of the long marches from Virginia would be revealed on the morrow.

Before long, the darkness enveloped the blue columns as they tramped in the dusty track. As they approached Gettysburg, the 11th's Regimental Sergeant Major, George Stouch, was no doubt excited. Before the war, he had been a druggist in Gettysburg and probably relished the thought of being able to visit family and friends when the next fight was over. Welcome as the idea was, the visit was going to have to wait, for the regiment was heading into a terrible fight. The pace was grueling, but by midnight they had reached Bonaughtown, a small cluster of houses four miles from Gettysburg, where they made camp.[90]

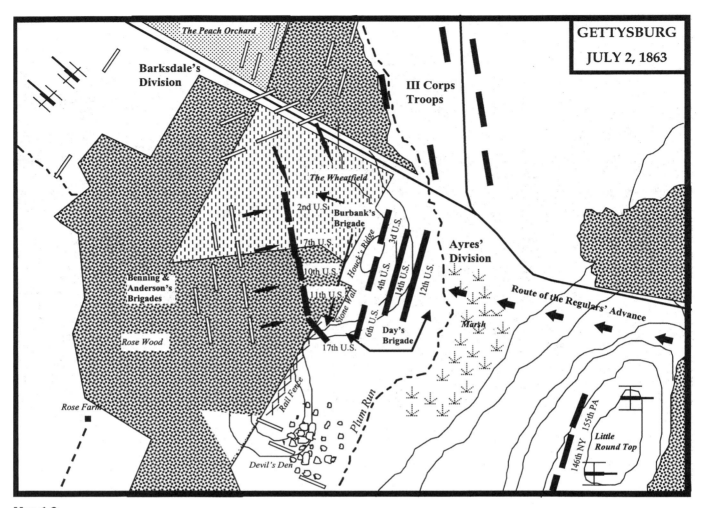

Map 1-9.

The respite from the long, dusty march was brief. About 3:30 a.m. on July 2, the entire brigade broke camp and moved to Powers Hill, a position about a mile and a half southeast of Gettysburg near the army's artillery park. About dawn, the brigade was formed in battle lines to the southwest of the XII Corps, and twenty men from each regiment were thrown out as skirmishers into a wood. Beyond the wood could be seen the pickets of the enemy in the distance. The brigade was ordered forward about 7:00 a.m., and advanced through the wood until it reached the far side, along Cemetery Ridge opposite the Peach Orchard. At this location the 2nd Brigade began a heavy but long-range skirmish with rebel sharpshooters, during which a small number of casualties was sustained. At 10:00 a.m., after about two hours of sporadic shooting, Colonel Burbank received orders to move his brigade to another position about two miles to the southwest near the Taneytown Road east of Little Round Top. On arrival there, the 11th lay idle for the next several hours, resting from their forced march of the previous day.[91]

The men lay in the July heat, listening to the sounds of battle as combat raged to the north. Suddenly, about 5:00 p.m.,

Brigadier General Romeyn B. Ayres, now commanding the 2nd Division (Sykes had been appointed to take the V Corps several days earlier when Meade assumed command of the army), received urgent orders to move his division to the summit of Little Round Top. The regulars quickly fell into line.[92]

The men of the 11th Infantry advanced toward the hill looming before them and listened to the cannonade. Surely they were about to join a terrible fight. As they approached the hill, the rapidity of the crackling rifle fire increased markedly. A staff officer rode up to Colonel Burbank urgently directing him "to move forward with the utmost dispatch." The brigade commander gave the order to move at the "double quick" to the north end of Little Round Top. The tired men struggled to run uphill in the sultry heat, but finally made it to the north slope of the hill, where it joins Cemetery Ridge. Arriving there, the brigade was deployed into a battle line to the right of the 3rd Brigade, which had arrived only a short time before, having tied in their flank with the 1st Division at the south end of Little Round Top.[93]

From those heights, the men could see across the marsh-like Plum Run valley to the Wheatfield and the Devil's Den. Little did they know that they were about to make history in a desperate fight between those two now-famous landmarks.[94] The 2nd Division was in the line of battle on the corps' right end, filling in the space that should have been filled by Major General Dan Sickles' III Corps. The V Corps had arrived just in the nick of time, for as soon as the 1st Division was in place, the Alabama troops of Brigadier General Hood's division swarmed up Little Round Top only to be repulsed several times by the division. That action culminated with the valiant charge of the 20th Maine.

Meanwhile, the fighting raged at the Devil's Den, the Wheatfield, and the Peach Orchard. Absorbed by the spectacle, the men of the 11th Infantry watched Sickles' III Corps receive hammer-like blows from Longstreet's I Corps. In an effort to bolster the III Corps' crumbling left flank, Ayres was ordered to advance the 2nd Division forward about 5:30 p.m. to attack into the teeth of the Confederate regiments between the Devil's Den and the soon to be famous Wheatfield. The division moved forward in column, with the 2nd Brigade leading. Burbank advanced his brigade with the 17th, 11th, 10th, 7th, and 2nd Regiments of U. S. regulars on line, left to right. As if on parade, the regulars advanced down Little Round Top and across the ankle deep muck of Plum Run, all the while receiving fire from the Confederates sheltered in the rocks of the Devil's Den, and from a low rise to their front—Houck's Ridge. The 2nd Brigade successfully pushed forward to a position on Houck's Ridge covered by a rail fence and a low stone wall and forced the enemy from those positions, "driving them back in a bloody charge."[95]

The 2nd Brigade halted at the stone wall and formed a battle line with the 17th Infantry, refused on the left, and the 11th holding a recessed portion of the wall to the 17th's right. On line to the 11th's right were the 10th and 7th Infantry Regiments, and finally the 2nd Infantry holding the right flank. Colonel Hannibal Day's 1st Brigade formed in reserve positions behind the 2nd Brigade, laying somewhat exposed on the side of Houck's Ridge. To the front of the regulars lay the Rose Wood, through which Colonel Edward Cross' brigade of II Corps troops were now fighting their way back to safety. To Cross's front, Brigadier General George T. Anderson's Georgians were pressing the federals back, but the regulars could not fire for fear of hitting Cross's men until they were clear of the front. As Cross cleared out, Ayres ordered the 2nd Brigade forward into the woods. Burbank ordered the brigade to conduct a half left wheel, pivoting on the 17th Infantry. After making the difficult swinging maneuver, regimental commanders had just enough time to redress their battle lines, then almost immediately began to volley into Brigadier General Henry L. Benning's Georgians, now coming up. Not expecting to run into another Union line, the Confederate line shuddered, then was pushed back.[96]

The 11th Infantry was now formed on line, positioned entirely in Rose Wood. The brigade battle line now extended from the Wheatfield on the right, to a shallow gully near the Devil's Den where the 17th Infantry anchored the left. Near the left of the 11th's line was a cluster of rocks (which can still be seen today near the 5th New Hampshire monument) that provided a portion of G Company with sparse cover. Sergeant Major Stouch positioned himself near these rocks. The regiment now reloaded and waited, but the hiatus was brief.

After the regulars had driven Benning's units out of Rose Wood, they in turn were attacked in the right flank by Brigadier General William Barksdale's Mississippians sniping from the Peach Orchard, while two new brigades under Brigadier General James B. Kershaw and Brigadier General P. J. Semmes added their weight to Anderson's and Benning's brigades renewing their attacks on the brigade front. For some thirty minutes, the 11th Infantry traded blows with the 1st Texas, 3rd Arkansas, and the 2nd, 15th, and 17th Georgia Regiments. In this attack, Lieutenant Colonel William T. Harris, commander of the 2nd Georgia, fell to the regulars' guns as he attempted to cheer his troops forward.[97]

The initial successes in Rose Wood were soon wiped away, however. On the regulars' right, all Union resistance suddenly broke, as Brigadier General W. T. Wofford's Georgians came howling through the Wheatfield. This attack placed Wofford's men in the right rear of the 2nd Brigade. The 10th, 16th, and 18th Georgia Regiments crashed into the flank of the 2nd U.S. Infantry, while Benning's and Anderson's brigades once again pressed their assault home in front. The 2nd Brigade was now in danger of becoming entrapped. Bloody close-in fighting ensued, and the regulars suffered numerous casualties from cross-fires. Unable to get the 1st Brigade into position to support the 2nd Brigade, Ayres had only one option. He ordered both brigades to withdraw through the open ground of the Plum Run Valley back to their previous positions on Little Round Top.

Directing the volleys of his battle line in the smoke-filled Rose Wood, Major Floyd-Jones received the orders to move to the rear. While the 17th Infantry to their left fought desperately to hold the flank at the rail fence, the major passed the order, and the men of the 11th began to retire to the stone wall just as a force of Confederates slammed into their backs. Turning to fight with bayonets and musket butts, several G Company men near the pile of rocks were roughly seized and made prisoner by troops of the 10th Georgia, including Sergeant Major Stouch, lieutenants Lemuel Pettee and Mathew Elder, and the company first sergeant, Levi Price. Suddenly, these men now had to scramble to the other side of the rocks to keep from being hit by friendly fire.[98]

The remainder of the regiment rolled over the stone wall and turned to volley into their pursuers. Captain Thomas Barri, a company commander highly regarded by his men, was directing the move of his company to the wall when he was wounded and fell. In spite of the heavy smoke and confusion in the wood,

Lieutenant Herbert Kenaston went to Barri's aid and began to carry him to safety. Just before they reached the wall, however, both were hit by rebel fire. Several men climbed over and quickly pulled the two to safety, but Kenaston died just as his men laid him against the stones. Despite Kenaston's heroic effort, Barri himself lived only long enough to be evacuated to the division field hospital.[99]

At the wall, the 11th held firm to provide the regiments on the right sufficient time to clear the wood and form up. To the rear, the men of the 1st Brigade watched in admiration. One later wrote, "The 2nd [Brigade] still stood to our front. Then their right yielded to the advancing rebels. The left (I believe it was the 11th [Infantry]) which was right in our front, held splendidly and poured two volleys into the enemy."[100]

Using the precious seconds provided by the 11th's stand, the other regiments of the brigade were able to claw their way back through the woods to the stone wall, where they formed up and set off for the far side of the valley. Although the withdrawal was conducted "in good order," Major Floyd-Jones reported that in those few minutes nearly half the regiment was lost to enemy fire. As they moved back through the valley, the men of the 11th Infantry not only received withering fire from the Wheatfield and Rose Wood to the rear, but also from Hood's Texans, who poured it on from the Devil's Den, now on their right. The agonizing return across Plum Run is a testimonial to the professionalism and discipline of the regulars during the Civil War. A soldier of the 155th Pennsylvania on Little Round Top watched the entire episode and was awestruck:

> A good view of that portion of the field, when not obscured by the smoke of battle, was afforded. The two small brigades of United States regulars of Ayres' Division had advanced beyond the position of the One Hundred Fifty-fifth on Little Round Top, toward the Wheatfield… to support General Sickles. The regulars fought with determined skill and bravely for nearly an hour, and then reluctantly fell back as if on drill, but sharply and bravely contesting every foot of the ground. These things I saw, and I am glad as a volunteer, to bear tribute to the United States regulars.[101]

The withdrawal by the regulars in the face of the enemy at Gettysburg stood in stark contrast to the shameful retreats conducted by some volunteer troops at places like Bull Run and Chancellorsville. As much of the army watched, the regulars moved with the parade ground precision and the iron discipline for which they were known. Another observer wrote that the "regular troops once more justify their old reputation; not a single man has left the ranks, and they allow themselves to be decimated without flinching."[102] For once, this discipline may have been their undoing, for it gave the rebel infantry plenty of easy targets—and they made the most of it. Colonel W. W. White,

commanding the 7th Georgia Infantry in this action, remarked of the fighting at Plum Run, "The loss of the enemy here was very great."[103]

The regulars literally paraded back to their start point on Little Round Top, leaving hundreds of bodies strewn in their wake. Many were killed outright, others wounded, then shot down again as they struggled through the sucking marsh. Reaching Little Round Top, the severely depleted division reformed battle lines facing the enemy, and took the opportunity to take revenge on the troops that had whittled their ranks on the way back from Houck's ridge. In concert with the rest of the V Corps troops on Little Round Top, the regulars helped repulse the final attacks of the day. They then began to take stock of their losses.

The division's casualties were horrendous. The 2nd Brigade's losses were so frightful that they were pulled out of the line altogether and moved to a camp on the reverse slope of the hill. Having gone into the fray with about 952 men, 447 of them were dead, wounded, or missing by that evening. Of eighty officers in the brigade, forty-one were killed or wounded, of which ten were in the 11th Infantry. In all, the regiment had twenty-five officers and 261 enlisted men engaged. Of these, five officers and sixteen enlisted men were killed or mortally wounded, five officers and eighty-five men wounded, and nine missing in action.[104] As things turned out, Sergeant Major Stouch was not among the missing. In the counterattack by the Pennsylvania "Bucktails" through Rose Wood, his captors broke and ran. Realizing that they had left their prisoners, rebels soon turned and attempted to shoot them. Once again, Stouch and the others had to scramble to the other side of the rocks, but not before he and Price were wounded and Lieutenant Elder was killed. To Stouch and Price's good fortune, the Bucktails swept past the rocks, and the cluster of G Company soldiers were able to get back to the regiment.[105]

The 11th remained in the brigade camp behind Little Round Top that night and throughout the next day but did not engage in any more fighting at Gettysburg. It did receive, however, some of the incoming fire from Confederate cannon set too high to support Pickett's famous charge on July 3, though no casualties were sustained.[106]

The regulars of the 2nd Brigade once again received high praise for their performance, but it came at high cost. Colonel Sidney Burbank, commanding the brigade, wrote to Sykes that, "The conduct of both officers and men in this severe contest was deserving of all praise, and was all I could wish."[107] Though they had suffered terribly in the fight, the losses sustained by the 11th Infantry were not in vain. Their efforts, along with the rest of the 2nd Brigade, saved several Union regiments from almost certain capture or destruction in the Rose Wood. It could even be argued that the regulars' timely arrival at the Rose Wood prevented the complete rout, or possibly even the destruction, of the III Corps by Hood's and McLaws' Divisions as they rolled up Sickles' flank. They certainly bought time for

Brigadier General Samuel W. Crawford's Pennsylvania Reserves (3rd Division, V Corps) to make their successful counterattack.

No fighting occurred on the 4th of July, but neither was there any great Independence Day celebration. Men of the regiment were afforded the opportunity to find and bury their dead. While the armies licked their wounds, Meade and Lee decided on what to do next. Lee chose to depart. On the evening of July 5, the Army of the Potomac began the wary pursuit of Lee's army. The 11th Infantry marched toward Williamsport, Maryland, and arrived there on the 10th. En route to Williamsport, Major Floyd-Jones took sick leave on July 8 and turned over command, once again, to Captain Russell. As it turned out, however, he was never to return, and the regiment lost their beloved "old man." Floyd-Jones had been the man who was largely responsible for preparing the 11th U.S. Infantry for war. He had led it through its severest trials and tribulations, and he had become respected and admired by his troops. But in late August, he was directed to take over command of the regimental recruit depot at Fort Independence. In September, he was further promoted to the richly deserved rank of lieutenant colonel, but the promotion came with a transfer to the 18th Infantry. Concurrently, he was appointed to command the fortifications of Boston Harbor.[108]

At Williamsport, the regiment conducted picket duty until the 14th, when they resumed the march and continued south through Berlin, Manassas Gap, Richardstown, and Warrenton, where they arrived on July 27. During the month of July, the 11th Infantry had marched a total of 216 miles.[109]

The regiment performed picket duty near Warrenton until August 14. It was then marched to Bealeton Station and entrained for Alexandria, Virginia, where it remained until the 19th. While at Alexandria, Major General Henry W. Halleck wired Ayres to coordinate with the Quartermaster's Department for transports and embark his division "immediately" for travel to New York City. During the month of July, several severe riots had broken out over the calls for new drafts of men to support the war effort. The city was inadequately secured by an unreliable police force, which was too small and untrained to handle such large mobs. After a number of violent clashes with police and some New York militia cavalry on July 16, the mob was all but in control of the city.

After the initial problems with the rioters on the 16th, a handful of regulars from the 8th Infantry were called out from Fort Hamilton to help the local authorities. These men were casuals, but all were battle-seasoned veterans who had been wounded in scrapes in Virginia, and they had no sympathy for the draft dodgers and their sympathizers who now rioted in the streets. The 8th regulars were moved to 22nd Street to recover the body of a cavalry sergeant who had been brutally beaten to death by the mob. The bloody scene did not endear the rioters to the troops. As they attempted to recover the body, the mob moved in and shots rang out. Without hesitation, the com-

mander gave the order to fire, and a volley cut down a number of rioters. The troops were then given the command to fire at will, and the regulars began to drop men at a rapid pace. Still not satisfied, the commander had the troops fix bayonets and charge the mob. Anyone resisting arrest was skewered by the veterans. In the space of about two hours, hundreds of the rioters were killed and wounded by this small company of the 8th Infantry, and the rioting abruptly ended—not just that day but from that point on.[110]

Even though things became relatively calm, violence could have broken out again at any time due to the raw emotions engendered by the draft. The commander of the Eastern Department asked for more troops to help keep the peace and so Ayres' division was given the task. Boarding the steam transports *Daniel Webster* and *Mississippi*, the 11th Infantry sailed up the East Coast. The trip was uneventful, save for the number of seasick soldiers "heaving Jonah" over the rails due to the rolling of the ship. A traffic accident also occurred: on the 19th, an unladen schooner attempted to take a tack in front of the bow of the *Webster*. She did not make it, however, and the *Webster* rammed her amidships, sinking her in short order.[111]

The regiment disembarked on the 20th at the Port of New York on its first visit to a duty station with which it would later become very familiar in the 1920s and '30s. At the port, hundreds of curious New Yorkers gathered to watch these new troops disembark and move into the city. It was apparent to them that these men were hard-core veterans. The ragged uniforms and rough countenances on their deeply lined, dirty faces meant that these units were not to be trifled with. As the bullet-torn colors were unfurled, and the citizens read, "Second U.S. Infantry," "Seventh U.S. Infantry," "Eleventh U.S. Infantry," they instantly realized just how true that was. More regulars! The word spread rapidly through the city, and the town became almost placid. After tangling with one company of regulars on the 16th, nobody was about to tempt a whole division of these fellows.[112]

While at New York, the soldiers of the 11th made camp initially at Madison Square Garden, then moved to Jones' Woods near the bank of the East River at 71st Street. During their short stay in the city, the 11th Infantry, along with the other regular regiments, was given a complete new issue of uniforms and equipment. Their camps quickly became models of military discipline, as inspections, formations, guard mount, and evening parade were instituted. But all was not spit and polish and army garrison routine. The troops were also afforded several chances to go on pass into the city. The men of the 11th Infantry undoubtedly took these opportunities to pull out all the stops and enjoy themselves, for they knew it was only a matter of time before they were back in the fight. And so it was.[113]

On August 30, 1863, Major Jonathan W. Gordon arrived to join the regiment. Major Gordon had been the commander of the 2nd Battalion, the Regimental Recruiting Service, and the

Recruit Depot at Fort Independence after the 11th Infantry left in late 1861. Now, as the senior field officer from the regiment available for duty, he assumed command.[114]

While the 11th was in New York, the War Department decided to keep the most worn-out regiments of regulars out of battle until such time as they could be rebuilt by recruiting efforts. As a result, the Regular Division ceased to exist on September 11. The remaining regiments were reorganized into the 1st Brigade, 2nd Division, V Corps (the Regular Brigade) and now consisted of the 2nd, 3rd, 11th, 12th, 14th, and 17th U.S. Infantry Regiments.

After ensuring that New York would remain calm, the brigade, under the command of Colonel Burbank, departed New York on the 12th and moved to Amboy, New Jersey, by steamer, then back to Washington by rail. The regiment bivouacked at Camp Ellsworth, near Washington, until the 21st, then moved to Culpeper, Virginia, where it rejoined the 2nd Division, V Corps. With the exception of a division review for General Meade and Secretary of War Edward Stanton on September 28, the regiment performed guard duties the rest of the month.[115]

The following month, the regiment was involved in the Bristoe Campaign, otherwise known as the "Campaign of Maneuvers." On the morning of October 10, the men were issued eight days rations before moving out for Beverly Ford. Over the next ten days, they participated in a bewildering series of exhausting marches and countermarches between Culpeper, Beverly Ford, and Centreville, as Lee and Meade attempted to maneuver their armies to gain an advantage over one another. The 11th Infantry finally went into camp near New Baltimore on October 22 without engaging the enemy.[116]

The regiment pulled picket duty until November 5 when it moved to Three Mile Station in preparation for another fight. The V and VI Corps were directed by Meade to seize the ford on the Rappahannock River at Rappahannock Station on November 6, and on the following day, the 11th Infantry was involved in the general assault. Though some of the fighting was heavy, especially for the VI Corps, the regiment lost only one soldier killed and one wounded.

Having successfully forced the crossing, the V Corps went into camp near Kelly's Ford as Meade pondered the next move for the Army of the Potomac. He decided he would once again attempt to flank Lee's army by crossing the Rapidan. This time, however, instead of heading east toward Fredericksburg, his plan was to strike southwest into the heart of Virginia, forcing Lee to come out and fight him on unprepared ground. On November 26, the V Corps set out on their march, passed through Paoli Mills, and crossed the Rapidan at Culpeper Mine Ford about 10:30 a.m. Delayed at the ford because of problems with the crossings by the rest of the army at Germanna Ford, the corps resumed its march and went into camp at Wilderness Tavern that night.[117]

The following day, they reached Parker's Store and, after a minor scrape with Confederate skirmishers, went into positions near New Hope Church. On the 28th, there was a general advance along the line, and it was found that Lee's troops had vacated their positions. After moving some two miles west, the federals found the Army of Northern Virginia dug in on high ground manning the west bank of Mine Run. The remainder of the day and that night was spent reconnoitering the rebel positions and preparing for an assault on the 29th. But upon seeing the formidable defenses in front of the V and VI Corps, Meade delayed the attack and sent the II Corps to find the enemy's left flank. Gouverneur Warren, now commanding the V Corps, found what he believed to be a weakness in Lee's positions and reported it to Meade, who then sent out orders for the assault to begin the following day. However, upon closer examination the next morning, Warren decided that the position was much stronger than originally thought and the attack was canceled. Believing that Lee's position was impregnable, Meade ordered a withdrawal of the army to the vicinity of Rappahannock Station.[118]

Another futile effort to defeat Lee had ended. After another month of marching and high hopes, Lee had once again outmaneuvered the Army of the Potomac. Though the 11th Infantry was involved in several skirmishes near Mine Run, it suffered only one man wounded and two missing.[119]

The regiment moved to Catlett Station on December 2, then to Bealeton Station, Virginia. While at Bealeton Station, a soldier, Private John McMann, previously found guilty of desertion, was shot by firing squad. His is an interesting tale.

Private McMann took leave of the 11th Infantry on May 15, 1863, just after Chancellorsville when the regiment was camped at Aquia Creek. McMann was described as a "hard case," but "hard luck" might have been a more apt description. After deserting, he decided to re-enlist as a substitute and had the misfortune of being sent as a replacement directly back to B Company, 11th Infantry, his original unit. Upon his arrival on September 24, he was recognized immediately by Lieutenant Irwin B. Wright, who brought the charges of desertion on McMann. A court-martial was convened November 5, and that court found him guilty of desertion and sentenced him "to be shot to death by musketry." The sentence was directed to be carried out on Friday, December 18. Private Pettit described the incident:

An occurrence took place in this Division last Friday between the hours of 12 and 1 o'clock P.M. which you will no doubt read of in the newspapers. Viz: the shooting of John McMahn [sic] of our regiment (and of our old company) for desertion. The whole Division turned out under arms and were formed into a square to witness the execution. I was on guard and also on post at the hour and had not a fair sight at it for a few obstacles but it was quite near and I heard the volley. All the rest of the guard not on post were taken out to see the example.[120]

The regiment moved to Bristoe Station on December 27, where it camped on Kettle Run for the next five days. It was then ordered back to Alexandria on January 1 to perform rail guard duties for the winter. [121]

Major Gordon was placed on special duty with the War Department in January, and Captain Francis M. Cooley, the senior company commander, took command.[122] Because of the small size of their assigned regiments, the 1st Brigade (the regulars) and 3rd Brigade, 2nd Division were consolidated and became the 4th Brigade, 1st Division on March 23, 1864. This brigade now consisted of the 2nd, 11th, 12th, 14th, and 17th U.S. Infantry Regiments, two New York Zouave regiments, and two Pennsylvania regiments. The 4th Brigade moniker lasted only about a month before it was redesignated as the new 1st Brigade, and the regulars were now once again under Ayres' command.[123] The division was under the command of another Old Army regular, Brigadier General Charles Griffin, who, like Ayres, had originally been an artilleryman.

During its stay in Alexandria, the 11th Infantry was encamped in Sibley tents near the train station. The regiment was selected to replace a volunteer unit performing security duties for trains on the Alexandria and Orange Railroad from Alexandria to Culpeper. Along the route, a great number of thefts occurred on the trains, prompting the detail of units to deal with the problem. The thieves were identified by J. H. Devereaux, superintendent of the U. S. Military Railroads, as teamsters, soldiers, and even some of the guard units themselves. The guard units were replaced and a short time later Devereaux, in a letter to the quartermaster of the Army of the Potomac, stated, "There is no fault to be found with the present train guards, and the Eleventh U.S. Infantry are especially effective."[124] General Sykes also wrote that "Numerous statements have come to me that the railroad has never been better guarded than now." Perhaps the reason lay with General Sykes's directives in his Circular No. 4, dated January 18, 1864. In short, he said:

> The Orange and Alexandria Railroad is the means of supply for the Army of the Potomac. The supplies passing over it keep that army alive. The safety of the road, its material, and what it transports should be to the troops assigned for its protection a sacred duty....The commanding officers of the Eleventh U. S. Infantry and the Eighty-third Pennsylvania Volunteers will be held responsible that their officers and men perform their duty on the trains as soldiers. Sentinels on the cars and all along the railroad will be instructed to fire upon and kill, if possible, any and all persons attempting to steal property from the trains."[125]

To perform the train guard duties required fully one half of the regiment each day. The regiment was down to about 200 officers and men when it arrived at Alexandria, but by the time they departed, it had been strengthened to 345.[126] The 11th Infantry would need the extra men, for it was about to enter the period of the war where it would sustain its heaviest casualties. Relieved of its train security duties on April 29, the regiment moved to Bealeton Station that day, where it rejoined the V Corps to prepare for Lieutenant General Ulysses S. Grant's Overland Campaign.

The Wilderness
May 4-7, 1864

On May 1, the regiment marched to Brandy Station, and two days later joined the Army of the Potomac at Culpeper. From there, the V Corps led the army's advance south into the Wilderness in an attempt to force the Army of Northern Virginia into a decisive open-field battle. Crossing Germanna Ford on May 4, Griffin's 1st Division, marched to Wilderness Tavern and headed west on the Orange-Fredericksburg Turnpike to provide the army with a blocking force should Lee's troops attack from that direction. After advancing about a mile, Griffin stopped the division, while the remainder of the V Corps assembled in the fields about the tavern and went into camp. Ayres' brigade traveled slightly farther west on the pike, and threw up light breastworks and a picket line.

Early on the morning of May 5, Griffin was ordered to push the 1st Division west, still performing a blocking mission, while the rest of the V Corps moved on the road to Parker's Store on its way south out of the Wilderness. Griffin had two brigades parallel the turnpike through the dense woods on both sides of the road; Brigadier General Joseph J. Bartlett's brigade on the south and Ayres' brigade on the north. Forward of the struggling columns, the brigade commanders had deployed skirmishers, and it was they who first came upon Saunders' Field and detected the skirmish line of Major General Edward "Allegheny" Johnson's Division of the II Confederate Corps advancing east on the pike. Griffin's men began a brisk fire with the gray-clad men across the field, and soon the firing was general. Both sides halted and threw up breastworks. There, the regulars stood fast, waiting for word on what to do next.

Having received the report of the initial contact, Meade ordered Warren to attack down the turnpike about 7:00 a.m. to crush Ewell's forces. Griffin, after observing what appeared to be the Confederates' own preparations for an attack, recommended that the V Corps attack be delayed. Warren agreed and sent a courier to Meade. After some consultation on the matter, Warren was overruled by Meade and Grant, and the V Corps was ordered forward.[127] Ayres received the order and prepared the regulars to advance.

The "Regular Brigade," as it was now called, was not actually composed of just Regular Army units by this time. In addition to the regiments listed above, there were four volunteer units from the previously disbanded 3rd Brigade that were assigned to Ayres. These were the 140th and 146th New York

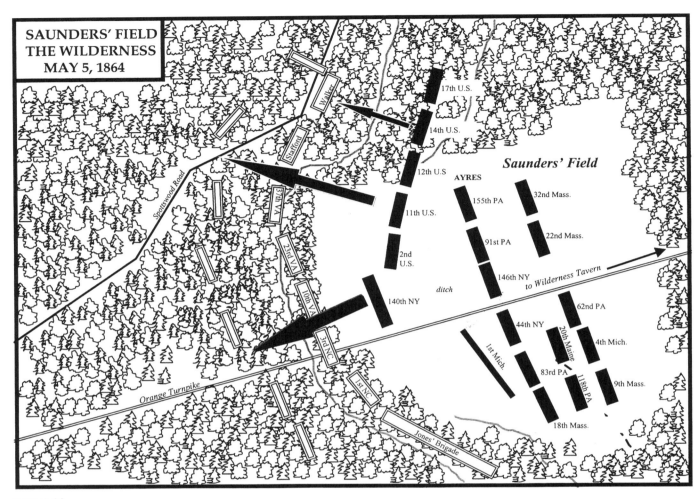

Map 1-10.

Volunteers, both Zouave units, and the 91st and 155th Pennsylvania Infantry Regiments. Like the regulars, these regiments had been whittled by combat down to about two hundred or fewer soldiers each. Because of their diminished numbers, all were lumped in with Ayres to give his command combat power that equaled something akin to an actual brigade of three full regiments.

The delays caused by the generals' discussions and message traffic caused the 1st Division's attack to be delayed until about 1:00 p.m. When the final decision came down, Ayres' command was formed along the wood line in two lines, with the regulars in the first line on the right and the 140th New York on the left. The second line was composed of the 155th Pennsylvania, the 91st Pennsylvania, and the 146th New York, right to left. With the turnpike forming the left boundary for the brigade, Ayres gave the command. On the right, the regulars advanced across Saunders' Field as if on parade:

And as the Second, Eleventh, Twelfth, Fourteenth, and Seventeenth regulars are advancing in the open field

under heavy fire, let me say that a steady orderly march like that is what calls for fine courage. It is easy, my friends, to break into a wild cheer, and at the top of your speed be carried along by excitement's perilous contagion even up to the enemy's works. But to march on and on in the face of withering musketry and canister, as the regulars are doing now…I say, that is a kind of courage which sets your heart abeating as your eye follows their fluttering colors.[128]

Steadily the units advanced against a hail of fire to their front until reaching mid-field, where the leading units had to negotiate a small streambed. As they stepped across, the New York Zouaves began to speed forward, just as the regulars began to receive fire from the right front. The early charge by the 140th New York, coupled with a slight drift to the right by the regulars in facing this new threat, caused a gap to appear between the two formations. Both groups launched into unsupported assaults that would have fateful effects.

The regulars advanced into the woods at the far side of the

field and initiated a bayonet charge that drove part of Brigadier General George H. Steuart's Virginians and the famous Stonewall Brigade out of their works and pushed them to the rear. Energized by their success, the regulars scrambled over the works and continued to a second defensive line. Here, the regulars drove into the retreating Virginians again, but things began to unravel. Coming up on the regulars' right flank were Louisiana troops of Brigadier General James A. Walker's brigade. A hand-to-hand melee broke out in which bayonets, clubs, fists, and other useful weapons were used freely. Meanwhile, on the south side of the pike, Bartlett's brigade had even greater success than Ayres' and had pushed deep into Major General Robert E. Rodes's Division; but to Bartlett's south the 2nd Division, V Corps, which had been supporting on the left had already been driven back. Griffin's entire 1st Division was now in great peril.

As had happened to the regulars at Chancellorsville, not ten miles away and a year before, closing in on both flanks of their division were not the two supporting Union divisions, but fresh brigades of rebels now intent on destroying it. Ayres' brigade formation had become dangerously ragged while struggling in the woods and its now unsupported flanks were quickly rolled up by the Confederate counterattack. The 11th and 12th Infantry Regiments had penetrated the deepest into the enemy lines and were now gravely at risk. They began fighting their way back to Saunders' Field in small groups, desperately forcing their way through the closing cul-de-sac. To further hamper their efforts, fires had broken out in the woods, which threatened to burn them to death if Johnson's men did not get them first.[129]

At the time of the Confederate counterattack, an incident occurred that caught the attention of Captain Cooley and several of the regiment's officers. As the fighting intensified, the fire threatened to burn to death soldiers too wounded to move out of harm's way:

A young English officer of the 11th, Lieutenant Wright Staples, had recently joined from staff duty still wearing a gray slouch hat, typical of nonregulation attire worn by staff officers. While endeavoring to stabilize his company, a soldier of the 12th mistook him for a rebel and shot him squarely in the back, mortally wounding him. Lieutenant John Patterson, of the same regiment [the 11th], passed his stricken compatriot on his way to the rear in what was rapidly becoming a stampede, when Staples hailed him for assistance. Flames were creeping toward the helpless man, prompting immediate aid from Patterson. Getting his hands under Staples' arms, he began to drag him out of danger, assisted by Sgts. John White and John Birmingham, both of the 11th. Together they carried him back through the tangle, laying him behind a breastwork for cover. [130]

What is not clear from the vignette above is that Patterson was able to accomplish this feat while under heavy fire from the pursuing Confederates. Although Patterson's efforts to rescue the young officer appeared successful, Staples died in his arms just after reaching the breastwork. For this heroic attempt to save a stricken fellow soldier, Lieutenant Patterson was later awarded the first Medal of Honor to be earned by a member of the regiment.

The trials of Ayres' brigade were not over. The men still had to cross back over Saunders' Field with the pursuing Confederates firing into their backs. Unlike Gettysburg, however, the officers had lost control of their units in the thick woods, so the men streamed across in clusters rather than in formation. Reaching the safety of the east side of the field, Ayres and the remaining leaders quickly rallied the men to prepare breastworks to repulse a Confederate counterattack that was sure to come; but the attack never transpired. Under orders from Lee not to become decisively engaged with the V Corps, Ewell ordered his men to entrench where they were to wait for Longstreet's I Corps to reinforce the army. Moving into positions with the brigade on the south side of the pike near where they had camped the night before, the 11th Infantry spent the remainder of the day digging entrenchments and preparing breastworks as the VI Corps came up on the 1st Division's right.

The following morning, at about 2:30 a.m., the 1st Division moved forward to the edge of Saunders' Field and entrenched at positions from where the division had advanced the day before. Now, however, Bartlett's brigade was on the north side of the pike and Brigadier General Jacob B. Sweitzer's 2nd Brigade held the south side. Ayres' brigade prepared positions behind Sweitzer. The 11th Infantry, once again, dug in and threw up breastworks to backstop the 2nd Brigade should the Confederates break through.

Farther south that morning, Hancock's II Corps was making a successful drive against A. P. Hill's III Corps. Just in time to prevent a disaster for Hill, Longstreet's I Corps surged up the Orange Plank Road and smashed into Hancock. Longstreet soon discovered a weakness in the Union left flank along an abandoned rail bed and moved units to exploit it. Brigadier General James Wadsworth's division had been detached from the V Corps to support Hancock's endeavor and Hancock quickly directed Wadsworth to plug the gap. Wadsworth personally went forward to direct his troops in blunting Longstreet's attack and was killed, but his attempt was rewarded, as the federals were able to hold the line.

Meanwhile, the 11th Infantry had spent the remainder of the early morning skirmishing with Ewell's troops and fighting forest fires started by the gunfire. Ayres pushed the 2nd, 12th, and 14th Regiments out about 10:00 a.m., while the 11th and 17th continued to reinforce the regulars' breastworks, as they expected a Confederate counterattack at any time.[131] In fact, a brief Union cannonade began near the regiment about 7:00 o'clock that morning to drive off what was thought to be the attack, but which turned out to be nothing more than an aggressive line of Confederate skirmishers. That brief incident was the last contact made by the regiment during the battle.

In the heavy fighting in the Wilderness, the regiment's casualties ran high: a total of sixty-six of their number were lost. The 11th lost two officers killed and two wounded; and nine enlisted killed, thirty-three wounded, and nineteen missing.[132] The tough battles ahead would further degrade the regiment's strength.

The 7th of May was spent further improving defenses, but the battle was essentially over. The two armies were getting nowhere, and the generals commanding looked to their maps for other possibilities. Grant and Lee both recognized that the crossroads at Spotsylvania Court House was a key conduit to Richmond. Whoever held it had a clear road to the Confederate capital, so Meade ordered Warren's V Corps to lead the army south along the Brock Road. The 11th Infantry departed their positions about 8:30 p.m. on May 7 and headed for Spotsylvania.

Spotsylvania Campaign
May 8-20, 1864

Trudging down the Brock Road in the inky blackness of the Wilderness, the men of the 11th Infantry moved like zombies. It was an aggravating march. The column moved accordion-like, but never stopped long enough for the men to lie down for rest. Sometime after midnight, they passed the crossroads at Todd's Tavern; then they inexplicably halted again. Forward of the V Corps, the Union cavalry of Brigadier General James H. Wilson was struggling to work through obstacles along the Brock Road emplaced by Fitzhugh Lee's rebel cavalry. Engineers worked to clear the obstacles, as detachments of cavalry were sent forward to reconnoiter the road. Just north of the Alsop Farm, Wilson's troopers found Lee's cavalry defending a line of breastworks across the road, which further impeded the federal advance.

Wilson could not budge the rebel cavalry and requested assistance from the V Corps infantry. About 7:00 a.m., Warren's lead division, the 2nd, led by Brigadier General John C. Robinson, advanced and pushed the rebel horsemen back, albeit slowly. At the Alsop Farm, the Brock Road split into two parallel lanes for about a half mile before rejoining near the Spindle House. Warren directed Robinson onto the eastern leg and Griffin's division onto the western leg, then continued the advance until a line of what was believed to be Confederate cavalry was detected on a rise called Laurel Hill, south of the Spindle farm. Warren ordered Robinson's division forward to take the hill on the east side of the Brock Road, then he returned to bring up the 1st Division. Finding Griffin, Warren directed him to attack along the west side of the road.

As Griffin's division deployed into Spindle's field before Laurel Hill, the lead elements assumed positions on the hill to receive the federal attack. Simultaneously, the remaining infantry of Major General Richard H. Anderson's I Corps (Longstreet had been wounded in the Wilderness) hurried south along Old Court House Road to reinforce the lead regiments. Warren, wisely, did not want the enemy to have time to strengthen his defenses, but in his haste, was about to launch an uncoordinated, two-division attack, believing that the works in front only held Confederate cavalry.

About 8:30 a.m., Bartlett's 3rd Brigade was brought on line first with its left flank bordering Old Court House Road. On the east of the road, Robinson's men were already moving forward to assault the rebel right flank. One of Robinson's brigades, the Maryland Brigade, advanced on the west side of the road in front of Griffin's division. In the meantime, Ayres' brigade began to form on Bartlett's right, but in the haste of the moment, the 3rd Brigade moved forward in the wake of the Marylanders before Ayres finished his formation. Sweitzer marched his 2nd Brigade to the right and formed on the regulars. By then, Griffin had given the order to assault the Confederate positions at Laurel Hill, and shortly thereafter, the charge went forward across the Spindle field.[133]

The Spindle field was then, and is now, a wide open pasture about five hundred yards square bordered by the Brock road on the east and woods on the other three sides. It has undulating ridges and drainage that cut across its length east to west. In some of the low areas, small stands of trees provide some concealment. As a body of troops approaches the south side of the field, it must expose itself to volleys of fire until dropping into the next swale, below the defenders' view. The low areas provide an attacker with cover until reaching the ridge upon which the Spindle farmhouse was situated. Once on that ridge, the defender has a clear field of fire of about 150 yards to stop a determined charge. At Laurel Hill, Anderson's men would consistently make the best of that killing zone over the next two weeks.

The regulars' attack that morning of May 8, at least to one observer, was "handsomely made, and, driving the Confederates, reached the burned [Spindle] house." While the regulars were en route to the Spindle House, the remnants of the Maryland and Bartlett's Brigades, their assaults broken, began streaming through Ayres' lines. One of the Maryland regiments had actually reached the rebel line and penetrated but could not hold, and was now driven back with heavy losses. To the east of the road, the rest of Robinson's division had also met with repulse, and he, himself, had been wounded. Reaching the Spindle House, the tired troops of the 11th Infantry and the other regulars began a brisk fire, firing from the reverse slope of the ridge. Griffin's command was now only 150 yards from the enemy trenchworks, but he realized that even if his men could carry them, they would be unable to hold them without any support on the right and left. Griffin ordered the division back to the tree line where his units had launched their attack and began to build breastworks.[134]

Warren fed his next two divisions into the fight about 10:15 a.m., and much like the attacks of 1st and 2nd Divisions, his was conducted piecemeal. And, like the attacks before, the

3rd and 4th Divisions were repulsed with heavy loss. By noon, Spindle's field was dotted with blue-uniformed bodies that lay blackened and bloating in the hot May sun.

Meade issued orders to renew the attack at 1:00 p.m., but because of the extended fighting in the Wilderness, the dusty all-night march along the Brock Road, and the unusually hot weather, the troops were exhausted. It took hours longer than usual to get the men ready for the assault. The V Corps finally attacked late in the afternoon, but the effort was half-hearted, and achieved little success before being stopped again. The corps then entrenched and generally improved its positions throughout the night and all day May 9, while Grant sent the II Corps across the Po River on the V Corps' right to try and flank Anderson's position on Laurel Hill. Ponderous movement on the part of II Corps allowed Lee to react quickly and Grant changed his mind about the flanking move. He now wanted to conduct a three-corps attack at 5:00 p.m. on May 10.

Earlier that day, Warren convinced Meade that an earlier attack by V Corps on Laurel Hill would likely succeed because Anderson had thinned his line to face Hancock's II Corps. Meade authorized the mission, and the V Corps was ordered to attack the Confederate lines in a frontal assault. As the 11th Infantry charged to the attack about 4:00 p.m., it quickly became apparent to all that Warren's assessment was in error. Some 1st

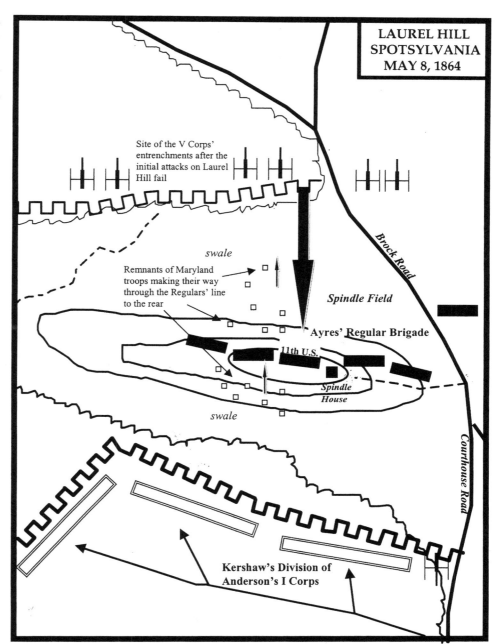

Map 1-11.

Division elements actually made it to the rebel works, but again the assault was made to no avail. Though the Union troops made progress and forced some rebel elements from their entrenchments, the well-planned Confederate fires gradually drove them out, and the bruised V Corps was forced back to its entrenchments. The 11th Infantry was particularly hard hit in this attack. Of some 230 remaining in the regiment, eighty-four were killed or wounded. One of the wounded was the able Captain William B. Lowe, commander of B Company.[135]

The 11th of May was spent by both armies recuperating and

jockeying for position. Early on the stormy morning of May 12, however, the 11th Infantry took part in a V Corps fixing attack at Laurel Hill against Anderson's I Corps, while Major General Winfield Scott Hancock's II Corps attacked the "Muleshoe" salient in the rainy, foggy, darkness. After the II Corps began its big assault that morning, the V Corps commenced supporting attacks at 9:15 a.m. to hold Anderson's men in place to prevent them from counterattacking Hancock's troops.

About 10:00 a.m., Griffin's 1st Division advanced over the same ground they had now twice traversed. The conditions could hardly have been worse. In a torrential downpour, the regulars could hardly make any headway as they slogged through the muddy, open field, under heavy fire from their front. Before reaching the Spindle House, they, and the rest of the 1st Division, were caught in a severe crossfire and driven back to their positions. But the II Corps attack was successful in retaining a portion of the Confederate line in the salient. The fighting was fierce and bloody all day long, and casualties were heavy, especially at the infamous "Bloody Angle." Eventually, the attack lost momentum, but Hancock's men heroically held on to much of what they had captured under the most horrific circumstances, weltering in mud, rain, blood, and gore.

During the day, Lee had directed the construction of a new line behind the Muleshoe, and the next morning about 3:00 a.m., the weary men of Ewell's II Corps slipped quietly away into the next line. The guns were more or less silent on May 13, both armies being exhausted from the fighting the day before. This was also true of the Regular Brigade. At this point, the 11th Infantry had dwindled to 139 officers and men. Replacements were not keeping up with the losses, and it was not clear how long the regiment could continue to fight under such circumstances.[136]

On the 13th, Meade ordered Warren's V Corps to march to the east and attack into the Army of Northern Virginia's right flank, where he believed Lee's defenses were weak. That evening, Ayres' brigade led the corps on a circuitous march to a position on the rebels' right flank. After another dreary all-night march in heavy rain, the regiment found itself only as far as the Fredericksburg Road by first light the following morning. The march had been made through broken terrain (there were no roads), mud, and flooded creeks that further taxed the tired troops. By the time the corps was concentrated on Lee's flank on the afternoon of the 14th, Meade determined it was too late and canceled the corps attack.

That afternoon, however, a sudden rebel attack forced Colonel Emory Upton's brigade out of a position that both sides had identified as a useful early-warning post. The sudden assault almost nabbed General Meade, who had been there visiting Upton's troops. Ayres' brigade was given the task of retaking the slight rise, and at about 7:00 p.m., the regulars counterattacked furiously in revenge for the losses suffered in their futile assaults the days before. Observing the action, Charles A. Dana, the assistant secretary of war, was impressed and reported to the secretary of war that "Ayres, with his brigade, very handsomely carried [the position] again."[137] The enemy realized their mistake and quickly vacated the area. Thus ended the 11th Infantry's combat actions around Spotsylvania. As in the Wilderness battle, the regiment's casualties were once again severe. Though only one officer was wounded, the enlisted men suffered seventeen killed, one hundred wounded, and ten missing. On the night of May 20, 1864, the V Corps began another march southward through Guiney's Station toward Richmond.[138]

Battle at North Anna River (Jericho Mill)
May 23-26, 1864

Warren's corps moved south, passing through Guiney's Station about 3:00 p.m. on the 21st. Upon crossing the Mattaponi River, it halted to hold the bridgehead against Confederate attack, thereby allowing the rest of the army to cross the next day. That night, the regulars camped at the Catlett farm, not half a mile from the Chandler House where "Stonewall" Jackson had died after his wounding in the Battle of Chancellorsville. About 10:00 a.m. on the 22nd, the V Corps pulled out of Guiney's Station and headed southwest through the junction at Madison's Ordinary, then turned west and marched to the Telegraph Road, where, once again, the corps headed south. Griffin stopped his division about 3:00 p.m. that day and encamped at Bullock's Church, near the home of Dr. Joseph Flippo, a close personal friend of Robert E. Lee. The march had been a relatively easy one, and the men settled down in a relaxed atmosphere. One soldier of the 140th New York wrote home: "Here things are jolly, bands of music play …all sufferings are forgotten for the moment."[139]

The next morning, Griffin's division took up the lead, with Sweitzer's brigade in the van, followed by Ayres' regulars, then Bartlett's brigade. The division reached Mount Carmel Church about 9:00 a.m. and halted for two hours, while Warren pondered where to cross the corps over the North Anna River. A runaway slave was brought to Warren and the man told the general that there was a ford up the river at Jericho Mill where the corps could cross infantry easily, but a bridge would have to be put in to cross artillery and the trains. Warren immediately dispatched Griffin to the ford and notified Meade and Grant.[140]

Grant was happy to hear of Warren's find, because it had now become apparent to him that Lee intended to defend the river along the Telegraph Road. Grant wanted the V Corps to seize the crossing, then drive southeast to force the Army of Northern Virginia away from the river, a move that would, in turn, allow the Army of the Potomac to cross unmolested. Grant ordered the II Corps to attack Chesterfield Bridge in order to would draw Lee's attention away from Jericho Mill.[141]

Jericho Ford sits between two relatively steep bluffs. On each side, the road enters and exits the ford paralleling the river as it climbs or descends the bluff. Because the north side of the bluff is somewhat higher than the south, it dominates the flat open pasturage on what was the Confederate side until the field reaches a tree line. When Griffin's men reached Jericho Ford on the North Anna River on the afternoon of May 23, they found the crossing undefended, and Griffin immediately ordered Sweitzer and Ayres to cross. To preserve the condition of their precious shoe leather, many men removed their brogans before wading the river. Lieutenant James P. Pratt of E Company described what followed:

> We crossed the North Anna yesterday afternoon. It was waist deep and very swift, with a rough bottom, and the

crossing was very difficult and slow, a squadron of cavalry dashed ahead of us. Our division was the first of the army across, and as soon as they reached the top of the high precipitous bank of the river, commenced a brisk fire. All out of breath, half the command barefoot, we formed and advanced a mile in splendid line, and then held the ground while other troops crossed.[142]

On the far side of the ford was a brigade of South Carolinians under the command of Colonel Joseph Brown. The brigade, from Major General Cadmus Wilcox's Division, A. P. Hill's III Corps, had been sent west to Noel's Station to cover the Confederate left flank and watch Jericho Ford. Pickets posted on the north side of the woods detected the federal troops as they crossed. They opened fire on the federals as they appeared over the edge of the bluff.

After moving through the ford and up to the plateau, Sweitzer threw out the 22nd Massachusetts as skirmishers and advanced his brigade to the far woodline, driving in the rebel pickets. Sweitzer then held in place as the regulars reached the open plain. There, they found Ayres shouting "Rally on the flag, boys!" and, machine-like, the regulars formed for battle, then drove into the rebel skirmishers on the left. Ayres threw out the 14th U.S. and 91st Pennsylvania, then both brigades advanced into the woods to their front. Moving to positions

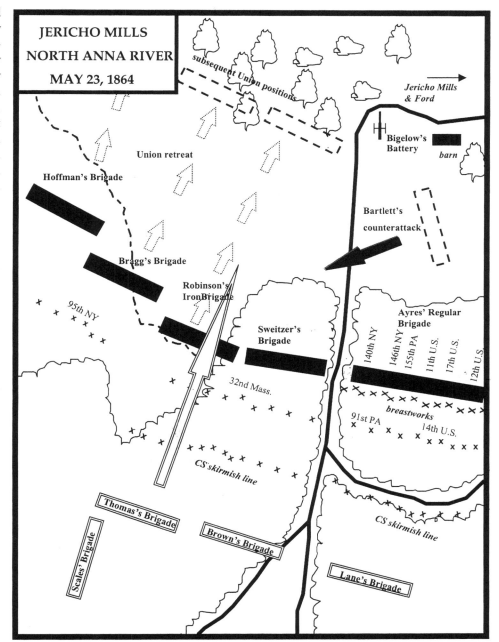

Map 1-12.

well into the stand of timber, the two brigades halted and immediately began chopping trees and digging entrenchments.[143]

As the regulars dug in, Bartlett's brigade went into position as a reserve behind Griffin, and two more V Corps divisions crossed over to the south side. The 3rd Division took up positions to the left of Ayres and completed the line to the river. The 4th Division, however, chose to remain down near the ford to cook their dinners. This left the Union right open,

which almost had disastrous consequences.

By 4:15 p.m., a 160-foot pontoon bridge was built, and artillery trundled across to the south side. The corps' three rifled cannon batteries were posted on the high ground on the north side of the river to overwatch the open plain. With artillery and infantry in position to hold the bridgehead, the V Corps prepared to cook dinner.[144]

As the V Corps settled into their new positions, Hill ordered the rest of Wilcox's Division to attack the federals at the ford. An erroneous report from Fitzhugh Lee's cavalry told Wilcox that the enemy force consisted of only two or three infantry brigades. In reality, Wilcox was unknowingly about to attack three federal divisions (about fifteen thousand men) with his six thousand troops. About 5:30 p.m., Union pickets reported heavy dust being kicked up on the road to Hanover Junction. Reports went to the rear, but no one seemed to be too excited about it. Warren, meanwhile, remained in his tent writing letters to his wife. Over in Ayres' area, the men of the 11th Infantry were in the process of cooking dinner. They were not going to miss an opportunity for a hot meal, because they did not know when they might enjoy another.

Suddenly, a great rebel yell pierced the evening air and gunfire exploded to the regulars' front. Peering to the far side of the wood, they could see a huge gray line heading right for them. The troops of Sweitzer's and Ayres' brigades, unstacked their weapons, leapt to their works, and commenced a heavy fire against Brown's South Carolinians and Brigadier General James H. Lane's North Carolinians. To the rear, Cutler's 4th Division scrambled to grab their rifles and set out to reach the high ground on the corps' right where it should have been all along. But as the division deployed to advance, the two brigades forming Wilcox's left wing crashed into the Pennsylvania Bucktails and the "Iron Brigade," driving them back toward the river. Many of these men broke and fled down the bluffs, heading for the pontoon bridge, and the onrush of refugees now hindered additional forces from reaching the south side to help.[145]

On the federal right, only one brigade held. Sweitzer's brigade also fell back, though in good order. Only Ayres now held in the center. The attack had interrupted the men's evening meal, which upset them in no small way. According to one account, the regulars, angry over their lost suppers, "waited until the Confederate line came within pointblank range and then opened fire with a vengeance."[146]

Back on the Union right, three batteries pulled into position amidst the shaken 4th Division. The presence of the artillery heartened the men, and soon many stragglers who had fled to the bluffs gathered their courage and returned to the fight. The 4th Division was now able to hold short of the ford. The actions of the artillery combined with a flank attack by Bartlett's brigade into the rebel left routed the two Confederate brigades facing the 4th Division. In front of the regulars, the line firmly held back the two Carolina brigades, both of which suffered heavily. According to John C. White of the 11th Infantry, "Our own steady and continuous vollies…created a slaughter, rarely to be seen." Having sustained heavy casualties in their own assaults at Saunders' Field and Laurel Hill, the regulars now had the grim satisfaction of dishing out the punishment for once. As the rebels retreated to Noel's Station, federal officers led a rousing cheer which echoed through the woods "in a tremendous roar of victory."[147]

Though the fighting was heavy, the 11th Infantry lost only three killed and seven wounded. The steadfast performance of the regiment earned the men of the 11th Infantry a note of congratulations in General Meade's order of the day.[148]

The following day, Warren found that Wilcox had disappeared from his front. So the V Corps continued its movement southeast until it came upon the new Confederate line extending southwest from Ox Ford across the Virginia Central Railroad to the South Anna River. Warren deployed his corps facing A. P. Hill's III Corps, with the 1st Division on the right of the line. The 11th Infantry occupied entrenchments and breastworks adjacent to Anderson's Station on the rail line, but only for the next couple of days.

The Army of the Potomac skirmished with Lee's troops through May 26, but Grant decided not to continue to attack the virtually impregnable rebel positions at the North Anna River. Instead, he ordered the army to move southeast once again and the 11th Infantry finished this march very near Mechanicsville, where it had fought its first battle two years before.

Cold Harbor (Bethesda Church)
May 30-June 6, 1864

Along with the 1st Division, the 11th Infantry led the V Corps on its march toward Hanovertown. The regiment crossed the Pamunkey River there on May 28 and continued the advance toward Mechanicsville. It crossed Totopotomy Creek on the 29th, and encamped near the Via house that evening. As part of a general reconnaissance by the 1st Division on the 30th, Ayres' brigade moved west on the Shady Grove Church Road behind Sweitzer. About 3:00 p.m., Sweitzer's brigade encountered skirmishers from Major General George E. Pickett's Division of Anderson's I Corps. Pushing the rebels back, Sweitzer's men continued forward until reaching a clearing where they were brought under fire from artillery near Hundley's Corner. Sweitzer had found the Confederate main line.[149]

Griffin deployed his brigades along the Shady Grove Road, with Bartlett to the north of Sweitzer, and Ayres refused his line back to the east to tie in with Crawford's 3rd Division. Meanwhile, Crawford sent a brigade to reconnoiter south along the Walnut Grove Road to its intersection with the Old Church Road. Just as it reached the intersection, it was struck by Rodes's division charging up the Old Church Road in an attempt to find the V Corps left flank. The federal brigade was quickly routed and flew headlong up the road toward Beaver Dam Creek. Upon seeing the fleeing brigade, Colonel Charles Wainwright, chief of the V Corps artillery, sped away to find his batteries and bring them forward to bolster the line.[150]

Rodes's division continued northeast up the Old Church Road while, Major General Stephen D. Ramseur's Division swung north and headed for Crawford's line. The switch in attacking forces gave Crawford time to pull his brigades north of Beaver Dam Creek and form a battle line. Additionally, Wainwright arrived with three batteries which he placed into position near the Bowles house. Soon, Ramseur's men attacked the patchwork line.

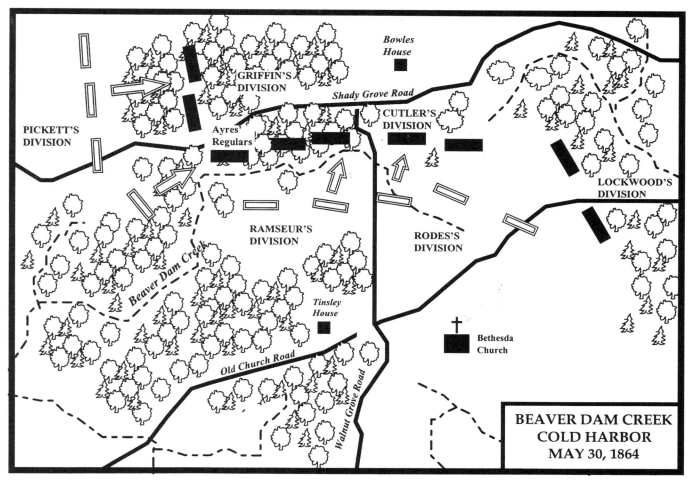

Map 1-13.

As Crawford's men received the brunt of the attack, Ayres' troops were able to provide supporting fires to their left front. The combined efforts of Ayres, Griffin, and Wainwright's artillery held Ramseur in check. Along the Old Church Road, the 2nd Division stifled Rodes's attack in that direction. About 6:00 p.m., Early renewed the attack against the V Corps with Gordon's Division, which had just arrived on the field. Ramseur pushed forward again, but by then, Crawford and Griffin's troops had had time to improve their works. The federal fire was incredibly destructive. Caught in the cross-fire of artillery, Crawford's infantry, and Ayres' regulars, the Confederate attack melted away. One of Ramseur's brigades lost three hundred of five hundred men engaged.[151]

Over the next two days, most of the fighting in the Cold Harbor area occurred south of Bethesda Church. As the Army of the Potomac shifted south, the V Corps shifted slightly also. The 1st of June found the corps in positions centered on the Old Church Road about a half mile west of Bethesda Church. To the north, Hancock's II Corps was directed by Meade to march south to participate in a three-corps attack to be conducted on June 2. The night of June 1, Hancock pulled out, but

Major General Ambrose E. Burnside did not get word that the II Corps was leaving the army's right flank until the following morning. Therefore, Burnside's IX Corps would have to perform a daylight withdrawal to refuse the army's right flank for protection. Early was looking for just such an opportunity and was quick to order an assault against the IX Corps when he realized it was pulling back late on the morning of June 2.

About 1:00 p.m., Warren observed dust clouds to his northeast and accurately guessed that Early was about to launch into the retreating IX Corps. Taking a great deal of risk, Griffin shifted his division to help fill the gap between him and the flank of Burnside's left-most brigade. The move now created another dangerous gap between the regulars and Bartlett's brigade to the northeast. About 2:00 p.m., covered by a driving thunderstorm, Early's entire corps fell on the hapless IX Corps and Griffin's division. Gordon's Division drove headlong into the gap between Ayres' and Bartlett's brigades. Supporting Gordon to the west, Ramseur's Division pushed toward the regulars down the Old Church Road. Soon, the line became a swirling battleground as friend and foe commingled in a desperate struggle.

The position had become untenable, and the order was given to fall back to a new line near Bethesda Church. On Ayres' right, Gordon's troops were successful in capturing a fairly sizable chunk of the 91st Pennsylvania. The 11th Infantry did not go unscathed either. In the confusion of the fight many men did not get the order to fall back, and dozens (mostly of F Company) were captured. As Ayres' men withdrew, the brigade on his left and Bartlett's brigade fell back as well, and the line was finally solidified virtually on the grounds of the church. By the time that Griffin organized the new position, Early's men had had enough and the attack dissipated.[152]

Though the 11th suffered only one officer and six enlisted wounded at Bethesda Church, forty-three men were listed as missing and were later determined to have been captured during the fight that day. Among the captured was Private Ira S. Pettit, who was shipped to Andersonville Prison in Georgia. Unlike Fort Independence, Andersonville was not a "delightful place" and Pettit died there of tuberculosis the following October.[153]

The regiment constructed breastworks at Bethesda Church and remained in this position until June 6, after which they marched six miles and camped near Allen's Mill. On the 11th, the regiment again took up the line of march. This time it would take them to Petersburg.

Petersburg Campaign
June 15-October 30, 1864
Crossing the Chickahominy River on June 12 at Long Bridge, the regiment turned west with the V Corps and moved to a blocking position near Riddell's Shop until the remainder of the army was across the river. Closing with the army, the corps camped near Charles City Court House on the 13th. The night of June 16, the 11th Infantry crossed the James River on transports and arrived in front of Petersburg at daybreak on the 17th.[154]

The 18th of June witnessed the first attack of the 11th Infantry at Petersburg, this time against the veterans of General P. G. T. Beauregard. The attack jumped off at 4:00 a.m. and made surprising progress. Surprising that is, in that Beauregard had repositioned his troops about a mile closer to Petersburg under the cover of darkness the night before. Upon arrival at the empty Confederate trench line, commanders set to work preparing for the next advance to the new rebel positions. The chore took too much time, and Beauregard was reinforced in the meantime by the arrival of A. P. Hill's corps. The Union attack that afternoon was poorly coordinated and beaten back with heavy losses. The 11th Infantry was ordered to prepare entrenchments that night, and occupied a position southeast of Petersburg between the Jerusalem Plank Road and the Norfolk and Petersburg Railroad until June 28, when the regiment was relieved and moved into a camp on the Avery Farm, about a mile to the rear.[155] During the month, the Regular Brigade was transferred back to the 2nd Division, when Ayres was promoted to command that formation.

Battle of the Crater
July 30, 1864
The 11th Infantry remained on the Avery Farm during July and improved their new entrenchments. On July 29, they were moved forward to support the IX Corps in a unique attack scheduled for July 30. The 48th Pennsylvania Veteran Volunteers, a unit composed primarily of coal miners, burrowed under the rebel lines and set off several tons of explosives, blasting a five hundred-foot gap in the enemy defenses. Because of several poor decisions and poorer execution, the IX Corps botched a golden opportunity to successfully seize Petersburg. The regiment, along with the rest of Ayres' 2nd Division, was positioned in a railroad cut as a reserve, ready to support the IX Corps. Ayres, watching the operation with intense interest, and noting that the attacking force was bogging down, requested Grant to let his division secure the gap, confident the regulars could do the job. But the commanding general declined, saying, "It is too late," and the regulars were not committed to the fight. The regiment returned to its camp that night.[156]

During the early part of August, the regiment once again went through the process of rebuilding, although the final results were less than satisfactory. It received a mixed reinforcement of draftees and volunteers that increased the regimental strength, but only to 206 officers and men. Many of the draftees were the dregs and malcontents of the type who had rioted in New York City the previous fall. In short, they were not the caliber of men who had originally volunteered to enlist in the 11th Infantry. But, with the time they had available, the regimental NCOs instituted the merciless discipline and indoctrination that the regulars were noted for. Through such techniques, the sergeants worked to bring the new men up to the standards expected of regulars. They would need it, for the next battles would severely test them.[157]

Battle of Weldon Railroad
August 18-21, 1864
Two weeks later, the regiment, now temporarily commanded by Captain Joshua S. Fletcher Jr., was dispatched with the V Corps on a mission to seize a portion of the Weldon and Petersburg Railroad south of Petersburg near Globe Tavern. The intent was to cut off that supply route into Petersburg from the rest of the South. Early on August 18, the Regular Brigade (now under the command of Colonel Joseph Hayes, formerly of the 18th Massachusetts) advanced toward the railroad. Trudging five miles west on poor trails and through hot, steamy woods, the brigade struck the line about 10:00 a.m. at Globe Tavern, also called the "Yellow House" because of its bright color. Startled by the huge column of federals emerging from the woods, the few Confederate pickets who guarded that portion of the line bolted to the rear.[158]

As the 1st Division began ripping up the rails, Ayres' 2nd Division took up hasty defenses about five hundred yards north

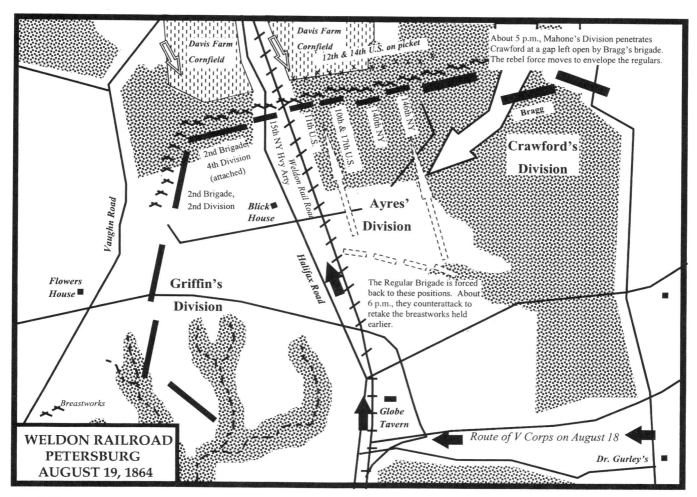

Map 1-14.

of the tavern, straddling the railroad with the Regular Brigade on the right, the 15th New York Heavy Artillery and the 3rd Brigade on the left, and the 2nd Brigade on the far left, connected to elements of the 1st Division. The 11th Infantry's left was the railroad embankment, and the remaining twenty-five men of the diminutive 10th Infantry were on the regiment's right. The remainder of the regulars was posted to the east of the 10th Infantry. About noon, skirmishers from the 140th New York and the 12th U.S. went forward (followed by the Regular Brigade in battle line), advanced about three quarters of a mile through an open field, then disappeared into a wood and dense undergrowth north of the tavern. The sharp crackling of a firefight began to build in front of the brigade as the skirmishers bumped into the pickets of Confederate forces in the vicinity of the Davis Farm. Moving at the double-quick, the regulars arrived on the far side of the wood where the brigade held in place.[159]

As anticipated, the enemy reappeared in force and formed up in two lines before the regulars, as rebel artillery wheeled into place and opened a preparatory fire for the counterattack.

They were troops of Harry Heth's division, and they charged through the Davis cornfield, successfully forcing the retirement of the 12th U.S. and 140th New York back to the safety of the 146th New York's battle line. Captain Fletcher ordered the 11th Infantry forward and, supported by the 5th New York, the two regiments poured a heavy volume of fire into Heth's flank, forcing his troops to retreat back through the cornfield with heavy losses.[160]

To ensure that the rebels could not rebuild the road, the regiment remained in position near the Davis farm, guarding the line and building breastworks during the night of August 18-19. After spending most of the 19th ripping up rails and improving defenses, the V Corps was attacked about 4:15 p.m. by Brigadier General William Mahone's division. Locating a gap in the federal line, Mahone's Virginians swept through and bypassed the Pennsylvania Reserve Brigade of Crawford's 3rd Division, now posted to the right of the Regular Brigade. In the ensuing attempt to fall back, friendly units masked the fire of those to the rear, causing much confusion, and the 1st Brigade was forced to withdraw by the press of the onrushing rebels. In the history of the V Corps, the writer described the resulting scene: "The 10th, 11th, 12th, 14th, and 17th regiments of regulars, which were posted in the front line of works on the right of the railroad, were rapidly enveloped, and many of the regiments, especially the 12th and 14th, were forced to fight their way through, losing by this means heavily in prisoners."[161] Of the action, Captain Fletcher explained that the regiment was located

> in nearly the same [positions] as on August 18, 1864, when we were again attacked by a heavy force, and the troops some distance on our right were driven back, we were again flanked and compelled to fall back to the left and rear, where the regiment reformed and advanced to retake the ground lost, we advanced through the woods in our front, on the east side of the Railroad and remained at the north edge of the woods until relieved by other troops at about 10:00 P.M.; the regiment then fell back to the positions they had occupied in the morning, and remained until August 20, 1864.[162]

Fletcher's description of the action is somewhat sanitized, as he failed to mention the desperate fighting his men had to do just to survive. Having flanked and overrun the Pennsylvania Reserves, Mahone's men now swept toward the railroad in an attempt to get behind the 1st Brigade's battle line. Another version of the actions of Fletcher and the 11th adds details:

> Captain Fletcher held the 11th steady, insofar as he was able, surrounded as he was, until the guns opened up on friend and foe alike, tearing crimson lanes through the screaming crowd. Up on the line, canister rattled against the barricades, pitilessly mowing down many of the 11th who stood by their colors planted on the works. Dozens were already being led away as prisoners toward the Davis Farm, while rebels groped through the smoke in search of other victims.[163]

Hayes was captured attempting to reach the brigade line, so command of the Regular Brigade devolved to Colonel Frederick Winthrop of the 5th New York. To save the brigade, Winthrop ordered the commanders of the 12th and 14th U.S. to hold the breastworks while the remainder of the brigade fought its way to the rear. The 187th Pennsylvania was ordered forward to save the regiments at the barricades, but their valiant effort went largely for naught, as the two forward regular units had all but evaporated by the time the 187th reached them, most of their troops having been killed or captured. Fletcher was able to fight his way back with the other regiments, rallied his men and, with a rush, counterattacked into the now disorganized Virginians, driving them out of their hard-won position.[164]

Though all regular regiments fought with extreme valor that day, the 11th U.S. seems to be the one unit that held the rest of the 1st Brigade together as a fighting force, such as they were able to manage in the melee. Colonel Francis Winthrop, in his report of the action that day singled out the acting regimental commander of the 11th Infantry: "While awarding great praise to every one of my regimental commanders, I cannot but mention the name of Captain J. S. Fletcher, commanding the 11th Infantry, for the skill and calmness with which he maneuvered his regiment, although for a long time the only officer remaining with it."[165]

General Hill's troops returned for a more determined effort on the 21st but only attained lesser results. The Confederates assembled a strong assault force that made several desperate attacks on the regiment to dislodge them from their positions. The 11th had made good use of their time by building breastworks while guarding the railroad and, as a result, they were able to drive the rebels back each time, though losing several more men to heavy cannon fire. The operations to take the Weldon Railroad had succeeded, but only at great cost to the Regular Brigade. In addition to the loss of its commander, the brigade lost 480 men of the 916 who entered the contest. The regiment alone lost six killed, thirty-two wounded, and fifty-one missing of the 206 who participated, a 43 percent casualty rate.[166]

The casualties sustained by the 11th Infantry since the 1864 campaign began had been extreme. Since the fighting in the Wilderness, it had dwindled to only seven officers and 133 men in spite of the new arrivals in early August. To replace some of the losses, Company H, 2nd Battalion, arrived from Fort Independence in late August under the command of Captain James M. Cutts. Cutts had been wounded during the June 18 attack on Petersburg and had apparently been sent back to Fort Independence upon recovery to bring this new unit down to join the regiment. For his actions in leading his troops through the Wilderness, at Spotsylvania, and during the Petersburg Campaign, Cutts would later become the regiment's second Medal of Honor winner. The arrival of Cutts's Company H brought the regiment back up to just over two hundred officers and men for the next round of battles.[167]

Poplar Springs Church (Peeble's and Pegram's Farms) September 30-October 1, 1864

Throughout September, the 11th Infantry continued to improve its defenses and guard the railroad, but late in the month they were ordered to move forward as part of a general corps advance. The regiment participated in several sharp actions near Poplar Springs Church, assisting in General Warren's effort to punch a hole in the Confederate lines and cut Boydton Plank Road, another key rebel supply route into Petersburg and Richmond. On September 30, the 1st Brigade participated in the 2nd Division attacks on the Confederate entrenchments around Peeble's Farm. The brigade was directed to advance from near Fort Wadsworth, northwest along the Poplar Springs Road, then northeast on the Squirrel Level Road, where it linked up with the 3rd Brigade, 1st Division. There, the regulars relieved the 3rd Brigade of possession of Fort Bratton, recently vacated by the 4th North Carolina Cavalry.[168]

Captain Cooley selected positions to the west of the fort supporting the 15th New York Heavy Artillery. The 5th and 146th New York Regiments were in Fort Bratton itself, the 14th U. S. Infantry to the east of the fort, and the 17th U. S. and 140th New York were held in reserve.[169] About 9:00 o'clock the following morning, their nemeses from the initial Weldon fight, Harry Heth's North Carolinians, attacked in pouring rain in an attempt to retake the fort but were severely mauled by the heavy fire from the regulars and New York infantrymen. The Tarheels were followed by Brigadier General James J. Archer's Virginians, then by Brigadier General Joseph R. Davis's Mississippians, in piecemeal attacks that were also beaten back with severe losses. General Heth soberly declined to attempt further assaults against the position.[170] The 1st Brigade's endeavors at Fort Bratton ensured that the Union positions won at Peeble's Farm the day before remained secure and were integrated into the federal lines.

Battle at Hatcher's Run (Boydton Plank Road) October 27-29, 1864

After the actions at Fort Bratton, the regiment returned to the vicinity of Globe Tavern. From October 4th to the 27th, the regiment remained in their old barricades by Weldon Railroad building strength. Early on the 28th, the Regular Brigade advanced to the salient won at Poplar Springs Church to participate in the attack to cut the Southside Railroad. Grant wanted to seize the line to prevent supplies from getting into Petersburg and Richmond.

In what was to be the last real combat action for the 11th Infantry in the Civil War, Captain Cooley advanced the regiment as far as Hatcher's Run, moving into positions to support the main attack. By this time, however, the regiment, as well as the rest of the Regular Brigade, had ceased to be a unit capable of heavy fighting. Few of the old soldiers from the early days remained. Most men were draftees who were not of the fighting caliber of their predecessors. As a result, the regulars were essentially spectators in this last action and suffered no casualties. At Hatcher's Run, the 11th Infantry was in a supporting role and mostly watched as the troops of the II Corps conducted the main effort. A few rounds were fired as their active field service as a combat unit sputtered to a close. The 11th Infantry remained at that position until it was pulled out of the line with the remainder of the Regular Brigade and relieved from assignment to the Army of the Potomac on November 1, 1864.[171]

The regiment was ordered to report to Major General Benjamin F. Butler, commander of the District of New York, for duty suppressing disturbances that might occur as a result of the presidential elections that month. The regiment moved to City Point and, on November 3, embarked on the *Admiral DuPont*, a captured blockade runner. The *DuPont* sailed that day and arrived at New York Harbor the next. The troops remained on board until the 6th, when they disembarked and proceeded to Fort Hamilton for billeting. After a short period of pulling guard duties at polling places, resting, and receiving recruits from Fort Independence, Cooley received a warning order to move again.[172]

On November 18, Major General John A. Dix, commander of the Department of the East, received a request from Grant to spare a regiment of regulars to report for special duties to Major General Lew Wallace, commanding the Middle Department. Dix replied that the 8th and 11th Regiments, now consisting of a total of six hundred men, were about to embark, and that he would provide them orders to report to Wallace. The two regiments were sent by steamer to Baltimore, and marched from there to Annapolis, Maryland, where they arrived on December 5. At Camp Parole, the 11th Infantry was assigned to the Infantry Brigade, VIII Corps, commanded by Colonel Adrian Root. Company C was detached for service with the District of the Eastern Shore for a short period for special duties.[173]

The regiment was at Annapolis for only five days when Lieutenant Colonel T. S. Bowers (Grant's adjutant general) wired General Wallace requesting that a regiment of regulars be made ready for immediate duty at Grant's headquarters at City Point, Virginia. Wallace replied that he could have one ready in forty-eight hours. Wallace selected the 11th Infantry and had his adjutant notify Colonel Root to prepare the regiment for movement. In his telegram to Colonel Root, Wallace's adjutant stressed that the request was direct from Grant and that Root's quartermaster should make immediate arrangements for the transportation of the 11th. Despite the urgency of the message, the regiment inexplicably remained at Camp Parole through December and into late January. Finally, on January 27, the 11th Infantry was transferred to City Point, Virginia, and assigned to perform guard duties for Grant's headquarters and other duties to include guarding secret dispatches on the mail boats from City Point to Washington, D.C.[174]

In early March 1865, a new commander took charge of the regiment. Captain Alfred E. Latimer assumed field command of the 11th from Captain Cooley, who had led the regiment through the bitter last days of their participation in Grant's campaigns through Virginia. Latimer, West Point class of 1853, had been at Fort Independence as commander of the recruit depot and superintendent of the Regimental Recruiting Service after Major Floyd-Jones was placed in command of Boston's harbor defenses. He would command the regiment for the next six months.[175]

On March 16, General Meade wired Grant to request the return of the 11th Infantry to the Army of the Potomac. Meade stated that he needed the regiment for provost duties and to form a part of his reserve for what would prove to be the last battles of the war. Grant approved the request and, on March 18, Captain Latimer reported for duty to Brigadier General George N. Macy, the provost marshal for the Army of the Potomac.[176]

On March 25, sometime before 5:00 a.m., Captain Latimer was notified to move the regiment to the vicinity of the IX Corps. Heavy firing was coming from that direction and the 11th Infantry and the 3rd Pennsylvania Cavalry were to position themselves to be able to help control a breakthrough or, potentially, participate in a counterattack. What had caused the commotion was the seizure of Fort Stedman by Major General John B. Gordon's division. Latimer moved the 11th forward to support the effort to retake the fort, but it was recaptured by the time the regiment arrived. In the afternoon, as the regiment was preparing to resume its provost duties, Generals Grant and Meade escorted a visitor about the field of battle. It was the president, and the 11th Infantry was turned out to honor him. Few of the men who had been present the last time the regiment paraded for Lincoln at Fredericksburg remained in the ranks now. After the formation, Latimer took charge of eighty-five officers and 2,005 rebel troops captured when Fort Stedman was retaken, and escorted them back to City Point, where they were handed over to another provost regiment.[177]

On March 29, the regiment departed City Point to follow the army's westward swing around the right flank of the Petersburg defenses. The regiment's mission was to guard the army's supply train and to continue escorting prisoners to the holding pens at City Point. That night, Latimer bivouacked the regiment at Perkin's House and departed at 1:00 p.m. the following day in a cold spring downpour. Two days later, the regiment was with the trains near Dinwiddie Court House, still cold, wet, and muddy. On April 2, they moved through Dabney's Mills and camped at the Cummings House that evening.

About 10:00 p.m., a fierce struggle began for possession of the Southside Railroad, Petersburg's last conduit for supplies from the rest of the Confederacy. By 11:00 a.m. the following day, the line was cut. The Army of Northern Virginia had to abandon Petersburg and Richmond, or they would simply be starved out in a couple weeks at most. The Union forces succeeded in capturing over five thousand prisoners in the battle, and the regiment started back with them for City Point that day. Upon arrival, the prisoners were put aboard boats for shipment north.[178]

With the exception of a short period guarding the army's wagon trains near Jetersville, Virginia, the regiment remained at City Point with the 14th Infantry until April 8. Two days earlier, Lieutenant Colonel T. S. Bowers had queried Grant whether to return the two regiments to Meade's control and was initially directed to have them report to Meade. However, the following morning, Grant countermanded the order and directed them to move by rail to Petersburg, and from there to Burkeville, Virginia, where Grant's headquarters was located.[179] Grant knew that the war was all but over, and he wanted to have as many of the regular units as was possible present for the final act.

On April 8, Latimer received orders to proceed to Grant's headquarters as soon as possible. His men entrained at City Point at 3:00 p.m. that afternoon and proceeded through Petersburg, arriving at Sutherland Station at 8 o'clock that evening. It was as far as they could go because the train's conductor feared that the line ahead was not safe for travel at night. The next day, as Grant and Lee were meeting at the McLean House at Appomattox Court House, the regiment's train was moving toward Wilson Station, where the regiment remained that night. On the 10th, the regiment began marching to Appomattox, arriving there on the morning of April 12, in time to witness the Army of Northern Virginia surrender arms and colors. Appropriately, the men of the 11th Infantry were able to participate in this historic conclusion of four long years of bitter struggle.[180]

The regiment remained in the Appomattox area supervising the destruction of the surrendered equipment and the signing of the required parole papers by the ex-Confederate soldiers. A short time later, the regiment was returned to the control of the Army of the Potomac provost marshal and then, in turn, transferred to a cantonment (soon to be named "Camp Grant") in Richmond, Virginia, where it arrived on May 6. There, it would remain for the next five years, performing guard and general occupation duties in connection with Reconstruction.[181]

During the war, the 11th Infantry had built an impressive record. Along with the other Regular Army regiments in the Army of the Potomac, the 11th Infantry had marched untold miles, fought in eight major campaigns and numerous other battles and skirmishes, helped save the Army of the Potomac from disaster on several occasions, and had successfully performed virtually every task it was assigned. Only when other units failed to come up on the flanks, or otherwise properly support the regulars, was it ever driven back. Its sacrifices were largely unknown by the public and rarely covered by newspaper reporters, who preferred to cover the "glorious exploits" of their respective state volunteers. A Boston reporter happened to chance upon the diminished brigade of regulars shortly after the battles around Bethesda Church, and after hearing their story related by not only the regulars themselves but corroborated by their loyal volunteer brethren from the 2nd Division (who, by then, were regulars themselves in all but name), he captured the essence of the regulars' efforts during the fierce battles of the Wilderness, Spotsylvania, and Cold Harbor—and in many ways their performance during the entire war:

> Ayres' regulars lost in one-half hour one-fourth of their number—a stern initiation to a campaign which 80 days have not ended....At Spotsylvania...again the regulars and their companion regiments are put into the thickest and again acquit themselves as the bravest, and again are more than decimated....At Cold Harbor...proportionate loss, which fell again most heavily upon Ayres' brigade—indeed the losses in this brigade have been exceptionally severe in nearly every engagement. Since Cold Harbor the brigade had borne its share of the marching and fighting.

Its losses since the 5th of May now amount to something over 2,000 including over 70 officers—2,000 from one brigade in one campaign! Had all the army suffered as severely, the entire loss would be fully double what it is....

Such then, is an adequate sketch of the services, the battles and losses of one brigade. I do not hold it up as unparalleled; on the contrary, it is but one of many, between whom no distinctions may be made. But I have thought it worthwhile to note the deeds of these regulars, not for the sake of the officers, but that of the rank and file, who, not accredited to any particular State, have lost, perhaps, something of the recognition due them....In no soldierly quality has there been a shade of difference, fighting side by side as they have been, between regular and volunteer. After three years of such war, who shall claim better training, more veteran skill, than those who responded to its first blast and have not faltered until this day?

At present, the brigade,—remember its style, First Brigade, Second Division, V Corps, when you come to read accounts of succeeding battles,—like most of the army, is in that admirable condition best described by one word, *effective*.[182]

The price of victory was high for the men of the 11th Infantry. Combat cost the lives of eight officers and 117 enlisted men. The regiment suffered over 350 officers and men wounded in action and an additional 158 were listed as missing or captured. An additional two officers and eighty-six enlisted men died from disease.[183] The regiment compiled one of the highest casualty rates in the Union Army, presaging a recurring pattern in the wartime experiences of the 16th Infantry. Regardless of the numerical designator, "11th" or "16th," this regiment would usually be in the thickest of fighting.

Over the next twelve years, the 1st Battalion, 11th Infantry, would undergo two major reorganizations that would ultimately result in its redesignation in 1869 as the 16th Infantry. The regiment would also participate in the onerous duties of occupation forces throughout the South during the Reconstruction era. Their experiences during Reconstruction would try the leaders and soldiers of the regiment in ways that, at times, seemed more difficult than facing the rifles of their recently defeated foe.

Officers' Row at Fort Concho, Texas, c. 1885

Chapter Two
Reconstruction, Reorganization, and Redesignation

These troops in Nashville...have conducted themselves in such a manner that the prejudices engendered by the war have been entirely dispelled.
Nashville Republican Banner, April 20, 1875

The great conflict concluded between the North and South in April 1865 transitioned into a period of friction and strife that still affects the United States in many ways. The 11th Infantry participated in several key events of the period that illustrate the difficulties encountered in trying to perform the essentially nonmilitary functions expected of the army in the South during a period of shrinking budgets and downsizing.

The Congress's desire to shift money to other programs by demobilizing the huge Civil War army into a smaller, but still effective, military force resulted in two major reorganizations of the Regular Army during the Reconstruction period. The second of these reorganizations resulted in the 11th Infantry receiving its present designation as the 16th Infantry. The reorganization also resulted in a much smaller postwar regular force than originally envisioned, and made the missions assigned to the army virtually impossible to fully carry out.

From a peak strength of about fifty-seven thousand in 1867, the army dwindled to a force of about twenty-six thousand and remained at that level until the Spanish-American War.[1]

But in May 1865, the great Union Armies had not yet felt the budgeteer's ax. To celebrate their victory of arms over the Confederacy, the Army of the Potomac and the armies of the Western Theater paraded for two days down the streets of Washington. The Army of the Potomac marched on May 23, but the 11th Infantry was not present in the ranks of the Provost Guard Brigade, nor of the grand old V Corps. The regiment, along with several others from George Sykes's old Regular Division, had already been sent South on the mission that would hold its attention for the next twelve years.

In late May, the 11th Infantry was assigned temporarily to the XXIV Corps for occupation duty in Virginia. Along with the 4th and 14th U.S. Regulars, it was formed into the 2nd Brigade of the 2nd Division. This arrangement was short-lived as the XXIV Corps was discontinued on July 10, 1865, and the 11th Infantry was then reassigned to the newly formed District of Henrico in the Department of Virginia. In addition to the 11th, the district, which included the former Confederate capital of Richmond, was garrisoned by the 3rd U.S. Artillery, 24th Massachusetts and 100th New York Infantry Regiments, 4th Massachusetts Cavalry, and the 25th and 43rd U.S. Colored Troops. The August 5, 1865 *Army and Navy Journal* reported that "this force, though numerically small is, as will be seen, of superior character."[2]

At this point, the 11th Infantry was quite large compared to its average wartime strength. Having fought as a single battalion throughout the war, enough men had finally been recruited to expand it into something that more closely resembled its authorized regimental structure. It now consisted of three battalions, each with eight companies lettered "A" through "H." Though authorized over 2,400 officers and men, the regiment's strength stood at only 835 assigned personnel; the 1st Battalion had recovered from losses to a strength of 200, the 2nd Battalion had 290, and the 3rd Battalion was in relatively good shape with 345 troops.[3] Many of these men were soldiers who had been recently mustered out of the service with state units but who found that the army life appealed to them and joined the regulars.

The 11th was posted to Camp Grant in Richmond and was the U.S. government's most potent and visible symbol of restored power in the former Confederate capital. Initially, all battalions were stationed at Camp Grant; however, as the demands of Reconstruction grew, the 3rd Battalion was eventually posted to other towns and cities throughout northern and central Virginia. Colonel Ketchum was still the nominal head of the regiment but remained on detached service in the adjutant general's office in Washington. He would remain so until March 15, 1869, having never actually commanded the regiment in the field or in garrison, except perhaps on ceremonial occasions.[4]

Actual command of the regiment initially fell to Captain Latimer, who performed this duty from March 1, 1865, through November of the same year. Following him as commander were Major Daniel Huston Jr. (November 1865 to January 1866) and, finally, Lieutenant Colonel (and Brevet Major General) Robert S. Granger. Granger was an old West Pointer who had served in the Seminole War and the War with Mexico. He had fought Indians in Texas for twelve years and was captured by Confederate forces in April 1861 near Indianola as the 3rd U.S. Infantry prepared to sail for the East Coast. After his parole, he served in Kentucky, commanded a division of the Army of the Cumberland and several districts under Union control in Tennessee and northern Alabama until the end of the war. He assumed control of the regiment in January 1866 and remained in charge until the reorganization of 1869.[5]

Many of the wartime officers were still with the regiment. Captains Charles S. Russell, Henry L. Chipman, Francis M. Cooley, Alfred E. Latimer, and Joshua S. Fletcher Jr., all of whom commanded the regiment during the war, were now company commanders in one of the three battalions. In addition, its two Medal of Honor winners, Captain James M. Cutts and 1st Lieutenant John H. Patterson, were still assigned. All of these officers, though still captains, had been breveted to lieutenant colonel or colonel for wartime service. In fact, of the fifty-three officers who served with the 11th in combat during the Civil War, twelve were breveted to higher ranks. This was the fifth highest number of brevets in the nineteen regular regiments. Unfortunately, several of these officers would be lost to the regiment in the 1866 reorganization.[6]

The primary role of the army during the initial stages of Reconstruction was one of restoring law and order. In most areas of the South, the civil authorities were nonexistent or were unable to contend with the rash of problems that occurred as a result of the lack of a strong government or police force. As a result, the 11th Infantry found itself in the role of policeman in a district initially hostile to its presence.

One of the regiment's first missions was to guard polling places in and around Richmond for the elections of October 1865. Because of the recent defeat of the Southern cause and the influx of candidates proclaiming their pro-Union sympathies, the potential for significant problems rose. In response, the department commander, Major General Alfred Terry, directed his commanders to take stringent measures to prevent civil disobedience. Latimer prepared for the worst by stationing troops at key locations throughout Richmond and at polling places. However, the visible presence of the armed troops ensured that the elections were conducted in relative peace, and no military intervention was required.[7]

Shortly after the elections in October, false rumors began to circulate among the ex-slaves in the district that the government would soon be giving away farm land. Believing that this rumor might prove disastrously provocative, General Terry quickly dispatched officers throughout the department to meet with groups of ex-slaves. There was a particularly large group near Richmond to which officers of the 11th Infantry were sent. After the meeting, threats of a "grand negro uprising," scheduled for after Christmas, surfaced. Terry's response to the group leaders was pointed. He simply threatened direct military action if an uprising occurred. The regiment prepared to deploy to the field in late December and remained on alert through the early part of January, but the uprising never materialized.[8]

In the early days of the occupation, with Virginia's economy shattered by war, many of the state's citizens were destitute, prompting Terry to order food to be distributed to these unfortunates. With the return of Virginia's soldiers to their farms, the economy slowly recovered so that, by November, the department commander suspended the issue of food to all areas save the District of Henrico (Richmond proper). That district was still unable to feed itself because the transportation system was not yet sufficiently recovered to adequately supply the city. Moreover, in the countryside shiftless ex-Confederate soldiers and former slaves had taken to stealing crops from regional farms, further exacerbating the food supply problem. A number of officers were detailed to investigate the thefts, among them the 11th's Captain Edward R. Parry. Parry quickly identified the culprits and arrested most of them in short order. Though this effort was successful, the depredations still continued, albeit at a much slower pace.[9]

By January 1866, the requirements of Reconstruction prompted the department commander to restation troops to other locations in Virginia. The 1st and 2nd Battalions remained at Camp Grant; however, the 3rd Battalion was selected to reposition its companies to Lynchburg, Charlottesville, Danville, Bristoe, and Fredericksburg. In July the manpower requirements produced by these moves resulted in the superintendent of the General Recruiting Service in New York sending enough recruits to bring the regiment up to full strength. Some 861 recruits soon joined the 11th's ranks, swelling the regiment to over 1,700 men and officers—a massive unit when compared to the Civil War regiment averaging 200 to 400 men.[10]

This influx of recruits was indicative of a general expansion of the Regular Army, necessitated by the concurrent demands of Reconstruction in the East and problems involving Indians in the West. Accordingly, beginning around September 1866, the number of infantry regiments was increased from nineteen to forty-five. But this boost in army strength was more apparent than real. The Old Army regiments, numbered 1 through 10, retained their prewar organization of one battalion of ten companies. The 11th through the 19th Regiments were reorganized on the same pattern, with the first battalion of each taking the regiment's number, and the second and third battalions splitting off to become individual regiments with their own numerical designations.

Thus, on December 5, 1866, the 1st Battalion of the 11th Infantry Regiment was redesignated the new 11th Infantry, the 2nd Battalion was redesignated the 20th Infantry, and the 3rd Battalion was redesignated the 29th Infantry. Colonel Ketchum held nominal command of the new 11th Infantry, although Lieutenant Colonel Granger retained actual command at Camp Grant. The 11th now consisted of one battalion of ten companies, Companies I and K being raised at that time to bring the regiment up to the same strength as the Old Army formations.[11]

The jump in actual strength of the army was accompanied by an increase in duties associated with the occupation of the South. Dissatisfied with President Andrew Johnson's lenient approach toward the conquered states, the radical Republicans who dominated Congress began undermining the commander in chief's control of the army. The Congress, therefore, enacted a series of "Reconstruction Acts" designed to place the South under direct military control. The first of these acts, passed in March 1867, created five Military Districts and abolished the Division of the South and its subordinate departments. The Department of Virginia thus became the First Military District.

Although the duties of the federal troops in the South increased significantly after 1867, the 11th Infantry found little to do in and around Richmond. Other than general police duties, which decreased as the civil authorities in the area became more organized, and with the exception of routine events such as courts-martial and transfers of companies to many of the towns that the old 3rd Battalion (now 29th Infantry) had occupied before departing for other stations, the remainder of the regiment's stay at Camp Grant was uneventful.

Contemporary issues of the *Army and Navy Journal* indicate that a high number of courts-martial were convened during this time. Typical of the types of charges brought forward was that of Second Lieutenant Samuel Graham and another officer. It appears that Graham was charged with "conduct prejudicial to good order and discipline" and "conduct unbecoming of an officer." Their crime was that they fraternized with enlisted men while drinking in a public bar and rode a carriage through town while intoxicated. Lieutenant Graham's fellow officer was additionally charged with making a false statement. The sentence was forwarded to the president for action, with the recommendation that Lieutenant Graham's dismissal from the service be suspended for six months "in hopes of amended behavior." His companion was not so lucky, as he was "cashiered from the service."[12]

By early 1869, the 11th Infantry was still headquartered in Richmond with six companies, one of which (H Company) was the guard force at Libby Prison. Of the remainder, two were at Camp Schofield in Lynchburg, and one each at Warrenton and Marion. This was the disposition of the 11th Infantry when it received orders in February for transfer to Texas to relieve the 15th Infantry. However, those orders were revoked, and new ones received, that directed the regiment to proceed to the Fourth Military District to be consolidated with the 34th Infantry. The regiment departed in late February, and the 44th Infantry relieved them of their posts in Virginia.[13]

Once again, the army was being reduced because of budgetary constraints imposed by Congress. In the reorganization of 1869, the infantry was reduced to twenty-five regiments by the consolidation of units. The unit with which the 11th was consolidated, the 34th Infantry, was constituted in May 1861 as the 3rd Battalion, 16th Infantry. Like all 3rd Battalions of the "New Army" regiments, the 3rd Battalion was raised late in the war, this one being formed at Madison Barracks, New York, in April 1864. It is unlikely that any of its companies saw combat during the war, as the 3rd Battalions were intended for recruit depot duties only. In August 1865, the Regular Brigade in Major General George H. Thomas's Army of the Cumberland was discontinued, and the 16th Infantry was sent to Nashville, where it was later joined by the 3rd Battalion. That battalion

was headquartered in Nashville with all companies except E Company, which was on duty in Chattanooga.[14]

In the reorganization of 1866, the 3rd Battalion was redesignated the 34th Infantry and remained at Nashville, but by March 1867, the 34th began to transfer companies to occupy posts in Mississippi for Reconstruction purposes. In May, the headquarters and four companies were removed to Grenada, Mississippi, and the remainder of the companies were spread throughout the state, two each to the towns of Columbus, Corinth, and Holly Springs. The companies of the regiment were transferred to other locations, frequently to meet the requirements of its mission. As a result, the locations of the companies were significantly changed by March 1869 when the 11th arrived to consolidate.[15]

The integration of the two regiments began on March 3, 1869 at various posts in Mississippi and Tennessee by meshing like-lettered companies. The senior company commander retained command, and the positions of the regimental adjutant and quartermaster were retained by the officer holding that job in the 34th and 11th Infantry, respectively. On April 6, the headquarters of the 11th Infantry was consolidated with that of the 34th Infantry at Grenada, Mississippi, and the unit was redesignated the 16th Infantry Regiment.[16]

Colonel Galusha Pennypacker, colonel of the 34th Infantry, became the regimental commander of the new 16th Infantry. Pennypacker was well known throughout the army for his leadership and heroism during the Civil War. In 1861, at the age of sixteen, Pennypacker enlisted in the 9th Pennsylvania Infantry. When that regiment was mustered out, he raised a company of the 97th Pennsylvania, which he commanded in 1864 at the age of nineteen. In January 1865, the young colonel led his regiment in the successful capture of Fort Fisher in North Carolina, a feat for which he received the Medal of Honor in 1891. During that fight, he was hit four times and received wounds that would affect his health for the rest of his life. His leadership was rewarded with the brevet promotion, at age twenty, to brigadier general, which made him fully three years younger than George Custer (usually thought to be the army's youngest general) at the time of his promotion to brigadier general. At the time of his promotion, Pennypacker became the only general officer who was not old enough to vote for the president who appointed him. Now, in 1869, he was the youngest regimental commander in the U. S. Army. He would remain the commander of the 16th Infantry for fourteen years.[17]

Many of the officers who had served with the old 11th U.S. Infantry during the war were now gone because of the reorganizations in 1866 and 1869. Only Captains Francis M. Cooley and Joshua S. Fletcher Jr. remained. Granger was still the regiment's lieutenant colonel, but the new major was William P. Carlin, a brevet major general, who had fought with the Civil War 16th Infantry in the Western Theater. Included in the new additions to the regiment were Captain Hugh Theaker (a future commander of the regiment) and Lieutenant

Frederick Rosencrantz, a Swedish immigrant who was a well-known and loved member of the regiment for many years.[18]

The consolidation of the two regiments was difficult on the officers and men. Having been brought together from two distinct parts of the country, there were few, if any, prior acquaintances among the officers. The "old soldiers," moreover, had fought in two distinctly different theaters of the war, and harbored all the jealousies that entailed. In short, there was little in common among the members of the two regiments. Colonel Pennypacker immediately recognized this and

care was taken by the new commander to remedy and allay any discordance that might exist. Frequent visits were made to all the posts both by the colonel and his staff, and by reason of these visits one of the chief disadvantages was in a short time overcome. The company officers became thoroughly acquainted with the headquarters of their regiment and an *esprit-de-corps* soon commenced to show itself, which gives to the regiment to this day a distinctive reputation.[19]

Having overcome the potential disharmony in the new regiment, the officers and men of the new 16th Infantry settled down to that "most disagreeable and unmilitary duty" that both of the old regiments had already experienced—Reconstruction. Much of what they settled down to was the same activities that they had left in Virginia. For example, C Company, under the command of Captain Fletcher, was ordered to Tuskegee, Alabama, to provide polling place guards for the October 8, 1870 elections. Fletcher, ably assisted by Lieutenant Rosencrantz, ensured that the elections proceeded without incident, and the company subsequently returned to its station at Aberdeen, Mississippi.[20]

Unlike Virginia, the Deep South was a hotbed of Ku Klux Klan (KKK) activity, and the efforts to suppress that organization constituted a major part of Reconstruction duties for occupying federal troops. On October 27, 1870, a large portion of the 16th Infantry began an expedition to assist U.S. Marshals in making arrests, enforcing revenue laws, and suppressing the KKK. An ad hoc battalion commanded by Major Carlin and consisting of Companies B, E, F, G, I, and K boarded trains at home stations and assembled at Huntsville, Alabama. Stopping off for brief periods at Tuscumbia, Alabama, and Atlanta and Forsyth in Georgia, the battalion finally arrived in South Carolina, where the major Klan problem was located.[21] In South Carolina, the battalion did most of its work in cooperation with U.S. Marshal Louis E. Johnson and the troops of the 18th Infantry and 7th Cavalry. Having deputy marshals attached, one to each of two companies, Major Carlin directed his troops to fan out to Columbia, Lawrenceville, and Newbury to round up several hundred suspected Klansmen. Most of these men were ultimately tried and convicted in U.S. District Court in Columbia. While the expedition took two months to complete,

the 16th Infantry was successful in breaking the power of the Klan in South Carolina. Later, the regiment would deal with the Klan elsewhere.[22]

About this time, elements of the regiment also participated in the so-called Brooks-Baxter Affair in Little Rock, Arkansas. The trouble started with the November 1872 gubernatorial election, when Elisha Baxter, of the Stalwart Party, was elected in a close contest. The Republican candidate, Joseph Brooks, refused to accept the results and finally, in April 1874, demanded a ruling on the election from the Pulaski County Circuit Court. Tempers began to flare, and Company I was dispatched to join C Company, already stationed in Little Rock, to discourage a clash between the two parties.[23]

On April 15, Brooks was declared the winner, but Baxter refused to yield control of the statehouse. Brooks thereupon directed a force of about 250 armed men to surround the capitol, forcing Baxter to leave. Both parties then appealed to the federal authorities. The appeals were turned down by the U. S. attorney general for legal reasons, and concurrently, the War Department directed the commander on the scene, Captain Thomas E. Rose of C Company, to remain neutral, except in cases "to prevent bloodshed or collision of armed bodies." As the two armed camps assembled their forces, Rose prepared for the worst. On the 17th, he moved his two companies into a position between the two contestants and warned Brooks and Baxter that he was prepared to take stringent measures if they clashed or interfered with federal troops. When President Grant learned that Rose's telegrams to the War Department were being intercepted, he ordered the captain to seize the telegraph office in order to secure the lines of communication. Additionally, on April 20, Company D departed Humboldt, Tennessee, to further reinforce Rose.[24]

Real trouble threatened to boil over on the 21st, when H. King White, a Baxter supporter, marched an ad hoc regiment of some two thousand armed black field hands to Baxter's headquarters at the Anthony House. Rose deployed two companies to face them down and directed White to disperse. After an incident occurred in which Rose rode his horse over a couple of White's men, Rose and White began to argue. Shortly thereafter, shots were fired and White's "regiment" scattered, but not before several of the men were wounded. Rose then moved detachments to key intersections throughout Little Rock, and further trouble was prevented.[25]

Things remained tense but relatively quiet for the next two weeks until May 7, when a fire fight broke out between the two parties. A group of Baxter's men were traveling on a boat on the Arkansas River when they were ambushed by Brooks's men. The battle cost twenty killed or wounded before it ended, but the wheel of justice was turning. On May 15, The U. S. attorney general, after much deliberation, rendered an opinion that Baxter was the legitimate governor of Arkansas, and Grant then officially recognized him.[26] Rose was then directed to support and protect the Baxter administration, and the Brooks faction subsequently melted away. By May 26, Company D was back at Humboldt.

The requests for assistance from the army by the civil authorities during this period of Reconstruction in the Fourth Military District were quite frequent. Sometimes, the requests were for large incidents, such as the Brooks-Baxter Affair, which held the nation's attention; at other times, the requests were for smaller affairs, such as the temporary move of K Company in August 1874 to Monterey, Kentucky, to protect deputy U. S. marshals in the performance of their duties.[27] Most of the latter cases usually put the men of the 16th Infantry in direct confrontation with the Ku Klux Klan.

One such challenge arose that same August in Humboldt. After returning to Swayne Barracks in Humboldt from their adventure in Little Rock, D Company was transferred to Jackson, Mississippi, on June 23, 1874. A small detachment stayed to guard military property left at the barracks. The lieutenant left in command at Swayne Barracks reported to regimental head-quarters on August 23 that the situation was deteriorating in the county since the departure of troops. The blacks in the area were being mistreated by certain whites who had been identified as members of the KKK. Meanwhile, the civil authorities were unable or unwilling to restore order and the few troops at the bar-racks had come under attack by rifle fire at night.

On August 24 the lieutenant requested reinforcements from the department headquarters, stating:

The whole country around are under arms on account of killings of some Ku Klux by Negroes saturday last. The Ku Klux Klan had been riding in large numbers for the last two weeks. Parties have fired into [our] camp at night. Threats made to attack us. All approaches to the garrison are watched by our pickets every night. Colored people are driven from home and work. Some shot. All in the gar-rison are worn out from the constant night watching and fatigue.[28]

Orders were telegraphed that day to the regiment, and G Company was dispatched to Humboldt, arriving the following day by train. Though the Klan in Humboldt was quieted by the arrival of the troops, the problem was not solved in other parts of the state because of the lack of enough troops and law enforce-ment officials. In his annual report to the secretary of war, Brigadier General Alfred H. Terry, commanding the Department of the South, stated that he felt that the problem was exacerbat-ed by the location of the U.S. Commissioners and U.S. Deputy Marshals. He recommended that they be located in communities where troops were stationed so that they could conduct their work more promptly and, therefore, more effectively.[29] Another major political problem that had the potential to flare into open conflict was the insurrection of the "White League" in New Orleans in September 1874. The league had been formed in Opelousas, Louisiana, in April 1874, with the intent of unseating the radical Republican governor of the

state, William P. Kellogg. The White League was formed into essentially military-type suborganizations by "Colonel" Fred N. Ogden, a supporter of John McEnery, who was Kellogg's rival. The troubles came to a head in September when the league attempted to acquire weapons to force an overthrow of Kellogg. The New Orleans police sought to prevent the league's efforts and were successful in seizing several covert arms stores. The police also caught wind that a boatload of rifles was being shipped from the St. Louis Arsenal and attempted to prevent the weapons from landing in the hands of the White League.[30]

These actions resulted in a large gathering of leaguers on September 14, who publicly declared McEnery as the new governor. McEnery's running mate, D. B. Penn, formally declared the formation of the Louisiana State Militia, which was quickly organized from the White League. At the time of the gathering, Brevet Major General William H. Emory, com-mander of the Department of the Gulf, had only sixteen soldiers stationed in New Orleans, hardly a sufficient number to prevent the overthrow of Kellogg. Meanwhile, Ogden exploited the situation by preventing access to the docks so that when the boat with the rifles arrived, his men could acquire the weapons. That afternoon, thirty-five hundred state troops and the met-ropolitan police—all under the command of James Longstreet, formerly a general in the Confederate Army—moved to route Ogden's troops and seize the weapons. Street fighting broke out, but Longstreet's force failed in their attempt, leaving a total of thirty-one dead and seventy-nine wounded (including Longstreet) on both sides.[31]

Kellogg was forced to leave New Orleans, but not before he appealed to Grant for troops. Emory was aware of the impending clash and had already sent troops from Holly Springs, Mississippi, to prevent a battle, but they arrived too late. Emory also ordered Colonel Pennypacker to New Orleans to take charge of the military affairs there on the 16th. Pennypacker took Companies D and F with him to New Orleans to reinforce the companies of the 2nd and 18th Infantry Regiments already sent on the 14th. In the face of this challenge from federal troops, McEnery backed down, and Kellogg was restored to power. However, Republicans throughout the state had also been thrown out of power, so federal troops continued to arrive and were posted to other cities to restore the rightly elected offi-cials. Eventually, Company G also ended up in New Orleans and H Company was posted to Baton Rouge. In all, twenty-six com-panies of troops from the Division of the South were sent to Louisiana to restore order by the end of September.[32]

Though the problems associated with the White League continued, the companies of the 16th began returning to their home stations in October, leaving the security of the city in the hands of other regiments. Colonel Pennypacker did not depart until late October, but with his departure came a tribute to him from the New Orleans *Times-Picayune* that was typical of the accolades he and the 16th Infantry seemed to receive wherev-er they went:

Colonel G. Pennypacker, for sometime past commanding the U. S. troops in Louisiana, left last evening under orders to resume his post at Nashville. His high reputation is sufficient guarantee that the official duties devolving on him have received faithful and efficient administration. In his relations with our people he has at all times, under all circumstances, been the modest and considerate gentleman. We wish well and kindly for Colonel Pennypacker wheresoever he may go.[33]

The activities of the 16th Infantry during their tour in the South did not all revolve around Reconstruction duties. The companies of the regiment participated in community assistance efforts, their own military training, goodwill events with their recent enemies, and even funeral escort duty for several well-known generals, not to mention all the mundane housekeeping duties and off-duty entertainments that all regiments engage in to help pass the time.

In October 1871, Mrs. O'Leary's cow kicked over a lantern in her barn and started the Great Chicago Fire—or so the story goes. Because of the vast devastation and prevalence of looting, the city authorities requested assistance from the army. General Sheridan's headquarters for the Division of the Missouri, sent to Chicago in the wake of the fire, responded by assembling companies from the 5th, 6th, and 9th Infantry Regiments in the city. To prevent the weakening of the Indian-fighting army out West, companies from the Division of the South were also called, and the 16th's E Company was deployed from its post at Louisville, Kentucky. After helping to restore order and protect public properties, the company returned to Louisville on October 24th.[34]

Apparently the men of E Company were the regiment's firefighters. The *Army and Navy Journal* for April 18, 1874, reported that the citizens of Lancaster, Kentucky (the company's station at the time), rendered their thanks publicly to the officers and men of the company for their efforts in putting out a major fire that occurred there on the 1st. The fire had threatened to burn a large portion of the town but, because of the fast action of E Company, the town was spared severe damage. The paper also pointed out that the company had fought fires in the town on three earlier occasions.[35]

In late January 1872, Major General Henry Wager Halleck died at his home in Louisville, Kentucky. Halleck had served as the general in chief of United States armies from 1862 to 1864 and, as such, played a significant role in the prosecution of the war against the Confederacy. With the promotion of Grant to that position in 1864, Halleck was made chief of staff to President Lincoln until the end of the war. Apparently the closest unit available, the 16th Infantry was therefore selected by the secretary of war to travel to Louisville and perform the funeral escort duty for the general.[36]

Four years later, the secretary of war directed the regiment to provide the funeral detail for Brevet Major General

Gordon S. Granger. Granger had served in Texas with the 3rd Infantry in the early days of the Civil War. He was captured by Confederate troops as his regiment attempted to escape after Texas seceded. He was eventually paroled and later served in a number of commands in the Western Theater of the war. At the time of his death, Granger was colonel of the 15th Infantry in Santa Fe, New Mexico. His body was railed to Lexington, Kentucky, where Colonel Pennypacker, the band, and four companies of the regiment performed escort duties at Granger's funeral.[37]

Throughout the Reconstruction period, Pennypacker's war wounds still caused him frequent discomfort. After suffering from several health problems in the fall of 1871, Pennypacker was granted a leave of absence on the recommendation of army surgeons. On December 12, 1871, Lieutenant Colonel James Van Voast, second in command, was ordered to take station at Nashville to assume command of the 16th Infantry during the commander's absence. After a short stay at his hometown of Chester, Pennsylvania, Pennypacker left for a more lengthy stay in Europe. While in Europe, a rumor began circulating through various papers that the regimental commander, who happened to be a bachelor—and a sought-after one at that—was soon to be married to one Miss Katie Putnam, a well-known American actress. Pennypacker read about the rumor in a newspaper and wrote back to the adjutant asking him to refute the rumor, as it was not true. The confusion apparently came as a result of the fact that the two were acquainted and happened to leave for Europe at about the same time.[38]

What was to be a one-year leave of absence stretched to almost two, but Pennypacker finally rejoined the regiment on October 21, 1873. Pennypacker's efforts to establish a good rapport between the people of Nashville and the 16th Infantry met with as much success as it had in New Orleans. In February 1875, the city council planned a grand celebration of Washington's birthday and invited the 16th to participate. Companies F and G and the band, which garrisoned the city, marched in the parade, and the band serenaded the citizens at a gala later that evening. The Nashville paper reporting the festivities complimented the regiment, even as it unknowingly foretold the departure of the 16th, when it stated, "The military are very popular here and their removal would generally be regretted. General Pennypacker and Captain Richards especially have won the friendship and esteem of the community."[39]

A similar testimony that shows how far the regiment's efforts went to restoring relations with people who were once their enemies came two months later when the 16th Infantry conducted a parade for the governor of Tennessee on April 11th. After the parade, Colonel Pennypacker held a reception in the regimental headquarters for the governor and key citizens of the city of Nashville. The *Nashville Republican Banner* reported:

During the stay of these troops in Nashville which has been since the war, they have conducted themselves in such a manner that the prejudices engendered by the war have been entirely dispelled, and both officers and men stand in high esteem among those who know them.[40]

Though the regimental headquarters had moved only once, from Grenada, Mississippi, to Ash Barracks in Nashville in 1871 (and remained there for five years), the company stations were anything but stable. For example, during the period January 1871 to May 1876 the following moves are indicative (but not all-inclusive) of the movement of the companies to perform Reconstruction duties:

March 9, 1871	I Company	to Meridian, MS
June 9, 1871	K Company	to Tallahasee, FL
June 23, 1871	I Company	to Oxford, MS
October 1871	E Company	to Chicago, IL
October 24, 1871	E Company	to Lancaster, KY
December 12, 1871	I Company	to Jackson, MS
August 12, 1872	H Company	to McComb, MS
October 17, 1872	H Company	to Jackson, MS
January 2, 1873	A Company	to Lebanon, KY
May 3, 1873	H Company	to Monroe, LA
June 1873	B Company	to Jackson, MS
September 6, 1873	K Company	to Frankfort, KY
May 5, 1874	K Company	to Monterey, KY
September 17, 1874	D Company	to New Orleans, LA
September 17, 1874	F Company	to New Orleans, LA
October 1874	H Company	to Baton Rouge, LA
October 1874	A Company	to Lebanon, KY
October 4, 1874	F Company	to Nashville, TN
October 4, 1874	G Company	to Somerville, TN
October 11, 1874	D Company	to Jackson, MS
November 1874	B Company	to New Orleans, LA
November 1874	E Company	to Humboldt, TN
November 11, 1874	K Company	to Frankfort, KY
November 18, 1874	G Company	to Humboldt, TN
November 18, 1874	A Company	to Memphis, TN
November 22, 1874	B Company	to Jackson, MS
November 25, 1874	D Company	to Humboldt, TN

The stability of the home station of the regimental headquarters came to an end on May 27, 1876, when the 16th Infantry was transferred to Newport Barracks in Louisville, Kentucky. The regiment's tenure at Newport Barracks was highlighted only by Colonel Pennypacker's appointment to temporary command of the Department of the South. He was designated by the War Department to take command on July 1 after Major General Irwin McDowell departed to assume command of the Military Division of the Pacific. Colonel Pennypacker turned over command of the department to Brevet Brigadier General Thomas H. Ruger on September 8, and departed with the regimental headquarters for its new station at Mount Vernon Barracks, Alabama, on September 25.[41]

The 16th Infantry's stay at Mount Vernon Barracks was also short, as the regiment was summoned once again to New Orleans to stave off trouble associated with the elections that November. The commander of the Department of the Gulf, Major General Christopher C. Augur, asked for and received reinforcements to protect the state Election Returns Board, and the 16th Infantry arrived in New Orleans in early December.

On December 22, the board certified Republican victories at all levels in the state, results that the Democrats vociferously contested. The Democrats claimed that ex-Confederate General Francis T. Nicholls was the true winner of the gubernatorial election, and a situation arose that was similar to the problems between Kellogg and McEnery only two years earlier. This time, however, the discontent was more noticeable in the outlying parishes. In Monroe, a force of five hundred well-armed Democrats threatened to install Nicholls supporters in local offices in spite of the presence of Captain Clayton Hale and his company of the 16th Infantry.

Throughout the early months of 1877, as the political machinations continued, the regiment kept the peace in the city, preventing the type of direct street conflict that had occurred in 1874. Finally, in April, after Rutherford B. Hayes assumed the presidency and, through political "horse-trading" so typical of the time, the outcome was decided in favor of the Democrats. The need for the regiment to keep peace in New Orleans passed.[42]

Need for the regiment had sprung up elsewhere, though. The gathering of the Sioux and Northern Cheyenne had precipitated a major uprising in the spring and summer of 1876, and the combined force of these two tribes had given Major General George Crook's column a mauling at the Rosebud River on June 17. On June 25 a combined force of Sioux and Cheyenne warriors utterly defeated Lieutenant Colonel Custer and the 7th Cavalry at the Little Big Horn. Settlers in the West had frantically called for protection against Indian depredations, and all available cavalry and most infantry had been moved farther west to better intercept the roaming bands of warriors. This action had left many posts guarded by small caretaking detachments entirely inadequate to protect the posts, much less the surrounding settlements. As a result, the 16th Infantry was ordered to Kansas to reinforce the 4th Cavalry and occupy stations in that state.

In May 1877, new orders sent the regiment by train to Kansas City. After a brief stop at Fort Leavenworth, the regiment continued on to Junction City, Kansas, where the regimental headquarters and Companies A, C, and H detrained and marched to Fort Riley, their new duty station. The remainder of the regiment was spread out across what constituted the Department of the Missouri, with stations at Fort Wallace and Fort Hayes in Kansas, and at Fort Sill and Fort Reno in the Indian Territory. The transfer of the regiment to the Department of the Missouri began its mission with the Indian-fighting army that would span the next twenty-odd years.

K Company, 16th Infantry Regiment, with Geronimo (seated top row, second from left, in dark vest), October 1886

Chapter Three
The Indian Wars

The men of that regiment were the most gentlemanly and orderly bunch of soldiers [I have] ever seen.
Tom Allen, citizen, Junction City, Kansas, 1877

The 16th United States Infantry disembarked from the Kansas Pacific train at Junction City, Kansas, on a still, hot day in early June 1877. As the troops stepped out onto the dusty siding, the NCOs barked orders to get the troops into formation to begin the six-mile hike into Fort Riley, the regiment's new headquarters. There to welcome the troops, were members of the community, curious to see the new outfit. Yet they were also somewhat dubious, as Junction City had seen units come and go over the past thirty years. In that time elements of the 5th, 19th, and finally the 23rd Infantry Regiments had occupied Fort Riley, then departed one after the other as the exigencies of the Indian campaigns called them away. Now the troops of the 16th had arrived, but how long would *they* stay? As it turned out, for the next three years.

Similar to the dispersion of subordinate companies that the regiment experienced during Reconstruction duties, the 16th Infantry was posted to several small forts in Kansas and the Indian Territory shortly after its arrival at Fort Riley. The headquarters, band and Companies A, C, and H remained at Riley, while Company F was posted to Fort Wallace and Company G to Fort Hayes in Kansas. Companies B and D were posted to Fort Sill, Companies E and I to Fort Reno, and Company K to Fort Gibson in the Indian Territory. The disposition of the companies remained thus during the stay in Kansas with the exception of the transfer of G Company to Fort Wallace in October 1878 and the transfer of D Company to Fort Gibson on February 28, 1880.

The men of the 16th quickly discovered that a soldier's life on the frontier typically entailed lengthy periods of seemingly endless boredom punctuated by rare moments of excitement, exhilaration, or sheer terror. For the next twenty-one years, the regiment would spend its time conducting a host of duties, few of which had to do with Indian fighting. Most of its time was spent performing routine post housekeeping duties, infrequent training exercises, and refurbishing existing post facilities that were often below acceptable standards required by army regulations. To break the monotony, there were infrequent forays against hostile Indians, performance of routine patrols to outlying base camps, and the usual off-duty entertainments that soldiers are historically adept at locating.

Though the soldiers of the 16th Infantry were certainly no different from other soldiers, the regiment quickly developed a rapport with the citizens of Junction City and established a reputation for sobriety and courtesy. Probably conditioned by the need to establish good relations with the local citizenry in their Reconstruction duties in Nashville, New Orleans, and elsewhere, their efforts to get along with the Kansans prompted a prominent Junction Citian, one Mr. Tom Allen, to remark that "the men of that regiment were the most gentlemanly and orderly bunch of soldiers [I have] ever seen." Colonel Pennypacker, as in Nashville and New Orleans, also quickly became a favorite in local social circles. An article from the *Junction City Union* in which he was described as "that chivalrous and knightly soldier...Colonel of the Sixteenth" went on to speculate on his latest pursuit of "amour," as he was still, and would be until his death, a bachelor.[1]

Before the troops at Fort Riley had really settled in, the post experienced one of those severe lightning storms for which central Kansas is noted. During the storm, Stable No. 4 was struck by a bolt that set it afire. In spite of efforts by soldiers to put out the flames, the building was a total loss. Destroyed in the fire was a considerable amount of hay, horse feed, an ambulance, and a horse-drawn water tank—but fortunately, no horses. Shortly thereafter, the bridge connecting the post with Junction City fell into the Republican River as a herd of cattle was crossing it. As the bridge had been built by a company that had long since gone out of business, the troops of the 16th were put to work building and maintaining a "temporary" ponton bridge to secure passage to the town. The state of Kansas was unable to replace the span until six years later.[2]

On July 21, union leaders of the Socialist Workingman's Party in St. Louis, Missouri, rallied rail workers to strike over pay and working hours and then, in coordination with some of the city's unemployed, took control of the city. Local police and the state militia were too intimidated to intervene, so the secretary of war ordered General Pope, the department commander, to send troops to restore control and protect federal property. As a result, within a month of their arrival at Fort Wallace, the men of Company F were en route to perform strike duty in St. Louis. On July 24, the company boarded a train and proceeded to Jefferson Barracks, Missouri, where they

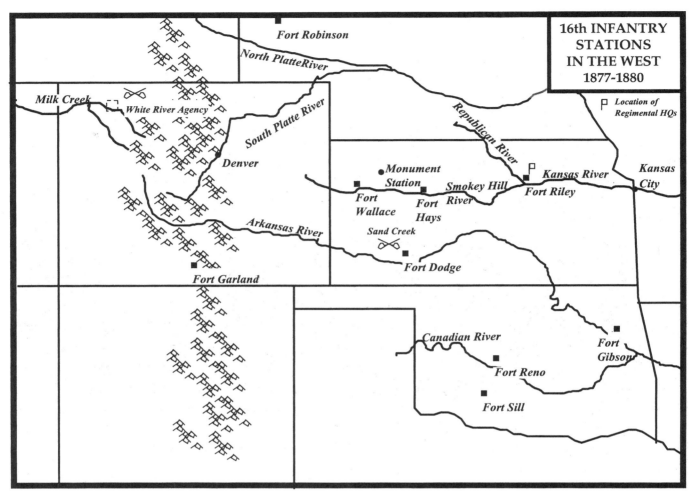

Map 3-1.

disembarked and prepared to confront the strikers. Along with companies of the 19th and 23rd Infantry Regiments, F Company encamped at the old arsenal near the barracks, as the city officials, buoyed by the arrival of four hundred sun-bronzed regulars, began negotiations with the now-cowed labor leaders.[3]

The problem did not end there, for strikers were also active across the river in East St. Louis, Illinois. Rioters had seized the Eads Bridge spanning the Mississippi River between the two cities on July 26, as well as the yards of two railroads then in federal receivership. Because the yards were technically the property of the federal government, the troops of the 23rd Infantry marched across to retake the bridge, while soldiers of F Company and the 19th Infantry, landed on the east side to seize the yards. There, they joined with the 23rd Infantry, and as before, there was no resistance from the rioters. The presence of four hundred well-armed and aggressive troops occupying the rail yards intimidated the laborers and the strike came to an end on August 2.[4] With things back to normal in St. Louis, Company F returned by train to Fort Wallace on August 10.

The following month, the 16th Infantry received orders to

deploy companies to search for a band of marauding hostiles. To ensure a wide area of coverage, Pennypacker ordered four companies to provide a net, albeit a loose one, from central to western Kansas, and south to Fort Sill in the Indian Territory. The four companies, D, F, G, and H, converged toward Fort Wallace, but in spite of their efforts, they detected no Indians. The search was not in vain, however, as they did capture several men wanted for train robbery.

In late September, Lieutenant Leven C. Allen, with a detachment of ten men, set out from Fort Hays for Buffalo Station. The detachment was aware of the potential for Indian trouble and the proximity of men who had recently robbed the Union Pacific Railroad. En route, they encountered the desperadoes. After a sharp skirmish, Allen's men killed two, captured several others, and recovered seventy-five pounds of gold. The detachment returned as heroes to Fort Hays on September 29, their normally dull lives somewhat enlivened for the time being.[5]

Following that episode, the regiment settled into the daily grind of routine duties. After an uneventful fall and winter, in

May 1878 the regiment was ordered to send details to the abandoned posts of Fort Harker and Larned to scrounge lumber, hardware, and anything else of utility. Having no further use for these stations, the army wanted to salvage anything usable before turning them over to the Department of the Interior.[6]

A humorous incident occurred the following month that belied the regiment's reputation for sobriety and may be indicative of the efforts of the soldiers to relieve their boredom. In early June, the companies at Fort Riley held a review for Colonel Pennypacker. The day was hot and apparently a number of the Irish and German troops were suffering from hangovers from the previous evening's bout with the bottle. Their commander, Major Samuel A. Wainwright, decided to pass the troops in review at the double time. Unable to keep up, the drunkards began to fall out here and there. Understandably, Pennypacker was embarrassed by the condition of his command and quickly convened a general court-martial to investigate the incident and restore sobriety to the command.[7]

In July 1878, Bruce Palmer Sr. was born to Lieutenant and Mrs. George Henry Palmer of F Company at Fort Wallace. This event began a longstanding association with the 16th Infantry Regiment by the men of the Palmer family, a tradition that would last until 1955 when George Palmer's grandson would assume command of the regiment. More will be heard from them later in the regiment's history.[8]

Cheyenne Campaign
September 7-October 17, 1878

The activities of the regiment in Kansas were not all dull and routine. As in any army, the primary duty of an infantry unit is to engage the enemy in battle and destroy, capture, or otherwise defeat him. The 16th Infantry's first engagement with Indians occurred in September 1878. On September 7, a band of Northern Cheyenne under Dull Knife and Little Wolf escaped from the Cheyenne and Arapaho Agency near Fort Reno in the Indian Territory in an effort to return to their homelands in the Tongue River area. The 4th Cavalry was sent to round them up, but Dull Knife was able to evade the horse soldiers. As the band crossed into Kansas, Companies A, F, G, and H were dispatched to western Kansas to intercept them.[9]

Working in conjunction with the 4th Cavalry, A Company was deployed near Fort Dodge, Companies F and G were in the field near Fort Wallace, and Company H was positioned near Monument Station. On the evening of September 21, Company A and a squadron of the 4th Cavalry engaged the Cheyenne along Sand Creek near Fort Dodge. After a sharp but inconclusive fight in which several soldiers and Indians were killed or wounded, Dull Knife again slipped away and headed north. Almost a week later, but only thirty miles away, the band ambushed the 4th Cavalry at Punished Woman's Fork near Fort Wallace. Killed in the action was Lieutenant Colonel William H. Lewis, the 4th Cavalry's executive officer. Companies F and G of the 16th, remaining in the field, pursued

the Cheyenne into the Sand Hills region of western Nebraska. Company G followed the Indian trail up the north fork of the Smoky Hill River, north to Beaver Creek and to Driftwood, Nebraska, finally reaching the Republican River on October 3. In spite of its efforts, Company G made no further contact with the Indians. About two weeks later, Dull Knife's band was captured by the 3rd Cavalry and incarcerated at Fort Robinson, Nebraska, where the Cheyenne's famous breakout would occur three months later.[10]

Ute Campaign
November 1879-April 1880

After the excitement with the Cheyenne, the next call to arms did not come until a year later. During the summer of 1879, Nathan C. Meeker, the agent for the White River Agency in northwestern Colorado, had nervously requested troops to bring order to the rowdy elements of the Ute tribe under his charge. His eccentric ideas and ways of dealing with the Utes had caused much unrest. On September 10, the local chief, Douglas, roughed up Meeker and threatened the whites at the agency. Meeker, quite ruffled, wired for help.

A mixed column of infantry and calvary was promptly formed with orders to proceed to the agency's relief. Departing on the 16th, the column, commanded by Major Thomas T. Thornburgh, comprised elements of the 4th Infantry and 5th Cavalry drawn from Forts Fred Steele and D.A. Russell in Wyoming. On October 29, the column halted en route while Meeker and Thornburgh parlayed with the Ute chiefs. The latter agreed to behave as a condition for keeping Thornburg's troops off agency land, but no sooner had the deal been struck than Thornburgh ordered his column forward to set up camp near the reservation. An armed response from Utes, who judged Thornburgh to be in violation of their agreement, was swift in coming. The ensuing battle, fought at Mill Creek, was a day-long affair in which Thornburgh was killed, thirty-three soldiers were killed or wounded, and twenty-three Utes were slain. In the meantime other Utes, believing they had nothing left to lose, slaughtered Meeker and all the whites at the agency, except for Meeker's wife and daughter.[11]

The army rapidly deployed reinforcements to Colorado from all over the West. The 16th Infantry was ordered to send two companies to help in the effort. Company F, at Fort Wallace, entrained to reinforce Colonel Wesley Merritt's 5th Cavalry and was present when that unit occupied White River Agency after the massacre. Company C entrained at Fort Riley and moved to Fort Garland, Colorado, where it came under the command of Colonel Ranald Mackenzie and his 4th Cavalry. For the next few months, these two companies participated in rounding up Utes thought to be guilty of various crimes and generally enforcing peaceful conditions. Their mission complete, the companies returned to home station the following spring.[12]

Late in the autumn of 1879, a beloved member of the regiment succumbed to "Father Time." Lieutenant Fredrik

Rosencrantz, a long-time member of the regiment, died on December 7, and was buried with full military honors in the Fort Riley cemetery. This colorful character was rumored to have been from the same House of Rosencrantz featured in Shakespeare's play "Hamlet." Before leaving Sweden, he had served in the Royal Swedish Horse Guards, where soldiering apparently got into his blood. After immigrating to the United States, he eventually ended up on the staff of the Army of the Potomac, rising to the rank of brevet major during the war. He chose to remain in the army after the war and spent most of his career in the 16th Infantry. Apparently, he was highly thought of in the Swedish Horse Guards as well, for sometime after his death, a brass tablet was purchased by his old comrades in Sweden, shipped to Fort Riley, and mounted on a wall in St. Mary's Chapel, where it can still be viewed as of this writing.[13]

Starting in March 1880, the 16th Infantry entered a period of increased activity, as a necessary response to the Cheyenne and Ute flare-ups of 1878 and 1879 respectively. Patrols and related expeditions would continue through the end of the year, as the following survey of month reports shows:

Mar. *Company F:* detachment conducted scout vicinity Fort Wallace. Distance of scout ninety miles.

Apr. *Company A:* detachments conducted scout vicinity central Kansas. Distance of 1st scout 198 miles and 2nd scout 78 miles.

Company F: detachment conducted scout vicinity Fort Wallace. Distance of scout eighty miles.

May *Company G:* departed Fort Garland, Colorado, May 17 for field service with Ranald Mackenzie's command at Gunnison County, Colorado. Established camp at Cline's Ranch. Distance marched 241 miles.

Company F: departed Fort Wallace, May 28, for field service at Middle Park, Colorado.

Company D: departed Fort Gibson, Idaho, I.T., at one o'clock P. M., May 28, for field service in New Mexico, per telegraphic instructions received from Headquarters, Department of the Missouri, dated May 26 and May 28, 1880. Arrived Belen, New Mexico at 3 P.M., June 1. Distance traveled by rail 1,081 miles.

Company H: departed Fort Riley at five A.M. May 29 for field service in New Mexico in compliance with S.O. No. 113, Headquarters, Department of the Missouri, dated May 26, 1880. Distance traveled by rail 937 miles.

June *Company A:* detachment conducted scout vicinity central Kansas. Distance of scout 251 miles.

Company H: departed La Junta, Colorado, June 1 en route to New Mexico, and arrived at Fort Craig, New Mexico, June 12. Departed Fort Craig June 15 for service in the San Mateo Mountains and established camp at Nogales Springs June 16. Distance marched 131 miles.

Company G: departed Cline's Ranch June 1, and arrived at the Uncompahgre River near Los Pinos, Colorado where it joined Mackenzie's command on the 2nd. Distance marched 39 miles.

Company D: departed Belen, New Mexico June 7 and arrived at Fort Craig, New Mexico June 12. Departed Fort Craig June 15 for service in the San Mateo Mountains and established camp at Nogales Springs June 16. Distance marched 116 miles.

Company F: arrived at Middle Park, Colorado, and established camp sixteen miles west of Hot Sulphur Springs, Colorado, at the mouth of Troublesome Creek June 9.

Company C: departed camp at Cochetopa Pass, Colorado, June 11, and arrived at the Uncompahgre River near Los Pinos, Colorado, where it joined Mackenzie's command on the 15th. Distance marched 120 miles.

July *Company A:* detachment conducted scout to Arkansas City, Kansas. Distance of scout 289 miles.

Company C: conducted scout in southwestern Colorado. Distance of scout seventy-five miles.

Company G: conducted scout in southwestern Colorado. Distance of scout ninety-three miles.

Company H: departed camp at Nogales Springs July 3 en route to Fort Craig, New Mexico, where it arrived same date. Distance marched 25 miles.

Company D: departed camp at Nogales Springs July 21 en route to Fort Bayard, New Mexico, for field service with Major [Albert P.] Morrow's command. Distance marched 185 miles.

Aug. *Company A:* detachment conducted scout in south central Kansas.

Company E: conducted repair work of telegraph lines along the Central Kansas Railroad.

Company G: conducted scout in southwestern Colorado. Distance of scout forty-eight miles.

Company D: departed Fort Bayard, New Mexico, August 1 en route to Knight's Ranch, New Mexico, where it arrived August 4. Distance marched forty-two miles.

Company H: departed Fort Craig, New Mexico, August 8. Detailed to provide protection for engineers conducting a survey for the route of the A.T. & S.F. Railroad into Arizona. Established camp at Stage Pass in the Goodsite Mountains, New Mexico, August 30. Distance marched 130 miles.

Sept. *Company H:* departed Stage Pass September 17 on engineer escort duty to Sonora, Mexico. Distance marched sixty-one miles.

Company D: departed Knight's Ranch September 19 for field service with Colonel George P. Buell's command in his foray into Mexico to track down Victorio

Oct. and his band of Apaches. Distance marched 219 miles.

Companies F and G: returned to Fort Wallace, Kansas.

Company D: departed Slocum's Ranch in Mexico October 1 with Buell's column and arrived at Fort Craig, New Mexico, October 29. Distance marched 370 miles.

Company H: departed Sonora, Mexico October 18 on engineer escort duty. Arrived at Camp L. A. Rucker, Arizona October 30. Distance marched 297 miles.

Nov. *Company D:* departed Fort Craig, New Mexico, November 1 and arrived at Fort Gibson, I.T., November 4. Distance traveled by rail 1,173 miles.

Company H: relieved from escort duty November 13 by K Company, 15th Infantry. Proceeded to Fort Craig, New Mexico, where it arrived November 30. Distance marched 323 miles.[14]

By the end of 1880, the Indians had been largely swept from the plains, and the need for large forces in Kansas, Nebraska, and the Dakotas was greatly diminished. However, the depredations by the Apaches still occurred at an alarming rate in Texas, New Mexico, Colorado, and Arizona. Therefore, Colonel Pennypacker received orders to send companies to various locations to help subdue hostile Indian tribes in those areas. One by one, the companies were ordered south and west, so that by the end of May only the headquarters, band, and staff personnel remained at Fort Riley. As noted above, Companies D and H were sent by rail to New Mexico in May to help subdue Victorio and his band of marauding Apaches.[15]

In late July 1880, Victorio and his band of 150 warriors entered Texas after being chased out of Mexico by the Mexican Army. Looking for water, they attacked a detachment of the 10th Cavalry led by the regimental commander, Colonel Benjamin Grierson, at Tinaja de los Palmas in Quitman Canyon, then melted back across the border. This incident began a series of running battles. On August 2, Victorio's warriors reentered Texas and were quickly detected by the Buffalo Soldiers, but successfully slipped away. The 10th Cavalry and its attached infantry again skirmished with the Apaches on August 6, after which Victorio reentered Mexico to escape the U. S. soldiers. By September, Colonel George P. Buell had gathered enough troops (including Company D, 16th Infantry) to enable him to cross his force into Chihuahua to operate with the Mexican Army in pursuit of Victorio. He did so but, predictably, the local Mexican commander changed his mind and ordered Buell's column out of the country before they were able to catch the Apaches.

The temporary American military presence in Mexico did not go for naught, however. Buell's actions gave the Mexican Army the impetus to do more about the problem with Victorio. As a result, the Mexicans redoubled their efforts and on October 15 they cornered the Apache chief. After a sharp fight, Victorio and sixty Apaches were killed and the remnants of his band were captured.[16]

In early November, Colonel Pennypacker received orders to once again transfer the entire regiment, this time to posts in west Texas to reinforce army efforts to provide security against the Apaches. Originally, his orders were to relieve the 10th Cavalry at Fort Davis, but upon the arrival of the headquarters and several companies in San Antonio, the orders were changed. The commander of the Department of Texas at this time was Major General E. O. C. Ord, an old friend of Pennypacker's from the war. Ord decided to place Pennypacker in charge of the "Post at San Antonio" (soon to be renamed Fort Sam Houston) and directed him to have the Headquarters and H Company (arrived from Fort Craig, New Mexico, on December 18) take station at the same post. The remainder of the regiment took station as follows: Companies A, B, C, and F at Fort Concho; Companies D, G, I, and K at Fort McKavett; and Company E at Fort Davis. This disposition changed slightly the following April when the regimental headquarters transferred to Fort McKavett so that Colonel Pennypacker could better control the activities of the regiment.[17]

By the time the 16th Infantry took station at Forts Concho and McKavett, the period of the posts' usefulness for defense or even as bases of operations against Indians had already passed. After the defeat of the Comanches in the Red River War of 1874-75, most of the hostile activity lay much farther west and into New Mexico. Less than a year after the regiment's arrival in west Texas, the new department commander, Brigadier General Christopher C. Augur, wrote in his annual report to the secretary of war: "It is not believed that any military post will be longer needed south of the Texas and Pacific Railway except those that bear on the defense or protection of the Rio Grande. Forts Concho, McKavett, and Stockton are thus rendered unnecessary."[18]

As a result of this report, General Sheridan issued orders for the abandonment of all three posts in 1882. However, there was not enough billeting to take care of all the companies in the remaining forts in west Texas. Therefore, the department commander decided to keep Forts Concho and Stockton open until such time that new barracks could be built at Fort Davis, the post designated to receive the regiment. In the summer of 1882, the regimental headquarters was transferred to Fort Concho. All companies at Fort McKavett, except D Company, were also transferred away by October, with two going to Fort Davis, two going to Fort Concho, and one to Fort McIntosh in Laredo. Company D was detailed to remain behind to salvage the post and transfer the materials to Concho. On the morning of June 30, 1883, the colors were not hauled up the flagpole at Fort McKavett. Instead, D Company was formed and began a long march to its new station at Fort McIntosh, thus ending the fort's thirty-one years of service to the army and Texas.[19]

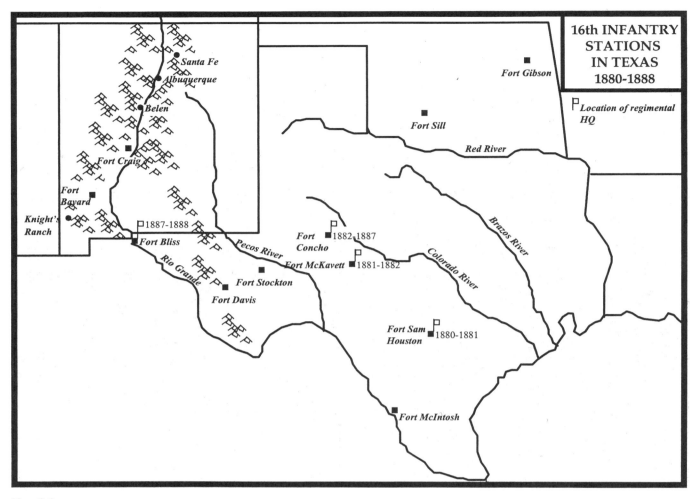

Map 3-2.

Not long after the arrival of the regimental headquarters at Fort Concho, Pennypacker's old war wounds troubled him anew to the point that he requested and received a three-month leave of absence. He left Fort Concho in August 1882, returning home to recover in the presence of family and friends in Chester, Pennsylvania. He was never to rejoin the regiment. His leave was extended so that he could travel to Europe for treatment, but apparently the trip did not alleviate his health problems. He was finally ordered to report before a retirement board in April 1883 and directed to be retired in July, thereby terminating the military service of the regimental commander who commanded the 16th Infantry longer than any other in its history.[20]

During Pennypacker's absence, the executive officer, Lieutenant Colonel Alfred Lacy Hough, ably commanded the regiment. Hough had been commissioned by the governor of Pennsylvania in 1861 for federal service and had served with distinction with the 19th Infantry during the war. After the war, he chose to remain in the army and secured a Regular Army commission. Pennypacker's retirement made a vacancy for a new colonel, but it was not to be Hough. Instead, Colonel Matthew Blunt was selected to fill the vacancy and command the 16th Infantry.

Blunt was a New Yorker who had graduated from West Point as an artilleryman in 1853 but served with the 12th U. S. Infantry in George Sykes's Regular Division during the Civil War. In fact, Blunt had commanded the 12th U. S. from Second Bull Run to Gettysburg and had won brevets up to the grade of colonel for his valor and courage under fire. After the war, he briefly commanded the 7th Infantry at Tallahassee, Florida, and was assigned as an assistant inspector general for the Department of the Cumberland in 1869-70. In October 1874, he was promoted to lieutenant colonel and assigned to the 25th Infantry, a post he held until he was promoted to colonel.[21] He took charge of the 16th Infantry on July 3, 1883, and would retain command for the next eleven years.

The decision to move the regiment to Texas was based in part on the decreased hostile activity in Kansas and the Victorio uprising in New Mexico. The move was not necessarily intended to put the 16th Infantry in the line of fire, but rather to free up other units to prosecute the campaigns against Geronimo in

New Mexico and Arizona. However, by the time the regiment arrived, Indian activity in west Texas had almost ceased. The period 1884-85 was so calm, that General Sheridan, in his annual report to the secretary of war, wrote: "The Department of Texas…has had an unusual quiet during the year. Furnished one quarter of its troops to aid in the protection of New Mexico from the Apaches, and all it could spare for operations in the Indian Territory."[22]

The lack of hostile Indian activity demonstrated that the army had been successful in taming the Wild West. However, the "quiet" that accompanied the success resulted in its own set of problems for the 16th Infantry. The first of these was desertion. During the period 1880-88 the regiment's average strength was thirty-five officers and 430 enlisted men. During the same period, losses due to desertion averaged forty-six men a year, or a little over 10 percent. While this seems quite high, the regiment actually had one of the lowest desertion rates in the army during that time. Conversely, the reenlistment rates in the regiment were among the highest in the army and were the highest for all white regiments in 1882 and 1884.[23]

These trends in the 16th Infantry can be attributed in large part to two factors. First, the quality of leadership in the regiment was good. The officers and NCOs were generally long-service men. They had been with their units for years, many since the reorganization of 1869, and they were experienced in using techniques that minimized discontent among soldiers. Second, duty in Texas, while boring at times, was relatively comfortable. The men did not have to spend long winters on the wind-swept prairies of Kansas or at isolated posts in the northern plains, where contact with civilians and the outside world was infrequent. The posts in Texas were located on stage routes or rail lines that brought a fair amount of contact with civilization. Additionally, each post had its own "Army Town" that offered some of the pleasures, albeit limited, that soldiers tended to pursue.

The commander of the Department of Texas, Brigadier General David S. Standley, attributed the high desertion rates in the army out west to two problems. First was the poor quality of food. This was particularly true in Texas, where the relatively warm temperatures year round encouraged the growth of bacteria in food, causing frequent illnesses in soldiers. The problem was somewhat alleviated later by providing ice-making machinery to Texas posts.

The second reason for desertion was the wool uniforms issued to the troops. While wool uniforms were fine for troops located in the northern posts such as Fort Abraham Lincoln or Fort Yellowstone for year-round wear, they were very uncomfortable in the heat of Texas summers, especially on campaign. Standley recommended a linen uniform for summer wear to relieve the discomfort experienced by the troops. Standley's recommendation was accepted, but development and testing of this uniform was slow, and the new uniform was not officially adopted until October 1888, after the 16th had been trans-

ferred to Fort Douglas, Utah.[24]

In spite of the lack of activity from hostiles, the 16th Infantry kept up patrolling activities in west Texas to ensure that any Indians roaming the area knew that the army was alert and prepared to act, or react, when, and wherever, necessary. West of Fort Concho were a number of subposts that were occupied, virtually on a constant basis, by companies or detachments of the 16th Infantry. These were Camp Elizabeth, located on the North Concho River nine miles northwest of the current town of Sterling City, Texas; Camp Charlotte, located on the Middle Concho River due west of San Angelo; and Grierson's Spring, located near the present town of Big Lake, Texas. The regiment used these camps as patrol bases from which the companies could easily foray into areas traditionally used by war parties.

A description of a typical tour at one of these subposts was rendered in a report dated March 24, 1881, from Lieutenant Isaac O. Shelby, in temporary command of A Company after that company's three-month stint at Grierson's Spring and Camp Charlotte. The company, consisting of Shelby and forty enlisted men, departed Fort Concho on December 21, 1880, and arrived at Grierson's Spring on Christmas day. Shelby wrote:

> The written and verbal instructions of the Commanding Officer of the District (Colonel Grierson, commanding the District of the Pecos) required me to leave a non-commissioned officer and three men at Camp Charlotte as a detachment of observation and to guard public forage, and with the remainder of the Company to take station at the Sub-Post of Grierson's Spring and scout the country frequently from thence well on to Camp Charlotte on the east, Pecos River on the west, old Camp Lancaster on the South, toward Castel Gap on the northwest, protect the Stage line and U.S. Mail from roving bands of whites and Indians and furnish such escorts for passing Government trains as were required.[25]

Lieutenant Shelby went on to say that during their tour "the Company scouted by detachments over ten hundred and seventy six (1076) miles of territory and…marched [a total of] twelve hundred and thirty six (1236) miles; that the country over which the Company and its detachments moved was quiet and that no traces of Indians or other marauders were discovered."[26]

In addition to the patrols, the men were put to use in other activities as well. Improving the subposts to make them more livable occupied most of the soldiers' time. During one of their tours at Grierson's Spring, F Company built several stone structures for storage and temporary defense. They also built a stone house for the company commander to reside in during their stay at Camp Charlotte. At Grierson's Spring, Company A built a stone kitchen and a bake house while they were there.

The regiment was put to use improving the sparse infrastructure in west Texas as well. A telegraph line was built by the 16th Infantry between Forts Davis, Concho, and Stockton, improving communications between those distant locations. Company F assumed the role of engineers and built a road between Colorado City, the railhead from which Fort Concho received supplies, and Camps Elizabeth and Charlotte in order to make resupply of those posts easier. Companies A and I were detailed to guard railroad crews as the Texas and Pacific Railroad was being built through west Texas.[27]

During the periods when their company was at home station at Fort Concho, the soldiers of the 16th Infantry had the opportunity to visit "the little town across the river" called San Angelo. While San Angelo offered many attractions to soldiers, the town was not always a safe place to seek them. A series of incidents occurred in January 1881 that give an insight into the town's dangers. These same events also give us a rare glimpse of the probably limited, but nonetheless real, camaraderie that developed between white soldiers of the 16th Infantry and black soldiers of the 10th Cavalry, while stationed together at Fort Concho.

The town of San Angelo was in its early stage of development and, as can be expected, consisted largely of saloons where the dregs of frontier society congregated to sate their desires for booze, women, and gambling. Because of these rough-hewn frontier types, violence and shootings in the town were frequent. On January 20, 1881 two soldiers from Fort Concho were killed in the saloon of John Nasworthy, an ex-sergeant, now barkeeper. A hooligan by the name of P. G. Watson, just arrived in San Angelo, decided for some reason to pistol-whip a Buffalo Soldier from E Troop, 10th Cavalry. Another soldier, T. Pinder from F Company, 16th Infantry, came to the aid of his fellow soldier but was quickly shot in the chest by Watson, who then also killed the other soldier. Friends rushed Watson to his horse, and he escaped. No one else lifted a hand to stop him. The lack of any real effort to catch the culprit on the part of the townspeople or law enforcement officers further exacerbated the already deep ill will the men of the garrison felt toward the town.[28]

Ten days later, on January 30, a young black trooper named William Watkins, also from E Troop, was shot and killed for no apparent reason by Thomas McCarthy on the street in front of a dive called Wilson's Saloon. Watkins' body lay in the street for some time before anybody bothered to report the incident. When the sheriff and a constable arrived, no one claimed any knowledge of the incident, although McCarthy was arrested later.[29]

The second killing was more than the troops could bear, and they resolved to do something about it. Colonel Grierson took extra precautions, such as holding additional roll calls and placing more sentries on guard at the fort, to prevent the troops from wreaking havoc on San Angelo. But one evening in the second week of February, the roll call after taps revealed a large number of men from both regiments absent. Meanwhile, a group of soldiers had pried open their arms racks and slipped into town to right some wrongs. Shortly after nine o'clock on the night of February 10, this group, about 130 strong and consisting of both black and white soldiers, showed up at the jail and demanded that the prisoner be turned over to them. Upon discovering that McCarthy was not there, they occupied Mrs. Tankersley's hotel, where McCarthy had been known to stay. When learning he was not there either, the soldiers found and held Sheriff J. D. Spears, telling him that he would die if he did not divulge the prisoner's whereabouts. Then, with the sheriff in tow, they searched the town and made threats that the town would be gutted if anybody attempted to stop them. After the passage of two tense hours an armed guard detail under Lieutenant Millard F. Eggleston, 10th Cavalry, arrived from the post. Upon seeing the detail entering town, the mob rapidly broke up and filtered back to the fort without having captured their man—and without having caused any real damage either.[30]

Not all of the excitement that the 16th Infantry experienced in Texas happened to the companies at Fort Concho, McKavett, and Stockton. After Fort McKavett closed in 1883, Companies D and E were transferred to Fort McIntosh in Laredo under the command of Captain Hugh Theaker. Their mission was to patrol the Texas border and prevent cross-border smuggling, livestock rustling, and general lawlessness. But occasionally, the duties involved something more interesting.

A local election took place in Laredo in April 1886 to select certain municipal officers. Many of the members of both parties were Mexican, and a dispute soon arose over who the winners were. The war of words soon became a war of bullets, but as long as the fighting was confined to the residents of Laredo, the garrison at Fort McIntosh, by law, could not interfere. However, when Mexicans from Nuevo Laredo began sending boatloads of armed men across the river, the dispute became an invasion of United States territory, and the post commander, Lieutenant Colonel R. F. Bernard of the 8th Cavalry, was promptly notified. Assembling the two companies of the 16th Infantry, Bernard moved them at the "double quick" into Laredo. Before the armed Mexicans could organize and seize any buildings, they were confronted by one hundred blue-clad soldiers bearing down on them. Resistance immediately crumbled, as the invaders dropped their weapons and threw up their hands or slipped away. Bernard had the soldiers round up the Mexicans and send them back across the river without weapons. Bernard's quick action protected the citizens from violence and prevented the possibility of fire and pillage. He and the soldiers of the 16th Infantry were personally thanked by the governor of Texas and the secretary of war for their prompt and effective actions to restore the peace in Laredo.[31]

Through much of 1885 and the first eight months of 1886, infantry and cavalry troops under General George Crook, and later General Nelson A. Miles, pursued Apache bands under Geronimo and a few lesser chiefs in New Mexico, Arizona, and Old Mexico. Finally, worn out, starving, and down to just a few warriors, Geronimo surrendered to Miles at Skeleton Canyon near Fort Bowie, Arizona, on September 4, 1886. Geronimo and a number of the other chiefs were put on a train to be imprisoned in Florida, but because of a disagreement between President Grover Cleveland and Miles over the details of the conditions of the surrender agreement, the chiefs were ordered to detrain at the Post of San Antonio, which they did on September 10. Company K, 16th Infantry, was detailed as the guard force while the Apaches were held in the "Quadrangle" at the post. On October 22 however, after a little over a month at San Antonio, Geronimo and his band were reloaded on a train, and K Company provided the guard detail that escorted Geronimo on his journey to Fort Pickens, Florida.[32]

In his report to the secretary of war for 1886, Major General Alfred H. Terry noted, "The year has been lacking in events in the Department of Texas."[33] This may have been true in terms of Indian activity, but the summer of 1886 brought a sea wind of change for the regiment and heralded the beginning of the end of the 16th Infantry's tour in Texas. On June 30, the orders issued back in 1882 for the abandonment of Fort Stockton were finally carried out, and Companies I and K were transferred to Fort Davis and San Antonio, respectively. Both Fort Stockton and Fort Concho had lived out their usefulness for the army, but had been kept open because there was no place else to quarter companies in the state. Nonetheless, with four new troops of cavalry being transferred to the Department of Texas that summer, the department commander decided to keep Fort Concho open a short while longer. However, with the new barracks at Fort Bliss, Fort Davis, and the Post of San Antonio completed that fall, the Headquarters and Companies B and H of the 16th Infantry were transferred from Fort Concho to Fort Bliss in January 1887, leaving only Companies C and F at Concho.[34]

The only other event of note for the regiment in 1887 was a drill meet at Paris, Texas, in June. Companies A, G, and K traveled to this meet, which was attended by elements of the 3rd and 8th Cavalry Regiments as well. No record exists as to the success of the regiment's participants, but it is interesting to note how fast the hard-bitten frontier Indian fighters were transformed into spit-and-polish parade-ground soldiers. Texas had indeed been tamed. The days when troops in Texas were needed to protect the frontier had passed. So it was no surprise when Colonel Blunt received General Order No. 20, dated April 13, 1888, directing that the 16th Infantry be transferred to the Department of the Platte. Further instructions from the department commander directed Colonel Blunt to proceed to take station at Fort Douglas and to detail four companies to occupy Fort Duchesne on the Uintah River.

In May, the regiment, less the Headquarters and Companies B and H, was assembled at San Antonio to prepare for the move to Utah. The Headquarters and Companies B and H departed El Paso by rail and arrived at Fort Douglas on May 30. The remainder of the regiment boarded trains in San Antonio on the 28th and arrived at Fort Douglas on June 2. Shortly after arrival, Companies A, C, F, and K, under the command of Lieutenant Colonel Hough, made the 156-mile march to Fort Duchesne, arriving there on June 19.[35]

The regiment's new mission was to oversee the restless Uncompahgre and White River Utes, the same Indians who had risen against Nathan Meeker at the White River Agency ten years before. But by the time the 16th Infantry settled in at their new posts, these Indians showed little inclination to cause problems and posed little threat to surrounding communities. The regiment's main activity, therefore, was improving the dilapidated conditions of the posts where they were stationed.

Fort Douglas, named after Senator Stephen A. Douglas, was established by Colonel Patrick E. Conner and the 3rd California Infantry in 1862. The stated reason for its establishment was to protect the overland mail and telegraph lines from the Indians. But it was also built to keep an eye on the Mormons, who were not trusted by Secretary of War Edwin M. Stanton. After the Civil War, the central location of the post warranted its retention, and a series of different units occupied it prior to the 16th Infantry's arrival. But those units suffered through their tour at the fort because of the War Department's inadequate funding for its upkeep. In September 1889, the department commander, Brigadier General John R. Brooke, reported his concerns to the secretary of war, relating, "Fort Douglas is rapidly deteriorating and cannot be kept in proper repair with the small allotments made available."[36]

The regiment's other station, Fort Duchesne, was in even worse condition than Fort Douglas. Established by Major Frederick W. Benteen, of Little Big Horn fame, on August 20, 1886, it was situated on the Uintah River, three miles north of its juncture with the Duchesne River. The post was purposely located on the Uintah Agency to be within rapid striking distance should hostilities break out. Because of its isolated location, little in the way of creature comforts or even premanufactured construction materials were available. As a result, many troops lived in what were essentially log huts. General Brooke's report about Duchesne stated that the quarters were "of a most temporary and inadequate character" and recommended money for improvements.[37]

Unfortunately, Brooke's request was not acted upon. Instead, Fort Duchesne was ordered to be abandoned—but not for three more years, so the companies there suffered through bitter winters in spartan conditions. On September 4, 1891, Companies B, D, and G (which had replaced the previous companies earlier so that the misery could be shared) departed Fort Duchesne to take permanent station at Fort Douglas with the rest of the regiment. Company I remained to salvage the post and marched away on February 3, 1892. The consolidation of the 16th Infantry at Fort Douglas did not remedy the quartering problem. Now, instead of log huts, four companies were billeted in tents. Anxious to get his troops out of the tents, General Brooke once again urgently requested money to improve the existing barracks and to build new barracks. Additionally, money was requested for the post sewer system,

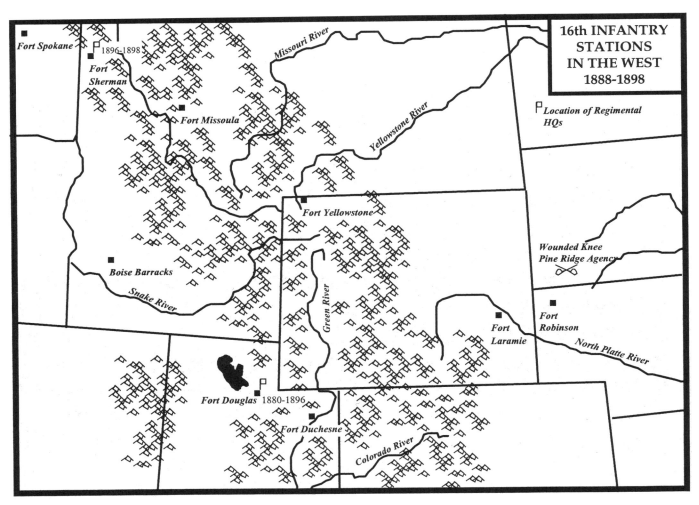

Map 3-3.

which was in bad shape and a potential health hazard.[38]

The urgency of the situation finally brought some action, but tardily. About the time the regiment was getting ready to leave Fort Douglas in September 1896, Brigadier General Frank Wheaton, the new department commander, reported that on his recent inspection he "found the post and garrison in a highly creditable state of efficiency and a most marked improvement since [his] inspection of the previous year." He also remarked that $5,000 was finally provided for the much-needed repairs to the sewer system. The barracks and officers quarters he found to be very good, but still "insufficient for the size of the garrison."[39]

The quartering woes not withstanding, the regiment still had its duties to perform, and one of the tasks that the 16th Infantry was selected to test was an experiment in turning Indians into soldiers. In the summer of 1890, Companies I and K of all line regiments were inactivated consequent to a downsizing of the army. The following year, the idea of enlisting Indians into regular units was adopted for test purposes. Indian scouts had been members of the U.S. Army for many years, but this plan called for enlisting Indians from various tribes and forming them into companies and troops in infantry and cavalry regiments of the Regular Army. The 16th Infantry was selected to be one of the regiments to test the idea, and Company I was directed to be reactivated and recruited to full strength with Brule Sioux from the Rosebud Agency.[40]

The initial results of this experiment were promising. While many of the troops scoffed at the idea of trying to make soldiers of Indians, they soon had reason to reconsider. A small detachment from Company I under the command of Lieutenant Lewis S. Sorley was given the mission of tracking down an escaped prisoner. With little in the way of clues as to where the prisoner might be, the Indians quickly tracked him down and turned him over to the authorities, thereby earning the grudging respect of the once-dubious regulars.[41]

In his report to the Secretary of War for 1892, General Brooke wrote:

I do not deem it wise to attempt further enlistments of Indians up to this time, but shall do so should a favorable opportunity occur. There are at this time four companies of infantry and one of cavalry in the department. As far as can be judged, the experiment of making soldiers of Indians promises success.[42]

However, just the following year he wrote:

The principal problem with Indian soldiers is that they don't speak English. They have a natural dread of ridicule on account of mistakes made in their attempts to speak the language. The ultimate success of the experiment depends on the Indian soldiers themselves.[43]

And finally:

There are only four companies of Indian infantry and six troops of cavalry left in the U.S. Army. The lack of knowledge of English, restlessness, unfamiliar environments and new habits contributed to failure of the program. Continued service will benefit neither them nor the Army.[44]

A short time later, orders went out to discharge the Indians. Company I was skeletonized but not inactivated. The officers and NCOs remained assigned to the company for a time in anticipation of reactivating it in the future. But no such orders were forthcoming, and the officers and NCOs were eventually reassigned.[45]

Pine Ridge Campaign (Wounded Knee)
January 1-23, 1891
On December 31, 1890, the regiment received orders from the Department of the Platte directing that four companies proceed to Fort Robinson, Nebraska, to participate in the containment of the "Ghost Dance" uprising. The Ghost Dance was the brainchild of a Paiute shaman named Wovoka. This medicine man's new religious doctrine was seized upon by some plains tribes, especially the Sioux, and used by rebellious chiefs and leaders to whip up certain elements of the tribes to a fighting pitch. The dance and "Ghost Shirts" were supposed to protect these Indians from the white man's bullets and allow them to defeat him in battle. Many Indians slipped off their reservations, and one group of Miniconjou and Hunkpapa Sioux under Big Foot headed for the Pine Ridge Agency to link up with the Oglala after the attempted arrest and death of Sitting Bull by reservation police on December 15. This was the band of Indians who were overtaken by the 7th Cavalry near Wounded Knee Creek in South Dakota, and with whom fighting broke out on December 29, 1890, resulting in the last major battle between the U.S. Army and Native Americans.

At the time of the Wounded Knee clash, the overall situation was extremely tense on all of the reservations in the northern plains. While minor incidents between Indians and whites broke out here and there, the potential for a major outbreak of

violence was imminent as the anger of the Indians came to the boiling point. In anticipation of further fighting, on January 1, Companies D, E, G, and H boarded the Union Pacific in Salt Lake City and arrived at Fort Robinson on the 3rd to assist in forming the second ring of troops around the Pine Ridge Agency. The following day, Companies D and E, under Captain Henry C. Ward, traveled by rail to Chadron, Nebraska, and from there marched to Adalon, going into camp just southwest of the Pine Ridge Agency. On January 5, Companies G and H, under Major John B. Parke, proceeded from Fort Robinson by rail to Oilrich, South Dakota, and camped there. Both elements were positioned to reinforce units already cordoned around the Indians at Pine Ridge.[46]

The situation remained tense for the next two weeks, but the tension gradually faded, as perceptive and thoughtful Indian leaders convinced their hotheaded braves of the futility of fighting such an overwhelming force. The ad hoc battalion under Major Parke saw no action but stood in readiness to respond if a battle developed. The battalion remained in position until January 19. By that time, the Ghost Dance rebellion had failed, and the Indians were once again under control. The companies returned to Fort Robinson and from there boarded a train to Fort Douglas, arriving home on January 23.[47]

Thus ended the 16th Infantry Regiment's contribution to the taming of the West. In reality, the regiment's role in the big picture was a minor one. Other regiments had experienced a great deal more combat and glory and had done more to bring the chapter of Indian warfare to its final conclusion. But the men of the 16th Infantry, who suffered through long winters on the wind-swept plains, lived in inadequate quarters on isolated posts, and marched hundreds of miles across hot west Texas deserts in anticipation of facing a marauding band of fierce warriors at any turn, felt that at least they did their share of the work. Though their actual combat with Indians was relatively limited, their efforts to provide security for settlers and railroad workers, and build roads and telegraph lines, accomplished as much as any other regiment to bring civilization to what were once the most dangerous areas of the American West.

The final major event of the regiment's tour at Fort Douglas occurred in the summer of 1894. That spring, coal miners in Colorado, Arizona, and New Mexico were discontented with their working conditions. This discontentment boiled over in July, and a call by those states' governors went out to the War Department for assistance. Brigadier General M. D. M'Cook, commander of the Department of Colorado, ordered the dispatch of two companies of the 16th Infantry to quell disturbances by coal miners associated with the railroad strike at Grand Junction, Colorado. The two companies arrived at Grand Junction at 6 p.m. on July 9 and immediately took possession of the rail yards. The following day, a company was directed to proceed to New Castle where miners were interfering with the movement of coal trains in that town. As at Grand Junction, the arrival of the troops eliminated interference with rail operations and ended the miners' threatened violence. After several days of martial law, the miners stopped their troublemaking, and the companies returned to their home station.[48]

In late summer of 1896, the final phase of the 16th Infantry's service in the Indian pacification effort began. War Department General Order No. 43, dated September 18, directed the transfer of the regiment to the Department of the Columbia. The regimental headquarters and Companies C, D, F, G, and H were posted to Fort Sherman at Coeur d'Alene, Idaho, under Colonel Hugh A. Theaker, the new regimental commander; Companies B and E were posted to Fort Spokane, Washington under Lieutenant Colonel E. M. Coates; and Company A was posted to Boise Barracks under Major William H. McLaughlin. From the beginning, it was apparent that the regiment would not be stationed at these posts for long. In 1897, Brigadier General Henry C. Merriam, the department commander, wrote, "Forts Spokane and Sherman, although new, may be said to have already fulfilled their mission. Boise Barracks has lost its strategic importance and suggest [its] possible early abandonment."[49] As it turned out, the regiment was not stationed in the "Great Northwest" for long—but not for reasons associated with the strategic importance of these posts.

The 16th Infantry was relatively inactive for the eighteen months it was at these stations. After its arrival, the Department of Colorado held a track and field meet in Denver. The team from the 16th Infantry competed against the teams from seven other regiments in the department and took first place overall.[50] While it is commendable that the regiment won, the fact that the department had the time to plan and execute such an activity reinforced the feeling that the Indian wars were truly at an end. The U.S. Army was now without an immediate real world threat for the first time since its inception in 1776. This situation would not last long, however, for trouble was brewing in different parts of the world that would start the regiment on an adventure encompassing a series of small wars and relatively short tours at distant posts.

The event that started the regiment on its next adventure occurred on Cuba when, on the night of February 15, 1898, the U.S.S. *Maine* blew up in Havana Harbor under mysterious circumstances. The anti-Spanish press in America reinforced the rumor that the cause was a Spanish mine or some other "infernal machine." A Spanish diplomat's insult of President William McKinley just prior to the incident made it easier to whip the American people into a fighting mood after the *Maine* disaster. Calls for war and revenge echoed through the halls of Congress and, on April 11, the president finally declared war. The declaration of war started the 16th Infantry on its way south and eventually put it in harm's way against its first foreign enemy.

Troops of the 16th Infantry crouch to avoid the fire coming from San Juan Heights

Chapter Four
Foreign Adventures

The dash and spirit displayed by the 6th and 16th regiments of infantry, which came under my observation, were marvelous. I never saw troops fight better.

Count von Goetzen
German Military Attaché to the U.S. Army, at San Juan Hill, July 1, 1898

The call for war in the winter and spring of 1898 was too much for politicians to resist, so the country committed itself to armed conflict with Spain. The realization of the inevitability of the war was not lost on Colonel Theaker, and he began preparing the regiment for movement. The lazy days of garrison routine were fast coming to an end for the 16th Infantry, and no one was surprised when orders were received on April 15 to move to the concentration point at New Orleans. However, before the regiment entrained for the Crescent City, the orders were changed to move to Camp Thomas, Georgia, where the Regular Army infantry, cavalry, and artillery regiments were to concentrate so they could train together before overseas deployment.[1]

The regiment departed in two elements, on April 17 and 22. By the last day of the month it was assembled in one location for the first time since October 1896. Camp Thomas, located on the Chickamauga battlefield, was named for Major General George H. Thomas, the "Rock of Chickamauga." The regiment was encamped close to the location where the Civil War 16th Infantry (no relation to our regiment) withstood the assaults that earned Thomas his sobriquet.[2]

At Camp Thomas, the regiment was briefly attached to I Corps, but the stay in northwest Georgia was short and left little time for training. On May 10, Brigadier General John R. Brooke, the I Corps commander, was directed to send the 16th Infantry, along with four other infantry regiments, to Tampa, Florida, to reinforce Major General William R. Shafter's V Corps. The regiment broke camp on May 12, marched to Ringgold, Georgia, and entrained for Tampa, arriving there on the 14th. At Tampa, the 16th Infantry was brigaded once again with its old comrades from Civil War days, the 6th Infantry, and with the 71st Infantry, New York National Guard. Together, these regiments formed the 1st Brigade, 1st Division, V Corps. Brigadier General Hamilton S. Hawkins, who had briefly commanded the 16th Infantry in 1894, was the brigade commander.[3]

Like the stay at Camp Thomas, the time spent in Tampa was short. The McKinley administration, originally committed to waiting for an autumn invasion of Cuba, after the peak danger periods of yellow fever and malaria, reversed its decision and endorsed an immediate invasion. The switch was brought about by several factors. First, the navy pushed for an early inva-

sion after their easy victory over the Spanish squadron at Manila Bay and the Spanish fleet's failure to challenge the U.S. blockade of Cuba. Second, a new assessment by McKinley's medical advisors determined that the original survey of the dangers of yellow fever infestation were overstated and that an invasion in the spring could be mounted without massive numbers of troops contracting the disease. And finally, on the diplomatic level, the administration feared that if it waited, Spain might succeed in getting other European powers to intervene on its behalf. Thus on May 2, General Miles was directed to mount an invasion at the earliest possible occasion.[4]

So the rush was on. On June 7, 1st Lieutenant John E. Woodward, acting regimental adjutant, received orders from General Miles's aide to the effect that "all troops not on board transports at daylight would be left as [the] fleet pulled out" the next day. At this time, the regiment had only seven wagons, so all tentage was left, and the remaining equipment was mostly hand carried by the troops to the railroad siding. Loading began at 2:00 in the morning of June 8, and the train pulled into Port Tampa at 5:00 a.m. Three hours later, the regiment began embarking on the USCT *San Marcos*. The whole loading operation, from bivouac to boarding, was a testimony to poor planning and poorer execution. Woodward recalled that the episode "was a horrible experience. I am afraid for many. A disgrace to our staff Dept certainly, but being one of the 1st Regiments in that morning, we fared much better than the rest."[5]

At this time, the strength of the regiment was twenty-three officers and 664 enlisted men, or about half of its authorized peacetime strength. Orders published by the War Department on April 27 had authorized the Regular Army to reorganize its regiments under the new three-battalion, twelve-company, table of organization. However, as a result of the McKinley administration's urging to begin the invasion promptly, the recruits enlisted to raise these new companies were destined not to join their regiments until after the fighting was concluded. The 16th Infantry would fight this war in the old ten-company configuration, but with two companies, I and L, still inactive.[6]

The troops waited on board the *San Marcos* for the next six days while the remainder of the invasion force was transported to the port and loaded. Finally, on June 14, all was ready, and the fleet of transports set sail. On June 22, the force arrived off the southern Cuban coast at Siboney, about ten miles to the southwest of Santiago de Cuba, the V Corps' ultimate objective. Remaining idle on board for two days, the regiment finally disembarked at Siboney on June 24, and went into camp near that point.

Later that day, elements of the regiment were ordered to move into a reserve line to protect the encampment. As the troops were moving up, they noticed wounded American troops being carried back toward the transports. Soon, word filtered down that Teddy Roosevelt's 1st U.S. Volunteer Cavalry had been in a scrap and had lost fifteen killed and forty-nine wounded. Rumor had it that the regimental commander, Colonel Leonard Wood, had also been killed in the fight. Suddenly, the real meaning of what the war in Cuba might entail began to hit home to the troops.

Upon reaching the military crest of the ridges overlooking the encampment, the troops fell to the ground, exhausted by the steamy tropical heat. The 1st Battalion was ordered back to camp, but the 2nd Battalion remained on outpost duty on the high ground that night.

The next day, the regiment moved to another camp about a mile and a half west of Sevilla, where it entrenched. While encamped at Sevilla, G Company was briefly detached to support other units in a minor reconnaissance in force. The regiment remained there until the morning of June 27, when the entire brigade marched toward Santiago, led by the 16th Infantry. The route took the brigade through the bottom of a rather large valley, thick with tropical undergrowth and dense, green foliage on the hillsides. The intense heat and humidity was hard on the unacclimatized men, but the move was made slowly and without a great deal of straggling. After moving about six miles, the troops halted and, once again, went into camp.

From this camp the troops could see part of the defenses that ringed Santiago, including the hill they would soon storm. That day, Lieutenant Woodward wrote in his diary that on the "Height on the hill to our right are two blockhouses and it is said that they are still held by the Spanish and are used as signal towers….Had a splendid view of the valley in front of us and the defensive lines of Santiago, at least part of them. It looks like a tough nut to crack, but if they go at it right it will come." The

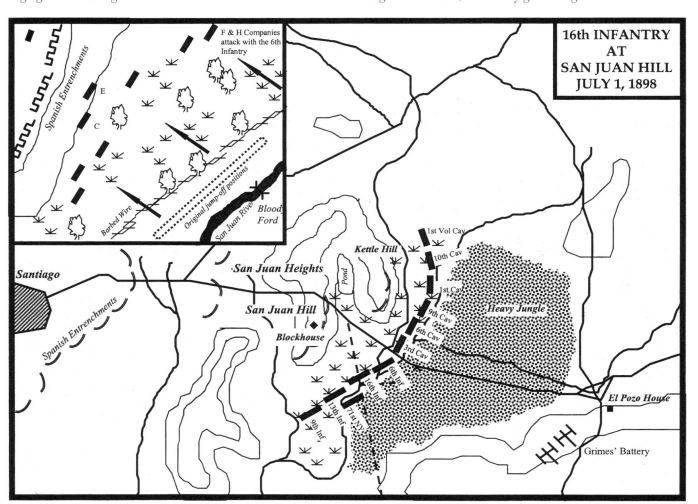

Map 4-1.

men of the 16th Infantry would soon have the opportunity to play the role of nutcracker.[7]

Santiago
July 1-17, 1898

As the buglers sounded reveille at 3:30 a.m. July 1, the troops of Hawkins's 1st Brigade began to stir. Anticipation filled the air as the troops went about their preparations to move. After a hastily prepared breakfast, the brigade moved toward Santiago at 5:00 a.m. The brigade order of movement placed the 6th Infantry in the lead, the 71st New York second, and the 16th bringing up the rear. The immediate objective of the 1st Division was to assault San Juan Hill. Nearby, a few hundred yards northeast of San Juan Hill, was Kettle Hill, the objective of Brigadier General Joseph "Fighting Joe" Wheeler's cavalry division.

Defending the hills around Santiago was the Division Santiago de Cuba, a mixed force of Spanish regulars sent over from the Home Army in Spain to suppress the insurrection, units of the Spanish Colonial Army, and Cuban loyalist volunteers. The division was commanded by General Arsenio Linares Pombo, and consisted of twelve infantry battalions, a battalion of mounted rifles, four cavalry squadrons, a battalion of mountain artillery, sappers, a telegraph company, and a few support and supply units.[8] An impressive force on paper, the division had no experience in sustained combat, lacked the cohesion that comes with training, and had little time to repair its deficiencies before the V Corps arrived at Siboney. Nonetheless, the Spaniards had prepared trenches, blockhouses, and other defensive positions, and cleared fields of fire along the avenues of approach to the city before the arrival of the Americans on the outskirts of Santiago. And they were prepared to inflict as many casualties as possible on the detested "Americanos."

The 1st Brigade's route of march was a narrow trail that caused the column to move sluggishly, as the humid, oppressive summer heat began to make itself felt. With B Company, commanded by fifty-eight-year-old Captain George H. Palmer, in the lead, the regiment's advance was slow and tedious. After passing the 1st Division Field Hospital, the column rested in place for about an hour, then resumed the march. At 7:00 a.m. another thirty-minute halt was made about a mile east of a trail junction that was the site of an old sugar refinery called the El Pozo House. Here, the troops were ordered to leave their packs to lighten their load and reduce fatigue. Continuing the march, the regiment passed the El Pozo House and quickly came under fire from Spanish cannon and rifles. The fight was on.

Orders came down the line for the regiment to move up to support the now-engaged 6th Infantry. To accomplish this, the men had to pass the cowering troops of the 71st New York, who were laying flat in the path to avoid Spanish bullets. The narrow trail was so cramped with prone soldiers that the regiment had to pass through the New Yorkers by stepping over them in single file. Having gotten past the 71st New York, the men of the 16th found themselves on a winding trail that proved difficult to follow because of the numerous tracks that intersected it. At times unable to distinguish trail from intersecting track, some elements headed off down the latter, causing them to become separated from the main body of the regiment.[9]

Constant fire from unseen Spanish riflemen made matters worse for the troops. The volume of enemy fire steadily increased and, with thick foliage on either side barring the way to off-trail deployment, casualties began to mount. The dense undergrowth further stymied the Americans by screening the Spaniards from anything in the way of accurate return fire. Recalling the bullets and shrapnel that raked their line, one of the regiment's officers later wrote, "It was a jungle of death. We were under this severe fire which seemed to be coming from all directions."[10] It became apparent to the men of the 16th Infantry that a Signal Corps observation balloon moving with their column was inadvertently pinpointing their location to the Spanish troops. The balloon was removed, but the damage had been done: the Spaniards knew where the Americans were and had a pretty good idea where they were going. The regiment pushed along the trail for another hour and a half before turning onto another trail leading westward to the San Juan River.[11]

The river generally flowed from north to south, perpendicular to the regiment's line of march. Upon reaching the river, the various companies of the regiment began fording at separate points. At one location, which became known as "Bloody Ford," the regiment took many of its casualties as Companies A and D moved across. Captain Theophilus W. Morrison, commanding D Company, was struck by rifle fire at this ford as he led his troops across. Morrison had been with the 16th Infantry since April 1869, twenty-nine years in the same regiment. Though he was the regiment's only officer killed in action that day, many others would be wounded before it was over.[12]

On the far side of the San Juan, officers and NCOs labored to get six companies of the 16th Infantry into battle lines for the eight hundred-yard assault up San Juan Hill. Once in position, the fatigued troops threw themselves down in a sunken road to rest and to take cover from the rifle fire. The scorching heat and humid conditions were also taking a heavy toll on the men. In his after-action report, Colonel Theaker recalled, "On reaching this point, the command being almost exhausted and myself entirely so, we rested about fifteen minutes."[13]

For some reason, Companies F and H had been diverted from the regiment by Lieutenant Woodward, who was now an acting staff officer with the 1st Brigade. Woodward linked them up with the 6th Infantry on the left, and they would make the charge up the hill with that regiment. Once the 6th and 16th Infantry Regiments were ready, General Hawkins and Brigadier General Jacob F. Kent, the 1st Division commander, arrived and ordered the assault to go forward. It was about 2:00 p.m.[14]

As the regiment moved out, it quickly encountered a barbed-wire obstacle that checked its advance. The obstacle consisted of six wire strands and was strongly anchored, primarily to trees and an overgrown hedge. Beyond the fence was a relatively steep, open slope covered with high grass through which the regiment had to advance. The San Juan Hill blockhouse stood in plain view on the hill beyond the open ground. For about fifteen minutes, the troops worked their way through the obstacles under increasing volumes of fire. Using bayonets and rifle butts, they attempted to break the wire and uproot posts.

As the troops struggled to get through the wire, U.S. artillery, especially a battery under Captain George S. Grimes near the El Pozo House, began to find the range of the Spanish entrenchments. The artillery fire initially caused much confusion in the regiment when some of the rounds landed within its ranks. At one point, Captain Charles H. Noble, leading the 2nd Battalion—which was now half way up the slope—received word from Colonel Theaker to fall back. But Theaker was well to the rear, unable to see the guns and thus to make a proper assessment of the situation. The messenger told Noble that "The Colonel says that is a Spanish battery and orders you to fall back." Noble was stunned. He was reluctant to withdraw after going so far, but as Theaker was nowhere to be found—Noble would later claim that Theaker had just "disappeared"—he had no choice but to return with his men to the foot of the hill. There he located a better approach to the top, but in doing so he lost valuable time in making his assault.[15]

By then, the regiment had broken into small groups moving independently of each other. Little remained of what could be called an "assault line." Spanish fire became so intense that company commanders and their troops both realized that they could no longer wait for the regimental commander to organize and lead them in a mass attack. Separately, companies began to charge up the hill, firing as they advanced, without stopping to take up support positions.[16]

Leading the regiment's attack was E Company under Captain William C. McFarland. McFarland's actions that day were related in an article in the *Army and Navy Journal:*

Here it was that Captain McFarland rushed to the front, and, sword in hand, urged his men up the hill under a withering fire. When about fifty yards from the blockhouse a shell from Grimes' battery exploded right over Captain McFarland, Lieutenant Ord, Sergeant Spears, Sergeant Boone, Corporal Fleming, and Private Goode. Lieutenant Ord was knocked down and Captain McFarland was struck in the head and fell forward, the blood streaming from his wound. Sergt. Boone rushed to him and helped to bind up his head with what is known as the emergency bandage. They were standing in wild grass up to their necks, and the officers in charge of the battery could not distinguish them even with their glasses. McFarland sprang to his feet and put his hat on his sword and waved it to notify the battery to cease firing. All of this was in a perfect rain of Mauser bullets.[17]

Under Captain McFarland's leadership, E Company was the first unit to storm the top of the hill and root out the remaining Spanish defenders who had not already fled to the next line of defenses.

To the right of E Company, Company A, under Lieutenant Richard R. Steedman, made for the hill as well. They, too, had a harrowing charge. Steedman recalled,

Our lines were scattered somewhat in moving forward, owing to distance passed over, steepness of slope, and the enemy's fires. Our foremost men were delayed a few moments near the crest of the hill from our artillery fire and from orders sent us [from Theaker], but continued the assault, and were among the first to gain the top directly in front of this trench, so that as we gained the crest many of our men had to step over this trench filled with dead and wounded [Spaniards].

Gallantry under fire was not in short supply in the 16th Infantry that day. Two trumpeters from the regiment had been detached to act as couriers for General Hawkins. These men were Private Henry C. Schroeder of G Company and a Private Doras from C Company. General Hawkins, concerned that the advance might falter due to difficulties with the wire obstacle, directed these two to blow the trumpet call for "Forward" to urge the assault troops on. The bugle call, of course, brought a hail of rifle fire each time it was sounded. Schroeder was particularly aggressive in his efforts, but somehow came through unscathed. At the urging of the trumpeters, the men continued to make their way through the wire and up the hill. Schroeder was awarded the Silver Star for his heroism that day.[18]

During the movement up the trail, the regimental color sergeant from F Company was struck and killed. Corporal William G. Van Horne seized the color and fell in next to Sergeant John P. Diehl, who carried the national color. Originally supposed to move with F Company (the color company), the two became separated and ended up with H Company and made the attack up San Juan Hill with that unit. The color bearers carried the colors furled until reaching the summit, where they shook them out and waved them furiously. However, for twenty minutes after the capture of the summit, the troops on the top continued to receive fire from friendly units to the rear that were still moving to get to the top. Sergeant Diehl began to move along the crest waving the U.S. color to signal the units to cease firing. A short time later, Lieutenant John F. Preston Jr. did the same with the regimental color and, finally, the friendly fire ended.[19]

Upon reaching the summit, Captain Samuel R. Whitall, commanding H Company, directed his men to seize the blockhouse and the immediate surrounding area. Having done so, the H Company troopers opened a brisk fire on the retreating Spaniards, who were now in the process of moving to the next trench line toward Santiago. By about 3:00 p.m., all companies of the 16th Infantry were on the hill and preparing the position for defense. Theaker and Hawkins arrived about thirty minutes after the crest was secured.

After the capture of the hill, Major William H. McLaughlin gathered Companies B, C, and H and, about 4:30 p.m., moved them into position on a ridge to the south of the blockhouse. These troops provided supporting fire for the 10th Infantry's attack on a trench line about four hundred yards away. This attack was completed in the dark, and units began entrenching and improving existing trenches. The remaining units of the 16th moved to join McLaughlin's force that night, while Roosevelt's 1st Volunteer Cavalry came over from Kettle Hill and began to improve positions on the 16th's right, on San Juan Hill itself.[20]

Construction of the forward entrenchments was completed about 3:00 a.m. on July 2, and Companies B, G, and H occupied the position with the remaining companies stationed behind in support. At dawn, Spanish troops delivered a heavy fire that continued in spasms throughout the day. In the trenches, Captain William Lassiter, commanding G Company, was wounded by rifle fire, only one of several casualties incurred during the day. About 10:00 that night, Spanish troops made a determined assault against the regiment but were handily defeated by superior American marksmanship.[21]

The regiment manned these positions until July 10, when it was moved to a position about one and a half miles northeast of the city of Santiago itself. There it was detailed to protect three batteries of artillery (Haine's, Parkhurst's, and Hamilton's Batteries) engaged in the bombardment of the city. It remained in those trenches until July 17, when the Spanish surrendered.[22] The fighting in Cuba was over.

Despite a disorganized assault and the absence of the regimental commander and the leadership he should have provided for the charge on San Juan Hill, the performance of the 16th Infantry at Santiago was superb. Only a cohesive, well-disciplined unit could carry out such an attack under those conditions. Theaker, fifty-eight years old at the time of the battle, was physically incapable of providing the leadership required of the situation. He gave confused commands at times and did not place himself where he could effectively control his unit and properly assess the situation. Instead, the attack was led by seasoned company commanders, some not too much younger than Theaker, largely acting independently, and was carried out by the zeal of young and healthy, though inexperienced, soldiers who instinctively knew what had to be done and acted accordingly. This combination of factors made the difference between success and failure that day.

The regiment paid a price for its success, however. During the campaign, it lost one officer and thirteen enlisted men killed, and six officers and 109 enlisted men wounded in action. The company commanders were particularly hard hit, with five of eight commanders being killed or wounded. In addition to the death of Captain Morrison of D Company, the following company commanders were wounded: Captain George H. Palmer,

B Company; Captain W. C. McFarland, E Company; Captain Thomas C. Woodbury, F Company; and Captain William Lassiter, G Company. Thus, the 16th Infantry suffered more casualties from enemy action than any other regiment in Cuba.[23]

The regiment's fighting abilities did not go unnoticed. Observing the charge on July 1, Count von Goetzen, the German military attaché to the U.S. Army in Cuba, remarked that "the dash and spirit displayed by the 6th and 16th regiments of infantry, which came under my observation, were marvelous. I never saw troops fight better." In his otherwise praiseless report of the action that day, Colonel Theaker accurately wrote, "When all did so well it would be difficult to specify particular acts of gallantry." In confirmation of that remark, of the approximately five hundred officers and men who made the assault that day, forty-nine members of the regiment were commended by name in the War Department General Orders No. 15 dated February 13, 1900.[24]

After the war, controversy arose over who did what at San Juan Hill. The capture of the hill and blockhouse were clearly the results of efforts by the 16th and 6th Infantry Regiments, though the 13th Infantry later attempted to claim credit for the capture of the blockhouse proper. Of course, the newspapers of the time had erroneously given sole credit for the capture of San Juan Hill to Roosevelt's "Rough Riders," even though they made their main assault up Kettle Hill (after which they went on to San Juan Hill).

As to which of the two regiments, the 6th or 16th, actually captured the blockhouse, no one will probably ever know, though the route taken by the 16th was more direct to that location. The 6th Infantry tried to claim their colors were first on the hill because the 16th's were not seen. The 16th's colors, however, were furled until the bearers reached the top, which led General Hawkins to weigh in on the controversy, stating that the flag incident "contrasts unjustly to the Sixteenth." Colonel Theaker also asserted unequivocally that "the colors of the Sixteenth Infantry were the first colors on the hill" and two other commanders, among the first troops on the hill, staunchly supported his assertion.[25]

Captain Noble later urged Colonel Theaker on several occasions to submit a more detailed report on the regiment's actions to get them on the record. Theaker refused to do so. One is tempted to wonder why. Perhaps it was he could not provide a precise report because he was not actually present in the charge and final assault on the hill, and was embarrassed to admit his whereabouts when his regiment was doing its job. This seems even more plausible when one considers the fact that McLaughlin assumed effective field command of the regiment on July 3 for the rest of the campaign. Theaker retired from the army less than six weeks later. Nevertheless, Noble did make the effort to complete the record by submitting a supplementary report to the War Department in December 1898. In his mind, there was no doubt that the 16th Infantry took the blockhouse and was first on the hill. He wrote:

The colors of the Sixteenth Infantry were first on the hill and planted there, to denote our victory and our position. In justice to the officers of the regiment and the request of some, I submit this report. It seems to me right and my duty to do so as the senior officer present during the battle. I beg to insist that this report and the reports of the several company commanders should govern for the action of the Sixteenth Infantry on this day of victory.[26]

During their three weeks on occupation duty, the units of the V Corps were rapidly decimated by yellow fever and various maladies brought on by heat, poor food, and a host of other causes. General Shafter had been sending daily reports of the problems to the secretary of war. The secretary, in turn, informed the president of the difficulties, and soon after, McKinley directed that the troops be brought home immediately. The 16th Infantry was marched to Santiago on August 8, and boarded the USCT *Grand Duchesse* for the return trip to the United States. On August 10, the ship set sail, arriving at Montauk, Long Island, New York, on the 15th. The regiment was detained in a yellow fever isolation camp for several days, then moved to Camp Wikoff, near Montauk, for rest and recuperation.[27]

During the campaign, reinforcements for the regiment began arriving in Cuba. The influx of new recruits was a result of the general recruiting efforts back home to increase Regular Army units to the authorized strength for a three-battalion regiment. On July 13, Companies I and K (the former inactive since the release from active duty of the company's Sioux troopers in 1892), were reactivated near Santiago with men from B, C, and H Companies and seventy-nine new recruits. Rounding out the new 3rd Battalion, Companies L and M were newly constituted and activated at Camp Wikoff on September 13 and 14 respectively.[28]

The 16th Infantry remained at Camp Wikoff until September 19. On that date, the regiment departed for Jersey City, New Jersey, where it would board trains bound for Alabama. A humorous incident occurred when the regiment was marching through New York City en route to the ferries that would take it to Jersey City. Most newspaper accounts of unit actions in Cuba covered the much embellished "deeds" of the "glorious" Volunteer and National Guard regiments, giving the public the idea that, once again, as during the Civil War, the volunteer and militia soldiers led the way in the heaviest and most important actions. A woman, one of a large crowd watching the 16th Infantry march by, vigorously waved and hollered at the troops. As the troops were passing, she called out, "Are you boys from the New York Guard?" Tired of the attention heaped upon the volunteers and clearly remembering the "heroic" actions of the 71st New York in Cuba, one soldier dryly answered, "No Ma'am, I'm just another goddamned regular."[29]

The new temporary station was Camp Wheeler near Huntsville, where the 16th Infantry began the process of rebuilding its strength and efficiency after the losses it suffered in Cuba. While at Camp Wheeler, the companies of the regiment took turns pulling provost duties in Huntsville to help local authorities keep the peace between soldiers and civilians. Company K, under the command of Captain Beaumont B. Buck, was sent to Camp Thomas at Chickamauga to restore order and protect government property there. Soldiers of the 9th U.S. Volunteer Regiment (Immunes) became defiant and restless waiting to be discharged. The arrival of K Company quieted the unruly troops, and good order and discipline, such as they were, were restored.[30]

In mid-January 1899, orders arrived directing the transfer of the 16th Infantry to stations in the Department of the Missouri. The Regimental Headquarters, Band, and Companies B, E, H, and L entrained for Fort Crook, Nebraska, on January 25, arriving there three days later. On February 11, Companies F, I, and M proceeded to Jefferson Barracks, Missouri, where they joined G Company, which had arrived three days earlier. By March 10, Companies A, C, D, and K had assembled at Fort Leavenworth, Kansas.[31] But the regiment's stay at these old posts was short-lived, for trouble was brewing in the Philippines.

After the United States declared official possession of the Philippines and its intention to maintain political control over the archipelago, "insurrectos" under the leadership of Emilio Aguinaldo began active operations against the American occupation forces. Against a force of forty thousand insurgents, Major General Elwell S. Otis, commanding general of the VIII Corps, had only twenty-one thousand U.S. troops. A call went out for reinforcements to crush what eventually became known as the Philippine Insurrection.[32] In accordance with War Department General Orders No. 35, dated March 3, 1899, the regiment was ordered overseas for its second war on foreign soil in less than a year.

Shortly after the receipt of the orders, the regiment underwent its third change of command since San Juan Hill. The new commander, Colonel Charles M. Hood, took charge on May 5. Hood had joined the Union Army in August 1861 and had served in the 31st Ohio Infantry, working his way up to sergeant. The Governor of Ohio commissioned him a second lieutenant on February 3, 1864, and he finished the war in the 31st Ohio as a captain. After the war, he secured a commission in the Regular Army and was assigned to the 41st Infantry and later served with the 24th, 7th, and 19th Infantry Regiments before assuming command of the 16th.[33]

The various elements of the regiment entrained for San Francisco in late May after preparing for their impending deployment during the winter and spring. The regiment departed on the USAT *Grant* on the 30th. Enjoying a brief but blissful two-day stopover in Honolulu, they arrived at Manila on June 26 "after a pleasant, but uneventful trip." The regiment, now consisting of thirty officers and 1,295 enlisted men, disembarked on July 1 and remained at Malate Barracks in Ermita. On July 5, they were assigned their initial mission. Around

Manila was a line of entrenchments that protected the capital against insurgent attacks. The 16th Infantry, now assigned to the 1st Division, VIII Corps, relieved a shaky volunteer outfit of that duty and occupied the line from the pumping station at El Deposito, east of the city, to Malabon to the north. The headquarters was set up at La Loma Church, in the center of the line. While occupying the position, the regiment engaged in aggressive patrolling and outpost duties, maintaining a visible presence that the insurgents were reluctant to test.[34]

Though the units were authorized to put up tents to make this duty more bearable, it rained constantly, making the mission trying. The mission became even more stressful due to the fact that, when the regiment arrived in the Philippines, over half of its enlisted men were relatively new recruits who had signed up after the Cuban campaign. In spite of this, the 16th Infantry developed a reputation for steadiness with the leaders of the VIII Corps. Therefore, on August 2, the regiment was relieved of its assignment to the 1st Division and brigaded with the 9th and 12th Infantry Regiments in "Fighting Joe" Wheeler's 1st Brigade, 2nd Division, VIII Corps.[35] The following day, the regiment was relieved of its positions by the 25th Infantry and it, in turn, relieved the 13th Minnesota Volunteer Infantry of the vital mission to protect the Manila & Dagupan Railroad.[36]

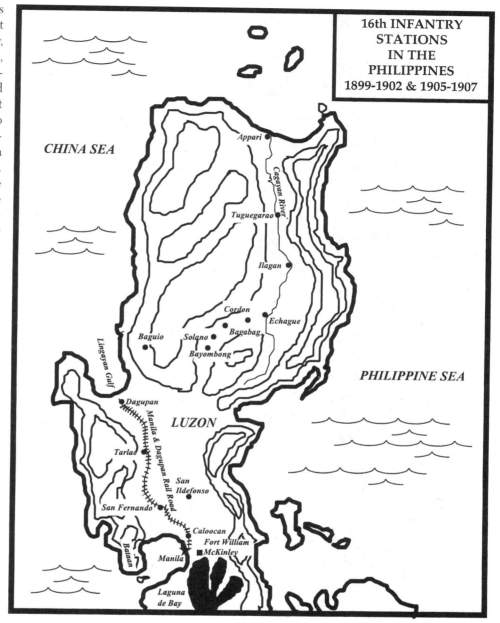

Map 4-2.

The Manila & Dagupan Railroad was the line of communication and supply for Major General Arthur MacArthur's 2nd Division, which was operating in the northern portions of the island of Luzon. As such, it was imperative that the rail line remain open. Therefore, the regiment had to maintain heavy guard forces at key points, such as bridges and chokepoints, and conduct aggressive patrolling operations along its entire assigned section of the route to prevent attacks or sabotage. The regiment's portion of the line ran from Manila in the south to San Fernando at the northern terminus. Companies were located at various villages along the route starting at Caloocan just

north of Manila and ending with an ad hoc battalion consisting of Companies B, E, H, and L, concentrated as a reserve at San Fernando.[37]

The insurgents here wasted no time in testing the new troops along the line. They immediately began taking potshots at the outposts and patrols that moved between key points. They were particularly active at night, usually by attempting to tear up sections of railroad. On the night of August 12, a detachment from Company I stumbled upon a group of *ladrones* (Filipinos of Spanish descent) prying up the rails near Bigaa and opened fire, killing one and driving off the remainder. The same day, the reserve battalion was called out to rescue a surrounded detachment of the 36th U.S. Volunteers fighting near Bacolor. Two days later, a detachment of troops from Companies F and I, under Lieutenant Jack Hayes, scrapped with a force of about 330 insurgents, under the command of "General" Pio de Pilar, who were intent on cutting the line near Guiguinto. The enemy force was driven off, leaving behind three killed and five wounded at no loss to Hayes's command.[38]

The reserve battalion was dispatched to assume control, temporarily, of the District of Cavite on September 5. The 1st Montana Volunteer Infantry was being relieved of that duty as they were about to go home, their volunteer period of service over. The reserve battalion was, in turn, relieved on September 25 and the companies redeployed along the line: B Company to Santo Tomas, E Company to Alapit, H Company to Malolos, and L Company to Calumpit.[39]

Insurgent activity along the railroad consisted of small unit actions, and almost nightly pinprick attacks punctuated by occasional determined enemy efforts. It was an experience not unlike that which future 16th Infantrymen would face in Vietnam. The tactical environment and the regiment's endeavors can best be appreciated by a listing of the following extracts from the *Annual Report of the War Department, 1900*:

Sep 8, 1899	Dets. Cos. G and M discovered and removed an "infernal machine" (mine) on the track just before a troop train passed.
Sep 9, 1899	Dets. Cos. G and M skirmished with insurgents along the rail line.
Sep 13, 1899	Co. G opened fire and drove off a party of insurgents on the line near La Lamboy Convent. Discovered and removed an improvised mine on the track.
Oct 6, 1899	Co. K skirmished with insurgents near Polo. No casualties.
Oct 9, 1899	Det. Co. D skirmished with insurgents at Maucauayan.
Oct 9, 1899	Band and Co. A attacked by insurgents near Caloocan. Armed with rifles from A Company, elements repulsed the attack. No casualties.
Oct 9, 1899	Co. A discovered telegraph wires down and track torn up near Marilao Bridge.
Oct 10, 1899	Co. D attacked by insurgents at Meycauayan. No casualties.
Oct 10, 1899	Co. K on patrol near Novaliches captured three insurgents and revolutionary government documents. No casualties.
Oct 12, 1899	Co. H skirmished with insurgents at Bagbag Bridge near Calumpit. Attack repulsed. No casualties.
Oct 15, 1899	Guard detail from Co. F skirmished with insurgents near Guiguinto. Telegraph found wire cut and quickly repaired. No casualties.

Oct 16, 1899	Track guard detail from Co. I fired upon by insurgents at Bigaa.
Oct 16, 1899	Patrol from Co. F, making morning checks of track line, fired upon by insurgents near Guiguinto. One KIA, one WIA.
Oct 17, 1899	Guard detail from Co. D skirmished with insurgents at Marilao Bridge.
Oct 17, 1899	Patrol from Co. M frees three Spanish soldiers who had been prisoners of war of the insurgents for fifteen months.
Oct 18, 1899	Co. K on patrol near Polo captured one insurgent, 50 rounds of Remington ammunition, and 5 bolos. No casualties.
Oct 18, 1899	Det. Co. F skirmished with insurgents near Guiguinto. One WIA.
Nov 3, 1899	Patrols from Co. D, making morning checks of track line, discovered insurgent party of 20 waiting to ambush train. Several insurgents wounded, no friendly casualties.
Nov 7, 1899	Co. K fired upon by insurgents at Polo. No casualties.
Nov 8, 1899	Bridge guard, Co. I fired upon by insurgents at Bigaa Bridge. No casualties.
Nov 9, 1899	Co. D fired upon by insurgents at Meycauayan. No casualties.
Nov 11, 1899	Det. Co. K engaged insurgents 1 mile west of San Mateo. Engagement spanned 1 hour, 30 minutes. One insurgent KIA. One soldier WIA.
Nov 21, 1899	Det. Co. K skirmished with insurgents at Obando.
Nov 22, 1899	Dets. Cos. A, C, and K under Captain Beaumont Buck engaged insurgent force of approximately 1,000 at San Mateo. Enemy had fortified the village with bamboo defenses some 12 feet high. Upon attacking the town, it became evident to Captain Buck that the insurgent force was disciplined and not disposed to retreat. As enemy fire intensified, Captain Buck was compelled to withdraw. Three WIA. Enemy casualties unknown.[40]

The foregoing incidents kept the men of the regiment active, but Colonel Hood, who wished to exercise the regiment in a large-unit operation, requested and was granted permission to participate in a convergence of forces under Major General Henry W. Lawton on San Miguel de Mayumo. The plan called for the 35th U.S. Volunteers and the 16th Infantry to advance on San Miguel from two different directions, squeezing the so-called insurrecto force of General Pio de Pilar between them. For the expedition, Colonel Hood selected H Company and one twenty-five-man platoon from each of the other companies except A Company. Taking only a platoon per company allowed the regiment to continue to provide security at all points on the rail line. Also under Colonel Hood's command was a battalion of the 3rd Infantry consisting of A, B, and C Companies; L Battery, 3rd Artillery, operating as infantry; fifty men of C Company, Macabebe Scouts; and a detachment of troops from the Hospital Corps. Additionally, three 1.3-inch guns and one 1.65-inch Hotchkiss mountain gun were attached to Hood's force. Interestingly, the Hotchkiss was manned by a contingent of 16th Infantrymen commanded by Lieutenant Guy G. Palmer, the son of Captain George H. Palmer, commander of B Company during the campaign in Cuba. In all, Hood had nineteen officers and 773 enlisted men in this expeditionary command.[41]

Assembling at Baliuag, the force departed on December 4 and headed up the Maasim-San Ildefonso Road. Shortly after crossing the Maasim River an insurgent outpost was encountered and quickly driven off. Approaching San Ildefonso, the enemy was located manning entrenchments on a hill overlooking the town. The artillery detachment was brought up and conducted a preliminary preparation of the enemy positions at about 10:20 a.m. At 10:45, a battalion of the 16th under Captain Walter A. Thurston and the attached battalion of the 3rd Infantry under Captain Arthur Williams began an assault of the trenches. The 3rd Infantry advanced toward the hill on the left side of the road while Thurston's battalion deployed on the right. Another battalion of the 16th under Major Joel T. Kirkman moved up the road in column to reinforce the main attack and, after about an hour of hard fighting, the insurgents were routed. The hatband of a mortally wounded insurgent found in the trench confirmed that the routed enemy unit was the 2nd Battalion of Bulacan Infantry. Hood's force suffered five wounded during the fight, but the Filipinos had nine known killed, and it was suspected that a greater number of wounded and killed had been carried from the field. After seizing the trench line, the American force provided a decent burial for the Philippine dead.[42]

The following day, the 2nd Battalion, Bulacan Infantry, reappeared north and east of the town, evidently intent upon retaking it. Hood had other plans, however. Taking personal charge of the 3rd Infantry elements and the 2nd Provisional Battalion of the 16th Infantry, he launched an attack on the insurgents at 9:30 a.m. Supported by Palmer's "artillery," the American force bounded north toward the enemy while, simultaneously, the 1st Provisional Battalion, 16th Infantry, under Major Kirkman, advanced toward the enemy's left flank. Hood's elements ran into heavy fire after advancing about a mile, but having already deployed, they returned the fire while they moved "through rice swamps and across ridges." The actual firing lasted only twelve minutes before the insurgents retreated. While supporting the main attack, Kirkman's battalion was in turn assaulted by a large Philippine element and forced to stand fast, but Hood's attack drove the insurgents from Kirkman's front.[43]

Kirkman's battalion remained in position after the battle as a security force, while the remainder of Hood's command returned to its positions in San Ildefonso. About two hours later, however, the same insurgents circled behind Kirkman's battalion and began another assault, Colonel Hood, hearing the firing, immediately moved out with his forces to reinforce Kirkman, but by the time he arrived, the 1st Battalion had driven off the enemy. Though only four enemy dead were found on the field, Hood's report stated that the insurgent losses were again believed to be much higher.[44]

Hood received orders from the department commander on December 6 to return to Baliuag. The command moved out, retracing its steps to its start point. Nearing the Maasim River, the lead elements ran into an ambush. Deploying rapidly, H Company swept through the enemy and routed them, killing ten and capturing seven, as well as confiscating numerous weapons dropped by the fleeing insurgents. Riding on horseback, Colonel Hood and his adjutant, Captain Thomas M. Moody, each captured an insurrecto. The regiment arrived at Baliuag that afternoon and remained there until orders arrived from the department headquarters on December 9 directing Hood to cooperate in a joint movement on San Miguel.[45]

Having received intelligence that the insurrectos had reoccupied San Ildefonso, the command left Baliuag on December 10 and halted early the following morning at the same positions they had occupied on December 4. Hood's second attack on the town almost mirrored his first. At 3:50 a.m. on the 11th, the 1st and 2nd Provisional Battalions under Major Henry C. Ward moved to conduct a flanking attack from Kirkman's old positions east of the town. The battalion of the 3rd Infantry and the Macabebe Scouts deployed to the left and right of the road for their assault. At 5:56 a.m., the artillery opened up, firing a preparatory barrage before Ward's attack. Sure that Ward was in place by then, Hood ceased the barrage and, as if by magic, Ward's force immediately sprang to the assault and swept into the town. Ward's elements succeeded in killing thirteen insurgents, and wounding or capturing nine others. At 8:40 a.m., Hood continued the march to San Miguel and linked up with the 35th U.S. Volunteers there at 2:00 p.m. The regiment encountered no further resistance.[46]

Thus ended the 16th Infantry's major campaign in the central Luzon area. After arriving back at their various company stations, the regiment was relieved of the guard mission for the Manila & Dagupan Railroad on December 19 and ordered to northern Luzon, where Aguinaldo was rumored to be operating. Having established "an enviable record for steadiness, efficiency, and bravery," the regiment departed from Manila on Christmas Eve. The Headquarters, Band, and the 1st Battalion sailed on the SS *Uranus,* the 2nd Battalion on the SS *Francisco Reyes,* and the 3rd Battalion on the SS *Venus.* The regiment arrived at Aparri two days later and disembarked there and at Lalloc. Station assignments were designated as follows: Headquarters, Band, and 1st Battalion stationed at Aparri; the 2nd Battalion with Companies G and H at Ilagan; Companies E and F at Tuguegarao; and the 3rd Battalion two hundred miles to the south in Nueva Viscaya Province.[47]

Luzon 1899-1901

While the 1st and 2nd Battalions disembarked at their new stations, the 3rd Battalion experienced a difficult time making its way to its posts in the interior. Departing Lalloc in cascoes (a large canoe-like boat) on January 4, it took twenty-three days of hard rowing up the Cagayan River to get to Echague, in Isabella Province, 125 miles from Aparri. Along the way, low water, sandbars, and rapids were frequently encountered. Some days, the battalion failed to make more than a mile. After arriving at Echague on January 27, the battalion marched seventy-five miles through the mountains to Bayambong in Nueva Viscaya Province. From there, the battalion split up and, by means of improvised ferries, bull carts, pack animals, and native carriers, took station as follows: Company I to Bagabag, Company K to Solano, Company L remained at Bayambong, and Company M to Cordon in Isabella Province.[48]

Once at their new duty stations, the companies of the regiment settled into a routine of guard duty, scouting, and interrogating the local peons about insurrecto activities. It did not take long for rebel resistance to erupt. The first of many sharp actions started at the end of February, and continued over the next fifteen months. On February 26, a detachment of twenty men from G Company, under Lieutenant Ernst Hagedorn, was patrolling eighteen miles northwest of Aparri when it was suddenly attacked by a large group of Igorrotes. Hagedorn's men quickly rallied and drove off the insurgents after killing twenty-five of them. The only American casualties were a Private James Reasack, who was wounded, and Lieutenant Hagedorn's horse, which was killed. Interestingly, the injuries were inflicted not by bullets but by lance thrusts.[49]

On the 28th a detachment of forty-five men from C Company, under Lieutenant Englebert G. Ovenshine, was dispatched to investigate reports of armed insurgents organizing and drilling near Lalloc. En route to the scene on March 1, Ovenshine's detachment encountered a band of about three hundred insurgents near Cullit, and a sharp exchange of gunfire ensued with those rebels lucky enough to have rifles. The detachment drove them off after several hours of fighting, suffering one killed and two severely wounded.[50]

That same week, the regiment received reports that "Chinos" (Filipinos of Chinese ancestry) were being attacked and driven from the village of Abulug about fifteen miles up the Cagayan River from Aparri. The night of the 28th, B Company, led by Major Ward, boarded two steam launches and a cascoe intending to land at Linao across from Aparri. From there, the company would move on foot upstream to Abulug. As the largest launch approached the far shore, however, it ran aground on a sandbar. While its crew struggled to free the boat, the other launch was overturned by heavy swells, and its troops, now in the water, fired several rounds to signal for help. Thus alerted, a party of insurrectos entrenched near the river

bank at Linao opened fire on the troops in the grounded launch, immediately wounding several men, including Ward. In response, the men in the cascoe, which was close to shore, jumped over the side into shallow water and, using their boat for cover, returned fire at the rebel entrenchments. By this time the command had become separated. All elements struggled to get ashore in the dark, with only the men on the cascoe, under the command of Quartermaster Sergeant Charley B. Chaney, managing to land on the Linao side. After unloading their supplies, they moved to positions from where they could pour fire on the enemy trench. After a sharp fight, Chaney's men routed the rebels, killing nine and capturing two others, both wounded. The remaining 16th Infantrymen were able to assemble the following morning and return to Aparri.

Casualties in the Cagayan River fight amounted to one killed and eight wounded (including Ward). In addition two men were missing, presumed drowned.[51]

Such actions typified the fighting during the regiment's Philippines tour. Most engagements involved patrols of ten to forty-five men, and occurred when the detachment walked into an ambush or encountered large but poorly led and equipped groups of insurrectos. Usually the latter quickly lost the will to fight after suffering heavy losses, inflicted by the superior marksmanship of the smaller but more aggressive American infantry units.

Sometimes, however, the fights were quite desperate in nature. Such was the case on September 14, 1900, when a slumbering detachment, outposted at Carig, was attacked by 350 to 500 insurgents at 6:00 a.m. Commanding the detachment was Sergeant Henry C. Schroeder, the one-time 16th Infantry bugler who had won the Silver Star for heroism at San Juan Hill in Cuba. His force consisted of seventeen men from L Company and six men and a corporal from D Company. Surprised while still in their bunks, the men were quickly organized for defense by Schroeder. Tumbling into any available position affording cover, they commenced a heavy and accurate fire that quickly repulsed the enemy's initial attempt to overrun them. But the rebels were determined to defeat the "Americanos" and did not break off the engagement, despite possessing only about fifty rifles between them. Soon, one American was killed and Sergeant Schroeder was severely wounded. Schroeder stayed at his post to direct his unit's actions, his steadfast leadership inspiring his men to resist continual enemy assaults on their position. Finally, after four hours of fighting, Schroeder ordered his men to attack. Amazed at the temerity of the Americans, the insurgents were driven off, leaving thirty-six dead on the battlefield. An additional ninety rebels were wounded, many of whom (it was later learned) succumbed to their injuries.[52] For his superb leadership in the face of adversity and overwhelming odds, Sergeant Schroeder was awarded the Medal of Honor, becoming the regiment's third member to be so recognized.

The small yet frequent scraps with the insurgents were not the only challenges confronting the soldiers of the 16th

Infantry. The jungles of northern Luzon presented their own difficulties, particularly to the soldiers of the 3rd Battalion. Upon arriving at their new stations in the Bayambong Valley in February, the battalion was in good shape overall. Because of the environment, however, its condition soon changed for the worse. In the humid climate, food swiftly spoiled and already frayed uniforms rotted. Sanitation was especially problematic—the natives had no concept of it—and, as a result, water sources were usually polluted with human or animal waste, or both. Malaria was prevalent and other diseases abounded. The extreme difficulty in travel from Aparri meant that supplies were slow in coming, often forcing the men to eat local fare. This always involved a degree of risk—the quartermaster could not know how the food had been handled before purchasing it.

In late March, Major Robert A. Brown, the inspector general of the 2nd Division, VIII Corps, was sent on a fact-gathering mission into the Cagayan Valley, primarily to reconnoiter the supply routes and inspect the functioning of the supply system. What he found, however, was the 3rd Battalion in a state of rapid deterioration. At Solano, the headquarters for the battalion, he received a written report from Waller H. Dade, the regimental assistant surgeon, who gave the following account:

When the men arrived at Solano they were in fairly good condition, excellent in fact, considering everything they had undergone since January 4. This status was maintained until about the 10th of the present month, when it seemed as though the entire command was sooner or later to be prostrated. The first death occurred on the 4th, at Cordon, a private of Company K dying of chronic dysentery after protracted illness. The second died at Solano on the 5th, of acute Bright's disease, a private of the same company. The men then seemed to lose all energy, appetite, and interest in everything. Malarial fever in some form or other affected more than 50 per cent of the entire command, continuing to grow worse until about the 20th, when the hospital was overcrowded. The steward, hospital corps privates, and extra help were worked to point of complete exhaustion from doing constant duty day and night. From a simple form at first, the fever seemed to take on the pernicious type, becoming the most fatal condition due to malarial poisoning I have ever seen. Strong healthy men would be assigned a cot at sick call in the morning only to be found a cold pulseless corpse at night.[53]

The conditions were similar for all companies except M Company at Cordon, which apparently escaped the pestilence owing to its location north of the mountains that spanned the valley south of that town. Dade's sick report from late March showed that of 320 men in the battalion, 169 were ill from various causes but mostly from disease. Accordingly, Major Brown

made several recommendations to ease the trials of the battalion, to include an immediate increase in the amount of safe food, serviceable clothing and equipment, and medical supplies being transported to the area. He also recommended the consolidation of the battalion at Echague and Cordon to get them out of the worst areas. This recommendation was eventually implemented, but the battalion had to be withdrawn that autumn and replaced by the 1st Battalion because of the severely depleted ranks in the hapless 3rd.[54]

In May 1901, the last engagement against the insurgents by a unit of the regiment occurred near Solano. A detachment of ten men, under Captain William O. Johnson, conducted a patrol in the mountains north of the town. Failing to make contact, Captain Johnson sent a six-man patrol under Sergeant Sawyer toward the village of Tuas on May 9. There, they ran into a small group of rebels and engaged them, killing two and capturing one rifle.[55] Thus ended the active operations against the insurrectos. By this time, Aguinaldo had been captured, the insurrection was losing steam, and the countryside was becoming pacified. The next phase of the regiment's activities began, that of assisting the newly assembled civil governments forming at the village, town, and district levels.

The 16th Infantry was now strung out 250 miles along the Cagayan Valley, with garrisons in the main towns. It was responsible for preserving the peace and administration of three provinces (Cagayan, Isabella, and Nueva Viscaya), which equaled one-third of the land area on Luzon Island. To support the pacification effort, Colonel Hood directed his regiment to assist local officials in holding elections, to aid municipal governments, and to provide police services to maintain order. Meanwhile, the soldiers also went to work building schools and teaching classes to the children. Officers were appointed to act as judges to prosecute common crimes until the civil governments could take over those responsibilities. Debts incurred by the regiment for the purchase of food, building rental, supplies, and so forth, were quickly paid off. As a result of the regiment's efforts, the people of northern Luzon came to trust and respect the intentions of the Americans, and the original reasons for the insurrection were largely forgotten. The districts under the administration of the 16th Infantry had become the most orderly on the island by the fall of 1901.[56]

The mission of the regiment in the Philippines was now complete. The conditions in the Cagayan Valley were anarchic when the troops arrived. The Port of Aparri had been blockaded; insurgents, robbers, and ladrones terrorized the populace; and no government functioned to provide order. Over a seventeen-month period, Colonel Hood's men worked hard to overcome and correct these problems. As an official assessment of the regiment's performance noted, "The tact, perseverance, and kindness of the regiment had born fruit...The regiment left the island with a most enviable record in every respect."[57]

Orders arrived in March directing the 5th Infantry to relieve the 16th of the Cagayan Valley posts late that spring. The

16th Infantry was ordered back to the United States to take station at Fort McPherson, Georgia. In June, the regiment assembled at Aparri and sailed—less Companies B, G, H and M—on the USAT *Logan* on the 12th. Arriving at the Presidio of San Francisco on July 8, the regiment remained there for a week before departing on troop trains, less 1st Battalion, for Fort McPherson. Upon arrival, the regiment relieved the 23rd Infantry of the post. Meanwhile, the 1st Battalion was ordered to Fort Slocum, New York, where it was to perform drill and training duties for the recruit depot there. The companies remaining in the Philippines sailed for the United States on the USAT *Lawton* on July 14 and traveled to the posts of their respective battalions.[58]

For the next fifteen years, the duties of the regiment were generally peaceful and, with some exceptions, unremarkable. Its duties, however, would take the men of the regiment to seven different stations in three countries, where environments would span from temperate to tropical, from frozen tundra to desert. In short, the regiment's duty, while short on action, was long on travel, training, and routine.

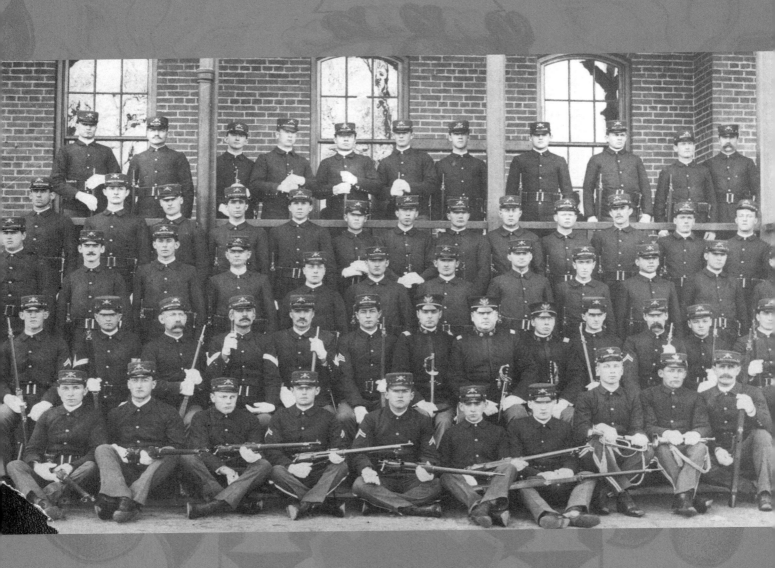

Troops of G Company, 16th Infantry, at Fort Crook, Nebraska, *c.* **1907**

Chapter Five
American Travelers

The two battalions of the 16th Infantry stationed here are in a high state of efficiency. There is an unusually large number of officers present for duty with their companies, and the good effect of their presence was observed at every stage of my inspection.

Major General Charles G. Morton,
Department of the Missouri
Inspection Report 1908

Fort McPherson, Georgia, was a welcome change from the jungles of northern Luzon. Though heat and humidity were still a problem, the disease, pestilence, and other dangers found on the Luzon were all but nonexistent. The regiment had arrived in the Philippines with over thirteen hundred officers and men. Because of losses from combat, disease, and expired enlistments, the regiment had dwindled to a strength of thirty-seven officers and 944 enlisted men when they left. By June 30, 1903, the regiment stood at forty-one officers and 613 enlisted men, its pre-Spanish-American War strength.[1] Although fewer in number, the men of the 16th Infantry would soon have an opportunity to rest, refit, and enjoy the pleasures to be found in nearby Atlanta. But the charms of that city would have to wait as the regiment set out almost immediately to re-hone those skills necessary to the infantry.

In August, the 2nd and 3rd Battalions road marched their companies to the target range at Waco, Georgia, a distance of fifty-five miles. Over the next six weeks, the companies were staggered to fire every ten days or so, as the range could handle only two companies at a time. Upon arrival, the troops set up tents, then underwent the various tasks associated with the marksmanship training of the period. The regiment was armed with the Krag rifle at this time, but was soon issued the new Springfield M-1903 rifle, which quickly became popular with the troops. This training routine was repeated by all companies each year at Waco, usually in May or June.[2]

In October, the venerable Colonel Hood was promoted to brigadier general and retired from the service. Colonel Hood, who had led the regiment through the Philippine Insurrection, was popular with the officers and men of the 16th and sorely missed after his departure. To replace him, Lieutenant Colonel Butler Price of the 4th Infantry was promoted to colonel and assumed command on November 4, 1902. Colonel Price was the last of the Civil War-era commanders. He had been commissioned in the 2nd Pennsylvania Cavalry in December 1861 and mustered out in January 1865. Returning to the army in May 1866, he served in the 4th Infantry for the next thirty-four years until assigned to the 16th.[3]

Ten days later, the new colonel assembled his regiment in full marching order and led them on a sixty-three-mile practice march to Hampden, Georgia, returning to post on November 18. Now that the regiment was fit and qualified with their weapons, they settled into routine garrison duties until the following May when companies once again conducted their annual trek to the range at Waco.[4]

After completing the annual target practice, companies of the regiment were dispatched to locations all over the South to assist in the training of various National Guard units. That summer, 16th Infantrymen trained the state troops of Georgia, Florida, Alabama, South Carolina, and North Carolina. The training of these militia units was a relatively new mission of the Regular Army dictated by the requirements of the Dick Act, which intended to make the National Guard better-equipped and trained for war. It was also a mission that the 16th Infantry would conduct every summer at Fort McPherson; and, indeed, virtually every summer it has had elements stationed in the United States up to the present day. In response to the efforts to provide good training to the guard units, the companies of the 16th received "high praise of their drilling, discipline, and methods of castramentation [techniques of establishing an encampment]."[5]

Concurrent with the marksmanship training of the 2nd and 3rd Battalions at Waco each May, the 1st Battalion traveled to Sea Girt, New Jersey, to conduct target practice. However, unlike their counterparts at Fort McPherson, the men of the 1st Battalion had no National Guard training requirement. The battalion's mission at Fort Slocum was to conduct basic training for recruits at the recruit training depot at that post. To accomplish that task, the battalion was reduced to a cadre of officers, noncommissioned officers, and a few privates per company. As the unit received new enlistees, the companies were filled with recruits who were trained in the School of the Soldier by the company cadre. Upon completion of this training, the troops were shipped off to fill the ranks of other infantry regiments. The battalion performed that mission until relieved in August 1904.[6]

Following the summer training of the various National Guard units, the regiment typically underwent an annual inspection by a team from the Department of the Gulf. In November 1903, Major General Henry C. Corbin, the department commander, personally headed the inspection team, and all units of the regiment were rated "very satisfactory," the highest rating that could be awarded. The inspector's report stated: "An unusual [high] state of efficiency in instruction, discipline, and readiness was reported by the inspector-general of the division at Fort McPherson, Ga., commanded by Colonel Butler D. Price, Sixteenth Infantry."[7]

Whereas 1903 was a relatively uneventful year for the 16th Infantry, the following year was highlighted by several special events that spiced up what was becoming a humdrum routine. On January 20, K Company was sent to Columbia Arsenal, Tennessee, to provide a guard force for that installation. Though it was an uneventful tour, it gave the men of that company a break away from their home station. They returned to Atlanta in July in time to join the regiment at annual target practice at Waco. After the training of the militia, the 16th Infantry was directed in September to proceed to Manassas, Virginia, to participate in the maneuvers of the Department of the Gulf. There, the 1st Battalion, now filled to peacetime strength with personnel, joined the regiment for the field training. Actually, the 16th Infantry did not function as a regiment, but was split up and attached to several separate commands. The 1st Battalion was attached to the 2nd Brigade, 1st Provisional Maneuver Corps; the 2nd Battalion to the 3rd Brigade; and Companies E and F were assigned provost guard duties at the town of Manassas. The maneuvers were highly successful and gave commanders the chance to operate units at a higher level of command and support than usual. After the maneuver, the 1st Battalion returned with the regiment to Fort McPherson to take permanent station there in late September.[8]

Shortly after returning to home station, the regiment underwent the annual Department inspection, this time conducted by Major General Adna Chaffee, commander of the Atlantic Division. The results of the inspection reported that "the excellent condition of the regiment was all that could be desired." The inspection was followed by the Department of the Gulf's Annual Athletic Meet in October, in which elements of twelve units participated. The 16th Infantry representatives did extremely well, winning twelve first place awards, four second place, and four third place finishes out of the twenty-three events.[9]

On November 19, the 2nd and 3rd Battalions traveled by rail to Jefferson Barracks near St. Louis to perform guard duties in connection with the Louisiana Purchase Exposition. Prior to beginning guard duties, the battalions conducted a series of exhibition drills, one of which was performed by the 2nd Battalion for His Imperial Highness, Prince Fushima of Japan. The battalion apparently impressed the young prince, who gave it his personal commendation for its performance.[10] Several days later on November 26, President Theodore Roosevelt arrived to visit the Exposition. The regiment turned out en masse for the honor of providing the presidential guard force during his visit. The remainder of the time at St. Louis was rather uneventful. Guard duty was conducted for several buildings and exhibits, including the Exposition Headquarters, for-

eign displays, and the U.S. State Department's exhibit. An account of the tour stated that "the guard duty was most rigorous on account of the area guarded, the number of posts, and the fact that one half of the guard was posted a distance of a mile from barracks, thus preventing their going to barracks for meals."[11] To make matters worse, the enlistments of a sizable number of men, most of whom had joined for service in the Philippines, expired while they were at St. Louis. The promise of furloughs upon return to Fort McPherson was not a sufficient enticement to get many of the men to reenlist and only about 10 percent, mostly noncommissioned officers, signed for another hitch. The guard duties at St. Louis were completed about the end of December, but the regiment did not depart for Fort McPherson until January 27.[12]

In April, the regiment underwent another inspection and a review by Major General James F. Wade, the new Atlantic Division commander. Immediately following the inspection, Colonel Price received General Order No. 8, Department of the Gulf, directing the 17th Infantry to take station at Fort McPherson and for the 16th Infantry to entrain for the Presidio in San Francisco on May 20 to prepare for movement back to the Philippines. Arriving on three different troop trains, the regiment debarked at the Presidio on May 27, boarded the USAT *Sheridan* on the 31st, and departed at noon that day. Sailing by way of Honolulu and Guam, the *Sheridan* arrived at Manila Bay on June 26. Disembarking the following morning, the regiment, less 2nd Battalion, traveled by cascoes to Fort William McKinley at Rizal, nine miles southeast of Manila. Concurrently, the 2nd Battalion traveled by cascoes to Malahi Island in Laguna de Bay to garrison that island and provide guards for the prison there. Upon arrival, the regiment was assigned to the Philippine Division commanded by Major General Henry C. Corbin, under whom the regiment had served while at Fort McPherson. It was further assigned to the Department of Luzon, commanded by Brigadier General Tasker H. Bliss.[13]

The 16th Infantry's second tour in the Philippines was not to be as exciting as its first. Other than the usual inspections, target practice, and garrison duties, the regiment had few remarkable events about which the men could write home. The following list of events sums up most of the regiment's activities while in the Philippines the second time around.

1905

July 4	The 1st Battalion conducted Independence Day parade in Manila.
July 29	Regiment, less 2nd Battalion, reviewed by Brigadier General W. S. Edgerly, Commander of the Department of Luzon.
August 7	The 3rd Battalion paraded in Manila in honor of the U.S. Secretary of War.
August 9	Regiment, less 2nd Battalion, reviewed by the Secretary of War and Major General Corbin.

September 24	Typhoon hit Malahi Island, destroying the barracks and a great deal of other government property.
October 7	The 2nd Battalion, less Company E, transferred to Fort McKinley. Took over duties at that post as stockade guards.
December 1	The 2nd Battalion relieved of duties as stockade guards.
December 2-9	Company A conducted 71-mile reconnaissance of the trails and villages surrounding Fort McKinley.
December 26	Colonel Cornelius Gardner assumed command of the 16th Infantry.

1906

January 2-20	Regiment, less 3rd Battalion, conducted annual target practice.
January 20	The 1st Battalion assigned to stockade guard duties.
January 13	Regiment reviewed by Admiral Sir Henry Noel, British Navy, and Major General Corbin.
January 31	Company E completed salvage operations at Malahi and is transferred to Fort McKinley.
February 16-March 8	The 3rd Battalion conducted annual target practice.
March 19	The 1st Battalion relieved of duties as stockade guards.
May 3-6	The 3rd Battalion conducted 30-mile practice march up the Mariquina Valley.
May 19	The 3rd Battalion assigned to stockade guard duties.
May 21-26	Companies B, E, and H conducted 125-mile practice march with Philippine Scouts units from Los Binas, Cavite, PI.
June 29	Regiment inspected by Major General J. F. Weston, commanding Department of Luzon.
August 13	The 2nd Battalion transferred to Camp Bumpus near Tacloban, Leyte Island, to conduct operations against the Pulajanes.
September 19	Companies A, B, D, and I assigned to stockade guard duties.
October 19	Companies A, B, D, and I relieved of duties as stockade guards.
November 24	Company K returned from detached service to San Mateo as guard force.[14]

As noted above, Colonel Cornelius Gardner assumed command of the 16th Infantry on December 26, 1905. Gardner, born in the Netherlands in 1849, was appointed to West Point from Michigan and graduated in 1873. After being commissioned in the 19th Infantry, Gardner spent the next twenty-five years in that regiment in various assignments in Colorado, Kansas, and Texas. He was assigned to command of the 31st Michigan Volunteer Infantry in April 1898, in which capacity he served until the following May. Two months later, he was assigned as colonel of the 30th U. S. Volunteer Infantry. Gardner led that regiment throughout its Philippine service and participated in General Schwan's expedition to the southern provinces of Laguna, Batangas, Cavite, and Taybayas in January 1900. Mustered out of volunteer service on April 15, 1901, he served as governor of Taybayas Province for a year before being assigned to command the 1st Battalion, 13th Infantry. He was promoted to lieutenant colonel on February 18, 1903 and spent most of the next two years at Fort Snelling, Minnesota, with the 21st Infantry until returning to the Philippines with that regiment in February 1905.[15]

In the summer of 1906, troubles brought on by the Pulajane tribesmen on Leyte Island boiled over, causing Major General Corbin to direct a battalion of infantry to that distant location to quell the problem. The unit selected was the 2nd Battalion, which received Special Order 192 on August 12, directing it to depart on August 13. The following day, the troops boarded the USAT *Kilpatrick* in Manila Bay and sailed the 462 miles to Leyte, disembarking at Tananan at 9:30 a.m. on the 16th. The battalion established Camp Bumpus near Tacloban as its main base camp. From August through November, the companies of the battalion conducted aggressive patrolling activities, but no engagements occurred. To better secure the areas for which the 2nd Battalion was responsible, the companies were deployed in December as follows: Company E at Dagami, Company F at Abuyog, Company G at Tolosa, and Company H to Burauen.[16] By February 1907, the original troubles had subsided and the 2nd Battalion was ordered back to Fort McKinley. On the 28th of that month, the battalion was assembled at Tacloban, and on March 2, loaded onto the USAT *Magdalannes*. Arriving at Manila Bay March 5, the battalion disembarked and traveled to Fort McKinley.[17]

Upon return to Fort McKinley, the 2nd Battalion found that the reinforced brigade to which the 16th Infantry was assigned had a new commanding general. In January, Brigadier General John J. Pershing had assumed command. Pershing had previously served in the Philippines, establishing a reputation for dealing effectively with the various tribes in the islands. As the 16th Infantry's higher commander, he now set out to train his units in brigade-level operations. This was an unusual twist for the peacetime U.S. Army, especially those units in the Philippines that were used to conducting operations at the company, troop, and occasionally, battalion levels. The regiment spent little time under Pershing's command, however, for on May 24, 1907, General Order No. 113 was issued, directing that the regiment return to the United States to take station at Fort Crook, Nebraska. It would not be the last time the 16th Infantry would serve under Pershing, however.[18]

On August 15, 1907, the men of the 16th boarded the

USAT *Sherman* in Manila Harbor for a month-long voyage that took them first to Nagasaki, Japan, then back to the United States. Disembarking at the Presidio on September 16, the regiment, less the 1st Battalion, boarded trains the following day en route to Fort Crook. The fifteen officers and 186 enlisted men of the 1st Battalion concurrently boarded a train bound for Fort Logan H. Roots, Arkansas, to take permanent station there under the command of Major James K. Thompson. By September 24 all elements had arrived at their new posts.[19]

The regiment's tour at these posts quickly settled into the routine it had experienced at Fort McPherson. For the next two years and nine months, the men of the 16th would participate in annual target practice, long cross-country marches, annual department inspections, and the training of the National Guard units of Nebraska and Arkansas. However, departures from the routine occurred just often enough to make life at least moderately interesting for the average 16th Infantryman. The first such departure came shortly after arrival at the new duty stations. The ensuing episode harkened back to the final days of the "Wild West" era and is probably the last instance of active operations by the U.S. Army against American Indians.

In the summer of 1906, while 16th Infantry was still stationed in the Philippines, the regiment's old wards from Fort Douglas days, the unhappy White River Utes from the Uintah Reservation, defied the government yet again by leaving their designated lands in eastern Utah. Subsequently rounded up by the cavalry, they were escorted first to Fort Meade, South Dakota, in November, then to the Cheyenne River Indian Reservation in South Dakota, arriving there on July 2, 1907. Still discontented, the Utes started disturbances the following October, prompting the dispatch of three troops of the 2nd Cavalry from Fort Des Moines, Iowa. The problems persisted into November and the remainder of the 2nd Cavalry was ordered to Gettysburg, South Dakota, and held there in readiness to act against the Indians should fighting break out.[20]

In late November, four companies of the 16th Infantry were also ordered out to support the operation. Company K was sent to Fort Des Moines to guard that post during the 2nd Cavalry's absence, while Companies I and M were sent to Gettysburg to protect the expedition's base camp and guard the field supply depot established there. The troops of L Company were temporarily divided among the other three companies to flesh them out for field operations. Shortly after their arrival, the troops of M Company were redeployed to the Indian River Agency to provide protection to the Indian Bureau agents and their workers. The show of force by the combined efforts of the 2nd Cavalry and the 16th Infantry had a distinct calming effect on the Utes. So much so that by December 20, all companies were back at Fort Crook.[21]

Their Indian fighting days over once and for all, the men of the regiment resumed their post routine. However, on the afternoon of May 12, 1908, that routine was shattered when a tornado swept through Fort Crook. At 5:35 p.m., the tornado touched down near the post and headed for its buildings. Although the regiment suffered no serious injuries, the buildings in the path of the twister sustained heavy damage and many of the fort's old oak trees were uprooted. The roof of the post hospital was ripped off, and nearly all buildings suffered varying degrees of damage. The post quartermaster estimated the cost at $100,000 to rebuild or repair the damage.[22]

Apart from the annual target practice and road marches, the men of the 16th participated in three unusual exercises during their tour at Fort Crook. One entailed night operations conducted by the 1st Battalion at the local training area near Little Rock, Arkansas, on June 28-30, 1908. The exercise was unusual in that units of the U.S. Army rarely conducted night operations during this period. The other two events were the maneuvers late that summer at Fort Riley, Kansas, followed immediately by a march to St. Joseph, Missouri, for participation in a "military tournament."[23]

War Department General Order No. 84 directed that "Camps of Instruction" be conducted by Regular Army units throughout the United States during the summer of 1908. The order stated that the maneuvers were to provide a scheme of instruction that would approximate field service under wartime conditions. The commander of the Department of the Missouri directed that available units in the department participate in maneuvers in September at either Fort D. A. Russell, Wyoming, or Fort Riley. The 16th Infantry, ordered to assemble in its entirety at the Fort Riley exercise, departed July 30, less the 1st Battalion, which had left on the 21st, having a longer distance to travel. At Fort Riley, the regiment joined the 13th Infantry; 2nd Cavalry; 7th Cavalry; batteries of the 3rd, 5th and 6th Field Artillery Regiments; two companies of the 3rd Battalion, Engineer Corps; and Company A, Signal Corps, all under the command of Brigadier General John B. Kerr. The maneuvers lasted a month and included some of the rarely attempted combined arms operations conducted by the U.S. Army before World War I.[24]

After the maneuvers, the regiment (less the lucky 1st Battalion, which boarded a train for Fort Root on September 10) was attached, along with the 13th Infantry, to a provisional brigade commanded by Colonel Gardner. The brigade was, in turn, attached to a provisional division organized for the military tournament in St. Joseph. The division was marched overland to St. Joseph in what was considered to be the largest such movement of troops since the Civil War. After arrival at Camp Everett Peabody on September 8, the division units participated in a series of competitive events of which the results, unfortunately, went unrecorded. The maneuvers and tournament concluded, the regiment marched back to Nebraska, where it paraded for the citizens of Omaha on September 29 before arriving home at Fort Crook for a well-deserved rest.[25]

In terms of training, there was less activity in 1909 than in the previous year, the major event being the provisional brigade maneuvers at Camp Corse in Des Moines, Iowa, and at Fort

Omaha in September and October. Units of the 1st Battalion, however, participated in two notable events. The battalion, less Company C, railed to Vicksburg, Mississippi, to act as the guard of honor for the unveiling of a monument dedicated to General Stephen D. Lee, C.S.A., on June 12. The following October, Companies C and D were selected for the honor of providing the presidential guard for President Roosevelt's visit to Little Rock on the 24th.[26] The regiment ended the year on a high note, receiving a commendation by the department commander after his annual inspection on December 20. After giving only a satisfactory report of the regiment for the 1908 inspection, General Morton reported:

> The post is in excellent condition. The Commanding Officer, Colonel Cornelius Gardner, 16th Infantry, has given its affairs an economical and careful administration. The two battalions of the 16th Infantry stationed here are in a high state of efficiency. There is an unusually large number of officers present for duty with their companies, and the good effect of their presence was observed at every stage of my inspection.[27]

The previous year's inspection report was lukewarm at best. Whatever the reasons for that report, it must have been in large part due to the fact that there had been ninety-nine deserters from the regiment that year. The number had dwindled to thirty-eight for 1909, which in today's army would still provide more than enough reason for firing the commander![28] In the army of that time, however, it was a relatively low desertion rate, at least for a stateside unit. General Morton's last statement above was probably a veiled reference to the improvement in morale experienced since the previous year, which had resulted in the lower desertion rate.

An interesting side note in the history of the 16th Infantry was the adoption in 1907 of the regiment's first coat of arms and motto. Executed in the so-called hodgepodge design common to regimental heraldry of the era, the 16th Infantry's coat of arms was flawed by the inclusion of honors won in the War of 1812 and the Mexican War by 16th Infantry Regiments that bore no relation to the current organization. The coat of arms consisted of a shield divided into six sections (see appendix). In the upper right section was the red cross of Saint George (War of 1812) on a white background; in the upper right, the flag of Mexico (Mexican War); in the middle left, a Confederate battle flag (Civil War); in the middle right, on a white square, a golden sun with rays and a Sioux wigwam signifying the "Sun Woman" (Indian Campaigns); in the lower left section, the coat of arms of the Kingdom of Spain (Spanish-American War); and, in the lower right, a quartered square with the volcano of Mayon in the upper right and lower left quarters, and the Katapunan emblem (Philippine sun symbol) in the upper left and lower right quarters (Philippine Insurrection). The crest consisted of a gold, sixteen-pointed star on which was super-

imposed a red, five-bastioned fort (the badge of the 1st Division, V Corps, to which the regiment was assigned at San Juan Hill), surmounted by crossed rifles, all above a wreath (rope) of blue and white, the infantry colors. The motto *Semper Paratus* was Latin for "Always Prepared"; but the actual rendering of the motto, as interpreted by contemporary members of the regiment was intended to be "Always Ready." The pamphlet listing the officers and NCOs of the regiment dated August 1, 1909, contains the description of the coat of arms and interprets the motto as such; therefore it is how the motto should be expressed by members of the regiment today.[29] Due to the mishmash nature of these old coats of arms, none from any regiment survived World War I. When distinctive insignia (popularly misnamed "unit crests") and coats of arms were officially authorized for adoption by army units in the early 1920s, the only aspects of the old 16th Infantry design to make it into the new design were the V Corps badge and the regimental motto. More on that design later.

On October 28, 1909, Colonel Gardner was notified via War Department General Order No. 215 that the 16th Infantry would be recruited to maximum authorized strength, relieved at Fort Crook by the 4th Infantry, and transferred to posts in Alaska in June 1910. In accordance with directives in General Order No. 24, Department of Missouri, the troops of the regiment boarded trains at 2:00 p.m., June 22, and started for the West Coast. All elements arrived at Seattle on June 27, boarded the USAT *Buford* that day, and set sail at 12:45 p.m. on June 29. The *Buford* arrived at Haines, Alaska, on July 3. The following day, the regimental headquarters, staff, band, Companies F, G, H, and K, and the Machine Gun Platoon disembarked to take station at Fort William H. Seward (see map 5.1). The Machine Gun Platoon, organized at Fort Crook, Nebraska, in 1908, was a new unit which, unknown to the 16th's soldiers, heralded a much more destructive form of warfare that many would experience less than a decade later. The remainder of the regiment was taken to other locations on the *Buford* and took station as follows: Companies A and L at Fort Gibbon (disembarked at Fort St. Michael and traveled up to Fort Gibbon via the Yukon River on the USS *General Jeff C. Davis*); Companies B and E at Fort Davis; Companies C and I at Fort Liscum; and Companies D and M at Fort St. Michael. All elements were at their new posts by August 1.[30]

The units of the regiment went into target practice shortly after their arrival at the new posts. They had not had the opportunity to conduct their annual shooting back at Forts Crook and Root, and they had to act fast before the winter weather prevented them from completing this task. Additionally, several units conducted conditioning marches before the snows arrived. Typical was the Machine Gun Platoon's 144-mile hike to and from Porcupine, Alaska, September 25-30.[31]

The assignment to Alaska was, in part, responsible for a further dramatic decrease in the number of desertions in the

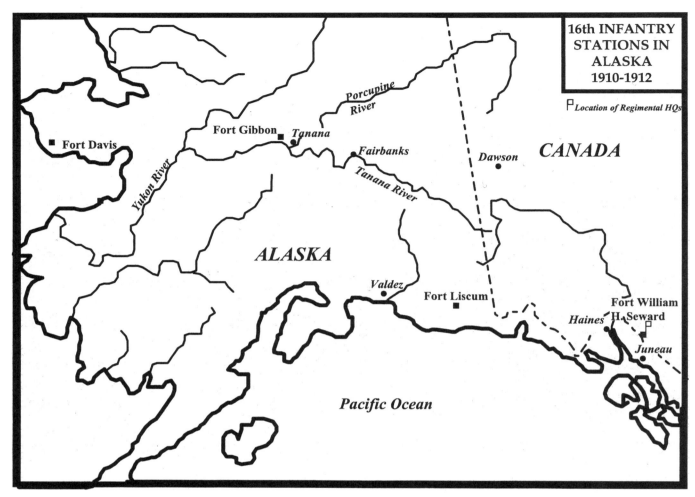

Map 5-1.

regiment. For the year 1910, the adjutant reported only nine desertions. Oddly, one of those deserters was an officer, 1st Lieutenant Daniel E. Shean. Shean must have decided that he did not belong in the wilds of Alaska, as he "went over the hill" before the move north and was dropped from the rolls on January 12, 1910. Another loss to the regiment, although not from desertion, was Major Beaumont B. Buck. Buck had been with the regiment since before the Spanish-American War and had commanded K Company during the Philippine Insurrection. He would later have the regiment under his command again during World War I when it was occasionally attached to the 2nd Infantry Brigade, 1st Division, which he would command. Joining the regiment was Major Charles S. Farnsworth, who would command the regiment briefly in 1914. Farnsworth was one of two 16th Infantry commanders who would be promoted to major general and appointed as the chief of infantry during the period prior to World War II.[32]

Life in Alaska for the members of the 16th Infantry was spartan. For six months out of the year (roughly October through April), the weather ensured that the main activity of the troops was surviving the cold. Secondary efforts were surviving the monotony of duty and canned food. The winters at all posts were cold and dreary, but for the soldiers at Fort Gibbon, in the interior of the territory, the isolation was most difficult. The fort's barracks, clustered around a parade field on the bank of the Yukon River, housed two companies of the 16th Infantry even though they were barely adequate for one. The post's primary mission was as a station for the Alaska communications system, operated by a tiny Signal Corps detachment there. By October, the river would begin icing up, forcing the steamboats to remain downstream for the winter, and with them went daily contact with the outside world, save what news came over the Signal Corps radios. Meanwhile, the snow began to fall and so did the temperatures.[33]

The nearest town was Tanana, at the confluence of the Tanana and Porcupine Rivers. Its main street consisted of a row of typical frontier businesses: a hotel, restaurant, barber shops, dry-goods merchants, and the like. Though the street was unpaved and often muddy, the town boasted a boardwalk that allowed the citizens to keep their shoes clean.[34] The town offered little recreation for the soldiers, other than cheap liquor that was purchased in vast quantities to help fight boredom. That caused other problems, however.

Mail came in overland from Fairbanks by dog sled and was rarely less than thirty days old. Fresh food could not be brought in, so canned food was the order of the day, save fresh moose meat, which was plentiful. When eggs could be had, it was not unusual for them to cost two bits a piece (about $3.00 in today's money). Entertainment came in the form of dances attended by the town's few unmarried or otherwise unattached women (whose physical attributes, one suspects, probably left much to be desired), boxing smokers, card games (yes, and gambling), bowling, and even a few of the new-fangled moving picture shows. Though it was very cold, outdoor sports—mostly dog-sled races—were popular as well. The post quartermaster had a number of dogs for the purpose of transportation in the winter months.[35] These teams were regularly raced for exercise, when not engaged in actual duties.

For all outdoor duties the troops of the 16th Infantry wore clothing known in the jargon of the time as "Alaskan Issue." An Alaska veteran, writing for the *Infantry Journal* in 1937, observed that

[T]his outfit, though decidedly effective in providing protection against the elements, could scarcely be classed as rakish. Reading from top to bottom the principal items included: fur caps, flapped for face protection; heavy outer coats over the thick breeches; long woolen stockings worn over the breeches legs and rolled below the knees; and moccasins with thick felt insoles. In damp weather we wore mucklucks [sic], but these were not often necessary, for Alaskan snow is unusually quite dry. Ordinary shoes were out, for leather froze as hard as a brick. The moccasins were quite comfortable in spite of their lack of heels. A soldier in this get-up looked about as military as a Maori chieftain.[36]

With the spring came the thawing of the ice and snow. In late July 1911, an unusually warm spring and early summer caused a higher degree of thawing of a glacier near Valdez. Water from the glacier flooded the streams that flowed into the town and threatened great damage. For three days, the men of Companies C and I fought the floods and successfully prevented a major catastrophe for the townspeople. That same month, however, Companies F, G, H, and K had a different problem—that of fighting a forest fire that threatened the town of Haines. Together with the citizens of that town, they successfully subdued the flames.[37] Meanwhile, with the thaw also came clouds of mosquitoes, which, at times, gave the men reason to wish for the snows to return!

The austere environment of Alaska helped keep the regiment's desertion rate low. For 1911 the regiment lost only three men to desertion despite the less than favorable duty conditions. Of course, where would one go if one did desert? Oddly enough, two of the deserters were from L Company, at isolated Fort Gibbon. The low rates should have contributed to high marks on the annual inspections conducted by the department inspector general, but the annual reports prepared for the regiment for the two years spent in Alaska only mention that the inspections took place and failed to include the usual glowing remarks about readiness and suchlike. Perhaps it was all the officers and men could do just to take care of their routine duties under such trying conditions.[38]

On the other hand, reports from the citizens of Alaska were favorably disposed toward the performance of the 16th Infantry during its tour in the territory:

Reliable citizens of Tanana and vicinity exhibit no hesitancy in stating that the reputation of the Fort Gibbon command is better than any other stationed here within their knowledge. Similar reports come from other parts of Alaska relating to the regiment in general. It must be a source of pride to the Regimental Commander, Colonel Gardener, and every member of the Regiment that it is unexcelled in discipline and general efficiency.[39]

Pursuant to Special Order No. 94, Western Division, dated April 20, 1912 the 30th Infantry was directed to relieve the 16th Infantry of the north country posts. The following June, the companies of the regiment were assembled at the coastal posts, where they embarked on the USAT *Sheridan* over the last two weeks of the month. Weighing anchor on July 1, the *Sheridan* sailed for the Presidio via Unalaska, Dutch Harbor, and Tacoma. Arriving at the Presidio on July 22, the troops began disembarking at their new duty station about noon. The following day, Colonel Gardner assumed command of the Presidio and, in a move not unusual for the army of that time, another officer was appointed as acting commander—even though Colonel Gardner was listed as regimental commander on the official rolls. Colonel Charles G. Morton was attached to the regiment to command for a period of about two months during the department maneuvers in August.[40]

Morton's stint as commander was destined to be short, however, as he was detached and relieved as commander pursuant to War Department Special Order No. 210 on September 16. In the interim, the executive officer, Lieutenant Colonel Chase W. Kennedy, was appointed acting commander.[41]

Other changes were in store for the regiment as well. Apparently, the 16th Infantry was authorized a special table of organization for its duty in Alaska. For example, a "Mounted Scouts" detachment was extant in the regiment upon arrival at the Presidio. To bring the regiment into compliance with standard tables of organization for infantry regiments, the following consolidations were directed by Regimental Special Order No. 45: the enlisted personnel in the "Mounted Scouts" were transferred to Company K, Battalion Headquarters Detachments were transferred to Company L, and the Machine Gun Platoon was transferred to Company M. All transfers were completed on August 1. Four days later, ninety-five recruits arrived from Fort Slocum to bring the remaining companies up to higher levels of personnel fill in time for pending field exercises.[42]

The department maneuvers, which lasted from 10 through 23 August, were really no more than a glorified road march. Assigned to the "Blue Brigade," the regiment was marched on the 11th to Cavalry Flats near the Presidio, where the brigade was concentrated. Over the next week, the brigade marched a route that took it through Colma, Milbrae, Redwood City, and San Jose, arriving at Coyote, California on August 20. For two days at Coyote, the regiment maneuvered with the Blue Brigade in a series of exercises that culminated in the regiment's movement back to the camp at Coyote. There, the regiment participated in a field inspection conducted by Major Alonzo Gray, the department inspector general, after which they made the return march to the Presidio, having covered a total of 129 miles round-trip.[43]

The early months of 1913 saw the regiment undergo several changes of command, beginning with the departure of Lieutenant Colonel Kennedy for the General Staff School at Fort Leavenworth on January 7. Assuming temporary command was Major William C. Bennett, who remained in charge until April 3, when Colonel George Bell Jr. was attached to command. The following month, Colonel Gardner, having formally commanded the regiment for seven and one half years, was relieved, and Colonel Bell was officially assigned as commander.[44]

Bell had been appointed to West Point in 1876 and was commissioned in the 3rd Infantry four years later. In that regiment, he served on the frontier in Montana and later at Fort Snelling, Minnesota, until his promotion to captain and transfer to the 1st Infantry in April 1898. On July 3, 1898, he participated in the attack on El Caney with the 1st Infantry and served in that regiment in the Philippines until being detailed to the inspector general's department in August 1907. He served in that capacity in the Philippines and in Texas until being assigned to command the 16th Infantry.[45]

In 1912, the Army General Staff organized the mobile forces of the army into sixteen divisions, of which four were Regular Army and twelve were National Guard units. Those regular units on the West Coast were to be organized into elements of the 3rd Division. In accordance with War Department General Order No. 9 dated 6 February 1913, the 16th Infantry was assigned to the 8th Brigade commanded by Brigadier General Walter S. Schuyler. Once again brigaded with the regiment were their old comrades from the charge up San Juan Hill, the 6th Infantry. Also assigned to the brigade was the 12th Infantry.[46] This reorganization was part of the army's first real attempt to maintain standing mobile forces larger than the regiment in peacetime, and the 16th Infantry would remain so assigned until its participation in the Punitive Expedition into

Mexico three years later.

The remainder of the regiment's stay at the Presidio was relatively uneventful, save for a stint fighting forest fires on Mount Tamalpais and in Marin County, August 7-12, 1913. The rest of the stay consisted primarily of the usual marches, target practice, inspector general visits, and the receipt and training of the 433 recruits received during the year.

In February 1914, command of the 8th Brigade passed from Brigadier General Schuyler to an old acquaintance of the regiment, Brigadier General John J. Pershing. At the time a routine event, "Black Jack" Pershing's tenure as brigade commander would eventually prove hugely consequential for the entire regiment, affecting its service and performance in the First World War.

Only two months after assuming command of the 8th Brigade, Pershing received orders to rush his units to the border in response to rumors that Francisco "Pancho" Villa was going to raid El Paso, Texas. Pershing selected the 6th and 16th Infantry Regiments for the mission and thirty-five hundred troops entrained for Fort Bliss on April 24. Arriving in El Paso on April 27, Pershing found that the two regiments of the 8th Brigade could not be quartered at Fort Bliss, as it was already crammed with the troops of three cavalry regiments, the 20th Infantry, and the 6th Field Artillery. Instead, the new arrivals were housed at a temporary cantonment called Camp Cotton, located at 7th and Cotton streets in El Paso proper.[47]

Camp Cotton was situated on the Rio Grande River near the city race track. From the camp, one could easily survey the Mexican city of Juárez and the blue mountains beyond. Over the next two years, troops of the 16th Infantry frequently crossed the international bridge into Juárez to sample the pleasures and otherwise enjoy the entertainments of the border town's fleshpots. In the same period they would also be affected by problematic relations between the United States and Mexico, particularly as manifested by political instability in Mexico's neighboring state of Chihuahua.

To maintain good relations with the local inhabitants of El Paso and the citizens of Juárez, Pershing paraded the entire complement of troops under his command through El Paso for "Army Day," June 14. Leading the parade was the 6th, 16th, and 20th Infantry Regiments, followed by the troops of the 12th, 13th, and 15th Cavalry Regiments, and finally the horse-drawn guns of the 6th Field Artillery. Interspersed throughout were regimental bands playing favorite martial music and popular tunes of the day.[48]

The regiment settled into the routine of the border army. Practice marches, small unit field problems, target practice, and garrison duties alternated with patrol stints on the border. Typically, this border patrol duty was assigned to two companies at a time for one-month periods. The patrol area for the 16th Infantry was a stretch of the border from the Hart's Mill cement plant to the viaduct west of El Paso. The duty could be actionful and even dangerous at times. For example, during the month of July, the regiment's patrols captured numerous Mexican irregulars on U.S. soil, and relieved them of some thirty-seven rifles.

That summer, Pershing watched with interest the events in Europe leading to the mobilization of European armies and, finally, open hostilities between the Triple Entente and the Triple Alliance. Sensing that the United States might eventually be involved in the war, Black Jack took his units to the field in October and November to conduct a series of maneuvers. The exercises were clearly influenced by the combat operations occurring in France, insofar as they were closely modeled on swift, maneuver-style warfare. Little did anyone in the American army anticipate the vicious trench warfare that was evolving even at that time. The weather during the field training was cold and blustery but mercifully dry. The clouds of fine dust, kicked up by the winds as the troopers ran through their paces, brought its own miseries that the regiment would suffer in spades two years later in Mexico.[49]

Shortly after returning from the field, an emergency arose that illustrates why the regiment was deployed to the border in the first place. During much of the regiment's stay in El Paso, nearby Juárez was the scene of frequent fighting between various Mexican factions, usually followers of Pancho Villa and Venustiano Carranza. The battling factions kept the Americans on edge with recurrent gunfights that sent stray bullets zinging into the Texas town from across the river. Sometimes the shots were purposely aimed into American territory and even at Americans themselves. On January 29, 1915, for example, Private William B. Warwick of G Company, while sitting in his tent at Camp Cotton, was instantly killed when a stray bullet struck him. A regimental board of inquiry determined that the round came from the Mexican side of the river, but predictably, no action was taken by Mexican authorities to arrest the perpetrator.[50]

Tensions were exacerbated by rumors then being circulated by Mexicans about raids or invasions into the United States at this location or that. One such story came to Pershing's attention toward the end of August 1915. On the 25th, a rumor was passed by an informant who stated that Mexicans of the Huerta-Carranza-Colorado faction, called the "Nationalists," were preparing an "uprising" into El Paso from across the river. After checking other sources, the general felt the hearsay was solid enough that he deployed the 16th Infantry to close the international bridges into Juárez. Additionally, all other troops were recalled to their encampments and held in readiness for action. The raid never materialized, however, and the troops were stood down.[51]

Though concern remained that revolutionary fighting could break out again at any time, the 8th Brigade generally assumed a passive posture, allowing units time to pursue activities that relieved some of the tension and provided entertainment. Sports, as usual, were high on the list of preferred pastimes. Oddly, one sport that caught on at Fort Bliss was soccer.

The post athletic and recreation officer organized a league in which the 16th Infantry team became the champions. The prize was the opportunity to compete against the winners of a league in El Paso. That team was the Empire Soccer Club, which the novices of the 16th Infantry trounced in the championship game.[52]

On November 25, 1915, Colonel William H. Allaire took command of the 16th Infantry. Commissioned into the 23rd Infantry from West Point in 1882, Allaire had served with the 23rd in Texas, the Philippines, and New York until September 1907. For the next four years, he served as the military attaché to the American Embassy in Vienna, Austria. He returned to the states in October 1911 and commanded a battalion of the 4th Infantry at Fort Crook. For a period of eight months, beginning February 1915, he commanded the 8th Infantry in the Philippines before being assigned to command the 16th Infantry.[53]

Mexico 1916-1917

During the various Mexican revolutions of 1910-17, numerous men vied for power. Eight-time president Porfirio Díaz was removed from office by Francisco Ignacio Madero who, in turn, was forced out by Victoriano Huerta, and later assassinated. This cold-blooded act caused four men, Venustiano Carranza, Álvaro Obregón, Emiliano Zapata, and Pancho Villa, to join forces, and they, in turn, overthrew Huerta in 1915. The United States decided to recognize Carranza as the de facto president of the Mexican government, which immediately displeased Villa, and he declared himself against the new government. After a series of defeats at the hands of the Carranzistas, Villa and his men began taking desperate measures.

On January 10, 1916, a group of bandits, purportedly Villa's men, stopped a train near Santa Ysabel in the state of Chihuahua and removed eighteen Americans, mostly mining engineers, and murdered them in cold bold. As word of the murders filtered back to El Paso, American blood began to boil and once again Pershing recalled the troops of the 8th Brigade to their camps and held them in readiness for trouble. When the bodies of the engineers arrived in El Paso on January 13, riots broke out. In their anger, Americans began to search the city to find Mexicans on whom to vent their wrath. In a predominantly Hispanic city (it did not matter whether they were American citizens or not), finding a person of the appropriate heritage to thrash was not difficult. In the rapidly deteriorating situation, the local police lost control, and troops were summoned to assist the local authorities in restoring order.[54]

At 11 o'clock that night, Pershing declared martial law in El Paso. Four companies of the 16th Infantry were dispatched to restore order to the downtown area, where most of the street fights were taking place. Lines of troops, four abreast, double-timed through the town and systematically swept people along, driving them out of the trouble areas by force of numbers and intimidation. With the establishment of sentries at street corners and the town squares, it was made evident to all that the troops were in charge and not to be trifled with. The problems quickly died down and by the following morning, the 16th Infantry handed over a docile city to the police.[55]

After this incident, rumors began to circulate that Villa—who denied any complicity in the murders—was planning a raid on the American side of the border. The Mexican commander of the Juárez garrison sent notice of Villa's supposed intentions to Pershing, but the warning was ignored as just another in a series of baseless rumors. No one seriously believed that the Mexican bandit would dare to invade the United States.

Those doubts were erased on the night of March 9, 1916, when five hundred or more Mexicans raided the town of Columbus, New Mexico. Though they caught the American garrison by surprise, what the invaders did not count on was the rapid response of the 13th Cavalry troopers stationed there. Bailing from their bunks and securing their weapons while still wiping the sleep from their eyes, the cavalrymen—many of whom were shoeless and clad only in their underwear—assembled a disjointed but nonetheless very effective defense of the town. By first light, seven troopers had been killed and five wounded, but sixty-nine bandit bodies were found scattered throughout Columbus. Detachments of the 13th Cavalry mounted up at dawn to conduct a pursuit and, over the next six hours, engaged the bandits several times as they fled over the border. Running low on water and ammunition, the cavalry finally turned north and crossed the border back into Columbus, leaving a trail of at least seventy more dead Villistas. In the several engagements with the 13th Cavalry, Villa's men suffered 190 killed and an unknown number of wounded (many of whom subsequently died).[56]

Reaction to the raid was swift. President Wilson directed Pershing to organize an armed force with the "sole object of capturing Villa and preventing any further raids by his bands...."[57] Within two days, Pershing had assembled an ad hoc division for that purpose. Designated the "Punitive Expedition," it comprised two brigades of cavalry and one of infantry. The 1st Provisional Infantry Brigade, organized at Columbus under the command of Colonel John H. Beacon (commander, 6th Infantry), was really nothing more than the 8th Brigade, less General Pershing and staff (see map 5.2). The brigade's units consisted of those in the old 8th Brigade (the 6th and 16th Infantry Regiments), as well as the attachment of Companies E and H, 2nd Battalion, Engineers. The very afternoon of the raid, the brigade units were rushed by rail to Columbus and, at precisely 1:05 p.m. on March 15, the 16th Infantry trudged across the border in pursuit of Pancho Villa.

The regimental color guard of the 13th Cavalry (which, because of the regiment's performance two days earlier, had been selected to lead the eastern column across the border) crossed the international boundary earlier at 12:13 p.m., followed by additional cavalry, the two infantry regiments, artillery, and the supply train. The men of C Company had the good for-

tune to be detailed as guards for the supply train and so were able to ride on the wagons of the 1st and 2nd Wagon Companies, while the rest of the 16th Infantry walked. The first day, the column reached Palomas, an almost deserted adobe village of thirty huts scattered about a small spring, and made camp for the night. The night was bitterly cold and the men found the water frozen in their canteens the following morning at reveille. At 7:30 a.m., the column continued south for twenty miles to Boca Grande without incident. Due to the more rapid advance of the mounted elements, the infantry fell behind. The column passed through high rolling country, then entered a canyon that lead to the day's bivouac site where the cavalry, artillery, and wagons had already arrived.[58]

For the next three days, the troops of the regiment marched south into the interior of Chihuahua, winding their way through Ojo Federico, Capuchin Pass, and Corralitos Ranch. On March 22, the regiment reached Casa Grandes and remained there for a month, conducting patrols and performing routine duties. During the stay at Casa Grandes seventy-four recruits arrived and began their orientation to real soldiering. On April 22, the regiment continued its journey deeper into the hinterland of Old Mexico: while the 1st and 2nd Battalions headed for Colonia Dublán, the balance of the regiment marched toward Namiquipa. The regiment reunited on May 5 at San Gerónimo Ranch, where it remained conducting company-sized forays into the surrounding country before moving to Namiquipa on May 30.[59]

The nights were exceedingly cold, the days hot and dusty. Water, moreover, was scarce and the terrain unusually rough. In spite of these conditions, the soldiers were itching for a scrap with the bandits, and morale remained high. As Pershing motored along in his staff car en route to Namiquipa, he was accompanied by Frank Elser, a reporter from the *New York Times*. Elser described the scene as they approached Namiquipa:

As we neared the place we could hear men's voices singing. Presently over a rise in the road a column of marching troops swung into view. They were the 6th and 16th Infantry. Behind them came the guns and ammunition carts of the 4th Artillery. As the men recognized Pershing they broke into a cheer. My throat hurt; we knew what their exultant thought was. They had hiked miles until their dogs hurt, and at last they were going to see action. It was war and the cavalry wasn't going to hog it all. Pershing's lips went into a tight smile and he saluted.[60]

In spite of what the men of the 16th Infantry wished at the time, this trip *was* to be almost entirely a cavalry show. For the infantry, it was to be ten months of relative boredom under trying field conditions. In addition to the difficult march into Mexico, another indicator of the conditions under which they would operate came on March 23, three days after arrival at the

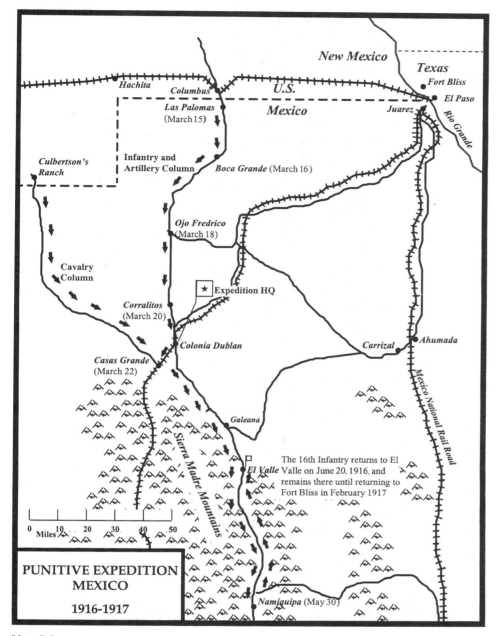

Map 5-2.

Within the map:

New Mexico

Texas

Fort Bliss

El Paso

U.S.

Juarez

Mexico

Rio Grande

Hachita

Columbus

Las Palomas
(March 15)

Culbertson's
Ranch

Infantry and
Artillery Column

Boca Grande (March 16)

Ojo Fredrico
(March 18)

Cavalry
Column

★ Expedition HQ

Corralitos
(March 20)

Colonia Dublan

Casas Grande
(March 22)

Carrizal

Ahumada

Galeana

Sierra Madre Mountains

Mexico National Rail Road

The 16th Infantry returns to El
El Valle Valle on June 20, 1916, and
remains there until returning to
Fort Bliss in February 1917

0 Miles 10 20 30 40 50

PUNITIVE EXPEDITION
MEXICO
1916-1917

Namiquipa (May 30)

tions. Colonel Harrell was notified to pull the 16th Infantry out of Namiquipa to a new camp to cover the entrance to the valley road that headed south into the Sierra Madre mountains.

On June 19, the regiment once again broke camp and trudged to El Valle, where it would remain for almost the rest of its time in Mexico.[62] As the men settled into their new surroundings, their camp came to resemble the winter quarters of the Army of the Potomac around Falmouth in the winter of 1863—without trees, however. In his book *Chasing Villa*, Frank Tompkins described a typical camp of the Punitive Expedition:

> The camp was most uncomfortable, due to high winds, frequent dust storms, tropical heat of summer, freezing cold of winter, deep mud in the tropical downpours, and swarms of flies. The soldiers had no tents except the shelter half each man carried with him. The men soon set to work to build adobe walls on which they placed their shelter halves as roofs. Considerable ingenuity was shown in making cots and other "furniture" for camp comfort.[63]

After the arrival of the troops, the regiment's wagons, field desks, kitchen utensils, and other equipment arrived. The men built adobe kitchens for the cooks, and sheltered messing areas, so they might have the small luxury of eating their meals out of the rain and sun. With few tactical duties to perform, the troops found ways to amuse themselves by forming sports teams. When the mundane training requirements were met for the day, the men played baseball or other organized activities to kill time. Without real soldier work to keep the men busy, one would guess that discipline might have faltered, yet Colonel Tompkins reported:

> Under these conditions the discipline should have suffered, but quite the contrary the men were cheerful, well behaved, and ready at all times to respond to any demand

base camp. That day, an infamous "Blue Norther" of unusual strength blew in, causing a severe dust storm. Sand made its way into food, bedding, and clothing. The command's water froze, causing further discomfort. Fortunately, the storm was short-lived and warmer conditions returned, but it was only the first of many instances of nasty weather.[61]

Pershing's efforts to capture or kill Villa had so far met with no success. By June it was evident to the general that the Punitive Expedition would not complete its mission easily or quickly. As a result, he ordered the redeployment of forces to provide maximum coverage and security of the area of opera-

their General might make upon them. During their entire time in Mexico no one of the command was guilty of anything that could bring discredit upon the Expedition.[64]

The 16th Infantry continued months of guard duty, marksmanship, and short patrols around the desert wastes of El Valle while U.S. and Mexican officials attempted to come to agreement on how to deal with Villa and get the American troops out of Mexico. In early 1917, however, the diplomatic situation between the United States and Germany had deteriorated to the point where the Germans announced that they would begin unrestricted submarine warfare against all shipping in war zones, even against the vessels of neutral countries. Concluding that renewed diplomatic relations between the U.S. and Mexico would ultimately resolve the issue of Villa, and that conflict with Germany was inevitable, President Wilson recalled the Punitive Expedition from Chihuahua. On February 5, 1917, the dusty doughboys of the 16th Infantry trudged back across the border at Columbus. In town, a reviewing stand had been set up and the entire column passed in review for General Pershing. From there, the regiment boarded trains and proceeded to take station at Camp Cotton.

On February 23, the British government released the infamous "Zimmermann Telegram," revealing Germany's attempt to join hands with Mexico in a war against the United States. This revelation, along with the loss of American ships and lives over the next six weeks, drove the president to ask Congress to declare war. The public outrage of Americans compelled their representatives to comply with the president's request, and a declaration of war was issued on April 6, 1917.

That month, Secretary of War Newton D. Baker recommended to President Wilson that Pershing head the American Expeditionary Forces (AEF) to France. Wilson agreed, and Pershing was directed to assemble a division for movement overseas as soon as practicable. Along with Colonel Malvern Hill Barnum, a West Point classmate, he selected four infantry regiments as the nucleus of the new division. The first of these was the 16th Infantry, the regiment with whom Black Jack had suffered the hardships in Mexico, the good times in El Paso, and the privations of Philippine duty. Along with the 18th, 26th, and 28th Infantry Regiments, the 16th would be integrated into the "1st Expeditionary Division" (later shortened to "1st Division") for service in France. This stroke of good fortune began an association between the 16th Infantry and America's premier division which has lasted over eighty years.

With the other three regiments, the 16th Infantry would write a new chapter in its story, a chapter that began as the regiment prepared to head east for Hoboken, New Jersey. The 1st Division had been ordered to assemble at that East Coast port to prepare for the voyage overseas. While the regiment busied itself at El Paso for its next big adventure, General Pershing and the AEF staff had already arrived in France for initial consultations with the Allies and had firmed up plans for the arrival of the 1st Expeditionary Division. Soon, the 16th Infantry would sail for the port of St. Nazaire, France, and would not return to the United States until it was over, "Over There."

REPATRIATED FRENCH WOMEN, THELONNE, ARDENNES AND SOLDIERS OF THE 16TH INF.

16th Infantry doughboys in Thelone, France, November 7, 1918

SEMPER PARATUS

Chapter Six
"Lafayette, We Are Here!"

There is, to my thinking, nothing finer in this world than the self-effacing role of the private soldier of infantry, and nowhere in this war has this private soldier of infantry been truer to his Country's expectations of him than in the Sixteenth Infantry.

Brigadier General Frank Parker, Commanding General, 1st Division

May 1917 found the men of the 16th Infantry Regiment in a canvas cantonment called Camp Newton D. Baker. Located near El Paso and overlooking the town of Juárez, it was sited on a sandy mesa where the West Texas winds often kicked up dust and sent it swirling through the tent flaps and into everything the soldiers owned.[1] Still, the troops were happy to be there. Anything beat the searing hot summer days and bitterly cold winter nights of El Valle, Mexico. After almost a year south of the border, Camp Baker was a comparative paradise. The enticements of the two border towns and the lazy routine of camp life upon their return were sorely welcomed changes, but it soon became apparent that the good times were to be short-lived.

That month, the camp was rife with scuttlebutt that the regiment was to go overseas to France. Suddenly, the camp became an ants' nest of activity. Men began scrambling back and forth. New issues of equipment were drawn and physical exams were conducted. Organized training with the rifle and bayonet increased, and physical training was reinstituted on a daily basis. New contingents of men arrived to swell the ranks of the depleted companies. Many of these men were regulars, or "old dogs," from other units who had volunteered to transfer to one of the regiments deploying overseas. However, most were faces fresh off the farm or straight from inner city neighborhoods, enthusiastically responding to the patriotic calls to fight the dastardly "Hun." Eager for adventure, they readily signed the recruiting papers and were soon on their way. The effect of the influx of all these troops, however, was to transform the 16th Infantry from a relatively small, close-knit team of field-hardened professionals into a collection of men that could be called a regiment only because they wore the same uniforms and shared the same unit designation.

The officers and NCOs of the 16th Infantry were determined to make soldiers of their men before departure. But having only six weeks to accomplish what normally would take at least a year, the end result was not impressive. Nevertheless, on June 3, the regiment boarded trains in El Paso and headed east. Though ordered to take precautions to conceal their movement, the troops were in such a festive mood over their impending enterprise that they chalked slogans such as "Can the Kaiser" and "Bound for Berlin" on the sides of the rail cars.[2]

While en route to New York City, a rather mundane administrative action occurred at the War Department that had a long-term effect on the 16th Infantry. Without realizing it, the clerk typing the orders assigning the regiment to the 1st Expeditionary Division on June 8, 1917, established a regimental-divisional relationship that has become the strongest and proudest association in the United States Army. Except for the period 1959-63 when infantry divisions were reorganized under the "Pentomic" concept, there has always been an element of the 16th Infantry assigned to the "Big Red One."

Upon arrival in New York, the regiment was brigaded with the 18th Infantry Regiment and assigned to the 1st Infantry Brigade under the command of Brigadier General Omar Bundy. Bundy had commanded the 16th Infantry in 1914-15, and he was delighted to have his old regiment again under his command. The hastily organized camps built in the New York area rapidly filled with the troops of the 1st Expeditionary Division, which was authorized twenty-eight thousand men. Despite the recent influx of new men, however, the 16th Infantry was still not up to full strength. Authorized 112 officers and 3,720 enlisted men—to be organized into three battalions of four companies each, a machine-gun company, supply company, and a medical department detachment—the regiment would sail with only 73 officers and 2,563 enlisted men.[3]

Under the cover of darkness on the night of June 9-10, the bulk of the regiment boarded the USCT *Saratoga* at Hoboken, New Jersey, while the regimental headquarters, band, and Companies A, B, C, E, and F embarked on the USCT *Havana*.[4] The ships lay at the docks for three more days, however, because the transports had to wait for the arrival of an escort of warships. Finally, on June 14, the convoy, consisting of four destroyers, the cruiser USS *Seattle*, and twelve transports carrying the advanced units of the 1st Division, departed for France.[5]

The voyage was largely uneventful until the night of June 22, when the convoy was attacked by a German U-boat about 10:15 p.m. The torpedoes were apparently aimed at the *Saratoga*, but due to the zigzag efforts of the ships' captains, the deadly projectiles streamed past the transports, leaving only bubbly, phosphorescent wakes that harmlessly dissipated in the waves. Three nights later, the convoy slipped quietly into the harbor at St. Nazaire, France, and dropped anchor.[6] On the gray, drizzly morning of June 26, the units of the 1st Division began to unload at the docks. First to go ashore was the 28th Infantry, the 1st Division headquarters, and the 16th Infantry. Initially, no one was there to greet the ship except for a small cluster of American officers who critically observed the actions of the troops as they formed up on the docks. The old-timers in the 16th Infantry quickly noticed one of the officers in particular, one for whom they had grown especially fond, despite his stern demeanor.

> They saw standing on the dock a tall man in khaki staring intently at them. So straight he stood, so narrowly he surveyed the ranks that old Mexican veterans pegged him immediately—JJP. They knew, some of those men, that the Punitive Expedition troops were now called "Pershing's Darlings," a sobriquet their general did not deny but which perhaps counted as a mixed blessing. He did stare hard![7]

The 1st Division would always be Pershing's favorite, but as will be later seen, the general's favoritism would prove a mixed blessing indeed. Initially, for some in the division, leaders and soldiers alike, Pershing's uncompromising pressure to meet high standards seemed excessive, but when the realities of trench warfare and the need to cooperate with the battle-hardened Allies struck home, it became apparent that his unwavering commitment to discipline and excellence was designed to ensure victory on the battlefield. If he could help it, Black Jack was going to make sure that the American army performed better than the European armies in the field and, to that end, he had determined that the 1st Division was going to set the standard for the rest of the American Expeditionary Forces (AEF).

While the sergeants dressed the ranks and the first sergeants took roll, the French townspeople hardly noticed these fresh-looking soldiers. At first, they seemed unaware that these new troops were about to head for the front to fight in the trenches. Perhaps they had seen too many of their own march off to die, and this was their way of dealing with reality. Then someone noticed something different about these men. They were huge; they were jovial; there was a confidence and swagger about them that the French had not seen in three years. Then it struck them. Perhaps it was the language these men were speaking or the colors they unfurled. No matter: they suddenly realized that these were Americans!

Word began to spread through the city that the Americans had arrived! People, mostly the young and old, ran to the docks and crowded the streets to see the "amis." Soon the crowds were cheering and expressing their joy at the arrival of the 1st Division. By now, the troops were ready. Someone, perhaps Colonel Allaire, ordered the band to play, and with the nation-

al and regimental colors waving and music wafting through the air, the 16th Infantry staged an impromptu parade through St. Nazaire on its way to Camp Number 1.[8]

Camp Number 1 was a hastily built cantonment located three miles from St. Nazaire. Constructed by German POWs, at the time of the arrival of the 1st Division the camp was a squalid mudhole.[9] In describing the regiment's first home away from home, the regimental chaplain related: "The Regimental Commander's cot stood in several inches of mud, and other things were in keeping. Very early in their foreign experience the doughboys grew accustomed to such disagreeable conditions, and took them as a matter of course."[10]

Private Tom Carroll of F Company remembered Camp Number 1 as "poor accommodations and lots of confusion...." He also recalled the persistent rain and the compound's barbed wire fence, built to keep the men confined in the camp. The troops, however, took advantage of the fact that there were no guards posted and easily slipped through the fence to go into town. Of course, a fair number of them became inebriated on the local wine, and one, a sergeant, was caught by the F Company commander attempting to bring two bottles of this precious commodity into the camp. Thereafter, guard posts were established and the forays into town lessened considerably.[11]

The regiment was at Camp Number 1 for less than a week when word came down that a battalion was to travel to Paris to parade through the city on the Fourth of July and participate in the formal French ceremonies welcoming the American Expeditionary Forces. The 1st Battalion was initially chosen for the parade duty, but when two cases of measles were discovered in A Company, the battalion was quarantined and 2nd Battalion was chosen in its stead. The 2nd Battalion boarded trains to Paris early on the morning of July 2. On a stop at Nantes that day, the battalion disembarked and held an impromptu parade through the town, much to the delight of its citizens.[12]

The 2nd Battalion arrived in Paris at 7:45 a.m. on July 3. Under a bright-shining morning sun, the Americans disembarked and marched through streets lined with crowds of enthusiastic Parisians. The regiment's immediate destination was Caserne de Reuilly, where they would be comfortably billeted in an ancient stone barracks that previously housed the French 163rd Infantry Regiment. The officers were put up in some of the finest hotels in the City of Lights. That evening the officers were feted with a banquet at the Cercle Militaire, while many of the men were chauffeured through the city to see the sights.[13]

The Americans also took time to shine brass, polish boots, and otherwise prepare for the next day's big event. The troops were up at 3:30 a.m. on the 4th and given a breakfast of rolls, jam, and coffee. Falling in for morning formation at 6:30 a.m., the troops were accounted for and loaded on trucks for the trip to Les Invalides, the old soldiers' home that houses the tomb of Napoleon Bonaparte.

The troops unloaded near that famous landmark and began their procession, with the battalion commander and staff leading the way, followed by the inimitable 16th Infantry Regiment Band and finally by the companies of American doughboys who had come to France to help "make the world safe for democracy." The first stop was the quarters of General Pershing, a yellow stucco building on the Rue Constantine, where the band delighted him with its strains. The battalion then passed through the imposing iron gates of Les Invalides. At the so-called Court of Honor, the battalion participated in a lengthy ceremony in which French soldiers presented Pershing and the regiment with banners. Capping this event were welcoming speeches by President Raymond Poincaré and Marshal Joseph Joffre.[14]

Initially, the idea of this parade through Paris was not warmly received by Black Jack. It was his fear that the soldierly bearing that only becomes instilled in men after many months of training would be lacking in this collection of troops that had been thrown together in time to ship out for France. His great concern was that these American soldiers would inspire only ridicule from the French people because of their poor marching skills, their inability to perform the manual of arms in a snappy manner, and their rumpled uniforms. After all, most were not much more than civilians in uniform. In short, Pershing feared that the Americans did not look and act like *soldiers!*. But he also felt that the appearance of American troops in Paris might be just the tonic the French needed to buoy their flagging spirits. Perhaps, he thought, the French would not notice or care about the Americans' marching deficiencies. So the general reluctantly gave his approval. Ultimately, he was right: the men did not look like polished soldiers. But he was also right about the French people; they went mad with joy![15]

Departing Les Invalides in the early afternoon, the regiment set out on a five-mile march to their next destination, Picpus Cemetery and the grave site of the Marquis de Lafayette. As the troops wound their way through Paris, marching past the Tuileries, the Place de la Concorde, and swinging on to the Rue de Rivoli, they were joined by the French 230th Territorial Regiment. Along the way, the Parisian crowds marching along became ever larger as the spectators on the walks cheered, shouted, laughed, and wept. The women were especially friendly, pushing into the ranks to kiss the big "amis" and press flowers into their hands, hats, cartridge belts, and rifle barrels. Many linked arms with the Americans and walked with them, speaking excitedly. Most of the soldiers, lacking fluency in French, hadn't the faintest idea what, exactly, the women were telling them, but even so, the meaning was clear: "Thank God you Americans have arrived!"[16]

Pershing, in the meantime, had been riding in a French military touring car. Forced by the crowds onto side streets, the vehicle paralleled the battalion's parade route, allowing the general to observe the joyful spectacle. Like his men, he was impressed by the enthusiasm of the French. Remarking on this supposedly martial event in his memoirs, he humorously noted that the troops were so festooned with blossoms that "the column looked like a moving flower garden."[17]

After covering five miles in the hot July sun, the 2nd Battalion arrived at Picpus Cemetery thirsty and dusty but motivated by the exhilaration of the Parisians. As the men were formed for the ceremony, the crowd pushed its way into the small graveyard. With Lafayette's grave and several speakers to their front, the men were put at ease. Several French orators proceeded to thank them and America for their contribution to the defense of France, after which several American speakers also made remarks. Even General Pershing, at the urging of the American ambassador, Brand Whitlock, made a brief statement. But it was Colonel Charles E. Stanton, whom Pershing had requested to give the formal address, who uttered one of the most memorable lines of the war. After waxing eloquently for several minutes in impeccable French, the good colonel, as if to reinforce the notion that America was over there to repay the debt of France's timely intervention in the American Revolution, ended his remarks with that famous declaration, "Lafayette, we are here!"[18]

Upon returning to the barracks that evening, the battalion was assembled in the compound of the Caserne de Reuilly for a ceremony. There, the outfit was presented a special gift by a group of American citizens in appreciation for the 16th Infantry's presence on French soil. It was a "husky young lion cub."[19] Perhaps it was given in hopes that the regiment would fight like lions in their upcoming battles. In fact, the 16th Infantry would eventually become a superb fighting outfit, but before that could happen, the regiment had to receive something else: combat training.

Before the lucky 2nd Battalion traveled to Paris, Colonel Allaire had already received orders to move the regiment to its training camp. In compliance with those orders, on July 5, the 2nd Battalion loaded the infamous "40 & 8s" and traveled to the Gondrecourt Training Area in the province of Lorraine. The remainder of the regiment left St. Nazaire on July 12 by train and journeyed to Gondrecourt, where it rejoined the 2nd Battalion on July 14.[20]

The regiment was not initially billeted in a camp, but in the homes, barns, and outbuildings around the tiny villages of Demange-aux-Eaux, Delouse, and Abainville. Sometime later, most of the men were moved into an actual camp consisting of small barracks. These "Chambourcy billets" were described as "...rough new barracks of an uncommonly flimsy type that offered special interest to visitors. These buildings were constructed of thin boards not tightly joined and it [was] apparent that they [had to] be strongly reinforced by tar paper or some other material before they [could] be made suitable for winter occupancy."[21] Living in these barns and barracks was bad enough, but that summer was unusually rainy. That, coupled with the early onset of cold weather, made for some trying training conditions.

At Gondrecourt, the regiments of the 1st Division went through a systematic training program with seasoned troops of

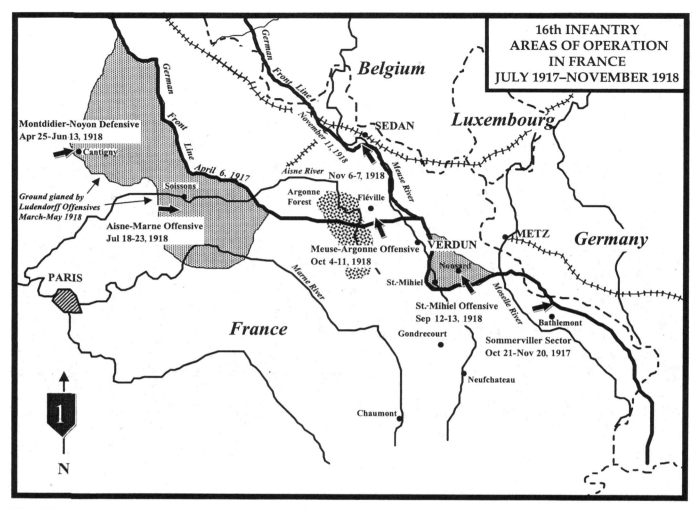

Map 6-1.

the French Army as instructors. Detailed for training with the 16th Infantry were units of a distinguished division—the 47th Chasseurs Alpins, ominously nicknamed the "Blue Devils." This unit had had extensive combat experience and was more than willing to teach the doughboys the hard lessons of trench warfare. The two units soon struck up strong and "very cordial" relations, with the Americans being somewhat in awe of what these tough little *poilus* knew and were willing to share.[22]

The first phase of the training program would last through August and focus on physical conditioning, learning the individual skills necessary for fighting and surviving on the Western Front, and small-unit exercises. In September the Americans would graduate to a regimen of company and higher-unit collective training. Finally, in October, the 1st Division would send regiments into quiet sectors of the line to acquaint the doughboys with the realities of trench warfare. A typical training day in August consisted of first call at 5:30 a.m.; reveille at 6:00 a.m.; drill, marches, or physical training at 7:00 a.m. This was followed by a full day of skills training that included instruction on rifle marksmanship, bayonet, grenades, gas masks, and

the French "Chauchat" light machine gun. By September, the companies and battalions were practicing assault tactics and the defense of trench lines.[23]

As the instruction progressed, Pershing made frequent visits to the division to inspect training. His standards were high for the AEF, and, initially, he did not like what he saw. On one inspection, he noted "sloppiness in dress and performance." A young officer on Pershing's staff, George Patton, attended the inspection and later wrote that the "men did not look smart, officers are lazy, troops lacked equipment and training, [and] were listless."[24]

In addition to rather frequent visits from Pershing, the 16th Infantry received numerous other visitors of note during its stay at Gondrecourt. On September 6, the third anniversary of the Battle of the Marne, the 1st Division was reviewed by French President Raymond Poincaré and several French generals. The parade ground (selected by none other than Captain George C. Marshall, the 1st Division's acting chief of staff) was a muddy mess. Furthermore, it was located on the slope of a hill, which made it difficult for the troops to remain dressed while marching. The less-than-acceptable performance of the 1st Division infantry regiments, coupled with the fact that the French officers accompanying Pershing on the inspection were clearly unimpressed, embarrassed the chief. The general's reaction was swift. He quickly let the division chain of command know what he expected and that he would accept nothing less.[25]

Those officers who had shown themselves unable to make the grade were removed. The remaining officers and NCOs also felt the pressure and, naturally, the pressure was in turn applied to the troops. Soon, as the training became more intense, the men began to look and act like professional soldiers. More important, they became proficient with their equipment and weapons. The chasseurs noted that the doughboys had become particularly good at throwing grenades and in marksmanship with the Chauchat. The barracks, too, began to shape up, as the NCOs bore down on cleanliness and standardization. On the next visit, things had improved considerably. Accompanying Pershing this time were Generals Pétain and Castlenau, and by the end of the inspection, the generals were in high spirits over what they had observed. In short, the regiment had made a "most creditable appearance," and the general headed back to his headquarters at Chaumont quite proud of his men.[26]

On the 15th of the following month, the 16th Infantry was reviewed by Pershing and then General of Division (later, Marshal) Ferdinand Foch on the plateau of St. Joirre. The regiment was in fine form, and the two generals were pleased with the inspection. As a gesture of his appreciation, Joffre presented each officer in the 16th Infantry with a wristwatch or pipe.[27] Shortly after this parade, the regiment's mascot custodian, one Private Smolley of G Company, reported that the lion cub, unaccustomed to the cold weather, had died from pneumonia. There was no time to lament the loss, as rumors swept through the billets at Demange about the regiment's impending departure to the front. On October 20, 1917, rumor became reality as the regiment formed in full marching order and tramped the muddy roads to the Sommerviller sector.

Sommerviller Sector
October 21-November 20, 1917
The town of Sommerviller was the designated logistics base for the 1st Division's first tour in the trenches. It was located in a quiet portion of the front where no significant actions had occurred since 1915. The 16th's share of the division's sector was just east of the tiny and thoroughly devastated village of Bathlèmont.

The last phase of the training plan called for each battalion of the four 1st Division regiments to occupy a stretch of trench for ten days and nights, under French control. So, on the evening of October 21, while the rest of the 16th Infantry stayed near Nancy back from the front, the 1st Battalion marched an additional eleven miles, filing past Einville, Maix, Valhey, through little Bathlèmont and into muddy rat-infested trenches on a desolate hill. The positions they inherited from

the French were a "morass of mud and debris from disuse." Facing them was a mile of "no man's land," within which was located the Bois de Benamont. Beyond that were the lines of the German 1st Landwehr Division, outlined by belts of rusty barbed wire and tanglefoot. To the south about two miles was the Rhine-Marne Canal.[28]

The 1st Battalion's stay in the trenches was relatively uneventful, the major event being the firing of the first American shot of the war into German lines by Battery C, 6th Field Artillery, on October 23. During daylight, the men became accustomed to the sights and sounds of the battlefield and, at night, they went out on patrols into no man's land with French guides, crawling up to within a few yards of the enemy's wire obstacles, only to crawl back to their own lines.[29] And so it went for ten days.

On November 1, Colonel John L. Hines arrived at the regimental PC (command post) to assume command of the 16th Infantry from Lieutenant Colonel Frank A. Wilcox. Wilcox had commanded the regiment since August 25, when Colonel Allaire had been promoted and assigned to be the provost marshal of the AEF. Hines was an 1891 graduate of West Point. After being commissioned in the 2nd Infantry, he spent his early years at posts in Nebraska until shipping out for Cuba in June 1898. Like most of his classmates after the Spanish-American War, he spent several years in the Philippines interspersed with assignments in the States. In August 1914, he was assigned as the acting adjutant of Pershing's 8th Brigade in El Paso and performed that duty with the Punitive Expedition. In May 1917, he traveled with the AEF headquarters as the assistant adjutant general, a position he held until assigned to take over the 16th.[30]

Known as "Birdie" by his West Point friends because of his springy, bird-like step, he was a tall and gangly, but cheerful, forty-nine-year-old West Virginian. He had been selected for command of the 16th Infantry to get the regiment straightened out. Though it had made a lot of progress at Gondrecourt under Wilcox's hand, it had not reached the levels of proficiency expected by Major General William L. Sibert, the 1st Division commander. Indeed, following his initial inspection shortly after his arrival Hines found the regiment's men "dazed or asleep....They did not seem to realize that the were on the verge of a big war."[31] It was not long before realization hit home in the hardest of ways.

On the cold evening of November 2, the men of the 2nd Battalion donned their packs and, with the help of guides, made their way forward to the regiment's sector of trenches to relieve the troops of the 1st Battalion. Company F occupied a position designated Strong Point Artois, which was about to become a scene of tragedy and heroism. Among the men of Company F were Private Thomas F. Enright from Pittsburgh, Pennsylvania, a former cavalryman on his third enlistment; Private Merle D. Hay of Glidden, Iowa, who had volunteered in the initial patriotic rush to join the coast artillery, but ended

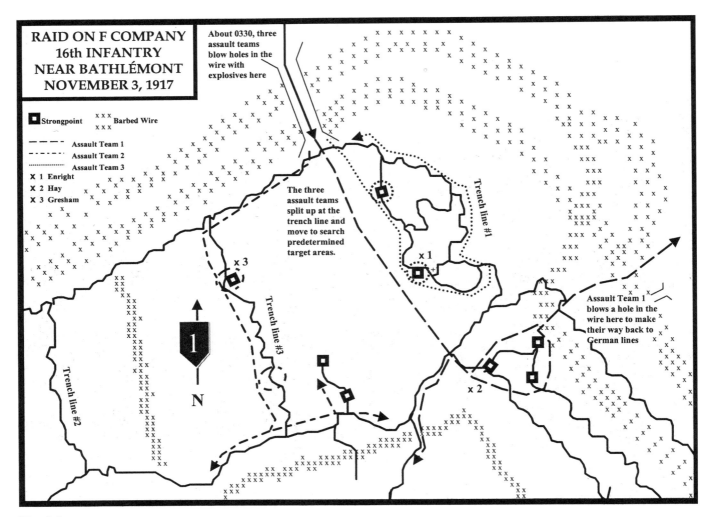

RAID ON F COMPANY
16th INFANTRY
NEAR BATHLÉMONT
NOVEMBER 3, 1917

■ Strongpoint ××× Barbed Wire
×××
– – – – Assault Team 1
– · – · Assault Team 2
· · · · · · Assault Team 3
X 1 Enright
X 2 Hay
X 3 Gresham

About 0330, three assault teams blow holes in the wire with explosives here

The three assault teams split up at the trench line and move to search predetermined target areas.

Trench line #1

Assault Team 1 blows a hole in the wire here to make their way back to German lines

Trench line #3

Trench line #2

Map 6-2.

up in the 16th Infantry; and their squad leader, Corporal Bethel Gresham of Evansville, Indiana, a veteran of the regiment's excursion into Mexico to chase Villa.[32]

In inky darkness beneath a cloudy sky the battalion took up positions in their muddy gash in the earth. The relief was uneventful and, with the exception of an occasional rifle shot, the sector was initially quiet. Then, at 3:45 a.m., the earth erupted in the blinding flashes and stupendous roar of a box barrage that isolated F Company. As the troops cringed in the mud, a raiding party of 213 men from the 7th Bavarian Landwehr Regiment made their way across "no man's land" toward F Company. As they reached the trenches, Gresham encountered one of the Germans aiming his Mauser rifle at him. Thinking the man was one of his fellow 16th Infantrymen, the corporal shouted, "Don't shoot. I'm an American!" The rifle cracked and Gresham crumpled into a pile, shot between the eyes. "I'm shooting every damned thing in sight tonight!" came the reply in "guttural, broken English."[33]

Nearby, Private Hoyt Decker saw an American soldier,

illuminated by flares and shell bursts, engaged in a desperate hand-to-hand struggle with two Germans. Decker thought the struggling man was Private Merle Hay. Before Decker could go to the man's assistance, he was shot twice and captured. After some fifty minutes, the artillery fire faded, and the German raiding party made its way back with twelve prisoners from F Company. Meanwhile, the remainder of the 2nd Battalion, recovering from the initial shock of the raid, responded to their orders for a counterattack by climbing out of the trenches and moving forward into no man's land. But, absent any real plan of attack and with dawn graying the sky, orders were sent to fall back to the trenches, and the men made their way back to their positions.[34]

In the trenches, the men found the bodies of the three men killed in the raid—Gresham, Enright, and Hay. Hay was found face down in the mud of the trench, his throat cut and a .45 pistol still firmly in his grip. Those who saw him thought that he had indeed been engaged in a terrific fight. Not far away lay Gresham and Enright. Enright also had his throat cut, the wound so deep that his head was almost severed. Gresham had been shot twice, once in the forehead and again in the throat, and had collapsed on the fire step. Scattered about the F Company positions were several rifles, helmets, and other pieces of equipment abandoned by the Germans, evidence that the 16th Infantry had at least wounded, and maybe killed, several of the raiders in return.[35]

November 3, 1917, was a gray, dreary day—the day America had finally been blooded in the ground war in Europe. The German raid had been almost perfectly carried out. Curiously, it was later discovered that it was a French deserter in Bathlèmont who, through some surreptitious means, had notified the Germans of the time and location of the relief by the 2nd Battalion, thereby ensuring that the Huns would have an absolutely green American unit opposing them.

The following morning, Gresham, Enright, and Hay were buried in Bathlèmont with full military honors rendered by an assembly of their buddies in F Company and a detachment of poilus from the French 18th Division. General Bordeaux, commander of the 18th Division, was on hand to give the eulogy. In his concluding remarks, he stated:

> Thus the death of this humble corporal and these privates appeals to us with unwonted grandeur. We will, therefore, ask that the mortal remains of these young men be left to us forever. We will inscribe on their tombs, "Here lie the first soldiers of the United States to fall on the fields of France for justice and liberty!" The passer-by will stop and uncover his head. Travelers and men of heart will go out of their way to come here to pay their tributes. Private Enright, Corporal Gresham, Private Hay! In the name of France, I thank you. God receive your souls. Farewell![36]

The 2nd Battalion remained in the line for an additional nine days. The only other incident of note came on the night of November 9, when the battalion repulsed a second raid. Then it was the 3rd Battalion's turn. By late November, all battalions of the 1st Division had rotated through the trenches, and on the 20th, the 16th Infantry returned to its billets at Gondrecourt. For the next two months, the division continued its training in rather severe weather conditions. Snow had begun falling and with it the temperatures. There was a shortage of wood and coal for heaters, as well as forage for the unit's horses. Nevertheless, training intensified in preparation for the 1st Division's next mission—independent operations in the trenches. This time, the division would control its own regiments and field artillery battalions.[37]

The regiment's losses during its initial combat in France were four killed and twelve wounded.[38] It was ready for the next phase of training.

Throughout December, the regiment continued to conduct training in trench warfare at Gondrecourt. During the month, the regiment under went an organizational change when the Training Battalion, 16th Infantry, arrived from Camp

MacArthur at Waco, Texas. This organization, consisting of nineteen officers and 740 enlisted men, had been undergoing machine-gun training for several months. On December 16, the men of D, H, and M Companies were distributed among the remaining rifle companies, and the 1st, 2nd, and 3rd Machine-gun Companies of the Training Battalion became the new D, H, and M Companies, respectively.[39]

Ansauville Sector
January 15-April 3, 1918

Arrival of new helmets and gas masks confirmed the scuttlebutt that the time to move was soon, and on January 15, 1918, the regiment formed up on the muddy roads around Gondrecourt for the thirty-two kilometer march to Sorcy. Carrying full packs, personal gear, and comfort items they were loath to leave behind, the men were further weighed down by rain-soaked overcoats. The day was bitterly cold and windy, which added to the misery as they slogged toward their destination. Foot problems abounded because of the wet conditions, and men steadily fell out of the march, unable to continue. Those that made the march were grateful to reach the barns and outbuildings of Sorcy that night, and get out of the wind and bitter cold.[40]

Three nights later, the 1st Infantry Brigade began relieving the crack 1st Moroccan Division of its positions. The 16th Infantry began its relief operation on the evening of the 19th, replacing the 8th Zouaves and the French Foreign Legion. Initially, the brigade was under operational control of the French 69th Division, but on the 30th, the 1st Division headquarters assumed tactical control of its units for the first time in a combat zone.[41]

The Ansauville sector, located about twenty miles northwest of Toul, was not the quiet area that Bathlèmont had been, yet still not as bad as the hot combat zones that the regiment would experience later. Heavy patrolling was the order of the day, and shelling of the lines was "frequent enough to make it interesting." Here, the regiment experienced its first gas attack. Initially nervous about the possibility, the men practiced masking so frequently that by the time a real attack occurred, it was somewhat anti-climactic.[42]

Illustrating the conditions under which the regiment labored at Ansauville, Major General Charles P. Summerall wrote of the division's experiences:

> The sector became very active and many casualties were suffered. Both the enemy and the Division carried out raids in force in which prisoners were captured and men were killed and wounded. Mustard gas was freely used by both sides and large numbers of men were quickly disabled in gas attacks. Flame throwing caused serious losses. The billets were often shelled and bombed and the casualties were serious....The artillery and infantry learned mutual confidence and the Division became a united team. All labored under great strain and realized

the grave responsibility that rested upon them.[43]

It was during the latter part of the regiment's stay in these trenches that the incident that became known as the "Fizzle Raid" took place—or rather did not take place, at least when it was supposed to. After several weeks of planning and rehearsals, a raiding party from the 16th Infantry was poised in the forward trench line on the evening of March 3, intent on seeking revenge for the Bathlèmont raid. Assembled to watch the action were Major General Robert L. Bullard, the division commander; Brigadier General George B. Duncan, the brigade commander; and none other than Black Jack Pershing himself. The scene was one of tension. The troops were nervous, but ready. Men crouched in their trenches waiting word to slip quietly over the top. As H-hour passed early on the morning of March 4, the generals grew impatient. No artillery preparation fires erupted. No flares were fired. "What's the problem?" one of the generals demanded. A pause ensued, then aides scrambled to find out the cause. Soon, the word came back. Squads from the 1st Engineers had just concluded that their Bangalore torpedoes were defective, and without them, it would be impossible to ensure a breach in the enemy's barbed wire. The raid was canceled.[44]

Orders came down the first week in March that the 2nd Brigade would relieve the 1st Brigade on March 9, but the date set for the second raid attempt was the 10th, so the men of the raiding party were to stay behind to execute the mission. This time, the foray went off without a hitch. At the arranged moment, the artillery laid a superbly executed box barrage on the targeted raid area, and eighty-two picked men under a captain known as the "Daredevil of the Regiment" swept across no man's land. Into the Hun trenches they went, shooting and bayoneting anybody they found. They took no prisoners. Upon finishing their business, the raiding party made its way back to friendly lines, having suffered only four wounded. Gresham, Hay, and Enright were avenged, and the men of the 16th Infantry gained considerable confidence in their ability to attack and defeat their German opponents.[45]

After coming out of the line, the regiment was billeted behind the Toul sector. For the next three weeks, as 2nd Brigade did their stint in the line, 1st Brigade troops were given passes to visit neighboring French villages. The men of the 16th Infantry had the opportunity to visit Aix les Bains, while some of the officers traveled to see Nice. All who had the chance to go reported a delightful time, but the trips were cut short by the first of the so-called Ludendorff Offensives, which began on March 21. As the situation on the Montdidier front worsened, the division received orders to prepare to move. On April 1, the 26th "Yankee" Division relieved the 2nd Brigade, and the 1st Division entrained for Gisors, forty miles northeast of Paris.[46]

At Gisors, the 1st Division was held in reserve, ready to launch into the line should the Germans achieve a break-through near Montdidier. Though the war raged to the east, the area around Gisors was a picturesque isle of calm. Unscarred by the ravages of war, the lush countryside here was in stark contrast to the devastated areas the men had recently occupied. The regimental headquarters was established at the Château Boury, a mansion built by François Monsart, the architect and builder of Louis XIV's palace at Versailles. The 3rd Battalion officers were also billeted in a beautiful 11th century château owned by a French cavalry officer.[47]

In early April, Colonel Hines received word of his promotion to brigadier general and reassignment to command the 1st Brigade. Replacing him in command of the 16th Infantry was Colonel Harry A. Smith, one of Hines's West Point classmates from 1891. Smith had spent several years in the Philippines right after the Spanish-American War with the 5th Infantry and had transferred with the regiment to the Presidio of San Francisco in 1902, where he spent another five years. In an unusual career pattern for the time, Smith spent the years 1907 to 1914 at Fort Leavenworth, first as a student, then as an instructor. From 1914 until 1917, he was assigned as the adjutant for the 5th Brigade at Galveston, Texas, then as an inspector general in China and the War Department. In early 1918, Smith spent time as a liaison officer with the British XV Corps, then as an instructor in the AEF school system before being assigned to command the regiment.[48]

While at Gisors, the officers of the division were assembled for a pep talk from Pershing. Clearly understanding the seriousness of the situation for the French Army, Pershing had agreed to commit three U.S. Army divisions (1st, 26th, and 42nd) to support the defensive operations blocking the German advance on Paris, and the 1st Division was to conduct the corps' main effort. In his speech to the officers, the general emphasized the "grave responsibility of the Division and the opportunity to establish the reputation of the American troops."[49] The meaning of Pershing's discourse was not lost on the officers of the 1st Division, and they determined that, come hell or high water, the "Fighting First" would establish a good reputation. In the succeeding months, they indeed achieved their goal.

Though the Gisors interlude was enjoyable, the exigencies of the war required the return of the 1st Division to the line. About the middle of April, the regiment conducted another long march to its next position near Picardy. Passing through Beauvais two days later, it soon arrived at Ansauville-Gannes, where it remained for several days. Approaching the Montdidier salient, the men could hear the guns at the front. During the night of April 24, the regiment went into the line near the Belle Assises Farm.[50]

Cantigny Sector
April 25-June 8, 1918
On April 20, the 1st Division was assigned to the French VI Corps and received orders to relieve elements of the 45th and 162nd Divisions in the Cantigny sector. The 1st Infantry Brigade

was selected to perform the relief, and the 16th Infantry was assigned that portion of the sector from Bois Celestin to the Bois de Fontaine. The 18th Infantry was on the regiment's left, beginning at the Bois de Fontaine and extending north to Bois St. Eloi, which included the town of Cantigny.[51]

The Belle Assises Farm was located some twenty-five hundred meters to the south-southwest of the town of Cantigny. Most of the regiment's line was located on a forward slope that extended east through an open field that had been the farm's wheat field in peaceful times. When the 16th assumed control of the trenches in this sector, they found them to be little more than ditches quickly scraped in the soil by desperate poilus attempting to blunt the German offensive. No barbed wire or other obstacles existed to slow an attack. The positions lay exposed to artillery and to sniper fire that was particularly irksome in daylight hours. The men could barely move in daylight for by doing so, they brought much unwelcome attention from the "boche" across the way in Cantigny.[52]

The regimental PC was established at Broyes and assumed control of the sector at 10:00 a.m. on April 27. The 16th Infantry had deployed two battalions forward, and one was held in reserve to the rear. Distributed throughout the sector were teams from the 1st and 2nd Machine Gun Battalions and elements of the 1st Engineers. The engineers were especially welcome as the infantrymen struggled to improve their defensive positions and prepare a main line of resistance to the rear over the next several weeks.[53] The ability to stand up, dig, string wire, and otherwise improve the trenches at night was a welcome respite for the men:

> It was a relief to get out and work at night, and there was plenty to do. For instance, there was no way to get from the Belle Assizes Farm to Broyes without passing along a road which was under full observation and direct fire of the enemy. One night four companies and two companies of engineers were told to make a communications trench. They worked like beavers. Had they been discovered at work, one thousand men might easily have been wiped out in a few minutes. But the dawn next day saw the trench stretching for a kilometer and a half, apparently the work of magic.[54]

The day-to-day existence of the men was nearly unbearable. Rations had to be transported forward on two-wheeled carts to points behind the main line. From there, chow was carried into the trenches in mermite cans, but by the time it arrived, meals were cold. Water was in short supply; often, men had to make one canteen last two days. Artillery fell upon the positions frequently, a seeming constant rain of metal that inflicted numerous casualties. But the most distressing problem was the inability to evacuate the wounded until nighttime. The torture of watching and listening to the suffering and moans of the injured soldiers as they lay in the heat or rain made life particularly horrid.[55]

The conditions forward of the Belle Assise Farm were such that many who suffered through this period referred to the Montdidier defensive "as a fiercer strain upon their nerves than even Soissons or the Argonne." However, release from the anxiety of Belle Assise came on the night of May 14-15 when the regiments of the 2nd Brigade relieved the 16th Infantry of its sector. The regiment, less 1st Battalion, was moved to rest positions in and around Froissy about twenty-five kilometers west of Cantigny, while the 1st Battalion was kept in division reserve around Chepoix. The rest was well-deserved and well-needed, but it was only a matter of time before the regiment was back in the fight. Soon, Colonel Smith was ordered to relieve the battered 28th Infantry of their recently hard-won positions east of Cantigny and, accordingly, on the nights of May 30 and 31 the doughboys of the 16th filled the trenches as the men of the 28th Infantry filed out of the line, grateful to be headed to the rear.[56]

Two days later, Smith directed the 3rd Battalion to straighten out their portion of the line. Reportedly, the directive to the battalion commander was, "Don't bring on a fight: don't have casualties, but straighten out the line." The method to fulfill the order was developed by two enterprising lieutenants who led their units forward shellhole by shellhole some one hundred yards during the night of June 1 and dug in. The following two nights, the process was repeated so that by dawn of June 4, the line had been advanced three hundred yards, "right under the very noses of the Boche," and without a single casualty.[57]

Montdidier-Noyon Defensive (Coullemelle Sector) June 9-13, 1918

In anticipation of the next big push by the Germans, the 1st Division reorganized its line on June 6 to integrate all its regiments into the sector and defeat the expected attack. The 16th Infantry shifted slightly north to assume control of the Coullemelle sector on June 9 while the 28th Infantry reassumed control of the Cantigny sector. The line was formidable, with two battalions up and one back throughout the 1st Division zone. Patrolling was increased, and battalions were rotated on a regular basis. But the effect of the constant artillery bombardment on the infantry was nerve-racking. Adding to the stress were the sounds of heavy fighting to the north (then to the south), the anticipation of an attack on their own positions, and the Americans' first experience with a concerted mustard gas attack against the 16th Infantry:

> It was a weird sensation, as one poked one's head out of a dugout, to hear the distant bells ringing, the whistles blowing and the strident din of the Klaxon sounding, and to see along the line the lurid light of green flares, all announcing the gruesome fact that the air was no longer fit to breathe, but was being transformed into a poisonous and deadly vapor. The Yankees were not panic-stricken as

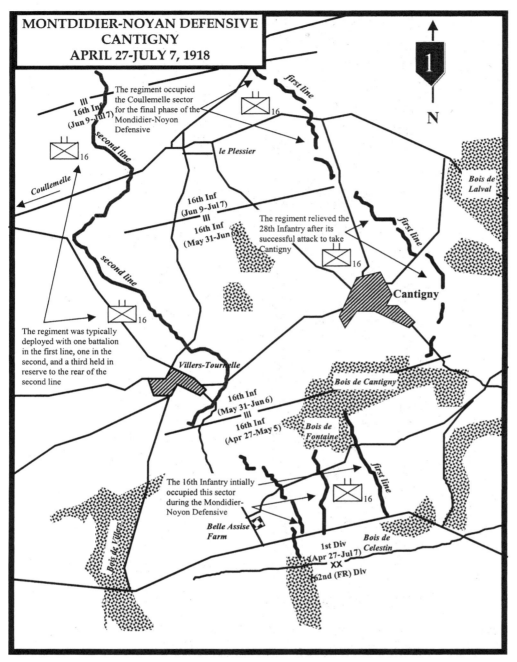

**MONTDIDIER-NOYAN DEFENSIVE
CANTIGNY
APRIL 27-JULY 7, 1918**

The regiment occupied the Coullemelle sector for the final phase of the Mondidier-Noyon Defensive

16th Inf
(Jun 9–Jul 7)

The regiment relieved the 28th Infantry after its successful attack to take Cantigny

16th Inf
(Jun 9-Jul 7)

16th Inf
(May 31-Jun 6)

le Plessier

Bois de Lalval

Cantigny

The regiment was typically deployed with one battalion in the first line, one in the second, and a third held in reserve to the rear of the second line

Villers-Tournelle

Bois de Cantigny

16th Inf
(May 31-Jun 6)

16th Inf
(Apr 27-May 5)

Bois de Fontaine

The 16th Infantry intially occupied this sector during the Mondidier-Noyon Defensive

Belle Assise Farm

Bois de Villers

1st Div
(Apr 27-Jul 7)
XX
152nd (FR) Div

Bois de Celestin

Map 6-3.

the Boche expected. They had learned how to meet these attacks. They acted like lightning. They did not adjust their gas masks. They just dove into them. Though the gas shells kept thudding into the sector for two days, they held fast and suffered few casualties.[58]

The men of the 16th Infantry did not just lie there and take this abuse, however. When opportunities appeared to strike back, they acted. On the evening of the Fourth of July, a

patrol from Company L, led personally by Captain H. S. Young, formed for a raid to celebrate Independence Day. After crossing no man's land, the patrol discovered a German raiding party just assembling for its own operation, apparently intent on spoiling the Americans' national holiday. Quickly springing into action, the doughboys attacked, scattering the Germans and capturing three prisoners including the unit officer, "from whom they gained valuable information." For their bravery that night, Young and his men were cited by the division commander in general orders.[59]

On the night of July 7, the poilus of the 152nd Division relieved the 16th Infantry of their sector, and the regiment moved to a rest area west of Froissy.

The expected blow did not fall against the Americans. It fell, instead, against the French First and Third Armies southeast of Cantigny, between Montdidier and Noyon. The 1st Division was held in readiness at Froissy for several days, but the 16th Infantry saw no further combat in the Cantigny sector. During these two campaigns, the regiment suffered a total of 669 casualties, of which 155 were killed or mortally wounded.[60]

Boarding trains, the 1st Division was transported to Chantilly north of Paris to rest and refit for future operations. The 16th Infantry was billeted in and around Rouvres and had the luxury of enjoying the excellent baths and spas of that town. The troops also took the opportunity to organize athletic competitions, some of which were attended by old Black Jack himself.

While at Rouvres, Colonel Francis E. Bamford assumed command of the regiment. Bamford had started his army career as an enlisted man in the 2nd Infantry and had succeeded in rising to the position of sergeant major of that outfit. In 1893, he was commissioned and transferred to the 5th Infantry. He was transferred to the 28th Infantry and promoted to major in 1901, and was still serving with that regiment when appointed to command the 16th Infantry on July 11, 1918.

Bamford received orders to move the regiment to Meaux and to concurrently send a company to Paris to march in the Bastille Day parade. The men from Company L, 3rd Battalion, were the lucky fellows who received the latter mission. On July 14, 1918, doughboys of the 16th Infantry once again paraded through the streets of Paris to the delight of the French people.[61] This time, however, they presented not the appearance of untried rookies but the spit, polish, and discipline of professionals steeled in the ways of modern war.

When Company L departed Paris, it linked up with the regiment at Meaux in time to receive orders to move once again. Loading up on camions on July 15, the regiment was spirited to a new division assembly area in the forest of Compiègne. On July 16, the gray morning skies hung low with dark clouds heavy with moisture. Rain began to fall, then pour on the men as they prepared for the next fight. This contest was to be dif-ferent, however, for the regiment was to participate in its first major offensive operation.

Aisne-Marne Offensive (Soissons) July 18-23, 1918

On the night of July 17, the regiment formed on a muddy lane in the middle of a dark forest. The movement was executed during a violent thunderstorm and pouring rain, with brilliant flashes of lightning continuously rending the blackness, providing illumination for the men to find their way. The regimental chaplain recalled:

Of all nights of the war, the one that stands out most vividly in the memory of the 16th Infantry is that black night of storm and tumult which resembled Dante's Inferno. Rain fell in torrent after torrent, vivid lightning flashes zigzagged across the sky. Thunder rolled through the hills. The powers of Heaven were shaken. It was a night of horror, yet one of glory. All nature was travailing in pain, as though it were the birth of a new day for humanity.[62]

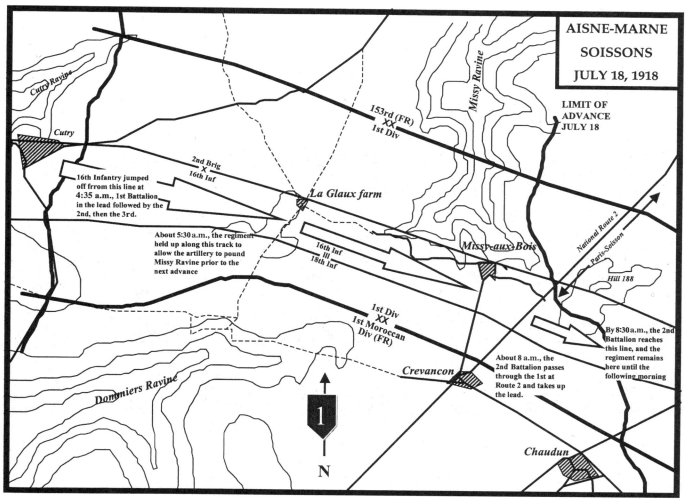

Map 6-4.

Made visible by the lightning flashes, long, brown columns of soldiers toiled forward in the muck, clogging a road already congested by the damage and debris of war. The columns proceeded in fits and starts, their accordion-like movements caused by the halting efforts of the lead elements to negotiate a nightmarish realm of shattered wagons, shell holes, shredded barbed wire, dead horses, and occasionally live horses driven mad by artillery fire. On and on the men struggled, through a seemingly endless night, with the officers urging them to make haste in order to make their jump-off positions before dawn. And make it they did—but just barely.

The regiment's attack was to be part of the French XX Corps' counteroffensive to reduce the German salient between the Aisne and Marne Rivers. The mission of the corps was to advance eastward to cut the rail line servicing the German units in the vicinity of Soissons. The 16th Infantry was in the middle of the 1st Division sector, with the 18th Infantry on the right and the 2nd Brigade on the left. The French guides had led the regiment through what was left of Couvres-et-Valsery and up a slope to the north-south road that served as the jump-off line. Just before dawn the rain stopped and the sky cleared. A red rocket was sent up to signal the beginning of the barrage.[63] It was soon followed by the distant rumble of the heavy guns and the screech of shells passing overhead. The battle had begun.

At 4:35 a.m., the battalions of the 16th Infantry—the 1st leading, the 2nd following, and the 3rd in brigade reserve—launched forward over the road and into the vast wheat fields beyond. Though it was later determined that two French deserters had warned the Germans about the impending attack an hour before, the barrage and the follow-on waves of infantry caught most of the enemy units by surprise. Preceded by a rolling curtain of steel, the 1st Brigade, supported by tanks, swiftly overran the initial enemy positions and advanced two kilometers to a small farm track running north from the La Glaux farm, the division's first objective. Having suffered only minor casualties, the regiment held in place for twenty minutes as the artillery pummeled defenses along the Missy Ravine. Columns of field-gray infantry could be seen retreating in the distance. In the midst of all this, a rabbit scampered across the field to avoid the advancing doughboys, and several took potshots at it.[64]

The line began to advance again, and by 7:30 a.m., the 16th Infantry had captured Missy-aux-Bois and advanced beyond to the division's second objective, Route Nationale 2, the main road from Paris to Soissons. This push had not been as easy as the first. In their efforts to seize Missy-aux-Bois, the 1st Battalion had taken heavy casualties from machine-gun fire originating from the Missy Ravine in the 2nd Brigade sector north of the village. The 26th and 28th Infantry Regiments, moreover, had been held up in their attempts to advance through the ravine by numerous well-placed machine-gun nests and artillery masterfully positioned in the depression. The 16th's partners in the 18th Infantry had kept pace and concur-

rently reached Route 2, but the 1st Moroccan Division, to their south, also had been stymied in its advance. The 1st Brigade was now well forward, with its flanks dangerously dangling.[65]

Extraordinary courage was needed to overcome the enemy's resistance this day, and many rose to the occasion. After his commander had been shot during the advance, 1st Lieutenant George T. Phipps of Evansville, Indiana, assumed command of his company. As he led the company to plug a dangerous gap in the battalion's flank, a machine-gun bullet shattered his right elbow. But in spite of this painful wound, Phipps stayed with his unit. After discovering he was the ranking officer on the field, Phipps then assumed command of the 1st Battalion. Holding up the battalion was a stubborn strong point. Phipps led the battalion on an attack that eliminated the position before he was finally evacuated from the field. He was later awarded the Distinguished Service Cross.[66]

Back with the regimental PC, Lieutenant Colonel James M. Craig, the regimental executive officer, pondered what to do upon learning that the 1st Battalion's officers were all down, and decided he had go forward to take command. Dodging bullets and artillery, he made his way to the hapless unit. His presence worked like a tonic on the troops, and they responded with drive and determination, advancing under the most trying conditions to Route 2.[67]

Route 2 was a tree-lined roadway running across an open ridge line that extended southwest to northeast. The battered lead battalions of the 16th and 18th Regiments hunkered down behind the roadside, which afforded some cover, as the follow-on battalions moved forward to launch the next attack. Heavy machine-gun fire swept the road, and artillery fell all around as the passage of lines was effected. Advancing across the road and into the fields beyond, the 2nd Battalion immediately began to take heavy casualties. Within a short period two companies were shattered, with most of their men killed or wounded. In one of these companies, the command had devolved onto a buck sergeant.

When his platoon leader was hit shortly after crossing the road, Sergeant Jerry Sullivan of Barre, Vermont, assumed command. Leading his platoon from F Company on a route that allowed them some cover, Sullivan's men were able to surprise and capture a battery of 77mm guns that had held up the company's advance. Killed shortly thereafter, Sullivan was awarded the DSC for his actions.[68]

Company E also had its heroes. Private Fred G. Soucy of Lewiston, Maine, and two buddies crept forward to clear out a machine-gun nest that was holding up the company. Before reaching the position, his two friends were killed. Enraged, Soucy charged the emplacement, killing the five-man crew and capturing the gun. Sergeant John Bobo also single-handedly wiped out a machine-gun position holding up E Company. He then gathered up two squads and assaulted a strong point, netting 125 prisoners and twelve machine guns! Unfortunately, the brave sergeant was killed shortly after this feat. Both men

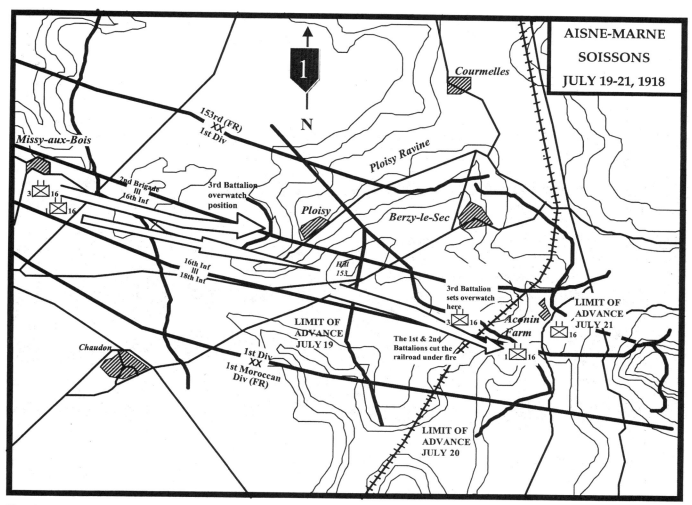

Map 6-5.

earned the DSC for their bravery.[69]

Despite the losses, the 2nd Battalion continued its advance, and with the 1st Battalion, 18th Infantry, successfully flanked a key German position, killing, capturing, or driving out its defenders. By 8:30 a.m., the regiment had reached its final objective of the day in the fields north of Chaudon.[70]

Throughout the remainder of the day, the 2nd Battalion was pounded with artillery as its men struggled to improve the trenches they had captured. That evening, all units were informed that the 1st Division would push on to take its final objective, Noyent-et-Aconin, beginning on the following day. Still under the command of Lieutenant Colonel Craig, the 1st Battalion, now actually in better shape than the 2nd, pushed beyond the line at 4:45 a.m. on the 19th to continue the assault. Following it was the 3rd Battalion, which had been released from brigade reserve and was now in support of the 1st Battalion's attack. As the 1st Battalion battled its way east, the 3rd Battalion swung northeast and came up on line. Overlooking the Ploisy Ravine, the 3rd Battalion established a

temporary blocking position on the regiment's open north flank to protect the advance against counterattacks.[71]

In the 3rd Battalion, the last of H Company's officers were wounded as it moved forward, leaving 1st Sergeant Edward A. Coyle in command. Regrouping his now unsure troops, Coyle skillfully led the company in an attack to seize a piece of needed terrain for the blocking position. Constantly leading from the front, his example encouraged the troops to continue the advance against great resistance. Just as the company reached the position, the courageous first sergeant was struck down by a hail of machine-gun fire, but his men were successful in taking the ground.[72]

On the right, the 1st Battalion's advance was held up by a number of machine-gun nests, one of which wounded Lieutenant Colonel Craig. He refused to be evacuated and continued to lead his men on. Despite mounting losses, Craig was able to get the battalion to continue to claw its way forward until the enemy guns forced a halt. Determined to reduce the machine-gun positions, Craig assembled several volunteers to go with him to locate and, if possible, rout the troublesome Huns. The small group was successful in knocking out several nests, and their efforts allowed the battalion to again move forward. Shortly after they restarted the advance, Craig was instantly killed in a burst of fire from another position. The effect of Craig's death prompted the men of the 1st Battalion to redouble their efforts "to humble the Boche."[73]

To reduce the numerous machine-gun nests, a few tanks were belatedly brought forward but, after only minor successes, most were knocked out by antitank fire. To compound the regiment's problems, German planes flew numerous missions, bombing and strafing the troops, which added to their misery.[74]

The advance on the 19th was hard going, with the 16th Infantry pushing only two kilometers farther east by 5:30 that afternoon. The 1st and 3rd Battalions dug in at a position centered on Hill 153, the limit of advance that day. To the north lay the 26th Infantry, which had now come on line by occupying Ploisy, and to the south lay the 18th Infantry. The regiment's flanks were secure.

Orders went out for the next push. The 1st and 2nd Battalions, with B Company, 1st Engineers attached, were to advance at 2:00 p.m. the next day to cut the railroad. After a two-hour barrage, the 1st Division attacked across the front. The 16th Infantry moved off of Hill 153 at the appointed time and advanced eastward against little opposition. Reaching the bluffs above the railroad, the doughboys proceeded down the slope when, suddenly, the earth around them erupted, blowing dirt and bodies into the air. The German artillery spotters held them in plain view, as did the machine-gunners, who also opened a heavy fire. The railroad embankment at the foot of the bluff offered their only chance of survival, so they dashed down the hill to this sanctuary. The battalions rapidly consolidated their positions and dug in to repel counterattacks, while the 3rd Battalion moved to a narrow point on the bluffs above, which provided overwatching fires for the rest of the regiment.[75] At the embankment, accountability efforts revealed that little more than 100 men remained in the 1st Battalion of the over nine hundred who had started three days before.[76]

By the evening of July 20, the XX Corps' mission had been completed. The 16th Infantry had cut the rail line, and the Germans had begun evacuating the Aisne-Marne salient. But the hard fighting was not over. That night, the XX Corps issued orders for the 1st Division to secure a line from Berzy-le-Sec to Buzancy and the 16th Infantry was ordered to jump-off at 4:45 a.m. on the 21st. At the announced hour, a rolling barrage began to cover the advance of the 1st Brigade. Though by then thoroughly bruised, the 1st Battalion led off the attack, followed by the 2nd and 3rd Battalions. Pushing forward under heavy resistance, the regiment captured the Aconin Farm and continued on to cut the Soissons–Château–Thierry road.

Like the three days previous, the fighting on the 21st was desperate. Only fierce determination and heroism would carry the day and, in the 16th Infantry, both were abundantly present.

In the 1st Battalion, a brand new 2nd lieutenant, Cyril Carder of Corning, New York, had been wounded in his back and arm but still refused to be evacuated. He continued to lead his unit forward, repeatedly exposing himself to intense enemy fire until he was killed by a machine gun. In the 2nd Battalion, Corporal Andrew Denn of Albany, New York, took command of an E Company platoon and led it against a German machine-gun nest. Although wounded in the effort, he continued on until he personally killed the gun crew. Corporal George R. Mitchell of Holdridge, Nebraska, took command of Company F after all its officers and sergeants were dead or wounded and led it through the day even though he himself had been wounded. First Sergeant Stallard Trower of Parksville, Kentucky, commanded Company I that day. The First Sergeant of F Company, Antony Scanlon of Lost Creek, Pennsylvania, assumed command of the entire 2nd Battalion and reorganized it while under fire after all the officers had become casualties.[77]

Many of the regiment's noncombatant soldiers also performed heroically. In five days of battle, Private Joseph H. Burchfield repeatedly recovered and treated wounded comrades while exposed to heavy enemy fire. Then he too was wounded as he made his way through a barrage to treat a wounded man in the front line. Chaplain Earl H. Weeds of Athol, Kansas, was constantly forward and under fire with the front-line troops. He was seen frequently providing first aid, praying over the severely wounded, and cheering up those who had been hit as they lay in the mud awaiting evacuation.[78] Despite exposing himself to great danger on numerous occasions to help his fellow soldiers, the chaplain came through the battle unscathed. Perhaps it was the good Lord Himself who protected this brave man of the cloth from harm.

About 11:00 that morning, a detachment of twelve F Company men, led by Corporal Mitchell, attempted to cross a small open valley, when the group was pinned down by severe small-arms fire. Corporal Alfred J. Buhl of Chicago, Illinois, was hit in the elbow and all but two of the others were soon killed or wounded as well. Spying Mitchell lying in the mud, shot through both legs, Buhl crawled over and dragged the man to safety. Three days previous, Buhl had carried his platoon leader twelve kilometers to a field hospital to save that man's life. Now, he threw Mitchell over his shoulder and carried him five kilometers to an aid station, all the while losing blood from his own arm wound. Upon reaching the aid station, he discovered that his clothes and pack had been pierced thirty-eight times by enemy bullets.[79]

Grinding forward an additional kilometer, the 16th Infantry fought its way to the final objective, a hill northwest of Buzancy, where it dug in to consolidate its gains. Once again, the Germans responded with heavy artillery fire that fell regularly throughout the rest of the day on the new positions.[80]

The remainder of the 1st Division regiments had reached their final objectives by that afternoon as well, and orders went out for the "Fighting First" to be relieved by the 15th Scottish

Division the night of July 22-23. The 22nd passed with a great deal of firing, but little movement, as both sides were relatively spent. That evening, the jaunty Scotsmen began arriving in the doughboys' trenches and inquiring, "Where is the bloody shooting gallery at?" The men of the 16th were content with letting the Highlanders find that out for themselves.

When the 1st Battalion filed out of its positions it numbered only forty men.[81] The other battalions had fared better but still paid a terrible price. Total losses in the five-day battle were 455 killed or mortally wounded and 1,205 wounded, resulting in a 50-percent casualty rate—the regiment's highest since Gettysburg.[82] Every battalion commander and the regimental executive officer had been killed or wounded. With so many junior officers cut down, it was not unusual for companies to fall under the command of sergeants or corporals and, in at least one case, a private. In all, casualties to the 16th Regiment constituted fully one third of the 1st Division's final toll in dead and wounded, a figure indicative both of the battle's savagery and the regiment's prominent role in the fighting.

Uncommon valor was a common virtue in the 16th Infantry at Soissons. No fewer than forty-five men earned the Distinguished Service Cross in those five bloody days. Many others earned lesser awards; all were heroes. Though the regiment would undergo other difficult trials during this war, none would be as intense as the five days of the Aisne-Marne offensive.

At great cost in lives and leadership, the 16th Infantry had performed superbly. In doing so it had contributed mightily to upholding the reputation of the "Fighting First" as the AEF's shock division. In recognition of its achievements and sacrifices, General Summerall cited the regiment in General Orders No. 41, August 2nd, 1918:

> [F]or distinguished conduct in attaining all objectives in the advance between July 18th-22nd, inclusive, and for exceptional aggressiveness in advancing a battalion into the enemy's territory without immediate support, while sustaining heavy losses, on July 21st, thus facilitating the operations along the entire front of the Division.[83]

After Soissons, the next show would be a cakewalk.

Saizerais Sector
August 7-24, 1918

Immediately upon leaving the line, the 1st Division was dispersed in and around Dammartin-en-Goele for a short respite. A week later the division entrained for yet another destination. The weary men of the 16th Infantry were hoping for furloughs in Paris, but it was not to be: their trains were headed south toward Toul. En route they glimpsed the Eiffel Tower; and this, as it turned out, was all they would see of the City of Lights. After only five days at Brouley near Toul, the regiment moved first to Port-à-Mousson, and then to the front lines in

Saizerais (St. Jacques) sector, where they relieved troops of the 2nd Moroccan Division on August 4-5. Compared to their recent experiences at Soissons, this stint in the line was a vacation. The sector consisted of lush green woods, babbling brooks, and the occasional shell lobbed their way to remind them that they were still engaged in a war. The regiment suffered only ten casualties during the stay at Saizerais.[84]

On August 6, Colonel Leroy S. Upton took command of the regiment from Colonel Bamford, who was promoted to brigadier general to take command of the 2nd Infantry Brigade. Upton was in command for only three weeks before being promoted and assigned to command the 57th Infantry Brigade. Command subsequently devolved upon the executive officer, Lieutenant Colonel Edward R. Coppock, on August 26. Like Bamford, Coppock had been a sergeant before being commissioned from the ranks as a lieutenant in F Troop, 3rd Cavalry, in 1901.[85] At some point in his career, Coppock decided that the infantry was for him and left behind the "Life of Riley." Unknown to him, he would soon be responsible for leading the regiment to singular achievement during the Meuse-Argonne campaign and through some of the bloodiest fighting of the war.

Relieved of the Saizerais sector by elements of the 90th Division on August 23, the regiment moved to the Vancouleurs Training Area, bivouacking near Pagny le Blanche Côte. Replacements poured in to fill the decimated companies for the next major offensive, which was fast approaching. The influx of so many new arrivals with battle pending meant that there could be no rest for the men of the 1st Division. Instead they were put through intensive training aimed at bringing them back up to the performance level expected of the AEF's premier shock formation. The new men had much to learn in very little time. Their preparations included a division-size rehearsal on ground similar to that over which it would soon attack. The maneuver was observed by Major General Joseph T. Dickman, commander of the U.S. IV Corps, to which the "Fighting First" had been attached for the upcoming St.-Mihiel offensive.

St.-Mihiel Offensive
September 12-13, 1918

On the afternoon of September 1st, Lieutenant Colonel Coppock was ordered to prepare for immediate movement to a new location. With nightfall, columns of khaki-clad doughboys were soon winding their way through the region's hills and dales to a new assembly area in the woods between Counieville and Raulecourt. Reaching their destination before first light, the doughboys quickly settled in for a week of further tactical training, with an emphasis on maneuver, marksmanship, and the use of grenades. Finally, on the night of September 11, the regiment was ordered forward to a jump-off line near Rambucourt. Reaching the jump-off line, the doughboys hunkered down to await the start of the inevitable barrage.

The St.-Mihiel salient had been selected by Pershing as the objective for the first major American offensive of the war,

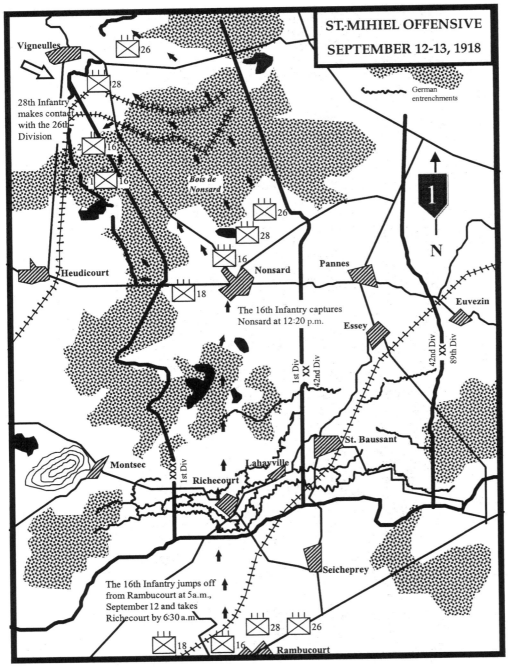

ST.-MIHIEL OFFENSIVE
SEPTEMBER 12-13, 1918

German entrenchments

Vigneulles

28th Infantry makes contact with the 26th Division

Bois de Nonsard

Heudicourt

Nonsard

Pannes

Euvezin

The 16th Infantry captures Nonsard at 12:20 p.m.

Essey

42nd Div

89th Div

1st Div

42nd Div

St. Baussant

Montsec

Lahayville

Richecourt

1st Div

The 16th Infantry jumps off from Rambucourt at 5 a.m., September 12 and takes Richecourt by 6:30 a.m.

Seicheprey

Rambucourt

Map 6-6.

on the right of IV Corps. The main blow would be delivered by I and IV Corps, with the latter advancing across the Woëvre Plain to the vicinity of Vigneulles, there to effect a juncture with V Corps driving down from the northwest. The IV Corps, commanded by Major General Dickman, was composed of three divisions, with the 1st Division on the corps left, the 42nd "Rainbow" Division in the center, and the 89th Division on the right.

The division's plan of attack called for the 1st Brigade to hold the western half of the division sector with the 18th Infantry on the left and the 16th Infantry on the right, while the 2nd Brigade (26th and 28th Regiments) advanced on the right flank of the 16th Infantry. In this scheme the 1st Division, out of all the Allied formations, had the most ground to cover before linking up with V Corps elements.

The 89th Division had already occupied the outpost line when the 1st and 42nd Divisions moved to their jump-off line on the night of September 11. By 1:00 a.m. on the 12th, the outposts had withdrawn and the American preparatory artillery fires began to fall.

The barrage lasted four hours, during which the doughboys of the 16th Infantry huddled in their trenches waiting for the flares that would signal them to "go over the top." Finally, about dawn, the streaks of colored rockets shot up to signal the advance, and over the troops went, surging toward the town of Richecourt. In the path of their advance was a stream rumored to be electrically wired by the Germans. Several officers plunged into the water and the troops, emboldened by the example, followed on the heels of their officers. There was no electrical current, but several men drowned in the crossing. On the far side, companies regrouped and within a short time had captured Richecourt, along with

to be carried out by the First U.S. Army. Organized on August 10, the First Army was under Pershing's direct command and, at the time of the offensive, comprised three American and one French corps. Moving around the salient from the northwest to the southeast, these corps were disposed as follows: V Corps in the topmost (northern) position on the salient's west side; French II Colonial Corps below V Corps, covering the tip of the salient; IV Corps on the south side, next to the French; I Corps

several machine-gun teams.[86]

Pushing through the town, the regiment fanned out into the fields beyond and advanced as if they were on an Infantry School demonstration maneuver. Having thus far suffered only light losses, the regiment continued to its next objective, the village of Nonsard, which it entered exactly on time at 12:20 p.m. There, it was forced to hold in place for three hours while the artillery struggled over bad roads to move forward. About 3:30 that afternoon, with the artillery finally in position to provide needed indirect fire support, the men of the 16th drove on against relatively light resistance, advancing north to cut the rail line running through the Bois de Vigneulles. The doughboys were past the railroad by 8:30 p.m., making contact with the 26th Division before dawn the next morning.[87]

The First Army attack had effectively cut off the salient and captured some sixteen thousand German prisoners, 443 artillery pieces, and liberated 240 square miles of French territory. Rightfully proud of his men's contribution to this victory, Coppock moved the regiment to a bivouac site in the woods south of Nonsard on the 13th. There he was pleased to learn that the regiment had only suffered twenty-two killed and 111 wounded in the offensive. This relatively good news was soon dampened by the cold, miserable rains that began to soak the troops, who had no tents, blankets, or coats.

On the 16th, none other than "Black Jack" himself showed up to voice his appreciation for the regiment's performance. Speaking to the assembled officers and men, he told them, "Remember that you belong to the First Division, a combat, shock division. I hope you will now be able to take a well-earned rest, but the war is not yet won; we might need you; when the crisis demands it, I shall call upon you."[88]

True to his word, Pershing was soon to call upon them again. In early September, the Allied commanders in chief agreed on plans to undertake joint offensive operations of massive size and scale. With the British attacking in Flanders and two French Armies attacking on the Champagne front, the American First Army would advance north through the Argonne Forest and along the Meuse River. The AEF's objective was the Carignan–Sedan–Mézières railroad, the main German supply line which, when cut, would render the enemy's position in that part of eastern France untenable.

On 10 September, U.S. divisions began taking over positions from French units along a line running roughly from Binarville, in the west, to just south of Damvillers, in the east. The 1st Division was ordered to begin movements to position itself behind the main American line after completing its actions at St.-Mihiel.[89]

On September 20 the 16th Regiment moved by truck from Nonsard to Souilly. Bivouacking in the woods, the troops immediately began assault training for the next big push. While at Souilly, a short civilian in a derby hat stepped off a train that had stopped near the regimental camp. He began to wander through the camp, talking to the troops to see how they were

doing. When he inquired of soldiers from Supply Company if their living arrangements were comfortable, one soldier bellowed, "Comfortable, hell! How can a fellow be comfortable sleeping on the ground in weather like this, with one blanket?" The diminutive gentleman happened to be Newton D. Baker, the secretary of war, but he took all such criticisms in stride. Shortly afterward, General Pershing appeared with his côterie of aides, and no doubt, the pucker factor suddenly increased significantly. However, the visit went well and the distinguished guests were later serenaded by the superb 16th Infantry band. The officers were assembled for a short visit with the secretary and Pershing, during which Baker praised both the 1st Division and 16th Infantry.[90]

Meuse-Argonne Offensive
October 1-12, 1918; November 5-8, 1918

A massive artillery barrage on the morning of September 26 heralded the beginning of the great Meuse-Argonne offensive. Nine U.S. divisions jumped off to begin what would be the final campaign of the war for the American forces. Initially held in First Army reserve, the 1st Division was ordered to positions west of Verdun on the evening of the 27th. The 16th Regiment marched all night, arriving near Verdun on the morning of the 28th. After spending a rainy day listening to the sounds of the great fight raging in the distance, the men loaded into trucks in the predawn darkness of the 29th and drove to Neuvilly, arriving around first light.

In the initial advance, and notwithstanding unusually tough opposition, the divisions of the I Corps managed to push the line four miles closer to Sedan. The resulting losses and inadvertent intermixing of divisions, however, required the corps to halt and bring in fresh units. Consequently the 1st Division, while at Neuvilly, was assigned to the I Corps, which in turn ordered the division to move up to Charpentry to relieve the 35th "Santa Fe" Division.

A relative newcomer to combat, the 35th Division was hard pressed in fighting where it was matched against veteran German formations such as the crack 1st Guards Division. Overcoming such divisions was a job that could only be performed by an exceptionally well-trained and high-spirited unit. That unit would be the "Fighting First."

General Summerall was directed to drive his division up the east side of the Forêt d'Argonne in order to cut German supply routes and thereby force the enemy units holding the forest to abandon it. The division's role was key to an operation which, if successful, would allow the First Army to continue its advance. On the 30th, the 3rd Battalion set out on foot for Charpentry, followed in turn by the 2nd and 1st Battalions.[91]

The regiment passed into a narrow valley about dark and began to see the effects of the fight on the men of the 35th. The 35th Division appeared fairly beaten. Upon his arrival at Charpentry, Coppock described the conditions he found about the town as "an awful mess."[92] But his veterans of the Soissons and St.-Mihiel were not concerned. The regimental chaplain described the attitude of the men of the 16th Infantry as they moved up to relieve the Missourians:

> One boy [from the 35th Division], with a wild light in his eye, told of the terrors up yonder on the hills, summing it all up by saying: "Oh, it's one hell up there." "Cheer up," came the prompt response from the ranks of the Sixteenth, "We were fighting the Boche before the Draft Board ever gave you a number."[93]

That night the regiment effected the relief of units of the 35th, taking up positions in the hills and ravines around the village. The positions were largely protected from enemy direct fire but not artillery, so Coppock established the regimental PC in a small stone house in Charpentry.[94] Although situated in a little valley behind the lines, the town was not beyond the reach of German artillery, which bombarded it frequently. The regiment hunkered down for the next four days, enduring numerous barrages aimed at breaking up and otherwise hampering I Corps' efforts to resume the offensive.

In the early morning hours of October 1, the Germans began a systematic barrage using mustard and phosgene gas shells. That night, the regiment suffered seventy casualties from gas. This same shelling caused the agonizing death of six of the regiment's twelve horses and over one hundred horses across the entire division. In all, some 3,470 gas shells of various types were fired into the 1st Division sector from October 1-4, inflicting over nine hundred casualties to the division before beginning its assault on the morning of the 4th.[95]

The 16th Regiment was actually scheduled to start its next push on October 3, but elements were active before that date. On the morning of October 2, the 3rd Battalion advanced five hundred yards into the next ravine to the northwest and dug in. Patrols sent forward soon determined that the regiment now faced the depleted but dangerous 5th Guards Division. It was going to be a tough fight. The men prepared to attack on the morning of October 3, but poor road conditions prevented the resupply of the division's artillery units, forcing the infantry to spend another miserable night in the line.[96]

Coppock received new orders on October 3 to advance to objectives just to the north of the village of Fléville early the following morning. The 16th Infantry Regiment was about to engage in one of its hardest fights of the war, and achieve a singular honor for which its members will be forever proud.

Fléville

On the morning of October 4, the troops crouched in their holes while suffering yet another HE-mustard bombardment. This one was particularly heavy, inflicting 192 casualties to the regiment before the Americans could even begin their assault. At 5:25 a.m. the American counter barrage erupted, shaking the

very ground where the men lay. Intermixed with the HE were smoke rounds that created a screen behind which the infantry could advance. At about 6:30 a.m., Coppock, though suffering from illness, led the 3rd and 2nd Battalions over the top (the 1st Battalion was in division reserve). Almost immediately the 3rd Battalion, with its commander, Major William F. Harrell, leading the way, ran into heavy machine-gun fire. It was as "though by magic, every wooded ridge bristled with hostile machine-guns, and from every hilltop for miles around Boche cannon belched forth their deadly fire."[97]

Opposing them were the Elisabeth and Tauentzien Regiments of the 5th Guards Division. These crack units were arrayed in depth, with their outpost line only some six hundred meters from the 16th's jump-off line. Behind the outpost line, in the woods on Montrebeau Hill and extending southwest to the Aire River, was the enemy's main defense line, which was backed by a series of reserve positions leading almost back to Fléville and occupied by six companies of the Elisabeth Regiment plus a battery of guns. Though worn by the previous days' combat, the troops of the 5th Guards Division were still capable of the fierce, determined resistance expected of a guards division, as they were to prove against the 16th Infantry that day.

The ground between the jump-off line and Fléville consisted of a series of ridges that ran essentially east to west. Between each ridge line was an open valley, about one hundred to two hundred yards across; none of the valleys offered much in the way of cover or concealment. German units defending the area had superb fields of fire—a perfect killing zone. Knowing that the battalion had to get through this belt quickly given the difficult nature of the terrain, Harrell went forward under intense fire to his most advanced elements, which had become disorganized. He rapidly sorted them out and personally led them in a rush to carry the initial positions. The rest of the battalion followed, and soon the lead companies of the Elisabeth Regiment cracked; but not without Major Harrell's being wounded, which forced his evacuation from the field. He became one of twenty-one 16th Infantrymen to earn the Distinguished Service Cross that day. Within the hour, the 2nd Battalion commander was wounded, and most company commanders were also wounded or killed.

Now under the command of Captain William R. McMorris, M Company commander, the 3rd Battalion cleaned out Montrebeau Wood and continued the advance toward the Exermont Ravine sometime after 7:00 a.m. Close behind in support was the 2nd Battalion, now under Captain Oliver Allen. After crossing a small ravine, the 3rd Battalion drifted northwest and, as it reached the top of the next ridge, began receiving fire from Ferme des Granges. The farm was actually outside the 1st Division sector, but McMorris nonetheless directed his men to clear it out. As the 2nd Battalion came up and supported from the ridge, McMorris's men routed at least two companies of the Elisabeth Regiment. The fight over Ferme des

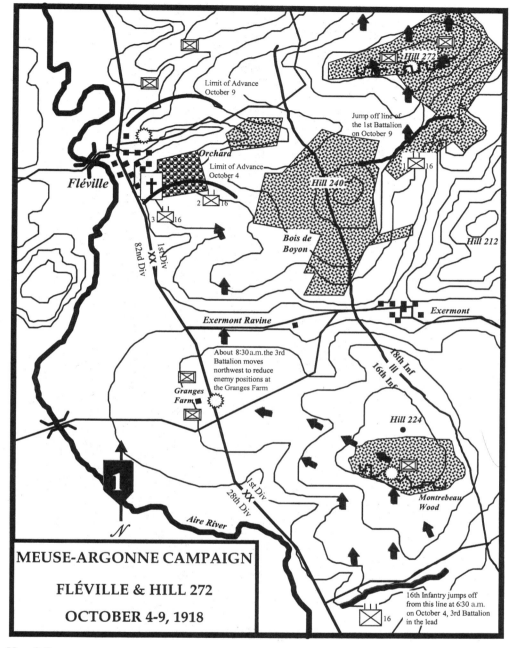

Map 6-7.

entry in the *Journal of Operations* kept by Lieutenant A. B. Butler, aide-de-camp to Major General Summerall, described the scene:

> The fields between the Exermont Ravine & our jumping off line are covered with the dead bodies of men of the 35th Div which fell back across it. Many of these had on their first aid bandages, showing they had been wounded & died after falling back. The Bosch does not look after our wounded.[98]

Those same fields were now strewn with many wounded and dead doughboys of the 16th Infantry. This time, however, the Hun would fail to recover the ground. The men of the 16th were not about to allow a repeat of the tragic events experienced by the 35th Division.

Arriving at the heights above Fléville, Coppock ordered the regiment to push on to the town. Moving through a large orchard, the 3rd Battalion rolled past the cemetery, down the side of a draw, and fought its way into Fléville. McMorris led the battalion through the debris-filled streets and out the north end of town, where it seized a small ridge to prepare for the inevitable counterattacks. The regiment was now two kilometers farther north than both the 18th Infantry, its right-flank unit, and the 28th "Keystone" Division on the left. In other words, the 16th Infantry had punched a deep salient into the German lines and now had to fight in three directions.

Granges slowed the advance again, and the regiment completed that job in the late morning. Proceeding beyond the farm, Coppock directed the regiment to cross Exermont Ravine and occupy the high ground on the far side. From that location, the regiment could make its final drive to take Fléville.

The route over which the 16th Infantry advanced was strewn with the bodies of American soldiers. The slain doughboys belonged to the 35th Division, which had attacked and then withdrawn over the same ground several days before. An

From the west, the 3rd Battalion received long-range fire across the Aire River from those German units that were not yet distracted by the 28th Division. Similarly, from the east, enemy units in the 18th Infantry zone turned their attention on the Americans north of Fléville. From the front, the battalion began to receive counterattacks from the fresh 37th Division.

During these attacks, numerous acts of bravery were performed by men of the 3rd Battalion. Company M's first sergeant, Edward E. King of Dayton, Ohio, led his unit through the morning's machine-gun and artillery fire after Captain McMorris had assumed control of the battalion. After ensuring that his men were in good positions, he grabbed several doughboys and took them forward to locate machine guns that were raking the company line. Successfully locating three separate positions, he and his men pounced on each and killed, wounded, or captured all the crews.[99]

Nor was King Company M's only hero on October 4. No fewer than six of its members earned the DSC that day. One of them, Sergeant Joseph W. Bradford of Brockton, Massachusetts, wiped out two machine-gun nests by gathering men from several squads and leading them against the guns. Another, Corporal Daniel C. McAuliffe of Butte, Montana, achieved a similar feat, and was severely wounded in the process.[100]

Corporal Fred M. Schultz from New Buffalo, Michigan, led his squad in capturing a field gun that had been particularly effective in knocking out the tanks that were attempting to support the infantry. The squad flanked and captured the gun's crew, after which Schultz singlehandedly killed the operator of a machine gun that had supported the gun. Schultz was wounded in the action, but insisted on helping two of his men back to the aid station.[101]

Heroes emerged in other companies as well. In Company I, Private George Van Buren of Valatie, New York, was hit twice in the advance toward Fléville but continued to advance with his platoon. Wounded for the third time, he fainted from exhaustion. Regaining consciousness, he struggled forward and found his company digging in to repel a counterattack that commenced shortly after he arrived. Van Buren was struck a fourth time as he helped fight off the attack. Gamely sticking to his position, he remained in the line until ordered to an aid station.[102]

During the early stages of E Company's progress that day, Sergeant Ben Dickens was severely wounded but stayed with his company. Upon learning that all the company's officers were down, he took command and led the men to support positions in the orchard above Fléville. There, he directed his company's repulse of a nearly overwhelming counterattack, though he was barely able to walk.[103]

Perhaps the day's saddest incident involved Sergeant Major George P. Storm. A native Pennsylvanian, Storm was one of the few long-service "Old Army" NCOs remaining with the regiment and was popular with officers and men alike. His presence was felt all over the battlefield that day. Moving with the 3rd Battalion PC, he volunteered to carry a message through heavy artillery and machine-gun fire. Successfully accomplishing that task, he stopped to aid several wounded men and detailed some of the lesser injured to escort prisoners to the rear. The battalion PC having moved forward in the meantime, Storm, after seeing off the wounded, made his way through "violent fire" to the new position where the battalion

was consolidating. He immediately set out to assist the other battalion leaders in preparing the defenses and was killed by shellfire as he made his way to the main positions. At the time of his death, the sergeant major had served twenty-nine years and ten months. In less than two months, the war would be over, and Storm would have been eligible for retirement.[104]

About noon, Coppock received orders from the 1st Division to pull the 3rd Battalion off the high ground north of Fléville and consolidate on the ridge south of town. The forward positions and the town itself were to be the target of a heavy HE and gas barrage. Complying with the directive, the battalion moved back through Fléville about 1:00 p.m. and took up positions in the orchard overlooking the town. Nearby, the 2nd Battalion was already digging in.

Coppock now took stock as the battalions prepared their positions. He determined that, of the twenty officers and 800 men of the 3rd Battalion who had jumped off that morning, only two officers and 240 men remained. In all, this had been a bloody day for the battalion, and a difficult day for Coppock and his staff. Moving with the 2nd Battalion, the regimental PC had been twice hit by HE and gas shells, yet somehow managed to carry on.

In the evening Coppeck established his PC in a "little cut" on the next ridge back from the orchard and pondered the situation.[105] It was precarious: the 2nd and 3rd Battalions were still surrounded on three sides as result of the failure of the 28th Division and the 18th Infantry to come up on the regiment's flanks. Losses had been heavy, and the artillery fire on their positions was constant. The 16th Infantry was on a thin string as night crept over the field.

"Clear and cold last night, but with a dead man's blanket I fared fairly well in a hole on a hill side," Coppock noted in his October 5 diary entry. The regiment would be required to hold their gains for the next seven days, until the rest of I Corps had fought its way up to the final objective line. It was an anxious time for the men of the 16th Infantry. At one point, with casualties mounting under the constant hammering of enemy artillery, General Summerall contacted Coppock over the field phone: "Can you hold on?" the division commander asked. "We will hold on," Coppock assured him.[106] As revealed by Coppock's diary entries for the following days, the situation was difficult and fraught with tension:

Sun., Oct. 6 The 18th Infantry is making every effort to come up on our right. The men are dug in like prairie dogs. I have a hole like the rest. We come out at night. The Boche fire all kind[s] of things at us, but are afraid to come after us.

Mon., Oct. 7 Cold rain. Sleeping or trying to sleep, on wet clay. This is not an old man's game. I have an awful cold or gas. My men are wonderful. Only half the regiment left. They just hammer all day and most of the night. Our mission is to hold until the balance of the division can come up. The 28th Inf Division on our left failed to come up. They are being relieved by the 82nd Inf Division.

Tues., Oct. 8 The way the officers and men are dropping out is awful. Today the regimental commanders were assembled and told that one more effort is to be made by the Division. All of our reserves go in, even using the Engineers as riflemen. My reserve battalion, the 1st, is attached to the 18th Infantry, and leads off tomorrow on the right. I am to hold our advance point with the 3rd Battalion.

Wed., Oct. 9 Foggy till noon. This place was one hell last night, Big 6 inch HE fell on our positions at intervals all night. Gassed twice. Masks saved us. We are part way up on a rocky hill side. Escaped the worst of it. The concussion gave us all headaches. Attack going slowly but surely. There has been an awful fight, but the 16th carried the day.[107]

The October 7 relief to which Coppock refers was followed by the attack of the 82nd Division on Châtel Chehéry and Hill 180, two German strongpoints that had prevented the 28th Division from coming up on the regiment's left flank. This successful assault cheered the men of the 16th, who had a panoramic view of the fight as it played out before them. The left flank of the 1st Division, and therefore that of the 16th Infantry, was now secure. This action left only the regiment's right flank open. The problem of the right flank was partially corrected when the 18th Infantry took most of Hill 240 in the Bois de Boyon on October 5, but it would not be fully secure until Hill 272 was taken.

Hill 272

On Hill 272, before which the 28th Infantry had been stalled since October 5, German positions constituted the last major obstacle between the 1st Division and its final First Army objectives. A division boundary change on October 8 placed Hill 272 in the 18th Infantry's sector, where that regiment was ordered to mount an attack the following day. The division reserve, which consisted of none other than the 1st Battalion of the 16th Infantry, was attached to the 18th Regiment and assigned to capture the hill.[108]

The night of October 8-9 was very cold and hard on the troops in the line. That night, a green troop assigned to the Machine Gun Company, Private Herbert L. McHenry, received a lesson in battlefield etiquette:

Me and Burhead stumbled over a dead soldier. I suggested to Burhead [that he] take the dead man's blanket. Burhead said, "If you take that blanket, I will kill you. Let the dead soldier have his blanket." Right there I learned the

feeling of the old experienced soldier toward a dead soldier, whether friend or foe, as we both saw that dead soldier was a German. Later this respect for the dead soldier was further shown me this morning when a soldier of our platoon, Donald M. Farnsworth of Portic, Kansas, passed that dead soldier as he lay under his blanket. As Farnsworth passed that soldier, he stopped and seriously said to him, "Buddy, if I had known you had that blanket last night, I would have borrowed it from you, but I sure would have returned it this morning. I sure did need it last night."[109]

On the morning of October 9, a thick fog, typical for that time of year, blanketed the Argonne's tortured landscape. Major Charles W. Ryder had placed his battalion in attack positions in a narrow wood five hundred meters south of Hill 272. The 1st Battalion was arrayed with Company C in the west and B in the east as the assault companies. In close support was Company D, drawn up behind C, and Company A, behind B. Ryder's PC was situated in the middle. The attached Machine Gun Company was on Hill 240, from which it would support the assault. Just before the men went over the top, the Germans got an inkling that something was brewing and fired a barrage where they suspected the support companies would be. Companies D and A were jammed up so close behind the assault companies, however, that the rounds fell harmlessly behind them.[110]

At 8:30 a.m., the guns of the 1st Field Artillery Brigade began their massive preparatory fires. Up and over the men went and disappeared into the swirling fog. Shortly after the advance began, C Company began to receive direct fire from Hill 176 to the west. Part of the company wheeled left to return fire and protect the flank of the battalion as it progressed farther north. In the fog contact between assault and support companies became impossible, but all continued until they reached the base of Hill 272. Ryder had accompanied Company D to the hill and, upon arrival, ordered it to hold while he checked on the status of the rest of the battalion. Amazingly, the companies all arrived at the base of the hill and were on line in the order of D, C, A, and B.[111]

Ryder issued verbal orders to his commanders to seize that portion of the hill to their companies' direct front, then fan out to take the top and far side of the promontory. Struggling through the fog, small groups of infantrymen began picking their way up the hill and taking out German positions one by one. Men worked their way between positions and came at the enemy from all angles. As result of these infiltration tactics, Hill 272, which had been the division's stumbling block for four days, fell to the 1st Battalion by 11:00 a.m.[112] Once again, the 16th Infantry had succeeded where others had failed.

But taking that hill was not the end, for the 1st Battalion doughboys then raced down the far side of the hill and fought their way to the Côte de Maldah, the I Corps' final objective:

Crawling up a ravine, they outflanked the machine-guns

and captured these cannon, and there [on the Côte de Maldah] they established themselves and prepared to receive counter-attacks. Soon 150 Boche, armed with machine-guns, laid claim to the hill, and after they were repulsed a second attack followed. When the Huns had been convinced that the hill belonged once and for all to the Americans, nothing remained for these gallant victors to do but sit down and pass the time by getting shelled twenty-four hours a day.[113]

Courage and fortitude were as prevalent in the 1st Battalion's assault on October 9 as when the regiment conducted its attack on the 4th. Private Arthur S. Long hailed from Roberts, Montana, and was a member of D Company. As his company made its way up Hill 272, a 77mm gun was employed in direct-fire mode against it. Long rose to the occasion and, armed with an automatic rifle, singlehandedly assaulted the position and captured the crew, thereby enabling D Company to take the ground.[114]

Not too long after D Company captured the Côte de Maldah, a transplanted Scotsman from Glasgow, Sergeant George King, was sent out with his squad on a reconnaissance patrol. Encountering machine-gun nests, the patrol went to ground—all except King. The plucky Scot drove on ahead by himself and killed the gunners of at least two guns. The patrol was able to finish its job and get back unscathed.[115] Both Long and King earned the DSC that day.

While the 1st Battalion was taking Hill 272, Coppock sent the 3rd Battalion forward once again through Fléville and occupied the ridge north of the town that had been the farthest limit of advance on October 4. The following day, October 10, the "Fighting First" was to make its final advance of the first phase of the Meuse-Argonne campaign. This presented a problem for the 16th Infantry, which had lost so many men in the initial push to Fléville and in the subsequent counterattacks and gas barrages. The regiment was close to being combat ineffective. More men were required for the 16th to achieve its objectives. Coppock made his way back to the regimental rear areas and asked for volunteers to fill his depleted ranks. Quite a few rear-echelon types readily stepped forward to take their chances in the front line with their infantry comrades. A few were stragglers, but most were cooks and mule drivers.[116] At 7:00 the next morning, patrols were pushed out from both the regiment and the 1st Battalion.

The intent of this operation was for the patrols to move forward and make contact with the enemy, thereby identifying weak spots for attack by the follow-on units. It was soon evident to the patrols that the German positions were vacated, and the enemy was falling back to the next defensive line, the "Kriemhilde Stellung." The 2nd and 3rd Battalions advanced to a ridge line and consolidated positions just southwest of Sommerance after brushing away pockets of resistance put up by the German 32nd Infantry Division. Meanwhile, the 1st Battalion probed forward to the Ravin du Grasfaux, due east of Sommerance. Resistance there was light also. Soon, orders came down to Coppock to turn over his positions to the 82nd Division. At 4:10 p.m. the relief was complete, and the regiment began to move to the rear. The 1st Battalion was relieved of its positions by the 42nd Division the following day.[117]

The regiment trudged back over the terrain on which it had shed so much blood. Going into the fight, it had numbered sixty-nine officers and 3,650 men. When it came out only thirty-two officers and 1,799 men remained.[118] The files of muddy, exhausted, khaki-clad doughboys wearily plodded through Fléville, Baulney, Charpentry, and on to Varennes, where they went into a "cheerless bivouac" to take stock of their losses.

The regiment (not to mention the entire division) had once again performed superbly. A German lieutenant colonel, captured on Hill 272 by the 1st Battalion, confirms this assessment in an after-battle report given to his captors. As recorded in *The Sixteenth Infantry in France* (page 40) the colonel stated:

Following this barrage closely were the troops of the First Division. I saw them forge ahead and knew that all was lost....Yesterday, I knew that the First Division was opposite us and I knew that I would have to put up the hardest fight of the war. The First Division is wonderful, and the German Army knows it. We did not believe that in five years the Americans could develop such as the First Division. The work of its Infantry and Artillery is worthy of the best army in the world.

On several occasions during and after the battle, General Summerall praised the 16th Infantry's performance. And well he might. While going up against the veteran 5th Guards Division, it was the only regiment of the entire First Army to reach its assigned objective during the first day of renewed offensive operations on October 4. It is to commemorate that achievement that the regiment, to this day, still holds October 4 sacred as its "Organization Day."

For two days at Varennes, the regiment waited for trucks to haul the men to their next training camp and rest billets at Marats le Grande. But the trucks never arrived, compelling the men to march to their destination, arriving on the 13th. The regiment remained at Marats le Grande for eight days, all the while receiving untried replacements. The new men were trained by the veterans, who realized that the "Fighting First" would soon go back into the line. On October 25 the regiment loaded on trucks and traveled to Recicourt Wood, where replacement operations and training continued.[119]

On October 23, Colonel William H. Harrell assumed command of the regiment from Lieutenant Colonel Coppock. Harrell was only thirty-nine years old, young for a full colonel. Born in South Carolina, Harrell had joined the army first as an enlisted man, then was commissioned from the ranks in 1903. In fifteen years, he had risen from 2nd lieutenant to colonel, taking command of the regiment as it prepared to go into its final phase of combat in the Great War.

By October 31, the First Army was ready to continue operations to cut the Carignan–Sedan–Mézières railroad. The following day, the First Army jumped off with I Corps on the left, III Corps on the right, and V Corps in the center. The attack achieved immediate success, and by November 4 had pushed the Germans beyond the Meuse River. The 1st Division was once again held in reserve during the initial stages of the fighting. Because of its tremendous élan and esprit, the reliable "Fighting First" was deemed most useful as a shock division, to be committed at a battle's critical point. The V Corps, to which the division was now assigned, soon had need for its services.

Sedan

The 16th Regiment moved to Gesnes on November 1, then marched all night to the Bois de la Folie, arriving the next day. Two days of rest in the woods were followed by another cross-country night march. By November 5, the regiment was in Bois de la Buzançy, tucked up behind the 2nd Division. A little after noon that day, the 1st Division received a warning order to prepare for an advance toward Mouzon on the Meuse River. By 4:00 p.m., the division's units were on the Beaumont-Stonne road, moving toward the objective. The division was supposed to relieve the 80th Division of its sector the next morning, taking positions between the 77th Division on the left and the 2nd Division on the right.[120] An order that evening, however, changed the whole nature of the operation and began a tangle of confused events culminating in a potentially disastrous but ultimately humorous episode for the 1st Division.

About 7:00 p.m., the V Corps received a message from the First Army that Pershing "desired that the honor of entering Sedan should it fall to the American Army." The attack was to be made by the I and V Corps, yet "boundaries were not considered to be binding." At 5:30 a.m. on the 6th, the 1st Division passed through the 80th Division outpost line running from Yoncq to Beaumont and headed northeast. On the right was the 2nd Brigade, in the middle was the 18th Infantry, and on the left was the 16th Infantry, drawn up in a column of battalions in the order 1st, 2nd, and 3rd. The regiment easily advanced through Yoncq and reached the Meuse at Autrecourt about noon, where it dug in.[121]

It wasn't until the afternoon of the 6th that the First Army orders of the previous day finally reached Colonel Harrell. The orders came by way of the 1st Division, arriving in the form of the division movement plan. And therein lay a problem. Where the army orders did not specifically direct the 1st Division to take Sedan, the division orders did. Clearly, Brigadier General Parker thought the "Fighting First" was responsible for seizing the city. Thus the movement plan directed the division to advance on Sedan in five columns, in doing so passing across the 77th and 42nd Divisions fronts, and arriving on the high ground south of Sedan on November 7, preparatory to the city's capture.[122]

Deployed on the division's far right (east) flank, the 16th Infantry columns were to advance on two axes. Starting from its positions around Autrecourt the 1st Battalion, designated Column No.1, would march up the Meuse River Valley; at the same time the remainder of the regiment, designated Column No. 2 and comprising the 1st Battalion, 5th Field Artillery, and Company A of the 1st Engineers, would move from Autrecourt to Wadelincourt via Raucourt, Haraucourt, and Thelonne. At Wadelincourt, Column No. 2 would link up with the 1st Battalion to attack Sedan. The remainder of the division would advance on three separate routes to the west.[123]

By 8:30 p.m. on November 5, the units had been assembled, briefed, and started on their way. As the columns groped along the dark trails and roads, the doughboys were chilled by a fine drizzle that soaked their heavy wool overcoats, making them heavier still. The 1st Battalion pushed on rapidly despite the hindering effects of frequent shelling, long-range machine-gun fire from across the river, and minor pockets of resistance. Bypassing the latter, the battalion passed through Remilly at midnight, reaching Allicourt about 2:00 a.m., where it encountered the enemy. Challenged by sentries, the lead men sprang to the attack and quickly overcame their opponents, killing several Germans and capturing several more. The remaining Germans wisely retreated toward Sedan. Driving on to Pont Maugis, the Americans entered the south side of the village just before dawn and ran into intense fire in their attempt to clear it. Next, fierce hand-to-hand fighting broke out, but the Germans would have little of that and they retreated. Before long, the battalion had secured most of the village and had captured a German wagon train. The Germans then infiltrated back into the town at various points. The fighting was not coordinated and the 1st Battalion was becoming disorganized. Furthermore, the battalion's way was now barred.[124]

After struggling to force a way through to the west, the commander ordered the battalion to a ravine south of Thelonne through which he knew the regiment must later pass. Turning south, the 1st Battalion took up positions in the ravine after dawn and waited for Colonel Harrell and the rest of the 16th.

Meanwhile, the other column, though confronting less opposition, had difficulties in navigating its way through the dark, damp night. The 2nd and 3rd Battalions moved out about midnight and lost contact with each other during the move. The 2nd Battalion crept into the gulch south of Thelonne about 5:00 a.m., where it was joined by the 1st Battalion coming in from Pont Maugis. The 3rd Battalion moved to a wooded area nearby, but it did not make contact with the rest of the regiment and so missed the subsequent action. Harrell, with the headquarters element and A Company, 1st Engineers, moved about dusk on the 6th, but this group did not make it to the ravine until about 7:00 the next morning.

As the various elements of the 16th Infantry made their way into the Thelonne Ravine, reports from companies of the 168th Infantry began to filter in to the command post of the

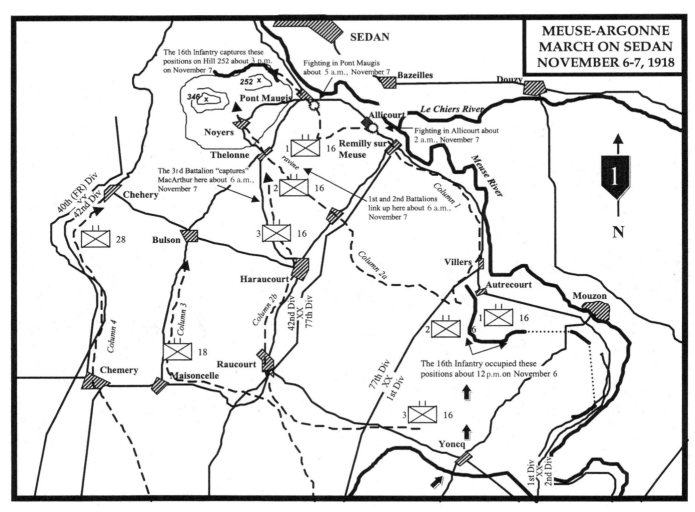

Map 6-8.

84th Infantry Brigade of unknown American troops moving across their sector. Brigadier General Douglas MacArthur, the brigade commander, was perplexed by this report and was unable to get any answers as to who they were. Leaving his headquarters, he went forward to reach the 168th's command post to prevent fratricidal shooting and to identify the unit. At the Beau-Menil Farm northeast of Bulson, MacArthur was "captured" by men of the 16th Infantry, and thereby determined that it was the "Fighting First" that was boldly driving through his area. At first, the men thought the general was a German officer because of the distinctive floppy hat and flowing scarf that he habitually wore. The doughboys forced him to accompany them to their battalion PC, where his true identity was learned. Needless to say, he was then "released amid a profusion of apologies."[125]

Having collected two of his three battalions, Harrell quickly developed a plan for an attack on Hill 252 to the north of Pont Maugis. This high ground was important for several reasons. First, it would flank and cut off the enemy units that had

held up the 1st Battalion's advance. Second, it was the intermediate objective assigned to the regiment for the Sedan operation. Finally, it was an excellent observation position and jump-off point for the regiment's assault on the French city. About 9:00 a.m., the regiment launched its assault.

Consisting of six companies (two companies from the 1st Battalion had become separated in the night fighting before Pont Maugis) and A Company, 1st Engineers, Harrell's attack force began advancing across two miles of rolling terrain. About 11:00 a.m., the regiment was held up by heavy machine-gun fire in the vicinity of Noyers. Patrols were sent forward and, by noon, had driven off the enemy. Without indirect fire support and against heavy machine-gun fire and shelling, the 16th Infantry pushed on through the Ruisseau de Thelonne and Noyers. The engineers, on the right flank, swerved east, captured Pont Maugis, and with massed rifle fire, suppressed two 77mm guns across the river that were being used in the direct-fire mode against the regiment. With the engineers thus engaged, the men of the 16th swept inexorably up the hill, capturing it in a rush about 3:00 p.m. Reaching the summit, they dug in and were pounded by heavy artillery fire the rest of the day.[126]

Sedan is a mere twenty-five hundred yards from Hill 252. The ancient city's church spires and other buildings were clearly visible to the men of the regiment, now occupying positions at the crest of the hill. But the honor of taking Sedan would not be theirs. The commander of the nearby French 40th Division, made hopping mad by the prospect of Americans liberating the city, sent a hotly worded message up his chain of command, protesting the 1st Division's encroachment on what he regarded as his prize—a French prize. Similar protests were voiced by virtually every general officer on the I Corps chain of command, including MacArthur, 42nd Division commander Major General Charles T. Menoher, and Major General Joseph T. Dickman, the corps commander. These and others complained vigorously to Lieutenant General Hunter Liggett, commander of the First Army, about the "Fighting First's" actions. Diplomacy prevailed and Summerall ordered the 1st Division to back off.

French troops subsequently relieved the 16th Infantry of Hill 252 about 2:00 a.m. on November 8. The Americans proceeded to their assembly area near Maisoncelles, little realizing, as they trudged wearily in the dark, how remarkable were their achievements in the final stages of the "Great War." In the past seventy-two hours they had advanced seventy-one kilometers, getting closer to Sedan than any other American unit. And they had done so with almost no sleep, under frequent fire, while suffering only twenty-nine killed and 152 wounded.[127]

Though many French and American commanders found them objectionable, the 1st Division's actions at Sedan amused Pershing, who refused to take seriously the idea that someone should be punished for the episode. Instead he praised his favorite division for its "fine spirit."[128] It was this battle that prompted General Pershing to issue General Orders Number 201, in which he remarked of the 1st Division, "The Commander in Chief has noted in this Division a special pride of service and a high state of morale, never broken by hardship or battle." Because the regiment bore the brunt of the fighting in this action, General Orders Number 201 may be considered to primarily apply to the 16th Infantry.

When they pulled out of the line, it was not apparent to the men of the 16th Infantry that they had just seen their last day of combat in the Great War. Even so, the doughboys were sure that it would not be long before the war ended. The morning of November 11 found the regiment marching in the Bois de Folie near Buzançy. As the doughboys slogged along, a rumor that the armistice had been signed circulated among them, but the thunder of big guns could still be heard in the distance. Then, about 11:00 a.m., the men noticed that the firing had ceased. The regimental chaplain remembered the reaction of the tired men:

Even when all were convinced that it was really true, that the war was for the time being at an end, there was no outburst of enthusiasm. The numbing effect of battle made it hard for the men to adjust themselves at once to the thought of victory and peace. But that night, for the first time since they had been in France, the men could light their campfires. So they celebrated by piling high the fagots. As it grew darker, flares and rockets began to go up, and there was a regular Fourth of July celebration. The officers at Regimental Headquarters built an enormous fire in the fireplace of the old farmhouse which they occupied, and gathered around for a pleasant evening, telling stories and singing songs far into the night.[129]

Five days later, the division was ordered to begin its movement into the Rhine Valley to take up occupation duties as part of the new Third Army. On the morning of November 17, the tired doughboys filed out of a "chilly, wind-swept hillside" bivouac near Eix and began the long march to Coblenz. Trudging along the roads, they were greeted with smiles by displaced Russians, Romanians, and Italians, and cheered lustily by the villagers of Lorraine as they passed through dirty, war-torn clusters of buildings that were once the pride of the province.

Once through the devastation of no man's land, the march was rather pleasant. The regiment reached Mercy le Haute on the 18th and found the villagers supremely friendly. So friendly, in fact, that the doughboys stayed another day. The following day, the regiment entered the Grand Duchy of Luxembourg. On the 23rd, they reached the city of Grevenmacher across from Pallien on the German frontier. Here, they were met at the gates of the city by a crowd, including the town fathers and a band playing "Yankee Doodle." Harrell proceeded to parade the 16th Infantry through the town, led by the colors and regimental band. The German Army at this time was under orders to evacuate the Rhineland in accordance with provisions of the armistice, but was slow to move. To prevent any untoward incidents, the 1st Brigade was held at Grevenmacher for a week while the Germans continued to pull back east of the Rhine. During this stop, the brigade commander, Brigadier General Frank Parker, ordered a brigade formation in the town square to celebrate Thanksgiving 1918.[130]

Occupation Coblenz Bridgehead
December 1, 1918-August 15, 1919

On December 1, the 1st Brigade crossed the Saar River into Germany, leading the American army's advance to the Rhine. The 16th Infantry marched along the west bank of the Moselle River while the 18th Infantry marched along the east bank. For a week and a half the Americans followed the river's winding path through the narrow corridor of the beautiful Moselle valley, marching jauntily through one small village after another. Passing through the picturesque mountain town of Trier, they reached Coblenz on the 12th. At Coblenz, where the Moselle flows into the Rhine River, the 1st Division was relieved from the IV Corps and assigned to the III Corps, which had the mission

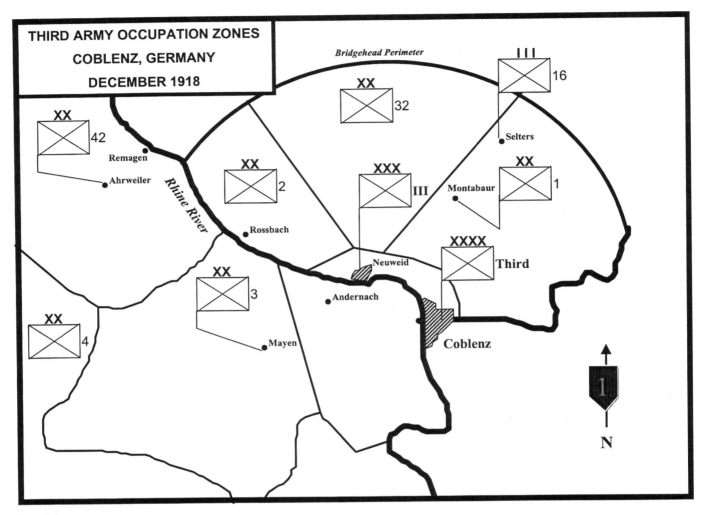

Map 6-9.

of occupying the bridgehead on the east bank of the Rhine.

At 8:30 a.m. on December 13, the 16th Infantry crossed the Rhine River at Coblenz on a pontoon bridge built by the 1st Engineer Regiment. In spite of the cold, drizzly rain, the troops marched forward with "the band playing and colors flying," looking every inch the combat veterans they were. Observing the regiment as it passed, General Parker turned to Colonel Harrell and remarked: "In all my military experience, I have never seen an outfit in better condition. I have not one word of criticism."[131]

The regiment's assigned occupation station was the little town of Dernbach. As well, subordinate units of the 1st, 2nd, and 3rd Battalions initially took up stations at Leuterod, Dernbach, and Hohr. The 1st Division's position was organized in three concentric arcs extending eastward from Coblenz. Each regiment occupied a section of the division line. The 16th Infantry's three battalions were echeloned, with the 1st Battalion occupying the outpost line centered on Leuterod, the 2nd Battalion occupying the main line of resistance centered on Dernbach, and the 3rd Battalion occupying the reserve

line centered on Hohr. The three battalions took turns manning these lines over the next several months.[132]

The men settled into what became essentially a garrison routine. Drill, marksmanship, and small tactical maneuvers were soon resumed as peacetime training pursuits.[133] The fact that the Germans had only recently been their enemies became hazy in the minds of men who, despite rules against fraternizing with the locals, began to seek more interesting pursuits. The Germans themselves took an interest in the Americans and found that these big, husky soldiers were as genuinely friendly as they appeared. The initial tension between Americans and Germans soon gave way to rather amiable relationships, at best, to mere refusal to associate, at worst.

The defensive posture of the AEF units in Coblenz was not entirely without reason, however. The German government had not ratified the peace terms offered by the Allies and, until they did, the Allied and German armies were technically still at war. In addition to other active measures, the regiment conducted daily patrols between the town of Rossbach and the

2nd Division positions at Hilgert. As AEF units were pulled out of the line to be sent home, the division assumed responsibility for an ever-increasing zone of occupation. Consequently in April the 16th Infantry moved its PC to the town of Selters, where it could better manage the now considerably expanded area under its control.[134]

The 1st Division performed frequent practice alerts during this period. In doing so, it aimed to achieve the twofold objective of keeping the soldiers in a high state of readiness, and in emphasizing American military resolve to the Germans even as American units were being pulled away. In May, the division was ordered to the field for maneuvers in the vicinity of Ellehausen-Wittgert. The maneuvers gave units the opportunity to train new soldiers in the conduct of field operations (which even the veterans had not performed since November), while providing the division staff and subordinate commanders with the opportunity to exercise the deployment plan for advancing farther into Germany should the peace negotiations break down.[135]

In mid-June, it appeared that an advance into Germany might become necessary. The negotiations at Versailles were going badly, with the German government resisting acceptance of the peace terms. German units were reported by intelligence sources to be moving into Westerberg and Herborn east of Coblenz. On June 23, 1919, the 1st Division issued an operation order to alert units to begin the advance "on order." The division was to move east with the 1st Brigade on the left and the 2nd Brigade on the right. The 1st Brigade mission was to seize railyards and telegraph facilities at Wetter. The order seemed imminent, but in late June the peace terms were signed and the division stood down.[136]

Shortly before the 1st Division was notified that it was to return to the United States, General Summerall was informed that the French nation desired to recognize a number of units for their superb performance in the recent effort to free French soil. A formal ceremony was planned and, on July 18, Marshal Pétain, hero of Verdun, came to Coblenz. With the 16th, 26th, and 28th Infantry Regiments drawn up in formation, the marshal and General Summerall came forward to each regiment's colors and decorated them with the French fourragère and the Croix de Guerre with Palm.[137] These were the highest awards that France bestowed on foreign military units and represented the deep appreciation that the people of France felt for the American efforts on their behalf. The United States had at long last paid the debt owed France for its vital support in America's War of Independence.

At the ceremony, Marshal Pétain congratulated Colonel Harrell on the superb record of the regiment and described the 16th Infantry as "tres magnifique, tres gallant, et tres brave." The French Army citation for the 16th Infantry stated:

[A] superb regiment which has always given an example of impetuosity and admirable courage as part of the First American Division, it has been able to force all to admire this unit which was the symbol of a nascent army. After having distinguished itself at Menil-le Tour and at Cantigny, it behaved gloriously in the counteroffensive of July 18th, 1918 south of Soissons, where, after a long march it fought for five consecutive days and captured very important [materiel] and numerous prisoners.[138]

The 1st Division remained in Coblenz until August 1919. On July 29, the division received its final movement orders home from Headquarters, American Forces in Germany. Departing from Coblenz on August 15, the 16th Infantry traveled by train through Belgium, then through Arras and Amiens to the French port of Brest. On August 23 the division boarded the steamships *Amphion, Freedom, Suwanee,* and *Marica* for the voyage home.[139]

The World War I record of the 16th Infantry is impressive. In the two years and three months it served overseas, over ten thousand men served in its ranks. Its total casualties numbered 3,389 wounded and 1,037 killed or mortally wounded. Its troops were the first Americans to arrive in France, the first to enter combat, and the first to suffer casualties from enemy action. Further, the regiment was among the first units to enter Germany, and among the first to cross the Rhine. It never failed to take an assigned objective (on scheduled time, no less) and never yielded any ground gained. In recognition of its excellent service in France, General Parker paid the following tribute to the 16th Infantry:

There is to my thinking, nothing finer in this world than the self-effacing role of the true private soldier of infantry, and nowhere in this war has the private soldier of infantry been truer to his Country's expectations of him than in the Sixteenth Infantry. All Honor, then, to these men, and to those gallant officers and non-commissioned officers, who have taught, inspired and led these private Great Hearts in the van of the American Expeditionary Forces.[140]

Back in the United States, the 16th Infantry would enter an era of service that would be at once peaceful yet frustrating. Even as the great American Expeditionary Forces had begun arriving on home shores, the Congress was already cutting back on military expenditures and pressing military leaders for rapid demobilization of the bulk of the nation's armed forces. Contrary to the provisions of the National Defense Act of 1920, political leaders would institute severe budget cuts that resulted in drastic reductions in U.S. military power, until the army was ranked seventeenth in the world in terms of overall strength. Over the next twenty years army leaders at all levels would be challenged to the utmost to provide realistic training for the soldiers under their command. The 16th Infantry's experience was to be primarily one of training with inadequate means and troops, coaching and mentoring National Guard and Organized Reserve units, and otherwise enjoying the sidewalks of New York.

Regimental honor company at the New York World Fair, 1939

Chapter Seven
The Sidewalks of New York

The conduct of officers and men in the performance of the duty was such as to excite the admiration and respect of all classes of citizens and was in keeping with the best traditions of the Army of the United States.
Rotary Club of Charleston, WV

November 28, 1919

After the war, most Americans wished to get things back to normal as quickly as possible. They wasted little time in this effort. By July 1921, the bodies of Bethel Gresham, Tom Enright, and Merle Hay had been returned to the United States and buried in their respective hometowns. Once household names, they would gradually be forgotten. Three months later, the Unknown Soldier was laid to rest at Arlington National Cemetery. But the economy was booming, times were good, and nobody wanted to think about war. The last one had been won, but with a horrific cost in blood. People believed, however, that there would never be another like it. "A war to end all wars, so let's get on with business" was the prevailing attitude. "The business of America is business" President Calvin Coolidge would soon say. Even so, America was proud of her soldiers' accomplishments and took the time to honor her heroes. Even as the last of America's combat divisions was at sea, on its way back from occupation duty in Europe, plans were in the works to celebrate its homecoming.

The ships carrying the 16th Infantry steamed into the Port of New York on September 3, 1919. The men of the regiment crowded the rails to get a good look at Lady Liberty; for many, it was one of the most welcome sights they had ever seen. Indeed, it was a sight many soldiers had thought they would never live to see. Relatively few of the men who had viewed the statue on the 16th Infantry's outbound journey were still with the regiment. The ships silently slipped past Governors Island and nudged up to the army piers at Hoboken, where those who did remain had departed for France almost two and a half years before. Soon, hundreds of doughboys in olive-drab uniforms streamed down the gangplanks. With little delay, the troops boarded trains for the short trip to Camp Merritt, New Jersey, where the 1st Division was temporarily billeted.

About a week before the division landed at Hoboken, the division commander, Major General Edward F. McGlachlin Jr., had arrived in New York at the head of a contingent of officers from each of his subordinate units. Meeting with New York City authorities, the soldiers and civilians set about planning the arrival and reception of the "Red One." The plan called for a parade down Fifth Avenue from 110th Street to Washington Square. Unlike the previous homecoming parades

conducted by New York's own 27th and 77th Divisions, this parade would consist of the entire twenty-eight thousand men of the "Fighting First," as well as the division's complement of horses, caissons, artillery, and other equipment. Early on the morning of September 10, the 1st Division loaded on trains for New York, and by 10:00 a.m. all units were in position and the parade began.[1]

Leading the procession was "Black Jack" Pershing himself, mounted on his favorite charger, "Kidron," followed by the AEF staff and a composite unit of men from the 2nd, 3rd, 4th, 5th, and 6th Divisions. Then came the 1st Division with General McGlachlin and the division staff, the 1st Engineers, and the 1st Infantry Brigade Headquarters. Next came the 16th Infantry, led by its commander, Lieutenant Colonel Clarence Huebner. The remainder of the division followed: infantry, artillery, and support units. The reviewing stand was at 84th Street and held such notables as Secretary of War Baker; General Peyton C. March, the army chief of staff; and Major Generals William L. Sibert, James W. McAndrew, and the 16th Infantry's former commander, "Birdie" Hines. In a second stand was Pershing's family and Senator Francis E. Warren, the general's father-in-law. Cheering onlookers thronged both sides of Fifth Avenue along the entire parade route, forming a crowd estimated in the hundreds of thousands. The parade was a big success, and the soldiers were impressed by the warm reception. The *New York Times* described the event as "the most impressive military function ever seen in the United States."[2]

The 1st Division departed Camp Merritt on September 15 and proceeded to Washington, D.C., where it staged another triumphal procession on the 17th. The division took the same route down Pennsylvania Avenue that the Army of the Potomac had trod during the Grand Parade of the Union armies in May 1865. The procession began at the Peace Monument at the foot of Capital Hill and continued down Pennsylvania to 15th Street, where the troops marched through a replica of the Arc de Triomphe. The reviewing stand was located in front of the White House, at the same location where President Andrew Johnson had stood to review the Army of the Potomac some fifty-four years before.[3] The reviewing party included Vice President Thomas R. Marshall, Secretary Baker, General March, numerous members of Congress, and foreign diplomats. Once again, grateful crowds cheered the ramrod straight soldiers of the "Red One," the cream of America's army. The ovation was described to be as great as that which the division received in New York. The soldiers were given strict orders not to look at the crowds as they marched, which gave them a serious demeanor not lost on the onlookers who remarked on their stern countenances.[4]

After the parade, the division moved to Camp George G. Meade, Maryland. There, those soldiers considered "emergency period" men (those enlisted only for war service, not in the Regular Army) were given their final outprocessing papers and physicals, and discharged from the service. Most were glad to leave and proud that they had done their duty. But even those who could not wait to go home no doubt felt twinges of regret brought on by leaving trusted comrades with whom they had suffered so much. The separation of these men severely depleted the ranks of the 16th Infantry. From a wartime strength of nearly three thousand officers and men, the regiment dwindled to fewer than one thousand.

The stay at Camp Meade was brief. On October 2, the regiment entrained for the journey to their next post, arriving at Camp Zachary Taylor, Kentucky, on the 4th. As they debarked from the train, few, if any, 16th Infantrymen noted that this date marked the first anniversary of the regiment's hard-fought victory at Fléville. Forming up at the platform, the troops marched to the cantonment area and were assigned to several of the large wooden temporary barracks of the standard wartime design.

Camp Taylor, located five miles southwest of Louisville, was one of the many wartime cantonments that sprang up around the United States to house the new "National Army" divisions. It had been the training camp of the 84th Division before its departure for overseas duty, and it served as the demobilization station for that division and elements of the 89th and 92nd Divisions.[5] Soon, the almost deserted post came to life with thousands of men proudly sporting the new "Red One" patch on their shoulders.

The 16th Infantry had hardly settled in when Colonel Harrell received orders on October 24 to prepare the regiment for movement to Charleston, West Virginia. In response to a coal miners' strike scheduled for November 1, Governor John J. Cornwell appealed to Major General Leonard Wood, commander of the Central Department, for troops to be dispatched to prevent violence in the coal fields. The governor was still able to legally request federal troops under the wartime emergency provisions referred to as "direct access," which were to terminate at the end of 1919. State governors were granted this power during World War I when the National Guard was in federal service, and briefly after the war until the guard could be reconstituted.[6]

The first nine hundred men of what was called the "provisional regiment" began movement from Camp Taylor on October 31 and, by the following day, all units were closed on their stations. The regimental headquarters was located at Charleston, along with Companies A, B, C, D, and E. The remaining companies of the 16th were sent to the small mining town of Clothier. Some 350 officers and men of the 18th Infantry were attached to the 16th for this mission, and these were sent to the town of Beckley. Additionally, troops of the 26th and 28th Regiments, attached to the provisional regiment, garrisoned other small towns and brought the total strength of Harrell's command to twenty-five hundred soldiers. Upon arrival, Colonel Harrell issued his units instructions for the enforcement of martial law.

The primary martial law tasks of the regiment were to ensure continued operation of the mines in the Guyan Valley and of the Norfolk and Western Railroad that serviced the fields. Soon after the troops took up stations in their respective areas, it became apparent to the organizers of the striking miners that to engage in any threatening acts so long as these troops were present was not a good idea. Machine guns were set up at key locations from which they were able to sweep likely riot locations. The troops, moreover, made themselves readily visible by frequent and armed foot and motorized patrols through the area. For two weeks, the pressure was kept up until mine owners and representatives of the United Mine Workers agreed to solutions that resolved the problems initially prompting the strike. On the 16th, Harrell ordered all units in outlying towns back to Charleston, and by November 18 the provisional regiment was on trains rumbling back to Camp Taylor.

The performance of the regiment in West Virginia received good marks. General McGlachlin received several letters of appreciation for the regiment's work. General Wood wrote, "Please extend my thanks to Colonel Harrell and the officers and men of his command for the excellent and satisfactory manner in which they performed the duty assigned them. The conduct of the troops won the good will of all classes and added to the prestige of the Regular Army." The state adjutant general remarked, "Their conduct was without reproach during their entire tour of duty....I am safe in saying that every law-abiding citizen in the state of West Virginia joins me in expressing our gratitude to Colonel W. F. Harrell, 16th Inf., and the officers and men of the Provisional Regiment." The Rotary Club of Charleston passed a resolution stating, "The conduct of officers and men in the performance of the duty was such as to excite the admiration and respect of all classes of citizens and was in keeping with the best traditions of the Army of the United States."[7]

The performance of martial law duties was not an uncommon activity for the post-World War I Regular Army, and the 16th Infantry had its share. In early 1920, an African-American man was arrested in Fayette County, Kentucky, under suspicion of having raped and murdered a ten-year-old white girl. In the racially charged climate of the times, many whites, convinced that the man had committed the act, threatened to lynch him. The trial was held in Lexington and a small contingent of the

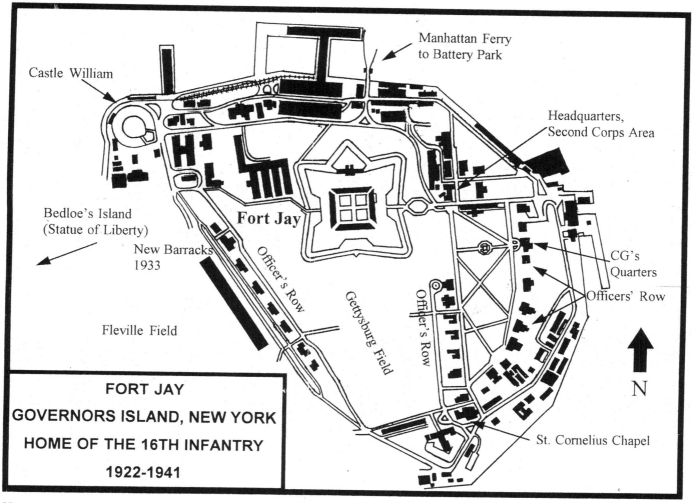

Castle William

Manhattan Ferry
to Battery Park

Headquarters,
Second Corps Area

Fort Jay

Bedloe's Island
(Statue of Liberty)

New Barracks
1933

CG's
Quarters

Officer's Row

Officers' Row

Gettysburg Field

Officer's Row

Fleville Field

St. Cornelius Chapel

N

FORT JAY

GOVERNORS ISLAND, NEW YORK

HOME OF THE 16TH INFANTRY

1922-1941

Map 7-1.

Kentucky National Guard was called out to provide protection and keep order about the courthouse. On February 9, the man was brought into town to stand trial. A guilty verdict was rendered that same morning, and a mob gathered, intent on carrying out justice in its own way. The situation soon spun out of control, and the guardsmen opened fire, killing five rioters and wounding eighteen. Governor Edwin P. Morrow requested federal assistance.[8]

General Wood directed the 1st Division to assist the National Guard, and by 1:00 p.m. that day an ad hoc force from the 2nd Infantry Brigade under Brigadier General Francis C. Marshall was en route on the Louisville and Nashville Railroad. Upon arrival General Marshall immediately declared Fayette County under martial law. Forming his troops in a skirmish line, Marshall ordered the unfurling of "Old Glory" and ordered an advance down Water Street. By their very appearance, the soldiers signaled the crowd that they meant business and would not back down. The streets were promptly cleared of rioters, and the troops easily took control of the courthouse. Unwilling

to scrap with this new group of soldiers, the now-tamed mob respectfully kept their distance from the regulars sent into their midst, and no untoward incidents transpired.[9]

The following morning, a battalion of the 16th Infantry arrived to reinforce the 2nd Brigade units. These men were quickly assigned routine patrol duties, working in conjunction with the local law enforcement agencies. That evening, 2nd Brigade units escorted the condemned man to the Eddyville State Penitentiary and left Lexington under the control of the 16th Infantry.[10] After six more days, General Marshall deemed it unnecessary to continue martial law, and the remainder of the battalion loaded up and returned to Camp Taylor.

That summer, the regiment, along with the 26th and 28th Infantry Regiments, traveled to Camp Perry, Ohio. These units were assigned the duty of supporting the annual National Matches for marksmanship. Their duties consisted of building camp areas, setting up and running ranges, and other support functions. The matches lasted from July 20 to August 28, and the regiment returned to Camp Taylor on the 29th. Upon arrival, the men learned that they were soon to be transferred to Camp Dix, New Jersey, with the rest of the 1st Division.

The reasons for the transfer of the division to Camp Dix were twofold. First, the War Department declared Camp Taylor to be surplus, and it was going to be offered up for sale. Therefore, space had to be found to house the division, and Camp Dix seemed to be the right place.

Why Camp Dix was the right place to station the "Fighting First" was the second reason for the transfer. Since early 1919, the War Department had been groping with how the postwar U.S. Army would be organized. The efforts of the General Staff resulted in the provisions of the 1920 National Defense Act. This document organized the army into three distinct components: the Regular Army, the National Guard, and the Organized Reserve. On the macro level, the continental United States was to be divided into nine "Corps Areas" that would replace the old department system. The allotment of states to the Corps Areas was based on the idea that they would be approximately equal in population. In terms of the mobilization of tactical units, each Corps Area would organize two corps (for example, the Second Corps Area would organize the II Corps and the XII Corps). The lower numbered corps consisted of one Regular Army and two National Guard divisions. The higher-numbered corps consisted of three Organized Reserve divisions. The 1st Division was selected to be the Regular Army division for the Second Corps Area, which consisted of New York, New Jersey, and Delaware. Camp Dix was the only cantonment in the Corps Area that could hold the entire division.

The regiment boarded trains at Camp Taylor on September 14, and rolled into Camp Dix at Wrightstown, New Jersey, two days later. Like Camp Taylor, Dix had been a National Army cantonment for the 78th "Lightning" Division during the First World War. It had also served as the demobilization station for that division in 1919, as well as for numerous other outfits arriving home from France.

Upon taking up residence in Camp Dix, the men of the 1st Division were put to work renovating the camp's dilapidated infrastructure. The barracks had fallen into disrepair and the area was in general need of policing. Trash was picked up, grass and shrubs cut and trimmed, and buildings painted and repaired. Soon, the garrison began to take on the customarily smart appearance of a cantonment occupied by soldiers of the famed "Red One."

Almost immediately following the transfer of the 1st Division to Camp Dix, the division staff laid plans to conduct the first of what would become an annual reunion in the "Red One" during the interwar years. The first reunion occurred November 10 and 11, 1920, and attracted some ten thousand veterans and their family members, as well as friends of the 1st Division. The evening of the 10th, the entire division put on a night "sham battle" at the amphitheater at Marne Hill for the entertainment of the veterans and thousands of other guests, including Pershing himself. It was described as a "titanic spectacle," complete with blank ammunition, searchlights, tanks, and star shells fired by the artillery. The following day, the division conducted a parade led by Pershing, and the division veterans were invited to march in the parade with their old outfits.[11] This, too, became a custom during the "Old Army" years, which, like so many of those old 1st Division traditions, has fallen by the wayside since World War II.

At Camp Dix, the regiment was still grossly understrength. Despite recruiting drives implemented when the regiment was at Camp Taylor, most companies were actually the size of platoons. As a result, in the autumn about half of the companies were reduced to cadre-level manning (company commander, first sergeant, supply and personnel clerks), and the men were transferred to other companies to bring them to something that more closely resembled company-strength. A new recruiting drive was started and slowly the empty companies filled with new troops.

With the influx of new men, the regiment was forced to begin "school of the soldier" training, consisting of drill, wear of the uniform, barracks maintenance, personal hygiene, and marksmanship training. This kind of training was good for the new men, but the sprinkling of old soldiers only chafed under this kind of work. None had received any really useful field training since the war. The regiment had ceased to be a combat-ready organization.

In July 1920, Colonel Harrell relinquished command of the regiment, and Major Thomas J. Strangier was appointed as acting commander. Strangier undertook corrective measures for the regiment's lack of combat readiness, instituting a training program aimed at getting the men into the field. Strangier had good intentions but, in the view of some old soldiers, his execution was flawed. For example, attack problems were conducted on open terrain rather than in the camp's swamps, thickets, and wooded areas. One veteran, reminiscing about the training at Dix, recalled, "I thought that when training to fight, we should train on ground like that on which fighting was most likely to occur. And if past experience, past and present, was an indicator, the site of combat would not be on easy ground."[12]

On December 1, 1920, the six-month regime of acting commanders ended when Colonel Francis E. Lacey Jr. arrived at Camp Dix to take permanent command of the 16th Infantry. By then Lacey, an 1889 graduate of the U.S. Military Academy, already had thirty-one years of army service under his belt, exclusive of his years as plebe and cadet at West Point. Assigned to the 1st Infantry Regiment in the autumn of 1889, he remained with that unit through the Spanish-American War, transferring to the 23rd Infantry as a captain in 1899. Like many officers of his generation, Lacy served in the Philippines, although his tour of seven years (1900 to 1907) was longer than most. Upon his return to the United States he attended school at Fort Leavenworth and the War College, then served with the 18th Infantry in Hawaii. Service as inspector general of the VII Corps during the First World War was followed by assignment to the office of the army chief of staff, where he served from June 1919 to November 1920.[13]

In the summer of 1921, the regiment was assigned to provide training assistance to the National Guard, Organized Reserve, Citizen's Military Training Camps (CMTC), and the Army Reserve Officers' Training Corps (ROTC). It was a mission the 16th Infantry would perform almost every summer for the next twenty years. The regiment's main duties in this regard consisted of preparing barracks areas, assisting with supply accountability and issue, and running marksmanship ranges. At summer's end, upon completing the annual training assistance mission, the regiment underwent some brief training of its own, then returned to Camp Dix and the routine of garrison life until the following summer.

A second winter at Camp Dix passed, and with warmer weather, the green hues of spring returned to the training areas. Soon, rumors began floating around camp that the division was going to be transferred yet again. Sure enough, orders arrived directing the movement of the division, but this time the units of the "Fighting First" would be farmed out to many of the old, tiny posts that dotted the landscape of the upper East Coast. The 1st Infantry Brigade drew a plum garrison assignment in New York City. The 16th Infantry, less the 3rd Battalion, was directed to take station at Fort Jay on Governors Island, New York Harbor. The 3rd Battalion was to transfer to Fort Wadsworth on Staten Island when that post was vacated in September. The 16th's sister regiment, the 18th, was posted to Forts Slocum, Schuyler, and Hamilton. The remainder of the division was garrisoned in small posts ranging from Fort Ethan Allen in Vermont to Fort Hoyle in Maryland.

On June 7, 1922, the 16th Infantry (less the 3rd Battalion, which remained behind to garrison Camp Dix), formed up on the company streets and began the march to its new station. Over the next two days it took a winding course through the New Jersey countryside, passing through Imslaytown and Long Branch before arriving at Sandy Hook on the 10th. There, the men boarded ferries at Fort Hancock and were transported across the straits to their new home.

After arriving at the docks of the island, the troops scrambled off the ferry, formed ranks, and marched through the imposing sallyport of this historic post. Governors Island had been a military station since 1755, when the 51st Colonial Militia Regiment of the British Army had been garrisoned there. The star-shaped fortress of Fort Jay was constructed in the 1790s in anticipation of war with France and became a federal military installation in 1800. It was renamed Fort Columbus in 1808, because of John Jay's unpopularity over the treaty he brokered with England in 1795. In 1904, however, Secretary of War Elihu Root directed the post be renamed Fort Jay. The island had been used as the springboard for the 22nd Infantry's seizure of German ships in New York harbor only minutes after the United States declared war in 1917.[14] That regiment had recently vacated the post and its quarter-

master, and that of the 16th, had been busy counting and signing over property over the previous several days in anticipation of the 16th Infantry's arrival.

Governors Island was paradise compared to the 16th Infantry's stations of the past eight years. Indeed, it provided the regiment with its first permanent barracks since leaving the Presidio of San Francisco in 1914. Besides the old coastal fortifications of Fort Jay and Castle William, the island post consisted of spacious brick barracks, large officers' quarters, a well-manicured polo field that could double as football and baseball fields, and a splendid view of the Statue of Liberty, who held high her golden torch less than a quarter mile away. Most important to the troops, the excitement of Manhattan was a two-minute ferry ride away.

Though many regiments had come and gone at historic Governors Island, it did not take the 16th Infantry long to put its stamp on it. Soon, roads on the island were renamed for Gresham, Enright, and Hay. Other roads were named for Lieutenant Colonel Craig, Captain Harry Kimmell, 2nd Lieutenant Cyril Carder, and several other 16th Infantry heroes from World War I. The piers were redesignated Soissons and San Juan Docks. Polo was played on Gettysburg Field, and reviews were held on Fléville Field. Other redesignations included the Argonne Heights golf course, St.-Mihiel Park, and Sedan Point.[15] When visitors came to the home of the 16th Infantry, they were surrounded by reminders of its history.

In many ways, life at Fort Jay in the 1920s and 1930s was stereotypical of the old "brown shoe army." Because of typically small peacetime budgets, the opportunity for substantive training was limited. Therefore, soldiers' time was consumed by garrison duties, sports, recruiting, and ceremonies.

Garrison duties at Fort Jay were not particularly onerous. A typical day started at 5:30 a.m., and reveille was sounded at 6:00 a.m. At reveille, the regiment would form up for the raising of the colors, and the "top kicks" would call roll. After announcements, the troops were marched to breakfast. At 8:00 a.m., the work day started. The mornings were generally spent in close order drill, calisthenics, equipment maintenance, classes, or soldier schools. From roughly September to May, the afternoons were often spent doing "extra duty" or other details directed by the first sergeant, or, for those soldiers with athletic skills, participation on one of several regimental sports teams. Other activities included "beautification" projects, inspections, and guard duty.

Guard duty at Governors Island was an important affair. Soldiers detailed to guard duty turned out in crisp uniforms and highly glossed shoes, competing for the coveted position of "Colonel's Orderly." This title ensured that the soldier would not have to walk a post that day. The competition was especially keen during the winter months, when bitter winds blew in from the sea and made walking a post truly miserable. As part of guard mount, the sergeant of the guard formed the detail in front of the regimental headquarters for the inspection by the officer of the day, after which the squad would be marched to their posts around the island. Guard posts included the Governors Island ferry docks, the regimental stables, the quartermaster warehouse, and the ammunition storage area. Regardless of location, each guard post had a superb view of the New York skyline and most overlooked the Statue of Liberty. Both sights were particularly mesmerizing during the hours of darkness. The lights from the tall buildings and from the ships departing and arriving at the port of New York certainly made guard duty for soldiers at Fort Jay a more enjoyable task than what troops experienced at places like Fort Meade, South Dakota, or at Fort Missoula, Montana. In reality, there was little danger from which the post had to be guarded, but guard duty was a way that soldiers, especially new men, were trained in the importance of vigilance, regardless of the military situation.

"Spit and polish" were important cultural aspects of the Old Army. Men usually continued to reenlist in the same outfit and, over the years, tended to develop a deep pride in their regimental membership. This pride manifested itself in a number of ways, not the least of which was the sharp appearance of members when in uniform. This was particularly true of the men of the 16th Infantry, who typically wore their uniform when off post in the city. They knew they not only represented the U. S. Army to the public but, even more, they represented the 16th Infantry Regiment—"the best damned outfit in the whole damned army."

In the mid-1920s, something new was added to the uniform of the 16th Infantry that increased pride then, and is still a source of pride today. The troops already wore the coveted "Red One" and the French fourragère on their left shoulder, but on July 23, 1923, the quartermaster general of the army approved the design of the regiment's new coat of arms. Based on the coat of arms of the village of Fléville, the shield consisted of a blue and white vair background, over which was superimposed a crossed bolo knife (the Philippine Insurrection), an arrow (Indian War service), and a red five-bastioned fort that represented the corps badge for the 1st Division, V Corps, in the Spanish-American War. The crest consisted of a devil's trident behind a sheaf of wheat, both superimposed over the white Maltese cross of the Civil War 2nd Division, V Corps. The cross symbolized the regiment's service in the Army of the Potomac, while the trident and wheat recalled the regiment's bloody and heroic efforts to save the III Corps between the Devil's Den and the Wheatfield at Gettysburg. The basic design of the shield was incorporated into a distinctive unit insignia and approved for wear by the men of the 16th Infantry on February 20, 1925.[16]

When the War Department approved the adoption of coats of arms for regiments in 1920, the action also prompted the redesign of regimental colors. The old regimental color was merely an updated version of those that had been carried by infantry regiments since the Civil War. The new version incorporated a regiment's coat of arms into the national seal and placed it on a silk color background of that arm: blue for infantry, yellow for cavalry, red for artillery, and so forth. On January 4, 1924, the 16th's commander, Colonel Charles Gerhardt, held a regimental review to retire the old color and and christen the new color that proudly bore the arms of the regiment. The regiment was formed in Battery Park in New York City and reviewed by Gerhardt and the 16th's old wartime commander, Major General Hines, who presented the new color and assisted in placing it on the staff. After brief remarks by Hines, the regiment was ferried back to Governors Island and assembled in the Chapel of St. Cornelius the Centurion. A contemporary article in the *Infantry Journal* described the scene:

> The new colors were placed on the altar by Chaplain Edmund B. Smith and blessed—consecrating the colors and those who serve it to uphold the traditions of the regiment, the country and its proud name, and the liberties of its citizens. The chaplain then received the old color for preservation and display in the chapel, where it joins over 100 colors of various units of the army dating back to the very first organization of the United States Army….General Hines then spoke a few words to the regiment, impressing on each member that these battle-scarred colors were worthy to join in the assembled colors of other wars and other periods of the country's struggles and progress through the loyal service of the men who had fought, bled, and died for their country under its folds.[17]

Not all of the regiment's activities while stationed at Fort Jay were routine. For example, on the afternoon of July 10, 1926, a bolt of lightning set off a series of explosions at the Lake Denmark Naval Arsenal in New Jersey. The explosions were caused by the detonation of 16-inch naval shells stored at the arsenal, and in a matter of minutes, twenty-one people lay dead and a huge fire raged out of control. A request for assistance arrived at Headquarters, Second Corps Area, at Governors Island, three hours later at 8:30 p.m. The Corps Area commander, General Summerall, designated Brigadier General Hugh A. Drum, commander of the 1st Division, as the disaster scene commander. Drum immediately set out for Lake Denmark, but just before leaving, he sent word to the 16th Infantry to send a disaster assistance detail to the arsenal as quickly as possible.[18]

This was not an easy task; July 10 was a Saturday. Moreover, it was a payday weekend. Most of the troops were on pass to spend their money in the big city. But, somehow, the officer of the day was able to round up seven officers, 155 men and seven old Liberty trucks. By 11:00 p.m., this provisional battalion rolled off the ferry at Battery Park and made its way through Manhattan to the Barclay Street ferry. The convoy encountered a street cleaner partially blocking the road just before reaching the ferry. The officer in the lead truck dismounted to get the operator to move his contraption, but the man refused, saying he had to let his hoses dry. The officer explained the emergency, and the man still refused. At that, the officer strode back to his truck and ordered the convoy forward, destroying the hoses as seven heavily-laden Liberty trucks rolled over them.[19]

Upon crossing by ferry into Jersey City, the trucks picked up a police escort. At each change in jurisdiction, a new police escort replaced its predecessor. As the detachment approached Dover, New Jersey, "a ghastly red hue tinged the horizon. It was like a threatening dawn and the intermittent sound of exploding shell fire told the troops that they were approaching the scene of disaster." About 2:00 a.m., the trucks rolled into Dover, where the men dismounted. The officers took off on a reconnaissance while the men were served coffee and doughnuts by some of the local maidens. The girls were naturally attracted to these armed and tough-looking men in uniform who possessed such serious faces. Batting their eyes, these "frail and anxious inquirers" sought the opinions of these "experts" and, of course, "Expert opinions were given."[20]

When the officers returned from their reconnaissance, they posted their men at strategic posts around the arsenal to keep the thousands of sightseers away from danger. Reporters and press photographers, appearing on the scene by the dozens, were among the most persistent interlopers. Throughout Sunday and Monday, the shells exploded and prevented the approach of firefighters. By Tuesday morning, however, the explosions had ceased, and search parties went in to locate bodies. Firefighters, meanwhile, moved in to extinguish the remaining flames. Heavy rains assisted the firefighters' efforts and, by Tuesday night, the fires were either out or under control. The need for troops to control crowds had passed by that evening. The next morning, the men were loaded into trucks for the trip home, and the convoy arrived at Governors Island on Wednesday night.[21]

The next exciting event found the soldiers of the 16th actually engaged in firefighting. Though most of the barracks at Fort Jay were large brick structures, they were meant to house only about a battalion's worth of soldiers. When the regiment moved from Camp Dix in 1922, two understrength battalions were billeted at Fort Jay, while the 3rd Battalion moved to Fort Wadsworth in September of that year. As a result of the overcrowding at Fort Jay, several companies of the regiment could not be housed in the main barracks. For example, B Company garrisoned Fort Wood on Bedloe's (Liberty) Island in 1922-23 and performed guard duties for the Statue of Liberty. Company E performed that duty in 1923-24, and A Company was stationed there in 1924-25. In 1925, the 1st Military Police Company occupied Fort Wood, and A Company was transferred back to Fort Jay. The only quarters available however, were decrepit tarpaper-and-wood barracks built for temporary use during the First World War. So in May 1925, A Company joined the Service Company, Headquarters Company, and the Band in what were known as the "splinter barracks."

Early on the morning of January 6, 1927, Private Claude Wallace, who happened to be awake, spotted flames in one of the buildings. Wallace responded by waking Bugler Charles Shore. Shore rushed out into the bitterly cold air in his underwear, and sounded "Fire Call" into the megaphone, as Wallace made his way through the buildings waking the others. Soon, entire companies turned out to fight the flames, initially under the command of privates, then first sergeants, and finally officers. Colonel Edward Croft, the regimental commander, notified the city authorities, and not long after, city fireboats appeared to assist in dousing the flames. But their help was too late in arriving. All four of the old structures were gutted. Not only were the barracks for A Company, Service Company, Headquarters Company, and the Band destroyed, but the Disciplinary Barracks workshops were also burned.[22]

Of course, this disaster further exacerbated the housing problem, which saw the newly homeless troops quartered in the YMCA building and other locations. But the debacle turned out to be a blessing in disguise. The War Department had wanted to tear down those old buildings since the war, but was prevented from doing so by budgetary constraints. Now, there was no choice. That year, Congress placed money in the army budget for billets on Governors Island, and soon, plans were drawn up for new barracks. One set of plans was bizarre. It envisioned a complex that resembled a medieval castle, complete with turrets and drawbridges. Cooler heads prevailed, and construction began in 1931 of more conventional barracks designed to house the entire regiment.

In early 1933 construction of the new barracks was completed. Fort Jay was now capable of housing all units of the regiment, and it wasn't long before the 3rd Battalion moved in. For the first time in over ten years, the entire regiment was quartered at one station, and the 16th Infantry's commander, Colonel Joseph A. Marmon, directed that the regiment hold a review to mark the occasion. On March 18, the regiment formed on Fléville Field in front of the new barracks, with a gap left in the formation for the 3rd Battalion to occupy. At the bugle sound of "Adjutant's Call," Major Norman Randolph marched the 3rd Battalion into the gap, thus heralding the regiment's reunification. The reviewing officers for the parade were Major General Dennis E. Nolan, Second Corps Area commander, and Rear Admiral Reginald R. Belknap. Both subsequently expressed complete satisfaction with the regiment's performance.[23]

An aspect of garrison life in every army unit is the emergence of "characters" who, by dint of their personalities and behavior, enliven what might otherwise be an intolerably dull routine. The 16th Infantry certainly had its share of characters. Among the most memorable during this period was a certain Sergeant Casey. A member of the regiment since 1917, Casey had joined up with the 16th somewhere between Fort Bliss and Hoboken, supposedly after going AWOL from a circus—because, it was said, he wanted to see the world. His buddies were eager to help him in this regard, smuggling him aboard ship as a stowaway just before the regiment sailed for France. This unconventional boarding procedure was necessitated by the fact that he was a small black-and-white mutt. His caretakers always claimed that Casey, who not yet a sergeant, was one of the first members of the regiment to descend the gangplank at St. Nazaire and set foot (or paws) on French soil. He had stayed with his buddies through the fighting in France and the occupation on the Rhine. He was a fond and familiar sight on Governors Island, known for his cheerful disposition, happily greeting every soldier he met with a wagging tail and bright eyes. In recognition of his faithfulness, Casey was promoted to the rank of sergeant and given his own pup tent [sic] to sleep in. One morning in early September 1925, however, Sergeant Casey was nowhere to be found. Had the little fellow gone AWOL again?

That morning, the regiment formed on the post's main street as the first chill breezes of autumn blew across the island. The long khaki lines stood at rigid attention and "Present Arms!" was ordered. Meanwhile, a bugler played reveille, and "Old Glory" was gracefully raised to the top of the pole. First sergeants began to call roll, but when the name "Sergeant Casey" was called, the usual bark was not heard. This was extremely unusual, as Casey had made every formation for years and had learned to answer to his name. This was the first time that anyone could remember that he had not been present for formation, and many began to rubberneck as the name was called out the second time. "AWOL," came a reply. At the conclusion of the formation, many wondered where the old boy had gone. A search of the orderly room and the back dock of the mess hall turned up nothing. Some surmised that he had finally figured out a way to get on the ferry and was probably gone for good.

Later that day, a company mail orderly en route to the post office walked past Sergeant Casey's pup tent. Looking inside, he spied the little dog curled up in the back of the tent. He called to him, but there was no answer. Casey had died in his sleep. So, the little soldier had not abandoned his buddies after all but had stuck with them to the end! The news spread through the regiment and many men felt a tug in their hearts. Even grizzled veterans of France experienced that familiar lump in the throat and a welling in the eyes when learning of Casey's demise. Soon a request was forwarded to the regimental commander for a formal military funeral. The "old man" loved Casey too and readily granted permission.

On September 5, the entire regiment formed to give Sergeant Casey a last salute. A casket for Casey's mortal remains was fashioned by the shop on post and borne to the grave site on a caisson, accompanied by troops marching in procession as a guard of honor. A twenty-one gun salute was rendered as Casey was laid to rest. The inscription on his headstone stated, "Sergeant Casey, U.S.A. He was only a dog, but he did his bit." The editor of the *New York Times,* impressed that a dog should be so honored, put an account of the funeral on the newspaper's front page.[24]

Another notable in the 16th Infantry during this period was Henry R. Vandercook of Tennessee. Twenty years old when he joined the army in 1920, Vandercook was assigned to D Company, 16th Infantry, at Camp Taylor. By 1924 he was D Company's First Sergeant, rising to that rank in a mere four years—an unprecedent achievement in an army where it could take ten years to make corporal.[25]

In contrast to Vanderhook, and not unusual for the 16th Infantry, there were men of long service such as Master Sergeant Claude L. Ensign. Ensign enlisted in 1898 and joined the regiment in 1912, serving in the Punitive Expedition and in five World War I campaigns. When he retired in 1928 after a total of thirty years of army service, a parade was held in his honor at Fort Jay.

Master Sergeant Ole Anderson joined the army in 1900 and was assigned to L Company in 1909. He reenlisted in that company seven times, serving in Alaska, on the Punitive Expedition, and in World War I. Like Vanderhook, he served a thirty-year hitch; and, like Vanderhook, his retirement in February 1930 was an occasion for a parade, held by the 3rd Battalion at Fort Wadsworth.[26] These are but two examples of the many soldiers who spent a goodly portion of their adult lives in the 16th Infantry Regiment.

Private Henry G. Keefer, from Scranton, Pennsylvania, was another special 16th Infantryman. He joined the regiment at Fort Jay in 1925 after serving six years in the merchant marine. He was assigned to Service Company and had been in the army only a few months when he was faced with an emergency that required his quick action. In November 1925, while aboard the ferryboat *General Otis* en route from New York City to Governors Island, he observed a man falling from the vessel into the icy waters of Upper New York Bay. Leaping overboard, the courageous private rescued the man, saving his life. Keefer's heroic deed might have earned him the Soldier's Medal, but no one thought to recommend him for the award. Subsequently transferred to Fort Sam Houston, he returned four years later to Governors Island as member of the Disciplinary Barracks Guard Detachment, and was involved in another dramatic incident.

In December 1929, several military prisoners were unloading coal at Pier A on the island. Suddenly, one of the prisoners grabbed a shotgun from a guard and leaped onto a tug moored at the pier and barricaded himself in the forecastle. The sentries fired several shots at the man but failed to hit him. Keefer heard the shots and, though not on duty, grabbed a gun from one of the guards and went after the man. While both guards and prisoners watched, Keefer made his way forward to the front of the boat where the prisoner lay in wait with his shotgun at the ready. Though the man had a clear field of fire, the spunky private shouted, "Put your hands up in the air and come out on deck before I blow your head off!" Evidently, the man believed Keefer and did not have the guts to fight it out; a short time later, out he came with hands high. Unknown to the man, but well known to Keefer, was the fact that Keefer's gun was jammed and he could not have returned fire. This time, Keefer was awarded that long overdue Soldier's Medal.[27]

As in any unit in the Old Army, sports were a major pastime for the troops of the 16th Infantry. Proximity to the city afforded many opportunities to attend professional baseball and football games, rather than listen to them on radio. At least as popular, if not more so, were intramural games and matches between companies and other regiments.

Football was a regimental passion. The units of the 1st Division had a football league in which units hotly competed for the Cooper Trophy. Now, this was not the tag or flag football played by army units today. This was gridiron war, played in full pads and helmets, where the old saying, "If you can't beat 'em, hurt 'em," was taken to heart. To win for the regiment was everything, and the 16th Infantry wanted to win. The team was called the "Jaybirds," and, though the name sounds tame today, they proved their grit on the field. The team was so good, that it was not unusual for them to scrimmage against the New York Giants from time to time.

The Jaybirds typically played against teams from the 18th Infantry, 1st Tank Company, 1st Signal Company, 1st Brigade Headquarters Company, and Coast Artillery units in the New York City area. But the real competition was generally with the 1st Engineer Regiment from Fort DuPont, Delaware, which had won the Cooper Trophy in 1936. The team of New York's Own won the Cooper Trophy the following year, however, in a hard-fought game against the "Redlegs" from Fort Hoyle, Maryland. The Jaybirds were coached by Captain Thomas M. Crawford and led by Lieutenant "Woody" Stromburg, the 1936 team captain of the West Point football team. As ten thousand spectators watched, Stromburg romped the length of Ebbets Field in Brooklyn and secured an 8-0 victory, thereby winning the championship of the Second Corps Area for the 16th Infantry.[28]

The team evidently became overconfident after their win against the artillerymen, for the following week the Jaybirds were trounced by the team from Fort Hamilton 28-0. Nevertheless, the Fort Jay team went on to win the Cooper Trophy for the next two years, and went undefeated in 1939. Their winning record may have continued into 1940, for the magazine Our Army reported that the Jaybirds had defeated the tough 62nd Coast Artillery team from Fort Totten 9-0 that November.[29]

Marksmanship, like football, was a regimental forte. Though there were times when shooting scores fell short of excellence, by and large the 16th Infantry was the "shootin'ist" regiment in the "Red One." Each year, the men of the regiment participated in the standard round of marksmanship qualifications, and other team and individual sport shooting competitions. Qualification shooting was generally conducted on ranges at Camp Dix in the Spring, while competition firing was done on indoor ranges at home station. The competition shooting was conducted either shoulder to shoulder or by postal matches.

In the mid-1920s, the regiment's record was unimpressive. In 1926 and 1927, for example, it came in third out of the four infantry regiments in the division. For the 1928 target season, however, the regiment was number one and had seven companies that qualified 100 percent of their men with the 1903 Springfield rifle, as compared to only three, four, and two for the 18th, 26th, and 28th Infantry Regiments, respectively. All regimental machine gunners, 37mm gunners, and trench mortarmen qualified that year, as well as 93 percent of those soldiers armed with pistols.[30]

In 1929, the Infantry Journal reported that the 16th Infantry had the best overall marksmanship scores of all thirty-seven infantry regiments in the U.S. Army. The regiment qualified 100 percent of its riflemen, machine gunners, cannoneers (37mm guns), and trench mortarmen. Additionally, the regiment had the highest average rifle qualification score and achieved an average of 297.2 points per man.[31]

The regimental small-bore team coached by Lieutenant P. H. Kron also had a banner year. The team took first place in the division competition by shooting a total of 2,581 points out of a possible 2,800.[32] That April, the team defeated squads from the 3rd and 29th Infantry Regiments, and followed that feat by besting thirty-two teams from across the Second Corps Area. This last event netted them the title of the National Rifle Association Champion Gallery Rifle Team for the Second Corps Area. Later that spring, these shooters trounced the teams from the 4th and 7th Infantry Regiments. The team went on to win eleven of twelve matches during the 1930 season and came in second in the only match it failed to win.[33]

That same year, the Howitzer Platoon reported that for the fourth year in a row, 100 percent of its gunners qualified with their weapons. The achievement is more impressive when one notes that all gunners achieved the rating of Gunner, First Class, or better, during the same period.[34] The following year, 1931, Company E won first place in the 1st Division for company-sized units, and a squad under Corporal Edward M. Fitzgerald from I Company went on to win the national title of the "Chief of Infantry's Combat Team" that same year.[35]

Though army life in the 1920s and 30s was not particularly rigorous, and there was plenty of opportunity to participate in sports and other pastimes, men in the civilian world were not necessarily knocking down doors to enlist. The 1920s was a decade of prosperity, pacifism, and generally good times. It was hard to convince young men to commit themselves to a regimented lifestyle. This was especially true for units in the New York City area. Though the population density was high, so too were the job opportunities in the bustling metropolis. Naturally, recruiting was difficult and, therefore, taken seriously by everyone from the regimental commander down.

In 1920, the army established a recruiting system that gave each infantry regiment a geographical area, generally one state, from which to recruit. Because they were stationed at

Camp Taylor at the time, the units of the 1st Division were given those states near Kentucky to recruit from, and the 16th Infantry was allotted the state of West Virginia. That system was soon abandoned as impractical due to the frequent moves by the various regiments around the country. Upon assignment to Fort Jay, the regiment absorbed a number of men from the 22nd Infantry who had not been transferred with that regiment to Fort McPherson, Georgia, but the 16th was still well short of its authorized peacetime strength. So, in December 1922, Colonel Gerhardt committed his troops to a recruiting drive in the city to fill the ranks.

On the cold morning of January 3, 1923, six hundred men were ferried to Battery Park, and from there, marched up Whitehall Street and Broadway, with the band playing and flags flying, all the way to city hall. Waiting for them there was a huge crowd of New Yorkers, curious to see the parade of troops, and Murray Holbert, the president of the City Board of Aldermen. While the men stood in mass formation before the steps of city hall, their frosty breaths clung to the cold air like so many steam vents, Holbert addressed the soldiers to express the city's support for their efforts. After Holbert's remarks and encouragement, the regiment was broken up into four-man teams and assigned recruiting sectors all over the city. The 1st Battalion teams were assigned to Manhattan, the 2nd Battalion to the Bronx, and the 3rd Battalion took station in Brooklyn. The recruiting effort continued for the next week with the goal of recruiting 250 men. The results of the first day's endeavor, reported in the New York Times, netted forty-four new recruits for the 16th Infantry. However, only nine were accepted for service.[36] The New York Times did not report the final tally, but given the results of the first, it is doubtful the goal was reached.

Some eighteen months later, the regiment's strength had dwindled again. By then, five hundred men were needed to flesh out the 16th Infantry just to meet peacetime authorizations.

Colonel Stanley H. Ford, regimental commander, was inspired by the successes of the 2nd Division's recruiting in Texas, and decided to give it a go in New York. This time, however, he determined to attempt a statewide drive in which only two hundred men would be recruited from the city and three hundred from the rest of New York state. This drive began on August 5, but apparently it was not successful either, for on September 9, the New York Times reported the opening of a second drive in which the regiment was attempting to recruit four hundred from the city alone.[37]

One recruit netted in the drive that autumn was Wilhelm Giesecke. Giesecke had had an interesting life before settling for a stint at Fort Jay. During the Great War, he had been a gunner on a German battleship and had participated in the Battle of Jutland. Shortly thereafter, he transferred to the submarine service, becoming a U-Boat crewman. On Good Friday 1918, his submarine was forced to the surface by a British destroyer after suffering damage in an attack. Once on the surface, Giesecke and several other crewmen leaped into the sea before

the submarine sank. He was rescued from the icy waters by the crew of the British destroyer and later made his way to the States after the war.[38]

The recruiting drives of the 1920s seemed to consistently fall short of the mark. Part of the problem was due to the previously noted poor living conditions for some units, and part was that much of the soldiers' time was spent in renovating the old posts they occupied in 1922. The posts had suffered neglect during the war years and took some time to get back into shape. By the late 1920s, however, army-wide morale had improved, and especially in the 1st Division. As the Infantry Journal reported in 1929:

> The 1st Division is sharing in the upward trend of morale that has been noticeable in the Regular Service for some time. An important indication of this is that the number of court-martial trials in the division is becoming smaller. For 1929 it was 500 less than in 1927. The improved morale of the division has not just happened. It is the result of careful planning and hard work. All posts of the division have been put into shape again after having become down at the heel during the war. Now that the work is done the amount of fatigue is greatly reduced and there is time for more military training and for athletics and recreations....Modern barracks are nearing completion in some of the divisional posts and are under construction in others.[39]

The improvements noted above not only increased the morale of the regiment, they also contributed to greater recruiting success in the 1930s—though the onset of the Great Depression was a factor in bringing more men into the army. Regardless of the reasons, by January 1936, the U.S. Army Recruiting News was able to report that the New York Recruiting District was having outstanding success bringing in new recruits in a special drive held from July through September 1935. The report stated that the 16th Infantry, which had a substantial number of men out helping to recruit, gained 361 new men, which was more than any other unit in the district.[40]

In addition to the drives, there was a marked upward trend in volunteer enlistments, by men who didn't need the prompting of recruiters. One such volunteer was the diminutive Henry S. Orten of Hoboken, New Jersey. Seventeen years old and just a little over five feet tall, Orten strolled into the recruiting office at 39 Whitehall Street in Manhattan, was examined and accepted, and offered duty with the coast artillery, military police, or the infantry. When told that an infantry unit was stationed on Governors Island within a short distance of his hometown, and therefore near his girlfriend, Orten determined to join "New York's Own." Handed his enlistment papers, he was told to report to the South Ferry at the Battery for transportation to his new home.

Standing at the dock near the ferry were two 16th Infantry

soldiers on military police duty, who checked passes and otherwise assisted soldiers and members of the public. Orten eyed them as he approached, and it seemed to him that the man in charge, a corporal, was the epitome of a soldier. The man was Corporal William McLaughlin, a self-confident, well-built, tough soldier who wore his uniform like a glove. McLaughlin was a native of Brooklyn and had joined the army when he was sixteen years old. On this day, he was all of twenty; but to Orten, he appeared to be a much older and experienced man. As Orten sauntered up to the men, McLaughlin gazed upon him in return. Sheepishly, Orten offered his papers to the corporal, who looked at the documents, frowned, then sized up the recruit standing in front of him. Shaking his head, he turned to his fellow MP, and, in his inimitable Brooklyn accent, growled, "What the hell is this army coming to?" That was Henry Orten's introduction to the 16th Infantry, and his acquaintance with a man Orten would later discover was exactly the soldier McLaughlin appeared to be.[41]

Ceremonies consumed much of the time and energy of the regiment during its stay at Governors Island. The regiment participated in these events so often that it developed a reputation in some circles for being a "show regiment" rather than a combat unit. Given the lack of training dollars in the 1920s and '30s, however, it was a reputation that probably fit most infantry units at that time. At Fort Jay, ceremonial events tended to be one of three kinds: organization days, parades, and reviews.

Following World War I, the War Department instituted a program requiring each regiment to declare a date considered important in its history. The date could be the actual unit activation date or a date that had other special significance (such as dates of battles), and would be considered the unit's "Organization Day." On January 17, 1920, Lieutenant Colonel Charles W. Ryder, executive officer and acting commander, replied to the War Department that October 4 would be the regiment's Organization Day to commemorate the 16th Infantry's singular achievement in capturing Fléville in 1918.[42]

Throughout the period between the wars, Organization Day was celebrated almost religiously in the 16th Infantry. Though it occurred only once a year, much time went into its planning and execution. The earliest account of this annual event is found in the *New York Times* in 1923. The celebration was held at Governors Island and was attended by Brigadier General William S. Graves, commanding general of the 1st Division, and over seven hundred spectators. The regiment was drawn up on Fléville Field, where Colonel Gerhardt administered the oath of office to all officers and enlisted men to impress upon them the importance of their service to the country. The adjutant followed by reviewing the regiment's history; then General Graves addressed the troops on the significance of the day. Gerhardt and Graves then participated in a brief ceremony, in which the general attached the campaign streamers to the regimental color. Following the review, the troops engaged in intramural sports, ate a picnic dinner and,

later that evening, attended a dance and vaudeville shows on post until "Taps" recalled them to their barracks.[43] Though few enlisted soldiers were married in those days, families of both men and officers were invited to attend. Sweethearts and friends from across the bay were also welcomed.

There was no Organization Day per se in 1924, which is not to say that there was no celebration. Indeed, October 4, 1924, was a special day in the history of the regiment, one that saw the 16th Infantry participating in ceremonies attendant to the unveiling of the 1st Division War Memorial in Washington, D.C. Two days previously, some forty-two officers and 1,120 enlisted men of the 16th and 18th Infantry Regiments boarded the USAT *St. Mihiel* in New York Harbor and sailed to the nation's capital. From the landing dock, the regiments moved to Fort Washington, Maryland, where they were billeted for their stay. On the morning of October 4, the 16th and 18th Infantry Regiments, both understrength, formed a single composite regiment and marched to the monument, which had been erected near the Ellipse. There, the composite regiment was formed before the grandstand, upon which stood President Calvin Coolidge, Major General Summerall, and numerous dignitaries. After the requisite oratory by Coolidge and Summerall, the massed bands of the 16th and 18th Infantry Regiments played "America." Then, Private First Class Dan Edwards, a Medal of Honor recipient and a true American hero, unveiled a gleaming white column upon which stood the bronze angel of "Victory." On the base was inscribed the names of division soldiers who had been killed in action or had died of wounds during the Great War. The monument was a fitting tribute to the thousands of 1st Division men who had given their best, and their all, in the service of the United States; and its unveiling was an appropriate way to celebrate the regiment's Organization Day.[44]

The pattern for Organization Day was generally set by the 1923 festivities. The succeeding celebrations varied only in size and number of activities. The 1925 Organization Day, for example, varied little from that of 1923. The main change was that the noncommissioned officers assumed command of the regiment and led it through the review. It was a novel twist and one that became a common sight at a number of 16th Infantry reviews during the period.[45]

Reviews were also a common activity of the 16th Infantry. These were generally conducted for arriving or departing commanders or for the retirement of long-service men. On one occasion, the regiment went further than expected. In November 1926, Major General Summerall, Commanding General of the Second Corps Area, received orders to become the chief of staff of the army. Summerall had been the wartime commander of the 1st Division and, though he was a hard-driving commander, the troops knew he loved the "Fighting First" and were glad to have the old boy around on Governors Island. The headquarters for the Second Corps Area was located just a short distance from the regimental area and General

Summerall undoubtedly felt somewhat nostalgic on the morning of November 19 when he walked over to Fléville Field to take this last review as the Second Corps Area commander. Upon completion of the review, the entire regiment marched with him down to the docks to see him off at the ferry. As the ferryboat pulled away, the band played "Auld Lang Syne."[46]

In April 1933, Secretary of War George H. Dern traveled to New York City for a meeting with executives from the Panama Railroad Company. Headquarters, Second Corps Area, tasked the 1st Division to support the secretary's visit, and the 16th Infantry was chosen as the support unit. The meeting was held at Park Avenue and 66th Street in the city, and cooks from the regiment were detailed to go over to the armory of the 7th New York Regiment to prepare the luncheon meal. The executives did not get the pheasant under glass they might have been expecting. Instead, they received standard army fare—pork chops, "slum rice," applesauce, and other army delicacies. The secretary seemed satisfied, however, and after the meeting ended, he was ferried to Fort Jay for a regimental review. He concluded his visit by inspecting the troops, facilities, and barracks at Fort Jay. The secretary was well pleased with the regiment.[47]

Three other notable garrison activities were "sham battles," "Transportation Shows," and "Field Days." Conducting sham battles for public entertainment was nothing new for the 16th Infantry—the regiment had conducted such a battle at the 1920 reunion of the 1st Division. When Colonel Croft was asked by the Army Relief Society to help raise money for the organization, he agreed to stage a public event designed to draw a crowd. The date set for the event was June 15, 1928. It featured a parade by the 107th Infantry (the old "7th New York") in their gray uniforms, a cavalry demonstration by troops of the 101st and 102nd Cavalry Regiments, and music provided by the bands of the 16th Infantry, 18th Infantry, 62nd Coast Artillery, and the U.S. Military Academy. The highlight of the entertainment, however, was to be the reenactment of the Battle of Fléville and the seizure of Hill 272 by the men of the 16th Infantry.[48]

A humorous incident occurred during the planning and execution of the event. The New York Times reported a story that the regimental executive officer, Lieutenant Colonel H. Clay Supplee, had difficulty locating farm animals for replicating the farms of Fléville. Not surprisingly, he had to travel outside the city to find the needed animals. When the Society for the Prevention of Cruelty to Animals (SPCA) caught wind of the plan to use animals, it lodged a protest, declaring that the animals might suffer pain in the sham battle or "mental anguish" from hearing the blanks fired. Supplee assured them that the animals would not suffer "one moment of pain."[49]

On the big day, twenty-five thousand New Yorkers paid to see the show. New York Governor Alfred E. Smith officiated as the guest speaker for the opening ceremonies, which were attended by Major General Hanson Ely, commander of the

Second Corps Area, and Major General William M. Haskell, commander of the 27th Division, New York National Guard. After the parade of the 107th Infantry and the cavalry demonstration, the 16th Infantry went into action. Supported by the guns of the 104th Field Artillery, the infantrymen began their attack on a replica of Fléville built on the polo grounds. As they advanced, tanks from the 1st Tank Company rumbled up to support with machine-gun fire. Planes of the 5th Observation Squadron from Mitchell Field on Long Island simulated German aerial attacks, as the antiaircraft guns of the 62nd Coast Artillery banged away in response. Artillery pits, dug to simulate impacting artillery rounds, exploded and added to the mosaic of sight and sound that thrilled the audience. "Refugees" fled the scene with their animals as the 16th Infantry approached. The village was taken by a final bayonet charge and, upon the fall of the town, the regimental band struck up "Over There" as the finale.[50]

The battle was a great success, and the Army Relief Society was pleased with the money raised. Lieutenant Colonel Supplee's troubles with the animals were not over, however; one of the goats, loaned by a "patriotic individual" from Staten Island, disappeared during the battle. Supplee sent out search parties of soldiers to locate the missing animal, but to no avail. A reporter from the Times questioned Supplee about the billy's fate, no doubt to see if any foul play was afoot. When asked what his thoughts were on the problem, with tongue in cheek Supplee simply replied, "It gets my goat."[51]

At 8:30 a.m. on June 23, six days after the sham battle, Corporal William Quinn of F Company was walking by the docks when he decided to get a drink of water from the fountain there. As he bent over to get a drink, his attention was suddenly attracted to movement not a yard away. It was the goat. "Well! And where in the name of Château-Thierry have you been, me bucko?" Quinn asked the goat, which responded by running off to seek protection under the docks. Quinn hollered to several other F Company men, who came to his assistance. They succeeded in cornering the goat, but two of them had to crawl under the dock to finally capture it. Much to the executive officer's relief, the goat was returned to its owner, and the SPCA's inquiries were no longer a concern.[52]

The event staged for the Army Relief Society the following year was the Battle of Cantigny. Both the 16th and 18th Infantry Regiments participated, making the show much bigger than its predecessor. The program was similar to the year before, but was stretched over two days.[53]

On November 11, 1929, the 16th Infantry took part in another sham battle, a reenactment of the capture of Exermont by the 18th Infantry. Held at Fort Hamilton, the battle was part of the eleventh annual reunion of the 1st Division veterans, and over two thousand of them made their way to New York to participate. This show was an even bigger affair than those staged at Governors Island, with the entire 1st Brigade and detachments of all units of the division involved. The supporting elements were essentially the same as described for the Fléville event, but, in a new twist, the men of the 16th Infantry were dressed as German soldiers. They had to oppose the American advance, and, to no one's surprise, they came out second best.[54]

The regimental "Transportation and Horse Shows" were also big affairs for men of the 16th. This was especially the case for those in the Service Company and in the heavy weapons companies (D, H, and M) because of the high density of draught animals in those units. These shows were held up to three times a year and consisted of a series of inspections and competitions to determine the best team in each category. The event generally began with the mules and equipment drawn up for inspection on Fléville Field. The equipment included the supply wagons from each company, machine-gun carts, and field kitchens. In later years, the formation included the motor trucks and motorcycles of the regiment. Each piece of equipment was inspected for serviceability and cleanliness, the mules and horses for health and grooming, and the soldiers for appearance and knowledge. After the formal inspections the judges moved on to the gymkhana, where mule racing, mounted wrestling, mounted tug-of-war, and engine trouble-shooting races were judged. There was even a contest for buglers, but as one wag observed, "it was probably the only time in the history of the Army that a bugler received a smile and a ripple of applause for blowing 'reveille.'"[55]

Whereas the Transportation Shows gave the support soldiers an opportunity to show their stuff, "Field Days" were a big event for all soldiers of the regiment. Field Days started off with a barracks inspection in the morning, followed by an in-ranks inspection and review. The formal portion of the activity was followed by a series of intramural competitions: football, baseball, basketball, and shooting. Individual awards were given for the "Best Turned Out" (uniform and equipment) soldier and team trophies for the company teams that won the sport competitions. The "Best Turned Out" company won the most highly coveted award, however, which was a simple blue "pennant" (streamer). The pennant was awarded for the highest combined scores in the inspections, marching, and various competitions, and was carried on the company's guidon until the following Field Day.

Soldiering at Fort Jay offered many attractions not available to the average soldier of the 1920s and '30s. In addition to having a front row seat for observing the New York City skyline, there were the entertainments of the city itself. Baseball games were especially popular. The city boasted three professional teams—the New York Yankees, New York Giants, and Brooklyn Dodgers—and tickets to the games were available to servicemen at reduced prices. There was also the Giants football team, and the Rangers and Americans hockey teams. Boxing matches at Madison Square Garden featured eminent pugilists such as Joe Louis, Jim Braddock, Max Schmeling, and Lou Ambers. Soldiers also took ferries to Brooklyn to visit the world-famous Coney Island amusement park, or traveled on excursion boats up the majestic Hudson River to view the beautiful terrain and regal mansions along its banks. For those soldiers with sophisticated tastes (and, to be sure, there were some), Broadway's show lights beckoned. There were also the New York Public Library, Museum of Natural History, and numerous art galleries.[56] Of course, there were more prurient pursuits, and the troops availed themselves of these as well.

The soldiers of the 16th Infantry were highly regarded by the citizens of New York. In part this sentiment was attributable to the efforts of the various commanders of the regiment, who had done so much to foster good public relations. However, it was also attributable to the fact that many men in the regiment originally hailed from one of the five boroughs. Indeed, the recruiting drives of the 1920s and '30s tended to give the regiment a distinctly New York flavor. In any event, the regiment soon became known affectionately as "New York's Own." In response to this genuine feeling of acceptance, it was only natural that the regiment would adopt the well-known tune, "Sidewalks of New York," as its regimental song, which it retains to this day.

Hardly a week went by during the interwar years without the 16th Infantry participating in some sort of activity in the city. Among the most popular with New Yorkers was the ceremonial guard mount held every Sunday evening in Battery Park on Manhattan's southern tip, just across from Governors Island. Performed to the accompaniment of the regimental band, the ceremony inevitably drew large crowds.

A special guest at one of the ceremonies was the then-famous child movie star called "Baby Peggy." Her real name was Diana Serra Cary, and she was the first famous child actress and easily the most popular of young stars in the silent movie era. By the time of the "talkies," she had become too old and her mantle was assumed by stars such as the Little Rascals and, later, Shirley Temple. Baby Peggy celebrated her fifth birthday with a publicity tour to New York City. She began the day at a large banquet in the ballroom of the Biltmore Hotel, and went from there to the Gimbel Brothers' toy store to hand out scores of Baby Peggy dolls to her fans. She was then taken to Battery Park, where the 16th Infantry performed a review in her honor. Upon conclusion of the review, Baby Peggy was made the honorary "Daughter of the Regiment" and presented a regimental crest by Colonel Gerhardt.[57]

Parades were frequent and provided an excellent opportunity for the regiment to shine. New York's annual Armistice Day and Fourth of July parades always included a contingent from the 16th. In June 1923, a battalion of the 16th marched in opening ceremonies for Jersey City's newly built Pershing Field; the following spring found the regimental band and a detachment of troops up in the Bronx, parading at Yankee Stadium on opening day of the 1924 baseball season.[58]

Sometimes a parade failed to go according to plan. In 1928, the Veterans of Foreign Wars requested 16th Infantry participation in a parade to celebrate the 106th birthday of

Ulysses S. Grant. The regimental contingent was to form at 116th Street and Broadway and, led by the band and the color guards of the 16th Infantry and the VFW, the troops would march to Grant's Tomb, located on the Upper West Side at Riverside Drive and West 122nd Street. As the men were assembling, however, Captain Daniel Kelleher of the New York Police Department ambled up to the parade leaders and informed them that the city had refused to issue the requisite march permit. Barred from using the streets, the soldiers and VFW members strolled along sidewalks to their destination, where General Peter Traub and VFW Commander Jean A. Brunner awaited them on the speakers' platform. Traub and Brunner were both thoroughly surprised to see a mob of men sauntering up to Grant's Tomb in no apparent formation or order. Incensed, Traub remarked to a reporter:

> There surely must be some mistake. In all my forty years in the United States service I have never before heard of such a thing....I could hardly believe my eyes when I saw men walking along the sidewalk to the stand with the United States colors furled under their arms and the band walking silently alongside them. If the Police Commissioner gave orders to stop the parade, then it surely must have been one of those mistakes due to a lack of understanding.[59]

General Traub went on to say that he had never heard of a case, in any city, where permission for regular troops to parade, no matter what the occasion, had been denied.

As it happened, the permit was ordered withheld by no less a personage than New York City Mayor James J. Walker. Two weeks earlier, a speaker at a ceremony held by the Sons of Union Veterans of the Civil War had criticized the mayor, first for attending the unveiling of a Confederate memorial, and later for allowing the the great-grandson of Robert E. Lee (who was also present at the unveiling) to participate in a welcoming ceremony for the German liner *Bremen*. Walker decided to punish the VFW for the speaker's comments, even though the VFW was in no way associated with the Sons of Union Veterans.[60]

Providing guards of honor for distinguished visitors to New York was another duty the regiment frequently performed on the city's behalf. In 1927, the 16th provided both honor guard and escort for General Wilhelm Heyes of the German Troop Office (in actuality, Germany's discreetly renamed General Staff, outlawed by the Versailles Treaty); in 1931, it provided the honor guard for Japan's Prince Takamatsu and his wife.[61]

Also in 1931, the regiment was selected to provide the guard of honor for Marshal Philippe Pétain and General Pershing, who were attending a ceremony commemoration the sesquicentennial of the victory at Yorktown. The guard, along with the band and the color guard, formed at Pennsylvania Station to meet Pétain's train; upon the marshal's arrival, the band struck up a rousing march, and the crowd, stirred by the music, cheered Pershing and his guest. After the customary oratory and other welcoming formalities had been dispensed with, Pétain and Pershing went to the Waldorf-Astoria Hotel, escorted by the regiment's guard detachment.[62]

The regimental band was especially busy during the inter-war years. As already mentioned, the band participated in numerous parades, guard mount ceremonies, and recruiting drive galas. When the Princeton University ROTC corps of cadets passed in review before Major General Frank R. McCoy, Second Corps Area commander, the band provided the music. During the summer months, it could be heard on Monday, Tuesday, and Thursday evenings, performing free for the public on Governors Island.[63]

In the 1930s, the band also had its own weekly radio program on WYNC, playing popular and martial music on broadcasts heard throughout the state. In 1934, Warrant Officer Harry Bradley, the assistant band leader, received a letter from one of the program's many listeners, Mrs. Charles Streeman of Oswego. Requesting that the band perform certain old tunes— "Philadelphia," "The Caliph of Bagdad," "Austrian Reveille," "The Huguenots," and the grand march from *Il Trovatore*— Mrs. Streeman informed Bradley that her father had been the 16th Infantry's band leader from 1870 to 1895; what is more, her father had directed the band in the playing of the aforenamed pieces in concert on October 17th, 1886, shortly after Colonel Blunt had taken command at Fort Concho, Texas. She went on to write:

> [T]hrough your kindness Mr. Bradley, I will again listen to a concert rendered by the dear 16th Infantry Band, a repetition of one led by my father, Arthur Fuessal at this very old Fort, way back in 1886. The concert took place at 4 p.m. on [the] parade ground....I can picture it all, the men on the barrack's porches; the Colonel with friends on the veranda; the band with little iron music racks; my dear father with baton in hand leading; what happy recollections this programme will recall. Words cannot describe my appreciation of your kindness in this matter.[64]

Little favors like these further endeared the regiment to the people of the New York City area.

A city like New York has no shortage of interesting events. There was always some big exhibition or celebration going on, and the regiment was frequently involved in some manner. In the summer of 1932, the city hosted the George Washington Bicentennial Exhibition to celebrate Washington's 200th birthday. As part of the event, Company A set up a model military camp in Bryant Park on 40th Street, just off Times Square. The troops built an orderly tent city along one edge of the park and set up displays near a replica of the old "Federal Hall," which had served as the first War Department building and was the site of Washington's first inauguration. The 1st Division's 1st Tank Company displayed a Renault tank, and the 62nd Coast Artillery from Fort Totten set up one of its 3-inch antiaircraft guns. Additionally, several old and new artillery pieces were on display, and the camp had a small theater where one could view the latest Army News Service film clips as well as silent and "talkie" films. Admission was free to the theater and all the displays.[65]

Duty at the camp proved a mixed blessing for the troops. On the one hand, it entailed only light chores plus the opportunity to roam the city when not on duty; on the other hand, it afforded the soldiers little privacy or creature comforts. Bathroom facilities were nonexistent: the troops had to load on Liberty trucks and travel to a nearby YMCA for showers. The mess hall was an open-air affair and, when in operation, there was no shortage of the ubiquitous "knights of the road" panhandling for hand-outs. A few bums even brought their own plates.

Additionally, the exhibition occurred shortly after an incident involving U.S. Army troops and members of the so-called Bonus Expeditionary Force. The latter, also known as the "Bonus Army," was a group comprising some twelve to fifteen thousand impoverished World War I veterans. Starting in the spring the veterans, with their families in tow, had descended on Washington, D.C., to demand immediate payment of military service benefits. On July 28, following Congress's refusal to meet their demand (payment was scheduled until 1945), many veterans rioted, and army troops were sent to expel them from their ramshackle encampment on the Anacostia River.

In New York, representatives of the Communist Party, seizing upon this episode as an opportunity for progandanzing, set up soapboxes across the street from Company A's tents to harangue "fellow workers" about the evils of war and the need to organize to fight against war. When the little band of Communists first showed up outside the camp it was thought that troops might have to expel them too. However, it soon became obvious that they were not going to be a problem, and that their real aim was to sell Communist Party tracts. Thereafter, the troops settled down and did what soldiers generally did in such circumstances—they took bets on how many tracts would be sold. Someone figured out that the twenty-one different observed speakers had managed to sell a grand total of three tracts at a nickel a piece.[66]

The years that the 16th Infantry spent at Fort Jay saw many changes in the regiment. Though many of the enlisted men spent year after year in the regiment, the officers came and went. This was especially true of the regimental commanders. Unlike the pre-Great War commanders, who often spent five years and more in command, the "old man" of the 1920s and '30s averaged only two years as the colonel of the regiment. Interestingly, few of the regimental commanders of this period were West Pointers. In fact, only three of the twelve commanders from 1920 to 1940 were Military Academy graduates, whereas virtually all of the regimental executive officers were.

Colonel Charles Gerhardt assumed command from Colonel Lacey on September 1, 1922. Gerhardt was an 1887 graduate from the academy and served initially with the 8th Infantry at Fort Assinniboine, Montana. With the 8th Infantry he had participated in establishing the cordon of units surrounding the Pine Ridge Agency following the Wounded Knee incident in December 1890. During the Spanish-American War, he served with the 23rd Infantry in Cuba and then accompanied that regiment on its subsequent tour in the Philippines. During the Great War, Gerhardt commanded the 4th Infantry Regiment and was promoted to brigadier general to command the 183rd Infantry Brigade in early 1918. After the war, he commanded the 36th Infantry at Fort Snelling, Minnesota, and attended the Army War College before assuming command of the 16th Infantry.

Gerhardt was succeeded by another academy man, Colonel Edgar T. Collins. Collins, however, never actually joined the regiment, though he was officially appointed as commander on September 1, 1924. He was promoted to brigadier general within a month of his assignment and reassigned elsewhere.

Colonel Stanley H. Ford was the next commander. He had been commissioned after receiving a degree from Ohio State University and assigned to the 16th Infantry in July 1898, a few days after the regiment's charge up San Juan Hill. He went with the regiment to the Philippines, and was promoted and transferred to the 25th Infantry in June 1899. After three years in the Philippines, he returned to Fort Sill, where he was selected to attend the General Service and Staff School at Fort Leavenworth in 1904. During the next four years he served with the 5th Infantry at Plattsburg Barracks, New York, and in Cuba. While in Cuba, he became involved with quartermaster duties and as a result served in that capacity for four years, including a tour on the Quartermaster General's staff in Washington, until 1912. In 1914, he was ordered to Tientsen, China, where he served with the 15th Infantry there until World War I. During the war, he served in several capacities, including as an observer with the British 39th Division, and as chief of staff of the 27th Division during its entire tour of combat duty. After the war, Ford attended the War College and was assigned as the chief of the Military Training Section of the War Plans Division in the War Department.[67] He was serving in the latter capacity when ordered to assume command of the 16th Infantry on December 11, 1924. Ford would later command the 1st Division in 1936.

The next two commanders both had the honor of being selected to be chiefs of infantry in the 1930s. Colonel Edward Croft, who commanded the regiment from December 20, 1926, to June 26, 1928, had commanded the 95th Division during the World War. He went on to become the army's premier infantryman in 1933. Croft's successor, Colonel Stephen O. Fuqua, commanded the regiment from June 26, 1928, to March 27, 1929. Fuqua was a long-time member of the 16th Infantry and a World War I "Red One" veteran. Interestingly, Fuqua preceded Croft as the chief of infantry.

Colonel Albert S. Williams next commanded the 16th Infantry. One of the few officers who had the honor of commanding the regiment twice, he first took command in May 1929, but for a period of only ten months. He next commanded the regiment from September 1, 1934, to July 1, 1937. Those who remember him recall that he was a strict disciplinarian. Williams once upbraided a young lieutenant for merely having his hands in his pockets.[68]

The commander of the regiment in the interim of Williams's two tours was Colonel Joseph A. Marmon. Marmon's claim to fame was his marriage to the actress Pauline Frederick. A humorous incident involving Marmon and his famous wife occurred not long after they were married. One weekend, the regiment was staging a review that the colonel's lady was to attend. As she drove up to a road block en route to the reviewing stand, she encountered Private Martin "Paddy" Roughn efficiently manning his post. She demanded to be allowed through, but Roughn refused, having no clue as to who she was. An argument ensued, and the sergeant of the guard sauntered over to sort things out. The good sergeant quickly identified the colonel's lady and let her pass, much to her relief and to the sergeant's embarrassment.[69]

In addition to changes in command, the regiment also underwent several organizational changes between the wars. The first of these reorganizations involved the headquarters, and the headquarters companies, of the battalions. In a move that seemed to indicate a return to the prewar days, when there was no fixed battalion headquarters, the headquarters and headquarters companies were demobilized on September 6, 1922. This was apparently an economizing measure on the part of the War Department. The battalion commanders were assigned directly to the regimental headquarters, and the men from the headquarters companies were distributed among the companies of the regiment. The War Department soon realized that the move was a mistake and, a month later, the headquarters of the battalions were reconstituted, but consisted of only the commanders and two or three staff officers per headquarters.[70] The battalion headquarters companies, however, were not reconstituted until the eve of World War II.

Another change that occurred almost concurrently with the demobilization of the battalion headquarters companies was the partial inactivation of the howitzer company. The latter had been added to infantry regiments in 1920 so that howitzers might accompany attacking infantry. It had been a known shortfall during the war that infantry had no "hip pocket artillery" immediately responsive to their needs. The howitzer company was the solution. In reality, however, this misnamed organization was actually armed with one-pounder cannon and Stokes mortars and, by 1932, rearmed with 37mm cannon and 81mm mortars. On September 14, 1922, the howitzer company was reduced to one platoon, also an economy-minded move.

The next change involved the band. Before World War I, the band had been a separate organization but, at some point, apparently during the war, it had become an element of the Service Company. For some reason, the adjutant general of the army directed that bands once again be made separate units. This directive took effect on July 13, 1927.[71]

During the war, many commanders recognized the need for greater infantry mobility on the battlefield. Though not used as combat vehicles, trucks provided some of that mobility, particularly when moving troops behind the lines or moving some of the heavier equipment (e.g., machine guns). The truck was clearly superior to the horse in most leaders' minds. Trucks did not have to waste much space carrying their own fuel; they did not consume fuel when not in use; and they were quickly repairable when damaged. Trucks, moreover, did not take six months to "make" and a year to grow and train, like the horse. However, trucks were expensive, and the army was not rich.

By the early 1930s, logistical planners in the army realized that trucks, in the long run, were actually more cost effective than horses and mules, and began to replace animals with vehicles. Back in the fall of 1927, the 16th Infantry and several other infantry regiments had been partially motorized on a temporary basis for tactical experiments. During the 1st Brigade annual maneuver in September at Camp Dix, the motorized 16th Infantry had maneuvered against the 18th Infantry, with encouraging results.

Based on positive reports from such exercises, the War Department began to take small steps toward motorization. In April 1932, 180 mules and the wagons of the 16th Infantry's Service Company were replaced by trucks, trailers, and motorcycles. The mules in the headquarters and machine-gun companies were retained to haul ammo trailers and pull gun mounts, leaving only thirty-four mules and twenty-four horses in the regiment. Just three years later, in March 1935, the *New York Times* trumpeted, "16th Infantry Formally Marks the End of Horse Transport," when the regiment loaded up on trucks for the trip to Camp Dix for that summer's training activities. Just the week before, the remainder of the regiment's mules and horses were transferred to other units, and new trucks were issued.[72]

This new form of transportation required new means of training and maintenance. Gone were the curry combs, anvils, and pitchforks of the old days. Now, photographs of cutaway engines, diagrams of the four-stroke process, and wiring diagrams lined the walls of stables, now used as maintenance bays for vehicles, with tools, oil, and spare parts replacing bins of grain and hay.

To train the operators of these new machines, the regiment organized a motor school at Fort Jay under the supervision of Captain Charles Carlton, the Service Company commander. Having established the school in the Service Company's garage, Sergeant Peter Sikola, the regimental motor sergeant, acquired several demonstration motors to use for training. The soldiers Sikola trained were largely unfamiliar with motor vehicles. As a result, most of the classes focused on basic concepts of motor functions, maintenance, practical driving skills, and convoy procedures. Traffic cops from the New York City Police Department were also invited in to teach vehicle laws and basic traffic safety procedures.[73]

The motor school was a relatively unique idea and was thought to be the only regimental school of its type then in existence. It is also indicative of the drive, spirit, and ingenuity that the leaders of the regiment demonstrated toward training in general during this period, particularly in light of the minuscule budgets provided to the army. Drive and spirit in peacetime training is a hallmark of the 16th Infantry that has existed in the regiment up to the present day, and it certainly was in evidence in the 1920s and '30s.

The typical training year in the 16th Infantry began just after the regiment's return from Camp Dix in the fall. During late fall, the training focus was on individual, crew, and squad skills. Close order drill, crew drills, and inspections were the routine. This training was followed by unit schools, specialty skill schools, and platoon drills during winter months. Springtime brought theoretical marksmanship training in preparation for actual range firing. In May and June, "target practice" and weapons qualification was conducted at Camp Dix. Some years, marksmanship training was delayed until August or September, after training assistance to the reserve components was completed. Often, the machine-gun companies traveled to Pine Camp, New York, to conduct their qualification training on the excellent machine-gun ranges there. After marksmanship training was completed, a portion of the regiment generally stayed at Camp Dix to support the training of the infantry regiments of the 77th and 78th Divisions and the infantry ROTC camp or to run the CMTC. The training support of the reserve components was usually followed by the maneuvers of the 1st Infantry Brigade in August or September, and sometimes as late as October. The cycle would then begin anew.

The annual summer training at Camp Dix was the training highlight of the year. Typically, the scenario had several companies move to Dix in mid-May to set up the tent cantonments for the reserve component camps and prepare to receive the incoming personnel for inprocessing. In the 1920s, the regiment conducted the ninety-mile move to Camp Dix by marching. Typically, units moved by ferry to Fort Hancock on Sandy Hook and camped there the first night. The following day, they began a four-day march to Camp Dix via Monmouth and Imslaytown. By 1933, however, the journey was conducted in only one day—by truck.[74]

The infantry ROTC units from the Second Corps Area began to arrive in late May, and these camps generally lasted until late July. Support for the ROTC included the setting up and operating of weapons ranges, the cooking of meals, stocking of supply rooms, and other support duties. Though they set up the camps for them, soldiers of the regiment had little direct contact in the training of ROTC cadets. Most of the training was conducted by the officers and NCOs assigned to the various participating schools.

In contrast, the CMTC camps were run primarily by the officers and NCOs of the regiment, at least in the 1920s. As a group they comprised the cadre for the candidate companies and conducted all classes and field training. The individual cadres were there when the candidates went to bed at night, and they got them up in the morning. By the 1930s, however, the regiments of the 77th and 78th Divisions began to take turns every other year operating the CMTC camps. Because the CMTC camps lasted six weeks, it took two regiments of reserve officers to operate a single camp. One regiment ran the camp for three weeks, then the next regiment arrived to complete the final three weeks. It was a good system for training the reserve components. It gave the reserve officers practical experience in training troops, and it gave the CMTC candidates leaders who were more patient in dealing with young men who had not yet committed themselves to the rigors of long-term military service. Through it all, the regulars of the 16th Infantry were there to help both regiments of reserve officers and the transition of responsibilities between the two at mid-camp.

The 1935 camp is a good example of how the system worked. In early July, some 2,079 CMTC candidates arrived at the Camp Dix railroad station. There to greet them was Colonel Williams and the 16th Infantry Band. After the regimental commander's official welcome, the candidates were inprocessed by the officers and NCOs of the 16th, then organized into an infantry regiment of twelve companies. The regulars assigned barracks, issued uniforms, conducted classes on the wear of the uniform, and then turned the regiment over to the officers of the 305th Infantry, 77th Division. For the next three weeks, the reservists trained the candidates in one of the three courses, Red, White, or Blue. An individual was assigned to a course depending on whether it was the first, second, or third time he had been to a camp. The fourth-year students acted as unit officers and assistant instructors under the tutelage of their reserve officer counterpart. After three weeks, the 308th Infantry arrived and took over the reins. Upon conclusion of the camp, the regiment held a graduation review, and the fourth-year students were commissioned into the Organized Reserve as second lieutenants.[75]

The training relationships that the regiment had with the 77th and 78th Divisions were cordial. This was a time when military service was considered a patriotic duty, even among the wealthy, who could have easily avoided military service. As a result, both divisions had their share of important personages. For example, the division commander of the 77th Division was none other than Brigadier General Cornelius Vanderbilt, the business tycoon. Another was Colonel Julius Ochs Adler, commander of the 305th Infantry and general manager of the *New York Times*. Not only did members of the regiment train with these two divisions, they socialized with them as well. This was particularly true of the 77th Division, as it was located in New York City. It was not unusual for the officers of the 16th Infantry to be invited to attend various 77th-hosted regimental and division dinners at Christmas and on other occasions.

In addition to aiding the Organized Reserve units with CMTC training and providing logistic support, the 16th Infantry provided other training assistance to the 77th and 78th Divisions. An unusual but not rare method of aiding reserve officer summer training was for the officers of one of the reserve regiments to assume command of one of the 16th's battalions. The 305th Infantry trained with this method in the 1928 camp. In August of that year, forty-four officers of the 305th marched a battalion from New York City to Camp Dix in August and engaged in ten days of training.[76]

The National Defense Act of 1920 was responsible for this unusual training method. By law, the Organized Reserve could fill 100 percent of the authorized spaces for officers in any reserve unit, but could enlist soldiers to fill only 33 percent of the authorized enlisted spaces. Men who held commissions in the World War and the ROTC and CMTC programs kept the officer spaces largely filled in the 1920s and 30s, but there was no mechanism to recruit and train enlisted men for the Organized Reserve. Only enlisted personnel leaving the active army were eligible to join the reserve, which kept the Enlisted Reserve Corps strength down to an average of about three thousand men nationwide in the 1920s and '30s. As a result, reserve units had a difficult time adequately training for their wartime mission. This provision was politically motivated, of course, and ensured that the Organized Reserve posed no threat to the National Guard's status as the first-line reserve force for the army.

In the five years before World War II, training for the 16th Infantry and the army took on a more serious flavor. In 1935, the United States was five years into the Great Depression. Adolf Hitler was only two years into his leadership of the Third Reich, but already his actions and comments had startled the powers of Europe, though he had not yet jolted them to the realities of what was coming. Japan was still on relatively good terms with the United States, but even so the U.S. Navy was slowly preparing for war with that nation. Many military planners believed that war with Japan, while not inevitable, was very likely at some time in the future. The planners looked over the War and Navy Departments' "Color Plans" and revised them into what eventually became the "Rainbow Plans" of the late 1930s. All of these activities prompted Congress to allocate money for the upgrade of aircraft and the expansion of the Army Air Corps, the provision of new ships for the navy.

For the army, assistance came in the way of funding for major maneuvers and command post exercises. Starting in 1935, the War Department was allocated enough money to conduct an army-level command post exercise in one army area and a full-fledged army maneuver in another each year. The department's long-range plan was to conduct a command post exercise in each of the four army areas once every four years (rotated from year to year), followed by a full-blown maneuver in that army area in the next fiscal year. This allowed the three components (Regulars, National Guard, and Reserve) in each army area to train together on a fairly regular basis and give army and corps area staffs experience in the mobilization and management of large bodies of troops.

The First Army maneuver of 1935 was held at Pine Camp, New York (now Fort Drum), August 17-31. It was the first of the annual large-scale army exercises held each year before World War II. According to the First Army training memorandum issued for the operation, the stated objectives of the maneuver were: "to test the ability of the First Army to concentrate simultaneously…prepare for field service, train all echelons in logistics, and provide combined field training for all components of the First Army."[77] The participating units were the 1st Division of the Regular Army; the 26th Division, Massachusetts National Guard; the 27th Division, New York National Guard; the 43rd Division, National Guard of Connecticut, Rhode Island, Vermont, and New Hampshire; and the 44th Division, New Jersey National Guard. Individual officers of the 76th, 77th, 78th, 79th, 97th, and 98th Divisions of the Organized Reserve also participated, performing umpire, staff, and support duties. In all, about thirty-six thousand troops took part, making this the largest peacetime exercise ever held in the United States up to that time.

For the first time in several years, the entire 1st Division was concentrated in one location, in an assembly area at Gates Corners, northwest of Carthage, New York. The maneuver's first two exercises involved only National Guard divisions, but Exercise No. 3 was all Regular Army, predominantly involving the 1st Division. The division mission was to move from the assembly and attack a defending infantry regiment located at Pitcairn, twenty-five miles away. What made this attack unique was that the 16th Infantry units were moved by trucks to their jump-off lines near the enemy.

As the lead vehicles neared the dismount point, an umpire stepped out and halted the column. He informed the lead officer that if the column proceeded past that point, the unit would suffer 10 percent casualties in men in equipment. The officer replied, "Done!" and sped forward, followed by the rest of the column. The unit dismounted much nearer the objective than the script called for, and the regiment attacked sooner than the enemy expected. Owing to the rapid move and the bold decision by the lead commander, the regiment secured its objectives and the exercise ended several hours earlier than planned.

The next two exercises involved the provisional I and II Corps in a force-on-force scenario. The 1st Division, reinforced with the mechanized reconnaissance elements of the 1st Cavalry Regiment, the tanks of the 67th Infantry (Tanks), and the 62nd Coast Artillery, was attached to the II Corps for Exercise No. 4, then transferred to the control of the I Corps for the final two-day exercise.

During a break between exercises, Major General Lucius Holbrook directed the bands of the division to conduct concerts in various towns in the area for public relations purposes. The 16th Infantry Band, under the leadership of Warrant Officer William C. White, conducted a concert in Watertown on August 23. The performance was held in the city park and several hundred citizens attended. The efforts of the band were well-received and reduced much of the anxiety local people had about having so many troops in the area.[78]

After the First Army maneuvers, the regiment returned to Fort Jay to begin its typical winter garrison regimen. The following February, another thirty-year man retired from the regiment. On the 28th, Master Sergeant Robert Sadusky, of the regimental Headquarters Company, was tendered a regimental review. Sadusky had served with the regiment in Mexico and in World War I. He had served in eight battles during the war and had been awarded the Distinguished Service Cross for heroic exploits in combat.[79]

A month later, the regiment paraded on Fléville Field for Major General Frank S. Parker's retirement. Parker had commanded the 1st Infantry Brigade in many of the regiment's actions in World War I and commanded the 1st Division during the Sedan drive. He was once again leaving command of the "Red One," and it was the 16th Infantry that he chose to see him off at the end of his career.[80]

The new division commander was the regiment's own Stanley H. Ford, now a major general. However, Ford was in command for only six months before the regiment paraded for his departure on September 28, 1936. Unlike his predecessor, Ford was not retiring; he was taking command of the Seventh Corps Area at Omaha, Nebraska. In this parade, "New York's Own," 850 men strong, passed in review (as prescribed in the new infantry drill regulations) for the very first time using the massed block formation that is the basis of drill still used in the army.[81]

The summer of 1937 was the three hundredth anniversary of the settlement of Governors Island. Colonel Williams ensured that the 16th Infantry was in the middle of the planning and participation of the island's Tercentenary Celebration. First was a parade for the public at Fléville Field on June 18. This event was followed by a mechanized demonstration performed by the 1st Cavalry Regiment (Mechanized).[82] This was the first time New Yorkers had seen the army's mechanized force and they were impressed by the performance.

The day following the demonstration by the 1st Cavalry, the 16th Infantry passed in review for Williams, who had been ordered to the University of Pennsylvania to be the P.M.S.& T (Professor of Military Science and Tactics).[83] Taking his place as regimental commander was Colonel Karl Truesdell, who assumed command at a July 3 review. Like many of the regimental commanders of the 1920s and '30s, Truesdell started his career as an enlisted man. After achieving the rank of sergeant, Truesdell was commissioned a second lieutenant of infantry in

1904. He served first in the infantry and then was transferred to the Signal Corps in 1912. In 1918, he went to France and served initially with the 33rd Division. He also served with the 26th Division and was ultimately assigned to the "Fighting First," with which he participated in the Cantigny, St.-Mihiel, and Meuse-Argonne campaigns. After the war, he attended the Staff School, the War College, and the Naval War College and, from 1932 to 1935, he served as executive officer for the 15th Infantry in Tientsen, China.[84] As commander, Truesdell led the regiment on its next major maneuver.

Early on the morning of September 2, 156 trucks and other vehicles, loaded with the troops of the 16th Infantry, were ferried across to Manhattan en route to summer maneuvers. From Manhattan, the convoy of vehicles made its way across the George Washington Bridge into New Jersey. A reporter observing the movement described the motorized regiment as a "snappy appearing, fast moving outfit" as it made its way across the city. The convoy motored to Indiantown Gap, Pennsylvania, which was normally the summer training site for the Pennsylvania National Guard. For the next two weeks, however, the Gap was the maneuver ground for exercises involving units of the 1st Division. This maneuver was special because it was the first time in several years the entire 16th Infantry had been assembled for tactical exercises. Usually, one company or another, or even a battalion, was left behind to watch the fort or conduct some other training activity, while the remainder of the regiment participated in the annual 1st Brigade autumn maneuvers.[85]

The highlight of this maneuver was an all-night movement and dawn attack made by the regiment against fixed defenses. The enemy was the 18th Infantry, which was dug in and conducting aggressive patrolling operations to prevent a surprise attack. Moving into an assembly area just before dawn, the regiment, with the 6th Field Artillery in support, was successful in taking its objectives. The operation almost failed, however, when the patrols of the 18th Infantry discovered the attack in its early stages.[86]

Arriving back at Fort Jay on September 16, Captain Edward J. O'Neill of Company F and Warrant Officer White of the Band were notified of a special mission. The two units were to comprise the honor guard for President Franklin D. Roosevelt's visit to Poughkeepsie, New York. The president was traveling to that city to help celebrate the 250th anniversary of its founding. In late October, the contingent, which also included the regiment's Drum and Bugle Corps, traveled to Poughkeepsie to serve as the president's escort. The visit was a hit with the residents of the city and was, no doubt, also a memorable occasion for the participating troops of the 16th.[87]

At the end of the month, all 1st Division units in the New York City metropolitan area were assembled at Fort Hamilton for the retirement of yet another division commander. This time, the review was for Brigadier General Perry Miles, who retired on October 31. Colonel Truesdell, as senior regimental commander, acted as the commander of troops for the occasion. Because Fort Hamilton was relatively small, the chief of staff decided to have only a portion of each of the units represented at the review. To represent those divisional units that were located outside the New York City area, the unit colors for the review were carried by soldiers of the 1st Infantry Brigade.[88]

On April 1, 1938, Colonel Truesdell was promoted to brigadier general and relieved of 16th Infantry command. The regiment conducted the customary review to give the new general a send-off to his new command, the 12th Infantry Brigade at Fort Sheridan, Illinois. Upon the review's conclusion, Truesdell gave his eagles to Lieutenant Colonel James L. Bradley, the regimental executive officer, and now, temporary commander of the 16th, in anticipation that he would soon need them. Present for this ceremony was old Colonel Harrell, who had retired as the regimental commander in 1920. Interestingly, Harrell had been Truesdell's first sergeant in the 73rd Coast Artillery Company when Truesdell had enlisted in 1901.

The annual summer training cycle followed close on the heel of Truesdell's departure. On May 23, Companies D, H, and M motored to Pine Camp for the 1st Division machine-gun and howitzer school. This annual camp had been established several years before to train the division's heavy weapons gunners. Gunners from all four regiments attended the training concurrently and participated in shooting competitions with the various weapons.[89]

Just before the remainder of the regiment departed for Camp Dix that summer, a memorial mass was held at Governor's Island on May 29 for the deceased members of the regiment. The New York National Guard's 165th Infantry, the old "Fighting Sixty-ninth," was invited to attend. This regiment was predominantly composed of Irish-Catholics from Brooklyn, and many men of the 16th Infantry came from the same neighborhoods. In all, some eight hundred men from the 165th and five hundred from the 16th Infantry attended the service.[90]

A week later, the new regimental commander arrived to take command from Lieutenant Colonel Bradley. He was Colonel Charles H. Rice, a West Point man. After his graduation from the academy before the World War, Rice had served with the 7th, 6th, and 1st Infantry Regiments at various locations in the United States. Overseas, Rice fought with the 4th and 90th Divisions in the AEF. Between the wars, he served as the G3 of the 7th Division; commander of the 2nd Battalion, 38th Infantry; and executive officer of that regiment. Rice had been an advisor to the Washington National Guard's 41st Division before coming to Fort Jay.[91]

In September 1938, the 1st Brigade conducted what was to be its last peacetime maneuver at Camp Dix. The exercise matched the 16th and 18th Infantry Regiments in a force-on-force battle. In one exercise, the 16th Infantry was ordered to attack the 18th in a situation reminiscent of its assault the year before at Indiantown Gap. This time, however, the 1st Tank Company was attached for the mission. Under near-wartime conditions, the 16th made its attack in protective masks through dust, smoke, and tear gas. With the tankers in support, the outcome was in little doubt, and the regiment carried the position. After the field training, Brigadier General Walter C. Short, the new division commander, inspected the regiment's camp. The general stated he was very impressed with the layout and later issued a commendation for the regiment's superior appearance.[92]

The year 1939 was to be a watershed for the 16th Infantry, in that a series of events unfolded that started it down the path to war. Though the attack on Pearl Harbor was still two years away, international tensions were mounting. Yet Americans were still hopeful that that the European powers would be able to come to terms with Adolf Hitler. Many people in Europe earnestly desired peace, but leaders, such as Winston Churchill and Franklin Roosevelt, felt that it was best to be prepared in the event that war did come. Not surprisingly in the circumstances, the king and queen of England accepted an invitation to attend the New York World's Fair in June 1939. It was deemed an opportune time to nurture the good relations established between the two countries in World War I.

To support the visit of King George VI and his queen, the 3rd Battalion motored home from Fort Dix on June 2. The battalion had been at Dix since April 23 conducting annual marksmanship training and preparing to support the Organized Reserve and CMTC camps. After a hurried evening of shining shoes and brass, pressing uniforms, and cleaning weapons, the battalion was loaded on boats to Fort Hancock the next day. The battalion and band met the royal couple for their arrival at New York Harbor amid the roar of cheering fans, the pomp and splendor of flags and banners, and the airs of patriotic music. Over the next week, the detail provided the military guard and escort for the British royals during their stay in the city.[93]

The regiment also formed the "World's Fair Detail." This detail, made up of hand-picked men from companies of the 16th Infantry and the regimental band, performed guard duties, exhibition drills, and ceremonies at the fair. It was as much a recruiting and publicity detail as anything, so the troops were selected to present the best possible appearance to the public. The men were slim, about the same height, and wore tailor-made uniforms. They were billeted in tents at the fairgrounds and had open access to the city when not on duty. Therefore, they were also allowed to take civilian clothes so that if they got drunk or into fights or other troubles downtown, people would think they were civilians.[94]

After the visit by the British royals, the regiment embarked on a series of maneuvers and exercises that kept it busy for the next year. These exercises were part of the U. S. Army's preparation, however unapparent to many of those involved, for the coming war. The first of these operations was the second First Army Maneuver, the first having occurred in 1935 at Pine Camp. This time the exercise took place in Clinton County, near Plattsburg in upstate New York.

Departing on August 3, the 2nd Battalion led the regiment's move to the maneuver area. The 1st Battalion arrived on August 7, and the remainder of the regiment rolled into camp on August 11. The regiment's camp was located at Silver Lake near Hawkeye, New York.

The training plan for the 1939 First Army maneuver differed from the 1935 exercise in that it was planned to start with small-unit exercises and culminate with more realistic large-unit force-on-force scenarios. The previous exercises had been relatively undemanding for the troops involved, but this maneuver would tax everyone, especially the soft National Guardsmen.

The period of August 13 through 15 was set aside for units to arrive, set up base camps, and conduct preliminary garrison training and "hardening marches." The next two days were given over to regimental maneuvers, followed by two days of brigade force-on-force maneuvers. Following a weekend break (August 19 and 20), the first corps-level maneuver kicked off. It lasted until August 22. August 23 through 25 was the grand finale in which the 26th, 27th, 43rd, and 44th Divisions of the "Black" First Army attacked the "Blue" Provisional Corps, comprising the 1st Division, 18th Infantry Brigade, and the 7th Cavalry Brigade (Mechanized).

The morning of August 23 found the 16th Infantry in an assembly area southeast of Redford, New York. Its mission was to conduct a movement eastward to gain contact with a Blue force that was moving to seize the Redford-Saranac area. The regiment jumped off about 10:00 a.m., with the 13th Infantry on the left and the 18th Infantry on the right, and swiftly headed down a route that paralleled the Salmon River. About noon, the lead elements ran into Black units that were soon identified as elements of New Jersey's 44th Division. The regiment deployed and took up defensive positions, but was soon pressured on the right by elements of the New York 27th Division. The regiment held against the attempted breakthrough by the combined efforts of the guard units.

After the initial halt in its forward movement, the regiment was able to continue to move east later in the afternoon. It was subsequently learned that a wide turning movement conducted by the 7th Cavalry Brigade into the rear of the 27th Division had caused a general withdrawal of the Black forces, allowing the Blue units to advance without any break in momentum. The evening of August 23 found the 1st Division along a line due south of Cadyville, marking an advance of about five miles.

The following morning, the National Guard divisions attacked all along the line and began to push the 1st Division and the 18th Brigade back toward Saranac. The heaviest attacks fell on the 16th Infantry in the 1st Division sector and on the 5th Infantry in the 18th Brigade sector. Both the 16th and 18th Regiments successfully side-slipped an intended envelopment by executing rapid forced marches out the danger area. The attack continued throughout the day and, by 6:00 p.m., the Blue units had been forced back to almost to the previous day's start-

ing point. The exercise ended with the National Guard troopers convinced that they had once again whipped the regulars.

General Fredrich von Boetticher, the German Army's liaison officer in the German Embassy in Washington, DC, was an invited observer to the First Army maneuvers. At the conclusion of the maneuver, von Boetticher, in reference to the division's quickness and mobility in making its attacks and escapes, complimented the "Red One" by remarking that "this division moves like a German unit."[95]

The men of the regiment arrived back at Fort Jay on August 30 to begin what they thought would be their routine fall and winter garrison activities. But this was not to be. Hardly had they arrived at Governors Island when two orders came down in quick succession that would have a significant impact on them, and on the 1st Division. The first order directed the "triangularization" of the Regular Army's infantry divisions. This meant that the division would lose one of the infantry regiments that had helped it build the superb reputation it enjoyed. The relieved unit was the 28th Infantry, and while the division was sad to see the "Black Lions of Cantigny" go, the men of "New York's Own" were glad to know they would not have to remove the highly coveted "Red One" from their left shoulders.

The reorganization also required other changes in the division. On October 11, HHC (Headquarters and Headquarters Company, 1st Infantry Brigade, was inactivated, and HHC, 2nd Infantry Brigade was relieved from assignment to the division. Concurrently, the divisional artillery, quartermaster, and medical regiments were reorganized into battalions. In short, the Regular Army divisions were pared down from the massive twenty-eight thousand-man "square" divisions of World War I to a slimmer, more mobile outfit of three regiments totaling sixteen thousand men. The advantages of this new organization would soon become apparent in the next phases of training.

The second order directed the temporary transfer of the 1st Division to Fort Benning, Georgia, to participate in maneuvers to test the new triangular organization. After implementing the changes in the new tables of organization, the 1st Division embarked on the trip to the piney woods post along the Chattahoochee River. On November 1, the regiment's advance elements, consisting of twenty officers and 630 men of the 1st Battalion, boarded the USAT *Republic* in Brooklyn and departed that same day for Charleston, South Carolina.[96] The 3rd Battalion and Service Company departed for Georgia by motor convoy on November 6, and finally, the regimental headquarters, medical detachment, and most of 2nd Battalion left for Charleston, also by transport, on the 15th. By November 19, all elements of the regiment had arrived at their new, though temporary, home.[97]

"Home" was a camp in a new cantonment area at Fort Benning. Known as Harmony Church and built on a site hastily cleared of tall Georgia pines by details of the 24th and 29th Infantry Regiments, the camp was a makeshift affair where the troops were quartered in pyramidal tents with wooden floors. This was definitely not Governors Island. Harmony Church had the crude look and feel of a lumber camp. Tree stumps were still much in evidence, the smell of fresh-cut pine filled the air, and the weather was getting cold. Brigadier General Truesdell, the assistant division commander, later remarked, "Winter in a pyramidal tent is no picnic, not even in Georgia, and the winter of 1939-1940 was one of the coldest. Harps Pond froze over solidly."[98]

The division arrived to find the camp only partially completed by the troops at Benning. Mess halls and other auxiliary facilities had to be built by the men of the 16th Regiment after they occupied the camp. Henry Orten, who by then had been in the army all of three or four months, was working on a construction detail when he looked down the road and saw a group of new recruits marching into the regimental area. He looked closer and, fixing his gaze on one of the new recruits, said to himself, "That looks like,…nah, it can't be." Then, suddenly and to his disbelief, he realized that recruit was his sixteen-year-old brother, Charlie!

After a short but happy reunion, Orten found out that his kid brother had been assigned to L Company, so he decided to take him over to his outfit. When they got there, Orten learned that Charlie's squad leader would be none other than Corporal McLaughlin. Escorting Charlie into the squad tent, they found McLaughlin there, and in his usual irascible mood. Orten told McLaughlin that Charlie was his new squad member. The corporal eyed little Henry and snapped, "Scram kid, we don't need no [news]papers in here today!"[99]

Training at Harmony Church began almost immediately. It started with the "School of the Soldier" to bring the new men in the regiment up to individual standards. Gradually, the scale of training increased and the tempo quickened, with exercises expanding from the squad level then to include platoons, companies, and, eventually, entire regiments. The units also made good use of Benning's excellent ranges, which accommodated all types of weapons. In some cases, new ranges had to be built from scratch to accommodate the needs of the division, as Fort Benning's existing ranges still had to support the training activities of the Infantry School as well.[100]

It was at Fort Benning that the 1st Division pioneered the "combat team" concept that was adopted by the army for operations in World War II. Later termed "regimental combat team," this formation comprised an infantry regiment, reinforced by a field artillery battalion, an engineer company, a medical company, signal detachments, and—depending on the mission—other assorted arms and support units. These attachments became more or less permanent and, in the 1st Division, were actually made official. Combat Team 16 (CT 16), for example, comprised the 16th Infantry; the 7th Field Artillery Battalion; Company A, 1st Engineers; Company A, 1st Medical Battalion; and a detachment from the 1st Signal Company. These units were habitually part of CT 16 for the duration of World War II and until the development of the "Battle Group"

concept in the so-called Pentomic Era (1957-63). These combat team relationships were institutionalized in the division Standing Operating Procedure (SOP) adopted on January 6, 1940.[101]

As spring approached, the division engaged in a series of exercises designed to prepare it for the IV Corps maneuver in April. One operation pitted the 1st Division in an attack against a combined force of the 24th and 29th Infantry Regiments, which defended a position with one flank anchored to the Chattahoochee River and other flank wide open. Advancing up to 150 miles at night in a series of truck-borne movements, the division was able to get a substantial part of its combat power on the open flank. As a light frontal attack pinned down the defenses, the main assault force rolled up the positions from the flank and rear.[102]

The following month, the newly activated 5th and 6th Infantry Divisions arrived at Fort Benning to form the IV Corps. The corps was organized under the command of Brigadier General Walter C. Short, who had been, up to that point, the 1st Division commander. Truesdell now took command of the "Red One" and led it through the next series of training events, which was aimed at readying the two new divisions for the Louisiana maneuvers, upcoming in May. On April 13, the entire corps, forty-one thousand men strong, moved to the field for division-on-division operations.

During the exercise, a reporter from the *New York Times* who covered the training activities of the 1st Division described his impressions of the "new warfare":

> Lacking the color of 1916-18, when marching soldiers went into battle in closer formation, the troops have reverted to the Indian manner of fighting from ambush. Soldiers spaced several yards apart move through the underbrush as the advance or retreat takes place, while the heavy guns and howitzers of the field artillery of the First, Fifth, and Sixth Divisions shoot from the rear.[103]

Later in the action, the 1st Division was attacked by the 6th Division and pushed back to the vicinity of Cuesseta, Georgia, near the south boundary of Fort Benning. In the late afternoon, the division counterattacked. With the 16th Infantry conducting the main effort, it first stopped the "Sightseeing Sixth" cold, then drove it back in places.[104]

On one of the many long marches during this exercise, Henry Orten found a discarded newspaper along the road. A headline announcing the fall of France was accompanied by a photograph of attacking German panzers. A short time later, several tanks from Major General George S. Patton's 2nd Armored Division rolled up and went into position next to his squad. Impressed with the great steel beasts, he remembered looking at his rifle and wondering, "What the hell am I going to do [with this] against these guys?" The same question would be raised by many 16th Infantry soldiers in July 1943 when, at the start of the Sicily campaign, the tanks of the Hermann Goering

Panzer Division tried to drive them back into the sea.[105]

Upon completion of the training at Benning, the IV Corps was ordered to move to the Louisiana Maneuver area for operations against the Provisional IX Corps, consisting of the 2nd Division and the 1st Cavalry Division. About the beginning of May, the 5th and 6th Divisions proceeded to Louisiana and were soon engaged in operations against the IX Corps. The 16th Infantry departed Fort Benning on May 7 and traveled by truck to Louisiana. Just as units were pulling into bivouac on the evening of May 9, General Truesdell received orders to launch an attack into the flank of the enemy corps. The division was not scheduled to enter the maneuver area until the following day but, nonetheless, attack orders were issued on the move, and the "Red One" continued to roll directly into the flank of the enemy. The resulting clash ended with the 1st Division reaching its assigned objectives—and another mark in the "win" column.[106]

For the next three weeks, some seventy-six thousand men of the two corps simulated combat in in the forests of central Louisiana under close-to-wartime conditions. The training was tough, and it revealed many of the shortcomings that resulted from twenty years of budgetary neglect. Senior leaders knew that the division needed more and better training, but even so, at the end of the exercise, the men were in top spirits and morale was high. And rightly so, for the regiment, as well as the rest of the division, had done extremely well given the often obsolete equipment and inferior resources then available. At the end of training critique, Major General Walter Krueger, commander of the provisional IX Corps, showed that he was impressed with the "Red One's" performance when he remarked that, during the training, his corps "was the guinea pig for the 1st Division."[107]

Though morale was high, the men were ready to go home. After six months in Georgia and Louisiana, ostensibly quartered in tent cities but actually spending most of their tour on exercises in the field, the troops were tired and ready for some leave-time in the big city. Clothing was badly in need of mending, and equipment required extensive maintenance or replacement. In late May, the regiment was ordered to return to Fort Jay, and on May 28, over sixteen hundred officers and men on 298 vehicles started a seven-day trip back to Governors Island. Among them were several hundred Southern recruits who had joined the regiment while it was below the Mason-Dixon Line.[108]

Henry Orten remembered these Southerners with affection: "There were Rebels in the outfit. In fact, my best friend was a Southerner…Some of them had joined [us] before Fort Benning as well as after. There were lots of Rebels in the [prewar] army. The backbone of the United States Regular Army was the poor Southerner, even back then. They were good soldiers too, I'll tell ya. I always liked the rednecks."[109] Though these men altered the demographic make-up of the 16th Infantry, it was still considered "New York's Own," and the Southerners were just as excited to return to New York City as the natives.

Arriving at home sweet home on June 4, the men of the regiment once again gazed upon their favorite lady, standing on her island in New York Harbor. After a few days of cleaning equipment and preparation, the regiment was assembled on Gettysburg Field for a formal change of command review on June 8. The incoming commander was Colonel Paul W. Baade, a 1911 graduate of West Point. Baade had been the regimental executive officer since August 1939 and, in an unusual progression of command for peacetime, now took command of "New York's Own."[110]

Hardly were the men ensconced in their neat, clean barracks when they heard scuttlebutt that the regiment was to participate in the First Army maneuver in upstate New York in August. In the six weeks that followed they both rested and busied themselves with refitting and refurbishing for the next big show. On August 5, 1940, the regiment boarded ferries to take the by-now familiar ride through New York Harbor to New Jersey, then motored to its assembly area at Winthrop, New York.

As usual, the 1st Division was expected to set the performance standard for the other units participating in the exercise. It all began with the setting up of the regimental cantonment areas. Brigadier General Walter C. Short, the division commander, directed that the camps be erected using aiming circles, or like methods, to ensure that the tents were neatly aligned. The men were quartered in pup tents; the officers were granted the luxury of sleeping in pyramidal tents.[111] Under the watchful eye of seasoned NCOs, the camps went up with the precision expected of the Regular Army.

The training consisted of a series of exercises that steadily increased in size and complexity. After initial shakedown events at the company and battalion levels, the training increased to regimental, brigade, and division levels and culminated in a massive corps-versus-corps maneuver. The 1st Division was on the northern flank of the II Corps and attacked against the 26th Division.

Toward the end of the stay in upstate New York, President Franklin D. Roosevelt made a tour of all the divisions to see the men in training and address as many of them as possible. The 1st Division was assembled at the campus of St. Lawrence University for the president's visit. After the president's departure, the weather turned chilly for August. One morning just before heading home to Fort Jay, Lieutenant Eston White woke to discover a thin layer of ice in a collapsible bucket used for shaving.[112]

The regiment loaded into trucks for the trip back to Fort Jay. Wartime budgets had not yet caught up with the needs of the army, so many soldiers rode home on trucks rented from civilian companies. A squad from E Company had the misfortune of riding on an old rattletrap with the label "Joe's Ice Truck" painted on its side. Just outside West Point, the convoy proceeded down a long hill and, unfortunately, the brakes on the truck not only gave out but caught fire as well. The quick-thinking driver of a Greyhound Bus pulled in front and allowed the truck to run into his rear bumper. He then used his own brakes to stop the runaway. Spectators stopped and ran over with fire extinguishers to put the fire out. Luckily, nobody was hurt, but that was the end of the line for Joe's truck.[113]

The First Army maneuver behind them, the men of the 16th Infantry arrived back at Fort Jay on August 27. Now, it was hoped they could relax and resume their normal garrison routine. At first things appeared to be headed that way. After recovery operations ensured regimental equipment was returned to tip-top shape, the men were given opportunities to go on leave or pass, but it was not long before the hopes for a routine garrison period were dashed.

In September, President Roosevelt called the National Guard to one year's active duty. On October 15, the Second Corps Area directed that fifty-five hundred men, all draftees with a three-year service obligation, would be assigned to the 1st Division to bring it up to wartime strength. Of these, the 16th Infantry was to receive about fifteen hundred recruits. At the same time, the 1st Division was alerted to assemble at Fort Devens, Massachusetts, in February to concentrate the division for additional training and to expedite the basic training of the new recruits.[114]

Two changes to the regimental structure occurred before the movement to Fort Devens. The first of these was the organization of the Antitank Company on October 1, 1940, under the command of 1st Lieutenant Charles J. Denholm (antitank companies had been added to the tables of organization (T/O) of infantry regiments as a result of lessons learned during the maneuvers in Georgia, Louisiana, and New York). Second, a sad event occurred that brought an end to seventy-nine years of service with the 16th Infantry—the regimental band was ordered to be inactivated effective January 6, 1941. The previous year, the band had barely dodged a separation from the regiment when it had been ordered to be relieved and redesignated as the Station Band, Fort Jay, on October 13, 1939. That order was rescinded on March 18, 1940, and it appeared that the band would remain with the regiment permanently. But the next order was final, and the 16th Infantry Band was inactivated.[115] The band had inspired the men of the regiment in many tight spots during the Civil War and had brought them hours of pleasure during tough times on the plains, in the Philippines, and in Alaska. Now it was gone, and another piece of regimental history and tradition was lost for good.

In those days, soldiers could enlist for a one-year hitch. Municipal judges in New York often dealt with delinquent neighborhood toughs and gang members by giving them the option of joining the army or going to jail. Naturally, most such miscreants chose to wear the uniform, and a number of them ended up in the 16th Infantry. The regiment's instrument for turning these tough guys into soldiers was a recruit training company run by a certain hard-nosed lieutenant, one Charles H. "Batshit" Horner. Horner's odd moniker reflected his standard (and frequent) response to situations and statements that he found objectionable: "That's batshit!" He and his NCOs usually succeeded in making soldiers out of their problem recruits. However, just about the time the regiment returned from upstate New York, a large group of delinquents was delivered to the recruit company courtesy of the New York court system. It proved too much for the company to handle and, in consequence, some of them they were able to make it through the training without really accepting the responsibilities of being a soldier, or without being weeded out of the army.[116]

Just after the regiment's return to Fort Jay, the 3rd Battalions of the 16th and 18th Infantry Regiments were selected to be the amphibious training units of the 1st Division. Both battalions were to be brought up to wartime strength for the training, which was to occur over the next several months. In order to bring each unit up to full strength, the other two battalions of their respective regiments were directed to provide men to flesh out their 3rd Battalion. Naturally, the 1st and 2nd Battalions of the 16th Infantry gave up their undesirables and, not surprisingly, many of the soldiers who had made it through the recruit company without adapting to military discipline were the very ones who were now concentrated in the 3rd Battalion. This situation, coupled with the personality of the 3rd Battalion's commanding officer, created difficult circumstances for the next year or so until the incorrigible ones had finally been weeded out, or had been transferred out of the regiment.[117]

On December 2, the 3rd Battalion departed Fort Jay for temporary station at Edgewood Arsenal to begin amphibious training. The remainder of the regiment passed through the portals of Fort Jay on the cold, gray day of February 24, en route for station at Fort Devens, where the entire 1st Division was assembling. It was to be the last time the men of the regiment would serve at Fort Jay. No longer would they be parade ground soldiers, nor would they "trip the light fantastic on the sidewalks of New York." Gone were the days of spit and polish, regimental reviews, and parades down Broadway. The days of summer camp at Camp Dix and leisurely field training in the cool autumn of the Atlantic seaboard were a thing of the past.

Instead, they would soon be earnestly engaged in learning ways to attack enemy positions and defend friendly ones. They would learn how to push themselves harder than they believed they could. They would learn how to use every weapon available to efficiently kill the enemy. In short, the regiment was now embarking on a journey that would lead them to the serious business of waging war. Little did they know upon leaving Fort Jay that cold winter morning that the 16th Infantry would soon be fighting its way across the battlefields of North Africa, Sicily, France, and Germany.

16th Infantry at Omaha Beach, D-Day, June 6, 1944

Chapter Eight
The Big One

You are one of the finest regiments in the army. I know your record from the day you landed in North Africa and through Sicily. I am beginning to think that your regiment is a sort of Praetorian Guard which goes along with me and gives me luck.

General Dwight D. Eisenhower, July 2, 1944

The federalization of the National Guard, the call to active duty of thousands of Organized Reserve officers, and the institution of a peacetime draft all served to reinforce the growing feeling among Americans that it was only a matter of time before the war raging in Europe would be their fight too. Indeed, the rapid activation of new units in the army, the establishment of new air corps bases in the Caribbean and northern Atlantic, and the institution of navy patrols in the western half of the Atlantic seemed to signal that the United States was preparing to enter the fray. By the same token, however, American involvement did not seem imminent. There was no consensus for it. So, the preparations continued.

Army planners believed that, in the event that the United States entered the war, the introduction of American soldiers onto continental Europe or Africa would require amphibious assaults. An increased emphasis was therefore placed on amphibious assault training. Accordingly, the 3rd Battalion, 16th Infantry, and the 3rd Battalion, 18th Infantry, were sent to Edgewood Arsenal near the Maryland shore toward the beginning of December 1940. The battalions were billeted in pyramidal tents in the camp normally used by ROTC cadets and CMTC candidates during the summer. Though the tents were equipped with Sibley stoves and wooden floors, the bitterly cold weather ensured that life in eastern Maryland would be uncomfortable. The amphibious training made it even more so.[1]

The 3rd Battalion, 16th Infantry, was under the command of Lieutenant Colonel Ray Cavanee, a stern martinet with flaming red hair. A World War I veteran with a battlefield commission, he had been transferred to the battalion after a tour of duty managing the disciplinary barracks at Fort Leavenworth, Kansas. Described by one lieutenant as "one of the meanest officers I've ever served under," he was a hard drinker who chewed out lieutenants for the smallest infractions. Noncommissioned officers also disliked Cavanee because he required officers to perform many of the NCOs' traditional duties and responsibilities. Unpopular with the troops as well, Cavanee related to them as if they were the prisoners he had been commanding at the disciplinary barracks.[2] Nonetheless, he pushed the battalion hard to master boat operations.

For the most part, the training at Edgewood took place along the banks of the Gunpowder River, which emptied into Chesapeake Bay. The training would later strike the participants as laughably amateurish compared to the real thing, but for now it was the best training available. The boats, for example, were of the "Lapp-streak" type (of various sizes), and had been borrowed from an ocean liner in drydock. Actually, they were rowboats, eight oars to a boat, and most held about fifty soldiers. Because there were not enough boats to load the whole battalion for a simulated landing, one or two companies would load up, row out into the river, turn around, and then wade ashore. Then the second wave loaded up and rowed out to do the same, until all the troops had gone through the drill.[3]

To make matters worse, the water was so cold that the troops were issued hip-waders so they would not suffer hypothermia when wading ashore. Once again, however, there were not enough waders to outfit all the men, so the exercise came to a halt while the first wave took off their waders and gave them to the second wave, who then put them on before rowing out, and so forth.[4] It was the kind of tedious exercise that irritates soldiers. One imagines that they began to wonder just what kind of idiot was in charge of such a screwed-up operation.

After the completion of the training at Edgewood, the two battalions and some division support elements were organized into the 1st Division Task Force under Brigadier General James G. Ord for Army-Navy Joint Exercise Number 7. For this exercise, the selected units were to participate in a mock invasion of Culebra Island near Puerto Rico. The task force traveled to the Brooklyn Army Base near the end of December and loaded on the USAT *Chateau Thierry* in New York Harbor. Joining the 1st Division troops on the *Chateau Thierry* were two batteries of the 99th Field Artillery Battalion, a mule-drawn, pack howitzer outfit. One of the batteries was commanded by an obscure young captain named William O. Darby. Darby, of course, later made American military history leading the famed ranger battalions in the Mediterranean theater. Sailing in late December, the ship joined a large naval task force that included marines, and traveled to Puerto Rico.[5]

The operations off Culebra were only marginally more polished than the exercises at Edgewood. This time, the troops climbed down rope ladders into forty-one-foot navy motor launches, typically used to transport sailors about the harbor when their ships were in port. Like the landing craft used at the Gunpowder River, the launches were essentially lifeboats, each holding about fifty-four troops. But these boats were motorized, and the troops did not have to row them. However, the launches frequently got stuck as they ran onto the beach, which, in turn, forced the troops to waste time pushing them off the sand before moving inland. The operation also included some of the new "Higgins" amphibious craft. These boats were the forerunners of the famed LCVP of World War II fame, but lacked the familiar drop-down ramp in front. They were smaller than the launches, about thirty-six-feet long, and held about thirty soldiers.

The task force actually participated in two landing exercises at Culebra, separated by a five-day voyage. In addition to the landing exercises, the commander of the naval task force trained his command in convoy and fleet operations. This required the men of the 3rd Battalion to pass several idle days at sea, while the fleet steamed around the Atlantic and the Caribbean. On February 6, the 1st Division Task Force landed for the second time at Firewood and Mosquito Bays on the southwest side of the island. After a short boat ride across the brilliant-blue, crystal-clear waters of the bay, the 3rd Battalion landed at Beach C-2. Initially, the troops milled about the beach, pushed the boats off the sand, leisurely organized squads and platoons, and transloaded equipment between men. Finally, the troops pushed inland to take their objectives, two hills about a kilometer from the beach. This they accomplished that day, but for the troops it must have been quite a lark. There was no opposition, except notionally; the weather was beautiful compared to the East Coast winter they had just experienced near the Chesapeake; and the island was a tropical paradise. Warm sunshine and cool ocean breezes made the movement to the hills little more than a nature hike and, once there, there was little for the troops to do except relax and pretend they were establishing a beachhead defense line.

The amphibious operations in the Caribbean were nonetheless useful to the two 1st Division battalions. While the training was not up to the level of professionalism that the division would later achieve, it was a good start. Critiquing the exercises, Lieutenant Colonel George P. Hays, the Task Force G3, concluded that a well-trained company with artillery support would have prevented a successful landing under real combat conditions. He also perceived three primary weaknesses in the operation. First, he believed that the landings needed to be conducted over a wider front to prevent the stacking of units as waves of troops came in. Second, troops must be trained to rush ashore and seize inland positions, not mill about on the beach. Third, initiative and personal leadership must be fostered in small-unit leaders assigned to amphibious units: "In many cases, these leaders, instead of acting on what they see, using their own judgment, simply wait orders from a higher commander or staff officer which would often result in heavy casualties. But if they act on their own initiative, they should

report [their actions] to the next higher C.O."[6] Hays's observations were prescient. Just how prescient would be made evident on a cold, gray morning on another beach, thousands of miles away, and three years later.

Its training completed, 1st Division elements reembarked on the *Chateau Thierry* in mid-February and headed north to Boston. Just above Cape Hatteras, the ship steamed into a severe storm that nearly proved its undoing. Pounded by huge waves and gale-force winds, the ship rolled violently as it struggled to make headway, achieving a mere two knots while causing much seasickness and raising fears that it might break apart. Those fears were heightened when numerous items of equipment, strapped to the upper decks, burst their bonds and were swept overboard.[7] The ship survived, however, and on February 19, the units disembarked at Boston and traveled to Fort Devens the same day. There, the 3rd Battalion prepared the cantonment area to receive the rest of the regiment from Fort Jay.

In the fall of 1940, selective service men (draftees) began to arrive at Fort Jay to flesh out the 16th Infantry to war strength. Before long, the regiment had swelled to 3,297 officers and men. Similar to its situation at the beginning of World War I, the regiment was a rather small nucleus of Regular Army troops surrounded by a vast pool of drafted men and volunteers who were hardly soldiers. Additionally, the new men were not the New Yorkers and New Jerseyans who had largely composed the regiment for the last twenty years. The northeastern flavor of the outfit was rapidly evolving into a cross-section of Americans, though the metropolitan-area soldiers would remain a sizable minority well into World War II.

For many soldiers in the outfit, especially the Southerners, the winter of 1941 at Fort Devens was a difficult time. That winter was one of the severest in memory, with heavy snows and bitterly cold temperatures. Luckily, the 1st Division had been moved into recently constructed wooden barracks that would become typical of the World War II design. Therefore, the billeting, while not the comfortable brick barracks of Fort Jay, was a far cry from the tent cantonment that the 3rd Battalion experienced at Edgewood Arsenal.

Though the barracks provided fair accommodations, the post itself was a poor place to train an infantry division. The maneuver area was too small and the ranges inadequate to support the variety of weapons in the arsenal of a modern regiment—much less an entire division. Why Devens was chosen and not Fort Dix, the division's traditional training area, was puzzling for some. The division commander, Major General Donald Cubbison, wondered, too, and came to the conclusion that it was politics, not military necessity, that sent the "Fighting First" to Massachusetts. Nevertheless, in 1st Division style, the officers and men rolled up their sleeves and set to work to hone the division into a sharp instrument of war. It was a difficult process.

Part of the difficulty was the command relationships

arranged for the 1st Division. Originally assigned to the II Corps in the War Department's mobilization plan, the division was reassigned to the VI Corps when that headquarters was transferred to Fort Devens in November 1940. However, because the "Red One" was designated by the Army Ground Forces as the army's strategic response division, it was not beyond GHQ to issue orders directly to the division. Exacerbating the problem, the division was also attached to the navy in May 1941 as a component of the I Amphibious Corps for training operations, which, in turn, drove the unit's training schedule. All three headquarters considered the division as their own.[8] It was a classic example of the violation of the "unity of command" principle. As a result, Cubbison and his staff were often pulled in three directions. At the least, it was an aggravating situation.

On July 11, 1941, the regiment formed for yet another change of command ceremony. Taking command was Colonel Henry B. Cheadle, a 1913 graduate of the Military Academy. During the First World War, Cheadle had served as an observer with several British and French Divisions and then returned to Camp Dodge, Iowa, where he served the remainder of the war as a machine-gun instructor. After several infantry assignments (in the Philippines; at Fort Eustis, Virginia; and at Fort Missoula, Montana), Cheadle served on the Eighth Corps Area staff at Fort Sam Houston, Texas, in 1934-38. He was the military attaché to Japan and Spain in 1938-40 and then was assigned to the 18th Infantry as its executive officer before coming to the 16th Infantry.[9]

After its arrival at Fort Devens, the 1st Division began to send battalions to Buzzard's Bay, Massachusetts, for additional amphibious training. One battalion at a time conducted the training, which usually lasted about two weeks, then was replaced by the next battalion in line. Some units did not get the chance to conduct the actual practice landings because of the severe winter weather. Subsequent to the training at Buzzard's Bay, a flood of volunteers and draftees arrived to swell the ranks of the division.

Each regiment spent the spring and early summer putting their new men through basic training and a series of small unit exercises that increased in complexity and size from squad to company level. About mid-June, the regiment was alerted, along with the rest of the 1st Division, for a joint amphibious operation with the 1st Marine Division at New River Inlet (now Camp Lejuene, North Carolina) in July and August 1941. A month later, the regiment moved to Boston and loaded on board the USS *Wakefield* for the voyage south. Arriving off the coast opposite Onslow and Hurst beaches in late July, the assault fleet anchored about twelve thousand yards off shore.

The plan called for the division to land in a column of regiments, CT 26 landing first, followed by CTs 16 and 18. The "Blue Spaders" went in on time and landed at Beaches C and D at Onslow. Upon receiving the required signals, the men of the 16th Infantry clambered down cargo nets into bobbing Higgins boats to make the approach to shore.

The landings were not without mishaps and trials. Several men were injured, some critically, while exiting the boats. Some severely strained their backs by jumping into the surf with heavy equipment loads. Others received broken bones from dismounting to the front, as the boat continued forward. Several suffered injuries as waves caused the bow to come down on their legs or body. Still others were injured when the tide caused boats to swing around and smash into the troops wading in the surf. At least one man from the 16th Infantry drowned. But the vast majority made it to the beach unharmed.

Once ashore, the regiment made its way forward, into the swamps immediately behind the beach area. Along with the muck, mire, and stumps that the men stumbled over, mosquitoes swarmed about the troops, causing them more misery. Beyond the swamps, the regiment encountered a canal and seized several previously selected crossing points, continuing its advance inland. Once the objectives were reached, the regiment was directed to conduct a withdrawal under pressure back through the marshes, in the darkness. The regiment successfully performed the operation and assembled on the beach—but only after a night of great difficulty and confusion.

This exercise was conducted not too long after the British Army's experience at Dunkirk, so the final phase of the training required the troops to guide landing craft to the beach, board the craft, and return to the transport. Arriving at the ship, the tired, mosquito-ravaged troops scaled the cargo nets and thankfully plopped themselves into any available space where they could dump their gear and go to sleep. While not a flawlessly executed operation, the mission had been accomplished.[10]

Still, a great deal had been learned about amphibious operations and soldiering. The regiment was evolving from a group of citizen soldiers into a professional infantry unit. To further mold his disparate organization into a team, Colonel Cheadle directed that the regiment celebrate Organization Day once it arrived back at Fort Devens. As before, this event served as an opportunity to initiate the new soldiers to the great history and traditions of the 16th Infantry Regiment and the 1st Division. The celebration began Friday evening, October 3, with an enlisted man's dance at the Hostess House on Robbins Pond. The following day, the regiment formed on the main parade at Fort Devens at 10:00 a.m. and proceeded to conduct a review for the many invited guests, many of whom were former members of the regiment, to whom a special tribute was made. After Colonel Cheadle's remarks and the reading of the regimental history, it was announced that four men, still assigned to the 16th Infantry, had served with the regiment in World War I: Lieutenant Colonel Wilson M. Spann, the executive officer; Master Sergeant McKinley L. Fuller; Staff Sergeant Harry L. Rosen; and Sergeant Walter P. Steele. Interestingly, these men were recognized as those "who served with the Sixteenth during the *last war*" [italics added].[11] The Second World War had yet to begin for the United States, but the apparent attitude in the 16th Infantry was that it was only a matter of time before the country was involved in the next one.

Organization Day was a pleasant interlude to the breakneck pace the regiment had experienced since the spring, when the weather had allowed the resumption of training. But unknown to the troops, General Cubbison was trying to get the 1st Division reinstated on the troop list for the First Army maneuver in North Carolina. The problem was that the navy was reluctant to relinquish control of the division, stating that it might be needed for rapid deployment for an emergency situation. Due to intercepted diplomatic traffic between the Japanese government and its ambassador to the United States, it appeared that war was a real possibility, and the navy announced that the "Fighting First" would not be released from its control. Only after the maneuvers started did the navy relent, and then only under the stipulation that the 1st Division could be recalled immediately for deployment.[12]

On October 15, the "Red One" rolled into the Carolina maneuver area and rejoined its old commander, Major General Truesdell, now commanding the VI Corps. The regiment bivouacked at Samarcand, North Carolina, and for the next six weeks, prepared, then participated in, this exercise, which consisted of three corps and over 295,000 soldiers. The regiment participated in four separate corps- and army-level exercises that culminated with the impressive First Army GHQ Maneuver that pitted the First Army (I and VI Corps) against the IV Corps.

In the first phase of the operation, on November 16, the division was initially held in reserve by the "Blue" First Army, as the VI Corps attempted to conduct crossings of the Pee Dee River. The crossings were opposed by the 4th Division of the "Red" IV Corps and air-support units of the 3rd Air Support Command.[13]

The day before the operation, the 3rd Battalion, 16th Infantry, was tasked to conduct a boat assault of the river near Monroe, North Carolina, ostensibly supporting the VI Corps push, and then move to hide positions on the east bank of the Pee Dee. A reconnaissance of the crossing site located a point where the battalion could cross in knee-deep water. The crossing was set for early the next morning, but as the day dawned, it was apparent that the river had risen significantly, causing a corresponding increase in the current speed. The wily Red commander had coordinated to get the dam operators upstream to increase the flow of water downstream to impede a crossing. Lieutenant Colonel Cavanee checked the proposed fording site and called off the operation fearing the needless loss of men. Instead, the battalion rejoined the regiment, crossing on a pontoon bridge on the afternoon of the 16th.[14]

That evening, the 1st Division was released to the VI Corps and moved to the far west flank of the First Army line. The following day, the division jumped off against the left flank of the 4th Division, pushed hard all day, and advanced twenty miles, causing the Red forces to refuse the entire left portion of their line. Over the next several days, the 1st and 2nd Armored Divisions demonstrated their mobility and speed but were not decisive against the infantry-heavy First Army. The final drive of the 1st Division on the first phase of the maneuver ended on November 21 with the victorious First Army in Monroe and the "Red One" mopping up the remnants of the 1st Armored Division, which had been trapped behind the advancing Blue forces.[15]

The second phase began on November 25, and once again, the 1st Division found itself in reserve. The division remained in reserve until the morning of the 27th, when it was committed to the west flank of the VI Corps. Advancing rapidly down the Van Wyck-Lancaster Road, the division achieved a major breakthrough and headed for the Red headquarters at Camden, South Carolina. The 16th Infantry easily sliced through the 4th Division elements attempting to stop the 1st Division's advance, and after a push of about twenty miles, the regiment was held up by umpires just south of Lancaster at dusk. That evening, General Drum ordered the division to attempt an encirclement of the 2nd Armored Division the following day, then to continue the drive for Camden. However, during the night, the 2nd Armored Division reoriented, and at first light, counterattacked the 1st Division's positions in Lancaster instead. The attacks were unsuccessful, but they did keep the "Red One" from advancing on the IV Corps' headquarters. The exercise terminated that afternoon.[16]

Several days later, the 16th Infantry loaded trucks for the long convoy to Fort Devens. The regiment had done well, morale was high, and everybody was looking forward to returning home and maybe some Christmas leave. On December 6, the regiment rolled into Devens and began the tasks of recovery. Weapons cleaning, tent maintenance, vehicle maintenance, and accounting for equipment was the order of the day. The unit area was bustling with activity that it had not experienced since the regiment left two months before. The following day was Sunday and everybody was looking forward to sleeping late.

Though the sleepy camp stirred late that morning, Sunday, December 7, was a duty day. Troops went about their chores and continued the process of cleaning up and repairing vehicles and equipment used in the recent maneuvers. That afternoon, radios began blaring the news of the Japanese attack on Pearl Harbor. Before long, the news swept through the post.

Lined up on the sidewalk in front of the personnel building that afternoon were scores of men slated to receive their discharges that day. Supervising the process was Master Sergeant James Lipinski, regimental S1 NCO. Lipinski heard the report of Pearl Harbor on the radio and quickly headed over to the regimental headquarters, where he informed Colonel Cheadle and Captain Frederick W. Gibb, the S1. Gibb quickly directed Lipinski to stop the discharges. The sergeant wisely strolled past the men and quietly told the personnel officer the situation. The officer immediately ceased the operation and informed the troops that they were now extended "for the duration."[17]

Suddenly, Christmas plans seemed less important. For some, the realization that the country was at war seemed surreal; for others, it was all too real. Sunday night, just before midnight, General Cubbison received a call from the War Department that illustrated the confusion and intensity of the situation just after Pearl Harbor. A "high official," obviously under some strain, called Cubbison and asked how soon the 1st Division could depart for the west coast and what equipment it needed for combat operations. Cubbison assured him the "Fighting First" could be en route the following day and that the 1st Division was equipped to exit the trains fighting if necessary. "Thank God!" came the reply. It was, Cubbison later wrote, "The most fervent statement I have ever heard."[18]

The division did not get orders for the west coast, but for Camp Blanding, Florida, instead. On February 18, 1942, the regiment boarded trains, less those who traveled in the regiment's motor convoy, and arrived in Florida five days later. Camp Blanding was a National Guard mobilization camp located near Jacksonville, Florida. The camp was currently occupied by the soldiers of the 36th "Texas" Division, who, like most Texans, figured they were the toughest sons of bitches that ever carried a rifle. Proud of their military prowess and Lone Star heritage, the "T-Patchers" were determined to let others know they ran the show at Blanding. For example, when frequenting the enlisted clubs, the Texans required everybody in the place to stand at attention and take off their hats when "The Eyes of Texas" or "Deep in the Heart of Texas" played on the jukebox. Well, that idea did not appeal to the predominantly Yankee 16th Infantry. In no time, fights broke out between the Texans and the men of the "Fighting First," and animosity built as one side or the other came out the winners. The military police did not like the situation in the least because, as often as not, they, too, received their share of bumps and bruises in the melees.

Major General Fred L. Walker, commander of the 36th Division, arranged for a get-together of the officers of the two divisions. At the gathering, toasts were made by the assistant division commanders for each other's division. Brigadier General Terry de La Mesa Allen, assistant division commander (ADC) for the 36th Division, toasted the 1st Division, and Brigadier General Theodore "Teddy" Roosevelt Jr., ADC of the "Red One," toasted the Texas Division. Walker capped the toasts with, "To the 1st and 36th Divisions: May their luck be as great as their glory." The band then broke into a medley of the "Sidewalks of New York" and "The Eyes of Texas," and officers of both divisions mixed and mingled and enjoyed the evening.[19]

Only two days later, Cubbison sent for Walker and informed him that there had been fights between the soldiers of the two divisions. He demanded that Walker order his men to stop the altercations, to which Walker replied that he would if the 1st Division soldiers were ordered to stop referring to the Texas troops as "that damned national guard." He later wrote, "I did not tell Cubbison, of course, but I had told my men not

to take any insults from the 1st, and they have taken me at my word." He also mused, "I guess we should have arranged a 'get together' to promote friendliness between the enlisted men of the two Divisions last weekend also."[20]

The war was starkly evident for some soldiers while they were at Camp Blanding. Lieutenant Eston White remembered going down to the beach at Jacksonville, Florida, and seeing burning ships torpedoed by German submarines just off the coast. U-boat crews called this period the "Happy Time," due to the ease with which they sank American shipping. Virtually any stretch of the Florida coast frequently revealed great billows of black smoke marking the graves of merchant ships. The nearness of the war prompted the division to require each regiment to have a battalion on standby alert to react to potential German incursions along the north Florida coast.[21]

One event for the regiment that harkened back to its Fort Jay days was a division review conducted on May 1, 1942. The review was held for none other than General George C. Marshall, the army chief of staff, to give him an opportunity to closely inspect the division for which he had served as the G3 in World War I. Also accompanying Marshall were Major General Leslie J. McNair, the chief of the Army Ground Forces, and Field Marshal Sir John Dill, the head of the British contingent of the Combined Chiefs of Staff. After the review, the generals observed several demonstrations put on by the soldiers to show their training progress.

Training at Camp Blanding consisted of jungle training, marksmanship, squad and platoon tactics, and extended road marches. One march for the 3rd Battalion was particularly memorable. When the regiment arrived in Florida, the weather was still relatively cold, but before long, temperatures went up dramatically. To make matters worse, the regiment was still outfitted with the brown, wool field uniform, which was great for cold New England winters but too warm for the tropic-like Florida weather. Even so, Cavanee decided he would take his battalion on a twenty-mile march through the Ocala National Forest. The rapid pace of the march and the heavy uniforms proved too much for many men, who fell out from exhaustion. For a part of the distance, Brigadier General Roosevelt, with his distinctive limp, marched along with the men, which further endeared him to them but did little to alleviate their predicament. After a while, Teddy left, and not too long after, Terry Allen, now a major general and commander of the 1st Division, pulled up to the sweating, ragged column of overheated men and demanded: "Who in the hell is in charge of this mob?" He was informed and sped off to find Cavanee. Not long after this march, Cavanee disappeared and Frederick Gibb, now a major, took command of the 3rd Battalion. Morale improved significantly thereafter.[22]

The regiment's stay at Blanding was short. On May 18, the division was transferred temporarily to Fort Benning to conduct a series of live-fire demonstrations with the 2nd Armored Division for a contingent of generals and important government leaders. The action included the participation of several of the new A-20 attack bombers, which dropped live ordnance. While there, the division was billeted in its old cantonment area at Harmony Church, which was now, not so affectionately, called "Dysentery Hill."[23]

The stay at the Infantry Center was even shorter, and the 1st Division entrained for the Indiantown Gap Military Reservation on June 6. At Indiantown Gap, the regiment made its final preparations for overseas deployment, ridding itself of excess property and acquiring the latest combat equipment. On June 21, the regiment received orders to prepare a battalion to accompany the division advanced party to England. The 2nd Battalion, commanded by Major Joseph B. Crawford, was selected, and on July 1, the division advanced party left Indiantown Gap for New York Harbor. At New York, the battalion embarked on two British transports, the HMT *Maloja* and the HMT *Duchess of Bedford*.[24]

Upon arrival in Liverpool, England, the troops of the advance party traveled by train to Tidworth Barracks to prepare for the reception of the remainder of the division. At Tidworth, they designated company and regimental billeting areas and coordinated for food, fuel, ammunition and other supplies. On August 2, the 16th Infantry joined the "Fighting First" on board the HMS *Queen Mary* and sailed the following day for Scotland. After an uneventful but crowded trip, the regiment debarked at Greenock on August 7. Meeting the division at the port was a Scottish bagpipe band and, to the troops' delight, the ship was unloaded to the "wild skirling" of the pipes.[25] The regiment remained near Glasgow that night and entrained for Tidworth Barracks the following day.

Tidworth Barracks was an old cavalry post located near Salisbury, in southern England. The post consisted of rather comfortable brick billets, headquarters buildings, and a station hospital. For the next month, it would be the scene of intensive training by the men of the regiment in preparation for their first combat operation. While the staff developed its plan for the mission, the companies began a series of long conditioning marches, calisthenics, weapons training, marksmanship, and demolitions. Squad, platoon, and company exercises were conducted first during daylight, then at night, to accustom the troops to operations in darkness.

The regiment subsequently moved by train to the British Combined Operations Training Center at Rosneath, Scotland, in mid-September to conduct amphibious training in preparation for Operation Torch, the invasion of Algeria and French Morocco. For the next thirty days, the troops were relentlessly drilled in all aspects of amphibious warfare on ships docked on the Firth of Clyde. Foul weather added to the realism and difficulty of training the units. Most of the training consisted of loading ships and debarking into assault craft using cargo nets. On the night of September 27-28, the regiment made a practice assault landing on the Inverchaolain Peninsula.[26] One participant described the action:

A final training exercise involved a night landing, in full field uniform including overcoats. It was raining and everybody was wet. [After the landing] we had to climb up a steep hillside onto a long plateau where the water in places was ankle deep and then converge on a town several miles away for return to our ship. The exercise lasted most of the following day and we were a wet and bedraggled bunch of soldiers when we finally returned to the ship.[27]

The troops then returned to Rosneath for additional training. On October 15, the regiment boarded two ships; HMT *Warwick Castle* and the already familiar *Duchess of Bedford*, and participated in a final landing exercise conducted at Loch Linnhe on October 18-19. After this exercise, the ships assembled with the invasion fleet in Greenock Harbor, Scotland, and waited. Finally, on the night of October 26, the fleet weighed anchor and slipped quietly into the Atlantic.[28]

Algeria-French Morocco Campaign
November 8-11, 1942

At the beginning of November 1942, Germany's war with the Soviet Union was entering its eighteenth month with no end in sight. By then Axis forces had overrun most of the Soviet Union's western regions and the northern half of the Caucasus but, significantly, had failed to capture Leningrad, Moscow, and Stalingrad. Meanwhile, Stalin had been prodding the Western Allies to open a "second front" to relieve Axis pressure on the Soviet Union. President Roosevelt promised Soviet Foreign Minister Vyacheslav Molotov that this would be accomplished before the end of the year. American military planners, led by General George C. Marshall, wanted the next major offensive in the West to be a direct assault on Europe, preferably in the form of a cross-Channel invasion of France in 1943. The British, however, opposed such an operation, believing that it was beyond Allied capabilities. A compromise was reached—instead of France, the Allies would land in Morocco and Algeria and advance into Tunisia as part of a larger effort to drive the Axis from North Africa. The proposed undertaking met with Roosevelt's approval, inasmuch as it satisfied his desire to keep the United States focused on defeating "Germany first" while fulfilling his promise to the Soviets to open a second front.

The invasion was to consist of three task forces: Western, Center, and Algiers. The 1st Division comprised the main effort, the Center Task Force, which drew the assignment of capturing the city of Oran.

Opposing the 1st Division was the French Army's Oran Division, a colonial unit consisting mostly of native troops commanded by French officers. Its estimated strength was 18,200 officers and men, including support troops. The French division was organized with two infantry regiments, a squadron of mechanized cavalry, an artillery regiment, and an attached battalion of the French Foreign Legion. The unit defending the 16th

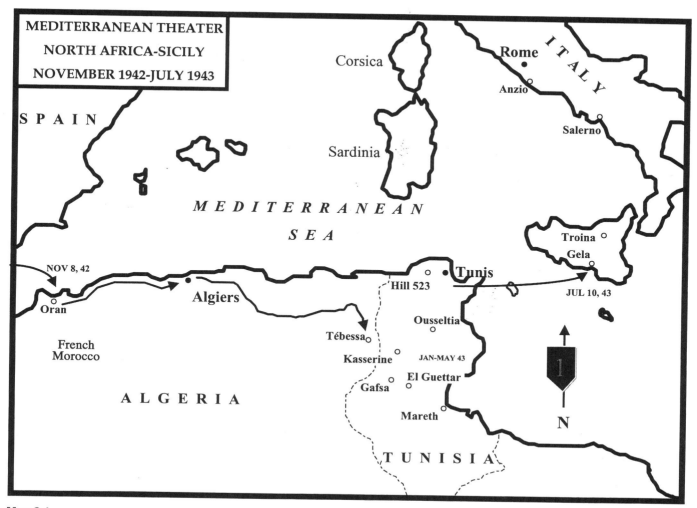

Map 8-1.

Infantry's landing area was the 2nd Régiment Tirailleurs Algeriens, supported by three batteries of the 1st Groupe Régiment Artillerie d'Afrique. Regimental intelligence summaries in late October indicated that the Oran Division had been in a state of readiness since October 10 and that the French anticipated an assault soon against Algeria, probably at Dakar or Algiers. The formation of mobile detachments in the Oran Division in late October led intelligence officers to believe that the French High Command would conduct guerrilla warfare if assault landings were successful in securing the Oran area. The summary cautioned commanders that the landings and the advance on Oran would likely be opposed.[29]

The plan for the 1st Infantry Division landings in Algeria called for three distinct assaults. Armored Task Force Green was to land at Beach X near Mersa Bou Zedjar, the 26th Infantry at Beach Y at La Andelouses, and the 16th and 18th Infantry Regiments were to assault Beach Z just southeast of Arzew. Armored Task Force Red (Combat Command B, 1st Armored Division) would also land at Beach Z, once it was secured by the infantry. The 1st Ranger Battalion had missions to take out coastal batteries on Cape Carbon and in the city of Arzew. The 509th Parachute Infantry was to jump in and seize the Tafaraoui airfield at first light. Once ashore, the armored task forces were to advance to the airfield and link up with the paratroopers, while the infantry were to cut off Oran from any reinforcements and capture the city. The primary objective was to capture the port facilities of Oran intact, so they could be used to support further American thrusts into eastern Morocco and Tunisia.[30]

The 1st Infantry Division was organized into the "combat team" configuration for Operation Torch. Combat Team 16 (CT 16) consisted of its usual elements and, at least for the amphibious phase of Torch, also included two batteries of the 105th Coast Artillery Battalion (AA), the 1st Recon Troop, and the 3rd Battalion, 351st Engineer Shore Regiment.[31]

The Center Task Force arrived in the Gulf of Arzew just before midnight November 7 and began preparations for the landings. During the approach and subsequent preparations for the landing, the men of the 3rd Battalion had the opportunity to listen to the Army-Notre Dame football game broadcast over the ship's address system.[32] The 2nd Battalion was even luckier. The master of the *Duchess of Bedford*, Captain Busk-Wood, opened up the ship's aft bar for men to get a drink before the invasion.[33] By midnight, the assault troops of Lieutenant Colonel William A. Cunningham's 1st Battalion and Gibb's 3rd Battalion were on landing craft circling in the inky blackness, waiting for the signal to go in.

The loading operation was not a smooth one for Sergeant Major Lipinski, now regimental sergeant major. In charge of two important radio operators and several men from the advanced command post (CP), Lipinski and his detail loaded into a boat for the move to shore. Unfortunately, one of the boat davits failed to release, and Lipinski and his troops were dumped into the Mediterranean. Pulled aboard, he and the men were quickly refitted with new gear, and the detail with the precious radios was loaded aboard the next landing craft going ashore. The coxswain gunned the engine, and the craft raced off into the night to link up with the first wave. Unable to locate the other craft, the coxswain headed for the shore, thinking that the others had already gone in. On reaching the beach, Lipinski, the radio operators, and the rest of the men on the craft trotted ashore against no opposition. The craft pulled away, and suddenly, the men realized that there were no other troops in the area. They had apparently landed before the rest of the assault forces! Lipinski quickly moved the men to a wadi for protection and waited for the rest of the assault force to arrive.[34]

Finally, the signal came, and the rest of the boats headed for shore. The troops were tense with anticipation. No one knew whether the French were going to fight them or welcome them. At 1:00 a.m., the initial wave landed on beaches Z White (3rd Battalion) and Z Red (1st Battalion) and moved rapidly inland to seize St. Leu. The troops encountered no opposition on the beaches. The 1st Battalion then fanned out to capture Demesme and advance on Port-aux-Poules, while Gibb led the 3rd Battalion inland down the road to Ste. Barbe-du-Tlelat, then veered west to seize Fleurus. The French offered only light opposition against the 3rd Battalion, and by 7:45 a.m., Fleurus was in Gibb's possession.[35]

As their comrades advanced inland that morning, the men of the 2nd Battalion, under Major Joseph B. Crawford, had remained aboard ship as the floating reserve for the 1st Division. Anxious to get into the fight, Crawford moved his battalion ashore about 10:00 a.m., without orders. When this was discovered by division headquarters, the battalion was released from reserve and sent along the same route as the 3rd Battalion toward Fleurus. Meanwhile, Gibb was moving on Ferme Arzeleff against scattered resistance, and Cunningham had pushed on to attack La Macta and seize the highway and the railroad bridges to the east. Cunningham's men were ordered to hold those bridges to prevent expected French reinforcements from Mostaganem and Perreguax from reaching Oran.[36]

At La Macta, the 1st Battalion ran into heavy resistance from the 2nd Régiment Chasseurs d'Afrique, an Algerian regiment. The battalion's lead elements were ambushed entering the town and a general engagement ensued. Having dropped off C and D Companies at St. Leu and Port-aux-Poules, and Company A at En Nakala, Cunningham had only Company B and Headquarters Company for the fight. Nevertheless, he ordered the two companies to conduct a coordinated attack, and supported by the guns of Battery A, 7th Field Artillery Battalion, and the HMS *Farndale*, succeeded in overcoming resistance by 1:30 p.m. The battalion secured the bridges by 2:00 p.m.[37]

That evening, there was little doubt about the final outcome of the fighting around Oran. Yet the French were not finished. The 18th Infantry was stalled on the road to St. Cloud by the 6th Régiment Tirailleurs Algeriens and the battalion of the Étranger Infantrie (Foreign Legion). About dark, Company K was detached to the 18th Infantry for an early morning assault on the town the next day. Meanwhile, the 3rd Battalion had moved north at 10:00 p.m. to cut the road behind the Algerians to prevent their escape.[38] Moving along the road flanking St. Cloud, however, the lead company of the 2nd Battalion was mortared by the French. Lieutenant Fred Hall, leading the point element, remembered that his men "took cover in the ditches along both sides of the road. There was an eerie glow from the ditch opposite me. One of the mortar shells had cut the electric light wire overhead and the live wire had fallen into the [rain-filled] ditch killing four of my soldiers. These were our first casualties."[39]

On the morning of November 9, the 1st Battalion held blocking positions at La Macta-En Nakala, the 2nd Battalion at Fleurus-Le Grand, and the 3rd Battalion astride the Oran-St. Cloud road. The 3rd Battalion received sporadic fire during the day, and infiltrating Algerians attempted to cut the 1st Battalion off from the beaches. However, after several brief but sharp firefights, Cunningham's men drove off the infiltrators. That afternoon, elements of the 6th Armored Infantry and the 19th Engineers arrived to relieve the 1st Battalion, allowing it to join the regimental attack on Oran.[40]

About 3:00 p.m. on November 9, Colonel Cheadle received orders to take Oran "at all costs." Cheadle planned for a two-pronged assault. The 3rd Battalion, reinforced by the Antitank Company; Company A, 1st Engineers; and the 5th Field Artillery Battalion, were to advance toward Oran down the St. Cloud road. The 2nd Battalion, reinforced by a battery of the 5th Field Artillery, and the newly returned K Company, were to move along a parallel road running from Fleurus to Assi Ameur into Oran. At 5:00 p.m., the regiment jumped off.

On the outskirts of Arcole, five miles east of Oran, the 3rd Battalion ran into substantial resistance, but overcame it by about 11:30 p.m. Just after midnight, the French laid a heavy barrage on both columns, and the 2nd Battalion experienced heavy machine-gun fire at Ferme St. Jean Baptiste as well. The columns halted in place as patrols reconnoitered to pin-

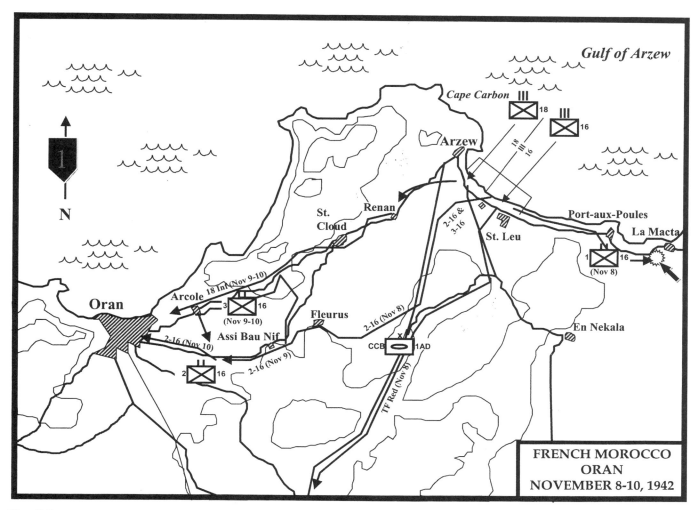

Map 8-2.

point the enemy positions. About 3:30 a.m., a staff officer from division headquarters found the 2nd Battalion and directed Gibb to rejoin the regiment on the 2nd Battalion route. The 18th Infantry had finally bypassed St. Cloud and was moving up to join the assault on Oran, and it would need the road that Gibb's battalion was using. Somewhat disgruntled, Gibb located a lateral road and began the journey south to link up with the regiment.[41] By 6:00 a.m., the battalion had reached the new route but had been under mortar and artillery fire almost the whole way.

Oddly, the position the 3rd Battalion had to relinquish to the 18th Infantry was almost at the Oran city limits and was better situated for the assault than the direction from which the regiment was now approaching the town. To make matters worse, the 3rd Battalion was to enter the new route behind the 2nd Battalion but ended up between Crawford's men and a battalion of the 2nd Régiment Chasseurs d'Afrique, which held a strongpoint near the village of St. Eugene, just as heavy firing broke out. Gibb's men now were pinned down between the two

forces as the fire passed over their heads. The fighting persisted at St. Eugene for six hours, as the 2nd Battalion leapfrogged forward through a series of farms, reducing one position after the other with the assistance of Cannon Company. Finally, the French troops were compelled to submit, and 308 chasseurs surrendered to the 2nd Battalion.[42]

After its relief at La Macta, the 1st Battalion had been trucked to link up with the regiment, and by 10:30 a.m., November 10, the regiment had been consolidated. Colonel Cheadle issued an order for the 1st and 2nd Battalions to take Oran, with the attack to begin about noon. The assault was to be supported by the 5th Field Artillery and Cannon Company, with the 3rd Battalion in reserve. The attack kicked off on time, and within an hour, all resistance within the city had ended.[43] Oran was in American hands.

The campaign, although brief, had cost the regiment twenty-five men killed and seventy-nine wounded. It was a relatively light tally compared to what was to come. Nonetheless, the men were proud of their work, and morale was excellent. The following day, the regimental headquarters was moved to St. Louis with the Service Company, Medical Detachment, and Antitank Company, providing local security. The 1st Battalion was moved to Tafaraoui airfield to secure it from air assault, while the 2nd Battalion was billeted at the so-called Casa Nuef, the barracks for the local garrison at Oran, and tasked to provide law and order in the city. Meanwhile, the 3rd Battalion was bivouacked at Fleurus with the 7th Field Artillery.[44]

In late December, the 16th Infantry received a new commanding officer. He was Colonel d'Alary Fechet, a West Point graduate from the class of 1912. During World War I, Fechet had served with the 2nd Division. Assigned initially to the 23rd Infantry, he took command of the 5th Machine Gun Battalion in January 1918 and led it through its campaigns until he was severely wounded during the Soissons offensive. A war hero, he was awarded the Chevalier of the Legion of Valor and the Croix de Guerre by the French government, and the Distinguished Service Cross. After the war, he stayed with the 2nd Division until assigned as the military attaché to Japan in 1924. He then attended the Infantry School, the Command and General Staff School, and the War College, and served in the 30th Infantry at the Presidio of San Francisco. In 1932, he was serving as the PMS&T (professor of military science and tactics) for Claremont College when he was retired for disability. After he left the service, Fechet became the principal of a children's day school, a vocation that would have unfortunate consequences later when interacting with his soldiers. In May 1940, he was recalled to active duty to be the PMS&T of the University of California until he received orders to become the military attaché to Great Britain in January 1942. He was assigned as the deputy chief of staff, 1st Infantry Division, in August 1942 and was in that assignment when he was assigned to command the 16th Infantry.[45] Although a good friend of Terry Allen's, he would prove to be an unpopular commander.

For two months, the regiment remained in the Oran area on occupation duty. Despite the recent fighting, however, the local population was generally friendly. One officer later wrote, "One of our objectives was to make friends with the French and convince their forces to join us. In a display of solidarity, we held a Thanksgiving Day parade and French units marched with us."[46]

One duty performed by the battalion garrisoned in Oran was guard duty, and among the various posts to be guarded was the "Villa Rosa," a popular whorehouse in the city. The task was not to prevent the soldiers from going in, rather it was to ensure that the business operated smoothly, without interference from drunken or otherwise troublesome soldiers. Other than a rotation of battalion duties in December, the regiment's only other major activity was training. During the first week in January, a regiment from the 34th Infantry "Red Bull" Division relieved the 16th Infantry of the positions around Oran. The regiment then began a two-week truck and rail journey that ended at Guelma, Algeria, on January 23.

Tunisian Campaign
January 23-May 9, 1943

The Axis situation in North Africa in January 1943 was not good. Field Marshal Erwin Rommel's German-Italian Panzer Army, which included the famous German Africa Corps (Deutches Afrika Korps or DAK), was reeling from losses inflicted by Montgomery's Eighth Army. Rommel's men were indeed tired, but they still had plenty of fight, and they soon demonstrated that to the novice American soldiers.

As Axis forces withdrew eastward, their lines of communication contracted, facilitating the supply of frontline units. The Allies, with their lengthening lines of communication, suffered accordingly. In the next series of actions involving the 16th Infantry, resupply problems had a deleterious effect on the regiment's combat performance. These problems were exacerbated by a deployment that saw the 1st Infantry Division split up and committed piecemeal along a two-hundred-mile front, much to the dismay and opposition of Terry Allen. The 16th Infantry was placed under the operational control of the 36th British Brigade, which, in turn, was under the control of the French XIX Corps—a difficult logistics situation, to say the least.

Ousseltia Valley

The newly constituted Fifth Panzer Army, under General Jürgen von Arnim, was wreaking havoc in the XIX Corps' zone, and in response, the II U.S. Corps ordered elements of the 1st Infantry Division committed piecemeal to various French and British commands to help stop the onslaught. On January 24, Cunningham's 1st Battalion was dispatched by the II Corps to link up with Combat Command B (CCB), 1st Armored Division, located near Ousseltia village. Upon arrival, the battalion moved into defensive positions but was not engaged. On the 26th, the regiment, less the 1st and 3rd Battalions, was ordered to the Siliana Valley, where the 1st Battalion was to rejoin it. As the regimental headquarters moved toward Siliana, the 1st Battalion and CCB, supported by the 7th Field Artillery Battalion, conducted a sweeping movement to contact into the Ousseltia Valley, forcing the enemy to withdraw with little resistance. After completion of the sweep, the 1st Battalion secured positions on the northern end of Djebel Serdj (Serdj Mountain), facing east across the valley.[47]

The regiment next shifted its direction of travel, linked up with the 1st Battalion in the Ousseltia Valley, and moved into positions on Djebel Serdj. Meanwhile, the 3rd Battalion dug in on the right (southeast) of the 1st Battalion. For the next several days, the regiment conducted reconnaissance patrols to develop routes and locate attack positions from which to counterattack enemy units that might attack down the Siliana Valley.

In the meantime, on January 27, the 2nd Battalion was attached to the British 36th Brigade to replace one of its battalions that had been detached to the British V Corps. The brigade's mission was to hold two major routes that led into the center of the XIX French Corps sector. The 2nd Battalion was

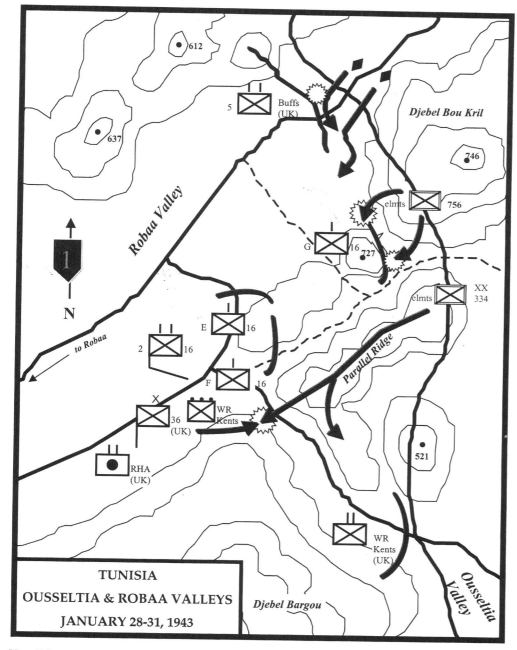

Map 8-3.

727, known as "Conical Hill," with one company providing the 2nd Battalion's attached forward observers (FO) with a protected observation post to survey the Robaa Valley, the northern Ousseltia Valley, and Djebel Bou Kril, the latter believed to be occupied by German troops. That night, G Company, under the command of Captain Carl Steuzel, and an attached heavy machine-gun platoon from H Company, stealthily moved forward and occupied the hill without incident.[49]

When a company supply jeep, sent during the night to Steuzel's position, failed to show up, Steuzel went forward at dawn to look for it. While walking down a mule trail in search of the lost vehicle, he was killed by machine-gun fire that also wounded his driver as the latter was dragging Steuzel's body back to their position. That afternoon, a patrol from F Company was sent up a parallel ridge that overlooked both Hill 727 and the location where Captain Stuezel was killed. The patrol ran off the enemy machine-gun crew and discovered a great deal of enemy activity on the far side of the ridge. The patrol reported the situation, but the information was interpreted by the battalion and brigade intelligence officers as either a relief in place or a withdrawal. In fact, the patrol had observed the enemy's preparations for a major attack against the 36th Brigade and Conical Hill.

Conical Hill was well situated as an observation post, affording Americans unobstructed views of the enemy's main positions and the routes leading to them. But the hill was not big enough to accommodate a reinforced rifle company, and the American positions on it were vulnerable to fire from the heights of the parallel ridgeline to the south. The Germans realized that Hill 727 could prove a major problem to their operations if it were left in American hands, and they quickly

trucked to its destination, arriving after a rainy night's journey to take up positions as the brigade reserve on the south side of the Robaa Valley. The British commander, Brigadier "Swifty" Howlett, positioned Crawford's men where they might support either the "Buffs" (the Royal East Kent Regiment, blocking the road from Pont du Fahs to the northeast) or the Royal West Kents (straddling the road leading from Ousseltia to the southeast).[48]

On January 28, Howlett ordered Crawford to occupy Hill

resolved to retake it.[50]

Early on the cold, misty morning of January 31, fighting opened in front of the Buffs when a German armored force pushed southwest down the road toward Robaa. From a position behind and to the left of Conical Hill, then-Lieutenant Colonel Crawford watched the distant battle unfold, fascinated by the sight of British antitank guns spewing white puffs of smoke as they engaged the enemy tanks. Suddenly, black puffs appeared over Conical Hill, indicating that G Company was taking airbursts from an artillery bombardment. Soon, the telephone line went dead and the men of G Company were in a fight for their lives.[51]

With enemy artillery and mortars pounding Conical Hill, G Company troopers pressed deep into their holes to escape the bombardment. Tracers from enemy machine guns crisscrossed overhead and ricocheted off the rocky hillside. Then, as Stuka dive bombers screamed down on the British artillery, suppressing the guns and depriving the Americans of both their direct support and counterbattery fire, German mountain troops of the 756th Gebirgsjäger Regiment conducted a frontal attack against G Company's stout defenses. Forced from their positions, a number of American troops fell back to the forward slope of the ridge on which E and F Companies had organized their defenses. To the men on that forward slope, the remainder of G Company, stranded on Conical Hill, appeared to have been cut off or captured. To the south, troops of the German 334th Infantry Division massed on the parallel ridge ominously flanking Hill 727, but instead of sweeping into G Company's rear, the Germans pushed along the ridgeline to the forward positions of F Company.[52]

Elsewhere, the Buffs had held their own and destroyed several tanks, including at least two of the new Panzerkampfwagen (PzKw) Mark VI "Tiger" tanks. The West Kents, however, were cut off by the German assault along the parallel ridge. A counterattack by a reserve platoon from the West Kents, reinforced by Crusader medium tanks, failed to dislodge the Germans. Even so, the Germans did not consolidate their gains and soon withdrew.[53]

Upon the enemy's departure, the Americans sent patrols to Conical Hill, where they expected to find a few defeated survivors of G Company. Instead they discovered that the hill's defenders had thrashed the Gebirgsjägers, inflicting heavy casualties on the enemy force, especially among the officers. But G Company, although victorious, had also suffered heavily, taking nearly one hundred casualties. With only forty effectives (officers and men) remaining, G Company was pulled out of the line and placed in reserve to refit and reconstitute. Several days later, Crawford received orders to rejoin the regiment in the Ousseltia Valley.[54]

By the time the 2nd Battalion linked up with the regiment, the 1st Division had reestablished control over its elements and had the mission of defending a forty-mile arc between Kairouan, Pichon, and Ousseltia. For the next ten days, the reg-

iment spent a relatively quiet time in positions on Djebel Er Rihana, on the eastern side of the valley. On February 19, positions were re-established at the 1st Battalion's old positions on Djebel Serdj, on the west side of the valley. The following day, Fechet had his regiment on the road as the lead element for the division's move to the Kasserine area.

Kasserine Pass

On February 14-15, the 1st Armored Division had been severely handled by elements of Arnim's Fifth Panzer Army at Sidi Bou Zid, at the western end of Faid Pass, and the II Corps ordered the 1st Infantry Division to help plug the holes. The division detached CT 18 to the 34th Infantry Division to help block penetrations driving north out of Sbietla, and CT 26 (TF Stark) was deployed to cover Kasserine Pass to prevent elements of Rommel's Afrika Corps, now organized into a *Kampfgruppe* (battle group) and attacking from the south through Gafsa, from advancing through the pass to Tébessa or Thala. Meanwhile, the 26th Infantry (minus two battalions), under the command Colonel Alexander N. Stark Jr., had been attached directly to Major General Lloyd Fredendall's II Corps for the defense of Kasserine Pass. On February 17-18, Fredendall undertook to strengthen Starks's regiment by giving the latter elements of the 19th Engineer Regiment, the 33rd Field Artillery Battalino, and the 805th Tank Destroyer Battalion. Stark arrived at the pass early the following morning to find the 19th Engineers busily preparing defenses on the southwest half of the pass, and his own 1st Battalion preparing the northeast half. The defenses were only partially completed when the initial probing attacks by the German 33rd Reconnaissance Battalion began at 10:00 a.m.

Reports from the 33rd revealed to Rommel that the pass was too strong for a recon unit to seize, so he committed two battalions of the DAK to punch through during the night. Probing attacks by German infantry occurred throughout the night of February 19-20. A full-scale fight had developed by early the following morning.

Concerned that he would be delayed too long at the pass, Rommel committed both the DAK and the 10th Panzer Division to penetrate TF Stark, drive into the heart of the valley beyond, and continue the attack toward Tébessa. By late afternoon on the 20th, Starks's defenses had been shattered and Rommel's troops were moving northwest from the Bou Chebka Pass and along the road to Tébessa.

Allen ordered Fechet to move CT 16 by truck from Ousseltia to Bou Chebka on February 20 to link up with elements of the 1st Armored Division and the French Constantine Division defending the area of Djebel Chambi, near the village of Kasserine.[55] A short time after the regiment's arrival that afternoon, Crawford's 2nd Battalion was attached to CCB, 1st Armored Division, under the command of Brigadier General Paul McD. Robinett. At dusk on February 20, Robinett ordered the 2nd Battalion to establish blocking positions that covered

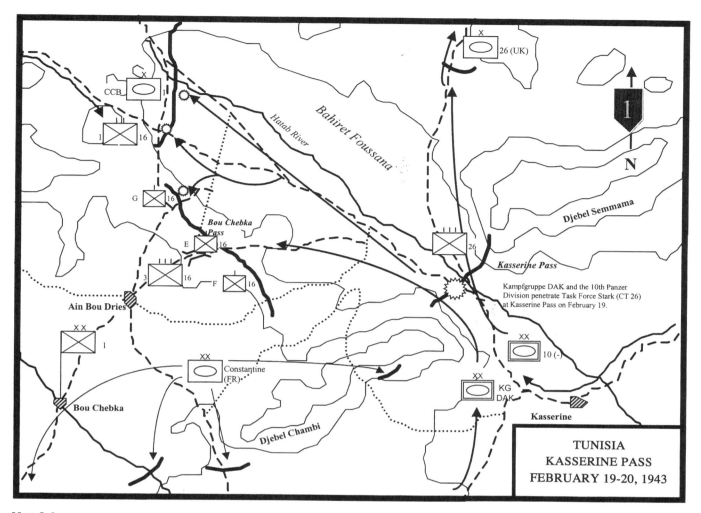

Map 8-4.

the trails leading west onto the plateau of Bou Chebka Pass toward Ain Bou Dries. Once there, Crawford made contact with the elements of TF Stark that had been pushed out of Kasserine Pass the day before and took up positions on their left. With an attack imminent, all units worked feverishly to dig in along the lip of the Bahiret Foussana.[56]

Company E was positioned astride the road leading through the Bou Chebka Pass; G Company held positions to the north of the pass, protecting batteries of the 33rd Field Artillery; and the remaining elements were placed to the south. All faced east across the valley. To reinforce Crawford, Allen directed Fechet to position a battalion in reserve behind the 2nd Battalion, and to send another battalion to defend the passes at Djebel el Hamra. Fechet sent the 3rd Battalion, under the command of Lieutenant Colonel John H. Mathews from the first of the year, to set up just east of Ain Bou Dries, where three trails converged leading west from the Bahiret Foussana valley. This location enabled Mathews to reinforce Crawford to the north, center, or south, and to backstop any enemy elements

that made it through. Cunningham's 1st Battalion was sent on a long motor march from Bou Chebka through Tèbessa and Haidra to a dismount point north of Djebel el Hamra. From there, the battalion deployed in combat formation and cautiously approached the designated defense area at dawn, expecting to retake it by force, only to discover that the 13th Armored Regiment already held the position.[57]

During the hours of darkness on the night of February 20-21, only a few scattered shots indicated there was any enemy activity at all. However, the scouts of the 33rd Reconnaissance Battalion, the eyes and ears of Kampfgruppe DAK, lurked in the valley. But they failed to detect the rather extensive efforts of CCB and the 2nd Battalion to cover the passes and reported incorrectly to Rommel that the passes were only lightly defended. That was what Rommel wanted to hear. He ordered the DAK, commanded by General Karl Buelowius, to seize the northern pass through Djebel el Hamra to protect his west flank, while the 10th Panzer Division, conducting the main effort, attacked to seize Thala. At 2:00 p.m., Kampfgruppe

DAK rolled through the Foussana Pass heading for its objective, but by 4:30 p.m. it had run into heavy artillery and tank fire from the 13th Armor and four massed howitzer battalions. The attack ground to a halt at 6:00 p.m., still four miles beyond Djebel el Hamra.[58]

During the night of February 21-22, all battalions of the regiment continued to improve their defenses. The weather had turned worse; cold, oppressive rains made the night miserable, but it caused more problems for the Germans than the Americans. The predawn darkness of February 22 found the Panzer Grenadier Regiment Africa struggling through the rugged terrain in a heavy downpour, trying to locate and attack the passes held by the 1st Battalion at Djebel el Hamra. Their attack was launched in a thick fog against the northern portion of the 2nd Battalion line held by G Company near the Bou Chebka Pass. The Germans forced G Company out of its position on Hill 812, and five guns of Battery C, 33rd Field Artillery, were abandoned to the enemy. By 9:00 a.m., however, the fog had dissipated, exposing the panzer grenadiers who were unable to advance any farther due to the pounding meted out by the division's artillery and the direct fire of the rest of the 2nd Battalion.[59] The grenadiers were pinned down.

Around 11:00 a.m. on the 22nd, the 1st Battalion, 8th Panzer Regiment, and the Italian 5th Bersaglieri Battalion pushed north into the 1st Battalion area, attempting to take the correct object at El Hamra pass and concurrently relieving the pressure on the now-beleaguered panzer grenadiers. By noon, however, this effort against Cunningham's infantry and the 13th Armored Regiment was also stopped cold. Throughout the morning, Allen had attempted to direct Fechet to retake Hill 812, and he was finally successful in reaching him in the early afternoon. Fechet, in turn, ordered Mathews' 3rd Battalion to attack the hill and the 2nd Battalion to provide support. At 4:00 p.m., the attack finally jumped off. Aided by tanks of G Company, 13th Armor, the 3rd Battalion drove the enemy off the hill and recaptured the guns of the 33rd Field Artillery. This attack inflicted heavy casualties on the panzer grenadiers and caused them great confusion and disorientation. A subsequent drive pushed many of the enemy troops north into the 13th Armor's lines, and over three hundred Germans were captured.[60]

Throughout the 22nd, Rommel's forces encountered stiffening resistance along all routes exiting west and north of the Bahiret Foussana Valley. The DAK had been bloodied by the combined efforts of the 16th Infantry and CCB, which were defending the northwest and western passes. About the same time, the 10th Panzer Division's drive on Thala was blunted and turned back by the 26th British Brigade. By late afternoon, Rommel realized that further efforts were not likely to achieve a breakthrough, and he decided to fall back. His orders to do so went out that night.

The following morning (February 23) the 16th Infantry, supported by a tank-infantry task force of the British Grenadier Guards, counterattacked across the Bahiret Foussana valley to retake the Kasserine Pass. Only light resistance was encountered from German stragglers, who had been separated from their commands and had failed to join the retreat when their units had moved through the pass the night before. Thus, the 3rd Battalion easily pushed through the gap to occupy positions on Djebel Ed Jebbas, located some three kilometers south of the pass. The 1st Battalion secured the western half of the pass, while the Guards task force took up positions on the shoulder of Djebel Semmama in the east. Shortly thereafter, the 2nd Battalion relieved the Grenadier Guards of their positions on Djebel Semmama.[61]

Unlike much of the II Corps, the 16th Infantry, in its first major challenge from the dreaded "Desert Fox" and his famous Afrika Corps, had at least bloodied the Germans. The fighting at Kasserine Pass proved a valuable experience for the men of the 16th Infantry, who learned a great deal about how the German soldier fought and how to defeat his attacks. In doing so they also learned that the troops of CT 16 were every bit as good as those of the famous Africa Corps, and that Rommel himself could be defeated. Most importantly, they learned that armored assaults against dug-in infantry were not likely to succeed, if the defenders fought skillfully. It was a lesson that would serve them in good stead a few months later in Sicily.

But the fighting had been costly. The regiment now needed replacements and time to refit. Many of its troops were wearing British uniforms issued when their own had worn out during the fighting in the rough terrain of the Ousseltia Valley. On March 1, the 60th Infantry (9th Infantry Division) relieved CT 16 of its positions in the Kasserine Pass, and the regiment joined the rest of the "Red One" in a rest area at Marsott, Tunisia. For ten days, the regiment rested, refitted, and conducted training at Marsott.

On March 10, Allen received orders to capture the French garrison town of Gafsa. The capture of the town was to support a link-up with General Bernard Montgomery's Eighth Army, pushing northwestward from the Mareth Line. In short, the capture of Gafsa signaled the beginning of the last phase of the struggle for North Africa.

Gafsa-El Guettar

The impending assignment for II Corps was known by the unlikely moniker of Operation Wop. The corps mission was to push down the Feriana-Gafsa road to seize Gafsa, then send forces toward El Guettar and Maknassy to threaten the communications lines of the Fifth Panzer Army that held the Mareth Line. The Eighth Army's push northwest and the II Corps' drive east were to effect a link-up after the Mareth Line was broken. The capture of Gafsa would provide a depot area and forward airfields for Montgomery's command from which it could support itself for future joint operations toward Tunis and Bizerte. The attack was also designed to draw away reserves from the Mareth Line, which had not yet been broken by the

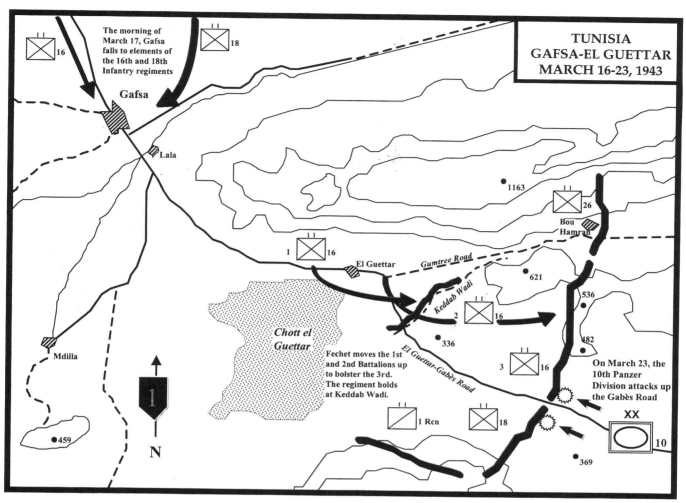

Map 8-5.

Eighth Army.[62]

The 1st Infantry Division drew the assignment of capturing Gafsa. Gafsa was an ancient town, long known as an oasis along the caravan routes skirting the northern edge of the Sahara Desert. French colonial forces had garrisoned the town for decades. Military intelligence sources now reported the Gafsa area as held by the Italian Centauro Division. The 1st Division plan was to attack the town from the northwest: CT 16 would attack directly into the town along the Feriana-Gafsa road, with the 1st Ranger Battalion advancing on the regiment's right and the Blue Spaders of the 26th Infantry on the left. The 18th Infantry was the division reserve.

On receiving the warning order for Operation Wop, Fechet dispatched a reconnaissance party to scout assembly areas where the regiment would dismount for the attack on the town. On March 11, the division was moved farther south to El Meredj; then next day it returned to its previous locations near Bou Chebka. Additionally, several days before the attack, the 1st Engineers were sent to clear the roads to Gafsa, removing

thousands of mines along the way. The engineers remained in positions along the road to ensure the way was not re-mined before the division made its final move.[63] All this activity did not escape the notice of the Italians in the Gafsa area, and it was assumed by the Americans that the enemy would be in a state of high alert when the attack was launched.

"Red One" troops were subsequently heartened to learn the Italians were pulling out of the Gafsa area. Therefore, on the rainy night of March 16, the regiment loaded in trucks at Bou Chebka and made the forty-five mile drive to its assembly areas unopposed and without major mishap. Though the move was made rapidly and efficiently (the assault units were in position well before the 6:00 a.m. LD time), the actual jump-off was pushed back to 10:00 a.m. on the 17th. The delay was caused by the inexplicable tardiness of the air bombardment ordered to soften up the defenses, even though it was obvious by 8:00 a.m. that the Italians were giving up the town.[64]

About midmorning, the aircraft finally showed up, dropped their bombs on the now-undefended target, and sped away. Shortly after the air strike, the regiment moved out with the 3rd Battalion on the left, the 1st on the right, and the 2nd in reserve. Against almost no opposition, I Company entered the town about twenty minutes after noon, pushed through, and linked up with troops of the 18th Infantry—the latter having approached Gafsa using a route that deposited that regiment on the east side of the town in an attempt to cut off the enemy's escape route.[65]

The 16th's regimental chaplain at this time was the incomparable Lawrence E. Deery. "Father Deery," as he was known, was a hard-drinking, hard-nosed Irish-American Jesuit from the boroughs of New York. The day of the attack on Gafsa also happened to be St. Patrick's Day, and Father Deery was not going to let a little war interfere with this important Catholic feast day. He vowed that he would preside over a St. Patrick's Day mass at the first opportunity. In fact, the town had been in American hands no more than an hour before the chaplain was preaching his homily.[66]

The good priest was a popular member of the 16th. Not satisfied with just giving the last rites for the dead and dying of the command, Father Deery was often seen helping with the digging of graves and the tender preparation and burial of his beloved comrades. He had been awarded the Silver Star for valor during the operations in Algeria: on November 9, during the 3rd Battalion actions near St. Cloud, he had gone forward to the front lines and assisted two wounded soldiers in crossing several fields covered by enemy machine-guns. After delivering the men to an aid station, he returned to the front, making his way through enemy lines to bring water to some 3rd Battalion soldiers. His willingness to do more than what was expected of a chaplain endeared him to the men of the regiment.[67]

After taking Gafsa, the 16th became the division reserve. Colonel Fechet was directed to occupy blocking positions astride the Gafsa-Maknassy Road to the east of the village. This position was located so that a force could easily defend the approaches to Gafsa on either the road to Maknassy or the road to Gabès. Mathews' 3rd Battalion drew the blocking assignment, while Crawford's 2nd Battalion occupied positions in the oasis. Cunningham's 1st Battalion garrisoned Gafsa and provided security for the new airstrip under construction there.[68] The remainder of the division continued its push toward El Guettar on the night of March 20 in heavy rains that now seemed continuous. The following day, the attacks carried the 1st Division to the foothills of the Djebel el Mcheltat against half-hearted resistance from the Centauro Division.[69] One officer remembered this attack well:

My company's first objective was to clear out some Italian positions reinforced by German artillery. We began a night attack across fairly open ground. The small-arms fire was intense, but we finally penetrated the Italian line. Lo and behold, the Italians began to surrender coming out of their positions with bags in their hands looking for passage

to the USA. This infuriated us because we figured as prisoners of war, they would get home [to the USA] before we would. It also infuriated the Germans who held Italians in low esteem and began firing on their surrendering allies.[70]

To consolidate the division's gains, Colonel Fechet was directed to assume a sector of front that placed the 3rd Battalion squarely between the 18th Infantry and the 26th Infantry. The battalion's right flank lay on the El Guettar-Gabès road and extended north through the foothills to link up with the 26th Infantry.

That evening, General Buelowius sent the 10th Panzer Division to counterattack and seize Gafsa. The 10th Panzer was a seasoned outfit with a proud battle record. In addition to its superb record in North Africa, the unit had played a vital role in the Battle of France in 1940. It was the fast-moving 10th Panzer that had slipped so rapidly through the Ardennes to take Sedan before French defenses could properly organize.[71] This feat allowed German forces to rapidly cross the Meuse River and bypass much of the Maginot Line.

On the morning of March 23, the famous division was attempting to perform a similar feat. By 5:00 a.m. the division's lead elements were spraying the southern slopes of Djebel el Mcheltat with tracers as they conducted a reconnaissance by fire, probing for a weak spot to break through. The men of the 3rd Battalion, reinforced by elements of the 601st Tank Destroyer Battalion, resisted vigorously.

As the fight at El Guettar grew hot, the 3rd Battalion received numerous artillery barrages that caused the veterans to cringe in their holes and rattled the nerves of the replacements. Down in the L Company area, Henry Orten shared a foxhole with one of the new soldiers. The intense artillery fire caused the man to break down and soon he was crying from fear. Once the fire slackened a bit, Orten attempted to steady the man by offering him a cigarette and talking to him. Hearing the exchange below him, Sergeant McLaughlin, now the acting platoon leader, popped out of his hole and walked down to the two men's position. Amidst explosions from artillery shells and streaking tracers, McLaughlin looked at the two soldiers, frowned at the scared man, and growled, "So what the hell do you want? Every day's just like the Fourth of July!"[72]

After the morning fog had burned away, Buelowius, from his CP on Hill 369, observed his panzers now methodically pressing their attack against the 3rd Battalions of both the 16th and 18th Infantry.[73] Concerned about his left flank, Mathews contacted Fechet to alert him to the German counterattack. Fechet, in turn, alerted Cunningham and Crawford, then sent the 2nd Battalion to take up positions on Mathews' left. Fechet then directed the 1st Battalion to occupy reserve positions in the Keddab Wadi, behind the main line, in case a breakthrough occurred down the road. Detrucking his troops at the fork of the Gafsa-Gabès and "Gumtree" roads, Crawford led the 2nd Battalion into positions beside the 3rd Battalion as the battle raged.[74]

The brunt of the assault fell on Mathews' men and the 3rd Battalion, 18th Infantry. Fifty tanks of the 7th Panzer Regiment, reinforced by the troops of the 69th and 86th Panzer Grenadier Regiments, fought tenaciously to dislodge the soldiers of the "Fighting First." Reinforced by the 5th Field Artillery Battalion, firing in the direct-fire mode against the panzers, the 16th Infantry slowly gave ground until reaching the Keddab Wadi. Once there, the line stiffened, and no further ground was given.[75]

After heavy fighting, the morning's attack by the 10th Panzer was finally held, but not until several guns of the 32nd Field Artillery Battalion had been overrun. Ordered to counterattack and retake the guns, Crawford directed E Company to conduct the mission. A little after noon, Captain Maynard W. Files pushed E Company southeastward to Hill 483 and recovered the guns before they could be destroyed by the Germans. By then, the remaining elements of the 10th Panzer Division had pulled back.[76]

Intelligence reports concluded that the 10th Panzer would try another push that afternoon, so the forward units prepared to receive the blow. The German counterattack came about 6:30 p.m., but the combined effects of concentrated artillery, antitank weapons, and machine-gun fire from the 16th and the 18th Infantry doomed the enemy effort.[77]

Over the next several days, the regiment remained in positions along the Gafsa-Gabès road until ordered to advance on Djebel el Mcheltat. The seizure of the djebel was supposed to set up conditions for the 1st Armored Division to punch deep into the enemy's rear areas. On the morning of March 28, the regiment jumped off from the Keddab Wadi and advanced four miles over rugged terrain, headed for its objective, Hill 482. The progress was unbearably slow. The regiment advanced wadi by wadi, ridge by ridge, working its way east, and suffering casualties for every yard it gained, including Lieutenant Colonel Cunningham of the 1st Battalion. The move was hampered by a lack of accurate topographic maps and the enemy's surveillance of the entire route. By day's end, the hill remained in the hands of the 48th Pioneer Battalion.[78]

That night, the 2nd Battalion attacked a well-defended intermediate objective reinforced with barbed wire and artillery. Crawford's men took the position, but were, in turn, pushed off by a combined tank-infantry counterattack. The battalion lost Captain Files, and an entire platoon from E Company was captured in the counterattack. The next morning, the position was carried again by a combined assault by the 1st and 3rd Battalions, but once again, at a high cost in casualties to both units.[79]

In the meantime, Fechet's men were losing confidence in their commander. In part this attitude was attributable to the stress of combat. But Fechet's unfortunate way of dealing with soldiers was the primary factor. The regimental commander had demonstrated several irritating personal quirks and poor leadership techniques from the beginning of his command. For example, he had the aggravating habit of addressing men as if they were his former kindergarten wards. He woke troops in the morning by gently prodding them as if they were children. On one occasion, German infantry and tanks were spotted rolling toward the regiment's defensive positions. A captain who had been observing the enemy scrambled into the regimental CP and notified Fechet of the oncoming force. Rather than moving out to check the spot report, Fechet chastised the officer for not wearing his helmet and field gear, told the man to put on his equipment, and then come back in to render a proper report. He waited for the officer to come back in the correct uniform before hearing the report; all the while, the German tanks rumbled closer to the regiment's positions. Fechet's neurotic obsession with being properly uniformed once prompted him to place a dishpan on his head when his helmet was lost. Such odd behavior caused more than just those in the regimental headquarters to believe that Fechet was unfit for command.[80]

Even Terry Allen had come to believe he may have made a mistake in assigning Fechet to command the 16th Infantry. Fechet's penchant for frontal attacks, despite the high casualties these entailed, was, in Allen's view, one of many indicators that his friend was still locked in a World War I mentality. He simply could not adjust to the modern battlefield. Still, not wanting to interfere with a regimental commander's prerogatives, he let Fechet have his way.

On March 30, the regiment again ground forward, attempting to take Hill 482 by frontal assault. Colonel Fechet decided that he and his staff were going to be up front with the lead elements of the 2nd Battalion as they began the push that morning. Of course, this was no place for a regimental commander and his staff to be in a deliberate attack, and the decision was to have bad consequences later in the morning. Company E led the attack, and as it crossed an open plain just before the foothills to Djebel el Mcheltat, the unit was pinned down by enemy rifle, machine-gun, and artillery fires. On the flank, F Company received the same treatment and suffered over fifty casualties, including the loss of its commander, Captain George J. Heil.

By noon, it was evident that the 2nd Battalion could not do the job alone and Fechet ordered a renewed frontal attack, à la World War I, with an additional battalion at 2:00 p.m. Colonel Stanhope Mason, the division chief of staff, called the regimental headquarters before the attack to get an update on the regiment's situation. Lieutenant Colonel Thomas Wells, regimental XO (executive officer) and an acquaintance of Mason, answered the call and despairingly told him that "they were going to take the objective, even if the costs might be heavy." Wells's agitated tone caused the chief of staff to be concerned that Fechet was about to get a lot of men killed.[81]

Mason took this information and informed Allen of his concerns, and further recommended that the division commander call off the attack. Allen, also visibly disturbed, called

Fechet, who immediately tried to convince the CG to allow the attack to proceed. Stating that "the honor of the regiment" was at stake, the regimental commander believed that the 16th Infantry would never regain its confidence if it failed to take Hill 482.

Allen uneasily agreed to the request, under the condition that the entire regiment went forward. Mason recalled that after his decision, Allen was still upset: "General Allen fussed and fumed, lit one cigarette after another, was beside himself with anguish over a situation which he saw as an either/or proposition—either he summarily relieved Fechet after countermanding his order to attack or let it go and hope for the best, the latter not being very likely."[82]

Fate was about to take a hand, however. In the ensuing battle, Fechet's elbow was shattered by a bullet, wounding him seriously and ending his tenure as regimental commander—much to the relief of more than one member of the regiment and General Allen as well. When the report of Fechet's wounding came over the division net, Mason remembered:

General Allen's obvious relief brought on by this turn of events…All tension was gone. He even had a faint smile on his face as he directed the attack to be called off at once…General Allen relaxed and we all went about our normal duties. But before I left General Allen, he told me that he prayed hard and earnestly to the Lord (and I don't think General Allen was a very religious person) for a solution and that the Lord had answered his prayers. No matter whether it was the Lord or just pure chance, the problem of Colonel Fechet and his WW I sense of regimental honor was immediately and completely solved.[83]

Unfortunately, Captain Brosokas, the regiment's veteran intelligence officer, was also wounded and evacuated.[84] For the time being, Lieutenant Colonel Wells took command of the regiment, while Allen began the search for a new commander.

Meanwhile, approaching from the northwest, Colonel George A. Taylor's 26th Infantry finally wrenched Hill 482 from the 48th Pioneer Battalion, but it too suffered heavy casualties in the effort. That evening found the 16th Infantry in wadis at the base of the djebel, taking account of its men and equipment and reorganizing for further combat. The mission had been accomplished, and the 1st Infantry Division had opened the way for the 1st Armored Division's advance—or so it was believed. Inexplicably, the 1st Armored moved only astride of the "Red One" before it too was stopped. Further attacks to the east were apparently necessary to ensure the armored division's breakthrough.[85]

On March 31, the 1st Battalion, now under the command of Lieutenant Colonel Charles J. Denholm (he had previously been the battalion's XO), continued the advance eastward over the southern reaches of the djebel. With the 3rd and 2nd Battalions following in echelon, the regiment reached the

Guetteria Valley the next day, after which enemy resistance all but ceased. Intelligence soon reported that the enemy was in flight because the Eighth Army had finally pierced the Mareth Line and captured Gabès.[86] Thus ended the bloody fighting in the rugged djebels around El Guettar.

The regiment soon returned to the Gafsa oasis for rest and reorganization, but the stay there was short-lived. By April 13, the entire division was reassembled at Marsott and prepared for the final drive to take Tunisia. While resting at Marsott, the regiment received its next regimental commander, Colonel George A. Taylor, West Point class of 1922, and late of the 26th Infantry.

Taylor's first assignment in the U.S. Army was to the 23rd Infantry at Fort Sam Houston, Texas. His career had featured an unusually long string of infantry assignments: 35th Infantry in Hawaii, 1924-27; 4th Infantry, Fort Lawton, Washington, and Fort Abraham Lincoln, North Dakota, 1927-28; 30th Infantry, Presidio of San Francisco, California, 1928-33; and the 38th Infantry, Fort Douglas, Utah, 1934-37. Not until Taylor attended the Command and General Staff School at Fort Leavenworth (1937-38) did he have a break from troop duty. Immediately following C&GSS, he was assigned to the 57th Infantry Regiment, a Philippine Scout unit at Fort William McKinley in the Philippine Islands. Upon returning from the Philippines, he was the S2 for the 1st Battalion, 16th Infantry, for about four months in early 1941; then he was assigned as a tactics instructor at the Infantry School at Fort Benning. In January 1942, he was transferred to the staff of Admiral Bennett, commander of the Advanced Echelon, Amphibious Forces, Atlantic Fleet. From there, in October 1942, he moved to the staff of the commander of the Naval Operating Base in Oran. In February 1943, he was assigned temporary command of the 26th Infantry. He was reassigned to the 16th Infantry on April 20, 1943, to replace Fechet.[87]

With the Eighth Army's penetration of the Mareth Line and the American victories at Gafsa, Maknassy, and El Guettar, the final stage of the Tunisian campaign was at hand. Even so, Axis forces in Tunisia, though roughly handled, were still full of fight, as they demonstrated over the next several weeks.

Mateur

For the next push, the U.S. II Corps was repositioned on the Allied extreme northern (left) flank, preparatory to a drive on Bizerte that would also serve to cover the advancing British V Corps on its immediate right. Setting forth from central Tunisia, II Corps traveled on four routes leading through the rear of the First British Army, with the 1st Division accomplishing this difficult move on April 18. The "Red One" assumed control of II Corps' central sector, an area consisting of hilly terrain running from Kef el Goraa (Hill 575) southeast for five miles. The 34th Infantry Division was on the division's left, the 1st Armored Division on its right.

The 1st Division was to conduct the II Corps' main effort for this offensive. Its initial mission was to seize the high ground running northeast between the Sidi Nasr-Mateur Road and the Tine River Valley. The corps' final objective was to take the city of Mateur.[88]

Facing the "Fighting First" was the 334th Infantry Division. Formed in Germany the previous autumn, this unit was relatively new to the Tunisian campaign. Behind the 334th, however, were the tough paratroopers of "Barenthin" *Fallschirmjaeger* (parachute) Regiment. Both units were in relatively good shape and had not suffered the pounding other Fifth Panzer Army units had taken during the previous six weeks.

The terrain that these units defended was less rugged than that of the El Guettar or Ousseltia Valley areas. The hills were characterized by relatively gentle slopes with little vegetation on top for concealment. Some slopes, however, were covered with olive groves, and the valley floors were a patchwork of farm plots, usually covered by waves of golden wheat. The hills, while pleasing to view, especially dressed in the green shades of spring, were actually intricate complexes of mutually supporting enemy positions that often had to be attacked simultaneously if units were to be successful in taking assigned objectives. Additionally, the relatively open terrain made it easy for enemy forward observers to bring indirect fire on an attacking force.[89]

The 16th Infantry was once again the main effort in the initial division attack on a series of hills six hundred to one thousand meters east of the line of departure. The 26th Infantry was to conduct a supporting attack in the north to take Hill 575, while the 18th Infantry attacked Hills 407 and 350 to the south. The regiment's mission was to assault Hill 400, a major hill with a series of smaller hills surrounding it. On April 23, the attack kicked off after a heavy artillery preparation.[90]

The regiment easily advanced across the gently sloping terrain until nearing two small but fiercely defended hills, designated 394 and 469. The 1st and 2nd Battalions, which had taken turns moving in the lead, eventually pushed past the hills, leaving their capture to the 3rd Battalion, now commanded by Lieutenant Colonel Charles P. Stone. The battalion was halted by tenacious resistance from Hill 394's defenders, assisted by fire support from their comrades on the adjacent Hill 469 (also known as Djebel Berboukr). Colonel Taylor, realizing that the hills could not be taken individually, ordered simultaneous attacks on both by the entire regiment.[91]

An incident occurred this day that is at once humorous, tragic, and indicative of how the misinterpretation of a combat situation can cause unintended consequences. After the attack began that morning, efforts to speed up the regiment's forward movement drew criticism from a high-ranking visitor to the 1st Division, Lieutenant General Leslie J. McNair. McNair arrived in the 2nd Battalion's area to personally assess its attack:

F Company was pinned down on the ridge in front of us. General McNair wanted to see the action, apparently believing we weren't being aggressive enough. By exposing himself on the ridge, our position was subjected to artillery fire during which he was wounded and our F Company First Sergeant was killed. I remember the General's aides bringing him off the hill into a jeep and speeding away to the Bn Aid Station. So much for him.[92]

The advance continued on the 24th, with the 1st Battalion taking most of the day to fight its way to the top of Djebel Berboukr. Casualties mounted from enemy resistance, but friendly artillery also inflicted over seventy casualties on the 2nd and 3rd Battalions during the day. The seizure of Djebel Berboukr by the 1st Battalion eliminated supporting fires against the 3rd Battalion's assault on Hill 394, and late that afternoon, that position also fell to the 16th Infantry.[93]

The division had finally reached the initial objective line. Colonel Taylor held a conference that evening with his staff and battalion commanders. After describing the day's events, he went on to say that, during the day, the "16th was the only regiment in the division to do any fighting, and this in the face of an entire German division." He concluded his little speech, "The commanding general made a visit to the CP today and he said you ought to be proud of the regiment. He said he is very proud of it."[94]

With the arrival of the 34th Infantry Division, the 1st Division's sector was narrowed, and the 16th Infantry went into division reserve for the next drive east. The division jumped off on the 25th, but the enemy had withdrawn to the east, leaving behind hundreds of booby traps and mines in his wake. Meanwhile, the 18th and 26th Regiments crept cautiously eastward, and by 8:00 p.m., the lead elements had reached Djebel Touta and the southwest end of Djebel Sidi Meftah. The division continued its advance on April 26, with patrols from the Blue Spaders making as far east as the Sidi Nsir-Chouigui Road. The "Red One" was now owner of the ground due south of Djebel Tahent (Hill 609)—the complex of hills considered to be the linchpin of German defenses west of Mateur. Hill 609 was also the main objective of the "Red Bull" Division to the north. That night Colonel Taylor was alerted to prepare the regiment to support the 34th Division's attack on Hill 609.[95]

Hill 523

The regiment moved to the northern flank of the division zone and pressed eastward, taking Hill 529 on the 27th, but the efforts of the 34th that day failed to make it to Djebel Tahent. The next morning found the 1st and 2nd Battalions between Hills 531 and 455 and attempting to seize Hill 523. But they could move only under severe direct and indirect fires. Struggling forward in the dry, still heat, moving boulder to boulder, ditch to wall, the dogfaces of the 16th Infantry advanced slowly, and then only after killing the stubborn enemy paratroopers or forcing them to abandon their positions under direct fire and grenades.[96] It was the grimmest, bloodiest kind of work. But like Hill 609 to the north, Hill 523 still remained

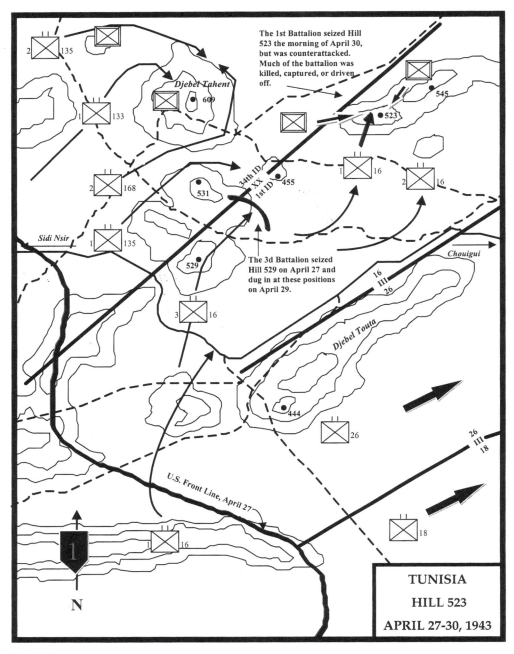

Within the map:

The 1st Battalion seized Hill 523 the morning of April 30, but was counterattacked. Much of the battalion was killed, captured, or driven off.

Djebel Tahent

609

2 � 135

1 〖〗 133

2 〗 168

Sidi Nsir

1 〗 135

531

34th ID
XX
1st ID

455

523

545

1 〗 16

2 〗 16

Chouigui

16
III
26

529

The 3d Battalion seized Hill 529 on April 27 and dug in at these positions on April 29.

3 〗 16

444

Djebel Touta

〗 26

26
III
18

U.S. Front Line, April 27

1

N

1 〗 16

〗 18

TUNISIA

HILL 523

APRIL 27-30, 1943

Map 8-6.

attack on Hill 531 that succeeded in gaining the southern ridge.[97]

Lieutenant Colonel Denholm (since promoted from major) received orders to take the lead that evening and issued his own assault order. Approaching the hill from the south, the battalion crossed the LD at 12:45 a.m. in the blackness of an overcast, drizzly, moonless night. The line of troops snaked forward, with A Company in the lead, followed by B, Headquarters, C, and finally D Company. The move to the assault position was only about one kilometer, so Denholm halted movement after six hundred yards and called for smoke rounds to mark the flanks of the hill. Satisfied he was on track, Denholm resumed the advance. A couple of scouts from A Company actually made it up to the crest of the hill undetected and discovered that it was defended by only fifty to seventy paratroopers with no obstacles to impede the assault.[98]

Deploying two platoons on line, Company A charged the hill and made it about halfway up before being forced to go to ground by the alerted enemy. The company quickly set up and provided supporting fire for the rest of the battalion. Denholm directed B Company to shift right and sweep the crest from the east and C Company to move up behind Company A, then shift left to sweep the north side of the hill from the west. The maneuver was accomplished as planned. The troops moved forward, position to position, and reduced the enemy with rifles, grenades, and even knives. By 4:45 a.m., the defenders were either dead or in full flight to the rear, save for eleven paratroopers who chose to surrender.[99]

Denholm had less than an hour before daylight, so he scrambled to direct the consolidation of his position. The ground was so rocky that foxholes were out of the question; the

in enemy hands.

Stone's battalion continued to grind forward after nightfall, attempting to take Hill 523, while the 1st Division Artillery pummeled the position, but morning found the hard-bitten paratroopers still controlling its crest. By the 29th, it was apparent to the corps and division commanders that the key to taking Hill 609 was Hill 523. The 2nd Battalion was spent, so Denholm's 1st Battalion drew the task of throwing the Germans off 523. But first, the 3rd Battalion conducted a supporting

best the men could do was to throw up prone fighting positions with rocks. To make matters worse, only one mortar section of D Company made its way to the objective. The remainder of the company, and therefore the majority of the battalion's heavy weapons, was separated during the night move and never joined Denholm's men on the hill.[100]

At daybreak the men realized, to their horror, that their new location was exposed to the observation and fire from adjacent enemy positions, notably on Hill 609. The attack had succeeded in interposing the battalion between the German positions around Hill 531 to its west, and other enemy elements farther east. The Barenthin Regiment could not tolerate an American battalion in its midst—the GIs would have to be driven off. Soon, the 1st Battalion began to receive small arms and indirect fire and, before long, both Denholm's artillery radios were destroyed; he now had no way to direct counterfires.[101]

Around 10:00 a.m., a 75mm assault gun on a piece of high ground to the west, in the direction of Hill 531, began lobbing shells into Denholm's positions. This gun and accompanying artillery fire kept the soldiers' heads down, thereby covering the approach of a German counterattack. Company C was hit particularly hard, losing all but four men of its 1st Platoon to shellfire. Aware that the company had been weakened, the rugged German paratroopers felt their way forward and assaulted its flank with machine pistols and hand grenades. Though the Americans fought tenaciously, often hand-to-hand, most of the men in the remaining two platoons were killed or captured.[102]

With the battalion's defenses unhinged by the loss of C Company, it was inevitable that the Germans would regain Hill 523 one position at a time. Denholm could have retreated, but instead chose to hold his ground. By noon, the force defending the crest had been reduced to the remnants of two platoons from A Company, and Denholm, recognizing the futility of continued resistance, surrendered. Denholm and his men were immediately hustled off the hill, and with them went the German troops who took it.[103]

Company D and men from the other companies now regrouped and counterattacked the hill. Surprisingly, the crest was regained with ease; the paratroopers were gone. Throughout the day, the remnants of the 1st Battalion, now down to about 225 men, maintained a precarious hold on the positions at the crest and western base of Hill 523. With help from friendly artillery, they beat back two counterattacks. Around 5:00 p.m., a company of tanks from the 1st Armored Regiment attempted to relieve the pressure on the 1st Battalion, but pulled back after losing four tanks to antitank fire. The Germans were obstinate, launching yet another counterattack that night. By 2:00 a.m. May 1, the crest of Hill 523 was once again in enemy hands.[104]

The 1st Battalion's heroic struggle to control Hill 523 proved a major distraction to the Germans, preventing them from adequately supporting their main defenses on Hill 609. The brief occupation of Hill 523's crest by Denholm's men

allowed the 34th Infantry Division to finally capture Hill 609 on May 1. At daylight on May 2, the only enemy presence in front of the 16th Infantry was a number of German stragglers coming in to surrender. The loss of Hill 609 had caused the remaining German units to pull back to the next line of resistance. The bloody fighting in this sector was over.

For their actions at Hill 523, the men of the 1st Battalion earned the regiment's first Distinguished Unit Citation of World War II. Their efforts had been costly. In assisting the 34th Division, the battalion lost thirty-three men killed, fifty-nine wounded, and 150 men captured, including Lieutenant Colonel Denholm.[105]

In the days following the capture of Hills 523 and 609, enemy resistance in Tunisia swiftly collapsed, with the remaining Axis forces surrendering on May 13. The end of the North African Campaign found the 16th Infantry in an assembly area southwest of Mateur, resting, reequipping, and receiving replacements. While there, the regiment buried those from its ranks who had made the ultimate sacrifice. The interment ceremonies included a memorial service, held in a wheatfield and attended by the entire regiment, with Colonel Taylor and Chaplain Deery presiding.[106]

The regiment's respite was short-lived. On May 13, the regiment began a four-day, 823-mile journey to another camp at St. Leu, near Arzew, not far from where the regiment had begun its North African odyssey only six months previous.[107] Nine days later, the regiment moved the short distance to the Fifth Army Invasion Training Center at Port aux Poules to begin amphibious refresher training in preparation for its next operation, the invasion of Sicily. In addition to the amphibious instruction, other courses were conducted at the Invasion Training Center that included "rifle and mortar ranges, street fighting, methods of reducing pill-boxes…combat exercises, and night problems. Training methods were unusually good, and the program was well-planned."[108]

The tent camp at Port aux Poules was located on high ground less than two miles from the Mediterranean Sea. The bare rocky soil, coupled with the dry, hot wind that blew dust into everything, made life at the camp unpleasant; but these conditions were somewhat ameliorated by swimming parties to the Mediterranean, and organized sports, movies, and stage shows.[109]

The amphibious training was conducted by battalion landing teams, one at a time. Each battalion, along with its attached units, boarded transports, moved out into the Mediterranean, turned around, and performed a simulated assault landing on the beach between Arzew and Mostaganem. During the time it was at Port aux Poules, General Marshall visited the regiment again and observed it going through its paces.[110]

On June 9, the Cannon Company, Antitank Company, Service Company, and the regiment's motorized elements departed St. Leu for a new camp at Staouli, twelve miles from Algiers. Two days later, the rest of the regiment boarded the

USS *Elizabeth Stanton,* USS *Samuel P. Chase,* USS *Betelguese,* and USS *Thurston* at Arzew and sailed for Algiers, arriving there on the 13th. Over the next eight days, the men of the 16th Infantry continued to participate in conditioning marches and loading exercises, and, on June 21, the entire 1st Division loaded on ships for an amphibious training exercise called Operation Conqueror. The convoy departed on June 23, and the landings were made at Sidi Feruch just after midnight against the "enemy" British 46th Division. The landings generally went well, and the division pushed back the Brits to successfully establish a beachhead by 2:40 p.m.[111]

On June 27, the 3rd Battalion, Cannon Company, and Antitank Company sailed for Tunis on board LCIs. The remainder of the 16th Infantry did not begin loading operations in Algiers Harbor until July 4, when it began embarking on the USS *Elizabeth Stanton* and USS *Thurston* in final preparation for invasion of Sicily, now labeled Operation Husky.[112]

Sicily Campaign
July 9-August 17, 1943

The decision to invade Sicily was made well before the Allied victory in North Africa was finalized. In January 1943, President Roosevelt, Prime Minister Winston Churchill, and the U.S.-British Combined Chiefs of Staff met at Casablanca in French Morocco to formulate long-term strategy for the defeat of the Axis. After much debate, the conferees determined that the invasion of Northwest Europe, across the English Channel, was not feasible until the spring of 1944. For the time being, and in keeping with Churchill's preference for a southern approach through what he had dubbed Europe's "soft underbelly," the Mediterranean Theater would remain the focus of Allied operations. Accordingly, Sicily would be the target of their next major effort, and planning for the invasion of that island was well advanced before the fighting in Tunisia had ended.[113]

Operation Husky would mark the combat debut of the I Armored Corps, commanded by then-Lieutenant General George S. Patton. Patton's corps headquarters was designated to command the Operation Husky forces (which included the U.S. II Corps commanded by Major General Omar Bradley). To avoid the confusion of having a corps commander working for another corps commander, Patton's I Armored Corps headquarters was scheduled to be deactivated on invasion day and immediately reactivated as Headquarters, Seventh Army.[114] The 1st Infantry Division remained under II Corps' control for the operation.

Sicily was a natural interim objective for the invasion of Italy (discussed at the Trident Conference in May, the decision to invade Italy was made at the Quadrant Conference in August). The island was only some ten thousand square miles (about the size of Vermont), but ranges of small, rugged mountains lined the northern half of the island and ran diagonally southeast, making for difficult terrain on which to fight. The

German and Italian units on Sicily were determined to use the terrain to their advantage.

Sicily was defended by the Italian Sixth Army, consisting of the XII Corps in the west and the XVI Corps in the east. The Sixth Army, though nominally Italian, consisted of both Italian and German divisions. Several of the divisions that defended Sicily were considered elite units and had seen heavy fighting in North Africa. The foremost of these units were the Italian 4th (Livorno) Division and the German Hermann Göring Panzer Division.

The Hermann Göring Panzer Division, under the command of Major General Paul Conrath, was technically a Luftwaffe unit. Most of the division's combat elements had been shipped to North Africa and had experienced major fighting in the closing weeks of the Tunisian campaign. The division's elements in Tunisia had been severely mauled, and as a result, they were returned to Italy in poor shape. Reconstitution was accomplished using the division's uncommitted units and refitted with Luftwaffe troops from Germany, Holland, and France for service in Sicily.[115]

Though it was a panzer division, its infantry regiments were nominally parachute (*Fallschirmjaeger*) units, which made the division an odd combination of tank and airborne elements. In a postwar interview, Conrath stated that although the division was at full strength in personnel and equipment, its training level was insufficient due to the time available to train the new troops before commitment at Gela.[116] Even so, the division was an elite unit expected to fight desperately to ensure that no shame or dishonor fell on its namesake. The 16th Infantry would face both the Livorno and Hermann Göring Divisions in its actions in Sicily.

Colonel Taylor and his staff received the conceptual scheme for the invasion of Sicily in early June and set to work preparing an assault plan for the regimental combat team. As finalized, the plan called for the 1st Battalion to land at Beach Red 2, and the 2nd Battalion to land at Beach Green 2. The 3rd Battalion was to be held in corps reserve for the initial stages of the operation. Once ashore, the regiment was to push north, making contact with Colonel James M. Gavin's 505th Parachute Infantry Regiment. The 505th was to be dropped about five to ten miles north of the beaches to prevent or slow the movement of tanks from the Hermann Göring Panzer Division to the invasion beaches. Once the link up was effected, the paratroopers and the 16th Infantry were to take the Ponte Olivo airfield from the east.[117] By July 6, preparations were complete, and the convoy sailed to rendezvous with other ships from Tunis.

Over the next two days, the convoy assembled west of Sicily, then steamed southwest toward Malta. On July 8, the men, who had been kept in the dark as to their next mission, were issued handbooks on Sicily and briefed on the plan. Equipment checks and mission brief-backs were conducted to ensure that the regiment was ready for the invasion. As the fleet approached the island, rough weather churned the sea, and the ships plowed through six- to nine-foot swells that caused much seasickness among those aboard. For a time, it seemed the landings might be canceled because of the heavy seas. However, before midnight on July 9, the seas calmed somewhat, and the men began moving to the gunwales, climbing over the side, and lowering themselves into the bobbing landing craft at the bottom of the cargo nets. Despite the choppy water and black night, the men of the "Red One" efficiently and methodically loaded into their boats and mentally prepared themselves for the rush ashore.[118]

At 12:57 a.m., the landing craft of the first wave were lowered away. In the subsequent movement to the assembly area, it took over an hour to gather the boats, but once assembled, the initial wave of the 16th Infantry headed northeast to the landing zone. At 2:43 a.m., the first assault elements of Combat Team 16 touched shore. Lieutenant William T. Dillon described the experience:

My LSVP was the left-most boat nearest to Gela, about 1-1 ½ miles away. I was on the left front of the boat with 3 abreast. The 2 [soldiers] on my right carried a roll of chicken wire to get over barbed wire entanglements. The boat hit a reef and the front went down. I jumped off to the left and the [machine-guns] opened up on shore. This is where Dubiac had his trigger finger shot off. I still don't know how many were killed or wounded in the LSVP. The water was about waist deep on the reef but came up to your neck before you reached shore. After you hit the beach there was barbed wire. I hit the sand and crawled under the barbed wire for about 10 ft when 6 grenades landed almost on top of me. I could see the top of a pill-box on the sky line and every time I moved a couple more grenades came over....Then a black shadow of a small boat about the size of a PT boat came coasting between me and the reef. I decided that the enemy wouldn't move while the boat was there so I backed out from under the wire and hauled ass out of there....I later found 66 small holes in my shirt, one splinter through my upper lip and lodged against my front tooth, one cut the arm off my glasses on the right temple and one went into the hollow of my throat—it's still there.[119]

Though Dillon received a tough welcome to the beaches of Gela, the initial waves of the 1st and 2nd Battalions generally met little resistance, though there was a scare caused by searchlights that lit up the craft as they were approaching the shore. The initial wave rapidly pushed inland against feeble opposition, but subsequent waves struck serious resistance from bypassed positions of the Italian XVIII Coastal Defense Brigade. The opposition from the Italians was supported by artillery and mortar fire until the cruiser USS *Boise* and the destroyer USS *Jeffers* fired several accurate salvoes to silence the enemy resistance.[120]

As the 26th Infantry and the 1st Ranger Battalion operated to the west to take the city of Gela, Denholm's 1st Battalion and Crawford's 2nd Battalion slipped past the Biviere Ponds and moved north to cut the coastal rail line, then northeast along Highway 115 toward the Piano Lupo road junction to link up with the 505th Infantry. About midmorning, the lead elements, still southwest of the junction, experienced a probing attack by twenty Renault light tanks from an Italian mobile defense group. It quickly became evident that the paratroopers had not accomplished their mission.[121]

The tanks were detected heading south from Priolo by the lead elements of the 1st Battalion. The battalion's forward observers (FO) called for fire, and the USS *Jeffers* responded by knocking out two of the tanks. Pushing on, the Italians turned southwest at Piano Lupo onto Highway 115. Just after proceeding down the long, shallow slope from Piano Lupo towards Gela, the tanks ran into the infantrymen of the 16th, armed only with rifles, machine-guns, and hand grenades. No elements of the Antitank or Cannon Companies were yet ashore, but the feisty soldiers were still able to take out two more tanks and disorganize the Italian advance. Without any infantry support of their own, the tankers began to feel vulnerable and retreated.[122]

Despite this initial scare, Taylor pressed his troops forward, and by noon, Denholm's men were at the Piano Lupo junction, yet no contact was made with any sizable group of paratroopers. What the 1st Battalion did encounter was a series of pillboxes and defense positions manned by the 49th Coastal Defense Battalion. Taylor directed Denholm's men to clear the junction, while Crawford's men assumed defensive positions on the high ground to the northwest. The 1st Battalion started to work and shortly after beginning operations, a map annotated with the enemy positions was captured that facilitated Denholm's efforts to reduce the strongpoints. By the end of the afternoon, about two companies of the Italian 49th Coastal Defense Battalion had been captured or killed by the 1st Battalion's efforts to take the Piano Lupo crossroads.[123]

Meanwhile, back on the beach, Lieutenant Dillon had reported to an aid station to have his wounds treated. In addition to his wounds, the grenades had also caused him to have a loss of hearing: "I told this [doctor] that I couldn't hear anything with my left ear. He took a look and said I had a ruptured drum but that eventually I'd probably be able to hear. I [then told him that] I couldn't even hear myself toot. He said he couldn't give me anything to make me hear better, but he could [sure] give me something to make me toot louder. Never heard that one before."[124]

As night settled in, the regiment was in firm possession of Piano Lupo. Before long, however, Taylor received orders to push on toward Niscemi, the 16th Infantry's initial objective. The 2nd Battalion was the unit closest to Niscemi so, about midnight, Crawford led out with G Company on the west side of the road and Companies E and F on the east. About 4:00 a.m., Crawford's men reached their intended positions about three miles to the north of Piano Lupo. For some reason, G Company departed from its assigned position and returned to Piano Lupo. Upon this discovery, Crawford was forced to move E and F Companies around 5:30 a.m. to a pleasant little orchard-covered ridge on the west side to cover the road where G Company should have been. Denholm's men, who had assumed positions about a quarter mile to the south of Crawford, defended positions covering the road at Casa del Priolo.[125]

Before Crawford and Denholm departed for the new positions, a column of over thirty enemy tanks had been reported along the road coming south out of Niscemi, only five miles to the north of where the two battalions were now digging in. Taylor expected a counterattack the following morning and he was not incorrect in his assessment.[126]

Gela Tank Battles

Inexplicably, the Sixth Army issued no orders for the Hermann Göring Division to attack on July 10. Poor relations between Conrath and his nominal superior, General d'Armata Alfredo Guzzoni, and their respective staffs prevented them from developing effective defense plans before the invasion, and counterattack plans afterward. Nevertheless Conrath issued orders to his units to attack the American beachhead and drive the invaders into the sea.

Prior to the Allied invasion, Conrath had to detach Kampfgruppe Schmalz as a counterattack force to oppose any invasion in the vicinity of the Gulf of Catania. Separated from the division by some forty road miles, Kampfgruppe Schmalz consisted of a panzer grenadier regiment, reinforced by two companies of tanks, an artillery battery, and the divisional engineer battalion; fully a third of the Hermann Göring Panzer Division. Soon after the landings, the Kampfgruppe was committed in the British zone and no longer available to Conrath.

Down to only two-thirds of a division, Conrath nevertheless planned a two-pronged attack scheduled for July 11. The first, an infantry-heavy force built around the 1st Hermann Göring Panzer Grenadier Regiment, would advance from Caltagirone, through Biscari, to the beaches in the 45th Infantry Division area. The other force, composed primarily of the Hermann Göring Panzer Regiment, would attack from Caltagirone through Niscemi, turning southwest onto Highway 115, to destroy the beachheads east of Gela.[127] Reconnaissance elements, lightly reinforced with tanks, pushed out that evening, made contact with the 16th Infantry, and continued skirmishing throughout the night of July 10-11, attempting to develop the American positions.

The main attack was supposed to kick off at 8:00 a.m. on the 11th, but because of poor road conditions the main forces of the Hermann Göring Panzer Division were unable to get into positions on time. Sparring between the American infantry and German tankers broke out at first light in front of the 2nd Battalion, and later in the 1st Battalion sector, resulting in American casualties and a few German tanks knocked out during the morning. Finally, about 1:00 p.m., the Germans and Italians attacked all along the 1st Infantry Division front. On the left of the 16th Infantry, Mark III and IV tanks of the panzer regiment's 2nd Battalion broke through the 26th Infantry and rolled to within fewer than two thousand yards of the beachhead, creating a dire situation for the "Red One."[128]

Meanwhile, at least forty Mark IV tanks of the regiment's 1st Battalion rumbled into Crawford's men. Fighting desperately with bazookas, rifle grenades, and two or three almost useless 37mm antitank guns, the 2nd Battalion was slowly driven back into the 1st Battalion positions, where fighting had also been heavy. Earlier that morning, small panzer detachments had sidestepped the 2nd Battalion and attacked the 1st Battalion positions. During these initial actions, Denholm was seriously wounded while personally manning one of the antitank guns and was evacuated. Command of the battalion now devolved to Major Edmund F. Driscoll.

The 3rd Battalion, which had been under the command of "Batshit" Horner since Stone was wounded in the latter days of the Tunisian campaign, had been brought up the evening before to reinforce the regiment and assumed positions covering the Piano Lupo junction south of the 1st and 2nd Battalions. Even with the addition of Horner's men, the regiment's situation was serious. The 2nd Battalion was pushed back to positions west of the road around Hill 172, and the 1st was across the road and to the east. Two of the 37mm antitank guns had been knocked out, and casualties were mounting. Taylor, to bolster the confidence of his men, sent out a message stating: "Under no circumstances will anyone pull back. Take cover from the tanks, but don't let anything else through. Cannon Company is on its way. Give orders for everyone to hold positions."[129]

In accordance with the landing plan, Cannon Company was not scheduled to land until late on July 11. With the attacks of the 10th and the probing actions by tanks that night and into the morning of the 11th, Taylor had bombarded division with urgent requests for some kind of antitank support. The initial response was indirect fire from the 7th Field Artillery and from the USS *Boise*, which kept the tankers buttoned up, but failed to severely deplete their numbers. Bazookas worked, but one had to allow the tanks to approach very close before using them. To make matters worse, when the Cannon Company actually came ashore the afternoon of July 11, it was landed on one of the 45th Division beaches because of the congestion on the 1st Division landing areas.[130]

Instead of charging off to support the regiment, the Cannon Company was initially directed to engage enemy tank forces that had broken through to the Gela plain and threatened the 1st Infantry Division's beaches. Firing some twelve hundred rounds, the company singlehandedly blunted the attack and destroyed numerous enemy tanks in a forty-five minute period. That mission accomplished, the company sped off to assist the

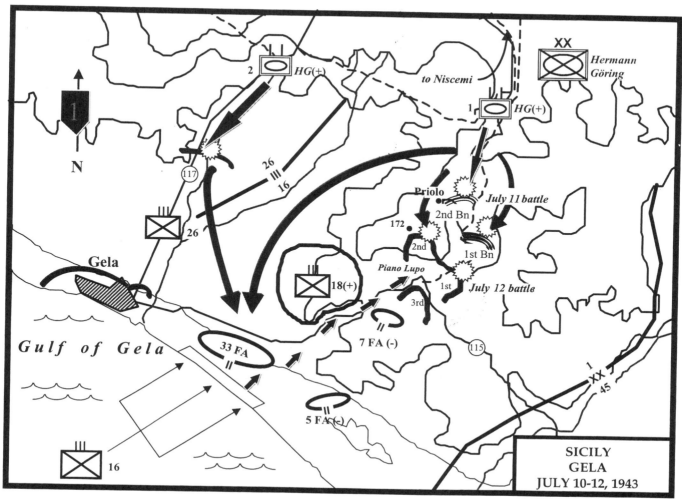

Map 8-7.

men up north.[131]

Up to this point, the regiment had been able to hold off the tanks because Conrath had, quite inexplicably, launched his tanks into the 16th Infantry without infantry support. With no panzer grenadiers to protect them, the German tankers were vulnerable to the American infantrymen who were brave enough to get in close for a kill. By 7:30 p.m., this situation had changed. Some twenty truckloads of enemy infantry were observed dismounting on the flank of the 2nd Battalion, followed by another thirty-five truckloads a short time later. Infantry was also appearing to the regiment's front. The situation had now become critical. Against a combined infantry-armor attack, the regiment was bound to be driven back or destroyed.[132]

In a scene reminiscent of a Hollywood movie, the Cannon Company arrived like the cavalry to save the day. Just after the enemy jumped off and advanced down the road, the halftracks of the Cannon Company pulled into overwatch positions and began blasting the surprised panzers. With machine-like pre-

cision, 105mm and 75mm cannon boomed rapidly and accurately. Caught in relatively open terrain, the Mark IV tanks became easy prey for the cannoneers, who destroyed about fifteen of them in a matter of minutes. Surprised by the intensity of the fire, the German attack melted away.[133]

During the day, one of the surreal incidents that often punctuate the reality of war occurred to four medics of the regimental aid station, all from the state of New York: Staff Sergeant Earl Wills Cahoes; Technician Fifth Grade William Larson, Story City; Technician Fourth Grade, John Packard, Highland Falls; and Private Robert Holden, Rochester. That afternoon, First Lieutenant Fred Thomas, a platoon leader with the 82nd Airborne, walked into the aid station and said, "There are two wounded American soldiers and one badly hurt Jerry in a house a couple of miles behind German lines, but I can take you right where they are. Can you come with me?" Wills looked at the officer hesitantly, then stammered, "Yeah, sure, I'll go." The three other men volunteered as well. Piling into two jeeps, the five soldiers sped down the road, right into the German lines. Upon arriving at an old farm house, Thomas said, "This is the place." Walking into the front room, the medics were astonished to find eight paratroopers and two German soldiers, all still armed, drinking wine, sharing a meal, and laughing heartily.

As the medics stood there dumbfounded, Thomas grinned and motioned them into the room where the wounded men lay. The two German soldiers walked over and had a few words with their comrade, reassuring him that everything was going to be okay, then strode out of the house. After tending the wounds, Wills directed his medics to load up the injured men for evacuation to the rear, but Thomas stopped him and said, "Wait a minute, you guys are in a pretty hot spot." Wills, already somewhat nervous about the strange situation, froze in fear. The lieutenant grinned again and informed him, "There are two Mark VI's parked in the orchard right in front of the house with their 88s covering the exit. I have to get their permission before we can leave." Wills stood there, utterly confused as the lieutenant went outside. In a few minutes, Thomas returned and informed the medics: "It's O.K. now. You can put them into the jeep. And, in case you're stopped by German patrols, the password is 'German-Lisso.'"

This was too much for Wills. "What the hell goes on here, sir?" he snapped at the lieutenant. "Who's crazy?" Thomas smiled broadly, then explained the story.

That morning the paratroopers had brought their two wounded men to the cottage for shelter and decided to avail themselves of the owner's food before moving on. As they ate, two German soldiers walked in and stated, in English, that there were two tanks hidden in the brush, aiming at the house. The tanks were immobilized, but the guns worked just fine. The German then proposed a "gentleman's agreement." It seemed that they, too, had a wounded buddy, but because their outfit was pulling out, their aid men were nowhere near, and they wanted medical care for him as soon as possible. If one of them would go and get an American aid team to treat and evacuate their man, they would release the paratroopers from captivity, and the two groups would go their separate ways. Thomas agreed to their proposal. It was either that, he figured, or be captured or killed along with his men.

"There must be no funny business," the German admonished. "Everybody must give his word of honor as a soldier and a gentleman." And, just in case, he stated he would hold Thomas's platoon captive until he returned. Wills was amazed. His detail loaded up the injured soldiers and returned to the aid station without incident. After relating the story to Captain John Lauten, the regimental S2, the captain eyed him with doubt. "It's true!" Wills insisted. When the regiment pushed forward a day or so later, Lauten made it a point to stop by the cottage. Sitting out in the orchard were two partially camouflaged Tiger tanks, just as Wills had described. "Isn't it crazy?" Lauten muttered.[134]

That night, intense patrolling revealed that the panzer grenadiers had positioned themselves on the regiment's flanks, and tanks remained in position to the front. At daylight, July 12, the 1st and 2nd Battalions began receiving mortar and small-arms fire as the next counterattack developed. It was a two-pronged effort with a tank-infantry team pushing down the Niscemi-Piano Lupo Road and another team, which included at least six Mark IV tanks and five Mark VI Tiger tanks, driving west into the 1st Battalion along the Vittoria-Gela Road. By this time, however, the regiment had been reinforced by the Antitank Company and some M4 Shermans from the 70th Tank Battalion attached to the 1st Division.[135]

The force moving down the Vittoria Road was successful in breaking through the 1st Battalion and reaching the Piano Lupo intersection, but by noon, three of the Tiger tanks had been destroyed, another disabled, and two Mark IVs set ablaze. The other attack was less successful, though it did disable Lieutenant Colonel Crawford early in the fight. Long-range fires continued to harass the enemy tankers that afternoon, and it was becoming apparent that the Germans' morale was shot and their aggressiveness badly blunted.[136] Failing to break through to the sea, and with his division flanked by American advances on the east and west, Conrath decided to go on the defensive until he could reunite his entire division.

The regiment, now supported by additional tanks, began to counterattack north towards Niscemi. The fight along the road was tough, with the Germans contesting the regiment's advance from strongpoints along the way. When division plans for the 18th Infantry to relieve the 16th changed on the evening of July 12, Taylor ordered his men to continue the advance through that night. Finally, patrols sent out to determine enemy intentions on the morrow found that the Hermann Göring Panzer Division had pulled out. The beachheads were finally safe.[137]

During the night, the 3rd Battalion, now in the best condition after the battering the 1st and 2nd Battalions had received, took the lead. Shortly before 10:00 a.m. on July 13, G Company moved into Niscemi against sparse resistance and secured the regiment's initial objective. The regiment remained in Niscemi until the following day when Taylor ordered it forward to regain contact with the Hermann Göring Division. Over the next day and a half, the men advanced against light opposition. Occasionally contact was made with tanks that lobbed shells their way, but the advance continued for some fifteen kilometers until K Company reached a point just southwest of Caltagirone. The advance was halted there, and the men of the 16th boarded trucks just before midnight on July 15 to move to another sector for a new mission.[138]

By morning on July 16, the 16th Infantry was near Mazarino, in reserve behind the 26th Infantry. After midnight, the regiment jumped off, moving through Barrafranca, with the 3rd Battalion leading. Against slight resistance, Pietraperzia was occupied during the morning, but pushing on toward Caltanisetta, the lead element found the bridge across the

Salso River blown up by retreating German sappers. Taylor was ordered to cross the river that night and seize the high ground on the far side. By holding the high ground, the regiment could provide cover for the engineers to construct another bridge so artillery and supply vehicles could continue to support the advance.[139]

Enna-Sperlingua-Nicosia

In the darkness of July 17-18, the 1st and 3rd Battalions crossed the Salso River against light opposition and gained the far ridge beyond without great difficulty. The engineers, meanwhile, constructed the bridge, and the drive toward Enna continued. Holding the line west of Enna was a new foe, the 15th Panzer Grenadier Division, commanded by Major General Eberhard Rodt. The 15th Panzer Grenadier Division was an experienced outfit that had participated in the fighting in Egypt and Libya against the British. In the final stages of the Tunisian campaign, it had sustained heavy casualties, but had been reconstituted by consolidating its old regiments with those of the ad hoc Sicily Division in late May 1943.[140] Now refitted, the division prepared to confront the units of CT 16 and the "Red One."

On July 18, the 70th Tank Battalion advanced ahead of the regiment east along Highway 117 in an attempt to reach Enna, but was driven back with substantial losses from antitank fire. Infantry would have to take the town, and CT 16 got the nod.

That afternoon, Taylor pushed patrols out eastward to determine the enemy's positions, and on the 19th the regiment began a general advance with the 1st and 3rd Battalions in the lead. Under heavy artillery and mortar fire, the troops made progress all day against generally light opposition, and by evening, Horner and Driscoll's men occupied the high ground southeast of Enna, overlooking the town. The following morning, the 3rd Battalion entered the town virtually unopposed and accepted the surrender of dozens of Italian soldiers. Pushing through the town, the 2nd Battalion went on to seize Calsibetta, and the Intelligence and Reconnaissance (I&R) Platoon made contact with the 26th Infantry to the north that afternoon.[141]

Over the next five days, the regiment remained in positions in and around Enna as the II Corps reserve until ordered to move to an assembly area southeast of Gangi on July 25. The 26th Infantry, meanwhile, had been pushing down Highway 120 in an effort to take Nicosia, but Kampfgruppe Fullriede of the 15th Panzer Grenadier Division had held up the Blue Spaders at Hill 962, about three miles northwest of the little town of Sperlingua. On the morning of July 25, Bradley released the 2nd and 3rd Battalions from corps reserve to Terry Allen to support the 26th Infantry. Taylor was ready and had started preparations for the attack.[142]

Taylor had previously kicked out reconnaissance patrols and the I&R Platoon that morning toward Nicosia in anticipation of orders for the attack on Sperlingua. Early the next morning, the I&R Platoon discovered an enemy platoon on Hill 1333, and the 2nd Battalion was sent forward to take the hill. After a three-hour advance and assault, about twenty German troops were driven from well-prepared positions, leaving the high ground to the 2nd Battalion. That evening, the 3rd Battalion passed through the Blue Spaders and jumped off to attack Sperlingua.[143]

The attack was a pincers-type movement. The 18th Infantry went along a route north of Highway 120 to attack Sperlingua from the north, while the 3rd Battalion, followed closely by the 2nd, moved south of Hill 962 to approach the town from the south.

The attack proceeded in the dark, and after capturing some forty German and Italian troops, the 3rd Battalion was hit by heavy fire from enemy positions north of the road. Simultaneously, the 2nd Battalion was stopped by equally heavy machine-gun fire from high ground to its front. Driven back, Horner's battalion on the north and Mathews' battalion to the south picked their way forward all day on the 27th, as the 1st Division Artillery fired concentrated target groups on enemy positions.[144]

By that evening, the 18th Infantry moved up on line with Horner's men and held in place. At 8:30 p.m., thirty-two Stuart tanks of the 70th Tank Battalion and a platoon of Shermans of the 753rd Tank Battalion rumbled past the tired dogfaces and took the German positions under direct fire. Spraying their death-dealing ordnance across the enemy positions, the tankers severely rattled the panzer grenadiers in their holes. Heavy German artillery fire finally drove off the tankers with a loss of two light tanks, but the armored thrust had had the desired effect. Patrols pushed out by the 3rd Battalion before dawn on July 28 found the enemy had withdrawn.[145]

About 8:30 that morning, L Company led the 3rd Battalion into Sperlingua, while the 2nd Battalion moved along the high ground to the south to protect the regiment's relatively open flank. In heavy rains and against sporadic sniper fire, Taylor pushed the regiment forward until Company I entered Nicosia about 10:00 a.m. Nicosia was defended by elements of the Italian Aosta Division, whose troops put up stiff resistance, especially on the high ground north of the city. However, the advance of the 18th Infantry to the enemy's north combined with the rapid depletion of ammunition, the mud and slime caused by the wet weather, and sagging morale induced the local Italian commander to finally surrender along with seven hundred of his troops.[146]

As the 2nd and 3rd Battalions consolidated their gains in Nicosia, Taylor moved Driscoll's 1st Battalion through to advance on Cerami to the northeast. Preceded by the I&R Platoon, the 1st Battalion trudged along Highway 120 that afternoon, but traveled only two miles before the I&R Platoon was stopped by machine-gun fire. Driscoll deployed the battalion and maneuvered his companies against the enemy positions. The battalion was successful in knocking out several machine-guns and capturing a few Germans before darkness

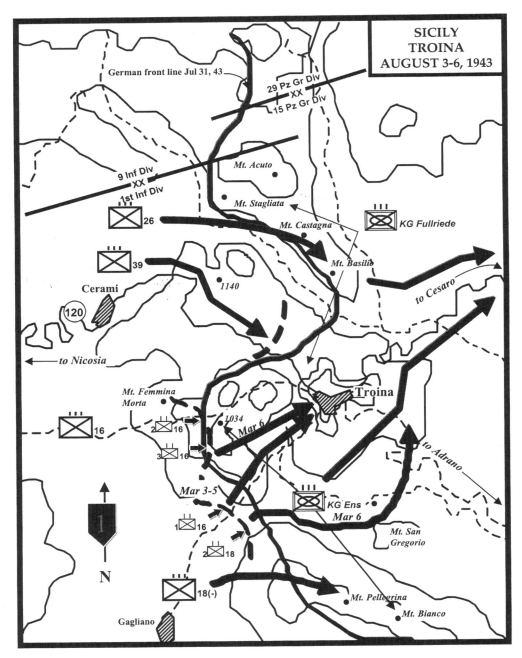

Map 8-8.

Troina

By this time the II Corps G2 had determined that the enemy was forming a new defensive line. Evidence of the "Etna Line" had been materializing since July 22, and intelligence officers believed this line was only an intermediate position until a final, and more concentrated, line could be developed behind it. The Etna Line ran roughly from the south side of Mount Etna to Gerbini, northwest to Troina, and almost due north to the coast near San Fratello. Troina appeared to be the keystone of this defense, and the 1st Infantry Division headed straight for it.

Facing the 1st Division in its sector were elements of the hapless Aosta Division, and now, the entire 15th Panzer Grenadier Division. General Rodt had finally regained operational control of the second half of his division, Kampfgruppe Eins (104th Panzer Grenadier Regiment with attachments), and he placed this unit to defend Monte Bianco and Monte Pelligrino to the south of the town and some elements on Hill 1034 due east of Troina. To the north, he placed Kampfgruppe Fullriede (129th Panzer Grenadier Regiment with attachments) to defend Monte Basilio and Monte Stagliata. These units formed a textbook, bowl-shaped defense that looked across a treeless plane to the west—which was the route that the Americans would have to traverse to take the town.[148] Rodt intended to make the "Red One's" efforts to take Troina as difficult as possible.

General Allen planned to take Troina with a two-pronged attack, using Colonel H. A. "Paddy" Flint's 39th Regimental Combat Team (which had been attached to the 1st Division until the remainder of the 9th Infantry Division arrived at the front) to attack down Highway 120 through Cerami and into Troina. To support that movement, the 26th Infantry was to

ended operations. The following morning, the battalion continued its efforts against elements of Kampfgruppe Fullriede, which occupied favorable positions on the high ground to the east. One by one, however, the machine-gun nests and fighting positions were reduced or captured, which allowed the 2nd Battalion to pass through to continue the attack. By dawn of July 30, Mathews' battalion held the ridgeline fronting the Cerami River just south of Highway 120.[147] The regiment had set up the conditions for an attack towards Troina by the 39th Infantry.

push south of Cerami and into Troina from the southwest. This plan was temporarily scrapped on July 31 when the 39th Infantry, after jumping off, enjoyed a cakewalk into Cerami. Indeed, that evening, intelligence officers at II Corps believed that Troina was not heavily defended. Thus, Allen changed the plan for the 39th RCT to continue the push into Troina on August 1. Flint's troops would attack without the support of Combat Team 26, which now seemed superfluous given the ease with which the 39th Infantry had captured Cerami.[149]

The 39th RCT's attack toward Troina, however, did not go well. The 3rd Battalion, after advancing just one kilometer north of Highway 120, was turned back by small arms and a heavy artillery barrage fire. To the south, the 1st Battalion had better success. It reached Hill 1034, just two miles west of Troina, but was later driven off by counterattacks by Kampfgruppe Eins.[150] Additional efforts by the 39th RCT on August 2 confirmed that Troina was heavily defended. Allen now believed it would take a major push to win the town. He next ordered the 39th RCT to continue the drive down Highway 120, while CT 26 was directed to circle north to take Monte Basilio and cut the German supply route to Cesaro, east of Troina. Combat Team 16, with 2nd Battalion, 18th Infantry attached, was to jump off from behind Monte Femmina Morta; two battalions would take Troina, and the other two battalions would drive south of the town to cut the road to Adrano and seize Hill 1056 on the east side.[151] This would cut all lines of supply to the 15th Panzer Grenadier Division and force its destruction or withdrawal.

Just after midnight on August 3, CT 16 moved out on its mission. Leading off was Mathews' 2nd Battalion, and at 3:00 a.m. the remainder of the regiment followed. Close behind Mathews, in support, was Horner's battalion. To the south was Driscoll's 1st Battalion, and on Driscoll's right was the 2nd Battalion, 18th Infantry, which pushed up the road from Gagliano towards the high ground to the south of Troina. By first light, Mathews' and Horner's men were pushing up the slope of Hill 1034 against steadily intensifying small-arms and mortar fire. With daylight came improved visibility, and the two battalions were soon pinned down on the slope. Despite the efforts of the officers and NCOs to keep the assault moving, it became obvious that any concerted rush would meet with serious casualties. Neither Mathews nor Horner could move forward, nor could either move to the rear.[152]

Seeing the precarious situation of the 16th Infantry, Allen ordered Taylor to move Driscoll's battalion and the 2nd Battalion, 18th Infantry, to take the slopes south of Troina. He hoped this drive would focus the enemy's efforts to the south and relieve pressure on Mathews and Horner. Before the attack diverted the Germans' attention, however, Kampfgruppe Eins counterattacked the exposed battalions on the slopes of Hill 1034 with tanks and infantry. The situation became desperate. Taylor quickly reacted and called upon the division artillery for indirect fire-support against the counterattack, and soon, every

available tube within range had shells screaming into the clusters of assault troops. The artillery fire, coupled with tenacious fighting by the infantry, broke the panzer grenadiers' efforts.[153]

The commander of Kampfgruppe Eins, Colonel Eins, was not through, however. Around 3:00 p.m., he threw another two hundred troops at Mathews and Horner. This attack fell primarily on the 2nd Battalion, and soon Companies E and F were each whittled down from their nominal strength of between 120 and 180 men to about 45 effectives. The two battalions moving up from the direction of Gagliano were also stalled. To the north, the attacks by Combat Teams 39 and 26 make no progress against Kampfgruppe Fullriede. The division had run into a solid wall of well-placed Germans who were willing to stand and fight it out.[154]

During the evening of August 3, Allen decided to bring in the entire 18th Infantry for the attack. With Driscoll's battalion attached to the 18th, the regiment would take over the southernmost portion of the sector and continue to press the south end of Kampfgruppe Eins, while the 26th Infantry would continue its swing north in continuation of the previously planned pincers movement. Meanwhile, Combat Teams 16 and 39 would keep up the frontal pressure.

Little success was achieved on August 5 as the attacks continued. Efforts by Mathews and Horner to gain control of the rest of Hills 1034 and 1006 were stifled by the aggressive counterattacks of Kampfgruppe Eins. No real success was achieved anywhere on the division front, but the continual grinding of the "Red One's" attacks wore down Rodt's men. Gradually, cracks appeared in Rodt's defenses. The Germans had stopped the advance of the 1st Infantry Division, but Rodt, knowing that his men could not withstand another day of hard fighting against the "Big One," requested permission to withdraw. His request was granted, and the 15th Panzer Grenadier Division pulled out on the night of August 5-6 to defend a line closer to Cesaro.[155]

That night, troops of the 16th Infantry noticed enemy resistance slackening. Patrols pushed out and encountered only sporadic rear-guard actions against their movements. By early morning, patrols from the 3rd Battalion picked their way into the devastated town only to find a few German defenders, and even they were soon on their way. The other battalions moved toward Troina, but their speed in doing so resulted in one of the more common tragedies of World War II. Air Force attack aircraft had been scheduled to hit the German positions around Troina that morning, but CT 16's rapid advance put the 1st and 3rd Battalions in close proximity to the now-empty enemy holes by the time the planes arrived on station. Soon the men of those battalions found themselves under attack by their own warplanes. They suffered several casualties to bombs and strafing fire, but even so, Troina was in the hands of the 3rd Battalion by 9:50 a.m.

Happily, the 1st Infantry Division was now ordered to hold in place pending the arrival of the green 9th Division. This was great news for the soldiers of the "Fighting First," and they were elated. After slugging it out on the line since July 10, everybody felt it was time for some well-deserved rest and relaxation.

Then came the shocking news that the division's top commanders, Terry Allen and Teddy Roosevelt, had both been relieved. The men of the "Fighting First" were stunned. Rumors flew: some said Patton's supposed dislike of Allen had finally resulted in the latter's dismissal. Others speculated that Allen's superiors were dissatisfied with the division's performance. Divisional pride had taken a severe blow.

But it was Omar Bradley, not Patton, who dismissed Allen and Roosevelt. His reason for doing so was attributable in large measure to an episode in Oran, following the Axis surrender in Tunisia. It so happened that 1st Division troops, returning to the city after the fighting had ended, found their access barred to local clubs and service installations by Army Service Forces (ASF) units. Enraged, the front-line troops went on a rampage: numerous fistfights ensued and many of the rear-echelon troops were beaten up. Requests from Bradley to discipline the troublemakers met with a lukewarm response from Allen, provoking Bradley's anger. The subsequent theft by Red One troops of vehicles and supplies belonging to other units, plus Allen's tolerant (even approving) attitude toward the overall cocky demeanor of his men, further strained the command relationship. Early in the Sicilian campaign, Bradley decided to relieve Allen. Bradley also resolved that Roosevelt had to go because the troops' strong attachment to him would be detrimental to a new commanding general's efforts to get the division to shape up. (The source for the preceding is Omar Bradley himself, writing in his autobiography, *A Soldier's Story,* 1951).

In truth, the division had performed superbly under Allen's leadership, but Bradley may have made the right move for both Allen and the division, even if it might have been for the wrong reason. By the time of his dismissal, Allen had commanded the division for well over a year. The strain of preparing the division for combat, two amphibious invasions, two major campaigns, along with the pressure to maintain the good reputation of Pershing's favorite division, had taken their toll on the flamboyant cavalryman. Allen was tired, and it was the right time for him to take a rest, and for a new commanding general to take over and lead the division on its next mission. The 1st Infantry Division would go into its next fight under Major General Clarence R. Huebner, a man the troops initially disliked but whom they would later affectionately nickname "The Coach."

On the afternoon of August 7, Generals Allen and Huebner journeyed to the regimental command post in Troina. Allen was accompanying the new commander on an inspection of units and was introducing Huebner to his subordinate commanders before turning over command of the division. To the assembled regimental officers and a representative sampling of NCOs, Allen told them: "…the Battle of Troina was by far the toughest battle we've had—far tougher than any in Africa. I'm proud of the tenacity of the 16th…[and of] the indomitable spirit each man has shown and is still showing. You are to be

congratulated for a truly great performance."[156] Praise like that made Allen's relief that much harder to take.

In some ways, the assignment to the "Red One" was like old-home week for Huebner. Starting at private, Huebner had served in the 1st Division in every grade except brigadier general. He had also briefly commanded the 16th Infantry in the late summer and early autumn of 1919. Though he would never be as popular with the men as Allen, he would eventually gain their grudging respect by diligently preparing the division for its most grueling fight ever.

With the battlefront moving ever closer to Messina, the regiment boarded trucks for Randazzo on August 14. The following afternoon, Taylor and Father Deery held a memorial service for the 16th Infantry soldiers who had died in Sicily. A few days later, as the II Corps reserve, the entire 1st Infantry Division went into bivouac sites on the slopes of the famous volcano, Mount Etna. There, hot showers, hot meals, and relaxation were the order of the day. On August 20, the regiment moved to Licata for more "R & R." However, the rest was punctuated by periodic formations, events common to armies even in wartime. On August 27, the division was formed to hear a speech by Patton. The occasion was his apology for recently slapping soldiers at hospitals for what he considered cowardice. Captain Fred Hall remembered the event:

> Close by our area was a hillside which formed a natural amphitheater at the bottom of which had been built a platform for staging various events. The division was gathered on a hillside and addressed by General Patton who congratulated us for a job well done and then apologized for what had transpired and his regret at his action. He was not popular in the First Division and his appearance was greeted with stony silence.[157]

At this point, many "Red One" men believed that Patton had been responsible for Allen's relief. This may explain, in part, the men's reaction to the general.

Five days later, the regiment held a retreat and awards ceremony to recognize soldiers for their deeds in the recent fighting. The ceremony was attended by General Huebner, who pinned the awards on the soldiers. Additionally, the men of the division were treated with a USO show. The show was a hit with the troops and starred the popular Bob Hope, Frances Langford, and Jerry Colonna, and various lesser-known entertainers.[158]

Entertainment aside, in September, the "Coach" reinstituted basic skills training, and to the cocky combat veterans, the training was an irritant they could do without. For the next month, basic rifle marksmanship, instruction in drill and ceremonies, wear of the uniform, hand salutes, guard mount, and "showdown" inspections were the order of the day. The training also included coordination of artillery fires with the infantry. Though not popular with the old soldiers, the training had its purpose and helped to integrate the replacement soldiers into the regiment—and there were lots of them.

While the regiment was bivouacked at Licata, the Fifth Army invaded Italy on September 9. The members of the "Red One" soon learned that the 36th Infantry Division was the main assault force at Salerno and had suffered the same kind of massive tank counterattack the 1st Division had received at Gela. Upon hearing the news, instead of reflecting on the common experience of the two divisions, Henry Orten wondered if the Texans were having any trouble getting the Germans to stand up and take off their hats when "Deep in the Heart of Texas" was played.[159]

On September 11, the regiment, less A and B Companies, was moved to a bivouac and training site at Palma di Montechiaro. The two companies that remained behind were detailed for airport security missions; A Company was sent to Licata Airport and B Company was sent to the Gela airfield. The rest of the regiment continued to perform basic training, guard duty, local defense patrols, and practice motor marches at Palma di Montechiaro. The 3rd Battalion, however, did get to enjoy a three-day pass to Palermo. Early October saw more of the same, only the autumn rains had arrived as well.[160]

By this time, it had become evident that the division was about to move again. Sure enough, movement orders arrived the second week of October, and the advanced party traveled to the port of Augusta on October 15. Six days later, the regiment followed on trucks. On October 23, the troops and equipment loaded aboard the HMT *Maloja* and set sail for England. Except for a brief stop at Algiers on the 26th, and passage through the Straits of Gibraltar on the 29th, the voyage was uneventful. After almost two weeks at sea, the HMT *Maloja* arrived at Liverpool, England on November 4, but the regiment remained on board until the following evening when it debarked about 9:30 p.m.[161]

Boarding trains that night in Liverpool, the regiment railed to Dorsetshire in south England, where the subordinate units were billeted as follows:

Regimental Headquarters and Headquarters Company	Beaminister
Antitank Company	Beaminister
Cannon Company	Beaminister
Medical Section	Beaminister
Service Company	Bridport
1st Battalion	Lyme Regis
2nd Battalion (less E and G Companies)	Bridport
E and G Companies	Walditch
3rd Battalion (less K, L, and M Companies)	Litton Cheney
K Company	Abbotsbury
L Company	Long Brady
M Company	Bexington

The billeting of the regiment remained the same throughout its second stay in England, with the exception of the transfer of F Company to West Bay in Dorset in late November. The remainder of the month was spent in setting up the unit camps and resuming the training, begun in Sicily, on fundamental soldier skills. Additionally, soldiers were granted leaves to visit many of the historic, and for some soldiers, the more infamous, sites in "Merry Olde England."[162]

The training in December included an increase in basic weapons marksmanship and a graduation to squad- and platoon-level exercises. A great deal of range time was spent on individual weapons such the M-1 Garand rifle, M-1 carbine, BAR, .45-caliber pistol, and hand-grenade, as well as crew-served weapons including the .30- and .50-caliber machine gun, 60mm and 81mm mortar, and 2.75-inch rocket launcher ("bazooka"). Bayonet training was instituted to build aggressiveness in the soldiers. Each rifle platoon was required to conduct one night problem per week in addition to other squad and platoon exercises. The cannon and antitank platoons underwent an intensive training cycle, culminating in a four-day, live-fire problem.

Though the training tempo increased, Colonel Taylor ensured that the men had an opportunity to enjoy more festive diversions as well. The recreation facilities in the Dorset camps were abundant, and the men were given every chance to use them. The regiment celebrated Christmas and New Year's, albeit with a twinge of homesickness in most cases. Nonetheless, at the end of 1943, the regimental commander reported the 16th Infantry's situation: "Morale good, food excellent."[163] Except for rotation home, what more could a soldier ask for?

The first month of the new year saw a continuance of the small-arms range firing, but platoon training shifted to "assaulting fortified positions and street fighting." Cannon Company spent January 4 through 9 on ranges in Wales. Meanwhile, conditioning marches were extended to as long as fifty miles. The three battalion headquarters staffs also conducted command post exercises (CPX) in preparation for the regimental CPX in February. The highlight of the month was a regimental formation at Bridport on January 16. On that date, General Sir Bernard Montgomery addressed the men at the cricket grounds in that town.[164]

Another upward shift in training complexity occurred in February. On the 4th, Colonel Taylor held a regiment-wide CPX to get the combat team's subordinate elements used to working together in a tactical environment. It had been six months since the last time the units had practiced communicating with strict tactical radio procedures. New personnel and equipment, coupled with the rustiness of the old-timers who had been with the regiment in North Africa and Sicily, prompted Taylor to begin whipping the regimental communications network into shape for the next big event.

On February 8, CT 16 traveled to Braunton, County of Devon, for a period of intensive assault training. At the U.S.

Army Assault Training Center in Devon, battalions ran through their paces, attacking fortified strongpoints and conducting preliminary beachhead operations. Here, training in demolitions, bangalore torpedoes, flamethrowers, organization of assault teams, and minefield clearing techniques gave the troops some indication of the types of missions they were soon likely to encounter. The instruction at the assault center was capped by battalion landing team exercises on the 24th. Two days later, the regiment was back in Dorset, conducting recovery operations in preparation for the next big exercise.[165]

That exercise was Operation Fox, which was to be held on March 11. Planning for the exercise had begun long before that date. Back when the regiment was at Braunton, Taylor and Major Carl W. Plitt, S3, had been ordered to report to the 1st Infantry Division headquarters at Blandford on February 22. There, they were given the preliminary operations plan for Operation Overlord, the invasion of Normandy.[166] From that point on, everything the regiment did was geared toward the accomplishment of its D-Day task. Operation Fox, which was designed to simulate Overlord, was the initial exercise to prepare the 16th Infantry for the most challenging mission in its already storied existence.

Combat Team 16 (now consisting of the 7th Field Artillery Battalion; Companies A and B, 1st Engineer Combat Battalion; and Company A, 1st Medical Battalion) boarded trains the morning of March 8 and traveled to the port of Weymouth, where it boarded the assault ship USS *Barnett*. For the next two days, the men went through boat drills, while officers and key NCOs were briefed on the plan and their responsibilities. The *Barnett,* and several other assault ships pulled out of the harbor early on March 11 and moved a short distance up the coast to a landing beach opposite the town of Strete at Slapton Sands. The town was CT 16's objective, and after a relatively uneventful landing, the town was "captured." This operation was supposed to be a full-scale rehearsal for the landing at Omaha Beach, but there were three major exceptions. First, nobody was shooting at them as they landed; second, the men performed no demolitions or live-firing; and oddly, for this exercise, the 116th Infantry went in on the left of the 16th Infantry.[167]

Upon the conclusion of Fox, the regiment returned once again to Dorset and continued its intensive training program. Range firing, calisthenics, and extended marches were emphasized, but time was made available for recreation also. During April, two important visitors came to Dorset to talk to the men of the regiment. The first was General Dwight D. Eisenhower, the Allied supreme commander. He addressed the men at a formation on the Bridport cricket field and also participated in an awards ceremony in which a number of 16th Infantrymen were decorated. The second visitor was Lieutenant General Omar N. Bradley, commander of the U.S. First Army, who addressed the regiment's officers at the Church Hall in Bridport.[168]

As April passed, the regiment prepared itself for the next big show, Operation Fabius I. This exercise was designed to simulate the regiment's D-Day mission as closely as possible. On April 25, the 16th Infantry moved into pyramidal tent camp at Martinstown that served as the marshaling area for the operation. After six days of pre-landing preparations, on May 1, the troops boarded the attack transports USS *Samuel B. Chase,* USS *Henrico,* and HMT *Empire Anvil* at Weymouth. Combat Team 16 spent two days aboard ships before arriving off Slapton Sands with the rest of the "invasion fleet."[169]

The regiment came ashore about 7:30 a.m. on May 4, and the landings went smoothly and on schedule, despite rough seas and rain. The regiment moved inland to secure initial objectives, which were captured the following day. After securing their objectives and digging in to repel counterattacks, units were notified of the exercise termination and moved back to Dorset. Unlike Fox, this time the 16th Infantry went in on the left of the 116th Infantry, just as it would in Operation Neptune, the actual D-Day landings.[170] The final plans were solidifying, and the big day for the 16th Infantry was fast approaching.

Arriving back at Dorset on May 7, the men turned to final preparations for the invasion. For the next ten days they were busy waterproofing vehicles, packing and crating equipment, turning in excess supplies, marking vehicles and equipment, and cleaning up the camps in and around Dorset. On May 17, CT 16 moved to marshaling camps, or "D-Camps," to be positioned for efficient loading for D-Day. On May 28, CT 16 units were reorganized into their invasion organizations, which were based on landing craft assignments and "assault teams." Just the act of forming these teams greatly increased the men's anticipation of the imminent invasion. The regiment's monthly historical report for May 29 reported: "…morale of men on fighting edge." Two days later, the men boarded ships at Weymouth and their morale was reported as "extremely high." The men of the 16th Infantry were ready for D-Day.

Normandy Campaign
June 6-July 24, 1944

Operation Overlord is probably the single greatest military operation ever attempted. In less than twenty-four hours, the combined efforts of American, British, and Canadian military forces were able to secure five beachheads in France, usually against fierce opposition, and land about 175,000 ground troops, who began the roll-back and ultimate defeat of Adolf Hitler's Third Reich.

Overlord was the result of two years' work by Allied planners. Originally conceived in 1942, the plan went through a number of alterations before the final version began jelling in early 1944. Overlord actually consisted of several subplans, of which Operation Neptune was the invasion phase. Neptune called for Allied landings on five beaches in Normandy. At the eastern end of the invasion area lay the three British-Canadian beaches of Gold, Juno, and Sword, in the vicinity of Caen, that were to be invaded by the British Second Army. To the west lay the sector of the U.S. First Army, which consisted of two beaches. Utah beach, at the base of the Cotentin peninsula, was the VII Corps' objective. In the center of it all lay Omaha beach, the V Corps' D-Day objective.

The Omaha landings called for two reinforced regimental combat teams from the 1st Infantry Division to land on a stretch of beach that extended from the village of Le Grand Hameau, in the east, to Vierville-sur-Mer in the west. The assault units selected for the Omaha operation were the 16th Infantry and the 116th Infantry (attached from the 29th Division). The 16th Infantry would go in on the eastern (left) half of the beach, and the 116th on the west. The 16th Infantry's half of Omaha beach was further divided into two subsectors or zones: Fox Green in the east and Easy Red in the west, next to the 116th Infantry's sector. The assault battalions designated to take these subsectors were the 3rd and 2nd Battalions respectively. The 1st Battalion was slated to follow the 2nd onto Easy Red.

The 16th Infantry's sector of the beach was some three kilometers long and extended from Le Grand Hameau to St. Laurent-sur-Mer. Both towns lay about two kilometers inland. The beach consisted of a band of fine brown sand, one to four hundred yards wide at low tide, before abruptly changing into a rocky shale seawall. Beyond the shale lay a meadow-like shelf, with marshy ground in some places, sand dunes in others. About one to two hundred meters wide, the shelf transitioned into rocky bluffs that ascended sharply for about forty meters. Fortified with pillboxes and entrenchments, enemy positions on the bluffs were ideally situated for beach defense, providing open fields for grazing and enfilading fire from the assortment of small arms, automatic weapons, and light and medium artillery with which the Germans were equipped. The beaches and the water approaches offered additional hazards in the form of barbed-wire entanglements, mines, and landing craft obstacles. As conceived by the defenders, Omaha beach was to be a veritable slaughterhouse for an amphibious assault force.

The bluffs were cut by three deep ravines that furnished natural ingress from the beach onto the plateaus above. The eastern-most exit was designated F-1 and was the least-useful route for military traffic, although it did have the advantage of a fork through which traffic could be directed toward Le Grand Hameau or Colleville-sur-Mer. A ten-foot-wide tarmac road designated E-3 ran through the center ravine and provided a direct route to Colleville-sur-Mer, a primary D-Day objective for the 16th Infantry. E-3 was considered the best of the three exits. Through the western ravine ran E-1, an eight-foot-wide sand road that led to St. Laurent-sur-Mer, an objective of the 116th on D-Day. One of the specified tasks for both the 16th and the 116th Regiments was to open these exits to allow vehicular movement onto the high ground.[171]

Once on the high ground, the terrain transformed into relatively flat farmlands, lush with the green hues of springtime and freshly planted crops. Crisscrossing the farmers' fields were thick hedgerows that marked the ancient boundaries for each plot of land. For defending troops, they provided excellent cover and concealment. An average commander with average troops could turn these belts of hedgerows into superb defensive positions. An imaginative commander with elite troops could make them a costly objective for any foe, as the men of the 1st Infantry Division would soon find out.

Complicating the difficulties facing the invasion troops was the weather. For several days before the invasion, a storm buffeted the English Channel. Overlord planners had decided that the landings would be made about dawn on a day when low tide occurred about 5:30 a.m. The intent was to ensure that the landing craft could reach the beach without having to steer around, or worse, run into the mine-tipped underwater obstacles that had been emplaced by the German defenders. Of course, that also meant that the men would have farther to run or crawl to get to the shelter of the shale seawall. Given the phases of the moon (which affected tidal highs and lows) and sunrise limitations (which coincided with low tide), planners determined that the window for the landings in June 1944 had to be on June 5, 6, or 7. When bad weather forced his cancellation of the landings on the 5th, Eisenhower made the risky decision to go on the 6th, when there was a slight chance that the weather would improve.

The enemy facing the Allied effort in Normandy was Army Group B, commanded by the 1st Infantry Division's old foe from North Africa, Erwin Rommel. Now a field marshal, Rommel had assigned the mission to defend the vicinity of the Normandy area to his Seventh Army. The defense of the Utah and Omaha beaches was assigned specifically to the LXXXIV Corps. The latter was composed of three "static defense" divisions and two "attack infantry" divisions. The main German forces in the Omaha beach area were the 716th Infantry Division (static defense), and the 352nd Infantry Division (attack infantry).[172]

The 716th Infantry Division constituted the primary beach defense force facing the British beaches and Omaha. Commanded by Lieutenant General Wilhelm Richter, the 716th had been formed on April 3, 1941, in Bielefeld, Germany. In May, it transferred to Rouen, France, and began training as a static coast-defense division, which gave its leaders and men three years to learn their mission area and prepare defenses. The division headquarters was relocated to Caen in March 1943, where it remained until shortly after D-Day. The division consisted of the 726th and 736th Infantry Regiments, and the 1716th Artillery Regiment. Attached to the 716th were the 441st and 642nd *Ost* (East) Battalions, so-named because they were composed mostly of Russians and Poles. At the time of D-Day, the 726th Infantry Regiment, less its 2nd Battalion, was attached to the 352nd Infantry Division. The 2nd Battalion formed the divisional reserve. Both the 726th Infantry Regiment and the 642nd East Battalion manned the main beach defenses that the 16th Infantry Regiment would have to fight through. The 736th was responsible for the defense of the British beaches near Caen. As the artillery unit for a static defense division, the 1716th had third-rate equipment, and many of those guns had been placed to cover the beaches in direct-fire mode. Therefore, the 352nd Artillery Regiment from the 352nd Division was attached to the 716th to support the fighting in the areas just beyond the beachhead.[173]

In support of the 716th Division was the 352nd Infantry Division. Its mission was to counterattack penetrations beyond the beachhead area and destroy, capture, or throw the invaders back into the sea. Commanded by Lieutenant General Dietrich Kraiss, the 352nd was formed on September 22, 1943, in Le Desert, France. It transferred to the Caumont area in France that November and began training as an attack division. The division headquarters was relocated to St. Lô in April 1944, where it remained until the Allied breakout in July. The division consisted of the 914th, 915th, and 916th Infantry Regiments; the 352nd Fusilier Battalion; 352nd Jaeger (Antitank) Battalion; and the 352nd Artillery Regiment. On D-Day, the 915th Infantry Regiment formed the LXXXIV Corps reserve; the 914th Infantry Regiment was prepared to counterattack in the 736th Infantry Regiment's area, in the 116th Infantry's sector; and the 916th Infantry Regiment was positioned behind the beach defenses that the 16th Infantry Regiment would encounter. As already stated, the 352nd Artillery Regiment was attached to the 716th Division.[174]

The Allies did not know that the 352nd Infantry Division was anywhere near Omaha beach on D-Day. This, despite the fact that Allied military intelligence had been tracking all German Army units in Normandy very closely and, on D-Day, had developed a remarkably accurate picture of where every unit was, down to the battalion level and, at times, even to the company level. In January 1944, the 352nd was identified in reserve positions around St. Lô, and Allied planners believed it was still in those positions at the time of the landings. In February, however, Rommel had inspected the Normandy units and concluded that the division was located too far to the rear for the purpose of repelling an Allied invasion. He ordered the division forward and, in March, the 352nd redeployed in the Omaha Beach vicinity—a movement that was not detected by the First Army's military intelligence community.

Interestingly, the redeployment of the division *was* known to the Allied high command from secret "Ultra" intercepts. In *Cross-Channel Attack,* Gordon A. Harrison wrote:

Brigadier Williams, G-2 of 21 Army Group, has said since the war that just before the invasion he did find out about the 352nd's presence on the coast but was unable to inform the troops....This is partially confirmed in a 21 Army Group Weekly Neptune Review #17 of June 4 which warned: "It should not be surprising if we discovered that it (the *716th Division*) had two regiments in the line and one in reserve while on its left *352nd Division* had one regiment up and two to play."[175]

This was indeed the disposition of troops on June 6, and

it meant the 16th Infantry was not attacking merely portions of one fixed and undermanned static defense regiment, but would instead face four battalions of combat troops. The decision not to inform the troops was to have dire consequences for the 16th Infantry on D-Day.

Another potential threat to the 16th Infantry was the 21st Panzer Division. Located between Caen and Bayeux, this division—Rommel's only armored reserve in the Seventh Army's area of operations—was capable of reaching the Omaha beachhead in two hours or less. Knowing this concerned Taylor and his staff, who clearly recalled their brush with tanks at Gela.

Given the difficult mission ahead, Combat Team 16 was significantly reinforced for the operation. Its task organization for D-Day was as follows:

Under Combat Team Control:
   HHC, 16th Infantry
   Antitank Company
   Service Company
   741st Tank Battalion (Duplex-Drive)
   (less B and C Companies)
   197th AAA Battalion (SP)
   1st Engineer Combat Battalion (less Companies A and B)
   20th Engineer Combat Battalion (less Company A)
   37th Engineer Shore Battalion
   (less Companies A, B, and C)
   Company A, 1st Medical Battalion

1st Battalion Landing Team ("Red Team")
   Cannon Company
   1 Platoon, Company A, 1st Engineer Combat Battalion
   1 Platoon, Company A, 20th Engineer Combat Battalion
   Company C, 37th Engineer Combat Battalion
   Elements, 5th Engineer Shore Brigade
   2nd Battalion Landing Team ("White Team")
   7th Field Artillery Battalion (in direct support)
   Company B, 741st Tank Battalion (Duplex-Drive)
   Company A, 1st Engineer Combat Battalion
   (less one platoon)
   Company B, 37th Engineer Combat Battalion
   Elements, 5th Engineer Shore Brigade
   Company A, 81st Chemical Weapons Battalion
   (4.2-inch mortar)

3rd Battalion Landing Team ("Blue Team")
   62nd Field Artillery Battalion (SP) (in direct support)
   Company C, 741st Tank Battalion (Duplex-Drive)
   Company A, 20th Engineer Combat Battalion
   (less one platoon)
   Company A, 37th Engineer Combat Battalion
   Elements, 5th Engineer Shore Brigade
   Company C, 81st Chemical Weapons Battalion
   (4.2-inch mortar)

In addition to the main combat units listed above were a host of small detachments from the signal corps, medical corps, military intelligence, civil affairs. There were also several liaison elements from the 1st Division, 50th (Northumbrian) Division, and the V Corps.[176]

Each Battalion Landing Team (BLT) had specific requirements on D-Day. The 3rd BLT, still under the command of Lieutenant Colonel Horner, had the mission to land at beach Fox Green, and reduce the defenses in that zone to allow the follow-on forces of the 1st Division to land unimpeded. After clearing the defenses, the battalion was to open exits E-3 and F-1, move to capture the villages of Le Grand Hameau, La Vailee, and Ste. Honorine-des-Pertes, then dig in and prepare to repel counterattacks. Additionally, Horner had to ensure that contact was made with the 231st Brigade, 50th Northumbrian Division, which was to land at Gold beach to the east and be prepared to pass the 26th Infantry through to continue the attack.[177]

On the right of the 3rd BLT, the 2nd BLT's mission was to land at beach Easy Red. The 2nd BLT was now under Lieutenant Colonel Herbert C. Hicks, who had taken command back in August 1943, just after the end of the Sicily campaign. Hicks's team was to reduce the beach defenses in its zone, open exit E-1, then continue south to capture the town of Colleville-sur-Mer. Additionally, the battalion had to gain and maintain contact with the 116th Infantry to the west. Finally, he had to be prepared to pass the 1st BLT through to continue the attack.[178]

The follow-up force was the 1st BLT, still under the command of Lieutenant Colonel Driscoll. Initially the combat team reserve, Driscoll was to pass through the 2nd BLT and attack to seize the villages of Formigny and Surrain south of Colleville. He, too, was to maintain contact with the 116th Infantry to the west and with CT 18, once it came up on the battalion's right. From positions at the two villages, the 1st BLT could cover by fire the valley leading to Bayeux. Additionally, Driscoll was to seize several bridges near Trevières and establish roadblocks against armored counterattacks from the 21st Panzer Division.[179] All these missions were thoroughly briefed and analyzed by regimental leaders once the 16th Infantry went into isolation before the invasion.

On May 17, the regiment moved to D-camps southeast of Dorset, nearer to the twin ports of Weymouth and Portland. The move was the first clear indicator that the long-awaited invasion of Europe was about to begin. While in the D-camps training continued, but it tended to focus on the more mundane tasks, such as long road marches and cleaning weapons, while the officers pored over maps, aerial photographs, and mock-up models of the landing and objective areas.

Being in the D-camps gave the men a sense that the "big show" was coming soon. To keep morale high, the troops were allowed frequent passes into surrounding towns. The passes, combined with fair weather and decent food, did the trick and kept the men in good spirits.

On May 24, the camps were sealed and access to them severely restricted. Two days later, the men were briefed on their mission and issued combat jackets. On May 27, the regiment displaced to marshaling area D-4, where the companies were reorganized into their assault sections and billeted by landing craft loads.[180] For the D-Day operation, the infantry companies were reorganized from the standard four-platoon organization into five assault sections and one headquarters section. Each section was intended to be a self-contained, mini-assault team, capable of independent operations until it could reach the high ground, where the company would reorganize into its normal configuration. Each team consisted of about thirty-five men with machine-guns, 60mm mortars, flamethrowers, demolitions, and bangalore torpedoes, in addition to the standard M-1 Garand rifles, BARs, grenade launchers, carbines, and other weapons infantrymen normally carried. Each section was expected to be able to penetrate the wire and mines, make its way to the enemy defenses, reduce them, and establish temporary defenses while the company assembled. The section leader was usually a seasoned lieutenant, with a tech sergeant as his second in command.

On the 31st, the troops were moved to Weymouth and Portland to load onto assault ships. The advance CP and the 2nd BLT boarded the USS *Henrico* at Portland, the 3rd BLT boarded the HMS *Empire Anvil* at Weymouth, and the 1st BLT and the regimental headquarters boarded the USS *Samuel Chase*, also at Weymouth. This move created excitement and anticipation, and the morale of the regiment was reported as "extremely high" and "on fighting edge."[181]

The regiment remained on board for the next six days, waiting for the final word to go. There was little to do now except clean weapons, write letters, and wait. Some soldiers went topside at every opportunity to get fresh air but also to marvel at the assemblage of ships. Technical Sergeant Donald Wilson of Lakeland, New Jersey recalled the scene:

> It was truly massive and it occurred to me that this same scene must be taking place in a number of British seaports. That it was happening in broad daylight, not really far from Fortress Europa, was absolutely astounding. Surely they [the Germans] must know, but where were they? Surveying this panorama convinced me that victory would ultimately, unquestionably, be ours.[182]

On Sunday, June 4, Chaplain Deery celebrated mass on board the 1st Division headquarters ship, USS *Ancon*. One would surmise there were probably more worshipers than usual that Sunday morning. Clearly, this was the long awaited "big show," a contest that many would not survive, and it seemed like a good time to get right with God.

Finally, the signal came, and at 9:00 p.m. on June 5, the ships steamed out of the harbor and joined the huge invasion fleet assembling in the North Sea. As the fleet sailed south, a vast armada of planes carrying three airborne divisions winged

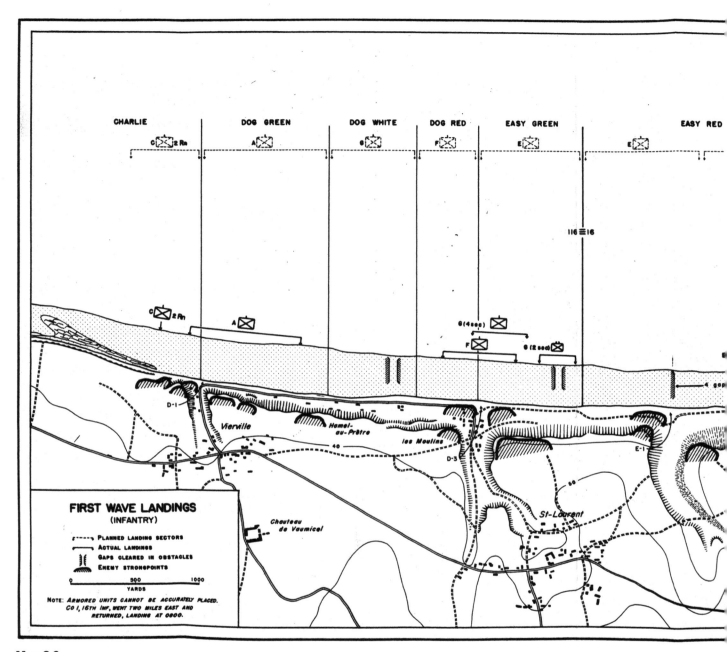

Map 8-9.

its way to the drop zones behind the beaches. There was no turning back; the invasion was on.

D-Day
June 6, 1944

About 1:00 a.m. on June 6, the vessels carrying the V Corps arrived at their designated spot and dropped anchor some twenty-three thousand yards (twelve miles) off the Normandy beaches. Few of the assault troops were comfortable enough to get any sleep, and they were about to get a lot less comfortable. About 3:15 a.m., the troops of the 2nd and 3rd Battalions were alerted to move to the gunwales, and began the tedious process of loading the landing craft. The procedure was made more difficult by rough seas resulting from the storm that had passed through just the day before. Upon reaching the gunwales, soldiers climbed over the side and carefully made their way down the rope nets. Near the bottom of the net, they had to time the moment they dropped into the craft below as the boat pitched and bobbed in the swells. Slowly, but efficiently, the 16th Infantry was loaded and soon on its way to shore.

On board the landing craft, the coxswains, commanding the array of LCVPs, LCAs, LCTs, LCMs, and other vessels,

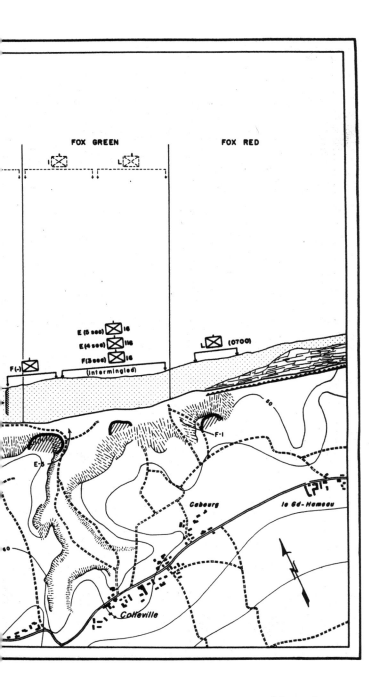

lessen the effects of seasickness. Soon, he felt almost normal.[183]

The men reacted differently to the ride. Some were extremely anxious; others were fascinated by the experience. One recalled:

> At some unseen and unheard signal, our landing crafts moved from line astern to line abreast. Then suddenly, throttles opened wide and the race to shore was on. To the right and left of my boat, a line of assault craft plunged forward, pushing crests of white water ahead of them. I know that the Light Brigade and Pickett's Charge flashed through my mind at that beautiful moment. It was pure excitement! The thrill, the exhilaration of the experience was, and remains to this day, indescribable, yet palpable.[184]

Leading the assault troops onto the beach were the "Duplex-Drive" (DD) tanks of Companies B and C, 741st Tank Battalion. These M4 Sherman tanks were designed to float by the use of a canvas barrier that encircled the vehicle. Carried aboard LCTs, the tanks went into the water about 5:50 a.m. and started toward the beach. The high swells, however, were too much for the water barriers erected around the vehicles' hulls, and soon the tanks, one by one, slipped beneath the waves. Those crews lucky enough to escape did so by piling into inflatable rubber rafts, colored yellow for easier rescue.

Meanwhile, the LCVPs with Companies I, L, E, and F began the twelve-mile trip to the beach. As they sped south, the comforting boom of fourteen-inch guns from the battleships USS *Texas* and *Arkansas* sounded in the distance as the ships began pounding the beaches. Added to the naval gunfire were the bombers of the Ninth Air Force, which started hitting targets, mostly beyond the beach as it turned out, about 6:05 a.m. Fifteen minutes out, the boats passed the yellow dinghies of the tank men. Many of the assault troops believed the men in the rafts were downed airmen. But soon, it dawned upon them that they were the DD men, and that the tanks would not be on the beach to assist in reducing the German defenses. In fact, only six of the thirty-two DD tanks made it to the beach that morning.

About the same time the lead boats passed the unfortunate tankers, three LST rocket ships, standing nearby, loosed their deadly loads in a spectacular pyrotechnic display. To the chagrin of the assault troops, however, the rockets fell harmlessly into the water or well inland, but not on their intended target—the beach defenses.

H-Hour: The Landings, 6:30-7:00 a.m.
2nd Battalion Landing Team

It was not apparent yet, but the landings had already gone awry. The 2nd Battalion's first wave was heading not for Easy Red, but for the dead center of Fox Green. About five hundred yards offshore, the LCVPs carrying Companies E and F began to receive machine-gun, mortar, and antitank fire. Here and

guided their boats into ever-growing assembly circles, going around and around for the next two hours or more. The men packed in the holds were jostled about and drenched with spray as the boats made their way through the heavy seas. The constant motion, combined with the nervous waiting, made the men sick, and many vomited. Captain Karl Wolf from Wethersfield, Connecticut, an "extra officer" riding in one of the 3rd Battalion headquarters boats, recalled that he felt queasy and, observing other men retching, he quickly began vomiting too. After emptying his innards in a plastic bag, he swallowed three Dramamine tablets, which had been issued to

there, a boat was hit by direct fire. While some hits caused superficial damage, others caused numerous casualties or sank the landing craft. About two hundred yards from shore, the LCVPs stopped and lowered their ramps. Immediately, small arms and machine-gun fire, which had been peppering the raised ramps, now tore through flesh and bone as men tumbled, staggered, and leapt into the frigid water. The water was about chest deep at this part of the beach. With bullets zipping into the water and mortar rounds exploding around them, the men pushed their way forward among the mined stakes, hedgehogs, and other obstacles. To the troops who had to make their way through that hell, the beach obstacles were a mixed blessing. On the one hand, they prevented the LCVPs from making it all the way to the beach; on the other, the obstacles provided the men with some protection as they fought their way ashore against heavy seas and German small-arms fire.

Company F, under the command of Captain John G. W. Finke, entered the water at about 6:40 a.m. Finke's boat and the 1st Section landed about on target near the boundary of Easy Red and Fox Green. The rest of the company, however, landed about four hundred yards too far to the east, on Fox Green.[185] Once ashore on Fox Green, the troops had to move across a no-man's land that offered little cover, other than that provided by the obstacles, until they reached the seawall about two hundred yards inland (at low tide). Fearful of the dangers this movement entailed, many men remained in the cold water, causing the follow-on boatloads to pile up to the rear. Debarking behind F Company came five sections of men from Captain Ed Wozenski's E Company and four sections of troops from the badly misdirected E Company, 116th Infantry. The situation on Fox Green in front of exit E-3 quickly deteriorated as hundreds of soldiers, their units hopelessly intermingled, struggled forward under heavy enemy fire.

Technical Sergeant Wilson struggled ashore with several of his men and made it to an obstacle on the beach. He looked back at his boat and saw that it had been hit and was burning. The coxswain's body was draped over the steering wheel, and another man was hung up on the side of the craft. His body "swayed back and forth as the boat drifted on the swells." Wilson watched as several riflemen tried to zigzag their way across the beach, but by the time they made their second stop, enemy gunners cut them down. "Joe Spechler took off with a twenty-five pound TNT satchel charge in his hand and another on his back. He ran some thirty yards and exploded—obliterated as little bits of the burlap used to strap the TNT blocks together, fluttered down and lay smoldering in the sand."[186]

To the west of Finke's headquarters element and 1st Section, the 1st Section of E Company, under First Lieutenant John Spalding from Owensboro, Kentucky, went into the water about 6:45 a.m., about where F Company should have landed. Spalding recalled, "Because we were carrying so much equipment and because I was afraid that we were being landed in deep water, I told the men not to jump out until after I had test-

ed the water. I jumped out of the boat slightly to the left of the ramp into water about waist deep." His men followed, making their way forward through heavy small-arms fire. On the way in, however, they encountered an underwater runnel that they had to cross by swimming, it being too deep for their feet to touch. Inflating their life vests, he and his men swam across the depression, but in doing so, lost much of the equipment they needed to reduce enemy positions and obstacles; flamethrowers, mortars, bazookas, and ammunition went to the bottom.[187]

At water's edge, the 1st Section took their first casualties: Private William C. Roper, shot in the foot, and Private First Class Virgil Tilley, hit by shrapnel in the shoulder. Spalding looked around for recognizable features and spied a demolished house, one that he believed to be a landmark that he remembered from the briefings. About this time, he noticed other troops moving across the beach: "They were too waterlogged to run, but they went as fast as they could. It looked as if they were walking in the face of a strong wind." The section made its way to the shale, bypassing a particularly active pillbox on its left. The 1st Section of E Company had made it to a position about halfway between exits E-1 and E-3 and ran into a concertina obstacle. Here, Spalding's men prepared to breach the wire with bangalore torpedoes.[188]

3rd Battalion Landing Team

The landings of the 3rd BLT were also in trouble. Captain John R. Armellino's Company L in the 3rd Battalion first wave experienced a series of misfortunes. Just after debarking from the *Empire Anvil*, the 4th Section's boat was swamped and went to the bottom. The heavy seas then caused the company to begin its approach late and it did not land until 7:00 a.m. Approaching the shore, the 1st Section's boat was struck twice by artillery, which inflicted some nineteen casualties. When they went into the water, Armellino's men discovered that they were about four hundred meters to the east of their intended landing site (where the jumbled units of the 2nd BLT now struggled to get ashore). For once, this was a fortunate turn of events in that the defenses where L Company landed were not as strong as others on the beach. Armellino was able to get 123 men of the 1st, 2nd, 3rd, and 5th Sections to a sheltered spot under the cliffs, where he immediately began organizing them for an assault on the enemy strongpoints. He had lost sixty-four men before reaching the cliffs.[189]

At the time, I Company had still not landed. Under the command of Captain Kimball R. Richmond, a popular officer from Windsor, Vermont, the company had transloaded into LCAs that morning, and at the appropriate time, had headed for shore. As their boats approached the beach, Richmond became aware that they were nowhere near his assigned sector. He deduced that they were actually approaching Port-en-Bessin, well to the east of Fox Green, and ordered the coxswains to pull back out to sea. Swinging to the west, I Company headed for the correct beach, but en route, the LCAs carrying the

4th and 5th Sections were swamped by the high swells. Company I was now down to four boats. Richmond contacted Horner by radio and informed him of the problem. Horner then radioed Captain Anthony Prucnal, commander of K Company, to take over I Company's missions.[190]

By 7:00 a.m., only three of the four assault companies were ashore, and only one, L Company, was relatively intact.

The Second Wave and Penetration 7:00-9:00 a.m.
2nd Battalion Landing Team

As the men of the 16th Infantry fought their way across the beach, the attached support units also attempted to do their jobs, with varying success. About 7:00 a.m., eight tanks of the 741st Tank Battalion were landed by LCTs. They were welcome reinforcements, but several tanks stalled upon landing, and most were knocked out within a short time. Also ashore were the troops of the 5th Engineer Special Brigade, who were attempting to blow up and remove obstacles to clear the beach for the landing craft. Engineers' casualties, especially among the leaders, were tremendous because of the nature of their work on the exposed beach. Within a short space of time, the brigade commander, brigade S2, and S3 were all killed, leaving a leadership vacuum that was never adequately filled during the day. The engineers' efforts were further hampered by the loss of clearing equipment, demolitions, and rapid destruction of those few bulldozers that were actually landed.

By 7:00 a.m., many men of E and F Companies were still pinned behind tetrahedrons—and the tide was rising. Still, a many others had made it to the seawall, albeit with severe casualties. Upon reaching the wall, many of the men were forced to field strip their weapons to clean them before they would fire. This was a particularly difficult task to accomplish while lying behind the wall, as bullets zinged overhead, and mortar rounds exploded on the beach. After gathering men who had made it to the wall, small-unit leaders of E Company began a lateral movement to the right in an attempt to move to the proper landing area. As groups made their way westward, they picked up additional E Company men and troops from other units willing to brave the fire, and made it to the company's intended landing point:

> Here the men were pinned down by fire. A 7-yard beachhead was established. By this time, the beachhead was blocked by the crowding of personnel onto the 7-yard penetration. Shoulder to shoulder the men lay prone on the pebbles, stones, and shale; some personnel laid in a prone position on the beach with bodies half inserted in the water. Landing craft disgorged more troops onto the 7-yard beachhead.[191]

Casualties mounted as more men from the succeeding waves crowded the area, attempting to find shelter.

The three F Company sections, still intermixed with E

Company men from the 16th and 116th Regiments, were opposed by three pillboxes, a bunker, and at least four machine-guns that covered an antitank ditch at exit E-3. Individually and in small teams, the troops overcame their initial shock and began fighting back. Staff Sergeant Raymond F. Strojny of Taunton, Massachusetts, grabbed a bazooka from one of his wounded men and made his way forward toward a pillbox. Taking careful aim, he launched a round into the gun slit, setting the position on fire. An F Company mortar man, Staff Sergeant Kazemir J. Pizo of Brooklyn, New York, set up his 60mm tube and soon rained rounds on another part of the same German strongpoint. After running out of rounds, he and several other NCOs led an attack on the trenches and captured fifteen enemy soldiers.[192]

To the west, Captain Finke with the rest of F Company was able to get his headquarters and the 3rd Section to the seawall directly below the strongpoint his company was assigned to reduce. His command, now diminished to about forty soldiers (not including those sections farther east) was armed primarily with rifles. Like many troops on that desperate morning, Finke's men had lost most of their special equipment on the way in. With this force, Finke faced a position consisting of an antitank gun, three pillboxes, and a casemated medium artillery piece. Unable to respond with heavy weapons, Finke's outfit was soon pinned down by machine-gun and sniper fire.[193]

Still father west, Spalding's troops had gathered enough bangalores to attempt a breach. Staff Sergeant Curtis Colwell and other men assembled the tubes and pushed them toward the wire. Soon, a blast erupted and a gap appeared. By ones and twos, the section made its way through the gap and safely to the demolished house that Spalding had previously noted on the way in. There, Staff Sergeant Philip Streczyk of New York, Spalding's section sergeant, left with Private Richard J. Gallagher of Brooklyn, to conduct a recon for a route off the beach. As the two men departed, Spalding looked down the beach to his left and observed a horrific spectacle. The pillbox that his section had bypassed earlier was now firing directly down the length of the landing areas, and Spalding watched helplessly as troops of F Company were mercilessly mowed down. "There was nothing we could do to help them," Spalding later lamented.[194]

About 7:00 a.m., G Company, the 2nd BLT's second wave, approached its correct landing area on Easy Red. Commanded by Captain Joe Dawson from Waco, Texas, G Company would figure prominently in the fighting for Colleville later in the day. Just two hundred yards from shore, one of the company's boats capsized and dumped its human cargo into the surf. The remaining craft, however, were able to drop ramps directly onto the beach, and men scrambled to reach the shale. It was 7:10 a.m.

Like the preceding wave, G Company was met with a hail of fire. Leading his men onto the beach, Dawson, his communications sergeant, and another soldier ran forward just

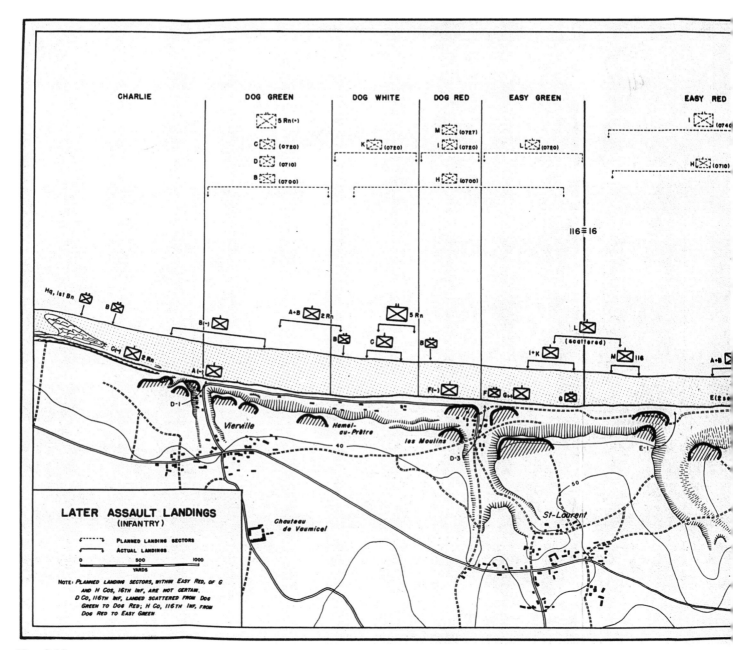

Map 8-10.

before their LCVP was hit by artillery. No one else made it off the boat. One of the men killed was Dawson's naval fire control officer, who carried the radio for controlling naval gunfire support once the unit was inland. The navy was to act as the regiment's artillery until the 7th Field Artillery Battalion landed later that morning. The loss of the radio was to have tragic consequences later that day.[195]

Struggling under their heavy equipment, some G Company men ran all the way to the shale, some went from obstacle to obstacle, some never made it. Upon reaching the shale, Dawson and his men found disorganized remnants of F

Company and E Company, 116th Infantry. Most were without leaders, and few appeared to be doing much about getting off the beach. Some had made it forward of the shale into the shelf area beyond the seawall, but many of those lay dead or wounded. Those who were still alive were pinned down by small-arms fire. Dawson quickly reorganized his company, and soon machine-guns and mortars were in action against the German positions on and below the bluffs. Through the efforts of junior officers and NCOs, an increasing volume of fire built against the German defenses. The rest of the 16th Infantry was finally beginning to fight back!

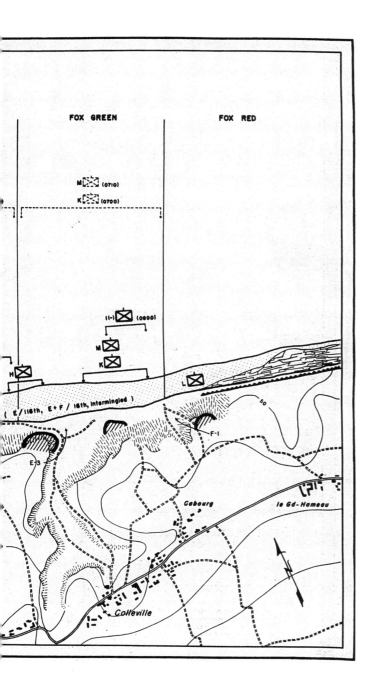

upward through antipersonnel mines and intense small-arms fire. Miraculously, nobody was hit or injured. Of the episode, Spalding later remarked, "The Lord was with us and we had an angel on each shoulder on that trip."[197]

Luck did not hold out for Spalding's section, however. Wounded in quick succession were Sergeant Hubert Blades, Private First Class Raymond Curley, and Sergeant Grant Phelps, all hit by a machine-gunner who fired from a foxhole above them as they ascended the trail. Near the top, Spalding and his men rushed the position, and the enemy soldier threw up his hands and shouted "Kamerad!" hoping to be spared. Realizing they needed him for intelligence, Spalding decided to save the man—despite his men's feelings to the contrary. It turned out he was Polish, not German, and was willing to talk. More importantly the 16th Infantry now had men on the top of the bluffs. It was about 9:00 a.m.

Not long after Spalding had reached the top, G Company followed Baldridge up to Dawson's location. Dawson now decided to move forward to reconnoiter the trail.

> Just about as I got near the top of the ridge I could hear voices, and suddenly I heard a machine gun. I looked up and sure enough, just above me was a machine gun, a German machine gun. And they couldn't see me because I was about six feet below them....I took two grenades and armed them and threw them into the machine gun nest that they had, and that silenced them.[198]

Dawson's men then scrambled to the top of the bluff.

Landing behind G Company, the 2nd Battalion's heavy weapons unit, Company H, under Captain Robert Irvine, landed on Easy Red about 7:30 a.m. They, too, received concentrated fire as they debouched onto the beach. Irvine's machine-gunners set up their guns and promptly directed them against a strongpoint facing Fox Green. But they, in turn, were pinned down by enemy gunners.

Coming in about the same time as H Company was the 2nd Battalion headquarters boat carrying Hicks, Major William R. Washington (battalion XO), Captain Fred Hall (S3), First Lieutenant Neville Chandler (S2), the operations and intelligence sections, FOs from the 7th Field Artillery, and assorted headquarters personnel. The boat dropped its ramp close to shore, but the men still had to wade through water and obstacles before reaching the beach. Once there, they made a mad dash to the seawall, but of twenty-eight men only fourteen arrived unscathed. Among those who did were Hicks, Washington, and Hall. The latter recalled:

> The beach was in a state of confusion. We landed at a point east of our designated landing area. We were under small arms and artillery and mortar fire. It was apparent that the naval and air bombardment preceding the landing had had little effect. Once ashore, it was a matter of

Off to his right, Dawson spotted some troops pinned down near the demolished house and ordered his company to move in that direction. Dawson soon located a narrow path through the minefields and wire and took Private Frank Baldridge from Quitman, Arkansas, with him to check out the trail. Halfway up the bluff, Dawson encountered Spalding and his E Company section. Dawson sent Baldridge back to bring up the company, as Spalding's men led the way up to the top.[196]

Meanwhile, Gallagher had returned from his recon and led Spalding's section up a trail Streczyk had found in a defile going to the top of the bluffs. In single file, the men climbed

survival, but I was so busy trying to round up unit commanders to organize their men to move along and eventually off the beach, there wasn't much time to think except to do what had to be done.[199]

Adding to his dismay, Hall sensed that the crowded conditions on the beach would serve to increase casualties; as more men came ashore and the tide rose, the troops made for a more concentrated target. Additionally, the landing craft had difficulty navigating past wrecks and returning boats, which slowed them down and increased their vulnerability to fire. Hall recalled that "some of the boats were taking direct hits. I watched one LCI coming in with troops unloading on ramps on each side. The ramps were raked with small-arms fire as the soldiers came down. There were many casualties. It was pretty bad."[200] But Hall did not have time to ponder the tragedy. By mid-morning, Hicks, Hall, and the 2nd Battalion CP moved toward the route taken earlier by Spalding and G Company.

Regimental Advanced Command Post
About the time Dawson's G Company made its way across the beach, the regimental advanced command post drew near Fox Green to the left of E Company. Commanded by Lieutenant Colonel Mathews, the regimental XO, the CP consisted of 102 men loaded on an LCM. Also on board were elements of the S1, S2, and S3 sections, the regimental communications section, and the entire I&R Platoon under Lieutenant Hill. At 7:20 a.m., about 150 yards from shore, the ramp dropped and the I&R Platoon plunged into the surf. Almost instantly, Hill's men were raked with machine-gun and small-arms fire. Struggling forward as fast as their heavy loads allowed, the men made for nearby obstacles, seeking cover, while the CP and communications people followed. Among the first casualties in the water was Lieutenant Colonel Mathews, killed by a burst of fire. Ducking from obstacle to obstacle, the two groups (Hill's men plus the CP and its attached communications unit) made their way forward in the chilly water, but thirty-five were killed or wounded before reaching the beach. Once on the beach, the CP personnel found "dead, wounded, and disorganized personnel, under constant enemy concentration of fire."[201]

Jim Lipinski, now promoted to warrant officer and assigned as the assistant S1, went into the water with several of his men from the S1 section. Making his way through the obstacles and onto the beach, he arrived at the shale with only three men left from his section. Keeping his wits about him, he began assembling as many CP personnel as he could find, moving them to the right, linking up with E Company, and setting up the advanced CP. After locating only a handful of CP men, including Chaplain Deery, the group warily made its way westward until they reached E Company, losing another S1 man en route.[202] There, they ran into the men of at least three companies, all bunched up as they desperately sought cover from the murderous fire.

By the time the regimental advanced CP landed, the combat team had five companies and hundreds of engineers, tankers, and other support troops ashore. In addition to the handful of destroyed tanks, the beach was littered with bulldozers, halftracks, weapons carriers, and other vehicles. Few were operational and troops were drawn to the disabled vehicles like magnets, using them for cover. The sparse cover available was crammed with soldiers just trying to stay alive. The masses of huddled men made excellent targets for those German machine-gunners who could place fire on them. As additional waves came in, the problem was compounded, and casualties rose.

Little by little, however, brave men overcame their fear and began to battle their way forward, either individually or in small groups. The mostly leaderless troops of the 5th Engineer Special Brigade mounted bulldozers and began to clear away obstacles. Those without dozers used explosives. Under seemingly impossible conditions, the engineers cleared several lanes, suffering 50 percent casualties in the process.

Medics performed miracles amid the rising tide and enemy fire. Many were killed or wounded while trying to save other men's lives. The medical personnel on Omaha beach exemplified the biblical adage, "Greater love has no one than this, that he lay down his life for his friends."

Just about any survivor from Omaha beach can relate a story of some courageous dogface who braved the fire to plunge into the surf and rescue a buddy from the rising tide. Private E. E. Nikkel recalled no fewer than five men from the I&R Platoon—Privates Jim Hair, Louis Schroedert, Ed Wagner, John Irvan, and Boyd Klingaman—who each performed this feat, not once, but repeatedly on that beach. Others who attempted it were often wounded or killed attempting to save another man.

The loss of Mathews, the cramped conditions on the seven-yard beachhead, the constant enemy small-arms fire, and soaked, inoperative radios, made it impossible to set up the CP to provide command and control of the troops on the beach. Individual initiative and small-unit leadership would be needed to win this fight. To the Allies' good fortune, the 16th Infantry had a great deal of both on that day.

One example is that of Technician Fifth Grade John J. Pinder Jr., a radioman from the regimental communications section. Entering the water about one hundred yards from the shore, Pinder struggled under the weight of one of the command post radios as he made his way forward under intense fire. Hit by small-arms fire only yards from his boat, he somehow held his radio out of the water as he struggled through the surf. Once ashore, he linked up with the CP; then, after refusing first aid and despite being weakened by loss of blood, he went back into the water three times to retrieve other pieces of communications equipment. Returning from his third trip, he was hit in both legs by machine-gun fire but made it back to the CP, where he assisted in setting up the radios. While engaged in this effort, he was struck a third time and killed. For his extraordinary courage and will to accomplish the mission, Pinder became the 16th Infantry Regiment's fourth Medal of Honor recipient.[203]

Resolute courage was a common virtue on Omaha beach on June 6.

3rd Battalion Landing Team

The reserve company of the 3rd Battalion, Captain Anthony Prucnal's K Company, arrived at its intended landing site on Fox Green at 7:05 a.m., only five minutes late. Unlike most companies that day, Company K soldiers walked onto the beach high and dry, all six boats arriving intact. Like all the other companies, however, the troops were met by heavy gunfire as they scrambled from their landing craft and charged across the sand. They bounded to the shale embankment, arriving relatively unscathed, but soon casualties mounted, especially among officers. The XO was wounded early in the fight. As he attempted to reorganize his dispersed company, Prucnal was mortally wounded, probably by a mortar round that also killed the wounded XO. Two other officers were killed or wounded before K Company got off the beach.[204]

Artillery and mortar fire was particularly heavy in K Company's area. Private First Class Roger L. Brugger of Clyde, Ohio, scrambled off his boat and headed straight for the shale. Under the protection of the seawall, Brugger looked back in time to see the boat he had just left explode when an 88mm shell hit the engine compartment. A short time later, another boat came in, and Brugger remembered: "As the guys came running to the wall, one guy got a direct hit with a mortar shell and all I could see of him were three hunks of his body flying through the air."[205]

Coming in fifteen minutes after Company K, the battalion's heavy weapons company, M Company, under Captain Emil Edmonds, reached Easy Red with few casualties. Following Company M by about forty minutes was Richmond's I Company. Finally arriving after their unintended detour to Port-en-Bessin, the company's four remaining boats approached Fox Green about 8:00 a.m. Richmond's boat struck a mine about four hundred yards out, and the survivors, Richmond among them, had to swim ashore. Meanwhile, the 1st Section's boat hung up on an obstacle, then withdrew. The 2nd and 3rd Section boats were both severely damaged by artillery or mines. Those I Company soldiers who survived unwounded made their way to the shale, where Richmond and three lieutenants scraped together a handful of men from L, K, and M Companies. Richmond's ad hoc force then began to return fire on enemy positions.[206]

Meanwhile, many of the M Company troopers, after reaching the seawall, had collapsed next to a jumble of infantrymen and engineers hugging the ground. After catching their breath and preparing their weapons, Edmonds' machine-gunners sprang into action and silenced a pillbox. Through strenuous efforts, Edmonds' leaders were able to emplace the guns to

support assaults on both the E-3 and F-1 strongpoints.[207] In fact, that was exactly what L and K Companies were preparing to do.

Out on the water, Horner could see that his men were largely pinned down on the beach by the strong defenses. Remaining on board his LCA, Horner and his naval observer contacted a destroyer to come to the 3rd Battalion's assistance and soften up some of the more stubborn positions. As Horner attempted to direct the ship's fire, the destroyer came in so close to shore that many, including Horner, thought that the ship was going to run aground. After pummeling the positions, the ship pulled away, having destroyed several of them, and relieving a great deal of pressure on the 3rd Battalion troops ashore.[208]

Down on Fox Red, Armellino's L Company went into action to reduce the strongpoint on the east side of exit F-1. Luckily, the company was able to round up a couple of operational tanks. Making the most of this rare asset, Armellino personally directed the tankers' fire, repeatedly exposing himself to enemy gunners. Before long, the gallant captain was seriously wounded and out of the fight, and Lieutenant Robert R. Cutler Jr., the company XO, assumed command.[209]

Cutler ordered the 2nd Section, under First Lieutenant Jimmie W. Monteith, to move up a small draw to attack a set of pillboxes on the bluffs to the east of exit F-1. The 3rd section was to advance on Monteith's right, and the 5th would follow in support. Meanwhile, the 1st Section, under Lieutenant Kenneth J. Klenk, was to move laterally on the beach and attack its original objective, the strongpoint on the west side of the exit F-1 draw. On the way in, Klenk's LCVP took two direct hits from artillery or antitank fire that wounded several of his men. Several more were killed or wounded on the beach, leaving Klenk with twelve men. Klenk led his reduced section toward its objective.

En route, Klenk picked up elements of two leaderless sections of E/116th and integrated them into his command. From positions along the dune line between exits E-3 and F-1, Klenk's ad hoc outfit laid down a base of fire on the easternmost E-3 strongpoint and provided Company K, now ashore and advancing into the draw, covering fires for their movement. Klenk maintained this fusillade until smoke from grass fires obscured his men's vision. He then decided to assault the strongpoint, using the smoke as cover. A five-man team moved forward to clear a way through the wire and mines but was pinned down. Klenk's section, along with newly arrived reinforcements, came to the rescue. Mortars fired on the enemy trenches, and one soldier summoned a tank that added its weight to the effort. Soon, the 1st Section took the position, capturing thirty-one Germans and killing several others. Just after the fight, Klenk was joined by much of K Company and more troops of the 116th on the high ground above the E-3 draw.[210]

Like so many other things that morning, getting up the draw was no easy task, but Sergeant Russell Richert of K Company remembered an incident that illustrates the difficulty and the potential danger:

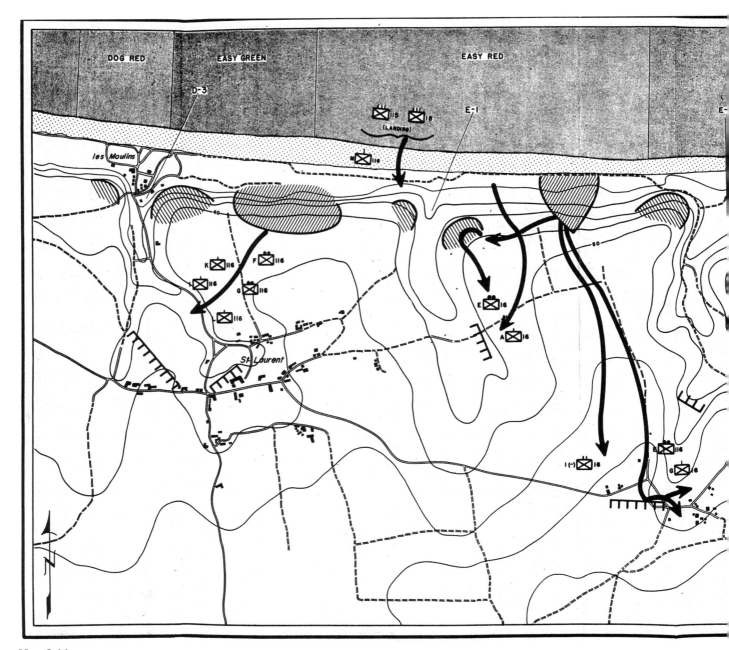

Map 8-11.

We were going up through the draw. I remember going up through that. We could see mines laying around, and I don't know if it was me or the fella in front of me. He was an Italian boy by the name of Nick Barbiari; he was a big Italian kid. We had them assault vests on and he had his entrenching tool covering the back of his neck....Either he or I must have set it off. It was a "Bouncing Betty" and it exploded right in my face. To this day I can remember the white flashes, the black streaks, and the orange and yellow. What saved us was...they had a hinge on 'em. The trip wire set them off and they come up, maybe four feet,

and then explode. I think this hinge must have been in my direction. Nick took the blast in his back. It took the shovel off at the swivelhead; tore it off. His pack was shredded. But 'cha know, he and I walked out without a damn scratch.[211]

The 3rd Battalion CP boat, carrying Karl Wolf, arrived at Omaha at about 8:15 a.m. The craft also carried Major Eston White, now the battalion XO; Captain Alan Morehouse, S1; and the CP personnel. As the ramp went down, bullets ripped into the packed craft; Morehouse was killed instantly by fire as he

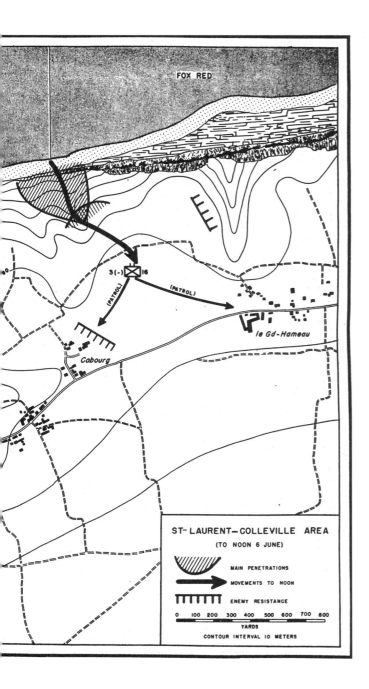

clouds of blood billowing from their bodies. Wolf decided that the spot was not a safe place after all and continued to move forward.[212]

Once on the beach, Wolf and the others discovered that they were surrounded by men wearing 29th Division patches. Only then did they realize that the CP group had not landed at Fox Green but at least two thousand yards too far to the west, almost due north of St. Laurent. Unable to move forward, the group dug in for protection. Just then Wolf observed an LCI pull close to the beach and drop its troop ramps. The first dozen men trundled off one ramp and went straight to the bottom in what proved to be deep water before the ship's skipper realized what was happening. Wolf and several others threw ropes to the hapless men, but most drowned, pulled under by their heavy loads and unable to inflate their life belts—which they had worn under their equipment, where the belts could not be inflated.[213]

After holding in place for a time, White concluded that the CP group had to make its way down the beach to link up with the rest of the 3rd Battalion. Wolf helped gather the ten or twelve men he believed remained of the group and began moving eastward. The trip, though harrowing, was punctuated by a humorous incident: "We crawled at first, and crouched, and ran at times," Wolf recalled;

> Every once in a while, enemy fire would make us stop and lie in the sand. One time after stopping, I felt someone shaking my leg. The Dramamine had finally kicked in and I had fallen asleep on the beach with enemy machine-gun fire going over my head. I finally woke up when a soldier behind me shook my leg. I soon realized what had happened and continued on. I suspect the men behind me who didn't know anything about my having taken [the pills] thought I was a pretty cool customer under enemy fire if I could take a nap under those conditions.[214]

Back at Fox Green, about the same time Klenk began his move on the strongpoint, Culter's other three sections were penetrating the beach obstacles almost directly below the defenses at F-1. Sergeant Wells's squad of Monteith's section made its way through two minefields and three bands of concertina wire to lead L Company up the defile on the east side. At the head of the draw, Monteith's 2nd Section set up a hasty defense to cover the approach of Cutler and the other two sections. To the west of Monteith, the 3rd Section, under Lieutenant Williams, also blew gaps in the wire and advanced on the west side of the defile. Against sporadic fire and without casualties, Williams, too, made it to the high ground at the head of F-1. The two sections linked up and continued to advance south until they crossed a heavily mined road. There, Cutler ordered them to set up defensive positions and contacted the battalion CP. It was 9:00 a.m.[215] Two major penetrations had now been made through the defenses on Omaha.

tumbled into the water.

Unloading almost on the boundary of Easy Red and Easy Green, the remaining troops of the CP element started the long wade to shore under fire. Moving diagonally to his right, Wolf joined up with two men who sought cover behind a hedgehog. The two had been held up by machine-gun fire to their front and were waiting for the fire to let up. Wolf felt relatively safe—until he spotted the tell-tale pattern of machine-gun bullets stitching the water toward his hedgehog. He reflexively ducked behind the obstacle. When he looked back, he saw other two men floating away, both face down in crimson

1st Battalion Landing Team

The CT 16 reserve, Driscoll's 1st BLT, was scheduled to follow the 2nd onto Easy Red beginning at 7:40 a.m. Right on time, at the correct location, Captain James L. Pence's A Company landed just to the east of exit E-1. Lieutenant William Dillon, now company XO, remembered the experience:

We were to land on a high ebbing tide at 7:30 A.M.—for once the LCVP was on course. I looked over the ramp and could see the little valley which was to be on our right, but I could also see that the Engineers hadn't been there to blow the Teller mine ramps about 600 yards from the beach. By now we were getting all kinds of fire. I didn't look back, but there wasn't a foot print in the sand, nor a dead man on the beach and we were supposed to be the second wave. Where was the first wave of troops?[216]

Of course, the 2nd BLT was well to A Company's left, so no troops had arrived on Dillon's part of the beach. Captain Pence, on the other hand, had landed farther east than Dillon, and there he found elements of the 2nd BLT still pinned down on the beach. Organizing his command, Pence sent orders for his troops to pass through the 2nd BLT, breach the wire and mine belt, and get to the high ground. Just past the shale, Dillon and several men encountered a concertina apron that could not be bypassed. After assembling three bangalore torpedoes, the team pushed the assembly through the wire and blasted a gap "big enough to drive a truck through." The time was about 8:30 a.m.

Passing through the gap, they advanced through a pond of stagnant water filled with bulrushes before being held up by a water-filled antitank ditch. The ditch was too deep to wade, so the men inflated their life vests and paddled across, only to enter a minefield on the far side. Here, Dillon lost two men to mines and small-arms fire. After the section gingerly picked its way through the mines, a runner informed Dillon that Pence had been wounded. Command of A Company had now devolved to him. "I knew then why I'd been made First Lieutenant on the beach in England," Dillon recalled. "As I lay there, I realized that now I was responsible for [175] men, or what was left of them."[217]

Ahead lay strong German defenses and more minefields, but Dillon knew he could not turn back. An able hunter in happier days, Dillon studied the ground and spied a faint trail winding its way through the mines and up the bluff. Crouching forward, he made his way up the path for some distance when he heard a loud explosion behind him. Looking back, he saw that one of his young troops had followed him and tripped a mine, blowing his leg off at the knee. The man was only one of forty-five A Company troopers to trip a mine, or take a round before reaching the heights that day. Returning to the company, Dillon led the command up the trail to the top without further incident.[218]

To the east of A Company, C Company landed at Easy Red, on the boundary with Fox Green, about 7:50 a.m. Commanded by Captain Victor Briggs, C Company encountered the same intense artillery and small-arms fire as the other five companies that had already landed in that vicinity (E, F, G, H, and E/116), many of whom were still pinned down at the seawall in a disorganized, intermingled mass of troops. On the way in, the 2nd Section's boat was hit by artillery or antitank fire, resulting in numerous casualties. Crossing the beach, the company was pinned down intermingled with the collection of previously landed soldiers and also pinned down by the enemy fire. Later that morning, Briggs was able to move his company to the bluffs, probably over the same route taken by Spalding and G Company.

Twenty minutes after A Company landed, Captain Thomas Merendino's B Company landed at Easy Red and made it ashore in relatively good order. Upon reaching the shale, the leaders rapidly reorganized the company, and soon began efforts to penetrate the wire obstacles to their front. Some elements of the company were able to use gaps blown by A Company, but others made their own.[219]

A team led by Staff Sergeant Harley Reynolds was held up near the wire by intense fire. As the team watched, a man unknown to Reynolds crawled forward with a bangalore torpedo to blow a gap. Once the charge was set, the man pulled the fuse but failed to move away from the blast area. Reynolds recalled that the man just looked back at him and "gave me a look I'll never forget. I think he knew he was going to die…and he did." The blast rent a sizable hole in the obstacle. Using smoke grenades to cover the team's advance, Reynolds was up like a shot and led his section through the gap, the first man through the wire on that part of the beach.[220]

Meanwhile, B Company's 3rd and 5th Sections pushed beyond the wire, only to enter a minefield below the strongpoint on the bluffs at E-1. Pinned down by rifle and machine-gun fire, the sections suffered numerous casualties before moving on. The men headed east about four hundred meters until they found the trail previously used by Spalding's section a short time earlier. Using that route, Merendino moved B Company onto the bluffs above Omaha and again reorganized the remnants.[221]

Regimental Headquarters and Special Units

Following the first and second waves of the 1st BLT, Driscoll, his battalion headquarters, and D Company, landed at Easy Red between 7:45 and 8:00 a.m. Following them was the LCM carrying the regimental main CP and Colonel Taylor. An "Old Army" soldier, Taylor was then forty-seven years old and had served twenty-two years as of that month. He had been in command for over a year, and had led the regiment through much of North Africa and all of Sicily, and had overseen a meticulous training program in Britain in preparation for this mission. He knew the regiment's capabilities and, based on its past performance, was confident that it would perform this mission as well. Given the regiment's state of training, and the expected level of naval fire and bombing support to soften the enemy defenses, it is doubtful that Taylor expected to find his men in the predicament he encountered on the beach that morning.

Wading ashore about 8:10 a.m., Taylor sensed an impending disaster. By that time, the entire regiment and some elements of the combat team were ashore, but no penetrations had yet been made in the defenses. Men were bunched up and there appeared to be little or no forward movement; and there were no functioning units above the section level. Realizing that only extraordinary exertions by the leaders could salvage the landings, Taylor called as many of the company and battalion commanders as he could find to the forward CP, and directed them to help get the men reorganized and off the beach in any way possible. Then, he, and they, spread out to personally assist units to reorganize and move forward. When word came that Spalding's penetration had been achieved, he was up and urging the more reluctant men to move to the high ground, saying, "If we're gonna die, let's die up there!" To another group, he is reported to have said probably the most memorable lines of D-Day: "There are only two kinds of people on this beach; the dead and those who are about to die. So, let's get the hell out of here!"[222]

Cannon Company, under Captain Thomas N. O'Brien, was scheduled to arrive in three elements on Easy Red. The halftracks would land at 7:30 a.m., the cannon at 9:30 a.m., and the trucks at 1:00 p.m. Unlike the rest of the regiment, Cannon Company was loaded aboard LCTs (which carried halftracks, trucks, and crews) and on LST *376* (which carried the company's 105mm cannon). After Sicily, the company had turned in its halftrack-mounted 105mm cannon and was now equipped with six 105mm cannon towed by halftrack prime movers.

The two LCTs carrying the prime movers approached (off-course) Fox Green at about 7:30 a.m. Both were hit repeatedly by antitank and machine-gun fire that killed or wounded several men. The boats withdrew, but one successfully landed three halftracks an hour later, and the other landed its three halftracks at 1:30 p.m. Four of the six vehicles were eventually destroyed on the beach by direct fire.

The cannon crews and their equipment fared even worse. The six cannon were each loaded on a DUKW amphibious truck for the trip into the beach. About 9:00 a.m., the DUKWs drove off the front end of LST *376*, some twelve miles off shore, and headed for Easy Red. Problems arose immediately. Because of the steep angle of the ramp and the load weights, the DUKWs partially flooded as they entered the water. When their bilge pumps failed to drain the water fast enough, the engines on two DUKWs stopped altogether, causing them to sink. Two other DUKWs sank en route to the rendezvous area, and one more sank in the heavy seas before reaching the beach. At Easy Red, Cannon Company was down to one unserviceable gun.

With Cannon Company unable to perform its role as the regiment's indirect fire force, Captain O'Brien temporarily reorganized the company as a rifle unit, and attached the outfit to the 1st Battalion.[223]

For the D-Day assault and subsequent drive to the inland objectives, Antitank Company (consisting of two AT platoons) was task-organized with one platoon each attached to the 2nd and 3rd Battalions. Both platoons came ashore with their respective battalion's reserve company. The company headquarters was scheduled to land at Easy Red at 8:30 a.m. but actually came ashore at Easy Green in the 116th Infantry's zone. The headquarters group made its way six hundred yards eastward, picking up two gun squads from the 2nd Battalion along the way, and set up its initial CP near the E-1 draw. The rest of the AT guns were landed in front of E-1 about 11:00 a.m. The company then reorganized before starting the move inland.[224]

Like Antitank Company, Service Company also landed at Easy Green about 8:30 a.m., but it quickly became pinned down under intense small-arms and artillery fire. The regimental S4, Major Leonard C. Godfray, accompanied the unit ashore, but while attempting to lead several men from the S4 section across the beach, he was cut down by machine-gun fire. Taking charge, Second Lieutenant Donald Balyeat had led Service Company and the S4 section through the minefields, up the bluffs, and inland by 10:30 a.m.

The men of CT 16's attached medical company had an especially difficult time at Fox Green. Grinding ashore at 8:35 a.m., LCI *85*, with A Company of the 1st Medical Battalion aboard, met with a hail of antitank and machine-gun fire. Several large-caliber shells (probably 47mm) slammed into the ship's forward hold, killing and wounding a number of men. The ship's captain backed away from the shore and attempted to land again at another location. On its second approach, the ship happened to pull in near to where Technical Sergeant Wilson had gone to ground:

> I saw an LCI approaching shore, large red crosses painted in white circles on the hull and superstructure. As it drew closer, I could see a line of medics on the port side of the deck, from bow to stern. Medics were badly needed on Easy Red! After beaching, the narrow gangplanks were lowered and several personnel made their way up to the sand and staked down some sort of cables stretching back to the ship. The crewman on my side almost made it back, but suddenly collapsed in the sand. Then an antitank shell struck the hull next to the port gangplank, blowing it away so that it just dangled in the water. The Jerry gunner then raised his barrel and put one right down the deck, followed by a couple more....The explosion sent medics and their gear flying in all directions. I vividly recall seeing a cloud of white bandages floating down into the smoke on deck.[225]

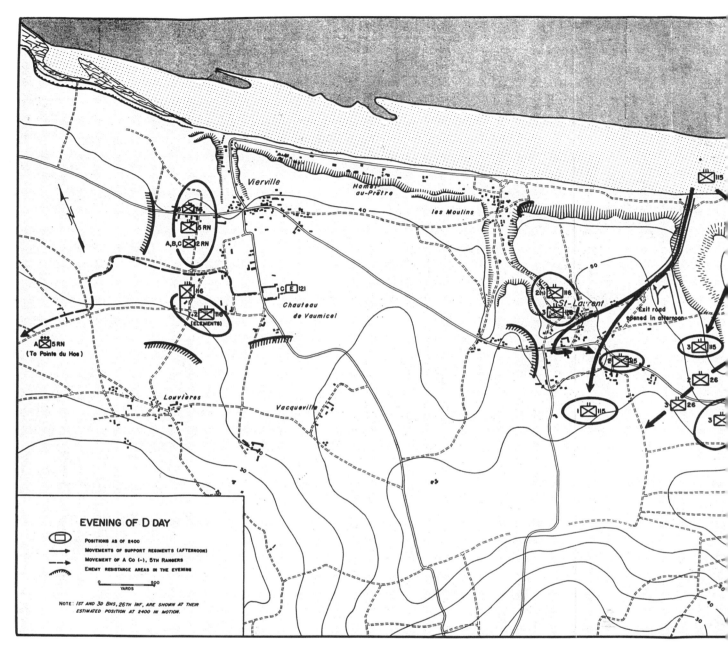

Map 8-12.

Once again the ship backed away, but the German gunner continued to pummel it, this time sending three more rounds into the hull, setting the ship afire. A courageous destroyer captain directed his ship to steam by and pound the AT position with 40mm and five-inch naval guns. This action silenced the stubborn German AT crew, but not before their marksmanship wreaked havoc with the LCI and the medics. The damage suffered by LCI 85 caused the ship's captain to evacuate the remnants of the medical company to the USS *Samuel Chase*.[226]

After reorganizing on the *Chase*, the company transloaded to an LCM, and finally came ashore at 5:00 p.m. Further

tragedy struck upon their second landing, when several more men were killed and wounded by artillery fire. The remnants of the battered company finally linked up with the regimental aid station. Despite their own terrible experiences that day the medics immediately went to work caring for and evacuating the regiment's wounded.

Expanding the Beachhead 9:00-4:00 p.m.
2nd Battalion Landing Team

By 9:00 a.m., CT 16 had achieved two penetrations of the German defenses. Soon, hundreds of men found their way

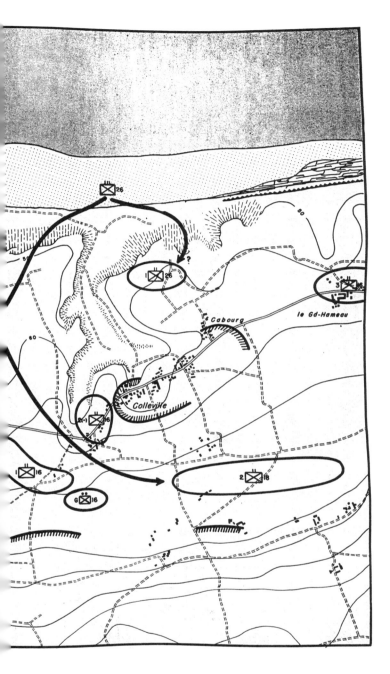

learned that the sixteen Germans held another position nearer the draw. He asked Blue for support in taking the position:

> As we went up in this direction we hit a wooded area. We found a beautifully camouflaged trench which ran in a zig-zag fashion, but we were afraid to go in. We went along the top of the trench spraying it with lead. We used bullets instead of grenades, since we had very few grenades, and thought that the bullets would be more effective. We did not fix bayonets at any time. We turned to the right and hit [another] wooded area; got no fire from there, so we yelled to Lieutenant Blue to shove off and he started for Colleville.[227]

Moving west along the bluffs toward the east side of the E-1 draw, Spalding's 1st Section headed for St. Laurent to establish contact with the 116h Infantry. They were now in hedgerow country and were already developing overwatch methods to advance from position to position. After capturing a German machine-gun crew, and crossing through two minefields, the section reached the defenses on the bluff top overlooking the draw. It was an extensive, well-fortified position but largely undefended by now. The lieutenant was about to drop a grenade down a bunker ventilator when Sergeant Streczyk halted him. Firing three shots, the sergeant yelled in Polish and German for the men to surrender. Out came four men carrying three wounded comrades.

Their first Polish prisoner had given Spalding good information, for it had brought the section into the rear of the German strongpoint. After using the communications trench to approach the Germans below them, the section was able to capture seventeen prisoners, an 81mm mortar position, and an antitank gun after a short firefight.[228]

Using virtually the same route that the 1st Section had blazed, more troops of E Company, led by Captain Wozenski, made contact with Spalding near the strongpoint about 10:45 a.m. Wozenski informed the lieutenant that his mission was changed and that his section would go with the rest of the company to link up with the remnants of the 2nd Battalion near Colleville. With only thirty men, including Spalding's, Wozenski now headed for Colleville.

Meanwhile, by 11:00 a.m., Dawson's G Company, and a handful of other men from E Company, had made their way south to a position at the road junction of Le Bray, near the western end of Colleville. Standing under a large oak tree in the yard of a wildly ecstatic French woman, Dawson held a conversation with a local villager to get intelligence on the number of Germans in Colleville. About that time, Major Washington joined up with the company and listened to the discussion. The villager told Dawson that there were two hundred Germans defending the town, but Washington did not believe him. Pulling Dawson aside, the battalion XO told him, "That guy's putting you on. He was sent out here to feed you a bunch

through the gaps to drive on to their assigned objectives. Indeed, the men who had led the way were already reducing the defenses on the bluffs or heading for the two main objectives, Colleville and Le Grand Hameau.

At the time of his ascent, Lieutenant Spalding did not know it, but his dangerous trek up the bluff had been supported by direct fire from G Company. Soon, Dawson's men were following Spalding's section up the trail, and the company's lead platoon leader, Lieutenant Blue, made contact with Spalding just below the top. Just before Blue arrived, Spalding had finished interrogating the Polish POW, from whom he had

of crap. Just take your company and go on in there and clean 'em out."[229] Little did Washington realize that the Frenchman was correct.

Soon, C Company came up and went into position on Dawson's right. With C Company holding the Le Bray road junction, Dawson decided to take his 1st, 2nd, and 5th Sections to seize Colleville, the 2nd Battalion's main D-Day objective. The group jumped off at 1:00 p.m., 1st Section leading, and made it to the church on the west end of the town. Dawson took a sergeant and a rifleman into the church to clear it and as soon as they passed through the door, the Germans inside opened fire on them. The private was killed but Dawson and the sergeant eliminated three German infantrymen in the sanctuary and a forward observer in the steeple.[230]

Stepping out into the courtyard, Dawson was signaling to bring up the rest of his men when a sniper sent a round through the butt of his carbine, shattering it and sending lead fragments into his leg and knee. The 1st Section subsequently came up, occupied the church, and opened a heavy counterfire. Within minutes, however, three more of Dawson's men were killed and two wounded. In the meantime, the other sections took up positions in and around a walled French farmhouse. Soon, the company was experiencing a concerted counterattack. Doggedly holding on to its foothold in town, the company repulsed the enemy's efforts, then moved forward to clear out the remaining resistance, killing or capturing twenty-six Germans. G Company had been successful in taking the western reaches of the town, but it was soon surrounded. Dawson organized an all-around defense and waited for reinforcements.[231]

Pinned down on the beach until just before noon, Finke and his first sergeant, Ted Lombarski, could round up a grand total of ten unwounded men from F Company. With this force, Finke moved up the bluffs. Given the diminutive size of his company at this point, Finke decided to use his remaining men as a security force for the battalion CP. Lombarski took three of the men to post them on the CP's left flank, and while the detachment made its way through the hedgerows, it ran into a nest of enemy resistance and a firefight developed. Finke sprinted forward to help out the detachment.[232] Technical Sergeant Wilson, just coming up from the beach, heard the firing and moved to the sound of the guns:

> Hustling along, we came to a side road running inland. The firing we heard was coming from down that road. Rounding a slight bend, we came upon First Sergeant Ted Lombarski, with a radioman and a rifleman, hovered around our company commander, Captain Finke, who was badly wounded and bleeding profusely from a number of places. Apparently during the fire fight we heard, he had stepped on an anti-personnel mine....A couple of others from some other unit came along, including a medic who began to take care of the CO. Finally, Captain

Finke looked up at Lombarski and said, "Sergeant, take over the company."[233]

Lombarski led F Company, now down to seven men, to Colleville. Splitting up on either side of the road, the little band made its way along the winding farm trail lined on both sides with signs reading "Achtung! Minen!" Approaching a couple of farm buildings, the men were temporarily pinned down by enemy fire, but after two of the defenders were killed, the remainder fled, leaving the buildings to Lombarski and his troops. Lombarski pushed his men down the road. Rounding a bend, they saw the church at Colleville-sur-Mer. Company F, or what was left of it, had reached its objective.[234]

The rest of the 2nd Battalion was just as determined to make its way to Colleville. By 11:00 a.m., Hicks, Hall, and the battalion headquarters personnel had moved through the gap blown earlier by Staff Sergeant Streczyk and made it onto the bluffs. Moving inland through hedgerows, Hall set up the battalion CP in a clump of trees, while Hicks went forward to check on the progress of his battered battalion. By 1:00 p.m., remnants of H Company had arrived nearby and set up their mortars to support the efforts to take Colleville. About the same time, Wozenski and Spalding arrived at the forward CP and contacted Washington. After a quick consultation, Wozenski had Company E take up positions in the ditches and hedgerows west of Colleville. The badly depleted battalion was now concentrated some eight hundred yards northwest of the town.[235]

3rd Battalion Landing Team

After the harrowing journey down the beach, White, Wolf, and the CP crew finally joined up with elements of the 3rd Battalion about noon. Soon after, they reported to the 3rd Battalion CP, which had been set up in the F-1 draw. There, they learned that, despite heavy casualties, the companies had made it off the beach and were progressing inland toward the battalion's objective, Le Grand Hameau.

Despite the losses to I Company, Richmond and his three surviving lieutenants gathered as many unwounded men as they could find and had moved up the F-1 draw. At the head of the draw, he found L Company, still behind their hastily prepared defenses, and assumed control of them from Lieutenant Cutler about noon. Just before Richmond's arrival, Cutler had sent a three-man patrol from the 5th Section, consisting of Privates Mielander, Butt, and O'Dell, to recon Cabourg to the southwest. While waiting for the patrol to return, Richmond and his leaders reorganized the fragmented units into a composite company in preparation for the move into Le Grand Hameau. About 1:00 p.m., however, a counterattack hit their position, attempting to overrun Lieutenant Monteith's 2nd Section.

Monteith, a young Virginian who hailed from the little hamlet of Low Moor, had already had a busy day. Down on the beach, he had moved up and down the shale, reorganizing his section without regard for his personal safety. At one point, he had led a couple of tanks across a minefield on foot and, while exposed to heavy fire, directed them into firing positions, from where they destroyed several enemy emplacements. After his section had seized the position at the head of the F-1 draw, he directed the establishment of their defenses on the high ground. When the counterattacks came against L Company, he continued to ignore his own safety by repeatedly crossing a two hundred-yard stretch of ground between fighting positions to "strengthen links in his defensive chain." The German infantry eventually surrounded Monteith and his men, but the lieutenant determined to break out and link up with the rest of L Company. As he led his men out of the encirclement, Monteith was cut down by fire and killed instantly. For his heroism that day, Monteith earned the regiment's fifth Medal of Honor.[236]

After coming up the E-3 draw, Brugger's section of K Company made its way toward Le Grand Hameau:

> We had to crawl through the hedgerows to get from one field to another. The French farmers used these as fences. In the corners there would be openings and the Germans had set up machine guns to fire [through] these openings. We'd give each other covering fire to make the machine gun crew keep their heads down, then 3 or 4 of our men would dash through the openings. As we crawled through these hedgerows, we would have to crawl over the dead and wounded.[237]

1st Battalion Landing Team
Upon reaching the hedgerows on the bluffs, Briggs reorganized C Company. While the reorganization was in progress, Briggs's men captured several Germans, whom he sent to the rear. Pushing south in tandem with B Company, Briggs's men moved through farm fields and hedgerows for about one thousand meters inland. At the "Manor House," located about five hundred meters west of Colleville, Briggs stopped the company and conducted an additional reorganization. At this point, B Company came up on Briggs's left flank. Briggs now attempted to push on, but just after the company passed the manor house, it was stopped cold by machine-gun fire, and Briggs ordered his men to dig in.[238]

After reaching the bluffs, Merendino's B Company also moved south, coming up on C Company's left flank. En route, Merendino's men cleared out several isolated enemy riflemen and machine-gun nests from the hedgerows as B Company headed for a crossroads five hundred meters west of Colleville. The company arrived there about 1:00 p.m., just as G Company was making its initial advance to the church. Merendino placed his men in position between Dawson's troops on his left, and C Company on his right. Behind Merendino, Dillon brought up A Company.[239]

Through losses and breaks in contact, Dillon's company was now down to two reduced sections. Advancing toward high ground well to the west of Colleville-sur-Mer, the company encountered numerous pockets of resistance and machine-gun nests, and systematically reduced them with maneuver, bazookas, rifle grenades, mortars, and small-arms fire. The fighting was sharp, and the company lost two more lieutenants, an NCO, and ten enlisted men killed or wounded. Approaching the rear of B Company, Dillon was ordered to stop and dig in. Soon after the company began digging, Lieutenant Frank Kolb arrived to assume command. At this point, only thirty men remained, although additional men from the missing sections made their way to the position throughout the rest of the day.[240]

Around 9:20 a.m., D Company, commanded by Captain Polydore "Pop" Dion, finally landed at Easy Red. Dion's troops moved to the shale with relative ease compared to the previous companies and prepared to support the remaining assault troops on the beach. Presently, the 2nd Machine Gun Platoon and the mortars opened fire on enemy emplacements only seventy-five yards away. Upon learning the location of a cleared route, Dion moved the company topside about 10:45 a.m. and advanced toward Colleville. Reaching a point about a half mile northwest of the town at 1:00 p.m., Dion contacted the rear of the 1st Battalion which was already in dug-in positions.[241]

Consolidation of Regimental Objectives
4:00 p.m. June 6 to 6:00 a.m. June 7
3rd Battalion Landing Team
In Le Grand Hameau, Richmond had gathered 104 men from Companies I, L, and K and organized them to defend the village from counterattack. The remnants of the 1st and 2nd Sections of K Company were with Richmond in the town, while Lieutenant Hallisey, with the 3rd, 4th, and 5th Sections, had occupied Cabourg by 2:00 p.m. and had dug in there. In groups of twos and threes, additional men from K Company made it into positions in or near the village by that evening. By dark, the company had suffered fifty-one casualties of 180 men assigned.

Edmonds had picked up a few men from Headquarters Company on his way up the bluffs, and had pushed M Company forward in an attempt to link up with Richmond. One heavy machine-gun section under Lieutenant Lazo went into position on the bluffs above the beach and protected the regiment's left flank until the following morning. The remainder of the company pushed through to join Richmond in Le Grand Hameau after being held up by mortar and small-arms fire.[242]

By 4:00 p.m., the 3rd Battalion firmly held the town and some additional positions three hundred yards to the east. That night, three platoons of the 745th Tank Battalion rumbled into Richmond's positions. The young captain proceeded to place each tank to reinforce his positions. Throughout the night and into the next morning, little knots of men, who had been separated from their companies during the chaos on the beach, made their way to the battalion area and found their units—further adding to the battalion's still small numbers.

2nd Battalion Landing Team

With the tattered remnants of E Company now numbering only fifty men, Ed Wozenski made his way south toward Colleville. Moving through snipers and dodging artillery fire, he led the company on a relatively easy sweep through the fields northwest of the town without losing a single man. On the other hand, the headquarters section, whom Wozenski was escorting, was pinned down on several occasions. Arriving at the Colleville-St. Laurent road, Wozenski placed two depleted sections under Lieutenant Huch into position on G Company's right flank. From there, the rest of the company dug in to the west, and a battalion line of resistance gradually formed.[243]

With the tiny remnant of F Company, 1st Sergeant Lombarski set up in defensive positions for the night near Colleville. Eight more men showed up before midnight, nearly doubling the size of the outfit.

After being surrounded, G Company's plight worsened when friendly naval gunfire began leveling the town about 4:00 p.m. In accordance with the naval gunfire plan, the navy had been scheduled to shell Colleville earlier that morning, but because of limited visibility, the bombardment had been delayed. Now, the ships' spotters could see the town and began pounding it to bits, not knowing part of it was held by Americans. Dawson's fire control officer had been killed on the beach, and he now had no way to contact the ships. His frantic efforts eventually succeeded in stopping the shelling about 5:00 p.m., but not before seven more of his men had been killed or wounded.[244]

The 2nd Battalion was unable to totally secure its D-Day objective, Colleville-sur-Mer. Given the tremendous pounding it took on the beach and the casualties it suffered en route to the town, it is a wonder that the leaders of the battalion were able to get it as far as they did. Despite enemy resistance, severe casualties, the congested beach, confusion, and even friendly naval fire, Dawson, Wozenski, Lombarski and a handful of surviving lieutenants and NCOs were still able to lead their men under fire and seize the west end of the town against heavy odds.

1st Battalion Landing Team

Of CT 16's three battalions on D-Day, the 1st came through the least marred. As a result, Driscoll was able to organize and conduct the most coherent battalion-level operations on the afternoon of June 6. Each of the three rifle companies made its way south toward the battalion objective on the high ground southwest of Colleville. Merendino's B Company led the battalion attack through the hedgerows past the Colleville-St. Laurent road. Company C cleared the fields to the west, and A Company followed in Merendino's wake. By 1:00 p.m., the lead elements of B Company crossed the Colleville-St. Laurent road, and immediately, the battalion was held up by stiff resistance from a wooded area to the southwest.[245]

As B Company supported their movement by fire, Briggs's C Company advanced into the woods and, before long, the German force melted away. Driscoll again ordered the battalion forward, now with C Company on the left (east) flank, B on the right, and A Company following. Arriving at the battalion's D-Day objective, the high ground overlooking Surrain, Driscoll organized the position with A Company on the left, C in the center, and B on the right. Captain Dion detached D Company's machine-gun platoons, one each, to B and C Companies and emplaced the mortar platoon at the center-rear of the sector to support the line units. Tied in on A Company's left flank was a section of G Company and elements of E and F Companies.[246]

By nightfall on June 6, a regimental line of sorts had been established. The 1st Battalion was in a relatively well-organized and coordinated position southwest of Colleville and was prepared to defend against counterattacks. The 2nd Battalion remnants held the western end of Colleville and were tied in with Driscoll's men near the crossroads by the manor house. The 3rd Battalion, located five kilometers to the northeast of 2nd Battalion, held its D-Day objective, Le Grand Hameau, and was preparing defensive positions. To the east of the 1st Battalion, the 2nd Battalion, 18th Infantry, had come up and assumed positions on the high ground south of Colleville. Just to the northwest of B Company, the 3rd Battalion, 18th Infantry was digging in.

The 1st Infantry Division's line on the night of June 6-7 was roughly in an arc from Le Grand Hameau west to Verville-sur-Mer. In the 16th Infantry's sector, all three battalions of the 16th and 18th Infantry Regiments were in the line, as were two of the 26th Infantry. The 1st Battalion, 26th Infantry, was held in reserve just north of Cabourg. By midnight, the beachhead, while still precarious and by no means a solid wall of combat power, was rapidly hardening into a stubborn, coherent defense manned by the veterans of the "Big Red One."

The morning of June 7 was cloudy and cool. The heavy fighting from the day before had evolved into uncoordinated counterattacks against the division front. Leaders at all echelons busied themselves attempting to round up men separated from their companies, strengthening defenses or moving forward, resupplying food and ammo, and generally continuing the fight. General Huebner, escorted by several officers from his staff, was also out trying to gauge the strength, morale, and dispositions of his subordinate units. Just after dawn, the general entered the 2nd Battalion CP, looking for the regimental headquarters and Colonel Taylor. Fred Hall greeted Huebner and volunteered to take him over to the regimental CP:

> I walked them [Huebner and his staff] back to the top of the bluff and pointed out the regimental CP below. I looked at the beach. It was crammed with disabled boats, tanks and vehicles, men and supplies. There was an aid

station. There was constant movement of men and vehicles on a narrow beach. Visibility had improved and I could see other ships at sea. I turned around and never went back.

Actually, Hall did go back. He went on to say, "Forty years dims the memory. My wife and I walked Easy Red Beach in May 1982. It was soon enough to return."[247]

Of all the many accomplishments of the 16th Infantry since 1861, most would agree that D-Day stands out as its greatest achievement. The level of sheer violence and stubborn resistance that the men had to endure and overcome has rarely been experienced by American arms and never exceeded on such a scale. As testimony to what a close-run thing it was, General Bradley, commanding the First U.S. Army Forces going ashore at Omaha and Utah Beaches, had contemplated the diversion of follow-on phases for Omaha to Utah beach. On board heavy cruiser USS *Augusta* that morning, he stood by helplessly as two assault regiments struggled to secure a beachhead. Disjointed reports confirmed to him that a crisis was building on the beaches. Despite excellent planning and exhaustive training and preparation, the Omaha landings nearly ended in failure. Why?

First, although the plan was a good one, it lacked the flexibility needed to react to unanticipated conditions. The air and naval bombardment utterly failed to soften the beach defenses. The plan, moreover, contained no measures for additional preparatory fires if the bombs missed the defenses or the rockets fell harmlessly into the water. When the initial assault waves encountered greater resistance than expected, the follow-on waves were often landed at the same locations where hundreds of troops were already pinned down, rather than moving to other areas on the beach where resistance was weaker or had been reduced.

Intelligence planners had failed to track the movements of the 352nd Infantry Division in a timely manner. As a result, the 16th Infantry faced about half of the 726th Infantry Regiment, the 439th Ost Battalion, and at least the 2nd Battalions of the 915th and 916th Infantry Regiments on D-Day. Instead of a favorable three-to-one, attacker-to-defender ratio, the regiment contended with a ratio of three to five—odds definitely not recommended by the Infantry School. Furthermore, the intelligence estimates stated that enemy morale was low, yet Colonel Charles H. Coates, a member of the War Department Observers Board, in his report of the operation, wrote:

Despite advance intelligence information [to the contrary], their morale was exceptionally high, and they fought with great zeal. When forced back from the cliff, they took cover in the ditches and hedge-rows on the plateau, falling back slowly and in good order, in such a manner that each ditch became a line of defense. Several such groups refused to fall back and had to be killed

before their positions were taken. A number of them remained behind in wooded areas as snipers and extracted a high toll before they were located and killed.[248]

Against this kind of resistance, it is a wonder that the 16th Infantry got off the beach at all. But it did get off the beach, and it went on to take two of its three D-Day objectives. To what can the regiment attribute its successes? The answer lies in training, small unit leadership, and the individual initiative of American soldiers.

Colonel Taylor, his battalion commanders, and their executive officers were all over the beach that day, braving the same fires and suffering the same deprivations as their men. Taylor's personal efforts to get the men moving and off the beach, Hicks's movements to the front to check on the progress of his units, and Horner's efforts to personally direct a destroyer's broadsides into enemy strongpoints were all significant. The regiment's success, however, was due to the sergeants, lieutenants, captains, and, at times, even privates, who took control of the men around them and made things happen. The breaching of wire obstacles, blasting of gaps in minefields, and reduction of enemy positions were accomplished largely by men who got up and led others forward, despite the long odds against them. Regardless of who the leader was or what company he may have belonged to, when men saw leadership, they responded to it, and success generally followed.

Even when designated leaders were either absent or incapacitated, private soldiers often took charge and did what had to be done. Despite 50 percent casualties and the loss of many officers and NCOs, engineers continued to clear the beach of obstacles, usually under heavy fire. Medics crawled from one wounded man to another, desperately attempting to save lives, and often losing their own in the attempt. Other aidmen risked their lives by repeatedly going into the surf and pulling in drowning or wounded men. While some soldiers froze in fear on the beach, many demonstrated extraordinary courage. Through it all, the regiment made progress because brave men did what had to be done—without waiting for orders! Coates summed it up concisely, saying: "the three prime reasons for the 16th Infantry's successful landing [were]: LEADERSHIP, SMALL UNIT FIRE AND MANEUVER, AND 'GUTS.' "[249]

As a result of the Red One's actions on D-Day, General Bradley's displeasure with the 1st Division (because of its conduct after the Tunisian Campaign) had been wiped away. Writing in *A Soldier's Story* of the unexpected presence of the experienced 352nd Division as the defender of Omaha Beach, he observed that

Had a less experienced division than the 1st Infantry stumbled into this crack resistance, it might easily have been thrown back into the Channel. Unjust though it was, my choice of the 1st to spearhead the invasion probably saved us Omaha Beach and a catastrophe on the landing.

The regiment overcame huge obstacles, but it paid a high price for its achievements. By the end of D-Day, of some thirty-six hundred personnel assigned, the regiment had suffered 971 casualties, or about one in every four of its men. A total of thirty-eight officers were killed, wounded, or missing. Among the slain were the regimental XO, the S4, and the K Company commander. The commanders of Companies A, F, G, H, and L were wounded. All of F Company's officers were killed or wounded. About the same numbers of other lieutenants and NCOs were also killed and wounded.[250] The distribution of casualties in the respective units by D+2 were as follows:

	Officers			Men			
	KIA	WIA	MIA	KIA	WIA	MIA	Total
HHC, 1st Battalion	0	4	0	0	33	11	48
A Company	0	2	2	3	34	27	68
B Company	0	0	0	0	16	31	47
C Company	0	1	0	3	14	10	28
D Company	0	0	0	0	9	28	37
(Total 1st Bn)	0	7	2	6	106	107	228
HHC, 2nd Battalion	0	0	0	0	12	20	32
E Company	1	1	1	6	78	42	129
F Company	1	2	4	6	36	64	113
G Company	0	2	0	4	28	26	60
H Company	0	1	0	3	22	8	34
(Total 2nd Bn)	2	6	5	19	176	160	368
HHC, 3rd Battalion	1	1	1	0	5	3	11
I Company	0	0	0	26	42	32	100
K Company	3	0	0	7	38	22	70
L Company	0	3	0	5	52	18	78
M Company	0	0	0	0	20	24	44
(Total 3rd Bn)	4	4	1	38	157	99	303
Regimental HHC	1	0	4	0	9	5	19
Service Company	0	0	0	0	0	0	0
Antitank Company	0	1	0	2	16	4	23
Cannon Company	0	1	0	0	9	20	30
Medical Detachment	0	0	0	0	1	0	1
(Total Regt'l Troops)	1	2	4	2	35	29	73
Totals	7	19	12*	65	474	395*	972

Total KIA	72
Total WIA	493
Total MIA	407*

Total Casualties 16th Infantry: 972 (945 on D-Day alone)
*Most of these men were later identified as KIA.

When men fell, others stepped forward to take their place and advance. After all, there was really no other choice. Once they had secured their D-Day objectives, the men of the 16th Infantry still had a war to fight.

The fighting for the 16th Infantry Regiment did not end at dark on D-Day. That night, determined counterattacks by elements of the 352nd Infantry Division were directed primarily against the 18th Infantry and Driscoll's 1st Battalion. Because the divisional front was tenuous, each battalion sent patrols between positions to maintain contact and detect enemy units attempting to infiltrate between the 1st Infantry Division troop locations. By the morning of the 7th, Colonel Taylor had regained effective control of the regiment, and soon units were actively conducting mop-up operations between the front and the beaches.

Meanwhile, the regiment became the division reserve, as the 18th Infantry advanced south on the right and the 26th Infantry drove south on the left. Though the combat team was in reserve, that did not mean that it was out of contact with the enemy. In fact, the regimental CP, located on the bluffs just up from the beach, was still under fire during the morning of June 7. At one point, Jim Lipinski was standing outside the CP discussing something with several troops. One of the men, an old master sergeant, had made a wisecrack that caused everybody to laugh, when suddenly the man's lower jaw was shot away.[251]

The danger did not end merely because the front had moved south. Many of the German defenders were isolated in the beach areas after the 18th and 26th Infantry continued its advance, and they now remained to be killed or captured. About 7:30 that morning, Fred Hall observed a column of fifty-two Germans coming in under the guard of three men. It turned out that the three soldiers escorting the POWs were Privates Mielander, Butt, and O'Dell from L Company, who had disappeared on the patrol into Cabourg the day before. After they had been captured, Mielander started talking to his captors and convinced at least one, probably a sergeant, to give up. Apparently, the Polish sergeant shot the German commander and helped convince the rest to surrender to the three Americans. That morning, the privates proudly brought in their catch.

To the east of Le Grand Hameau, Horner pushed the 3rd Battalion toward Port-en-Bessen to make contact with the 50th (British) Infantry Division. Mounted on tanks from B Company, 745th Tank Battalion, K Company rolled down the coastal road and made contact with the 50th Division's 231st Brigade. By the end of the day, the 18th and 26th Infantry Regiments were well to the south of the regiment, leaving CT 16 to mop up bypassed positions, some of which resisted ferociously.

Despite the continuation of fighting in virtually every direction, Horner, Eston White, and several of the 3rd Battalion staff officers accepted an invitation to share dinner with a French farmer on the evening of June 7. Horner left the battalion's mascot, "Dagwood," in his jeep while he and his officers went in to enjoy the meal. Dagwood was a russet-brown, medium-sized bowser that someone on the staff had adopted back in North Africa. The dog had been with the battalion in Sicily and was smuggled aboard ship for the trip to England. He was fond of riding on Horner's jeep and generally slept in Horner's quarters, wherever that might be. As a result, the battalion commander had become rather fond of the mutt.

Inside, the officers enjoyed a dinner of omelets and cider, followed by after-dinner drinks of Calvados, the local applejack brandy. After conversation and a number of toasts, the commander determined that it was time to leave and thanked the farmer and his wife for their hospitality. Stepping outside the old stone cottage, Horner discovered that Dagwood was nowhere to be seen. Conducting a search for the dog, he became very agitated. The officers believed the dog had probably run off for good and had just convinced Horner to give up the hunt, when Dagwood suddenly reappeared, trotting down the road with his tongue hanging out. It soon became obvious to all that the little rascal had become the first in the regiment to make a "French Connection" on the Continent since World War I.[252]

Over the next three weeks, CT 16 remained in division reserve as the "Red One" ground its way through the hedgerows. While CTs 18 and 26 stayed up front, the regiment protected the division's flanks and rear and maintained contact with units of the British Second Army to the east. Though there was not any heavy fighting for the regiment, there were daily skirmishes and clashes with bypassed enemy positions.

The First Army was steadily moving southward, but the Cotentin Peninsula still had not fallen. The port of Cherbourg, still in enemy hands, was desperately needed by the First Army after its artificial port ("Mulberry") was wrecked by a four-day storm that struck the English Channel on June 19. The trickle of supplies, compounded by the stiff resistance of Rommel's troops in northern France, ensured slow going. By the end of June, Cherbourg was invested, and the 1st Infantry Division was in defensive positions north of Caumont.

While the regiment was defending the Caumont sector, Eisenhower took the opportunity to visit and present some well-deserved awards. On July 2, on the lawn of a grand old château, under a stand of stately elms, Taylor assembled all the men he could gather that had earned the Distinguished Service Cross and the Legion of Merit on D-Day. Twenty-four officers and enlisted men were all that could be brought together for the ceremony; the rest were dead or hospitalized. In attendance with Eisenhower were Bradley, Huebner, and Major General Leonard T. Gerow, the V Corps commander.

After personally pinning the awards on their chests, Eisenhower gathered the men around him:

> I'm not going to make a speech, but this simple little ceremony gives me the opportunity to come over here, and through you, say "Thanks." You are one of the finest regiments in our army. I know your record from the day you landed in North Africa and through Sicily. I am beginning

to think that your regiment is a sort of Praetorian guard which goes along with me and gives me luck. I know you want to go home, but I demanded if I came up here, that you would have to come with me. You've got what it takes to finish the job. If you will do me a favor when you go back, you will spread the word through the regiment that I am terrifically proud and grateful to them. To all of you fellows, good luck, keep on top of them, and so long.

The regiment remained in defensive positions near Caumont for the next eleven days and conducted aggressive patrolling. On July 12, the division was alerted that it would be pulled out of the line and relieved by the 5th Infantry Division. On the following day, the 2nd Infantry Regiment took over CT 16's positions.

Upon its relief by the 2nd Infantry, the regiment moved to a rest camp at Colombières. There, on July 14, Colonel Taylor received a well-earned promotion to brigadier general and became the assistant division commander of the 4th Infantry Division. Replacing Taylor was Frederick Gibb, who had left command of the 3rd Battalion in December 1942 to be the 1st Division G3. Gibb would command the regiment through the rest of the war.

Though it was termed a "rest camp," the stay at Colombières was more of a pause in operations to refit, reequip, and provide replacements for the "Red One" after its tough fight through the hedgerows. The refitting of the division was also more than a routine replacement operation, for it had been selected to play a pivotal role in an impending mission that was designed to end the hedgerow-to-hedgerow slugfest that the troops of the First U.S. Army were experiencing. On July 12, the day before the 1st Division was pulled out of the line and sent to Colombières, Bradley presented to his staff and corps commanders the concept of what became known as Operation Cobra.

Campaign for Northern France
July 25-September 14, 1944

Frustrated by the high casualties and slow going through the hedgerow country, Bradley sought a major breakthrough to end the bloody stalemate. Ideally, he also wanted to destroy or capture the bulk of the LXXXIV Corps, now under the command of Lieutenant General Dietrich von Choltitz, which had been effectively opposing the First Army's advance. Studying his maps, his eye fell on the rolling terrain south of the St. Lô-Pèriers road. The area had a good paved-road net that supported east-west and north-south movement. Also, the fields of the hedgerow system there were much larger and gave the enemy less favorable defensive opportunities than the areas behind the beaches. In addition, the ridgelines ran east-west, a direction that favored an attacker who desired to cut in behind the opposing enemy force. If Bradley could push a force rapidly down the St. Lô-Coutances road to the sea, he could cut off and potentially capture the bulk of the LXXXIV Corps, which consisted of eight battered, but still effective, divisions numbering some forty thousand men.

The divisions composing the LXXXIV Corps included: the 243rd Infantry Division, 91st Infantry Division, 2nd SS Panzer Grenadier Division, 17th SS Panzer Grenadier Division, 5th Fallschirmjaeger Division, Panzer Lehr Division, 353rd Infantry Division, and the 275th Infantry Division. The latter two divisions were respectively the LXXXIV Corps and Seventh Army reserves. In the ensuing battle, the Panzer Lehr Division and the 2nd and 17th SS Panzer Grenadier Divisions would be the main forces opposing the 16th Infantry's advance.

The plan, as finally developed, called for fighter bombers and medium bombers of the Ninth Air Force and heavy bombers of the Eighth Air Force to conduct a massive carpet bombing of a twenty-five hundred-by-six thousand-yard box of terrain just south of the St. Lô- Pèriers road, about three miles west of St. Lô. This bombardment would primarily fall on the Panzer Lehr Division, which faced the 9th and 30th Infantry Divisions. Just after the last bombs fell, the VII Corps, under Major General J. Lawton Collins, would swiftly push through the dazed troops of the Panzer Lehr Division and establish a salient, with the 9th Division holding the western shoulder, the 30th Division holding the eastern shoulder, and the 4th Division pushing straight south to the vicinity of Carantilly-Canisy. Following the 4th Division, the 2nd and 3rd Armored Divisions would push toward Coutances and swing south, then west, to surround the city from the south. The 1st Infantry Division, with Colonel Truman E. Boudinot's CCB, 3rd Armored Division, attached, would push into the salient, pass through the 9th Division at Marigny, and drive down the St. Lô-Coutances road to take a series of three hills, the last being at the village of Monthuchan. The capture of these objectives would set the conditions for an advance of the VIII Corps, acting as a hammer to capture, or destroy, the German units against the 1st Infantry Division anvil.[253]

The 16th Infantry Regiment's mission in all this was to follow CT 18's attack on Objective #1 (the high ground in the vicinity of Camprond), relieve CT 18 of Objective #1 and organize it for defense against German units attempting to flee south. The regiment was also to maintain contact with CT 18 as it headed for Objective #3 (the high ground in the vicinity of Monthuchan, just northeast of Coutances), and contact with CT 26 when it seized Objective #2 (the high ground in the vicinity of Cambernon). For this mission, CT 16 consisted of its usual attachments, plus a battery of the 103rd AAA Battalion, two tank destroyer companies, a heavy mortar company, and the 745th Tank Battalion (less two companies). Colonel Gibb intended to use the 745th as a covering force in the CT's advance.[254]

This, then, was the mission of the 16th Infantry in the great Normandy breakout. However, as always in warfare, the enemy had the opportunity to vote on the plan, and the resulting operation would not unfold as neatly as it appeared on paper.

Coutances

The campaign to establish the Normandy lodgment ended on July 24, 1944, with the beginning of Operation Cobra. Originally scheduled to begin July 21, Cobra was postponed for four days because of heavy rains in the area of operations. Meanwhile, the entire combat team had moved into its attack positions behind the 9th Division on the 21st and so remained in place in the mud and mire waiting for the clouds to dissipate. Finally, just after midnight on July 25, the VII Corps sent a teletype message to all subordinate units that D-Day, H-Hour, was 11:00 a.m. on the 25th.[255]

About 10:15 that morning, the first of some fifteen hundred B-24 and B-17 bombers began their bomb runs over the "Bomb Saturation Area" in front of the 9th and 30th Divisions. Despite the fact that the two divisions had pulled back those units closest to the target area, an unfortunate accidental triggering of a bomb load by one bomber group sent hundreds of bombs crashing primarily into the lines of the 39th, 119th, and 120th Infantry Regiments, killing 111 men and wounding another 490. In addition, Lieutenant General McNair, who had apparently forgotten the lesson he had learned in North Africa about standing too close to the front, was well forward watching the bomb run when one of the bombs hit near him, reportedly blasting him and his driver into pieces. Upon hearing the news of his death, several men remembered McNair's stop at the regiment's front lines in North Africa, and the resulting injury to him and several of the regiment's soldiers as a result of his visit. One man, who had watched McNair's actions on that occasion, felt little compassion for the general on this one, stating, "I felt bad about our troops who were killed and injured by our own bomber strike in Normandy," he wrote, "but not for General McNair."[256]

Notwithstanding the bombing debacle, the 4th, 9th, and 30th Divisions jumped off about 11:30 a.m. Though the bombardment had had great effect, destroying or decimating many elements of the Panzer Lehr Division, the units conducting the initial breach through the target area almost immediately ran into opposition, some light, some heavy. The 30th Infantry Division, for example, was able to advance toward the St. Lô-Coutances road, contending with only minor pockets of resistance which it was able to clean out rather easily. The 9th Division, on the other hand, had great difficulty in advancing toward its objective, the town of Marigny. The capture of this crossroads was key to the follow-on exploitation forces that were to blast down the St. Lô-Coutances road to establish the blocking positions behind the LXXXIV Corps. By the night of July 25, the VII Corps had advanced only about one to two miles along the front, and no clear penetration of the German defenses had been made.[257]

It was not until the following day that the effects of the bombardment became evident. After their resistance on the 25th, the German line began to crumble, and the front directly forward of the 30th Division gave way on the 26th. This

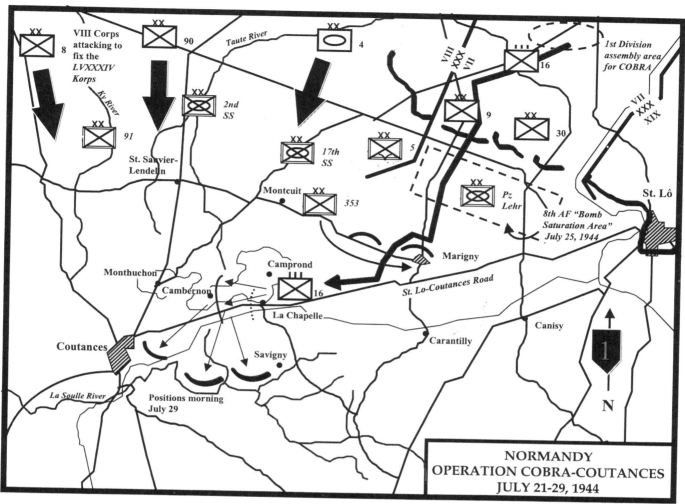

Map 8-13.

opening gave Collins the opportunity to launch the 2nd Armored Division toward its objectives to the south and southeast. But the 9th Infantry Division was still experiencing tough opposition in its efforts to secure Marigny. Collins had already determined that if the VII Corps was to take the town and have any chance to bag the LXXXIV Corps, he had to commit armor, and therefore, had notified Huebner the evening before to clear the road to Marigny. Huebner, in turn, gave the 18th Infantry, supported by Boudinot's CCB, the mission.[258]

On the morning of the 26th, the 18th Infantry entered the line between the 9th and 30th Divisions and pushed south toward Marigny. All day, the 18th advanced against troops of the 353rd Infantry Division and elements of the 2nd SS Panzer Division, but by nightfall, it was still a mile north of the town. There, the regiment was held up by several Mark IV tanks and 75mm antitank guns despite efforts by CCB to flank the enemy position.

Meanwhile, the "hammer" of Bradley's great offensive, the VIII Corps, had already begun its drive south, but because

Collins' plan to launch a powerful armored drive toward the west remained thwarted, no "anvil" was in place with which to smash the enemy units north of Coutances. Huebner knew that he had to break through and do it fast or the entire LXXXIV Corps would slip through the First Army's grasp. He therefore resolved to launch Boudinot's CCB to seize Comprond on the morning of July 27, by bypassing Marigny. The 18th Infantry would remain to take Marigny that morning, but the 16th Infantry would pass through, following the route of CCB, and instead of relieving the 18th Infantry at Camprond, would advance along the St. Lô-Coutances Road to seize the high ground northeast of Coutances (Objective #3).[259]

Having located a bypass to the west of Marigny, Boudinot's combat command pushed through light defenses on the morning of the 27th and drove down the road toward Coutances against sparse opposition until it reached its objective. But resistance by the 353rd Division at Marigny continued to stymie the 18th Infantry throughout the night of July 26-27, until early morning, when the town was finally occupied.

Coming up behind the 18th and CCB was Horner's 3rd Battalion, waiting to advance. Gibb ordered the remainder of the regiment to remain in the assembly area to avoid clogging the road until a hole was cleared through the German line in the vicinity of Marigny. About 11:00 a.m. Horner's men were still two kilometers north of the town, when they turned off onto the dirt trail that CCB had used to bypass Marigny. Pushing on toward the Coutances road, they encountered an enemy force of about one hundred infantrymen, reinforced with a Mark IV tank and an antitank gun. This force held up Horner until just after dark, when the 3rd Battalion struck the road and turned west. At 9:51 p.m. and 10:13 p.m. respectively, the 1st and 2nd Battalions were ordered to take the same route as the 3rd Battalion and head west for Objective #3.[260]

What made the passage past Marigny that night so impressive was that two-thirds of CT 16 was able to pass unmolested through a three hundred-meter gap in the German defenses. The Germans had managed to retain control of the Marigny crossroads by placing direct fire on it from the high ground southwest of the town, so moving through the town was out of the question. Additionally, units of the 353rd Infantry Division and two companies of the 2nd SS Panzer Division still held a line west of the town through which CCB and the 3rd Battalion had already passed. Between these two units, there was now only the three hundred-yard gap through which the rest of the regiment would have to pass to make it to the St. Lô-Coutances road and link up with the 3rd Battalion. In the dark, troops of the 1st Engineer Battalion worked with bulldozers along the trail to ready it for the passage of the regiment's vehicles and follow-on units. Oddly, the Germans were uninterested, or more likely, too exhausted, to interfere with the work, and before dawn, Gibb's combat team had quietly slipped between two strong enemy positions and was pushing down the road toward its objective.[261]

The early morning light did not bring all good news for Gibb, however. Though the 3rd Battalion had penetrated about seven kilometers west of Marigny to La Chapelle, the rest of the regiment was slowed up by the stubborn resistance of the 353rd Division. Gibb reported to the G3: "Situation confused. Traffic rotten. Movement to La Chapelle impossible at this time. Tanks double-banked on road. Receiving enemy artillery fire. Request notification of CCB intentions. Enemy confused, but present." As the regiment ground toward Coutances, it passed hundreds of dead German soldiers and twisted, burning vehicles littering the way. It seemed that the enemy should be in total flight, but opposition was actually increasing. By now, the Germans had discovered the danger to the LXXXIV Corps and were attempting to hold open routes of escape to the south. In addition, the VIII Corps was now actually pushing the enemy out of the sack, and time was slipping away.

By 8:00 a.m., Driscoll's 1st Battalion had passed through La Chapelle and ran into heavy resistance near La Groudière. From this point on, the advance toward Coutances degenerated into the familiar hedgerow-to-hedgerow fighting. As Driscoll advanced on La Groudière, Hicks's 2nd Battalion came up on the left, and these two battalions in turn came up on Horner's left. The fighting along the regimental front became general and though it advanced beyond La Groudière, it did so only through the assistance of heavy concentrations of tank, mortar, and machine-gun fire and help from the fighter-bombers of the Ninth Air Force. The troops CT 16 was now encountering were those of the 2nd SS Panzer and the 17th SS Panzer Grenadier Divisions, who fanatically fought for every yard of ground. Indeed, though Major Plitt had reported to the Division G2 that morning that the enemy defenses appeared to be folding, by the end of the day, CT 16 had suffered its most severe casualties since D-Day.[262]

By nightfall of the 28th, the regiment had gained only twenty-five hundred yards since first encountering the determined enemy around La Groudière. Night patrols sent out by the 1st and 3rd Battalions determined that the enemy was still forward in defensible positions, though they also discovered that the strongpoint that had caused the 1st Battalion so much trouble contained only enemy dead and a couple of knocked-out tanks.

The discovery by 2nd Battalion patrols that night gave Gibb another option. The patrols revealed that the areas south of the St. Lô-Coutances road were relatively free of Germans. When this was reported to division, Gibb was instructed to swing the regiment south and establish a defense line on the high ground above the La Soulle River. By this time, units of the VIII Corps had already captured Coutances and objective #3 anyway, so it was now necessary to reorient the 1st Division.[263]

Gibb issued the appropriate orders, and the following morning the regiment jumped off against light opposition. By 3:00 p.m., the regiment was deployed along the La Soulle River. It remained there for only a few hours when orders came down for Gibb to assemble the regiment at St. Denis-le-Gast, some ten miles southeast of Coutances. A new mission for the regiment and the division was about to unfold, and the drive on Coutances was over.

Bradley's ambitious goal to capture or destroy the LXXXIV Corps was not successful. When the operation was completed, the bulk of the German units were able to escape, but the damage to the LXXXIV Corps was still considerable. It had suffered losses of men and materiel from which it would never recover. The breakthrough achieved by Cobra also set up the breakout from the Cotentin Peninsula by Patton's newly activated Third Army less than a week later and was the springboard from which the Allied forces would now go on to free France. The 16th Infantry's participation in Operation Cobra, while not entirely successful it its ultimate objective of cutting off Coutances from enemy retreat, did result in the capture and destruction of hundreds of enemy troops and their equipment. Though it fell short of taking its final objective, the regiment's performance was praiseworthy, especially given the mud, rain, and cramped road conditions it had to contend with. The regiment's advance down the Coutances road drew enemy forces away from both the VIII Corps' push south as well as the 2nd Armored Division's attack on Canisy and Pont Bracard. In short, CT 16 had been instrumental in helping create the conditions for the 12th Army Group to begin the drive across France.

Mayenne-La Ferté-Macé

For the next several days, the "Red One" advanced against relatively light resistance; the combat team moved south and southeast, meeting minor pockets of Germans, most of whom surrendered easily. On August 1, a surprise raid by the Luftwaffe hit the regimental CP and several combat team units, causing moderate casualties. CT 16 continued south to Le Quesinere and Le Mesnil-Rouges, where it halted to await orders. There, the regiment became the division reserve and moved out on August 3 as the covering force for the division's right flank. The division crossed the Sée River that day and continued south and east until August 5, when the combat team was assembled near Buais. There, Gibb received orders to participate in a division attack to the southwest to seize Mayenne.

The following morning, CT 16 led the division in an attack toward the town, anticipating a tough fight, but the I&R Platoon went all the way to Mayenne without opposition. Gibb quickly moved units to establish support positions on the west bank and secure the bridge across the Mayenne River. Meanwhile, the regiment was formed in a semicircle facing the east, with the 3rd Battalion holding the bridge on the north, the 1st Battalion facing the town of Aron across the river to the east, and Hicks's battalion holding positions in the town and to the south.

Once in the town, it gradually became apparent to all that the division had moved so rapidly that it had cut off a sizable number of enemy troops from the 9th Panzer Division and other German units, who now had no way across the river except the bridges at Mayenne and Ambrières-le-Grand. Additionally, to the east, in and around the town of Aron, the rest of the 9th Panzer Division was in position to resist the advance of the 1st Division and to help their comrades fight their way back across the river.

On the night of August 6, German units made a determined effort to break through against Horner's men at the bridge. While artillery and mortars pounded Driscoll's 1st Battalion across the river, a mixed force of tanks and infantry attacked the 3rd Battalion. Soon, ground fighting developed forward of the 1st Battalion and then from what seemed to be all directions. The regiment was apparently surrounded! Despite heavy German small-arms and indirect fire, all elements of CT 16 held against the assaults. By morning, the attacks tapered off, and patrols were sent into Aron to assess the situation. They discovered a heavy concentration of German troops believed to be preparing to support a push against the 1st Battalion. For the next several days, the regiment braced for a major counterattack, but it never came.[264]

The German High Command in the West was now aware that a large portion of its forces were in great peril. The Seventh Army, commanded by SS General Paul Hauser (who had recently commanded the II SS Panzer Corps), was fighting for its life. By stubbornly resisting in the Mortain-Vire area, Hauser had allowed the flanks of his army to be rolled up by Montgomery's 21st Army Group to the north and Bradley's 12th Army Group to the south. The 1st Infantry Division's rapid drive on Mayenne and Ambrières-le-Grand had become part of an effort to form a large bag of the Seventh Army. By August 8, Patton's Third Army was driving east; on August 11 it turned north to draw tight the strings of the bag. The opening through which the Seventh Army might escape was rapidly closing between Falaise and Argentan.

To help ensure that Hauser's troops would not escape the trap, Bradley ordered Lieutenant General Courtney H. Hodges, the new commander of the First U. S. Army, to fix the II Fallschirmjaeger Corps, the LXXXIV Corps, and the LVIII Corps to prevent them from running out the far end of the bag while Patton cut them off from the rear. The 16th Infantry's part in this great effort was an attack toward La Ferté-Macé. This maneuver would, in turn, allow the regiment to fix, capture, or destroy elements of the 9th Panzer and 10th SS Panzer Divisions. The regiment's primary objective for this mission was the seizure of the high ground northeast of La Ferté-Macé. The 3rd Battalion was assigned that specific task. The 1st Battalion's mission was to take the town of Les Roussiers, just north of the 3rd Battalion's objective, and the 2nd Battalion was to protect the regiment's right flank during the movement, and attack the town of Le Mesnil-de-Briouze. In the line of march between Mayenne and La Ferté-Macé were two large forests that Major John Lauten, the regimental S2, reported as heavily defended by the enemy (according to information provided by the division G2). The night of August 13, Horner's men led the attack northeastward.

Contrary to the division's intelligence reports, Horner's men encountered only scattered resistance through the Andaine Forest and the Bois (forest) de la Ferté, but did have to do some hard fighting to take their objective at La Sauvagère. In doing so, the battalion lost three officers and nineteen men. Passing through the 3rd Battalion, Hicks's men encountered several tanks opposing their advance. These were quickly knocked out by an attached platoon from the 745th, and the 2nd Battalion took Le Mesnil-de-Briouze with no problems after that. Driscoll's men made a superb attack on Les Roussiers while it was still dark and netted over one hundred prisoners, thirteen half-tracks, and one tank, and destroyed eleven other half-tracks with bazookas. The following day, patrols from the 2nd Battalion made contact with the British 50th Division, and on August 18, the bag was closed. The Seventh Army had been largely destroyed, which created a distinct resistance vacuum on the Western Front. The race to the West Wall began.[265]

For the next several weeks, the fighting for the 16th Infantry was relatively light, as it participated in the dash across France to the border of Germany. After a rest at La Fertè-Macè, the regiment boarded trucks on August 24 and convoyed 150 miles to Lardy, just south of Paris. Soon, orders came down from VII Corps for another drive east. The 1st Division was to advance on the corps' left flank, and CT 16 was assigned to be the division's left-most unit to maintain contact with the V Corps during the attack. On August 27, the regiment jumped off and moved through the French countryside against little opposition—and to the delight of the townspeople whom they liberated. On August 30, the regiment arrived at the battlefield of Soissons, where their predecessors had paid such a terrible price in flesh and blood only twenty-six years earlier. Some units set up in positions overlooking the church at St. Pierre-Aigle, where the regiment had established its command post during the World War I battle.[266]

Mons
Over the previous two weeks, Bradley's 12th Army Group had swept all before it. His opponent, Field Marshal Walter Model, now commanding Army Group B, was unable to establish a viable defensive line along the Somme River and decided he must fall back to the West Wall, the famed "Siegfried Line." Bradley now saw another opportunity to cut off a large chunk of the German ground forces, and he ordered Hodges to turn the First Army north and cut off the Fifth Panzer Army. Hodges, in turn, gave the V Corps and Collins' VII Corps the mission. If the maneuver was conducted correctly, the VII Corps would cut off, capture, or destroy two panzer and eight to ten infantry divisions in the Mons-Maubeuge area.[267]

Collins' orders to his division commanders called for the 3rd Armored Division to drive north on the Avesnes-Mons highway, with the 1st Infantry Division in close support. The 9th Division would stay to the east to guard the corps right flank, and the 4th Cavalry Group was ordered to screen the gap between the 9th Division and the Third Army as the corps turned north. If successful, the resulting maneuver would crush the trapped Fifth Panzer Army units against the XIX Corps.

The maneuver began on August 31 as the corps shifted direction at Laon, but within two days, the V Corps had to pull up short because of gasoline shortages in the First Army. Hodges also ordered the VII Corps to halt, but Collins did not get the word until after the lead combat command of the 3rd Armored Division had taken Mons against light opposition on the evening of September 2. At the same time, the 1st Division had followed and entered Avesnes. At first, it appeared that the trap had not been sprung.

In reality, however, elements of the LVIII Panzer Corps, II SS Corps, and the LXXIV Corps, all under General Erich Straube, had been trapped by the VII Corps southwest of Mons. Straube, LXXIV Corps commander, had assumed command of the other two corps when he, and they, had been cut

off from communications with their army headquarters. Straube had rightly guessed that his ad hoc force was in peril of being surrounded and began an organized a retrograde movement to escape the trap. He started too late, however; his forces ran straight into the 1st Infantry and 3rd Armored Divisions.[268]

The troops that the 3rd Armored Division had encountered between Maubeuge and Mons were the advanced elements of the German breakout force headed east for Charleroi. The combat command in Mons was now cut off from the rest of its division. Upon the discovery of this force, Huebner ordered a battalion of the 26th Infantry to fight its way through to Mons, followed by the remainder of that regiment, and sent the 18th Infantry to the northwest to seize Bavai. This was accomplished the morning of September 3.

About 2:00 p.m. that day, Gibb called his battalion commanders to the CP near Maubeuge to receive an attack order. It was apparent from the attack of the 26th Infantry that the entire area between Maubeuge and Mons was thick with German units attempting to flee the trap. Gibb directed Driscoll and Horner to push east along the road toward Givry, then north along the highway to Mons. Hicks's 2nd Battalion was ordered to clear the Bois de Laniers along the Bavai-Binche highway, then link up with the regiment back toward the east. The 3rd Battalion, 18th Infantry, had already passed through these woods, but German units had been reported infiltrating through them, and the 2nd Battalion was to block, capture, or destroy them.[269]

After returning to the battalion CP, Hicks ordered Joe Dawson, now the 2nd Battalion XO, to move the battalion to the mission area. Earlier, F Company had been sent on a separate mission, and Hicks went to find the company with the expectation of returning with it to link up with the rest of the battalion. Taking charge, Dawson mounted the battalion on trucks, tanks, tank destroyers, and anything else that would move and set out for the Bois de Laniers. At the south edge of the woods, Dawson sent G Company north to block the Bavai-Binche highway and ordered E Company to cut the road at Gognies farther east. Company H and the headquarters remained at the south edge and took up hasty defense positions. Dawson awaited the arrival of Hicks and F Company, but soon, all hell broke loose.

As G Company approached the highway, men could see some burned-out hulks of German vehicles blocking the way that had earlier been hit by fighter-bombers. Unable to pull onto the road, the company dismounted, and the 2nd Platoon made its way forward to investigate the wreckage. The men discovered that it was a much larger convoy than they had thought, and it completely blocked the highway. Just as the 2nd Platoon crossed over to the north side of the road, gunfire broke out from all directions. Within seconds, all three platoons were engaged in hot firefights with disorganized clumps of enemy troops who had been surprised by the presence of the Americans. The combat was at close quarters, with hand

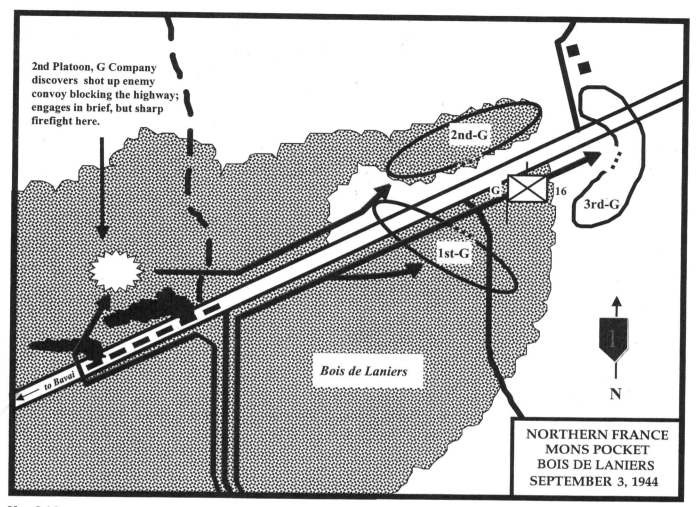

2nd Platoon, G Company discovers shot up enemy convoy blocking the highway; engages in brief, but sharp firefight here.

2nd-G

G 16

3rd-G

1st-G

to Bavai

Bois de Laniers

N

NORTHERN FRANCE
MONS POCKET
BOIS DE LANIERS
SEPTEMBER 3, 1944

Map 8-14.

grenades and Tommy guns being particularly effective. However, the fight had gone out of the Germans, and before long, they began to surrender in droves. Just as a group of POWs was sent to the rear and the company continued the move toward its intended positions, the situation would repeat itself. After sending hundreds of prisoners to the regimental POW pen located in a rock quarry near Maubeuge, G Company finally set up blocking positions, with 1st Platoon covering the highway west toward Bavai, the 3rd Platoon toward Binche, and the 2nd covering the company perimeter to the north.[270]

Meanwhile, Wosenski's Company E had arrived safely at Gognies. Turning north at the crossroads, Wosenski headed for the Bavai-Binche highway, some six hundred yards away. Just as he topped a hill, he spied a German convoy stopped on the road only 150 yards away. Not yet detected, Wosenski immediately ordered 1st Platoon to dismount and attack along the east side of the road; he ordered the 2nd Platoon, with the light machine-gun section attached, to attack along the west side; and the 3rd Platoon was directed to remain in the town

and watch the company's rear. The 60mm mortar section set up near the town to provide indirect fire. Wosenski sent two tank destroyers to set up a blocking position in the town and the other two to support the attack down the road. Just as the two platoons jumped off, firing erupted in all directions.

The 1st and 2nd Platoons almost immediately ran into a stiff firefight to the front. In the town, the 3rd Platoon discovered that many of the houses held Germans who had been hiding in the cellars. This made for the uneasy realization that the enemy were among them already. Fortunately, the Germans were so disorganized and confused that they gave up readily after only slight resistance. Still, the fighting north of the crossroads went on for about two hours and firing was quite heavy at times. Just before dark, the 1st and 2nd Platoons were able to push on and reach the highway. By then, the Germans there had had enough, and they too began to surrender in bunches. Soon, the company had charge of over three hundred POWs, and the commander ordered no more to be taken that night.[271]

No too long after the two rifle companies departed, fight-

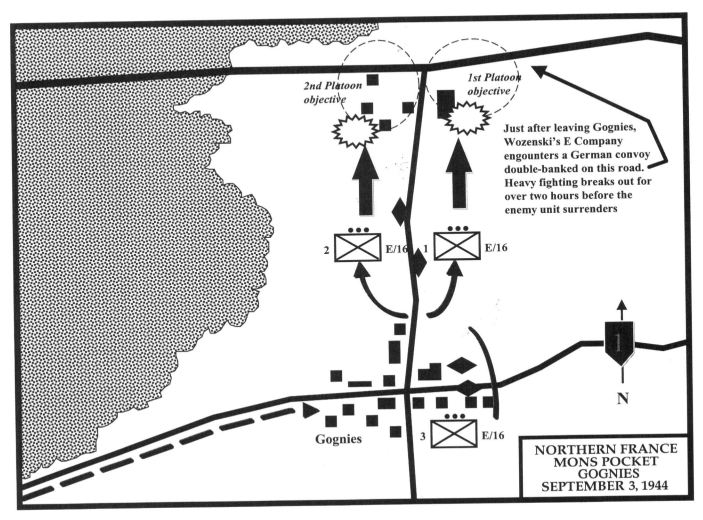

2nd Platoon objective

1st Platoon objective

Just after leaving Gognies, Wozenski's E Company engounters a German convoy double-banked on this road. Heavy fighting breaks out for over two hours before the enemy unit surrenders

2 E/16

1 E/16

Gognies

3 E/16

1

N

**NORTHERN FRANCE
MONS POCKET
GOGNIES
SEPTEMBER 3, 1944**

Map 8-15.

ing had erupted at the battalion CP area as well. As if by design, enemy troops appeared in several directions, but this movement was quite unintentional. The CP group and H Company immediately opened fire, but as in the other instances, the Germans they encountered had little will to fight and soon began to surrender. Oddly, the first prisoners taken by the headquarters element were captured by four cooks. Before long, clerks, mechanics, and even CP personnel were taking prisoners. Dawson ordered a temporary holding area set up with barbed wire, and it soon filled with POWs. Combined with the prisoners coming in from the other companies, the compound became too small to hold them all, and Dawson had to begin sending detachments of one hundred prisoners under guard to the division POW pen at Maubeuge.[272]

Meanwhile, Hicks was not able to locate F Company until he found them in Mons, where they too had taken a number of prisoners and turned them over to the 3rd Armored Division. By the time Hicks and F Company rejoined the battalion on September 5, the action at the Bois de Laniers was over.

The regiment's actions at Mons had been decisive. By the time the 1st Division finished policing the area, the 6th Fallschirmjaeger, 18th Luftwaffe Field, 47th Infantry, 273rd Infantry, 348th Infantry and 712th Infantry Divisions had disappeared from the German order of battle. Over twenty-five thousand Germans had been killed or captured. The 1st Division alone was credited with capturing 7,500 Germans, of which the 2nd Battalion was credited with capturing 3,256. Many of the captured Germans were senior officers who expressed surprise at the speed with which the 1st Division was able to cut them off. At the time of their capture, they had orders to retreat to the Siegfried Line, but now, Model was tens of thousands of men short with which to man it. Even so, the fight to break the West Wall would prove to be a long and costly battle.

Aachen

The advance through France had been a cakewalk compared to what the men of the 16th Infantry had experienced between D-

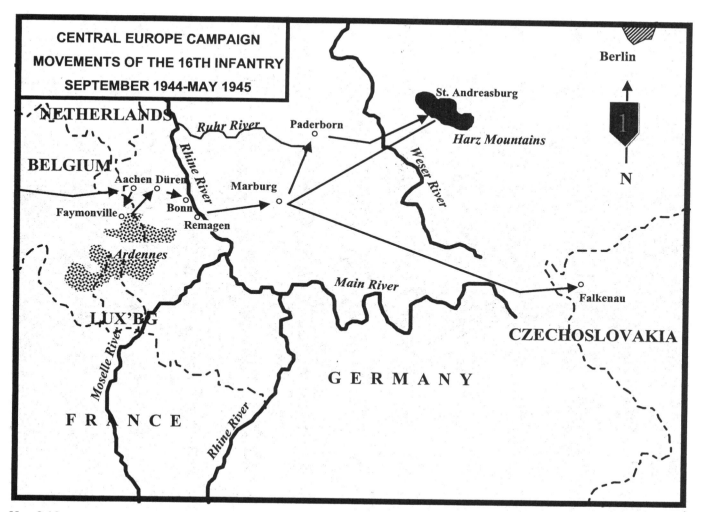

CENTRAL EUROPE CAMPAIGN
MOVEMENTS OF THE 16TH INFANTRY
SEPTEMBER 1944–MAY 1945

Map 8-16.

day and Mayenne. Enemy opposition had crumbled, one position after another, and the Germans seemed incapable of establishing a firm line anywhere. Their morale, moreover, had obviously plummeted. For the average American dogface in the European Theater of Operations in August 1944, the most common sight of the enemy was one of hands held high, often with a scrap of white cloth on a stick. To many 16th Infantrymen, it seemed as though the war would be over by Christmas if not sooner, but here and there, indicators appeared that the Germans had fight left in them. The first of these indicators came east of the little Belgian town of Herve.

The VII Corps' northerly attack into Mons now placed it squarely west of the ancient German city of Aachen, but lack of gasoline and other supplies forced it to remain in place for several days as the First Army adjusted its lines. After helping to reduce the Mons pocket, the 16th Infantry conducted a seventy-six-mile move by trucks to Huy, Belgium, on September 7, and remained there in a defensive posture until September 10. That day, the regiment made another move to Herve, located a

few miles from the German border. Once in Herve, Gibb received orders from the 1st Division to conduct a reconnaissance-in-force to test the outer defenses of the Siegfried Line. Gibb issued the order for the 1st Battalion to lead the regiment into the Aachen Municipal Forest, and on September 11, the regiment moved forward. After experiencing heavy artillery fire and increased enemy resistance in the woods that day, Driscoll's men secured objectives around Henri Chapelle that evening and prepared to probe forward again the following morning.

At 8:00 a.m. on September 12, the 1st Battalion pushed eastward toward the German frontier. Unlike the encounters of the previous few weeks, the advance through the forest was difficult. Against well-emplaced fighting positions, reinforced with logs and overhead cover and manned by troops who firmly resisted, the 1st Battalion's advance was slow and costly. By noon, Gibb had thrown Horner's battalion into the fight on Driscoll's right, and with the additional firepower, the German defenses were reduced at a faster rate. Before nightfall, C Company attacked and captured several pillbox positions, thus

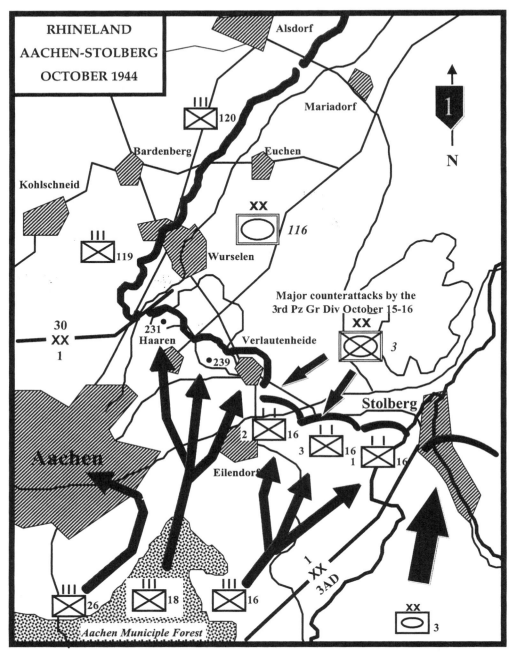

Map 8-17.

forcement of the line by units shipped in from central Germany and the Eastern Front would turn the First Army's fight to reach the Roer River into a bloody, three-month slugfest in the cold, damp forests and gray rubble of destroyed villages along the German frontier.

One reason for the sudden change of attitude on the part of the Wehrmacht troops was that they were now fighting in direct defense of their homeland. Always considered a good fighter up until the July breakout, much of the German soldier's stubborn fighting ability that the American soldier had come to grudgingly respect, now returned. In fact, at times the resistance appeared fanatical. Adding to the determination of the German soldiers facing the 1st Infantry Division was the fact that they were defending the city of Aachen, the birthplace of Charlemagne, and one-time capital of the Holy Roman Empire. Over the past one thousand years, thirty-two German emperors and kings, including Charlemagne, had been crowned in the large Catholic cathedral in the center of the city. Referring to the importance of the city as a symbol, Charles B. MacDonald wrote, "Hitler himself often prophesied that his empire, like Charlemagne's, would last a thousand years. To strike at Aachen was to strike at a symbol of Nazi faith."[274] There was little doubt that Aachen would be staunchly defended.

Other than its symbolic importance, Aachen was relatively unimportant, but it remained a significant obstacle to the VII Corps' eastward movement. Located in a low area, it sat squarely between two belts of the Siegfried Line. The first belt was designated the Scharnhorst Line, the second the Schill Line. These belts consisted of a series of mutually supporting concrete pillboxes, reinforced with log dugout positions, minefields, and so-called dragon's teeth antivehicle obstacles. To

becoming the first U. S. Army unit to seize German soil in wartime.[273]

The fighting in the Aachen Municipal Forest proved to be tough going indeed, and was a precursor to the kind of combat that awaited the U.S. Army as it attempted to roll into the German heartland. Buoyed by the great losses suffered by Army Group B since late July, some in the American high command figured that the Siegfried Line was merely an undermanned shell of a defense that would be easily cracked. Though there was some truth to that perception early on, rapid rein-

the rear were numerous artillery pieces and mortars, all of which formed a formidable defense if properly manned.

To the south of Aachen was a relatively open area, dotted with villages and towns, called the Stolberg Corridor, which led directly to the Roer River to the northeast. Although generally free of trees and crossed with a good road net, the villages provided the corridor defenders with natural defense positions from which to resist attacking forces. Additionally, the number of villages and towns congested the area to the extent that they made the corridor anything but a straight shot to the Roer River.

To the south of the Stolberg Corridor lay the Hürtgen Forest, a thickly vegetated area of rolling hills and cross-compartmented gullies and streams. The woods primarily consisted of tall firs and old-growth hardwoods that provided defenders with cover, concealment, and materials for fighting positions. The trees were also a curse because they caused rounds hitting high in the branches to throw shrapnel down into the foxholes of otherwise safe infantrymen. Only one main road cut through the forest and that was well to the south of the 1st Infantry Division sector. Units fighting in the forest would have to pack food, ammunition, and supplies along foot trails or, if they were lucky, a jeep trail, making the processes of combat that much more difficult

Facing the 1st Infantry Division in Aachen and the Stolberg Corridor on September 12 was the LXXXI Corps, under Lieutenant General Friedrich August Schack. The corps consisted of three badly mauled divisions and a hodgepodge of unit remnants. The once-excellent 116th Panzer Division defended Aachen proper. Nicknamed the "Greyhounds," the 116th had fought with great agility from Normandy back to the West Wall, one of a few German divisions that had acquitted itself well in the great retreat. It now had no panzer regiment (which had been destroyed in the retreat across France), and its two panzer grenadier regiments were reduced to about half strength. For its mission of defending Aachen, it had been reinforced with three Luftwaffe fortress battalions and now consisted of about seven thousand men. The second force was the 9th Panzer Division, which had been severely thrashed by the 16th Infantry at La Ferté-Macé. The division had been reinforced by the ten tanks of the 105th Panzer Brigade but was still so weak that it carried the title "Kampfgruppe 9th Panzer" on the German battle maps. This outfit was given the responsibility of defending the Stolberg Corridor. In addition to these units, Schack had been promised the 394th Sturmgeschutz (assault gun) Battalion, the rejuvenated 12th Infantry Division, and two other fresh divisions. All were to arrive within the next several days.[275]

Realizing that the lack of supplies might immobilize his corps, Collins was able to get Hodges to agree to a reconnaissance-in-force to the Siegfried Line on September 12, with the hopes that he would be reinforced with supplies for an exploitation if he broke through. Collins, like many others, felt that the West Wall was weakly defended and a push now might create a gap through which the rest of the army could pour. He knew the route through Aachen was too difficult to force, as was the Hürtgen Forest to the south, so he determined to send the 1st Infantry Division into the Stolberg Corridor to isolate Aachen and force a way through the Scharnhorst Line. He would then sling the 3rd Armored Division forward to seize Düren on the Roer plain, while the 1st Division cleaned up Aachen. If the going was found to be too tough, the 1st Division would be in a position to partially surround the city, while the 30th Infantry Division of the XIX Corps would complete the encirclement of the city on the north side. The 1st Division would then reduce the city's defenses. The 3rd Armored Division, meanwhile, would seize Eschweiler and hold until the infantry came up to help force a way through.[276]

Huebner's plan for the 1st Division's role was for the 18th Infantry to approach Aachen from the west and isolate the city from that direction. Then, the 26th Infantry was to isolate Aachen on the south side and prepare to take the city. The 16th Infantry's mission was to penetrate the Scharnhorst Line and attack to seize the high ground on the east side of the city.[277] The "reconnaissance-in-force" rendered by the 1st Battalion—during which it entered Germany on September 12—was the beginning of Collins' efforts to break through the West Wall.

Despite the regiment's initial success in taking a portion of the German defenses in the Aachen Municipal Forest on September 12, there was still no penetration of the line. Collins, therefore, shifted the corps' efforts from a reconnaissance-in-force to a full-fledged attack. He ordered Huebner to send one regiment to support an attack by the 3rd Armored Division that would attempt to break into the Stolberg Corridor on September 13 in the vicinity of Ober Forstbach-Schmidthof-Rott. Huebner selected the 16th Infantry for the mission and directed Gibb to continue the advance through the forest toward Ober Forstbach, on CCA's left, while the rest of the 3rd Armored Division attacked northeastward toward the town of Stolberg. Once through the Scharnhorst Line, the 16th was to swing northeast and seize the high ground around Eilendorf.[278]

Jumping off about dawn on the 13th, the 2nd and 3rd Battalions advanced along the north shoulder of CCA against stiff resistance, while the 1st Battalion, already forward of the other two, sustained severe counterattacks most of the day. By nightfall, the 3rd Battalion had fought its way past roadblocks, obstacles, and small detachments using effective delaying tactics to approach, but not penetrate, the dragon's teeth near Ober Forstbach. The 3rd Armored, however, had penetrated the dragon's teeth, but only with severe losses in men and tanks. Collins directed the attack to continue the following day.[279]

On September 14, CCA attacked, made it to the outskirts of Eilendorf, and held in place for the 16th Infantry to come up. Concurrently, CT 16 launched a coordinated combat team attack, capturing numerous pillboxes, and penetrating the Scharnhorst defenses. The regiment pushed all day, through Ober Forstbach and Brand, but fell short of reaching Eilendorf.

Continuing the assault the following day, the 2nd Battalion entered Eilendorf before noon and seized the high ground west, north, and northeast of the town. By the end of September 15, Aachen was surrounded on three sides, and the 1st Infantry Division had completed the first phase of its mission.[280]

After CT 16 seized the high ground east of Aachen, Brigadier General Doyle O. Hickey, commanding CCA, continued the drive on Eschweiler and attempted to pierce the second belt of the West Wall, the "Schill Line." Anticipating trouble reaching that objective, Hickey had requested and received infantry reinforcement in the form of Captain Charles H. Cunkle's Company A. Just as he anticipated, Hickey's command ran into stiff antiarmor defenses as it skirted Stolberg on the north side. As the lead tank battalion proceeded toward an intermediate objective, the "Geisberg" (Hill 228), it soon lost eight tanks from seven well-concealed antitank guns on and near the hill. Hickey then launched A Company toward Hill 228, and after the fiercest fighting the regiment had experienced so far in this phase of the battle, Cunkle's men captured the Geisberg before nightfall. More importantly, the loss of that hill effectively cut any contact between the 116th and 9th Panzer Divisions, and disrupted the LXXXI Corps' defenses.[281] The remaining defenses of the Schill Line were hardly substantial, and the way to the Roer River seemed within grasp.

Rhineland Campaign
September 15-December 15, 1944
By the nightfall of September 15, the LXXXI Corps was teetering on the brink of disaster. Stretched to the limit by attacks in the Stolberg Corridor and the combined efforts of the 1st and 30th Infantry Divisions to surround Aachen, Schack's troops appeared about to crack. The 116th Panzer Division was down to only sixteen hundred combat troops, two Mark IV tanks, one Mark V Panther tank, one assault gun, and four guns of the 394th Sturmgeschutz Battalion. Kampfgruppe 9th Panzer was only slightly better off with twenty-five hundred troops, thirteen Panther tanks, twelve assault guns, and fifteen antitank guns.[282]

The new variable in the situation, however, was the arrival of the newly rebuilt German 12th Infantry Division on the morning of September 16. Nicknamed the "Wild Buffaloes," the 12th Division was an old army outfit that had seen extensive combat in Poland, France, and on the Eastern Front. Almost destroyed in the fighting around Mogilev during the summer of 1944, the division was pulled back into Germany and was rebuilt with the men and equipment of the partially active 549th Infantry Division. Colonel Gerhard Engels, an officer who had served on Hitler's personal staff as an adjutant, was appointed the new commander. Now numbering some 14,800 men, it had been fully outfitted with mostly new equipment and reinforced with the 102nd Sturmgeschutz Brigade to make up for shortages in assault guns.[283] The Wild Buffaloes were ready to get into the fight, but as things turned out, they would not be employed in the way Engels envisioned.

Engels, concerned about the reports he had received of the situation around Aachen, requested and received from Schack a promise not to commit the 12th Division piecemeal (since it would arrive, unit by unit, over the next two days). Schack broke that promise almost right away, when the 27th Fusilier Regiment arrived at Juelich early on September 17. As they disembarked at the station, Schack sent the regiment on a two-pronged attack into the Stolberg Corridor. One battalion was launched against elements of CCA, near Eschweiler, the other was ordered to attack the 16th Infantry positions near Verlautenheide. The command was on the road immediately, and before dawn, was ready to attack.

Bursting out of a wooded area east of Eilendorf, the 27th Fusiliers "charged in well-disciplined waves with fixed bayonets."[284] An impressive sight, no doubt, but also a perfect target for the concentrated machine-gun, mortar, and artillery fire of the 16th Infantry. The counterattack fell particularly heavy against Wozenski's E Company. The company had been partially overrun in a counterattack the day before and now was threatened with destruction. Only after close-in fighting, often with hand grenades, was the attack of the fusiliers shattered and finally thrown back with heavy losses. The 27th made an another attempt that afternoon, but it, too, was repulsed with severe casualties.

The 12th Division's other two regiments, the 48th and 89th Infantry Regiments, were also sent into piecemeal attacks as they arrived that day, and received similar treatment from units of the 3rd Armored Division and the 9th Infantry Division. One battalion of the 89th Regiment was down to one hundred men by the end of the day. By the time Engels arrived to take field command of the Wild Buffaloes, the division had been virtually wrecked in fruitless attacks against the VII Corps.

Despite its severe losses, the advent of the 12th Infantry Division in the Stolberg area did have some positive effects for the LXXXI Corps. Over the past five days, the VII Corps had experienced substantial losses as well, but Collins had no fresh divisions to throw into the fight. The lack of supplies and the efforts of Engels' men now prompted Collins to consolidate his gains and switch over to the defense, at least temporarily.

For the next couple of weeks, the VII Corps was stalled in the Stolberg Corridor while it waited for the XIX Corps to complete the encirclement of Aachen. The mission to encircle and reduce Aachen had always figured in the First Army's plans. Now that it was apparent that no easy breach was going to be made in the West Wall, and supplies were not immediately available for a major offensive, the seizure of the town became a high priority.

What this meant for the men of the 16th Infantry was several weeks of defending against the fanatical counterattacks of some of the best troops then available to the Third Reich. Dug in on positions stretching from near Verlautenheide to Stolberg, the regiment was pounded by some of the heaviest artillery barrages it experienced during the war. Until it was captured by the

18th Infantry on October 8, Hill 239 (better known as "Crucifix Hill") provided German spotters with a clear view of the regiment's defenses, enabling them to direct artillery fires with deadly accuracy. In the circumstances, the men of the 16th had little choice other than to dig deeper and hunker down in their holes.

Compounding the troops' misery was the cold, rainy, weather. The inevitable losses from trenchfoot and other weather-related maladies thinned the regiment's ranks. The combination of bad weather and constant bombardment proved too much for a few men, who went mad and had to be evacuated.

It should be noted, however, that CT 16 was not idle during this phase. On September 20, Gibb directed the 1st Battalion to attack and seize the town of Stolberg. Having lost three hundred men in five days, every rifle company was down to about half strength, so L Company, 18th Infantry, was attached for the mission. Though Stolberg was by then essentially a pile of rubble, the defending 12th Infantry Division offered stubborn resistance. From the start, A and C Companies were hardly able to move; while B Company made only moderate gains, and did not quite reach the town. The attack resumed on the 21st, and after bitter house-to-house fighting, the 1st Battalion occupied the town by the end of the day.[285]

For the next two weeks, the regiment held in position while the XIX Corps conducted its assault on the West Wall defenses. Major General Charles H. Corlett, the XIX Corps commander, assigned the mission to the 30th Infantry Division, which scheduled its attack for October 7, hoping to link up with elements of the 1st Division at Würselen, northeast of Aachen.[286]

While the VII Corps prepared for its next move and waited for the XIX Corps to move into position, the LXXXI Corps, now under the command of General Friedrich J. Koechling (who replaced Schack in late September), was receiving reinforcements to replace the battered divisions in and around Aachen. The most recent arrival was the 246th Volks Grenadier Division, commanded by Colonel Gerhard Wilck. The 246th had relieved both the 116th and 9th Panzer Divisions of their sectors, including Aachen, in late September, and those divisions were pulled back into Germany for refitting. In an amazingly short time, the 116th Panzer Division had been rebuilt and now stood at some 11,500 men, but it still possessed only forty-one Mark IV tanks. Koechling had been promised the return of the 116th at the earliest possible time. He had been promised the twelve-thousand-man 3rd Panzer Grenadier Division as well. Both divisions were en route to the LXXXI Corps when the 30th Division launched its October 7 attack to reach Würselen.[287]

The 1st Infantry Division's responsibility in this final encirclement effort was to attack Würselen from the southwest and link up with the 30th Division forces there. Huebner gave the

18th Infantry that job, and alerted the 26th Infantry to prepare to attack Aachen proper once the 246th Volks Grenadier Division was cut off from the rest of the LXXXI Corps. The 16th Infantry was to remain in positions in the vicinity of Verlautenheide-Eilendorf-Stolberg to perform the threefold mission of defending against enemy efforts to prevent the final entrapment, maintaining contact with the 3rd Armored Division, and protecting the 1st Division's right flank. On October 7, the 30th Division and CT 18 started their respective attacks toward Würselen, and after three days of unexpectedly hard fighting, they united at the Ravelsberg (Hill 231) on October 10. The reduction and capture of Aachen by the 26th Infantry began the next day.

The same day that the 1st and 30th Divisions linked up at Hill 231, the 3rd Panzer Grenadier Division and the hastily rebuilt 116th Panzer Division arrived to reinforce Koechling. The 3rd Panzer Grenadier Division, commanded by Major General Walter Denkert, was initially given the mission to widen the supply route into Aachen, but the mission was changed to a counterattack to break the encirclement when the German commander realized the route into the city had already been closed by the 18th Infantry. For the next several days, reports filtered into the 1st Infantry Division headquarters of the presence and build-up of the 3rd Panzer Grenadiers east of Verlautenheide and Eilendorf.[288]

Meanwhile, the 16th Infantry had spent the previous three weeks reinforcing and improving its defenses northeast of Aachen. After its initial attacks on Eilendorf in mid-September, Gibb had deployed the combat team with Driscoll's men in positions near Stolberg, Horner's troops held the line at Eilendorf, and the 2nd Battalion held the far left of the line on a ridge between Verlautenheide and Eilendorf.

The ridge between Verlautenheide and Eilendorf was some two thousand yards long, and faced northeastward toward a wooded area that provided a concealed approach from the vicinity of Eschweiler. Dawson recalled that "it was a very vital thing that we maintain" the ridge, for its loss would allow the Germans to reoccupy Crucifix Hill and reopen the supply line into Aachen. The high ground overlooked a wide meadow that an attacking force would have to cross before it reached the base of the ridge, unless it used a railroad cut leading directly into the I Company area. For three weeks, companies of the 2nd and 3rd Battalions had held that ridge and had suffered numerous probing attacks and artillery barrages. Now, the men braced for a ground attack. "Situation reports showed a growing enemy build up beyond the woods," recalled Sergeant Don Wilson of F Company. "We knew they were coming....Their artillery barrage…[continued] for an hour or more. It was later reported that over 3,000 rounds fell in our area. Amazingly, we only had two fatalities. When the barrage lifted, we could hear them singing rousing marching songs as they came through the woods."[289]

About 10:00 a.m. on October 15, the fresh troops of the

29th Panzer Grenadier Regiment, supported by ten to fifteen Tiger tanks of the 506th Panzer Battalion, rolled out of the railroad cut and converged on the boundary between the 2nd and 3rd Battalions.[290] Holding those positions were Dawson's own G Company and Richmond's I Company. Within thirty minutes the situation was desperate, with both companies on the verge of being overrun. Gibb and Eston White (the regimental S3 since replacing Plitt on August 5) coolly worked to get support up to the two beleaguered units, first dispatching several tank destroyers from the 634th Tank Destroyer Battalion, then requesting air support through division. By 1:00 p.m., however, all communication had been lost with the companies, and it appeared that a breakthrough had occurred. The fighting now spread to E and F Companies, further indicating that G and I Companies were overrun.[291]

Through heavy artillery fire, the troops of the 3rd Panzer Grenadiers continued their advance, intent on throwing the 16th Infantry off the ridgeline. The 29th Panzer Grenadier Regiment had indeed overrun G and I Companies, and Tiger tanks roamed at will among the American positions. But the men in the holes were still fighting. As his troops desperately battled the grenadiers, Gibb continued to call for air support to help stop the onslaught. Finally, at 1:45 p.m., P-47s of the 492nd Fighter Bomber Squadron arrived to blast a concentration of thirty German vehicles and strafe the accompanying German troops. By 2:00 p.m., the tough fighting on the part of the men of the 2nd Battalion, in combination with the air strike and the superb fire of seven field artillery battalions, broke the 3rd Panzer Grenadier Division's attacks.[292]

But Denkert was not done, launching several attacks against the 16th Infantry through the night of October 15-16. By the light of flares, Dawson's men received another determined assault by a company of grenadiers, reinforced with tanks, who succeeded in reaching G Company's defensive line in the dark. Dawson called for artillery on his own positions, and still another company of grenadiers got into the 2nd Battalion lines. The fighting was intense, but the men of G Company held:

> Though Germans were all among the foxholes and the enemy tanks perched little more than twenty-five yards away to pump fire into the holes, the men held their positions. Had it been daylight, the sight of some withdrawing might have infected the others; as it was, the men stayed, basically unaware of what the overall situation was. Out of little clumps of resistance and individual heroism they fashioned a sturdy phalanx.[293]

Bleeding from a head wound received when a mortar round struck his farm house CP, Dawson developed a plan to crush the attack. First, he moved several tank destroyers in to engage the enemy tanks in the G Company positions. Once the tank destroyers were in place and engaged, he called for additional artillery fire. The combined fires of artillery, tanks, and infantry drove off the panzer grenadiers. In the morning light, the men of G Company counted some forty German bodies strewn about their positions.[294]

Denkert's men attempted several more attacks throughout the day on October 16, but the 2nd Battalion consistently beat them back with heavy losses. In the evening, the 3rd Panzer Grenadier Division finally broke off its attacks. Having lost almost one-third of its combat strength in just over two days of fighting, it needed to reorganize. Some 250 dead panzer grenadiers lay in front of the G Company positions. Next door, Sergeant Wilson surveyed the scene and remembered the thrashing F Company had suffered on the beaches of Normandy: "By dawn it was all over. I walked out in front of our lines, toward the woods. There was not a single German soldier more than twenty yards beyond the trees. Fires were still burning in the trees and among the bodies. Jerry had lost hundreds of people. I felt somehow satisfied that an old score had been settled."[295]

The 3rd Panzer Grenadiers made at least two more attempts to break through the 16th Infantry on October 18 and 19. But their efforts were in vain, and on the morning of October 21, Colonel Wilck, now commander of all forces in Aachen, surrendered his remaining troops to the men of the 26th Infantry. It had taken the Blue Spaders four days of hard fighting to capture the city, but the fighting would have been harder still had it not been for the success of the 16th Infantry and 18th Infantry in blocking German efforts to support the city's garrison. For their part in the fighting at Verlautenheide ridge, G and I Companies received Presidential Unit Citations.

Though the first major German city had fallen, it was a somewhat hollow victory, for ancient Aachen was virtually destroyed in the process. Like a sign from God, however, the ancient cathedral still stood in the center of the devastated city, intact and only lightly scarred. The cathedral later became a scene of much wonder when townspeople observed General Hodges, escorted by his staff, respectfully enter the sanctuary, kneel, and offer a prayer of thanksgiving. Hitler had always contended that a German was too good to kneel for anyone or any reason, and now the citizens of Aachen watched as the commanding officer of the army that had conquered their city humbled himself before God.[296]

In his efforts to prevent Aachen's capture, Model had used up several divisions, and had lost between forty-five and seventy tanks in its defense. In addition to their killed and wounded, the defenders also lost some 11,600 troops to capture. While this was a substantial loss in manpower, it may have been a greater psychological blow; for by now, even the most fanatic soldiers of the Reich realized that Germany was unlikely to win the war. Even so, there was plenty of hard fighting to be done, especially over the next three months. The time bought by the LXXXI Corps in September and October enabled the West Wall fortifications to be reinforced by addi-

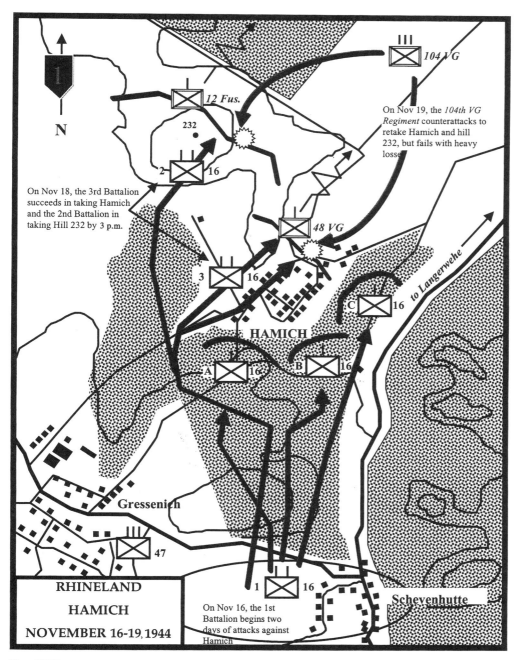

On Nov 19, the *104th VG Regiment* counterattacks to retake Hamich and hill 232, but fails with heavy losse

On Nov 18, the 3rd Battalion succeeds in taking Hamich and the 2nd Battalion in taking Hill 232 by 3 p.m.

On Nov 16, the 1st Battalion begins two days of attacks against Hamich

RHINELAND
HAMICH
NOVEMBER 16-19, 1944

Map 8-18.

and less interested in the conduct of the war," and the battalion executive officer felt obliged to bring the problem to the attention of the regimental commander. Gibb agreed that it was time for Hicks to go and pulled him out of the line. Ed Wozenski, now a major, took temporary command of the 2nd Battalion.[297]

After the stiff fighting at Verlautenheide, the regiment experienced only sporadic contact for the next two weeks. This relative lull in the fighting allowed Gibb to start rotating battalions through a rest area at Brand, about a mile to the rear, beginning with the 2nd Battalion on October 22. Each battalion got about four days out of the line to rest, shower, and eat a hot meal. On November 9, the entire regiment was relieved of its positions near Stolberg by the 104th Division's 415th Infantry, as part of a division move to the rear. The regiment assembled in Brand and continued to receive replacements to make good the losses sustained at Verlautenheide-Stolberg.

The delays caused by the lack of supplies siphoned off by Operation Market-Garden to the north may have allowed the Germans to further strengthen their defenses along the Siegfried Line, but Collins had not given up on the idea of achieving a breakthrough in the Stolberg Corridor. He planned to do that by sending the 1st Division to seize the Hamich ridge—supported by attacks of the 104th Division through the Eschweiler-Weisweiler industrial complex to the north—and the 4th Division through the Hürtgen Forest to the south. With the ridge in the 1st Division's hands, the corps would be poised to spring toward the Roer River valley.

The Hamich ridge extended from the vicinity of Schevenhutte northwestward toward Eschweiler. The dominant height was Hill 232, a superb artillery observation position.

tional troops, and allowed the Germans more time to further improve defenses in places like the Hürtgen Forest, among other places.

Hamich

By the end of October, a number of men in the regiment, and especially in the battered 2nd Battalion, had cracked under the strain of heavy combat. That battalion's commander, Herbert Hicks, had begun to act oddly and showed signs of combat fatigue. One of his officers described his behavior as being "less

From there, German forward observers could rain down indirect fire virtually anywhere in the Stolberg Corridor. Its capture was paramount to the success of 1st Division operations up to and beyond the Hamich ridge. Hamich, a little village of about thirty houses located southeast of Hill 232, would also figure prominently in the forthcoming operation.

Facing the 1st Division's sector was an old adversary, the 12th Division, now given the honorific title "Volks Grenadier" by Hitler for its efforts around Aachen. Still commanded by Engels, now a general, it was down to only 6,381 troops. It was scheduled to be pulled out of the line for refitting in preparation for the Ardennes counteroffensive, but was held in place until a replacement division became available for its relief. The division's 48th Panzer Grenadier Regiment held the Hamich ridge.[298]

Huebner's plan for this attack called for the attached 47th Infantry Regiment to seize the town of Gressenich, while Boudinot's CCB cleared the Stolberg Corridor to the left of the 47th Infantry, up to Scherpenseel. The 26th Infantry would jump off from Schevenhutte to attack along the east side of Weh Creek to take the village of Heistern, the Laufenberg castle, and ultimately the towns of Jungersdorf and Langerwehe. The 16th Infantry was tasked to assault the Hamich ridge and seize Hill 232 and the village of Hamich proper. The combat team would then continue attacking north to take the Rösslerhof castle, and finally, Luchem. The seizure of these objectives would bring the 1st Infantry Division to the Roer plain.

Bad weather continued to cause problems for the 16th Infantry.

Conditions were miserable and the weather was cold and rainy, and our soldiers had little shelter from the elements. We now began to have problems with trench foot. Our soldiers were outside in the cold and wet, their shoes were not waterproof and once they were soaked, it was virtually impossible to dry them out. The best we could do was to get dry socks and shoes and to get the soldiers to work together as buddies massaging their feet to get their circulation going. This was a serious problem.[299]

Making matters worse was the difficult terrain between the jump-off line and Hamich. Eston White, who replaced Plitt as the regimental S3 in August, recalled:

In preparation for that attack by the regiment, I made a reconnaissance of the regimental front, which was terrible terrain. Not only was it wooded, but it was hilly. A terrible place to make an attack. Personally, I felt that the attack at this time, in that particular area was very ill advised, but I was only a regimental operations officer.[300]

His concerns, as it turned out, were valid.

Gibb's plan to take the Hamich ridge called for the 1st Battalion to take the lead and seize the village. The 3rd Battalion would follow the 1st and break off to capture Hill 232. The 2nd Battalion would remain in reserve but, if necessary, it would come up on the 3rd Battalion's left to help take the hill. On November 10, the three battalions moved into an assembly area west of Schevenhutte and spent the next five days preparing for the attack. For some of the more fortunate troops, houses were commandeered and men rotated through them so they could warm themselves and dry their feet.

At noon on November 16, following a massive air and artillery bombardment of the attack route, Driscoll's 1st Battalion, led by Companies A and C and supported by a platoon of Sherman tanks from the 745th Tank Battalion, jumped off near Schevenhutte and moved into the Hürtgen Forest. Almost immediately, they encountered intense resistance in the wooded, hilly terrain. The Germans occupied numerous expertly constructed, log-reinforced emplacements, forcing the battalion to reduce each emplacement in turn—a grueling task, made harder still by the hindering effects of mud and cold. By 3:15 p.m., Driscoll's men had reached the edge of the woods overlooking Hamich and were preparing to take the village. But the assault was delayed by counterattacks by 48th Volks Grenadier Regiment. During one of these attacks, Captain O'Brien, the Cannon Company commander, was killed.[301]

At dusk, Driscoll brought up B Company for what he intended to be the final assault on Hamich. He decided to attack despite the absence of the supporting tank platoon, which had met with slow going on the forest's windy, muddy trails, and had been further delayed by enemy resistance at Gressenich. Moving out of the woods, his men started to approach the village across open ground. They didn't get far: the Germans blasted them with an assortment of weapons, including rapid-fire antiaircraft guns and 210mm artillery. With casualties mounting, the attack was called off and the battalion retired to the wood line, where it dug in for the night.[302]

Late the next morning (November 17), the U.S. 47th Infantry Regiment, which had jumped off at the same time as CT 16 the day before, finally took the town of Gressenich, opening a route to bring up the tank platoon. The Shermans rumbled through Gressenich and proceeded to link up with the 1st Battalion that afternoon, allowing Driscoll to launch a coordinated tank-infantry assault on Hamich. The attack failed—even with the aid of tanks the battalion, weakened by heavy casualties, was unable to force the enemy's defenses. That night, Gibb contacted Horner and changed the latter's mission from seizing Hill 232 to capturing Hamich. The next morning, a squadron of P-47s flew in to help break up the German defenses and after a heavy artillery concentration along the ridge—especially on Hill 232—the 3rd Battalion, less I Company but reinforced by tanks and tank destroyers, swept across the open ground about 8:00 a.m. and entered the village.

After eight hours of tough house-to-house fighting, the 3rd Battalion was in possession of all but a few houses on the village's north side.[303]

Meanwhile, Gibb had ordered the 2nd Battalion to seize Hill 232. After fifteen battalions of artillery pounded the objective with an impressive time-on-target concentration, the battalion burst out of the woodline at 2:00 p.m. and rushed the hill. It quickly fell to the Americans: many of the defenders, troops of the 12th Fusilier Battalion, had been killed in the preliminary bombardment, and the survivors were too stunned by the shelling to offer any resistance.

The 16th Infantry now held most of the Hamich ridge, but its possession was to be bitterly contested the rest of the day and that night. In the woods southeast of the village where it had supported Horner's attack on Hamich, the 1st Battalion was soon counterattacked by elements of the 48th Panzer Grenadiers. On the right flank of the regiment's positions lay Captain Briggs's C Company, which had less than seventy men remaining of the 160 that had jumped off the day before. Among the casualties was Briggs himself, killed by one of the deadly tree bursts that took the lives of so many men during the Hürtgen fighting. Manning a C Company position on the left flank of his platoon, Technical Sergeant Jake W. Lindsey helped Lieutenant James Wood supervise the preparation of his platoon's defenses. The company had lost thirty-four of forty men killed or wounded since the day before; Wood was now the leader of a six-man platoon, including him and Lindsey.

About 2:00 p.m., the platoon was hit by a counterattacking company of grenadiers, reinforced by five tanks. Lindsey first drove off the tanks with rifle grenades after they had approached to within fifty yards, then repelled six assaults by enemy infantry. Wounded in the knee, he turned his fire on an eight-man squad attempting to set up a machine-gun position not more than fifty yards away. Bleeding and out of ammunition, Lindsey jumped out of his hole and attacked the Germans with his bayonet, killing three, capturing three, and driving off the other two. In front of the platoon position lay some one hundred dead panzer grenadiers. Lindsey was credited with killing ten of them with his rifle, seven with grenades and three with his bayonet. For his heroism that day, Lindsey was awarded the regiment's sixth Medal of Honor.[304]

The counterattacks against the 1st Battalion were equally severe elsewhere. The battalion had jumped off with about 160 men per company; by that evening, A Company was down to 100 men, and B and C Companies were each down to about seventy men. Additionally, the regiment had lost two company commanders killed in action: C Company's Captain Briggs and Cannon Company's Captain O'Brien. In Hamich itself, Horner's men were still rooting out enemy troops from the cellars of several houses.

Model could not afford the loss of the Hamich ridge, so he sent the LXXXI Corps a fresh division to take it back. Entering the lines facing the 1st Division's sector on November 18 was the 47th Volks Grenadier Division, commanded by Lieutenant General Max Bork. Though the 47th was close to full strength, it had been rebuilt by the reassignment of men from the navy and the Luftwaffe, and from the assignment of seventeen- and eighteen-year-old draftees and a few veterans from the Eastern Front. Moreover, its newly formed infantry regiments had completed only six weeks of training; its artillery regiment, one week. However, the division would soon demonstrate that its training deficiencies were more than offset by the fighting spirit of its men.[305]

The division's first assignment was to retake the Hamich ridge (specifically Hill 232) and the village of Hamich. Bork gave the job to the 104th Volks Grenadier Regiment, commanded by Colonel Josef Kimbacher. Down to only two battalions, Bork assigned one battalion to take Hill 232; the other was to attack and seize Hamich. Each battalion was to be reinforced with armored vehicles of the 116th Panzer Division. The regiment's two battalions moved to assembly areas near Hamich in the predawn darkness of November 19, where they would rendevous with the elements of the 116th Panzer Division preparatory to their attack. But a lieutenant who was leading a column of the 116th's tanks and halftracks to link up with the battalion slated to attack Hill 232 lost his way en route to the assembly area. Instead he accidently guided the force down a trail toward Hamich—and C Company. After a brief firefight, the lieutenant discovered his error and turned the force around, only to bump into the 3rd Battalion when the column blundered into the village itself.

The column had just reached the edge of the village when Horner's men, alerted by the column's earlier contact with C Company, opened fire and called for artillery support. As Horner's troops scurried for cover in the houses, artillery began to land among the German vehicles. While the halftracks retreated, several tanks pushed on and entered the village, and began to prowl the streets and spaces between the buildings. At least two lumbered into shell craters from which they could not extract themselves, but others continued to look for targets. One Tiger tank pulled up next to a house occupied by Sergeant Carmen Turchiarelli from K Company. Turchiarelli grabbed a bazooka and scrambled upstairs to a second-story window. From this vantage point he fired his weapon into the open turret hatch of the tank, killing the crew and disabling the vehicle. Lacking infantry support, the rest of the tanks fled back toward the north, leaving their unfortunate lieutenant-guide to be captured.

About 5:30 a.m. the two battalions of the 104th pushed off on their attacks. The battalion assaulting Hamich, supported by eight tanks, hit the 3rd Battalion again, but Horner's men readily repulsed this effort before dawn. To the north, the other battalion, absent the tanks that had blundered into Hamich earlier, launched its drive from the woods east of Hill 232. As they crossed the open ground before the 2nd Battalion, the Americans opened fire with devastating effect, killing and wounding hundreds of the volks grenadiers in short order. In one attacking company, only the commander survived unhurt.[306]

Meanwhile, the 26th Infantry struggled to seize its initial objectives to the east of Weh Creek. Against fresh units of the 47th Volks Grenadier Division in the forest, the 26th Regiment fought its way two miles northeastward, just short of the Laufenberg castle, by November 19. After four days of struggle, the two regiments gained a few more miles of German territory. But they suffered over one thousand casualties, and had failed to break through to the Roer.

Rösslerhof

For the second phase of this offensive, Huebner ordered the 18th Infantry to take the towns of Wenau, Heistern, and Langerwehe, attacking between CTs 16 and 26. While the latter focused on Jüngersdorf and Merode, the16th Infantry was to continue attacking on the left to cut the Weisweiler-Langerwehe highway and seize Luchem. To achieve that goal, the regiment first had to capture the high ground around the Rösslerhof castle.[307]

The approach to the castle was difficult. As described by Charles MacDonald, it

> took the form of a parallelogram bounded on the southwest by the Hamich ridge, on the northwest by the Inde River, on the northeast by the Weisweiler-Langerwehe highway, and on the southwest by the Weh Creek. The parallelogram embraced the purlieus of the Hürtgen Forest. A nondescript collection of farms, villages, industrial towns, railroads, scrub-covered hills, and scattered but sometimes extensive patches of woods, this region would offer serious challenges to an attacker, particularly during the kind of cold, wet, weather late November had brought. Indeed, these troops who would fight here where the Hürtgen Forest reluctantly gives way to the Roer plain would experience many of the same miseries as did those who fought entirely inside the forest.[308]

The 16th jumped off for the attack on the castle as soon as Wenau fell to the 18th Infantry on the afternoon of November 19. With the U.S. 47th Infantry covering its left flank, CT 16 easily reached the Bovenburger Wald (forest) about two miles from the castle. There it held in place until the 18th Infantry could take Heistern, thus denying German artillery spotters the clear view that town afforded of the 16th Infantry's sector. After a two-day battle with the 115th Volks Grenadiers defending Heistern, CT 18 captured the town, opening the way for Gibb to attack the Rösslerhof November 21.

The Rösslerhof castle sat on high ground near the northern edge of the next stand of forest beyond the Bovenburger Wald. The combat team would have to cross open terrain to enter the next forest, the Wilhelmshohe Wald, then attack through that forest to reach the castle. Just to the north of the castle, about one-half mile away, was the Aachen-Düren railroad, and a mile beyond that was the Weisweiler-Langerwehe highway. Defending the Rösslerhof and its surrounding high ground was Kampfgruppe Eisenhuber, a patchwork of remnant units from the bruised 47th Volks Grenadier Division.[309]

On November 21, the 2nd Battalion attacked northward and entered the Wilhelmshohe Wald, where the defenders halted its advance. The following day, the regiment remained in place while their artillery dueled with German batteries. Finally, on November 23, the 2nd and 3rd Battalions launched a coordinated attack that seized the high ground, after which K Company captured the Rösslerhof at dusk. All though the night, the 3rd Battalion, in positions around the castle, repulsed strong counterattacks while the 2nd Battalion prepared for a morning assault aimed at cutting the highway.[310] The 2nd Battalion attacked at 7:30 a.m., gaining only a few hundred yards of German territory before its advance was halted by heavy enemy artillery fire.

The fighting around the Rösslerhof was vicious. Casualties among leaders had been high since the beginning of the campaign; and for the 3rd Battalion companies holding the castle and the surrounding terrain, leader casualties had been particularly heavy. The night before the Rösslerhof attack, Gibb went to the extreme expedient of assigning his division liaison officer, Lieutenant Oswaldo Ramirez of Mission, Texas, to K Company as a platoon leader. After taking communion with Chaplain Deery the next day, the understandably nervous Ramirez made his way forward with ammunition, rations, and eight replacements for the company. That evening, after leading his detachment on a perilous journey through shellfire that splintered trees like toothpicks, Ramirez located Captain Everette Booth, the K Company commander, in the castle's basement. Descending a ladder into the basement, Ramirez found the CP crowded with wounded men who were unable to be evacuated in the constant barrage. Booth was concerned with how long his men could hold, but he was happy to see Ramirez and the replacements.

Booth quickly briefed the lieutenant and assigned him to take charge of the platoon protecting the approaches to the castle. Booth then told Ramirez to link up with his forward observer, who would take him down to his position. Grabbing the FO, Ramirez climbed the basement ladder, but just as he reached the top, a shell hit the castle right over his head and sent him and the FO tumbling to the floor, knocking Ramirez unconscious. When he came to, Ramirez was directed by Booth to wait until morning to link up with his platoon.

By the following morning, the intense shelling had ceased. Booth and Ramirez went out to check on the men and ascertain damage. Strewn about the hill were the bodies of American and German soldiers, many of them killed in the previous day's attack. Ramirez later recalled that many wounded GIs had bandaged themselves and stuck to their positions, gamely waiting, ready to continue the fight.[311]

After only a week of combat against the 1st Infantry Division, the 47th Volks Grenadier Division had been devastated. Because of the losses it had suffered in that short time, it could no longer be considered a full-strength division, forcing its redesignation as "Kampfgruppe"—a fate reserved for only the most battered units. Even so, it had prevented a breakthrough by the 1st Division. The 1st Division G2 section later complimented the 47th Volks Grenadier Division in its monthly enemy activities report as being "the most suicidally stubborn unit this division has encountered on the continent."[312]

By this time, additional reinforcements for the LXXXI Corps were necessary, and they came in the form of the 3rd Fallschirmjaeger Division. Nearly destroyed in the fighting at St. Lô during the Allied breakout, this division was subsequently sent to Holland to rebuild. Its replacements were mostly inexperienced men and boys, some as young as sixteen, and all recruited from the *Hitler Jugend* (Youth) organization. They were described as being "short on experience, but long on Nazi ideology." Apparently full of military ardor, this parachute division entered the line in front of the 16th Infantry on November 26. Though German paratroopers had the reputation of being tough fighters, just applying the name to a group of conscripts does not confer toughness, at least in this instance. As a result, this division failed to acquit itself as well as its predecessors in the fight against the "Red One."

On November 27, Driscoll's battalion was scheduled to support an attack by CT 18 on Langerwehe, that regiment's final objective for this offensive. The 1st Battalion's objective was the town of Gut Merberich, and its attack jumped off at first light, with artillery fires preparing the way. Paratroopers from the 3rd Fallschirmjaeger Division arrived in Gut Merberich just before the barrage started, and were in no way ready for the concentrated fire. Terrified by the rounds that were suddenly and unexpectedly exploding in their midst, the troopers scrambled to find cover in basements and culverts. Driscoll's men followed on the heels of the barrage and entered Gut Merberich virtually unopposed, capturing the town and most of the paratroopers, some sixty in all. Referring to the performance of his new charges, a captured German NCO, hardened by his experiences on the Eastern Front, wryly commented that "the iron in the hearts of these kids turned into lead in their pants."[313] From Gut Merberich, the 1st Battalion advanced on Langerwehe and, in cooperation with CT 18, captured that town the evening of November 28.

Luchem

By November 28, the 1st Infantry Division line stretched from near Merode to the Frenzerberg castle, but it lagged behind the line of the 104th Division to the north. Collins wanted the line straightened and, to that end, ordered Huebner to take the town of Luchem. Gibb assigned the job to Driscoll. Over the next three days, patrols scouted toward Luchem to reconnoiter routes, locate enemy positions, and observe enemy activities.

The patrols determined that the town was defended by about two companies of paratroopers, one company each from the 8th and 9th Fallschirmjaeger Regiments, supported by mortars and no more than three tanks. There were few mined areas, and the paratroopers had erected a roadblock on the road that led into the town from Langerwehe.[314]

When the 1st Battalion was pulled out of the line on November 19, it had fewer than 380 men remaining from an authorized strength of over 800. While in reserve, its losses were made good by the arrival of some four hundred untried replacements, which meant that the battalion had more green soldiers than veterans for the attack on Luchem. This alone, Driscoll realized, was cause for concern; the fact that the attack was to occur at night in wintry weather only increased the potential for failure. To compensate for the lack of experience in his battalion, Driscoll secured a platoon each of M3 Stuart tanks, M4 Shermans, and M10 tank destroyers (in each instance, one platoon comprised four vehicles), as well as a platoon from the regimental AT Company. Driscoll hoped that the added firepower of these units would bolster the confidence of the new men.[315]

Driscoll received the attack order on December 2. Calling his key leaders to his CP about noon that day, he issued his plan. Companies A and B would lead the attack, A on the right, B on the left, with C in reserve. Company A, commanded by Captain Stanley Winters, would take the south and eastern part of the town. Company B, under Captain Frank Kolb, was to move west of Luchem, secure support positions at, and cut, the Autobahn, then secure the west and northern sections of town. Driscoll attached the Stuart tanks to Winters and the tank destroyers to Kolb. All else remained under battalion control. "Surprise is our biggest asset in taking this town," stated Driscoll, "so we're not laying on any artillery preparation." Considering the fanatical defense the Germans had been putting up since Aachen, this raised a few eyebrows. Driscoll went on to explain that there would be "curtain fires which will be laid on to box the town as soon as we contact the enemy and start our push into town."[316] After Driscoll laid out the rest of the details for indirect fire support, he described the logistics and communications plan, then asked for questions. Line-of-Departure time was set for 6:00 a.m. on December 3.

The following morning, a patrol from A Company departed early and quietly eliminated an outpost—six men with a machine gun—in the path of the company's advance. Company B also sent out a patrol that reduced a similar position. The rest of the men of A and B Companies, crouched in their positions west of Langerwehe, nervously waited for the final order to move. Right on time, the companies jumped off in the foggy darkness and headed north. The weather was cold, and a light drizzle further added to the men's discomfort as they spread out and proceeded across the flat open terrain.

About forty-five minutes later, the two companies slipped past the outposts destroyed by their patrols and continued on to

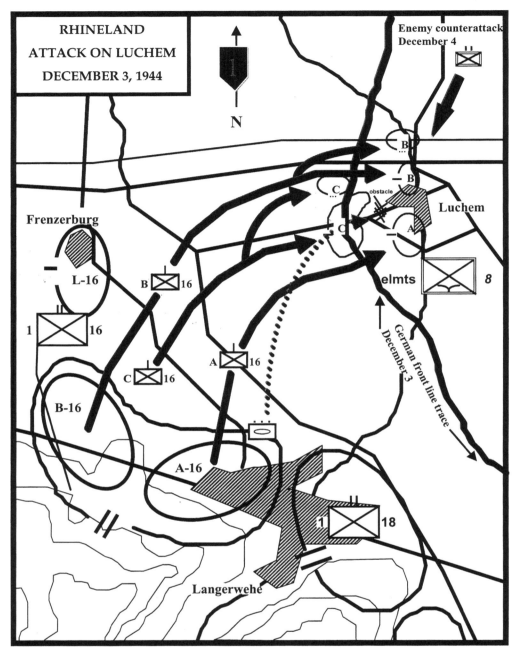

Map 8-19.

Luchem. The following tanks and TDs passed through the busted roadblock and peeled off into the streets. The tank assault was too much for some paratroopers. With American infantry behind them, and now tanks in front of them, many surrendered without firing a shot.[317] Others, however, fought back.

For the next hour and a half, both companies methodically cleared cellars and houses against occasionally stiff resistance. The major trouble Winters and Kolb experienced was actually from bypassed positions on the outskirts of Luchem. Both companies ended up turning platoons around to fight these positions. In one scrap, Private Robert T. Henry's platoon was held up by machine-gun emplacements armed with a total of five guns. Henry, one of the green troops experiencing his first taste of combat, volunteered to take out the positions. Attempting to race across 150 yards of open terrain, he was struck by a burst of fire about halfway across. Bleeding profusely, he staggered forward in a determined effort to finish the job, but was mortally wounded only yards from the enemy nest. However, the young soldier's determined attack unnerved the defenders, who abandoned their post. As they fled, the other men in Henry's platoon leapt to the attack and captured or killed every one of the Germans. Henry's action made it possible for his comrades to seize and advance beyond a tough position without further casualties. For his bravery he was awarded the regiment's seventh Medal of Honor.[318]

With assistance from the tanks and TDs, position after position was destroyed or captured. One machine-gun position in a culvert near the Autobahn caused Kolb's men a great deal of problems, but it was soon silenced by a hail of grenades. Within seconds, about seventy paratroopers poured out of the

their objectives, Winters' A Company entering Luchem undetected as Kolb's B Company reached the Autobahn. Company B then turned to enter the town from the west, also unobserved. About 7:30 a.m. both companies sent platoons forward to clear the town, just as the artillery curtain descended to cut off the German defenders. Concurrently, Driscoll ordered the tanks and TDs forward as support, and all eight vehicles rumbled out of Langerwehe, headed for Luchem. After crossing the fifteen-hundred meter open area at a gallop, the lead tank crashed through the roadblock at the town's entrance and rolled into

culvert like so many stirred-up ants. Scrambling over the Autobahn embankment to the north side, they ran directly into the waiting guns of B Company's overwatch platoon. All these Germans were either captured or killed..[319]

The battle was going well, so Driscoll moved his CP into Luchem and co-located with Winters' CP. By noon, the town was secure, and by 3:00 p.m. Driscoll had brought up C Company to set up a 360-degree defense. The battalion now held Luchem with A Company holding the east and northeast sector, B Company holding the north and northwest sector along the Autobahn, and C Company holding the south and west. The tanks, AT guns, and machine-guns were sited to meet the inevitable counterattack, and patrols were sent forward in anticipation of the enemy's reaction.

That night, minor clashes flared up at various points around the perimeter as enemy units probed for weak spots and approach routes. The Germans returned in force the following afternoon. About 2:30 p.m. on December 4, six German assault guns took up defilade positions and began lobbing rounds into Luchem to soften up the American positions. Two hours later, the enemy assault force, comprising two companies of paratroopers, was spotted assembling in a draw north of the town. Supporting artillery, called to break up the troop concentration, responded too slowly, firing just as the Germans came boiling up out of the draw. To the Germans' dismay, however, the American artillery was quick to adjust, and soon rounds were decimating the attackers. Only about thirty of these men made it through the barrage, and most of these were cut down by small-arms fire before reaching the town.[320] By 5:45 p.m., it was all over. Luchem remained in American hands.

Recalling his men's performance at Luchem, Driscoll later stated, "This was one of the best-executed attacks the battalion ever made. The whole operation worked like clockwork, and if I had to do it all over again, I'd use precisely the same tactics."[321] Despite the inexperience of most of the 1st Battalion's men, and the difficult weather conditions and open terrain, the battalion was able to carry out its mission almost exactly according to plan. In seizing the town, Driscoll's men captured almost two hundred Germans, destroyed six tanks and, in conjunction with artillery fire, killed, wounded, or captured another two companies of the 8th and 9th Fallschirmjaeger Regiments. Most of the credit for the battalion's success goes to the experienced officers and old soldiers of the battalion, who took a bunch of green troops and got them to perform like veterans. Thus, within a thirty-six-hour period, the battalion had destroyed or captured enemy forces almost equaling its own strength—an impressive performance indeed.

In some ways, the attack at Luchem was a fitting way to end the Siegfried Line Campaign. It was the kind of attack that the First Army commanders had hoped to launch at the campaign's outset. Hodges, Collins, and Huebner had all wanted to breach the West Wall in one fell swoop. However, when Eisenhower shifted the supply priority to Montgomery's 21st Army Group, the First Army was forced to conduct limited attacks against the Siegfried Line defenses. Too much time was spent trying to breach the line using economy-of-force measures, which allowed the Germans to reinforce the line despite the massive losses they had suffered since June 6. As a result, what should have been a one-week effort stretched into a battle lasting a full three months.

The good news was, the 1st Infantry Division had chewed up or destroyed three divisions (12th and 47th Volks Grenadier, 3rd Fallschirmjaeger), and severely damaged elements of several others. But the victory was costly for the Red One: in the bitter fighting between September 12 and December 9, some 3,352 men of the division were killed, wounded, or captured; of that total, 1,221 had belonged to the 16th Infantry. Through a great deal of suffering, the division had finally reached the Roer valley, and it seemed a time for a period of refitting was appropriate. On December 5, however, CT 16 pulled out of its positions around Luchem and Gressenich and moved to relieve the 60th Infantry (9th Division) of its sector at Rötgen. It remained in that sector for five days, until it was relieved by the 309th Infantry (78th Division) on December 11. The combat team was finally sent to a rest camps at Verviers and Herve in Belgium for long overdue rest, replacements, refitting, and retraining.

The stint at Verviers was a welcome change for the men of the 16th Infantry. For over two months, they had borne the brunt of heavy fighting in the cold, wet Hürtgen Forest. Now they were billeted in dry, warm buildings with clean bunks and hot showers. It was a well-earned reward for their efforts in October and November. In the words of John Baumgartner:

> Casualties had been very high, shell fire had decimated companies; counterattacks had taken heavy tolls; it had been a time of terrible battle: a time to try the soul of a great combat unit. Through the days and nights of fierce battle to the south and east of Aachen, through the costly, unrelenting fight for the Hamich area, through the frightful shelling with the terrific losses from tree bursts in the Hürtgen forests around Hamich, the 16th had continued to press forward, or if unable to advance, to hold its dearly purchased ground. If ever a regiment deserved a rest, it was this prime fighting outfit.[322]

In addition to the warmth and dryness, a number of the soldiers received an additional reward. Those who had been with the regiment in North Africa and Sicily had earned enough points to be rotated back to the States. Though all of these men were happy to be going home, no doubt many of them felt pangs of sadness, even some guilt, for leaving their friends behind. There is a close bond among combat soldiers: the product of shared danger and privation. It is a connection fully understood only by those who have shared the frontline experience, and it generally proves to be lifelong. Breaking those ties, particularly when it means leaving one's buddies at the front, almost always arouses sadness and guilt after the initial elation over going home had passed. At a time when morale should be high due to the expectations of more comfortable surroundings, there is, in reality, a dampening effect on veterans when they leave, as well as on those who remain behind.

Two soldiers who remained were privates Kenneth A. Lees and John J. Wendland of I Company. On their first night in Verviers, however, all they were anxious to share was the experience of consuming a little liquor to get the war off their minds. Attempting to get into the local pub, they found it packed, so they ended up in the town square debating what to do. One of them noticed that mass was starting in the town's Catholic church and suggested they go to the service. "It's something to do," one said, and in they went.

The mass was conducted in Flemish, but still made a great impression on the men. They participated fully in all the liturgical rites, even taking communion. The mass had ended when it became evident to them that they were only GIs in the church. As they left the sanctuary, the priest, an old, gray-haired gentlemen, asked them in impeccable English if they would wait a few moments until after he saw off the parishioners. They did, and when he returned, he introduced himself as Father Michel and requested that they join him in his rectory. To this, they also agreed.

At the rectory, the two men and Father Michel gathered in the priest's study, sitting around a warm fire while talking over a wide range of topics and enjoying a few glasses of wine. It was certainly a different kind of evening from the one Lees, Wendland, and their buddies had envisaged when they first started out. After several hours of pleasant conversation, Father Michel offered to provide them with rosaries, St. Christopher medals, and the like, should they be interested. They replied they would appreciate these items, and the priest said he would have them delivered to the soldiers. As they were standing in the door, Father Michel invited them back any time, and the two men trudged through the snow, returning to the cozy little schoolhouse where Company I was billeted.[323]

The departure of the North Africa and Sicily veterans from the 16th Infantry resulted in the loss of a wealth of combat experience, wisdom, and leadership. These losses, coupled with the influx of additional replacements, prompted Colonel Gibb to develop training plans to prepare the regiment for its next round of combat. The training was to start the day after the regimental awards ceremony, on December 16. That day, however, men could hear the rumble of battle to the southeast of Verviers. Rumors began to circulate about a breakthrough by the Germans. Soon, a warning order arrived to prepare to move the regiment south. All the training Gibb had planned for his new soldiers would now have to be conducted "on the job."

That afternoon, Wendland, Lees, and the others dropped by the church to let Father Michel know they were moving out. He was already aware of the breakthrough by way of the civil-ian grapevine, and presented several rosaries and St. Mary medallions to the men. He also told them that he would pray for them and include them in his general intercessions of every mass "until this war was over." The following day, these five men, as well as the rest of CT 16, boarded trucks that took them south to build a defensive line near Robertville, Belgium.

Ardennes-Alsace Campaign
December 16-January 25, 1945

The event that caused the early departure of the regiment from Herve and Verviers has since become known as the "Battle of the Bulge," but to the German soldiers conducting the mission, it was known by its codename Wacht Am Rhine ("Watch on the Rhine"). The plan for the offensive took form in the mind of Adolf Hitler back on September 16 when, during a situation briefing at the Wolf's Lair (Hitler's headquarters in East Prussia), the Führer announced that he had decided to launch a counteroffensive through the Ardennes with the military objective of seizing Antwerp and cutting off British forces in the north. The political objective was to create battlefield circumstances that would induce the Western Allies to seek a separate, negotiated peace, thereby creating a rift between the Western Allies and the Soviet Union and, not incidentally, enabling Germany to turn full-force on the Soviet Union. Accomplishing this aim, however, would require the rebuilding of the battered German armies on the Western Front. Plans were rapidly developed to this end, which included provisions for the recall and rehabilitation of several SS panzer divisions from the Eastern Front to spearhead the offensive.

The zone of the Ardennes through which Hitler intended to launch his offensive extended from Monshau, Belgium, in the north to just south of Etterlbruck, Luxembourg, in the south. The major commands selected to conduct Wacht Am Rhine were the Sixth Panzer Army, commanded by Colonel General Josef "Sepp" Dietrich; the Fifth Panzer Army, commanded by General Hasso-Eccard von Manteuffel; and the Seventh Army, commanded by General Erich Brandenberger. The armies constituted Army Group B, under Field Marshal Walther Model's overall command. (Fifteenth Army, commanded by Lieutenant General Gustav-Adolf von Zangen, was part of Army Group B but did not participate in the offensive.)

Dietrich's Sixth Panzer Army was situated in the northern sector of the zone and was to undertake Army Group B's main effort. Its mission was to penetrate the American front, cross the Meuse River at or near Liège, then turn north and attack toward the Albert Canal and the final objective, Antwerp. Manteuffel's Fifth Panzer Army in the center would attack due west toward Namur, where it would cross the Meuse. From there it would turn north to support Dietrich's attacks toward Antwerp, and protect the German left flank of the penetration. Brandenberger's Seventh Army, composed almost entirely of leg infantry divisions, was responsible for protecting the Fifth Panzer Army's left flank from counterattacks by Patton's Third

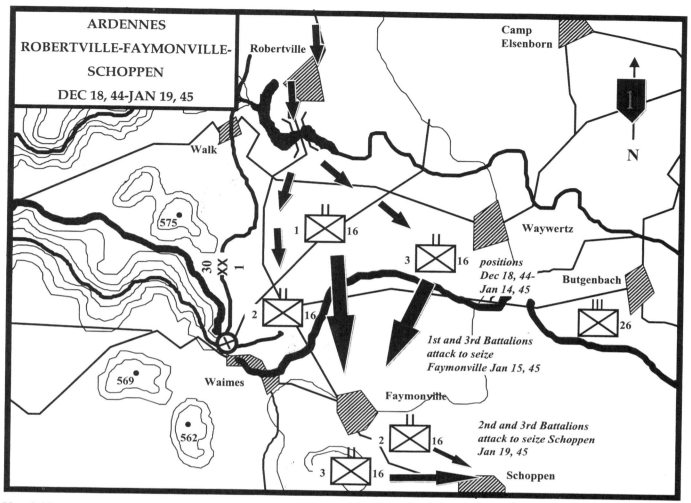

Map 8-20.

Army to the south.

The area in the Ardennes selected for the main push by the Fifth and Sixth Panzer Armies was held by Hodges' First Army, specifically the V and VIII Corps. Badly bruised in the autumn fighting along the Siegfried Line, both corps had been relatively dormant since the end of November when the Hürtgen Forest finally fell. The area the Germans had targeted for their primary thrust was now held by the battered 28th Infantry Division and several new divisions, which had been assigned to their respective sectors—which, it was thought, would remain fairly quiet—to initiate them to combat. Additionally, the First Army zone had been broadened to accommodate Eisenhower's decision to make the 21st Army Group's offensive the main effort in September; as a result, units held frontages that were doctrinally too wide for their capabilities under normal combat situations. In short, the conditions for an attack through the Ardennes were about as favorable for the Germans as Hitler could have hoped.

The spearhead for Wacht Am Rhine would be the I SS

Panzer Corps of the Sixth Army. Commanded by Lieutenant General of Waffen SS Hermann Priess, the I SS Panzer Corps consisted of the 1st SS Panzer Division, 12th SS Panzer Division, 277th Volks Grenadier Division, and the 16th Infantry's nemeses from the fights around Aachen and Luchem, the 3rd Fallschirmjaeger and 12th Volks Grenadier Divisions. The corps' mission was to first punch a hole through the sector held by the 99th Infantry Division with the three infantry divisions, after which the 1st and 12th SS Panzer Divisions would advance to seize crossings over the Meuse River. The II SS Panzer Corps, composed of the 2nd and 9th SS Panzer Divisions, would pass through Dietrich's troops on the Meuse River line and speed northwest to seize Antwerp. Once through the 99th Infantry Division, the 3rd Fallschirmjaeger, 12th Volks Grenadier, and 277th Volks Grenadier Divisions were to hold the shoulder of the penetration to forestall an Allied counterattack into the Sixth Army's right flank. By early December, all the pieces of the complicated plan were essentially in place. Now, it was just a matter of waiting for the weather to turn bad enough to negate Allied air superiority. That opportunity came on the morning of December 16.

At 7:00 a.m. that day, following a preparatory artillery barrage, troops of the 277th Volks Grenadier and 12th Volks Grenadier Divisions charged through the woods into positions held by the 99th Division's 393rd and 394th Infantry Regiments, along the line of Lanzerath-Losheimergraben-Krinkelt. By noon, the 99th's reserves had all been committed, and the division was engaged in bitter fighting as the lead elements of the I SS Panzer Corps tried to punch through. Requests went out to the VII Corps for reinforcements and, by midnight, Major General Clift Andrus (who had assumed command of the 1st Infantry Division on December 11), had dispatched the 26th Infantry to Camp Elsenborn, Belgium, and alerted the 16th and 18th Infantry Regiments for movement on the morrow. As it turned out, CT 16 did not move for two days.

About 6:30 a.m. on December 18, CT 16 proceeded to Robertville, twenty-two miles to the southeast of Verviers. The night before, German paratroopers had reportedly been dropped along the routes from Verviers to block reinforcements from that direction, but they were unable to effectively coordinate their effort. As a result, the combat team was able to make it to Robertville unchallenged. From Robertville, the 2nd Battalion, now under the command of Lieutenant Colonel Walter H. Grant, was sent to Waimes and deployed on the regiment's left flank, where it linked up with the 120th Infantry Regiment of the 30th Division. To the east, the 3rd Battalion deployed along a line with L Company in Weywertz; I Company, dug in on high ground, covered a couple of demolished bridge sites along a tributary of the Amblève River; and K Company positioned itself just southeast of Robertville. The 1st Battalion went into reserve positions near Robertville.

Once in Weywertz, Captain Bouchard, L Company, assigned sectors to his three platoons. About 3:00 p.m., Private Oliver A. Carey was assigned his position and told to dig in. The area was eerily quiet; there had been no sign of enemy activity and Carey's buddy doubted the Germans were anywhere near. After struggling to dig a foxhole in the frozen ground, Carey and his partner were told to move their gear into a house with the rest of his squad, then go get evening chow. He and his squad members had just returned to the house from the chow line and were sitting down to eat, when in walked five very young German soldiers who demanded "Hands up!" Not inclined to argue with the five machine pistols leveled at them, Carey and his buddies were marched back to German lines. The enemy was indeed out there.[324]

Lieutenant Colonel Horner learned the same lesson when he went into Waimes. About mid-morning, two Germans (apparently from the 1st SS Panzer Division), one a captain, the other dressed as an American soldier, walked into a school house and captured the 47th Field Hospital that was stationed there. As the medical personnel were loading their patients in ambulances for the journey into captivity, one of the ambulance drivers escaped and alerted other American troops on the outskirts of town. Soon, three half-tracks with quad-50 machine-guns rolled into the schoolyard and scared off the two Germans. Horner arrived a short time later and directed the evacuation to continue, but this time in the opposite direction.[325]

Once in position, the regiment sent reconnaissance patrols toward the south and west. The 2nd Battalion patrolled into Malmèdy, where they made contact with the 120th Infantry. A 1st Battalion patrol also made contact with the 120th Infantry in Walk, and the 3rd Battalion contacted the 26th Infantry's right-flank units in positions west of Butgenbach. Gradually, noises and other indicators revealed the enemy's presence in the area, but no appreciable contact was made with the Germans that day or night.

On the 19th, E Company pushed out from Waimes to scout into Faymonville. As the company approached the town, it received fire from several locations, revealing that the Germans held the town. In fact, subsequent patrols determined that the town was teeming with enemy troops and tanks and, as the company pulled back to Waimes, artillery fire was directed into the town to disrupt the enemy activities.[326]

While no major contact was made on the 19th, the Germans in Faymonville began probing actions that night. First, a patrol explored I Company positions at the bridge sites and, after being driven off, scouted K Company positions to the west. Later, E Company reported enemy activity to its front. Near midnight, a force estimated at about two companies rushed the 1st Platoon of I Company. Fierce fighting broke out at close range as small groups of enemy soldiers attempted to infiltrate the 1st Platoon's defenses. Two Sherman tanks came up the road and helped I Company drive off the attack. At about the same time, L Company was also hit with an attack, but in both cases the enemy was repulsed.[327]

The enemy force building in the Faymonville area was part of the 3rd Fallschirmjaeger Division. After the bloody nose they received from the 16th Infantry at the Rösslerhof and Luchem, one might well imagine that the paratroopers were unhappy to learn that their old foes now faced them again at Faymonville. Unhappy or not, over the next several days, the paratroopers conducted probing actions all along the regiment's line. On the 21st, the 26th Infantry received a severe attack by the 12th SS Panzer Division, which was trying to break through the regiment's front. With the help of twelve battalions of artillery, CT 26 was able to beat back the assaults. The failure by the enemy to achieve a penetration prompted Gibb to speculate that the next effort would be made against the 16th Infantry. Accordingly, an alert went out along the line to the 16th.

A minor attack hit Company F late in the morning on the 22nd, followed that evening by a stronger effort against the 3rd Battalion. In both instances, the enemy was repulsed. And so it went for the next several days: probes here, small attacks there, but no concerted efforts against CT 16. As each hour passed and the Americans built up their defenses, the Germans' chances of successfully attacking the 16th Infantry waned. Each day saw additional mines emplaced, wire obstacles strung, and fields of fire improved. Over the next three weeks, the regiment conducted heavy patrolling in the snow and ice, but combat was limited mainly to clashes between opposing patrols and the occasional probe.

The winter of 1944-45 was one of the coldest and snowiest ever recorded in Europe. The severe weather was responsible for as many casualties in CT 16 as enemy action—maybe more. By January 8, the snow had become so deep and troublesome that 1st Division engineers had to use bulldozers to keep open the vehicle supply lines into the regimental areas.

While the 3rd Fallschirmjaeger Division made their desultory efforts against the 16th Infantry, to the south of the 1st Division line, the Battle of the Bulge raged at St. Vith, Bastogne, Stoumont, and hundreds of other locations. One by one, the attacks were defeated. By mid-January, the Fifth and Sixth Panzer Armies had shot their respective bolts, and were fighting desperately for their very survival.

On January 15, the 12th Army Group began a general counteroffensive designed to cut off the German salient and crush the forces trapped between the First Army on the north and the Third Army on the south. The 16th Infantry's initial objective in this drive was the town of Faymonville. About 5:00 a.m. that morning, the regiment jumped off in deep snow. The 1st Battalion's objective was the town itself; the 2nd Battalion would advance on the left in support of the 1st Battalion's attack. The 3rd Battalion advanced between the 2nd Battalion and the 18th Infantry, which had come up on CT 16's left flank. Before Driscoll's men entered Faymonville, severe fire stopped Company A in the fields to the north. Meanwhile, Companies B and C were able to reach the town. A house-to-house battle ensued, lasting all day, through the night, and into the following morning.

While the 1st Battalion battled to take Faymonville, I Company dug in to the east to prepare for counterattacks. Stumbling upon a shell hole right where they were ordered to dig in by a stand of woods, Lees and Wendland began to dig the hole deeper and turn it into a fighting position. Gravitating to the position, the three other men who had spent the evening at Father Michel's rectory joined Lees and Wendland and dug their holes next to the post. Artillery began to fall in the area, and as it became heavier, the men dug faster. Suddenly, a shell shattered a tree standing above the holes and sent shrapnel into all three positions. Wendland's leg went numb and he realized that he had been wounded. In calling to the other four men, he determined from their responses that they had also been wounded by the shellburst. No one could move to the rear for aid because of the continued shelling. The men lay in the bitter cold all day. As each hour passed, the danger grew that one or more of them would die from loss of blood or exposure. In the end, however, all survived to be evacuated to a field hospital that evening. It seemed to the men that Father Michel's

prayers for their survival had been heard.[328]

Once Faymonville was cleared by the 1st Battalion, the 2nd Battalion was ordered to continue the advance and seize Schoppen to the southeast. Grant proceeded toward Schoppen, but after the battalion entered a wooded area half-way to the village, it stumbled into fierce resistance on three sides and was forced to withdraw. The following day, no effort was made to advance, but the 1st Battalion moved farther south to position itself west of Schoppen. Gibb ordered Horner to take Schoppen on the 18th, and the following day the 3rd Battalion attacked in a driving blizzard with the 2nd Battalion in support. Making their way through heavy snowdrifts while the wind drove snowflakes into their faces, Horner's men wearily forced their way into the town. The severe weather conditions turned out to be an ally of the battalion, however, as it allowed them to reach Schoppen without being detected. Karl Wolf (now commanding I Company) recalled:

We had a platoon of medium tanks assigned to the company. The tanks with their tracks had no problem with the snow. I remember riding on the back of one of the advanced tanks. We did not fire artillery before the attack and, with the wind blowing in our faces, the Germans could not hear the motors of our tanks. They didn't expect we would be attacking in such miserable weather."[329]

The Germans holding the town were hunkered down trying to stay warm and were unaware of the 3rd Battalion's presence until it was too late. Before noon, the town was captured, and K Company secured the high ground to the south.

The weather was terribly hard on the troops. Though some were able to get inside captured houses, others were forced to man positions in the bitter cold. A wounded soldier who was not located quickly by aid men or his buddies often froze to death.

The night Schoppen fell, Wolf made his way back to the 3rd Battalion CP in a jeep. Passing by the woods where the 2nd Battalion had been ambushed two days before, he heard a noise and ordered his driver to stop: "Sure enough, an NCO stumbled [out of the woods] in bad shape. He was almost incoherent. His legs were frozen to the knees and he had no feeling in them. I believe he had been walking around in circles for over a day. We took him back and had the medics evacuate him, but I am sure he lost his legs."[330]

As the 3rd Battalion attacked Schoppen, the 1st attacked south toward Elbertingen, and the 2nd pushed south to the Amblève River. Once along this line, CT 16 held in place until January 23, when the direction of attack shifted east toward the West Wall. Over the next five days, the regiment continued to push east against limited resistance, taking the towns of Modersheid, Mirfeld, and Valender. The combat team remained in the vicinity of Valender until February 5. On that date it was transported north, back through Robertville, Eupen,

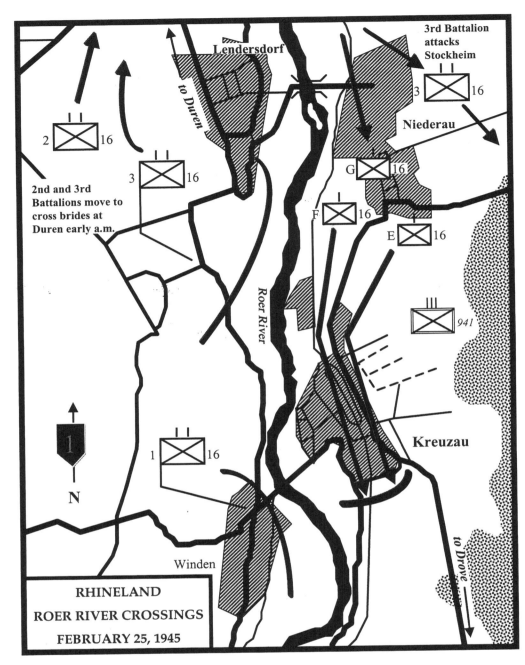

Map 8-21.

stand on Elsenborn Ridge, backed by the veteran 1st and 2nd Infantry Divisions, as anything. Their actions on the ridge were largely responsible for the I SS Panzer Corps' failure to break through to the Meuse River. Too much of the I SS Panzer Corps' combat power had been depleted by its efforts to break through the 99th and the 2nd Divisions. Had that breakthrough occurred, the American position at Bastogne would have been a great deal more tenuous, and likely would have fallen, possibly resulting in a different conclusion to the campaign.

Rhineland Campaign (Phase 2)—Roer River

The new regimental line centered on the town of Winden and overlooked the Roer River. The area on the opposite shore was dominated by high ground to the south of Kreuzau and defended by elements of the 353rd Infantry Division. The Germans defending the zone through which the 1st Division would have to attack had had several months to reconnoiter and prepare their positions to repel an attack from across the Roer. Though the defenses were well-built and situated, and would likely cause the devastation of a force attacking frontally, Gibb had no plans to oblige his foe if he could avoid it.

For three weeks, Gibb and his staff developed plans to conduct an assault crossing of the river. Upstream from Winden, however, were the dams across the Roer from which the Germans had increased the flow of water, raising the river levels. Additionally, by mid-February, the snows had mostly turned to rain, causing the river to remain at consistently high levels and thus preventing an easy crossing. After toying with several ideas—one featuring the construction of assault bridges, others, a crossing by assault boats—Gibb settled on a plan that called for the 2nd and 3rd Battalions to force a bridge at Düren, in the 8th Infantry Division's sector, on

and Gressenich, and relieved the 13th Infantry near Schevenhutte, where the 16th had begun its attack on Hamich two and a half months before.

For the 16th Infantry, the Battle of the Bulge was over. The fighting to hold the northern shoulder was important to the overall victory in this campaign. Much has been written about the desperate fighting at St. Vith and the 101st Airborne Division's stand at Bastogne. Those units deserve high praise for their deeds, but in reality, the ultimate American victory was as much the result of the green 99th Infantry Division's heroic

February 24. Once across the bridge, Grant's 2nd Battalion would attack south to take the Kreuzau defenses in the flank, while Driscoll's 1st Battalion would feint an assault crossing to draw attention, then support the 2nd Battalion's attack from the high ground across the river, just north of Winden. The 7th Field Artillery Battalion would also lay down a steel barrage east and south of the town to isolate it from reinforcements. The 3rd Battalion (now commanded by Ed Wozenski, who had taken over the battalion on February 5 when Horner became the regimental executive officer) would follow the 2nd Battalion across the bridge, then drive east to seize an area of wooded hills southwest of Stockheim, thereby protecting the 8th Division's right flank. Once Kreuzau fell, the 1st Battalion would cross on a footbridge hastily thrown across the river at Kaufferath.[331] From there, CT 16 would continue its drive east.

After suffering through several Luftwaffe attacks on the night of February 24-25, the 2nd Battalion began crossing the bridge at 8:30 a.m. By 9:30 a.m., the 3rd Battalion had also crossed, and by noon, both battalions were assembled near Niederau and ready to attack. At noon, Grant's men moved south out of Niederau: Company E with an attached platoon of Shermans on the left, Company F on the right, and G Company in reserve. The two companies crossed a large open field where they were exposed to direct observation and fire. So focused were the defenders toward the 1st Battalion's feint to the west, however, that Grant's troops were not engaged until a machine-gun located in the ruins of an old factory building opened up on them when they were only 150 yards from the edge of the town.

Smothering that position with return fire, both companies bounded forward and were at the first stretch of houses in a flash. Using the main road south through town as a boundary, the two lead companies advanced, encountering pockets of opposition and sniper fire. In response, the E Company commander called the Shermans forward, and the tankers blasted any position that offered resistance. The companies continued to move through the town, encountering no opposition until they came abreast of the road leading across the river into the 1st Battalion's area. Ater clearing three-fourths of the town, both companies ran into a second, more determined, line of positions.

Grant moved his troops on line and developed a heavy volume of fire against the German positions. The tank platoon and two tank destroyers also added their weight to the effort. The overwhelming firepower was too much for the defenders, who broke off and retreated to the southeast toward Drove. By 5:00 p.m., the town was in Grant's hands, and he prepared for a counterattack. It never came. Instead, Grant ordered G Company to continue the advance on Drove. By 7:30, that town, too, was in American hands. The attack had cost the 2nd Battalion fewer than ten casualties, and Grant's men had killed fifteen Germans and captured fifty-one, all from the 941st Infantry Regiment.[332]

Meanwhile, Wozenski's attack in the hills did not go as well. Though the 3rd Battalion seized one hill with ease, the failure of the 8th Division troops to take Stockheim caused Wozenski's men a serious problem. They were being picked off by German defenders in the town, which was outside the battalion's sector. The battalion could do little except return fire at the town.

The 16th Infantry made small attacks to the southeast for the next two days while the remainder of the 1st Infantry Division crossed the Roer. On February 26, Gibb received orders to attack and seize Vetweiss the following day. Vetweiss was an important road hub needed by the division for further advances to the east. After Stockheim fell, the 2nd Battalion took Soller by 2:00 a.m. on February 27 and, a few hours later, B Company seized Frangenheim to the southeast of Soller. Vetweiss was the next town to the east and Gibb assigned Wozenski's battalion to capture it.

The way to Vetweiss lay across twenty-five hundred yards of open fields, where an attacking force would be in full view of the town's defenders. Wozenski directed I Company to take Vetweiss, and held K and L Companies in readiness if I Company ran into trouble.

After receiving the battalion order, Captain Wolf issued his plan to his platoon leaders about 7:30 a.m., February 27. He directed his platoon leaders to mount their men on the company's attached armored vehicles for the advance into Vetweiss. The 3rd Platoon, mounted on M-10 TDs, would advance on the north (left); Wolf and the 2nd Platoon would ride M4 Shermans in the center; and the 1st Platoon, riding on M3 Stuarts, would advance on the south. The latter would also be responsible for peppering a stand of woods to the south, the suspected location of enemy AT positions. Once at the edge of town, the troops were to dismount and each platoon would secure a portion of the town in coordination with their armored platoons. After giving his orders, Wolf and the platoon leaders reviewed the plan by viewing the route of advance from an attic in the town of Soller. From there, they could see the entire route into Vetweiss. Promptly at noon, a twenty-minute barrage by the 7th Field Artillery Battalion began falling on the objective.[333]

As the barrage pounded the town, Wolf ordered the tanks forward. Within three hundred meters of the start, it became apparent that the recent snows and rain had saturated the fields, and the tank destroyers began to bog down on the left. The drivers attempted to swerve back onto the road leading to Vetweiss, but before any reached it, all four TDs had stuck fast. As the 3rd Platoon dismounted and headed for Vetweiss, the other two platoons ground forward, the light tanks spraying the woods with machine-gun and 37mm fire as they went.

About seven hundred meters from the town, the light tanks also began to bog down in the fields and the company began to receive AT fire. To the rear, one of the mired tank destroyers was hit and went up in a ball of fire. The crews of the TDs had abandoned their vehicles rather than keeping up a steady fire on the town as directed. This, in turn, allowed the

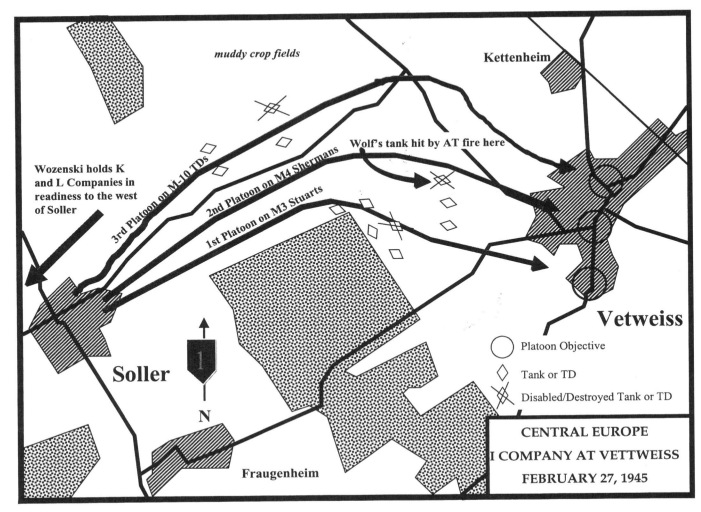

Map 8-22.

enemy AT gunners to shoot at their targets without fear of return fire.

As a result, the lead Sherman, on which Wolf happened to be riding, was struck and set on fire: "I was standing on the deck directly above where the [shell entered the fuel tank and set off an explosion]. A close call! All of us on the outside were burned to some extent, but not seriously. The tank platoon leader, gunner, and assistant gunner were seriously hurt with broken bones and burns. The driver and assistant driver never got out alive."[334]

Wolf was thrown from the tank and, though dazed, gathered his uninjured men and continued the push toward Vetweiss. As he reached the town, he realized that he was accompanied only by a light machine-gun team and his XO, Lieutenant William Jackson, and one platoon leader, Lieutenant Lee Stockwell. To make matters worse, the mired tankers mistook them for Germans and began to spray their area with suppressive fire. After signaling the tankers to shift fire, Wolf collected knots of men as they straggled in and sent them by platoon groups to take their objectives. Somehow, two Shermans

freed themselves and finally joined Wolf at the edge of town. By 1:45 p.m., I Company held most of the town, despite the great difficulties it had encountered. The rest of the 3rd Battalion joined it a short time later to consolidate the company's gains.[335]

Over the next week or so, CT 16 advanced through the Rhineland, seizing the towns of Gladbach, Luxheim, and Eggersheim. On March 3, the regiment reached Weilerswist, then pursued the retreating foe through Trippelsdorf, Metternich, Hemmerich, and Kardorf, reaching Waldorf on March 6. The 1st Infantry Division advanced all along the line, with the 16th Infantry in the center, the 18th on the right, and the 26th on the left. As the regiment approached the Rhine River, rumors circulated that the 16th would be assigned to take the city of Bonn. Nonetheless, the drive continued, and the men, bone-tired of walking and fighting, plodded eastward until the regiment reached a line running from Alfter to Roisdorf. Since February 25, CT 16 had advanced thirty miles. In ten days, it had advanced farther than it had in the previous five months.

Bonn

In the VII Corps' advance on the Rhine River, the 9th Infantry Division was originally assigned to take Bonn. Then the 9th Armored Division shifted its drive south toward Remagen, and the 1st Infantry Division's sector suddenly widened to include the city. At 2:20 a.m. on March 7, orders confirmed the rumor that Bonn was to be CT 16's responsibility.

Enemy resistance in the advance on the Rhine had been desultory, but as the American army approached the river, opposition to the advance began to stiffen. Many German units were still on the west side of the Rhine, and the few bridges still standing had to be safeguarded until the bulk of the troops and equipment could be evacuated. The bridge in Bonn still stood, though it had been wired for demolition by troops of the 6th Engineer Regiment. Defending Bonn proper were an estimated six hundred troops, a force that consisted of the 253rd Replacement Training Regiment, as well as several flak detachments that had previously defended the city's industrial areas from aerial bombardment. Additionally, the tough fighters of the infamous 1st SS Panzer Division *Leibstandarte Adolf Hitler* (Adolf Hitler Lifeguard) were reported to be in the vicinity of Bonn. Colonel Gibb was unconcerned, however, as he was aware the 1st SS had been gutted by the fighting near Stavelot and La Gleize during the Battle of the Bulge. But even when the 1st SS was in its prime, the men of the Big Red One had proved more than a match for Hitler's best.

Upon receipt of the orders to attack Bonn, Gibb directed his battalion commanders to keep pushing to get as close to the city as possible for the jump-off. By 2:00 p.m. on March 7, the 1st Battalion was in Waldorf, the 2nd was just northeast of Bornheim, and the 3rd was occupying Roisdorf and Alfter, just four kilometers from the west edge of Bonn. CT 16 was still occupying the division's center sector. By dark, the 1st Division was poised to reach the Rhine the following day.

Gibb gave his order to seize Bonn late on the evening of the 7th. Wozenski's 3rd Battalion was to advance on Bonn at 4:00 a.m., March 8, approaching the city down the highway from Roisdorf to the northwest. Driscoll's 1st Battalion, on Wozenski's right, was to approach Bonn from the west via Dransdorf, on the road leading to Bonn from that town. Grant's 2nd Battalion, as reserve, was to follow the 1st Battalion into the city. Each battalion was to form a column of men and vehicles and head straight down its respective road. Like the attack on Luchem, there was to be no artillery preparation. Gibb expected that the lack of any preparatory fires would give the combat team the element of surprise. Once in Bonn, the 3rd Battalion was to seize and occupy the northern part of the city, and the 1st Battalion was to occupy the center, opposite of the Rhine river bridge. The 2nd Battalion would occupy the western third of the city once it came up later in the morning. The 18th Infantry would take the southern fringes of Bonn.

At 4:00 a.m. on March 8, the 3rd Battalion jumped off, K Company leading, followed by I and L. Each company marched down the road in a column of twos, intermixed with a tank and TD platoons. After moving about two kilometers, flares lit up the sky, but since there was no reaction from the soldiers marching along, any enemy watching apparently determined that the column consisted of their own troops moving toward the Rhine to escape the advancing Americans. Machine-gun positions to the south ignored the column and fired off to the west, or sent the stream of bullets harmlessly above the men's heads.

The sense that the Germans were unaware that the long column of troops was composed of Americans became apparent as outpost after outpost was surprised, disarmed, and forced to fall in and march along. At one point, men from K Company picked up a sentry who had been guarding a bivouac site. About an hour later, I Company captured the relief sentry at the same location. Entering the city, the lead platoon of K Company marched down darkened Köln Strasse (street) side-by-side with a detail of German soldiers moving to its post. Rather than open fire and alert the enemy to their presence, the platoon leader just let the detail march along. Just before the platoon turned off toward its objective, one of the enemy troops, seeing one of the new M4E8 Shermans (probably confused into thinking it was friendly because of the muzzle brake on its 76mm gun), yelled across the road, "Welche Panzerdivision ist dieser?" (Which armored division is this?). No one answered. The company just turned left onto Rosental Strasse, and the enemy detail marched off into the night, blissfully unaware that they had come very close to capture—or worse.[336]

As the lead elements marched into the city center, it was eerily quiet. By 5:30 a.m., K Company had reached its assigned objective with hardly a shot fired. Lieutenant Robert Smith and Sergeant Jacks moved down to the edge of the Rhine and discovered, incredibly, that the bridge was still intact. About the same time, however, the troops of the 253rd Replacement Training Regiment finally realized that they had a large American force in their midst, and all hell suddenly broke loose. As rifle and machine-gun fire broke out, several German tanks and assault guns moved into predetermined blocking positions on Rosental and Romer Strassen to protect the approaches to the bridge. A short time later, a flood of German vehicles, filled with troops, pushed into the town from the north, desperately racing for the bridge. The 3rd Battalion's own tanks and TDs went into action, and within an hour had knocked out a Mark VI Tiger, an 88mm AT gun, and eight trucks and smaller vehicles. Not surprisingly, the traffic stopped.

Marching into the city on Herr Strasse, I Company followed K into its assigned objective and joined the fight about 6:30 a.m. About two hours later, L Company also reported that it was in position as well. By that time, it was apparent that the 3rd Battalion had stirred up a hornet's nest. The fighting in the streets of Bonn was confusing and deadly, especially for the Germans. At one point, a sedan carrying a German officer was shot up by the platoon sergeant from 1st Platoon, I Company.

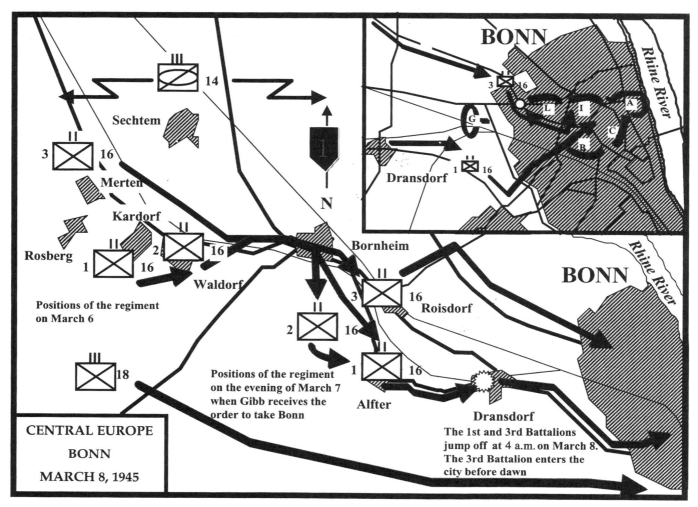

Map 8-23.

After the car rolled to a stop, the dead officer was still sitting up in the rear, looking as if nothing had happened. About thirty minutes later, an enemy tank pulled onto Köln Strasse, and the tank's commander, thinking the car was an American vehicle, fired two rounds, one of which took the officer's head off. The headless officer remained a rather macabre sight that day as fighting swirled around the vehicle.[337]

By 8:30 a.m., A Company from Driscoll's battalion had reached its assigned objective to the south of the 3rd Battalion. It linked up with K Company and extended the line southward along the river. Company C, which had encountered heavier opposition in its approach to the city, was held up again by stiff resistance at Bornheimer Strasse about 10:00 a.m. The company was not be able to break through this position for nine hours. Once they were able to continue to move, however, the men of C Company took up positions that night to the southwest of Company A. Captain John Lycas, the commander, happened to set up his CP that evening in the house where Ludwig van Beethoven was born.[338]

The 18th Infantry, which had been assigned the mission of taking the southern half of Bonn, also encountered a great deal of opposition to its advance, and was not able to secure its objectives until about 6:00 p.m. Additionally, the 2nd Battalion had been held up outside of Roisdorf. Through all this, the bridge, miraculously, was still not blown.

Here was a golden opportunity to get across the Rhine without a great loss of men. Gibb reported to division that the Bonn bridge still stood, and General Andrus responded by ordering the 26th Infantry forward to seize it. The Blue Spaders were directed to pass through the 16th and rush the bridge, but while they were en route, the bridge collapsed in a huge explosion about 9:30 p.m. Bonn had fallen, but a division other than the Red One would reap the glory of seizing a Rhine River bridge.

The next morning and early afternoon were spent mopping up the city. The task was not too difficult, as most of the enemy troops remaining in Bonn knew they had been cut off by the destruction of the bridge and saw little purpose in further resistance. Ultimately, some seventeen hundred Germans were captured. The 16th Infantry's own losses were remarkably light: only six killed, fifty-one wounded, and three missing in action.[339]

The success of the attack on Bonn was remarkable given the condition of the men. By all standards, the morale of the American troops should have been poor. They had been driving hard since crossing the Roer River twelve days earlier. The last four days and nights, they had been on the attack continually and almost always in the rain. In addition, few men had succeeded in getting more than an hour or two of sleep. By one account, they were "haggard and unshaven. Weary eyes were sunk deep into faces that were masks of fatigue and strain." A platoon leader, Lieutenant John Baumgartner, who had joined the 3rd Battalion just before the attack, described his new outfit as a "company of walking dead men." But given the prospect of seizing Bonn by surprise and possibly crossing the Rhine without delays and static fighting (which had been their lot over the past five months), the men responded with "the élan of a rested, fresh veteran unit."[340] The replacements who had filled the regiment after the bloody fighting in the Hürtgen Forest and the Bulge had become superb soldiers, just like their predecessors who had established the regiment's reputation in North Africa, Sicily, and Normandy.

Though the regiment's personnel losses since the beginning of December had not been at the levels sustained during the bloody battles around Aachen and in the Hürtgen Forest, the numbers killed, wounded, or incapacitated by the severe weather and illness had reached a critical stage. Meanwhile, the 12th Army Group was not receiving enough infantry replacements from the United States and was unable to maintain units even near full strength. As a result, Bradley looked for other remedies to the manpower shortage. One entailed the deactivation of certain antiaircraft units and using their personnel as infantry replacements (since the Luftwaffe was all but destroyed).

Another option was to ask for volunteers from all-black engineer and quartermaster units. This was an unprecedented move in the segregated army of that era. In reality, however, it was only another step on the long road to full integration in the army, mandated by President Truman just three years later. As a result, in March 1945, a platoon of black soldiers was assigned to the regiment. Fred Hall remembered:

After a period of training, one platoon was assigned to each regiment of the division. The 16th Infantry platoon was assigned to "B" Company which furnished an experienced white platoon leader and platoon sergeant. It gave "B" Company an extra platoon and it wasn't long before it was committed to combat. These soldiers fought hard and well and suffered many casualties. We were proud to have them as part of the 16th Infantry.[341]

On March 10, most of the regiment was pulled back to a rest area near Bonn. Two companies from the 2nd Battalion were sent to relieve the 32nd Cavalry Squadron of a sector along the Rhine River near Waldorf. Meanwhile, news filtered in that the 9th Armored Division had captured the Ludendorff Bridge at Remagen and troops were pushing through to the other side of the Rhine. The 1st Infantry Division would soon move to the Remagen bridgehead in preparation for a big breakout. On March 15, Gibb received orders to move, and on the 17th, the 1st Battalion crossed the Rhine at Remagen. The remainder of the combat team crossed the next day. Interestingly, Remagen was only fifteen miles north of where the regiment had been stationed for occupation duty after World War I.

Central Europe Campaign
March 25–May 11, 1945

Within days after CT 16 crossed the Remagen bridgehead, nine divisions of the III, V, and VII Corps stood poised for a massive drive eastward to Giessen. But Bradley refused to allow the First Army to attack until Montgomery's 21st Army Group had completed its own crossings of the Rhine. On March 19, Hodges learned from Bradley at Luxembourg City that the First Army's restrictions would be removed on March 25. Hodges returned to his headquarters and prepared his staff for the new offensive.

In the Remagen bridgehead, the VII Corps held the northern zone of the First Army sector, the III Corps held the center, and the V Corps held the south. The 1st Infantry Division occupied the northernmost sector of the VII Corps zone. Facing the 1st Infantry Division was the LIII Corps, commanded by one of Germany's best panzer generals, Lieutenant General Fritz Bayerlein. The LIII Corps consisted of the 11th Panzer Division, then considered the Fifteenth Army's best unit, and the partially rebuilt but still potent Kampfgruppe Panzer Lehr Division. Because Model believed that the main drive of any American breakout in the Remagen bridgehead would proceed northeastward toward the Ruhr valley, Bayerlein's LIII Corps was given the lion's share of Fifteenth Army tanks. Once again, the 1st Infantry Division would be facing the most powerful force in the entire First Army sector.[342]

Unfortunately for Model, Hodges had no intention of attacking toward the Ruhr; instead, he planned to drive due east. The VII Corps' mission was to drive along the south side of the Sieg River, destroy all enemy forces in the zone, cross the Dill River, and head for Marburg. The 1st Infantry Division, reinforced by CCR, 3rd Armored Division, had the far left sector of the VII Corps zone, while the 104th Infantry Division, commanded by Terry Allen, advanced on the right. On March 25, the First Army began its long awaited offensive.

Ruhr Pocket

In reality, the offensive had already started for Combat Team 16, which had been grinding its way forward since March 20 on the far left of the division zone. In essence, the 16th Infantry held the left flank of the entire First Army. For the previous five days, the regiment had attacked through wooded hills and deep draws, seizing numerous towns and clearing the flanks of the 3rd Armored Division as the latter drove eastward. Along with the rest of the 1st Infantry Division, it had succeeded in expanding the Remagen bridgehead in the face of stubborn armored counterattacks conducted by the 11th Panzer Division. As part of the First Army offensive, on March 25, CT 16 continued the push eastward, capturing no fewer than thirty towns in five days. On March 30, the regiment was ordered to move to Büren and establish blocking positions. A new mission for the 1st Division, indeed for the entire VII Corps, was about to unfold.

The combined attacks of the First Army to the south of Düsseldorf and the Ninth U.S. Army to the north had created a new opportunity for the American forces. As the two armies pushed east, the better part of the Fifteenth and Fifth Panzer Armies of Army Group B and two corps of Army Group H were encircled in an area extending from Düsseldorf-Cologne to Paderborn. On the morning of March 31, the combat team motored over one hundred miles to Büren, led by the tanks of the 3rd Armored Division, which slashed their way northward to block the retreat of German units in the Ruhr pocket. At Büren, the regiment made contact with the 8th Armored Division, Ninth Army, and went into defensive positions. The Ruhr pocket was sealed.

Intelligence officers believed the pocket held between thirty and fifty thousand enemy soldiers. In reality, over three hundred thousand German troops were caught in the trap, and the 1st Infantry Division now stood square in their path to freedom. On April 1, the regiment attacked northeastward toward Paderborn and drove forward against light opposition. By the end of the day, the 1st Battalion was in positions around Steinhausen, the 2nd Battalion had seized Geseke, and the 3rd Battalion had organized a defense on the towns of Weine and Barkausen.[343]

The following day, a breakout was attempted in the vicinity of Geseke, but the 2nd Battalion was successful in containing it. The regiment also captured several aircraft, twenty locomotives, and one hundred railroad cars near Steinhausen, but the heavy fighting from the expected German breakout never materialized. Instead, for the next five days, the regiment engaged in patrolling and some light fighting. The German Army seemed to have lost its will to fight. The mop-up of the Ruhr pocket was left to other units and the 1st Infantry Division was pulled out of the line for another mission.

On April 6, CT 16 moved to assembly areas near Brakel and prepared to conduct an assault crossing of the Weser River opposite Furstenburg. On the 7th, teams went forward to reconnoiter the crossing sites, while the 5th and 7th Field Artillery Battalions moved into positions to support the crossing. At 3:00 p.m. on April 8, the 1st and 2nd Battalions launched their assault boats in broad daylight. On the far side of the river were tough SS troops. In what could have been a bloody affair, the two battalions crossed with the assistance of smoke and direct artillery fire, and readily captured their objectives on the high ground around Furstenburg. Resistance by the SS was negligible: even the soldiers of that vaunted organization were beginning to lose heart. On April 9, the combat team continued its push east even as the 3rd Battalion was alerted for a special mission. The following day, the regiment was relieved by CT 26 and went into division reserve, while the 3rd Battalion, attached to the 4th Cavalry Group, drove eastward toward the Harz Mountains.

Harz Mountains

While the Fifteenth U.S. Army reduced the Ruhr pocket, the First and Ninth Armies had pushed eastward toward the Harz Mountains in central Germany. Rising some three thousand feet above sea level, the Harz Mountains were the primary obstacle in the two armies' advance across the northern plains toward Berlin. A pagan stronghold in the early Middle Ages, it had, more recently, become a tourist retreat. Now the mountain refuge became the assembly area for the newly constituted Eleventh Army as it prepared to conduct a major counterattack. The Eleventh Army consisted of about seventy thousand men and was directed to organize in the Harz and await the arrival of the Twelfth Army. The two forces, once united, were to attack eastward to relieve Army Group B, trapped in the Ruhr pocket. Instead, the Eleventh Army was itself about to be surrounded by the U.S. First and Ninth Armies, in the same manner they had cut off the Fifteenth and Fifth Panzer Armies. The First Army, and specifically the VII Corps, passed the mountains to the south and pressed the Eleventh Army from that direction, while the Ninth Army's XIX Corps attacked from the north.[344]

The 1st Infantry Division approached the Harz Mountains on April 11 from the direction of Clausthal at the western end of the salient, and in conjunction with the 9th Division to the southeast and the 330th Infantry Regiment to the northeast, began to pressure the trapped German forces. The 16th Infantry, less the 3rd Battalion, followed in division reserve until April 12, when it passed through elements of the 104th Division and entered the dark wooded hills near Herzberg. One soldier later described the setting:

> Many of the ingredients for a grim struggle to the death were present in the Harz—a trapped enemy, harsh, sharply etched terrain cloaked by dense woods, caves, mines, and winding roads that could be readily blocked at defiles, stream crossings, and almost anywhere else within the woods.[345]

Another wrote:

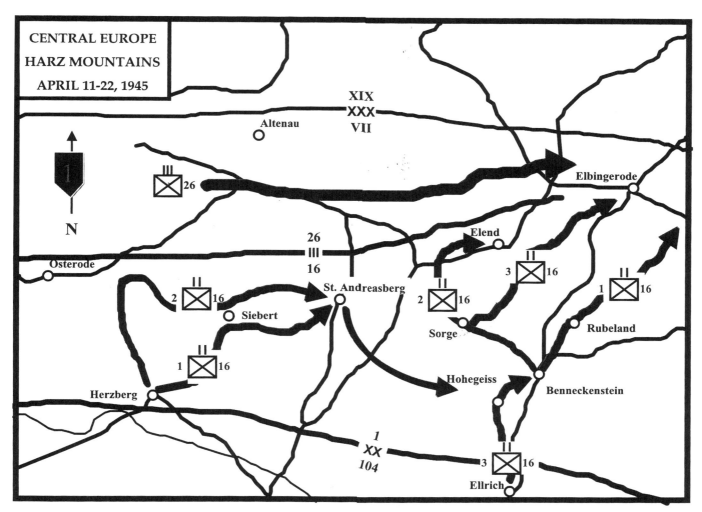

CENTRAL EUROPE
HARZ MOUNTAINS
APRIL 11-22, 1945

Map 8-24.

Some days, the going was so hard over rough mountainous terrain that 500 yards an hour was the limit for foot troops, even when unopposed. In the heavily forested mountains, road blocks were particularly effective. Sometimes the enemy would have blown trees down across the road for hundreds of yards. The terrain offered perfect positions for hundreds of strongpoints.

The conditions and terrain reminded the men of the Hürtgen Forest, and many believed that the regiment was in for another bloody fight. But combat in the Harz would not replicate the earlier battle. But this is not to say that the combat team had an easy time. Several engagements ensued against stubborn troops fighting last-ditch delaying actions that resulted in numerous casualties. One of these battles was the fight to reach St. Andreasberg.

After Wozenski's 3rd Battalion was attached to the 4th Cavalry Group, Gibb had requested to have that unit returned to the regiment. He had determined that the conditions facing the 16th Infantry in the Harz Mountains required all three battalions for the combat team to perform effectively. The request was denied, and instead the 4th Cavalry Group, with the 3rd Battalion still attached, was given the mission to push north on Highway 4 to seize the towns of Ellrich and Hohegeiss.[346] This mission, however, did place Wozenski's men in the sector to CT 16's right flank. With the regiment attacking east and the 4th Cavalry Group attacking northwest, the two forces would converge near St. Andreasberg.

Meanwhile, Gibb had ordered Driscoll to attack Herzberg and Grant to take Lonau. On the afternoon of April 13, both towns fell to the regiment. Pressing on along the narrow roads that wound through the mountainous terrain, the 1st Battalion ran into stubborn opposition near Siebert. On Driscoll's right, the 3rd Battalion was also held up south of Hohegeiss by well-placed strongpoints. All battalions hastily went on the defensive for the night, and sent out bazooka teams and patrols to take out dug-in tanks and other key positions in their way.

On April 14, Gibb ordered Grant to take the high ground

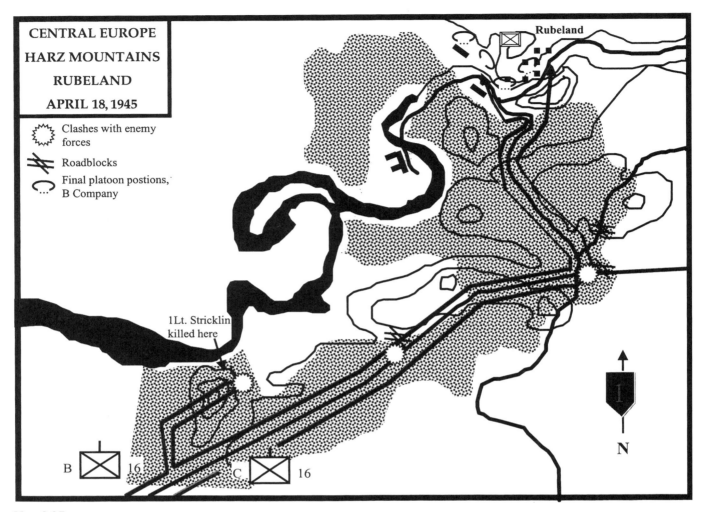

CENTRAL EUROPE

HARZ MOUNTAINS

RUBELAND

APRIL 18, 1945

Clashes with enemy forces

Roadblocks

Final platoon postions, B Company

Rubeland

1Lt. Stricklin killed here

B 16

C 16

1 N

Map 8-25.

north of St. Andreasberg, and gave Driscoll the mission to seize the town itself. The patrols sent out by Driscoll the night before had reduced the tanks and roadblocks, but only with difficulty. Early that morning, the 1st Battalion moved easily past Siebert, but while pushing down the road it again ran into tough resistance that slowed the advance to a crawl. The 2nd Battalion had slightly more success, but only by reducing stubbornly held roadblocks was it able to approach St. Andreasburg. By late afternoon, both battalions were on high ground overlooking St. Andreasberg, still several hundred yards to the east.

From their vantage point west of the town, Driscoll and Grant observed German troops pulling out of St. Andreasberg, raising hopes that the Americans might take the town without much fighting. Advancing under a heavy artillery barrage, the 2nd Battalion and supporting tanks of the 745th Tank Battalion fought their way into the village, which by this time had been largely evacuated. Enemy snipers were particularly active, however, and the men had to warily pick their way through the rubble to clear the town. After numerous casualties the 2nd

Battalion finally cleared St. Andreasberg shortly after midnight.[347]

Farther east, Wozenski, in coordination with the 4th Cavalry Group, was continuing the drive on Hohegeiss. After encountering several strongpoints reinforced with tanks and SP guns during the day, Wozenski's troops finally captured Hohegeiss in a textbook attack that evening.[348]

The following day (April 15), the 2nd Battalion pushed past St. Andreasberg toward Hohegeiss, while Wozenski now veered east with the 4th Cavalry Group to attack Sorge. Over the next two days, all elements continued to advance east against varying degrees of resistance.

On April 17, the 1st Battalion received orders to attack Rübeland. That day, P-47 pilots had reported seeing a large enemy force fleeing east from Tanne, toward Rübeland. General Andrus ordered Gibb to stop and, if possible, destroy the enemy column. Early on the morning of April 18, Driscoll loaded his men on to trucks, tanks, and TDs for the trip to Benneckstein, the line of departure. Attached to the battalion was one platoon of Shermans from the 745th Tank Battalion, and one platoon of M10s from the 634th Tank Destroyer Battalion.

At 7:00 a.m., the battalion jumped off with B Company on the left of the road leading towards Rübeland, C Company on the right, and A Company trailing in reserve. Company C was to push east to clear the road, then, upon reaching an intersection due south of the town, turn left and assault the town from the south. Company B's mission was to advance across country and hit the town from the southwest.[349]

About 8:15 a.m., B Company began its cross-country trek, but was soon slowed by stands of densely packed fir trees. One account stated that the advance of both companies was "hampered by the thick woods, underbrush, and sections of soggy swamp ground. The woods brought memories back to some who had seen action in the Hürtgen Forest."[350]

Some forty minutes later the company emerged from the woods into a large clearing on top of a hill. As the lead elements were crossing the open area, they were met with a stream of machine-gun tracers. After the company returned fire, the enemy fusillade ceased as suddenly as it began. Lieutenant Lawrence Stricklin, the company commander, went forward and yelled out for the enemy to surrender. He was promptly shot through the heart. The executive officer, Lieutenant Harvey Hanna, summoned forward by the radio operator, took immediate command. Hanna, unable to contact Driscoll, consulted with Captain John Lycas, C Company commander, and decided to return to the road and link up with C Company for the push down the road.[351]

Upon reaching Lycas's position, Hanna lead B Company on the north side of the road, while C Company pushed on the south side. After B Company flanked a position troubling C Company's advance, both units ran into a strong roadblock at the intersection where the force was to turn north. The resistance here was described as "fanatical" and was so fierce that it led some to believe the enemy troops were drunk. Point-blank canister fire from the tanks and machine-gun fire did not seem to faze the Germans, much less diminish their zeal to fight. Hanna set up supporting fires, while two platoons from Lycas's company assaulted the position and finally cleared it. The force then turned north toward Rübeland.[352]

Shortly after this episode, P-47s suddenly appeared and began to strafe an unseen foe on the advancing units' flanks and up ahead, in the town itself. Pushing another kilometer north from the crossroads, the force encountered additional resistance, but in each case it was feeble. The POW catch was beginning to grow. At one point, 114 Germans meekly surrendered to B Company without a fight. Almost immediately after these men gave up, Hanna's troops discovered over one hundred enemy vehicles in a camouflaged motor park in the woods along the road.[353]

As the two companies approached the town, a terrific volume of small-arms fire greeted them from the high ground surrounding it. Four Shermans were brought up, and from positions along the twisting road that led into the town, began to pummel enemy positions in and around the village, while the infantry maneuvered to enter it. On the far side of the creek running through the town, P-47s continued to bomb and strafe hidden enemy concentrations. Unknown to the two company commanders, enemy reinforcements were struggling mightily to reach the beleaguered town, and the planes were successfully keeping them at bay.[354]

About 6:20 p.m., both companies reached the south edge of town. Lycas peeled off to take the eastern half of town, while Hanna attacked the west. Leading the B Company assault through Rübeland was the all-black 3rd Platoon. Enemy resistance was heavy in the village, but by using "infiltration, ducking, dodging, [and] house-to-house combat methods," the 3rd Platoon cleared the western part of the town up to an old concrete bridge. Meanwhile, the platoon had unknowingly advanced with their right flank exposed to an enemy force of over one thousand troops. Nonetheless, in the process, they had cleared the part of town south of the river and captured over fifty prisoners.[355]

At this point, the 3rd Platoon took up overwatch positions covering the bridge. The bridge was too narrow to get vehicles across, so the company was going to have to clear the north side without tank support. Supported by the covering fires of the 3rd Platoon, the 1st Platoon charged across and advanced northwest, followed by the 2nd, which drove due north, and finally by the 3rd, which headed to the northeast to establish contact with C Company. This attack broke the back of all resistance in Rübeland. The Germans began surrendering in droves, and by the end of the day over eight hundred had given up to B Company alone. The 3rd Platoon netted the biggest fish of the day, an admiral who claimed he was in charge of shipbuilding and naval inspection. By 9:30 p.m., the town was securely in the hands of the 1st Battalion.[356]

On the same day, to the south, the 2nd Battalion attacked to seize the town of Rothehütte. At 7:00 a.m., the battalion jumped off from Sorge in a heavy drizzle and thick fog. Led by F Company, the battalion headed north to establish contact with the 26th Infantry in Elend; then it was to turn east for the attack on Rothehütte. Attached to the company was one platoon each of Shermans and M10 TDs. Following a road and a railroad line that led to Elend, the company immediately ran into resistance from dugouts. The F Company troopers soon policed up eight Germans and left two dead in their positions. From this point on, the movement to Elend became one surrender ceremony after another. Company F captured no fewer than 171 enemy troops and two field hospitals in the six kilometers to Elend, encountering little determined resistance along the way.[357]

Reaching Elend, the company made contact with the 26th Infantry, but hardly had it arrived when it was ordered to continue the advance on Rothehütte, fifty-five hundred meters to the east. While G Company advanced along a road to the south and E Company advanced in the center, F Company headed east along the road going directly to the town. About fifteen hundred meters from Elend, F Company encountered a Tiger II tank with its gun zeroed in on the road. After the tanks and TDs made two attempts to knock out the German tank, a 7th Field Artillery FO immobilized it with indirect fire but did not kill it. Finally, a pilot in a Cub liaison plane was able to direct artillery precisely on top of the vehicle, killing its commander and wounding the rest of the crew. The pilot then brought fire on three more Tigers in the town, disabling one and driving off the other two. With the assistance from the FOs, E and G Companies easily went on to capture Rothehütte.[358]

By the end of the day on April 18, the regiment had netted 1,911 POWs. Resistance in the Harz was clearly crumbling, and over the next four days, the POW haul for CT 16 was over six thousand enemy troops. By April 22, with the Harz area largely mopped up, the 1st Infantry Division was pulled out of the line and sent 120 miles to Marburg for several days of rest and recuperation. The respite did not last long, for on April 26 CT 16 was alerted for a move southward. The following day, the 1st Infantry Division was relieved from assignment to the First Army and reassigned to Patton's Third Army, which was driving southeastward into Czechoslovakia. Boarding any available trucks and vehicles, the men of the regiment were transported southward to Selb, where the 2nd and 3rd Battalions went into assembly areas, and the 1st Battalion assembled at Asch, just across the border in Czechoslovakia. As the combat team's attached units motored to Selb the following day, the three battalions relieved units of the 97th Infantry Division of their defensive positions.[359]

For the next eight days, the regiment conducted aggressive patrolling into Czechoslovakia and made several company-size attacks to seize towns forward of the division area. On May 5, Berlin fell to the Russians, and the Red Army was fast approaching the regiment's positions from the east. German opposition was dissolving across the front, but intelligence garnered from Czech citizens indicated that there was still a large body of Germans in the country's interior that was willing to fight. That day, Gibb received orders to continue the advance eastward and to capture any remaining German units or, failing that, force them to fight.

"The Last Kilometer"

At 6:00 a.m. on the wet, misty morning of May 6, CT 16, three battalions abreast, advanced eastward to its objective, Falkenau, some thirty kilometers away. The 1st Battalion pushed on against little resistance until noon, when it struck a detachment of marines from the battleship *Admiral Scheer*. Fighting with determination, the marines inflicted twenty casualties on B Company, including one officer and three men killed. The 2nd Battalion lost one killed and seven wounded in their advance that day. The 3rd Battalion also encountered stiff

resistance at Kulsam. By the end of the day, the regiment was still fifteen kilometers from Falkenau and had suffered a total of fifty-one casualties. As it turned out, these were the last battle casualties of the war for the 16th Infantry.

At 6:00 a.m. on May 7, the regiment jumped off on its last attack of World War II. It had advanced for a little over two hours when Gibb received a radio communication from the 1st Infantry Division: "Cease all forward movement" crackled over the net and instructions to organize defensive positions followed. The German high command had reached an agreement with the Allies for unconditional surrender, and all American units were to accept the surrender of enemy troops in their respective sectors. Gibb directed the orders to be forwarded to the battalions. To Ed Driscoll, who had been with his battalion since the beginning of the war and had seen so many of his men killed and maimed over the past three years, the order was the best thing he ever heard. His reaction? "It's about goddamn time!"

The World War II record of the 16th Infantry Regiment is one that few units can approach and even fewer, if any, can surpass. During its 443 days of combat, three assault landings, and eight campaigns, the men of the regiment earned six battalion-level and three company-level Presidential Unit Citations (PUC); the entire regiment earned the PUC for its actions at Normandy. Service Company and the Medical Detachment earned Meritorious Unit Commendations. The regiment was twice awarded the French Croix de Guerre with Palm. That achievement, coupled with the two Croix de Guerre awarded in World War I, allows members of the regiment to wear the Medaille Militaire Fourragere, one of only four units in the United States Army so honored. The Belgian Army also cited the 16th Infantry twice for actions at Mons and Malmèdy and also awarded the regiment its fourragere. In addition, four men of the regiment earned the Medal of Honor, three posthumously. Eighty-seven men were awarded the Distinguished Service Cross, thirteen posthumously, and three earned it thrice. This tally was fully half of the DSCs awarded in the 1st Infantry Division in World War II. The Silver Star was awarded to 1,926 men, 217 of whom won it two or more times; 2,828 won the Bronze Star; and 6,896 earned the Purple Heart.

Such laurels won in battle are only earned through blood and sacrifice, however, and the men of the 16th Infantry paid dearly for their honors. The regiment suffered over seventy-five hundred casualties in World War II. The tally was:

	Officers	Enlisted
Killed in Action:	48	1202
Wounded in Action:	262	5384
Missing in Action:	20	612

In short, the regiment had once again fought its nation's war with valor and courage. It contributed as much as, if not more, than any unit its size to the final victory in Europe. Now, like its Great War predecessor, the 16th Infantry would have to work diligently to keep the peace in an occupied Germany. Unlike their regimental ancestors, however, these men were to perform this duty for the next ten years, a period during which they would see their former enemies become essential partners in the North Atlantic Treaty Organization (NATO) in its efforts to contain the Soviet Bear during the Cold War.

Crossing of the Moselle River, July 1959

Chapter Nine
The Cold Warriors

Your regiment has few equals in any army.
Major General Thomas S. Timberman, October 19, 1951

The morning of May 9, 1945, dawned cool and fair, but there was still tension in the air. For the soldiers of the 16th Infantry Regiment, there was no real sense that the great endeavor called World War II was over; nor was there any impression that the fighting had really ended. There was little elation, no celebrations. The long months of hard combat had left most soldiers drained of the emotional and physical energy needed to get worked up about the end of the war. Many of them had seen buddies killed and maimed, and if they were elated about anything, it was the fact that they had made it through the ordeal at all.

Not a few officers and men also realized that there was still a difficult job ahead. While demobilization was right around the corner for many soldiers in the European Theater of Operations (ETO), others did not have enough points to go home. Many men would be transferred to units slated to participate in the invasion of Japan; others would be assigned to occupation duties in Germany and Austria. Among the senior leaders of the Big Red One came the realization that somebody was going to have to oversee the demobilization of the German armed forces, provide security for occupation forces and installations, and ensure an environment that allowed for the stabilization of German society until local, state, and eventually, national government officials were elected and assumed responsibility for running the country. Until the Germans could rebuild their governmental infrastructure, the occupying forces would have to fill the vacuum, and the 1st Infantry Division was one of several divisions selected to perform the role of occupation force. As things would turn out, it would be the only occupation division remaining in Germany after 1948.

For the next thirteen years, the 16th Infantry Regiment performed essential roles in the occupation mission. It began the period as conqueror and policeman but, as the Soviet threat developed to the east, the men of the regiment transformed into protectors, and eventually, allies, of the German people.

The regiment would also experience a great many changes to its organization during the next twenty years. It would undergo a fairly radical transition to the "Battle Group" concept that eliminated the traditional regimental structure, and evolve from there into the basic organization still in use today—that of the independent battalion attached to flexible brigades.

Through this period of change, the soldiers of the 16th Infantry continued to train and prepare for the next mission, whatever it might be and wherever it might take them.

But all this lay in the future. The immediate postwar mission for the regiment in Germany was to oversee the demilitarization of the German XII Corps.

By the end of the first week of May 1945, the XII Corps was tightly squeezed between Patton's Third Army moving southeast, and the Russian 102nd Corps advancing to the northwest. When the war officially ended, the 16th Infantry received orders to occupy a thirteen-kilometer sector along the Ohre River, from Frazensbad to Karlsbad, in Czechoslovakia. Forward of the regimental sector were tens of thousands of German soldiers waiting to surrender. In anticipation of the demilitarization mission, Colonel Frederick Gibb set up the combat team headquarters in Frazensbad, where it would remain for the next month executing the requirements of Operation Eclipse. Eclipse called for ETO units to accept the surrender of German army and air force units, disarm and demobilize them, and separate SS and Nazi party members from the whole. The ETO units were also to repatriate Allied POWs to their home countries, control travel between occupation zones, and generally assist military government activities.

Well before the official German surrender on May 9, the enemy was increasingly giving up in great numbers. Most Germans were anxious to surrender to the American army rather than be taken by Soviet forces. Under Russian captivity, they believed their very lives would be at risk. But as Eclipse was implemented the morning of May 9, a controversy arose over whom these enemy soldiers (caught between the Soviets and the American Third Army) were to surrender. The Germans were desperately attempting to move into American lines to give up, and the Big Red One was prepared to accept them.

A day or so earlier, General Andrus had directed the construction of a huge POW pen at Hof, which V Corps had approved as processing point for German prisoners. However, at 10:30 a.m., the plan was suddenly changed when a V Corps staff officer informed the 1st Division G3 that German troops were no longer allowed to enter friendly lines, stating: "They will have to be processed forward of our front lines."[1]

This change to the plan sent ripples of confusion up the

chain of command to General Andrus himself, who became frustrated about the situation and contacted Huebner (commander of V Corps since the previous December). Huebner changed his directive: "Don't let them through…handle those you have in your areas and that is all. Do whatever you want, shoot if you have to, but don't let anymore in. I don't give a damn how many are out there. The Russians will be coming along and let them take them.…I want the Russians to get in there and take care of what is out in front." Andrus informed Huebner that George Taylor, now the assistant division commander, had gone forward that morning and "talked to them [the Germans], and they don't have much food. They don't have much of anything." Huebner's reply was, "I don't have any help for you."[2]

It seemed, then, that the Big Red One's recent enemies were to be left to the mercy of the Red Army. Before receiving the orders to the contrary from Huebner, Gibb and White (who was regimental S3 once again after returning from attending the Command and General Staff School, or C&GSS) drove out to a German headquarters located an in old castle about four miles east of Falkenau to coordinate the surrender and movement of a large number of German soldiers to a POW pen in Cheb. Upon arrival, White recalled seeing a number of women and children on the castle grounds, no doubt family members of the German staff in the headquarters. Shortly, Gibb, White, Lieutenant General Fischer (the German commander), and his chief of staff, Colonel Karlson (who spoke fluent English) met in the courtyard to work out the details. There, an unlikely scene developed as two American and two German officers labored together to work out road march tables for the passage of German units through American lines to the POW cage. After completion of the march tables, Gibb informed the general that half of the German force command would surrender to the Russians and the other half to the Americans. Upon conclusion of their work, Gibb and White piled into the jeep and headed back to Falkenau.

On the road to Falkenau, however, the two Americans happened on a jeep-load of rough-looking Russian troops, wearing a mixture of Soviet and German uniforms. Gibb stopped to ask the Russians what they were doing in the U.S. sector and, after contacting division by radio, told White to take the Russians and head back to the castle. Gibb had just received the order to keep the Germans out of American lines.

White dutifully escorted the Russians to Lieutenant General Fischer at the castle. There he informed Karlson of the orders Gibb had received and that all the Germans were now to turn themselves over to the Red Army. This information spread rapidly among the German civilians. White heard screams and wails of anguish from the women. He knew it was time to leave, and he did, quickly, leaving the Germans in the charge of the Russians.

In one instance, however, a great number of Germans were able to avoid captivity under the Soviets because of the actions of a young lieutenant in the 5th Field Artillery Battalion.

Lieutenant John F. Rummel encountered a long column of German trucks filled with dispirited troops slowly making their way back to Germany and captivity. Rummel realized that these men needed to be rounded up and not allowed to roam freely behind American lines, so he contacted the 16th Infantry to set up a concentration area at an airport near Eger. The regiment accomplished this task and shortly thereafter thousands of POWs streamed into the compound. Rummel later claimed that some four hundred thousand men were eventually corralled there. Although this figure is doubtful, the total was certainly high. Rummel went on to say that "several years later, I learned that General Patton had given orders that all Germans were to be turned back to the Russians. I am certain that if that had been done, they would have been slaughtered."[3] Indeed, many men of the German armed forces who came under the control of the Red Army never made it back home alive. The realization of this possibility was prevalent among many U.S. soldiers, and it tended to color the interaction between them and Soviet troops.

Relationships between the Soviets and the officers and men of the 16th Infantry ranged from suspiciously cordial to restrained hostility. In one incident, General Andrus invited his Russian counterpart from the Soviet division opposite the 16th Infantry to a dinner at a hotel in Franzensbad, where Gibb had set up the combat team CP. When the Russian commander arrived, his armed escort immediately posted security around the area with "tough-looking squads of machine gunners," apparently because he mistrusted American allies. In another instance, the Russians, unwilling to care for a number of wounded German soldiers, forced the latter into the American lines without authorization.[4] Though most disputes were resolved without great difficulty, the frequent contacts between the American and Soviet soldiers increased tension levels for various and sundry reasons. Fred Hall recalled:

> There was an air of distrust in these contacts. It has been said many times, and it is true, that the attitude of our veteran soldiers was disappointment we were not going to occupy Berlin, and as we probably would have to fight the Russians some day, we might as well get the job done now.[5]

Despite the unease caused by the interaction between the two armies, the 16th Infantry worked steadily and methodically to achieve the objectives of Operation Eclipse. By June 5, the mission had been completed. During the month-long effort, the 16th Infantry processed some fifty thousand German POWs and repatriated over fifteen thousand Allied POWs. The regiment was alerted for a change of station, and on June 7, the 79th Infantry Division relieved the Big Red One of its sector in Czechoslovakia. The following day, the regiment motored to its next duty station at Bamberg, Germany and, in turn, relieved the 8th Infantry Regiment of its occupation duties in the Landkreis ("county") of Bamberg and Hochstadt.

The regimental headquarters was stationed in the city of

Bamberg; however, the companies, at this time, were predominantly posted to outlying towns:

Regimental Headquarters
and Headquarters Company   Bamberg
    Antitank Company   Bamberg
    Cannon Company   Bamberg
    Medical Detachment   Bamberg
    Service Company   Bamberg
1st Battalion HHC   Hochstadt
    A Company   Muhlhausen
    B Company   Schlusselfeld
    C Company   Weisendorf
    D Company   Herzogenaubach
2nd Battalion (complete)   Bamberg
3rd Battalion HHC   Hirschaid
    I Company   Bamberg
    K Company   Burgebrach
    L Company   Strullendorf
    M Company   Hallstadt

For the next eight months, the principal duties of the regiment were guarding POW cages, displaced person (DP) camps, and ammunition dumps, and manning traffic control points throughout both Landkreisen. To accomplish these tasks, the AT Company was reorganized as an ad hoc military police company, and the men of Cannon Company was pressed into service as camp guards and administrators for the POW camp in Bamberg. The remainder of the companies performed traffic control point, POW work detail, and ammo dump guard duties.[6]

The POW camp run by Cannon Company held some thirty-two hundred prisoners, all of whom had to be interrogated (and processed for further jail time if they were SS or Nazi Party members) and, eventually, released to go home. Most of the POWs were employed regularly on work details to rehabilitate the U.S. kasernes (post or barracks) in the area, remove trash and rubble, remove wrecked or captured military equipment to concentration points, or work on such projects as bridge construction and road repair. The prisoners were cooperative, and no reports of violence against American troops were recorded during the regiment's stay in Bamberg. There was an average of two escapes per day from these work details, however.[7]

Relations with the local population were good, at least overtly. Occasionally, however, buildings or vehicles were vandalized. In other instances, soldiers arrested civilians for singing nationalistic and Nazi songs, an act strictly forbidden under the martial laws of occupation. The most serious incidents reported while the regiment was stationed in Bamberg involved German women, who were threatened with harm by young German men for dating Americans. To some degree, these resentments were offset by the regiment's efforts to help clear rubble and compile a winter reserve of fuel wood for the citizens of the Landkreis during the summer and fall of 1945.[8]

As the U.S. Army in Europe continued to redeploy units back to the states for demobilization, the remaining divisions picked up larger areas of responsibility. In November, several 16th Infantry units changed locations as the regiment's area of responsibility expanded. The 1st Battalion moved its headquarters to Mellrichstadt and the 3rd Battalion relocated to Hammelburg Lager. Company E picked up the responsibility for security of a DP camp in Schweinfurt, while the 3rd Battalion assumed responsibility for a POW compound and a civilian intern (CI) camp in Hammelburg. The 1st Battalion was also deployed along the border with Czechoslovakia in the Landkreises of Mellrichstadt and Konigshoefen and manned twenty-four posts to control cross-border traffic. By this time, the regiment had charge of twelve POW, DP, and CI camps with an inmate population of over 19,300 persons. The area of responsibility had expanded from two Landkreis to twelve.[9] To complicate matters, the expansion of duties and obligations came at a time of turbulent command assignments.

Beginning on September 23, the regiment was assigned the first in a series of short-term regimental commanders. On that date, Colonel Gibb departed and "Batshit" Horner assumed command for the next fifteen days. Then, on October 8, Colonel Adna C. Hamilton took over; but he, too, departed on November 10, after which the executive officer, Lieutenant Colonel Emanuel M. Robertson, assumed command for the next two months. During this period, despite the fluctuation in commanders, the regiment was able to build better relations with the Red Army along the border.

In November, the assumption of responsibility for the border posts from the 102nd Infantry Division put men of the 16th Infantry back in close contact with their Soviet counterparts. Though suspicions remained, efforts on the part of the various regimental commanders established several reciprocal policies between the two forces. For example, since there was no clear demarcation line between the two Allied zones, soldiers on both sides frequently strayed into the other side's area of occupation. The agreement reached between the 16th Infantry and the units of the CII Corps stipulated that the errant soldier(s) be peacefully retained at a guard post until the other side could be contacted, and a representative, usually a junior officer, sent to identify the stray and escort him back to the friendly zone. Even with these joint agreements, there was still friction between the two former Allies, even to the point of creating some interesting speculation on the part of the German people.

One of the duties of the regimental S2 at this time was to glean information from the local populace to reduce black market activities, resurgent Nazi movements, and the like. The S2, Major Herbert B. Allen, used the military police, traffic control points guard, POW guards, and guards at the border posts to question German civilians, as well as displaced persons, about the "latest rumors" and public opinion. The January 4, 1946, *Weekly Counterintelligence Report* illustrates the sense there was something amiss between the two recent allies, as per-

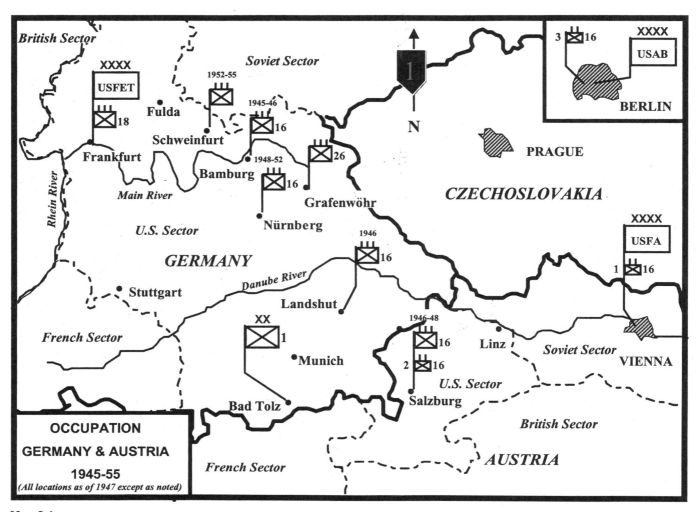

Map 9-1.

ceived by the civilian population. The following are examples from the December 1945 period:

> It is rumored among German civilians that there is open warfare between the Americans and Russians in the border between occupation zones.
>
> Outbreak of war between the Western Allies and the USSR is imminent. It will be touched off by the current Russian-Turkish disagreement and German troops will be used to fight with Allied forces against the Soviet Union.
>
> Originating supposedly in the Russian zone of occupation, the following rumor was heard: In the vicinity of Willmars, former SS troops are now serving in the United States Army and are wearing American uniforms.[10]

The contacts with the German civilians and DPs also provided information regarding other activities about which the S2 was interested in gathering intelligence. These included information on the so-called Werewolf Nazi youth groups and black market activities.

The Werewolf organization was supposedly composed of Nazi-indoctrinated teenagers, ex-members of the Hitler Youth, and demobilized soldiers, presumably SS, who were dedicated to continuing the war using the methods of an underground resistance movement. The existence of this organization was known well before the war ended, but it never caused much of a problem at any time during the occupation period. Nonetheless, American occupation forces took it seriously, at least for the first six months or so after the end of hostilities, and made a concerted effort to identify members and arrest them. Though there were indications of underground activity in the Bamberg area, it never appeared to be organized.

Of more concern to the 16th Infantry military police in the Bamberg area was an active black market. The main items of trade, at least during this period, were cots, blankets, field jackets, and GI food, namely, C, K, and Ten-in-One rations. To catch violators, teams composed of troops from the provisional regimental military police company, reinforced by men from the military government, counterintelligence detachments, and the United Nations, conducted so-called Swoop operations on suspected residences and locations.

These operations met with varying degrees of success and usually netted a few blankets and some cans of food, but rarely discovered large caches of pilfered military items.

Probably the major event involving the 16th Infantry military police during the stay at Bamberg was the escape of two convicted soldiers from the regimental stockade in late October. Rather than leave the area, Private Ernest Brewer and a Private Montorano attempted to remain in Bamberg and were occasionally reported by their ex-buddies who spotted them on the streets of the city. On one occasion, specifically November 16, they were seen joy-riding in an old olive drab sedan. The MPs gave chase but failed to apprehend them. Two weeks later, on December 2, Brewer was shot and killed by a military police guard near the regimental headquarters, and six days later, Montorano was arrested and imprisoned.[11]

Occupation duties took a toll on the combat readiness of the regiment. Combat readiness was further degraded by the frequent rotation home of soldiers with high points and the inability of the replacement system to make good these losses. For example, by July 1, 1945, the regiment's strength had dropped to 1,442 troops from a wartime high of about 3,400. The vast majority of the losses were from "high point men." By September 8, the regiment had grown to 2,730 assigned personnel but then lost another 500 soldiers by the end of that month.

The replacements seemed to come in two categories: soldiers who were combat veterans from other units that were being disbanded or sent home, or new men who had just completed basic training. The veterans stayed just long enough to get enough points to go stateside, which left the regiment filled largely with novice soldiers led by the die-hard professionals who had decided to make the 16th Infantry home after the war was over. As a result, the regiment, while performing its military police/occupation duties with its usual efficiency, was woefully unprepared for combat. In March 1946, Major John Finke, now commanding the 3rd Battalion, estimated that "assuming that this battalion will be at full strength on July 1, 1946, and we will be permitted to initiate a coordinated Training Program for the Battalion, it is felt that in approximately four (4) Months of intensive training this unit will be able to be considered fully operational."[12] In short, it would not be until November 1, 1946, that the unit could be ready for combat. That assessment was roughly applicable to the rest of the 16th Infantry as well.

Given its occupation duties, training was next to impossible for the regiment to conduct at any level except perhaps individual and squad. For example, in the second week of February 1946, only 510 men in the regiment were available for training on a daily basis. This was typical of the occupation period. The daily guard, military police, and housekeeping requirements

required 1,538 soldiers. When one considers that most of the duties required twenty-four hour shifts, many of the men available for training on one day pulled a twenty-four-hour shift the next. Also, men were frequently siphoned off for "hey you" occupation tasks mandated by higher headquarters. In one instance, the XV Corps headquarters commandeered a replacement package of men, destined to flesh out the depleted ranks of the regiment, to perform guard duty at its headquarters for an indefinite period of time.[13] All of these distractions ensured a severe degradation of the regiment's combat readiness.

Combat, however, was probably one of the last things on the minds of most officers and men, even though the potential for armed clashes with Soviet troops was far from remote. There were just too many occupation duties to perform. Organization Day was apparently not even remembered that first year after the war. However, the regiment did take the time in November to recall its achievements during the conflict. On November 28, a composite company of eighty-four men traveled to Nürnberg for an observance hosted by the Belgian government. There, at the renamed Soldiers Field (formerly the Nürnberg Stadium), troops from the 1st and 9th Infantry Divisions participated in a ceremony in which both formations were awarded the Belgian Fourragere for their service at Mons and in the Battle of the Bulge.[14]

Unlike the good old days at Fort Jay, the advent of a new regimental commander in January 1946 was heralded with little ceremony. Colonel John R. Jeter, a man respected for his fairness and moral leadership, assumed command of the 16th Infantry that month.

As 1946 dawned, the need for a strong occupation force in Germany was rapidly decreasing. The situation had evolved to the point where military government units were performing most of the necessary administrative duties. One service the German people were still unable to perform, because they had no national government to coordinate it, was that of a national police force. Though local police had resumed duties associated with crime control, they could not coordinate police functions between states, nor did they have control over the national borders. These functions were largely performed by occupation units such as the 16th Infantry. To relieve combat units of some of the police and border patrol duties, Headquarters United States Forces European Theater (USFET) authorized the formation of the United States Constabulary. The Constabulary was to be organized in the spring of 1946 using the 4th Armored Division as the base force.

To release that division from its occupation duties so it could reorganize and train for its new role, the 1st Infantry Division was sent south to take over the 4th Armored Division's sector of the border with Austria. The 16th Infantry Regiment's piece of that mission was to take over the sector between Simbach and Finsterau from CCB. On February 25, the 2nd Battalion relieved CCB of its area, and on February 28, the regiment was relieved by the 15th Infantry of the posts around

Bamberg and established its new headquarters at Landshut.[15]

The movement to Landshut was conducted by motor convoy and rail and was completed without incident. Upon occupation of its new posts, the regiment was deployed as follows:

Regimental Headquarters and Headquarters Company	Landshut
Antitank Company	Passau
Cannon Company	Deggendorf
Medical Detachment	Landshut
Service Company	Landshut
1st Battalion (complete)	Landshut
2nd Battalion	Vilshofen
E Company	Simbach
F Company	Griesbach
G Company	Pocking
H Company	Freyung
3rd Battalion (less I Company)	Deggendorf
I Company	Straubing

At Landshut, the duties of the regiment changed little from those at Bamberg. Essentially, they consisted of guarding two POW compounds; two CI camps; three SS hospitals; thirty-two small DP camps consisting mainly of Russians, Ukrainians and Poles; military police duties; and manning sixteen border posts with the Soviet zone of Austria. These duties were rotated among the three battalions so that no one unit always performed the worst details.

The occupation experience in Landshut was much like that in Bamberg, but there were some significant differences. For example, the postwar resistance effort was distinctly evident. As reported by the S2, there was frequent cutting of phone lines between the regimental and battalion headquarters and those to the outlying companies. On March 24, 1946, a motorized curfew patrol from E Company was fired on from a dwelling on the outskirts of Presiting, but a search of the house came up with nothing. There was no indication that the Werewolf band was active in the Landshut area; other groups similar to the Werewolves—notably the Eidelweiss and Diamonden organizations—were the most likely culprits. There was also increased raiding by inmates of certain DP camps on other camps and on German civilians. Both of these problems greatly increased the workload of men performing military police duties.

Relations with the Germans in the Landshut area were at once better and worse than those in Bamberg. While the Germans appreciated the police and protection that the Americans provided, there were those among them who still harbored Nazi sympathies—a source of friction between the local populace and the Americans. The relaxation of non-fraternization rules and the corresponding increase in relationships between soldiers and local girls increased the problem. Fights between soldiers and young German men became more common in Landshut. The increase in contact between the

soldiers and German girls also caused a significant growth of venereal disease, which continued to be a health problem for the regiment for the entire occupation period.

The relations with the Russians at the new duty station continued to be a mixture of cordiality and mistrust. Opposite the regiment's border sector was the Soviet 48th Cavalry, apparently the reconnaissance unit for the 15th Infantry Division. Because a clearly delineated no-man's-land had yet to be established between the two countries, illegal and accidental border crossings were frequent. The crossings were primarily characterized by raids by DPs from Austria into Germany, schnapps-buying trips into the American zone by Soviet soldiers, or soldiers accidentally wandering into the wrong zone while sightseeing. The same procedures used to repatriate lost soldiers at Bamberg were coordinated with the 15th Infantry Division as well. Contact points were set up at Mellrichstadt and Ober Kappel, and there were frequent opportunities to use them.

On March 8, 1946, the Soviet border guards seized three Bavarian border police at Frohnan, disarmed them, and took them into Austria. The Russians claimed that the men had been seized because they (the Soviets) had no knowledge of German police being allowed to carry weapons. A meeting between representatives of the 48th Cavalry and 16th Infantry to discuss the incident resulted in "the most satisfactory of any conducted with Russian forces to date. The Bavarian Policemen were given their arms and returned to the border."[16]

Less than two weeks later, on March 22, border guards of F Company picked up two soldiers of the 48th Cavalry who had wandered into the American zone near Wegscheid. The two were questioned and then turned over to their unit at the nearest contact point. Six weeks later, on May 10, three Red Army soldiers were captured by F Company near Post No. 31. The men were held overnight and returned to a Soviet officer at Ober Kappel the following day. In apparent retaliation, five Soviet soldiers crossed the border and disarmed two F Company guards and attempted to force them back into Austria. While the Soviets fired several shots at them, the two men somehow escaped, then fled back to the Austrian side of the border. The following day, Lieutenant Lawrence Kolb, the F Company commander, met with the Soviets at their border post and recovered the two weapons.[17]

Such incidents continued to fuel rumors among Germans that war between the Anglo-American alliance and the Soviet Union was only a matter of time. Coupled with the Germans' increased interest in politics brought about by their spring elections, and Winston Churchill's famous "Iron Curtain" speech (at Westminster College in Fulton, Missouri, in March 1946), the rumors actually increased morale among what should have been a war-weary people. Regarding Churchill's remarks, the Counterintelligence Report for March 29, 1946, related that "civilians are taking a great interest in the speeches made by Winston Churchill in America. Some comments to the effect that Churchill's stand resembles that of Hitler's was heard. In general, the Germans were pleased with any derogatory remarks against the Russians."[18] The Germans perceived (correctly) that the tensions between the former allies would shorten the period of occupation, and hasten the day when they might return to the family of responsible nations.

Despite rumors and tensions, cooperation continued in varying degrees between the 16th Infantry and its Soviet counterparts across the border. The regiment's participation in Operation Taper was an example of such cooperation. Taper entailed the repatriation of Russian, Ukrainian, and other Soviet DPs to the Soviet zone of occupation. This cooperation was not always appreciated by all concerned, especially by some of the repatriates. In May 1946, Major Finke oversaw the loading of several trainloads of Soviet DPs from the camps around Deggendorf. One train departed on May 9 without incident, but a shipment on May 13 was short four escapees who refused to return to the Soviet Union. By the time the train departed at 2:00 p.m., one man had attempted suicide by cutting his throat, and before the train arrived at Hof to be turned over to the Russians the following day, two others had attempted to escape by jumping. In the attempt one man was killed, the other severely injured with a skull fracture.[19]

By July 1, 1946, the United States Constabulary had completed its reorganization and deployment and was prepared to take over all constabulary missions. On that date, the 16th Infantry was relieved of its constabulary duties. Concurrently, Finke received an alert to consolidate the 2nd and 3rd Battalions with the regiment at Landshut. This move was accomplished by the end of the month. It was a short-lived posting for the 3rd Battalion, which moved again on August 27, this time to Weilberg.

With the reduction of most of the regiment's constabulary missions, Jeter increased the level, frequency, and sophistication of training for his subordinate units. On July 8, the regiment embarked on an intensive training program that included squad and platoon tactics, range firing, scouting, and patrolling. The renewed emphasis on training was a welcome change for all concerned, but it was soon interrupted by new occupation requirements. The entire 1st Battalion was committed to building a camp for nine thousand infiltrees in August, and sizable details were required to assist in clearing the Hungarian DP camp at Pocking and for guards at the two SS hospitals and the enemy materiel depot at Landshut. Because of these duties as well as daily housekeeping requirements, the regiment was able to engage only about 6 percent of its troops in training in the late summer and early autumn of 1946.[20]

The continuing demobilization and return of organizations back to the United States required units of the 1st Infantry Division to take over ever-larger areas of responsibility. The reduction of U.S. Army units in Europe during the summer of 1946 prompted the division to alert Colonel Jeter for a regimental change of station to Austria in October. This next move, however, would drastically affect the 16th Infantry's nascent

efforts to regain combat readiness, for the regiment was to be split up among three different locations. The regimental headquarters, 2nd Battalion, and special companies were to be transferred to the vicinity of Salzburg and assigned to the Area Command Land Salzburg. The 1st Battalion was to be assigned to the Vienna Area Command in that city. The 3rd Battalion was to transfer its men to the 1st and 2nd Battalions and be reduced to cadre strength. The cadre were then to be assigned to the Berlin Command and transferred to take over the 3rd Cavalry Squadron. There, the cavalry unit would be reorganized into infantry and become the new 3rd Battalion. For the next twenty-one months, the 16th Infantry would not function as a regiment, per se, but as three separate battalions controlled by three separate commands.

The 1st Battalion was the first to go, departing on October 11 for Vienna by rail and motor convoy. The following day, the 3rd Battalion, reduced to a cadre of seven officers and sixteen enlisted men, boarded a train for Berlin. On October 18, the regiment's advance party departed for Salzburg, followed by the rest of the headquarters and the 2nd Battalion on the 19th.

En route to Austria, the regiment was embroiled in a situation emblematic of the security climate in the immediate postwar period. During the stay at Bamberg, the regimental headquarters had hired several DPs to perform housekeeping and clerical tasks. One of those employees was a young Polish girl, Maria Clara Recken. Recken hailed from Lwów, the chief city of Galicia, until 1939 a Polish province dominated by a Ukrainian majority. After the war, the city, along with the rest of Galicia, had been transferred to the Ukrainian SSR and given the Ukrainian name of Lviv. Recken had been hired as a maid to perform cleaning and maintenance jobs around the headquarters, and soon became known as "Ronny" by the headquarters personnel. While doing her work, she eventually caught the eye of the assistant adjutant, Jim Lipinski, who began to date her secretly and in violation of the nonfraternization rules. When the regiment moved to Landshut, she and several other DPs went with the regiment and, while there, she and Lipinski began to discuss the possibility of marriage. Then orders came for the move to Austria.

Lipinski was on the horns of a dilemma. He did not want to leave Maria in Landshut, but because she was a DP, he could not legally take her to Salzburg. He decided to smuggle her across the border. Riding in the back of Lipinski's jeep, Ronny covered herself with a sleeping bag, and Lipinski placed duffle bags and other equipment on top of her, providing additional concealment. Approaching the border post with Austria, it became apparent to Lipinski that U.S. MPs and Austrian border guards intended to search all vehicles passing through. Thinking fast, Lipinski jumped out of his jeep just as they prepared to search it and faked a severe toothache: "Does anybody have any bourbon or whiskey?" Lipinski yelped; "I got a bad tooth and it's killing me!" One of the guards replied in the affirmative and hustled off to find the bottle. Lipinski then demanded, "Where's the nearest dental clinic? I've got to get there as soon as possible!" One of the soldiers blurted out its location, then Lipinski took a big swig of booze, thanked the man in feigned anguish, piled into the jeep, and ordered the driver to move out. He later married Ronny and brought her home to the United States.[21]

Technically, the regiment's mission in Austria did not entail occupation duties, though it was referred to in that vein. The official diplomatic line was that Austria was not an occupied country, but a liberated one. Though it had been liberated, it still required a treaty with the United Nations before it would be free to run its own affairs. Until then, Austria was to be governed much like Germany. To that end, it was divided into four administration zones, each governed by one of the four major powers. The U.S. zone was essentially the central portion of the country, with the Soviet zone to the east and the British and French zones to the west. The U.S. zone was further divided into two area commands, Area Command Land Salzburg and the Vienna Area Command. Upon arrival at their respective posts, the 1st and 2nd Battalions of the 16th Infantry became the principle combat elements of the United States Forces in Austria (USFA), commanded by General Mark W. Clark. The other major unit of USFA was the 4th Constabulary Regiment, headquartered at Linz.

Performing occupation duties in Austria before the 16th Infantry arrived was the 5th Infantry Regiment, which was scheduled for inactivation on November 15. For the next three weeks, Colonel Jeter oversaw the transition of responsibility for kasernes, equipment, and duties from that regiment. By the inactivation date, the 16th Infantry had assumed those responsibilities and incorporated the residual troops from the 5th Regiment that were not scheduled to rotate home. The influx of men from the 5th Infantry brought the 2nd Battalion close to its authorized strength.

The overall situation in Austria was better for the troops than it had been in Germany. First, Austria had not experienced the level of devastation that Germany had, so just its appearance alone was more attractive. Second, the food situation was a significant improvement, which had a corresponding effect on morale in general. Additionally, clean, healthy, off-duty activities for the men were more available. For example, there were three movie theaters in the Salzburg area, one of which held one thousand soldiers and had two showings nightly and four different shows weekly, compared to the single five hundred-seat theater in Landshut. There were also rest and recreation (R&R) trips to Paris, London, the Riviera, and other interesting locations.[22]

The 1st Battalion situation in Vienna was considered the better of the two assignments in Austria. Upon arrival, most of the battalion was billeted in Stifts Kaserne on Mariahilferstrasse, while A Company occupied a barracks on Bastienstrasse, and B Company at Haubenbiglgasse. When it left Landshut, it consisted of twenty-three officers and 611 men, but temporarily shot up to forty-nine officers and 1,245 men when it was consolidated with the 1st Battalion, 5th Infantry. At that strength, the battalion could afford to give each man one day on and one day off when he pulled a twenty-four hour duty (usually several two- or four-hour shifts). By the time the battalion had dwindled to authorized strength in early 1947, that schedule had changed to three days on, one day off.[23]

At first, the duties for the 1st Battalion in Vienna seemed a lot like those it had performed in Landshut. The battalion had to man twenty-three "targets" or guard posts throughout the city and its suburbs. Posts comprised a variety of locations, to include the rail head at Althanstrasse, the USFA airstrip, the SS stockade, the headquarters of the Vienna Area Command, hotels, schools, and a doughnut bakery. Duties required 293 soldiers per day, not including housekeeping requirements, so once again training took a back seat to occupation requirements.[24]

There was a new duty associated with the mission at Vienna that the battalion did not have in Germany—that of ceremonial troops for Headquarters, USFA. The battalion got its first taste of that role on October 21 when it conducted a formal retreat parade at the USFA Headquarters. This was a weekly mission that was assigned as a permanent detail to A Company for the first several months that the battalion was in Vienna. Later, other companies were detailed to perform the task as well.[25]

In Salzburg, the 2nd Battalion was billeted at Camp Truscott, actually situated in the suburb of Glasenbach, four miles southeast of the city. The Service and Antitank Companies were posted to a small kaserne in Salzburg proper, and Cannon and F Companies were assigned barracks in the town of Hallein. Like the 1st Battalion, duties for the 2nd Battalion in Salzburg seemed to be nothing more than the occupation mission it had left in Landshut. The battalion had to provide guards for thirty-five targets for which it had responsibility. The guard duties included an SS hospital, three DP camps, two POW cages, and a military stockade with which it shared guard responsibilities with the 505th MP Battalion. The battalion formally assumed responsibility from the 5th Infantry for these posts at midnight on October 28.[26]

The 2nd Battalion in Vienna, like the 1st Battalion, also had to perform ceremonial duties upon occasion. The first of these was for a visit by Lieutenant General Clark to Salzburg on November 5. Meeting the general at Franz Joseph Bahnhof that morning was the 16th Infantry Honor Guard and the bagpipe band inherited from the 5th Infantry.

The band was a big hit with Clark and his wife, as well as with soldiers' families. It became a tradition for the band to meet dependents on the train as they arrived from the states or from some other post. The band was also popular with the troops, who were always ready for something different to distract them from the boredom of occupation duty.

Fortunately, the off-duty opportunities for the 2nd Battalion soldier were good. For those soldiers who were athletically inclined, there were two gymnasiums, a football stadium, tennis courts, and a swimming pool at Camp Glasenbach. The Special Services also offered skiing, ice skating, and hunting opportunities. The club system was excellent, with no fewer than three officers' clubs, two senior NCO clubs, and eleven enlisted men's clubs. One of the senior NCO clubs was renamed the "Fort Jay Club," no doubt by the old timers in the regiment.[27]

In late November, the regiment underwent its first major postwar reorganization. On the 30th, the 16th Infantry lost two of its wartime stalwarts when the Cannon and Antitank Companies were inactivated. The men from Cannon Company were transferred to F Company, and the Antitank men went to H Company. Additionally, the regimental medical detachment was expanded and reorganized as Medical Company, 16th Infantry. Though technically still part of the regimental tables of organization, the inactivated companies were determined to be unnecessary for peacetime duty. The inactivations were also carried out in anticipation of a forthcoming reorganization of U.S. Army infantry regiments (the new TOEs then in development).

While the regimental headquarters and 2nd Battalion settled in at Camp Glasenbach, the 3rd Battalion grappled with organizational problems of its own. When the cadre arrived at Berlin, it assumed control of the troops of the 3rd Cavalry Squadron stationed at Roosevelt Barracks. The officers and men of the old 3rd Battalion, who transferred with the colors and records to form the new battalion, were all combat veterans with the regiment during the war. The group included Karl Wolf, who was now the battalion S3. As veterans of the wartime 16th Infantry, they were somewhat anxious to imbue the regimental traditions and esprit into the new unit. Unfortunately, the 3rd Cavalry was not exactly an elite outfit, judging by the men who composed it in October 1946. The following excerpt from the battalion's December *Report of Operations* sheds light on its failings:

> The delinquency rate remained high and many cases were referred to Courts Martials. The majority of all offenders were under 20 years of age and in most cases had been drinking at the time the delinquency occurred. Determined efforts to rid the battalion of misfits, etc., have been carried out through Section VIII proceedings and reduction boards. V.D. continued to be the only serious medical problem confronting the battalion and there was an increase in December.[28]

The disciplinary levels of the Berlin troops in the autumn of 1946 were a far cry from what was expected of the 16th Infantry. Under the leadership of the regimental old timers, the men of the 3rd Battalion gradually achieved the high standards and discipline expected of Berlin Command soldiers that would become well-known throughout the army in later years. By the 1960s, soldiers headed for Berlin were expected to be among the army's best. They had to be because they were America's most visible representatives to the communist world. A soldier in Berlin who exhibited poor discipline was quickly bounced out of the command and sent back to West Germany. There was no fooling around with a man who did not want to be part of the best, and it all started with the 16th Infantry in October 1946.

Disciplinary problems in the 16th Infantry were not limited to the 3rd Battalion. All units experienced them over the next two years, as unit strengths continued to fluctuate and the quality of recruits remained generally low. For example, Captain Edward J. Geaney, S3 of the 1st Battalion in 1947, reported, "It is a known fact that a large percentage of the personnel comprising today's army do not possess the necessary aptitude for military service. The 1st Battalion, 16th Infantry, like most other units has been burdened with its share of this type of personnel." Lieutenant Colonel John Speedie and his leaders took actions to fix the problem by eliminating undesirable soldiers from the army, sending poorly educated soldiers to night schools, reducing incompetent NCOs, and increasing the number of courts-martial to punish those men who failed to stay in line. Those court-martialed men were assigned to the battalion's hard-labor detail.[29]

Part of the disciplinary problem was due to the boredom engendered by the continuing guard duties. Since their arrival in Vienna, the men of the battalion spent the vast majority of their time pulling guard on the twenty-three guard posts around the city. Their schedule was essentially one day on and one day off. This problem was partially remedied by the establishment of an Austrian Civilian Guard, which took charge of many posts. Also, the battalion was able to eliminate other posts, and still others were consolidated. By the end of September 1947, the guard requirements were reduced to ninety-four men a day, which meant that a man pulled duty one day and would not have to perform it again for three more days.[30]

A slight influx of personnel to the battalion also helped the situation to some degree. Authorized thirty-seven officers and 837 enlisted men on July 1, 1947, the battalion had thirty-two officers assigned but only 556 enlisted men, of which only 515 were available for duty. That summer, the battalion had a net increase of fifty-three men, a welcome addition to the guard ranks.[31]

These improvements prompted two major changes during the summer of 1947, the first of which was the consolidation of the battalion at Stifts Kaserne. That August, A Company and the battalion S4 section were moved from other locations in the city to the battalion home post, which significantly increased the administrative efficiency of the battalion. The second change was the most welcome, for it heralded a gradual shift toward the regiment's proper mission—training for combat.

The decrease in guard requirements freed up time for Lieutenant Colonel Speedie to conduct unit field training. After an initial period in July when soldiers were put through classes on basic skills, the training shifted to twenty-four-hour company exercises focused on field craft and pre-marksmanship training. By September, the entire battalion went to the field for additional tactical training and also trained on marksmanship and range firing crew-served weapons. The slight change in focus from occupation duties to field training significantly improved the soldiers' morale.[32]

The experiences of the 2nd Battalion in Vienna were similar to those of the 1st Battalion. Guard requirements, honor guard duties, and dwindling unit strength had caused morale to plummet after the first month or two in Salzburg. For example, during the month of February 1947, Captain Frederick H. Black, the regimental S1, reported that while 271 enlisted men were sent home to the states, the 2nd Battalion received only nine in return. Additionally, he reported morale of the 16th Infantry elements in the Salzburg area as only "fair." To make matters worse, the battalion went on a constant alert on February 20 that kept the men in the kaserne through at least the end of March. No free time off post was allowed.

This was followed by two incidents at camps in Salzburg. The first occurred at Camp Franz Joseph, the Jewish DP, on March 23. A riot by three hundred inmates erupted when two inmates were identified as former "capos"—Jewish men who had worked for and cooperated with the SS guard units for labor battalions at the infamous Buchenwald concentration camp. The disturbance was quelled when 16th Infantry guards entered the camp and separated the two men from their accusers. The second incident was a prison break at Camp Marcus Orr, the POW and War Crimes stockade. Both events caused a doubling of the guard requirements, which further diminished morale.[33]

In April and May, troop strength continued to decline, causing further strains. It should be noted at this point that the 2nd Battalion was actually composed of only three companies. Company F had been reduced to almost zero in personnel and then used as a holding company by Zone Command Austria (ZCA) for troops arriving in and departing Austria. In the latter part of the year, the company was even directly attached to Headquarters, ZCA, and became responsible for providing troops for the USFA commanding general's guard and motor pool operation. Still, by the end of May, morale was reported as "excellent" due to an increase in personnel and relief from several guard functions.

This trend continued through the summer of 1947 as additional guard duties were eliminated and training increased. The last inmates of the Jewish DP camp were shipped out in June and the camp was closed. As a result, the range firing instituted in March continued at an increased pace during the summer, especially with machine gunners. Alerts were instituted to deploy companies to the field on no notice, and field training was conducted with the 4th Constabulary Squadron. Little by little, occupation duties became less significant, and combat readiness assumed higher levels of importance.

The 3rd Battalion's experiences in Berlin were not unlike those of its two sister battalions. It performed guard duties at various locations in the city, including the Berlin Command Stockade, the Wannsee Internment Camp, and the headquarters for the Office of the Military Government of the United States (OMGUS). Additionally, the battalion provided guards to the famous Spandau Prison, where Germany's most infamous war criminals were held.

Like the 1st Battalion, the 3rd Battalion had to perform many ceremonial duties. Many of those duties were also performed by one unit, I Company. The company was reorganized to consist of an honor guard platoon and a fife and drum corps, organized to provide music for the events. The ceremonies were generally conducted for the U.S. Military Governor and Chief, United States European Command (EUCOM), General Lucius D. Clay, during his frequent visits to the city. Though his headquarters as EUCOM commander was in Heidelberg, his OMGUS office was in Berlin. When he was in town (and in fact, when he was traveling), the Honor Guard provided him with bodyguards. Additionally, I Company was responsible for conducting the weekly retreat parades at the OMGUS headquarters.

These parades often required the presence of the entire battalion and sometimes even other units of the Berlin Command. For example, on June 8, 1947, the battalion paraded for General Clay and Assistant Secretary of War John Petersen. At the end of the month, Clay showed up with Petersen's boss, Secretary of War Kenneth P. Royall. Other dignitaries for whom the battalion paraded at various times were General Eisenhower, General Bradley, Lieutenant General Curtis LeMay, and the RAF's Air Chief Marshal Sir William Shelton Douglas.[34]

A humorous incident occurred at a review for General Bradley in the summer of 1947, one that reflects the pride that the old-time 16th Infantryman had in his regiment. Bradley was on an inspection tour of units in Germany, and when he arrived in Berlin, he was treated to a review by the 3rd Battalion. During the inspection portion of the ceremony, Bradley spotted an old soldier in the ranks, one Sergeant Alter. Bradley liked to talk to men who had been in the army before the war, so much so, that he would actually break ranks to get to the man. So it was with Alter.

"Well, Sergeant Alter, when did you enlist?" Bradley inquired. "1937, sir," came his reply. "What outfit did you serve with during the war?" asked the general. "B Company, sir" Alter responded. Bradley, somewhat perplexed, said, "Yes, but what regiment?" to which Alter proudly answered, "Hell, this one, general. What other regiment is there in the U.S. Army!?" Bradley got a kick out of this and roared with laughter. He queried the man further by asking him, "Well Alter, in that case were you at Hill 609?" "Yes sir." "Well maybe you and I ran into each other on Hill 609?" Alter demurred, "No sir. When I was on Hill 609, there weren't nobody higher'n a second looey!" Silence ensued and the battalion commander cringed at Alter's answer, but Bradley roared with laughter once again.[35]

Unlike the other two battalions, the 3rd Battalion had the advantage of being able to trade off many of its guard posts with other units so that it might head to the field for training as a battalion. In early June 1947, the battalion increased the frequency of physical fitness training, range firing, and small-unit tactical training in preparation for a battalion field training exercise (FTX) at Grafenwöhr, Germany—known simply as

"Graf" to old soldiers. On June 10, the battalion's duties were handed over to the 16th Constabulary Squadron, and two days later, the battalion boarded a train and headed west.

The train arrived at Grafenwöhr the following day, and training commenced in earnest on the 16th. The training was designed to be incremental, from individual- to platoon-level range and tactical training. The first week was devoted to range firing with individual weapons; training with rifles, hand grenades, and bazookas; and road marches. Additionally, training consisted of night recon patrols and fast preparation of defense positions. This training was culminated by a battalion review and an inspection by the 1st Infantry Division commander, Major General Frank W. Milburn, who complimented the battalion on several points. The training progressed over the next two weeks from squad to platoon training in both the attack and defense. On July 7, the battalion returned to Roosevelt Barracks in high spirits. The battalion historian was able to report at the end of July that "morale was very high during this period, which was shown by the individual pride in the companies and the backing given to the units' training, activities, and sports."[36]

Sports comprised an important part of life in the 3rd Battalion. The battalion became established as a sports powerhouse the first year it was formed in Berlin. Its various sports teams, all designated the "Green Hornets," competed against all comers in every sport competition of the Berlin Command. The battalion football team was particularly good and went undefeated for the 1947 season. The basketball team went undefeated for 1946 and 1947.

At the beginning of 1948, the battalions of the 16th Infantry were making headway toward developing into combat-ready units despite the continuing occupation duties. However, guard duties were decreasing, DP and POW camps were closing, and personnel turnover with its associated turbulence was easing. The units could look forward to a better organized and more consistent training program. Meanwhile, the relationship between the USSR and its former allies, the United States and Great Britain, was deteriorating over questions of the future sovereignty of certain European nations and other disagreements. It was becoming apparent to many in the west that Stalin had no intention of giving up control of Poland, Czechoslovakia, the eastern zone of Germany, and other countries. As a result, the European Command finally began a series of initiatives designed to put all its units on a combat-ready footing.

The first of these initiatives to have an impact on the 16th Infantry was the increased emphasis placed by Headquarters, USFA, on the regiment's mission as the tactical reserve in Austria. For example, the quarterly report for the 1st Battalion, April-June 1948, stated that USFA's emphasis on the regiment's tactical proficiency was evidenced by "the continued reductions in guard commitments...by the increased interest and assistance of higher headquarters in furthering the training program; and by the establishment of one reinforced rifle company as an immediate reserve to be available for any assigned mis-

sion on one hour's notice."[37] Additionally, the 1st and 2nd Battalions of the regiment experienced increased alerts and spent more time in the field.

The expansion of combat-forward training activities signaled that the end of the regiment's occupations might be near. Indeed, it was. Because of the increased tensions with the Soviet Union, EUCOM directed the 1st Infantry Division to gear up and re-hone its combat skills, dulled by two and a half years of occupation duties. Frequent concentrations of all divisional units for joint training units would be necessary to accomplish that task. Therefore, in early 1948, EUCOM decided to bring back to Germany those elements of the 16th Infantry still in Austria. The regiment was to be relieved of all guard duties and reclassified as a tactical unit rather than an occupation unit. The means by which this was to be accomplished, however, were not as simple as convoying the regiment to its new duty station. Instead a new unit was to be activated and redesignated as the 16th Infantry.

On April 22, 1948, the 7892nd Infantry Regiment was activated in Frankfurt, Germany, under the command of Colonel Sterling A. Wood. The regiment, less the 1st Battalion, was billeted in the Area D Kaserne in Frankfurt. The 1st Battalion was billeted in Friedberg. The mission of the 7892nd was to take soldiers who had either been transferred into the regiment from units throughout EUCOM or sent from the United States as replacements and put them through basic training in individual skills, marksmanship, and the use of crew-served weapons. The soldiers were to be molded into a cohesive unit in less than three months—a difficult task for the best of leaders.

Unfortunately, the 7892nd had been used as a dumping ground for undesirables by the EUCOM units tasked to furnish soldiers. This made Colonel Wood's task exceedingly difficult But help was on the way. In Austria, the units of the 16th Infantry were preparing to be redesignated as the 350th Infantry Regiment, and the men had been informed that a new 16th Infantry was being formed in Frankfurt. Men who had served with the regiment during the war would be allowed to transfer to the new unit if they wished. Of course, there were not many of them left, but a handful volunteered to go, "Paddy" Roughn among them. Roughn had joined the regiment in 1933 at Fort Jay, and as the "old soldier," was given the honor of carrying the colors to Frankfurt. Just as the men of the 3rd Battalion had had to do in Berlin, these men would have to instill the traditions and history in its troops of the new 16th Infantry Regiment.

On June 15, 1948, in two separate ceremonies, the 16th Regiment in Austria was redesignated the 350th Infantry Regiment, and the 7892nd was redesignated the 16th Infantry Regiment. At the time of the redesignations, the new 16th Regiment's strength was ninety-seven officers and 1,990 enlisted men, less the 3rd Battalion.[38] After struggling to successfully rebuild the battalions in Austria to full-strength, motivated, and moderately well-trained units, the regiment was essentially starting over. It would be some time before the same level of camaraderie and readiness would be achieved in the new outfit, but little time was lost in getting started.

Toward the end of June, the 16th Infantry motored and railed to the training center at Grafenwöhr, where it joined the rest of the division on July 1 to begin the long process of fashioning a combat-ready organization. The regiment was billeted at Camp Omaha, where it remained for the next three and a half months, as it participated in a series of increasingly sophisticated training exercises.

The first month was spent beautifying Camp Omaha, preparing for the training exercises, and participating in several ceremonies. On July 7, two important events occurred. The first was the activation of the Provisional Heavy Tank Company. This unit was activated in anticipation of its eventual formal integration as part of the regiment. That same day, the regiment participated in a division review honoring the regiment's return to the division. In front of Under Secretary of the Army William Draper; General Sir Brian Robertson, CG of the United Kingdom's Forces in Europe; General Joseph P. Koenig, Commander of the French Occupation Zone; and General Milburn, Lieutenant General Clay formally presented the 16th Infantry's colors to Lieutenant Colonel Emanuel M. Robertson, the acting regimental commander. On July 20, training of the regiment began in earnest.[39]

The next three weeks of training focused on the regiment's subordinate elements. From July 20 through August 4, the line companies and special units conducted range training on all weapons in the regiment. The Service Company and unit motor elements conducted support activities, to include a division motor march designated Exercise Prime, August 6-7. From July 26 through 28, the regimental and battalion headquarters participated in Exercise Black, a division-level CPX.[40]

The day that Exercise Black began, the regiment welcomed its new commander, Colonel John P. Evans, who would become known as the "Great White Father" by the troops for his stature, white hair, and distinguished mien. Evans graduated from West Point in 1923 and spent the prewar years on a series of infantry assignments in the United States, the Philippine Islands, and Hawaii. He attended the Command and General Staff School in 1937-38 and, after a second tour with the Hawaiian Division, was assigned to the Infantry Replacement Training Center at Camp Wolters, Texas, just before Pearl Harbor. In 1943, he was assigned to the VIII Corps as the G3 and remained in that position throughout the war in Europe and until December 1945. Over the next three years, he served on the Army Integration Board; was G4, III Corps; and served as the senior instructor for Organized Reserve Corps units in Oklahoma. He was serving in the last capacity when he received orders in the spring of 1948 assigning him to command the 16th Infantry.[41] He joined the regiment just in time to participate in its most extensive peacetime training effort since the Carolina Maneuvers of 1941.

August was primarily devoted to small-unit training in squad and platoon tactics. The training phase culminated with Exercise Green, a company-level, graded event occurring August 23-25. This was followed by Exercise Gray (August 30-September 1), which was designed to exercise the newly reconstituted 16th Regimental Combat Team (RCT). The RCT consisted of its member-units from World War II, including the 7th Field Artillery Battalion; Company A, 1st Engineers; and Company A, 1st Medical Battalion. This last exercise served as a preliminary event to the regiment's participation in the big show, Exercise Normal. A EUCOM-level exercise, EUCOM saw the 1st Infantry Division maneuvering against the aggressors of the 6th Constabulary Regiment. For Exercises Gray and Normal, the 1st Parachute Battalion Group and the Royal Horse Guards of the British Army of the Rhine were attached to the regiment to serve as the missing 3rd Battalion.[42]

Exercise Normal kicked off on September 1, the same day that Exercise Grey ended. Evans was determined to whip the regiment into shape. To that end, he insisted on strict compliance with standard training procedures, such as maintaining blackouts, ensuring that troops didn't bed down where they might be run over by vehicles, and following sanitary guidelines. His failure to follow his own rules led to an unfortunate incident one night during the exercise. After consulting with his staff in the regimental CP, Evans excused himself to answer nature's call. Stepping out of his well-lit tent into pitch darkness, the colonel groped about in search of the latrine—but could not find it. Instead he selected a tree, and was relieving himself when a voice at his feet, speaking in a thick Spanish accent, calmly informed the colonel, "Hesscooze me sooer, but you peesin on me!"[43]

Upon the conclusion of the division exercise, the regiment underwent combat firing proficiency tests as a sort of graduation exercise. Upon conclusion of the training, Major Tracy L. English, the regimental adjutant, reported that the training "proved beyond all doubt that this regiment is capable of aggressive sustained combat against any determined enemy."[44] Later events proved that this was an overly optimistic pronouncement.

After the field training and proficiency tests, the regiment conducted post-field maintenance of weapons and equipment, and prepared to move to its new station in Nürnberg. Shortly before the move, two old friends rejoined the regiment under different names, as mandated by the new infantry regiment tables of organization. On October 10, the Cannon Company was reactivated, reorganized, and redesignated as the Heavy Mortar Company; and the Antitank Company was reactivated with the personnel and equipment of the Provisional Heavy Tank Company as Tank Company, 16th Infantry.

Additionally, the regimental Medical Detachment was expanded and redesignated as the Medical Company, 16th Infantry.[45] With these new configurations, the 16th Infantry was ready to move to its new home.

On September 27, the advanced party and the regimental headquarters departed Grafenwöhr for Furth Air Base near

Nürnberg. On their arrival, men of the advanced party split up and began the process of signing for billets and furniture, and otherwise preparing to receive the rest of the regiment. The stationing plan called for the headquarters and the regimental Headquarters Company, the Heavy Mortar Company (1st Battalion), and Service Company to be billeted at Furth Air Base, in Furth; the 2nd Battalion at Flak Kaserne in Zirndorf; and the Tank Company at Santa Maria Kaserne, also in Zirndorf. The units arrived at their respective kasernes on October 22.

Despite the training at Grafenwöhr, the new regiment remained ill-prepared for a combat role. In part this was attributable to high turnover in the NCO ranks. By the end of the year, many of the NCOs who had undergone the training at Grafenwöhr were scheduled for rotation back to the states. When they went home, they took their experience with them—and their replacements, if any, were less well-trained.

Another sign of the 16th Infantry's overall deficiency was the high number of disciplinary actions taken by the regiment (though this also meant that the chain of command was doing something about the disciplinary problems). For the period, the 16th Infantry recorded 185 courts-martial and ninety-two other disciplinary boards. Even so, the regimental report for the period indicated morale was improving. The Heavy Tank Company's report for the October-December period probably tells the real story: "This unit has progressed from a discontented, badly disorganized cadre to the status of a partially trained organization….The outlook for the future is a stringent policy of eliminating undesirables and an equally stringent training of the unit to better utilize the considerable power of this type of organization." Don Taylor, a platoon leader with the Tank Company at that time, recalled that once the "undesirables" were gone, "The Tank Company of the 16th Infantry Regiment was the best duty I ever had in my life. I look at the kids today and I can't imagine we were what we were. We were more cohesive than any other unit I've ever encountered."[46]

Additionally, the regiment underwent several inspections (including a division Inspector General (IG) inspection) in November and December. In each instance the regiment apparently received low marks, and a reinspection was scheduled for January.

Evans did not ignore these problems. He took measures to remedy the disciplinary situation, poor morale, and low training levels. First, he involved the regiment in activities calculated to improve the men's pride in their outfit. On October 28, the regiment held its first parade at Furth during which a number of men were recognized for their duty performances. This was followed by a motorized Armistice Day parade through Nürnberg on November 11. After the parade through town, Evans formed the regiment at Soldier's Field for a review by General Milburn and the two division's two brigadiers, John McKee and Ralph Canine. Additionally, the 1st Battalion conducted a review for Secretary of War Royall on December 29 during his visit to Bamberg as part of his EUCOM tour.

Typically, the soldiers griped about participating in such events, but they also turned out in their best regalia to look good for the audience. All of these ceremonies helped the men to function better as a team.[47]

Colonel Evans also encouraged sports as a way of building esprit in the regiment. He started a competition in November to come up with a regimental nickname that would be indicative of the regiment's character and history, yet also suffice as a sports team name. The name selected was "Rangers." It was picked from a pool of names submitted by the men of the regiment and chosen because it was "suggestive of vigilance, prowess, and spirit." It is a nickname that has stayed with the regiment to this day, although the Center of Military History refuses to officially recognize it.[48]

The new regimental commander did not let down on training and readiness after the 16th Infantry arrived at Nürnberg. One of the first actions Evans took was to establish an alert plan, under which the regiment was expected to roll to the field within two hours of notification. Next, an intensive training period to correct deficiencies noted at Grafenwöhr began on November 1, only one week after the regiment's arrival in Nürnberg. On November 23, an alert was called and the regiment moved to a concealed bivouac at Tennenlohe, the regiment's local training area. The emphasis of this training was on winter field craft, operations in blackout conditions, and local security measures by the troops. While this training was underway, the regimental and battalion command posts participated in a CPX. The training was short, only two days, and the regiment returned to its billets on the 25th.

Three weeks later, the process was repeated, only this time the regiment was deployed as part of a division exercise called Winter Prime II. By 3:15 p.m. on December 16, the regiment was closed on its assembly area and prepared to advance on Darmstadt, the notional objective. After twenty-four hours of operations in the snow, the regiment proved that its communications were functioning, both to higher and lower units, and that its men were ready to operate in adverse conditions. All of this was designed to further ready the division for the upcoming EUCOM exercise, Snowdrop, in January 1949.[49] In each of these events, the men of the regiment performed passably, neither encountering nor causing major problems.

While the regiment was reforming in Germany and participating in the training at Grafenwöhr, the 3rd Battalion continued its occupation duties in Berlin. About the same time the 7892nd Infantry was forming in Frankfurt, the 3rd Battalion was in preparing to go to the field. On April 1, the 16th Constabulary Squadron relieved the battalion of its guard duties, and Lieutenant Colonel Donald B. Miller took the battalion to the Grünewald ("Green Forest") near Berlin for a month's field training. The focus of the training was marksmanship proficiency, individual fire and maneuver, and squad tactical training. During the stint at the Grünewald, Miller took the battalion to Truman Hall (OMGUS headquarters) for a review by General Clay. Despite the fact that the men had been in the field that morning, Clay commented that the "high standard set by this parade would be used as an example for other units' future parades."[50] The battalion returned to its duties in Berlin about the time things were heating up between the Western Allies and the USSR.

The reassembly of the 1st Infantry Division during the spring of 1948 and the renewed emphasis on training, field work, and alerts all constituted a response to the increasingly strained relations between the United States and the USSR. Tensions were coming to a head over disagreements on many issues, the most immediate of which were the nature of the future national government for Germany and currency reforms in Berlin. The Soviets responded by closing all land and rail routes into the city in June 1948. General Clay's answer to the land blockade was Operation Vittles, popularly known as the Berlin Airlift. For the next eleven months, the 3rd Battalion took turns with other units in Berlin unloading food, medicine, and other supplies from thousands of Air Force cargo planes at Tempelhof Airfield to keep the city going. When the men were not pulling stevedore duties, they were often pulling security duties at the autobahn checkpoint at Helmstadt and "Checkpoint Charlie," staring down their Soviet counterparts.[51]

Though the battalion faced the possibility of open warfare on a daily basis, the unit still found time for less serious pursuits. During the last three months of the year, the Green Hornets won the Berlin Command baseball and basketball championships, while the bowling team moved up to first place by the end of the year. On December 10, I Company served as the honor guard at Tempelhof for a visit to Berlin by Secretary Royall and two congressmen. The battalion also hosted a series of Christmas parties on December 21-23 for the local German Youth Activities organization. Additionally in December, the 3rd Battalion provided the guards for Spandau Prison.[52]

The year 1949 witnessed an increased training tempo for the regiment. In early January, the 1st Battalion returned to Grafenwöhr for a week's training in night compass work, squad attack problems, familiarization firing, and operating in winter conditions. The battalion returned in time to participate with the entire Big Red One in Operation Snowdrop, starting on January 16.

On the morning of the 16th, the regiment was alerted, then rolled to an assembly area near Babenhausen. From there, Colonel Evans directed the battalions to assume defensive sectors along the Rhine River facing east. Like many exercises during this period, Snowdrop was not so much designed to rehearse the division units in general defense scenarios as it was to test unit alert plans and communications. The purpose was to determine whether the units could support themselves and operate in the cold German winters. The exercise ended January 23, and the regiment returned to home stations without conducting major tactical operations.

In March, it was the 2nd Battalion's turn to go to Grafenwöhr. The training plan was similar to that of the 1st Battalion, the difference being that the battalion spent over two months at Graf, part of the time conducting guard details for the post, and the rest in the EUCOM spring maneuver.

In April, the regiment was alerted and rolled to the field once again, this time for Exercise Showers, the EUCOM spring maneuver. This exercise took place near Neumarkt, and the regiment's initial mission was to provide cover for the withdrawal of the 2nd Constabulary Brigade across the Ludwig Canal. After the regiment successfully executed the covering mission, B Company conducted an assault crossing of the canal at Nerreth, as a feint aimed at drawing aggressor forces away from the main crossing effort at Neumarkt. The feint succeeded and the main crossing was forced by a tank-infantry team which was "extremely successful despite the fact that the majority of the riflemen were relatively inexperienced in tank-infantry tactics."[53]

Exercise Showers ended on April 25, but less than a month later, the 16th Infantry was again en route to Grafenwöhr for what was to become an annual summer event—several months of training with the 1st Infantry Division at Camp Omaha.

On May 20, the regiment entrained for Graf with the all-black 371st Infantry Battalion attached as its missing 3rd Battalion. Until July 2, the unit engaged in range firing of all weapons, including, for the first time, tank ranges for the Heavy Tank Company. While at Grafewöhr, the regiment participated in a division review to celebrate the 32nd Anniversary of the activation of the 1st Infantry Division in June. A series of sports competitions were held to celebrate the event and the Rangers came away with first place in the machine-gun contest.[54]

The division also solemnly observed the fifth anniversary of D-Day on June 6. In commemoration of the landings, Evans announced that the regiment's kasernes were officially renamed in honor of three valiant 16th Infantrymen who had given their all at Omaha Beach. Furth Air Base was redesignated Monteith Barracks after Medal of Honor winner Jimmie Monteith; Flak Kaserne was renamed Pinder Barracks after Medal of Honor winner John T. Pinder; and Santa Maria Kaserne was renamed Adams Barracks in honor of Private First Class John W. Adams, a member of H Company, who was posthumously awarded the Distinguished Service Cross for his heroic actions on D-Day. Evans further stipulated that other locations on the posts would be named for heroes of the regiment à la Fort Jay in the 1920s. He went on to rename the baseball field at Monteith Barracks for Corporal Stephen J. Mulhall, another deceased D-Day hero. The event concluded with a review honoring ten men who came ashore on D-Day and who still served with the regiment: Lieutenant Jimmie Parker, and sergeants Martin Roughn, Gus Kolowitz, Eugene Harrell, Ray Derry, Edward Lynch, Frank Petrosino, Lionel Pender, Dave Arangio, and Martin Vanoy.[55]

In late June the regiment ended its training period at Graf with a series of battalion-level combat firing proficiency tests. Upon return to home stations on July 2, the "Rangers" almost immediately took to the field near Erlangen for an exercise on defense of a river line. This training concluded with assault river crossings assisted by A Company, 1st Engineer Battalion.[56]

Three weeks later, the regiment returned to Graf and, from July 27 to August 5, served as umpires for the combat firing proficiency tests of the 18th and 26th Infantry Regiments. This was followed by regimental combat team operations from August 16 to 18, which in turn was followed by the division train-up for the EUCOM fall maneuver.

That maneuver, designated Exercise Harvest, began with an alert on September 2. At the time, the French Army's 5th Battalion, Chasseurs à Pied, was attached to the regiment as its third battalion. On September 4, the Rangers moved to an assembly area near Pfaffenhoffen and prepared to meet the aggressor force, composed of U.S. Constabulary units. Initially, the regiment conducted a delaying action, falling back as the "enemy" attacked. On September 10, however, the Big Red One went on the offensive, and the 16th Infantry attacked for the next six days. During the advance, the Rangers seized the bridge across the Danube River at Ingolstad and successfully captured its final objective near Grafenwöhr on September 16. Major General Milburn sent a letter of commendation to Colonel Evans to compliment him on the performance of the regiment: "Your energetic and forceful pursuit of the enemy during the evening and night of September 10," wrote the general, "caused him to retreat to his position north of the Danube River in a state of great demoralization."[57] The efforts of Evans to train the regiment and re-install pride and discipline in the 16th Infantry were paying off.

After the successes of Exercise Harvest, the regiment returned in a state of high morale to its home stations. To cap off the year's successes, Evans reinstituted a tradition in the 16th Infantry that had been dormant since before World War II. On October 4, the 16th Infantry celebrated Organization Day, an occasion last celebrated at Fort Devens in October 1941. That morning, the regiment kicked off the celebration with the traditional review, this time at Monteith Barracks, for Major General Milburn, now the deputy commander for U.S. Army, Europe; Major General John E. Dahlquist, the new division commander; and a host of other generals and dignitaries. After the pass-in-review, Evans assembled the regiment in a "U" formation and directed the regimental chaplain to give the invocation. In keeping with the tradition of Organization Days past, the regimental history was then read, followed by the presentation of a number of awards to men of the regiment and remarks by the regimental commander. A series of intercompany sporting and military events filled up the rest of the day. The celebration concluded with a "hop" at the serviceman's club that evening.[58]

The 1949 training year was culminated in early December with the 1st Battalion's return to Grafenwöhr. There the battalion conducted night exercises, squad and platoon problems, and familiarization firing, returning to Nürnberg just before Christmas.[59] Colonel Evans had made great strides in 1949

toward preparing the regiment for combat. The sophistication, frequency, and seriousness of the field training had helped to turn a group of hardheads and misfits into a fairly decent combat regiment. On several occasions, general officers had commended the 16th Infantry for its performance in the field. All these activities played a role in raising the morale of the men and their pride in the regiment. But there were other factors that contributed to the turn-around in morale.

Post life at Nürnberg, on those rare occasions when the regiment was at home, was filled with Fort Jay-like ceremonies, sports, and various other activities. In addition to the D-Day observance and Organization Day, the regiment had staged several parades and ceremonies. For example, on February 25, 1949, the entire regimental combat team turned out for a review for General Clay and Ambassador Robert D. Murphy during their visit to Nürnberg. On April 6, Army Day, the Rangers paraded through the city, then conducted a review for military dependents and the German citizenry at Soldiers Field. For Armistice Day in November, the 2nd Battalion held a parade for the citizens of Zirndorf, with the town's leading citizens watching from the reviewing stand.[60]

The adoption of the aforementioned Rangers nickname was but one way the postwar 16th Infantry distinguished itself from the prewar regiment. Another was the nicknaming of the 16th Infantryman's distinctive insignia ("unit crests") as "checkerboards" because of the blue and white vair on the shield. Finally, any soldier who served in the regiment at this time will swear up and down that the unit song was not "The Sidewalks of New York," but was "Roll Out the Barrel." The latter was unofficially adopted, no doubt, in recognition of the Rangers' most popular off-duty pastime. Not surprisingly, however, no one can remember actually passing in review to "Roll Out the Barrel."

During the year several improvements were made to post facilities, and these also helped to improve morale. In October, a new post chapel was completed at Monteith Barracks, replacing the academic building that had been used in that capacity. The men of the battalion took great pride in the chapel, and raised money to purchase seven stained-glass windows that commemorated the unit's fallen soldiers of World War II. Each window memorialized each of the line companies, Headquarters Company, and the Heavy Mortar Company (formerly Cannon Company).[61]

Another facility improvement was the conversion of an aircraft hanger at Monteith Barracks into the "finest gymnasium in EUCOM." The quality of the gym may explain, at least in part, why the Rangers basketball team won the division title that year. Additionally, 16th Infantry pugilists Jim Johnson and Pat Arellano won the 1st Division middleweight crown and the EUCOM bantam weight championship, respectively (the regimental boxing team, managed by Lieutenant Don Taylor, placed second overall in the division title matches). The hockey team also won first place in the division league.

Though its accomplishments in training and sports helped get the regiment back on the track to becoming combat proficient and well-disciplined, they did not eliminate disciplinary problems altogether. Excessive drinking and brawling in the off-post clubs continued to generate arrests, trading on the black market was rife, and venereal disease remained the foremost health problem. During the year, there were seventeen general courts-martial, 217 special courts-martial, and 298 summary courts-martial; some 150 men eliminated from the service by boards. The 1949 historical report stated: "In the matter of the high number of elimination boards, all tend toward the separation of undesirable personnel from the service, but at the same time, the figures indicate that an extremely poor quality of men were sent to the regiment. All too frequently, those who were eliminated, never should have been allowed to enter the service."[62]

As for the 3rd Battalion, it had spent the first seven months of 1949 embroiled in the Berlin Airlift crisis. Activities associated with the airlift occupied much of the battalion's time and energy, until July 29 when it was finally and permanently relieved of its duties at Tempelhof Field. Subsequently, the battalion was awarded the Berlin Airlift Device and cited in DA General Order 21, 1949, for its efforts—the only infantry unit to be so recognized.

Even during the airlift, the battalion still found time to participate in various ceremonies for OMGUS; it also guarded General Clay and his residence, and provided the guard detachment for Spandau prison from April through December. In March, the Honor Guard was relieved from I Company, redesignated the 7788th Infantry Platoon, and temporarily attached to the battalion. The platoon moved to McNair Barracks in August, taking with it many of the ceremonial and personal guard duties associated with General Clay and OMGUS.[63]

When the airlift ended, the battalion returned to the Grünewald to brush up on tactical and weapons skills. The emphasis was on range training in August and September; on tactical training in October and November; and on squad tactics in December. Concurrently with the squad training, the battalion commander, Lieutenant Colonel Keith H. Barber, held a CPX in the Grünewald to train his staff and subordinate commanders in communications and the orders process.[64]

Even with all the training in the second half of the year, the battalion did not ignore the sports program. Like the rest of the regiment, the battalion sports teams had become powerhouses in their area. The Green Hornets basketball team, for example, chalked up its third Berlin Command first place title in as many years and went on to win the EUCOM championship. Likewise, the baseball and softball teams won league titles in the Berlin Command.[65]

Similar to the rest of the 16th Infantry, Barber's command still had its share of disciplinary problems, and he, too, took appropriate actions to fix the problems. During the year, some 389 men were court-martialed and 80 were eliminated through boards. Most of the problems centered on AWOLs, drunk and disorderly conduct, assault on German nationals, and frequenting off-limits establishments. The last offense practically disappeared when the ban on such visits was lifted on almost all listed locations. The venereal disease rate was reported to be somewhat lower than the rest of EUCOM, but it was still apparent that even the Rangers in Berlin considered themselves ladies' men (though the term "lady" must be loosely applied!).[66] But the VD rate was not the only indication that the 3rd Battalion had established relations with the local populace.

The German Youth Activities program continued to be a popular activity of the battalion. During the months of July and August, the battalion hosted a summer camp for over three hundred German youths in the Grünewald. During the year, it sponsored movies and discussion programs at youth detention centers and orphanages, and the annual Christmas programs had become a popular annual event. For 1949, the battalion hosted parties and distributed candy and toys for over one thousand underprivileged German children.[67]

By 1950, the regiment had settled into a routine that it would follow, more or less, for the rest of its stay in Germany. In some ways, however, 1950 would be anything but routine. Because of worsening relations with the Soviet Union in 1949, the United States, Canada, and ten other European nations formed the North Atlantic Treaty Organization as a counter to the growing Soviet military threat to Western Europe. On the other side of the world, the communists had won the Chinese Civil War, and the Soviet Union was aiding a military build-up by the aggressive communist regime in North Korea. Things were heating up on the world stage.

At the close of 1949, the U.S. Army had only forty-one thousand troops stationed in Europe. The main combat units were the 1st Infantry Division and the Constabulary (which was not equipped for heavy combat operations). With the advent of the Korean War in June, the Department of Defense realized that America's armed forces were woefully inadequate to meet that war's requirements and other threats worldwide. Beginning in late summer 1950, EUCOM began an unprecedented build-up of ground forces in Germany. By the spring of 1951, the Seventh Army, V Corps, VII Corps, three more infantry divisions, an armored division, and appropriate numbers of support troops joined the Big Red One in the defense of Western Europe. By the fall of 1951, the U.S. Army would have 150,000 troops in Germany.

At the beginning of 1950, however, the Korean War and the subsequent buildup of U.S. forces were in the future, and the year began with the already established routines. One of the first events the regiment's reinspection by the division IG. The 1949 inspection had not been satisfactory, and Dahlquist directed the regiment to take corrective actions and be reinspected. The inspection lasted from January 7 to 14, and upon its conclusion, the IG remarked, "Never have I seen such improvement in an organization in such a short period of time. I feel that the accomplishment has been phenomenal." He went on to state that he believed that the regimental mess was the best in the entire division.[68]

The IG's remarks could be applied to the 16th Infantry Regiment's performance in virtually every area in 1950, whether in sports, discipline, or training. For example, despite the fact that the Rangers had only two battalions' worth of troops to draw on for team members (compared with the 18th and 26th Infantry Regiments, each with three battalions), they went on to win an impressive set of sports titles in the division and throughout Germany. The football team reestablished its winning ways in the tradition of the old Jaybirds when they took the division title. They went on to win the USAREUR championship for 1950. While the boxing team repeated as the runner up in the division competition, three of its members won the division titles in the bantam-, fly-, and middleweight divisions. Jim Johnson took the middleweight crown in the division for the second year in a row, then went on to win the USAREUR title. Likewise, the USAREUR bantamweight crown went to Sammy Price of the 16th Infantry. Price went on to become a member of the Britannica Shield and Pan-American Boxing Teams that year.

The track team won seven titles in the division championships, and John Culin went on to win the USAREUR high jump competition. The "provisional battalion" (Service, Tank, and Mortar Companies) won the division basketball league, and the bowling team broke all existing Nürnberg Post bowling records. Perhaps it was the regiment's superb athletic efforts that prompted USAREUR to designate it as the host regiment for the 1950 athletic year. As such, it hosted most of the division and European Command-level events during the year.[69]

With the improved performance of its athletes, the 16th Infantry experienced a corresponding decrease in disciplinary problems, though there was still much room for improvement in this area. The impression that morale was continuing to improve and that pride in the regiment was on the rise is further strengthened by the fact that over two thousand Rangers were members of the 16th Infantry Regiment Association, a chapter of the Society of the First Division. The chapter was active in conducting an extensive entertainment program during the year. It also sponsored what was probably the first organized pilgrimage by members of the regiment to Omaha Beach in June. Thirteen D-Day participants of the 16th Infantry who were still serving with the regiment, including John McCarthy, John Finke, and Paddy Roughn, traveled to Normandy and laid a wreath at the newly erected 1st Infantry Division memorial near the U.S. cemetery.

The regiment's combat readiness and training also improved considerably. Given the amount of time units spent in the field or on weapons ranges, this should come as no surprise. By this time, no-notice alerts were a routine event, held monthly, if not more frequently. The amount of time spent in the field on these alerts increased as well. The variety of training for the first few months of the year is apparent in the following:

Tank Gunnery	Heavy Tank Company	Grafenwöhr	January 7-21
CPX "SLEET"	Regtl/Bn CPs	Heilbronn	January 16-20
Sqd/Plt problems	1st Battalion	Tennenlohe	February 13-20
EIB Test	Regiment	Home Stations	February 21-23
Ranges/Co. problems	2nd Battalion	Grafenwöhr	Feb 27-March 10
Ranges	1st Battalion	Burgfahrenbach	March 1-30
CPX "SHAMROCK"	Regtl/Bn CPs	Speyer	March 15-22

On May 9, the regiment conducted its annual movement to Camp Omaha for spring and summer training with the 1st Infantry Division. The training began with a series of marksmanship events and competitions, and ended with 1st Battalion being named the best battalion in the division combat firing proficiency tests.

The range training was followed by a series of progressively larger unit drills and problems ranging from squad to company level. After the D-Day observance, the battalion attack and defense tests were administered from June 7 to 23. Once again, the 1st Battalion won top honors in the division in this event. The regiment returned to home stations the following day.[70]

The Korean War broke out just after the regiment returned to Nürnberg from Grafenwöhr. At first, most American GIs in Europe seemed relatively unconcerned. But as the situation worsened that summer and as military planners and intelligence personnel began to worry that the Russian bear might take advantage of Uncle Sam's distraction in the Orient, training intensified for the 16th Infantry.

On July 3, a coordinated training program began to prepare the regiment for Exercise Rainbow, the EUCOM annual training exercise. It started off with a "Watermanship" course, which would ensure that each man in the regiment could swim, and it culminated with a river crossing operation by the 2nd Battalion at Rottenbach, July 10-12. This was immediately followed by the 16th Infantry's first air transportability training, July 14-21. Toward the end of the month, the regiment returned to Camp Omaha., to prepare for Rainbow with the following series of exercises:

Attack problems	1st & 2nd Bns	near Mantel	Aug 3-5
CPX Rainbow	16th RCT	near Heilbronn	Aug 7-18
Defense problems	16th RCT	near Weiden	Aug 10-12
Roadblock*	16th RCT	near Erlangen	Aug 21-23
Tune-up*	16th RCT	near Forcheim	Aug 24-27
Live Fire exercises	Counterfire Platoon	Grafenwöhr	Aug 29-Sep 1
	B Company	Grafenwöhr	Aug 29-Sep 1

E Company	Grafenwöhr	Aug 29-Sep 1
F Company	Grafenwöhr	Aug 29-Sep 1
Hvy Mortar Co.	Grafenwöhr	Aug 29-Sep 1

*Division-level exercises

During this period, it became apparent that the 16th Infantry's hard work in sports and discipline was paying off in training. The RCT defense problem of August 10-12 was particularly successful—so much so that Brigadier General George W. Smythe, the assistant division commander, offered what was, for him, uncharacteristic praise for the officers and NCOs: "There couldn't be any compliment [other] than to say you were better than the other two regiments during the defensive problems."[71]

As had become customary, the EUCOM training exercise was the climax of the training year, and this one had several unique aspects. During Exercise Rainbow, the 16th Infantry was reinforced by the 3rd Battalion, 351st Infantry, from Trieste. The 3rd Battalion was airlifted from Udine, Italy, and transported a distance of 604 miles to an assembly area near Eberbach, Germany. The operation was a precursor of the air mobility concept and was successful overall, in spite of the fact that several soldiers were forced to parachute from one aircraft that developed engine trouble shortly after take-off.[72]

Upon conclusion of the training year, the regiment took time to wind down and focused on a few things other than training. On October 4, the Rangers once again celebrated Organization Day. This celebration included a special ceremony during which the flag from the citizens of Le Puy—presented to the 2nd Battalion at Les Invalides in Paris on July 4, 1917—was returned to the regiment. The flag had disappeared during the war and was all but forgotten. It was located in Pershing's possessions when he died in early 1950 and had been returned to the army. Upon its receipt, the adjutant general of the army inquired whether the regiment wanted the banner returned, to which Evans, of course, replied "yes." The division staff arranged for Lieutenant General Augustin Guillame, the commander of French occupation forces, to travel to Monteith Barracks to make the second presentation of the banner in the 1950 Organization Day ceremony.[73] Curiously, the flag has since disappeared.

Nine days later, the regiment underwent another change of command, as Colonel Evans departed to become the Chief, U.S. Military Liaison Mission, Soviet Occupation Zone. Replacing Evans was Colonel Charles H. Royce, a 1924 U.S. Military Academy graduate. During World War II, Royce had been an observer with the British Eighth Army in North Africa. After a short stint as a CGSS instructor, he went to the 44th Infantry Division to be the chief of staff. In 1944, he was reassigned to the IX Corps as deputy chief of staff, and stayed in that job through the Philippines campaign. In 1945, Royce became the IX Corps chief of staff, finishing the war in that position. In 1947, he was first assigned as the commander of the 325th Infantry at Fort Benning, then went to Fort Riley, Kansas, to become the chief of staff of the newly activated 10th Infantry Division. He was in the latter job when he received orders to take command of the 16th Infantry.[74]

At the same time of Royce's assumption of command, the 3rd Battalion in Berlin was preparing to join the rest of the regiment in Nürnberg. But just as had been done in 1946, only a small group of cadre, the records, and the colors would transfer back to the regiment. On October 16, the existing unit in Berlin was redesignated the 3rd Battalion, 6th Infantry and, one month later, Lieutenant Colonel William H. Birdsong and a small cadre of officers and NCOs assumed command of the new 3rd Battalion at Johnson Barracks in Furth. As before, the new 3rd Battalion was used as a dumping ground for undesirable soldiers from other units. Birdsong and his leaders faced a hard uphill climb to turn the new unit into a well-trained and disciplined outfit. The addition of the 3rd Battalion brought the 16th Infantry's troop strength up to 168 officers, 8 warrant officers, and 3,339 enlisted men, the highest since World War II.[75]

The respite after the EUCOM exercise in late September ended on October 25 when the regiment was alerted and rolled to the field for what was supposed to be an overnight deployment. Four days later the 1st Battalion returned to Grafenwöhr for training in squad and platoon problems and night patrolling, followed by the 2nd Battalion on November 5. This training was completed on November 11, and was followed by another alert on the 28th. The alert was inspected by the Seventh Army Commander, Lieutenant General Manton Eddy, who observed the regiment move out of its kasernes in a heavy rain, march fifteen miles, return to post, and prepare for motor pool as well as "junk on the bunk" inspections. The month of December was spent on ranges and conducting the by-now traditional Christmas parties for the children in the German Youth Activity.

The Command Report of the 16th Infantry for 1951 begins, "There were many things done exceptionally well, but of major concern were the things that could have been done better." It goes on to say that, "The most striking characteristic of the 16th Infantry Regiment has been its outstanding esprit-de-corps."

In the area of discipline, the regiment experienced what initially appeared to be a high number of courts-martial cases for the second year in a row. The Rangers racked up twenty-five general courts-martial, 325 special courts-martial, and 458 summary courts-martial in 1951. Except for an increase of the number of special courts-martial, the number of disciplinary cases was little changed from the year before. The increase in special courts-martial, however, was attributable to the addition of the new 3rd Battalion's statistics. Absent the latter, the regiment actually experienced a significant decrease in disciplinary cases in all categories except one, and only a slight decrease in that one.[76]

Training continued to be intense in 1951, with the Rangers spending nearly five months in the field on training exercises, alerts, and ranges. For example, the 1st Battalion spent 121 days at Tennenlohe, Grafenwöhr, or other field locations; the 2nd spent 156; and the new 3rd Battalion spent 165 days in the field. And these figures do not include the time that individual companies went to the field.[77]

The usual squad through battalion training problems were conducted during the winter and spring and culminated in the new Armed Forces Field Tests (AFFT) at Graf from May through July. Each battalion was put through a series of graded exercises designed to evaluate its performance on specific combat missions. The grading team from the 1st Infantry Division Training Headquarters (Provisional) noted several deficiencies in the regiment: the failure of squad leaders to exercise proper fire control procedures; weak troop leading procedures by platoon leaders and squad leaders; and the lack of understanding by squad, platoon, and company commanders of the capabilities and tactical employment of supporting weapons.

In spite of these problems, all three battalions received high ratings compared to the other infantry battalions in the division. At the end of the 1st Battalion's AFFT, in which it received a "superior" rating, General Dahlquist was briefed on its performance and reportedly remarked, "You can't be as good as the umpires say you are." But it was the 2nd and 3rd Battalions that went on to tie for the highest scores in the division—an impressive achievement for such a new battalion. After observing the 3rd Battalion on its attack problem, Dahlquist stated that the battalion's actions were "characterized by people who know how to fight a ground war."[78]

The fall exercises included corps-level maneuvers for the first time. The 1st Infantry Division had been assigned to the V Corps upon the latter's return to Germany the previous year, and with that headquarters, the division participated in Exercise Jupiter, September 26–30. The follow-on EUCOM exercise, Combine, held October 2–10, was the largest U.S. Army peacetime maneuver since before World War II. Over 150,000 troops participated, including the V Corps, VII Corps, 4th Infantry Division, 2nd Armored Division, the I French Corps, and troops from the British Army of the Rhine.[79]

The exercise kicked off on October 2 when the aggressor force, the III Mechanized Corps (played by the 2nd Constabulary Brigade) attacked the 1st Infantry Division, which held positions forward of the Main River southeast of Frankfurt. The 22nd Infantry, attached to the Big Red One from the 4th Division, conducted a covering-force battle and then withdrew through the 16th Infantry and across the river the following day. After holding until October 5, the Rangers withdrew to positions along the Main. Later that day, the 6th Ranger Company, acting as an aggressor unit, parachuted in and captured a bridge at Hanau in the 16th Infantry sector. The regiment quickly counterattacked and retook the bridge.

On October 6, elements of the aggressor 24th Airborne Division landed south of Aschaffenburg on the west side of the Main on October 6 to assist the 67th Light Infantry Division in capturing a railroad bridge over the Rhine. This move caused

much of the Seventh Army to pull back from the Main River positions. It appeared that the 1st Division might have to pull back across the Rhine the following day, but it held, as the I French Corps moved up to the south to counterattack on October 8. That day, the 16th Infantry moved to an assembly area to assist the French attack.

At 5:30 a.m. the following morning, the Rangers jumped off in support of the French effort. Attacking eastward, the regiment reached the Main near Aschaffenburg and prepared to conduct an assault crossing of the river to seize a bridgehead. With none other than General Dwight D. Eisenhower observing, the Rangers seized the far side and, by noon, had taken its objectives. There, it was forced to halt until the Blue Spaders captured their objectives. The latter were seized at 4:00 p.m. The push continued the following morning, and the exercise ended at 1:45 p.m. on October 10.[80]

The 16th Infantry had performed well. The men sensed this, and morale was high when the regiment arrived back at home stations. For the next several days, the troops conducted recovery operations and made preparations for the regimental birthday.

The 1951 Organization Day ceremonies were not held on the traditional date of October 4 because of the regiment's participation in Combine. Instead Organization Day was celebrated on October 19. Attending the affair was Major General Thomas S. Timberman, the new 1st Infantry Division CG. On his first visit to the regiment since taking command, Timberman was the honored guest at the traditional review. After the reading of the regimental history and before the pass-in-review, the general addressed the soldiers, complimenting them on their "superior performance" in the recent EUCOM maneuver. He reminded them, "Your regiment has few equals in any army." Subsequently Colonel Royce, soon to leave the regiment, told them, "We have, in the past year, been molded into a well-trained, hard-hitting, fighting force, and this could not have been accomplished without the sincere and active interest of each one of you here."[81]

In November, the 3rd Battalion celebrated the first anniversary of its return to the regiment with a parade staged by the battalion NCOs. On the reviewing stand as guests of honor were several World War II battalion veterans, including Lieutenant Colonel Ed Wozenski, who had commanded the 3rd Battalion from February 1945 to the end of the war. Wozenski had done well in the postwar army and was now commanding the 169th Infantry Regiment, 43rd Infantry Division. Also on the stand were Major Kimball Richmond, Major Finke, and Master Sergeant McCarthy.[82] Richmond had commanded I Company through D-Day until he was wounded in October 1944, and McCarthy had commanded M Company from December 1944 to June 1945, when he reverted to his enlisted grade in the postwar draw-down. John Finke, who had commanded two companies in the 2nd Battalion during the war, assumed command of the 3rd Battalion later that month.

On November 1, 1951, Royce departed to become the new

assistant division commander, and William W. O'Connor assumed command of the 16th Infantry. O'Connor was a West Point classmate of Royce's. During World War II, he had served as the chief of staff of the 76th Infantry Division, and was serving as the chief of staff of the V Corps when appointed to command of the Rangers.[83] He assumed command of the 16th Infantry at a time when there were significant changes in the wind.

The year 1952 was indeed a time of change for the regiment. The regiment would participate in army integration, see the departure of General Eisenhower from the army, and a move to a permanent new duty station. What did not change were the frequent alerts, good morale, and lots of time in the field.

In 1948, President Truman had signed the executive order directing the integration of the United States armed forces, but it was not until June of 1951 that the 16th Infantry began the process, and then only in driblets. During that month, the first black soldiers to serve with the 16th Infantry since 1945 were assigned to the regiment because of athletic abilities. Still, the integration of the 16th Infantry went relatively smoothly. Sergeant Charlie Silk, then a member of the regiment's Counterfire Platoon, recalled that

> integration really began in the 16th Infantry in 1951 with the integration of the athletic teams.…They started for the season of 1951 with the baseball teams. They brought some black players over that we had played against from the 122nd Trucking Company, and I guess [guys from] the other trucking companies went over to the 26th and then 18th Regiments. Then we began to integrate the basketball teams, and so on. To the best of my knowledge, it began through sports. I think if you were going to do something like that, it was an excellent way to do it. It made the whole process go more smoothly. I think by doing it that way, the other [white] soldiers in the regiment would see the regiment being represented by black players as well as the whites, and that way they were accepted more readily into the company, because they were able to show their playing skills.[84]

It was not until March 1952 that the 16th Infantry began to integrate in earnest. Instead of serving in platoon packages, black soldiers were assigned as individual replacements to all regimental units. The men came from the 370th and 373rd Armored Infantry Battalions, proud lineal successors of the World War I and II regiments of the same name.[85] Those units now passed into history.

The following month, K Company was railed to Aschaffenburg to participate in a farewell review for General Eisenhower. Representative units from all over EUCOM attended the ceremonies. The general's departure from the service signaled that the men who had led the army during World War II were fast departing the active-duty scene. Only seven years after the war, virtually all the theater, army group,

army, and most corps commanders were already retired. The men were sorry to see Ike go.

The arrival of two National Guard divisions in the spring and summer of 1951 to reinforce EUCOM caused a shuffling of units in Germany. As it became apparent that these divisions were going to stay for the long haul, the Seventh Army staff determined that further moves were necessary to better consolidate units into tighter divisional areas. Therefore, in May, Colonel O'Connor announced that the regiment would move to Schweinfurt in June.

On June 20, the troops of the regiment moved to bivouac areas to facilitate the turnover of Monteith, Pinder, Adams, and Johnson Barracks to the 169th Infantry. A short time later, the Rangers moved to Grafenwöhr for summer training. Upon its conclusion, the regiment moved into its new homes at Ledward (regiment minus) and Conn Barracks (Tank and Mortar Companies) in mid-July.[86]

The morale continued to be rated as excellent in 1952. One of the reasons cited is that the recreational facilities on the posts in Schweinfurt were as good, or possibly better, than those in Nürnberg. The kasernes boasted two large gymnasiums, two enlisted men's clubs, two bowling alleys, several PXs and snack bars, two theaters, and an excellent Special Service club. Another reason appears to be the venereal disease rate. While acquiring the disease did nothing to improve morale, no doubt the act of acquiring it did. In 1952, there were 269 new VD cases compared with only 89 in the previous year. An analysis showed that the rate soared after the move to Schweinfurt. Perhaps the "recreational facilities" in the city of Schweinfurt were better than those in Nürnburg as well, or it just might be the attraction of new fields to plow. Whatever the reason, it was clear that the men's morale was still up.[87]

One thing is certain: the men were not bored. Frequent alerts and field time saw to that. EUCOM had ordered increased vigilance in response to signs that the Soviets might take advantage of the situation in Korea. Now, when the regiment was alerted, instead of rolling to the field over night, it usually remained there for a week, sometimes two. By January, the regiment had one battalion on immediate alert at all times, and by the following August, the alert battalion remained in an assembly area in the field until relieved by the next battalion. Indoctrination classes on Soviet uniforms, equipment, and tactics also increased significantly.[88] International tensions made the average soldier focus even more on the training.

The first big exercise of 1952 was the 1st Division's Exercise Ferryboat in late March. This maneuver was a cold, wet, and miserable experience for the Rangers. The aggressor force was the 14th Armored Cavalry Regiment, which simulated a Soviet attack across the inter-German border. Taking up positions near Schney in a chilly spring rain, the RCT prepared defensive positions to ward off the blow. Unfortunately, the string of successes that the regiment achieved the previous few years was broken when the cavalrymen were able to break through, thus terminating the exercise early.

This lackluster performance was redeemed by several other training achievements during the year, however. During the AFFT cycle at Graf in June and July, the regiment's performance was equal to that of the previous year. Additionally, regimental marksman accomplished several conspicuous feats, the most notable being that of Corporal Joseph Zapata of Houston, Texas, who scored 639 of 640 points on the M-1 qualification course, a EUCOM record.[89]

Increasing Soviet-U.S. tensions struck home again during the regiment's Organization Day ceremonies. The celebration kicked off that morning with the customary review and transitioned to the field day activities. At 1:00 p.m., however, Colonel O'Connor received notice of an alert, and less than two hours later, the 1st Battalion, on alert status, marched out the gates for the assembly area, with the rest of the RCT following later that day.

While in the field in 1952, the RCT participated in Exercise Bell Hook, which consisted of two phases. The first phase was a division CPX held October 7-9, followed by a maneuver phase held October 15-19. At 12:45 a.m. on the 15th, the Rangers received a warning order for movement to new positions, and by daybreak, they were digging in positions on the west side of the Rhine. When the exercise ended on October 19, the 3rd Battalion remained in the field as the alert battalion while the rest of the regiment returned to home stations.

Throughout 1953 and 1954, the 16th Infantry Regiment's activities continued in pretty much the same pattern as 1950. There were frequent alerts, plenty of field time at Graf and Tennenlohe, and occasional breaks for recreational activities. With the death of Josef Stalin in March 1953, and as the Korean armistice took hold that summer, tensions between the United States and the Soviet Union began to ease. Though the Soviets protested the steady march toward formation of the Federal Republic of Germany and its military integration with NATO, they realized that there was little they could do about it. The resulting reduction of tensions caused alerts to be pared back to 1950 levels, though training continued to be paramount in USAREUR (Headquarters, U.S. Army Europe; redesignated as such from Headquarters, EUCOM, on August 1, 1952). The two National Guard divisions that had reinforced NATO in 1951 were redesignated as Regular Army formations and became a permanent part of the Seventh Army.

With the reduction of tensions in Germany, army planners looked for more efficient ways to rotate personnel to Europe. One solution was Operation Gyroscope, which called for the replacement of Europe-based divisions by stateside units approximately every three years. This system allowed every stateside division the opportunity to share in the burdens of European defense. Gyroscope appeared to be a more efficient way to rotate personnel, because, theoretically, it allowed soldiers who had spent several years working together and building well-trained units to remain together while they switched places with

like units from the states. It was hoped that this system would prove more efficient than the inherently disruptive individual replacement system. To test the new idea, the Department of the Army selected the 1st Infantry Division as one of two divisions to participate in the first Gyroscope. After serving thirteen years as an occupation force and defender of Western Europe, the Big Red One would come home in the summer of 1955.

The other division selected to participate in the rotation was the 10th Infantry Division, then stationed at Fort Riley, Kansas. During the second week of January, Colonel Kenneth Dyer, commander of the 86th Infantry Regiment, along with several of his staff officers and members of the division's advanced party, arrived in Schweinfurt. From January 12 to 14, Dyer and his officers coordinated with their counterparts from the 16th Infantry to plan the 86th Infantry's assumption of missions and occupation of Ledward and Conn Barracks, scheduled for June.[90]

Four months later, the 16th Infantry's advanced party departed in two sections, on May 2 and 8 respectively, for Fort Riley. Twenty days later, the 86th Infantry's advanced party arrived in Schweinfurt, and the process of inventorying and signing for billets, furniture, and equipment began. Upon completing the inventory, the two regiments began swapping locations. In mid-July, the Rangers were railed to Bremerhaven, Germany, and boarded the USS *Upshur* for the voyage home. In a scene reminiscent of the division's return from France some thirty-six years previous, after the First World War, the men of the Big Red One crowded the ship's rails as *Upshur* slipped past the Statue of Liberty.

After docking at Pier 4 of the Brooklyn Army Base, the division band strode down the gangplank and played as the colors of the 1st Infantry Division followed, fluttering in the cool ocean breeze. On hand to greet the ship were various dignitaries from the Defense Department, the city of New York, and the Society of the First Division, as well as five former division commanders—Allen, Huebner, Andrus, Milburn, and Dahlquist—and the current commander, Major General Guy S. Meloy. A citation for "distinguished and exceptional service" was presented to the division by the New York City administrator and, after several speeches, the entire division clambered down the gangplanks and sped off on thirty-day furloughs, after which they would to report to their new home at Fort Riley.[91]

Needless to say, Fort Riley had changed considerably since the 16th Infantry had served there in 1880. In the following decades, Riley had served as home to numerous cavalry regiments and the Cavalry School. During World War I, a subpost, Camp Funston, was built on the eastern reaches of the reservation as a "National Army" cantonment; it was rebuilt during World War II, to house new divisions mobilized for that conflict. In early 1941, Camp Forsyth, the Cavalry Replacement Training Center, was established on the western end of Fort Riley. After the demise of the cavalry branch at the end of the war, Riley became home to the Army General School and, in 1948, the 10th Infantry Division was reactivated there. For the next thirty-five years (excepting the division's five-year tour in Vietnam), the old post would serve as home to America's oldest and most decorated division.

In August 1955, the 16th Infantry Regiment moved into its new billets at Camp Funston. During the First World War, Funston was the mobilization center for the 89th Division, commanded by Major General Leonard Wood. Just before and during the early stages of World War II, the camp was briefly the home of the 2nd Cavalry Division when Terry Allen commanded that unit. Now, the units of the Big Red One took up residence there until a permanent, more modern troop area could be built on Custer Hill, with the 16th Infantry occupying the block of barracks located between 1st and 6th Streets and D and E Avenues.

Though duty at Fort Riley would be at a slower pace than that which the Rangers had experienced in Germany, there was plenty to keep them busy. The next ten years would see significant changes to the army and to the 16th Infantry. The advent of the nuclear weapons was driving the evolution of modern warfare and causing the development of new ideas and concepts. It had created new battlefield conditions, and the army had to be prepared to operate in such an environment; hence, between 1957 and 1963, the 16th Infantry underwent two major reorganizations to meet the conditions of modern war. It would also redeploy to Germany, but it would ultimately end up fighting in a kind of war that the army had not prepared to wage. Those changes were still in the future, however, when the regiment resumed training at Fort Riley. The first major training event for the 16th Infantry occurred in November 1956. During the period November 17-21, the 16th Infantry participated in Exercise Red Arrow, an exercise created to test the air transportability of an RCT in a simulated nuclear battlefield scenario. For this exercise, the regiment was organized under the RCT concept with its usual attachments, the 7th Field Artillery Battalion and A Company, 1st Engineers. Company A, 1st Medical Battalion, had been dropped from the RCT line-up when the regiment was still in Germany, and A Battery, 48th Antiaircraft Artillery Battalion, had been added.

Prior to the actual exercise, two thousand RCT troops spent several days at Marshall Field training to load C-119, C-123, and C-124 aircraft. On November 15 and 16, RCT units were transported to Smokey Hill Air Force Base in Salina, Kansas, and Olathe Naval Air Station in Olathe, Kansas, to prepare for the air movement back into the maneuver area on Fort Riley. On November 17, the lead infantry units were air-landed into Marshall Field, then air transported into the Fort Riley maneuver area by H-21 helicopters. Once landing areas were secured, other elements were inserted directly into dirt strips in the maneuver area, in the fashion of an assault landing.[92]

Over the next four days, the regiment conducted a series of attacks in icy, cold weather conditions across the rolling Fort Riley plains. The temperatures dropped to twenty degrees and were accompanied by snow and sleet, which caused more than

one Korean War veteran to remark on the similarities between the training exercise and that war. Despite the weather, morale remained high, as the 16th Infantry took on no less than seven aggressor battalions. At the end of the exercise, the division chaplain, Chaplain (Lieutenant Colonel) John I. Rhea, remarked that the spirit of the Rangers was "way up there. I met only a couple of men who complained."[93]

The following February, the 1st Infantry Division began the transition to the so-called Pentomic tables of organization. The development of the Pentomic concept was prompted by the conditions and tactical problems of the nuclear battlefield. Army planners believed that the old triangular division was both too cumbersome and too concentrated on the battlefield, hence exceedingly vulnerable to heavy casualties by a tactical nuclear strike. The remedy was to eliminate the three-regiment structure and reorganize the division into five "battle groups" that would be spread out over greater distances and, therefore, make a less-vulnerable target. The reorganization would have far-reaching effects on the 16th Infantry and other combat arms regiments throughout the army.

On February 1, 1957, the entire 16th Infantry, less Company A, was inactivated on paper. The regimental headquarters and the headquarters company reverted to control of the Department of the Army, and the Service, Heavy Mortar, Tank, and Medical Companies were disbanded. Companies B through M were redesignated HHC, 2nd through 12th Battle Groups. The HHCs of the 1st, 2nd, and 3rd Battalions were redesignated HHC, 13th through 15th Battle Groups, and Company A was reorganized and redesignated 1st Battle Group, 16th Infantry (1-16), the only remaining active unit. New subordinate companies were constituted to take the place of those redesignated as battle groups.

The foregoing actions were, of course, all on paper. The existing flesh and blood regiment was reorganized into a battle group by reassigning companies F through M to the 2nd Battle Group, 2nd Infantry, and reorganizing the remainder of the units into the 1st Battle Group, 16th Infantry. With the stroke of a typewriter key, the "regiment" ceased to exist as an active organization, and the remaining elements in the 16th Infantry were reduced from an organization of over three thousand men to one of about fourteen hundred.

Under the battle group TOE, the 16th Infantry consisted of a battle group headquarters, a headquarters and service company, a mortar battery, and four line companies, each with four rifle platoons and a weapons platoon. This organization was later modified to consist of a battle group headquarters and headquarters company, a combat support company, and five line companies, each with three rifle platoons and a weapons platoon. The span of control of three units at each level of command in the triangular concept had basically evolved to five in the Pentomic structure.[94]

The Pentomic structure also caused changes to the habitual task organizations adopted under the old RCT concept.

Now the "16th RCT" became a "task force" labeled "TF 1-16." Under the task force concept, the habitual task organization now became the following:

TF 1-16:
1st Battle Group, 16th Infantry
A Battery, 1st Battalion, 7th Field Artillery
B Company, 1st Medium Tank Battalion, 69th Armor
B Company, 1st Engineers
2nd Platoon, B Company, 121st Signal Battalion
2nd Platoon, A Company, 701st Ordnance Battalion

Occasionally, the 2nd Flight, Direct Support Platoon, 1st Aviation Company, was attached as well, but for only specific types of missions.[95]

One of the more interesting aspects of the restructuring to the battle group TOE was the addition of tanks and armored personnel carriers (APC) to the reconnaissance platoon. In November 1957, the platoon received two M-41 "Walker Bulldog" tanks and two of the new M-59 "low profile" APCs. Though the M-59 had a lower profile than its predecessor, the M-58, it was still a giant compared to the APCs that the 16th Infantry would later come to know. A short time later, four M-41s were also assigned to the assault gun platoon.[96]

After transitioning to the battle group TOE, Colonel Roy Doran, battle group commander and regimental commander since August 1956, moved the 16th Infantry to the field for three months of training in the Pentomic structure. A transportation battalion, equipped with enough M-59 APCs to fully mechanize at least one battle group (or one company per battle group), had been added, allowing a few elements of the 16th Infantry to operate as mechanized infantry for the first time.

While the battle group trained on the plains of Kansas, Colonel Doran was assigned another mission. In June, the 16th Infantry was to receive nine hundred soldiers to put through basic training and advanced individual training (AIT) for their eventual reassignment to the 8th Infantry Division in Germany. After rolling in from the field in late April, the unit went to work preparing instructors to train the recruits and set up the required training schedules. By early June, the Rangers were ready, and on June 12, the trainees arrived. About 180 were assigned to each company.

During their stay with the 16th Infantry, the trainees received superb training to ready them for duty overseas. They also participated in other regimental activities. For example, a week after their arrival, the entire battle group, trainees and members, were involved in the annual Army Day celebration. The battle group held a review during which the regimental history was read as battle streamers were added to the colors for each campaign. A series of sporting events followed.[97]

In July, Samuel Fuller, the Hollywood movie director, visited the division. Fuller, who had served with the regiment from Sicily to the end of the war, delighted in his association with the 16th Infantry and the "Big Red One," and he always found a way to mention the 1st Infantry Division in every movie he made. In one movie, a western, he even had a Big Red One patch inconspicuously scrawled on a fence post just to get his plug in for the division. While visiting his old outfit, Fuller announced that he was preparing to shoot a war movie called *The Big Red One* for release the following year.[98] It so happened, however, that twenty-five years would pass before the movie was made and released, with Lee Marvin in the starring role.

The recruits also had the opportunity to learn more about the regiment's history by visiting the 16th Infantry museum. Established under Colonel Duran's authority shortly after the regiment's arrival at Fort Riley in 1955, the museum held numerous mementoes of the 16th Infantry. Among the most valuable items was the Medal of Honor awarded to Henry Schroeder for his actions in the Philippines in 1900. Schroeder donated the medal, as well as number of bolo and krise swords, while visiting the museum in 1956.

Other items in the museum's collection included recently returned flags presented to the 2nd Battalion in 1917, and sports and marksmanship trophies from the 1920s and '30s. The collection grew continually with the frequent donation of other items. In October 1957, H. E. Powers of Poughkeepsie, New York, donated the regimental colors that Corporal William Van Dorne had carried up San Juan Hill. When the museum had received and installed the flag, Private Carlos O. Melendez, a native of Santiago, Cuba, and now a Ranger, stated, "Everyone in Santiago has heard of the Sixteenth. In the fifth grade, I was told of the famous charge. It is a thrill to see the actual flag!"[99]

The museum acquired other regimental treasures in February 1958. Master Sergeant James Greene, the museum curator, had somehow learned that Mrs. Carrie L. Hay, mother of Private Merle D. Hay, was still alive in Glidden, Iowa, and that she might be willing to donate a number of her son's mementoes from the regiment. Greene took off for Glidden and found Mrs. Hay. The latter was delighted that the regiment was still aware of her son's place in its history and was pleased to present a number of items to the museum, including Hays's coffin flag; a collection of poems written about Hay, Gresham, and Enright; and a miniature replica of the monument erected in France commemorating the sacrifice of the three men.[100]

In January 1958, the museum, along with the rest of the battle group, moved into new barracks on Custer Hill. These quarters had several advantages. First, they were the most modern billets in the army at that time, which meant they were comfortable and well-insulated from the cold of the hard Kansas winters. Second, they were on the highest ground around for miles. The World War II "splinter barracks" at Funston were located on the flood plain of the Kansas River, and were prone to flooding during periods of heavy rain. Finally, Custer Hill was right next to the best maneuver areas of the post. Now, it was just a short hike to the training areas.

Just after the move to Custer Hill, the army announced

that it was no longer feasible to rotate divisions to Europe under the Gyroscope concept, and that the rotations would be conducted at the battle group level. On April 3, 1958, the Fort Riley post newspaper, *The American Traveler*, informed its readers that, beginning in late 1958, the five battle groups of the 1st Infantry Division would rotate to Germany to replace the battle groups of the 8th Infantry. Additionally, the 1st Battle Group, 16th Infantry, would replace the 10th Infantry at Würzberg in early 1959.[101]

In May, the Department of the Army announced the formation of the "Strategic Army Corps" (STRAC). Intended as a rapid deployment force, the STRAC consisted of the XVIII Airborne Corps as the controlling headquarters, the 82nd and 101st Airborne Divisions, and the 1st and 4th Infantry Divisions. With the STRAC mission came an increase in air mobility training requirements.

The following month, the battle group, now under the command of Colonel Frederick W. Collins, participated in another air mobility exercise, not unlike that of Red Arrow two years previous. Dubbed Operation Ranger, the exercise was conducted June 9-12 and included a ground movement to Schilling Air Force Base in Salina followed by air load training at that site. Flown in on the C-123s of the 347th Troop Carrier Squadron from Pope Air Force Base, the Rangers were inserted into dirt strips at Fort Riley and went almost directly into action against an aggressor force.[102]

In August, the regiment was visited by Hans H. Rosencrantz, great-nephew of Frederick Rosencrantz, the beloved 16th Infantry officer who was buried in the Fort Riley cemetery in 1879. Members of the regiment escorted Hans to the grave site, then took him over to view the marble tablet dedicated to Rosencrantz in St. Mary's chapel on main post.[103]

December 1958 and January 1959 were times of great change, excitement and, in some ways, sadness for the 16th Infantry. On December 1, the command of the battle group passed from Colonel Collins to Colonel David S. Daley, a 1939 graduate of the Citadel. That evening, a formal dinner was held at the Custer Hill Service Club during which Colonel Collins said his goodbyes to the officers of the battle group, then handed over the silver baton of command to Daley. The presentation of the baton of command was a ritual that started in the early 1950s and ended soon thereafter, just before the 16th Infantry's deployment to Vietnam. The baton is now lost.

In January, the regiment lost two old friends. With the regiment's rotation to Europe pending, Paddy Roughn, then a chief warrant officer and battle group supply officer, decided that after twenty-five years with the 16th Infantry it was time to retire. Roughn's departure left Master Sergeant George C. Zares as the only remaining 16th Infantry D-Day veteran with the unit. Upon his retirement, Roughn still wore the same pair of 16th Infantry crests he had been issued at Fort Jay in 1933.[104]

January also saw the passing of Henry Schroeder, age eighty-three, who won a Medal of Honor in 1900 while serving

with the regiment in the Philippines. Upon receiving word on January 22 that Schroeder had died, a funeral detail from the battle group traveled to California to render him the final honors he richly deserved.[105]

By 1959, the units of the 1st Infantry Division had been home for over three years. It was time for the 16th Infantry to rotate back to Germany. On October 28, 1958, the division headquarters issued Movement Order Number 25 directing the battle group to report to the Brooklyn Army Terminal for shipment back to Germany on March 1, 1959. On March 5, the Rangers boarded the USNS *Darby* and, after nine days at sea, arrived at Bremerhaven on March 13. Upon debarkation, the 1st Battle Group, 16th Infantry, was relieved from assignment to the Big Red One and assigned to the 8th Infantry Division "Pathfinders." For the first time since 1917, the 16th Infantry was separated from the 1st Infantry Division.[106]

It did not take long for the 16th Infantry to make its mark in the 8th Division, however. In September 1959, the Rangers deployed to the field and underwent the new Army Training Test (ATT), which had replaced the AFFT. Although the troops were unfamiliar with the local terrain, they earned a superior rating for their performance and were cited by the V Corps commander for their efforts.

Notwithstanding the regiment's separation from the 1st Infantry Division, the rank and file continued to observe the traditions formed while the regiment was part of the Big Red One. For example, in July 1959, Lieutenant Colonel Quinton L. Gates, the battle group executive officer, accompanied by Captain David W. Affleck (Assistant S3), Private First Class Burt G. Laur (driver), and Private First Class Donald L. Andrews (interpreter), traveled to Fléville to ascertain whether the blue-and-white vair shield in the 16th Infantry coat of arms was inspired by the town's coat of arms. Additionally, the group wanted to let the town fathers know that the 16th Infantry was back in Europe, and that the unit wanted to maintain an association with the town for historical and social purposes. Though the connection between the regimental heraldry and the town's coat of arms shield was not confirmed, the trip was nonetheless considered a great success because of the good feelings the visit engendered between the Americans and their French hosts.[107]

The men's pride in the 16th Infantry was demonstrated in various ceremonies involving the battle group. For example, as part of the 1959 Patton Remembrance Day ceremonies in Ettlebrück, Luxembourg, the 16th Infantry paraded through the streets of that town in fine style. The town fathers were struck by the unit's appearance and soldierly bearing and requested Colonel Daley to have the battle group participate again the next year. He accepted and this parade became an annual activity for the battle group until it departed Germany in 1963.

Another indicator that the outfit had high morale and pride was its low AWOL rate. In the period August 28-February 28, 1960, for example, B Company had no AWOLs, an achievement that earned it a letter of commendation from the

USAREUR commander.

Just after the arrival of the 1st Battle Group in Germany, another event occurred that signaled the distinct change in the direction that regimental lineages were evolving in the United States Army. On May 1, 1959, the 3rd Battle Group, 16th Infantry (lineally, the old C Company), was activated with headquarters at the Lincoln W. Stoddard Reserve Center in Worcester, Massachusetts, under the command of Colonel Irving J. Yarock. The 3rd Battle Group was an Army Reserve unit assigned to the 94th Infantry Division. Like many reserve component units, most of the subordinate companies were scattered around the state. Thus, Combat Support and E Companies were stationed in Worcester with the battle group headquarters, and the remainder of the units were based as follows: A Company in Uxbridge, B Company in Dudley, C Company in Fitchburg, and D Company in Franklin.

Fortunately, most of these units were based relatively close to Fort Devens, which enabled Yarock to assemble the unit for training at higher collective tasks on a more frequent basis than most National Guard or Reserve units. As well, the battle group often held its weekend drills in the field at Devens rather than at hometown reserve centers.

The 2nd Infantry Brigade was also based at Fort Devens, and the battle group staff formed close ties with that unit. Units of the 2nd Brigade were helpful in providing assistance, information, and equipment to assist the 3rd Battle Group in its efforts to improve its combat readiness.

Though Devens was close at hand, the battle group typically conducted its Annual Active Duty Training (ANACDUTRA) at Pine Camp, New York (now Fort Drum), site of the 16th Infantry's 1935 maneuvers as part of First Army. For at least one year (1963), however, the battle group did perform its ANACDUTRA at Devens with the 2nd Brigade, 5th Infantry Division (organized from the 2nd Infantry Brigade in 1962).

The next major training event for the 1st Battle Group was USAREUR's annual winter maneuver, dubbed Wintershield II. For this second Wintershield exercise, sixty thousand troops of the Seventh Army deployed to the field to participate in repelling a simulated invasion of West Germany. The VII Corps and the German 11th Panzer Grenadier Brigade assumed the role of aggressor forces, against the defending V Corps (including the 8th Division and 1st Battle Group), 11th French Mechanized Brigade, and 14th Armored Cavalry Regiment. The exercise was conducted in Bavaria, between Hohenfels and Berlangendorf, during a stretch of severe winter weather. For its part in Exercise Wintershield II, the battle group won special praise from Lieutenant General Frederic J. Brown, who wrote to its commander, Colonel John Singlaub:

Your night attack to secure crossings at the Vils River was a model operation. In all instances the sound planning, practiced techniques, and professional execution marked your command as combat ready, physically fit and superbly trained. You and your command are to be commended for superior and noteworthy contribution to the overall success of the exercise. I am singularly impressed with the professional competence of your first class and famous outfit. You ably demonstrated your combat readiness.[108]

While the battle group was involved in Wintershield II, a certain Private John J. Copeland was en route to Baumholder. He arrived at Bremerhaven in early February, was processed through the division replacement company at Bad Kreuznach, then put on a train to Baumholder to join his new outfit. He recalled that he thought that he might be in trouble when he discovered that the train had to *back into the station* because Baumholder was literally the end of the rail line. He also noticed that there were still "a lot of pillboxes and dragon's teeth in the area." Assigned to the communications platoon in HHC, his concern was relieved when he soon realized he had joined a good unit:

When I arrived, the battle group had just returned from Wintershield II. Everybody, including me, was put to work cleaning, repairing, and putting the equipment back in good condition. They were good soldiers. Everybody was there to do an important job and they did it well....We had a great commander, Colonel John Singlaub. He was a West Pointer, and he had the respect of the men and he also respected us....Even though we were in the 8th Division, we learned all the traditions of the 16th while it served in the 1st Infantry Division. We kept them alive.[109]

In July 1961, B Company was selected to travel to Le Havre, France to participate in making Darryl F. Zanuck's movie *The Longest Day*. The troops had a good time mingling with actors Gregory Peck, Henry Fonda, and John Wayne, and they did such a good job that Zanuck wanted to pay them as extras. The new battle group commander, Colonel George H. Russell, intervened and turned down the offer by stating that the men were there to conduct amphibious warfare training and that they were already being paid by Uncle Sam. Needless to say, Colonel Russell was not popular with the B Company troops, at least for a day or two.[110]

The following month, while B Company was still in France, the Berlin Wall crisis erupted. General Bruce C. Clarke, USAREUR commander, ordered Major General Edgar C. Doleman, commanding general of the 8th Infantry Division, to send a mechanized task force down the autobahn through the East German sector to Berlin as a show of force to prove to the world, and especially NATO and Europe, that the United States was not going to back down. The troops of the 16th Infantry heard rumors that they would be the ones to go, but because B Company was still in France, the 1st Battle Group, 18th Infantry was selected instead.

The Berlin Wall incident sent shivers throughout the world. President Kennedy called up 120,000 troops, including two

National Guard divisions, to counter this threat from the Soviets. For almost a year, military forces on both sides were frequently on alert and always in a high state of readiness. The incident also set off a series of events that caused the Rangers a few problems.

About the time the Berlin Wall went up, a shipment of M-14 rifles arrived in Baumholder for the 1st Battle Group, which was to be the first unit in USAREUR to get the new rifles. Unit armorers had diligently prepared their old M-1s for turn-in and soldiers were already attending classes to learn how the new rifle functioned. But when the 18th Infantry was sent to Berlin, someone at higher levels decided to equip that unit with the new rifles instead.[111] This decision moved the 16th Infantry down the issue priority list to where the 18th Infantry had been.

In autumn 1962, the battle group's M-14s finally arrived and the armorers once again prepared the M-1s for turn-in. On October 19, the supply sergeants completed the turn-in process and the Rangers received their new rifles. Then, on October 22, USAREUR went on high alert because of the Cuban Missile crisis. The following day, the battle group was ordered to turn in the M-14s and redraw the M-1s because there was not enough M-14 ammunition in Europe to go to war![112]

Upon receiving the alert, all USAREUR units prepared to deploy to their wartime assembly areas. Colonel John J. C. Moore, the new battle group commander, called a formation for the entire unit and told the men, "Until further notice, there will be no more practice alerts. Next time you hear that siren, it is for real. Be prepared to move out and never come back." Copeland remembered that this period was particularly tense. All the vehicles were combat loaded with necessary ammunition, mines, and other equipment, normally issued only for training. Personal weapons were kept in wall lockers rather than the arms room, a highly unusual practice even in those days. Fortunately, the siren never sounded. But Rangers were ready to roll to their GDP (General Defense Plan) positions if the balloon had gone up.[113]

The GDP area for the 1st Battle Group at this time was the Fulda Gap, the most likely avenue of approach for an invading Soviet army. The unit's area was close to Wildflicken, and, as any USAREUR soldier who has had a GDP can testify, the troops of TF 1-16 knew theirs "like the backs of their hands." The battle group and company commanders, platoon leaders, platoon sergeants, and squad leaders spent many hours walking their ground looking for the best fields of fire, dead space, locations for crew-served weapons, and obstacle locations to develop a defensive position that would stop or at least slow invading Soviet forces. However, the battle group configuration made the job of defending such a large GDP difficult.

After the army reorganized to the Pentomic concept, it did not take long for many people to realize that the idea was flawed. The span of control was too large; the existing communications systems were incapable of supporting units over the required distances; and the U.S. Congress was leery of placing tactical nuclear weapons (the Davy Crockett missile system)

under the control of a sergeant at the company level. As a result, in 1963, the army began the process of another major reorganization, this time under the Reorganization Objective Army Division (ROAD) concept. This TOE called for a return of the triangular concept, albeit not to a fixed regimental structure. Instead, there were to be separate battalions that could be attached to one of three brigade headquarters to meet mission requirements. Though in peacetime a battalion's attachment to a given brigade would be habitual, even seeming to be permanent, in wartime that association would mean little as battalions would be swapped around as needed.

The first of the 16th Infantry units to reorganize to the new TOE was the 3rd Battle Group. On January 7, 1963, it was reorganized and redesignated as the 3rd Battalion at Worcester, and concurrently, it was relieved from the 94th Infantry Division and assigned to the 187th Infantry Brigade (Separate). Next to reorganize was the 1st Battle Group. The existing unit in Germany was reorganized and redesignated the 1st Battalion, 16th Infantry, on April 1, 1963, but the colors were shipped back to Fort Riley with a unit that had just completed a Long Thrust rotation. On April 25, the unit in Germany was redesignated the 1st Battalion, 13th Infantry, and the 1st Battalion was reassigned to the 1st Infantry Division.

Though the colors of the 1st Battalion, 16th Infantry, were once again with the Big Red One, the unit did not really exist. Technically it was active, but there were only a couple of soldiers assigned to keep it so. The full reorganization of the 1st Battalion would have to wait the reorganization of the 1st Infantry Division from the Pentomic TOE to the ROAD configuration and the return of the 2nd Battle Group from Germany.

On October 1, 1963, the 2nd Battle Group (old B Company) was activated by the reflagging of the 2nd Battle Group, 8th Infantry, at Wildflicken, Germany, and assigned to the 1st Infantry Division. The battle group was not immediately reorganized into the battalion configuration because of its ongoing participation in the Long Thrust X rotation to Germany. Long Thrust was a successor to Gyroscope and a precursor to the Reforger operations that would be instituted after the Vietnam War. That summer, in response to the Berlin Wall crisis, the battle group had deployed to Germany. There, it drew pre-positioned war stocks and participated in a series of tactical exercises, the last of which was Exercise Winter Track in January.[114] Upon the conclusion of that event, the 2nd Battle Group returned to Fort Riley.

The unit arrived on February 20, 1964, at Forbes Air Force Base in Topeka, where it was met by Major General Jonathan O. Seaman, the division commander. Upon arrival at Fort Riley, it immediately began reorganizing into two battalions. This was accomplished by splitting the battle group into two parts: half stayed with the new 2nd Battalion, and the other half went to the 1st Battalion. The reorganization was completed on March 2, 1964, when the 2nd Battle Group was redesignated the 2nd Battalion and the 1st Battalion was active with its full complement of troops.[115] Lieutenant Colonel Herman S. Napier was assigned as the 1st Battalion commander, and Lieutenant Colonel Joseph E. O'Leary was given command of the 2nd Battalion.

Both battalions were assigned to the 2nd Brigade at Camp Forsyth, commanded by Colonel James E. Simmons. Wasting no time, Simmons took the brigade on March 27. For the next week or so, both battalions trained intensively on night attacks, company defense problems, and—something new to the current crop of 16th Infantrymen—counterguerrilla operations.[116] Training in the latter would receive greater emphasis as the next year wore on.

In the spring and summer of 1964, the battalions of the 16th Infantry supported ROTC summer camp training for the first time. This activity would become a routine task for the 16th Infantry for many years afterward, except during the battalions' deployment in Vietnam. The 2nd Battalion also had the opportunity to run another group of recruits through AIT, an activity that took up most of that battalion's time that summer. Also that summer, the battalion conducted extensive rail load training at Camp Funston; prepared for the U.S. Strike Command's autumn exercise, Gold Fire I; and received a new commander, Lieutenant Colonel Lloyd L. ("Scooter") Burke.

Held in Missouri, Gold Fire I was designed to exercise portions of the STRAC forces for rapid deployment. For the exercise, the 1st Infantry Division, less the 2nd Brigade, was to be flown into airfields in and near Fort Leonard Wood. The 2nd Brigade, designated Task Force Sioux and consisting of the 1-16, 2-16, 1-26, and 1-28 Infantry battalions, was to sneak into the area by ground and act as aggressors against the rest of the STRAC forces. In late October, the division was airlifted to Fort Leonard Wood. Within a week, the 2nd Brigade had penetrated friendly lines by way of a night movement near Lebanon, Missouri. The movement was almost too successful, forcing umpires to halt the 2nd Brigade for six hours to prevent it from overrunning another of the division's brigades while it regrouped. The 1-16's performance was particularly noteworthy, earning Lieutenant Colonel Napier the Joint Services Commendation Medal later in June.[117]

In the spring of 1965, few if any soldiers at Fort Riley realized that the United States was about to become embroiled in a controversial war. In the 16th Infantry, activities continued to hum along just as before. In April, the 2nd Battalion celebrated its Organization Day (not to commemorate the regiment's achievements at Fléville, but rather to mark its first-year anniversary as a ROAD battalion). In May, the 1st Battalion sent two companies to Fort Leavenworth to help that post celebrate Armed Forces Day. But little by little, it became more apparent that the U.S. Army was going to send combat divisions to Vietnam, and that the Big Red One was going to be a part of this movement. In July, the 2nd Brigade received final orders to deploy to Vietnam, and by then everybody else knew that the rest of the division would soon follow.

Since 1945, the 16th Infantry had undergone a number of difficult changes and had been forced to operate in difficult conditions. Through the splitting of the regiment in 1946, the virtual ground-up reorganization in 1948, and the bewildering reorganizations from regiment to battle group to battalion TOEs, the officers and men of the regiment had attempted to preserve the standards, history, and traditions of the 16th Infantry. The history had indeed been preserved and high standards were always reestablished after a time—but, unfortunately, many traditions were lost, casualties to discontinuity caused in part by repeated reflagging, inactivation, and reactivation of units.

The problem of preserving traditions and tracing regimental history is exacerbated when two or more regimental units serve in separate divisions and fight in separate parts of the world. In essence, they evolve into different organizations with different histories, even though they share the same regimental number and unit insignia.

The cause of this confusion and numerous related problems are rightly attributed to the institution of the Combat Arms Regimental System and its successor, the U.S. Army Regimental System. Many in the army consider both bad ideas to begin with, and would prefer to maintain only one battalion of each regiment on active duty or in the reserves. This would ensure that more of the old units that have good combat histories can remain alive and, more important, will ensure that a regiment will only have one history to maintain. The 16th Infantry's experience in Vietnam and thereafter will serve to illustrate how difficult it is to maintain a regiment's history.

During the twenty-year interim between World War II and the war in Vietnam, soldiers of the 16th Infantry, indeed the entire U.S. Army, had been busy preparing to fight the Soviets on a European battlefield, possibly in an environment where nuclear and chemical weapons would be used. The most likely scenario also envisioned a motorized/mechanized slugfest against an enemy with tactics, doctrine, and equipment that American soldiers clearly understood and where the lines were clearly drawn. By and large, the sides were black and white—the good guys against the bad guys.

The soldiers of the combat division deployed to Vietnam in 1965 went into the fight with widespread public support. The attitude was, "We can accomplish anything in war; after all, didn't we win World War II? We can do it again, especially against a fifth-rate enemy like North Vietnam." But Vietnam was a different kind of war. There, the lines drawn for soldiers were blurred, literally and figuratively, and before long, the reasons for American involvement became just as fuzzy to many folks back home. After a time, the attitude of soldiers and units also changed. The American soldier went into the war with vigor and idealism, but many came out with great disillusionment, not only with the war, but with the army as an institution, and for some, even about the nation itself. Still, through it all, the men of the 16th Infantry would perform their duties with the efficiency, valor, and discipline expected of Big Red One soldiers.

1st Battalion machine-gun team, Vietnam, 1967

SEMPER PARATUS

Chapter Ten
Cold War Interlude—Vietnam

The NCOs and enlisted men performed like the truly magnificent soldiers they are
Brigadier General Bernard W. Rogers, March 1966

The morning of July 14, 1965, dawned humid, hot, and hazy as the USNS *Gordon* lay at anchor in the South China Sea near Cape St. Jacques, the colonial name for the South Vietnamese port city of Vung Tau. On board the *Gordon* were the troops and equipment of the 2nd Brigade Task Force, commanded by Colonel James E. Simmons. The task force, consisting of the 2nd Battalion, 16th Infantry; 1st and 2nd Battalions, 18th Infantry; 1st Battalion, 7th Field Artillery; and assorted brigade and division support units, had departed Fort Riley on June 24-25, traveled to the port of San Francisco, and sailed from that port on June 25. After almost three weeks en route and a brief stop at Qui Nhon to drop off the 1st Battalion, 18th Infantry, the *Gordon* dropped anchor in the calm waters off Vung Tau.

The Rangers unloaded the ship at first light and, once ashore, prepared for the movement to their base camp near Bien Hoa. The task force moved ashore by unloading the battalion's personnel into LSMs and then landing them on the beach near the town. Second Lieutenant Ed Coates of Norway, Michigan, remembered that the operation seemed like D-Day, but without the fight to get ashore:

> It reminded me of World War II only we didn't have any incoming fire. They threw the cargo nets over the side, and we climbed down the cargo nets with our field gear onto these little landing craft. Then went on the beach in the landing craft. There was a convoy of trucks there waiting to pick us up....There was some getting people organized, of course, and making sure we had everybody, and getting them lined up. Then we loaded our gear on the trucks, got on the trucks and off we went.[1]

From the Vung Tau airfield, the troops were airlifted fifty kilometers on C-130s to Bien Hoa Air Base, then trucked to their first home in Vietnam—Long Binh.

The events that culminated in the deployment of the 1st Infantry Division to Vietnam in 1965 had their genesis in France's failure to reassert its control over its colonies in French Indochina after World War II. Following the decisive defeat of the French garrison at Dien Bien Phu in 1954, Vietnam was divided into two zones at the 17th parallel, and elections were scheduled for 1956 to decide the question of reunification. In the meantime, Ho Chi Minh, leader of the Viet Minh (the organization that had defeated the French) established a Communist government in the north at Hanoi. At the same time, Ngo Dinh Diem, a Roman Catholic and former functionary in the French colonial government, gained control over the southern provinces by overthrowing the criminal rings that controlled them. Members of these gangs subsequently became the nucleus of the Viet Cong (VC).

A pillar of American foreign policy at this time was the containment of Communism, so the United States decided to bolster the fledgling Diem government and resist Ho's efforts to spread Communism over both zones. American aid initially consisted of economic support and military assistance in the form of the U.S. Army Military Assistance Advisory Group (MAAG), Vietnam. Through the efforts of the MAAG, the 150,000-man Army of the Republic of Vietnam (ARVN) was reorganized along U.S. lines and equipped with American equipment.

Despite American support of the South Vietnamese government, by 1964 the Viet Cong had built an alarmingly effective insurgency in the south. The VC's strength grew from five thousand in 1959 to about one hundred thousand in 1964. Additionally, for the first time, a few regular North Vietnamese Army (NVA) units had come south to assist the VC. As a result, the South Vietnamese Army, and its paramilitary auxiliaries, failed to cope with the increased level of enemy activity.

By the first half of 1965, the situation in the south had deteriorated to the point that ARVN battalions were consistently defeated by VC units that were, in turn, clandestinely supported by NVA troops. One officer working at J-3, Military Assistance Command, Vietnam (MACV) recalled:

> Really, the [South] Vietnamese were just getting chopped up badly and we were losing—during the spring and early summer of '65—we were losing an [ARVN] regiment or two it seemed like every week. Song Be [a provincial capital] was overrun and at Quang Ngai we lost what looked to be two regiments. Over near the Michelin [Rubber Plantation] they lost another regiment. It was really so bad that after the battle at Quang Ngai, which was in May of

'65, the Vietnamese II Corps commander said he wasn't sure he could get his troops to even go out and fight in their own operations.[2]

But help was on the way. After the Gulf of Tonkin incident in August 1964, President Lyndon B. Johnson obtained Congressional support to use all force necessary to protect American lives and provide for South Vietnam's security. To alleviate the deteriorating situation, Johnson sent in marines to protect Da Nang in March 1965; then he ordered the 173rd Airborne Brigade deployed to provide security to American installations around Saigon.[3] On May 22, 1965, the 2nd Brigade Task Force learned that it was to ship out to Vietnam. Its original mission called for the brigade to secure a major logistics complex at Qui Nhon in the II Corps Tactical Zone (II CTZ). However, the severe threat posed by recent VC attacks around Saigon prompted a change of mission, and on arrival, it was ordered to secure the city of Bien Hoa and the American air base there.

The 2-16's first base camp was located southeast of the air base at a crossroads called Long Binh. Situated between Bien Hoa and Saigon, the Long Binh base camp was little more than a jungle wasteland at the intersection of Route 316 (which led to Saigon) and Highway 15 (the route to Vung Tau).

Long Binh was located about twenty kilometers northeast of Saigon in the III Corps Tactical Zone (III CTZ), a significant location for guarding the northern approaches to the capital. In addition to securing Saigon, the 2nd Brigade's tactical area of operational responsibility (TAOR) (and later the 1st Infantry Division's as well) was initially the provinces of Tay Ninh, Binh Long, Binh Duong, Long Khanh, Bien Hoa, Gia Dinh, and the capital district. The TAOR included several key locations that would figure prominently in the battles to come. These included the so-called Iron Triangle, Nui Ba Den Mountain, the Michelin Rubber Plantation, and War Zones C and D. The two war zones were areas in Tay Ninh and Long Khanh provinces that the South Vietnamese government considered to be so fully under Communist control that it declared them "free fire" areas. Therefore, anything and anyone in these war zones was considered a legitimate target.

The brigade task force's initial missions were to finish building the base camp, clear the areas around the camps of secondary growth for fields of fire, and conduct security sweeps of the immediate areas around Long Binh and Bien Hoa. This meant that battalions would conduct local, small unit "search and destroy" (S&D) missions, at least initially. Larger unit operations would follow.

Luckily, the 2nd Battalion drew the site of an old French Army rifle range on which it would build the unit's compound. This meant that, unlike the rest of the units in the brigade, the Rangers had little jungle to clear before they could construct the compound. Upon arrival late on the afternoon of July 14, the troops of the battalion immediately went to work digging in

on the battalion's specified perimeter. "[T]here was a sense of urgency to set up, get stuff put away, and get dug in, and get some kind of [defensible] position before darkness," recalled First Lieutenant Kenneth M. Alderson of Madison, Tennessee. Lieutenant Colonel Lloyd L. "Scooter" Burke, the battalion commander, selected an old range building as the site of the battalion headquarters.[4]

Initially, the men built only foxholes and bunkers, but as the days passed, sandbags, concertina wire, anti-personnel mines, concrete, and tentage arrived for the troops to use for improving the compound. Eventually, they poured concrete slabs and erected GP Medium tents for sleeping quarters, but for the first several weeks at what became known as "Camp Ranger," the battalion essentially lived in fighting positions—at least when it was actually there.

The first night in what would become Camp Ranger was not calm, nor quiet. Several field artillery batteries spent all night firing registration rounds. On several places along the perimeter, nervous Rangers cut loose from time to time with single shots and bursts of automatic fire, most likely shooting at figments of the imagination. This type of firing was repeated on the second night, but on the third night, troops on the northern section of the 16th Infantry perimeter and those of the 18th Infantry on that battalion's southern section traded fire for several minutes before leaders in both battalions realized that their troops were shooting at each other. Burke and the Vanguard battalion commander quickly took strict steps to quash any possibility that such an event would occur again.[5]

At this time the 2nd Battalion consisted of a headquarters company and three rifle companies. In addition to the battalion staff sections, a support platoon, mess section, and other support elements, the headquarters company also included a reconnaissance platoon and a heavy mortar platoon (81mm mortar). Each of the three rifle companies (A, B, and C) consisted of three rifle platoons and a weapons platoon. The weapons platoon consisted of four 50-caliber machine-gun teams, a mortar platoon equipped with three 60mm mortars, and crews for several 90mm and 106mm recoilless rifles. In all, there were 829 officers and men authorized under this TOE.

This organizational structure soon proved to be too light in manpower and combat capabilities, so enterprising battalion commanders began to revise their battalion's organization based on experience and the exigencies of the situation. Typically, they would organize a fourth maneuver element by combining the recon platoon, the heavy mortar platoon, the antitank platoon, and the ground surveillance radar section into an ad hoc company. Given the relative uselessness of these kinds of units in Vietnam (save the recon platoon), battalion commanders found ways to equip these men with rifles, required them to leave behind their heavy mortars, recoilless rifles, and radar sets, and used them as security forces and as basic infantry soldiers.[6] This system was so successful that modified TOEs were established for infantry units in Vietnam. The army formally added

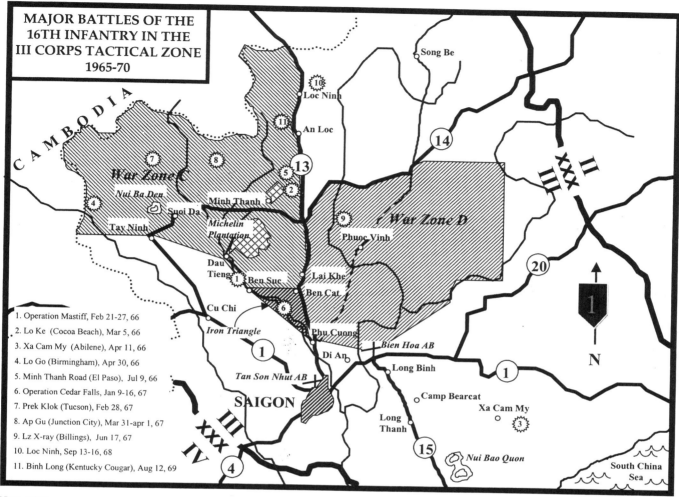

MAJOR BATTLES OF THE
16TH INFANTRY IN THE
III CORPS TACTICAL ZONE
1965-70

1. Operation Mastiff, Feb 21-27, 66
2. Lo Ke (Cocoa Beach), Mar 5, 66
3. Xa Cam My (Abilene), Apr 11, 66
4. Lo Go (Birmingham), Apr 30, 66
5. Minh Thanh Road (El Paso), Jul 9, 66
6. Operation Cedar Falls, Jan 9-16, 67
7. Prek Klok (Tucson), Feb 28, 67
8. Ap Gu (Junction City), Mar 31-apr 1, 67
9. Lz X-ray (Billings), Jun 17, 67
10. Loc Ninh, Sep 13-16, 68
11. Binh Long (Kentucky Cougar), Aug 12, 69

Map 10-1.

another line company (D Company) in 1967, and a specialty unit company (E or Combat Support Company) in 1969.

When the 2nd Battalion arrived in Vietnam, its commander, Lieutenant Colonel Lloyd L. Burke, was already a legend throughout the army. Burke had entered the service from his home state of Arkansas, and initially served as an enlisted man. He later earned his commission through OCS and went to Korea with the 1st Cavalry Division, where he commanded a company in the 5th Cavalry Regiment. Burke's officers and men respected his abilities as a soldier and a leader, and no one doubted his courage. He had won the Medal of Honor at Chong-Dong in October 1951 in desperate fighting. On the 21st of that month, Burke had led his company in an attack on several bunkers and personally wiped out three of them. While attacking the third position, he literally caught enemy grenades in the air and hurled them back into the bunker. At that point, his men were pinned down by fire, so he grabbed a machine gun, positioned it on high ground, and raked the enemy ranks, killing seventy-five North Korean sol-diers. Although wounded, he led his men forward with the machine gun and killed an additional twenty-five. This feat enabled his men to capture the company objective.[7] With his combat experience guiding his efforts, Burke had vigorously trained his battalion at Fort Riley to make it as ready as possible for the hardships he knew it would face in Vietnam.

Assisting Burke were four well-trained and professional company commanders: Captains Doyle Taylor, Clayton Johnson, and Robert C. Canady (commanding Companies A, B, and C, respectively). Commanding the Headquarters Company was Captain Thomas F. Eddy. Additionally, Burke had an excellent staff consisting of Major George Lokken, XO; First Lieutenant Norman Carlson, S1; Captain Walter Tomihiro, S2; Captain Robert Powell (soon to be replaced by Major Ted Westerman), S3; Chief Warrant Officer Third Class Jack E. Teegarden, S4; and Sergeant Major Chandler Caldwell, the battalion sergeant major. Together, these men had prepared the 2nd Battalion well for the tasks ahead.

At the time of its arrival in Vietnam, the battalion was

composed primarily of men who had volunteered for the army. In time, however, the ranks would have large numbers of draftees. As professionals, the veterans were proud of their membership in the 16th Infantry and the Big Red One, and their spirit proved contagious to the replacements who later joined the battalion. Their pride in service that set the foundation for the good morale and esprit-de-corps the 2-16 experienced throughout its stint in Southeast Asia, even in the confused and turbulent later years of the war.

The Rangers' initial mission at Long Binh was to help secure the Bien Hoa Air Base, conduct a mobile defense of the airfield, and undertake offensive counterinsurgency operations as directed. The mission also implied S&D missions, road clearing operations, and support of the Civic Action Program (CAP). The first combat operation of a 1st Infantry Division unit took place on July 22, when B Company conducted a search of areas northeast of the battalion base camp to detect VC infiltrators.

Defense
July-December 1965
In early 1965, General William C. Westmoreland, commander of the Military Assistance Command, Vietnam (MACV), realized that the most serious threat to the South Vietnamese government was the deteriorating situation in the III CTZ, especially in those areas around Saigon. Therefore, as American combat forces arrived in South Vietnam to stem the tide, the general placed them in base camps, strategically located in the provinces around the capital, from which they could prevent attacks on the city. After a unit had secured its immediate TAOR, Westmoreland planned to use those same base camps as springboards for large-scale operations to seek out and defeat VC main force units. While U.S. forces conducted initial defense and attrition operations, Westmoreland expected that ARVN units would move into training areas and be reinforced, reequipped, retrained, and otherwise prepared to reassume the offensive role. Later, again using American forces, Westmoreland planned to drive VC units into ever-smaller sanctuaries. Once they were concentrated, he expected to destroy them with the overwhelming combat power of combined U.S. and ARVN units.

Westmoreland's plan for the III Corps Tactical Zone included building a security belt with the 173rd Airborne Brigade and the 1st Infantry Division. Later, after the arrival of the 25th Infantry Division and 3rd Brigade, 4th Infantry Division, this security belt would be strengthened. The Big Red One's TAOR was essentially a triangular area north of Saigon that included Bien Hoa (2nd Brigade), Phuoc Vinh (1st Brigade), and Ben Cat (3rd Brigade). The 25th Infantry Division TAOR was to be the west area around Cu Chi; the 3rd Brigade, 4th Infantry Division, TAOR to the west of Dau Tieng; and the 173rd Airborne Brigade TAOR was to the east of Bien Hoa. The TAOR in which the battalions of the 16th Infantry operated was generally the same as the TAOR for the 1st Division.

The 1st Infantry Division TAOR was located partially in and to the east of War Zone C. It included many regions that would soon become well-known names to Big Red One soldiers: the Iron Triangle, the "Trapezoid," and the infamous Michelin Rubber Plantation. Splitting the TAOR almost in the middle was Highway 13. This road was division's main supply route (MSR), but it also served as a conduit for enemy offensives and resupply if not controlled. The terrain of the III CTZ was considered the most favorable in Vietnam for large-scale operations. The area was a transition zone between the swampy Mekong Delta to the south and the Central Highlands to the north. It consisted of jungled plains interspersed with gently rolling hills, and was cut by the Saigon River, which progressed northwest to southeast forming the basin toward which all other water courses in the region flowed. The III CTZ was, without question, a critical piece of terrain to both sides. Appropriately, the mission to protect it was assigned to the Big Red One.

Facing the 1st Division was a veteran VC unit, the 9th People's Liberation Army Force (PLAF) Division, commanded by Senior Colonel Hoang Cam. The division was activated on September 2, 1965, from the 1st and 2nd PLAF Regiments. These two regiments had been organized in 1961 and had fought in numerous engagements against the South Vietnamese Army, including the pivotal battle at Binh Gia village in December 1964. The 9th Division consisted of the 271st, 272nd, and 273rd PLAF Regiments, the 84A Artillery Regiment, and assorted combat support and service support units. It was the first Viet Cong main force division formed entirely in South Vietnam. Seasoned by years of combat, the troops of the 9th PLAF Division were tough adversaries. One American officer recalled of the VC soldier:

> I developed a tremendous amount of respect for the Viet Cong, [even] the little old guy down there who was a farmer by day then picked up his rifle at night....There were certain areas that we would go into and would fight certain regiments....You would know when you were against good people; mortar rounds would land at night in your area, and you would be probed. So, I respected the enemy. I tried to instill that respect in the soldiers, and cautioned them not to take this guy for granted...When you could see the diggings we saw, those tunnels, the trenches, the little makeshift hospitals, why, you can't help but respect this guy...He was tough.[8]

Although they led good fighters, the commanders of VC units, and later, those of NVA units as well, would rarely commit units larger than a company to combat, and then only when they felt they had a good chance to inflict substantial damage to an American unit. Additionally, like elsewhere in Vietnam, the 9th Division was reinforced by numerous local-force and guerrilla units (about thirty thousand troops) that conducted reconnaissances, ambushes, and partisan-like operations against vulnerable American locations. These were the forces that B Company set out to test on July 22, 1965.

That morning, Captain Johnson's B Company moved out of Camp Ranger and headed northeast toward the hamlet of Ga Ho Nai to conduct a sweep operation. The mission was to clear areas in front of the 2nd Battalion, 18th Infantry's perimeter of any VC personnel and positions. Lieutenant Colonel Burke participated in the action by riding above in a UH-1 "Huey" helicopter to assist the company's movement and provide the company commander with a view from the sky. About 3:00 p.m., as B Company scoured the ground below, two bulldozers working to clear out the jungle flushed two VC into the open. Burke spotted them and flew toward the spot where they had reentered the brush. He directed the chopper pilots to fly low over the place where he had last seen the enemy. As the craft passed over, a sharp explosion greeted them. A VC soldier had either thrown a hand grenade or fired a rifle grenade at the Huey, and the resulting blast severely injured Burke, Captain Powell, his S3, and Sergeant Major Caldwell. The chopper made it back to the air base, but Burke's and Powell's injuries were such that they had to be evacuated to the United States.[9]

Two days later, Lieutenant Colonel Y. Y. Phillips Jr., arrived from MACV headquarters to take command of the 2nd Battalion. Phillips (whose given name is actually the initials "Y. Y."), an affable, but demanding, officer from Nashville, Tennessee, was a twenty-one-year army veteran who had received his commission through OCS in 1945. En route to the Pacific as an eighteen-year-old lieutenant, Phillips had learned that he would be sent to Europe instead when news of the Japanese surrender arrived. There, he ended up in the 78th Division and briefly served with the 3rd Battalion, 16th Infantry, in Berlin for about three months, before returning to the states in January 1947.

Recalled to active duty in 1951 (the same month he graduated from Vanderbilt University), Phillips served at Fort Benning and later with the 24th Infantry Division in Korea after the armistice was signed. Following duty as an aide and executive to General Carter Magruder for several years in the Far East and the Pentagon, Phillips served with the 101st Airborne Division, earned an MBA at Syracuse University, and served a second tour in the Pentagon in the office of the Deputy Chief of Staff for Operations. He was serving as the executive officer to Major General William E. DePuy at J-3, MACV headquarters in Saigon when he was ordered to assume command of the 2nd Battalion.

Upon taking command of the battalion, Phillips sized up Burke's efforts in preparing the unit for its mission in Vietnam. He remembered:

I would have to say that my impression, and it proved later to be true, that the battalion was just in superb condition. It had professional officers, professional NCOs. Even the squad leaders and the riflemen were superb troops. It was just a pleasure to command and have men that responded immediately and so well without questioning everything. I believe at this stage of the war, the 2-16th was probably as good as any comparable combat unit in the world.[10]

For the rest of July and early August, the battalion continued to provide close-in security for the airfield at Bien Hoa and occasionally performed platoon- and company-size sweeps. It conducted its first battalion-level search and destroy mission on August 8-9, destroying several suspected VC dwellings and defense positions, but encountering no enemy resistance. The battalion spent the remainder of the month performing the airfield security mission (commonly referred to as the "Palace Guard") and S&D operations, mainly in the vicinity of Bien Hoa, Long Binh, and Long Thanh. The battalion had its first confirmed VC KIA on August 16. The tally would increase significantly over the next five years.

The next battalion-level operation was a search and destroy mission in the Long Thanh district southeast of Long Binh. Designated Operation Caoutchouc, this mission directed the battalion to conduct a sweep through Ap An Vieng village and the nearby rubber plantation, then move southwest to Highway 15 and capture, kill, or destroy any enemy personnel, equipment, and facilities.

Surprisingly, intelligence on the enemy in the area was fairly good. For example, the search area was known to be the AO (area of operation) of a forty-man VC platoon commanded by one Ly Khai. Ly's unit was armed with one Browning Automatic Rifle (BAR), a few submachine guns, and rifles. The unit was also known to operate by breaking up into four- to five-man squads to conduct ambushes in the AO. Ly Khai commonly used sentries disguised as fishermen to provide him with early warning of targets and enemy units. The intelligence report indicated that the VC base camp was in the vicinity of the sweep area, and its destruction was one of the battalion's primary objectives.

The battalion conducted this operation over three days in several phases. About 5:00 p.m. on September 8, A and C Companies trucked over two routes to jump-off points at Camp Bearcat, a Special Forces camp about fourteen kilometers southeast of Long Binh. The two companies dismounted there and moved along specified routes the following afternoon and night. Both companies were in temporary positions by 6:30 a.m., September 10. Canady's C Company and the Recon Platoon set up blocking positions on the southwest side of the plantation and prepared to net any VC attempting to escape the village in that direction. Captain Doyle Taylor's A Company occupied positions to the northeast and prepared to sweep the hamlet.

As A and C Companies occupied their positions that morning, B Company was airlifted to a blocking position on the north side of the An Vieng plantation to prevent escape in that direction. Once Captain Johnson's blocking position was established, Taylor's men moved into Ap An Vieng, conducted a house-to-house search, and assembled all civilians into the southwest corner of the hamlet. The company's efforts to move the villagers to the assembly area were assisted by a psychological operations (PSYOPS) team armed with bullhorns mounted on choppers. The team shouted instructions in Vietnamese to lessen the villagers' confusion in complying with instructions.

Once the civilians were assembled, members of the South Vietnamese National Police who had accompanied A Company, interrogated the villagers. The police efforts netted twelve suspected VC and three draft dodgers. The 2nd Battalion's success at Ap An Vieng ensured that it generally operated with National Police teams in the future. Over the next two days, the battalion conducted three more sweeps toward Highway 15, but it made no contact with Ly Khai, his platoon, nor the base camp.[11]

Conducting village "seals" was a common operation for infantry battalions in Vietnam, and during the following months, the 2nd Battalion conducted many of them. After targeting a VC-controlled village, the battalion would typically move under the cover of darkness into positions surrounding the village by 3:00 a.m. Once set, the troops had orders to engage any VC trying to get out of, or into, the village before dawn. This was a rather simple task. Since there was a dusk-to-dawn curfew, anyone caught outside was considered VC and captured or killed.

At daylight, one company with an attached National Police unit entered the village to conduct a thorough search for VC suspects and caches of food, ammunition, and weapons. Over the months, such tactics yielded hundreds of VC, VC suspects, and tons of supplies. This kind of operation did as much damage to VC infrastructure and resources as the more highly publicized S&D sweeps.[12]

Six days later, Colonel Phillips lead the battalion on another battalion S&D sweep, titled Operation Plumbob. On September 16, the battalion swept the AO near Tân Uyên and made contact with a VC platoon. While only two VC were killed, two wounded, and one captured, the battalion also destroyed a number of positions and bunkers. The mission revealed that the VC had been highly active in an area not previously thought to be troubled by enemy activity.[13]

About one week later on September 23, the battalion was engaged in sweep operations near Phu Cuong when Doyle Taylor's A Company ran into fierce resistance from a well dug-in VC unit. Elements of the company made four separate efforts to overrun a particularly tough enemy bunker, until Specialist Fourth Class Wayne L. Beck, a former telephone company employee from Newbury, Missouri, volunteered to knock out the position with a flame-thrower. The problem was getting close enough to do it. Under the covering fire of his buddies, Beck scrambled across open ground toward the enemy position but was struck in both legs by machine-gun fire and fell to the ground. He struggled to his feet, staggered forward under his

heavy load, and was hit again in the shoulder before falling next to the bunker. Pointing the nozzle of the flame-thrower into an opening, Beck loosed its deadly stream into the enclosure and incinerated twelve stubborn VC. Beck survived his wounds, and for his actions, the brave specialist earned the division's first Silver Star for valor in Vietnam.

For the next three months, the battalion primarily carried out security missions around Bien Hoa, but it did participate in two brigade-sized efforts: Operations Hopscotch and Bushmaster II.

Hopscotch was an operation north of Bien Hoa, in the Phuoc Vinh area, designed to clear the location for occupation by the 1st Brigade. The operation lasted from October 4 to October 25, and although the battalion made little contact with the enemy, it destroyed some 622 tons of rice, eleven trucks, and eleven base camps.[14] This operation gave way to Operation Bushmaster II in November.

As these operations were occurring, the American build-up in South Vietnam continued with the arrival of new units, including the rest of the Big Red One. About three months after the 2nd Brigade Task Force left Fort Riley, the rest of the 1st Infantry Division arrived in Vietnam. On October 9, 1965, the 1st Battalion, 16th Infantry, under the command of Lieutenant Colonel William J. Lober Jr., arrived at Cape St. Jacques with the other elements of the 1st Brigade on the USNS *Mann*. In an operation almost exactly like that of its brother battalion, the 1st Battalion debarked at Vung Tau and moved to its first base camp at Ben Cat in Phuoc Vinh province, twenty-eight kilometers northwest of Saigon.

Lober also had excellent company commanders and staff officers. The commanders were: Captain James Boccagno, Headquarters Company; Captain Edward Yaugo, Company A; Captain Robert A. McDonald, Company B; and Captain Homer S. Mapp, Company C. The staff consisted of the executive officer, Major John E. Morris; the S3, Major Walter G. Riley, and several others.

Like the 2nd Battalion, the 1st Battalion's initial activities focused on road clearing operations, Civic Action Program support, and S&D missions. The 1st Rangers were at Ben Cat for less than a month before participating in their first combat operation.

On November 14, the battalion was airlifted to a landing zone (LZ) south of the Michelin Rubber Plantation to conduct S&D sweeps in support of ARVN forces. This air assault was the opening gambit of Operations Bushmaster I and II.

Operations Bushmaster I and II
November 14-December 8, 1965

In October and November, intelligence reports indicated a significant increase in enemy activity in the Michelin Rubber Plantation-Ben Cat-Lai Khe area and the build-up suggested a possible attack on Lai Khe or Ben Cat. Major General Jonathan O. Seaman, commander of the 1st Infantry Division, received orders to support a search and destroy mission performed by the 5th ARVN Infantry Division operating east of the Michelin Rubber Plantation. The 5th Division's mission was to locate and destroy the 271st PLAF Regiment. Seaman directed Colonel William D. Brodbeck's 3rd Brigade (the "Iron Brigade") to support the ARVN troops by engaging the Phu Loi Battalion, thought to be operating due south of the Michelin plantation.

As part of the 3rd Brigade's efforts, 1-16 was assigned the mission to "destroy or capture Viet Cong personnel, equipment, supplies, and installations" in the vicinity southeast of Dau Tieng. Additionally, the battalion was to clear Highway 13 between Lai Khe and Ben Cat and provide route security for convoys moving along the division MSR. To ensure surprise, the battalion was airlifted to its AO.[15]

At 10:18 a.m. on November 14, B Company landed at the LZ and secured the area for the rest of the battalion. In less than thirty minutes, the rest of Lober's troops were on the ground and moving east. Almost immediately, C Company discovered a small base camp containing VC documents and a sewing machine used for making VC uniforms. Then, at 11:35 a.m., the company opened fire on three enemy troops wearing camouflage uniforms, but apparently missed them. This contact set the stage for the rest of the day. As A and B Companies searched fruitlessly throughout the morning and afternoon, the troops of C Company destroyed two tunnel complexes; captured considerable VC equipment, medical supplies, and documents; and killed five insurgents. They also wounded and captured three others. These were the first confirmed enemy casualties by a 3rd Brigade unit since its arrival in country. A and B Companies, on the other hand, had made no contact. The battalion, meanwhile, closed into a defensive perimeter about 7:00 p.m. and settled in for the night.

The action on November 14, proved to be the major event of the operation. For the next four days, Lober's men busied themselves with capturing and destroying several tons of rice and clearing booby traps along the route. They made no further contact with the enemy. The 1st Rangers linked up with 5th ARVN Division near Dau Tieng on the 19th.

On the morning of November 20, helicopters moved the battalion to Ap Bau Bang. There, Lober deployed his battalion to secure Highway 13 from Ap Bau Bang to a bridge on the highway south of the village. Although a convoy was severely ambushed along Highway 13 just north of Bau Bang that day, the portion of the route secured by the 1st Battalion was relatively quiet, with the exception of the detonation of a mine that destroyed a B Company vehicle and wounded three personnel. At 5:45 p.m., the battalion was released from the security mission and airlifted back to Ben Cat.[16]

Overall, the 3rd Brigade had good success in Operation Bushmaster I. The Iron Brigade units beat back the attack on the convoy near Trung Loi on the 20th and, by the end of the operation, had killed some 245 VC and destroyed numerous facilities and large quantities of supplies in the heart of the enemy's base camp areas.

But General Seaman was not done. Right on the heels of Bushmaster I, he ordered the initiation of Bushmaster II. Once again, the 3rd Brigade was ordered to support elements of the 5th ARVN Division, this time, the 7th Regiment. For this mission, Brodbeck's Iron Brigade was reinforced by Phillips's 2nd Battalion, which made Bushmaster II the first of several operations where both battalions of the 16th Infantry operated under the control of the same brigade.

On November 27, 1965, Lober was alerted to move 1-16 to the vicinity of the Michelin Rubber Plantation to support the 7th ARVN Regiment's efforts to clear the jungled area southeast of the plantation of enemy facilities. About 10:00 a.m. on November 28, the 1st Battalion was inserted into a LZ near Dau Tieng and moved directly into position on the flank of the ARVN unit. The battalion's mission was to conduct S&D sweeps in the Michelin Plantation initially, then operations in zone from the village of Xã Thi Tinh along Route 240 to Ben Cat.

On the following morning, the battalion flew into the airstrip at Dau Tieng and moved into the orderly rows of rubber trees searching for an elusive enemy. The 1st Rangers made no contact with the VC throughout the day and moved into a defensive position near Ap Sì 11 for the night. The following morning, Lober pushed his battalion west about five hundred meters, then north for another two kilometers. After troops from A and C Companies discovered a small, camouflaged tunnel system about 2:30 p.m., no other contact was made that day. The battalion went into its night defensive perimeter (NDP) about 5:30 p.m.[17]

As part of Bushmaster II, Brodbeck ordered Phillips's 2nd Battalion to "move to the Michelin Rubber Plantation to search [for] and destroy Viet Cong and their installations and materials." Phillips's mission was to commence two days into the operation; therefore, beginning at 8:30 a.m. on November 30, the battalion departed in four lifts from Bien Hoa Air Base to the vicinity of the plantation.

For the next seven days, both battalions, operating independently of each other, had minimal contact with VC, although several men were wounded from booby traps, including Captain Bob McDonald, the commander of B/1-16. At noon on December 7, Lober received orders from 3rd Brigade to link up with Phillips's 2nd Rangers, set up in a blocking position near Ap Nha Mat, southeast of the Michelin Plantation along Route 240. Colonel Brodbeck's intent was for the 1st Battalion to drive any retreating VC into the waiting guns of Phillips's men. Captain Lober's troops, meanwhile, swept through the zone and linked up with the 2nd Battalion, but once again, no contact was made with enemy units. En route, Company C discovered another extensive VC training camp but, due to the urgency of time in completing the sweep, only ammunition and supplies were blown up, and no attempt was made to destroy the tunnel system.[18]

That night, both battalions experienced minor sniper fire

and probing from enemy scouts but suffered no casualties. The following morning, S&D operations continued toward Ben Cat but were suspended about midmorning, and the battalions returned to their respective base camps.

The results of Bushmaster II for the Rangers were not significantly different from those of the previous operation. No major contact occurred with enemy units, but both battalions accomplished the destruction of VC training camps, mess halls, bunkers, and tunnels, and captured or destroyed large quantities of ammunition. It was a typical S&D mission in Vietnam—destruction of supplies and facilities but little contact with the enemy.

The early S&D missions in Vietnam could be frustrating. Colonel Phillips recalled, "Our biggest difficulty was locating the enemy to fight." On one mission, the battalion had been receiving harassing sniper fire but no major contacts. Phillips, frustrated by the enemy's sniping, began to lean on his company commanders for results: "I want to see some dead snipers," he ordered them. The following morning, Phillips was sitting on a log eating his breakfast, when he spied Captain Gerald A. Griffin, his A Company commander, bearing a load on his shoulders and walking toward him. As Griffin approached him, Phillips realized that he was carrying a dead VC. Walking up to him, the captain dumped the body in front of Phillips and said, "Well, I wanted you to see a dead sniper." Phillips chuckled and invited the captain to sit down and have breakfast. Griffin accepted, sat down on the body, and consumed his meal with Phillips, then picked up the unlucky VC and carted him back to the jungle.[19]

Phillips's 2nd Rangers returned to Long Binh on December 13. Three days later the Rangers went to the Long Thanh district with the 2nd Brigade for Operation Smash II.

During the operations around Bearcat, Captain Griffin's A Company was sent on an ambush operation near Long Thanh village. Two platoons departed Bearcat after dark and moved southeast to ambush positions near the village. En route, soldiers picked up two suspicious woodcutters, whom Griffin ordered bound, gagged, and taken along for the mission. Early the following morning, Griffin, his company now in position, initiated the ambush against a blue Land Rover vehicle that had no business being on the road at that hour. Upon searching the devastated vehicle, the troops found two bodies and a lot of VC documents. Further investigations that day determined that one of the dead men was the VC province chief for Phuoc Tuy province.[20]

In mid-December, the 2nd Battalion was able to stand down from combat operations long enough to celebrate Christmas and enjoy a visit from Bob Hope and other celebrities. The officers and men of the battalion celebrated Christmas that year in a variety of different ways. For example, Sergeant Major Caldwell, Lieutenant Norman Carlson, Staff Sergeant Jose Longeria, and Private First Class Bruce Fisher donated clothes, toys, and school supplies, paid for by men of the bat-

talion or donated by families in the states, to the Ke Sat Orphanage. Chief Warrant Officer Third Class Teegarden, Sergeant James Darby, and Specialist Fourth Class James Perry, sang Christmas carols to patients at the 93rd Evacuation Hospital. Many Rangers attended Christmas services at the recently built "Ranger Memorial Chapel." This chapel, which had been dedicated only a month before, was the project of soldier-bricklayer, Private First Class Edward Young, "engineer" Specialist Fourth Class John C. Prichett, and Chaplain Edward D. Nouchette. When the chapel was completed, Phillips and General Seaman dedicated it to 16th Infantrymen killed in action. Many of the men attending the services that Christmas had also helped build the church.

The soldiers had several special Christmas visitors as well. Many Rangers piled on trucks and went to Bien Hoa to see the Bob Hope Christmas show. At the end of the show the soldiers sang "Silent Night" with Anita Bryant.[21]

During the holiday cease-fire, a unique incident occurred that involved the troops of Captain Robert Canady's C Company. An ambush patrol of the 3rd Platoon, lead by Sergeant Everett Langston, reported movement of VC troops across their front. This movement was in violation of the cease-fire, so the patrol was given permission to engage. As the enemy element unknowingly crept into the patrol's kill-zone, the Rangers' guns erupted in a dazzling display of light, sound, and death.

After the firing had died down, the troops heard several men shouting something from the kill zone that sounded amazingly like English. In fact, it was. Langston ordered the assault team to sweep through the kill zone and, as they cautiously moved forward, they miraculously discovered five American civilians among the VC dead.

The men claimed they were construction workers who had been captured near Bien Hoa and were being moved to a VC sanctuary in War Zone D. They were bound with their hands behind their backs, and each had had a VC guard walking behind with orders to shoot the prisoners if they ran into trouble. Fortunately, only one of the guards was able to carry out these orders before being killed. One prisoner had been stitched up the back with a .45-caliber Thompson submachine gun, a weapon that the American infantrymen did not possess. This is the only known instance of American combat troops freeing captives of the VC in the field.[22]

Meanwhile, the 1st Battalion had returned to Ben Cat after Bushmaster II and spent their Christmas preparing to leave that post permanently. On December 29, the 1st Rangers transferred up the road to Lai Khe, which would serve as the unit's home for the remainder of its stay in Vietnam.

Counteroffensive
December 1965-June 1966
By December 1965, General Westmoreland believed that U.S. forces could begin counteroffensive operations the next spring,

when the arrival of additional units enabled him to take the initiative. The intent of the so-called Counteroffensive campaign was to keep the VC off balance while American forces built base camps and a logistics infrastructure to support large-scale offensive operations. Westmoreland initiated the Counteroffensive in the III CTZ with a series of small operations conducted in previously untouched strongholds of the 9th PLAF Division. The first of these was an operation by the 3rd Brigade called Operation Crimp, beginning January 6.[23]

That morning Lober's troops cleared and secured Highway 13 from Lai Khe to Ben Cat to ensure the safe passage of several convoys moving into the Crimp AO. Two days later the 1st Battalion was airlifted into LZ Jack, northwest of Cu Chi, to secure it for the insertion of other units. The LZ turned out to be defended, and one chopper was shot down coming in, but no casualties were sustained. After trading shots with the departing VC, the Rangers secured the LZ for the "Black Lions" of the 1st Battalion, 28th Infantry, who landed shortly after. For the next four days, the battalion conducted sweeps and performed blocking missions for other battalions, encountering little resistance. On the 12th, the 1st Rangers were released from Crimp and immediately began Operation Buckskin.

For Buckskin, the 1st Battalion mission was to conduct S&D operations in TAOR Alice, around Cu Chi, to engage VC and destroy their base camps. The operations were designed to throw the VC off balance while the 2nd Brigade, 25th "Tropic Lightning" Infantry Division, occupied its new base camp at Cu Chi. For the next three weeks, the battalion conducted numerous sweeps throughout Alice, destroying numerous base camps and gathering intelligence, while the Tropic Lightning soldiers occupied Cu Chi without harassment. In this operation the 1st Battalion destroyed a number of tunnels that honeycombed the Cu Chi area; killed an estimated twenty-one VC (four confirmed); and identified elements of the newly arrived L87 and 267 Main Force Battalions and the 506th Local Force Battalion.[24]

About the same time the 1st Battalion was finishing its sweeps of AO Alice, the 2nd Battalion was preparing to participate with the 2nd Brigade in Operations Mallet and Mallet II. The Mallet operations, interestingly, took the 2nd Brigade, now under the command of Colonel Albert E. Milloy, into an area east of Saigon not previously entered by U.S. forces. Intelligence reports indicated that up to six battalions of the Phu Loi Regiment and the Nhon Trach District Committee were operating in the area between Bien Hoa, Ba Ria, and Phuoc Le. The enemy units had not been particularly active, but they had been conducting harassment and collection of taxes against local peasants and kidnaping hamlet chiefs. The battalion mission on Mallet was to airmobile into LZ Spike near Phuoc An and drive north to seek out the Phu Loi Regiment. On January 28, the battalion was airlifted to LZ Spike.[25]

While the 1st Battalion, 18th Infantry ("Vanguards") held blocking positions to the north, the 2-18 and 2-16 pushed from Spike toward those locations but failed to make enemy contact.

Over the next week, the 2nd Brigade conducted local sweeps and ambush patrols but made few contacts with the enemy.

Having thoroughly searched the areas north of Phuoc An with limited results, Milloy kicked off Mallet II on February 7. Mallet II moved the brigade about twelve kilometers northeast to the vicinity of the Binh Son plantation to seek out the D800 Battalion and the Dong Nai Regiment.

That morning, Colonel Phillips's battalion trucked into an assembly area about six kilometers due south of the plantation, while the two Vanguard battalions trucked to their jump off positions in the plantation. The two battalions of the 18th Infantry conducted a S&D sweep south to Phase Line Trudy, while Phillips's 2nd Rangers established blocking positions along Trudy to form an anvil against which the Vanguards would hammer the VC units. Once again, however, the local VC commander refused to be brought to bay. Over the next week, the 2nd Brigade failed to make any significant contact with either VC unit. Phillips's battalion returned to Long Binh on February 15. Overall, the Mallet operations netted only forty-seven VC KIA against ten U.S. KIA, while destroying several small base camps and rice caches.

Perhaps the greatest accomplishment during the operation was less tangible than a body count. The 2nd Brigade "Operations Report on Lessons Learned" for Operation Mallet stated, "A by-product of Operation MALLET not shown in enemy losses is the tremendous boost in morale given to [South Vietnamese] government forces and officials in the area."[26]

Command of the 2nd Battalion passed to Lieutenant Colonel William ("Bill") Hathaway on February 17, 1966. Hathaway was a tall, genial soldier from Springfield, Virginia. He had attended the Virginia Military Institute for three years before dropping out and joining the Army. He had earned his commission through OCS and had served in numerous infantry assignments until arriving in Vietnam in 1965 with the Big Red One. A consummate leader, Hathaway held the respect of soldiers and officers alike. "Never said a bad word about anyone" is a common phrase those who knew Hathaway used in referring to him. "A real Southern gentleman" is another. Hathaway would be the battalion's longest serving commander in the Vietnam War.

Operation Mastiff
February 21-27, 1966

Ongoing division intelligence operations since the 2nd Brigade's arrival in Vietnam and Operations Bushmaster and Bloodhound in November and December reinforced the perceived modus operandi of the 9th PLAF Division. Intelligence summaries had accurately located all three regiments operating in War Zone C since at least November 1965, and they continued to remain in the immediate vicinity to the west and east of the Michelin Rubber Plantation. Additionally, several other units had been identified in the division TAOR. These included the 761st and 762nd PLAF Regiments, 241st Artillery Battalion, and the Phu

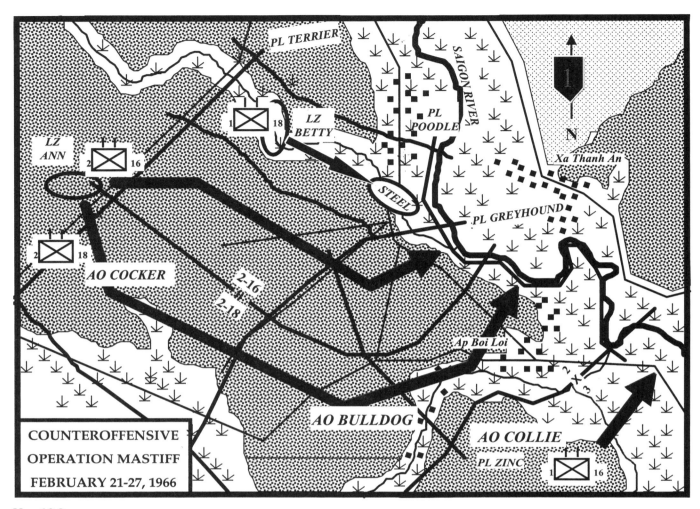

Map 10-2.

Loi Battalion. Because contact with these latter units was lost and reports indicated that the 272nd PLAF Regiment had been moving eastward, intelligence officers believed that these units and their supplies were probably migrating eastward from War Zone C to D. In an effort to disrupt VC infiltration routes between the two war zones, 1st Division commander Seaman, now a lieutenant general, initiated Operation Mastiff on February 21.[27]

The 1st Division mission for Mastiff was to conduct offensive operations with the 2nd and 3rd Brigades in the vicinity northwest of the village of Ben Suc, notorious as a VC support base. The division's AO was along the south side of the Saigon River, and the intent was to find and destroy any enemy units in the area and disrupt enemy infiltration operations into War Zone D. The 2nd Brigade was assigned the western sector of the division AO, and the 3rd Brigade was given the eastern sector. Both brigades had missions to conduct S&D operations using a blocking battalion and two sweep battalions.

Of the two, Colonel Milloy's 2nd Brigade had the more difficult mission. The brigade was to air assault into two LZs, Ann and Betty, along the line of departure (LD), phase line Terrier. The 1-18 Infantry had the mission to land in Betty and to move to set up the western blocking position (Steel). The other two battalions, 2-16 and 2-18, were to sweep through AO Cocker, then turn 90 degrees to sweep through AO Bulldog to the Saigon River (phase line Poodle).

Colonel William Brodbeck's 3rd Brigade was to perform an almost mirror-image operation but without the difficult 90-degree turn. The 1st Squadron, 4th Cavalry (nicknamed "Quarterhorse"), attached to the brigade for Mastiff, was to set up blocking position Paul in the east. The 1-16 and 2-2 Infantry would insert into two LZs along phase line Shepherd, then sweep through AO Collie to the river.[28] When all battalions were in their initial positions, the 1st Division would form a box around the area known as the Boi Loi Woods, with the river forming a closed lid to prevent any enemy infiltration through that direction. As the battalions closed in, the enemy would be concentrated with no means to escape and thus, forced to fight.

The operation went almost exactly according to plan, though it began with a tragic event resulting in the death of the Recon Platoon's popular platoon sergeant, Staff Sergeant James R. Ruthledge of Duncan, Oklahoma, on February 20. A heavy-set NCO who always had a cigar in his mouth, "like Sergeant Rock" one soldier recalled, Ruthledge was known for taking care of his troops. His dream was to go to flight school and be a chopper pilot. This day, however, his mind was on the mission ahead.

Specialist Fourth Class Robert Hoenig of Cooper, Texas, Ruthledge's radiotelephone operator, recalled that he narrowly missed suffering the sergeant's fate. "I had a minor medical problem and…told Sergeant Ruthledge, I had to run down to the medics right quick and get something taken care of and I'd be back." When he got to the aid station, the physician's assistant (PA), a warrant officer, told Hoenig that his problem was such that it would prevent him from participating in the next mission. Hoenig argued with the man, but the PA was adamant.

Hoenig returned to the Recon Platoon's tent and informed Ruthledge of the situation. "I'm six foot, two [inches tall]. Ruthledge was about five, seven; five, eight. And he looked around, lookin' for another RTO, and he chose Charles Rousseau—a hell of a guy. Rousseau was like about five, two."

The RTO position filled, Ruthledge moved the platoon over to the helipad, while Hoenig lay in his bunk. Hoenig could tell that the platoon was preparing to lift off because he could see the dust kicked up by the choppers. Suddenly he observed a fireball in the direction of the helipad. "What the hell was that?" Hoenig muttered to himself and hobbled over to the airfield gate as quickly as he could. When he inquired of the gate guard what had happened, he was told that two choppers had collided and all on board were killed.

About half hour later, several of the injured Recon Platoon troops were evacuated, Rousseau among them. Hoenig went over to the hospital to see Rousseau and found out what had happened. Rousseau explained that he was sitting with Ruthledge on the lead chopper, and the craft began to hover just after take off. The pilot of the second chopper was blinded by the dust thrown up by the first chopper, but he believed the lead craft had taken off and was still moving forward. Likewise, the second chopper continued to climb, but flew into the hovering lead craft. The second chopper's blade cut into the troop compartment where Ruthledge and Rousseau sat, taking the top of the sergeant's head off. "You're damn lucky you whadn't there," Rousseau told Hoenig, "because if you'd been sittin' there—the blade went right over my head. If you'd a been there, it'd took you off at the shoulders. It was bad. It was bad."[29]

The rest of the 2nd Battalion airlifted into LZ Ann at 9:00 a.m. on February 21 and began movement to the east. To the north, the 2-18 paralleled Hathaway's 2nd Rangers in AO Cocker, while the 1st Battalion, 18th Infantry, occupied blocking position Steel at the Route 238 bridge across the Rach Suot River. All day, resistance was light and only three VC were killed, as the two battalions swept to phase line Greyhound. The following day was similar to the first, except that the battalion overran and destroyed a VC hospital complex. On February 23, the battalion reached the Saigon River and was detailed by the 2nd Brigade to assist in removing by sampans tons of rice located in the sweeps of the two previous days. The effort to remove the rice went sour on the 24th, however, when the Vietnamese sampan operators abandoned their boats after several VC opened fire on them from the north bank. Air strikes subsequently sank the drifting boats, and the rest of the rice captured during the operation was destroyed on location so that it would not be recovered by the VC. On February 25, the battalion was airlifted back to Bearcat.

The Mastiff operations of the 1st Battalion were not unlike that of the 2nd, but with slightly more excitement. About 9:00 a.m. on February 21, the first lift of Lober's Rangers, consisting of A and B Companies and the mortar and recon platoons, hit the ground in LZ Hal. These units secured Hal for the second lift, consisting of C Company. Just prior to the arrival of C Company, six 82mm mortar rounds landed among the troops of A Company. No casualties were incurred, but it became evident to the Rangers that "Charlie" was indeed out there. Lober pushed his troops north into the jungle, and within minutes B Company was under sporadic fire. After killing one VC and wounding another (both of whom turned out to be female), the battalion pushed on to occupy blocking position Bill about 11:00 a.m. At Bill, Lober had his men dig in to establish an NDP. Several times during the afternoon and evening, the enemy probed the position. One enemy soldier was killed in these actions.

The following morning, 1-16 began its S&D sweep northward. Moving through dense, tangled brush, the Rangers made slow progress against light resistance. They discovered several rice and ammunition caches but made only infrequent contact with their shadowy foe. Then, at 1:40 p.m., VC soldiers command-detonated a claymore-style mine against C Company, killing four men and wounding four others. Two hours later, A Company discovered what appeared to be a regimental headquarters and mess hall, along with various supplies and equipment and nine thousand rounds of small arms ammunition. Company C subsequently discovered extensive trench and tunnel systems, and Company B came across a battalion base camp nearby. Due to B Company's desire to speedily engage the enemy, the captured ammunition and supplies were destroyed, but the facilities were left to be dealt with later.

As the Rangers pushed north, they contended with numerous booby traps. Prior to their efforts to get away, the VC had extensively booby-trapped facilities, supplies, and trails. The danger posed by these devices slowed operations, as men took time to locate, disarm, or otherwise dispose of the hazards. After a deliberate move, performed much more slowly than Lober desired, the battalion went into its NDP at 5:00 p.m.

The following day the 1-16 spent uneventfully in a nearby blocking position as the 2nd Brigade's 2-18 Infantry came up on the left in AO Bulldog. Unfortunately Lober had not been informed of the Vanguards' plan of action, so nothing was accomplished by the effort. After sitting in position all day vainly waiting for the 2-18 Infantry to drive the enemy into his sights, Lober returned his battalion to its previous night defensive position.

On February 24, Lober split up the battalion to begin the destruction of the facilities that had been discovered on the 21st. He sent A Company, still commanded by Captain Ed Yaugo, to demolish the regimental headquarters and B Company, under Captain Woody Koch, to raze the battalion base camp.

As A Company approached its objective, it bumped into a dug-in VC force, estimated at twenty men. Yaugo had one platoon lay down a base of fire, while he maneuvered the rest of the company to flank the VC position, but enemy troops, well-camouflaged and hidden in the trees, cut down five of Yaugo's men, killing two. After evacuating his three wounded troopers, Yaugo pushed on.

Discovering blood trails leading to the camp, Yaugo ordered his men to proceed cautiously. As they reached the camp, small arms fire erupted from an enemy force estimated at platoon strength. Instantly, A Company went into action. Three more of Yaugo's men were struck down, one mortally wounded, as the company assaulted the compound. In moments, the area was secured, but the VC had melted away. However, they did not get away unharmed. Numerous heavy blood trails and "hunks of flesh" indicated that at least nineteen enemy soldiers were hit by fire. Though no bodies were located, Yaugo estimated, based on counting blood trails and body parts, that his men had killed eight and wounded eleven. In return, he had lost three KIA and five WIA. Additionally, two men were wounded by booby traps as they searched the compound and prepared it for demolition.

Meanwhile, Koch's efforts to destroy the battalion base camp went off without a hitch. After completing that task, B Company discovered another VC camp as it was moving towards that evening's NDP. While Koch's troops were destroying the compound, they encountered several VC and a brief firefight ensued. After the scrap, the Rangers recovered two bodies and one wounded VC.

Over the next three days, the 1-16 made no further contact with enemy troops, but it did discover several small-arms ammunition and supply caches. On February 27, the battalion airlifted back to Lai Khe.

Operation Mastiff had achieved only limited success. The Big Red One had failed to corner and destroy a regiment of the 9th PLAF Division, a primary objective; moreover, the Americans had managed to kill only thirty enemy soldiers (with the 1st Battalion accounting for about a third of that number). On the plus side, the 1st Division had destroyed extensive enemy facilities and large quantities of supplies. Perhaps most

importantly, the leaders and men of both Ranger battalions had learned useful lessons about the logistics of jungle operations, fire-coordination planning, and adjacent-unit coordination. All these lessons came in handy in later operations.[30]

From March 1-5 the 2nd battalion participated in Operation Hattiesburg, south of Tay Ninh in the 25th ARVN Division's TAOR. The five-day operation was relatively uneventful, and the battalion sustained no casualties. During the operation, Captain Griffin's A Company, 2-16, was airlifted to a new base camp at Bearcat near Long Thanh in anticipation of the entire 2nd Brigade moving there. Theater engineers had been diligently working on this new camp and expected to complete it by late March. Griffin's troops went there to provide security for the engineers, to help in the construction effort, and to perform the role of advanced party for the rest of the battalion as it came in. In late March, the rest of the 2nd Battalion and the 2nd Brigade arrived at their new home at Bearcat.

Operation Cocoa Beach
March 3-6, 1966
While the 2nd Brigade participated in Hattiesburg, the Iron Brigade kicked off Operation Cocoa Beach on March 3. The intent, once again, was to draw the 272nd PLAF Regiment into battle. For this operation, Colonel Brodbeck positioned two infantry battalions (2-28 and 1-2) about six miles north of Lai Khe along the west side of Highway 13 to act as bait. He kept 1-16, now commanded by Lieutenant Colonel Lee S. Henry Jr., in standby reserve to assist either of the two bait battalions should the enemy decide to bite. To the commander of the 272nd Regiment, the Black Lions of the 2nd Battalion, 28th Infantry, apparently looked like a most tasty morsel, and on March 3-4 he marshaled his regiment and the D-61 South Ben Cat Company to crush the "unsuspecting" battalion.

Battle of Lo Ke
March 5, 1966
On March 3, the 2-28 Infantry moved into a position in the Lo Ke Rubber Plantation, located about one mile west of Bau Bang, and prepared a strong defensive perimeter. The troops dug well-placed fighting positions, expecting a heavy attack. The following day, S&D patrols were sent out to make contact and destroy whatever enemy troops and supplies could be found. As expected, that night the battalion received intelligence from the 3rd Brigade S2 that a regimental-size force was near Bau Bang, and the battalion went into full alert.

Early on the dark morning of March 5, an ambush patrol, led by Second Lieutenant Robert J. Hibbs, made first contact with an enemy company and inflicted heavy casualties on them. Hibbs then ordered his men back to the perimeter, but en route the patrol ran into another enemy company preparing to assault the battalion's battle position. The troops fought their way through, but Hibbs was killed while covering the retrograde movement.[31]

About 6:35 a.m. the main attack commenced on the 2-28's perimeter, with a battalion-sized force attacking on each side. Several attacks were sustained over the next three hours until 9:30 a.m., when the next major push came against the southern perimeter. The situation had become serious, so Brodbeck ordered the Rangers to the rescue.

Within sixteen minutes of receiving the order, A Company, now commanded by Captain Peter S. Knight, was in the air, winging its way to a LZ northeast of the Black Lions' position. Knight's troops secured the LZ and the remainder of the battalion came in seven lifts. By 10:55 a.m., the Rangers were sweeping southwest toward the 2-28's position. Almost immediately, Captain Homer Mapp's C Company engaged about thirty VC attempting to make their way out of the area. The fighting was brief and the company sustained one WIA. For the next several hours, each company made numerous sporadic, but sharp, contacts with enemy remnants as the VC attempted to escape to the north. In all, the battalion killed forty-five VC and located the bodies of another twenty, probably killed by air strikes or artillery. The Rangers also accounted for another ten known WIAs and three POWs. Remarkably, no additional casualties were sustained by the 1st Battalion.

One of the POWs was an eighteen-year-old boy named Truong Van Chuoi from Company C18/9000A, who claimed he had been forced to join the Viet Cong forces. His unit was a 250-man reinforcement unit that had come from Saigon four days before. The unit was some type of ordnance supply organization that had carried forty-eight .51-caliber machine guns and 420 other small arms up to Bau Bang to equip another unit that had never shown up at the rendezvous point.[32]

About 3:30 p.m., 1-16 entered the 2-28 Infantry's perimeter and broadened the existing position. For the next twenty-four hours, the battalion conducted recon patrols around the position, counting bodies, gathering intelligence, and destroying abandoned enemy equipment. At 5:00 p.m., March 7, Operation Cocoa Beach was terminated, and units returned to Lai Khe. The 272nd Regiment and D-61 South Ben Cat Company suffered a total of 199 KIA during the four-day operation.

Operation Abilene
March 30-April 15, 1966

Though most of the 1st Infantry Division's efforts had thus far been focused to the northwest of Saigon, enemy activities had been picking up in other parts of the III CTZ as well. In early 1966, intelligence efforts began to indicate a build-up of supplies in areas to the east of Saigon to support the 5th PLAF Division. The supplies were reportedly being stockpiled to support the division in an offensive against the capital. In response to this build-up, General Seaman ordered the development of plans for Operation Abilene. This operation was designed to be a spoiling attack to destroy the supplies and base camp areas supporting the 5th Division's attack. Additionally, during the operation, II Field Force engineers would clear a new supply route to the South China Sea.

The 1st Infantry Division's mission during Abilene was to find and destroy elements of the 5th and 94th ("Dong Nai") PLAF Regiments of the 5th Division and their base camps. The 3rd Brigade's portion of that mission was to operate in the southern half of the division TAOR. The Iron Brigade's area was designated AO Oregon. On March 30, C-130s airlifted the brigade from Lai Khe to the airfield at Vung Tau to stage for further operations. The following day, Lee Henry's 1st Battalion was airlifted into LZ Pendleton, four kilometers northeast of the Núi Dinh—Núi Bao Quon mountain complex. For the next two days, the battalion swept westward, just north of the twin mountains of Núi Toc Tiên and Núi Thi Vai, until it reached Highway 15, four kilometers south of Ph' My. It remained there until the 4th, when it was airlifted to the brigade CP location southeast of Xuyên Môc.

For the next five days, the battalion remained at the brigade CP location pulling security for the Iron Brigade Tactical Operations Center and the 2nd Battalion, 33rd Field Artillery. However, each of the three line companies performed independent airmobile insertions and sweeps at several locations in the eastern half of AO Oregon. The primary event of this period was B Company's capture on April 8 of two VC tax collectors (with the help of one of the local farmers).

On April 11, the battalion moved to LZ Butte and performed S&D sweeps near Núi Hôt for the next three days with minimal results. On April 14, Henry's 1st Rangers airlifted to Lai Khe after two weeks of fruitless searching.[33]

While the 1st Battalion's efforts during Abilene were largely barren of enemy contact, Colonel Hathaway's 2nd Battalion had a livelier time. The 2nd Brigade's mission was to conduct S&D operations in AO Nebraska, the northern half of the division's TAOR. On March 30, the 2nd Battalion was airlifted into LZ Norman, ten kilometers west of Xã Cam My, where, as the brigade reserve, it performed security for the 2nd Brigade CP and the 1st Battalion, 7th Field Artillery. The two battalions of the 18th Infantry conducted S&D sweeps to the south over the next several days.

On April 2, the 2nd Battalion, 18th Infantry, assumed the reserve mission, and Hathaway's 2nd Rangers were airlifted into the new 2nd Brigade AO, ten kilometers northwest of Xuyên Môc. From April 3 to 6, Hathaway's troops conducted sweep operations in that area.

About this time a comical incident occurred involving Hathaway and the A Company commander, Jerry Griffin. Hathaway had the battalion set up a NDP near a small village for a couple of days, while he waited for orders for the next mission. He and his sergeant major, Louis Guerra, accompanied by Griffin and his radioman, Private First Class Richmond K. S. Long, went into the village to look around. Out of the corner of his eye, Griffin noticed a flash dart out of a nearby hooch. It was a young boy, clad only in black pants, running for the nearby river. Griffin recalled thinking, "There is only one reason why

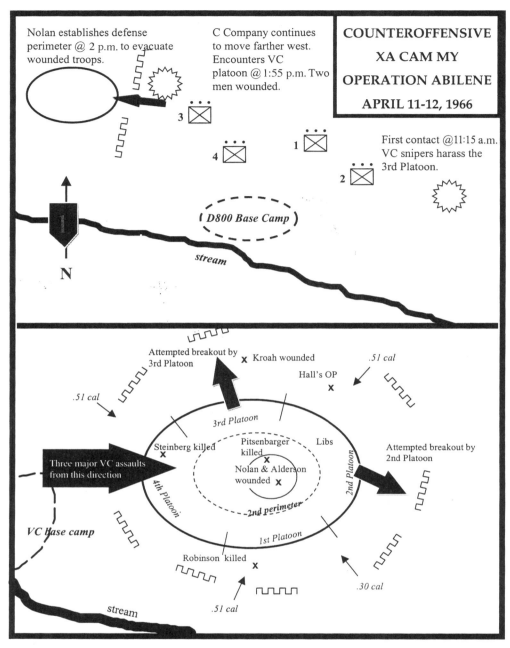

Nolan establishes defense perimeter @ 2 p.m. to evacuate wounded troops.

C Company continues to move farther west. Encounters VC platoon @ 1:55 p.m. Two men wounded.

**COUNTEROFFENSIVE
XA CAM MY
OPERATION ABILENE
APRIL 11-12, 1966**

First contact @11:15 a.m. VC snipers harass the 3rd Platoon.

3

4 1

2

D800 Base Camp

stream

N

Attempted breakout by 3rd Platoon

x Kroah wounded

.51 cal

Hall's OP
x

.51 cal

3rd Platoon

Steinberg killed
x

Pitsenbarger killed
x

Libs

Nolan & Alderson wounded x

Attempted breakout by 2nd Platoon

Three major VC assaults from this direction

4th Platoon

2nd Platoon

2nd perimeter

VC base camp

1st Platoon

Robinson killed
x

.30 cal

stream

.51 cal

Map 10-3.

a young Vietnamese in black pajama bottoms would run at the sight of Americans; and it wasn't because he wanted to tell his friends the good news about the arrival of the Americans. He was a damned VC for sure, because he was also carrying what looked like a weapon, and it wasn't hunting season." Griffin jumped into his jeep and pursued the boy, followed shortly by Hathaway and Guerra in another jeep.

As they approached the river, the boy leaped into the water, just as Griffin's jeep skidded to a stop. Hathaway had seen the youth go into the water as he hustled up to the bank. All waited

for the VC to surface. After a time, the battalion commander looked at Griffin and said, "I guess he got away." To which the company commander replied, "No, he's still in the river someplace. I'll make him surface." In seconds, a grenade was lobbed into the water, and up the VC came. The colonel, happy with this turn of events, then suggested, "Well, someone needs to go in and save him." To which Griffin incredulously replied, "Save him! Hell, I thought we were trying to kill him!" At this, Hathaway pushed the captain into the water, and Griffin dutifully pulled the boy to shore. Later, Griffin was given a big write up in the 2nd Brigade newsletter for this "humanitarian act," while Hathaway and the sergeant major insisted to everybody that the captain had "voluntarily" jumped in to rescue the boy.[34]

Meanwhile, on April 3, the battalion found and destroyed a base camp consisting of fifteen barracks. The following day, it captured and destroyed 350 tons of rice and ammunition. On April 7 and 8, the Rangers moved to the Binh Ba area and conducted a village seal in coordination with ARVN troops. The following day, the battalion returned to S&D operations.

By April 9, intelligence information from the division G2 indicated that, "It was becoming apparent that local force units presently operating in the area were scattered and disorganized with little capability to mount effective operations." Indeed, the G2 had information that the two VC main force regiments that the Big Red One was looking for were not in the province. However, there were also indications that one unit, the D800 Battalion, a unit subordinate to the 94th ("Dong Nai") Regiment, was still somewhere in the AO. On April 9, orders came in for another mission. Hathaway did not realize it then, but one of his units would find the D800 Battalion momentarily. The action would become the most significant event of Operation Abilene.

Battle of Xã Cam My (Courtenay Plantation)
April 11, 1966

The afternoon of April 10, 1966 was bright and sunny; appropriate weather for an Easter Sunday. That afternoon Company C, 2nd Battalion, 16th Infantry, found itself seven kilometers due east of the little village of Xã Cam My. Just north of Xã Cam My lay the Courtenay Rubber Plantation. While not as extensive as the Michelin Rubber Plantation, the Courtenay plantation and its surrounding areas offered the same kind of shelter that was ideal for VC units.

Company C, commanded by Captain William R. Nolan, consisted of 134 men distributed in four platoons and a headquarters element. That Sunday they occupied a temporary defensive perimeter on the edge of an open area. No other friendly units were nearer than about one thousand meters. As part of the plan for Operation Abilene, Lieutenant Colonel Hathaway had been directed to put his companies out in isolated locations with the intent of enticing the four hundred-man D800 Battalion to conduct an attack on one of them. Theoretically, each company was placed in a location where they could quickly move and provide mutual support. In reality, the thick jungle foliage and the lack of trails and LZs in the area prevented any rapid movement.

These actions were all in keeping with General DePuy's mandated techniques for waging war against the enemy. Typically, an enemy commander refused to engage an American unit unless he felt he had clear superiority in firepower and had a reasonable chance for success. Therefore, DePuy's technique was to entice the enemy to take on what appeared to be an isolated American unit. Once the VC were decisively engaged, U.S. artillery and air power would hammer them, and other U.S. units would surround them and pile on with superior firepower. In theory, DePuy's idea was a good one and was one of the few ways to goad the VC into a fight. If anything went wrong, however, such as a unit moving out of range of artillery support or out of reach of reinforcing units, dire consequences could result. That is what happened to C Company near the Courtenay Plantation the day after Easter 1966.

Nolan's unit was just finishing Easter services that afternoon when the chaplain spotted three VC clad in black pajama-style uniforms moving across the clearing about four hundred yards away. The chaplain called the troops' attention to the enemy soldiers, and Second Lieutenant John W. Libs of Evansville, Indiana, quickly reacted by calling on several of his men to come with him to go after the VC. Sergeant Lawson H. Passmore, a squad leader; Private First Class Phillip J. Hall, an M-60 gunner; and one other man, sprang to their feet and accompanied Libs. Firing as they went, the group attracted the attention of other troops, who also opened fire on the madly running enemy. Two VC went down, but the third made it to the wood line and disappeared.[35]

Arriving where the two VC lay, Libs found one dead, but the other was wounded and conscious. Before the man died,

Libs was able to extract some valuable intelligence from him. When he asked the company's South Vietnamese interpreter what the man said, the interpreter falsely told him that the dying VC stated he was from an independent unit. One soldier, however, knew some Vietnamese, and later pulled the platoon leader aside to tell him that the dying man actually said he was from the D800 Battalion, the very unit the Rangers were looking for. Libs informed Nolan of the information, and the company commander decided to move the company to a different NDP to prevent the enemy, now alerted to their presence, from easily finding them.[36]

Before nightfall, C Company received a heliborne visitor in the form of General DePuy. During his visit, DePuy explained to the officers the position they were in: "You guys are out here alone. By all intelligence, D-800 is nearby. Your chances of getting hit tonight are very good. Our artillery has you bracketed in."[37] Then, just as he had come, DePuy mounted his chopper and flew away.

After a tense night, April 11 dawned on C Company without any enemy contact, much to everyone's relief. About 7:30 a.m., the company shoved off in search of D800, led by the 3rd Platoon. The movement was unremarkable (with exception of the discovery of some abandoned trenches about 8:30 a.m.) until just after 11:00 a.m., when the 3rd Platoon, led by Second Lieutenant Martin ("Marty") Kroah Jr., made a brief, but sharp, contact with a couple of VC. Kroah's platoon made several more contacts and sightings in quick succession, but no firm firefights developed; so Captain Nolan decided to continue to push on.

The rest of the company was moving in the order of the company headquarters, 4th Platoon (Second Lieutenant George Steinberg), 3rd Platoon (Second Lieutenant Smith A. Devoe), and finally, Johnny Libs's 2nd Platoon. About 1:55 p.m., a VC force estimated at platoon strength fired on Steinberg's 4th Platoon and hit two men, forcing Nolan to stop the company. This would prove to be a mistake. Unknowingly, Nolan had led his company to within 150 meters of one of the D800 Battalion's base camps—and it was occupied.[38]

The VC used the time Nolan spent trying to medevac his unit's two casualties to surround the company. Libs, nervous and possessing a sixth sense after his many months in combat, anticipated the enemy's move and called Nolan on the radio. "Roll up the wagons now," he said. Nolan, a relatively new commander, had learned to listen to his senior platoon leader's advice, but he could not get the company into a well-organized, contiguous perimeter before D800 attacked.[39]

Phil Hall had not realized that the 2nd Platoon had formed a perimeter, and he had remained in an isolated position, separated from the rest of the platoon, when it moved to form the perimeter. Suddenly, he spotted several enemy troops, mostly clad in black but others in khaki. This meant that the VC were being led by tough NVA regulars, and that was not a good sign. Suddenly, realizing his danger, Hall retreated to the perimeter after felling a pajama-clad VC with his shotgun. He quickly informed Libs of his sighting.

Forward of the company, Lieutenant Kroah called for artillery to break up an enemy force massing to his front. Soon, shells from the 1st Battalion, 7th Field Artillery, the 16th Infantry's previously reliable Redlegs from Combat Team 16 days in World War II, came crashing into the jungle right on target. Kroah then radioed, "Fire for effect!" but rather than blasting the VC assault positions, the shells landed in his own platoon area, killing or wounding about seventeen Rangers.

When Kroah called off the artillery fires, the enemy used the lull to move in closer and pick off the Americans by sniping from the trees. By now, Nolan realized that he had led his company into a trap and decided to pull back before he was cut off. Kroah informed him that he was unable to pull back due to the large number of wounded and dead his platoon had already sustained. Nolan was apparently prepared to leave Kroah's platoon to its fate, but when the other platoons attempted to move, they were driven to the ground by intense small arms fire. It was too late. The bag was tied.[40]

About 3:25 p.m., air force rescue teams came in to evacuate the dead and the wounded, and miraculously, they were able to rescue twelve men from the hell hole that C Company's position had become. On the last attempt, one of the choppers was hit by fire, and the air force rescue man, Airman First Class William H. Pitsenbarger, waved off the chopper and elected to remain with Charlie Company. It was a brave act, but it would cost him his life (On December 8, 2000, Pitsenbarger was posthumously awarded the Medal of Honor in a ceremony at Wright Patterson Air Force Base in Ohio. Present at the ceremony were Pitsanbarger's father, John Libs, Phil Hall, Ken Alderson, and six other C Company veterans.)

Meanwhile, Nolan realized that the company had to break out if it was to survive, and told his executive officer, First Lieutenant Ken Alderson, to contact one of the platoons and direct it to conduct a breakout. If successful, the rest of the company would follow. However, right after he talked to Alderson, Nolan was wounded and lost effective command of the company.

By 5:00 p.m., the VC started mortaring the company perimeter. In response, the 1-7 Field Artillery pinpointed the mortars by counterbattery radar and blasted them into silence. Meanwhile, Kroah and Libs attempted another breakout. Kroah's 3rd Platoon tried to force its way through to the northwest while Libs's 2nd Platoon pushed southeast. Both efforts failed.

About 5:45 p.m. the VC pushed ten machine-guns, including at least two .50-calibers, into position to rake the now-battered company. Up above the desperate fight, Major Bibb Underwood, the battalion executive officer, assisted in bringing artillery in as close to the company's perimeter as possible. Libs and Alderson maintained contact with Underwood and asked where B Company was. The executive officer responded:

"Hang in there. We'll give you everything we've got. Bravo Company is still one thousand meters away." At this, Libs despaired. He knew that in this kind of jungle, it would take B Company hours to reach them. "They'll be too fucking late," Libs responded. "We'll be rotting in the jungle by the time Bravo gets here."[41] Charlie Company was on its own.

The afternoon wore on and dusk settled on the perimeter. By now, Kroah was wounded five times, and his platoon sergeant was dead. Steinberg, hit seven times, was also dead. Nolan was also out of action, and Alderson had been stunned when a VC bullet knocked his helmet from his head. Stretches of the porous perimeter were now held only by the dead and dying.

Over in the 1st Platoon, Sergeant James W. Robinson of Annandale, Virginia, was fighting with the heart of a tiger. Grabbing an M-79 grenade launcher, he effectively silenced several snipers that had caused numerous casualties in his platoon. Spotting two wounded men laying outside the line, he bravely bolted to them and dragged them into the perimeter and dressed their wounds. Throughout the day, he busied himself collecting and redistributing weapons and ammo and later dragged another man to safety, though he, too, was wounded in the effort. As he bandaged his own wounds, Robinson spotted the .50-caliber machine gun that had caused so much damage. He shouted to his troops, "I see the fifty! I'm going for it. Cover me!"

Out of M-16 ammo, Robinson grabbed two grenades off his belt and pulled the pins. Taking a deep breath, the sergeant made a mad dash at the gun; the whole time bullets were splashing around him. One tracer round set his pant leg on fire as he ran. Tumbling to the ground, he ripped away the burning pant leg, then jumped up again to finish off the gun. He made it to within thirty feet of the machine gun and lobbed the grenades into the position just as he fell dead from two .50-caliber hits in the chest. His aim was true, however, and the position erupted from the two grenades. For his indomitable courage that day, Robinson earned the regiment's eighth Medal of Honor.[42]

As darkness enveloped the battlefield, small arms fire slackened. Soon, VC women began searching the perimeter, stripping the American dead of weapons and ammo, and killing the wounded with a shot to the head. Libs attempted another breakout with his remaining troops, but the hail of fire again stopped his men in their tracks. One man, Private First Class Edward W. Reilly of Upper Darby, Pennsylvania, was mortally wounded in this fusillade and died in prayer, holding the small crucifix he habitually wore around his neck. Libs realized that if his troops were to have any chance now, he had to have artillery fire, and he had to have it all night long. Using a PRC-25 radio that Private Hall had found for him, Libs contacted Underwood and told him to bring artillery in all night as close to the perimeter as possible. He also requested and received flares to silhouette any movements made by the VC to mass for an attack.[43]

Meanwhile, back in the 3rd Platoon, Kroah, his medic, and his radioman, all three wounded, held each other's hands and recited the Lord's Prayer. For all they knew, they were the only survivors in the platoon. Playing dead, the three were searched by VC women looking for weapons and anything of value. The medic, however, did not play dead well enough and was shot in the head by one of the women.

About 9:00 p.m. Libs suddenly heard the voice of the turncoat South Vietnamese interpreter (the man who had lied to him about what the dying VC had said the day before) yelling to the VC. A South Vietnamese National Policeman who had also accompanied the company yelled to Libs that the man was telling the enemy where they were. The traitor was quickly shot down by a blast of "friendly" fire.

Up above, Underwood kept creeping the artillery barrage closer to the perimeter. Between the blasts, the screaming voices of wounded and dying VC came from the impact area.

As the indirect fire shook the area, spraying the Rangers with dirt and blasted foliage, Libs muttered to himself, "God bless you Bibb Underwood." He knew the artillery was preventing the enemy from massing for an attack. By this time the battle was over. The battalions of the 1st Division Artillery had fired over eleven hundred rounds to help save what was left of Charlie Company that night.[44]

And so it went, until everybody noticed the VC fire slacken. Alderson called off the artillery with the proviso that the batteries be prepared to continue at a moment's notice. On the perimeter, men scrambled to help their wounded buddies, redistribute weapons and ammo and plug holes in the line. They were painfully aware that the VC could resume their assault at any moment and that Charlie Company was on the verge of destruction. The badly wounded were dragged to the center of the position, but those wounded troops who could still fire stayed on the line.

For the next three hours, the area remained quiet. The survivors could hardly believe that the enemy had given up. Hopes soared as streaks of light to the east announced the dawn of April 12. About 7:15 a.m., First Lieutenant James Crocker, executive officer of Captain Juris Plakans's B Company, was the first of that company to make contact with the remnants of C Company. Plakans's company had arrived earlier in the night after hacking its way through a kilometer of heavy jungle and set up a NDP just within earshot of Nolan's beleaguered men. Plakans would have been there sooner, but Hathaway instructed him not to go into the C Company perimeter until daylight unless Nolan was still in contact.[45] The battalion commander wisely refused to risk the real possibility that the link up between the two American units would result in friendly fire casualties. Nevertheless, it is likely that the arrival of B Company was at least in part responsible for the D800 Battalion's retreat. After scrapping all day and night with one company of Rangers, the VC commander probably had no

desire to take on a fresh company of 16th Infantrymen.

Soon, a fleet of helicopters arrived with massive assistance. First in were the engineers, who cleared a LZ to get the casualties out. They were followed by medics, who went right to work patching up the wounded while they waited for a medevac. General DePuy also came in and queried Alderson and Libs, the latter engaging the division commander in a rather heated discussion. DePuy took the lieutenant's words patiently. After Libs explained the full story, he ended it with the comment, "You walked us right into a goddamn holocaust, general." DePuy replied, "Yeah, but there's no other way to get a goddamn fight going." Many years later, Libs realized DePuy was exactly right. Libs later remarked, "Thinking back on it now, I would have done it the same way if I were DePuy."[46]

For their efforts on April 11-12, 1966, C Company was awarded the Valorous Unit Award by the Secretary of the Army on April 23, 1968. But the honor came at a high cost. The company had suffered thirty-five killed and seventy-one wounded of the 134 that entered the fight, resulting in an 80 percent casualty rate. The D800 Battalion suffered forty-one KIA by body count; however, Lieutenant Colonel Hathaway later estimated that the enemy KIA count may have been as high as 150, though it is doubtful that the latter number can be accurate. Generally, the ratio for WIA to KIA ratios is three to one. Even if the former count is entirely accurate, that means that D800 suffered at least 160 casualties out of an estimated strength of about four hundred. Given the poor medical care the VC provided their soldiers, many of their wounded probably died later. Given the additional evidence accumulated over the next two days, Hathaway's determination that the D800 Battalion had suffered something more than 41 dead was probably accurate.

After C Company was evacuated, Hathaway doggedly pursued the injured D800 Battalion with A and B Companies. Hot on their trail, the 2nd Battalion pushed north. Along the way, numerous blood trails and bandages were discovered that led the Rangers to an empty bunker complex and base camp. That place, too, was littered with bloody bandages, but no bodies, dead or otherwise, were found.[47]

After two more days of searching, the Rangers made no further contact with VC units. On April 14, the rest of the battalion returned to its base camp at Bearcat.

Operation Birmingham
April 24-May 17, 1966

War Zone C lay in the northwest corner of Tay Ninh province adjacent to Cambodia, where no ARVN or allied forces had operated since 1961. It was predominantly an agricultural area that consisted of low flatland with gentle, almost imperceptible slopes, except for Núi Ba Den (which literally translated means "Mountain of the Black Virgin"), a single mountain jutting noticeably from the surrounding terrain. Heavy foliage in undeveloped areas provided ample and ideal concealment for VC units. There were numerous LZs in the area, however, that made it easier to get units into otherwise impenetrable locations.

Intelligence planners at MACV believed that the Central Office of South Vietnam (COSVN), the controlling headquarters of all VC units in the III CTZ, was located in War Zone C. The major ground unit that COSVN controlled in that zone was the already familiar 9th PLAF Division. Since War Zone C was also the base of supply for most VC units in Tay Ninh province, the enemy could be expected to fiercely defend their meager resources. Therefore, General DePuy intended to send all three brigades into War Zone C to destroy as much VC support infrastructure as possible and to find and destroy the COSVN.

For Birmingham, Hathaway's 2nd Battalion was placed under operational control (OPCON) of the 1st Brigade for the first time since its arrival in Vietnam. Commanded by Colonel Edgar N. Glotzbach, the brigade's mission was to operate initially in AO Buick, along the Rach Cai Bac River that bordered Cambodia. Colonel Henry's 1st Battalion, meantime, was to operate with Colonel Brodbeck's 3rd Brigade in AO Ford, south of Buick and due west of Tay Ninh.

On April 24, the 2nd Battalion entered the TAOR at LZ Red about twenty kilometers northwest of Tay Ninh. For two days, the battalion remained at Red as the brigade reserve, then on April 26, conducted a relief in place with another 1st Brigade battalion. For the next four days, the battalion worked in conjunction with Lieutenant Colonel Richard Prillaman's 1st Battalion, 2nd Infantry, performing S&D sweeps northward along the Rach Cai Bac River. The sweep was fairly unproductive until April 27, when Captain Griffin's A Company bumped into a small VC detachment and killed three soldiers early that afternoon. Soon after, the company located sixty-three tons of rice and discovered sixty-eight hundred black and khaki uniforms, and the recon platoon found and destroyed another nine tons of rice.

Two days later, the Rangers discovered another 108 tons of rice and a large field hospital complex along the banks of the Beng Go River.[48] The major event of Operation Birmingham occurred the following day.

Battle of Lo Go
April 30, 1966
Leaving Captain Plakans's B Company at the VC hospital, Lieutenant Colonel Hathaway pushed the 2nd Rangers north past the village of Lo Go on the morning of April 30. About 8:45 a.m., as it moved with the 1-2 Infantry, the battalion came under automatic weapons fire from the Cambodian side of the river. Apparently a VC unit was conducting a river crossing when the battalions arrived in the area. The 1-2 Infantry deployed in the direction of the river, and the heavy return fire from the two U.S. battalions caused the enemy guns to temporarily fall silent.

Meanwhile, the VC commander used the lull to attempt an encirclement of the 1-2 Infantry and that battalion soon became decisively engaged. As the fighting progressed, Colonel Prillaman's battalion was indeed partially surrounded by the enemy, as the VC pinned down the 1-2 Infantry from support positions across the river and moved a maneuver force to flank the Americans from a tree line to the northeast.

As he prepared to move north, Hathaway contacted Griffin to relieve the pressure on the 1-2 Infantry. Griffin moved out, and soon, troops from Second Lieutenant Ron Miles' platoon, which was in the lead, spotted the VC force in the tree line to the northeast that was now attempting to surround the 1-2 Infantry. Griffin's men stealthily moved eastward, then north, and successfully flanked the enemy. Once in position, Miles' platoon attacked and penetrated the VC line, while the rest of A Company rolled up the enemy's left flank. In their desperate efforts to escape, the VC soldiers set fire to the grass to slow the American advance.[49] In this engagement, A Company killed eight enemy troops and stumbled upon a company base camp that it also destroyed.

The rout of the VC force to the northeast allowed Prillaman's troops to now focus their attention solely on their assailants across the river, and they returned fire with a vengeance. Assaulting toward the river bank, the battalion killed forty-two VC on the east side of the river, and killed probably another seventy-five, whose bodies they could see heaped up on the banks and on the far side of the stream. Meanwhile, Hathaway's troops mopped up to the north and accounted for another four enemy in sporadic contacts in that direction. Others were killed as they attempted to swim to safety in Cambodia, but their bodies were swept down river.

In the five-hour battle, the two battalions had handed the enemy a severe defeat. The American units accounted for fifty-four confirmed VC KIA and upwards of one hundred dead that could either be seen laying on the Cambodian side of the Rach Cai Bac or identified from aerial photographs. These dead were later identified as belonging to the 3rd Battalion, 70th Security Guards Regiment, the COSVN's security and area control unit. The 1st Division intelligence officers were surprised that a single VC battalion would stand and fight so hard when outnumbered by American battalions. They theorized that it was probably sent to engage and delay the Americans while other units evacuated equipment and supplies to the safe haven of Cambodia. Regardless of the reason, the Battle of Lo Go was the largest single engagement during Birmingham.[50]

Two days of uneventful patrolling followed. On May 2, the 2nd Battalion airlifted to a large plantation area east of Tay Ninh for the next phase of Operation Birmingham. There, Hathaway's men stood down for twenty-four hours of maintenance before starting S&D sweeps to the southeast the following day. On May 5, in a pouring rain, the battalion attacked a suspected VC assembly area in coordination with the 2nd Battalion, 18th Infantry, but only light resistance was encountered. The next day, operational control of the Rangers was turned back over to the 2nd Brigade.[51]

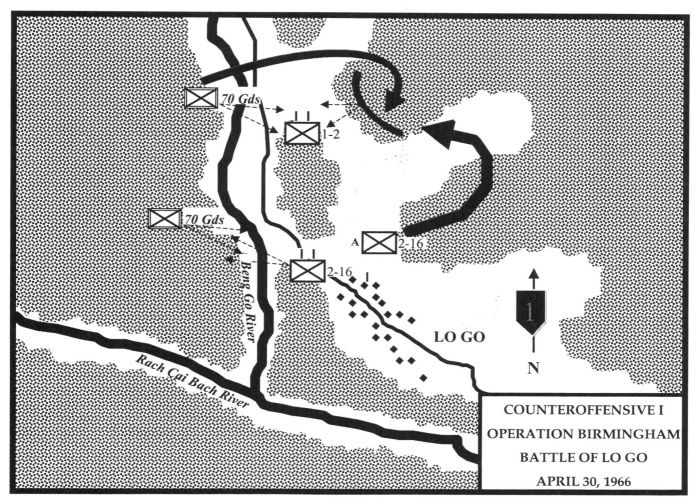

Map 10-4.

The experience of the 1st Battalion, 16th Infantry, during Birmingham was more dull than that of its brother battalion. On April 24, Henry's troops flew from Lai Khe to Tay Ninh in C-130s, then transloaded into choppers for insertion into the 3rd Brigade's Base 3, twenty kilometers west of Tay Ninh. At Base 3, the battalion assumed security for part of the perimeter with the 2nd Battalion, 28th Infantry. After only four hours on the ground, A Company killed one VC and captured three others inside the perimeter. Within minutes, Captain Woody Koch's B Company captured three more. By 5:00 p.m. that day, the battalion had rounded up an additional 152 VC suspects and turned them over to the brigade POW team.

On April 26, the battalion's only significant engagement during Birmingham occurred northwest of Base 3. C Company stumbled into a heavily fortified base camp held by about twenty-four VC. After a sharp firefight the company overran the position, killing ten enemy troops. Blood trails indicated another eight were wounded. The attack cost C Company four KIA and seven wounded in return.

From April 27 to May 2, the battalion engaged in a series of sweeps that failed to bring the enemy to battle but did result in the destruction of six base camps, five tons of rice, and one sampan. The battalion was airlifted out the following day and assumed the security mission for Camp Gordon J. Lippman for the rest of the operation.[52]

Meanwhile, from May 7 to 10, while the monsoons held forth in great volume, the 2nd Brigade operated north of Soui Da in an attempt to locate COSVN. The effort did not locate the suspected headquarters, and then the mission was called off early due to the heavy rains. Disappointed with the insignificant results, Milloy displaced his command to Dau Tieng to commence sweeps southeast along the northeast side of the Saigon River. However, as before, Hathaway's 2nd Battalion made little contact with the enemy for the next several days. On May 15, Operation Birmingham was terminated, and the 2nd Battalion returned to Camp Bearcat.

The overall results of Birmingham for the 1st Infantry Division were once again disappointing. The division failed to locate and destroy the COSVN. The VC did not aggressively defend their supply bases as expected, and the 9th PLAF Division skillfully avoided battle with the American forces. But the operation was not entirely void of results. Between the two 16th Infantry Battalions, the Rangers netted sixty-four enemy KIA, and they intercepted and destroyed tons of supplies. More importantly, the Big Red One effectively put COSVN on notice that its deepest recesses of War Zone C were subject to powerful incursions by the 1st Infantry Division.

Counteroffensive, Phase II
July 1966-May 1967

Most of the 1st Infantry Division's major operations in the first half of 1966 were designed to counter and roll back the increased enemy strength and activities in Tay Ninh and Binh Duong provinces northwest of Saigon. Though the units of the Big Red One were successful in locating and destroying numerous base camps, supply dumps, and tunnels, they still had not been successful in drawing the 9th PLAF Division out for a pitched fight. The reason: the VC division was preparing to conduct an offensive of its own in Binh Long province. Now it appeared that the 1st Division might soon get its chance to effectively engage its elusive foe.

Operation El Paso I, II, and III
May 19-August 24, 1966

While the division had been operating to the west in Tay Ninh province during Birmingham, U.S. intelligence collection efforts in the III CTZ indicated an ominous build-up of VC forces in Binh Long province. Indicators also suggested that COSVN was infiltrating reinforcement NVA units from the north. Information gleaned from a captured enemy notebook and other documents indicated that the 273rd PLAF and 101st PAVN Regiments were preparing an assault on the district headquarters town of Loc Ninh and on the nearby 5th Special Forces camp. The 271st and 272nd Regiments were also planning to support the attack by raiding villages to the southeast of Loc Ninh and by setting up blocking positions to ambush American reinforcements into the area. In response, the 1st Infantry Division G3 began developing plans for Operation El Paso, an ambush of the 273rd Regiment at Loc Ninh.[53]

The initial phase of Operation El Paso consisted of security for Loc Ninh and PSYOPS (Psychological Operations) to win over the local population, which had long suffered Communist domination. The PSYOPS also attempted to push the "Chieu Hoi" (Open Arms) campaign to convince VC soldiers to defect. This was accomplished by leaflet drops and loudspeaker exhortations from helicopters.

On May 19, Henry's 1st Battalion was airlifted into Loc Ninh by C-130s and moved immediately to the field south of the town. The following morning, the 2nd Battalion, 16th Infantry, attached once again to the 3rd Brigade, inserted into a LZ two kilometers northeast of the 1st Battalion. As a cour-

tesy, the LZ had been secured by Henry's recon platoon the night before. For the next five days, the Rangers aggressively patrolled around the town but made only one contact, which resulted in the only enemy KIA during the first phase of El Paso. On May 25, the 1st Battalion returned to Lai Khe, and the 2nd Battalion departed for Camp Bearcat. The 1st Squadron, 4th Cavalry (nicknamed the "Quarterhorse"), assumed the Loc Ninh security mission.[54] Once again, the 273rd Regiment had eschewed battle.

One week later on June 2, El Paso II began as a brigade-sized operation under control of the 3rd Brigade. Six days later elements of the 1-4 Cavalry and the 2-18 Infantry decisively engaged the 272nd Regiment along Highway 13 between An Loc and Lai Khe. After a pitched battle, the 272nd lost an estimated 250 killed and broke contact. The following day, El Paso II was elevated to a division-level operation, and the 1st Brigade deployed to Minh Thanh.

This time, Hathaway's battalion was attached to the 1st Brigade and was airlifted to Minh Thanh on June 9 and assigned the job of providing security for the 1st Brigade CP there. The 1st Battalion (OPCON to the 3rd Brigade at Loc Ninh airfield since June 6) had performed a similar mission during the initial stages of El Paso II.

Supply Base Raid
June 21, 1966

Colonel Hathaway's troops conducted S&D sweeps around Minh Thanh until June 20, when they received a change in mission. During Operation Birmingham in May, a VC defector, Nguyen Ming Nhut, reported a VC supply depot located a few kilometers west of the Michelin Rubber Plantation that contained some three million piasters' (about $25,640) worth of supplies. The camp was guarded by the eighty-man C65 Local Force Company and was considered a main support base for the 9th PLAF Division. Hathaway was directed to find and destroy it.

On the morning of June 21, the 2nd Rangers made a heliborne assault into a LZ near the site. Coming upon a hut, the lead company encountered six VC, and a brisk firefight ensued. One VC was killed, one captured, and two wounded. Pushing on, the battalion bumped into another VC detachment and killed one of them. Though a small camp was located and destroyed, the main depot was not located before nightfall, so the battalion coiled into its NDP.

The following morning, the 2nd Battalion, 2nd Infantry, was committed to the raid when it was discovered how extensive the supply depot was. Over the next six days, the two battalions exhaustively endeavored to destroy the spread-out installation and destroyed food, facilities, and military and medical supplies worth over 23 million piasters (about $196,500). During the raid, Hathaway's Rangers killed eleven VC and captured one thousand tons of rice, eight hundred sheets of tin, and other assorted weapons and supplies. On June 28, the 2-18

Infantry replaced the Rangers at Minh Thanh and the battalion returned to Camp Bearcat.[55]

While the 2nd Battalion conducted missions around Minh Thanh, Henry's 1st Battalion flew into Loc Ninh on June 6, and performed fire base security missions and conducted platoon- and company-size sweeps around the area for the next ten days. On June 17, the battalion moved to the Minh Thanh airstrip to provide security for the engineers improving the strip there. The battalion remained at Minh Thanh until June 23, when it returned to its home base. While the 1st Rangers were back at Lai Khe preparing for their next mission, the battalion took time out for a short ceremony to welcome a new commander. On June 26, 1966, Lieutenant Colonel Rufus C. Lazzell took command from Lee Henry.

For the next week or so, El Paso II was mainly a 1st Brigade operation as it continued to search for the elusive 9th Division. A major fight developed on June 30 when the 1-4 Cavalry struck the 271st Regiment at Srok Dong. The brigade piled on more units with the result that the 271st suffered almost three hundred KIA before it disengaged. The following day, the brigade repositioned to block the enemy regiment's withdrawal into Cambodia. On July 2, the 1st Battalion returned to Loc Ninh and rejoined the 3rd Brigade, when it was determined that the 271st Regiment was probably headed that way. Fruitless searches characterized the next six days' efforts, but on July 8, Lazzell's command was made OPCON to the 1st Brigade in anticipation of a major engagement.

Battle of Minh Thanh Road
July 9, 1966

The Battle of Minh Thanh Road started with a deliberate deception effort to trap a VC regiment. It worked beautifully. General DePuy directed Colonel Sidney B. Berry Jr., commander of the 1st Brigade, to develop the plan. Knowing of the VC's affinity for gaining early intelligence, Berry "leaked" the information that a supply convoy would move down the Minh Thanh road from Highway 13 to Minh Thanh at a given time. As anticipated, the commander of the 272nd PLAF Regiment received the information and moved to ambush the convoy. Little did he know that the "convoy" was going to be the heavily armored tanks and tracks of the 1-4 Cavalry, and the "supplies" were going to be heavy volumes of American ammunition. Thus, Lazzell's 1st Battalion was attached to the 1st Brigade to help trap the 272nd.

On the 8th, the battalion moved to Quon Loi to position itself for the operation. The following morning, the vehicles of the Quarterhorse moved out of An Loc, en route for Minh Thanh. About 11:00 a.m., two troops of the squadron had advanced to a point about halfway between check points Tom and Dick when they received heavy automatic and recoilless weapons fire. The VC had employed two battalions in a one thousand-meter-long ambush. As the Quarterhorse fixed the VC in position, Berry moved four infantry battalions into posi-

tion to ambush the ambushers. The 1st Battalion, 18th Infantry, moved northeastward from Minh Thanh to block the 272nd's right flank. Concurrently, the 1st Battalion, 28th Infantry, flew into a LZ on the left flank. These two battalions blocked in the regiment.

About noon, the 2nd Battalion, 2nd Infantry, moved up behind the cavalry to reinforce them and relieve some of the pressure. At 1:26 p.m., Lazzell's men began their air assault into LZ NC behind the VC ambush site to close the trap. Within an hour, the Rangers were on the ground. By this time, however, the VC commander must have suspected the danger, for his troops had broken contact and started moving northwest. Berry directed Lazzell to cut behind the fleeing enemy by moving on foot to LZ "N5." The movement through the jungle was excruciatingly slow due to the thickness of the foliage, but here and there, the battalion made contact with groups of VC desperately attempting to escape the sack.

As C Company led the battalion through dense bamboo thickets, it encountered an occupied base camp. The point man signaled to the platoon leader that he heard voices, and the company moved up on line to attack, but the VC opened fire first. "I hit the dirt behind a rise," Specialist Fourth Class Gaylord Courchesne recalled. "I was so close to one machine gun, I could hear the Viet Cong talking and changing ammo drums." Another soldier, Private First Class William Finley, remembered that, "They had me in a cross fire. I looked back and bullets were hitting the dirt within six inches of my feet. I couldn't move." The lead platoon was pinned down, and things started to get worse.

As the company commander, Captain Shelby Mott, moved up the rest of his unit to provide a base of fire, Lazzell also moved forward to control the battle. Closing in to C Company's position, Lazzell was struck in the left elbow by a .51-caliber round and had to be evacuated. Captain Ed Yaugo, now the S3, took command of the battalion.[56]

Yaugo directed Mott to pull back as he called for air support. Soon, aircraft were on station blasting the base camp and silencing the resistance. The Rangers then moved into the camp, destroyed its contents, and continued to move. By the time the battalion reached N5 about 5:00 p.m., the rest of the ambush zone had been swept by the 1-28 Infantry. The ambush was over. Before dark, Lieutenant Colonel George M. Wallace arrived to replace Lazzell in command of the 1st Battalion.

Over the next two days, the 1st Brigade units conducted sweeps to harass and pursue the decimated VC regiment. By the time the battle ended, the 272nd had lost almost three hundred KIA. It was later discovered that this loss came from only two of the regiment's three battalions.[57] On July 11, the 1st Battalion returned to Quon Loi.

The division conducted El Paso III from July 13 to August 24, and during this period, the 2nd Battalion played only minor roles such as guarding the 1st Engineers' efforts to rebuild a bridge along Highway 13 and guarding the 2nd Brigade CP at

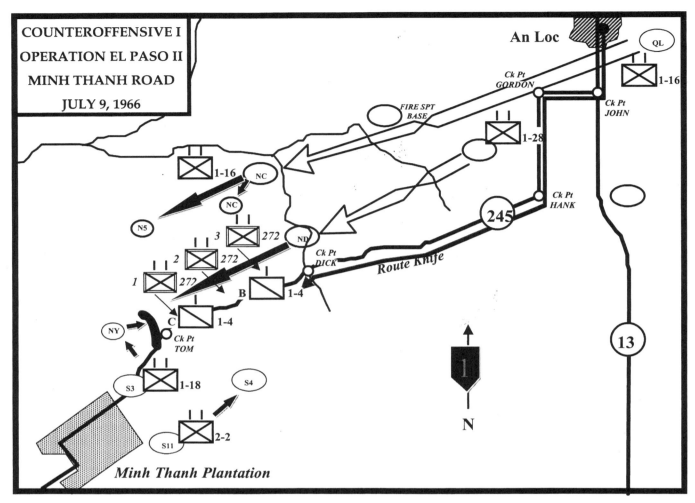

Map 10-5.

Quon Loi. Hathaway's men conducted numerous but profitless sweeps to make contact with VC elements. The amount of patrolling during El Paso caused Private First Class Fred Dunham to complain about his recruiters: "They [said] 'Join the Army and see the world.' I didn't know the trip would be made on foot!"[58]

El Paso was another successful operation for the Big Red One. While the 1st Infantry Division did not entirely destroy either the 271st or 272nd Regiments, much less the 9th Division, it did succeed in killing 855 enemy troops and wounding untold numbers of others, and effectively forcing Senior Colonel Cam to abandon his planned offensive in Binh Long province. Once again, Cam ordered his division to retreat into its Cambodian sanctuaries.

Operation Amarillo
August 1966
The 1st Battalion, meanwhile, did not participate in the last phase of El Paso because it was attached again to the 1st

Brigade for Operation Amarillo. The brigade was directed to clear and secure a section of Highway 16 about four miles east of Lai Khe for the safe passage of supply convoys. The road had been the scene of numerous ambushes and harassing raids by the VC Phu Loi Battalion, and Colonel Berry decided to pull together much of the same team that had been so successful the month before on the Minh Thanh Road to try to eradicate the troublesome enemy unit.

The mission kicked off on August 23, and for the next three days, two infantry battalions searched for the Phu Loi Battalion. On the 25th, the recon platoon from the 1st Battalion, 2nd Infantry, literally walked into the VC unit's base camp near Bong Trang. Unfortunately, the camp happened to be occupied at the time. The men quickly took refuge in a VC tunnel, called for artillery, and a violent battle commenced. Colonel Berry rushed the other battalions to the scene, including Colonel Wallace's 1st Battalion, which was airlifted to a LZ three miles east of Lai Khe and headed east to the sound of the guns. About 4:30 p.m., A Company, in the lead, ran into heavy resistance from VC forces armed with recoilless rifles and .50-caliber machine guns. Two platoons were mauled, and the company commander was killed. Nevertheless, the battalion continued to push eastward until dark.

Into the night and until the next morning, the battle raged as four U.S. battalions closed the ring. The 1st Battalion, 26th Infantry, was particularly successful in penetrating and overrunning key portions of the VC base camp. By the next morning, it was all over. All companies of the 1st Rangers had been in severe engagements, and during the brief operation, nine men had been killed and eighty wounded. Some of those casualties were the result of friendly air strikes and the crash of a helicopter. The battalion accounted for fifteen VC KIA by actual body count, but over 170 enemy soldiers were killed by the 1st Brigade out of an estimated 400 in the VC battalion. Given the estimated number of wounded, the Phu Loi Battalion almost ceased to exist.[59]

For the month of September, both battalions of the 16th Infantry were occupied mainly by base camp security and local search and destroy missions. From September 16 to 21, the 1st Battalion participated in Operation Danbury near Lai Khe, in which the main event of note was the capture of thirty-nine tons of rice. The mission was not without contact, as the battalion lost four men killed and twenty-seven wounded.[60]

Additionally, an event of note occurred at Lai Khe during the third week of September. Brigadier General John R. Deane Jr., the assistant division commander of the 1st Division, visited A Company, 1st Battalion. Deane had served in A Company as an enlisted man right after World War II, but he was not visiting for that reason. The general was there to award the Combat Infantryman's Badge to Staff Sergeant Jose Garcia. What made this a special occasion was the fact that this was Garcia's third award of the CIB. He had earned it two times previously, once in World War II and once in Korea.[61]

The 2nd Battalion, meanwhile, participated in sweeps to clear areas around the base camp at Bearcat. Then on September 20, the battalion permanently moved with the 2nd Brigade to the 1st Infantry Division's base camp at Di An, when the rest of the 4th Infantry Division arrived in country and took over Camp Martin Cox.

Operations Tulsa/Shenandoah
October 9-November 2, 1966

In early October, a VC defector informed division intelligence officers that the 272nd PLAF Regiment had moved into a base camp near Long Nguyen in Binh Long province. This information, combined with the increase of VC efforts to interdict and disrupt allied resupply convoys on Highway 13, caused Generals DePuy and Seaman concern. They feared that if the VC could effectively slow traffic on Highway 13, the enemy could exploit the propaganda value of the allies' inability to resupply units in the province and gain popular support.

DePuy developed a two-phase strategy to relieve pressure on the highway. First was Operation Tulsa, an eight-day effort to clear Highway 13, repair the road for heavy traffic, and ensure the passage of numerous convoys into Binh Long province. Assuming that increased convoy efforts would draw out the 272nd Regiment and other VC units to halt them, DePuy organized Operation Shenandoah, a follow-on reconnaissance-in-force (RIF) and S&D operation focused on securing the supply routes in the vicinity of Minh Thanh, An Loc, and Loc Ninh.[62]

On October 10, Colonel Sidney M. Marks, new commander of the 3rd Brigade, deployed three battalions along Highway 13 to safeguard it from enemy attacks, while Hathaway's 2nd Rangers remained at Lai Khe to protect that camp from attack. At the same time, Wallace's 1st Rangers swept and secured a section of Highway 13 between Ap Bau Bang and Lai Khe and destroyed an antipersonnel mine but encountered no resistance. For the next seven days, units strung along the highway cleared their assigned sectors each morning, encountering mines, booby traps, and spider holes, but rarely enemy soldiers. In one brief contact on October 13, Wallace flew into a LZ where one of his companies was engaged. As he directed the movement and evacuation of troops, the battalion commander was slightly wounded by grenade or mortar fragments but remained in the field despite the painful wound. Still, most days were rather tame, and each day, the supply convoys passed, largely unmolested, to their destinations.

During the initial stages of Tulsa, intelligence developments made it apparent that the 9th Division was staged in locations remarkably similar to those of the previous spring during Operation El Paso. The 272nd Regiment was confirmed to be near Long Nguyen, the 273rd along the Cambodian border west of Loc Ninh, and the 271st southeast of Tay Ninh along the Saigon River. Additionally, Colonel Cam could rely on reinforcement by the 101st PAVN Regiment, located on the west side of Highway 13, and the Dong Nai Battalion and remnants of the Phu Loi Battalion, on the east side. The positioning of the enemy units appeared to foreshadow another significant encounter between the Big Red One and the 9th Division.

But, alas, it was not to be. Over the next two weeks, all three brigades scoured the countryside north of Lai Khe and other parts of War Zone C, but except for a few minor scrapes with small groups of the enemy, no significant contacts were made. The 1st Battalion, attached to the 1st Brigade, conducted sweeps from October 17 to 29 with hardly any action whatever.

The 2nd Battalion, meanwhile, had been pulled away to participate in Operation Allentown. Operating along the Saigon River southwest of Di An in a search for the 271st Regiment, Hathaway's troops had slightly more success than their brethren in the 1st Battalion. Conducting several night ambushes along the river, the 2nd Rangers were credited with sinking several sampans but accomplished little else. On November 2, Shenandoah was ended, and all units returned to home stations.

Unknown to DePuy, Colonel Cam was purposely avoiding contact in order to prepare for a major battle. His superiors had ordered him to destroy a newly arrived American unit, mainly for propaganda purposes, and he could not afford to have his recent efforts to rebuild the 9th PLAF Division thwarted. This explains the Big Red One's frustrating experiences in October trying to find and bring to battle large enemy formations.

Operation Attleboro
November 4-24, 1966

After suffering severe defeats at the hands of the 1st Infantry Division in the late summer of 1966, General Nguyen Chi Thanh, COSVN commander, wanted a much-needed victory against U.S. forces in the III CTZ. In September, Nguyen learned that the inexperienced 196th Infantry Brigade, just arrived from the United States, had occupied the base camp at Tay Ninh. Here, he believed, was an excellent opportunity for a veteran unit to trap and crush some green newcomers and achieve a propaganda coup. Not surprisingly, Nguyen gave the mission to Senior Colonel Hoang Cam's 9th PLAF Division.

Although Cam's division had been fairly thrashed and weakened during the spring and summer scraps with the Big Red One, Nguyen still considered the 9th Division his most experienced and reliable unit. Throughout the summer and early fall, Cam had worked tirelessly to rebuild his division for further operations in War Zone C. By September, the 9th Division, reconstituted largely by NVA replacements, was once again capable of large-scale operations. Therefore, in October Nguyen directed Cam to seek out and destroy the 196th Infantry Brigade, as well as the 5th Special Forces camp at Suoi Da and several Civilian Irregular Defense Group (CIDG) posts in the province. Success in one or more of these efforts was sure to generate a great deal of political and propaganda value just before the South Vietnamese National Liberation Day on November 1 and the general elections in the United States on November 8.

Cam's plan involved three separate thrusts: The 272nd Regiment's mission was to attack the CIDG posts at Suoi Cao, thirty miles southeast of Tay Ninh City; the 101st PAVN Regiment, still attached to Cam from the 7th PAVN Division, was assigned the job of destroying the Special Forces camp at Suoi Da; and the 271st Regiment, the main effort, was to attack the 196th's base camp, then draw the unsuspecting American reaction force battalions into a trap and annihilate them.[63]

As the new unit in the field, the 196th Infantry Brigade had been attached to the 25th Infantry Division for combat operations. It was commanded by Brigadier General Edward H. de Saussure, a field artillery missile expert, who was uncomfortable with commanding an infantry brigade. Nevertheless, de Saussure initiated Operation Attleboro back in mid-September to conduct sweeps around the Tay Ninh base camp. The month-long series of sweeps were largely unproductive, and so, on October 19, de Saussure was directed to send a battalion to the vicinity of Dau Tieng to assist the 25th Division with conducting S&D missions there. That battalion discovered large supply caches on the 23rd, and de Saussure was authorized to expand Attleboro to a brigade-size mission on October 30. Three more battalions departed for Dau Tieng, leaving the Tay Ninh base camp defended by only the 3rd Battalion, 21st Infantry.

On November 2, the brigade conducted a complicated S&D sweep to the northwest of Dau Tieng and bumped into the 101st PAVN Regiment, apparently en route to attack the Soui Da Special Forces camp. The situation quickly went sour for de Saussure, especially since Colonel Cam now decided to direct more units of his 9th Division to attack the hapless 196th Brigade. On November 4, the 101st Regiment ambushed the 1st Battalion, 27th Infantry, pinned it down, and inflicted serious casualties. Meanwhile, de Saussure committed additional units into the fight in piecemeal fashion, and the effort went from bad to worse. Throughout the day, de Saussure had several visitors to his CP, including DePuy, and each visitor came away convinced that the 196th Brigade was not bungling the situation. The acting commander of the II Field Force, Major General Frederick C. Weyand, contacted General DePuy to get his read on the situation, after which, he directed DePuy to relieve de Saussure and have the 1st Infantry Division take over the operation that afternoon.[64]

As the 196th attempted to disengage from the enemy, DePuy moved the Big Red One into positions to take on the 9th Division. On November 5, he ordered Colonel Marks's Iron Brigade to the Suoi Da Special Forces camp and the 2nd Brigade, now under Lieutenant Colonel Sam S. Walker, to deploy to Dau Tieng.[65]

When he received DePuy's order to move the 2nd Brigade to Dau Tieng on the 5th, Walker selected Hathaway's battalion to move first to secure the staging area there. The 2nd Battalion arrived at Dau Tieng about 6:45 p.m. and formed a defensive perimeter to protect the entry of the rest of the brigade. The next battalion into Dau Tieng was the 2-18 Vanguards. The brigade's remaining battalion, 1-18, had been attached to Marks's 3rd Brigade, so the following morning, Wallace's 1st Battalion, 16th Infantry, was attached to the 2nd Brigade and sent to Dau Tieng. Consequently, for the entire Attleboro period, both Ranger battalions operated under the control of the 2nd Brigade.

At 1:50 p.m. on November 6, Wallace's battalion was designated as the brigade ready reaction force (RRF) and remained at Dau Tieng. The other two battalions (2-16 and 2-18) were ordered to insert into LZs northwest of Dau Tieng that afternoon. About 4:05 p.m., Hathaway's troops were picked up by UH-1 Hueys and winged their way to LZ Joe to begin S&D sweeps toward Objective Tango. Intensive artillery and air preparation fires blasted the areas around the LZ, but as the choppers approached, VC troops, apparently lying in wait, opened up with all they had. Leaning out the side of his "slick" (a transport Huey without armament), Staff Sergeant Ferrel Johnson eyed the spot were his company was to land. He recalled, "As soon as we were within range, the VC opened up on all sides with small arms and automatic weapons. They tried their best to keep us right on those choppers." But the enemy fire failed to stop the Rangers:

> The Rangers leaped from the helicopters and assaulted. "Everybody was on line and walking towards the bunkers. The VC really got shook up when we just walked right at them firing," said Private First Class Doug J. Landry. "Then a machine-gun opened up on us and Sergeant [Clarence A.] Newton and I started firing at it, but it just wouldn't quit. The VC machine-gunner got right on top of the bunker and aimed for our CO. He forgot to pay any attention to us—that was a fatal mistake."[66]

Once the entire battalion was on the ground, Hathaway had his troops conduct searches around the immediate perimeter. The effort recovered twelve bodies with their weapons, but the numerous blood trails indicated that VC casualties from the artillery fire were much greater than that. Nightfall prevented a more thorough search, and only enough time for the battalion to develop an effective NDP.

The following morning, Wallace's 1st Battalion also landed at LZ Joe and passed through the 2-16 en route for OBJ Tango to the northeast. Wallace's movement confirmed that many other VC were killed by the artillery preparation. The combined search efforts of both battalions revealed a total of sixty-five enemy KIA. By 1:05 p.m., Wallace was on Tango with no further contact. Both battalions conducted S&D sweeps throughout the day and each located a base camp and supplies, all of which were destroyed.

That night, a patrol from the 1st Battalion detained a man who turned out to be an enemy soldier. He had wandered into the patrol looking for a rice cache in the area that had already been policed on an earlier sweep. The man was later identified as a lieutenant in the 101st PAVN Regiment, the first indication that NVA regulars were involved in this operation.[67]

The following day (November 8), Wallace and Hathaway were both alerted for another air assault mission set for noon on November 9. This time, the 1st Battalion went into LZ Hotel first. As before, a concentrated artillery preparation preceded the insertion, but this time, the battalion went in with no resistance—at least initially. Only after the choppers began to lift off, did the VC respond, and then with only sporadic small arms fire. Once again, immediate patrols discovered a base camp that indicated recent occupation, and at one location, ten bicycles abandoned by their owners. About 3:00 p.m., the 2nd Battalion inserted into Hotel, followed by the 2nd Brigade tactical CP (TAC CP). The 1st Battalion assumed the north side of the perimeter, the 2nd Battalion the south, and both settled in to conduct a series of recon and ambush patrols that afternoon and evening. The brigade NDP was probed several times that night, resulting in several sharp bursts of fire around the perimeter. The light of the following morning revealed five enemy bodies. As on

the previous two days, the sweeps conducted on November 10 uncovered tunnels, ammunition, and other supplies but resulted in no significant contact with enemy forces. It seemed as if the enemy had just melted into the surrounding terrain.[68]

Additional efforts over the next two days still failed to lure the 101st Regiment into battle, so the 2nd Brigade withdrew both battalions and sent them back to Dau Tieng on November 12 for refitting and preparation for operations in another area. On November 13, Wallace's battalion reverted to being the brigade RRF, and Hathaway's troops were given the mission to cordon off and search the hamlet of Ben Cui II. That task was completed by 6:00 p.m. the next evening and resulted in the capture of twenty-seven VC and one enemy KIA. The battalion also discovered that the village was also a supply processing point for the 82nd Rear Service Group, a COSVN-level logistics command. While Company C remained to seal off that hamlet, Hathaway moved the rest of the battalion that afternoon to cordon and search Ben Cui III, but that effort resulted in only one VC prisoner. The battalion spent the rest of the day supporting a Medical Civic Action Program (MED-CAP) operation, whereby some 190 children and adult villagers were treated for various ailments by battalion medical personnel.

For the next two days (November 15-16), both battalions were used to secure stretches of Highway 239 to ensure a safe supply route into the Attleboro AO. This duty was followed by S&D efforts by 1-16 near LZ Pine and the reversion of 2-16 to brigade RRF until November 20. Over the next five days, both battalions engaged in several air assault operations followed up by S&D sweeps, but no further significant contact was made with the enemy.

The reason there was so little contact was because Senior Colonel Cam's 9th PLAF Division was in high gear, headed for the Cambodian border. The combined efforts of the Big Red One had resulted in 1,106 known enemy KIA, 300 of those accounted for by the battalions of the 2nd Brigade. What had started off as a gambit to severely defeat or destroy a green U.S. infantry brigade had ended as another severe thrashing of the 9th PLAF Division and its temporary withdrawal into Cambodian sanctuaries. The COSVN supply system and infrastructure also suffered significant losses.

In his after action report for Operation Attleboro, Colonel Walker also related that mechanized infantry could be used in the sparse jungle areas of Tay Ninh province, especially in the large rubber plant complexes. This recommendation would ultimately bear fruit in the 1st Division and would have an impact on the 1st Battalion, 16th Infantry—but not until two years later.[69]

Operations Fairfax/Healdsburg
November 29-December 5, 1966
Early December was a period of small unit operations for both Ranger battalions. The 2nd Battalion was selected to participate

in the high priority Operation Fairfax in central and western Thu Duc district just northeast of Saigon. Fairfax was a first-of-a-kind operation that paired three U.S. battalions each with an ARVN battalion in an effort to severely curtail VC operations in vulnerable areas close to the capital. Colonel Hathaway's mission was to work with the 30th ARVN Ranger Battalion in performing ambushes and S&D sweeps to destroy VC forces, guerrillas, and VC infrastructure in the district.[70]

For about a week, the two units set up numerous ambushes along trails and streams. In one instance, patrols from C Company waded to a large island in the Saigon River to set up a series of ambush positions. The island was known to be infested with VC during hours of darkness, and several were spotted in hasty departure as the troops made their way ashore. Unknown to the company commander, the river's level was affected by the coastal tide, and the island lay submerged under three feet of water for six hours of darkness. The unfortunate soldiers spent a miserable night, standing in hip-deep water, as mosquitoes and leeches had a banquet of Ranger blood.[71] About the end of December, 2-16 was relieved by another battalion and returned to its base camp at Di An.

While the 2nd Battalion was engaged in Fairfax, the 1st Battalion was participating in the Iron Brigade's Operation Healdsburg. The battalion's mission in Healdsburg was to conduct air assaults into Binh Duong province near Lai Khe and conduct S&D sweeps in the assigned AO.

On November 29, the 1st Battalion was airlifted to a LZ and commenced a seven-day operation that was a typically frustrating Vietnam experience for tens of thousands of American infantrymen. Over the next week, the battalion conducted another air assault, several S&D sweeps, and sealed and searched a village. Contact with the enemy was frequent, but light. Nevertheless, the contacts resulted in numerous U.S. casualties. At the end of the week, the battalion could account for seven VC KIA and thirteen captured, but the 1-16, in turn, suffered four KIA and twenty-five wounded. The battalion returned to Lai Khe on December 6.[72]

Five days later, the 2nd Platoon, C Company, under Second Lieutenant Ben Starr, was lured into an ambush while on a S&D sweep near Suoi Da. Of the thirty men in the platoon, all except two were killed or wounded, including the platoon leader. One of the first choppers on the scene was that of the 1st Division's new ADC, Brigadier General Bernard Rogers, who had the pilot land in the open area where the unit had been hit. While Rogers' driver assisted with the wounded and loaded several men on the general's chopper to get them to the nearest field hospital for care, Rogers discussed the action with the survivors.[73] Certainly, there was little the general could do to remedy the incident, but his presence on the field of battle so soon after the fight was no doubt appreciated by the men who survived.

An incident occurred about this time that humorously illustrates how rapidly things could change for a soldier in

Vietnam, and at the same time, shows a side of General DePuy not generally known. Captain Louis J. Murray Jr., of Raleigh, North Carolina, was a staff officer in the 1st Division G3 shop. One evening in December, he was preparing a briefing when he heard DePuy's voice come over the command net: "Get Murray ready to go," Murray recalled. "Thirty minutes later, I was [in command of] a company (A/1-16) out in the middle of nowhere. I remember a lieutenant [who walked up said], 'Sir, I'm sure glad you're here.'"

Murray went right to work:

That first night I was there, I checked the perimeter, and met my first sergeant, the platoon leaders, platoon sergeants, [and] walked around. I finally sat down to let the adrenaline come down a little, and it dawned on me; I'm supposed to meet my wife on R&R (rest and relaxation leave) tomorrow in Hawaii.

The next morning, a chopper flew over the company, then came in to land. It was Gen DePuy. Murray walked up to the general and saluted. DePuy asked him, "How are things going?" "Fine, sir," replied Murray, then gave DePuy a situation report. "It's a little different out here than where you were, isn't it?" DePuy inquired. "Yes, sir. It is," responded the captain. "Well, take care of yourself," cautioned the general, then he boarded his chopper for another destination. Murray later reflected that, "Here was a man running a division of 25,000 men, and he takes time to come out and see individual people."[74]

Operation Cedar Falls
January 9-16, 1967

As U.S. troop strength in South Vietnam continued to grow in late 1966, Westmoreland looked forward to the opportunity to conduct a multidivisional operation in the III CTZ to seek out and destroy enemy strength in areas where he had hitherto lacked the combat power to effectively attack. The II Field Force commander, Lieutenant General Seaman, wanted the initial strike to fall upon the Iron Triangle. This area had long been a base for VC logistics operations and was characterized as a "dagger pointed at Saigon." It was also suspected of harboring the headquarters of Military Region IV, a COSVN command and control cell that directed enemy military and political efforts against the Saigon-Gia Dinh capital region. Thus far, the Iron Triangle had only been lightly tested, most notably during Operation Mastiff almost a year before.

The mission of the II Field Force in Operation Cedar Falls was to attack the Iron Triangle and the Thanh Dien Forestry Reserve "to destroy enemy forces, infrastructure, installations and Military Region IV headquarters." Additionally the operation plan called for evacuation and resettlement of the area's civilian population elsewhere. The entire Iron Triangle was to become a barren wasteland to preclude its support of, and continued use by, the VC. General Seaman's planners

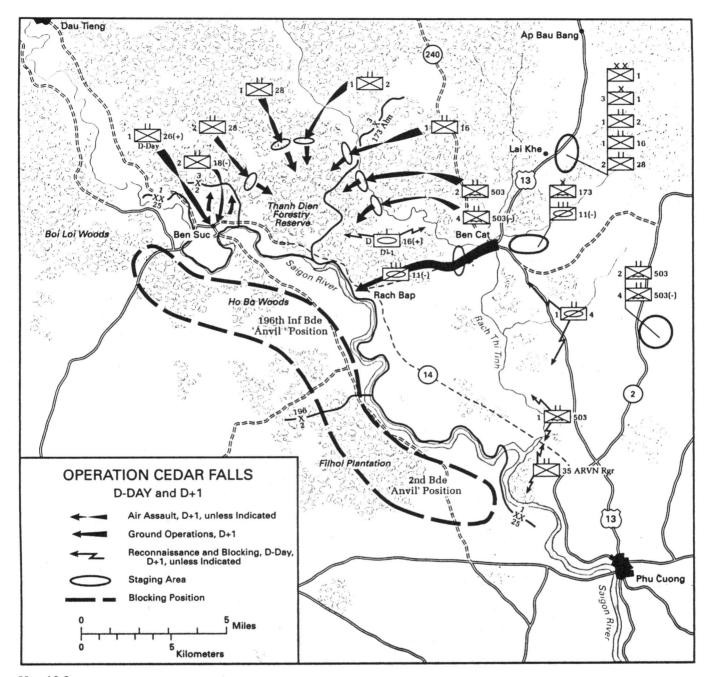

Map 10-6.

believed that the operation, if successful, would also trap and destroy the partially rebuilt Phu Loi Battalion, the 272nd PLAF Regiment (which was actually still in Cambodia reconstituting), and the 165A PLAF Regiment. The latter unit was also called the "Capital Liberation Regiment" and had the primary responsibility for operations in the Saigon area.[75]

The operation was an ambitious one. Seaman intended to use a massive "hammer and anvil" technique. The 2nd Brigade, 25th Infantry Division, and the 196th Infantry Brigade posi-

tioned on the south side of the Saigon River from Phu Hoa Dong in the southeast to the Boi Loi Woods in the northwest would form the anvil. The 35th ARVN Ranger Battalion; the 1st Battalion, 503rd Infantry; and the 1st Squadron, 4th Cavalry, would provide blocking positions on the southeast end of the north side of the river. The 2nd and 3rd Brigades of the 1st Infantry Division in the north and northwest and the 173rd Airborne Brigade to the east made up the hammer. By January 8, the anvil units were positioned waiting for the hammer to fall.[76]

On the morning of January 9, Lazzell (who had returned to command the 1st Battalion on November 28 upon Wallace's promotion to colonel) boarded his troops on slicks at Lai Khe and air assaulted into a LZ on the edge of the Thanh Dien Forestry Reserve, just west of the Thi Tinh River. As the Iron Brigade's left-most unit, 1-16 had the 173rd Airborne Brigade on the left and the 1st Battalion, 2nd Infantry, on the right. The battalion's mission was to conduct a S&D sweep to the Saigon River in coordination with the other "hammer" battalions.

The first day was uneventful, the only incident of note being enemy fire that struck the OH-13 helicopter on which Lazzell was riding. The craft was damaged badly enough to force its landing, but no one was injured. The battalion killed two VC that night in its NDP, but once again the following day was uneventful. For the next several days, the battalion provided security for "Rome plow" bulldozer teams that cleared hundreds of acres of jungle to destroy existing base camps and caches and prevent future use by the VC. Lazzell's troops remained in the field until January 16 and accounted for only five VC KIA and three captured, but they captured or destroyed some seventy-five tons of rice and several small base camps.[77]

In the middle of the deadly business of war, several humorous incidents occurred during the many Cedar Falls sweeps conducted by the 1st Battalion. As C Company moved through a thick jungle area, the point man happened upon a wounded VC, apparently abandoned by his buddies. The man had wounds in his chest, arm, and leg but was still defiant. As Specialist Fifth Class Richard Myers, a company medic from Jersey Shore, Pennsylvania, bent down to help the man, the VC spit in the medic's face. Myers' fellow medic, Specialist Fifth Class Harold Spain, tied a handkerchief around the man's head so he could not repeat his act. Bending over again, Myers went to work, when suddenly, the man bashed him in the nose with his good arm. Sergeant Leonard A. McManus held down the VC's arm, and Myers started bandaging again. Finally, Myers completed his task of mercy, and the prisoner was loaded on a medevac chopper. As the chopper pulled away, Private First Class William N. Stadelman remarked to Myers, "I wonder why they left him behind." "It's simple," the harried medic dryly replied. "He's got bad breath."[78]

In another incident, the A Company Commander, Lou Murray, recalled an incident involving his 3rd Platoon sergeant, Matthew Leonard of Birmingham, Alabama. "A great guy; always had something good to say," remembered Murray about Leonard. While out on a road clearing operation along Highway 13, Murray was contacted out of the blue by the ADC, Brigadier General James R. Hollingsworth. "Alpha 6, this is Danger 79, do you need anything?" The startled captain, never expecting to hear a general on his net, quickly replied, "No, I don't need anything." Hollingsworth responded, "Well if you need anything, let me know" as his chopper flew out of the area.

Leonard, a snuff dipper, heard this exchange and wandered over to Murray and said, "Sir, we aren't getting any

Copenhagen [tobacco snuff] in our sundry packs." Murray assured the good sergeant that if Hollingsworth "ever calls again, I'll mention that." The following morning, Danger 79 called again. This time, Murray told Hollingsworth of the problem. The captain could hear the ADC burst out laughing on the radio. "That evening," stated Murray, "when we got our resupply chopper bringing in the ammo, mortars, etc., and the mail, especially, here was a package of Copenhagen. Several cans of it. I said, Sergeant Leonard, there's your goodies. He was happy."[79]

While the 1st Battalion was participating in the opening stages of Cedar Falls, the 2nd Battalion was back in Thu Duc on its second stint with Fairfax. In mid-January the 2nd Rangers pulled out of Thu Duc long enough to change commanders from Hathaway to Lieutenant Colonel Bruce E. Wallace. The day following the 1st Battalion's return to Lai Khe, Wallace led the 2-16 on an air assault into the Iron Triangle near the village of Ben Suc. But like the 1st Battalion's efforts the previous week, those of the 2nd Battalion were just as void of significant accomplishment during the remainder of the operation.

The overall results of Cedar Falls, however, met Seaman's objectives for the operation. Some seven hundred VC were killed, and an equal number surrendered or were captured. The support infrastructure of Military Region IV was destroyed and the capture of several of that headquarters' camps generated a windfall of valuable intelligence about VC operations in South Vietnam. Additionally, the destruction of Ben Suc village, the evacuation of civilians from the Iron Triangle, and the work of the Rome plows, which leveled eleven square kilometers of jungle, made the vaunted Iron Triangle almost useless to the enemy for future operations against Saigon—at least for the time being.[80]

Operation Lam Son-Tucson D
February 16-18, 1967

By mid-January 1967, the 271st and 272nd PLAF Regiments had recovered enough to redeploy from Cambodia into War Zone C. MACV intelligence had located the 271st on the Cambodian border near Lo Go, and the 272nd had moved into the Michelin Rubber Plantation. The 9th Division's third regiment, the 273rd, was located outside of War Zone C, but two other units of interest, the 101st PAVN Regiment and the 70th Guards Regiment, were both in the war zone. The 101st, normally part of the 7th PAVN Division, had now apparently come under permanent control of the 9th. The 70th Guards, about which little was known, was COSVN's security unit. The presence of this unit attracted Westmoreland's interest.

In the fall of 1966, Westmoreland had directed the II Field Force to develop plans for a major operation in War Zone C to engage and destroy large portions of the enemy in that area and eliminate COSVN. A major victory in the war zone would allow U.S. and ARVN units "breathing space" to conduct meaningful pacification operations to win over the

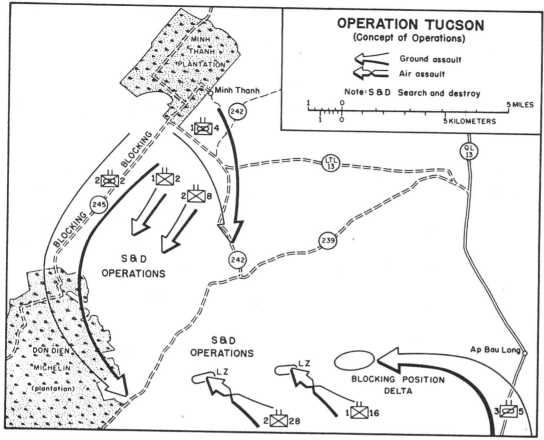

OPERATION TUCSON
(Concept of Operations)

Ground assault
Air assault
Note: S & D Search and destroy

Map 10-7.

conducted properly, Tucson would accomplish three objectives: deceive the enemy as to where the big hammer would fall; position 1st Division units to initiate Junction City; and drive the 272nd Regiment northwest, deeper into the trap with the 271st.[51]

The Big Red One launched Tucson on February 14 with the deployment of the 2nd and 3rd Brigades into the Long Nguyen Secret Zone in Binh Long province. This area was considered to be the 272nd's main base area and a supply route between War Zones C and D. The 3rd Brigade's mission was to conduct a reconnaissance in zone to locate and destroy enemy forces and bases.

At 11:17 a.m., February 14, Lazzell's 1st Battalion, operating as part of the 3rd Brigade, air assaulted into LZ 2, nine kilometers due east of the Michelin plantation. As was typical, the LZ had been prepared by heavy artillery concentrations, and the battalion landed without incident. The next three days were rather uneventful, save the battalion's discovery and evacuation of 470 tons of rice and the wounding of ten Rangers by an incoming mortar barrage. On February 17, the 1st Battalion was airlifted to posts along Highway 13 to conduct road clearing and security between Bau Long and Con Thanh. Lazzell's troops were now in position for Junction City.

Soon after Cedar Falls, the command of the 2nd Battalion changed again; this time the flag passed to Lieutenant Colonel Joseph R. Ulatoski. The battalion did not participate in Tucson in mid-February. Instead, 2-16 participated in Operation Lam Son 67 with the 2-18 Vanguards. Lam Son was the ongoing joint pacification support operation conducted between units of the Big Red One and the 5th ARVN Infantry Division in Binh Duong province. It was designed to attack local force units, destroy VC political infrastructure, and isolate main force units from supporting VC operations against civilians in the province. During Lam Son, the Rangers sealed the village of Tan Phuoc Khanh as part of the division's "Revolutionary Development"

peasants in the countryside in support of the South Vietnamese government. The operation he envisioned, Junction City, had been postponed by the need to first conduct Cedar Falls. By the third week of February, however, Westmoreland was set to kick off this new offensive.

Westmoreland wanted to position units in the TAOR in such a way that he could spring Junction City without arousing VC suspicions. Therefore, the two major units involved, the 1st and 25th Infantry Divisions, conducted separate deception operations to disguise their respective objectives. The 25th Division's effort, Operation Gadsden, began in early February, and placed the Tropic Lightning's units into War Zone C along the Cambodian border. The intent of Gadsden was to cause the 271st to move from the border area farther east into the Junction City target area.

The Big Red One's Operation Tucson began almost two weeks later and was designed to appear as if the major focus was on the 272nd Regiment in the Michelin Plantation area. The real targets, however, were both the 271st and 272nd Regiments and the COSVN headquarters. At the end of operations, Gadsden would place the units attached to the 25th Division (3rd Brigade, 4th Division, and 196th Infantry Brigade) in positions to block escape routes into Cambodia. If

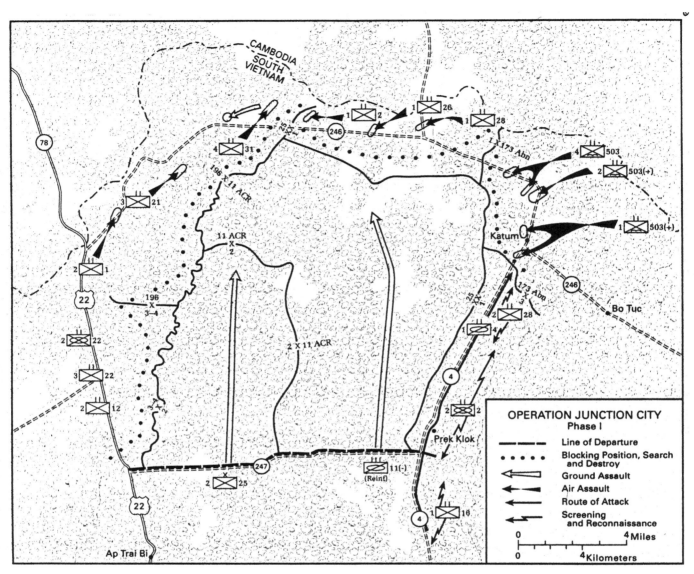

Map 10-8.

concept. On February 22, however, the 2nd Battalion was pulled out of Lam Son to participate in Junction City.

Operation Junction City
February 22-April 15, 1967

Junction City would be the largest single Allied operation in the Vietnam War. By the time it ended, it involved twenty-two U.S. infantry battalions, four ARVN infantry battalions, seventeen artillery battalions, four thousand air force sorties, and 249 helicopters, making it the largest air assault operation in history.

Once all units were positioned for Junction City, they formed a giant horseshoe. The attached brigades of the 25th Infantry Division formed the western blocking positions; the 1st Brigade, 1st Infantry Division, manned the northern positions; the 173rd Airborne Brigade took position in the northeast; and

the 1st Division's 3rd Brigade formed the eastern blocking positions. The hammer, located at the open end of the horseshoe to the south, was composed of the 2nd Brigade, 25th Division, and the 11th Armored Cavalry Regiment (ACR). Ideally, these two units would drive the enemy north into the guns of the battalions in the blocking positions.

On the morning of February 22, the blocking forces air assaulted into LZs on the perimeter of the horseshoe. Over the next three days, the hammer forces swept north, but the overall results of the 25th Division's big drive were unimpressive in terms of enemy contacts and KIAs. Only fifty-four VC were killed versus twenty-eight dead GIs. However, the destruction of facilities and captured rice and equipment was great.

Upon completion of the initial drive, Seaman directed all units to conduct thorough S&D sweeps in their respective

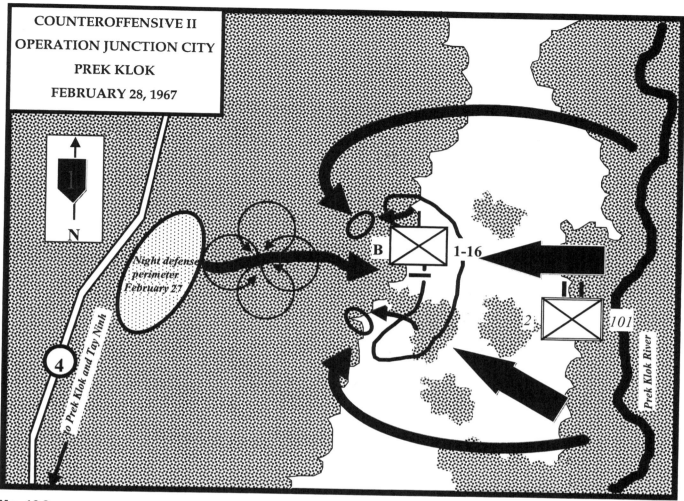

Map 10-9.

TAORs beginning February 25. In response to this massive offensive, General Thanh directed COSVN forces in War Zone C to strike back by ambushing small American units, especially supply convoys, along Route 4. This directive set the stage for a desperate battle and another Ranger's great acts of heroism.

Battle of Prek Klok
February 28, 1967

For the opening stages of Junction City, Lazzell's 1st Battalion constituted the 3rd Brigade's reserve. On February 23, 1-16 airlifted from Lai Khe to its reserve position at the Suoi Da base camp, where it was assigned part of the perimeter defense. That night, the A Company received an intense mortar barrage that killed two men and wounded five others including Lou Murray, the company commander. He remembered that the barrage was intense:

We [the battalion officers] had spent the day conducting an aerial reconnaissance of the area we were going to go

into. That evening, not too long after we had finished digging in, the rounds came in. A good friend of mine, Captain Bill Williamson, the B Company Commander, said that it looked like the Fourth of July. All of the rounds were concentrated in the A Company area. A piece of shrapnel hit me in the back of my head, and I was okay for a while. Some of my men later told me that they knew I was going when I told them to ensure that they continued to repair the rain damage to the fighting positions. Of course, it hadn't rained for months.[52]

On the 24th, the battalion was airlifted to form part of a screen line along Route 4, six kilometers south of Prek Klok. Lazzell's tasks were to secure a portion of Route 4, prevent VC units from escaping east, and perform S&D sweeps.

Other than receiving .50-caliber machine-gun fire from a friendly mechanized unit in the early morning darkness of the 25th, the next three days of Operation Junction City were rather uneventful for the 1st Battalion as it migrated northward from its initial LZ. The night of February 27, Lazzell pulled the battalion into a NDP along Route 4, just north of the hamlet of Prek Klok.

At 8:00 a.m. the following morning, B Company, under the command of Captain Donald S. Ulm, moved out of the perimeter on a S&D sweep. Its limit of advance was Prek Klok creek, about twenty-five hundred meters to the east. The company moved with platoons in column, as it struggled to break through the heavy foliage. The technique that Ulm used to conduct the search was to move about five hundred meters, stop, and send out small patrols in several directions using the "cloverleaf" search pattern.

By 10:30 a.m., the company had gone about one thousand meters when 3rd Platoon, in the lead, made contact with an enemy force to its front. Because the enemy force included at least three machine guns, Ulm deduced that it was more than one company in size. Indeed, B Company had run into the 2nd Battalion, 101st PAVN Regiment, en route to conduct convoy ambush operations along Route 4. Additionally, Ulm noted that his foe was not in prepared positions, which indicated a classic meeting engagement. The two units had literally bumped into each other on the move.

The 3rd Platoon was soon decisively engaged but unable to achieve fire superiority. Ulm's forward observer (FO) responded by calling heavy artillery fire on the enemy from the 2-33 Field Artillery at the Prek Klok fire base. About the same time, a division command and control chopper arrived to help coordinate air strikes against the enemy. About twenty minutes into the fight, Ulm lost contact with his 3rd Platoon, so he attempted to move the 2nd Platoon up on the 3rd's right and the 1st Platoon on the left. As the units moved into position, the area erupted in small arms and mortar fire, but miraculously, the company sustained few casualties, at least initially.[83]

Within minutes after making contact with the enemy, the 3rd Platoon Leader was wounded and incapacitated. Coming to the fore to fill the vacuum was none other than the platoon sergeant, Matthew Leonard. Leonard rallied his troops and repulsed the initial attack and then formed a defensive perimeter. Moving about the positions during a brief lull, he redistributed ammo and encouraged his men. While moving to another position, he spotted a wounded man outside the perimeter, bolted over to him, and dragged him back into the lines. An enemy bullet shattered his left hand during the effort, but Leonard continued his vigorous leadership. Soon, however, the enemy positioned a machine gun to sweep the entire platoon area. Meanwhile, the platoon's M-60 malfunctioned and the crew was killed or wounded even as Leonard attempted to help them clear the jam. In response, the sergeant assaulted the enemy machine gun himself and killed its crew. Severely wounded several more times, Leonard then crawled over to a tree, propped himself against it, and continued to fight until he died of his wounds. Leonard would become the 16th Infantry Regiment's ninth Medal of Honor winner.[84]

By 12:30 a.m., C Company had formed a 180-degree arc and reestablished contact with the 3rd Platoon. Within half an hour, movements to the west indicated to Ulm that the company was surrounded. The commander repositioned elements from the 1st and 2nd Platoons toward the threatened areas and formed a 360 degree perimeter. In doing so, however, the troops drew heavy, accurate fire from NVA regulars firing from well-camouflaged tree positions. Officers, NCOs, and anyone who attempted to show leadership drew fire, and many leaders went down, wounded or killed.

Ulm now directed air strikes on the heaviest concentrations of enemy fire. The air force responded by dropping highly effective cluster bomb unit (CBU) munitions, at times within thirty meters of the company perimeter. The combined effects of small arms fire, artillery, and air power finally took their toll on the enemy force, and by 2:00 p.m., the fighting died down to desultory sniper fire. By 3:00 p.m., all contact with the NVA unit was lost.

Soon, two companies of 1-16 were airlifted into a LZ about six hundred meters to the northeast of B Company's position. One company reached Ulm late that afternoon and helped the battered unit get to the LZ so its wounded and dead could be airlifted out. In all, Ulm's command had lost twenty-five men killed and twenty-eight wounded. In return, however, the 101st Regiment had suffered 167 known KIA.

The following morning, Brigadier General Rogers landed at the LZ and talked with the B Company men about their fight. He found that the artillery and air support rightfully received high praise. He also learned the details of the unit's actions. Impressed with the men's accomplishment, Rogers called the company together to tell them so. Among other things, he told them, "Although many of your leaders were wounded, the company never lost control of the situation. The NCOs and enlisted men performed like the truly magnificent soldiers they are...."[85]

Meanwhile, Ulatoski's 2nd Battalion was busy during Junction City as well. On March 21, the battalion was airlifted into LZ Charlie to conduct S&D sweeps in support of the 2nd Brigade's efforts to find and destroy the COSVN headquarters. Once into Charlie, the battalion cleared that location for use as an artillery fire support base (FSB), then swept south toward Route 246. The mission was uneventful over the next several days, until one morning when Captain Lloyd Gunn's C Company conducted a sweep just inside a wood line. There, a well-concealed machine gun opened up on the lead platoon. The point man took the full brunt of the initial burst and fell dead instantly. Behind him, the 2nd Squad went to ground and returned fire. The squad leader, Staff Sergeant Billy R. Hardigree, attempted to move his squad up, but this movement drew intense fire from his right front.

Realizing his element was outgunned, Hardigree calmly contacted his platoon leader, explained the situation, and requested permission to withdraw. The platoon leader, Second

Lieutenant Edward Pollack of Spring Valley, New York, granted permission, and shortly afterward, Hardigree's squad linked up with the lieutenant. Pollack then directed air and artillery strikes in the vicinity of the enemy.

After about fifteen minutes, Pollack lifted the fires and advanced toward the enemy positions with 1st Squad protecting his right flank. Private First Class Ronald Burns of Grossville, Tennessee, recalled what happened next: "When we tried to recover the body of our point man, 'Charlie' opened up on us again. We jumped into one of their own trenches and then really started pumping lead at them." After another intense exchange of automatic fire, the VC broke contact. Fortunately, there were no additional friendly casualties.

"It was getting late," Private First Class Ray Fisher, platoon RTO, later related, "and we had a long hike back to our [battalion NDP]. Our platoon took the lead and after walking about 800 yards, we again were fired upon by concealed Viet Cong." The platoon quickly spread out, and this time, achieved fire superiority. Pollack pushed the platoon forward, and as the men advanced, they picked off a VC who attempted to run. But the Rangers took casualties too, among them the platoon sergeant, as he successfully hurled a grenade to take out an enemy position. Another man was mortally wounded as he rushed an enemy bunker and routed the occupants, several of whom were cut down as they ran. As Staff Sergeant Clarence Tilley approached one wounded VC, the man attempted to kill him, but the VC's AK-47 jammed after a short burst of fire. Taking no chances, Tilley finished him off. That ended the contact.[86]

Company C returned to base camp just after dark carrying two dead and several wounded. They also brought with them three captured AK-47s that appeared to be new and well cared for. This was a new twist, as the VC were usually armed with SKS rifles or older weapons. It appeared that the local VC forces were being up-gunned.

Battle of Ap Gu
March 31-April 1, 1967

By the third week of March, the new II Field Force commander, Lieutenant General Bruce Palmer Jr. (who had commanded the 16th Infantry Regiment in 1954-55) had determined that the S&D efforts in the southeastern area of War Zone C were futile. Palmer was on the verge of abandoning them when new intelligence indicated that the 271st Regiment was moving toward Katum. The VC unit was traveling so fast that it dodged the 196th Infantry Brigade's effort to intercept it and continued eastward to attack FSB Charlie at Sroc Con Trang.

Meanwhile, Colonel James A. Grimsley Jr., commanding the 2nd Brigade, also sought to bring the 271st to battle. On March 30, he sent the Blue Spaders of the 1st Battalion, 26th Infantry, commanded by Lieutenant Colonel Alexander Haig, into LZ George in an effort to locate the elusive prey. LZ George was a dried up swamp located about two kilometers west of the hamlet of Ap Gu and one kilometer north of Route

246. The area was relatively open, tall grass, and surrounded by jungle. Upon arrival, Haig had his men search in a cloverleaf pattern around the area but they made no contact. The battalion dug in along a 360-degree NDP on the LZ that night.

The following day, the 1-26 conducted sweeps in all directions from the LZ. Probing about eight hundred meters north of George, the recon platoon ran into the 2nd Battalion, 70th Guards Regiment. Company B moved to help the beleaguered scouts but was also pinned down. Haig soon had a full-blown firefight on his hands, but he was finally able to disengage about 5:00 p.m. and returned to LZ George. There, his battalion reoccupied fighting positions they had previously prepared and waited for reinforcements.

The reinforcements came in the way of Colonel Lazzell's 1-16. On loan to Grimsley from the 3rd Brigade, the Rangers came into George about 5:00 p.m. that afternoon against a VC force that was watching the LZ. Private First Class John Vessello recalled that "It was hot the moment we hit the landing zone. They opened up on us even before we got out of the choppers."[87] After an aggressive sweep and a short, but fierce, firefight, the Rangers drove the enemy force off, then moved into a 360-degree defensive perimeter just to the northwest of 1-26's original NDP. After selecting his positions, Lazzell had his troops dig in because he anticipated a big fight. By evening, both battalions had established strong defensive positions using the newly developed "DePuy Bunker" that is now the standard fighting position of the U.S. Army.

After detecting the Blue Spaders' presence, COSVN redirected the 271st Regiment to attack LZ George in coordination with the 70th Guards. About 5:00 a.m. on March 31, enemy mortars began firing registration rounds in preparation for a major attack. By 5:15 a.m., over five hundred 60mm, 82mm, and 120mm mortar rounds had plastered both battalions, but no one was killed, thanks to the new bunkers. Immediately on the heels of the barrage came the ground attack, with the 271st hitting the Blue Spaders and the 70th Guards assaulting the Rangers.

Within minutes, Haig's line had been penetrated by the VC main attack in the C Company sector. Soon, the enemy was entering bunkers in the B Company sector as well, but the troops broke the attack, then assisted C Company and the recon platoon to form a new line. Meanwhile, Lazzell's men to the northwest successfully held the 70th Guards at bay. The Rangers' deadly fire cut down dozens of VC assault troops as they attempted to hit the battalion perimeter or flank the 1-26's position.

At first light, the air force joined the fight with CBU munitions. The air strikes, coupled with artillery support from FSB Thrust to the southeast, pounded the enemy formations. Soon helicopter gunships joined in, and the VC began to break contact. By 8:00 a.m., the attack was broken. Lazzell ordered the Rangers out of their holes and joined the newly arrived 1st Battalion, 2nd Infantry, in what turned out to be an unpro-

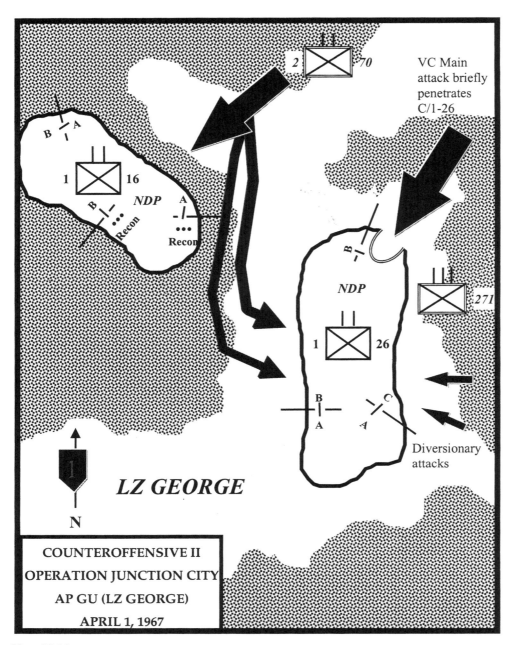

Map 10-10.

capturing 850 tons of food, and killing over twenty-seven hundred enemy soldiers and wounding untold others. The 9th PLAF Division had been severely mauled once again, along with several other VC and NVA formations. On the other hand, the 9th Division and COSVN were able to escape across the Cambodian border once more. This action, nevertheless, directly affected the enemy's ability to coordinate and control VC and insurgent activities in much of War Zone C, leaving a power vacuum that the South Vietnamese government could fill. It also disrupted COSVN's operational timelines because the command now had to spend energy overseeing the replacement of personnel and equipment lost in the campaign.[89] Still, II Field Force had failed in its efforts to destroy the main enemy headquarters and its primary fighting force in War Zone C, making Junction City something less than a complete victory.

The Rangers of both battalions could claim success. Between the two, the men of the 16th Infantry could claim a direct role in adding almost eight hundred VC to the overall II Field Force tally. With their hard won laurels in place, the Rangers returned to their respective base camps in mid-April, the 1st Battalion to Lai Khe and the 2nd Battalion to Di An.

ductive pursuit of the battered VC units. A subsequent sweep of the battalion defensive perimeters revealed 609 dead VC. This was accomplished at a total cost of seventeen KIA from the two U.S. battalions. Ap Gu was the biggest single victory of the operation.[88]

The Battle of Ap Gu also proved to be the last significant contact for any units involved in Operation Junction City, and by mid-April all 1st Division units had returned to their respective base camps. Overall, the troops of the Big Red One had a right to be proud of their efforts. They had assisted the II Field Force in destroying over five thousand enemy base camp structures,

The 2nd Battalion next participated in Operation Manhattan from April 23 to May 14. Its participation, however, was limited to providing security for various base camps and road-clearing missions. The battalion initially began the operation on loan to the 3rd Brigade and secured the brigade's base camp at Lai Khe until the end of the month. For the first part of May 1967, the battalion conducted security sweeps around the Bunard Base Camp and later provided security for lengths of Route 314 east of Phu Loi. During the period May 12-15, the 2nd Rangers secured FSB Bravo, and afterward, the Quan Loi Base Camp until the 25th.

Meanwhile, the 1st Battalion spent May providing security for the 1st Engineer Battalion as it built an airstrip at Suoi Da. Though the mission was generally uneventful, one patrol bumped into an enemy unit and sparked a hot firefight. Several men were wounded, but all were successfully evacuated by a medical evacuation (medevac) helicopter.

Counteroffensive, Phase III
June 1967-January 1968

The major II Field Force operations of the first six months of 1967 had successfully mauled the units of the 7th and 9th Divisions and Military Region IV, but with the advent of the rainy season in May, COSVN could be counted upon to use the bad weather to infiltrate reinforcements and supplies to replenish those lost in the fighting. Indeed, that spring, the II Field Force intelligence team detected an enemy buildup in War Zone D centered on the recently battered 271st PLAF Regiment.

The disposition of 1st Infantry Division units at this time called for the 1st and 3rd Brigades to continue offensive operations in and near War Zones C and D, while the 2nd Brigade conducted pacification operations around Di An. Thus, when General John H. Hay, the Big Red One's new commanding general, learned of the enemy concentration, he determined that he would strike first with the 1st and 3rd Brigades.

Operation Billings
June 12-17, 1967

The division's spoiling attack was labeled Operation Billings and called for the two brigades to conduct S&D missions north of Phuoc Vinh. On June 12, three battalions, under 1st Brigade control, inserted into two LZs about seven to ten kilometers north of the city. Concurrently, the 3rd Brigade inserted the 2nd Battalion, 28th Infantry, Black Lions, into a LZ at Chi Linh to secure a FSB there. The following day, Lazzell's 1-16 went into LZ Rufe, seventeen kilometers due north of Phuoc Vinh, and secured the site for the follow-on battalion, 2-28 Infantry, from Chi Linh. The two battalions secured the area around Rufe and dug in for the night.

The Battle at LZ Rufe
June 14, 1967

On the morning of June 14, Lazzell pushed B and C Companies out to the west of Rufe to seek out the enemy. Just after noon, C Company, commanded by Captain Stephen Weisel, spotted five VC soldiers about two kilometers southwest of the LZ, but they were not able to engage them. Two hours later, B Company, commanded by Captain Carroll R. Wilson, received sporadic small arms fire about one kilometer north of C Company. The firing was brief, then tapered off, seeming to indicate that the enemy had broken contact. Fifteen minutes later, however, Wilson's men were struck in full force, in the front and flanks, by a VC battalion. The company commander frantically brought artillery and air strikes to bear, as Lazzell ordered C Company to move to B Company's aid.

After the initial contact, Staff Sergeant Arturo T. Fuentes Jr. of San Antonio, Texas, a squad leader in B Company, rapidly deployed his men and effectively directed their fire at the attacking enemy. Disregarding his personal safety, the sergeant constantly shouted directions and encouragement to his men. He also frequently moved between positions and resupplied his troops with ammunition. At one point, Fuentes noticed an enemy squad attempting to flank his position, and without hesitation, he charged the VC force, firing his weapon and tossing grenades. He killed several of the foe before the others fled.

Fuentes next spotted a badly wounded machine gunner and moved to assist the man. En route, Fuentes himself was wounded and nearly blinded by an enemy grenade. Despite serious injuries, the sergeant crawled to the machine gun and opened a devastating fire on the enemy. Fuentes would later receive the Silver Star for his actions that day; it was his third Silver Star in six months.[90]

The fighting was desperate as B Company repulsed the VC assaults. By the time Weisel arrived at B Company's location after 6:00 p.m., the beleaguered unit had beat back the VC attack but had suffered six killed and fifteen wounded. A search of the area before dark revealed sixty-two enemy dead.[91]

The next two days of patrolling and sweeps were uneventful, and Hay believed that the 271st Regiment had moved about twenty kilometers farther north near a vast area of bamboo stands. One location, designated LZ X-Ray on operations maps, looked like a good place to insert a couple of battalions to search for the evasive prey. The first unit into the LZ on June 17 was Lazzell's 1-16.

The Battle at LZ X-Ray
June 17, 1967

The insertion into LZ X-Ray began at 7:30 a.m., and before noon, the 1st Rangers had secured the area. The landings were preceded by the usual preparatory artillery barrage and, as a result, the air assault was unopposed. As soon as Lazzell's battalion was on the ground, he moved it into the tree line and formed a perimeter around the entire LZ to wait for the Black Lions to reinforce him for the follow-on S&D mission. Just after the lead elements of the 2-28 landed, Lazzell received reports of VC moving toward the perimeter from the northwest. "We moved into an area where there was a clearing," recalled Private James Mauchline, a mechanic-turned-rifleman from Sterling Heights, Michigan. "We just started to dig in inside the tree line and got ambushed. 'All hell broke loose,' as the old saying goes."[92] About 12:45 p.m., the enemy attacked into positions held by the Black Lions of B Company. Lazzell had found the 271st Regiment.

The initial attacks against B Company, 2-28, were designed to fix that unit while other assault elements moved into position to attack elsewhere. About 1:00 p.m., fierce assaults were launched against A Company, 1-16, from the northeast. Soon pressed hard in the sectors held by A and B

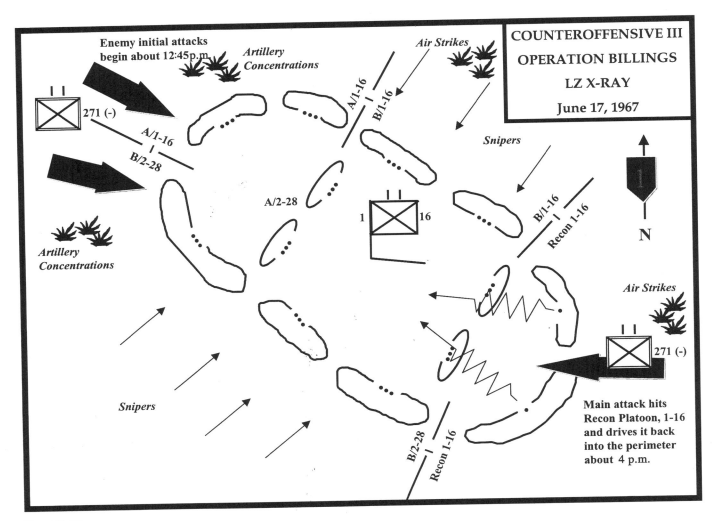

Map 10-11.

Companies, Lazzell called for heavy artillery concentrations and gunship support. The combined effects of the indirect fire and air power successfully defeated the attacks.

This victory was short-lived, as the VC then attacked the Rangers' recon platoon from the southeast. The Rangers in that sector responded with a withering fire that killed scores of enemy troops. "We were stacking them up like cord wood," one man later remarked, but this second attack overran the scouts. Only a few of them escaped to link up with other units on the flanks.

Initially, the contact appeared to be a chance encounter with VC local forces. Before long, however, the enemy effort took on the hallmarks of a well-planned and rehearsed ambush by a veteran force estimated to be at least two battalions. These troops were well-uniformed in khaki, wore steel helmets, and were equipped with the latest AK-47 assault rifles, which indicated they were not a local-force company. Their attack routes had been carefully marked, and they had moved quickly to engage the Rangers before the U.S. troops were able to dig in.

Soon, the situation grew serious and Ranger casualties

mounted. During the fight, a CH-47 Chinook helicopter, loaded with medical supplies attempted to land. Private Mauchline remembered that "it was shot up, but did land safely....They were looking for volunteers to run across this open field during this exact time and get [the] medical supplies. They were offering a Silver Star for anybody [who would try], but I wasn't into heroics. I stayed put where I was."[93]

For a time, it seemed that the enemy might break through to the center of the LZ, but air strikes by F-100s stabilized the situation by 3:00 p.m. Due to the heavy concentrations of small arms fire and air support, the VC commander decided that he had had enough and began to break contact under the cover of a two-hour mortar barrage. About 7:00 p.m., the division RRF arrived, but the battle was long over, and the Rangers had been severely handled. The battalion had lost thirty-five men killed and 150 wounded out of a field strength of about five hundred.

The 271st had not gotten away unscathed, however. A search of the area immediately after the fight revealed seventy-two bodies, and a sweep deeper into the AO the next day found twenty-six additional enemy KIA. Ultimately, there were 286 VC KIA reported, but this body count is open to speculation. For example, the only weapons that were recovered were two light machine-guns, a carbine, an RPG, and an AK-50.[94] But, Captain Lou Murray later recalled that "you couldn't use weapons count as an accurate way to measure the number of enemy KIA. The VC had a habit of dragging off bodies so you couldn't get an accurate count. If they couldn't drag off the bodies, they would certainly pick up the weapons if they were given the opportunity."[95] Given the fact that the 271st Regiment was able to break contact without the Rangers in pursuit, this makes the reported body count more plausible. Regardless of the final count, it is safe to say that the 271st received a bloody nose in its scrap with the 1-16.[96]

The following day, the 1st Battalion was airlifted back to Lai Khe, and its participation in Billings was essentially over. Meanwhile, Captain Ulatoski's 2nd Battalion had been conducting S&D operations in AO Strike during the early days of June, but on 11 June, the battalion was moved to Phuoc Vinh to support Operation Billings. For the remainder of the operation, the 2nd Rangers secured the airfield and support base at Phuoc Vinh, guarded the Song Be River bridge at Phuoc Hoa, and performed stints as the division RRF, though Ulatoski never received a call requesting his services.[97]

A week after returning to Di An, command of the 2nd Battalion was turned over to Lieutenant Colonel Stanley Parmentier. Almost immediately after taking the flag, Parmentier took the 2nd Rangers to the field to participate in Operation Lam Son 67, north of Saigon.

During the early stages of the war, infantry battalion commanders had recognized that the existing battalion TOE, with three line companies, was too light for the type of operations the units typically had to perform. The level of casualties sustained by units, the constant rotation of personnel, and the need for an additional maneuver element caused many commanders to form composite companies with their recon platoons and mortar platoons-turned-riflemen. In 1967, Westmoreland received permission to activate D Companies in all infantry battalions in Vietnam. On August 1, 1967, both Ranger battalions formed the new companies through the transfer of experienced personnel from other companies and groups of new soldiers just sent over from basic training centers in the United States. The units were put through a precise training program designed to prepare them for the rigors of combat in Vietnam.

Operation Portland
August 12-21, 1967

On August 9, the 1st Infantry Division G2 received intelligence that an unidentified enemy regiment, with between fifteen hundred and two thousand men, was in covered defensive positions southwest of An Loc along Route 245. Additional developments indicated that this was a well-equipped NVA unit, probably the 165th PAVN Regiment of the 7th Division.

Intelligence planners believed that the regiment could not be reinforced by the 141st Regiment in less than twenty-four hours, so General Hay decided to commit only one brigade to the operation initially. He directed the 1st Brigade to remain on standby in the event a second NVA regiment showed up. This decision committed Parmentier's 2-16 to guard the base at Quon Loi for the whole period. Hay gave Colonel Frank E. Blazey's Iron Brigade the nod to go in after the mystery unit and bring it to battle.

On the 12th, Blazey sent two battalions into a LZ southeast of the enemy force. First in was the 1st Battalion, 2nd Infantry, followed by Lieutenant Colonel Calvert P. Benedict's 1-16. Over the next ten days, the two battalions thoroughly swept the reported area but made no contact with enemy units. Evidence in the area indicated that the enemy regiment had not stopped but had simply passed through. Part of the failure to make contact may be explained by the fact that, for some inexplicable reason, Blazey had not utilized a blocking force, and the enemy unit had probably moved away from the U.S. battalions with ease.[98] This frustration with not being able to come to grips with the enemy would also be a hallmark in the next operation conducted by the Rangers, but not for other units of the Big Red One.

Operation Shenandoah II
October 1-15, 1967

The last major combat operation for both Ranger battalions in 1967 was Operation Shenandoah II. The 1st Infantry Division had not conducted a large-scale operation since Billings in June because the 9th PLAF Division, now commanded by Senior Colonel Ta Minh Kham, had gone to great pains to avoid contact and even detection since then. The VC colonel preferred, instead, to allow his division to recover from the beating it had taken earlier in the year, and he moved it to the vicinity of Dong Xoai. Likewise, Hay moved the 1st Infantry Division's headquarters from Di An to Lai Khe in September to get it closer to the combat areas between the two war zones.

In July, Colonel Kham sent the badly mauled 271st Regiment to the Long Nguyen Secret Zone (known to the VC as Base Area 255) to receive replacements and refit. After the regiment was rejuvenated, it was to rejoin the 9th Division for attacks in Binh Long province. General Hay, however, was determined not to allow the VC regiment any further respite from danger. On September 29, he sent the 1st Brigade into the northern area of the secret zone, and the following day, the Iron Brigade deployed in the southern half of the zone to search for the 271st Regiment.

At 10:00 a.m. on October 1, the 1st Battalion (under the command of Colonel Benedict since June 28) was airlifted to a rice paddy. As the troops bailed out of the choppers, they splashed into waist-deep water, then waded through the muck until they reached dry ground. Once out of the paddy, Benedict moved the battalion south through heavy foliage and bamboo thickets for about a kilometer. Arriving at a rubber plantation about six kilometers northwest of Lai Khe, his men cleared the area and established a new fire support base, Lorraine I.

Over the next two weeks, as several other 1st Division battalions engaged in hot firefights, the 1st Battalion conducted S&D sweeps along Route 240 making occasional contact with the enemy, but not fighting any major battles. The battalion did uncover many tons of rice, ammunition, and other supplies. One cache alone held thirty-five tons of rice, most of which was destroyed by burning it with gasoline. On October 16, the battalion returned to Lai Khe.

Upon the battalion's return to Lai Khe, it underwent another reorganization. That day, Company E, the battalion's new combat support company, was activated under the command of First Lieutenant Robert B. Durant. This new unit was formed by transferring the recon platoon, the heavy mortar platoon, and the ground surveillance radar section from the headquarters company and activating a new company headquarters to control the special units.[99]

Two days later, the battalion was committed to the 1st Brigade AO about twenty kilometers northwest of Lai Khe. For ten days, the battalion performed sweeps but encountered no enemy. On October 29, it returned to 3rd Brigade control and ended its role in Shenandoah II.

The relatively calm activities of the 1-16 Infantry during October belied the hard fighting going on elsewhere in the area of operations. Operation Shenandoah II resulted in the deaths of 957 enemy troops in a month of combat, mostly in the 271st and 272nd Regiments. The 1st Infantry Division lost 106 men to enemy action, and another 323 wounded.[100] While the Rangers came away relatively unscathed, they had harried the already over-taxed 271st Regiment, and helped to disrupt its reconstitution timeline.

During Shenandoah II, the 2nd Battalion provided security for FSB Normandy I until November 6. During this period, the battalion conducted squad-, platoon-, and company-sized ambushes and reconnaissance operations in areas about eight kilometers east of Ben Cat.

From November 7 to 19, the Rangers remained at Lai Khe pulling routine security missions for that base and participating in local pacification efforts as part of the newly instituted "Accelerated Pacification Campaign." On November 20, the battalion was airlifted to security positions to guard several artillery FSBs to the northwest, and remained there until returning to Lai Khe on December 6. Colonel Darrel L. Gooler's assumption of command of the 2nd Battalion on December 14 was the most significant event during the remainder of that month.

Tet Counteroffensive
January-April 1968
The 1967 battles in War Zones C and D had devastated the Big Red One's arch-rival, the 9th PLAF Division. By the end of

December, that division had withdrawn across the Cambodian border, once more to rebuild after suffering massive losses during the year. Senior Colonel Kham also began to prepare it for another mission, one that would probably be the most important of its existence—the Tet Offensive in February 1968. In the meantime, relative calm descended in the 1st Infantry Division's TAOR as a result, and the Big Red One used the lull to direct more attention toward pacification efforts.

By January 1968, the transition from large-scale combat operations to local RIF and S&D sweeps, conducted by platoons and companies, was well underway. When units were not conducting these small-scale combat missions, they were involved in pacification efforts.

For the month of January, Colonel Benedict's 1st Battalion spent most of its time performing security tasks for the Lai Khe base camp. On January 11-12, Benedict's troops sealed Ben Cui village, just southeast of Lai Khe. Setting up the blocking positions, battalion elements engaged in several brief firefights. One man was killed and two were wounded, but the Rangers killed nine VC and capturing thirteen, including assorted weapons and supplies.[101] The last event of the month was an air assault into AO Bluefield on January 18. Participating in S&D sweeps over the next four days, the battalion uncovered several tons of rice and two small base camps but made no contact with the enemy. The battalion returned to Lai Khe for the remainder of January.[102]

Similar to the 1st Battalion, Colonel Gooler's 2nd Battalion spent most of January performing security missions for base camps and FSBs. During the first three weeks of January, the 2nd Rangers operated out of FSBs Ranger III and Sicily VI. Here too, the 2nd Battalion troopers guarded engineers as Rome plows cut free-fire zones and roads. On the night of January 8-9, elements of the battalion ambushed and sank two sampans on the Thi Tinh River, south of Ben Cat. Toward the end of the month, however, the battalion was pulled back to the village of An My, about one mile north of Phu Loi.[103] The Rangers did not know it, but their move to An My was in response to directives from MACV to pull U.S. units closer to Saigon. Something big was in the wind.

Before the turn of the year, General Westmoreland had planned to conduct another multidivision operation in War Zone C to clear out remaining VC base camps there. However, information regarding a massive enemy build-up began to surface in December, and movements of VC and NVA units toward Saigon in January confirmed the hunch that the enemy was about to launch a major offensive, probably against the capital itself. Westmoreland decided to postpone the big operation in War Zone C and directed Lieutenant General Weyand, the II Field Force commander, to strengthen U.S. forces around Saigon. By the time the Tet Offensive got underway, more than half of the U.S. maneuver battalions in the III CTZ were already in position to block or defeat an enemy attack.

On the evening of January 31, 1968, Specialist Fourth

Class Dennis Mozee from St. Joseph, Missouri, was motoring south on Highway 13 on his way to the Long Binh base camp. Mozee had been drafted into the army and trained as a heavy maintenance mechanic. When he shipped out to Vietnam, he had been assigned to the 1st Division and ultimately to Headquarters Company, 2-16 Infantry, in September 1967. On the 31st, Staff Sergeant Lawrence Phillips ordered him to drive a deuce-and-a-half truck on a supply mission to Lai Khe. About dusk, and still about eighteen kilometers west of Long Binh, his co-driver, Specialist Fourth Class Smith, nicknamed "Smitty," told Mozee to pull the truck over to the side of the road.

"Something's not right," Smitty told Mozee. Mozee looked about the hazy horizon and to the southeast toward Saigon and Long Binh; he could see large flashes and bright lights streaking through the air. "Must be the New Year's celebration, man. You know, Tet," Mozee replied. "No it's something else," Smitty insisted, "Something's not right." Just then, as Mozee stared through the haze of the gathering dusk, he beheld an eerie sight. Not two hundred yards away, several dozen well-armed enemy troops appeared, literally out of the ground, and moved, ghost-like, toward some unknown destination. For some reason, they had no interest in the American truck sitting along the road. Not waiting for them to change their minds, Mozee gunned the truck to life and sped off to the east.

Arriving at Long Binh after dark, Mozee learned that the nearby ammunition dump had been hit by VC sappers. Apparently, there was VC activity everywhere. Stumbling into Mozee and Smitty after their return, Staff Sergeant Lawrence directed them to load up their truck with some unmarked supplies and carry them to a military police unit in Saigon as soon as possible. Once the deuce-and-a-half was loaded, the two departed and headed across the Dong Nai River bridge. As they approached Saigon, ever-increasing amounts of small arms fire erupted in all directions. Then the fire came closer to the road, and finally, bullets began coming in the direction of Mozee's truck. Mozee decided that the MPs did not need whatever it was he was carrying that badly and he turned around and returned to Long Binh.

"I knew they were shootin' at us, but it didn't seem like they were getting that close," Mozee recalled. As the truck reached the Long Binh compound, Mozee stopped the truck just outside. The gates were closed and appeared to have been damaged by a crash. There were no guards about, and he wondered what was going on. Turning to Smith, he asked him, "What do you think?" Just then, he noticed an odd pleading look in Smith's eyes; then Smith slumped over. As he grabbed Smith and attempted to help him, he realized the young soldier's shirt was soaked with blood. It was too late; Smith was dead. "That's what I remember about Tet," mourned Mozee. Something, indeed, had not been right that night.[104]

Back at An My, the 2nd Battalion had been alerted to the numerous attacks around Saigon. The area remained relative-ly quiet until February 1, when one of the Big Red One's old adversaries, the 273rd PLAF Regiment, ventured far from its normal AO to attack A and B Companies (then operating with the 1-4 Cavalry). A heavy firefight developed, but the 2nd Battalion prevailed, killing twenty-two VC and wounding many others. Continuing its sweep operations the following day, the infantry/cavalry task force killed another 372 enemy troops in heavy fighting. Additionally, the task force destroyed an enemy field hospital, overran an artillery battery, and wiped out the regimental commander and staff. The 273rd Regiment was essentially destroyed.[105]

Throughout February, the 2nd Battalion, less C Company, continued to operate in the An My-Di An area. Company C, meanwhile, was detailed to guard the critical Route 15 bridge only four kilometers from downtown Saigon. For the month of March, the battalion carried out mop-up operations and ambush patrols in the Phu Loi area. One ambush succeeded in killing twelve VC and capturing twelve others.

While the 2nd Battalion was busy around Phu Loi during Tet, the 1st Battalion remained at Lai Khe, and witnessed less of the major fighting associated with the enemy offensive. On February 22, however, elements of the battalion did engage portions of the 165th PAVN Regiment a few kilometers northwest of Tan Son Nhut Air Base. The firefight resulted in twelve NVA dead. Contact with the enemy also increased while the battalion was conducting security sweeps, resulting in thirty-four enemy KIA for the month.

For the first half of March, the battalion moved to Di An to conduct RIF missions for the division headquarters base camp. Operations at Di An were relatively tame, but the battalion succeeded in killing ten VC, suffering two killed and ten wounded in return. The 1st Battalion returned to Lai Khe on March 16, and five days later, the command passed from Benedict to Lieutenant Colonel Richard Eaton. By the end of March, the great enemy offensive was largely over.

The Tet Offensive of 1968 was the largest Viet Cong operation up to that date and for the rest of the war, at least when U.S. troops were involved. Initially, some eighty-four thousand VC and NVA troops attacked thirty-six of the forty-four provincial capitals and almost every airfield in South Vietnam. Most importantly, the VC mounted a major attack against Saigon, including the U.S. Embassy, the Presidential Palace, the ARVN Joint General Staff headquarters, and Ton San Nhut Air Base. While Tet would become a significant political victory for the Viet Cong, it was also a military disaster. Between January 31 and the end of February, the enemy had suffered forty-five thousand dead. Assuming the standard three to one ratio of wounded to killed, the VC and their allies ultimately sustained about 180,000 causalities. In one five hundred-man battalion of the 9th Division's 273rd Regiment for example, only forty-five men remained who were not dead or wounded.

Upon conclusion of the 1968 Tet Offensive, the Viet Cong as a military force was devastated and would never again be able to go toe-to-toe with American forces in the field. Unfortunately, the story of the scale of the VC defeat tends to be given short shrift in most histories of the Vietnam conflict. From Tet onward, the North Vietnamese regular army would be forced to take on ever-increasing responsibilities in prosecuting the war in the south.

While Tet was a military victory for the Allies, it was also a setback to the South Vietnamese government's pacification program as well. After the VC demonstrated their ability to strike directly at the heart of Saigon, many peasants in the countryside had even less faith that the central government could protect them. As a result, MACV determined to redouble its pacification efforts, especially now that the VC actually posed less of a threat than at any time since before the U.S. intervention.

Counteroffensive, Phase IV
April-June 1968
General Westmoreland designed Counteroffensive, Phase IV, to take back areas lost to the enemy during Tet. It began with a number of battalion-size attrition operations in the I CTZ in April 1968. The excellent success achieved by allied forces in that zone forced COSVN to shift its efforts back to the III CTZ in mid-Spring. Meanwhile, Operation Lam Son 68, a continuation of the South Vietnamese government's "Revolutionary Development" efforts in Binh Duong province, was suspended on March 10. Operation Quyet Thang commenced the next day.

Operation Quyet Thang
March 11-April 7, 1968
Operation Quyet Thang ("Certain Victory") was the 1st Infantry Division's effort to destroy VC and NVA forces attempting to exfiltrate from the Saigon area through Binh Duong province. Positioned in the southern part of the province, the 2nd Brigade controlled the operations of both battalions of the 16th Infantry. Colonel Gooler's 2-16 was deployed just east of Ben Cat in company-size blocking positions and Colonel Eaton's 1-16 conducted RIF efforts southeast of Phu Cuong. The key event of the operation for Gooler's troops came on the night of April 3-4 when the recon platoon ambushed a VC platoon and killed thirteen enemy troops. The tables were soon turned, however, when the scouts realized that the enemy unit was from an estimated battalion-size force that was now attempting to surround them. The scouts were soon heavily engaged, but Captain Gary Harr's A Company came to the rescue and broke the siege. Three days later, after almost no additional contact with the enemy, Quyet Thang ended and was followed by Operation Toan Thang, Phase I.

Operation Toan Thang
April 8, 1968-November 1, 1969
Major General Keith L. Ware, the new commanding general of the 1st Infantry Division, instituted a new division offensive on April 8. The effort was part of Toan Thang ("Complete Victory"), a joint operation conducted by the II Field Force and the III ARVN Corps to conduct rapid RIF incursions into suspected and known VC sanctuaries in the III CTZ. The operation was designed to take advantage of the VC power vacuum and to keep the enemy off balance after their thrashing during Tet. Toan Thang's long-term purpose (it would last until November 1, 1969) was to root out and destroy communist infrastructure, provide security for villages and hamlets, and assist the training of local defense units such as Popular Forces, Regional Forces, and the CIDG. Both battalions of the 16th Infantry would participate in the effort on several different occasions.

The Big Red One naturally focused its efforts on the TAOR in War Zone C and the area east to War Zone D. After the initial sweeps into the sanctuaries, the various units of the division turned to night ambushes along infiltration and supply routes. During the month of April, Eaton's 1st Battalion continued to perform security duties at Lai Khe until the 17th, when the battalion launched Operation Ao Duty 3. That morning, the battalion was airlifted into a LZ next to the Song Be River, about twenty kilometers north of Tân Uyên. Eaton spread out his companies, and all headed southwest, traveling across the bluffs that overlooked the river at that point. About 2:20 p.m., B Company made its way off the bluffs into a ravine about eighteen-hundred meters from the LZ, when the point man observed a lone VC. The man fled with the company following, but the Rangers soon ran into an unknown enemy force. When the company received intense small arms fire and RPG rounds, the commander called for air strikes and artillery. The enemy then broke contact, but not before B Company suffered nine wounded while inflicting only one KIA on the VC. The following day, two more contacts developed resulting in four VC KIA.

Over the next several days, the most significant event was a battle on April 22 near the initial LZ. Elements of the 1st Battalion came upon an apparently unoccupied base camp about 10:30 a.m. While conducting a search of the camp, the Rangers were attacked by the returning occupants just after 3:00 p.m. The assaulting VC were intent on retaining their camp, so Eaton brought up the rest of the battalion as well as artillery and mortar concentrations. The fight lasted until 6:30 p.m. when contact ended. Eaton pulled the Rangers into the battalion NDP to continue the sweep on the morrow.

The following morning, the battalion located an eighteen-bunker complex that was destroyed by the Rangers. The battalion also destroyed a cache of 120mm mortar rounds and several weapons and inflicted four known KIA on the enemy. After this fight, the battalion returned to Lai Khe. This S&D mission was typical of most operations that American infantry battalions conducted for the rest of the war. The following summary of the mission results illustrates how success was measured in a war in which holding terrain seized from the enemy was often irrelevant to calculating victory and defeat:

Enemy Casualties:
  VC KIA 15 (actual body count) 6 (estimated additional)
Captured Weapons and Ammunition:

AK-47 rifles	5
SKS rifles	2
Russian rifle	1
RPG rounds	23
AK-47 rounds	6,480
82mm mortar rounds	5
107mm mortar rounds	28
Chinese "claymore" mines	3
Grenades	12
10-lb homemade bomb	1

Captured Food, Clothing, and Equipment:

M-16 magazines	11
Documents	4.5 pounds
Field phones	4
Transistor radios	4
Typewriter	1
VC gas mask	1
Khaki uniforms	30 sets
VC "black pajama" uniforms	30 sets
Mortar tube cleaning rods	2
Mortar tube cleaning brushes	2
Ox cart	1
Medical supplies	miscellaneous[106]

At about the same time Eaton's men were destroying the bunker complex, Colonel Gooler's 2nd Rangers conducted a spectacular seal operation of Chanh Luu village, just east of Ben Cat. U.S. intelligence had long suspected Chanh Luu was an enemy supply base that actively supported VC operations in the Tet offensive. Gooler had been directed to seal it and clean it out.

The night of April 23, one of Gooler's companies moved into position around Chanh Luu. One of the unit's ambush positions soon encountered an enemy column consisting of over 250 well-armed troops who passed within ten meters of the well-concealed Rangers. Realizing that the VC force was too big to engage, the patrol let them pass, then reported to Gooler that the column had moved into the village. Gooler repositioned the company closer to the village and directed the airlift of another company into a LZ early the following morning.

At first light, one of the companies went into the village while the other remained in overwatch. Surprisingly, there was no resistance. Gooler's Rangers easily rounded up some 272 people, mostly young men, and with the help of the National Police, determined that 268 of them were VC soldiers. The Rangers also thoroughly searched all the hooches in the village and discovered a stash of about 275 pounds of rice per dwelling. The total haul was about six tons of rice, but oddly, only three automatic weapons and two grenades were found. Apparently the VC had hidden their weapons upon arrival in the village and the search teams were unable to find the storage location. Gooler's reaction to this otherwise successful operation was only the comment, "One day chicken, the next day feathers!"[107]

On May 5, COSVN launched the "Mini-Tet" offensive to attack Saigon, but this effort, too, was handily repulsed by II Field Force units. Ambush patrols continued to be the primary activity conducted by both Ranger battalions during the month of May in response to this offensive, but the low body count is indicative of the scale of disaster that had befallen the VC in February and March. For all their efforts, the 1st Battalion killed only one VC in May, while the 2nd Battalion accounted for only five. The following month, the battalions engaged in the same activities and garnered eleven and twenty enemy KIA, respectively.[108] Clearly, the enemy had been significantly weakened.

Counteroffensive, Phase V
July-November 1968

With Counteroffensive, Phase V, MACV began a nation-wide offensive to retake remaining areas that were under enemy control before Tet. In the III CTZ, Phase II of Operation Toan Thang began on June 1, and both Ranger battalions spent the better part of the next two months engaged in ambush patrols, RIFs, and road sweeps to support the operation goals. A mission late in June was typical of the Rangers' experiences during this period.

On June 26, Eaton's 1st Battalion airlifted into a LZ about seven kilometers south of the Michelin Rubber Plantation in support of Toan Thang. Over the next five days, the battalion conducted RIF and S&D sweeps. Enemy contact was light, but the battalion destroyed a significant amount of foodstuffs and some weapons, with a small base camp and many bunkers. With little more to be accomplished, Colonel Eaton returned the battalion to Lai Khe on June 30.[109]

A little over two weeks later, the 1-16 deployed to the field in response to information that elements of the 7th PAVN Division, commanded by Colonel Nguyen The Bon, were in base camps north of Tân Uyên. On June 17, the battalion inserted into a LZ about five kilometers south of the Song Be River, due south of the location where it had operated in April during Ao Duty 3. Three days of searching resulted in minor contacts and the capture of miscellaneous supplies, until C Company maneuvered into a base camp during a routine contact on the 20th. A firefight broke out with a reinforced company of the Dong Nai Regiment, later determined to be about one hundred strong. The remainder of the U.S. battalion closed in, and fighting lasted most of the day. The action resulted in three Rangers killed and fifteen wounded, but only three VC bodies were recovered.

Over the next two days, A Company searched the base camp and discovered more than three hundred bunkers and other facilities covering an entire grid square. Two VC from the

522nd Rear Service Group, an apparent caretaker unit in the complex, were killed during the sweep. During another sweep north of the big base camp on July 21, Eaton was severely wounded by enemy small arms fire and evacuated. Three days later, the battalion returned to Lai Khe, and Lieutenant Colonel Willard Latham took the flag.

The months of July and August were similar in activity and content for the soldiers of the 1st Battalion. Latham's troops conducted several air assaults in War Zone C, mainly in the area known as the "Trapezoid," located between the Michelin Rubber Plantation, the Saigon River, and Ben Cat. The 1-16 made numerous cat-and-mouse contacts with small detachments of the 5th PLAF Division; still, battalion S&D efforts resulted in only three NVA and seventeen VC KIA for the month.

The 1st Battalion returned to Lai Khe on September 8 and immediately stood down to prepare for a move to join the 9th Infantry Division south of Saigon. On 13 September, Latham's troops boarded Hueys at 12:55 p.m. for the trip to their new home at Dong Tam. Upon its arrival, the battalion was relieved from the 1st Infantry Division and assigned to the 9th Infantry Division. Concurrently, some sixty M-113s and numerous other tracked and wheeled vehicles of the 5th Battalion, 60th Infantry (Mechanized), under the command of Lieutenant Colonel Eric Attila, ground their way north to take up residence at Lai Khe. On its arrival, the 5-60th Infantry became the second of only two mechanized battalions now in the 1st Infantry Division.

Like the 1st Battalion, the 2nd Battalion conducted numerous ambush patrols and road sweep operations in July and August in support of Operation Toan Thang. Although the ambush operations in July only netted six VC, the Chieu Hoi ("Open Arms") program prompted significant numbers of defectors to surrender. Additionally, on July 12, Lieutenant Colonel Charles P. McLean assumed command of the battalion from Gooler.

The major event during August was the battalion's efforts to conduct another seal of Chanh Luu village. On August 1, B and D Companies teamed up with elements of the 11th ACR and the 1st Battalion, 8th ARVN Regiment, to isolate the town, but the efforts to seal the village precipitated a firefight. The ensuring battle and three-day seal resulted in eighteen VC KIA, one of whom was a VC general. Ninety-four other VC were captured, along with an unusually large cache of ammunition and weapons.

One month later, the battalion conducted a similar operation at Binh My, another suspected VC supply base. After the seal was complete, the battalion set up separate company NDPs near the village. That night, an ambush patrol from Charlie Company captured a VC soldier, and intelligence garnered from the man indicated that the VC were preparing to attack the company to retake the village. The patrol leader quickly pulled his troops out of their positions and led the way back to inform the company commander. Within minutes of acquiring this information, C Company came under mortar fire, and was then hit by an enemy ground attack. A combination of small arms fire and the excellent performance of the company's mortar platoon handily defeated the attack. Similarly, B Company was also hit by a mortar barrage, then assaulted by an enemy force estimated at one hundred men. The company drove off the attackers, killing at least six VC. Three VC were captured the following day by B Company S&D sweeps.

On September 11 and 12, the 1st Battalion, 2nd Infantry, and later, the 1st Battalion, 28th Infantry, was heavily engaged by elements of Colonel Bon's 7th PAVN Division near Loc Ninh. In one assault by the 1-28 Infantry on Hill 222, the NVA soldiers tenaciously fought to retain their position. The fighting became intensive enough that the 2-16 Infantry was suddenly pulled out of Toan Thang operations and sent north to assist the 1st Brigade.

Battle of Loc Ninh
September 13-16, 1968
By August 1968, the 7th PAVN Division had recovered enough from its Tet casualties to resume operations in War Zone D. Various indicators that month had revealed increased NVA activity in the areas north and east of Loc Ninh, and minor enemy scrapes with ARVN and U.S. units sweeping the area revealed the presence of the 141st and 165th Regiments setting up base camps and moving in supplies. In September, General Ware determined to send Colonel Fred Krause's 1st Brigade into War Zone D to find and engage the 7th Division. During the initial stages of this operation, the 1-2 Infantry made contact with the 141st Regiment on September 11.

At the time, Colonel McLean's 2nd Battalion was occupying semi-permanent NDPs, while engaged in pacification efforts in the vicinity of "Claymore Corners," well east of Lai Khe. McLean received a warning order about midnight on September 12 to be prepared to move to Loc Ninh the next morning. The series of events that followed illustrates how a unit can overcome difficulties and still perform its mission.

The mission called for the 2nd Battalion to insert into blocking positions north of the fighting on Hill 222 to catch any NVA units trying to exfiltrate north into Cambodia. However, the requirement put McLean and his unit into a logistics quandary. The battalion's base camp was at Di An, where the rear detachment remained, but the battalion had been operating out of Lai Khe for several months during Toan Thang. Additionally, C Company and a mortar platoon were operating near Phuoc Vinh and were supported from that base. Now the battalion would have to move way north and conduct support operations from Loc Ninh. Consequently the Rangers had to coordinate logistic support from four different locations.

At 7:00 a.m., McLean's TOC (Tactical Operations Center; the battalion's field headquarters element) and part of D Company moved by chopper to Quon Loi and awaited the arrival of A and B Companies. However, these two companies and the D Company mortar platoon were flown directly to Lai Khe. Specialist Fourth Class Robert B. Humphries recalled that the arrival at Lai Khe was somewhat ominous. "We flew into Lai Khe in helicopters and there must have been ten C-130s, the 'doughnut dollies,' the Big Red One Band, and cases of ammunition, and thought [to ourselves] 'This is not good.'"

The unit was transloaded into C-130s, and flown directly to Loc Ninh, not Quon Loi. Humphries remembered:

We had no idea what we were going to do, and they said, "Well, take a case of ammunition and get on the C-130," and we took off and flew forty-five minutes to an hour. I thought we were crashing; red lights went on and bells were ringing, and uh…we actually landed on a dirt road in Loc Ninh, just right outside of a Special Forces camp. [The landing area] was actually on top of a mountain too.[110]

Colonel Krause learned that the battalion had been split and persuaded the air force to transport the TOC and D Company to Loc Ninh by C-130 as well. Unfortunately, upon arriving in Loc Ninh, McLean discovered that the aircraft with the TOC, a rifle platoon from D Company, and the D Company commander had been diverted to Bien Hoa because of mechanical difficulties. McLean reorganized D Company by attaching the recon platoon and placing the company under the command of the senior lieutenant who happened to be the mortar platoon leader. All was done before noon.

The air assault was slightly delayed, but by 12:45 p.m., the rest of the Bobtail battalion was airlanded by the C-130s on the LZ, a strip of Highway 13, just few kilometers north of Hill 222. Moving off its LZ, the battalion elements consolidated, deployed directly into a rubber plantation, and moved south toward the planned blocking positions. This was no easy task because the battalion had not yet received maps of the AO. Arriving at the assigned location, McLean moved the Rangers into an eleven-hundred-meter-long blocking position, with Captain John W. Matthews' A Company in the west, Captain Glade M. Bishop's B Company in reserve, and the reorganized D Company occupying the eastern sector.

While D Company was deploying, an NVA force estimated at 150 men attacked troops of the recon platoon. After a sharp firefight, the enemy was repulsed and broke contact. Some time later, B Company in the rear was also hit, and for a time it appeared that the enemy was trying to surround the unit. Later events indicated the effort was merely a feint by the enemy unit to avoid decisive contact so it could retire to the northwest and the safety of the Cambodian border.

While the battalion was busy digging in, Colonel McLean sent patrols forward to determine what was to his front. The sweeps revealed twenty dead NVA soldiers, several weapons, and blood pools left by the wounded. Just before dark, A Company experienced probing fires from a small village to the southwest. The company returned the fire and pushed a sweep into the village, where two more dead VC were found with their weapons.

That night in the blocking positions was an eerie experience for the Rangers. In the distance, forward of A Company, peering through the light evening rain, the men observed bobbing lights. The lights turned out to be the torches, flashlights, and candles of NVA troops searching for their wounded and dead. A call to the nearest FSB brought artillery crashing into the vicinity, and not surprisingly, the lights disappeared.

The next morning, McLean was holding a meeting with his commanders, when he received a call from the recon platoon leader that 150 "friendly" troops were moving toward his location. The lieutenant reported that the unidentified troops waved as if in greeting and walked in the open directly toward his platoon. McLean recalled, "This seemed a little illogical to me. Although I had a fairly good fix on Defiant (the code name for 1-28 Infantry), which was a pressure force driving the enemy towards me, it was conceivable that possibly they had one unit moving rather rapidly in my direction." He directed the platoon leader to move forward and tell the unit to stand fast where they were. Approaching the unknown unit, the platoon leader was greeted with a hail of automatic weapons and RPG fire. It soon developed that this was a forward security unit leading casualty parties north to Cambodia.[111]

The NVA unit seized the initiative and struck the center of the battalion position, then sent flanking elements to both sides of the blocking position attempting to surround the battalion. When they realized that the 2-16 was too big for them to handle, the flanking elements broke contact and fled north. The fixing unit in front of the Rangers was pinned down, however. One cluster of about sixty troops, mostly litter bearers with patients (probably from the fighting around Hill 222), hustled for cover in a small clump of trees forward of A Company that had previously been targeted by artillery and the air force. Within seconds of their arrival, the stand of trees erupted in blinding flashes from the impact of 8-inch rounds, followed by 750-lb bombs. Though there was never an accurate body count taken, McLean estimated that twenty to forty NVA troops were killed in that incident.[112]

Soon after this contact, McLean directed D Company to sweep forward and assess the results, but he was almost immediately directed by Colonel Krause to move south and link up with the 1-28 Infantry. Matthews' A Company took up the lead, he but soon reported some suspicious movement (that turned out to be a herd of cattle). McLean moved forward and linked up with Matthews, then directed him to determine what was causing the cattle to move. Sure enough, when the herd moved into the open, behind it came a well-dispersed NVA platoon. Another strange encounter followed.

During the earlier encounter, the waving NVA troops apparently thought that the D Company soldiers were indeed friendly. Having spent the night in the rain-soaked red clay of

Loc Ninh, the American soldiers and their NVA counterparts were so muddy that both sides took on appearances that made it difficult to differentiate friend from foe. When this NVA platoon emerged from the rubber trees into the open, the leader could clearly see the American battalion command group, FOs, and Matthews standing in a cluster observing him too. McLean recalled,

> The [NVA] platoon leader, who was directing the movement of the force approaching us, leaned against a tree, stared directly at us, and then motioned his forces to come forward. Sensing that he took us for friendly [troops], we made no [radical] movement and permitted him to walk within 40 meters of our locations which placed him within 20 meters of the deployed riflemen. And at this time, the Company Commander…gave the order to fire.[113]

Mathews's line erupted in automatic fire, killing eleven of the enemy in seconds. The rest of the enemy platoon fled into the rubber trees followed by A Company for about four hundred meters. During the pursuit, the Rangers killed several more NVA, recovered numerous discarded weapons, and captured the platoon leader and one squad leader.

Compounding the enemy's confusion was the fact that the Rangers had removed their helmets during the halt, except the recon platoon, who wore "booney hats." The NVA soldiers also had no headgear or wore a hat similar to the booney hats. Thus, the enemy platoon was completely off-guard until it was too late to react.

After this action, McLean pushed the battalion south through a rubber plantation toward the link-up point some twelve hundred meters away. Just as Bishop's B Company, now in the lead, arrived at the correct location in the early evening, the point man spotted an enemy force of about fourteen men moving through the rubber trees and high grass on a route diagonal to the main body of Rangers. In the fading light, McLean brought up D Company on the flank of the NVA unit. From about forty yards away, the company opened fire.

A lively engagement ensued and continued into the enveloping darkness. The firing eventually ceased, and the battalion pulled into a defensive perimeter to wait for morning. The light of dawn on September 15 revealed that the battalion had actually entered an enemy base camp. The subsequent search located several bodies, along with more blood pools, cooking utensils, and much personal equipment and supplies. The disposition of the captured materials indicated that the enemy had been surprised and had fled in great haste.

For some reason, the 1-28 Infantry had not moved to the linkup site, so Colonel McLean continued moving south and contacted the Black Lions about noon. Upon linkup, Krause sent both battalions on a seventeen kilometer RIF toward Cambodia to sweep up scattered remnants of the 141st

Regiment. The battalion made only eleven kilometers that day, and the following afternoon, McLean's men were returned home to Di An for the first time in seven months.

McLean remembered this operation as a fine moment in the 2nd Battalion's history. Of the Rangers' accomplishments, he stated that "there was much pride in the battalion for having been thrown into an area [which was] pretty unfamiliar for them; with the battalion logistics spread all over South Vietnam and very sketchy briefings on what we were going to be doing; and to have come out of it so well."[114] On this last point McLean was modest. His battalion inflicted over fifty KIA on the 141st Regiment during the four-day operation, and suffered only two casualties in return, one of which was a snake bite.

The 2nd Battalion returned to Lai Khe in early October, but it was there for only twenty-four hours before conducting an airmobile insertion into the Trapezoid. Operating under the 3rd Brigade and with two other battalions, the Rangers spent a week conducting company-sized sweeps in search of the 101st PAVN Regiment. Though they made only fleeting contact with the enemy, the Rangers found plenty of evidence that "Charlie" had recently been in the area. Near the end of the battalion's stint in the field, one company located a half-mile-long base camp, estimated to be of division-size, complete with concrete bunkers, office spaces, showers, warehouses, and mess halls. The major cache yielded over four hundred pressure mines, seven hundred RPG rounds, one hundred mortar rounds, and other munitions.[115]

Upon arrival at Dong Tam, the soldiers of the 1st Rangers were not exactly given a warm welcome by the men who wore the red, white, and blue "butter cookie" of the 9th Infantry Division. The second night of the 1st Battalion's short stay at Dong Tam, the post soldiers' club featured a girlie show featuring some Australian beauties. The soldiers of the 1st Battalion were anxious to see the show and showed up in the bar still wearing the coveted Big Red One on their left shoulder. Naturally, this brought on a number of caustic remarks from the "Varsity" division men.

Of course, the "Rangers," proud of their association with the 1st Division, could not allow their ex-division's honor to be soiled, and presently, the entire club was a wild scene of flying knuckles, bloody noses, and screaming Australian women. Despite playing away from home against the hometown team, the Rangers bested the "butter cookie" grunts in grand style. They readily demonstrated that the Big Red One was the real varsity team in Vietnam, but their hard-fought victory came with a price. The next day, the 9th Division commander, Major General Julian Ewell, ordered Latham's troops out of Dong Tam and into the field. That morning, the 1st Rangers were exiled on an airmobile operation to the "Plain of Reeds" west of Dong Tam.[116]

For the five weeks it was assigned to the 9th Division (under the designation "1st Battalion, 16th Infantry") Colonel Latham's 1st Battalion conducted RIF and S&D missions in the swampy terrain of the Mekong Delta. Then, on October 21, the

1st Battalion colors were returned to the Big Red One. The same day, at ceremonies at Lai Khe, the 5-60 Infantry, now under the command of Lieutenant Colonel Donald C. Shuffstall, was redesignated the 1st Battalion, 16th Infantry (Mechanized). Concurrently, Latham's battalion became the new 5-60 Infantry in the 9th Division. In honor of the redesignation, Shuffstall adopted a new nickname for the 1st Battalion: "Iron Rangers." The new moniker was intended to combine the traditional regimental nickname with the fact that the 1st Battalion now performed its missions in M-113 armored personnel carriers.[117]

Counteroffensive, Phase VI
November 1968-February 1969

About mid-November 1968, MACV initiated the Accelerated Pacification Campaign (an invigorated Operation Lam Son) that was the essence of Counteroffensive, Phase VI. Battalion efforts throughout the III CTZ shifted from S&D Sweeps and RIFs to assisting ARVN units in securing areas to root out the VC political infrastructure in the hamlets and villages outside the larger cities. Basically, the process called for U.S. Army units to secure a given target area, then ARVN units, national police, and civil authorities would move in to screen the inhabitants. In this way, many VC soldiers, sympathizers, and political leaders were rooted out and imprisoned. The procedures were so successful that they formed the basis of most of the remaining ground operations for the 1st Infantry Division in Vietnam. After late 1968, only a few large-scale operations like those of 1966-67 would be undertaken.

On November 18, the 1st Battalion was assigned to the Accelerated Pacification Campaign. The battalion, like most units in this effort, had a dual mission. First, the Iron Rangers were to provide hamlet security by conducting combat operations in the target districts of Chanh Luu and An Dien (located in the "Iron Triangle"). Second, they worked to decrease VC influence over those areas by performing a multitude of civic action duties. For example, during the last two weeks of November, the battalion's medical platoon, supported by elements of the 1st Medical Battalion, treated over nine thousand villagers in Medical Civil Actions Program (MEDCAP) operations. The medics also conducted a midwife training program. The line troops, at least those not pulling security, helped build a school, a fish pond, and a marketplace in Chanh Luu. Others helped to construct FSB Riley next to the village and helped to organize and train Regional Force and Popular Force units in local security operations.

In early December, the 1st Battalion conducted a seal of An Dien village to root out suspected VC. Shuffstall's men also performed rice denial operations using RIF and night ambushes. On December 21, Captain Sherwood Goldberg's C Company, operating from positions along the Saigon River, ambushed and sank a sampan carrying supplies and rice to VC troops near the capital. The same day, Captain Roy May's B

Company killed two VC in an ambush and found two more bodies after a sweep the following day. All of these operations served to convince local villagers that they would be protected from the VC.

Meanwhile, Colonel McLean's 2nd Battalion had also been assigned to the Accelerated Pacification Campaign. For three months beginning November 1, the battalion operated exclusively under the 2nd Brigade in the southern Lam Son area, with the mission of interdicting enemy infiltration through the Phu Loi Gap and providing security in the target area of Quan Ban hamlet, near Di An. McLean's men occupied four Patrol Base/NDPs (Venable Heights, Palm Springs, Pagoda Inn, and Torch Hill) north of Di An to support Operation Lam Son 68. Throughout the area, the battalion set up a series of observation posts to watch over the farmers as they harvested, threshed, and transported their rice. More importantly, the OPs remained vigilant to ensure that the rice did not fall into the hands of the VC as the farmers transported their harvest to market. These pacification efforts paid off when villagers began to freely provide their guardian Rangers information concerning enemy intentions and identified several key people in the area who were VC sympathizers.

Tet 69 Counteroffensive
February-June 1969

The success of the Accelerated Pacification Campaign begun in November was amply demonstrated by the enemy's inability to stage another strong Tet offensive as they had done the year before. Through intensive intelligence efforts, the II Field Force was ready for Tet 69, and aggressive ground operations throughout the III CTZ ensured that the enemy was unable to mount a single potent major attack. Indeed, the operational report for this month stated that the 1st Infantry Division "experienced one of its least active months for some period in terms of enemy activity."[118] This did not mean that the Rangers were inactive; both battalions of the 16th Infantry were busy throughout the period conducting sweeps or providing hamlet security for the pacification campaign.

In late January, the division received intelligence of an enemy buildup in the Michelin Rubber Plantation, and the 1st Battalion was ordered to conduct a RIF to engage or disrupt enemy units staging in the area. On February 1, the Iron Rangers, less B Company, rolled out of Lai Khe, headed for the plantation. Shuffstall conducted seals of three villages with the assistance of the local Popular Force unit. Over the next six days, the battalion uncovered only small caches and destroyed several large bunker complexes. One find yielded thirty-six bicycles that the Iron Rangers donated to the children of An Dien village. The battalion then rolled back into Lai Khe on February 6, its mission completed.

Ten days later, the Iron Rangers moved to Thoi Hoa to participate in Operation Friendship. This mission required Shuffstall's troops to work with the 8th ARVN Regiment in patrolling that unit's pacification area. Both units performed daytime RIFs and nighttime ambushes and made contact with the enemy six times over the next eight days. Though the battalion suffered two KIA, thirty-six WIA, and eight APCs destroyed, its status report for the month of February stated that "casualties were light."

Operation Plainsfield Warrior
April 18-24, 1969

On April 18, the Iron Brigade commenced Operation Plainsfield Warrior in the Trapezoid. The brigade mission was to clear the area of communist infrastructure and influence to engage and, if possible, destroy the Trapezoid's habitual squatters, the 101st PAVN Regiment and the 83rd Rear Service Group. The 2nd Battalion, now under the command of Lieutenant Colonel Hugh S. Galligan since January, moved to the field from Venable Heights to participate in the action.

The first several days were relatively uneventful, but on April 22, the battalion, along with the 1-26 Infantry, marshaled at FSB Aachen for a new mission. Galligan's battalion was assigned to work with the 4th Battalion, 9th ARVN Regiment, in a seal operation of Binh Chua village, southwest of the Michelin Rubber Plantation. At 10:00 p.m., the force deployed by air and successfully sealed the village that night and the following morning. Contact was made with the enemy soon after landing, and by the end of the seal, thirteen VC were killed, six captured, two ARVN draft dodgers were arrested, and five weapons confiscated.[119]

On April 18, 1969, Lieutenant Colonel Kenneth G. Cassels assumed command of the Iron Rangers from Shuffstall. Two days later, the battalion was in the field on a new mission—to reopen Highways QL-14 and 311 from Dong Xoai to Song Be. This route traversed an area that had been under VC domination for the previous five years, and II Field Force was anxious to reopen it. For the next two months, the battalion provided security detachments for several U.S. and ARVN engineer companies in some of the roughest terrain in the III CTZ. These land-clearing companies operated Rome plows that cut two hundred-meter swaths along the sides of the road to make an ambush along the route a difficult proposition.

About every eight days, the Iron Rangers constructed a new fire support base from which artillery could help protect the clearing operations. Additionally, Cassels' troops conducted ambush patrols into the Phuoc Long Victory Gardens in late May and RIFs to the areas on the east side of Núi Ba Ra mountain. These ventures gave the battalion the distinction of being the first U.S. unit ever into these areas. When completed, the Song Be Road operation cost the battalion ten KIA, sixty-seven WIA, and ten APCs lost to enemy action, mostly to mines. On June 15, 1969, the first convoy from Saigon to Song Be ceremoniously rolled along the entire route unmolested, thus ending the domination of Phuoc Long province by the VC—or so it was believed.[120]

Summer-Fall 1969
June-October 1969

With the election of President Richard M. Nixon in November 1968 came several changes to U.S. policies in South Vietnam. Nixon had made a campaign promise to get the United States out of Vietnam "with honor;" so as part of that process, during the summer and fall of 1969, combat operations were increasingly turned over to ARVN units. A troop withdrawal schedule was drawn up and began with the 9th Infantry Division at Camp Bearcat in August 1969. Most of the enemy's efforts were directed toward ARVN units during this period, and he seemed content to avoid contact with U.S. units as the Americans began their withdrawal to the states.

On July 25, Lieutenant Colonel Hugh Patillo, the new commander of the 2nd Brigade, learned that his brigade would be responsible for hosting the first visit of President Nixon into a combat area in Vietnam. The division selected two companies to act as the honor guard and audience for the president, one of which was B Company, 1st Battalion, 16th Infantry, under the command of Captain Ernest L. Freeman.

On July 30, the president arrived at Di An, and drawn up in formation to greet him was Freeman's B Company and C Company, 1st Battalion, 18th Infantry. Upon mounting the grandstand, Nixon presented three soldiers with the Distinguished Service Cross, then motioned the troops to break ranks and crowd around him. After making a few remarks, and telling the soldiers of the American people's great admiration for their service, he waded into the crowd to shake hands and talk to the men. He took names and hometowns and interjected his own homespun greetings with pats on the soldiers' backs and a warm, "How are you?" The president's visit was greatly appreciated by the Rangers and the "Vanguards," and the president relished his chance to visit with them. Later, as he was leaving, Nixon waved at the men and said what they all hoped was true: "We'll see you home!"[121] In less than a year, it would be true for the Big Red One.

In July, the 2nd Battalion conducted S&D operations from FSB Lorraine near Lai Khe. In several minor actions, the battalion continued to attrit the VC C-61 Company and Ben Cat District Company. Early the next month, Lieutenant Colonel Joe G. Mears took over command from Galligan and was soon ordered to conduct road security operations along the Song Be Road. Now dubbed "Thunder Road" because of the enemy mortar, rocket, and mining activity and numerous FSBs along the way, the Song Be corridor road was constantly troubled by enemy efforts to interdict convoys and roll back the allied incursion into their domain. The 2nd Battalion performed convoy security missions along the route until it returned to Di An in September.

In late September, the 2nd Battalion moved again, this time from Di An to Lai Khe, and was assigned to the 3rd Brigade in early October. For the first time, both Ranger battalions were under the command of the Iron Brigade on a permanent basis, and the arrangement would generally remain so for the rest of the war.

Operation Kentucky Cougar
August 7-September 20, 1969

In early August, the 1st Division learned that its old nemesis, the 9th Division, now commanded by Senior Colonel Nguyen Thoi Bung, was preparing for a new offensive in Binh Duong province. By this time, the 9th Division had been reorganized and redesignated as a PAVN (NVA) division. After the massive casualties it suffered during the vicious battles in 1966 and 1967, and especially due to the division's disastrous efforts in the 1968 Tet Offensive, most of the original VC troops were gone and their replacements were all from the north.

The intelligence indicators were that Bung's division might strike areas along Highway 13 between An Loc and Quan Loi from bases across the border in Cambodia. That area was now the AO of the 3rd Brigade, 1st Cavalry Division, since that division had assumed responsibility for Binh Long province. When that shift in TAORs occurred, Colonel James Leach's 11th Armored Cavalry Regiment had been placed under the control of the 1st Cavalry Division. To counter the 9th Division's plans around An Loc, Major General Elvy B. Roberts, commander of the 1st Cavalry Division, initiated Operation Kentucky Cougar. In late July, Colonel Cassels' 1st Battalion was placed under the operational control of the 11th Armored Cavalry Regiment and moved north on Highway 13 to help the cavalry block the eastward movement of the 272nd and 273rd Regiments.

Battle of Binh Long Province
August 12, 1969

Over the next thirty days, the Iron Rangers fought two major actions and numerous minor engagements. The first major action was a battle five kilometers northwest of An Loc on August 12. For the five days prior to that mission, the 1st Battalion (for this mission consisting of the Headquarters Company, and A and C Companies only) was primarily utilized to secure a series of FSBs in areas between Quon Loi and An Loc. On August 10, a platoon from Captain Robert R. Olson's A Company, in coordination with an ARVN company from the 4th Battalion, 9th ARVN Regiment, conducted an air assault near An Loc. The combined U.S./ARVN force, accompanied by Colonel Cassels, went into a LZ defended by NVA troops. Cassels recalled that this landing was the "hottest LZ I was ever in. I'm sure the chopper took bullets as it rose from the LZ."[122]

Upon landing, the Iron Rangers immediately engaged an NVA unit and killed twenty-three of them. Four enemy soldiers were captured, and "singing like turkeys," indicated that units of the 9th Division were indeed moving into the area.

The next evening, Cassels assembled his battalion, less Olson's A Company, at FSB Allons II about eight kilometers north of An Loc, as the RRF for the 11th ACR. Given the diminished size of the Iron Rangers for this operation, Colonel Leach attached D Company, 5th Battalion, 7th Cavalry, that afternoon to Cassels to give him additional firepower. Even with the additional rifle company, Cassels commanded just over three hundred men for the impending operation.

While C Company guarded Allons II, Olson's A Company pulled security for FSB Thunder IV just northeast of An Loc. On the morning of August 12, Cassels was directed to bring his units to the vicinity of FSB Eagle II, there to counterattack an enemy force that had attacked the fire base a couple of hours earlier.

Moving in the darkness, the battalion's elements linked up at Eagle II about dawn without encountering the expected enemy resistance. Cassels then decided to move along the enemy's suspected withdrawal route to the southwest. The Iron Rangers moved out with Olson's A Company in the lead, Captain Phillip Greenwell's C Company following, and the troops of the 7th Cavalry riding on the tops of the C Company tracks (APCs).

Encountering a suspicious ford at a small stream, Olson's men took a great deal of time to reconnoiter the area before crossing. Cassels, impatient with the delay, moved forward to push the company across. With the battalion commander's urging, Olson finally moved A Company across the ford and Cassels' track joined the column about five vehicles back from the front.

After traveling about four kilometers, Olson's lead elements were hit by RPG and automatic weapons fire about 7:05 a.m. The first track in the column, the platoon leader's, was struck by an RPG round, and just seconds later, struck again by a 57mm recoilless round that killed the driver and set the vehicle on fire. The platoon leader was blown clear of the vehicle, but only slightly dazed. After the lieutenant made his way back to Cassels' track, the battalion commander directed him to mount another of his platoon's tracks and get a base of fire started at the enemy.[123] Within minutes, the Iron Rangers were engaged against a six hundred-man battalion of the 272nd Regiment.

Though outnumbered two to one, Cassels deployed the battalion to attack in a southerly direction, with C Company on the right, A on the left, and his command track between the two. The .50-caliber machine-guns laid down a base of fire, as the D Company grunts scrambled off the tops of the tracks and deployed forward. The infantrymen from A and C Companies also deployed and added their fire to that of the tracks, but the enemy fire steadily increased, and the advance of the battalion was stopped. Cassels called for air support and artillery.

After about forty minutes of intense fighting, Cassels' track, as well as those of the two mech company commanders, had been disabled by enemy fire. All three commanders scrambled to other vehicles to continue the fight. Soon, the enemy force attempted to flank the battalion, but the Iron Rangers countered the move and drove the enemy eastward in an attempt to drive them into a clearing where the choppers of the. 1st Cavalry Division's 2nd Battalion, 20th Field Artillery (Aerial Rocket) could attack the NVA troops.

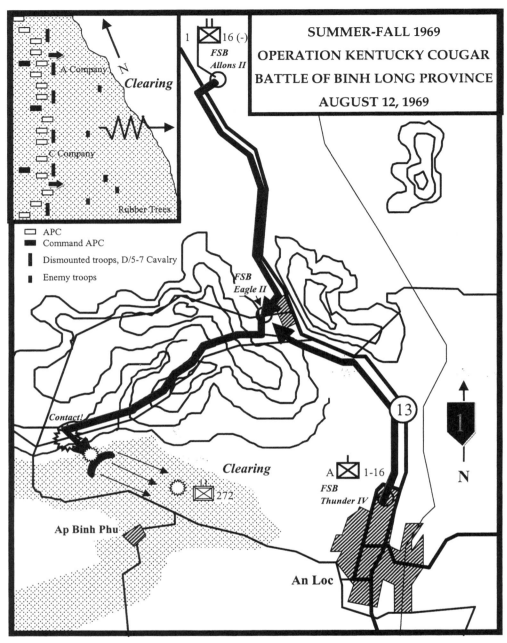

Map 10-12.

By noon, three more APCs had been knocked out of action, and the enemy continued the fight. About 2:00 p.m., the battalion's command and control chopper carrying the S3, Major James Harris, was shot down by a .51-caliber machine gun. Harris was subsequently rescued, and by 3:00 p.m., was back in the air helping to control the battle. Fighting continued until 4:00 p.m., when Leach directed the battalion to break contact. The subsequent sweeps located twenty-nine bodies of the 272nd Regiment and numerous weapons and ammunition. The fighting cost the Iron Rangers two KIA, twenty-seven wound-

ed, and five APCs destroyed.[124]

The other significant battle involving the Iron Rangers took place on September 5 as part of Operation Kentucky Cougar, with A and C Companies once again engaging a significant portion of the 273rd Regiment. About 1:30 p.m., the Battalion S2 and elements of the 1st Platoon, A Company, were dispatched to the 214th Regional Forces Company compound to conduct an interview of its members regarding an attack on its compound the night before. En route back to the battalion NDP at FSB Allons II, the platoon was ambushed and called for help. Cassels responded by mounting A and C Companies and heading for the ambush site. Approaching from the east, Cassels spotted the beleaguered 1st Platoon and deployed his companies on line with Greenwell's C Company to the right and A Company, temporarily under Second Lieutenant Willie D. Miller, to the left.

As some twenty or more M-113s went into action, the troops could see the gun flashes of many AK-47s engaging them to their left front. Once the linkup was effected, Cassels swung the two companies to the southwest and began effectively engaging the enemy. Greenwell's company received the majority of the rifle fire, and he gradually moved his unit forward to hose down the NVA positions with .50-caliber machine-gun fire. Meanwhile, A Company refused its left flank after receiving RPG-7 fire from across the road to its left; moreover, the company had not kept up with the forward movement of C Company. Before long, some of A Company's fire began to hit in and near Greenwell's tracks. Cassels, seeing the danger of fratricide, yelled at Miller over the battalion command net to pull A Company forward, but due to radio problems, the lieutenant was unable to comply until just before the action ended at 6:30 p.m.

The battalion had suffered two soldiers killed and fifty-four wounded in the fight. An investigation of the incident later revealed that no American troops were injured by friendly fire and that the majority of soldiers requiring medical evacuation suffered from ear damage from enemy rounds hitting their tracks. The damage to the 273rd PLAF Regiment was much greater, however; the Iron Rangers killed sixty-three of its soldiers.[125]

By the end of Operation Kentucky Cougar, the battalion had killed over 150 VC and NVA troops in some of the heaviest fighting of the year. These engagements were a major setback to the 9th Division and helped prevent its anticipated attacks on An Loc and Quan Loi, but they also cost the battalion four dead, sixty-two wounded, and eight APCs.[126] The enemy, however, claimed that the Iron Rangers had suffered a great deal more than that. In a radio broadcast by "Hanoi Hanna," the North Vietnamese stated that C Company had been entirely wiped out. Naturally, the troops of C Company thought this a "shameful bit of yellow journalism," and Staff Sergeant Sam Saliba penned a tune in reply, titled "Bandito Charlie's Here to Stay." Sung to the tune of "The Ballad of the Green Berets," some of the troops sang it over the company frequency in hopes that the VC were listening and would know that the "banditos" were still alive and well.[127]

On September 20, the 1st Cavalry Division terminated Operation Kentucky Cougar, and that night, the Iron Rangers rolled south on Highway 13 in a cold, soaking rain. As the Iron Rangers approached the north gate of Lai Khe after a long, wearisome road march, troops on the lead tracks heard band music. Then they spotted the new division commander, Major General Albert E. Milloy, the division staff, and the Big Red One band standing at the gates. Milloy and his staff were there to welcome the Iron Rangers home.[128] After their arrival, the troops found barbecued chicken, steaks, potato salad, and plenty of other food waiting for them.

The following day, Lieutenant Colonel David C. Martin, assumed command of the 1st Battalion from Cassels. Martin would be in command for only a week before the Iron Rangers rolled to the field again.

Operation Iron Danger
September 27, 1969-January 1, 1970

In August and September, division and brigade intelligence officers received evidence that much of the Dong Nai Regiment was moving south out of the Catcher's Mitt area toward Thu Duc and was now strung out between Tân Uyên in the north, and Chanh Luu to the south. The C-61 Local Force Company was reported to be located on the other side of Highway 13 about ten kilometers northwest of Ben Cat. Additionally, a POW from the 101st PAVN Regiment reported that his unit was now in the area of Michelin Rubber Plantation—Boi Loi Woods—western Trapezoid. This concentration of enemy forces would have once sparked speculation of a major attack in the area; however, intelligence from captured POWs and defectors from all three units indicated

that the enemy had no desire to make contact with U.S. forces. Their only objective was to find food. The pacification campaign was working—the VC and NVA forces were starving, but the Big Red One was not going to have any pity on them.

With Operation Iron Danger, Major General Milloy directed the first division-level operation of the year. For subordinate missions, he sent the 1st Brigade after the 101st PAVN Regiment in AO Argonne and the 2nd Brigade after elements of the Quyet Thang Regiment in AO Ardennes. The Iron Brigade was detailed to seek out and destroy a battalion of the Dong Nai Regiment near Bau Bang and the C-61 Local Force Company southwest of there. Colonel Elmer D. Pendleton, commander of the 3rd Brigade, directed Martin's 1st Battalion to find the Dong Nai elements and Mears's 2nd Battalion to attack the C61 Local Force Company.

Consequently, on September 27, Martin rolled the whole 1st Battalion out of Lai Khe and clattered up the Song Be road to seek and destroy elements of the Dong Nai Regiment. Operation Iron Danger was the first time in 1969 that the entire battalion had operated together since the beginning of the year. Every other time, one or more of the subordinate companies had been detailed to other missions when the Iron Rangers took the field.

Over the next month, Colonel Martin's troops searched in vain for the NVA regiment in the Catcher's Mitt, but the enemy was successful in avoiding a fight. The battalion's efforts were then refocused to the Trapezoid, south of the Thi Tinh River on October 22. By the end of the operation, on November 10, the battalion had failed to find the Dong Nai Regiment, but it did locate numerous caches of enemy equipment in both the Catcher's Mitt and the Trapezoid. In one instance, the battalion found enough weapons and equipment to outfit an entire NVA battalion.[129]

While the 1st Battalion was searching for the Dong Nai Regiment, the 2nd Battalion helped open a new FSB, dubbed Dominate, in the Rocket Belt in early October. For the next two months, Mears's troops protected resupply convoys from Lai Khe to FSB Dominate along Route 240. As December drew to a close, the battalion conducted S&D sweeps in the Deadman, the Rocket Belt, and T-Ten stream complex in efforts to mop up remnants of the C-61 Company. But like the 1st Battalion, it was unable to come to solid grips with the enemy. Still, a press release from this operation related the battalion's success against the C-61 Company's logistics:

> Once a formidable enemy, local force soldiers of the Ben Cat District, who have controlled several villages in the area for more than five years, have plummeted in strength to a force whose greatest concern seems to be getting something to eat....The men of this enemy force have been sustaining themselves on roots, leaves, and what little rice they could steal....By blocking all entry to the crop area and preventing local villagers from making "rice

runs" in ox carts to the guerrillas in outlying woods, the 2/16th has virtually starved the enemy into submission. Evidence of this is the increasing numbers of Hoi Chanh from the Ranger's area of operations.[130]

Winter-Spring 1970
November 1969-April 1970
Despite its best efforts in Iron Danger, the Big Red One failed to make significant contact with the enemy. In November 1969, however, MACV once again detected increases in enemy activity in the III and IV CTZs. The G2 section of the II Field Force had also picked up on the activity and determined that it probably heralded the onset of the next winter campaign. Though engagements between American and NVA units were light, the increase manifested itself by the NVA's intensified attacks and harassment of people in hamlets throughout the zone. American intelligence planners discerned that the pacification campaign was working. The initiative in swinging the villagers toward supporting the South Vietnamese government was in the allies' favor, and the enemy was desperately trying to reverse the trend. In terms of any direct military action, enemy tactics continued to be attacks against ARVN installations and avoidance of U.S. units. This was due to the staggering losses inflicted by vast American firepower and the U.S. units' willingness to engage in protracted firefights. The NVA and VC had a great deal less trepidation about fighting most South Vietnamese units.

Operation Toan Thang IV
January 7-February 1970
The 1st Battalion rolled in from Operation Iron Danger on January 4, and Martin was quickly alerted to prepare the Iron Rangers to participate in another mission. This time both battalions of the 16th Infantry were placed under the operational control of the 2nd Brigade to participate in Operation Toan Thang IV in Phuoc Tuy province, southeast of Saigon. The missions in Phuoc Tuy were to destroy NVA/VC units, prevent infiltration of replacements and logistics, and support ARVN pacification efforts in the province. Thus, Martin and Mears moved their battalions southeast to Phuoc Tuy province on January 7.

Martin moved the 1st Battalion to the vicinity of Camp Bearcat, where his men set up squad and platoon ambushes, performed security missions, and helped to construct FSB Dakota. Later in the month, the Iron Rangers joined the 8th Royal Australian Regiment and the 3rd Battalion, 46th ARVN Regional Forces, to secure and sweep the Núi Ba Quan Mountain range in the province. During the sweep, the battalion discovered several cavern complexes that showed signs of recent enemy occupation, but no contact occurred. The troops rendered the caves uninhabitable by drenching the interiors with CS (tear) gas.

The following month, the mixed U.S., Australian, and ARVN force continued its efforts in the dense jungles near Núi Ba Quan just east of Highway 15, and along the Thi Vai River. The riverine operations were particularly successful, oddly combining the mechanized Iron Rangers in cooperation with engineers operating "ski boats." On March 3, Martin was ordered to cease operations and return the 1st Battalion to Di An, where it would stand down for return to the United States.[131]

Vietnam-Era Service of the 3rd Battalion, 16th Infantry
The service of the 3rd Battalion, 16th Infantry, is almost forgotten in light of the combat efforts of its two brother battalions in Vietnam. The activities of the battalion were like most other reserve component infantry battalions during the period. Its monthly armory training focused on preparing the unit for its annual summer camp (ANACDUTRA, or "Annual Active Duty for Training"), generally held at Pine Camp, New York. The unit's 1966 camp was typical of its annual summer training throughout the 1965-70 period.

The battalion attended ANACDUTRA at Pine Camp during the first two weeks of August that year. The training was not onerous, but it was all real training—no beer in coolers, and suchlike. The events consisted of squad, section, and platoon-level Army Training Tests (ATT) for all line companies. Headquarters Company was evaluated on support operations, and the mortar platoons conducted live-fire training. Additionally, selected officers and NCOs staffed two recruit companies and conducted basic combat training for a host of reserve soldiers who had recently enlisted.

There were other events worthy of note for the battalion as well. On November 11, 1966, A Company marched in the annual Veterans' Day parade in Roslindale, Massachusetts, the company's hometown. In April of that year, the entire battalion participated in the posthumous presentation of a Bronze Star medal to the parents of Captain Paul Berthiaume, a battalion officer who had volunteered for active duty and had given his life in Vietnam. A similar ceremony was held later for Specialist Fourth Class David M. Vancellette, who also volunteered for active duty and died in combat.

Not all recognition activities were so somber. For example, in December 1966, Staff Sergeant Paul M. Rugg was recognized as the Reservist of the Year by the Vice Chief of Staff, General Creighton W. Abrams, at a dinner in Worcester.[132]

As the years of the war passed, the battalion partook in a host of other activities, some reflecting the best of times, such as the annual Veterans' Day and Memorial Day events; and some that contemplated the worst of times, like riot control training that could be used on college campuses. Regardless, the officers and men of the 3rd Battalion also served their country during the Vietnam War. Some enlisted to get extra money, others to avoid the draft, and still others put on the uniform merely because of the long-standing tradition of citizen-soldiery in the old Northeast. Whatever the reason, all served knowing that they too were subject to the call to arms should the nation require it.

Operation Keystone Bluejay
March 3-April 4, 1970

The 1st Infantry Division's plan to return to Fort Riley was dubbed Operation Keystone Bluejay and actually began on December 15, 1969, but the two battalions of the 16th Infantry did not begin stand down from operations until early March. The return of the Big Red One to the United States would not be the same as in the two previous wars. Unlike World Wars I and II, the division would not sail into port to be welcomed by brass bands and throngs of patriotic citizens waving American flags at the dockside as the soldiers strolled down the gangplank. No, this time the personnel of the 1st Infantry Division would be shipped home as individuals or reassigned to other units if they had not completed one year's service in Vietnam. By March 16, both battalions of the 16th Infantry were void of soldiers. Only the battalion records and colors remained, and those were deposited with the Headquarters, 1st Infantry Division, for shipment to Fort Riley. The hot war interlude in the Cold War was over; the Vietnam experience for the 16th Infantry Regiment ended almost without notice.[133]

Vietnam was a mixed blessing for the soldiers of the 16th Infantry. Both battalions performed up to the standards expected by the Big Red One and its history. But, depending on when one served there, Ranger veterans of that war have mixed feelings about its conduct and their role in it. Today, those who served in the early stages of the war from 1965 to 1968 believe that they were winning and that Vietnam was a "just war," fought for just reasons. Those who served afterward seem to have less belief in those notions. Still, members of both battalions added laurels to the regimental history, regardless of when they were in Vietnam, and most seem to have felt themselves fortunate to have served in the 16th Infantry and the Big Red One. Though both units, no doubt, had some disciplinary and drug problems, the high expectations of the officers and NCOs seem to have contributed to a lower incidence of discipline problems overall than most U.S. Army units' experiences in the latter stages of the war. At least that is the belief of those Rangers who served in the battalions at that time.

As in past wars, the performance of the two 16th Infantry battalions was solidly professional. In a war where success was measured by numbers, rather than ground gained, both battalions were successful. For example, from October 1965 until March 1970, the 1st Battalion inflicted at least 1,284 KIA on enemy units. The battalion also captured 330 NVA and VC soldiers, 1,571 AK-47 or SKS rifles, and almost two million pounds of rice. Given the 2nd Battalion's longer period of service, that battalion could claim comparable statistics, if not even more successes.

But the Rangers paid a price as well. The 1st Battalion suffered 328 officers and men killed in Vietnam, while the 2nd Battalion claims 234 members were killed in action. The 16th Infantry had two Medal of Honor winners, one from each battalion, and both were awarded posthumously. Hundreds of Rangers earned the Distinguished Service Cross and the Silver and Bronze Star medals. Still, in their own way, all who served in this controversial war were, and are, heroes, if for only answering their country's call, when others purposely chose to avoid service.

Half a world away, there came another call, one that would refocus the attentions of the Big Red One and the battalions of the 16th Infantry. Its new mission would require the regiment to face a former ally, the Soviet Union, across the fortified borders of a divided Germany. The division's attention would have to shift to a Eurocentric focus and require it to develop a rapid deployment capability and master the techniques of mobile warfare. This mission would be the 1st Infantry Division's focal point, and that of the 16th Infantry, for the next twenty years.

Troops of the 1-16 at Nürnberg Airport, 1970

Chapter Eleven
From the Heartland to Deutschland

We are proud of your work

General Carl E. Vuono, June 1989

On the morning of April 15, 1970, Major General Robert R. Linvill stood on a reviewing stand that had been erected on the Infantry Parade field at Camp Forsyth, Kansas, a World War II-era subpost of Fort Riley. He gazed down on a huge, grassy field made lush and green by winter snows and more recent spring rains. As a venue for polo matches from the 1920s through the 1940s, the same field had once resounded to the crack of mallets on small wooden balls and the thunder of galloping horses. It had long since been converted to a parade ground, with the old polo club on the west end reconfigured as an officers club. The field's east end sported rows of so-called splinter barracks, constructed during World War II and housing an entire brigade of troops. Drawn up before Linvill in parade formation was the 24th Infantry Division (Mechanized), nicknamed the "Victory" division, the unit he commanded.

It was a colorful tableau, the division's olive-green ranks contrasting with the field's bright green grass, all set against brown-gray backdrop of the distant Flint Hills. Interspersed among the ranks were unit guidons and flags—blue, red, yellow, orange, and green—snapping smartly in the cool prairie breeze. Also on hand was a crowd of spectators made up of military dignitaries, politicians, civilians, and the wives and children of the soldiers. They had all come to witness the transformation of the 24th Infantry Division into the "Big Red One."

In 1968, most of the Victory division had been moved from Germany to Fort Riley after the Big Red One had vacated the post to go to Vietnam. Its 3rd Brigade, however, had remained in Germany as part of the U.S. Army Europe (USAREUR). Because of this dual-based configuration and its recent return from Germany, the 24th Division was the natural candidate to be the rapid deployment force to USAREUR, a mission the Big Red One would now assume.

On this day, the 24th Division was to be reflagged as the 1st Infantry Division (Mechanized), ushering in a new era and new missions for the army's premier division. Standing in the formation at Camp Forsyth was the 1st Battalion, 19th Infantry, commanded by Lieutenant Colonel Louis J. Pistone. Upon the reflagging of the 1st Division, this battalion would become the 2nd Battalion, 16th Infantry. Two days later and half a world away, the 3rd Brigade, 24th Division, stationed at Sheridan Kaserne in Augsburg, Germany, was redesignated the 3rd Brigade of the Big Red One. At the same time, the 1st Battalion, 21st Infantry, commanded by Lieutenant Colonel David P. Thoreson, was reflagged as the 1st Battalion, 16th Infantry, and stationed at Sheridan Kaserne.[1]

These actions in mid-April 1970, which established the course of the 1st Division's future for the next twenty years, were in part driven by growing concerns that America's deepening involvement in the Vietnam War came at the expense of Western European security. With the bulk of the U.S. Army tied down in Southeast Asia, and therefore unable to respond quickly and massively to other crises, Western Europe had become increasingly vulnerable to the threat of Soviet aggression. The split-stationing of the 1st Division, a new focus on developing more efficient methods of rapidly reinforcing NATO units in Germany, and the changes in U.S. Army doctrine to incorporate new ideas about mobile warfare and the use of armored and mechanized forces, put the battalions of the 16th Infantry in the anticipated forefront of what many believed would be the next great European war.

In 1970, the U.S. Army Europe still consisted of the Seventh Army, the V and VII Corps, and four divisions—two armored and two mechanized. The Seventh Army's sector of the inter-German border was not significantly changed from 1955 when the 1st Division returned to the United States. The American zone extended from Kassel in the north down to the Austrian border. The V Corps was responsible for the Fulda Gap-Cheb area, the most likely avenues of approach for an invading Soviet army. The VII Corps, positioned in the more mountainous region of Bavaria, held a sector extending roughly from Nürnberg to Austria. The 3rd Brigade's station at Augsburg placed that unit firmly under the control of the VII Corps and, at least initially, USAREUR's war plans called for the remainder of the 1st Infantry Division to be employed in that sector as well. It was for this role that the troops of the 16th Infantry would prepare on yearly basis, until 1990.

From 1970 to 1990, most activities of the 16th Infantry's Regular Army battalions were linked to two key training events. Exercise Reforger (Return of Forces to Germany), conducted in 1969, would become the primary annual training event for the 1st Infantry Division, and the U.S. Army in Europe, during this period. Beginning in 1982, rotations to the National Training Center (NTC) at Fort Irwin, California, became the second major training event involving the 1st Infantry Division units (and, indeed, all Continental United States [CONUS] heavy combat arms units).

Generally speaking, most other training revolved around these two exercises. But the battalions of the 16th Infantry participated in numerous other events as well. These included special training situations, such as assistance to the National Guard and ROTC; "adventure training"; reorganizations and activations under the ineffective and detrimental U.S. Army Regimental System; the COHORT unit manning experiments; and plain, old-fashioned sporting and social events.

Reforger

The Reforger idea was not a new concept in 1969, when it was first conducted. Indeed, units of the 16th Infantry had participated in several variations of NATO deployment exercises in the 1950s and '60s, including Gyroscope and Long Thrust. However, Reforger differed from other exercises in that it was designed to rapidly reinforce NATO forces with CONUS-based units, not just rotationally replace units scheduled to return to the United States. The deploying units would draw prepositioned equipment, then exercise one of USAREUR's several operation plans in a force-on-force maneuver, usually involving several Allied units. The units would then clean up and turn in the European-based equipment and return home. All this was aimed at impressing on the Warsaw Pact (as well as NATO nations) that the United States was committed to defending Europe and could do so rapidly.

The first Reforger was conducted in January and February 1969 by the 24th Infantry Division. The participation of the 24th Infantry Division ensured that the Army's Fort Riley-based division would be the primary Reforger unit for the next eight years. The first exercise that the Big Red One participated in was actually the second Reforger, held in November 1970. From the time it was reflagged at Fort Riley in April until it departed Forbes Field in Topeka, all efforts of the division were concentrated on the deployment, the follow-on maneuver phase (designated Certain Thrust), and the redeployment to Kansas.

Typically, the 1st Infantry Division deployed on Reforger during the autumn, and by the end of its second deployment (Reforger III, October 1971), the division had worked out most of the problems associated with getting to Germany, drawing equipment, and preparing for operations. The army added a new twist for Reforger IV, however, when the deployment was skipped during the fall of 1972 and pushed back to the winter of 1973. The deployment went well and the weather was no hindrance to soldiers used to operating on the frigid Kansas prairies.

For Reforger V it was back to an autumn deployment, but in the middle of the operation, the 1973 Yom Kippur War broke out, causing concern at USAREUR that the conflict might ignite a larger war between NATO and the Warsaw Pact. Even as

USAREUR units went on high alert and deployed to the general defense positions, the 1st Infantry Division did not skip a beat. In the event that war did break out, the Big Red One would be needed in Germany, so it continued to focus on the upcoming mission. Lieutenant General (Ret.) Ronald L. Watts, then commanding the 2nd Battalion, 16th Infantry, recalled:

> In those days, we were going to Reforger every year. That was before they started rotating it around to other units, so the 1st Division was the Reforger division. And so you really trained all year, not just for the Reforger deployment, but [also] for the mission in Germany…We did not have METLs [Mission Task Lists] and things like in those days, but we had something pretty close to it, I guess, because we were focused on our wartime mission.…I don't believe [the October 1973 Yom Kippur War] had any impact on us. Obviously we were following it, but I don't believe it had any impact [on the 1st Infantry Division's ability to deploy and participate in Reforger 73].[2]

This focus on the division's primary mission was a trademark of the Big Red One for twenty years. Though the 2nd Battalion, and later the 5th Battalion, made numerous Reforger deployments, one example will suffice to describe the experiences of a generation of 16th Infantry soldiers who participated in the massive effort to practice reinforcing U.S. ground forces in Germany between 1970 and 1990. The 2nd Battalion's participation in Reforger 86 is at once a good example of the typical Reforger and, at the same time, an illustration of how the U.S. Army makes do when things do not go as planned.

In 1986, the 2nd Battalion was under the command of Lieutenant Colonel Michael V. Harper. For that year's Reforger, the battalion, as well as the rest of the Big Red One was to deploy to Germany in January. Winter Reforgers were becoming more prevalent by this time because the U.S. Army wanted to reduce maneuver damage to the German countryside. By January, German farmers would have already harvested their crops, and their fields would be frozen hard from winter temperatures. All of this combined to reduce the amount of maneuver damage and, more importantly, the amount of money Uncle Sam would pay the German farmers in compensation for destroyed crops.

Like other Reforgers, the division went through a series of train-up exercises (Manhattan and Casus Belli) to prepare the units for the deployment and follow-on exercise. To support the division's overall plan, Harper also set up myriad other training events to prepare the 2nd Battalion for the trip. These events included the standard medical checks, preparation of wills, new dogtags, and the like. Also included were USAREUR drivers training courses, and practice vehicle draws set up in the battalion's motor pool to simulate the draw of POMCUS (Prepositioning of Material from the Continental United States) equipment at a Combat Equipment Company (CEC) site. After several months of preparatory training, conducted coincidentally with EIB testing, FTXs, and other scheduled events, the troops of the 2nd Battalion processed through Craig Gym on Custer Hill in early January, boarded busses, and traveled to Forbes Field in Topeka. There, the battalion boarded several Air Force C-141 Starlifter cargo planes and took off for Germany.

The flight was long and boring. The soldiers were treated to the joys of "troop seats," a red nylon fold-down bench that ran the length of the aircraft on each side, and two rows of seats running down the plane's middle. Troops placed their rucksacks under the seat and were seated facing each other, knee to knee. The restroom was at the front of the aircraft, so anyone needing to use it in flight had to bull his way through a gauntlet of legs or literally walk above the center rows using the mesh seat backs to step on as he precariously tightroped his way forward. Those seated in the rear of the aircraft had the additional delight of experiencing the drafts of air, bitterly cold over the Atlantic at ten thousand feet in January, blowing in through the closed but inadequately sealed cargo doors.

After what seemed like an eternity, the planes finally landed in the Azores and the troops debarked. While air force ground crews refueled the aircraft for the next leg, the Rangers were herded into an old roller skating rink, where they stretched their legs, "took a whiz," and received some welcomed hot chocolate. Some two hours later, the men reboarded the C-141s and were soon winging their way to Ramstein Air Base, where the planes landed the next day.

From Ramstein, the battalion was bussed to the CEC site near Neureut, where the battalion's advance party was already preparing hand receipts for the draw. The draw process began almost immediately. In the next twenty hours, over two hundred vehicles, machine guns, mortars, tents, field kitchens, and numerous other items were issued. Because of the battalion's training back at Fort Riley, the draw went smoothly. As the draw neared completion, the battalion quartering party, under the battalion XO, Major Edward Buckley and Command Sergeant Major Gilbert Wrangel, departed for the battalion's sector of the 1st Division assembly area east of Germersheim. The rest of the battalion departed the next day in the predawn darkness to avoid interfering with German civilian traffic.

In a large wooded part of the initial assembly area, the battalion set up defensive positions and simulated the draw of ammunition from nearby ammunition supply points hidden in the German forest. Meanwhile, cooks broke out their kitchen trailers and fired up their stoves to ensure their proper functioning. Other soldiers went through function checks to ensure their equipment was in proper working order. Because of cold, wet weather, heaters were especially well examined. Unfixable equipment was returned to the CEC site, and new items issued if available. After several days of acclimating itself in the woods, the battalion received orders to move to the maneuver box.

The following evening, the battalion line companies, less their wheeled vehicles, moved to a nearby railhead and spent most of what proved to be a cold drizzly night loading their M-113 APCs and other tracked vehicles on rail cars for the trip east. The Rangers pitched in enthusiastically, anxious to get on with the maneuver. The troops accomplished all tasks efficiently and without injury, despite the dangers of light mist and ice. Before first light, the train pulled away, leaving the battalion's wheeled vehicles to road march to the Tactical Assembly Area (TAA).

The route to the battalion's initial TAA followed Autobahn 6 from just south of Heidelberg to Nürnberg, then turned north on Autobahn 9 for twenty kilometers, before turning onto a secondary road heading east for seventy kilometers to Wernberg. The TAA was located just east of a little German village called Oberkoblitz, only twenty kilometers from the Czechoslovakian border. The task was to get there in one piece—a major challenge, given the miserable weather conditions.

At first light, the battalion's wheeled vehicles departed in two convoys, the first under the command of Captain Steve Davis, the HHC commander, and the second under the battalion S4. The journey was harrowing and long, taking twenty hours to complete. The convoys made several halts en route to refuel vehicles and allow soldiers to relieve themselves. The refuel points were run by Bundeswehr (German army) support units using five-gallon cans. The small cans ensured a long refueling process which, in the circumstances of the cold, rainy weather, did not endear the Bundeswehr troops to the Rangers.

After refueling at Crailsheim, the two convoys drove over the Mittelfranken, a large, high ridge line between Ansbach and Nürnberg. As the vehicles approached the summit, the rain turned to snow and the roads became slick. About 4:00 p.m., some twenty minutes after reaching the top, the weather began to close in. Adding to the difficulties was rush hour traffic near Schwabach. An expensive, silver Mercedes pulled in front of the S4's vehicle and cruised along for several minutes as the convoy descended the Mittelfranken. Suddenly, the German vehicle's taillights came on, and the car slowed considerably, causing the S4's driver, Specialist Fourth Class Tim Mathis, to gently tap his brake pedal. Unfortunately, the Mercedes was slowing so fast that Mathis had to fully apply the brakes, which then caused the heavily laden quarter-ton trailer to pull the tail of the jeep around so that, within seconds, the vehicle was spinning around in circles on the icy autobahn, headed down the slope of the highway. Each time the vehicle swung around, Mathis saw the battalion's five-ton wrecker bearing down on them, unable to move to the next lane because of the heavy civilian traffic. Additionally, the wide-eyed mechanic driving the wrecker could not fully apply his brakes, for fear that a chain reaction smash-up would ensue. A disaster was in the making.

Fortunately, each time the vehicle swung around, the weight of the trailer pulled the jeep slightly to the right, so that after the fourth or fifth rotation, the jeep struck the gravel shoulder, though pointed the wrong way. There it immediately stopped with the trailer lined up perfectly behind. The wrecker rushed by, just missing the jeep, followed by the rest of the convoy, which pulled over to the right shoulder five hundred meters down the highway. Because of the rush hour traffic, nearly thirty minutes passed before Mathis got the jeep safely turned around and before the convoy was rolling again.

The convoy, already slowed by the weather, was now farther behind schedule. The convoy continued without incident through Nürnberg, then turned off onto the secondary road to Wernberg just after dark. The battalion was negotiating the Frankische Alb, another major ridge line, just as the weather worsened and falling snow slowed the convoy to a crawl.

Nearing one of the few intersections on the seventy-kilometer stretch of road, the convoy commander spotted hundreds of headlights and flashing yellow "whoopee" lights that indicated the presence of another convoy coming up on a road to the right. As the head of the Ranger convoy arrived at the intersection, the S4 could see by the bumper numbers that the other convoy was the Wisconsin National Guard's 32nd Infantry Brigade, another Reforger unit. The convoy was not on its assigned route, the convoy commander having turned onto the road to Wernberg only a minute or so before the 2-16 convoy reached the intersection. Had the Rangers not been delayed by the near-accident, their convoy would have arrived at the intersection well before the guardsmen. In the event, they were forced to stop and let the 32nd Brigade pull onto the road ahead.

For the next hour or so, vehicle after vehicle chugged by the waiting Rangers. The guard convoy looked like a gypsy caravan, with little organization. Maintenance trucks, jeeps, wreckers, mess trucks, fuelers—all seemed to be mixed together with no regard for company or section. One could only wonder how long it would take them to unscramble everything when they reached their assembly area.

Finally, at about midnight, the last brigade vehicle passed through the intersection, allowing the 2-16 convoy to continue its journey. At about 2:00 a.m., after driving some forty kilometers, the guard convoy turned off to the north. The Rangers now had the road to themselves, and passed through Oberkoblitz about an hour later. There, the convoy was met by the S4 NCO, Staff Sergeant Randy Messersmith, who led the vehicles to an open field bordered on three sides by tall firs. By this time the snow had stopped and the moon had poked through the clouds enough to bathe the fields and trees with light. It was a winter wonderland—but a cold one. When the snow quit falling, the temperature dropped.

With daybreak, the various vehicles belonging to the line companies were policed up by first sergeants and supply sergeants and sent to company assembly areas located north and east of Oberkoblitz. The battalion's tracked vehicles had made an uneventful train trip to Vilseck, where they were downloaded the day before and driven to the assembly areas. The headquarters vehicles, maintenance, mess, medical, scouts, and mortars moved from the field to an assembly area nearer Oberkoblitz, where Harper had established the battalion headquarters in the fire station.

For the next two days, the Rangers anxiously awaited the start of the exercise. The maneuver box was essentially the area marked by Marktredwitz in the northeast, Bamberg in the northwest, Nürnberg in the southwest, and the Oberpfülzer Wald in the southeast. Opposing the Big Red One for Exercise Certain Sentinel were the 11th ACR and the 1st Armored Division. Both sides champed at the bit, anxious to begin the "war." But it was not to be.

Unfortunately, the weather turned unseasonably warm. The snows began to melt, turning the fields into quagmires. Should tanks and tracks maneuver through them, the troops would spend more time digging them out when they got stuck than conducting the maneuver. More important to the budget planners at USAREUR, the muddy conditions meant extensive damage to farmers' fields and higher maneuver damage costs. The decision was made to modify Exercise Certain Sentinel.

Instead of an actual maneuver, the 1st Infantry Division conducted a "JeepEx." That is, battalion and company commanders moved along the routes of march, conducting their attacks in jeeps representing maneuver units. It was not a very realistic exercise and, needless to say, Harper and the Rangers were disappointed. After coming all the way to Germany to maneuver, the battalion instead spent the next two weeks in soggy assembly areas trying to stay warm and dry, while their commanders drove around the countryside simulating brigade attacks.

The only noteworthy event during the battalion's stay in Oberkoblitz was the visit to one of the companies by a group of Warsaw Pact officers, who were observers to Reforger and allowed by NATO to observe the maneuver. The visit took a humorous turn when the battalion's cooks baked a batch of cookies for the visitors, but some wag thought that Kool-Aid, rather than coffee, would be a good thing to wash them down. The cookies went fast, but nary a soul touched the ice-cold Kool-Aid.

Upon conclusion of the JeepEx, the battalion made a short trip to Hohenfels, the Reforger Redeployment Assembly Area (RAA) for that year. There the troops were assigned heated, open-bay billets, a welcome reprieve from the cold beet fields of Oberkoblitz. The Rangers immediately began the process of cleaning and repairing vehicles for the turn-in at the CEC site and cleaning their own equipment for the rigorous customs inspection that followed. Once through the inspection process, the battalion's home station equipment was packed in Conexes and loaded on trains for the port at Bremerhaven. The POMCUS vehicles and equipment were similarly cleaned, repaired, and loaded for rail shipment back to Neureut. The wheeled vehicles would be convoyed back to the CEC site on the autobahn.

On January 28, while the battalion was at Hohenfels, Harper met with battalion staff and company commanders gathered in the headquarters billets to discuss the RAA activities, the impending turn-in, and activities upon return to Fort Riley. As the commanders and staff seated themselves to start the meeting, Harper entered the room, visibly disturbed. The commander walked up to his place at the table, looked around the room, and announced that the space shuttle *Challenger* had exploded just after take-off and that all seven people on board were undoubtedly killed in the explosion. The people gathered in the room pondered the meaning of that news for a moment, and then began a serious, but subdued, staff meeting.[3]

Within three days, the RAA activities were complete and the battalion journeyed by rail and road back to Neureut for the turn-in. There, Harper directed that the sergeant major and the battalion's NCOs conduct the turn-in without officer involvement. Officers were to get involved only when necessary. In true 16th Infantry fashion, the Ranger NCOs tackled the responsibility with gusto and completed the turn-in without a hitch.

During the turn-in phase, many of the 2-16 soldiers visited German historical sites and shopping areas. In the mountain town of Trier, soldiers bought quality German goods, such as crystal, cuckoo clocks, and music boxes. Other soldiers went to Strasbourg, France.

With the turn-in complete, the battalion was bussed back to Ramstein in February, where the troops boarded aircraft for the trip home. This time, however, the Rangers drew a Boeing 747 instead of a C-141. In contrast to the C-141 flight to Germany, the trip home was relatively comfortable and warm. The plane landed at Forbes about 1:00 a.m., and by 3:00 a.m. the troops arrived back at Craig Gym, where they claimed their A and B bags, threw them over their shoulders and headed for the orderly room. Once all weapons and equipment was accounted for, Harper released the battalion. Reforger 86 was history.

Of course, any good soldier knows that exercises like Reforger do not just happen. A great deal of planning, coordination, and training occurs before a unit actually deploys. And so it was for the 1st Infantry Division. Over the twenty plus years that the Big Red One participated in various Reforger deployments, its division staff developed a number of documents and exercises to train and prepare subordinate units and staffs to rapidly and efficiently deploy to Germany to counter the Soviet threat.

A 1st Infantry Division Reforger exercise was driven by several documents that specified how the deployment, reception, movement to forward assembly areas (FAA), and maneuver was to be executed. The first of these documents was a two-inch-thick book that eventually evolved into something affectionately called "FRED," the Fort Riley Emergency Deployment plan. This publication outlined in great detail how the division would execute rail, air, and sea deployments from Fort Riley, and its contents was ingrained in most 1st Division soldiers, especially staff personnel.

As part of the training process to exercise the FRED, division units participated in several unannounced Emergency Deployment Readiness Exercises (EDRE) annually. Typically, a unit (normally one battalion) called out for an EDRE was alerted about 3:00 a.m. and directed to prepare for deployment. The exercise could be a deployment that actually sent a unit overseas, but usually it was a modified version, where the unit remained on post. The modified version usually tasked each company in the selected unit to perform some aspect of a full-up EDRE to exercise all areas of the FRED. These usually included a full equipment pack-out in Conex containers, a Preparation for Overseas Movement (POM) personnel processing station, movement of vehicles to the Camp Funston railhead and rail loading them onto flatcars, and perhaps movement of personnel to a range to draw ammunition and test fire individual and crew-served weapons. In some instances, elements would actually bus to Forbes Field, load up, and take a flight in a C-141, then return to Forbes.

Rail and air load training were frequent Fort Riley training events, and the Rangers, like most Fort Riley units, became proficient in these tasks. In preparation for Reforger, units also performed German rail-loading procedures, as the Deutsches Bundesbahn (the German national railroad) required a different tie-down process than that practiced in the U.S.

The capstone training event in preparation for Reforger was Operation Manhattan. This operation started out as a long road march exercise for training drivers and leaders to conduct convoy procedures over long distances. Manhattan eventually evolved to include a practice POMCUS draw in unit motor pools, POMs, rail and air load exercises, and a 120-mile road march east along I-70, south through Council Grove, west to Herrington, and back to the post.

To train the division's subordinate staffs in controlling the reception, deployment to forward assembly areas, and conduct of the initial combat operations, the division staff developed Exercise Casus Belli. This exercise, essentially a CPX, was conducted predominantly in Long Gymnasium on Custer Hill. In its early form, the exercise was conducted on large 1:50,000 map boards depicting that year's maneuver box in Germany and utilized unit counters moved around by battalion players. Meanwhile, the battalion staffs set up in cubicles that served as Tactical Operations Centers (TOC) and were hooked up to their various attachments and higher headquarters with field phones. In later iterations of the exercise, the battalion, brigade, and division TOCs set up in the field, and the tactical play was controlled by computers.

The foregoing details describe most of the processes and training that the 2nd Battalion, and later the 5th Battalion, had to go through to participate in Reforger exercises in Germany. The 1st Battalion, stationed with the 3rd Brigade (redesignated "1st Infantry Division [Forward]" in 1975), generally participated in only the maneuver phase of Reforger. The remainder of its training year was similar to the 16th Infantry Regiment's experiences when it was stationed in Germany in the late 1940s and early 1950s.

1st Battalion, 16th Infantry
Iron Rangers
1970-1990

Except for Reforgers, the primary training events for the 1st Battalion in the 1970s and 1980s were range firing at Grafenwöhr ("Graf"), maneuver training and ARTEP (Army Readiness and Training Evaluation Program, formerly the "Army Training Test") evaluations, and the not-too-popular, and all-too-frequent, "no notice" alerts.

Training at Grafenwöhr had changed a great deal since the regiment's last trip there in 1955. Whereas Graf was then both a range and maneuver complex, by the 1970s the caliber, range, and lethality of the army's weapons had increased to the point where Graf had become essentially, though not entirely, a huge range complex. A visit to Graf to shoot in the 1950s entailed range-firing of stationary small arms, machine gun, 60mm and 81mm mortars, and perhaps recoilless rifles. By the 1970s, a Graf rotation included visits to ranges for small arms, machine guns, track-mounted machine guns, 81mm and 4.2-inch mortars, Dragon antitank guided missiles (ATGM), and TOW ATGM. If an attached tank company went, planning included ranges for those weapon systems as well. Activity on the ranges included mounted, stationary, and moving target firing exercises, as well as mechanized infantry squad and platoon live-fire drills, where rapid dismounting and engagement of targets was part of the training.

A typical live-fire training rotation for the 1st Battalion took place at Graf in the spring of 1985. In April of that year, the battalion moved from Hohenfels, where it had just completed battalion-level ARTEP evaluations, and traveled to Graf to conduct a live-fire maneuver exercise. All the battalion's weapons systems were fired on the various ranges that ring the Graf range complex. The training also included live firing the battalion's TOW missile launchers and a rehearsal for a larger brigade exercise to take place in May.

That month, the 1st Infantry Division (Forward) conducted a brigade-level live-fire exercise at Range 301. This exercise was a little out of the ordinary in that it incorporated live air strikes by Air Force A-10s and AH-1 Cobra attack helicopters.[4]

Live-fire exercises of this sort tended to be the capstone event to a series of maneuver training exercises. The 1st Battalion's maneuver training generally consisted of three kinds: small-unit maneuver at the local training area (LTA), company- and battalion-level maneuver at Hohenfels, and large-scale maneuvers in the German countryside.

The most common form of maneuver training for the Iron Rangers was conducted at the 1st Infantry Division (Forward) LTA at Muensingen. The training at Muensingen was generally conducted at the company level or below and the maneuver space was large enough for company commanders to plan and execute squad-, platoon-, and company-level exercises.

The training that resulted in the brigade live fire at Graf in the spring of 1985 began with platoon-level ARTEPs at Muensingen that February. In extremely cold weather, each infantry platoon conducted defense, hasty attack, and deliberate attack missions. Engineer assets were also incorporated into the training to enhance the battalion's obstacle-breaching operations. The final exercise was a dismounted night attack against an entrenched opposing force (OPFOR).[5]

The next step in the maneuver training cycle was a rotation to the maneuver center at Hohenfels the following month for graded ARTEPs. Like a trip to Graf, a visit to Hohenfels was not accomplished by a quick drive on the autobahn. It involved complicated planning for railcars, convoy clearance, coordination for billets, ammunition, and a host of other minute details. Once the battalion arrived at Hohenfels, it typically signed for hard billets for two or three days before deploying to the field.

Both of the 16th Infantry battalions deployed to Hohenfels that March to be evaluated on ARTEP missions. Each battalion was evaluated on road marches, response to ambushes, attack missions, defense missions, and counterattacks. Apparently, the 1st Battalion did well on the ARTEP evaluations, for it went on to participate in the live-fire exercises at Graf that spring, as did the 4th Battalion.

The maneuver training cycle for the 1st Battalion in February and March 1989 was similar to the 1985 effort, with one major difference. When the 1st Battalion completed its training at the LTA, it went into the maneuver box at Hohenfels to take on the OPFOR at the new Combat Maneuver Training Center (CMTC), recently established at Hohenfels. The U.S. Army Europe's version of the NTC, the CMTC was a rigorous six-day exercise that taxed all aspects of the battalion's combat and combat support systems. The Iron Ranger battalion was the first USAREUR unit tested at the new facility, and was followed by the 4th Battalion.[6]

The last form of maneuver training conducted by the 1st Battalion was the most fun for the small-unit leaders and soldiers. These were the large-scale maneuvers conducted on the German countryside, such as Reforger and Harvest Trek. The units of the 1st Infantry Division (Forward) typically alternated years between being a player unit and running the Joint Visitors Bureau (JVB) for dignitaries visiting the maneuver area.

The first Reforger in which the Iron Rangers participated was Reforger II in November 1970. Dubbed Exercise Certain Thrust, the battalion, and the 3rd Brigade, joined the rest of the Big Red One for the maneuver phase of the event. From 1970 to 1983, this was the standard operating procedure for the 1st Division's participation in the Reforger maneuver exercise. Up to that point, the VII Corps wartime OPLANS (Operation Plans) had the 1st Infantry Division (Forward) forming a part of the rest of the Big Red One for every planned contingency. But increasingly, the brigade and its subordinate battalions were given missions that did not envision them operating with the parent division in wartime. Gradually, Oplans were changed to the point that the 1st ID(F) shared the name of the 1st Division, but would not operate with the parent unit in wartime. It literally functioned as a separate formation. This separation of the two 1st Division components evolved into other non-maneuver missions for the 1st Infantry Division (Forward) during some subsequent Reforgers. The most common of these missions was the operation of the USAREUR Joint Visitors Bureau.

The January 1986 Certain Sentinel exercise marked the first time the Iron Rangers formed the JVB. That year, the 1st Battalion was tasked to operate the JVB at Herzo Base, north of Nürnberg, for Reforger 86. As the JVB support unit, the Iron Rangers were responsible for preparing itineraries for dignitaries, coordinating the latter's visits with player units, and providing escorts for visitors. The dignitaries that year included numerous general officers, political leaders from several NATO nations, and even Warsaw Pact officers sent over as observers. The battalion performed this duty with such professionalism that General Glenn K. Otis, USAREUR commander, remarked that the battalion's JVB operation was the "best I have ever seen at a Reforger."[7]

During the following year's Reforger, the battalion stayed in garrison while its officers served as umpires for the exercise. In 1988, however, the battalion participated as a maneuver unit in Exercise Certain Challenge, the largest Reforger ever conducted. Over 103,000 American, 16,500 German, and 5,100 Canadian soldiers participated. The Big Red One from Fort Riley also joined in, but did not operate with the 1st Infantry Division (Forward) for the exercise.

In addition to rotations to Graf and Hohenfels and participation in Reforger exercises, the Iron Rangers participated in various other training events. For example, in February 1976, A Company was airlifted to Berlin to conduct "combat in the cities" training at the city's Military Operations in Urban Terrain (MOUT). Departing on February 10, the company spent two days climbing through windows and crawling through sewer lines in 3rd Battalion's "Doughboy City," a modern MOUT site built by the U.S. Army to simulate combat in Berlin.[8]

Another example of the variety of training conducted by 1st Battalion occurred on April 21, 1986. That day, C Company conducted a unique air assault training exercise. Without prior notice, the company was ordered to aerially insert into a target area, locate an enemy position, assault it, and extract a friendly POW held captive there. The troops were given only two and one-half hours to secure their weapons and field gear, conduct rehearsals, and load on CH-47 Chinook helicopters for the flight into the landing zone. Despite the lack of preparation time, the company executed the mission with few difficulties.[9]

In October 1987, about 200 Iron Rangers made up part of the 540-man contingent from the 1st Infantry Division (Forward) that joined Colonel Robert W. Higgins for Aferdou 87. This was a heavy brigade command post exercise conducted near Errchidia, Morocco, with the Moroccan Army. While the CPX was taking place with the headquarters elements, troops of the 1st Battalion ran several joint small-arms ranges with Moroccan Army soldiers.[10]

Given the Cold War and the positioning of Warsaw Pact forces right across the inter-German and Czechoslovakian borders, security was a major part of everyday life for USAREUR soldiers. Hence, like all combat arms battalions, the Iron Rangers performed guard duties at their Böblingen kaserne. They were also detailed to provide guard forces for other locations from time to time, such as the materiel depot at Miesau.

In November 1986, the Iron Rangers were chosen to provide the security force for a major ceremony at the EUCOM headquarters at Patch Barracks in Stuttgart. The increase of security was deemed necessary due to the high number of dignitaries attending the retirement ceremonies for the EUCOM deputy commander, General Richard L. Lawson. Such a gathering made a superb target for the notorious Red Brigades, a terrorist organization active in Germany at that time).[11]

In addition to guard duties, no soldier who served in a combat arms unit in Germany from 1948 to 1990 will ever forget the 3:00 a.m. sirens that signaled an alert. Rolling out of a nice warm bed in the dark, pulling on fatigues and battle gear, and tramping through the cold morning fog to the motor pool while lugging a .50-caliber machine gun over one's shoulder was on no soldier's list of fun things to do. Yet month after month, American soldiers consistently performed that task during the Cold War period.

Training and security details were not the only activities that kept the Iron Rangers busy in the 1970s and 80s. There were also other events, such as the restationing of the 3rd Brigade, sports, ceremonies, and adventure training, that occupied their time. Troops also had the opportunity to participate in several trips to historical places to maintain the battalion ties with the regimental history and the Big Red One.

The 3rd Brigade stay in Augsburg was short because of the selection of Munich as the site for the 1972 summer Olympic Games. To assist the German government in freeing up space in that city to support the games, the U.S. Army agreed to consolidate much of its Army Security Agency assets in Augsburg. This plan required most of the 3rd Brigade to move out of Sheridan Kaserne and restation its subordinate units in Göppingen and Böblingen. The Iron Rangers arrived at their new post, Panzer Kaserne, in Böblingen in April 1972, which became their home for the next twenty-two years.

Böblingen was the birthplace for another Iron Ranger tradition, the "Panzer Bowl." The idea behind the Panzer Bowl was generated in the Keller Bar of the Panzer Kaserne's officer's club in the late summer of 1976. Apparently several Iron Ranger officers antagonized a number of men from the 4th Battalion, 73rd Armor, in a boisterous argument over the "personal habits and preferences" of armor officers. To calm the two most vocal antagonists, Captain Greg Vuksich (1-16) and Major Dave Riggs (4-73), the Iron Ranger XO, Major Neal "Big Red" Seibert, suggested that the dispute be resolved by a mass duel—a flag football game between the officers of the two battalions. Hands were shaken and the Panzer Bowl was born.

The two sides agreed that the game would, when possible, be played on Thanksgiving Day so that the troops and families of both sides could attend. The two teams immediately set to work with the zeal of high school football players. On the Iron Ranger team, Captain Pat McCarron was selected to be the coach. Captains Vuksich and Warren Wilson were picked to be the defensive and offensive team captains, respectively. This leadership team strove to achieve victory against the tankers.

On both sides, wives and sweethearts volunteered to be cheerleaders. The "disinterested" armor and infantry officers of the 1st Infantry Division (Forward) staff were tasked to referee the game. The two battalions even lit bonfires, organized team breakfasts and parades with floats and bands, and marched around the Kaserne to drum up excitement and support for their teams.

Finally, the day of the first Panzer Bowl arrived on Thanksgiving Day 1976. It was a typically cold, wet, autumn day in Bavaria. The drizzle turned the field into a muddy morass, but both sides stuck gamely to their guns in the fierce gridiron struggle. Ultimately, the Iron Rangers were victorious, 12-6. A ceremony followed the game, at which Brigadier General John C. Faith, the 1st Infantry Division (Forward) commander, presented a trophy to the winners—a football-shaped coconut mounted on a scrap metal stand!

This first game set the standard for all following Panzer Bowls. Whichever side won, grunts or tankers, it was a hard-fought and hard-earned victory—there were no blowouts. The tradition lasted fifteen years, the last game being played on November 21, 1990. Ultimately, the Iron Rangers won eleven of the contests, lost three, and tied one. Honors for most games played by one soldier goes to Colonel Steve Wesbrook. In the first two contests, he was the S3 of the 4/73rd. In the 1984 and 1985 games he was the commander of 1/16th. Finally, he participated in two games as the 3rd Brigade commander, appropriately playing on each team for half the game.[12]

Another 1st Battalion tradition that originated at Böblingen was the use of the "Iron Ranger," an M-3 halftrack that had been with various units in Germany since the end of World War II. The vehicle had apparently fallen into the hands of the 1st Battalion upon the latter's reflagging from the 21st Infantry in 1970. The Iron Ranger assumed an almost iconic status for the 16th Infantry, and was seen in many battalion and brigade ceremonies and parades. Typically, the 1st Infantry Division (Forward) commander used the half-track for trooping the line in parades and reviews.

The 1st Battalion also started the "Project Partnership" program while at Böblingen. Project Partnership established a habitual training relationship between the 1st Battalion and the French Army's 5th Dragoons as well as the Bundeswehr's 501st Jäger Battalion. The joint activities conducted among these units included everything from mutual social events such as the annual spring "German-American Friendship Week," to combined field operations during Reforger. In August 1976, in preparation for the autumn Reforger, the Iron Rangers participated in an intensive series of combined exercises with the 501st Jäger Battalion at the Muensingen LTA. The high kill ratios subsequently achieved by the 1st Battalion during Reforger 76 were attributed, in part, to the 501st Jäger Battalion's AT Platoon, which operated with the Iron Rangers that year. In March 1978, the battalion competed with its two partner units in a series of marksmanship and tactical training events.[13]

In addition to joint training, the Project Partnership program was designed to build mutual trust and confidence among soldiers of NATO nations. Another goal was establishing closer ties at the national levels. On July 15, 1985, the Iron Rangers were invited to Wildermuth Kaserne to serve as the honor guard for a Project Partnership ceremony at that German installation. At that ceremony, the honorable Hans Haller, Lord Mayor of Göppingen, received the Project Partnership award for his efforts to maintain positive relations between the American military community and the people of his city. The ceremony was attended by Secretary of the Army John O. Marsh; Lieutenant General Hans-Henning von Sandrart, the Bundeswehr chief of staff; and the USAREUR commander, General Glenn K. Otis.

In addition to developing closer bonds with their Partnership units during the 1970s and '80s, the various Iron Ranger battalion commanders also took steps to preserve the regiment's history and traditions. Given the 1st Battalion's close proximity to battlefields on which the 16th Infantry fought in World War II, it was not unusual for commanders to find time in busy training schedules to take some of their subordinates to visit some of those sites.

In early 1974, for example, the Iron Rangers battalion commander, Lieutenant Colonel John E. Woolley, was directed to send an honor guard to Normandy for the thirtieth anniversary of D-Day. Woolley selected A Company for the job, and two forty-man platoons were provisionally formed for the occasion. The main ceremony was held at Omaha Beach and was attended by General Omar Bradley, who complimented the 16th Infantrymen on their appearance and bearing.

Ten years later, the battalion was once again directed to send a contingent to Normandy for the fortieth anniversary ceremony. This time, Lieutenant Colonel Steve Wesbrook selected E Company to represent the regiment. This ceremony was attended by President Ronald Reagan and French President François Mitterand.[14] The E Company soldiers no doubt relished the chance to stand on the very beaches that figured so prominently in their regiment's history and to serve as the guard of honor for the president.

In July 1988, Lieutenant Colonel Carl Baxley and the officers of the 1st Battalion traveled to Normandy for an officer professional development exercise. Accompanying them was retired Major General Albert H. Smith, honorary colonel of the regiment. The general, it will be recalled, had served as a company commander, battalion staff officer, and regimental S3 in the 16th Infantry during World War II. On this occasion he conducted a series of on-site lectures and presided over discussions with the battalion officers at Omaha Beach, Colleville-sur-Mer, St. Laurent-sur-Mer, and Caumont. The contingent participated in memorial ceremonies at those locations as well.[15]

Though the battalion took time to strengthen ties with its past, most of its attention was given over to the current mission. A major shift in the battalion's capabilities to successfully perform that mission occurred with the turn-in of its M113s in September 1989. That month, the Iron Rangers were issued and trained on the M2A2 Bradley Fighting Vehicles (BFV) at the Vilseck training center.

This increase of combat power came at a time when the probability that it would ever be used against the Soviet threat was drastically reduced. That fall, irresistible pressure for democratic reforms gripped East Germany and other Warsaw Pact nations bordering the West. Soon, rioting and civil unrest broke out, and eastern Europeans began to flagrantly disregard travel restrictions and, in a mass movement, began to flow across the borders, especially when Hungary announced that it would open its borders late that summer. On November 8, 1989, the Berlin Wall, and the evil and oppression it symbolized, figuratively crumbled into dust. Though not apparent at the time, these events were the death knell of the 1st Infantry Division (Forward) and its subordinate elements.

Not entirely aware of that their chief military threat was dissolving, the troops of the 1st Battalion continued to train for war. Starting in 1990, the Bush administration announced troop reductions in Europe to ease the Soviet Union's fears and to realize the supposed "peace dividend" that military downsizing would entail. Soon, rumors began circulating as to which units would be inactivated. Certainly, some believed, the army would not consider reductions of the Big Red One. Many 1st Infantry Division (Forward) soldiers took comfort in that thought and continued to conduct normal activities, certain that the unit's future was secure.

In June 1990, the 1st Battalion again sent a detachment of troops under its commander, Lieutenant Colonel Robert L. Moberly, to participate in another D-Day memorial ceremony. Moberly's group laid wreaths at the 1st Division's memorial at Omaha Beach and at the graves of Brigadier General Teddy Roosevelt and Jimmy Montieth. Moberly also used the opportunity to conduct professional development training by analyzing the actions of Joe Dawson's G Company on D-Day.[16]

Afterward, rumors flew that the 1st Infantry Division (Forward) might be deactivated. The 82nd Airborne Division's rapid deployment to Saudi Arabia after Saddam Hussein's invasion of Kuwait gave some the hope that all plans to inactivate units might be put on hold. But on September 20, 1990, the hammer fell. The 1st Infantry Division (Forward) received orders to stand down. The target date for the 1st Battalion, 16th Infantry, to inactivate was March 1, 1991, just six months in the future.

2nd Battalion, 16th Infantry
Rangers
1970-1990

The 2nd Battalion underwent numerous changes after its return from Vietnam. The 2nd Rangers remained active at Fort Riley for a little over four years until it was inactivated in August 1974. Less than two years later, the battalion was reactivated in a ceremony at Engineer Parade on Custer Hill on May 19, 1976. Under the command of Lieutenant Colonel Henry O. Johnson, the battalion's new life was brief, as it was inactivated again four months later on September 20 and redesignated the 1st Battalion, 28th Infantry.

Over three years would pass before the 2nd Battalion unfurled its colors again, this time in a ceremony at Camp Forsyth in December 1979. This event involved the reflagging of the 2nd Battalion ("Manchus"), 9th Infantry, previously a 2nd Infantry Division unit. It had been returned to the United States the previous year under President Jimmy Carter's efforts to reduce troop strength in Korea. But, on that cold December day, the Manchus became Rangers, though it took time for some of them to make the transition.[17] From that point on, the 2nd Battalion remained active until 1994.

The first major training event for the 2nd Rangers after its relocation to Fort Riley was a mechanized company live-fire demonstration performed for six hundred members of the Kansas American Legion in June 1970. This event was followed by intense training and preparation for the battalion's first Reforger that fall. According to the battalion's Annual Historical Report for 1970, the 2nd Battalion was the first maneuver unit to deploy on Reforger II, draw equipment, cross the LD, close at the RAA at Grafenwöhr, turn in equipment at the CEC site, and arrive back at Fort Riley.[18]

In June and July of 1971, the battalion participated in its first ROTC summer camp support. It was a mission at which the Rangers became adept over the years. In addition to no fewer than eight command post exercises, the battalion also participated that year in several field training exercises that culminated with its deployment on Reforger III, October 1-28.

In 1972, a forty-man platoon of specially selected volunteers from all elements of the battalion participated in a unique event called the "Arkansas River Trace," a rafting trip down that waterway. As conceived by Lieutenant Colonel William M. Hadley, the 2nd Battalion commander, the project would

allow the citizens of Colorado, Kansas, Oklahoma, and Arkansas a first hand opportunity to see the men of the 1st Infantry Division in action: It will provide them with a better understanding as to the Army and the programs the Army is developing to train and challenge the young men of today's generation. This project is designed to test the platoon's ability in all kinds of climatic conditions, contrasting terrain features, and water operations. It also develops stamina and durability...[19]

Two additional goals included training the battalion staff to plan and support long-term, long-distance operations and, in coordination with the Environmental Protection Agency, report the location of environmental hazards, unauthorized dumping of industrial waste, and trash piles along the river.

On April 15, 1972, the ad hoc platoon left Fort Riley and traveled to the headwaters of the Arkansas at Climax, Colorado. The soldiers arrived at Climax to find three feet of snow on the ground. After a day of preparation, acclimatization, and a cold night's sleep, the platoon began the journey by walking along the river, which at that point was little more than a trickle. The first day's hike resulted in sore feet and a few blisters, and there was an encounter with Flip Wilson, a popular comedian and television celebrity. Wilson spotted the troops and came over to chat with them briefly before they continued the trek to Granite, Colorado.

In the following week, the troops hiked to a point about ten miles north of the Royal Gorge, where they aired up three RB-15 rafts, entered the water, and rafted to Pueblo, Colorado. There, the troops linked up with a hometown recruiter from the division's 1st Battalion, 63rd Armor Regiment, and helped his recruiting efforts in the city. The platoon leader also decided to stay over an extra day in Pueblo because it was payday, and the money was burning holes in his men's pockets. This stopover ended the mountain phase of the trek.

The plains phase of the journey took the troops to Wichita via Dodge City. En route, the platoon overnighted in National Guard armories. Crossing into Kansas, the Rangers encountered a group of soldiers from Fort Carson on a similar journey. The Rangers were unimpressed with the so-called Mountain Post soldiers, who struck them as poorly disciplined and unsoldierly in appearance. The Rangers' low opinion of the Fort Carson soldiers was reinforced upon their arrival in Dodge City. It so happened that the Fort Carson group had gotten to the city a day early, staying in the local armory—and leaving the place in a mess. Fearing that the Rangers would do the same, the armory's guard commander initially turned them away. He only relented when the platoon leader offered to clean the armory to the commander's satisfaction.

The plains phase was anything but pleasant. Cold spring rain and, at times, snow, made the going difficult, but the troops pushed on. They soon learned that the Fort Carson troops had quit their effort, which stiffened the Rangers' resolve to complete the journey. The platoon marched from Dodge City through Great Bend, to Lyons, Kansas, where they spent a day helping that community in a civic-action project. The troops then marched on to Wichita.

From Wichita, the Rangers were able to raft the rest of the way to the Mississippi River. At stopovers in Oklahoma, they were feted by the townspeople in Ponca City and Tulsa and greeted warmly at all other stops. They paddled their rafts the entire way from Wichita to Tulsa, where they switched to outboard motors. On May 19, the platoon reached Fort Smith on the Arkansas border and, six days later, entered the waters of the "Father of Rivers." After six weeks and 1,270 miles, the Rangers had at last reached their destination.

The final report detailing the results of the trip gave the effort mixed reviews. While it appears that some good ecological data was provided to the EPA, it was difficult to determine the impact of the effort on recruiting. One positive aspect of the trip was that the Rangers self-discipline was much in evidence. The platoon leader laid down only two rules for the duration of the journey: be present for the morning formation and avoid trouble in off-duty activities. Neither of the rules was broken.

The other positive note of the Arkansas River Trace was the reaction of the civilians whom the men encountered. At the end of the trip, the assessment was that American citizens still liked and admired the U.S. Army. One Arkansas newspaperman was quoted as saying: "It is so good to see a group of Army men, with haircuts and in uniform, completing a long and arduous project like this. All we seem to be reporting on are longhaired radicals destroying some part or another of America without making any contribution at all."[20] The warmth and hospitality showed to the soldiers along the way no doubt reinforced their faith in America.

The year 1973 saw a great deal of activity for the 2nd Battalion. Lieutenant Colonel Ronald L. Watts took command in March and the battalion immediately started an Advanced Individual Training (AIT) cycle, which lasted through May. The battalion began with ninety-three AIT soldiers, twelve of whom had been recent residents of the U.S. Army Retraining Brigade at Camp Funston. The training was tough and demanding and only seventy-four men completed the course.[21]

That year was also highlighted by the battalion's participation in two Reforgers: Reforger IV in January-February, and Reforger V in October-November. In the past, the post-Reforger training period at Fort Riley was one of little activity. One of the few required tasks, typically, was the month-long dispatch of division soldiers to their hometowns to perform recruiting duties, for army in general and the 1st Infantry Division in particular. However, following Reforger V, the division commander, Major General Gordon J. Duquemin, pulled all his battalion and brigade commanders into the division conference room in December and stated that, "This time you're not going to sit back on your laurels and do nothing. This time, I want to see training…." This post-Reforger cycle was not to be a slack period and the CG's directive worked right into Ron Watts's plans for unit training:

What we [the battalion NCOs and officers] had done after Reforger was over and while we were cleaning up equipment, getting ready to redeploy, was to do a "bottoms up" review—what we'd call now a training assessment—and put together a training program before we ever redeployed. So we had that in place and we were going to kick it off the first Monday after New Year's. So when I listened to [the division commander's guidance], I said, "We're ahead of the power curve here."[22]

Right on cue, Watts took the Rangers to the field on the Monday after New Year's Day, right into a Kansas blizzard. The snow came down so thick that the battalion commander decided not to move the troops in their APCs, but to road march them to the field instead. "We were the only division unit in the field," Watts remembered, "and we all felt good about that." But, soon, Watts had cause to change his mind.

The CG flew out to the field that afternoon and located the battalion commander on a range. The division commander proceeded to chew Watts out for having his soldiers in the field in such cold weather. He demanded to know why the battalion was not in garrison and why Watts did not have troops out in their hometowns helping to recruit for the 1st Division. After dishing out this verbal reprimand, the CG boarded his chopper and flew off, leaving behind a befuddled battalion commander.

Dumbfounded by receiving such a reproach for doing exactly what he believed to be his most recent marching orders, Watts informed his brigade commander, Colonel Archie Brown, of the event and of his belief that the CG might relieve him. Although initially shocked, Brown told his battalion commander not to be concerned. A couple of days later, Watts queried Brown about the division commander's intent. Apparently the CG must had a bad day that Monday, because when Brown told the division chief of staff about the incident, the chief chuckled about it and replied that the CG had said, "Don't worry about it. Watts was doing what he ought to be doing." This came as good news to a relieved, but still rather confused, battalion commander.[23]

Early that year, army planners had determined that each division needed to be reduced from ten to nine maneuver battalions. The 1st Infantry Division selected the 2nd Battalion, 16th Infantry for inactivation. The 2nd Battalion was chosen because the 16th Infantry was the only regiment in the division that had two active battalions.[24] It was inactivated in August, and remained inactive, except for a brief period of four months in 1976, until December 16, 1979. It was then reactivated at Camp Forsyth as the 2nd Battalion, 9th Infantry, under the command of Lieutenant Colonel John P. Otjen. The 2/9th had been a leg infantry battalion assigned to the 2nd Infantry Division in Korea until ordered home in 1978 as part of President Jimmy Carter's troop withdrawal program. Eventually, it was decided to redesignate the battalion as the 2/16th Infantry, which entailed retraining the unit as mechanized infantry. Otjen set about doing just that in January 1980.

That month, the new Rangers deployed to the Fort Riley maneuver area to begin the process of molding mechanized soldiers. This training was paired with maintenance training on the battalion's new M113 APCs and preparation for the next month's Annual General Inspection, which the Rangers passed with flying colors.

In April, Otjen's command was tagged to participate in a "no-notice" EDRE exercise. That month, the Rangers were alerted and told to pack their bags and Conexes for a movement to Gowen Field, Idaho. After its arrival at Gowen Field, the battalion spent thirty days in the deserts of southwest Idaho, conducting mechanized operations and external ARTEP evaluations.[25]

After a summer of ROTC support, the battalion once again conducted a cycle of advanced individual training for a group of soldiers enlisted under the Cohesive Unit Program (CUP).

Under Otjen's successor, Lieutenant Colonel Karl H. Lowe, the 2nd Battalion continued to participate in the typical training activities required of Fort Riley units. That is until November 1981, when the first company of COHORT soldiers was assigned to Captain Michael Swanson's B Company. By the end of January 1982, all three line companies in the 2nd Battalion were COHORT units.[26]

During the early 1980s, the army looked for new and innovative ways to man the force. One of several options was the COHORT program. The COHORT (Cohesion, Operational Readiness Training) program was designed to build maximum esprit and camaraderie among soldiers who entered the army at the same time. It would do so by having a company of recruits go through Basic Combat Training (BCT) and AIT together, then serve out a three-year tour assigned to the same company at their duty post. To help maximize the COHORT program's potential for career-long unit esprit de corps, the army also adopted what proved to be the ill-conceived and ultimately ill-fated U.S. Army Regimental System (USARS).

USARS was designed to establish several battalions in selected combat arms regiments. Each regiment would have one or more (usually two) battalions at its regimental post and one or more (usually two) battalions overseas. The lowest numbered stateside battalion would function as the regimental headquarters for administrative purposes, such as coordinating regimental activities, assisting the honorary colonel of the regiment (a retired officer of some note in the regiment's recent past), and acting as custodians of the regiment's history, trophies, and other honors and memorabilia. Soldiers would be assigned to one of the regimental battalions on rotations overseas and then return to the regimental post for another assignment to a stateside battalion in the same regiment.

In support of this program, two more battalions of the 16th Infantry were activated on February 28, 1983. That day, at Göppingen, Germany, the 1st Battalion, 26th Infantry, was reflagged as the 4th Battalion, 16th Infantry, under the command of Lieutenant Colonel Joseph C. Arnold. The same day at Fort Riley, the 1st Battalion, 18th Infantry, was redesignated the 5th Battalion, 16th Infantry, under the command of Lieutenant Colonel Robert W. Higgins.

With these redesignations, the historical ties between the 18th and 26th Infantry Regiments, in place since 1917, were severed. The esprit de corps engendered by these associations was sacrificed to support what was good idea only in theory, and one that the Army as an institution never supported, especially in terms of resourcing and personnel management. As a result, USARS would bump along for the next decade or so, and never achieve anything it was designed to do.

Prior to the implementation of USARS, the new manning system it was designed to Support—COHORT—was well under way. The program had its origins in the 16th Infantry, when a company of COHORT soldiers arrived at Fort Riley in January 1983 and were assigned to B Company. Unlike USARS, COHORT was well thought out and thoroughly resourced, but it too had problems. Captain Thomas M. Carroll was the commander of B Company when the COHORT soldiers were assigned. He recalled:

I was assigned to the 2nd Brigade S3 shop and I was notified that I would be receiving [command] of a COHORT company.…During that time I was to develop a training plan for this company and for follow-on COHORT companies to be able to bring in an OSUT company from Benning and bring them through the training stages, from squad-, platoon- and company-level training.…They arrived in January 1983. There was not a lot of guidance [from the Infantry Center at Fort Benning]. I got some guidance from the battalion commander and the battalion S3.…[27]

To help him with the process of preparing the training plan and getting the barracks ready to receive the new soldiers, Carroll had a mixed bag of NCOs who had been sent over by other units, or who had been assigned directly as incoming replacements. Some were very good, others were average at best, and some had no business being NCOs.

Perhaps the advancement to NCO grades of this last group was unavoidable, because during the period of the late 1970s and early 1980s, the U.S. Army had many soldiers who had been recruited, despite low intelligence levels, in order to adequately fill the ranks. By 1983, many of these soldiers had become junior NCOs. At the same time, new recruits now faced a poor economy, and recent pay raises in the military, combined with excellent educational incentives, caused a renewed interest in military service by America's youth, with the result that army recruiters were instructed not to take anyone without a high school diploma. This led to the strange, and sometimes difficult, situation where new soldiers were being led by men who were less intelligent (sometimes by far), and often less motivated.

An additional problem with the COHORT program was the failure to plan for a large influx of married soldiers. Carroll stated:

The challenges we faced was trying to incorporate them and families into the Fort Riley community. My honest opinion was the fact that I do not believe that the division, and the local community, was prepared adequately to bring in families, and to inprocess entire families of a company of soldiers.…We did have a lot of challenges, both the officers and NCOs, in getting everything ready, and to help inprocess families, and to find housing and everything else.… [T]here were a lot of young families—young privates with young wives—living in trailer courts and things.[28]

COHORT had another problem—which soldiers to promote? Under the previous individual replacement system, new soldiers arrived at their first duty station at different times, so that there were frequently openings for promotions to Private E-2, Private First Class, and Specialist. At each of these ranks, however, there were fewer and fewer slots as the soldiers were promoted. Most soldiers in a COHORT company were quite competent and deserving of the next higher rank when they hit their minimum time in service for promotion. But only a few could be promoted. As a result, this system caused a great deal of frustration for soldiers who saw troops in non-COHORT units making rank sooner, at a swifter pace.

But COHORT's advantages outweighed its problems. The COHORT soldiers were motivated and functioned cohesively, the key to combat unit effectiveness. Kevin Richards, a lieutenant and platoon leader in B Company, recalled his first impressions of these soldiers when they arrived at Fort Riley:

I remember it was late January or early February when almost 200 new troops arrived at Camp Forsyth. I can remember it like it was yesterday. They were on a bus, still in their Class A uniforms, but still looking like soldiers. It was snowing. It was a neat sight to see. The soldiers were scrambling to get off the bus and into formation. They were very motivated and wanted to make a good impression on their new leaders.…[29]

Training COHORT companies was in many ways easier than training an individual replacement-type company. Because the COHORT soldiers arrived together from AIT, their only notion about how training should be conducted was to the high standards their drill sergeants had demanded. A soldier arriving in the unit through the replacement system often came from another infantry unit that may have used different techniques to accomplish a given mission. The unit from which he came may or may not have had higher or lower standards than his new unit. But almost without exception, that soldier believed his previous unit did things the right way, even though the "right way" was only one of several techniques that may be correctly applied to the problem at hand. The COHORT soldier, on the other hand, was almost an empty slate and was eager to learn from his new leaders. He carried no preconceived notions about which technique was the "right way."

COHORT soldiers were all at the same level of experience and thus required the same training, at least to a point. Their new leaders did not have to worry too much about planning various types and levels of concurrent training. Generally speaking, if one soldier needed to be trained on a specific task, they all needed it.

Another advantage of the COHORT system was that, by the second half of the company's life cycle, all of the problem soldiers had been reformed or removed from the army. The rest of the troops were well-disciplined and trained, and high levels of esprit and camaraderie were in place. A COHORT company at this stage was able to perform tasks that only well-trained, motivated troops could achieve. For example, Richards was the company executive officer of B Company during the last half of the company's life cycle. In preparation for a rotation to the NTC, Richards' new company commander decided to get "killed" to allow Richards an opportunity to run the company through one of four day-long training lanes. The exercise that Richards led the company through was an obstacle lane, built and defended by the 1st Engineers.

Assisting Richards in the operation were one experienced platoon leader and two new ones. One of these officers was fresh out of West Point and quite naive about the army. Still, with a few good NCOs, and great cooperation from a company of motivated COHORT soldiers, the new XO was able to maneuver the company to a dismount point with no losses. From there he moved them around the flank and eventually attacked the 1st Engineer defenses from directly behind the position. The defenders were stunned when about ninety soldiers eagerly swept across the objective, firing into their backs as they moved to the far side of the position. Every soldier who dismounted was present and accounted for on the objective. All had big smiles and knew they had done well that day.

Richards also respected the kind of initiative these soldiers had as well. During the first of their two NTC rotations, the B Company troopers were directed to dig in and defend a position on Furlong Ridge. Within a couple of hours, most of the soldiers had dug their positions armpit deep and to Fort Benning standards. The problem was that no overhead cover had yet been provided, and without that protection, the OCs would assess numerous casualties on the company if the position was hit by artillery. One soldier resolved to solve this problem. Richards recalled:

The kids had worked their asses off out there. It was 120 degrees and they were melting in their tracks. They were pretty-well dug in, but the class 4 [timbers, sand bags, concertina, etc.] hadn't arrived. I was up on the high ground and I noticed this one troop heading off in the distance toward an old outhouse. I figured he was going out there to take a dump. But before long, I noticed he was tearing this thing apart. He taken a crowbar out there, tore it down, and dragged the wood back to his position to cover

his hole. Nobody told him to do that. He just knew it had to be done. Incidentally, the class 4 did finally arrive, and the troops worked their asses off to get overhead cover on their positions until just before the attack. I don't think we lost anybody to artillery fire.[30]

In addition to training the influx of new COHORT soldiers, the 2nd Battalion participated in training support to the reserve components, a mission that the 16th Infantry had often performed during its days at Fort Jay. During this period, the 2nd Battalion maintained a summer training affiliation with the Kansas National Guard's 1st and 2nd Battalions of the 137th Infantry. For the summer of 1984, and again in the summer of 1985, the battalion dispatched a training support and evaluation group to Camp Ripley, Minnesota, to assist and evaluate these two battalions' Annual Training (AT). For both years, this group consisted of the battalion commander, Lieutenant Colonel Harper, the company commanders—including Captains Steve Davis, Donald Osterberg, William Rousseau, and John Powell—and several NCOs expert in TOW, 4.2-inch and 81mm mortars, and support operations.

Typically, each expert was assigned to their counterparts in the 137th Infantry to assist, guide, and evaluate the guardsmen during the two-week training event. Though the work could be long and tedious, it was made more enjoyable by good relations with the guardsmen and the cool summer weather. Only the massive number of mosquitoes made the time in the field unpleasant.

There was also time for less serious endeavors. On the weekend, in the middle of the AT, the Rangers had time for softball, sightseeing in the nearby town of Brainerd, and sampling "Beer Batter Walleye" dinners, a local specialty. For the more adventurous, there was the Camp Ripley stripper bar across from the main gate.

During the 1984 AT, a humorous incident occurred involving the Big Red One's ADC, Brigadier General Lloyd McHugh. McHugh, known somewhat affectionately as "Big Mac," had a reputation for being a no-nonsense field soldier. When it came to training, the general did not tolerate cutting corners or failures to meet ARTEP standards, and he was not the least bashful in informing a wayward soldier, NCO, or officer of such failures.

The major training event for that summer's AT was a squad movement-to-contact ARTEP exercise involving MILES-equipped troops and vehicles (MILES is an acronym for Multiple Integrated Laser Engagement System.) The problem was that one company evaluated by C Company's Captain John Powell had failed to properly prepare its MILES equipment. Additionally, the commander had unilaterally decided to disregard certain basic requirements, like uniform SOPs, wearing helmet chin straps down (instead of tucked under the camouflage band), and requiring his squads to move along covered and concealed approaches rather than straight down the road, and so forth.

As the first of this company's squads moved out that morning, Don Osterberg was watching it depart and knew that this substandard display of soldiering would catch McHugh's eye, provoking one of the ADC's well known tirades. After the squad had been gone for a while, Osterberg contacted Powell, who had gone forward to watch the initial contact. "Charlie Six, this is Alpha Six, has the first C Company squad arrived yet?" inquired Osterberg. "Alpha Six, this is Charlie Six, Roger," came Powell's response. Osterberg, wanting to know whether McHugh had started tearing into the National Guard commander about his soldiers' appearance and tactics, further asked, "Has the 'Big Mac Attack' begun?" A long silence held the airwaves, but Osterberg was insistent. "Charlie Six, has the 'Big Mac Attack' started yet?" "Uhhh…Alpha Six, this Charlie Six, negative, but I think it's about to," came the sheepish reply. Unknown to Osterberg, sitting in Powell's jeep next to the radio was the normally humorless McHugh, who had heard the whole conversation. McHugh gave Powell a serious look, then broke into a big grin, and climbed out of the jeep on his way to perform his "Big Mac Attack."

With the end of the AT came the frustrating experience of filling out the FORSCOM (Forces Command) Form 1-R, the guard unit's training evaluation. It was, in essence, a report card. A great deal of effort and wordsmithing went into preparing the evaluation. The difficulty came in balancing the need to fully reveal the problems that the unit should correct for the next AT, with the realization that the evaluated officers and NCOs could lose their jobs if the results were poor. In all, however, the Ranger experts generally agreed that most elements of the Kansas National Guard infantry battalions were in pretty good shape given that they only had thirty-eight days a year to train.

Like any good battalion, the 2nd Battalion developed traditions of its own to instill esprit de corps in its officers and men. The most notable of these traditions was the so-called Bonehead Award. The "award" was a large, scraggly old bone of indeterminate origin that someone—probably a second lieutenant—found in the Fort Riley maneuver area. Mounted on a wooden plaque, the bone had bits of dried flesh hanging from it, looking as though some scavenger had failed to properly finish its meal before being scared off. The award was presented at the monthly battalion officer's call (usually at the Officer's Club) to the battalion officer who had committed the most thickheaded act during the previous thirty days or so. The process of nominating the recipient required the accuser to stand up and relate to the gathered members a story about the nominee that had at least a grain of truth. Several nominations were always sure to be tendered.

Upon conclusion of the nominations, a vote was taken, and the winning officer was presented with the plaque. The so-honored officer had three responsibilities for the next thirty days, or at least until the next award ceremony was held. First, he had to display the plaque in a prominent location in his work place for visitors to gawk at. Second, he had to fix on the plaque a small brass plate inscribed with his name, month, and year of the award. And, finally, the officer had to safeguard the coveted trophy to ensure that it was not "lost" during his tenure, for if he allowed someone to walk off with the precious plaque, he would surely win the honor for the second time in a row.

In May 1987, the 2nd Battalion participated in the first of several visits to the city of Chicago for the annual Armed Forces Day parade. Lieutenant General Frederic Brown, commanding general of the Fourth Army at Fort Sheridan in Chicago, wanted active duty combat soldiers to participate in the city's parade. He asked for troops from the Big Red One, and the division responded by selecting the 2-16 Infantry, under the command of Lieutenant Colonel Joseph Terry, to march in the first of several annual parades.[31]

On May 2, some four hundred Rangers marched eleven blocks down La Salle Street in downtown Chicago amid cheering crowds of spectators. After the parade, 120 of the men attended a White Sox game at Comiskey Park, while others went to the downtown shopping district or the Six Flags amusement park north of the city. The trip was also an opportunity for the soldiers to learn more about the heritage of their regiment and division. The highlight of the trip was a visit to the 1st Division Museum at "Cantigny," the estate of the late Robert R. McCormick, in Wheaton, Illinois, a suburb west of Chicago. (McCormick, a former owner of the *Chicago Tribune*, had served with the 1st Division in World War I.) There, the troops saw numerous displays of uniforms, equipment, flags, dioramas, and other paraphernalia pertaining to the history of their regiment and division. The experience helped the soldiers understand what their predecessors had accomplished in World Wars I and II.

In all, soldiers are not particularly enamored of marching in parades. But most of the Rangers saw the utility in this particular event. Staff Sergeant Jesse Topasna probably said it best: "The way I see it, civilians don't really see us that often, This is our opportunity to come [to Chicago] and show that we're here for a purpose. We're the first to ever represent the division here and it's a privilege that our battalion was selected to come."[32]

The selection of the 2nd Battalion to be the 1st Division unit to attend the Armed Forces Day parade in Chicago was an honor earned by hard work. So it was too, for the 3rd Company, 362nd Panzer Grenadier Battalion, when it traveled to Fort Riley in March 1989. For a week, the German company trained with the 2nd Battalion in a series of problems on a field training exercise. The 3rd Company started the event by joining the Rangers on a twenty-five mile tactical road march along the old Highway 77 in the midst of an early spring snowstorm. Once in a tactical assembly area, the company was split—one platoon going with B Company to prepare a company defensive position, and the other two platoons with A and C Companies to prepare an attack on B Company's defenses. All engagements were conducted using MILES equipment to demonstrate to the soldiers of the 362nd the realism afforded by its use. The 3rd Company's executive officer, 1st Lieutenant Ulrich Wegert, led one of the platoon attacks against B Company's defenses and found out how real the MILES systems were and how good the Rangers were at fighting on the defense. After suffering heavy "casualties," the lieutenant told a reporter, "They had great positions and good obstacles, which gave us no chance."[33]

The following month, one hundred soldiers from C Company boarded aircraft to travel to Wallduern, Germany, for a similar training stint with the German Army. Though the week-long training period varied in content, the highlight was the soldiers' opportunity to compete for the Bundeswehr's Sports Medal. To win it, the troops had to conduct a two hundred-meter swim, a five-kilometer run, weight lifting, and several track and field events. When it was over, twenty-two C Company soldiers had earned the badge.[34]

In May, the 2nd Battalion, now under the command of Lieutenant Colonel Lawrence S. McAfee Jr., traveled to the Windy City once again for Chicago's annual Armed Forces Day parade. The trip was similar in all ways to the earlier visit, including attending a White Sox game and visiting Cantigny. Of the visit, McAfee remarked, "This is a way to reward good soldiers, and give them the chance to show the American public what the Army is all about."[35]

After concluding the summer routine of reserve component and ROTC advanced camp support, the Rangers turned much of their attention to that autumn's sports program. The fall football schedule was particularly competitive, and when the finals arrived in early November, the competitors for the post championship had boiled down to an all-Ranger super bowl—HHC, 2-16 Infantry, versus B Company, 5-16 Infantry.

The HHC team, dubbed the "Rude Dogs," was composed of several veteran members, including the coach, Sergeant Charles A. Countiss. The team had gone to the championship games for each of the previous three years, but each time had come up short. In the first of the two-game series, the "Devil Rangers" (the nickname for soldiers of the 5-16) jumped ahead early with a 20-6 lead in the first half, and went on to win even more convincingly. In the second game, however, the Rude Dogs managed a 20-14 win at the final whistle. The victory was enough to put the HHC team over the top in points for the post championship for 1989.

That same week, both of the 16th Infantry battalions' wrestling teams also took top honors in the post championship. In the final tally, the 2nd Battalion took the first place team trophy with four first-place wins and one second place in the individual matches, followed by the Devil Ranger team which won the second place trophy. The two first-place showings that week put McAfee's Rangers in first place for the Post Commander's Cup competition for that year.[36]

At about the same time the Rangers were winning laurels in the sports arena, they were also busy preparing for their next NTC rotation. In late November, the "Outlaws" of A

Company conducted a reverse cycle airmobile operation. For this exercise, the company commander used the daylight hours to plan and rehearse the mission; then, on the frigid night of November 7, the company was picked up by several UH-60 Blackhawk helicopters and inserted into an LZ on the Fort Riley reservation. The Outlaws then conducted several reconnaissance missions and a raid on an enemy position.

Over the next two days, the company conducted two more insertions and raids. Each time the Outlaws moved an average of four kilometers in the dark to strike enemy locations before withdrawing to a PZ (Pickup Zone) for withdrawal. Summing up the feeling of many soldiers, Specialist Robert Pepperdine, an A Company soldier, remarked that "this exercise gave me a feeling for the kinds of missions we'll have to do at the NTC....It's tough, but so are we."[37]

The following January, Pepperdine had the opportunity to see how tough they were when the Rangers conducted another rotation at the NTC. It was to be McAfee's last significant event as battalion commander, for at the end of the month, Lieutenant Colonel Daniel R. Fake took the colors.

The first half of 1990 was rather uneventful for Fake and his battalion. Most activities focused on typical training events. In July, however, Vice President Dan Quayle visited the Eisenhower Center in Abilene. On hand to greet him was an honor guard composed of the 2nd Battalion's D Company, lined up along the walk to a speaker's platform in front of the Place of Meditation.[38]

The next month, all eyes were on events in Kuwait, as the soldiers of the 2-16 Infantry, like so many Americans, watched on CNN the events related to the Iraqi invasion of that country. Still, Fake's training schedule continued unabated that month and into the autumn. As routine training activities continued, the soldiers watched unit after unit deploy to Saudi Arabia to support Operation Desert Shield, and many Rangers wondered how long it would be before the Big Red One would go over too. They would soon find out.

3rd Battalion, 16th Infantry
Maine Rangers
1970-1990

During the period 1970-1990, the reservists of the 3rd Battalion participated in a host of training events, and were involved in community service projects and public relations efforts. They also took part in monthly drills at their local Army Reserve centers, and ANACDUTRAs, usually at Fort Drum, New York (previously Pine Camp). The battalion would also undergo several reorganizations and relocation of units due to recruiting problems associated with the Vietnam drawdown. Additionally, to help overcome the stigma of Vietnam and the unpopularity of military service in the early 1970s, the 3rd Rangers spent a fair amount of time involved in an effort normally associated with the National Guard—community action.

The 187th Infantry Brigade's newsletter of the period, *The*

Quarterly Report, details several community action projects in which battalion units participated. For example, B Company (Brockton, Massachusetts), under the command of Captain Richard K. White, cooperated in a joint environmental project with students of the Social Science Department at Brockton High School in January 1974. Coordinated and supervised by Master Sergeant Russell Kahler and Staff Sergeant Jon Hinxman, the project entailed collecting discarded Christmas trees and transporting them to the coastal communities of Scituate and Plymouth. There, B Company volunteers helped to embed the dead conifers in the local beaches to help prevent erosion.[39]

The Combat Support Company (Worcester, Massachusetts), took a different approach to community outreach. The company commander, Captain Thomas White, and several NCOs jointly decided to form a drill team, a unit not commonly found in a combat unit. Clothed in army dress-blue uniforms and carrying M-1903 Springfield rifles, the team made its first public appearance in the Loyalty Day parade in Quincy, Massachusetts, on March 30, 1974. The team was evidently a big hit with the spectators, and the following autumn it performed the pre-game show for the New York Jets-New England Patriots football game in Patriot Stadium at Foxboro on November 17, 1974.[40]

That same fall, in October, Captain David H. Johnson's C Company (Fort Devens, Massachusetts) participated in the "Light a Light" fund-raising drive for the mentally retarded in Leominister. The troops gathered in the evening hours and, working in teams, visited participating homes to collect household goods for resale. The town then held a huge garage sale for the collected items, with all proceeds going to organizations and individuals involved in helping the mentally retarded.[41]

At about the same time as the "Light a Light" drive, C Company's Reserve Center at Fort Devens was renamed for Sergeant Major Gordon W. Burke. Burke had joined the army in January 1941 and was one of the rare soldiers who had served in both the Pacific and European Theaters during the war. Discharged from active duty in October 1945, he enlisted in the Army Reserve in 1948. By 1951, he was a first sergeant in M Company, 376th Infantry; three years later, he was appointed as the regimental sergeant major. He served as the 3rd Battle Group's only sergeant major and then as sergeant major for the 3rd Battalion until 1967, when he died suddenly in the field at Camp Drum at that summer's ANACDUTRA.[42]

By 1975, community action efforts notwithstanding, all units of the 187th Infantry Brigade (entirely located within the state of Massachusetts) had difficulty maintaining required manning levels. The unpopularity of military service after the Vietnam War, coupled with increasing economic growth and job opportunities, made service with the reserve components less attractive. By the spring of 1976, the brigade was manned at 50 percent of its authorized strength of about four thousand troops. Of the approximately 2,000 officers and men assigned to the 187th, only 1,066 made it to training at Fort Drum that summer.

In an effort to relieve the manpower crunch in Massachusetts and attempt to increase the brigade's personnel strength, the 94th Army Reserve Command decided to transfer the 5th Battalion, 5th Field Artillery, and the 3rd Battalion, 16th Infantry, to other parts of New England. In August 1976, the 3rd Battalion was relocated to Maine, with headquarters at Saco. The remainder of the battalion was distributed as follows:

Headquarters Company	Saco, Maine
A Company	Dexter, Maine
B Company	Rockland, Maine
C Company	Auburn, Maine
Combat Support	Rochester, New Hampshire

Except for the battalion Headquarters and Headquarters Company, the subordinate elements would remain at these locations for the next eighteen years. The Headquarters and Headquarters Company was moved twice, once to Portland in November 1977, and then to Scarborough in August 1978.

The 3rd Battalion, now under the command of Major Merle A. Taylor, soon resumed monthly drills at the companies' respective reserve centers. Community action projects were resumed and, before long, the battalion had taken on the nickname "Maine Rangers." Like their predecessors in Massachusetts, the men of the Maine Rangers soon became accepted, fully integrated members of the community at large. Their willingness to assist the community, especially in emergencies, won accolades for the 3rd Battalion. A notable example of rendering assistance can be found in the massive snowstorm that hit New England in February 1982.

That month, Rockland, Maine, was struck by heavy snows and high winds that caused severe drifting. The town was virtually immobilized. Not having a local National Guard unit, the town turned to the local Army Reserve unit, B Company, 3-16, under the command of 1st Lieutenant Jack M. Sherman. A local radio station news manager, Michael Gross, called Sergeant Arthur Robson to plead for help. Robson, a regulation-wise old soldier, informed Gross that only the president of the United States could call out the Army Reserve to help in civilian disasters—"That's the [National] Guard's job." Gross's heart sank. Robson then told the newsman that the regulations did not preclude reservists from *volunteering* to help.

Robson began contacting the members of B Company, and soon many of the unit's troops were digging people out of their homes, delivering medicine, and bringing in food and firewood to the elderly. This effort led B Company to organize the Reserve Enlisted Association (REA), which would become a part of the local Operation Helping Hand organization. The men even purchased a four-wheel-drive vehicle for future emergencies (regulations also prohibited the use of military vehicles unless approved at high levels). This turned out to be a prudent move, for over the next year, the REA helped out in at least four emergencies.

For the company's efforts to help the community, the city of Rockland turned out to issue citations to the battalion commander, Lieutenant Colonel John Buckley, and several of the most active members of the REA: Staff Sergeant Nathan Pierpont, Staff Sergeant Harry Fitzgerald, Sergeant Frank Malone, and Specialists Fourth Class Gary Fitzgerald and Brian Poland. Buckley also awarded these men the Army Achievement Medal.[43]

Cold weather operations were not unknown to the Maine Rangers. However, the Annual Training (AT, formerly ANAC-DUTRA) was usually performed in the pleasantly cool summers at Fort Drum. But for the 1983 camp, the entire 187th Infantry Brigade assembled at Camp Edwards, Massachusetts, to participate in Exercise Ready Spirit, February 19 to March 5. This exercise was part of the brigade's mobilization and deployment training program. Because the brigade's wartime mission was to reinforce and defend Iceland, it only made sense to perform the brigade's training during periods of cold weather.[44]

Buckley divided the 3rd Battalion's training into three phases: Phase I focused on rear area and fixed installation security missions; Phase II on company level area defense missions integrated with fire support; Phase III on reconnaissance, intelligence gathering, and economy-of-force operations. All missions were performed in the sort of weather the brigade could expect to experience in Iceland, should it ever deploy there. As a result, that year's AT (in which the 101st Airborne Division's 1st Battalion, 506th Infantry, also participated) proved to be among the most realistic training mission ever undertaken by the 3rd Battalion.[45]

In short, the 3rd Battalion conducted a host of training and community support activities in the 1970s and 80s, and performed them all in the best traditions of the 16th Infantry Regiment. As the 1990s approached, the battalion prepared for even more ambitious training opportunities; but, but as with all battalions of the regiment, that coming decade would bring unexpected events and changes.

4th Battalion, 16th Infantry
Ranger Forward
1983-1990

On February 28, 1983, the 1st Battalion, 26th Infantry, was reflagged as the 4th Battalion, 16th Infantry, at Göppingen, Germany, under the command of Lieutenant Colonel Joseph C. Arnold. This battalion initially took the nickname "Blue Devils" in honor of the 47th Chasseurs Alpins, the French regiment that trained the 16th Infantry at Gondrecourt during World War I.

Like the Manchus of the 1-9 Infantry, it took these ex-Blue Spaders a while to get used to being Rangers, but upon learning the 16th Infantry's history and experiencing its camaraderie, the troops of the 26th Infantry gradually came around in short order.

After their conversion to the 16th Infantry, the men of the 4th Battalion launched into a series of training events that occupied them the next year. The first of these events was a month-long field training exercise at the Muensingen LTA in June and July. Upon returning from this exercise, Company A deployed to Berlin's Doughboy City to participate in a MOUT exercise in August.[46]

September saw the battalion's participation in Reforger 83, Confident Exercise. As was sometimes the case in previous Reforgers, the battalion did not maneuver in 1983 but provided umpires and evaluators for the player units. This was followed in October by C Company's trip to the French Commando School. There, the company underwent a grueling ten days of training that included river crossings, close-in antitank tactics, and mountaineering.[47]

After the holiday season, the Blue Devils were supposed to participate in a 3rd Infantry Division exercise called Ranger Challenge, but unusually warm winter weather in January forced its cancellation. It was feared that, with the ground so soggy, the cost of maneuver damage to farmers' fields would be too high.

The following month, however, abnormally low temperatures and high snowfall struck the Combat Support Company while it was conducting interoperability training with the battalion's Project Partnership unit, the 231st Gebirgsjäger Battalion. The two units had traveled to the Reiteralp winter survival training area near Bad Reichenhall and encountered more than they bargained for. After the troops had learned how to build igloos and other snow shelters, a blizzard struck them with smothering, blinding snows and winds in excess of seventy miles per hour. A four-man team, consisting of Sergeant Jeffrey Grainers, Specialists Fourth Class Tim Flores and Wilson Morrow, and Private First Class Thomas Graham, went to work digging out their fellow soldiers buried under the deep snow drifts. Through these soldiers' fast action, the company suffered no injuries, and each soldier in Sergeant Grainers' team was awarded the Army Achievement Medal.[48]

After conducting a Level I gunnery training exercise at Graf in late February, the battalion transitioned to the new J-Series (Division 86) TOE in March. Under the J-Series TOE, the assets in the Combat Support Company, less the antitank platoon and all maintenance and mess teams from the line companies, were transferred to the Headquarters Company. The battalion gained a new rifle company, D Company, and the antitank platoon was beefed up to become E Company, an antitank organization. The intent of this TOE was to enable the army to counter the threat posed by the heavily armored and mechanized Warsaw Pact armies.

During the spring and summer of 1984, the new battalion commander, Lieutenant Colonel George S. Basso, led the Blue Devils through two maneuver rotations at Hohenfels. On the first rotation, Basso let the battalion's NCOs take charge of several operations and all of the cold-weather training. For the July rotation, the battalion acted as the OPFOR for the 3rd Brigade, 3rd Infantry Division. Upon conclusion of this training, the Blue Devils were commended by the 3rd Brigade commander for their work and described as a "very professional organization and a formidable opponent."

In Reforger 84, Certain Fury, the 4th Battalion, as part of the 1st Infantry Division (Forward), found itself in the unusual position of filling in as the 5th Infantry Division's 3rd Brigade, a position normally filled by the Louisiana National Guard's 256th Infantry Brigade. In spite of the fact that the opposing 3rd Infantry Division had all the latest in modern equipment (including the M-1 Abrams tank and the M-2 Bradley fighting vehicle), the M-60- and M-113-equipped battalions of the 1st Infantry Division (Forward) were ruled to have inflicted several defeats on the "Marne" men. Three months later, the 4th Battalion participated as umpires in the 1985 Reforger, JeepEx, as umpires.[49]

In late May 1985, C Company Blue Devils traveled to Verdun, France, with the 1st Infantry Division (Forward) commander, Brigadier General James B. Allen. At the American Meuse-Argonne cemetery, the battalion participated in commemorating the sacrifices of American soldiers at that year's Memorial Day ceremonies.[50]

The remainder of 1985 and the early months of 1986 were relatively slow compared to the previous two years. For the month of June 1985, the battalion performed guard duty for the large Miesau storage facility and, in October, the 4th Battalion's excellent cooks won the VII Corps' Phillip A. Connelly Food Service Competition.[51]

The first half of 1986 was taken up by preparation for, participation in, and recovery from range densities (i.e. weapons firing) at Graf in February, ARTEP evaluations at Hohenfels in April-May, and a 1st Infantry Division (Forward) density at Graf again in July. This training was followed by an unusual multinational exercise called Franconian Shield, September18-26. Conducted in Franconia and northern Bad Württemberg, Franconian Shield consisted of an exercise by the 1st Infantry Division (Forward), the III (GE) Corps, and the 1st French Armored Division. At its height, the exercise involved some fourteen thousand wheeled vehicles, thirty-four hundred armored vehicles, and 220 aircraft.[52]

In July 1986, Lieutenant Colonel W. Edward Shirron took command of the 4th Battalion. Apparently, Shirron did not care for the Blue Devil nickname and directed the adoption of a new nickname—Ranger Forward—in November 1986. Perhaps the old name reminded Shirron of the Blue Spader nickname of the previous battalion but, according to the battalion's assistant adjutant, 1st Lieutenant John Barrett, the new moniker was adopted to conform with the Ranger nicknames adopted by other units of the 16th Infantry.[53]

As the 1980s wore on, the 4th Battalion continued to prepare for its wartime missions. Along with the 1st Battalion, it participated in Reforgers 87 and 88, and deployed annually to Grafenwöhr and Hohenfels. In September 1989, the 4th Battalion also transitioned to the M2A2 Bradley Fighting Vehicles at the Vilseck training center.

When the Berlin Wall came down in November of that year, the Ranger Forward battalion, just like its brother battalion in the 1st Infantry Division (Forward), carried on as if a major threat from the East still existed. In February and March, the 4th Battalion conducted maneuver training in preparation for its first rotation to the Combat Maneuver Training Center (CMTC), USAREUR's equivalent to the NTC. While there, the troops were addressed by the USAREUR commander, General John R. Galvin. In his speech, Galvin addressed the concerns of the troops about which units would be inactivated. The USAREUR commander was not reassuring when he told them that "although some units would be inactivated, the decisions have not been made as to which units and when." In other words, all chips, including the two 16th Infantry battalions, were still on the table.

Nevertheless, the 4th Battalion carried on. On May 8, 1990, sixty-four troops of the Ranger Forward battalion, including its commander, Lieutenant Colonel Russell Honore, accompanied the 1st Infantry Division (Forward) commander, Brigadier General James Mullen, to a wreath-laying ceremony at the 1st Infantry Division memorial in Cheb, Czechoslovakia, for the forty-fifth anniversary of VE Day.

Escorted by the local Czech commander across the border from Bindlach, Germany, to Cheb, Honore recalled that after all those years of facing down the Warsaw Pact forces, "It was and eerie feeling crossing that line." At the border, the U.S. military attaché from Prague and a Czech military liaison officer joined the group.

At the 1st Infantry Division memorial, the Czech Army had drawn up an honor guard and band for the ceremony. Stepping off the busses, the Ranger Forward soldiers also formed a guard of honor, and Mullen and Major General Jiroslav Kinvel, commander of the Czech Western Military District, marched forward to place a wreath on the memorial. After the customary speeches, the officers attended a reception, while the soldiers had the opportunity to mingle with their Czech counterparts, drinking beer, swapping insignia, and touring the city. In all, it was a good opportunity for the 16th Infantrymen to build friendly ties with their former enemies.[54] The day passed quickly, and soon it was time to return.

At that juncture there occurred a tense incident reminiscent of countless Cold War confrontations between NATO and Warsaw Pact forces. Both the Czech and American state departments had approved the ceremony and General Kinvel had been assigned as the host. As such, Kinvel was responsible for ensuring the preparation of passes and related documents for the American contingent. Unfortunately, and unbeknownst to Mullen, the paperwork was never completed, leaving the American party without the documents required by the Czechs for cross-border travel.

It had proved easy to get into Czechoslovakia; getting out was another matter. When the visitors returned to the border to cross back over into Germany, the Czech guards, probably members of a new shift, were dismayed to find a group of American soldiers, accompanied by a brigadier general no less, on the "wrong" side of the international boundary. The guards refused to let the vehicles through. It was only after the Americans invoked General Kinval's name and the border guards made a few hurried phone calls, that the Czechs allowed their former enemies to pass through the checkpoint.[55]

The following month found Honore's battalion engaged in ARTEP evaluations at Hohenfels in their first rotation to the new Combat Maneuver Training Center. As the second unit ever to participate in a CMTC rotation, the Ranger Forward battalion was visited by the army's chief of staff, General Carl E. Vuono. A group of 4-16 soldiers were seated in a pleasant glade, and Vuono visited with the men, exchanged questions and answers. Upon conclusion of the visit, Vuono had one last question: "What are you going to do when you get back to garrison?" Not surprisingly, their reply was "Clean tracks!" With that Vuono grinned and departed, saying, "Listen troops, take care. We are proud of your work."[56]

In June 1990, the ever-proficient cooks of the 4th Battalion added new laurels to their achievements by winning the VII Corps' "Best Dining Facility" award. The following month, concurrent with the 1st Battalion's trip to Normandy, a 4th Battalion contingent traveled to Belgium to lay wreaths at the 1st Division memorials at Henri-Chapelle and Butgenbach. Honore also took this opportunity to conduct a professional development session at Hamich to study that battle and visit the location where Jake Lindsey won his Medal of Honor.[57]

At the start of August, the Ranger Forward battalion was functioning as the OPFOR for the 1st Armored Division at Hohenfels. Meanwhile, on August 2, Iraqi forces overran Kuwait. On August 20, both 1st Infantry Division (Forward) Ranger battalions sent soldiers to participate in the 1990 USAREUR Infantry Skills Competition. It was a squad from the 4th Battalion, however, that won the "Mystery Event," in which the unit captured an enemy held bridge.[58]

Exactly one month later, General Crosby Saint released the list of USAREUR units to be inactivated, and the 4th Battalion, 16th Infantry, was on the list. The target date was June 1, 1991.

5th Battalion, 16th Infantry
Devil Rangers
1983-1990

The same day that the 4th Battalion came into being, the 1st Battalion, 28th Infantry, was redesignated 5th Battalion, 16th Infantry, at Fort Riley, under the command of Lieutenant Colonel Robert W. Higgins. The battalion was assigned to the Big Red One's 1st Brigade, which used the tactical call sign Devil; therefore, the troops of 5-16 adopted the nickname "Devil Rangers."

Though active just over eight years, the 5th Battalion would participate in a wide variety of activities, including NTC rotations, Reforgers, COHORT, off-post training events, and training the National Guard.

The day that the battalion was redesignated as the 5-16 Infantry, Higgins was alerted to prepare his battalion for a deployment to Fort Drum, New York, to participate in a 1st Brigade field training exercise there. For thirty days, the Devil Rangers conducted force-on-force maneuvers and range firing for all weapons systems. After returning to Fort Riley, the 5th Battalion spent the summer performing evaluations or training support of several reserve component units, including the 32nd, 69th, and 205th Infantry Brigades at Camps McCoy, Funston, and Ripley, respectively.

That same summer, the battalion underwent several organizational changes as well. The first of these was the reassignment of the battalion from the 2nd Brigade to the 1st Brigade on June 17, 1983. The second was the reconfiguration of the battalion from an H-series to a J-series TOE, September 19-23, 1983.[59]

Like most infantry battalions in the 1980s, the Devil Rangers' main focus was preparing for rotation to the NTC. The 5th Battalion's first opportunity to go to the NTC came near the end of Higgins' tour as commander of the Devil Rangers. In August and September 1984, the 1st Brigade, under the command of Colonel William Mullens, along with the 5th Battalion, 16th Infantry, and the 2nd Battalion, 34th Armor, deployed to Fort Irwin, California, and engaged the dreaded OPFOR, otherwise known as "Krasvonians." The rotation turned out like almost all rotations in those days, with the battalion receiving a sound thrashing from the Krasvonian OPFOR.

It should be noted that opposing forces of the NTC, which represented the military might of the notional nation of "Krasvonia," consisted at this time of two maneuver battalions (one armored, one mechanized infantry) of U.S. Army soldiers. To realistically perform their role as a Soviet-style motorized rifle regiment, these battalions were thoroughly trained in Warsaw Pact tactics. Additionally, they were equipped with a number of actual Warsaw Pact armored vehicles, but the majority were U.S. vehicles modified to look like Soviet tanks, APCs, and reconnaissance vehicles.

Because the Krasvonians spend most of a given year performing their OPFOR mission, they are constantly improving as a team, developing superior unit cohesion and gaining battlefield experience the NTC rotating units (known as BLUE-FOR, for Blue Forces) normally lack. From repeatedly facing units employing the same U.S. Army tactics, the Krasvonians know exactly what to expect from their adversaries and how to counter their every move. As well, they are familiar with every rise and fold in the Fort Irwin terrain and are thus well-practiced at using the topography to their advantage. Consequently BLUEFOR soldiers, fighting well-trained foes on their home turf, find it very difficult to win even a single engagement, much less the majority of them.

Under Higgins' tutelage, and despite their second-place finish, the troops of the battalion came away with a much better appreciation for the requirements of being a combat soldier and for the myriad requirements of efficiently operating as a combined arms task force.

The battalion's next confrontation with the Krasvonians came in December 1986, when Lieutenant Colonel William R. "Ray" Lynch was in command. For this second rotation, the 1st Brigade deployed with the 1st Battalion, 34th Armor, to task-organize with the Devil Rangers. Though Lynch had built on Higgins' foundation, the battalion nonetheless, and quite typically, came out second best against the OPFOR.

The 1st Brigade's next deployment to the NTC once again employed the 2nd Battalion, 34th Armor, paired with the 5th Battalion under the command of Lieutenant Colonel Dwight B. Dickson. This rotation, conducted February and March 1988, continued to show improvement in the battalion's combat readiness. Dickson might have been able to demonstrate a significantly improved battalion during the next 1st Brigade rotation, but the division commander, Major General Leonard P. Wishart III, decided that the division's roundout battalion, 2nd Battalion, 136th Infantry, from the Minnesota National Guard, would go as the deploying infantry battalion.

Assigned as the division's fifth infantry battalion as part of the "Division 86" restructuring in the early 1980s, the 2/136th Infantry had been assigned to the 1st Brigade as its fourth maneuver battalion. Historically, the affiliate training unit for the guardsmen was the Devil Rangers, and each year the 5th Battalion would send a tailored package of trainer/evaluators to Camp Ripley to assist the guard battalion in enhancing its combat readiness. Partially as a result of the Devil Rangers' efforts over the years, this battalion did very well (especially given that it was National Guard and only trained thirty-eight days annually) during its training at the NTC.

The 5th Battalion's rotation to the NTC in February-March 1988 proved to be the harbinger of a busy year. After their return to Fort Riley in late mid-March, Dickson's troops barely had time to perform the customary post-field maintenance operations on vehicles and equipment before they were fully engaged in Operation Manhattan. This exercise was a bit different from previous ones in that the state of Kansas allowed the division to road-march more than just the wheeled vehicles on I-70 and state roads. As a result, the people of Kansas received the rare opportunity to see an entire division of tanks, APCs, and self-propelled artillery, as well as other tracked and wheeled vehicles, on the march.

Manhattan was followed by the second annual Armed Forces Day parade in Chicago, the first of several Devil Ranger visits to the city. In May, some 360 Devil Rangers traveled to the Windy City and marched through downtown to the strains of the 1st Division Band. Throngs of people lined the streets, shouting and cheering the soldiers of the 5-16. After the parade, the soldiers visited the First Division Museum at Cantigny.

The Armed Forces Day parade in Chicago, and the visit to Cantigny, would be an annual event for the 2nd and 5th Battalions for several years to come.

In July, Dickson moved the battalion to the new Multipurpose Range Complex (MPRC) for training. The MPRC, located in the northwest corner of the Fort Riley maneuver area, was designed to allow tank and infantry units to conduct realistic live-fire training. Over the four-day exercise, Dickson had his soldiers perform a variety of live-fire tasks, including mounted and dismounted maneuvers. It was the sort of training that had been sorely lacking in the training of mechanized infantry soldiers until the opening of the MPRC.

Just over a month later in September, the 5th Battalion deployed on Reforger 88. The soldiers did not know it, but this largest of all Reforgers was the last in which the Devil Rangers would participate as a full-strength battalion. The next version of the exercise the 5th Battalion participated would be, for the most part, a computerized command post exercise.

On April 13, 1989, Lieutenant Colonel Sidney F. "Skip" Baker Jr. replaced Dickson as commander of the 5th Battalion. Baker's first significant training event was already in the works when he assumed command. This event was an Expert Infantryman's Badge (EIB) test prepared and conducted jointly by the 5th Battalion and Lieutenant Colonel McAfee's 2nd Battalion, 16th Infantry. The highlight of this training for those few soldiers good enough to earn the EIB was an awards ceremony on April 28, at which the FORSCOM commander, General Colin Powell, presented the highly coveted badges to the men.[60]

During the EIB event, Baker sent A Company, under Captain John Schatzel, to the NTC to participate as an OPFOR unit for one rotation. This was a welcome adventure for those Devil Rangers: for once, they got to be the bad guys. In doing so, they learned a valuable lesson. As Schatzel observed, "This experience proved to us that the OPFOR is not invincible." That realization would become more apparent in the second decade of NTC rotations.

That summer, the Devil Rangers became the first Big Red One unit to receive the new M2 and M3 Bradley Fighting Vehicles. The vehicles and support equipment arrived over a two-month period, until the battalion had fifty-two of the new BFVs. Thus equipped, Baker now faced a training challenge. Over the next several months, he guided the battalion through the New Equipment Training (NET), oversaw its training for the challenges of a Level 1 gunnery exercise at the MPRC in January 1990, and, as a sort of capstone exercise, took them on a rotation to the NTC in March and April.

Baker requested assistance from an old friend, Colonel Jan Beers, who had commanded one of the first battalions to receive the BFVs several years before. Beers had established the standards for Bradley transition training while commanding a battalion of the 7th Infantry in the 3rd Infantry Division in Germany. Beers responded to Baker's request by sending him two large boxes of information. Baker and his staff pored over the AARs, studies, and other documents, and proceeded to develop their plan for NET training and reorganization of the battalion with fewer infantrymen.

Initially, the battalion received invaluable assistance from the Fort Benning NET Team. Although the transition period was short—just thirty-eight days—the switch to Bradley's went smoothly. Baker remembered that, "There were far fewer [problems] than I expected there were going to be coming out of an M-113 battalion…The NET team that came out of Fort Benning was exceptionally good. We had met with them prior to their ever starting the training and laid out the ground work. We simply made the plan and followed it."[61]

Baker followed this initial training with multiple trips to the field for maneuver training. The battalion also frequented Range 18, Fort Riley's "field fire" range, to prepare tank and Bradley crews for the major test at the MPRC. The training proceeded through the autumn of 1989 and into the winter of 1990 and concluded with a "Gauntlet" exercise before the battalion deployed for its next NTC rotation in March 1990.

Baker's rotation to the NTC was different from the others, due in part to his longstanding relationship with the division commander, Major General Gordon A. Sullivan. Baker had known the division commander since the days when Sullivan served as the chief of staff of the 1st Infantry Division (Forward) in 1970s. Now, Sullivan, in cooperation with the U.S. Army deputy chief of staff for operations, worked to get the Big Red One involved in a new concept at the NTC—a light/heavy rotation (a heavy task force attached to a light infantry brigade). He selected Baker's trip to the NTC to be the test rotation.

This meant that the 5/16th would not go with the 1st Brigade, as in previous rotations. Instead, Baker's troops were attached to Colonel Jeff Ellis's 1st Brigade, 7th Infantry Division (Light), which consisted of three light battalions of the 9th Infantry, a field artillery battalion, the brigade support battalion, and a portion of the 7th Division's support base units (signals, military intelligence, military police, logistics, etc.). Further, two companies from the 2/34th Armor were attached to the battalion to make it a balanced task force.

Although sound in concept, the new rotation was not without problems, particularly in the preparation phase. The 1st Brigade had only just returned to Fort Ord in late January from Panama, where it was involved in the effort to oust Panamanian dictator Manuel Noriega. With the NTC rotation scheduled for March, Ellis and his troops had little time to shift gears and refocus their efforts from actual combat in a jungle environment to participation in a desert scenario, laser-tag exercise. Additionally, Baker's command was unable to work with the brigade before joining it in the so-called Dust Bowl, the NTC bivouac area. The entire joint predeployment coordination consisted of one brief planning session at Fort Ord before the rotation.

In the field, minimal joint planning and the total lack of joint training translated into the light brigade's inability to adequately support a heavy task force, especially in regard to maintenance. The lack of heavy equipment transports and other direct support assets resulted in TF 5-16's maintenance status to drop to 60 percent of tanks and 70 percent of BFVs combat capable by Day 14 of the rotation.

Additionally, and as a direct result of the training shortfall, the light infantry commanders had no appreciation for the pace and scale of operations for a heavy task force. Baker recalled:

> We were making an attack through the Granite Pass. The plan was a good one—we were going to pass the task force through one of the battalions of the 7th Division, and they were going to clear lanes for us through Granite Pass, which had been obstacled. Well, the light infantry got up there on time, we crossed the LD on time, we get up there on time, and they've cleared the lane, sure enough. Unfortunately, the lanes were cleared on the perspective of a light infantryman. There was no way I could get my Bradleys and tanks through those [narrow] lanes. And so here we come, ripping through, getting ready to rip out the guts of the OPFOR and we come to a screeching halt right there at the obstacle.…[62]

Notwithstanding these problematic circumstances, the rotation achieved exceptional results. Baker, justifiably proud of his battalion's accomplishments, observed that "the intensity of the soldiers of TF 5-16 never slacked up. Their esprit de corps was top notch. The [brigade] commander…felt that their 'Never Say Die' attitude was the greatest."[63]

Upon the battalion's return to Fort Riley, some 120 Devil Rangers began preparing for the battalion's second Memorial Day trip to Chicago. After marching in the city's Memorial Day parade, the soldiers were at a Cubs game at Wrigley Field, followed by a barbeque hosted by the Society of the 1st Division at Cantigny.

As in the previous year's parade, the Devil Rangers were a big hit with the citizens of the Chicago, and with attending dignitaries as well. Among the latter was Major General (Ret.) Neal Creighton, who had formerly commanded the 1st Infantry Division in the early 1980s, and who was now the president of the Society of the 1st Division. Creighton was moved to write the division commander to compliment the battalion on the appearance and deportment of its soldiers.

The trip to Chicago was a fitting way for the Devil Rangers to start the summer. Besides the usual ROTC summer camp and reserve component support, the battalion could look forward to a slower pace, especially after going through the NET transition, Bradley gunnery, and the NTC. That was true until August when Iraqi forces invaded Kuwait. Suddenly, the more relaxed pace abruptly changed to a more hurried approach to training as the battalion began serious preparations for war.

Through the late summer and autumn of 1990 Baker and

his troops—who were then getting ready for a Level I gunnery at the MPRC in September—had been following the crisis in Kuwait. It soon became evident that the Big Red One would be going to Saudi Arabia. Baker recalled that, "We automatically assumed in August that the army would send the 1st Infantry Division. No matter who else they sent, they were going to send the Big Red One." Like their brethren in the 2nd Battalion, the Devil Rangers knew they were going for sure when the secretary of the army announced the deployment in November.

The Rangers at the National Training Center 1982-90

With the recall of American ground troops from Vietnam in the early 1970s, the U.S. Army quickly refocused on its primary Cold War mission, the defense of Western Europe. The war in Southeast Asia had been a "leg" (light infantry) war against a tough but nonetheless unsophisticated enemy. Ground commanders had concentrated on body counts and pacification efforts, and the combat units almost always enjoyed air, materiel, and fire superiority in most encounters with the enemy.

The defense of Western Europe posed different challenges. The armies of the Warsaw Pact nations were disciplined, well-equipped—and large. In a conflict with those armies, NATO forces would be outnumbered. Moreover, they would be fighting a war in which mounted combat, fast-paced and lethal, would predominate. Commanders and units would have to operate over long distances and perform complicated attacks, much of the time in darkness. The army of the mid-1970s was not ready for such a war, and its commanders knew it.

Several commanders sought to remedy the deficiencies of the post-Vietnam army. Among the most influential were General William E. DePuy, first commander of the U.S. Army Training and Doctrine Command (or TRADOC, established in 1973 at Fort Monroe, Virginia; General Donn A. Starry, DePuy's successor at TRADOC; and Major General Paul F. Gorman Jr., TRADOC deputy chief of staff for training. DePuy's experiences in World War II and later in Vietnam convinced him that the army needed a better way to train; to that end he set out to revolutionize the Army's training systems, as well as develop doctrine that would allow the army to "fight outnumbered and win" in what he termed a "come-as-you-are war." His efforts led to the publication of a new FM 100-5 *Operations* manual, the army's basic doctrinal guide, and the ARTEP training system.

Publications such as FM 100-5 were all well and good, but in themselves they did not and could not train the army for war. Combat battalions needed a place where they could perform the full range of tasks expected of them in a mechanized conflict, including live-fire exercises. DePuy's vision for a combined arms training center, Gorman's initial efforts to lay the foundation for such a training center, and Starry's implementation of DePuy's vision, all led to the establishment of the National Training Center (NTC) at Fort Irwin, California. The

product of what was rightly described as the "most costly single Army training initiative in peacetime history,"[64] the NTC has more than justified its cost, as evidenced by the U.S. Army's superb performance in Operation Desert Storm. Like so many soldiers who honed their combat skills in the powdery sands of the Colorado Wadi and on the basalt rocks of the "Whale"—famous, or infamous, terrain features at the NTC—the men of the 16th Infantry realized a tremendous increase in battlefield competence after a rotation through Fort Irwin.

The first NTC rotation for a 16th Infantry unit was that of the 2nd Battalion in August 1983. Most battalions that went to the NTC in those days underwent a grueling experience, not just from a well-trained OPFOR but also from the evaluators themselves. Not only did the BLUEFOR unit almost always receive a sound thrashing from the "enemy" force on the battlefield; the key leaders were then required to sit through the infamous After Action Review (AAR) following each battle. The AAR was an opportunity for the Observer/Controller (OC) team to bring the leaders into a van and, in no uncertain terms, flog the BLUEFOR leaders for their poor performance. The 2nd Battalion, during its first rotation to the NTC, received the full treatment, on the battlefield and in the AARs.

Nevertheless, each time a battalion went to the NTC, it came away a better unit; and the individual soldiers, NCOs, and officers all had a better idea of how to fight. Most of the insights gained from a rotation would then be applied to the battalion's home station training, or were carried away by the soldiers to be used again when they returned to the NTC, whether it was with the same battalion or not.

Similarly, each time a Big Red One battalion went to the NTC, the division staff got better at developing a predeployment training plan that prepared the battalion for its next trip to Fort Irwin. In the army scheme of things, each commander is responsible for training the forces up to and including forces that are two levels down from his position. Thus, a division commander is responsible for molding and training battalion commanders and their battalions. At Fort Riley, the 1st Infantry Division commander's staff developed an exercise, eventually known as Gauntlet, to prepare the two battalions that typically went on a rotation. A typical Gauntlet exercise and NTC rotation of the 1980s is exemplified by the experience of the 2nd Battalion in its February 1985 rotation.

After a summer and early fall of ROTC support, ranges, and platoon ARTEP evaluations, the 2nd Battalion, under the command of Lieutenant Colonel Mike Harper, was ready for the pre-NTC train-up (not yet called Gauntlet). For the impending rotation, the 2-16 Infantry was to be task organized with one of the 2nd Brigade tank battalions, the 3-37 Armor, under Lieutenant Colonel Brusitis. That battalion was to send two armor companies to TF 2-16, while the Rangers' D Company, under Captain Terry Gendron, and B Company were attached to Brusitis's command. Harper retained A Company, still under Don Osterberg, and C Company, an almost brand new COHORT unit, now under the command of Captain Bill Rousseau.

In the predawn darkness on a November morning, the Rangers rolled out of their motor pool on Custer Hill and road marched north around the Fort Riley impact area, then east to an assembly area just southeast of the town of Riley, Kansas. There, the battalion split up into companies, task organized into teams, and prepared the teams to run through four training lanes designed to train the teams on specific tasks. Over the next four days, each team negotiated lanes in which they had to perform a hasty daylight attack, a deliberate night attack, a team defense, and an obstacle lane prepared and defended by the 1st Engineers.

Meanwhile, TF 3-37 Armor moved to an assembly area in the northwest reaches of the post reservation, where it went into hastily prepared defenses. After a day spent drawing ammunition and MRE meals and testing radios, weapons, and MILES equipment, the 3-37 was ready for its first mission, a movement to contact.

The evaluators acting as OCs for the companies of the 2nd Battalion belonged to the battalion's sister unit, the 5-16 Infantry. The OCs went everywhere with their evaluees, including operations orders and AARs. The OPFOR was played by the 4-37 Armor, reorganized along Soviet lines.

Over the next four days, Brusitis's command negotiated three missions—movement to contact, deliberate attack, and defense—while Harper's battalion negotiated the four team lanes. At the end of the first four days, the two task forces switched assignments, with TF 2-16 taking on the 4-37th Armor while the TF 3-37 Armor teams negotiated the four training lanes.

The following illustrates how these lanes were conducted, as well as how effective the lane system could be in preparing a unit for its trip to the NTC and, ostensibly, for combat.

In an earlier train-up for another battalion's rotation several months before, Harper had chastised the B Company commander for his poor development of his team's battle position. Upon Harper's inspection, he had found that the commander had not sited his attached tank platoon well, failed to properly camouflage his positions, misplaced the few obstacles that were erected, and virtually ignored a flank avenue of approach into the company's defenses. Before these errors could be corrected, the OPFOR had attacked and had blown through the hole in the team's defenses on the open left flank. All the problems Harper pointed out and more came to light at the team's AAR that day. They were lessons not forgotten by the B Company commander or his troops.

On the second day of the team lanes in November, this same company drew the team defense lane. In a battle position at an old farmstead about fifteen hundred meters west of the reservation's "Four Corners" intersection, Team Bravo went to work digging in to defend against a battalion attack the following morning. The terrain was relatively open with little in the

way of concealment, but there was a superb kill zone that the commander chose to build his defense on.

Positioning his tank platoon in the center, with two-tank sections to the right and left to create a withering cross-fire, the commander then placed his two infantry platoons to hold the flanks. The infantry sent troops forward as OPs. On the left flank, on a ridge overlooking the position, the left platoon leader positioned a squad to drive off reconnaissance efforts and to act as early warning in case the OPFOR "cheated" and attacked from outside of the boundary prescribed by the division G3. On the right, in the most likely infantry avenue of approach, additional OPs were placed to watch that approach. Additionally, all vehicles and soldier fighting positions were dug in using engineer assistance and team soldiers. Forward of the battle position, Team B soldiers also emplaced a series of wire and mine obstacles to canalize the attacking force into the kill zone. It was a formidable position.

While the position was being built, an unknown captain, in standard army field garb, visited the battle position and briefly observed the team's efforts. After a few words with the company commander and the operations NCO about locating the battalion TOC, he sped off to the south and disappeared. At about the time the officer left, 1st Lieutenant Keith Cooper, the team's OC rushed up and asked the commander, "Do you know who that was?" The commander replied he did not. "I know him. He happens to be from the battalion that is acting as the OPFOR. That was the OPFOR commander that's going to oppose you tomorrow and he knows how you've arranged your position!"

This was bad news, but it also gave the team commander intelligence about the bad guys. The OPFOR commander was from a tank battalion that was known to have only one infantry company attached for the missions they were performing on four lanes. At best, the attack on the morrow would contain one platoon of infantry. The enemy assault would be predominantly tanks.

Quickly, the commander got his platoon leaders together and explained the situation and directed that the tanks be pulled back slightly to new positions that, happily, were later discovered to be better than the original locations. Dragon and LAW teams were sent forward to concealed positions further bolstering the team's AT potential. Meanwhile, the team's TOW section was moved from its original position to the high ground around the farmstead so that it be out of the artillery impact area when the barrage began. It could still reach out to kill the enemy in the primary kill zone or to the area west of the battle position in case the attack came from that direction. In its new position, the left tank section could also range that potential avenue of approach. The right flank was thoroughly obstacled and bounded by a "river" (old Highway 77).

Satisfied that his assets were in the best possible locations, the commander went out just before dark to check the battle position from the enemy's perspective. Forward, he found that the Dragon and LAW teams were in excellent positions and busily engaged in obstacle construction. The obstacles were indeed well-sited and according to commander's intent, though the soldiers had a long way to go and would have to work through the night to complete them.

Several positions were poorly camouflaged, with netting that did not conceal the vehicles underneath. This was the only problem the team commander discerned. He remedied the problem with a quick visit to those positions. Though far from complete, the overall battle position was developing into a credible defense. By dawn the following morning, all was set for action.

The actual attack was almost anticlimactic. About 8:00 a.m., the forward OPs reported reconnaissance efforts by the enemy, and soon two vehicles were destroyed by the LAW and Dragon teams. Within thirty minutes, a large formation of tanks was spotted rolling along the sector northwest of the team position. The enemy was attacking as expected. The TOW sections, DRAGON teams, and left tank section prepared to engage in that direction.

But then, at the OPFOR commander's signal, the attacking force turned east. It was a serious blunder—the turn was made too soon. Instead of crashing into the team's left flank, the enemy commander had unknowingly directed his command to drive directly into the battle position's kill zone. Had he struck the flank, Team B would still have been ready for him, but he might have succeeded in getting a few vehicles past the defense. But, now, within five minutes, the team's tank platoon, TOWs, Dragons, and LAWs destroyed some twenty tanks and six APCs, virtually annihilating the enemy force. The collection of OPFOR vehicles stood motionless forward of the team, with yellow lights flashing brightly in the early morning light. Clearly, B Company had learned something from its performance just a couple of months before.

The NTC train-up had prepared both battalions for the upcoming rotation, which started on February 21, 1985, when the 2nd Brigade rolled into the NTC's Dust Bowl. Harper's TF 2-16 was the first into the force-on-force phase of the rotation, while B and D Companies went to the live-fire with Brusitis's TF 3-37 Armor. In each of their first two missions against the OPFOR forces, the Rangers achieved a tactical draw. But their performance in the second mission was an improvement over the first. The same was true of the two 2-16 companies attached to Brusitis for the live-fire. The first live-fire mission, a defense, was actually a failure because of the faulty location of assets, so the battalion was "recocked" and executed a second defense. On this second attempt, the task force then rolled through the live-fire attack in good order, though too slowly.

The experiences of the two Ranger companies attached to TF 3-37 Armor for the force-on-force phase are illustrative of a unit's incremental improvements during a typical rotation. The first mission for the companies was a defense of the central corridor between Brown's Pass and Debman's Pass. The first

effort to defend this area ended in the task force, especially Team B, being penetrated and largely overrun. At the AAR, the brigade commander, Colonel Arthur Fintel, announced that the defense would be re-executed. Twenty-four hours later, and after some shifting of forces, repositioning of obstacles, and relocation of key weapons, the OPFOR attacked again. This time it was fought to a standstill.

Next on the agenda was a "reaction mission," which required movement by the entire task force within an hour after receiving an order to attack a certain objective—in this instance, Red Lake Pass. With no time for briefing platoon leaders, the teams rolled out of the central corridor, into the southern corridor, through the Whale Gap, and into a maelstrom of enemy fire. The task force was largely destroyed by OP "Bone" with the Rangers' Team B losing twelve of fourteen APCs within less than three minutes of penetrating the initial wire obstacle.

The task force was then pulled back to the west end of the southern corridor and ordered to conduct another attack, this time to secure the Whale Gap for a follow-on brigade attack. Brusitis's plan called for the infantry to dismount and execute a deliberate night attack, to be followed by the tank teams at first light.

For this action, Gendron's D Company would seize the "Whale," a large basalt hill mass east of the gap, while B Company captured the Furlong Ridge west of the gap. The two companies moved out around midnight, with Gendron's team in the lead, followed closely by the APCs of Team B. Both teams moved mounted, intending to find hide locations for the tracks where the troops could dismount and proceed by foot to conduct their respective attacks.

Team B troops reached its dismount point about 2:00 a.m. While Gendron's vehicles rumbled on in an easterly direction to D Company's dismount point, Team B's commander and most of his troops begin the long climb to Furlong Pass, also to the east (a small force, commanded by the company XO, Kevin Richards, stayed back with the APCs). Two hours later the dismounted troops of Team B had surmounted the high ridge dividing the southern corridor from the so-called Valley of Death. Visible on the low ground to the south of the Whale were a dozen or so flashing yellow lights—an apparent sign that Gendron's troops had already started taking out the OPFOR positions there. Some eighty B Company soldiers started their descent into the Valley of Death—and out of radio contact with TF 3-37.

They reached the valley floor just west of the gap by first light. The troops pushed hard and finally reached a little finger of high ground at the west end of the gap. Inexplicably, there was no opposition. The OPFOR had apparently pulled back. Nevertheless, the company commander had the 2nd Platoon secure overwatch positions in the direction of the Whale, while the 3rd Platoon was sent into the gap to start filling in portions of the tank ditch there so that the follow-on tank teams could punch through.

Meanwhile, the commander climbed back to the top of the ridge to restore contact with the task force commander. He notified Brusitis that the west half of the gap was secure and that it did not appear that the east half was occupied by either good guys or bad guys. Brusitis informed him that Team D had been heavily engaged the night before and had lost much of its combat power. Team B would now have to secure both sides of the Whale Gap. At the end of the conversation, the Team B commander looked over to the low ground south of the Whale and saw about a dozen APCs motionless in the open. He realized then that the flashing yellow lights from the night before were not OPFOR vehicles but those of Team D.

As his troops finished filling in gaps of the tank ditch, the commander moved the 2nd Platoon to the Whale to cover that side , while the 3rd Platoon secured the Furlong. As soon as the platoons reached their positions, the rest of TF 3-37 came barreling through the gap and briefly engaged several OPFOR vehicles to the northeast. Meanwhile Richards brought up the company's attached tank platoon and APCs and put them into link-up positions with their dismounted elements

The task force was soon reconstituted, and after a successful defense of the Whale Gap the following day, it was moved to an assembly area just east of Red Lake Pass. There, the task force was given another deliberate attack mission.

Initially, the task force was supposed to conduct an early morning attack against Hill 720, located at the east end of the central corridor. After a discussion with the task force S3, the B Company commander was given permission to conduct a thirteen-kilometer dismounted move to get into the enemy battle position from behind. Gendron's Team D would come up at first light the next morning to reinforce. For this final mission, the company lost its tank platoon but regained its third infantry platoon to bolster the assault.

That night, once again, the company made a long night march north through a rough wadi system. About 3:00 a.m., the column turned west and crossed the main north-south road on that part of Fort Irwin. Just after crossing, B Company encountered the enemy's laager position, but quietly crept past without being detected.

By 5:00 a.m., the commander had successfully positioned the company directly behind the enemy position just over the crest of the ridge so that it could not be detected. There, the commander held in place until just before dawn. As the sky began to lighten, the company moved forward over the top, three platoons on line, and almost immediately began to encounter enemy positions. Soon, the yellow kill lights on OPFOR vehicles began to flash. The enemy commander initially could not believe that a BLUEFOR dismounted unit had got into his position, but with his reinforced motorized rifle company rapidly suffering losses, he realized he had to take action or be completely destroyed.

After destroying seven BMPs and two tanks, the B Company troops were hit by a local counterattack from OPFOR infantry and the two remaining BMPs. The Rangers were soon pinned down. A rather rare (for the NTC) infantry-versus-infantry firefight broke out, with both sides attempting to outflank each other and concurrently sustaining heavy casualties. Just as it appeared that the OPFOR was gaining the upper hand, Gendron's Team D came crashing into the position "just like the cavalry," according to Brusitis, and it overran the remaining enemy opposition. Gendron then proceeded to hunt down the last two T-62s on the far side of the OPFOR position.

This was the last mission for those two Ranger companies at the NTC. Task Force 2-16 had experienced similar increases in tactical ability, with Don Osterberg's Team A conducting a particularly impressive night attack on his last mission of the rotation. However, while the Rangers' 1984 rotation to the NTC was relatively successful as early NTC rotations went, it was not perfect. Many techniques that are considered essential to a rotation today were lightly addressed or even ignored back then. Activities such as rehearsals were desirable, but it was believed then that there was no time for them in the NTC rotation schedule. Synchronization matrices were not thought of at the battalion level at that time. But a later generation of mechanized soldiers would find the time to do rehearsals and become more adept at using the skills and tools necessary to win in combat.

The combat training the U.S. Army's heavy maneuver battalions received at the National Training Center between 1981 and 1990 was superior to that of any modern army. Even so, and however realistic, the NTC experience was still just a simulation of combat. But the real thing would come soon. In August 1990, President George H.W. Bush responded to Iraq's conquest of Kuwait by deploying U.S. military forces to Saudi Arabia. Operation Desert Shield had begun, and Operation Desert Storm was on the horizon. The largely combat-inexperienced officers and men of the 16th Infantry, like the rest of the U.S. Army, were about to go head-to-head against men and forces that had been battle-hardened by years of combat against the Iranians. Desert Storm would be the test of just how good the U.S. Army's peacetime training system really was. It would also determine whether the battalions of the 16th Infantry could face off and defeat an enemy that was equipped and trained in the manner for which the Rangers had been preparing to fight against since 1970. The answer would be determined in a one hundred-hour duel in the desert wastes of Kuwait and Iraq.

General Schwarzkopf and Devil Rangers, Gulf War, 1991

Chapter Twelve
Desert Duels

I'm damned proud of you. That bastard picked the wrong fight!

Major General Thomas L. Rhame, March 3, 1991

Since shortly after World War II, the evening retreat ceremony at Fort Riley has been held in front of Summerall Hall. Originally the post hospital, Summerall Hall became the post headquarters in the 1950s. Since then, every day at 5:00 p.m., the garrison military police lower the flag as "To the Colors" is played. At that time, all traffic stops on Huebner Road, and soldiers in all vehicles get out and salute the flag.

On the evening of November 10, 1990, First Lieutenant Jay Mumford, Battalion S2 for the 2nd Battalion, 16th Infantry, was on his way home from work, listening to a CNN newscast on his car radio. He arrived in front of Summerall Hall just as "Retreat" was sounded. Mumford shifted into park and, with the engine and radio still running, emerged from his vehicle. "Retreat" was followed by "To the Colors." The lieutenant snapped to attention and saluted. Upon doing so he heard the newscaster announce that the Department of Defense had just declared that the 1st Infantry Division would be deployed to the Persian Gulf in support of Operation Desert Shield. "It was on CNN. It has to be true!" Mumford remembered joking to himself.[1]

That same afternoon, 2nd Lieutenant Doug Hughes, a platoon leader in D Company, was passing by his company dayroom when he poked his head in to see what was going on. Several of his soldiers were crowded around the television watching Wolf Blitzer on CNN. Hughes walked just as Blitzer announced that the Big Red One was going to the Persian Gulf. He recalled his soldiers' more somber reactions: "There wasn't a lot of whooping and hollering. Instead a quiet mood fell over the room as soldiers began to assess what the word, now finally out, would mean to them and their families."[2]

Most had anticipated the announcement. Many believed that, in the event of war with a nation fielding a conventionally equipped army, the Big Red One would surely be involved. The newscast only confirmed them in their belief.

The Iraqi army invaded and conquered Kuwait in early August 1990. President George H.W. Bush responded by dispatching the 82nd Airborne Division to Saudi Arabia, signaling American resolve to defend against further aggression. At first many hoped and felt that military action would not be necessary—that diplomacy could resolve the crisis. But diplomacy failed. Economic sanctions against Iraq were instituted and the

buildup of American forces in Kuwait continued. At the same time, the president began putting together a unique coalition of Middle-Eastern and European nations to oppose the Iraqis.

In Saudi Arabia the 82nd Airborne Division was soon joined by the 24th Infantry Division (Mechanized), the 101st Airborne Division (Air Assault), and the 1st Cavalry Division. These formations constituted the XVIII Airborne Corps. In October planners for Third Army and U.S. Army Central Command (CENTCOM) decided that the deteriorating situation in the region warranted the deployment of a heavy corps. Later in the month, VII Corps ("Jayhawks"), commanded by Lieutenant General Frederick Franks Jr. and based in Germany, was given the nod. A troop list that included the 1st Armored Division, 3rd Armored Division, and the 1st Infantry Division (Mechanized) was approved.

The 1st Infantry Division would deploy to Saudi Arabia without its third brigade, the 1st ID(F). The latter, replaced by the 2nd Brigade of the 2nd Armored Division, was tabbed for a support role. First it would assist in moving VII Corps out of Germany, then it would deploy to Dammam, Saudi Arabia, there to serve as a port handling unit for the incoming units—a humble but nonetheless vital mission.

Defense of Saudi Arabia
August 1990-February 1991

At about the same time that the Rangers at Fort Riley learned that the Big Red One was deploying to Saudi Arabia, VII Corps directed the 1st ID(F) to transfer equipment and personnel to deploying corps units, despite the fact that the brigade's subordinate units had already begun the process of inactivation. Company B, 1st Battalion, 16th Infantry, was further detailed to operate the railhead at Böblingen to assist units that needed to send equipment by rail to ports in northern Germany for loading on Saudi-bound transports. The operation, one account noted, was performed "in typical 'Iron Ranger' fashion…on schedule and without accident or injury." In two weeks, the company had loaded more than one thousand VII Corps vehicles.[3]

Deployment, November 1990-January 1991
4th Battalion, 16th Infantry

The 1st ID(F) mission to help move VII Corps out of Germany

soon changed to receiving corps units arriving in Saudi Arabia. In late November, the brigade received orders to set up the headquarters for VII Corps (Forward) in Dammam. On December 2, the 1st ID(F), consisting of Task Forces 4-16 Infantry and 3-34 Armor reinforced with many soldiers from 1-16 Infantry, began arriving in Dammam for Operation Desert Duty, the reception and onward movement (ROM) of VII Corps units into Saudi Arabia. The remaining soldiers of the 1st Battalion would spend the war inactivating 1st ID(F) units and performing security duties for the garrisons and family housing areas in Böblingen.[4]

In Dammam Colonel Honore's TF 4-16 organized port handling teams to receive equipment and materiel coming into the port. TF 4-16 also provided housing, life support, and security for some fifteen thousand soldiers in units temporarily encamped in and around Ad Dammam (upon receiving their equipment, the units would head west to a Tactical Assembly Area [TAA] in the Saudi desert).

When troops arrived by plane far in advance of their equipment, which was coming by sea, Honore's troops began to run into problems. Before long, instead of caring for fifteen thousand soldiers, Honore had the problem of housing in excess of thirty thousand Jayhawk soldiers. Scrambling to find shelter, TF 4-16 was soon billeting incoming troops in warehouses and tent cities that were literally erected overnight by the Ranger Forward battalion. Finally, the Saudi Arabian government provided the use of the Khobar Bedouin Village for housing the incoming soldiers of the VII Corps.[5] Soon known by the troops as "Khobar Towers," these high-rise apartments had been built by the Saudi government to lure Bedouins out of the desert to live a more comfortable existence in Dammam. The experiment failed when the Bedouins refused to leave their familiar nomadic lifestyle for the cushy, but confining, dwellings.

In addition to running the reception area, Honore's troops had to perform security missions for the billeting areas as well. Around Khobar Village, engineers threw up a berm, while the Rangers dug in fighting positions for guards and machine-gun crews. The troops strung triple-strand concertina wire and set up exit and entry guard posts. They also maintained roving patrols throughout the area.[6] These measures ensured that no serious threats were ever carried out against the ROM efforts of TF 4-16, nor against any of the units that passed through Dammam.

2nd Battalion, 16th Infantry

While the 4th Battalion was preparing to support ROM operations at Dammam, Lieutenant Colonel Daniel R. Fake's 2nd Battalion at Fort Riley was getting ready for the deployment and combat operations. In preparation for a scheduled rotation to the NTC in December, the 2nd Battalion had just completed a Gauntlet train-up exercise in October. Consequently, Fake's organization was intimately familiar with most of the attached units with which it would fight the Gulf War.

Theoretically, Colonel Fake's troops were already approaching peak performance as mechanized infantry soldiers, a big plus as deployment approached. Nevertheless, as always, there are some things a unit needs to improve upon, and Fake set about ensuring that his battalion's weaknesses were corrected before the movement. On November 14, he announced that the battalion's priority of work for the deployment was (in order): Nuclear, Biological, Chemical (NBC) defense training, repairing inoperative vehicles, maintaining operational vehicles, and painting the battalion's vehicle fleet in a desert-sand hue.

The battalion's 244 combat vehicles were painted with Chemical Agent Resistant Coating (CARC). Tracked vehicles received their coat at Building 8100, the main maintenance shop at Fort Riley. The HUMMVs were painted at the post auto craft shop, while all other wheeled vehicles were sent to various locations in Junction City.[7] After painting, bumper numbers and unit markings were reapplied. Finally, a large, black "V" was painted on every vehicle as a recognition device.

Fake was a stickler for clean markings, ordering the repainting of vehicles with markings that were in the least bit flawed. Some flaws were, in the opinion of many painters, quite minor and really beyond the notice of anyone but their battalion commander. But orders were orders, and the soldiers did as they were told. One soldier remarked, "we don't know if our efforts were appreciated, but we do know [that] we did a mighty fine job."[8]

The job was completed by Thanksgiving. Rail loading operations followed in early December. Throughout November, the Rangers had developed and modified load plans for vehicles, Conex inserts, and Milvans. They carefully packed and inventoried these items, then spent three days loading the battalion's tracked and wheeled vehicles and seven Milvans on trains bound for Beaumont, Texas.[9]

The battalion's advanced party left for Saudi Arabia on December 17. All remaining troops were given Christmas leave, which lasted through January 2, 1991. On January 5, the 2nd Battalion's main body processed through Craig Gym on Custer Hill, loaded on buses for the trip to Forbes Field in Topeka, and boarded contract airliners for Dahran.

5th Battalion, 16th Infantry

The deployment preparation experience of Baker's Devil Rangers was similar to that of Fake's 2nd Battalion. With the completion of the NTC rotation in March and the Level I gunnery exercise in September, the 5th Battalion was also approaching peak performance. Because of the 5th Battalion's high state of readiness, the division's G3, Lieutenant Colonel Terry Bullington, decided that other units were in more need of the training facilities than Baker's men. Therefore, he made some changes to the 5th Battalion's training schedule.

First, Baker's unit went through the gunnery exercise as a task force, not as a pure battalion. This training forced the unit's training and logistics planners to learn what it takes to integrate two tank companies into the gunnery exercise and support them in the field, not only with food and fuel, but with ammunition as well. Second, Baker's troops did not have the opportunity to execute Table XII, the capstone exercise in a Level I Gunnery event that pits a platoon against a large target array designed to replicate an enemy battalion. The planners eliminated Table XII so that so more units could get on the range before deployment.[10]

After the gunnery exercise, the already busy pace of events became frenetic. Task Force 5-16 performed a multitude of tasks, all designed to prepare the troops for deployment and combat. In Craig Gym, troops were herded through POM (Preparation for Overseas Movement) stations designed to ensure that their personal readiness items were in order. Dogtags were reissued, immunizations administered, government life insurance forms updated, teeth checked, powers of attorney made out, and wills prepared.

When personal readiness was not the immediate chore, the battalion focused on individual and squad proficiency tasks and vehicle maintenance. Following the gunnery exercise, Baker put his "dismounts" (dismounted infantry troops) through a squad proficiency course that included a live-fire exercise. To increase realism, he included fire and movement by the soldiers on the ground, as well as integrating fire support from a Bradley Fighting Vehicle (BFV) while the squad maneuvered.[11]

Like the 2nd Battalion, the 5th Battalion Devil Rangers had to have their 250 vehicles ready for shipment to Saudi Arabia. Paint and markings were applied, maintenance performed, and work completed to meet standards set by the U.S. Customs Service, the U.S. Navy, and civilian shipping firms. "It was a very, very hectic period," Baker recalled, [with] people working eighteen hour days. But we still managed to enjoyed ourselves. I don't think we drove soldiers into the ground like tent stakes."[12] After giving the troops time to be with their families over the Christmas holiday, the 5th Battalion boarded aircraft at Forbes Field in Topeka, and started its journey to Dahran.

Reception and Onward Movement
January-February 1991
2nd Battalion, 16th Infantry

The 2nd Battalion began arriving at Dahran on January 6. From there, the troops were shuttled to Khobar Towers to await the arrival of the battalion's equipment. In the interim, there was little for the soldiers to do other than "get accustomed to the strange odors on the wind" and note the utter lack of moisture in the Saudi Arabian climate. Companies soon began to perform roving squad-sized security patrols around the ten-square-kilometer complex to bolster the guard force provided by the already overstretched 4th Battalion.[13]

In the meantime, an unloading detail went to King Abdul Azziz Port, about twenty-six kilometers north of Dammam, to receive the battalion's vehicles. Upon the arrival of the ships carrying these vehicles, the troops quickly separated the wheeled from the tracked vehicles and organized them into convoys. The wheeled vehicles were driven to their destinations, but the tracked vehicles were moved on Heavy Equipment Transports (HET) in order to minimize damage to the paved roads.

On the afternoon of January 13, the first convoys departed for the initial assembly area at TAA Roosevelt. Riding on HETs was Captain Kirk Schleifer's E Company, the battalion's antitank unit, which would provide security at the assembly area. Over the next several days, the remainder of the battalion convoyed to TAA Roosevelt and prepared for future operations.[14]

The Allies had given Saddam Hussein, the president of Iraq, until January 16 to withdraw his forces from Kuwait. When he failed to do, the Allies launched air strikes against Iraqi targets. Thus Operation Desert Shield ended and Operation Desert Storm, the war with Iraq, began. At 3:00 p.m. the next day E Company moved north about eight kilometers to screen the task force TAA. The move was accomplished without radios and certain other equipment items, which had not been unpacked from their Milvans back in Dammam as a result of a logistical foul-up (all 2-16 units would experience the same problem during the next few days).

Previously, the brigade commander, Colonel Anthony Moreno, had decided that the 2nd Brigade would only task organize 2-16 Infantry and the 3-37 Armor. His third battalion, 4-37 Armor, was to remain purely a tank outfit. Thus, on January 19, A and D Company from 3-37 Armor were cross-attached to Fake's battalion. In return, Fake sent Captain Thomas Rouse's A Company and Captain Mark Hammond's D Company over to the armor battalion.[15] Later, B Company, 1st Engineer Battalion, was added to the task organization. This task organization caused the battalion to lose twenty-eight BFVs but, at the same time, gain the same number of M1 Abrams tanks. Upon completion of this swap, Moreno had two balanced task forces and one pure tank battalion for the impending operation.

Once the task force arrived at the TAA and the majority of equipment was on hand, Fake and his subordinate commanders conducted generic rehearsals at all levels. The Rangers engaged in this generic training almost constantly until the start of the ground war. On January 26, Fake received the brigade operations order. The plan required TF 2-16 to conduct a deliberate attack to penetrate enemy defenses along Phase Line Wisconsin. At Wisconsin, the task force would force four lanes through the Iraqi obstacle belt and then attack, in zone, to destroy enemy forces between Wisconsin and PL Colorado, then eventually to PL New Jersey.[16]

Once Colonel Fake had issued the task force order, his troops began to rehearse the mission specific tasks. They conducted their rehearsals under all conditions—daylight, night, mounted, and on foot. The soldiers made extensive use of terrain models and sand tables. In addition, Fake and his key leaders performed exhaustive "rock drills." Later, 2-16 performed mounted rehearsals on full-scale replicas of Iraqi defenses prepared by the engineers. The first efforts went poorly. Consequently, all went back to the basics to correct the problems. After a brigade "leaders only" rehearsal on February 7 corrected many misunderstandings, the task force performed another brigade-size full-up rehearsal the following day. This time, the operation went smoothly.

Moreno, satisfied that his subordinate elements were ready, canceled further training and directed units to perform an intensive four-day maintenance period. During the maintenance stand-down, troops had time to take care of personal business and purchase items from the mobile PX that was established in the back of one of the unit's cargo HEMMTs (a large cargo truck designed to carry ammunition). The HHC first sergeant, Stephen Hillyer, was responsible for keeping the PX restocked. Fulfilling that duty was no easy task. Hillyer recalled:

The only problem was that the PX warehouse was on a military base 150 miles away cross country over desolate desert, and the map that I had was a 1 over 1,000,000 scale, the kind of map a pilot in a very fast aircraft uses. The ironic part was that when it came to go get the PX items, all the Magellans (Global Positioning System (GPS) receiver) were given out. How did we get the 150 miles cross country to King Khalid Military City? Dead reckoning and a $3.00 wrist compass. It was a great boost to my morale when we managed to get there and back without getting lost. It's just ironic that the guys with the Magellans never went more than 5 miles from the assembly area and were able to use a $3,000 navigation system every inch of the way. 150 miles cross country and back in a HUMVEE and I was forced to use a three dollar wrist compass and a map for a 747 pilot![17]

Early on the morning of February 14, the entire 1st Infantry Division moved from TAA Roosevelt to occupy battle positions (BP) some 160 kilometers to the northwest. Upon conclusion of the move, the 2nd Battalion task force, now dubbed "TF Ranger," was in BP 12, located only thirty-five kilometers south of the Iraqi defenses. After four days of local patrolling in this battle position, the task force jumped northward a short distance to BP 22 on February 18.

At BP 22, the task force continued to prepare for combat operations. For several days, units test fired tank and Bradley main guns into the large nine- to twelve-foot dirt berm (that served as the boundary marker that separated Iraq from Saudi Arabia) to ensure that weapons systems were operational. Infantrymen, some fresh from Advanced Individual Training (AIT), others recalled reservists, poured into the battalion. Before long, all companies were over strength, but no one was

complaining. Anyone with a sense of history might have recalled that the regiment was similarly over strength on D-Day, with additional men added in expectation of heavy casualties on Omaha Beach. TF Ranger was expected to take heavy casualties breaching the initial Iraqi defenses, and it was believed that the extra troops were assigned for that reason.

On February 20, elements of the task force sent troops forward to the berm to ensure that the crossing sites, previously cut by the engineers, were clear of any enemy observation positions or other positions. The following day, Fake received a fragmentary order (FRAGO) that revealed the date and time of the attack—5:30 a.m., February 24.

5th Battalion, 16th Infantry

The arrival of the Devil Rangers in Saudi Arabia went smoothly. The main problems were the coordination of the arrival of soldiers coming by air and the equipment coming by sea, and the fact that the breech block mechanisms for the BFVs' Bushmaster 20mm guns had been removed (in accordance with shipping regulations) and packed separately before the vehicles had been loaded on board ship. Apparently, no one had briefed the division commander, Major General Thomas L. Rhame, about this detail and he subsequently "went incandescent" when finding out. The delay in locating and mounting the breech blocks was minor, and soon the battalion was the first to be ready to move to TAA Roosevelt.

Upon arrival at the TAA, Colonel Baker discovered that being first is not always good. Since his outfit was ready to go, the 1st Division called upon it to perform an inordinate number of "flex missions," which Baker described as "a nice euphemism for jump through your ass drills." These tasks required the Devil Rangers to respond to Iraqi moves, conduct reconnaissance missions, and other important tasks.[18]

After departing TAA Roosevelt, TF 5-16 assumed responsibility for a battle position three kilometers south of PL Vermont (the berm along Tapline Road), at 6:45 a.m. on February 18. Part of Colonel Lon E. Maggart's 1st "Devil" Brigade, the Devil Rangers were organized into two tank-heavy teams (A and D Companies) from 2-34 Armor, and two mechanized teams formed around the battalion's B and C Companies. In addition to the battalion's antitank unit, E Company, Baker also had D Company, 9th Engineers, attached.

Along PL Vermont, the task force was responsible for a six-kilometer front. TF 2-34 was to the west of the Devil Rangers, and the 2nd Brigade's TF 3-37 was to the east. Due to the relative inactivity of the Iraqi units to the north, Baker had the scout platoon screen the task force from the berm during the day. At night, a team, augmented by an E Company ITV (Improved TOW vehicle) platoon and two GSR (ground surveillance radar) vehicles, relieved the scouts and stood watch with integral thermal night sights. The engineers constructed twenty-six vehicle positions so that tanks and Bradleys could use their main gun and TOW systems to fire at the enemy over the berm if necessary.[19]

The first night, Captain Richard K. Orth's Team Alpha relieved the scout platoon and occupied positions on the berm for the surveillance mission. As night fell, the team commander reported visual contact with dismounted Iraqi patrols that seemed to be guided by artillery-fired illumination rounds. At about 9:30 p.m., the team commander called for mortar fire against the targets, and the results appeared effective. Four and one-half hours later, Team Alpha lookouts spotted several Iraqi soldiers three to four hundred meters in front of the berm waving a flag and banging on a metal object, apparently attempting to surrender. Once again the team commander called for mortar support, this time with illumination rounds. As each flare popped, however, the Iraqis would drop to the ground and hide. Despite repeated efforts to coax them into coming in, the Iraqis refused to come forward.

At about 4:20 a.m., Baker finally ordered the team commander to engage the enemy. Soon, small-arms fire of all calibers opened up on the hapless Iraqis. One man was observed to fall and remain motionless; the others quickly disappeared into a fold in the earth. The body of the fallen Iraqi lay motionless for over forty-five minutes, but a later scan of the area discovered that he had disappeared too. A subsequent daylight patrol to the site revealed trash and body waste, but no body and no blood.[20]

Over the next four nights, this scene was often repeated with some variations. On the night of February 22, however, three Iraqi soldiers succeeded in surrendering to Team Charlie. No other significant events took place before G-Day.

Enemy Situation

On paper, the Iraqi Army was a formidable force. Thought to be the fourth largest army in the world in 1989, it consisted of some fifty-six divisions, twenty-six of which were arrayed against the coalition forces. Facing the 1st Infantry Division across the Saudi-Iraqi border were the Iraqi 26th and 48th Infantry Divisions, units considered to be adequately equipped and trained to perform a static defense mission but woefully unprepared to take on the armored juggernaut that was about to descend upon them. The 48th Infantry Division was dug in parallel to the Saudi-Iraqi border about twenty kilometers north of the berm. Holding positions to the left rear of the 48th, was the 26th Division. When the attack finally started, the 1st Infantry Division would have to penetrate elements of both of these enemy divisions.

Behind the 48th and 26th Divisions, to the northeast in what became dubbed "Objective Norfolk," was the Republican Guards Tawakalna Division and elements of the 10th and 12th Armored Divisions of the Jihad Corps. All were positioned in Iraqi territory with the exception of the 10th Armored Division, which was just inside the Kuwaiti border. The Iraqi tank and mechanized divisions were considered to be Saddam's mid-level formations in terms of equipment, efficiency, and relia-

bility. Planners could count on these units being used as a counterattack force or second-line defense if the Iraqi infantry divisions along the Iraqi-Saudi border failed to stop the Coalition's initial penetration.

The Republican Guard divisions were Saddam's best. Originally raised as a special guard force for Saddam, in 1990 these units were expanded into several tank and mechanized divisions and organized into a corps directly under the control of the Iraqi high command. Most commanders and many of the troops manning these units were specially recruited from Saddam's home area of Tikrit, and as a result, they were fiercely loyal to him. He equipped them with the best equipment available and paid them much better than the rest of the army. For these reasons, Saddam expected a great deal more from these troops than he did from the main army forces.

Saddam's army, especially the Republican Guards, was equipped with some of the latest military equipment, mostly Soviet. While the Iraqi army's tank and mechanized divisions had about 250 older T-54s, T-55s and T-62s, the Republican Guard units were equipped with the T-72M1, a top Soviet export model. The Iraqi army was also equipped with a mixture of BTR-60, BMP, BMP-1, and other eastern block APCs. Iraqi artillery, however, was predominantly Austrian, French, and South African.[21]

In addition to the Iraqi Army, the troops of the 1st Division also faced the challenging Iraqi winter weather. Although the time of Rangers' arrival meant they missed the 120-plus-degree weather of the Saudi summer, they encountered frequent winter sandstorms that wreaked havoc with vehicles, radios, and other equipment. Often the visibility dropped to less than one hundred meters in such conditions. Though the days were warm, night often brought freezing temperatures. Rain was another frequent visitor during the desert winter and could quickly turn dry stream beds into raging torrents capable of sweeping vehicles and personnel downstream.

The terrain in the 1st Infantry Division's area of operation was relatively flat, open desert without major terrain features. The country posed no significant obstacles, except those that were man-made, between the berm and the division's ultimate destination, the Safwan-Kuwait City highway. The lack of major terrain features posed a serious navigation problem, rendering maps virtually useless. Satellite receivers, issued down to the platoon level, helped the troops find their way. Known by various names ("Magellan," "Slugger," and so forth), the receivers used the satellites of the Global Positioning System (GPS) to obtain a ground fix, thus enabling the vehicle-mounted navigator to accurately plot a course through the desert wastes.

In terms of defenses, the Big Red One faced two distinct Iraqi lines reinforced with obstacle belts north of the Tapline Road. The first of these lines was that of the 26th and 48th Infantry Divisions. This line, well laid out with tanks, antitank weapons, and infantry fighting positions, was sited to ensure interlocking and supporting fires. With the lack of vegetation and flat terrain, the Iraqi defenders had superb fields of fire to stop an attack. Forward of the line, Iraqi engineers had emplaced belts of antipersonnel and antitank mines and thickets of barbed wire. To the rear, the divisional artillery were positioned to provide a rain of steel to break up assault forces trying to break through.

The second defense line, manned by the Jihad Corps, was similar to the first, with fire trenches added. The latter were six feet deep, filled with crude oil from local wells, and positioned forward of and parallel to the defense trenches. Used effectively in the war with Iran, the fire trenches would prove an utter failure in Desert Storm. However, their uselessness was not apparent on the eve of battle, and the troops of the Big Red One regarded them with some trepidation.

Division Mission
Lieutenant General Frederick Franks, commanding general of the U.S. VII Corps, tabbed Rhame's 1st Infantry Division to carry out the initial penetration of the Iraqi defenses—a potentially difficult and dangerous undertaking upon which the success of VII Corps' attack, if not the entire Coalition offensive, hinged. After completing its mission, the division would temporarily revert to the corps reserve, preparatory to an anticipated role in the destruction of the Jihad Corps. In the coming battles the division's four assault battalions, including the 16th Infantry's 2nd and 5th Battalions, were expected to sustain severe casualties.

The division's mission was later modified when corps intelligence officers determined that the Iraqi defenses did not extend west of the corps front. Franks thereupon decided that the 1st Infantry Division and 3rd Armored Division should bypass the defenses to the west, and only the U.K. 1st Armored Division would pass through the gap opened by the Big Red One. Immediately upon completing their passage of the lines, the British would turn east and roll up the second-echelon defenses and block any attempted counterattacks into the corps' right flank.

The division's scheme of maneuver was developed by Lieutenant Colonel Bullington (G3), and his plans officer, Major Donald A. Osterberg. The plan called for the division to attack with Maggart's 1st Brigade on the left and Moreno's 2nd Brigade on the right. Maggart selected Baker's 5-16 Infantry and Lieutenant Colonel Patrick Ritter's 1-34 Armor to conduct the breaching operations. Both were balanced task forces, each with two tank and two mechanized companies, with an attached engineer company assisting in the opening and marking of the breach lanes. Maggart opted to keep Lieutenant Colonel Greg Fontenot's 1-34 Armor pure.

Moreno's task organization was not significantly different from Maggart's. He selected Fake's 2-16 and 3-37 Armor as the breach forces. He also organized them into balanced task forces and kept his reserve, the 4-37 Armor, as a pure tank organization.

In both brigades, the two breach elements would be followed by the pure tank battalions, which would each race through the breach to destroy Iraqi armored forces arrayed in depth. These battalions would then be followed by the 3rd Brigade, 2nd Armored Division, the division's third brigade, which had replaced the 1st Infantry Division (Forward) when it was decided to use that organization to support the VII Corps' deployment and reception. The 3rd Brigade would widen the penetration and guard against a counterattack. Once the British forces were through the breach, the division would reorganize and follow the VII Corps as the reserve.

These actions had been thoroughly rehearsed at all levels. On January 30, a division-level rehearsal saw the Big Red One breach a full-scale replica of the Iraqi defenses, followed by the 1st U.K. Armored Division's movement through the breach. By February 22, all units were ready for the ground war to begin.

Final Preparations
February 22-23, 1991
2nd Battalion, 16th Infantry
On the day that Team Charlie accepted the surrender of the three Iraqi soldiers, (February 22), all units received notification that G-Day was to begin at 5:00 a.m. on February 24. In the meantime Coalition warplanes and the Big Red One's artillery steadily pounded the Iraqi defenses, providing some measure of reassurance to the troops of the assault battalions. The impending operation was expected to be successful, but bloody.

Though the efforts by the air force and artillery had its consolations, many soldiers found greater comfort in making peace with their maker in the hours before the attack. As someone once said, "There are no atheists in a foxhole," and the soldiers of the 16th Infantry were no different. At the 2-16 Infantry's TOC on the evening of the 23rd, Chaplain Thomas MacGregor and troops of the regiments gathered for a final service before going into battle. Such scenes were prevalent throughout the American lines that night, despite the Saudi government's decree banning such religious observances. Indeed it was an activity that had been ongoing at military stations throughout the world for months before the fighting started. As the soldiers removed their Kevlar helmets and bowed their heads in prayer, a light drizzle fell.[22] The service soon ended and the soldiers went back to work, their souls cleansed, but the morrow's great undertaking was still much on their minds. TF Ranger was ready.

Liberation of Kuwait, February 24-28, 1991
Coming to Grips—February 24, 1991
2nd Battalion, 16th Infantry
Task Force 2-16 crossed the berm (Phase Line Vermont) at 5:02 a.m. on February 24 and rolled toward the LD with a five-kilometer front. The scout platoon screened to the Rangers' front, followed by Captain Horacio Schwalm's Team D (D/3-37) as the advanced guard. The remainder of the task force followed in a diamond formation. Task Force 3-37 moved on Fake's right, the

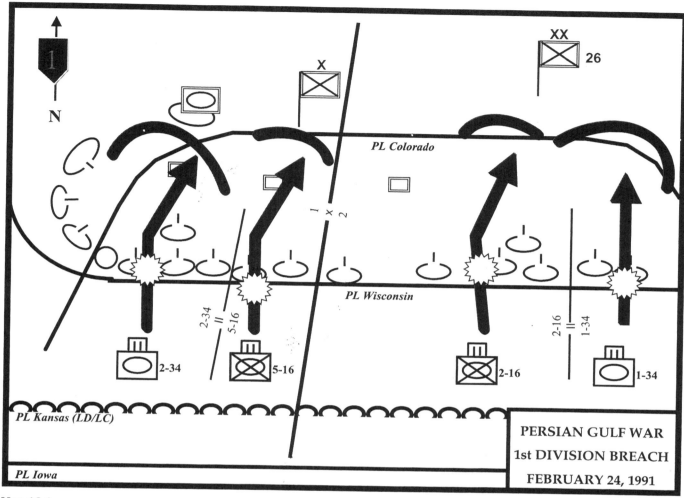

Map 12-1.

Devil Rangers on his left.

Thirty-six minutes after crossing the berm, the Rangers crossed the LD at PL Minnesota and, having made no contact, pushed on to PL Iowa. At 8:20 a.m., the scouts reported Iraqi infantry to the front, and the battalion's heavy mortar platoon responded by firing the first shots of Desert Storm for TF 2-16. Soon, Iraqi troops were surrendering in droves. The Rangers drove forward to PL Kansas. The task force encountered its first resistance about 10:00 a.m. when the advancing vehicles received small arms and machine-gun fire from an Iraqi infantry position. Realizing the futility of their efforts, the Iraqis soon surrendered.[23]

By 10:58 a.m., the Rangers had passed Kansas and pulled into hasty defense positions at PL Birch. Here, the task force was to remain in place and prepare to conduct the breach on the following morning, but the speed of the advance and light resistance convinced Rhame that the division could breach the Iraqi first line that day. He contacted Franks and requested that the Big Red One be allowed to do so.

5th Battalion, 16th Infantry

West of TF 2-16, beginning at 4:30 a.m., the M1 tanks and M2 Bradleys of Baker's Devil Rangers task force ground toward the berm in the misty drizzle. On Baker's left was 2-34 Armor; the 2nd Brigade was on his right. In front, the TF 5-16 scouts conducted a screen, with Captain James T. Nepute's Team D (D/2-34) just behind, acting as the advanced guard. "As we crossed the LD," Baker recollected, "there were an awful lot of tight lips and white knuckles. But there was nobody looking back over their shoulder wanting to run away and go home."[24]

Meeting only light resistance from elements of the Iraqi 110th Brigade (26th Division), the force pushed north into the enemy's security zone. When resistance developed, Bradleys fired upon the defenders to pin the Iraqi infantry down while plow tanks buried the position if the enemy troops failed to surrender. Seeing their comrades suffer such a fate prompted many Iraqis to quickly give in.[25]

The Devil Rangers reached PL Iowa at about 11:00 a.m. and held in place. Baker, in the meantime, sent the scouts forward to PL Plum to screen the task force while it halted. The 1st Division had seized the Iraqi security zone well ahead of schedule, reaching its first day's objective with virtually no casualties and plenty of daylight remaining.

Meanwhile Franks had received permission from CENTCOM's commander, General Norman H. Schwarzkopf, to proceed with an early breach. Franks set the time for 1:00 p.m. but later pushed it back to 3:00 p.m.[26]

On to the Breach—February 24, 1991
5th Battalion, 16th Infantry

About 11:00 a.m., Baker was summoned to the 1st Brigade TOC for a commanders' conference. Told by Maggart that the division would perform the breach at 3:00 p.m. that day, the battalion commanders briefly discussed the operation, then returned to their respective units, with Baker arriving at his task force TOC about 1:00 p.m. Meeting with his team commanders, Baker went over the revised plan of attack, informing them that their artillery preparation, scheduled for three hours on the following day, had been decreased to thirty minutes and would commence within the next hour and a half, at 3:30 p.m.

The team commanders were not heartened by this news. Before Desert Storm they had been told that, even with a three-hour artillery preparation, they could expect 40 percent casualties, especially if the Iraqis used chemical agents. But "Skip" Baker, a veteran of two combat tours in Vietnam, was dubious:

> I thought about it, and I pondered over it, and prayed about it, but I didn't think that was going to happen....You can't predict that kind of crap. There's no possible way. I mean, we could have gone up against a flippin' division and suffered no casualties whatsoever, or we could have run smack dab, headlong, into three of the Republican Guards divisions, dug in in prepared defenses, and ready to fight. And we could have been annihilated. But you can't think about that. That's not the game plan. The game plan is to go in, kick ass, take names, win the battle, win the war, do your job....[The casualty predictions] were a concern, but it wasn't one that was overwhelming.[27]

Still, the shorter artillery preparation phase no doubt caused some concern over whether it would be effective enough to counter the Iraqi commander's ability to lob chemical rounds into the breach sites. As it turned out, the 1st Division Artillery located and destroyed every remaining artillery piece of the Iraqi defenses forward of the division. The redlegs fired over eleven thousand rounds from tube artillery and 414 rounds of MLRS (Multiple Launch Rocket System), devastating the 48th Division's artillery and eliminating much of that division's ability to affect the Big Red One's next move.[28]

At 3:00 p.m., the Devil Rangers churned forward with Teams D and B (Captain Todd D. Smith) in the lead. Each team was responsible for creating two passage lanes through the obstacles and fighting positions. About one thousand meters short of the forward Iraqi defenses, the lead tanks dropped their mine plows and began to grind their way through the mine fields and wire entanglements, encountering only light resistance. Within forty-five minutes, TF 5-16 had four lanes cut, proofed, and cleared through the first defense belt. Follow-on teams quickly secured far-side objectives, in the process taking 160 prisoners.[29]

Once his units were through the breach, Baker called the fuellers forward to refuel the task force and directed his team commanders to prepare for future operations. At this time the Devil Rangers suffered their first casualty. At approximately 9:30 p.m., Private First Class Robert L. Daugherty, one of the fuel handlers, was severely injured by an exploding DPICM (Dual Purpose Integrated Conventional Munition) bomblet he had apparently picked up. Medics, believing Daugherty to be in a minefield, probed forward to reach him. He was soon evacuated to the battalion aid station, but despite the efforts of the medics and the physician's assistant, Daugherty died at about 11:30 p.m. It was a sad incident but, amazingly, the task force sustained no additional casualties.[30]

2nd Battalion, 16th Infantry

The biggest problem for Fake's troops—still poised between PLs Kansas and Plum—was the increasing number of Iraqi soldiers wanting to surrender. About 11:50 a.m., the E Company commander, Captain Kirk Schleifer, reported to Fake that he had just accepted the surrender of a well-dressed Iraqi lieutenant colonel and over 120 Iraqi soldiers, all that was left of one of the 48th Division's front-line battalions. The Iraqi commander, speaking in halting English, stated that he had buried 250 of his soldiers since the war had started, all of whom had been killed in Coalition air strikes and artillery bombardments. Soon, the POW problem became so acute that Fake directed his task force engineer to take his ACEs and throw up a rectangular berm to serve as the brigade POW pen.[31]

About 1:00 p.m., Moreno issued his subordinate commanders the FRAGO changing the breaching mission to 3:00 p.m.. Unlike Baker, Fake decided to refuel before the breach and called his fuellers forward. Meanwhile, Schwalm's Team A (A/3-37 Armor), as previously planned, moved forward to inspect the forward Iraqi defenses and, at 1:41 p.m., reported large numbers of concertina stakes but no wire. Further reconnaissance revealed that there were no mines or tank ditches to hinder the assault. By 2:20 p.m., the team pulled back to avoid the scheduled artillery barrage.[32]

At 3:08 p.m., Fake ordered the breach teams forward. Fear and dread gripped the troops, but none faltered. Within ten minutes, Teams A and D had cleared the first lanes through the first trench line, but the resistance here was more active than that which the Devil Rangers encountered.

About twenty minutes into the effort, a dug-in BRDM fired on Captain Kelly Morningstar's Team Delta. The company XO dispatched it with one 120mm round from his M1A1. Within an hour, the team had destroyed three more enemy vehicles, one being hit by a TOW from an ITV from over a mile and a half away.

Captain Scott Rutter's Team C reached the second trench line, turned east, and cleared that position of enemy resistance. Team D continued north about thirty-five hundred meters past the initial breach point, cut through the third trench line, then turned east and rolled up that position. Pushing through the lanes behind the breach teams came Teams A and B, which turned east and moved to positions to continue the attack in that direction. Schleifer's E Company moved to the north of the breach and set up in a designated support-by-fire position to protect what was now TF 2-16's left flank, as it made the big turn toward Kuwait. From this position, the AT company subsequently destroyed five additional armored vehicles, including a T-55, a ZSU 23-4 air defense vehicle, and two artillery pieces.[33]

By 5:15 p.m. Fake's units were set at PL Colorado, where they established security for the night. In twelve hours, the Rangers had traveled twenty-eight kilometers, captured six hundred enemy soldiers, breached the Iraqi main defense line, and destroyed numerous armored vehicles, but incredibly they had suffered no casualties. As darkness fell, the task force refueled, sorted and transported its prisoners to the brigade POW pen, and prepared for operations on the morrow.

Desert Storm—February 25, 1991
2nd Battalion, 16th Infantry

About 5:45 a.m. on February 25, the task force received a FRAGO to continue its attack east at 7:00 a.m. Like the day before, the advance was preceded by an artillery barrage, this time against the Iraqi 25th Infantry Division. Intelligence reports indicated that this division was better prepared than previously defeated 48th to resist an attack, and the information soon proved to be correct.

Fake started his command forward at 8:02 a.m. with the AT Company still guarding the left flank. Then came Teams D, C, and B, left to right, with Team A following in reserve. Within twenty minutes of the LD, elements began engaging the remnant bunkers and vehicles of the 48th Infantry Division. At 8:36 a.m., Sergeant Stephen Harriau, a track commander in 3rd Platoon, E Company, spotted what appeared to be a command bunker, festooned with antennas, and requested permission to fire on it. Given the go ahead, Harriau scored a direct hit on the position. Iraqi troops came pouring out of the bunker and ran to another bunker some distance away. The sergeant pulled up and prepared to launch a missile at the second position, when suddenly white flags appeared from its opening. Harriau checked his fire and went forward to accept the surrender of the commanding general of the 48th Division, ten other officers,

and 127 enlisted men. Sergeant Harriau and his crew had just eliminated the enemy division's command post.[34]

Continuing their advance, the lead elements confirmed by spot reports what Fake had learned earlier. At about the 93 northing (the 90-degree latitude line), tank and track commanders could see extensive defenses and wire obstacles about twenty-five hundred meters to the east. This was the beginning of the 25th Infantry Division's lines. Commanders called for fire on the position, but for some reason the division artillery was slow to respond. In the meantime Teams B and C engaged by direct fire what appeared to be a reinforced company.

The Iraqi soldiers facing Team C fiercely resisted the Rangers' attempts to root them out of their fighting positions. The fighting began in earnest at about 9:20 a.m. just as the artillery began falling on the enemy positions. Rutter directed his FIST (Fire Support Team) chief to shift the artillery fires and moved his company forward in the attack. There was no real contest. Bradley and tank fire, coupled with Vulcans raking the trench lines, soon induced the Iraqi infantrymen to give up. By 9:50 a.m. the fight was over and enemy troops, hands in the air, were streaming from of their positions.[35]

Around 11:00 a.m. Fake reported to Moreno that his task force had advanced fourteen kilometers and had reached PL New Jersey, the limit of advance. Meanwhile, the Iraqis continued to surrender in such numbers that they soon became a hindrance to further combat operations. Indeed, information received from the Big Red One G2 indicated that the 1st Division had captured over twenty thousand Iraqis in the first eighteen hours of operations.[36]

At 1:00 p.m., Fake pushed the scouts forward to screen the task force as it consolidated its positions. Six hours later at 7:00 p.m., the chemical threat status was downgraded to MOPP 1 (Mission Oriented Protection Posture), which allowed the relieved soldiers to climb out of their bulky, charcoal-lined suits. This was soon followed by a FRAGO ordering Fake to defend along PL Utah and placing TF 2-16 under the direct operational control of the VII Corps.[37]

5th Battalion, 16th Infantry

About 11:30 p.m. on February 24, Baker received an order directing him to attack to seize Objective 12K, a nondescript piece of terrain identified only by a "goose egg" on the task force operations map. Defended by the Iraqi 3rd Battalion, 110th Infantry Brigade, the objective was a series of trench lines and an extensive bunker system. Rejecting an earlier plan for hitting the position from the south, Baker and his S3, Major Brian R. Zahn, devised a scheme for attacking it from the north and issued a FRAGO to that effect at 1:30 p.m.

Prior to the LD time at 6:00 a.m., Baker had moved Captain Gerald N. Niland's E Company to a support-by-fire position overlooking the objective. Niland was to keep the enemy pinned down as Captain Orth's tank team and Captain Joseph F. Thompson's Team C approached the position. After

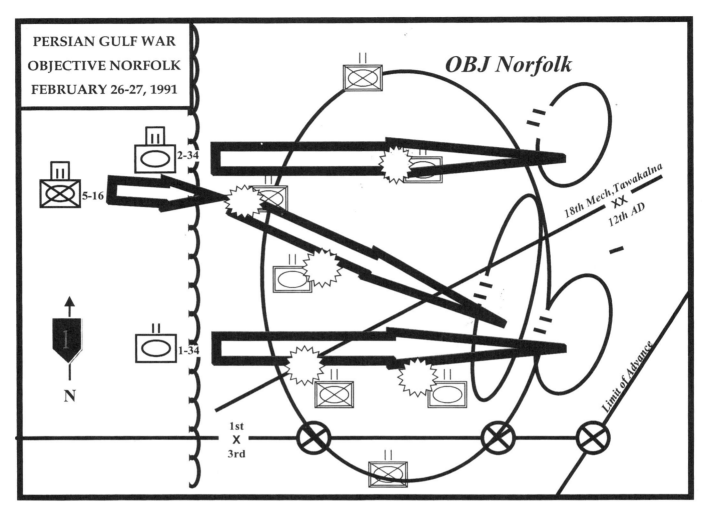

Map 12-2.

a delicate bypass movement around a portion of TF 2-34, Orth's Team A rolled through half of the objective, capturing only five prisoners—one whom was the brigade commander of the 110th. The position was so extensive, however, that the team was forced to halt and begin clearing operations before it could safely move on.

Meanwhile, Thompson's team came up on Orth's left and continued the attack into the objective. By 9:00 a.m., the position was secure. While infantry troops from the two teams destroyed enemy equipment and ACEs bulldozed the bunkers and trench lines, Baker moved the rest of TF 5-16 to Battle Position 160 to prepare for the next mission, Operation Jeremiah II—a massive attack by the Big Red One into the flanks of the Republican Guard units in Kuwait.

Baker received the FRAGO for Jeremiah II about 3:30 p.m. He began moving TF 5-16 east to a new jump-off point at 7:00 p.m. Arriving at the location around midnight, Zahn and the battle staff went to work refining the plans for the advance on the 26th.[38]

Desert Storm—February 26, 1991
2nd Battalion, 16th Infantry

After consolidating positions along PL Utah on the afternoon of February 25, TF 2-16 remained in place until the following morning, when Fake's troops began destroying captured enemy equipment, bunkers, and trench lines. For the next two days, the Rangers labored from dawn to dusk destroying Iraqi vehicles and artillery, filling in trenches, blowing up bunkers, radios, weapons, and rounding up Iraqi documents and prisoners for processing in the rear. Despite the dangerous work, the task force sustained only two injuries during period, both from DPICM munitions laying on the ground.

5th Battalion, 16th Infantry

At 1:30 a.m., Baker ordered his team commanders to position their units for the next attack. At 5:00 a.m., the Devil Rangers began movement to PL Hartz about sixty kilometers to the east. Following the brigade's direct support field artillery battalion, 1-5 FA, the task force carefully made its way forward in a driving sandstorm, reaching PL Hartz at 3:30 p.m. Shortly thereafter, the 1st Brigade TOC directed the task force to round up four to six hundred Iraqi soldiers who were waiting to surrender about four kilometers east of PL Hartz. Smith's Team B received the mission, and he sent his XO and a platoon to secure the demoralized mob.[39]

Battle of Objective Norfolk

By the morning of February 26, Coalition ground forces had been successful all along the front. Saddam's first-line divisions had been destroyed, captured, or immobilized. All that remained were the tank and mechanized divisions and the Republican Guards units in and near Kuwait. Though these divisions had been attrited by the air campaign, they were still relatively intact and waiting to give battle. In light of their past performance against Iranian forces, the guards could be expected to put up stiff resistance.

During the day, Maggart had received the FRAGO directing him to attack into the Republican Guard Tawakalna Division holding Objective Norfolk on the morning of the 27th. TF 5-16 received the FRAGO in turn, and Baker issued his FRAGO to the task force at about 5:00 p.m. The task force mission was to follow behind the brigade and in the center between TF 2-34 on the left and 1-34 Armor on the right as those two tank units passed through the 2nd Armored Cavalry Regiment (ACR). The brigade was then to blast its way through the Tawakalna Division and into the Iraqi reserve units.[40]

Barely ten minutes had passed before the brigade was ordered to execute the mission with an LD time of 5:30 p.m. instead of the following morning. Though still in the process of refueling, the Devil Rangers immediately began staging for the attack, but a misoriented engineer company and a wheeled vehicle convoy crossing to the front delayed the task force's departure by almost forty minutes.

Now fifteen kilometers behind the rest of the brigade, Baker led the task force forward in column at thirty-five kilometers per hour. The Devil Rangers pulled into the rear of the brigade formation about 10:30 p.m. and prepared to conduct a passage of lines through the 2nd ACR, which the lead 1st Brigade elements had already contacted. Once the passage was completed, what has since come to be known as "Fright Night" began.

The night of February 26-27 was relatively clear in terms of weather. The moon was up and provided some illumination of the battlefield. Visibility was obscured, however, by the haze from the many oil field fires set by Saddam's fleeing troops, and by the burning hulks left by the 2nd Cavalry in their initial fights with the Tawakalna Division at the 73 Easting. All these conditions combined to make this night a rather surrealistic experience and added to the anxiety of the troops of TF 5-16.

Because TF 5-16 was in the rear of the brigade movement, and initially behind Fontenot's TF 2-34, Baker ordered a "weapons tight" status on his force to ensure that there would

be no "friendly fire" incidents. This meant that the crews could open fire only after securing Baker's personal permission.

Because most enemy resistance that night came from dismounted infantry, the situation for the soldiers of TF 5-16 was especially tense. Gunners scanning the area viewed numerous potential targets in their thermal sights, but the enemy vehicles they spotted appeared to have been knocked out by the tank battalions that had already passed thorough, or seemed to have been abandoned by their fleeing crews. Nevertheless, small-arms fire erupted from various bunkers as the task force slowly ground its way forward. The task force quickly responded with coax machine guns and 25mm chain guns to suppress the enemy fire.

Because Ritter's battalion was a tank pure unit, with no infantry, it was unable to adequately clear the areas through which it passed. Baker therefore began to drift his task force southeastward to get in behind 1-34 Armor. The Devil Rangers cleared the way for the follow-on support units to safely pass, but it was a difficult task. In several instances, Baker had to dismount soldiers to root out resistance in trenches still defended by a few diehards. By the time dawn broke on the morning of February 27, the Devil Rangers had destroyed one T-55 tank, two BMPs, eleven BRDMs, sixteen MTLBs, and eleven trucks. They had also captured 144 Iraqi soldiers.[41] At about 9:00 a.m., the task force joined Fontenot's and Ritter's units on the far side of Norfolk.

Desert Storm—February 27-28, 1991

While TF 2-16, still near the berm, continued to destroy enemy equipment on the morning of February 27, the Devil Rangers pushed on to PL Milford, where it established hasty defense positions and resupplied and refueled the teams. Behind the 1st Brigade lay the smoldering remnants of the 8th Armored and 19th Mechanized Brigades of the Tawakalna Division. The remaining formations of the Jihad Corps lay ahead, but would prove to be a negligible threat in the hours to come.

Baker's task force began moving again at 10:30 a.m. Still operating in support of brigade, it advanced slowly throughout the day, policing hundreds of Iraqi prisoners en route. By 5:30 p.m., the task force had entered restricted terrain that was ideal for infantry attacks against mechanized forces, so Baker halted his command and directed his team commanders to set up a 360-degree defense with observation posts forward. The night of February 27-28 passed without incident, but the following morning hundreds more Iraqi soldiers approached the Devil Rangers, intent on surrendering. The task force soldiers simply ordered the Iraqis to march to the rear where follow-on units would accept their capitulation. In the meantime, Baker moved TF 5-16 out of the wadi system and ordered it into a tactical laager position to refuel and resupply. While executing this movement, word of the cease-fire came over the net.[42]

The 1st Brigade was soon ordered to move to an assembly area thirty-five kilometers to the east, arriving there about 5:30

p.m. That evening, since Fake's 2-16 was still destroying enemy equipment and vehicles near the initial breach site, the Devil Rangers were attached to the 2nd Brigade and ordered to link with that brigade near Safwan. There, Baker's men were to assist in securing the airfield at Safwan, where the cease-fire negotiations would be held with Saddam Hussein's representatives. The task force moved the morning of March 1 to link up with the 2nd Brigade three kilometers south of the Iraqi border near Safwan. Baker's command arrived at the airfield to assume the western sector at 3:00 p.m.[43]

Safwan

At 5:40 p.m. on March 1, Fake's TF 2-16 was reattached to the 2nd Brigade and arrived at the airfield, where it was to help secure the negotiation area. Moreno ordered the 2nd Battalion to secure the southern portion of the perimeter around the field, while the 5th Battalion secured the west. The 1-4 Cavalry, TF 3-37, and 4-37 Armor were directed to secure the remainder of the perimeter. By 9:30 p.m. all elements were in place.

That evening, Fake sent William's Team B to clear and secure the route into the airfield for the Iraqi negotiators. This was accomplished by the next morning, but the Rangers then received word that the talks were postponed until the following day.

On March 3, the negotiations were scheduled to start at the airfield at 11:00 a.m. with the 2nd and 5th Battalions providing much of the security for this historic event. As the Iraqi generals drove along the route that Team B had cleared for them to enter, they saw the team's BFVs menacingly parked along the route south of the runway and Fake's BFV with the battalion colors proudly wafting in the breeze.

Also parked along the route, guns facing toward the road, was TF 5-16's "Team Freedom" consisting of two tank platoons, two mechanized platoons, and one AT platoon, representing each of the team organizations of the task force. Baker also had his battalion colors flying from his command track. The two 16th Infantry battalions gave the Iraqi negotiators every sign that day that the U.S. Army had won the contest, and that the Rangers were ready and eager to resume battle if necessary.

The soldiers of Thompson's C Company, 5-16 Infantry, secured the actual site of the talks. These began as scheduled and lasted until 3:00 p.m., at which time the Iraqi generals were escorted back to Safwan and sent to tell Saddam the bad news about the outcome of the "Mother of All Battles."[44]

The war was over and the Rangers of both battalions almost immediately began their next task—the destruction of captured Iraqi equipment. Baker's troops concentrated on the positions around Jabal Sanam (Hill 138) overlooking the airfield, then pulled out to return to the 1st Brigade on March 5. For the next ten days, Fake's men continued the destruction efforts amidst rumors of additional fighting in Iraq and the possible resumption of hostilities.

On February 6, General Rhame visited his battalions. Arriving at TF 2-16's position, he gathered about one hundred TF 2-16 soldiers around Fake's communications track and talked to them about the war, the results, and their performance. He summed up his remarks by saying, "I'm damn proud of you. That bastard picked the wrong fight!"[45]

Homeward Bound

For the next two months the soldiers of both task forces were employed in the destruction of Iraqi equipment and ammunition, identifying and burying the enemy's dead, securing key locations, and finally, cleaning and packing unit equipment for the trip home. Early in April, the Devil Rangers were sent south to clear a path back through the minefields and prepare RDA (Rear Deployment Area) Huebner for occupation. On April 14, the division began traveling to Huebner, where equipment would be cleaned at temporary wash racks, inspected, and otherwise prepared for the final customs inspections at King Khalid Military City (KKMC). After a two-day trip that took them back through the very passages they had cut in the Iraqi defenses and the berm seven weeks before, TF 2-16 also arrived at Huebner on April 28 to begin recovery operations.

For the next ten days the troops pitched in to account for their equipment and prepare it for the rigorous customs inspections. Finally, on April 24, TF 5-16 departed for KKMC. Two days later, the Ranger advanced party traveled to KKMC, followed by the TF 2-16 main body on April 28.

Not so affectionately called the "MGM" due to its faint resemblance to the MGM hotel in Las Vegas, KKMC served as the last home away from home for both the 2nd and 5th Battalions before redeployment to Fort Riley. At KKMC the two task forces carried out the final maintenance, washing, inspection, and packing of vehicles and Milvans before loading them onto HETs for the trip to the port. By the first week of May they had loaded the last vehicles, and the troops settled in to await their place in the redeployment airflow. Finally on May 9 and 10, the Devil Rangers departed for Fort Riley, followed by the Rangers on May 11 and 12. The regiment's first tour in the Middle East had ended.

As in past wars, the troops of the 16th Infantry had a right to hold their heads high. Upon conclusion of hostilities, Dan Fake and Skip Baker wrote to the regiment's serving Honorary Colonel, Colonel (Ret.) Bill Hathaway, to report on the performance of their respective battalions. Fake wrote:

> The Battalion did exceptionally well. These young men never hesitated & had a clear focus. They upheld the proud tradition of the regiment and 2-16 Infantry....You can be proud of these young men, their moral fiber, and their willingness to accomplish any task. They are proud members of a regiment that [always] meets any task head on and performs well.[46]

Skip Baker was also proud of his troops:

The 5-16 is still very combat-ready; high morale and excellent discipline prevail. As our Colonel-of-the-Regiment, I want you to know that the soldiers of the 16th acquitted themselves courageously under fire and with dedication and honor. You have every right to be as proud of their performance as I am.[47]

The performance of all battalions of the 16th Infantry in the Persian Gulf War was indeed impressive. During the four-day conflict the Rangers of the 2nd Battalion had destroyed ten tanks, seventeen artillery pieces, and six APCs, and captured some thirteen hundred Iraqi soldiers. The Devil Rangers of the 5th Battalion accounted for six tanks, seventeen artillery pieces, and ninety-one APCs, and captured 996 Iraqis. Honore's 4th Battalion, while not involved in the fighting, helped to unload 152 ships, in the process handling 50,500 pieces of equipment and containers, and provided life support to over 107,000 soldiers.[48] At the same time the regiment suffered only three fatalities in the war. While any loss of life is a tragedy, on balance this was an enormous accomplishment relative to the casualties sustained by Rangers in past wars and the amount of punishment inflicted on Iraqi forces.

Much of the great success achieved by the U.S. Army in the Gulf War can be attributed to the training that units received at the National Training Center (NTC) for the previous eight years or so. The realistic scenarios, the well-trained opposing forces, and the hard work of observer/controllers to ensure that units were "getting it right" during their rotations through the NTC all contributed immeasurably to the army's ultimate achievements in the desert. The best tribute of how well the NTC did its job came from a soldier in the 5-16 Infantry after the war. He simply said, "Compared to the OPFOR at the NTC, the Tawakalna Division was a piece of cake."

In addition to being the final exam for the National Training Center's first decade of effort, the Gulf War was to be a test of the U.S. Army's AirLand Battle doctrine. It was also a test of an army that had been painstakingly built by generals who learned from mistakes made by the U.S. Army during the Vietnam, and post-Vietnam, eras. Rebuilt during the presidency of Ronald Reagan, the army was imbued with the "can-do" spirit and patriotism of that popular commander in chief. The efforts of the Reagan administration to help those generals rebuild and strengthen the American armed forces, combined with the acquisition of the latest and best equipment, recruitment of well-qualified men and women, superb training opportunities, and a renewed sense of self-worth and mission after the Vietnam War, cannot be underestimated when evaluating the performance of the army in Operation Desert Storm. These factors all helped to produce what was arguably the best army ever fielded by the United States and, arguably, by any nation at any

time in history. Four battalions of Rangers were part of that army and did their part to win that war, as well as to bring the Cold War to an end.

With the end of the Cold War, the wartime mission of the 1st Infantry Division became more ambiguous than it had been during the previous forty years. The division's focus was still Eurocentric, but with the caveat that it might have to deploy to the Middle East once again. With the continuation of the post-Gulf War drawdown and the advent of the Clinton administration, the 1st Infantry Division's focus become even less clear. Over the rest of the 1990s, the regiment underwent numerous changes and drawdowns ultimately resulting in only one battalion remaining in active service. Even so, the primary activities of the 16th Infantry during the final decade of the century would remain centered on training for NTC rotations.

1st Battalion, 16th Infantry
1991-1994

By 1990, the systems and ideas that had initially driven the concept of the United States Army Regimental System were dead. In addition, the army had dropped the COHORT system and personnel managers deemed the idea of regimental home-basing impractical. As a result, the concept of having multiple battalions of the same regiment on active duty no longer made sense. In addition, with the loss of several divisions from the force structure, the army stood to lose numerous old and well-decorated regiments from the active rolls.

Although the Gulf War had temporarily interrupted the inactivation of the 1st Infantry Division (Forward), the schedule called for the 1st and 4th Battalions to be chopped from the rolls as well. For whatever reason, the Department of the Army decided to keep the 1st Battalion on the active list and determined to reflag the 5th Battalion at Fort Riley as the new 1st Battalion. This change went into effect on July 15, 1991. At the same time the 1st and 4th Battalions in Germany were inactivated and the 5th Battalion at Fort Riley was redesignated as the new 1st Battalion. Lieutenant Colonel Frank J. Stone, a 1976 North Georgia College graduate, took command of the newly redesignated battalion.

The first major event in which the new 1st Battalion (still using the Devil Ranger nickname) participated was an Expert Infantry Badge test, run by the battalion and held at Devil Parade across from the 1st Brigade headquarters building. Involved in the test were soldiers from the 2nd Battalion, mortarmen of the division's four tank battalions, and the 1-4 Cavalry. In all, 365 soldiers tested their skills, but when it was over, only 49 received the badge from Major General William Hartzog, the new division commander, at Devil Parade. Of particular note was the accomplishment of Sergeant Barry Rush, a squad leader in Headquarters Company. His squad won the Squad High Percentage award. Rush was awarded an Army Achievement Medal; four of his seven squad members were awarded the coveted badge; all received a four-day pass.[49]

In October, the dismounted soldiers of D Company and the TOW crews from E Company conducted Operation Dragoneer. A seven-day exercise designed to prepare the troops for an upcoming NTC rotation, Dragoneer featured air assault missions into enemy rear areas to seize and hold chokepoints and other key terrain features. The troops were airlifted from Devil Parade to privately owned farmland along the Solomon River near Niles, Kansas. The use of an off-post site was an unusual aspect of the exercise. Since World War II, carrying out army operations on civilian land has become increasingly problematic, mainly because of opposition by landowners. In the countryside around Fort Riley, however, soldiers are generally well-received by the local populace, and this time was no different. "Two gentlemen pulled up in a pickup truck, very interested in what we were doing," stated Major Mark Landrith, battalion S3. "We happened to have a helicopter on the ground at the time. They checked it out and just wanted to know what we were doing....The attitude [of the local civilians] continued to be very supportive.[50]

Soon after Dragoneer, the battalion deployed to Fort Irwin for another NTC rotation. This was the battalion's first NTC rotation since the Gulf War, and although it had participated in the war (as the 5th Battalion), by this time it was an almost entirely different unit because of the rotation of personnel. Hardly anyone who had been with the unit when it was the 5th Battalion remained in key positions. The performance of the battalion at the NTC reflected its newness as a team. In addition to Colonel Stone's battalion, the brigade combat team consisted of the 2-34 Armor and a light infantry battalion from the 10th Mountain Division. Though exposing a few rough edges, Stone's troops came through the event a better outfit.

Over the next several months, the Devil Rangers went through a series of training events to file off those rough edges. The following September, the battalion went through another EIB test. This time 36 out of the 197 soldiers vying to earn the EIB won badges. Additionally, two 1st Battalion soldiers, Staff Sergeant Rob Cruce and Corporal Jason Brown, were respectively honored as 16th Infantry NCO of the Year and Soldier of the Year.[51]

In late October 1992, the battalion conducted a week-long Level III gunnery exercise, which was followed by a squad assault course in November. Shortly after these events, Colonel Stone was hit with two short-notice tasks that would have a significant effect on the 1st Battalion for the next year.

The first of these requirements was a return trip to the NTC. Originally scheduled to send about three hundred soldiers to augment the OPFOR in January 1993, that assignment had been canceled late that summer and new plans were laid out for that time period. Suddenly, the earlier requirement was resurrected by the III Corps in November, and Colonel Stone now had to revise his next quarter's training plan again to accommodate the mission. With the appropriate training plans and other preparations completed, the three

hundred-man Bobtail battalion deployed to Fort Irwin on January 5, and spent three cold and exhausting weeks performing as leg infantry with the OPFOR. Despite extremely cold and wet weather conditions that were unusual for the desert around Fort Irwin, the troops accomplished their missions with Devil Ranger gusto.

Stone received the second short-notice requirement just after the battalion returned from the NTC. In February, the commander was notified to put together a four-platoon, 125-man, leg infantry company to deploy to Saudi Arabia to perform a ground security mission for U.S. air defense units there. Stone selected Captain Stanley A. Smith's C Company for the job and directed that the battalion "dismounts" (those soldiers who rode in the back of the BFVs and had to dismount as regular infantry) from each company would form the bulk of the deploying organization. This decision meant that the Bradley crews of each company could stay together and maintain their crew gunnery proficiencies—all except C Company's crews, of course.

On March 23, the company processed through Craig Gym, and departed from Forbes Field in Topeka. Once in Saudi Arabia, C Company was attached to the 2nd Battalion, 7th Air Defense Artillery (ADA) as its security force. Smith split up his troops and deployed them to ADA sites in and near Dahran and Riyadh for the next five months, until the company's return in August.

Meanwhile, in Kansas, the rest of the battalion embarked on a very busy spring and summer schedule that culminated in the battalion's next trip to the NTC that autumn.

In April, the battalion negotiated a series of platoon-level ARTEP exercises in the cold, wet, and muddy environment of late winter snows. This was followed by a month-long Level I gunnery exercise in late April and May, and the dispatch of several teams in late May to support National Guard training at locations across the country, including Camp McCoy, Wisconsin, and Fort Carson, Colorado. The Fort Carson team provided training assistance to the 16th Infantry's perennial affiliation unit, the Kansas National Guard's 1st Battalion, 137th Infantry.

On June 18, 1993, command of the battalion was passed from Colonel Stone to Lieutenant Colonel William S. "Scott" Knoebel, a 1976 graduate of Norwich University. Almost immediately upon taking command, Knoebel and a team from the battalion deployed to Fort Stewart, Georgia, to support the summer training of the South Carolina National Guard's 218th Infantry Brigade.

Taking Captain Dave Grimm's entire A Company to act as OPFOR, Knoebel deployed about 180 officers and men to Fort Stewart on Operation Bold Shift. This force was divided into three training teams consisting of the B, D, plus HHC company commanders and selected officers and NCOs, and a rump battalion staff. The battalion's mission was to set up training lanes for the scout platoons of each of the three maneuver battalions in the brigade and train and evaluate those platoons. Over the next three weeks, Captains Steve Sabia (B Company), Tim

DeLass (D Company), and Bruce Gourlie (HHC) constructed training lanes, instruction areas, and sand tables; conducted rehearsals and classes; and put the three scout platoons through a series of thorough ARTEP exercises. They successfully executed the mission, with the result that three scout platoons were much better prepared to perform their wartime missions.

Upon returning from Fort Stewart, the 1st Battalion started a series of training events designed to prepare it for its next NTC rotation in October and November. Beginning in July, the battalion ran through company lanes, then participated in the capstone preparation event, Exercise Gauntlet, August 8-13. This exercise was conducted under the extremely rainy weather conditions during that summer of 1993. The ground became so soggy, that there were times when tanks became stuck on the *tops* of hills.

During one particularly violent thunderstorm, the battalion was scheduled to conduct a movement to contact. Just before the Devil Rangers were to jump off, the division TOC inquired of Colonel George W. Aldridge, the 1st Brigade commander, whether he wanted to call off or delay the attack. Aldridge contacted Knoebel to get his opinion, but the Devil Ranger commander demurred, stating that the attack would not be canceled in actual combat. Knoebel recalled that the discussion in the TOC and from company commanders was one of "let's get on with it and get going. Let's just do the best we can." At this point, he knew that the battalion had a lot of spirit and was ready to do their assigned missions under the toughest of circumstances. Minutes later, TF 1-16 crossed the LD.[52]

The battalion made its way south through rain and darkness to make contact with the OPFOR played by 4-37 Armor. Some elements got misdirected and moved in the wrong direction, and the operation did not appear to be going the way it should. But as the scouts made the initial contact with the enemy's defenses and company commanders got their bearings in the early morning light, units began to arrive at the correct assault positions. Soon, Captain Steve Sabia's B Company, the breach team, was busily cutting through the enemy's wire obstacles and getting elements to the far side to neutralize the enemy's overwatch positions. Unfortunately, the breach location, poorly selected by the battalion S3, was actually in the enemy's main kill zone, and "casualties" mounted rapidly as the flashing yellow lights that indicated a killed vehicle began to multiply. Nevertheless, the Devil Rangers continued to push.

Meanwhile, Brigadier General Huba Wass de Czega hinted to Colonel Aldridge that the outcome was obvious and the task force was going to fail, but the brigade commander refused to stop the play. "The battalion says they can do it," Aldridge told the ADC, "and they're still moving." Instead of halting the exercise, the brigade commander wanted to see how far the Devil Rangers could go.[53]

Though things did appear bleak, the heroic efforts of the B Company troopers paid off. Soon the attached tank teams, which also had heavy losses, were able to force a penetration into the enemy's rear areas. Though the losses were high, the battalion succeeded where the armored task force that previously tried the same mission had utterly failed. The success, which was really a tactical draw, gave the men of the battalion great confidence in their teamwork. Despite the bad weather that summer (along with accompanying clouds of mosquitoes), the Devil Rangers were able to achieve even greater success in each of their remaining missions during the train-up.

One incident occurred during Gauntlet that made Colonel Knoebel particularly proud of his soldiers and their willingness to take charge. Upon taking command, he perceived a lack of initiative among the NCOs and junior officers of the battalion, which he chalked up to their fear of doing something wrong. He began to emphasize to all his leaders, commanders, lieutenants, and NCOs alike, that everybody had jobs to do. Everybody had to "get into the fight" to make a battalion run as it should, and he encouraged commanders to make sure that it was their NCOs who took care of NCO responsibilities, not their officers. He also pushed company executive officers to take on higher levels of responsibility to relieve company commanders of administrative burdens.

In this effort, Knoebel had help from two superb soldiers. One was Command Sergeant Major Everett H. Tuxhorn Jr., the battalion's top soldier. Knoebel called Tuxhorn "the finest command sergeant major I've ever seen. He had never forgotten that he was a soldier first and foremost. He demanded high standards, yet he was a man of great compassion and character."[54]

And this was indeed true. Tuxhorn typically cared for his soldiers at the same time he was disciplining them. One night at the MPRC, there was a particularly violent thunderstorm with lighting, winds, and rain that rocked the gunnery tower. Climbing into his HUMMV, Tuxhorn drove out in the severe weather to check on the soldiers at the guard posts to ensure that they were not injured. At each station, he gave them instructions to remain in the middle of their guard shacks so that they did not touch the metal sides and told them that they were not to use their radios until the storm had passed in order to minimize the chance that they might be struck by lightening. Once the storm was over, however, he warned them, "You'd better have that damned radio on and making your [communications] checks right away." He added that if he had to come out there again to make sure they were not asleep or had forgotten to turn the radio back on, there would be hell to pay.

Knoebel also had an outstanding executive officer, Major Delane B. "Dee" Esplin. Esplin was a short man, but a giant when it came to work capacity. Working sixteen to eighteen-hour days, he was tireless in ensuring that the day-to-day operation of the battalion went as smoothly as possible.

These two men adopted Knoebel's approach and encouraged the battalion's NCOs and young officers to use their initiative and take charge of their responsibilities. Before long, sergeants began to realize that they did have authority, as well as responsibility, and that they would be supported by the chain of command in taking the initiative. The same became true of the battalion's junior officers.

Knoebel knew he was making progress in these efforts during the Gauntlet exercise in August. Due to the heavy rains that had by then lasted for weeks, the Republican, Kansas, and Smokey Hill Rivers overflowed their banks and threatened to flood out the homes of several Devil Ranger soldiers in Junction City and Manhattan. With the battalion in the field, several wives had no option but to call to the battalion rear detachment NCO in charge and ask for help. Even under normal circumstances, getting authorization to dispatch a vehicle off-post at Fort Riley was difficult, but the Devil Ranger NCO in the rear decided without authorization to send details of stay-behind soldiers loaded on "deuce and a half" trucks into town without authorization to aid the families of battalion soldiers. The NCO could have been reprimanded for the action, but he had made the right decision and Knoebel firmly supported him.[55]

Gauntlet proved to be invaluable for the battalion. After its conclusion, Knoebel's three key planners, the XO, S3, and CSM, went to work and developed a targeted training and administrative plan to get the battalion ready for the NTC that autumn. The first event was a Level II gunnery exercise.

The Devil Rangers rolled into the gunnery exercise in early September with the knowledge that they had done well during Gauntlet. The NCOs' and soldiers' new-found confidence in the battalion helped them to set several new division records for gunnery scores, particularly in the category of one thousand crews. Upon conclusion of this training, the 1st Battalion had set a new cumulative record for a battalion gunnery in the 1st Infantry Division.

A short respite followed, during which the troops achieved new laurels and relaxed a little before deploying in October on the 1st Battalion's next NTC rotation. Back in garrison, the Devil Rangers learned that they had won the brigade reenlistment award for that fiscal year. Additionally, the soldiers of the 1st Battalion went on to win the brigade sports day competition. Clearly morale was high.

During this respite, just before the deployment, the Devil Rangers held another session to present the not-so-coveted "Black Maltese" award at the Fort Riley Leader's Club. Named after the distinctive black Maltese cross that once adorned the rear sides of the 5th Battalion's APCs in years past, the Black Maltese was awarded in a similar vein as the 2-16 Infantry's "Bonehead" award. The award was a large black Maltese cross made of sheet metal, mounted on a wooden base, and adorned with small mementoes of some significance relating to the exploits of previous "winners" of the award. Each time the prize was awarded, the winner was required to add something to the maltese cross using glue, rivets, or some other semipermanent method. In addition, the proud holder of the cross received a small replica of the award, hung from a leather thong that had to worn about the neck for the next thirty days,

as the award itself was too cumbersome to carry around in the work areas. Typically, some poor lieutenant was stuck with the prize, and rarely a company commander. In the spirit of the occasion, commanders frequently conspired together to ensure that attention was deflected elsewhere, and they were usually successful.

With the conclusion of the rest-up period and the fun of the Black Maltese session behind them, the Devil Rangers deployed to the National Training Center in high spirits, ready to take on the vaunted OPFOR. The battalion arrived at Fort Irwin on October 20 and, as was customary, set up tentage in the infamous Dustbowl, which was now fitted with such "luxuries" as shelters with stand-up concrete tables for eating meals. Generally, however, the Dustbowl was just as miserable as in the past—rows of pup tents in the blowing sand and portable latrines that seemed to be a mile away at 4:00 a.m.

The first task facing the battalion was the vehicle draw. Due to turn-in difficulties faced by the previous rotation unit, many of the vehicles scheduled for issue to the 1st Battalion were not ready when the Devil Rangers started their draw. Additionally, Boeing, the contracting company that ran the vehicle maintenance yards, decided that over one thousand track shoes had to be replaced on the BFVs that were to be issued to the 1-16 Infantry before the vehicles could be released for training. Boeing offered minimal assistance, but in true "Ranger" fashion, the battalion pitched in and replaced the shoes over the next three nights, then went on to complete the draw on schedule.[56]

In the meantime, the Devil Rangers ran two brigade gunnery ranges before units went into the maneuver box to begin the rotation. The first was a MILES (Multiple Integrated Laser Engagement System) gunnery range and the second was a live test-fire range. Both of these ranges were built and ran by the battalion's very able Master Gunner, Staff Sergeant Daniel Willing. Willing constructed the MILES range on a low ridge north of the vehicle staging area, and within two days, had run fifty-four tanks and sixty BFVs through the range, while correcting all deficiencies associated with the MILES equipment.

Late the evening of the second day on the MILES range, Willing then led a convoy with a range construction detail through the central corridor northeast, up to a location known as the "Arrowhead," and built the brigade's live-fire range just northeast of that distinctive hill. Here, once again, Willing ran a smooth operation that ensured that all tanks and Bradleys of the 1st Brigade Task Force test-fired all weapons systems in one day.

At this point, the decision to send one company to Saudi Arabia really began to hamper the battalion. With one hundred of the 1-16's non-Bradley crew soldiers overseas, the battalion had to rely on sixty volunteers from the Arkansas National Guard's 39th Infantry Brigade. These troops were not mechanized soldiers, but straight-leg infantrymen, and few if any had ever undergone training on mechanized infantry operations. Under the guidance of Captains Rhett Russell and Dave

Rasmussen from the battalion's S3 shop, these Arkansas soldiers were put through a three-day crash course. Although the training time and resources available were far less than what Russell desired to get these men ready, his superb efforts resulted in their being able to perform at least the rudimentary tasks of mechanized soldiers.

First, the 1st Battalion had to go through the rotation's live-fire phase. About October 25, the Devil Rangers occupied defensive positions west of Drinkwater Lake in the NTC's northern corridor. Then, over the next couple of days, the battalion dug in and prepared for the attack. The following day, TF 1-16 executed an excellent day defense of the northern corridor. This was followed by a night defense of the same positions. In all the defense missions were very successful, though in one instance an enemy platoon was ruled to have broken through.

The day after the night defense, TF 1-16 conducted a passage of lines through Alpha-Bravo pass. They also conducted a movement to contact as its live-fire offense mission. Under the cover of indirect fire provided by the 1st Battalion, 5th Field Artillery, TF 1-16 deftly negotiated the enemy positions west of the pass in Echo Valley, swung north, and descended along the winding trail of another narrow pass called the "Escarpment." There, the task force reentered the northern corridor and advanced to the west end of the corridor to Leech Lake pass. By 5:00 p.m., the battalion had advanced elements into the valley beyond.

This successful attack was followed by a rather treacherous, all-night road march under a new moon. The battalion made its way through the Khyber Pass and ended its trek at an assembly area near McLean Lake. The following morning, to Knoebel's "utter disbelief," the entire task force had made it to McLean Lake without losing a vehicle. There, the task force transitioned to the force-on-force phase of the rotation.[57]

Transitioning to this phase held its own challenges. At McLean Lake, the battalion had to concurrently turn in all live ammunition, draw blank ammunition, receive its first mission, and prepare the operations order, all the while performing maintenance on weapons and vehicles and otherwise preparing for the next mission.

Another challenge was dealing with the NTC's mechanized infantry Observer Controller team dubbed the "Scorpions." The chief of the team (Scorpion 07) at this time was none other than that irascible old Ranger, Colonel Russell Honore. Knoebel recalled that Honore demanded high standards but was a fair judge. Now the Devil Rangers would fall under the "Ragin' Cajun's" scrutiny for the next ten days.

The first mission for Knoebel's troops in this phase was a movement to contact. That morning, the Devil Rangers raced past Crash Hill, through Brown and Debman Passes, over the Barstow Road, and met the OPFOR regiment between Hill 876 and the "Iron Triangle." When the battle was done, the 1st Battalion had destroyed virtually every OPFOR vehicle and still had over two-thirds of the battalion remaining.[58] It was an aus-

picious beginning to an unusual force-on-force rotation.

The second mission of the rotation was not to be quite so successful. In a deliberate attack, the task force moved from the Barstow Road along the central corridor and conducted an attack on enemy positions near Hill 720. In a scene reminiscent of its breach operation during the Gauntlet exercise, TF 1-16 cut a hole through the OPFOR's obstacle belt and penetrated about seven hundred meters into the enemy defenses with two tank teams before being destroyed.

Though technically a draw, this feat was quite rare for Blue Force units to achieve against the OPFOR. Of this attack, Colonel Knoebel stated, "The OPFOR standard was that nobody would ever penetrate their wire. They had an extremely high standard. We were not only able to penetrate their wire, but were able to get into their actual BPs (battle positions) before we were destroyed."[59]

The following mission was not a cakewalk either, but the result was sweet revenge. The Devil Rangers were given the task of defending Brown and Debman Passes. This was not an easy job because it called for the deployment of a covering force in the Colorado Wadi, a main defense between the North Wall and Brown Pass, and responsibility for the area back to Crash Hill. Essentially, TF 1-16 had to take up a defensive position sixteen kilometers deep and ten kilometers wide. For the mission, Knoebel pushed the scout platoon and Tim DeLass's Team D forward of the Barstow Road. Captain Fred Hoskins' E Company, dug in along the North Wall facing Brown Pass; Steve Sabia's Team B defending Debman Pass; and a tank team in the center of the valley floor composed the main defense line. Team Tank was the task force reserve and counterattack force. The trains were responsible for the areas to the rear toward Crash Hill.

The trains, under Esplin's control, actually had some capability to perform the rear area defense task because by this point, the task force had fallen to a seventy percent operational ready (OR) rate. In other words, out of twenty-eight tanks and forty-four BFVs, eight tanks and thirteen Bradleys were undergoing repairs at the maintenance point in the rear. The problem was, not all of them could shoot or move and those vehicles in the rear were not in the main line to defend.

Nevertheless, the following morning, the OPFOR fell against the task force defenses with five battalions. After DeLass's team withdrew to the main defenses, the OPFOR pushed through Brown Pass and immediately encountered Hoskins' E Company. Though putting up a good fight, Hoskins' force was almost wiped out and the OPFOR hugged the North Wall to try and slip around the task force's north flank.

DeLass, who had moved Team D into positions in the main defenses, now reoriented his unit and counterattacked northeast into the OPFOR units getting past the E Company remnants. But, given the weight of the enemy attack, DeLass's team was soon destroyed, but not before slowing the OPFOR enough to allow the task force to send in yet another counterattack. Team Tank, in the center of the task force battle position, soon took the enemy units under fire and took a devastating toll on the enemy.

About the time this was occurring, the OPFOR attempted two other approaches. The first was a battalion-size push to try to force Debman Pass, but Sabia's team was successful in beating back that assault. The second was an air assault to the rear of the battalion's defenses near the Chinaman's Hat. Fortunately, the battalion S3 had positioned his vehicle on high ground just to the rear of the defenses where he could observe both the main defenses and the rear areas toward Crash Hill. With the approach of the choppers, the S3's gunner, Dan Willing, went into action. In short order, the battalion master gunner single-handedly destroyed the entire air assault force, either in the air or once the troops were on the ground.[60]

As the battle reached its final stages, Knoebel launched Team Tank and Sabia's Team B into the remaining OPFOR echelon as it attempted to break through. But the final drive was in vain. Upon conclusion of the action, little remained of TF 1-16, but the OPFOR had lost five battalions. Only a reinforced platoon penetrated the main defenses, and part of that unit was eliminated by TOC personnel using Viper AT weapons. Despite the low OR rate, the Devil Rangers had fought the OPFOR to a standstill.

Task Force 1-16 concluded this successful rotation to the NTC with two brigade-level attacks during the last phase. The first of these attacks was another successful penetration of enemy defenses at the south side of the Colorado Wadi. The second was a brigade attack near Hill 876 that ended with both TF 1-16 and TF 1-34 fought to a standstill by an OPFOR that had grown tired of being whipped.

This rotation illustrates how far the U.S. Army had come since the early years of the NTC. In that early period, BLUEFOR units rarely defeated the OPFOR. By the mid-1990s, however, a BLUEFOR victory was not a rare event. Battle and training techniques that had received lip service in the 1980s were now practiced almost religiously. These techniques included procedures such as "rock drills," where the task force commander would literally walk his key leaders through the operation using synchronization matrices while walking on a large terrain model constructed for conceptual rehearsals. Mounted rehearsals performed by the key leaders in their vehicles would often follow the drills. Such techniques, which were rarely if ever performed in the 1980s, had become commonplace in the 1990s. As a result of what it learned, the battalion's next rotation would be even more successful.

Before leaving the NTC, Colonel Knoebel began the process of finally reestablishing the 1st Battalion's traditional nickname. During the battalion's earlier deployment to Fort Stewart for Bold Shift, the battalion S3 had informed Knoebel that the 1st Battalion's nickname had been "Iron Rangers," which it adopted in Vietnam. Furthermore, the battalion had never made the transition from Devil Rangers after its redesignation

from the 5th Battalion. Knoebel agreed that for historical reasons (and the fact that he liked the correct nickname better anyhow) it should be changed back to Iron Rangers and discussed the change with the brigade commander, Colonel Aldridge. Aldridge also agreed that it should be changed, but directed that this should occur until after he left command of the "Devil Brigade" the following May. Despite that restriction, when the battalion's sign on the famous rock pile near the front entrance to the NTC was repainted due to age, sand, and sun, it was the moniker Iron Rangers that adorned the rock. In May 1994, the 1st Battalion resumed the use of its traditional nickname.

Despite being involved in many training activities throughout the rest of 1994, Knoebel remained focused on preparing the 1st Battalion for its next NTC rotation.

2nd Battalion, 16th Infantry 1991-96

Upon their return to Fort Riley after the Gulf War, the Rangers of the 2nd Battalion spent the rest of May accounting for, cleaning, and turning in equipment for storage in preparation for block leave. At the beginning of June most Rangers departed on thirty-day leaves for hometowns throughout the United States to see loved ones and share their experiences with family and friends, while their vehicles were en route on board ships from the Middle East.

Upon the soldiers' return from leave, the battalion's vehicles still had not arrived on post. Also, because of the 1st Infantry Division's Gulf War deployment, it had been replaced by the 4th Division as the deploying unit for the 1991 Reforger. Additionally, after the war, many of the battalion's key leaders and soldiers were transferred out of the unit on normal rotation. In terms of teamwork, the 2nd Battalion was almost like a totally new unit. Colonel Fake realized the battalion would have to retrain, starting with the basics; as Major Richard Rachmeler, the S3, termed it, "the crawl, walk, run method."[61]

Having a new team to train, no Reforger mission to prepare for, and no vehicles and other equipment to train with, Fake decided that his soldiers would restart the training process with the competition for the EIB held at the 1st Brigade's Devil Parade. Over the month of August, the contestants were eliminated one by one until only thirty-four remained to receive the highly coveted award at the end.

Following the EIB testing, a Level I gunnery in September at Range 18 and the MPRC took place. During this training, two crews in the battalion's C Company fired perfect one thousand-point scores on Gunnery Table VIII. The winning crew, consisting of track commander 2nd Lieutenant Mike Pound and gunner Sergeant Tim McVeigh, took top honors by not only hitting all targets presented, but by doing it in less time than Staff Sergeant Anthony Palmer's one thousand-point crew.[62] The Level I gunnery exercise was followed by platoon-level ARTEP exercises near the close of the year.

Lieutenant Colonel Richard Gribling, who had been the

S3 of 2-16 Infantry in 1985-86, returned to assume the role of Ranger 6 on January 10, 1992. Assisting him were two capable officers, Major Mark Stevens, the S3, and Major Terry Gendron, the executive officer. Gendron had been the commander of 2-16's D Company at the same time that Gribling had been the S3.

Like all maneuver battalion commanders in the Big Red One at this time, Gribling stepped into a command of a unit with a very busy training schedule. His first mission as battalion commander was to lead the 2-16 Infantry as OPFOR troops against Frank Stone's 1-16 Infantry, as well as provide OCs for the 1st Brigade's Gauntlet exercise in March and April.

Later that spring, Gribling deployed a support and training evaluation group to Fort Stewart in June for the first of the Bold Shift exercises with the 218th Infantry Brigade. Like the Gauntlet exercise just completed, this operation required the deployment of elements to act as the OPFOR against the 1st Battalion, 118th Infantry, and an evaluation team of officers to act as OCs and evaluators.

In July the 2nd Battalion engaged in yet another EIB testing event. At the end of that year's testing, forty-nine Rangers received the EIB from Brigadier General Huba Wass de Czega, the Big Red One's ADC.

In August 1992, much of the 2nd Battalion deployed to the NTC to augment the 177th Armored Brigade (OPFOR), or concurrently, acted as OPFOR for TF 4-37 Armor's Gauntlet exercise in preparation for that battalion's upcoming rotation to the CMTC at Hohenfels in September. In what was to be a first-ever training event, a CONUS-based heavy battalion participated in a CMTC rotation as part of Reforger 92. Accompanying the 4-37 Armor were A and B Companies from 2-16 Infantry. By all accounts, this too was a successful rotation for the Rangers who participated.

Because the exercise that year was largely a computer-generated command post exercise, the 2nd Battalion's participation in Reforger was limited—apart from the two companies that deployed to the CMTC—to the battalion headquarters and a small support group from headquarters company. In the main, Reforger 92 was a successful operation for both battalions of the 16th Infantry. However, one tragedy marred the 2nd Battalion's participation. Early in the deployment, Specialist Jaymes D. Marshall was killed on the autobahn when he fell out of his HUMMV. He had fallen asleep without securing his safety strap and when the driver swerved to avoid a German driver, Marshall fell out, striking the road head first at about forty-five miles per hour.[63]

Following Reforger and the Christmas holidays, on January 10, 1993, the Rangers rolled to the field in bitter winter weather for two weeks of training preparatory for their next NTC rotation. "The post was closed due to the weather," Stevens said at the time, "but a foot of snow doesn't stop us."[64] Despite the snow and bitter cold, the battalion successfully completed the training and transitioned from this event to the customary

Gauntlet exercise in February and March 1993. From there, the battalion went on to its first NTC rotation under Gribling's command in May and June. Due to the command team's extensive work with each other over the previous year, Gribling, Gendron, and Stevens were able to execute, by all accounts, another remarkably successful 16th Infantry rotation.

In the very first force-on-force battle, for example, TF 2-16 had the mission to secure the "Whale Gap," a narrow opening between an imposing basalt and rock hill mass called the "Whale," and a thin ridge line known as the "Furlong." In a rapid movement to contact, the Rangers rushed to the gap, beating the OPFOR to the punch, and then proceeded to thrash the enemy with intense tank, Bradley, TOW, and artillery fire. It was the first time in eight years that a rotation unit had defeated the OPFOR in the opening engagement.[65]

As with Knoebel and his 1st Battalion, Gribling was given a second opportunity to take the 2nd Battalion through the NTC. He did so in May 1994 with the 4-37 Armor. Like the first rotation, the Rangers performed even better the second time around.

On January 7, 1994, Lieutenant Colonel Thomas M. Jordan took command of the 2nd Battalion from Gribling in a ceremony held in King Field House due to the winter weather. Over the next two years, the 2nd Battalion underwent much of the same training routine as in past years. Although training support to the ROTC was gone due to the inactivation of the Third ROTC Region headquarters and its attendant summer training camp held at Riley, the 2nd Battalion continued to support Bold Shift with the 218th Infantry Brigade and other National Guard units. Likewise, Reforgers were no more, but one or two NTC rotations during each battalion commander's tenure were the norm, and Jordan's time in command was no different.

Jordan's time holding the flag ended when Lieutenant Colonel Robert Rush assumed command in January 1996. Rush's command of the battalion was very brief, however, for four months later, on April 10, 1996, soldiers of the 2nd Battalion, 16th Infantry furled the battalion's colors for the third time in twenty-one years. The 2nd Battalion was no more. Like the 3rd, 4th, and 5th Battalions before it, the 2nd Rangers had become a part of history.

3rd Battalion, 16th Infantry
1991-94

The training activities for the 3rd Battalion in the 1980s had focused essentially on the Annual Training (AT) that it performed each summer at Fort Drum, New York. With the 1990s came new training opportunities, additional laurels to the battalion's accomplishments, and though the "Maine Rangers" may not have known it at the time, the budgeteer's postwar drawdown ax.

The first of the new training opportunities for the battalion's soldiers came in the way of a mission that was a sign of the times. With no Soviet Bear to threaten NATO, reserve components, like the Regular Army, had to scramble to find missions that made them a needed and relevant asset to the United States' defense posture. As a result, a company of the 3rd Battalion traveled to Arizona on a drug surveillance mission along the Mexican border in the autumn of 1991.

The mission lasted a month, or about two weeks longer than the normal AT period, and was an excellent training opportunity for the so-called Maine Rangers. During the deployment, the soldiers lived in the open and functioned as squad-sized reconnaissance patrols. The patrols would go out for several days at a time reporting suspicious activities to the local law enforcement agencies to investigate.[66]

After a year of monthly drills preparing for its next AT, the 3rd Battalion deployed to the Canadian Forces Base Gagetown in August 1992. There the Maine Rangers joined thirty-two hundred other soldiers from the 187th Infantry Brigade in a series of field training exercises. The battalion conducted a motorized road march to and from Gagetown from its hometowns in Maine.

Soon after this event, the battalion learned that it had won the Chief of Staff of the Army's Award for Maintenance Excellence for 1992. In his letter of congratulations to the battalion, Major General Roger W. Sandler, the Chief of the Army Reserve wrote:

> It gives me great pleasure to know that an infantry unit of the United States Army Reserve had achieved the high standards of maintenance excellence that this award represents. Your success is particularly satisfying when you consider that the 3-16 Infantry was selected as winner over all other USAR MTOE units in the intermediate category; and that you won this award in times of constrained resources.[67]

Declining resources for the Army also meant that such a large force structure in the active or reserve components could no longer be sustained. Thus the end of the Cold War sounded the death knell for many reserve component units, and in the Army Reserve, the separate infantry brigades were some of the first on the chopping block. After receiving its inactivation notification from the brigade headquarters, the soldiers of the 3rd Battalion began the almost year-long process of repairing and accounting for equipment and turning it in to various depots before the final inactivation ceremony.

That ceremony occurred at the 94th Army Reserve Command Headquarters at Hanscom Air Force Base, Massachusetts, on April 14, 1994. After thirty-five years of faithful service in the United States Army Reserve, the 3rd Battalion, 16th Infantry was gone. Still, the men of that organization left a legacy of service just as proud as that of their Regular Army brethren, even if their martial accomplishments were somewhat sparse in comparison.

What they can boast of is their direct service to their hometowns and the good relationships they fostered with the very citizens whom all American soldiers serve. The reserve component soldier is arguably the most visible representative of the armed forces to a majority of Americans. For the American public, the local army reservist and national guardsman give the U.S. Army a reality that is something more than a movie or television commercial. There can be no doubt that the Maine Rangers and their predecessors in Massachusetts did a fine job in representing the army and the 16th Infantry Regiment in their communities.

1st Battalion, 16th Infantry
1995-1999

After the Iron Rangers' very successful 1993 NTC rotation, Colonel Knoebel set to work preparing the battalion for its next rotation with a new command team, which included Major Paul Darcy, the XO, and Major Greg Legere, the S3. But the battalion soon ran into problems associated with the drawdown.

After General Hartzog's departure from the Big Red One, Major General Joshua Robles took command. Robles made it his personal mission to reduce training costs to the division by withholding money from training budgets, and challenging commanders to do less with more in this period of Army reductions. Unfortunately, the result was not a leaner, meaner force, but a force that was valiantly trying, but failing, to maintain high levels of proficiency with substantially fewer resources than were previously available. After a frank exchange of opinions between Knoebel and the division's chief of staff regarding readiness, the battalion received additional training dollars to correct training deficiencies revealed by Knoebel's assessments. With the additional money, Knoebel embarked on a new training effort to prepare for the battalion's next NTC rotation in February 1995.

The battalion's February 1995 rotation to the NTC was even more successful than the previous one. For example, during the live-fire missions that rotation, the Iron Rangers destroyed every target presented. On the first movement to contact mission, the battalion destroyed every OPFOR vehicle that opposed it. This time the battalion's maintenance status remained above 90 percent for the entire time it was in the field. The Iron Rangers made it look so easy that the new division commander, Major General Randolph House, was moved to say that the "1-16 was so confident in its abilities, it was moving through the NTC just having fun."[68]

The February 1995 NTC rotation was Knoebel's last major training event before giving up command to Lieutenant Colonel Robert W. Brown in June 1995. Arguably, it was during those years that the 1st Battalion reached its peak as a fighting outfit. Although the battalion has continued to prepare for its wartime missions and participate in NTC rotations over the next four years, it has done so in the face of ever-decreasing resources and uncertain wartime mission requirements. Brown and his successor, Lieutenant Colonel Frank Harmon, not only struggled to maintain crew and infantry skills during a time of fewer resources, but also during a period when America's sons have not demonstrated a particularly high propensity to serve the flag, resulting in empty ranks in the companies. The Iron Rangers, as well as the rest of the army, have also suffered from the lack of a well-defined threat. Without that threat, determining how to train has become more problematic. Indeed, battalion commanders and their staffs today are less sure of what missions their troops may be called on to perform and the levels of proficiency that must be maintained to carry out those missions. Therefore, army commanders have looked for other opportunities to employ soldiers, and for the time being, it appears that our army will be not utilized for preserving peace instead of making war.

In May 1999, Lieutenant Colonel Keith Lovejoy, the current commander of the 1st Battalion, 16th Infantry, assumed command of the remaining battalion of Rangers in the United States Army and immediately began preparation for a new kind of mission, similar to what other 16th Infantrymen have performed in the past: a peacekeeping mission. Though trained for war, the battalion was selected to reinforce the United Nations' Stabilization Force (SFOR) in Bosnia, and deployed in August 1999 on Operation Joint Forge, the ongoing U.S. peacekeeping mission in that country.

For this mission, Lovejoy commanded a twelve-hundred-man task force consisting of the entire 1st Battalion, two armored companies, and an engineer company. The task force was stationed as follows: at Camp Dobol, battalion headquarters, B and D Companies, 1st Battalion, 16th Infantry, D Company, 1-34 Armor, A Company, 1st Engineers; at Camp McGovern, A Company, 1st Battalion, 16th Infantry, A Company, 2-34 Armor, B Company, 1st Engineers; at Camp Demi, C Company, 1st Battalion, 16th Infantry, B Company, 1st Engineers.[69]

Since Task Force 1-16 has arrived in Bosnia, it has experienced few rewards and most of the frustrations that go with such service. Nevertheless, the Iron Rangers continue to soldier on in the best traditions of the 16th Infantry Regiment.

In truth, throughout the 1990s, all battalions of the 16th Infantry carried on the proud traditions and heritage of the regiment and maintained the high standards expected of the soldiers who wear the Big Red One. Today, as this is written, only the 1st Battalion remains to bear our nation's flag and regimental colors proudly. While serving in Bosnia, the Iron Rangers continue to add new laurels to the regiment as they attempt to bring peace and stability to that war-torn country. Peacekeeping service overseas is a mission that has become common for the U.S. Army in this post-Cold War period with its wars of separation and nationalism. It is a mission that tries the skills, discipline, and professionalism of the soldiers that have to perform it. By all accounts, the soldiers of the 16th Infantry in Bosnia are performing that mission with pride and professionalism, just as their forebears would expect.

Epilogue
"The Past is Prologue"

"As long as there is a United States of America, there will always be a "Big Red One."
—Gen. Gordon Sullivan

In many ways, the story of the 16th Infantry is the history of the U.S. Army since 1861. Ask a stranger on the street to name a famous American land battle from the Civil War onward, chances are he will name one that the regiment fought in. The 16th Infantry has fought in every one of the U.S. Army's major conflicts since 1861, except the Korean War. Of course, during that period, the Rangers were performing the vital mission of facing down the Soviet threat to Europe. The men of the 16th Infantry have loyally performed their duties in wartime and peacetime, and have consistently accomplished all that has been asked of them—and more.

Since the inactivation of the 2nd Battalion in 1996, there has been but one battalion of the 16th Infantry on active duty, and it still serves with the 1st Infantry Division. Perhaps this is as it should be. A modern infantry battalion consists of some 840 officers and men, about the average strength that the 16th Infantry Regiment has maintained throughout most of its existence, save in World Wars I and II, and the period of 1945-57. Without a formal regimental structure, having multiple battalions of the same name does little to engender esprit de corps for the "regiment" if the men who serve in them have only the regimental number in common. Indeed, the fact that each battalion adopted different nicknames in the post-regimental era highlights the fact that each was striving to be different, rather than endeavoring to build a common heritage. Even the traditions in each battalion went in disparate directions. For the sake of maintaining a common history, lineage, and traditions, one should hope that the current army policy of keeping only one battalion active in each regiment (and maintaining historical assignments to divisions for those units) will be retained from this point on.

By count, over thirty-five hundred members of the 16th Infantry Regiment have made the ultimate sacrifice in service to the United States of America since 1861. These men are generally unknown, unsung, and even unappreciated by many of the countrymen they served. But they are not forgotten by their regimental comrades. They are remembered and honored every Memorial Day at the 1st Infantry Division Monument in Washington, D.C., and other locations throughout the world. They are remembered by their comrades at the memorial service held each year at the reunion of the Society of the First Division. And they are remembered by their comrades who "reenlist" in the 16th Infantry each year by renewing their membership in the regimental association. These men join the association to keep their connection with the 16th Infantry alive. They relish the opportunity to reunite with their buddies, and through laughter, and sometimes tears, they gather to retell old war stories and listen to new ones. They are tales that only their peers can fully appreciate. When pressed, they will also tell others of the heroic exploits and honors, and, yes, even of the foibles and failures of the Rangers with whom they had the privilege to serve. Each story is a mini-chapter in the 16th Infantry's tale. Though it is up to the active duty soldiers to write new pages in the regimental history, it is the ex-Rangers who ensure that the regiment's story is told and that the soldier, past, present, and future, is not forgotten.

It is likely that in the future, the soldiers of the 16th Infantry will be in the thick of our nation's next war. Just as in the past, future Rangers will step forward to support and defend the Constitution and fight our nation's wars, with courage and honor. A famous general once said, "As long as there is a United States of America, there will always be a "Big Red One." Let us pray to God that there will always be a 16th Infantry Regiment, and brave, selfless, American sons who will rally to the colors and fight, whether the cause be popular or not, as long as it is right. Let us further pray that these men live up to the dedication and sacrifice of the Rangers who have gone before. If they do, America will continue to be in good hands.

"Semper Paratus—Always Ready".

Pictorial History

Civil War 1861-1865

Fort Independence, Massachusetts (c. 1934), birthplace of the 16th Infantry. Located on Castle Isle in Boston Harbor, Fort Independence served as the regimental depot of the 11th U.S. Infantry from 1861 until 1866. Note the similarity between the outline for the fort with the design on the current 16th Infantry regimental insignia.

1st Lt. Francis E. Brownell, 11th U.S. Infantry. Brownell became one of the war's first heroes when he killed the man who murdered Col. Ephraim E. Ellsworth in the famous incident at the Marshall Boarding House in Alexandria, Virginia. He was rewarded with a Regular Army commission in the 11th Infantry.

George H. W. Stouch, Sergeant Major, 11th U.S. Infantry (shown here as a Lt. in the 3rd Infantry). Stouch looked forward to his return visit to his howetown of Gettysburg, Pennsylvania, but instead of a family reunion, he was treated to hot combat and temporary capture in the Rose Wood on July 2, 1863.

Indian Wars 1877-1898

The renowned 16th Infantry Band on parade at Fort Riley, Kansas. The 16th Infantry, less several companies, served at Fort Riley from 1877 to 1880.

Officers' Row at Fort Concho, Texas, c. 1885. This West Texas post served as the headquarters for the regiment for five and a half years. Today, Fort Concho is a Texas state historical site.

K Company, stationed at the Post of San Antonio, was selected to perform the guard detail escorting Geronimo and his key lieutenants to be imprisoned at Fort Pickens, Florida, in October 1886. Geronimo is shown here, seated top row, second from the left, wearing a dark vest.

Fort Douglas, Utah, c. 1890. Fort Douglas served as the regimental headquarters post from 1888 to 1896. Part of the regiment served concurrently at Fort Duchesne, Utah.

Fort Duchesne, Utah, c. 1886. This view of the post shows the headquarters and officers' row. The troops' accommodations were not nearly as comfortable. One can easily discern the barrenness of this post. Fort Duschene now serves as the headquarters of the Uintah Indian Reservation.

A trooper from B Company strikes a martial pose for the camera, probably at Fort Spokane, Washington, shortly before the Spanish-American War. The newness of his uniform and equipment and his youthful appearance indicate that he is probably a new recruit having his picture taken to send home to his family. One wonders if he participated in the famous charge up San Juan Hill.

Fort Spokane, Washington, served as the home for Companies B and E just before the Spanish-American War.

Fort Sherman, Idaho, served as the 16th Infantry's last headquarters post before the regiment participated in the Spanish-American War. Duty here was pleasant and the tempo of life relatively slow. That all changed with the sinking of the USS Maine in February 1898.

Spanish-American War/Philippine Insurrection 1898-1902

Troops of the 16th Infantry crouch to avoid fire from San Juan Heights, July 1, 1898. They are near Bloody Ford and will soon cross to make the final assault.

The famous charge at San Juan Hill was led by the 16th infantry.

Major (ret.) Henry C. Schroeder, Medal of Honor winner for actions at Carig on Luzon, September 14, 1900. The photo was taken at Fort Riley in July 1956, when he donated his medal, which he is wearing at his neck, to the regimental museum. The medal is now in the collection of the Cantigny First Division Museum in Wheaton, IL.

This is an actual photograph of troops making the charge up San Juan Hill on July 1, 1898. Given the position of the soldiers, they probably belong to the 6th or 13th Infantry Regiment. The 16th Infantry, not visible, is located somewhere just to the left of the blockhouse.

Troops of the 16th Infantry in the trenches on San Juan Hill. The regiment attacked up the hill to the right of this location.

An unidentified 16th Infantry officer serving in the Philippines about 1900. Note the tropic uniform.

American Travelers 1903-1914

The troops of G Company pose in front of their barracks at Fort Crook, NE, c. 1907. It was at Fort Crook that the 16th Infantry first experienced the duties of training reserve component troops, a task with which the regiment would become very familiar from then on.

Punitive Expedition 1914-1916

The headquarters area of the 16th Infantry's new home at Fort Bliss, Texas, July 13, 1914. The regiment was sent to Texas in response to the threat of border incidents from warring revolutionary factions across the border.

Troops of the 16th Infantry gather for their evening meal at a temporary camp in Mexico.

Camp of H Company, 16th Infantry at El Valle, Mexico. Note the adobe walls and shelter-half roofs. The regiment's stay in Mexico was uncomfortable and boring. By all accounts, however, the men performed their duties well.

The tired doughboys of the 16th Infantry rest their aching dogs under a pleasant grove of trees during the initial march into Mexico. Though two regiments of infantry traveled into Mexico with Pershing, the Punitive Expedition was destined to be a cavalry show.

World War I

Soldiers of the 16th Infantry take a break at their billets in Dimanche. Upon arrival in the Gondrecourt training area, there were no barracks to house the division, so the troops were billeted in homes, barns, and other outbuildings.

Parade of the 2nd Battalion in Paris, July 4, 1917. By this time, the 16th Infantry was filled with many new men, and Pershing was at first reluctant to risk national embarrassment by having such green troops march through Paris. He needn't have been concerned—the Parisennes were ecstatic with the arrival of the Americans.

The regiment undergoes bayonet training at Gondrecourt under French tutelage, July 30, 1917. Note that the soldiers are still wearing campaign hats and retain the look of "green" soldiers.

One month later, troops rest between drills at Gondrecourt. By now, the men are beginning to look like combat soldiers.

It was not all work and no play at Gondrecourt. These soldiers found something in which to interest themselves only ten minutes after being paid, October 22, 1917.

By October the training at Gondrecourt had become much more sophisticated. Here the regiment participates in a live-fire exercise.

The first three members of the AEF killed in action in World War I:
Pvt. Thomas F. Enright, Corp. James B. Gresham, Pvt. Merle D. Hay, all
of F Company. They were killed during a trench raid on November 3, 1917.

Burial ceremonies for Gresham, Enright, and Hay in Bathlemont, France.

Troops of the 16th Infantry, probably the 3rd Battalion, in the trenches at
Gypse Hill, November 19, 1917.

Troops in the line near Ansauville. It was in this active sector, which the regiment occupied in January 1918, where the 16th Infantry, for the first time, experienced the kind of trench warfare with which it would become very familiar. Active patrolling across no man's land, raids into enemy lines, and gas warfare were the order of the day.

Now blooded veterans, the troops of the 16th Infantry pass in review at Gondrecourt, March 20, 1918. The reviewing party consists of (L-R): Maj. Gen. Hunter Liggett, Gen. John J. Pershing, Secretary of War Newton D. Baker, and the regimental commander, Col. John L. Hines.

A detachment of 16th Infantrymen at the ration break point near Pleissy, July 16, 1918, just before the great battle at Soissons.

Doughboys of the 2nd Battalion digging in behind a railroad embankment just north of Chaudon at the end of the first day's attack at Soissons, July 18, 1918. Soissons was the regiment's bloodiest battle in World War I.

The first day of the Meuse-Argonne campaign, the 16th Infantry was the only unit in the First Army to reach its objective—the village of Fléville. This scene shows the main road through Fléville looking from south to north. The doughboys of the 16th Infantry approached the village along the high ground to the southeast of this point.

Gen. John J. Pershing, AEF commander, and Maj. Gen. Charles P. Summerall, 1st Division commander, inspect the 1st Battalion near Nonsard, September 16, 1918. Pershing had stopped by to visit the 1st Division and tell the troops of his pride in their efforts at Soissons and St.-Mihiel. He also promised that he would soon call on them again.

Men of the 16th Infantry, under shellfire, rush through the streets of
Thelonne, France, during the drive on Sedan, November 7, 1918.

The church in Fléville looking from south to north from the vicinity of the
cemetery. The lead elements of the regiment would have entered Fléville
at about this point. The orchard where the main defenses were later
established was to the right rear of this point.

16th Infantry doughboys in Thelonne, France, November 7, 1918.
An old woman from the just-liberated village expresses her appreciation
to the soldiers.

French refugees watch the men of the 16th Infantry as they move up the road through the Bois de Boliers, November 9, 1918. In two days, the war would be over.

The 16th Infantry withdraws from the Sedan area, November 12, 1918. The war is over, but there is still a big job ahead.

Having marched through the Moselle valley, victorious doughboys of the 16th Infantry prepare to enter hard billets in Coblenz, Germany, December 11, 1918.

Capt. Earl Almon, commander, M Company, 16th Infantry, reads the order of the day to the burgermeister (mayor) and town crier of Leuterod, Germany, January 12, 1919. The 1st Division would remain on occupation duty until August 1919.

Gen. Pershing decorates the colors of the 16th Infantry at ceremonies held in Neuweid, Germany, August 3, 1919. In less than two weeks the regiment would be sailing home.

The 16th Infantry, led by Lt. Col. Clarence R. Huebner, marches through the Victory Arch in New York City, September 10, 1919, upon the occasion of the 1st Division's return from occupation duties in Germany.

Interwar Years 1920-1941

Governors Island c. 1922.

Fort Jay c. 1925. The 1st and 2nd Battalions were billeted in this old coast artillery fortification until 1933.

The regimental honor company performs a retreat ceremony at the Court of Peace during the New York World's Fair, fall 1939. Note that the troops are about the same height and build.

The Manhattan skyline from Governors Island. This is the view that greeted the regiment's sentries each night in the 1920s and 30s.

The eastern sallyport leading into Fort Jay. This is the view seen by the men in 1922 as they marched in to occupy their first permanent barracks since 1914.

Diana Serra Cary, a.k.a. "Baby Peggy," during her visit to New York City in 1923. The 16th Infantry's commander, Colonel Charles Gerhardt , named Baby Peggy as the first "Daughter of the Regiment" and presented her with a regimental insignia, worn on her fur scarf.

St. Cornelius Chapel, the primary house of worship for the heavily Catholic 16th Infantry while it was stationed on Governors Island. Note the numerous retired regimental colors hanging in the sanctuary. It was here that the regiment retired and displayed its World War I colors in January 1924.

Dedication of the 1st Division Memorial in Washington, DC, October 4, 1924. The entire 16th Infantry helped dedicate this impressive monument commemorating the more than three thousand comrades who made the ultimate sacrifice in World War I. Members of the Big Red One still remember their comrades here every Veterans' Day and Memorial Day.

The 16th Infantry parading on the sidewalks of New York. Frequent participation in the city's numerous ethnic and patriotic parades endeared the regiment to the city and greatly assisted the unit's ability to recruit. The regiment's efforts at good relations would earn it the sobriquet "New York's Own" during its tenure at Fort Jay.

The new regimental barracks (shown about 1960). Upon arrival at Fort Jay in 1922, the 16th Infantry, less the 3rd Battalion and one company, was billeted in Fort Jay. The rest of the regiment was housed at Fort Wadsworth and Fort Wood. With the opening of these barracks in 1933, the regiment was housed under one roof for probably the only time during its existence.

A bugler practices "Church Call" in preparation for an outdoor mass, spring 1938. Note the regimental coat of arms being used as the tabard for the bugle.

B Company marching to the parade field, spring 1938. The 16th Infantry was very much a "spit and polish" parade outfit during its stay at Governors Island. Note the appearance and step of these disciplined Regulars.

Contingent of specially picked men, selected to garrison Camp George Washington at the New York World's Fair, February 18, 1939.

The regimental cantonment at Harmony Church, Fort Benning, Georgia, March 1940. Note pyramidal tents and roads scraped in the Georgia sand.

Chow line in the field at Fort Devens, Massachusetts. The winter of 1941 was one of the harshest in memory. The poor weather, coupled with the poor training facilities, made the regiment's stay at Fort Devens less than productive.

Troops of the 16th Infantry conduct practice amphibious landings at Falmouth, Massachusetts, June 6, 1941. Note the lack of a bow ramp. Three years to the day, they would come ashore at another beach under much less favorable conditions.

Troops of the 16th Infantry at New River descending into an early Higgins version of the LCVP.

Soldiers of a 16th Infantry signal detachment set up an antenna on the beach at New River, North Carolina. Note the lack of security and the number of soldiers without helmets. As the regiment's draftees evolved into soldiers (and especially after the war began) casual scenes like this became nonexistent in training events.

A squad of 16th Infantrymen stroll off the beach to move inland on the attack at New River.

World War II

Field Marshal Sir John Dill talks with a 16th Infantryman during his visit to Camp Blanding, Florida, May 1, 1942.

The 2nd Battalion, 16th Infantry, marches through Kasserine Pass en route to Kasserine and Farrinana, Tunisia, February 26, 1943.

Following his battalion's capture on Hill 523, Lt. Col. Charles J. Denholm and his men were taken to Tunis and put on an Italian cargo ship for transport to a POW camp in Italy. After air attacks by Allied planes, Denholm and his men were able to gain control of the ship and return to shore. Denholm is shown here at the May 8, 1943, reunion with Col. George Taylor.

After capturing Nicosia, the men of A Company are shown here advancing on Troina on July 28, 1943.

Following six days of heavy fighting in the hills west of Troina, a patrol enters the town to clear out enemy snipers on August 6, 1943.

Capt. Kimball Richmond (left) briefs Lt. Gen. Omar Bradley on the conduct of I Company's small arms range in England in the spring of 1944. The 1st Division ADC, Brig. Gen. Willard Wyman, and Maj. Charles T. Horner, 3rd Battalion commander, stand to Bradley's left.

One of the most famous photographs of World War II. Here, men of the 2nd Battalion wade ashore into the maelstrom on Easy Red at Omaha Beach.

Troops of the 16th Infantry make their way forward with cover provided by one of the few dual-drive (DD) tanks that made it to shore that morning. Note the soldiers in the distance taking cover behind the shale seawall and others forcing their way forward toward the bluffs.

These soldiers are taking cover behind one of the many antiboat obstacles that littered Omaha beach. The man to the left (with the white semi-circle on his helmet) is one of the special engineer brigade soldiers assigned to blow lanes in the obstacles to clear the way for follow-on landing craft.

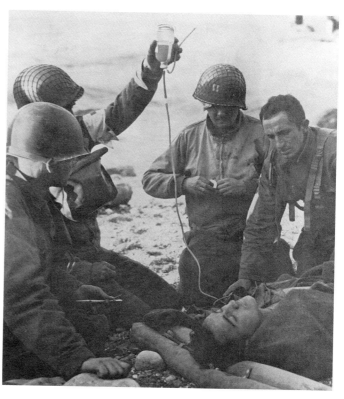

Medics treating 16th Infantry wounded on Omaha Beach. Though the infantry had a hard day on June 6, the medics sustained severe casualties as well. Through it all, they responded magnificently, disregarding their own safety to treat men who had fallen to enemy fire.

G Company, under Capt. Joe Dawson, reached this point at the western edge of Colleville-sur-Mer on the morning of June 6, (modern view). Dawson and two men cleared the church just before the unit was counterattacked by a strong German force. The company's primary defense was built around the farm buildings to the right.

Assault troops of the 3rd, 16th Int wounded while storming Omaha Beach, wait by the Chalk cliff for evacuation to a field hospital for further medical treatment. Colleville-Sur-Mer, Normandy, France 6 June.

3rd Battalion soldiers awaiting evacuation from Omaha Beach, June 6, 1944. Given their location under the bluffs at Fox Red, these men are most likely from L Company.

Gen. Dwight D. Eisenhower rewards his Praetorians, July 2, 1944. Here, Ike is pinning the DSC on Maj. Charles T. Tegtmeyer, the regimental surgeon. To Tegtmeyer's left are Capt. Joe Dawson and Capt. Kimball Richmond.

Troops of the 16th Infantry mounted on a tank of the 745th Tank battalion near La Ferté-Macé, France. At this point the regiment is racing forward to help close the gap of the Falaise pocket, August 1944.

Soldiers of F Company, 16th Infantry, moving through the Hürtgen Forest toward Hamich, Germany, November 18, 1944. The bloody fighting here was considered by many of the regiment's veterans as the toughest of the war.

C Company advances on Faymonville, Belgium, January 16, 1945. This attack signaled the Big Red One's initial efforts to begin recovering the territory lost to Hitler's legions in the Battle of the Bulge.

This captured German half-track was used by L Company as an ammunition carrier and sometime ambulance during the Ardennes campaign. It is shown here moving forward as the regiment advances on Schoppen, Belgium, January 22, 1945.

16th Infantry troopers moving into position in Bonn, Germany, February 1945.

Soldiers of B Company watch for enemy movement near the Rhine River bridge in Bonn, Germany, March 9, 1945. The capture of Bonn is considered to be the 16th Infantry's most successful attack in World War II.

From newly captured Wehrden, members of the 16th Infantry make an assault crossing of the Weser River to attack Furstenberg, April 8, 1945.

G Company moving through St. Andreasburg in the Harz Mountains, April 15, 1945.

Tanks of the 745th Tank Battalion provide cover for 16th Infantrymen in St. Andreasburg in the Harz Mountains, April 14, 1945. Resistance in the Harz Mountains at times rivaled that of the Hürtgen Forest.

Cold War I, 1945-65

The 16th Infantry Honor Guard greets General Sir John Steele, high commissioner of Austria, at the train station in Salzburg, Austria, August 20, 1947. This was one of the typical duties for members of the regiment while stationed in Austria in the late 1940s.

Soldiers of the 16th Infantry serving as guards at the Nürnberg trials in 1948.

The regiment formed an Honor Platoon from specially selected men to perform ceremonial duties. This unit, shown here with Col. John P. Evans, also performed guard duties associated with the Nürnberg trials in 1948.

The regiment's first home after reconsolidation in Germany in 1948 was an old Luftwaffe airfield in Furth, near Nürnberg. This scene shows the front gate at Furth.

Front gate to Ledward Barracks in Schweinfurt, Germany. This was home to the 16th Infantry from 1952 to 1955.

The 86th Infantry prepares to receive the 16th Infantry at Camp Funston, Kansas, May 14, 1955. The two regiments traded places as part of Operation Gyroscope.

An Ontos antitank vehicle from the 1st Battle Group, 16th Infantry, crosses a stream at Adershaufen, FRG, during Operation Winter Shield II, February 2, 1961.

Sfc. Luis Medina (center), B Company, 1st Battle Group, directs his men in setting up an antitank defense position near Vilseck, FRG. The troops were participating in Operation Winter Shield II in February 1961.

Aggressors of D Company, 1st Battle Group, prepare to attack, February 8, 1961, during Operation Winter Shield II.

Troopers of B Company, 1st Battle Group, advance through Rohrbach, FRG, February 8, 1961. The troops were acting as aggressors during Operation Winter Shield II.

Gen. Lucius D. Clay, commander of EUCOM, presents the 16th Infantry colors at Grafenwöhr upon the occasion of their return from Austria, July 7, 1948.

An M-59 APC from the 1st Battle Group conducts a crossing of the Moselle River in July 1959. During that summer, the 16th Infantry participated in extensive river crossing training using pontoon bridges and squad assault boats.

Corporal Champagne assembles a demolition charge as part of EIB testing in 1952.

A squad leader from C Company directs the loading of his men in an APC. This training was conducted to prepare the 1st Battle Group for its Army Training Test in September 1959.

Troops of the 1st Battle Group wait to board the USNS *Darby* at the
Brooklyn Army Terminal, March 5, 1959. The Rangers returned to Germany
as part of the Gyroscope Program and were assigned to the 8th Infantry
Division at Baumholder.

Maj. Gen. Chauncey D. Merrill, CG 94th Infantry Division, presents the
colors to Col. Irving Yeosock upon the activation of the 3rd Battle Group,
16th Infantry, at Worcester, Massachusetts, in May 1959.

Vietnam, 1965-1970

View of Camp Ranger, July 29, 1965. The 2nd Ranger's first home in Vietnam was built on an old French Army rifle range near Long Binh.

A mortar crew from HHC, 2-16 Infantry's heavy mortar platoon, August 3, 1965. Crew members left to right are: Pfc. John Lane, Pfc. Ronnie Fountain, Pfc. Edward Tuggle, Pfc. Troy Earnest, and Sgt. Dave Garterman.

2nd Lt. Harry E. Smith (right) gives Sgt. Shine a FRAGO during Operation Plumb Bob, September 16, 1965

Change of Command, 2-16 Infantry, February 1966. L-R: Col. A. E. Milloy, 2nd Brigade; Lt. Col. William S. Hathaway, incoming commander, 2-16 Inf.; Maj. Gen. Jonathan O. Seaman, CG, 1st ID; Lt. Col. Y. Y. Phillips, outgoing commander, 2-16 Inf.; CSM C. Caldwell, battalion sergeant major.

A machine gun team from A Company, 1st Battalion, on patrol northwest of Suoi Da during Operation Junction City, February 5, 1967. This scene illustrates the heavy jungle terrain that made the Rangers' mission of tracking down and engaging the enemy so difficult.

1st Lt. Edward Christianson calls for fire on a VC position after receiving
sniper fire during Operation Junction City, March 5, 1967.

APCs of the 1st Battalion provide security for engineer Rome plows,
May 10, 1969. The Iron Rangers spent two months on this mission,
which resulted in the successful opening of the Song Be Road from
Dong Xoi to Song Be.

Rangers of the 1st Battalion pinned down in a fire fight north of Phuoc
Binh, mark their position with smoke to identify their location to friendly
fighter-bombers. Operation Billings, June 15, 1967.

Rangers of the 1st Battalion on a search and destroy mission near Phuoc
Binh during Operation Billings, June 15, 1967.

Sgt. Jerry McDonald, HHC, 1st Battalion, 16th Infantry, prepares a C-4 charge to blow up VC bunkers near Soui Da, May 17, 1968. Though soldiers of both battalions of the 16th Infantry had their fair share of direct contact with the enemy, location and destruction of VC field facilities was a far more common activity for the Rangers in Vietnam.

The APCs of C Company, 1st Battalion, with troops of the 5th ARVN Division on board. The company provided lift to the ARVN soldiers to night ambush positions near FSB Allons, 1969.

Commanders and colors center, march! The Iron Rangers conduct a final
review at FSB Dakota before departure to the United States, March 4, 1970.

Lt. Col. David Martin, 1-16 Infantry commander, leads the Iron Rangers
out of FSB Dakota to take the battalion home to Fort Riley, March 4, 1970.

Cold War II, 1970-1990

Troops of 2-16 Infantry load up on a C-141 at Nürnberg International Airport at the end of Reforger II, October 31, 1970.

Sp4 Raymond Herringer and SSgt. O. C. Herring man an OPFOR position near Pfalzing, FRG, during Reforger III, October 8, 1971.

Soldiers of the 2nd Battalion afloat on their mission to travel the
Arkansas River trace, May 17, 1972.

M-113 and M-151 antitank jeep cross the highway on an attack
near Aub, FRG on Reforger IV, 1972.

Sp4 Eric Gear, 1st Battalion, 16th Infantry, mans his TOW
during Reforger IV.

Desert Storm, 1991

At the end of the Gulf War, both the 2nd and 5th Battalions were detailed as perimeter security units at the Safwan airfield. Here, Gen. Norman Schwarzkopf poses with Devil Ranger soldiers just after the peace negotiations there.

Both battalions of the 16th Infantry were equipped with the hard hitting M2 Bradley Fighting Vehicles (BFVs) during the Persian Gulf War.

Regimental Commanders 1861-1957

Commanders, 1st Battalion, 11th U.S. Infantry, 1861-1866

Maj. Delancey Floyd-Jones
May 1861-Jan 1863 &
Mar 1863-Jul 1863

Capt. Henry L. Chipman
Jan 1863-Mar 1863

Capt. Charles S. Russell
Jul 1863-Aug 1863

Maj. Jonathan W. Gordon
Aug 1863-Jan 1864

Capt. Francis M. Cooley
Jan 1864-Jun 1864

Capt. Joshua S. Fletcher Jr.
Jun 1864-Sep 1864

Maj. Daniel Huston Jr.
Nov 1865-Sep 1866

Commanders, 11th Infantry Regiment, 1866-1869

Col. William S. Ketchum
Sep 1866-Mar 1869
(nominal commander)

Lt. Col. Robert S. Granger
Sep 1866-Mar 1869
(commander in the field)

Commanders, 16th Infantry Regiment, 1869-1957

Col. Galusha Pennypacker
Mar 1869-Jul 1883

Lt. Col. James Van Voast
Dec 1871-Oct 1873

Lt. Col. Alfred L. Hough
Aug 1882-Jul 1883

Col. Matthew M. Blunt
Jul 1883-Aug 1894

Col. Hamilton S. Hawkins
Aug 1894-Sep 1894

Col. William H. Penrose
Sep 1894-Mar 1896

Col. Hugh Theaker
Mar 1896-Aug 1898

Col. William S. Worth
Aug 1898-Nov 1898

Col. Charles M. Hood
May 1899-Oct 1902

Col. Cornelius Gardner
Dec 1905-Jul 1912 &
Sep 1912-May 1913

Col. Charles Morton
Jul 1912-Sep 1912

Lt. Col. Chase W. Kennedy
Sep 1912-Jan 1913

Col. George Bell Jr.
May 1913-Jul 1914

Col. Omar Bundy
Sep 1914-Sep 1915

Col. William H. Allaire
Nov 1915-Aug 1917

Lt. Col. Frank A. Wilcox
Aug 1917-Nov 1917

Col. John L. Hines
Nov 1917-Apr 1918

Col. Harry A. Smith
Apr 1918-Jul 1918

Lt. Col. Edward R. Coppock
Aug 1918-Oct 1918

Col. William W. McCammon
Jun 1919-Aug 1919

Col. Francis E. Lacey Jr.
Dec 1920-Sep 1922

Col. Charles Gerhardt
Sep 1922-Sep 1924

Stanley H. Ford
Dec 1924-Aug 1926

Col. Edward Croft
Dec 1926-Jun 1928

Col. Stephen O. Fuqua
Jun 1928-Mar 1929

Lt. Col. Irving Phillipson
Mar 1929-Sep 1929

Col. Albert S. Williams
Sep 1929-Mar 1930

Col. William W. McCammon
Mar 1930-Jul 1932

Col. Joseph A. Marmon
Jul 1932-Jul 1934

Col. Albert S. Williams
Sep 1934-Jul 1937

Col. Karl Truesdell
Jul 1937-Apr 1938

Col. Charles H. Rice
Jun 1938-Jun 1940

Col. Paul W. Baade
Jun 1940-Jul 1941

Col. Henry B. Cheadle
Jul 1941-Jan 1943

Col. d'Alary Fechet
Jan 1943-Apr 1943

Col. George A. Taylor
Apr 1943-Jul 1944

Col. Frederick W. Gibb
Jul 1944-Sep 1945

Col. Charles T. Horner
Sep 1945-Oct 1945

Lt. Col. Emmanuel Robertson
Nov 1945-Jan 1946

Col. John R. Jeter
Jan 1946-Jul 1947

Peter P. Salgado
Sep 1947-Jun 1948

Sterling Wood
Jun 1948-Jul 1948

Col. John P. Evans
Jul 1948-Oct 1950

Charles H. Royce
Oct 1950-Nov 1951

Col. William W. O'Conner
Nov 1951-Feb 1953

Commanders, 16th Infantry Regiment, 1869-1957

Col. Bruce Palmer
Mar 1954-Jun 1955

Col. Samuel E. Gee
Jun 1955-Aug 1956

Col. Roy E. Doran
Aug 1956-Feb 1957

Photos unavailable

Colonel Montgomery C. Meigs	May 1861
Colonel Erasmus D. Keyes	May 1861-May 1864
Lieutenant Colonel Edmund Schriver	Jul 1861-Mar 1862
Captain William G. Edgerton	Sep 1864-Mar 1865
Captain Alfred E. Latimer	Mar 1865-Sep 1865
Lieutenant Colonel William McLaughlin	Jul 1898-Sep 1898
Colonel Clarence M. Bailey	Nov 1898-May 1899
Colonel Butler D. Price	Oct 1902-Dec 1905
Lieutenant Colonel Leven C. Allen	Dec 1905-Feb 1906
Major W. C. Bennett	Jan 1913-Apr 1913
Major Charles S. Farnsworth	Jul 1914-Sep 1914
Colonel Edwin A. Root	Jun 1915
Lieutenant Colonel Frank L. Winn	Jun 1915-Jul 1915
Captain Orrin R. Wolfe	Jul 1915-Aug 1915
Captain James N. Pickering	Aug 1915-Sep 1915
Captain Orrin R. Wolfe	Sep 1915-Sep 1915
Major George H. McMaster	Sep 1915-Nov 1915
Colonel Francis E. Bamford	Jul 1918- Aug 1918
Colonel LaRoy S. Upton	Aug 1918-Aug 1918
Colonel William F. Harrell	Oct 1918-Jun 1919, Oct 1919-Jul 1920
Major N. D. Bagnall	Aug 1919-Sep 1919
Major Thomas J. Strangier	Jul 1920-Oct 1920
Major Joseph H. Davidson	Oct 1920-Nov 1920
Colonel Edgar T. Collins	Sep 1924-Nov 1924
Lieutenant Colonel Nicholas Campanole	Sep 1924-Dec 1924
Lieutenant Colonel Sheldon W. Anding	Aug 1926-Dec 1926
Colonel Albert S. Williams	Sep 1929-Mar 1930, Sep 1934-Jul 1937
Lieutenant Colonel Joseph J. O'Hare	Jul 1934-Aug 1934
Lieutenant Colonel James L. Bradley	Apr 1938-Jun 1938
Colonel Charles H. Rice	Jun 1938-Jun 1940
Colonel Adna C. Hamilton	Oct 1945-Nov 1945
Lieutenant Colonel E. E. Cruise	Jul 1947-Sep 1947
Colonel Vernon P. Mock	Feb 1953-Mar 1954

Medal of Honor Recipients

1st Lt. John H. Patterson, 11th U.S. Infantry. Patterson was awarded the Medal of Honor for actions in attempting to save a wounded officer, Lt. Wright Staples, from the flames in the Wilderness, May 5, 1864.

Sgt. Henry C. Schroeder, L Company, 16th Infantry (shown here as a major), September 14, 1900. Leading only twenty-three men, Schroeder held off an attack by an estimated 400 insurrectos at Carig on Luzon Island in the Philippines. Though personally wounded and his command badly outnumbered, Schroeder led his men in an attack that completely demoralized the enemy and drove them off.

Tec. 5 John J. Pinder, HHC, 16th Infantry. Pinder repeatedly subjected himself to fire on Omaha beach, gathering communications equipment and ensuring that the regimental headquarters could communicate that day. He was wounded each time he went into harm's way. On the third trip, his luck ran out.

1st Lt. Jimmie W. Monteith Jr., L Company, 16th Infantry. Guiding tanks on foot while under fire, and leading his troops through wire, mines, and enemy resistance, Monteith was the epitome of a small-unit leader on D-Day. After securing positions on the bluffs north of Cobourg, Monteith was killed while leading his men out of an encirclement.

Sgt. Jake W. Lindsey, C Company, 16th Infantry. Lindsey became the regiment's sixth Medal of Honor winner when he single-handedly killed twenty German soldiers armed only with his rifle and a few hand grenades. He performed this feat while defending newly captured positions near the village of Hamich in November 1944. He is shown here on the steps of the U.S. capitol, just after being awarded the medal, by President Harry S Truman on May 21, 1945.

Pvt. Robert T. Henry, B Company, 16th Infantry. During the 1st Battalion's attack on Luchem, Germany, December 6, 1944, Private Henry volunteered to attempt the destruction of a nest of five enemy machine guns that had stopped the advance of his platoon. Armed only with his rifle and hand grenades, he sprinted toward the enemy position. Before he had gone half the distance he was hit by a burst of machine-gun fire. He staggered forward until he fell mortally wounded only ten yards from the enemy. Henry's single-handed attack forced the Germans to abandon their emplacement, allowing his company to reach its objective and capture key enemy defenses and seventy German prisoners.

SSG James W. Robinson Jr., C Company, 2nd Battalion, 16th Infantry. On April 11, 1966, Robinson's company was pinned down by a VC battalion near the Courtenay Plantation about fifty miles east of Saigon. Throughout that afternoon, he fought back with a grenade launcher, rescued two wounded men, and redistributed ammunition to his troops, but was wounded in the process. After spotting a VC .51-caliber machine gun that had inflicted heavy casualties on his platoon, he charged the gun with only two grenades and destroyed it, but made the ultimate sacrifice in the process.

PSG Matthew Leonard, B Company, 1st Battalion, 16th Infantry. When his platoon leader was killed in an enemy attack near Prek Klok on February 28, 1967, Sgt. Leonard quickly organized the platoon into a stout defense. Leonard moved about his men redistributing ammunition and encouraging them to fight. Wounded while rescuing one of his soldiers, he repaired the platoon's malfunctioning M-60 machine gun and was wounded a second time in the process. Just as he cleared the jam, he spotted an enemy machine gun, assaulted the position, and killed the crew. In doing so, he was struck a third time, this time severely. Last seen, he was manning the M-60 and continued to fight until he died of his wounds.

Appendices

Appendix 1
Medal of Honor Citations of the 16th Infantry Regiment

First Lieutenant John Patterson
May 5, 1864

Unit: 11th U.S. Infantry. *Birthday:* February 10, 1843. *Place of Birth:* Selkirk, New York. *Date of Death:* October 5, 1920. *Place of Burial:* Albany Rural Cemetery, Albany, New York. *Entered Service at:* New York. *Place of Action:* The Wilderness, Virginia. *Date of Issue:* July 23, 1897

Citation: Under heavy fire of the advancing enemy, picked up and carried several hundred yards to a place of safety a wounded officer of his regiment who was helpless and would otherwise have been burned in the forest.

Captain James M. Cutts
1864

Unit: 11th U.S. Infantry. *Birthday:* 1838. *Place of Birth:* Washington, D.C. *Date of Death:* February 24, 1903. *Place of Burial:* Arlington National Cemetery, Arlington, Virginia. *Entered Service at:* Providence, Rhode Island. *Place of Action:* The Wilderness, Spotsylvania, and Petersburg, Virginia. *Date of Issue:* May 2, 1891

Citation: Gallantry in actions.

Sergeant Henry R. Schroeder
September 14, 1900

Unit: L Company, 16th U.S. Infantry. *Birthday:* December 7, 1874. *Place of Birth:* Chicago, Illinois. *Date of Death:* January 26, 1959. *Place of Burial:* Fort Rosecrans National Cemetery, San Diego, California. *Entered Service at:* Chicago, Illinois. *Place of Action:* Carig, Philippine Islands. *Date of Issue:* March 10, 1902.

Citation: With twenty-two men, defeated four hundred insurgents, killing thirty-six and wounding ninety.

First Lieutenant Jimmie Montieth
June 6, 1944

Unit: L Company, 16th Infantry. *Birthday:* July 1, 1917. *Place of Birth:* Low Moor, Virginia. *Date of Death:* June 6, 1944. *Place of Burial:* A.M.B.C. Cemetery, Colleville-sur-Mer, France. *Entered Service at:* Richmond, Virginia. *Place of Action:* near Colleville-sur-Mer, France. *GO Number, Date:* #20, March 29, 1945 *Place of Issue:* Presented to Montieth's family by Brigadier General Frank Dorn in Richmond, Virginia.

Citation: For conspicuous gallantry and intrepidity above and beyond the call of duty on June 6, 1944, near Colleville-sur-Mer, France. First Lieutenant Monteith landed with the initial assault waves on the coast of France under heavy enemy fire. Without regard to his own personal safety, he continually moved up and down the beach reorganizing men for further assault. He then led the assault over a narrow protective ledge and across the flat, exposed terrain to the comparative safety of a cliff. Retracing his steps across the field to the beach, he moved over to where two tanks were buttoned up and blind under violent enemy artillery and machine-gun fire. Completely exposed to the intense fire, First Lieutenant Monteith led the tanks on foot through a minefield and into firing positions. Under his direction several enemy positions were destroyed. He then rejoined his company, and under his leadership, his men captured an advantageous position on the hill. Supervising the defense of his newly won position against repeated vicious counterattacks, he continued to ignore his own personal safety, repeatedly crossing the two or three hundred yards of open terrain under heavy fire to strengthen links in his defensive chain. When the enemy succeeded in completely surrounding First Lieutenant Monteith and his unit, and while leading the fight out of the situation, First Lieutenant Monteith was killed by enemy fire. The courage, gallantry, and intrepid leadership displayed by First Lieutenant Monteith is worthy of emulation.

Technician Fifth Class John J. Pinder Jr.
June 6, 1944

Unit: Headquarters Company, 16th Infantry. *Birthday:* June 12, 1912. *Place of Birth:* McKees Rocks, Pennsylvania. *Date of Death:* June 6, 1944. *Place of Burial:* Grand View Cemetery, Hanover Township, Pennsylvania. *Entered Service at:* Burgettstown, Pennsylvania. *Place of Action:* near Colleville-sur-Mer, France. *GO Number, Date:* #1, January 4, 1945.

Citation: For conspicuous gallantry and intrepidity above and beyond the call of duty on June 6, 1944, near Colleville-sur-Mer, France. On D-day, Technician Fifth Grade Pinder landed on the coast one hundred yards off shore under devastating enemy machine-gun and artillery fire, which caused severe casualties among the boatload. Carrying a vitally important radio, he struggled towards shore in waist-deep water. Only a few yards from his craft he was hit by enemy fire and was gravely wounded. Technician Fifth Grade Pinder never stopped. He made shore and delivered the radio. Refusing to take cover afforded, or to accept medical attention for his wounds, Technician Fifth Grade Pinder, though terribly weakened by loss of blood and in fierce pain, on three occasions went into the fire-swept surf to salvage communication equipment. He recovered many vital parts and equipment, including another workable radio. On the third trip he was again hit, suffering machine-gun bullet wounds in the legs. Still this valiant soldier would not stop for rest or medical attention. Remaining exposed to heavy enemy fire, growing steadily weaker, he aided in establishing the vital radio communication on the beach. While so engaged this dauntless soldier was hit for the third time and killed. The indomitable courage and personal bravery of Technician Fifth Grade Pinder was a magnificent inspiration to the men with whom he served.

Technical Sergeant Jake William Lindsey Sr.
November 16, 1944

Unit: C Company, 16th Infantry. *Birthday:* May 1, 1921. *Place of Birth:* Isney, Alabama. *Date of Death:* July 18, 1988. *Place of Burial:* White House Cemetery, Waynesboro, Mississippi. *Entered Service at:* Lucedale, Mississippi. *Place of Action:* near Hamich, Germany. *GO Number, Date:* #43, May 30, 1945. *Place/Date of Issue:* Presented to Technical Sergeant Lindsey by President Harry S Truman at a joint session of Congress on May 21, 1945.

Citation: For gallantry and intrepidity at the risk of his life, above and beyond the call of duty, on November 16, 1944, in Germany. Technical Sergeant Lindsey assumed a position about ten yards to the front of his platoon during an intense enemy infantry-tank counterattack and, by his unerringly accurate fire, destroyed two enemy machine-gun nests, forced the withdrawal of two tanks, and effectively halted enemy flanking patrols. Later, although painfully wounded, he engaged eight Germans, who were reestablishing machine-gun positions, in hand-to-hand combat, killing three, capturing three, and causing the other two to flee. By his gallantry, Technical Sergeant Lindsey secured his unit's position, and reflected great credit upon himself and the United States Army.

Private Robert T. Henry
June 12, 1945

Unit: B Company, 16th Infantry. *Birthday:* November 27, 1923. *Place of Birth:* Greenville, Mississippi. *Date of Death:* June 12, 1945. *Place of Burial:* Greenville Cemetery, Greenville, Mississippi. *Entered Service at:* Greenville, Mississippi. *Place of Action:* Luchem, Germany. *GO Number, Date:* #45, June 12, 1945.

Citation: Near Luchem, Germany, Private Robert T. Henry volunteered to attempt the destruction of a nest of five enemy machine guns located in a bunker 150 yards to the flank, which

had stopped the advance of his platoon. Stripping off his pack, overshoes, helmet, and overcoat, he sprinted alone with his rifle and hand grenades across the open terrain toward the enemy emplacement. Before he had gone half the distance he was hit by a burst of machine-gun fire. Dropping his rifle, he continued to stagger forward until he fell mortally wounded only 10 yards from the enemy emplacement. His single-handed attack forced the enemy to leave their machine-guns. During this break in hostile fire, the platoon moved forward and overran the position. Private Henry, by his gallantry and intrepidity and utter disregard for his own life, enabled his company to reach its objective, capturing this key defense and 70 German prisoners.

Staff Sergeant James W. Robinson Jr.
April 11, 1966

Unit: D Company, 2nd Battalion, 16th Infantry. *Birthday:* August 30, 1940. *Place of Birth:* Hinsdale, Illinois. *Date of Death:* April 11, 1966. *Place of Burial:* Clarendon Hills Cemetery, Westmont, Illinois. *Entered Service at:* Chicago, Illinois. *Place of Action:* near Xa Cam My, Republic of Vietnam. *GO Number, Date:* #35, September 13, 1967. *Place/Date of Issue:* Presented to Sergeant Robinson's family by Secretary of the Army Stanley R. Resor at the Pentagon on July 16, 1967.

Citation: On April 11, 1966, Company C, 2nd Battalion, 16th Infantry was engaged in fierce combat with a Viet Cong battalion. Despite the heavy fire, Sergeant Robinson moved among the men of his fire team, instructing and inspiring them, and placing them in advantageous positions. Enemy snipers located in nearby trees were inflicting heavy casualties on forward elements of Sergeant Robinson's unit. Upon locating the enemy sniper whose fire was taking the heaviest toll, he took a grenade launcher and eliminated the sniper. Seeing a medic hit while administering aid to a wounded sergeant in front of his position and aware that now the two wounded men were at the mercy of the enemy, he charged through a withering hail of fire and dragged his comrades to safety, where he rendered first aid and saved their lives. As the battle continued and casualties mounted, Sergeant Robinson moved about under intense fire to collect from the wounded their weapons and ammunition and redistribute them to able-bodied soldiers. Adding his own fire to that of his men, he assisted in eliminating a major enemy threat. Seeing another wounded comrade in front of his position, Sergeant Robinson again defied the enemy's fire to effect a rescue. In so doing he was himself wounded in the shoulder and leg. Despite his painful wounds, he dragged the soldier to shelter and saved his life by administering first aid. While patching his own wounds, he spotted an enemy machine gun which had inflicted a number of casualties on the American force. His rifle ammunition expended, he seized two grenades and, in an act of unsurpassed heroism, charged toward the entrenched enemy weapon. Hit again in the leg, this time with a tracer round which set fire to his clothing, Sergeant Robinson ripped the burning clothing from his body and staggered indomitably through the enemy fire, now concentrated solely on him, to within grenade range of the enemy machine-gun position. Sustaining two additional chest wounds, he marshaled his fleeting physical strength and hurled the two grenades thus destroying the enemy gun position as he fell dead upon the battlefield. His magnificent display of leadership and bravery saved several lives and inspired his soldiers to defeat a numerically superior enemy force. Sergeant Robinson's conspicuous gallantry and intrepidity, at the cost of his life, are in keeping with the finest traditions of the United States Army and reflect great credit upon the 1st Infantry Division and the United States Armed Forces.

Platoon Sergeant Matthew Leonard
February 28, 1967

Unit: B Company, 1st Battalion, 16th Infantry. *Birthday:* November 26, 1929. *Place of Birth:* Eutaw, Alabama. *Date of Death:* February 28, 1967. *Place of Burial:* Shadow Lawn Cemetery, Birmingham, Alabama. *Entered Service at:* Birmingham, Alabama. *Place of Action:* near Suoi Da, Republic of Vietnam. *GO Number, Date:* #9, January 9, 1969. *Place/Date of Issue:* Presented to Sergeant Robinson's family by Secretary of the Army Stanley R. Resor at the Pentagon on December 19, 1968.

Citation: Platoon Sergeant Matthew Leonard distinguished himself during combat operations with Company B, 1st Battalion, 16th Infantry, near Suoi Da, Republic of Vietnam, on February 28, 1967. His platoon was suddenly attacked by a large enemy force employing small arms, automatic weapons, and hand grenades. Although the platoon leader and several other key leaders were among the first wounded, Sergeant Leonard quickly rallied his men to throw back the initial enemy assaults. During the short pause that followed, he organized a defensive perimeter, redistributed ammunition, and inspired his comrades through his forceful leadership and words of encouragement. Noticing a wounded companion outside the perimeter, he dragged the man to safety but was struck by a sniper's bullet which shattered his left hand. Refusing medical attention and continuously exposing himself to the increasing fire as the enemy again assaulted the perimeter, Sergeant Leonard moved from position to position to direct the fire of his men against the well camouflaged foe. Under the cover of the main attack, the enemy moved a machine gun into a location where it could sweep the entire perimeter. This threat was magnified when the platoon machine gun in this area malfunctioned. Sergeant Leonard quickly crawled to the gun position and was helping to clear the malfunction when the gunner and other men in the vicinity were wounded by fire from the enemy machine gun. Sergeant Leonard rose to his feet, charged the enemy gun and destroyed the hostile crew despite being hit several times by enemy fire. He moved to a tree, propped himself against it, and continued to engage the enemy until he succumbed to his many wounds. His fighting spirit, heroic leadership, and valiant acts inspired the remaining members of his platoon to hold back the enemy until assistance arrived. Sergeant Leonard's profound courage and devotion to his men are in keeping with the highest traditions of the military service, and his gallant actions reflect great credit upon him and the United States Army.

Appendix 2
Lineage and Honors of the 16th Infantry Regiment

1861-1999

Lineage:

Constituted May 3, 1861 in the Regular Army as the 1st Battalion, 11th Infantry. Organized July 1861-February 1862 at Fort Independence, Massachusetts, and Perryville, Maryland. Reorganized and redesignated December 5, 1866 as the 11th Infantry. Consolidated March 28-April 6, 1869 with the 34th Infantry (See ANNEX) and consolidated unit designated as the 16th Infantry. Assigned June 8, 1917 to the 1st Expeditionary Division (later redesignated as the 1st Infantry Division). Relieved February 15, 1957 from assignment to the 1st Infantry Division and reorganized as a parent regiment under the Combat Regimental System.

Annex:

Constituted May 3, 1861 in the Regular Army as the 3rd Battalion, 16th Infantry. Organized in April 1864 at Madison Barracks, New York. Reorganized and redesignated September 21, 1866 as the 34th Infantry. Consolidated March 28-April 6, 1869 with the 11th Infantry and consolidated unit designated as the 16th Infantry.

Campaign Participation Credit:

Civil War
Peninsula
Manassas
Antietam
Fredericksburg
Chancellorsville
Gettysburg
Wilderness
Spotsylvania
Cold Harbor
Petersburg
Virginia 1862
Virginia 1863

Indian Wars
Cheyennes
Utes
Pine Ridge

War With Spain
Santiago

Philippine Insurrection
Luzon 1899

Mexican Expedition
Mexico 1916-191

World War I
Montdidier-Noyon
Aisne-Marne
St.-Mihiel
Meuse-Argonne
Lorraine 1917
Lorraine 1918
Picardy 1918

World War II
Algeria-French Morocco (with arrowhead)

Tunisia
Sicily (with arrowhead)
Normandy (with arrowhead)
Northern France
Rhineland
Ardennes-Alsace
Central Europe

Vietnam
Defense
Counteroffensive
Counteroffensive, Phase II
Counteroffensive, Phase III
Tet Counteroffensive
Counteroffensive, Phase IV
Counteroffensive, Phase V
Counteroffensive, Phase VI
Tet 69/Counteroffensive
Summer/Fall 1969
Winter/Spring 1970

Persian Gulf War
Defense of Saudi Arabia
Liberation of Kuwait

Decorations:

Presidential Unit Citation (Army), Streamer embroidered NORMANDY (16th Infantry cited; WD GO 73, 1944) Omaha Beach, June 6, 1944

Presidential Unit Citation (Army), Streamer embroidered MATEUR, TUNISIA (1st Battalion, 16th Infantry cited; WD GO 60, 1944), Mateur, Tunisia, April 29-30, 1943

Presidential Unit Citation (Army), Streamer embroidered SICILY (1st and 2nd Battalions, 16th Infantry cited; WD GO 60, 1944), Gela, Sicily, July 10-13, 1943

Presidential Unit Citation (Army), Streamer embroidered HÜRTGEN FOREST (1st and 2nd Battalions, 16th Infantry cited; WD GO 120, 1946), Hamich, Germany, November 16-26, 1944

Presidential Unit Citation (Army), Streamer embroidered HAMICH, GERMANY (3rd Battalion, 16th Infantry cited; WD GO 120, 1946), Hamich, Germany, November 16-26, 1944

Distinguished Unit Citation (Army), (Cannon Company, 16th Infantry cited; WD GO 60, 1944), Gela, Sicily, July 11-13, 1943

Distinguished Unit Citation (Army), (Companies G and I, 16th Infantry cited; WD GO 60, 1944), Eilendorf, Germany, October 15-17, 1944

Meritorious Unit Commendation, Streamer embroidered VIETNAM 1967-68 (2nd Battalion, 16th Infantry cited; WD GO 42, 1969)

Valorous Unit Award, (C Company, 2nd Battalion, 16th Infantry cited; DA GO 17, 1968), Courtenay Plantation

Valorous Unit Award, (A and D Companies, 5th Battalion, 16th Infantry cited; U.S. Army Forces Central Command, Permanent Orders 71-1, May 8, 1992), Objective Norfolk

Berlin Airlift Device, (3rd Battalion, 16th Infantry cited; DA GO 21, 1949), Berlin, Germany

French Croix de Guerre with Palm, World War I, Streamer embroidered AISNE-MARNE (16th Infantry cited; WD GO 11, 1924) France, 1918

French Croix de Guerre with Palm, World War I, Streamer embroidered MEUSE-ARGONNE (16th Infantry cited; WD GO 11, 1924) France, 1918

French Croix de Guerre with Palm, World War II, Streamer embroidered KASSERINE (16th Infantry cited; WD GO 43, 1950) Tunisia, February 1943

French Croix de Guerre with Palm, World War II, Streamer embroidered NORMANDY (16th Infantry cited; WD GO 43, 1950) France, 1944

French Medaille Militaire, Fourragere (16th Infantry cited; WD GO 43, 1950)

Belgian Fourragere 1940 (16th Infantry cited; WD GO 43, 1950)

Citation, Order of the Day of the Belgian Army for action at EUPEN-MALMÉDY (16th Infantry cited; WD GO 43, 1950)

Citation, Order of the Day of the Belgian Army for action at MONS (16th Infantry cited; WD GO 43, 1950) August-September 1944

Appendix 3
Heraldry of the 16th Infantry Regiment

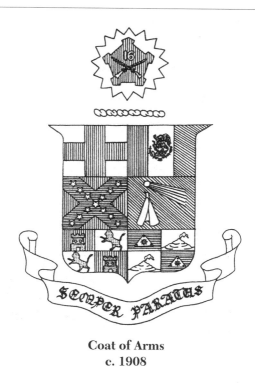

Coat of Arms
c. 1908

Motto: *Semper Paratus* (literally "Always Prepared"; more properly "Always Ready")

Symbolism: The coat of arms followed the "hodge-podge" design practice adopted by numerous regiments at the time. This design was faulty historically as it included honors won during the War of 1812 and the Mexican War by the 16th Infantry Regiments of those conflicts (but which have no relation to the current organization). The description of the design is as follows: the shield was divided into six sections; the upper left section was the red cross of St. George (War of 1812) on a white background; the upper right section was the design of the flag of Mexico (Mexican War); the middle left consisted of the Confederate battle flag (Civil War); the middle right was a white square on which was superimposed a golden sun with rays and a Sioux wigwam signifying the "Sun Woman" (Indian Campaigns); the lower left section was the design of the arms of the Kingdom of Spain (Spanish-American War); the lower right section consisted of a quartered square with the volcano of Mayon in the upper right and lower left quarters, and the Katapunan emblem (Philippine sun symbol) in the upper left and lower right quarters (Philippine Insurrection). The crest of the arms consisted of a gold, sixteen-pointed star on which was superimposed a red five-bastioned fort (the badge of the 1st Division, V Corps, to which the regiment was assigned at San Juan Hill), surmounted by infantry crossed rifles, all above a wreath (rope) of blue and white, the infantry colors. The motto *Semper Paratus* was Latin for "Always Prepared." The actual rendering of the motto, as interpreted by the members of the regiment of the time, however, was intended to be "Always Ready." The design was approved by the secretary of war in 1908 for wear as a mess jacket insignia and for use on regimental stationery.

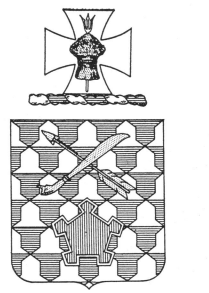

Distinctive Insignia

The distinctive insignia is the shield of the coat of arms. The sample of the insignia was approved November 24, 1926.

Coat of Arms

Shield: Vair *argent* and *azure*, in chief an Indian arrow and a Philippine bolo in saltire *or*, and in base, a five-bastioned fort *gules*, fimbriated of the third.

Crest: On a wreath of the colors *argent* and *azure*, on a cross pattée *argent*, a garb proper pierced by a devil's trident in pale *sable*, armed *gules*.

Motto: *Semper Paratus* (literally "Always Prepared"; more properly "Always Ready"), adopted 1907.

Symbolism: The shield is the fur vair, white and blue, from the arms of Fléville, France. This town was captured by the 16th Infantry on October 4, 1918 after very heavy fighting in the Meuse-Argonne campaign of World War I. The crossed arrow and bolo recall the regiment's fighting in the Indian Campaigns and the Philippine Insurrection. The five-bastioned fort was the badge of the 1st Division, V Corps in Cuba, to which the regiment was assigned during the fighting at San Juan Hill. The crest is the white Maltese cross of the 2nd Division, V Corps, to which the regiment was assigned during most of its campaigns in the Civil War. The sheaf of wheat superimposed over the trident represents the desperate fighting between the Wheatfield and the Devil's Den at Gettysburg, where the regiment lost approximately 50 percent of its effective strength in action with Confederate forces. The motto "Always Ready" has been used by the 16th Infantry since 1907.

**Coat of Arms
of
Nobel Nicolas Seigneaux De Lützelbourg
Lord of Fléville**

The arms of Nobel Nicolas Seigneaux de Lützelbourg from which members of the 16th Infantry used the vair portions to design the regiment's coat of arms in 1923. Little is known about this man, but he apparently was the lord of the Fléville area sometime before 1700.

(Drawing adapted from *L'Armorial des Pricipales Maisons et Families du Royume*, 1757)

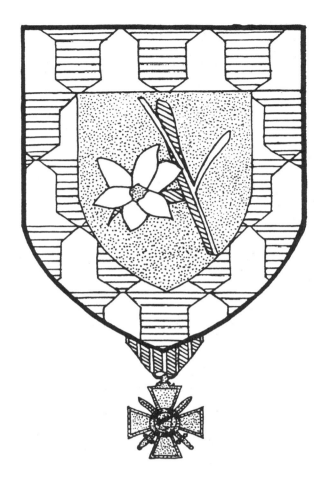

Coat of Arms of
The Town of Fléville, France
Adopted 1999

Shield: A Common Blue Eye blossom *azure* on a shield *or*, superimposed on a shield vair *argent* and *azure*. In base, a Croix de Guerre medal.

Symbolism: The shield consists of a gold shield bearing a *Common Blue Eye* (Sissi Rincium Montanum) flower, superimposed on a blue and white vair shield. The gold shield represents the *Canadian Goldenrod* (Solidago Canadensis) flower. These flowers are not native to France, but were the result of seeds given as a gift by an American doughboy to a villager from Fléville, France, during World War I. The seeds were subsequently planted, and today these blue and gold flowers grow wild throughout the Fléville area. The vair is from the arms of Nobel Nicolas Seigneaux de Lützelbourg. The French government awarded the Croix de Guerre to the town for its sacrifices in World War I.

Appendix 4
Battle Group and Battalion Commanders

16th Infantry Regiment
1957-present

Name	Dates	Remarks
1st Battalion, 16th Infantry		
Colonel Roy E. Doran	Feb 15, 57-Jan 58	Commander, 1st Battle Group
Colonel Frederick W. Collins	Jan 58-Nov 58	Commander, 1st Battle Group
Colonel David S. Daley	Nov 29, 58-May 60	Commander, 1st Battle Group
Lieutenant Colonel Cecil M. Curles	May 60-Jul 20, 60	Acting Commander
Colonel John K. Singlaub	Jul 20, 60-Jul 15, 61	Commander, 1st Battle Group
Lieutenant Colonel Condee C. Nason	Jul 15, 61-Aug 61	Acting Commander
Colonel George H. Russell	Aug 61-Jun 12, 62	Commander, 1st Battle Group
Lieutenant Colonel Condee C. Nason	Jun 12, 62-Jul 18, 62	Acting Commander
Colonel John J. C. Moore	Jul 18, 62-Apr 25, 63	Commander, 1st Battle Group
NA	Apr 25, 63-Mar 30, 64	Commander, 1st Battalion
Lieutenant Colonel Herman S. Napier	Mar 30, 64-Jul 23, 65	
Lieutenant Colonel William J. Lober	Jul 23, 65-Mar 11, 66	Commander during Vietnam
Lieutenant Colonel Lee S. Henry Jr.	Mar 11, 66-Jun 26, 66	Commander during Vietnam
Lieutenant Colonel Rufus C. Lazzell	Jun 26, 66-Jul 10, 66	Commander during Vietnam
Lieutenant Colonel George M. Wallace II	Jul 10, 66-Nov 28, 66	Commander during Vietnam
Lieutenant Colonel Rufus C. Lazzell	Nov 28, 66-Jun 28, 67	Commander during Vietnam
Lieutenant Colonel Calvert P. Benedict	Jun 28, 67-Mar 21, 68	Commander during Vietnam
Lieutenant Colonel Richard A. Eaton	Mar 21, 68-Jul 24, 68	Commander during Vietnam
Lieutenant Colonel Willard Latham	Jul 24, 68-Oct 21, 68	Commander during Vietnam
Lieutenant Colonel Donald C Shuffstall	Oct 21, 68-Apr 19, 69	Commander during Vietnam
Lieutenant Colonel Kenneth G. Cassels	Apr 19, 69-Sep 21, 69	Commander during Vietnam
Lieutenant Colonel David C. Martin	Sep 21, 69-Mar 11, 70	Commander during Vietnam
Lieutenant Colonel Louis J. Pistone	Apr 18, 70-Jul 7, 72	
Lieutenant Colonel William H. Wilcox	Jul 7, 72-Jan 9, 74	
Lieutenant Colonel John E. Wooley	Jan 9, 74-Jul 8, 75	
Lieutenant Colonel Donn G. Miller	Jul 8, 75-Dec 15, 76	
Lieutenant Colonel James A. Sullivan	Dec 15, 76-Nov 29, 78	
Lieutenant Colonel John A. Noble	Nov 29, 78-May 12, 81	
Lieutenant Colonel Terry A. Gordon	May 12, 81-May 30, 84	
Lieutenant Colonel Stephen D. Wesbrook	Jun 1, 84-Jun 24, 86	
Lieutenant Colonel Carl Baxley	Jun 24, 86-88	
Lieutenant Colonel Robert L. Moberly	1991	Commander during Desert Storm
Lieutenant Colonel Frank J. Stone	1993	
Lieutenant Colonel William S. Knoebel	Jun 18, 93-Jun 95	
Lieutenant Colonel Robert W. Brown	Jun 95-Jun 97	
Lieutenant Colonel Frank Harmon	Jun 97-Jun 99	
Lieutenant Colonel Keith Lovejoy	Jun 99-Present	

Name	Dates	Remarks
2nd Battalion, 16th Infantry		
Colonel William T. Gleason	Oct 7, 63-Mar 2, 64	Commander, 2nd Battle Group. Reorg and redes 2nd Bn Jan 20, 64
Lieutenant Colonel Joseph E. O'Leary	Mar 2, 64-Jul 64	
Lieutenant Colonel Lloyd L. Burke	Jul 64-Jul 24, 65	Commander during Vietnam
Lieutenant Colonel Y. Y. Phillips	Jul 24, 65-17 Feb 66	Commander during Vietnam
Lieutenant Colonel William S. Hathaway	Feb 17, 66-Jan 17, 67	Commander during Vietnam
Lieutenant Colonel Bruce E. Wallace	Jan 17, 67-Feb 67	Commander during Vietnam
Lieutenant Colonel Joseph R. Ulatoski	Feb 67-Jul 9, 67	Commander during Vietnam
Lieutenant Colonel Stanley J. Parmentier	Jul 9, 67-Dec 14, 67	Commander during Vietnam
Lieutenant Colonel Darrel L. Gooler	Dec 14, 67-Jul 12, 68	Commander during Vietnam
Lieutenant Colonel Charles P. McLean	Jul 12, 68-Jan 69	Commander during Vietnam
Lieutenant Colonel Hugh S. Galligan	Jan 69-Aug 69	Commander during Vietnam
Lieutenant Colonel Joe G. Mears	Aug 69-Jan 70	Commander during Vietnam
Lieutenant Colonel William E. Panton	Jan 70-Apr 16, 70	Commander during Vietnam
Lieutenant Colonel David P. Thoreson	Apr 16, 70-May 26, 70	1-19th Inf redes 2-16 Inf Apr 16, 70 at Fort Riley, KS
Lieutenant Colonel Kenneth M. Miller	May 26, 70-Jun 14, 71	
Lieutenant Colonel William M. Hadley	Jun 14, 71-Mar 14, 73	
Lieutenant Colonel Ronald L. Watts	Mar 14, 73-Aug 74	2-16 Inf inactivated Aug 74
Lieutenant Colonel Henry O. Johnson	May 19, 76-Sep 20, 76	2-16 Inf inactivated Sep 20, 76
Lieutenant Colonel John P. Otjen	Dec 16, 79-Jun 19, 81	Commander when 2-9 Inf was redes 2-16 Inf Dec 16, 79
Lieutenant Colonel Karl H. Lowe	Jun 19, 81-Sep 29, 83	
Lieutenant Colonel Michael V. Harper	Sep 29, 83-Apr 9, 86	
Lieutenant Colonel Joseph G. Terry	Apr 9, 86-Apr 7, 88	
Lieutenant Colonel Lawrence S. McAfee Jr.	Apr 7, 88-Jan 31, 90	
Lieutenant Colonel Daniel R. Fake	Jan 31, 90-Jan 10, 92	Commander during Desert Storm
Lieutenant Colonel Richard Gribling	Jan 10, 92-Jan 7, 94	
Lieutenant Colonel Thomas M. Jordan	Jan 7, 94-Jan 96	
Lieutenant Colonel Robert Rush	Jan 96-10 Apr 96	2-16 Inf inactivated Apr 10, 96
3rd Battalion, 16th Infantry		
Colonel Irving J. Yarock	May 1, 59-Jan 7, 63	Commander, 3rd Battle Group. Served with 1st Inf Div WW II
Lieutenant Colonel George F. Cooney	Jan 7, 63-Jul 68	
Unknown	Jul 68-Feb 21, 71	
Lieutenant Colonel William N. Grenier	Feb 21, 71-Jan 31, 73	
Lieutenant Colonel Eugene P. Riley	Jan 31, 73-Feb 1, 74	
Lieutenant Colonel Paul J. Provencher	Feb 1, 74-May 18, 75	
Lieutenant Colonel David L. Higgins	May 18, 75-Jun 30, 76	
Major Merle A. Taylor	Sep 20, 76-Mar 23, 77	Acting Commander
Lieutenant Colonel Carl R. Triebs	Mar 23, 77-Apr 30, 77	
Lieutenant Colonel George Darling	Apr 30, 77-Aug 10, 78	
Major Theodore N. Kaliveas	Aug 10, 78-Nov 30, 78	Acting Commander
Major Louis W. Austin	Nov 30, 78-Jan 1, 81	
Major Peter J. Deane	Jan 1, 81-Mar 4, 81	Acting Commander
Lieutenant Colonel John R. Buckley	Mar 4, 81-Mar 6, 84	
Major Robert T. Wright	Mar 6, 84-Jul 1, 85	
Major Robert P. Antoniuc	Nov 1, 85-Mar 17, 86	Acting Commander
Lieutenant Colonel Michael Severance	Mar 17, 86-Oct 16, 88	
Major Donald W. Lane	Oct 16, 88-Dec 1, 88	Acting Commander
Lieutenant Colonel Carl H. Sanborn	Dec 1, 88-Aug 22, 92	
Lieutenant Colonel Mark E. Hammond	Aug 22, 92-Apr 15, 94	3-16 Inf inactivated Apr 15, 94
4th Battalion, 16th Infantry		
Lieutenant Colonel Joseph C. Arnold	Feb 28, 83-Jun 7, 83	
Lieutenant Colonel George S. Basso	Jun 7, 83-Jun 5, 86	
Lieutenant Colonel W. Edward Shirron	Jun 5, 86-Jun 19, 87	
Lieutenant Colonel John W. May Jr.	May 19, 87-Jun 12, 89	
Lieutenant Colonel Russel L. Honore	Jun 12, 89-Jul 16, 91	Commander during Desert Storm. 4-16 Inf inactivated Jul 16, 91

Name	Dates	Remarks
5th Battalion, 16th Infantry		
Lieutenant Colonel Robert W. Higgins	Feb 28, 83-Oct 10, 84	
Lieutenant Colonel William R. Lynch	Oct 10, 84-Jan 6, 87	
Lieutenant Colonel Dwight B. Dickson	Jan 6, 87-Apr 13, 89	
Lieutenant Colonel Sidney F. Baker Jr	Apr 13, 89-Jun 25, 91	Commander during Desert Storm
Lieutenant Colonel Frank J. Stone	Jun 25, 91-Jul 16, 91	Commander when 5-16 Inf was redes 1-16 Inf at Fort Riley. 5-16 Inf inactivated Jul 16, 91

Appendix 5
Station List of the 16th Infantry Regiment

Dates	Elements	Station	Assignment/Remarks
May 14, 1861	Headquarters, 1st Battalion 11th Infantry	Fort Independence, MA	Organized
Aug 61	Company A	Fort Independence, MA	Organized
Aug 61	Company B	Fort Independence, MA	Organized
Aug 61	Company D	Fort Independence, MA	Organized
Aug 61	Company G	Fort Independence, MA	Organized
Oct 20, 61	1st Battalion, 11th Infantry	Perryville, MD	Dix's Division, Middle Department
Feb 15, 62	Company C	Perryville, MD	Organized
Feb 15, 62	Company E	Perryville, MD	Organized
Mar 9, 62	1st Battalion, 11th Infantry	Various locations in Virginia until Sep 11, 62	*Infantry Reserve Bde, Army of the Potomac Mar 62-May 62
*Reorganized into 1st and 2nd Brigades, 2nd Division, V Corps May 20, 1862			
Jul 5, 62	Company F	Harrison's Landing, VA	Organized
Jul 5, 62	Company H	Harrison's Landing, VA	Organized
Sep 11, 62	1st Battalion, 11th Infantry	Various locations in Maryland until Oct 30, 62	2nd Bde, 2nd Div, V Corps
Oct 30, 62	1st Battalion, 11th Infantry	Various locations in Virginia until Dec 16, 62	2nd Bde, 2nd Div, V Corps
Dec 16, 62	1st Battalion, 11th Infantry	Falmouth, VA except for several short periods in Jan, Apr, and May 63 until Jun 63.	2nd Bde, 2nd Div, V Corps
Jun 4, 63	1st Battalion, 11th Infantry	Various locations in Virginia until Jun 27, 62	2nd Bde, 2nd Div, V Corps
Jun 27, 63	1st Battalion, 11th Infantry	Various locations in Maryland until Jul 1, 63	2nd Bde, 2nd Div, V Corps
Jul 1, 63	1st Battalion, 11th Infantry	Gettysburg, PA until Jul 5, 63	2nd Bde, 2nd Div, V Corps
Jul 5, 63	1st Battalion, 11th Infantry	Various locations in Pennsylvania until Jul 14, 63	2nd Bde, 2nd Div, V Corps
Jul 14, 63	1st Battalion, 11th Infantry	Various locations in Virginia until Aug 20, 63	2nd Bde, 2nd Div, V Corps
Aug 22, 63	1st Battalion, 11th Infantry	New York, NY Departed Sep 12, 63	District of New York
Sep 14, 63	1st Battalion, 11th Infantry	Various locations in Virginia until Sep 63-Mar 64	1st Bde, 2nd Div, V Corps Jun 17, 64 1st Bde, 1st Div, V Corps Mar 64
Apr 4, 1864	3rd Battalion, 16th Infantry	Organized at Madison Barracks, NY	Became 34th Infantry 1866 Consolidated with 11th Infantry 1869

Dates	Elements	Station	Assignment/Remarks
Jun 17, 64	1st Battalion, 11th Infantry	Vicinity of Petersburg Departed Nov 1, 64	4th Bde, 1st Div, V Corps Mar 64-Apr 64 1st Bde, 1st Div, V Corps Apr 64-Jun 64 1st Bde, 2nd Div, V Corps Jun 64-Nov 64
Nov 6, 64	1st Battalion, 11th Infantry	Fort Hamilton, NY Departed Dec 3, 64	1st Bde, U.S. Troops, District of New York Nov 64-Dec 64
Dec 5, 64	1st Battalion, 11th Infantry	Camp Parole, MD Departed Jan 26, 65	Inf Bde, VIII Corps Dec 64-Jan 65
Jan 26, 65	1st Battalion, 11th Infantry	City Point, VA Departed Mar 65	Provost Guard Brigade, Army of the Potomac Jan 65-May 65
May 65	1st Battalion, 11th Infantry	Camp Grant, Richmond, VA	2nd Bde, 2nd Div, XXIV Corps May 65-Jul 65 Departed Feb 69 Department of Virginia Jul 65-Aug 66 Department of the Potomac Aug 66-Mar 67 First Military District Mar 67-Feb 69
Sep 21, 1866	3rd Battalion, 16th Infantry reorganized and redesignated the 34th Infantry Regiment at Grenada, MS. Regiment located as follows:		
	Regimental HQ	Grenada, MS	Fourth Military District
	Companies A & F	Columbus, MS	
	Companies B, H, & K	Grenada, MS	
	Companies C & G	Holly Springs, MS	
	Companies D	Greensboro, MS	
	Companies E & I	Corinth, MS	
Dec 5, 1866 Jan 1, 1869	1st Battalion, 11th Infantry reorganized and redesignated the 11th Infantry Regiment at Camp Grant, Richmond, VA.		
	Regimental HQ	Camp Grant, VA	First Military District
	Companies A-E, H	Camp Grant, VA	
	Company F	Warrenton, VA	
	Companies G & K	Lynchburg, VA	
	Company I	Marion, VA	
Mar 28-Apr 6, 1869	The 11th Infantry and 34th Infantry consolidated and designated the 16th Infantry at various locations in Mississippi and Tennessee as follows:		
Mar 1869-Aug 1871	Regimental HQ	Grenada, MS	Fourth Military District
	Company A	Natchez, MS	
	Companies B, E, & G	Jackson, MS	
	Companies C & F	Vicksburg, MS	
	Companies D & I	Grenada, MS	
	Company H	Lauderdale, MS	
	Company K	Corinth, MS	
Aug 1871-May 1876	Regimental HQ	Nashville, TN	Department of the South
	Companies A & E	Taylor Barracks, KY	
	Companies B & H	Jackson, MS	
	Company C	Aberdeen, MS	
	Companies D & I	Humboldt, TN	
	Companies F & G	Nashville, TN	
	Company K	St. Augustine, FL	
May 1876-Dec 1876	Regimental HQ	Newport Barracks, KY	Department of the South
	Companies A & K	Newport Barracks, KY	
	Companies B & F	Nashville, TN	
	Companies C & I	Little Rock Barracks, AR	
	Company D	Livingston, AL	
	Company E	Lebanon, KY	
	Company G	Chattanooga, TN	

Dates	Elements	Station	Assignment/Remarks
Sep 1876-Dec 1876	Regimental HQ	Mount Vernon Brks, AL	Department of the Gulf
	Companies A & F	Mount Vernon Brks, AL	
	Company B	Jackson, MS	
	Company C	Little Rock Barracks, AR	
	Company D	Livingston, AL	
	Company E	Mobile, AL	
	Company G	Baton Rouge Barracks, LA	
	Company H	Monroe, LA	
	Company I	Shreveport, LA	
	Company K	Huntsville, AL	
Dec 1876-May 1877	Regiment	New Orleans, LA	Department of the Gulf
May 1877-Jun 1887	Regiment	Fort Leavenworth, KS	Department of the Missouri
Jun 1877-Nov 1880	Regimental HQ	Fort Riley, KS	Department of the Missouri
	Companies A, C & H	Fort Riley, KS	
	Companies B & D	Fort Sill, IT	
	Companies E & I	Fort Reno, IT	
	Company F	Fort Wallace, KS	
	*Company G	Fort Hayes, KS	
	Company K	Fort Gibson, IT	

*Transferred to Fort Wallace, KS in 1878

Dates	Elements	Station	Assignment/Remarks
Nov 1880-Mar 1881	Regimental HQ	San Antonio, TX	Department of Texas
	Companies A, B & C	Fort Concho, TX	
	Companies D, E, G, H, I and K	Fort McKavett, TX	
	Company F	San Antonio, TX	
Mar 1881-Jul 1882	Regimental HQ	Fort McKavett, TX	Department of Texas
	*Companies A, B, C, & F	Fort Concho, TX	
	Companies D, E, G, I, & K	Fort McKavett, TX	
	**Company H	San Antonio, TX	

*These companies also garrisoned camps at Grierson Springs, Camp Elizabeth, and Camp Charlotte for one to six month periods.
**This duty was rotated with other companies of the regiment (F Company Nov 1880-Mar 1881; H Company Jan 1881-Dec 1881; G Company Nov 1882-May 1888; K Company Jul 1886-May 1888; A Company Sep 1886-May 1888; F Company Oct 1887-May 1888).

Dates	Elements	Station	Assignment/Remarks
Jul 1882-Jan 1887	Regimental HQ	Fort Concho, TX	Department of Texas
	Companies A, B, C, & H	Fort Concho, TX	
	*Companies D & E	Fort McIntosh, TX	
	**Companies F, I, & K	Fort Stockton, TX	
	Company G	San Antonio, TX	

*One of these companies was periodically stationed at Fort Ringgold on a temporary basis.
**One to two of these companies were periodically stationed at Fort Davis.

Dates	Elements	Station	Assignment/Remarks
Jan 1887-May 1888	Regimental HQ	Fort Bliss, TX	Department of Texas
	Companies A, F, G, & K	San Antonio, TX	
	Companies B & H	Fort Bliss, TX	
	Company C	Fort Concho, TX	
	Company D	Fort Ringgold, TX	
	Company E	Fort McIntosh, TX	
	Company I	Fort Davis, TX	
May 1888-Oct 1896	Regimental HQ	Fort Douglas, UT	Department of the Platte, May 1888-Jul 1893
	Companies B, D, E, G, H and I		
		Fort Douglas, UT	Department of Colorado, Jul 1893-Sep 1896
	*Companies A, C, F, & K	Fort Duchesne, UT	

*Transferred to Fort Douglas August 25, 1891.

Dates	Elements	Station	Assignment/Remarks
1892	Companies I & K	Fort Douglas, UT	Inactivated
Oct 1896- Apr 1898	Regimental HQ	Fort Sherman, ID	Department of the Columbia
	Companies C, D, F, G, and H	Fort Sherman, ID	
	Companies B & E	Fort Spokane, WA	
	Company A	Boise Barracks, ID	
Apr 1898-May 1898	Regiment	Camp George H. Thomas, Chickamauga, GA	I Corps

Dates	Elements	Station	Assignment/Remarks
May 1898–Jun 1898	Regiment	Tampa, FL	1st Bde, 1st Div, V Corps
Jun 1898–Aug 1898	Regiment	Cuba	1st Bde, 1st Div, V Corps
Jul 13, 1898	Companies I & K	near Santiago, Cuba	Reactivated
Sep 13–14, 1898	Companies L & M	Camp Wikoff, NY	Constituted and activated
Aug 1898–Nov 1898	Regiment	Camp Wikoff, Long Island, NY	1st Bde, 1st Div, V Corps Aug 1898–Oct 1898 2nd Bde, 1st Div, IV Corps Oct 1898–Nov 1898
Nov 1898–Jan 1899	Regiment	Huntsville, AL	1st Bde, 1st Div, IV Corps Nov 1898–Jan 1899 Provost Duties
Jan 1899–May 1899	Regimental HQ Companies A, C, D, & K Companies B, E, H, & L Companies F, G, I, & M	Fort Crook, NE Fort Leavenworth, KS Fort Crook, NE Jefferson Barracks, MO	Department of the Missouri
Jun 1899–Dec 1899	Regimental HQ Company A Company B Company C Company D Company E Company F Companies G & M Companies H & L Company I Company K	Caloocan, Luzon, PI Caloocan Santo Tomas Malabon Meycauayan Apalit Guiguinto La Lomboy Convent Calumpit Bigaa Polo	1st Div, VIII Corps Jun 1899–Aug 1899 1st Bde, 2nd Div, VIII Corps Aug 1899–Dec 1899
Dec 1899–Jul 1902	Regimental HQ 1st Battalion 2nd Battalion (-) Companies E & F 3rd Battalion	Aparri, Luzon, PI Aparri, PI Ilagan, PI Tuguegarao, PI Solano, PI	District of Northeast Luzon Jan 1900–Aug 1900 2nd District, Department of Luzon, Philippines Division Aug 1900–Jul 1902
Jul 1902–May 1905	Regiment (-) *1st Battalion	Fort McPherson, GA Fort Slocum, NY	Department of the Gulf Department of the East
*Joined the regiment at Fort McPherson in Aug 1904.			
Jun 1905–Sep 1907	Regiment	Fort William McKinley	Department of Luzon, Philippine Division
Sep 1907–Jun 1910	Regiment (-) 1st Battalion	Fort Crook, NE Fort Logan H. Roots, AR	Department of the Missouri Department of Texas
Jun 1910–Jun 1912	Regimental HQ Companies A & L Companies B & E Companies C & I Companies D & M Companies F, G, H, K & MG Platoon	Fort Wm H. Seward, AK Fort Gibbon, AK Fort Davis, AK Fort Liscum, AK Fort Saint Michael, AK Fort William H. Seward, AK	Department of the Columbia
Jun 1912–Apr 1914	Regiment	Presidio of San Francisco, CA	8th Brigade, 3rd Division
Apr 1914–Mar 1916	Regiment	Camp Cotton, El Paso, TX	8th Brigade, 3rd Division
Mar 1916	Regiment	Columbus, NM	1st Provisional Brigade Punitive Expedition
Mar 1916–May 1917	Regiment	En route, Mexico	1st Provisional Brigade Punitive Expedition

Dates	Elements	Station	Assignment/Remarks
May 1916	Regiment	San Geronimo Ranch, Mexico	1st Provisional Brigade Punitive Expedition
Jun 1916	Regiment	Namiquipa, Mexico	1st Provisional Brigade Punitive Expedition
Jun 1916-Feb 1917	Regiment	El Valle, Mexico	1st Provisional Brigade Punitive Expedition
Feb 1917-Mar 1917	Regiment	Camp Cotton, El Paso, TX	8th Brigade
Mar 1917-May 1917	Regiment	Camp Newton D. Baker, El Paso, TX	8th Brigade
Jun 1917-May 1917	Regiment	France	1st Division
Dec 1918-Apr 1919	Regiment	Dernbach, Germany	1st Division
Apr 1919-Aug 1919	Regiment	Selters, Germany	1st Division
Oct 1919-Sep 1920	Regiment	Camp Zachary Taylor, KY	1st Division
Sep 1920-Jun 1922	Regiment	Camp Dix, NJ	1st Division
Jun 1922-Nov 1939	Regiment (-)	Fort Jay, NY	1st Division
Sep 1922-Jun 1933	*3rd Battalion	Fort Wadsworth, NY	
Jun 1922-25	**Companies A, B, E	Fort Wood, NY (Liberty Island)	
1933-40	***Company A	Camp Dix, NJ	

*Transferred to Fort Jay in June 1933
**Each of these companies stationed at Fort Wood for about one year each 1922-25.
***Company A stationed at Camp Dix, NJ to administer/support C.C.C. camps.

Dates	Elements	Station	Assignment/Remarks
Nov 1939-May 1940	Regiment	Fort Benning, GA	1st Division
May 1940-Feb 1941	Regiment	Fort Jay, NY	1st Division
Feb 1941-Feb 1942	Regiment	Fort Devens, MA	1st Division
Feb 1942-May 1942	Regiment	Camp Blanding, FL	1st Division
May 1942-Jul 1942	Regiment	Indiantown Gap, PA	1st Division
Aug 1942-Oct 1942	Regiment	Scotland/England	1st Infantry Division
Nov 1942-Jul 1943	Regiment	North Africa	1st Infantry Division
Jul 1943-Nov 1943	Regiment	Sicily	1st Infantry Division
Nov 1943-Jun 1944	Regiment	England	1st Infantry Division
Jun 1944-Sep 1944	Regiment	France	1st Infantry Division
Sep 1944	Regiment	Belgium	1st Infantry Division
Sep 1944-Dec 1944	Regiment	Germany	1st Infantry Division
Dec 1944-Feb 1945	Regiment	Belgium	1st Infantry Division
Feb 1945-Apr 1945	Regiment	Germany	1st Infantry Division
Apr 1945	Regiment	Czechoslovakia	1st Infantry Division
Apr 1945-Jun 1945	Regiment	Franzensbad, Czechoslovakia	1st Infantry Division

Dates	Elements	Station	Assignment
Jun 1945-Nov 1945	Regiment (-) 1st Battalion	Bamberg, Germany Hochstadt, Germany	1st Infantry Division
Nov 1945-Feb 1946	Regiment (-) 1st Battalion 3rd Battalion D Company E Company Cannon Company	Bamberg, Germany Mellrichstadt, Germany Hammelburg, Germany Maroldweisach, Germany Schweinfurt, Germany Hammelburg, Germany	1st Infantry Division
Feb 1946-Oct 1946	Regiment (-) 2nd Battalion 3rd Battalion	Landshut, Germany Vilshofen, Germany Deggendorf, Germany	1st Infantry Division
Oct 1946-Jul 1948	Regimental HQ 1st Battalion 2nd Battalion 3rd Battalion Service Company Antitank Company Cannon Company	Glasenbach, Austria Vienna, Austria Salzburg, Austria Berlin, Germany Salzburg, Austria Salzburg, Austria Hallein, Austria	1st Infantry Division
Jul 1948-Oct 1948	Regiment (-) 3rd Battalion	Grafenwöhr, FRG Berlin, FRG	1st Infantry Division
Oct 1948-Jun 1952	Regimental HQ 1st Battalion 2nd Battalion *3rd Battalion Heavy Tank Company Heavy Mortar Company Service Company Medical Company	Monteith Barracks, Nürnberg, FRG Monteith Barracks, Nürnberg, FRG Pinder Barracks, Zirndorf, FRG Roosevelt Barracks, Berlin, FRG Adams Barracks, Zirndorf, FRG Monteith Barracks, Nürnberg, FRG Monteith Barracks, Nürnberg, FRG Monteith Barracks, Nürnberg, FRG	1st Infantry Division

*Transferred to Johnson Barracks, Furth, FRG Nov 15, 50.

Dates	Elements	Station	Assignment
Jun 1952-Aug 1952	Regiment	Grafenwöhr, FRG	1st Infantry Division
Aug 1952-Sep 1955	Regiment (-) 1st Battalion 2nd Battalion 3rd Battalion	Conn Barracks, Schweinfurt, FRG Ledward Barracks, Schweinfurt, FRG Ledward Barracks, Schweinfurt, FRG Ledward Barracks, Schweinfurt, FRG	1st Infantry Division
Sep 1955-Feb 1957	Regiment	Fort Riley, KS	1st Infantry Division
Feb 15, 1957	Regiment inactivated and integrated into the Combat Arms Regimental system.		

Battalion Station List, 1957-1999

Dates	Elements	Station	Assignment
1st Battalion			
Feb 1957-Mar 1959	1st Battle Group	Fort Riley, KS	1st Infantry Division
Mar 1959-Apr 1963	1st Battle Group	Baumholder, FRG	8th Infantry Division

Redesignated 1st Battalion April 1, 1963, transferred, less personnel and equipment, to Fort Riley, KS.

Dates	Elements	Station	Assignment
Apr 1963-Oct 1965	1st Battalion	Fort Riley, KS	1st Infantry Division
Oct 1965-Apr 1970	1st Battalion	Vietnam	1st Infantry Division
Apr 1970-Feb 1972	1st Battalion	Augsberg, FRG	1st Infantry Division (Fwd)
Apr 1972-Jan 1991	1st Battalion	Böblingen, FRG	1st Infantry Division (Fwd)
Jan 1991-May 1991	1st Battalion	Saudi-Arabia	1st Infantry Division (Fwd)
May 1991-Jul 1991	1st Battalion	Böblingen, FRG	1st Infantry Division (Fwd)
Jul 1991-Present	1st Battalion	Fort Riley, KS	1st Infantry Division (Mech)

Dates	Elements	Station	Assignment

2nd Battalion

Feb 1957-Oct 1963	2nd Battle Group	Inactive	

Activated by redesignating 2nd Battle Group, 8th Infantry October 1, 1963 at Fort Riley, KS.

Oct 1963-Mar 1964	2nd Battle Group	Fort Riley, KS	1st Infantry Division

Redesignated 2nd Battalion March 2, 1964.

Mar 1964-Jul 1965	2nd Battalion	Fort Riley, KS	1st Infantry Division
Jul 1965-Apr 1970	2nd Battalion	Vietnam	1st Infantry Division
Apr 1970-Aug 1974	2nd Battalion	Fort Riley, KS	1st Infantry Division (Mech)
Aug 1974-May 1976	2nd Battalion	Inactive	1st Infantry Division (Mech)
May 1976-Sep 1976	2nd Battalion	Fort Riley, KS	1st Infantry Division (Mech)
Sep 1976-Dec 1979	2nd Battalion	Inactive	1st Infantry Division (Mech)

Activated by redesignating 2nd Battalion, 9th Infantry December 1979 at Fort Riley, KS.

Dec 1979-Jan 1991	2nd Battalion	Fort Riley, KS	1st Infantry Division (Mech)
Jan 1991-May 1991	2nd Battalion	Saudi-Arabia/Kuwait	1st Infantry Division (Mech)
May 1991-Apr 1996	2nd Battalion	Fort Riley, KS	1st Infantry Division (Mech)

Inactivated April 10, 1996 at Fort Riley, KS.

3rd Battalion

Feb 1957-May 1959	3rd Battle Group	Inactive	
May 1959-Jan 1963	3rd Battle Group	Lincoln W. Stoddard	94th Infantry Division
	HHC	USAR Center, Worcester, MA	
	Company A	Uxbridge, MA	
	Company B	Dudley, MA	
	Company C	Fitchberg, MA	
	Company D	Franklin, MA	
	Company E	Worcester, MA	
	Combat Support Co.	Worcester, MA	

Reorganized and redesignated 3rd Battalion January 7, 1963.

Jan 1963-Aug 1976	3rd Battalion	Worcester, MA	187th Infantry Brigade (Sep)
	HHC	Worcester, MA	
	Company A	Roslindale, MA	
	Company B	Brockton, MA	
	Company C	Fitchberg, MA	

Aug 1976-Nov 1977	3rd Battalion	Saco, ME	187th Infantry Brigade (Sep)
	HHC	Saco, ME	
	Company A	Dexter, ME	
	Company B	Rockland, ME	
	Company C	Auburn, ME	
	Combat Support Co.	Rochester, NH	

Nov 1977-Aug 1978	3rd Battalion	Portland, ME	187th Infantry Brigade (Sep)
	HHC	Portland, ME	
	Company A	Dexter, ME	
	Company B	Rockland, ME	
	Company C	Auburn, ME	
	Combat Support Co.	Rochester, NH	

Aug 1978-Apr 1994	3rd Battalion	Scarborough, ME	187th Infantry Brigade (Sep)
	HHC	Scarborough, ME	
	Company A	Dexter, ME	
	Company B	Rockland, ME	
	Company C	Auburn, ME	
	Combat Support Co.	Rochester, NH	

Inactivated April 15, 1994 at Fort Devens, MA.

Dates	Elements	Station	Assignment
4th Battalion			
Feb 1957-Feb 1983	4th Battalion	Inactive	
Feb 1983-Jan 1991	4th Battalion	Göppingen, FRG	1st Infantry Division (Fwd)
Jan 1991-May 1991	4th Battalion	Saudi-Arabia	1st Infantry Division (Fwd)
May 1991-Jul 1991	4th Battalion	Göppingen, FRG	1st Infantry Division (Fwd)

Inactivated July 16, 1991 at Cooke Barracks, Goeppingen, GE.

Dates	Elements	Station	Assignment
5th Battalion			
Feb 1957-Feb 1983	5th Battalion	Inactive	
Feb 1983-Jan 1991	5th Battalion	Fort Riley, KS	1st Infantry Division (Mech)
Jan 1991-May 1991	5th Battalion	Saudi Arabia/Kuwait	1st Infantry Division (Mech)
May 1991-Jul 1991	5th Battalion	Fort Riley, KS	1st Infantry Division (Mech)

Inactivated July 16, 1991 at Fort Riley, KS.

Appendix 6
NTC and CMTC Rotations

16th Infantry, 1983-98

Battalion	Training Center	Rotation	Dates	Remarks
2nd Battalion	NTC	83-09	Aug 11-24, 83	with 4-37 Armor
5th Battalion	NTC	84-12	Aug 22-Sep 4, 84	with 2-34 Armor
2nd Battalion	NTC	85-06	Feb 21-Mar 12, 85	with 3-37 Armor
5th Battalion	NTC	87-03	Nov 22-Dec 11, 86	with 1-34 Armor
2nd Battalion	NTC	88-03	Nov 29-Dec 18 ,87	with 4-37 Armor
5th Battalion	NTC	88-06	Feb 25-Mar 15, 88	with 2-34 Armor
5th Battalion	NTC		March 1989	OPFOR Augmentation
1st Battalion	CMTC	89-01	March 1989	with 3-34 Armor
4th Battalion	CMTC	89-01	April 1989	with 3-34 Armor
2nd Battalion	NTC	90-04	Jan 3-Jan 26, 90	with 4-37 Armor
1st Battalion	CMTC	90-04	Mar 14-Mar 16, 90	
4th Battalion	CMTC	90-04	Mar 21-Mar 24, 90	
5th Battalion	NTC	90-08	Apr 9-May 2, 90	with 1st Brigade, 7th ID (L)
2nd Battalion	NTC	91-05	February 1991	with 3-37 Armor
2nd Battalion	NTC	92-06	Apr 2-Apr 29, 92	with 3-37 Armor
1st Battalion	NTC	92-09	May 25-Jun 21, 92	with 2-34 Armor
1st Battalion	NTC	93-04	January 1993	OPFOR Augmentation
2nd Battalion	NTC	93-09	May-Jun 1993	with 3-37 Armor
1st Battalion	NTC	94-02	Oct 21-Nov 19, 93	with 1-34 Armor
2nd Battalion	NTC	94-08	Apr 28-May 27, 94	with 4-37 Armor
1st Battalion	NTC	95-05	Feb 2-Mar 3, 95	with 2-34 Armor
2nd Battalion	NTC	96-01	Sep 30-Oct 27, 95	
1st Battalion	NTC	96-05	Feb 1-Mar 1, 96	
1st Battalion	NTC	97-05	Feb 1-Feb 28, 97	

Appendix 7
Distinguished Members of the 16th Infantry Regiment

Honorary Colonels of the Regiment

Major General Albert H. Smith Jr. (Ret.)
b: MD 1919   s: ROTC, The Johns-Hopkins University

Dec 23, 83-May 1, 90

16th Inf Regimental S3 in WW II
ADC, 1st Inf Div-Vietnam

Colonel William S. Hathaway
b: VA   s: OCS, (ROTC at VMI 3 years)

May 1, 90-Aug 31, 93

Commander, 2-16 Inf-Feb 66-Jan 67

Lieutenant General Ronald L. Watts (Ret.)
b: MO 1935   s: ROTC, Pittsburgh State University

Aug 31, 93-Sep 27, 96

Commander, 2-16 Inf-Mar 73-Jul 74
CG, 1st Inf Div-Jun 84-May 87
CG, VII Corps-Jul 87-Aug 89

Colonel (Ret.) Gerald Griffin
b: MD 1936   s: OCS, Fort Benning, GA 1959

Sep 27, 96-Present

Commander, A/2-16 Inf-Oct 65-May 66
S3, 2-16 Inf-May 66
ADC to Maj. Gen. DePuy-May 66

Honorary Sergeants Major of the Regiment

CSM Chandler Caldwell (Ret.)

May 1985-May 1988

CSM, 2-16 Inf-1965-66

CSM John Guerra (Ret.)

May 1988-Sep 1994

CSM, 2-16 Inf-1966-67

CSM Luis J. Landin (Ret.)

Sep 1994-Sep 1997

1st Sgt Lorenzo Cooper (Ret.)

Sep 1997-Present

1st Sgt, D Co, 1-16 Inf-1994-96

Distinguished Members of the Regiment

1984
Joseph T. Dawson, DSC
Service: World War II

Col. Herbert T. Hicks Jr., DSC
Service: World War II

Maj. Gen. Charles T. Horner Jr., DSC
Service: World War II

Col. William R. Washington, DSC
Service: World War II

Brig. Gen. Edward F. Wozenski, DSC *
Service: World War II

1985
Col. Bryce Denno, DSC
Service: World War II

Frank. J. Kolb Jr.
Service: World War II

2 Lt. Jake Lindsey, MOH
Service: World War II

Col. William J. Lober Jr.
Service: Vietnam

Maj. John D. Shelby Jr., DSC *
Service: World War II

1986
Maj. Gen. Theodore Antonelli
Service: World War II

Maj. Gen. Calvert P. Benedict
Service: Vietnam

Col. Everette L. Booth, DSC
Service: World War II

Col. John M. Brooks
Service: World War II

Victor P. Brosokas, DSC
Service: World War II

Col. Lloyd L. Burke, MOH
Service: Vietnam

Col. Kenneth G. Cassels
Service: Vietnam

Maj. Gen. Richard G. Ciccolella
Service: World War II

Richard H. Cole
Service: World War II

Capt. Polydore F. Dion
Service: World War II

Brig. Gen. Richard J. Eaton
Service: Vietnam

Lt. Col. Edwin W. Elder Jr.
Service: World War II

Lt. Col. John G. W. Finke, DSC
Service: World War II

Lt. Col. William Friedman
Service: World War II

Col. Hugh S. Galligan
Service: Vietnam

Lt. Col. Carl J. Giles Jr, DSC
Service: World War II

Col. Charles Hangsterfer
Service: World War II

Richard L. Harris, DSC
Service: World War II

Col. George J. Heil
Service: World War II

Dr. Milo H. Holden
Service: World War II

Robert M. Irvine
Service: World War II

Col. Donald T. Kellet
Service: World War II

Col. Robert L. Kestlinger
Service: World War II

James A. Krucas, DSC
Service: World War II

Maj. Gen. Willard Latham
Service: Vietnam

Brig. Gen. David C. Martin
Service: Vietnam

Col. David C. Milotta, DSC
Service: World War II

Col. Joe Mears
Service: Vietnam

William L. Nimmo Jr.
Service: World War II

Col. Stanley L. Parmentier
Service: Vietnam

Col. Y. Y. Phillips
Service: Vietnam

Col. Steven V. Ralph
Service: World War II

Col. Donald C. Shuffstall
Service: Vietnam

Maj. Gen. Albert H. Smith Jr.
Service: World War II

Maj. Gen. Charles P. Stone
Service: World War II

Brig. Gen. Joseph R. Ulatoski
Service: Vietnam

Maj. Gen. George M. Wallace II
Service: Vietnam

Col. Eston T. White
Service: World War II

John S. Winter
Service: World War II

Gen. James K. Woolnough
Service: World War II

CW4 James B. Lipinski
Service: World War II

CW4 Martin P. Roughn
Service: World War II

Samuel Fuller
Service: World War II

CSM John Guerra
Service: Vietnam

Lester R. Hudson
Service: World War II

John S. Hurkala
Service: World War II

Richard J. Myers, DSC
Service: Vietnam

Albert I. Nendza, DSC
Service: World War II

Andrew W. Parrish, DSC
Service: Vietnam

Joseph W. Pilck, DSC
Service: World War II

1st Sgt. Richard J. Ricioppo
Service: World War II

Arthur S. Tozar
Service: World War II

John H. Worbington, DSC
Service: Vietnam

1987
Dr. Noah Barysh
Service: World War II

Prof. Robert A. Brand
Service: World War II

Gen. Bruce Palmer Jr.
Service: Cold War 1954-55

Lt. Col. Karl E. Wolf
Service: World War II

1st Sgt. William J. Ashley
Service: Vietnam

John F. Connor
Service: Vietnam

1988
David C. Ballard Jr.
Service: World War II

Col. Ted Westerman
Service: Vietnam

1st Sgt. Nick D. Bacon, MOH
Service: Vietnam

CSM Chandler Caldwell
Service: Vietnam

CSM William B. Feely
Service: Vietnam

Edward F. Tatara, DSC
Service: World War II

1989
Capt. Martin L. Kroah Jr.
Service: Vietnam

John W. Libs
Service: Vietnam

Col. Bibb A. Underwood
Service: Vietnam

Phillip J. Hall
Service: Vietnam

John Souch
Service: Vietnam

1990

Col. Wendell W. Black
Service: Vietnam

Robert Canady
Service: Vietnam

Col. Gerald K. Griffin
Service: Vietnam

Col. William S. Hathaway
Service: Vietnam

Maj. Gen. Ralph C. Smith
Service: World War I

Col. Fred T. Wilson, DSC
Service: World War II

Sgt. Maj. William B. Arthington
Service: Cold War

Sfc. William T. McNeese
Service: Vietnam

MSgt. Joe B. Shine
Service: Vietnam

1991

No inductions in 1991 due to the Persian Gulf War

1992

Capt. Thomas E. Avery
Service: Vietnam

Col. Charles L. Cosand Jr.
Service: Vietnam

Lt. Col. Royce E. Pollard
Service: Vietnam

Wayne L. Beck
Service: Vietnam

Richmond K. S. Leong
Service: Vietnam

Buster E. Tiffany
Service: Vietnam

1993

Lt. Col. Edmund K. Daley
Service: Vietnam

Gen. William DePuy
Service: Cold War

Carl F. LeMier
Service: World War II

Col. Roger G. Seymour
Service: Vietnam

Lt. Gen. Ronald L. Watts
Service: Cold War

1994

Frederick Erben
Service: World War II

CSM Leonard P. Frusha
Service: World War II

Lt. Col. Fred W. Hall
Service: World War II

Simon S. Hurwit
Service: World War II

CSM Luis J. Landin
Service: Vietnam

Col. William S. Orlov
Service: Vietnam

Col. Doyle D. Taylor
Service: Vietnam

1995

Col. Kenneth Alderson
Service: Vietnam

Col. Michael V. Harper
Service: Cold War

Arnold R. Lambert
Service: World War II

John Willetts
Service: World War II

Col. Herbert M. Payne
Service: Vietnam

Lt. Col. Brian P. Zahn
Service: Gulf War

1996

Col. Edward J. Coates
Service: Vietnam

Lt. Col. James J. O'Donnell
Service: Gulf War

Lemuel C. Phillips
Service: World War II

Ronald J. Renne
Service: Vietnam

Charles E. Silk
Service: Cold War

1997

John E. Bistrica
Service: World War II

Charles Caldera
Service: Vietnam

1st Sgt. Lorenzo Cooper
Service: Cold War

George M. Gillespie
Service: World War II

Donald F. Shrake
Service: Vietnam

1st Sgt. Steve Stepro
Service: Cold War

1998

Col. Lester E. Barlow
Service: Cold War

Lt. Col. William M. Jackson Sr.
Service: World War II

Mr. Robert L. Brunelle
Service: Vietnam

Mr. Henry S. Orten
Service: World War II

Capt. James R. Kuechler
Service: World War II

Mr. John J. Copeland
Service: Cold War 1961-63

Mr. John B. Seville
Service: Vietnam

1999

Col. Sidney Baker
Service: Gulf War

Arthur Chaitt
Service: World War II

Col. Arthur Bakewell
Service: Cold War

Floyd Hayes
Service: Cold War

Maj. Louis Murray
Service: Cold War

Alvin Brown
Service: Vietnam

Steven M. Kellman
Service: World War II

2000

Joseph L. Argensio
Service: World War II

Donald Dignan
Service: Vietnam

Howell K. Bryant
Service: Vietnam

Lew W. Hosler
Service: Vietnam

Lt. Col. John F. McNulty
Service: Cold War

Lt. Col. Steven E. Clay
Service: Cold War

John F. Krolicki
Service: Vietnam

*Indicates 1st Oak Leaf Cluster
MOH–Medal of Honor
DSC–Distinguished Service Cross

Notes

Notes

Sources frequently cited and terms or phrases frequently used in these End Notes are identified by the following abbreviations:

AAR	After Action Report
A.E.F.	American Expeditionary Forces
ANJ	*Army and Navy Journal*
ANR	*Army-Navy Register*
ARN	*U. S. Army Recruiting News*
ARSW	*Annual Report of the Secretary of War*
ARWD	*War Department Annual Reports*
CG	Commanding General
CMH	U.S. Army Center of Military History
CT	Combat Team
1stID	First Infantry Division
GPO	Government Printing Office
HQ	Headquarters
IJ	*Infantry Journal*
MRC-FDM	McCormick Research Center, First Division Museum at Cantigny, Wheaton, Ill.
NYT	*New York Times*
OR	*The War of the Rebellion: A Compilation of the Official Records of the Union and Confederate Armies*
RCT	Regimental Combat Team
RG	Record Group
Washington	Washington, D.C.

Chapter 1—The Civil War

1. Francis B. Heitman, *Historical Register and Dictionary of the United States Army, from Its Organization, September 29, 1789, to March 2, 1903* (Washington: GPO, 1903; reprint, Frederick, Md.: Olde Soldier Books, 1988), 1:866.
2. John K. Mahon and Romana Danysh, *Infantry,* vol. 1, *Regular Army,* Army Lineage Series (Washington: GPO, 1972), 369; Robert W. Coakley, *The Role of Federal Military Forces in Domestic Disorders, 1789–1878,* Army Historical Series (Washington: GPO, 1988), 255–56; Gregory J. W. Urwin, *The United States Infantry: An Illustrated History, 1775–1918* (New York: Sterling Publishing Co., 1991), 93.
3. *Webster's American Military Biographies* (Springfield, Mass.: G. & C. Merriam Co., 1978), 278–79.
4. George W. Cullum, *Biographical Register of Officers and Graduates of the U. S. Military Academy at West Point, N.Y.: From Its Establishment, in 1802 to 1890,* 3rd ed., rev. and extended (Boston: Houghton Mifflin, 1891), 1: entry 671: Ezra J. Warner, *Generals in Blue: Lives of the Union Commanders* (Baton Rouge: Louisiana State University Press, 1964), 264.
5. Cullum, *Biographical Register,* 2: 171–72.

6. John H. Patterson and R. J. C. Irvine, "Eleventh Regiment of Infantry," *Journal of the Military Service Institute of the United States* 12 (1891): 372. Although Schriver had graduated from West Point in 1833, he had resigned from the service in 1846 and was president of the Rensselaer and Saratoga Railroad when in 1861 he volunteered to return to active duty.
7. John C. White, "A Review of the Services of the Regular Army During the Civil War," *Journal of the Military Service Institute of the United States,* 48 (1911): 241.
8. Ira S. Pettit, *The Diary of a Dead Man: Letters and Diary of Private Ira S. Pettit,…United States Army, during the War Between the States,* comp. Jean P. Ray (Waverly, Ia., 1976; reprint, Eastern Acorn Press, 1981), 137.
9. Patterson and Irvine, "Eleventh Regiment of Infantry," 373; U.S. War Department, Adjutant General's Office, *Official Army Register for 1863* (Washington: GPO, 1863), 41–42.
10. Timothy J. Reese, *Sykes' Regular Infantry Division, 1861–1864: A History of Regular United States Infantry Operations in the Civil War's Eastern Theater* (Jefferson, N.C.: McFarland & Co., 1990), 59.
11. U.S. War Department, *The War of the Rebellion: A Compilation of the Official Records of the Union and Confederate Armies* (Washington: GPO, 1880–1901), series 3, pt. 4, 25.
12. *Notes on the 16th United States Infantry,* 16th Infantry file, CMH, Washington, D.C., unpublished manuscript, n.d., 1. This manuscript is a synopsis from the regimental returns in RG 394.
13. Reese, *Sykes' Regulars,* 55.
14. Ibid., 56; Pettit, *Diary of a Dead Man,* 49, 62, 164.
15. Pettit, 63, 68.
16. Ibid., 61.
17. Patterson and Irvine, "Eleventh Regiment of Infantry," 373.
18. *16th Infantry Notes,* 1; Patterson and Irvine, "Eleventh Regiment of Infantry," 373.
19. *16th Infantry Notes,* 1.
20. *OR,* series 1, vol. 5, pt. 1, 19.
21. The "Old Army" regiments consisted of the 1st through the 10th Infantry Regiments, all of which had been in existence before May 1861. The "New Army" regiments were those numbered "11" through "19."
22. Patterson and Irvine, "Eleventh Regiment of Infantry" 373; *16th Infantry Notes,* 1.
23. Reese, *Sykes' Regulars,* 70–71.
24. *16th Infantry Notes,* 1.
25. *OR,* series 1, vol. 12, pt. 3, 313.
26. Reese, *Sykes' Regulars,* 73.
27. Patterson and Irvine, "Eleventh Regiment of Infantry," 374.
28. U.S. Military Academy, Dept. of Military Art and Engineering, *The West Point Atlas of American Wars,* ed. Vincent J. Esposito (New York: Frederick A. Praeger, 1959), 1:45 (hereinafter referred to as Esposito).
29. William H. Powell, *The Fifth Army Corps (Army of the Potomac). A Record of Operations during the Civil War in the United States of America, 1861–1865* (London: G. P. Putnam's Sons, 1896), 89.

30. *OR*, series 1, vol. 11, pt. 2, 349–50.
31. Powell, *Fifth Corps*, 110.
32. *OR*, series 1, vol. 11, pt. 2, 379.
33. Ibid., 375.
34. Alexander S. Webb, *The Peninsula—McClellan's Campaign of 1862* (New York: Charles Scribner's Sons, 1881), 151.
35. Ibid.
36. Powell, *Fifth Corps*, 150, 153–54.
37. Alfred Davenport, *Camp and Field Life of the Fifth New York Volunteer Infantry* (New York: Dick and Fitzgerald, 1879; reprint, Gaithersburg, Md.: Olde Soldier Books, 1992), 243.
38. Webb, *The Peninsula*, 166.
39. Powell, *Fifth Corps*, 189.
40. *16th Infantry Notes*, 1–2.
41. John W. Ames, "The Second Bull Run," *Overland Monthly* 8 (1872): 399.
42. Ibid.
43. Ibid., 400.
44. *OR*, series 1, vol. 12, pt. 2, 481.
45. Ames, "The Second Bull Run," 401.
46. Ibid.
47. *OR*, series 1, vol. 12, pt. 2, 496–97.
48. Ames, "The Second Bull Run," 402.
49. Ibid.
50. Ibid.
51. *Battles and Leaders of the Civil War*, (New York: The Century Co., 1887–88), 2:489.
52. *OR*, series 1, vol. 12, pt. 2, 485–87, 500.
53. Ames, "The Second Bull Run," 403.
54. *16th Infantry Notes*, 2.
55. Stephen W. Sears, *Landscape Turned Red: The Battle of Antietam* (New Haven: Ticknor and Fields, 1983), 278–80.
56. *OR*, series 1, vol. 19, pt. 1, 365.
57. Powell, *Fifth Corps*, 295–96.
58. *OR*, series 1, vol. 19, pt. 1, 365.
59. Ibid., 297–99.
60. *16th Infantry Notes*, 2.
61. Ibid.
62. Rufus F. Zogbaum, "The Regulars in the Civil War," *North American Review* 167 (1898): 24.
63. *16th Infantry Notes*, 2; *OR*, series 1, vol. 21, pt. 1, 428.
64. Reese, *Sykes' Regulars*, 169.
65. Ibid., 187.
66. Pettit, *Diary of a Dead Man*, 81.
67. *OR*, series 1, vol. 21, pt. 1, 429.
68. Ibid., 426.
69. Ibid., 428–29.
70. Ibid., 429.
71. Henry Steele Commager, *The Blue and the Gray: The Story of the Civil War as Told by Participants* (Indianapolis: Bobbs-Merrill Co., 1950), 320.
72. *16th Infantry Notes*, 3.
73. Reese, *Sykes' Regulars*, 193–94.
74. Pettit, *Diary of a Dead Man*, 81.
75. Ibid., 96.
76. Reese, *Sykes' Regulars*, 194–95, 379.
77. Pettit, *Diary of a Dead Man*, 115.
78. *16th Infantry Notes*, 3.
79. Esposito, *West Point Atlas*, 85.
80. Pettit, *Diary of a Dead Man*, 129.
81. Powell, *Fifth Corps*, 438–39.
82. Reese, *Sykes' Regulars*, 212–13.
83. Esposito, *West Point Atlas*, 85.
84. Reese, *Sykes' Regulars*, 217.
85. Ibid.
86. Pettit, *Diary of a Dead Man*, 130–31.
87. *OR*, series 1, vol. 27, pt. 1, 533, 539.
88. Ibid., 146–47.
89. *16th Infantry Notes*, 3.
90. Ibid.; Reese, *Sykes' Regulars*, 257.
91. *OR*, series 1, vol. 27, pt. 1, 644–50.
92. Reese, *Sykes' Regulars*, 240–41.
93. *OR*, series 1, vol. 27, pt. 1, 644.
94. Reese, *Sykes' Regulars*, 240–41.
95. *OR*, series 1, vol. 27, pt. 1, 644–50.
96. Reese, *Sykes' Regulars*, 245–47.
97. *OR*, series 1, vol. 27, pt. 2, 420.
98. Ibid., 250–51.
99. Ibid.; *OR*, series 1, vol. 27, pt. 1, 649–50.
100. Reese, *Sykes' Regulars*, 250.
101. Ibid., 251–53.
102. Ibid., 253.
103. *OR*, series 1, vol. 27, pt. 2, 397.
104. Ibid., pt. 3, 179.
105. Reese, *Sykes' Regulars*, 257.
106. Ibid., 258.
107. *OR*, series 1, vol. 27, pt. 1, 645.
108. *16th Infantry Notes*, 4; Cullum, *Biographical Register*, 2:172.
109. *16th Infantry Notes*, 4.
110. Reese, *Sykes' Regulars*, 283–89.
111. Pettit, *Diary of a Dead Man*, 157.
112. Reese, *Sykes' Regulars*, 286–88.
113. *16th Infantry Notes*, 4; *OR*, series 1, vol. 29, pt. 2, 52.
114. Heitman, *Historical Register and Dictionary of the United States Army*, 1:465; Pettit, *Diary of a Dead Man*, 159.
115. *16th Infantry Notes*, 4.
116. Pettit, *Diary of a Dead Man*, 172–73.
117. Powell, *Fifth Corps*, 580–82.
118. Ibid., 583–87.
119. Pettit, *Diary of a Dead Man*, 172–73; *OR*, series 1, vol. 29, pt. 1, 672, 683.
120. Pettit, *Diary of a Dead Man*, 93, 177, 356–59.
121. *16th Infantry Notes*, 4.
122. Ibid.
123. Frederick H. Dyer, *A Compendium of the War of the Rebellion* (reprint edition, Dayton, Oh.: Morningside Press, Broadfoot Publishing Co., 1994), 1:303.
124. *OR*, series 1, vol. 33, pt. 1, 377–78.
125. Ibid., 390–91.
126. Reese, *Sykes' Regulars*, 312.
127. Bruce Catton, *Grant Takes Command* (Boston: Little, Brown & Co., 1969), 187–88.
128. Reese, *Sykes' Regulars*, 303.
129. Ibid., 306.
130. *OR*, series 1, vol. 36, pt. 1, 123.
131. Ibid., 554.
132. Ibid., 141.
133. William D. Matter, *If It Takes All Summer: The Battle of Spotsylvania* (Chapel Hill, N.C.: University of North Carolina Press, 1988), 64-65; Powell, *Fifth Corps*, 634.
134. Ibid.
135. Reese, *Sykes' Regulars*, 312.
136. Ibid.
137. *OR*, series 1, vol. 36, pt. 1, 70. 138. Ibid., 149.
139. J. Michael Miller, *The North Anna Campaign: "Even to Hell Itself," May 21–26, 1864* (Lynchburg, Va.: H. E. Howard, 1988), 28–29, 47.
140. Ibid., 54.
141. Ibid., 55.
142. Reese, *Sykes' Regulars*, 312.
143. Miller, *North Anna Campaign*, 62.
144. Ibid., 63.
145. Ibid., 72–73.
146. Ibid., 73.
147. Ibid., 83.
148. Powell, *Fifth Corps*, 687.
149. Louis J. Baltz, *The Battle of Cold Harbor, May 27–June 13, 1864* (Lynchburg, Va.: H. E. Howard, 1994), 46.
150. Ibid., 46–47.

151. Ibid., 48–51.
152. Ibid., 126–28.
153. *16th Infantry Notes*, 5; Pettit, *Diary of a Dead Man*, 200.
154. *16th Infantry Notes*, 5.
155. Ibid.
156. Powell, *Fifth Corps*, 709–10.
157. Reese, *Sykes' Regulars*, 322.
158. Ibid., 326.
159. Ibid.
160. Ibid., 326–27; Powell, *Fifth Corps*, 712.
161. Powell, *Fifth Corps*, 714.
162. *16th Infantry Notes*, 7.
163. Reese, *Sykes' Regulars*, 330.
164. Ibid. *16th Infantry Notes*, 7.
165. Powell, *Fifth Corps*, 715.
166. Ibid., 723; Reese, *Sykes' Regulars*, 332.
167. Reese, *Sykes' Regulars*, 379, 396, 398.
168. Richard J. Sommers, *Richmond Redeemed: The Siege at Petersburg* (Garden City, N.Y.: Doubleday & Co., 1981), 259.
169. Ibid., 316.
170. Ibid., 335.
171. *16th Infantry Notes*, 5.
172. *OR*, series 1, vol. 43, pt. 2, 552; Lieutenant John S. McNaught, Diary, 1863–1865. Special Collections Library, Perkins Library, Duke University, Durham, N.C.
173. *OR*, series 1, vol. 43, pt. 2, 645, 852–53.
174. Ibid., 775–76; *16th Infantry Notes*, 5.
175. Cullum, *Biographical Register*, 1: 359.
176. *OR*, series 1, vol. 46, pt. 3, 3–4; *16th Infantry Notes*, 6.
177. Ibid.; McNaught diary.
178. Ibid.
179. *OR*, series 1, vol. 46, pt. 3, 595, 638.
180. Powell, *Fifth Corps*, 748.
181. *16th Infantry Notes*, 6.
182. Reese, *Sykes' Regulars*, 318.
183. Dyer, *Compendium*, 2:1712–13.

Chapter 2 - Reconstruction, Reorganization, and Redesignation

1. Maurice Matloff, *American Military History* (Washington: GPO, 1969), 282.
2. *OR*, series 1, vol. 46, pt. 3, 1314; *Army and Navy Journal* 2, no. 50 (August 5, 1865): 1.
3. *16th Infantry Notes*, 6.
4. Warner, *Generals in Blue*, 263–64.
5. Cullum, *Biographical Register*, 1: 562–63.
6. *ANJ* 3, no. 44 (June 23, 1866): 699.
7. *ANJ* 3, no. 9 (October 21,1865): 130.
8. *ANJ* 3, no. 41 (June 2, 1866): 649.
9. *ANJ* 3, no. 14 (November 25, 1865): 209.
10. *ANJ* 3, no. 22 (January 20, 1866): 343; *ANJ* 3, no. 48 (July 21, 1866): 759.
11. Mahon and Danysh, *Infantry*, 31–32.
12. *ANJ* 4, no. 36 (April 27, 1867): 566.
13. *ANJ* 6, no. 27 (February 20, 1869): 419; *ANJ* 6, no. 28 (February 27, 1869): 343.
14. *ANJ* 3, no. 3 (September 9, 1865); *ANJ* 3, no. 41 (June 2, 1866): 647.
15. *ANJ* 4, no. 37 (May 4, 1867): 582.
16. Theophilus F. Rodenbaugh, *Army of the United States* (New York: Maynard, Merrill & Co., 1896; reprint, New York: Argonaut Press, 1966), 630–31.
17. Warner, *Generals in Blue*, 365–66.
18. Rodenbaugh, *Army of the U.S.*, 630–31.
19. Ibid., 631.
20. *ANJ*, October 29, 1870, 167.
21. Rodenbaugh, *Army of the U.S.*, 631; "History of Company G, Sixteenth Infantry, Fort Crook, Nebraska, December 1, 1908," 1, unpublished manuscript, 16th Infantry file, CMH, Washington, D.C.
22. Coakley, *The Role of Federal Military Forces*, 312.
23. Ibid., 330.
24. Ibid., 330–31.
25. Ibid., 331.
26. Ibid., 332–33.
27. U.S. War Department, "Annual Report of the Secretary of War," *War Department Annual Reports, 1874* (Washington: GPO, 1874), 1: 48–49.
28. Ibid.
29. Ibid.
30. Coakley, *The Role of Federal Military Forces*, 324–25.
31. Ibid., 325.
32. Ibid., 326.
33. *ANJ* 12, no. 12 (October 31, 1874): 179.
34. *ANJ* 9, no. 13 (November 11, 1871): 205; *ANJ* 9, no. 14 (November 18, 1871): 215.
35. *ANJ* 11, no. 36 (April 18, 1874): 564.
36. *ANJ* 9, no. 22 (January 13, 1872): 352–53.
37. *ANJ* 13, no. 26 (February 5, 1876): 395, 397.
38. *ANJ* 9, no. 21 (January 6, 1872): 332; *ANJ* 10, no. 3 (August 31, 1872): 35.
39. Ibid., 27 February 1875.
40. *Nashville Republican Banner*, April 20, 1875.
41. *ARSW 1876*, 1:81.
42. Coakley, *The Role of Federal Military Forces*, 335–36.

Chapter 3 —The Indian Wars

1. Captain Woodbury F. Pride, *The History of Fort Riley* (Topeka, Kans.: Cavalry School, 1926), 178.
2. Ibid., 177.
3. Clayton D. Laurie and Ronald H. Cole, *The Role of Federal Forces in Domestic Disorders, 1877–1945* (Washington: GPO, 1997), 50.
4. Ibid., 52.
5. "Battle Participation of the 16th Infantry," unpublished manuscript, n.d., 16th Infantry file, CMH, Washington, D.C.; "History of Company G, Sixteenth Infantry, Fort Crook, Nebraska, December 1, 1908," 3, unpublished manuscript, 16th Infantry file, CMH, Washington, D.C.
6. Pride, *Fort Riley*, 177.
7. Ibid., 177–78.
8. Bruce Palmer Jr., *The Palmer Family and the 16th Infantry* (Fort Washington, Md.: 16th Infantry Association, 1987), 2 (December 12, 1887).
9. Robert M. Utley, *Frontier Regulars: The United States Army and the Indian, 1866–1891* (Lincoln, Nebr.: University of Nebraska Press, 1973), 283–4; Pride, *Fort Riley*, 178.
10. Harold W. Johnston, "A History of the 16th U. S. Infantry Regiment During the Indian Wars Period (1865–1891)," *Fort Concho Report* 19, no.4 (winter 1987–88): 4.
11. Utley, *Frontier Regulars*, 335–37.
12. Johnston, "16th Infantry During the Indian Wars," 6; Pride, *Fort Riley*, 180.
13. Pride, *Fort Riley*, 180.
14. "Battle Participation of the 16th Infantry."
15. Pride, *Fort Riley*, 180.
16. Utley, *Frontier Regulars*, 363-64.
17. Chester, Pennsylvania, newspaper clippings, November 23, 1880, and March 26, 1881, Colonel Galusha Pennypacker file, U.S. Cavalry Museum Archives, Fort Riley, Kans.
18. *ARSW 1881*, 1:129.
19. Charles M. Robinson III, *Frontier Forts of Texas* (Houston, Tex.: Lone Star Books, 1986), 46.
20. Chester, Pennsylvania, newspaper clippings, August 27, 1882, and July 4, 1883, Pennypacker file, Fort Riley, Kans.
21. Cullum, *Biographical Register,* 2:339.
22. *ARSW 1885*, 1:61.
23. *ARSW 1880–1888*, passim.
24. *ARSW 1884*, 1:126; Randy Steffen, *The Horse Soldier, 1776–1943: The United States Cavalryman—His Uniforms, Arms, Accoutrements, and Equipments* (Norman, Okla.: University of Oklahoma Press, 1978), 2:22–24.

25. Wayne Daniel, "The 16th Infantry at Fort Concho, 1881," September 14, 1882, unpublished manuscript, Fort Concho Museum, San Angelo, Tex.
26. Ibid.
27. Ibid.; Johnston, "16th Infantry During the Indian Wars," 11.
28. Johnston, "16th Infantry During the Indian Wars," 11–12
29. Ibid., 12.
30. Ibid., 13.
31. *ARSW 1886*, 1:125.
32. Johnston, "16th Infantry During the Indian Wars," 14.
33. *ARSW 1886*, 1:117.
34. *ARSW 1888*, 1:174.
35. Ibid.
36. *ARSW 1889*, 1:168.
37. Ibid.
38. *ARSW 1892*, 1:123.
39. *ARSW 1896*, 1:150.
40. *ARSW 1892*, 1:123.
41. Edward M. Coffman, *The Old Army: A Portrait of the American Army in Peacetime, 1784–1898* (New York: Oxford University Press, 1986), 260.
42. *ARSW 1892*, 1:123.
43. *ARSW 1893*, 1:132.
44. *ARSW 1894*, 1:69.
45. Ibid., 141.
46. "Battle Participation of the 16th Infantry," 4–5.
47. Ibid.
48. *ARSW 1894*, 1:139.
49. *ARSW 1897*, 1:108.
50. Coffman, *Old Army*, 357.

Chapter 4 - Foreign Adventures

1. Department of the Army, Center of Military History, *Correspondence Relating to the War with Spain, April 15, 1898 to July 30, 1902* (Washington: GPO, 1993), 1:7; Graham A. Cosmas, *An Army for Empire: The United States Army in the Spanish-American War* (Columbia, Mo.: University of Missouri Press, 1971), 107.
2. Unpublished and untitled manuscript, n.d., 16th Infantry file, CMH, Washington, D.C., 1.
3. Ibid.
4. Cosmas, *Army for Empire*, 121–23.
5. John E. Woodward Diary, Spanish-American War Survey Files, File 1898 W-1442, U.S. Army Military History Institute, Carlisle Barracks, Carlisle, Pa.
6. Cosmas, *Army for Empire*, 113.
7. Woodward diary; "Battle Participation of the 16th Infantry," 8; "16th Infantry," n.d., 1, unpublished manuscript, CMH, Washington, D.C.
8. Ron Field, *The Spanish-American War, 1898*, Brassey's History of Uniforms (Washington: Brassey's, 1998), 98.
9. Ibid.
10. Photocopy of a letter from Captain Charles H. Noble to the Adjutant General, U.S. Army, Washington, D.C., December 1898, 16th Infantry file, U.S. Cavalry Museum Archives, Fort Riley, Kans.
11. "16th Infantry," 1–2.
12. Ibid., 2.
13. *ARSW 1898*, "Report of the Major General Commanding the Army," Report of Colonel H. A. Theaker, Sixteenth United States Infantry, Fort San Juan, Cuba, July 5, 1898 (Washington: GPO, 1900), 1278–79.
14. Ibid.
15. Captain C. H. Noble to the Adjutant General, December 1898.
16. Ibid.
17. *ANJ*, September 10, 1898.
18. "16th Infantry," 4.
19. Ibid., 3.
20. Ibid.
21. Ibid.
22. Ibid.
23. Ibid., 2–3.
24. Ibid., 3–4.
25. Captain C. H. Noble to the Adjutant General, December 1898.
26. Ibid.
27. "16th Infantry," 4.
28. Ibid.
29. Ibid.
30. Ibid.; Beaumont B. Buck, "Military Service of Colonel Beaumont B. Buck, Infantry," unpublished manuscript, Beaumont B. Buck Collection, U.S. Cavalry Museum Archives, Fort Riley, Kans.
31. "16th Infantry," 5.
32. Matloff, *American Military History*, 337
33. Heitman, *Historical Register and Dictionary of the United States Army*, 1:539.
34. "16th Infantry," 5.
35. U.S. War Department, *Annual Reports of the War Department, 1900*, vol. 1, pt. 6 (Washington: GPO, 1900), 129.
36. Ibid., vol. 1, pt. 4, 290; "16th Infantry," 5.
37. "16th Infantry," 5.
38. Ibid.
39. Ibid., 6.
40. *ARWD 1900*, vol. 1, pt. 6, 141–47, 309–14, 403–17 passim.
41. Ibid., pt. 4, 22–23, 237.
42. *ARWD 1900*, vol. 1, pt. 6, "Report of an Expedition From Malolos to San Miguel de Mayumo…by Colonel Charles C. Hood," 614–61 passim.
43. Ibid., 617.
44. Ibid.
45. "16th Infantry," 7.
46. *ARWD 1900*, vol. 1, pt. 6, "Report of Expedition by Colonel Hood," 620–21.
47. *ARWD 1899*, vol. 1, pt. 6, 91; "16th Infantry," 7.
48. "16th Infantry," 8.
49. *ARWD 1900*, vol. 1, pt. 4, 777.
50. Ibid, 772.
51. Ibid; *ARWD 1900*, vol. 1, pt. 3, 24; *ARWD 1900*, vol. 1, pt. 4, 780–82.
52. U.S. Congress, Senate, Committee on Veterans' Affairs, *Medal of Honor Recipients, 1863–1978: "In the Name of the Congress of the United States"* (Washington: GPO, 1979) 380.
53. *ARWD 1900*, vol. 1, pt. 1, 180.
54. *ARWD 1900*, vol. 1, pt. 1, 180–82.
55. "Battle Participation of the 16th Infantry," 14.
56. "16th Infantry," 10.
57. Ibid, 11.
58. Ibid; *Correspondence Relating to the War with Spain*, 1345, 1355.

Chapter 5—American Travelers

1. *ARWD 1903*, vol. 3, 1–5.
2. "Regimental Record, 16th Infantry," unpublished manuscript, 16th Infantry file, CMH, Washington, D.C., 11.
3. Heitman, *Historical Register and Dictionary of the United States Army*, 1:806.
4. "Regimental Record, 16th Infantry," 11.
5. Ibid.
6. Ibid.
7. Ibid., *ARWD 1904*, 3:32.
8. Ibid.
9. Ibid., 12.
10. Ibid.
11. Ibid.
12. Ibid., 11–12.
13. "Continuation of Regimental Record, 16th Infantry, 1905," 16th Infantry File, CMH, Washington, D.C., 14; "Roster of Troops, Philippine Division, Manila, P.I.,1905," Combined Arms Resource Library, Fort Leavenworth, Kans.

14. Ibid., 14–15; "Continuation of Regimental Record, 16th Infantry, 1906," 16–17.
15. Cullum, *Biographical Register*, 3:221; 4:239; 5:209–10.
16. "Continuation of Regimental Record, 16th Infantry, 1906," 17; "Roster of Troops, Philippine Division, Manila, P.I. 1906," Combined Arms Resource Library, Fort Leavenworth, Kans.
17. "History of Company G, 16th Infantry, Fort Crook, Nebraska, December 1, 1908," 10, unpublished manuscript, 16th Infantry file, CMH, Washington, D.C.
18. Donald Smythe, *Guerrilla Warrior; The Early Life of John J. Pershing* (New York: Charles Scribner's Sons, 1973), 133.
19. *ARWD 1908*, 3:130.
20. Ibid., 107.
21. Ibid., 107–08.
22. Ibid., 105; "Continuation of Regimental Record, 16th Infantry, 1908," 1.
23. "Continuation of Regimental Record, 16th Infantry, 1908," 1.
24. Ibid., 2; *ARWD 1909*, 3:80–81.
25. *ARWD 1909*, 3:80–81.
26. "Continuation of Regimental Record, 16th Infantry, 1909," 2–3.
27. Ibid.
28. "Continuation of Regimental Record, 16th Infantry, 1908," 3; "Continuation of Regimental Record, 16th Infantry, 1909," 3.
29. "Roster of Commissioned and Non-Commissioned Officers of the Sixteenth U.S. Infantry, Fort Crook, Nebr., 1909," Buck Collection, U.S. Cavalry Museum Archives, Fort Riley, Kans.
30. "Continuation of Regimental Record, 16th Infantry, 1910," 1–2.
31. Ibid., 2.
32. Ibid.
33. Captain John M. Tatum, "A Spell on the Yukon," *Infantry Journal* 44, no. 1 (January–February 1937): 32.
34. Ibid.
35. Ibid., 34.
36. Ibid., 34–35.
37. "Continuation of Regimental Record, 16th Infantry, 1911," 1.
38. Ibid.
39. "Synopsis of an Outline History of the Sixteenth United States Infantry," unpublished manuscript, 16th Infantry History File, Reports of Operations, 16th Infantry, Records of the Adjutant General 1917–, RG 407, National Archives, Washington, D.C.
40. Cullum, *Biographical Register*, 6A: entry 2988.
41. "Continuation of Regimental Record, 16th Infantry, 1912," 2.
42. Ibid.
43. Ibid.
44. "Continuation of Regimental Record, 16th Infantry, 1913," 1.
45. Cullum, *Biographical Register*, 3:339; 4:335; 5:302.
46. Urwin, *United States Infantry*, 150.
47. Smythe, *Guerrilla Warrior*, 205; Leon C. Metz, *Desert Army: Fort Bliss on the Texas Border* (El Paso, Tex.: Mangan Books, 1988), 85; "Regimental History Sixteenth Infantry for 1914," entry 1568, 16th Infantry Histories, Regular Army Mobile Units 1821–1942, RG 391, National Archives, Washington, D.C., 1.
48. Metz, *Desert Army*, 85.
49. Frank E. Vandiver, *Black Jack: The Life and Times of John J. Pershing*, (College Station: Texas A&M University Press, 1977), 2:590.
50. *NYT*, January 30, 1915, p. 1.
51. Ibid., August 26, 1915, p. 3.
52. Metz, *Desert Army*, 88.
53. Cullum, *Biographical Register*, 3:364; 4:364–65; 5:345-46.
54. Metz, *Desert Army*, 88.
55. *Dallas Morning News*, January 13, 1916, p. 1; January 14, 1916, p. 1.
56. Colonel R. Ernest Dupuy and Major General William H. Baumer, *The Little Wars of the United States: A Compact History from 1798–1920* (New York: Hawthorn Books, 1968), 121–32.
57. Ibid., 132.
58. Colonel Frank Tompkins, *Chasing Villa: The Story Behind the Story of Pershing's Expedition into Mexico* (Harrisburg, Penna.: Military Service Publishing Co., 1934), 74–76.
59. "Regimental History Sixteenth Infantry for 1916," entry 1568, 16th Infantry Histories, Regular Army Mobile Units 1821–1942, RG 391, National Archives, Washington, D.C., 1.
60. Herbert M. Mason Jr., *The Great Pursuit* (New York: Random House, 1970), 142.
61. Smythe, *Guerrilla Warrior*, 225.
62. "Regimental History Sixteenth Infantry for 1916," 2.
63. Tompkins, *Chasing Villa*, 214.
64. Ibid.

Chapter 6—"Lafayette, We Are Here!"

1. Adolf A. Hoehling, *The Fierce Lambs* (Boston: Little, Brown & Co., 1960), 57.
2. Regimental chaplain, *The Story of the Sixteenth Infantry in France* (Frankfurt, Germany: Martin Flock, 1919), 8.
3. Hoehling, *Fierce Lambs*, 77.
4. Regimental chaplain, *Sixteenth Infantry in France*, 8; U.S. War Department, "A.G.O. Form 016, Unit Historical Data Cards for the 16th Infantry," 16th Infantry Regiment file, U.S. Army Center of Military History, Washington, D.C.
5. Regimental chaplain, *Sixteenth Infantry in France*, 8.
6. Ibid.; U.S. War Department, *World War Records of the First Division, A.E.F.*, vol. 16, "16th Infantry Regiment War Diary."
7. Frank E. Vandiver, *Black Jack: The Life and Times of John J. Pershing* (College Station, Tex.: Texas A&M University Press, 1977), 2:723.
8. Regimental chaplain, *Sixteenth Infantry in France*, 9.
9. Society of the First Division, A.E.F., *History of the First Division During the World War, 1917–1919* (Philadelphia: John C. Winston Company, 1922), 7.
10. Regimental chaplain, *Sixteenth Infantry in France*, 9.
11. Typewritten transcript of the diary of Private Tom Carroll, Company F, 16th Infantry, A.E.F., World War I, box 182, "1st Division 1920s, Misc.," MRC-FDM.
12. Captain Allen P. Kingman, "The 16th Infantry in Paris," *Infantry Journal* 31, no. 6 (December 1927): 638.
13. Regimental chaplain, *Sixteenth Infantry in France*, 9; *World War Records of the First Division, A.E.F.*, vol. 16, "16th Infantry Regiment War Diary"; "War Diary of 2nd Battalion, 16th U. S. Infantry," entry 1568, 16th Infantry Histories, Regular Army Mobile Units 1821–1942, RG 391, National Archives, Washington, D.C., 3.
14. Hoehling, *Fierce Lambs*, 90–91.
15. Donald Smythe, *Pershing, General of the Armies* (Bloomington, Ind.: Indiana University Press, 1986), 33.
16. Army Times Publishing Company, eds., *The Yanks Are Coming: The Story of General John J. Pershing* (New York: G. P. Putman & Sons, 1960), 66.
17. Ibid.
18. Vandiver, *Black Jack*, 2:724.
19. Hoehling, *Fierce Lambs*, 95.
20. Society of the First Division, *History of the First Division*, 8.
21. Vandiver, *Black Jack*, 2:764.
22. Regimental chaplain, *Sixteenth Infantry in France*, 11–12.
23. Ibid.
24. Vandiver, *Black Jack*, 2:764.
25. Ibid., 2:795-96.
26. Ibid., 2:764.
27. Regimental chaplain, *Sixteenth Infantry in France*, 13.
28. Hoehling, *Fierce Lambs*, 139.
29. Ibid., 146.
30. Cullum, *Biographical Register of the Officers and Graduates*, 6A:601.
31. Allan R. Millett, *The General: Robert L. Bullard and Officership in the United States Army 1881–1925* (Westport, Conn.: Greenwood Press, 1975), 323.
32. *World War Records of the First Division, A.E.F.*, vol. 16, "16th Infantry Regiment War Diary"; Hoehling, *Fierce Lambs*, 17, 71.
33. Hoehling, *Fierce Lambs*, 153–54.
34. Ibid., 154, 156.

35. Ibid., 156–58.
36. Ibid., 161.
37. Society of the First Division, *Memorial Album: Pictorial History of the 1st Division*, "The First Division in World War I," by General Charles P. Summerall (San Diego: Society of the First Division, 1946), 3.
38. American Battle Monuments Commission, *1st Division Summary of Operations in the World War* (Washington: GPO, 1944), 8.
39. Headquarters, 16th Infantry, General Orders No. 18, December 16, 1917, box 50A, entry 2133, 16th Infantry Correspondence, Records of U.S. Army Mobile Units 1821–1942, RG 391, National Archives, Washington, D.C.
40. Regimental chaplain, *Sixteenth Infantry in France*, 16–17.
41. Ibid., 17.
42. Ibid., 18.
43. *Memorial Album*, 3.
44. Millett, *The General*, 345.
45. Regimental chaplain, *Sixteenth Infantry in France*, 19.
46. Ibid.
47. Ibid. 20-21.
48. Cullum, *Biographical Register*, vol. 5, 1900-10 and vol. 6A, 1910-20, entry 3423.
49. *Memorial Album*, 4.
50. Regimental chaplain, *Sixteenth Infantry in France*, 22.
51. Battle Monuments Commission, *1st Division Summary*, 10–11.
52. Regimental chaplain, *Sixteenth Infantry in France*, 22.
53. Battle Monuments Commission, *1st Division Summary*, 11.
54. Regimental chaplain, *Sixteenth Infantry in France*, 23.
55. Ibid., 23.
56. Battle Monuments Commission, *1st Division Summary*, 15.
57. Regimental chaplain, *Sixteenth Infantry in France*, 24.
58. Ibid., 26.
59. Ibid., 26–27; *World War Records of the First Division, A.E.F.*, vol. 24, "Citations," 16th Infantry Regiment.
60. Battle Monuments Commission, *1st Division Summary*, 17.
61. Regimental chaplain, *Sixteenth Infantry in France*, 28–29.
62. Ibid., 30.
63. Ibid., 31; Battle Monuments Commission, *1st Division Summary*, 22.
64. Regimental chaplain, *Sixteenth Infantry in France*, 32.
65. Ibid.
66. Hary R. Stringer, ed., *Heroes All! A Compendium of the Names and Official Citations of the Soldiers of the United States and of Her Allies Who Were Decorated by the American Government . . . in the War with Germany, 1917–1919* (Washington, D.C.: Fassett Publishing Co., 1919), 315.
67. Regimental chaplain, *Sixteenth Infantry in France*, 28–29.
68. Stringer, *Heroes All!*, 381.
69. Ibid., 61, 371.
70. Regimental chaplain, *Sixteenth Infantry in France*, 33.
71. Battle Monuments Commission, *1st Division Summary*, 26.
72. Stringer, *Heroes All!*, 108.
73. Ibid., 109; Regimental chaplain, *Sixteenth Infantry in France*, 34–35.
74. Regimental chaplain, *Sixteenth Infantry in France*, 34.
75. Battle Monuments Commission, *1st Division Summary*, 28–29.
76. Regimental chaplain, *Sixteenth Infantry in France*, 34.
77. Stringer, *Heroes All!*, 120, 280, 394.
78. Ibid., 78, 409. Both Private Burchfield and Chaplain Weed were later awarded Distinguished Service Crosses for their actions at Soissons.
79. Typewritten transcript of the experiences of Corporal Alfred J. Buhl, Company F, 16th Infantry, A.E.F., World War I, Alfred J. Buhl file, MRC-FDM.
80. Battle Monuments Commission, *1st Division Summary*, 30–31.
81. Regimental chaplain, *Sixteenth Infantry in France*, 35–36.
82. Battle Monuments Commission, *1st Division Summary*, 33.
83. Regimental chaplain, *Sixteenth Infantry in France*, 40.
84. Ibid., 41.
85. Heitman, *Historical Register and Dictionary of the United States Army*, 1:327.
86. Regimental chaplain, *Sixteenth Infantry in France*, 43.
87. Ibid.
88. Ibid., 44–45; Battle Monuments Commission, *1st Division Summary*, 58.
89. Battle Monuments Commission, *1st Division Summary*, 60.
90. Regimental chaplain, *Sixteenth Infantry in France*, 49.
91. Ibid., 51.
92. Rexmond C. Cochrane, *Gas Warfare in World War I, Study No. 3*, U.S. Army Chemical Corps Historical Studies (Aberdeen Proving Grounds, Md.: U.S. Army Chemical Corps Historical Office, 1957), 5.
93. Regimental chaplain, *Sixteenth Infantry in France*, 51.
94. Ibid.
95. Diary of Major Edward R. Coppock, copy in 16th Infantry file, CMH, Washington, D.C.; Cochrane, *Gas Warfare in World War I*, 1.
96. Ibid.
97. Ibid.; Regimental chaplain, *Sixteenth Infantry in France*, 51.
98. Cochrane, *Gas Warfare in World War I*, 22.
99. Stringer, *Heroes All!*, 224.
100. Ibid., 67, 252.
101. Ibid., 350.
102. Ibid., 397.
103. Ibid., 123.
104. Ibid., 378; Regimental chaplain, *Sixteenth Infantry in France*, 54.
105. Regimental chaplain, *Sixteenth Infantry in France*, 53–54.
106. Ibid., 53.
107. Coppock diary.
108. Battle Monuments Commission, *1st Division Summary*, 73.
109. Herbert L. McHenry, "As a Private Saw It: My Memories of the 1st Division, World War," manuscript in the Herbert L. McHenry file, Military History Institute Archives, Carlisle Barracks, Pa., 62.
110. The Infantry Journal, *Infantry in Battle* (reprint, Washington: Center of Military History, GPO, 1997), 147–48.
111. Ibid., 148.
112. Ibid., 149.
113. Regimental chaplain, *Sixteenth Infantry in France*, 57.
114. Stringer, *Heroes All!*, 246.
115. Ibid., 224.
116. Regimental chaplain, *Sixteenth Infantry in France*, 54.
117. Battle Monuments Commission, *1st Division Summary*, 76–79.
118. Coppock diary.
119. Regimental chaplain, *Sixteenth Infantry in France*, 65.
120. Battle Monuments Commission, *1st Division Summary*, 81–83.
121. Ibid., 83–84.
122. Ibid., 85.
123. Ibid., 86–87.
124. Regimental chaplain, *Sixteenth Infantry in France*, 66–67; Battle Monuments Commission, *1st Division Summary*, 87.
125. D. Clayton James, *The Years of MacArthur*, vol. 1, *1880–1941* (Boston: Houghton Mifflin Co., 1970–1985), 1:233.
126. Battle Monuments Commission, *1st Division Summary*, 88–89.
127. Ibid., 93, 95; Regimental chaplain, *Sixteenth Infantry in France*, 68.
128. Edward D. Coffman, *The War to End All Wars: The American Military Experience in World War I* (New York: Oxford University Press, 1968; reprint, Madison, Wis.: University of Wisconsin Press, 1986), 352–53.
129. Regimental chaplain, *Sixteenth Infantry in France*, 71.
130. Ibid., 73.
131. Ibid., 74.
132. *World War Records of the First Division, A.E.F.*, vol. 10, "Field Orders of the 16th Infantry Regiment."
133. Regimental chaplain, *Sixteenth Infantry in France*, 75.
134. *World War Records of the First Division, A.E.F.*, vol. 10, "Field Orders of the 16th Infantry Regiment."
135. Ibid.
136. Ibid.
137. *ANJ*, September 6, 1919, 2.
138. *World War Records of the First Division, A.E.F.*, vol. 24, "Citations," 16th Infantry Regiment.

139. *NYT*, July 31, 1919, p. 15; "Adjutant General Form 016 Historical Data Cards," 16th Infantry Regiment file, U.S. Army Center of Military History, Washington, D.C.
140. Regimental chaplain, *Sixteenth Infantry in France*, 76.

Chapter 7—The Sidewalks of New York
1. *ANJ* (September 13, 1919): 54–55.
2. Ibid.
3. *NYT*, September 18, 1919, p. 17.
4. Ibid., September 20, 1919, p. 77.
5. U.S. War Department, *Order of Battle of the United States Land Forces in the World War*, vol. 3, *Zone of the Interior*, pt. 2, *Territorial Departments, Tactical Divisions Organized in 1918, Posts, Camps, and Stations* (Washington: GPO, 1931–1949; reprint, Washington: GPO, 1988), 893–94.
6. Laurie and Cole, *The Role of Federal Military Forces in Domestic Disorders*, 256.
7. *ANJ* (December 20, 1919): 487.
8. Ibid., 297–98.
9. Ibid., 298.
10. Ibid., 299.
11. *NYT*, November 11, 1920, p. 17.
12. Cullum, *Biographical Register*, 4: entry 3320; 5: entry 3320; and 6: entry 3320.
13. Donald D. Kyler, Company G, 16th Infantry, 1917–24, unpublished memoir, 1st Division Files, Military History Institute Archives, Carlisle Barracks, Pa., 148.
14. Robert B. Roberts, *Encyclopedia of Historic Forts: The Military, Pioneer, and Trading Posts of the United States* (New York: Macmillan Publishing Co., 1988), 555–56.
15. *ARN*, July 1, 1928 (Governors Island, N.Y.: U.S. Army Recruiting Service, 1928), 4.
16. Mahon and Danysh, *Infantry*, vol. 1, *Regular Army*, 369.
17. *IJ* 24, no. 3 (March 1924): 314–15.
18. *ARN*, August 1, 1926, 4.
19. Ibid.
20. Ibid.
21. Ibid., 4, 15.
22. *NYT*, January 6, 1927, p. 1.
23. Ibid., March 18, 1933, p. 8; March 19, 1933, p. 17.
24. "Sgt. Casey Gets Military Burial; 16th Infantry Sad at Buddy's Passing," *NYT*, September 5, 1925, p. 1.
25. *ARN*, February 15, 1924, 10.
26. *NYT*, July 16, 1928, p. 1; *Our Army*, March 1930, 32.
27. *ARN*, April 1, 1930, 6.
28. *ANJ* (November 20, 1937): 237.
29. *ARN*, January 1939, 16; *Our Army*, November 1940, 16.
30. *IJ* (March 1929): 310, 312.
31. Ibid., (August 1930): 185–87.
32. Ibid., (April 1929): 555.
33. *ARN*, May 15, 1930, 12; *IJ* (May 1930): 556.
34. *IJ* (April 1930): 435.
35. General Order No. 7, 1st Division, October 12, 1931; *IJ* (September–October 1931): 463.
36. *NYT*, January 3, 1923, p. 19; January 4, 1923, p. 40.
37. *NYT*, August 5, 1925, p. 21; September 9, 1925, p. 22.
38. *NYT*, November 30, 1925, p. 10.
39. *IJ* (March 1929): 309–10.
40. *ARN*, January 1936, 10.
41. Henry S. Orten, recorded interview by the author, July 24, 1998, Tropicana Hotel, Las Vegas, Nev.
42. U.S. War Department, "AGO Form 762, 16th Infantry Regiment," 16th Infantry file, CMH, Washington, D.C.
43. *NYT*, October 5, 1923, p. 21.
44. *ANJ*, August 30, 1924, 1274; *ANR*, October 11, 1924, 338–39.
45. *NYT*, October 6, 1925, p. 28.
46. *NYT*, November 20, 1926, p. 19.
47. Ibid., April 4, 1933, p. 7.
48. *NYT*, June 3, 1928, p. 14.
49. Ibid., June 6, 1928, p. 24.
50. *NYT*, June 17, 1928, p. 1.
51. Ibid., June 20, 1928, p. 28.
52. Ibid., June 24, 1928, p. 3.
53. Ibid., June 7, 1929, p. 20.
54. *Our Army*, December 1929, 30.
55. *ARN*, July 1, 1927, 7.
56. "Service at Governor's Island," *ARN* 17, no. 6 (June 1937): 11, 15.
57. *IJ*, (January 1924): 64–65.
58. *ARN*, June 1, 1924, 4.
59. *NYT*, May 7, 1928, pp. 1, 12.
60. Ibid.
61. *ANR*, April 18, 1931, 374.
62. *NYT*, October 24, 1931, p. 12.
63. *NYT*, June 30, 1934, p. 18; May 19, 1934, p. 36.
64. *ANR*, March 28, 1931, 291; Letter from Mrs. Charles Streeman to Warrant Officer Harry R. Bradley, July 31, 1934, 16th Infantry file, U.S. Cavalry Museum Archives, Fort Riley, Kans.
65. "That Camp on Broadway," *IJ* (November-December 1932): 417–20.
66. Ibid.
67. *ARN*, October 1939, 11.
68. Telephone interview by the author with Martin P. "Paddy" Roughn, March 21, 1988.
69. Ibid.
70. "AG Form 016," 16th Infantry Regiment file, CMH, Washington, D.C.
71. Ibid.
72. *NYT*, May 1, 1932, p. 16; March 18, 1935, p. 17.
73. *ARN*, June 1, 1936, 4.
74. *NYT*, September 3, 1926, p. 9; Roughn telephone interview, March 15, 1998.
75. *NYT*, July 7, 1935, sec. 2, p. 4.
76. *NYT*, August 12, 1928, p. 20.
77. *ANJ*, August 31, 1935, 1150.
78. *ANJ*, August 31, 1935, 1144.
79. Ibid., March 7, 1936, 564.
80. *NYT*, March 27, 1936, p. 3.
81. Ibid., September 29, 1936, p. 16.
82. Ibid., June 18, 1937, p. 23.
83. Ibid., June 19, 1937, p. 19.
84. *Who Was Who in American History—The Military*, (Chicago: Marquis Who's Who, Inc., 1975), 594–95.
85. *ANJ*, September 4, 1937, 1; October 23, 1937, 153.
86. Ibid.
87. Ibid., October 23, 1937, 157.
88. Ibid., November 6, 1937, 205.
89. *NYT*, April 22, 1938, p. 40.
90. Ibid., May 29, 1938, p. 5; May 30, 1938, p. 26.
91. Cullum, *Biographical Register*, 6B: entry 4573, 7: entry 4573, and 8: entry 4573.
92. *NYT*, September 27, 1938, p. 8.
93. *NYT*, June 1939, sect. 1, p. 3; *Report of Marches and Changes of Stations of the 16th Infantry, 1 January–31 December 1939*, 16th Infantry file, CMH, Washington, D.C.
94. Henry S. Orten interview.
95. *Memorial Album*, 44.1
96. *NYT*, October 31, 1939, p. 7.
97. "Changes of stations, 16th Infantry," 1939, 3, 16th Infantry file, CMH, Washington, D.C..
98. *Memorial Album*, 44.2
99. Orten interview.
100. Ibid.
101. Training Circular No. 2, HQ, 1st Infantry Division, "Standing Operating Procedure, 1st Division," January 6, 1940, in possession of the author.
102. Ibid.
103. *NYT*, April 19, 1940, p. 6.
104. Ibid.

105. Orten interview.
106. *Memorial Album*, 44.3
107. Ibid.
108. *NYT*, June 5, 1940, p. 12.
109. Orten interview.
110. Cullum, *Biographical Register*, 6B: entry 4984, 7: entry 4984, and 8: entry 4984.
111. Eston T. White, recorded interview by the author, July 25, 1998, Tropicana Hotel, Las Vegas, Nev.
112. Ibid.
113. Orten interview.
114. *NYT*, October 16, 1940, p. 10.
115. U.S. War Department, "AGO Form 762," 16th Infantry file, CMH, Washington, D.C.
116. White interview.
117. Ibid.

Chapter 8—"The Big One"

1. Blythe Foote Finke, *No Mission Too Difficult!: Old Buddies of the 1st Division Tell All About World War II* (Chicago: Contemporary Books, 1995), 11.
2. Orten interview; White interview.
3. Finke, *No Mission Too Difficult!*, 11–12.
4. Ibid., 12.
5. White interview.
6. Memorandum, Subject: Constructive Information on Landing Operations of 1st Division Task Force, February 3, 1941, file 301-3.9.1, Reports of Operations, 1st Infantry Division 1941–45, Records of the Adjutant General 1917–, RG 407, National Archives, College Park, Maryland.
7. White interview.
8. *Memorial Album*, 12.4.
9. Cullum, *Biographical Register*, 7: entry 5179, 8: entry 5179, and 9: entry 5179.
10. White interview.
11. "Sixteenth Infantry Organization Day," Fort Devens, Mass., 1941, Commemorative Pamphlet and Program, 16th Infantry Regiment Association Archives.
12. *Memorial Album*, 12.5.
13. Christopher R. Gabel, *The U.S. Army GHQ Maneuvers of 1941* (Washington: GPO, 1991), 136.
14. White interview.
15. Gabel, *GHQ Maneuvers*, 147–48.
16. Ibid.
17. James Lipinski, "Notes," provided to author, April 16, 1999.
18. *Memorial Album*, 12.5.
19. Fred L. Walker, *From Texas to Rome: A General's Journal* (Dallas, Tex.: Taylor Publishing Co., 1969), 66–67.
20. Ibid., 67.
21. White interview.
22. Ibid.; Orten interview.
23. White interview; Lieutenant Colonel Fred W. Hall Jr., "A Memoir of World War II," unpublished manuscript in the possession of the author, 3.
24. John W. Baumgartner et al., *The 16th Infantry, 1798–1946* (Bamberg, Germany: Sebaldus Verlag, 1946), 8.
25. Ibid., 9.
26. George F. Howe, *Northwest Africa: Seizing the Initiative in the West*, United States Army in World War II, The Mediterranean Theater of Operations (Washington: GPO, 1957), 63.
27. Hall, "A Memoir of World War II," 6.
28. Ibid., 71; Baumgartner, *16th Infantry, 1798–1946*, 10–11.
29. Intelligence Summary Number 1, HQ, CT 16, October 20, 1942 & Intelligence Summary Number 2, HQ, CT 16, October 24, 1942, Reports of Operations, 16th Infantry, Records of the Adjutant General 1917–, RG 407, National Archives, Washington, D.C.
30. Howe, *Northwest Africa*, 192.
31. Field Order No. 1, Operation Torch, Headquarters, 1st Infantry Division, October 10, 1942, photocopy located in file R-11291, Combined Arms Resource Library Archives, Fort Leavenworth, Kans.
32. Ibid., 193.
33. Hall, "A Memoir of World War II," 6.
34. James Lipinski, interview by the author, June 3, 1998, at 4524 North Pegram Street, Alexandria, Va. Lipinski also recalled that while he and his men waited for the rest of the regiment to land, they huddled in the wadi around one of the radios and listened to General Dwight D. Eisenhower's address informing the world of the North African invasion.
35. After Action Report, CT 16, November 21, 1942, box 5909, RG 407, NA
36. Howe, *Northwest Africa*, 208.
37. Ibid., 208–09.
38. AAR, CT 16, November 21, 1942.
39. Hall, "A Memoir of World War II," 6.
40. Howe, *Northwest Africa*, 217.
41. Ibid., 221; AAR, CT 16, November 21, 1942.
42. Ibid.
43. AAR, CT 16, November 21, 1942.
44. Ibid.
45. Cullum, *Biographical Register*, 7: entry 5039, 8: entry 5039, 9: entry 5039.
46. Hall, A Memoir of World War II, 6.
47. Howe, Northwest Africa, 381.
48. Major Donald T. Kellett, "The Action at Robaa," *Infantry Journal* 63, no. 3 (September 1948): 13.
49. Ibid.
50. Ibid., 14.
51. Ibid.
52. Ibid.
53. Ibid., 15.
54. Ibid., 16.
55. H. R. Knickerbocker, et al., *Danger Forward: The Story of the First Division in World War II* (Chicago: Society of the First Division, 1947; reprint, Nashville, Tenn.: The Battery Press, 1980), 62-63.
56. Howe, *Northwest Africa*, 460–61.
57. Ibid., 463.
58. Ibid. 461–62.
59. Ibid., 463.
60. Ibid., 464.
61. Baumgartner, *16th Infantry, 1798–1946*, 21.
62. Howe, *Northwest Africa*, 543.
63. Ibid., 547; Knickerbocker, *Danger Forward*, 65.
64. Howe, *Northwest Africa*, 543.
65. Knickerbocker, *Danger Forward*, 65–66.
66. Lipinski interview.
67. Ibid.; Silver Star Citation, Captain (chaplain) Lawrence E. Deery.
68. Knickerbocker, *Danger Forward*, 67–68.
69. Howe, *Northwest Africa*, 547.
70. Hall, "A Memoir of World War II," 9.
71. Knickerbocker, *Danger Forward*, 68.
72. Orten interview.
73. Howe, *Northwest Africa*, 560.
74. Knickerbocker, *Danger Forward*, 69.
75. Ibid.
76. Ibid.
77. Ibid.
78. Howe, *Northwest Africa*, 569; Baumgartner, *16th Infantry, 1798–1946*, 24–25.
79. Baumgartner, *16th Infantry, 1798–1946*, 24.
80. Lipinski interview.
81. Stanhope B. Mason, "Reminiscences and Anecdotes of World War II," unpublished monograph, MRC-FDM, 53.
82. Ibid., 53–54.
83. Ibid., 54.

84. Baumgartner, *16th Infantry, 1798–1946*, 25. During one of the author's interviews for this book, one former member of the regiment related the story that Colonel Fechet's performance had at this point become erratic and potentially dangerous to himself and his soldiers. Given that the advance had to be conducted over open terrain, Fechet's staff judged that that morning's attack was ludicrous, but Fechet's mind could not be changed. Father Deery was heard to make a remark to the effect that "Something has to be done about this!" Deery was then seen heading for Fechet's location with a carbine. The inference was that Deery had wounded Fechet to get rid of him as commander. This incident may only be anecdotal and apocryphal, as no other surviving members of the staff have confirmed the story, though several have heard it. One officer who was at the regimental command post that morning denies the validity of the story. It does, however, reflect the prevailing attitude that many people harbored toward Fechet as commander.

85. Ibid.

86. Ibid.

87. Cullum, *Biographical Register*, 7: entry 6925, 8: entry 6925, 9: entry 6925.

88. Howe, *Northwest Africa*, 613.

89. Ibid., 622.

90. Ibid.

91. Ibid., 625.

92. Hall, "A Memoir of World War II," 10.

93. Howe, *Northwest Africa*, 625.

94. Baumgartner, *16th Infantry, 1798–1946*, 28.

95. Howe, *Northwest Africa*, 626.

96. Baumgartner, *16th Infantry, 1798–1946*, 29.

97. Ibid.; Howe, *Northwest Africa*, 634.

98. Lieutenant Colonel Charles J. Denholm, Memorandum from Lieutenant Colonel Charles J. Denholm to Commanding Officer, 16th Infantry Regiment, May 11, 1943, Subject: Assault on Hill 523, Reports of Operations, 16th Infantry, Records of the Adjutant General 1917–, RG 407, National Archives, Washington, D.C..

99. Ibid.; Howe, *Northwest Africa*, 636.

100. Denholm, Memorandum, May 11, 1943.

101. Ibid.

102. Ibid.

103. Ibid.

104. Ibid.

105. Baumgartner, *16th Infantry, 1798–1946*, 30; Howe, *Northwest Africa*, 636.

106. Baumgartner, *16th Infantry, 1798–1946*, 32-33.

107. Ibid., 33.

108. Memorandum to the CG, 1st Infantry Division, Subject: Reports After Action Against the Enemy, Headquarters, 16th Infantry Regiment, August 18, 1943, Reports of Operations, 16th Infantry, box 5909, Records of the Adjutant General 1917–, RG 407, National Archives, Washington, D.C.

109. Ibid.

110. Ibid.

111. Ibid.

112. Baumgartner, *16th Infantry, 1798–1946*, 34.

113. Albert N. Garland and Howard M. Smith, *Sicily and the Surrender of Italy*, United States Army in World War II, The Mediterranean Theater of Operations (Washington: GPO, 1965), 1.

114. Ibid., 57.

115. Historical Division, European Command, Foreign Military Studies Branch, Hermann Göring Panzer Division in Sicily 1943, July 10–14, 1943, "Commentary," file N 17500.773-D, Combined Arms Research Library Archives, Fort Leavenworth, Kans., 2–3.

116. Ibid.

117. Ibid., 100.

118. Memo to CG, 1st ID, After Action Against the Enemy, HQ, 16th Infantry Regiment, 4–5.

119. William T. Dillon, "Pearl Harbor to Normandy and Beyond," unpublished manuscript, U.S. Army Military History Institute, Carlisle Barracks, Pa., 5.

120. Garland and Smith, *Sicily and the Surrender of Italy*, 139.

121. Ibid., 151. The regimental after action report estimated the number of tanks in the Italian attack at eleven; Memo to CG, 1st ID, After Action Against the Enemy, HQ, 16th Infantry Regiment, 5.

122. Garland and Smith, *Sicily and the Surrender of Italy*, 151–52.

123. Ibid., 152.

124. Dillon, "Normandy and Beyond," 5.

125. Garland and Smith, *Sicily and the Surrender of Italy*, 165.

126. Memo to CG, 1st ID, After Action Against the Enemy, HQ, 16th Infantry Regiment, 5.

127. Garland and Smith, *Sicily and the Surrender of Italy*, 148–49.

128. Ibid.; Baumgartner, *16th Infantry, 1798-1946*, 41.

129. Baumgartner, *16th Infantry, 1798-1946*, 41.

130. Colonel Bryce F. Denno, "Eight Ball Cannoneers," *Field Artillery Journal* 51, no. 1 (January–February 1983): 15; Garland and Smith, *Sicily and the Surrender of Italy*, 160.

131. War Department General Order Number 60, 1944, Distinguished Unit Citation, Cannon Company, 16th Infantry, Gela, Sicily, July 11–13, 1943.

132. Baumgartner, *16th Infantry, 1798–1946*, 41.

133. Ibid.

134. First Lieutenant Hubert Goldberg, "History of the Medical Detachment, 16th Infantry, November 1940 to May 1945," unpublished manuscript, section 1988.31, box 177, MRC-FDM, 8–10.

135. Memo to CG, 1st ID, After Action Against the Enemy, HQ, 16th Infantry Regiment, 6.

136. Ibid.

137. Baumgartner, *16th Infantry, 1798–1946*, 44.

138. Ibid., 46.

139. Memo to CG, 1st ID, After Action Against the Enemy, HQ, 16th Infantry Regiment, 7; Baumgartner, *16th Infantry, 1798–1946*, 49.

140. Ibid., 50; W. Victor Madej, ed., *German Army Order of Battle 1939–1945* (Allentown, Pa.: Game Marketing Co., 1981), 2:95.

141. Memo to CG, 1st ID, After Action Against the Enemy, HQ, 16th Infantry Regiment, 7.

142. Garland and Smith, *Sicily and the Surrender of Italy*, 314.

143. Memo to CG, 1st ID, After Action Against the Enemy, HQ, 16th Infantry Regiment, 8a.

144. Ibid.

145. Ibid.; Garland and Smith, *Sicily and the Surrender of Italy*, 314.

146. Memo to CG, 1st ID, After Action Against the Enemy, HQ, 16th Infantry Regiment, 8a.

147. Ibid.

148. Garland and Smith, *Sicily and the Surrender of Italy*, 335.

149. Ibid., 325, 331.

150. Ibid., 334–36.

151. Ibid., 338.

152. Ibid.

153. Ibid., 339.

154. Ibid.

155. Ibid., 344–46.

156. Baumgartner, *16th Infantry, 1798–1946*, 65.

157. Hall, "A Memoir of World War II," 14.

158. Ibid.

159. Orten interview.

160. 16th Infantry Regiment, *Historical Report for the Month of September 1943*, October 3, 1943, Operations Reports of the 1st Infantry Division, Records of the Adjutant General 1917–, RG 407, box 5910, National Archives, Washington, D.C..

161. Ibid., *Historical Report, October 1943*, December 1, 1943.

162. Ibid., *Historical Report, November 1943*, December 4, 1943.

163. Ibid., *Historical Report, December 1943*, January 14, 1944.

164. Ibid., *Historical Report, January 1944*, February 7, 1944.

165. Ibid., *Historical Report, February 1944*, March 4, 1944.

166. Headquarters, 16th Infantry Regiment, Comments and Criticisms of Operations Fox, Fabius I, and Neptune, June 30, 1944, Records of the Adjutant General 1917–, RG 407, box 5927, National Archives, Washington, D.C..

167. Ibid.

168. 16th Infantry, *Historical Report, April 1944*, May 9, 1944.
169. Ibid.
170. 16th Infantry, *Historical Report, May 1944*, undated; 16th Infantry Regiment, Operations Fox, Fabius I, and Neptune.
171. Major Carl Plitt, "History, CT 16 Invasion of France, S3 Combat Report, Covering Citation of the 16th Infantry for the Period June 6, 1944," Records of the Adjutant General 1917–, RG 407, box 5927, National Archives, Washington, D.C., 8.
172. Gordon A. Harrison, *Cross-Channel Attack*, United States Army in World War II: The European Theater of Operations (Washington: GPO, 1951), 254–57.
173. Madej, *German Army Order of Battle, 1939–1945*, 2:82; Harrison, *Cross-Channel Attack*, 254–57.
174. Ibid., 69.
175. Harrison, *Cross-Channel Attack*, 319.
176. Plitt, "History, CT 16 Invasion of France," 4–5.
177. Ibid., 6.
178. Ibid., 5-6.
179. Ibid., 6.
180. 16th Infantry, *Historical Report, May 1944*, not dated.
181. Ibid.
182. Donald E. Wilson, *D-Day Plus 18,262, 1944–1994*, 14, manuscript published by the 16th Infantry Regiment Association, 16th Infantry Regiment Association Archive, Fort Washington, Md.
183. Karl Wolf, "The War Years of Karl E. Wolf," unpublished manuscript in the possession of the author, 2.
184. Wilson, *D-Day Plus 18,262*, 17.
185. Plitt, "History, CT 16 Invasion of France," 3.
186. Wilson, *D-Day Plus 18,262*, 18.
187. Master Sergeant Forrest C. Pogue and Staff Sergeant J. M. Topete, transcript of an interview of Lieutenant John Spalding conducted at Herve, Belgium, February 9, 1945, E Company, 16th RCT folder, Military History Institute Archives, Carlisle Barracks, Pa., 3–4.
188. Ibid., 4-5.
189. Plitt, "History, CT 16 Invasion of France," 5–6.
190. Ibid.
191. Ibid., 2.
192. Ibid., 4
193. Ibid., 4.
194. Spalding interview, 6.
195. Transcript of an interview with Major (then Captain) Joseph T. Dawson (Ret.) conducted by Andy Rooney for CBS Television, April 29, 1984, Dawson file, MRC-FDM, 4.
196. Transcript of an interview with Major Joseph T. Dawson (Ret.) conducted by Dr. John F. Votaw, April 16, 1991, Dawson file, MRC-FDM.
197. Spalding interview, 7. Staff Sergeant Streczyk was later awarded the Distinguished Service Cross for his actions on D-Day.
198. Dawson, CBS interview, 5.
199. Hall, "A Memoir of World War II," 18.
200. Ibid.
201. Plitt, "History, CT 16 Invasion of France," 12–13.
202. Telephone interview of James Lipinski by the author, October 15, 1998.
203. Medal of Honor citation for Technician 5th Grade John J. Pinder Jr.
204. Plitt, "History, CT 16 Invasion of France," 10.
205. Transcript of Roger L. Brugger, K Company, 16th Infantry, 1942–44, D-Day Transcripts File, MRC-FDM.
206. Plitt, "History, CT 16 Invasion of France," 5.
207. Ibid., 11–12.
208. Transcript of an interview of Major General Charles T. Horner (Ret) conducted by Andy Rooney for CBS Television April 29, 1984, Dawson file, MRC-FDM, 4.
209. Plitt, "History, CT 16 Invasion of France," 6.
210. Ibid.
211. Russell Richert, interview by the author, July 25, 1998, Tropicana Hotel, Las Vegas, Nev.
212. Wolf, "The War Years of Karl E. Wolf," 3.
213. Ibid.
214. Ibid.
215. Plitt, "History, CT 16 Invasion of France," 7.
216. Dillon, "Normandy and Beyond," 11.
217. Ibid.
218. Ibid.
219. Staff Sergeant Harley Reynolds, videotaped comments of his experiences on D-Day. The regiment's after action report for D-Day states that the B Company headquarters boat was hit by artillery or antitank fire and sunk. This is apparently an error that has been confirmed by several men who were on the boat.
220. Ibid.
221. Plitt, "History, CT 16 Invasion of France," 16.
222. Ibid., 18; Stephen Ambrose, *D-Day, June 6, 1944: The Climactic Battle of World War II* (New York: Simon and Schuster, 1994), 356.
223. Plitt, "History, CT 16 Invasion of France," 20.
224. Ibid., 21.
225. Wilson, *D-Day Plus 18,262*, 20.
226. Ibid., 21.
227. Spalding interview, 8–9.
228. Ibid., 10–12.
229. Transcript of an interview with Colonel William R. Washington (Ret) conducted by Andy Rooney for CBS Television, April 29, 1984, Dawson file, MRC-FDM, 9.
230. Plitt, "History, CT 16 Invasion of France," 9; Dawson, CBS interview, 9.
231. Ibid.
232. Ibid., 4.
233. Wilson, *D-Day Plus 18,262*, 22. Finke had actually been wounded by a German mortar round fired from the position that Lombarski had just encountered.
234. Ibid.
235. Hall, "A Memoir of World War II," 19.
236. Medal of Honor Citation of First Lieutenant Jimmie W. Monteith Jr.
237. Brugger interview, 7.
238. Plitt, "History, CT 16 Invasion of France," 14.
239. Ibid., 15.
240. Ibid., 14.
241. Ibid., 16.
242. Ibid., 12.
243. Ibid., 3.
244. Dawson, Votaw interview.
245. Plitt, "History, CT 16 Invasion of France," 15.
246. Ibid., 16.
247. Hall, "A Memoir of World War II," 20–21.
248. Colonel Charles H. Coates, memorandum, "Operations of the 16th Infantry on the Normandy Beachhead, D to D+2," July 21, 1944, file N-7323, Combined Arms Research Library Archives, Fort Leavenworth, Kans.
249. Ibid.
250. 16th Infantry "Dagwood" Daily Casualty Report, June 6, 1944 to June 8, 1944, published in "Casualties 6-30 June 1944," 16th Infantry Regiment Association.
251. Lipinski interview.
252. Eston White, tape recording of his World War II experiences, located in the author's possession.
253. Martin Blumenson, *Breakout and Pursuit*, United States Army in World War II: The European Theater of Operations (Washington: GPO, 1961), 218.
254. Major Carl Plitt, "History of CT 16, Battle of Coutances," World War II Records of the 1st Division, 1940–48, Records of the Adjutant General 1917–, RG 407, box 5907, National Archives, Washington, D.C., 8.
255. 1st Infantry Division, G3 Report of Operations, July 1–31, 1944, Inclusive, World War II Records of the 1st Division, 1940–48, Records of the Adjutant General 1917–, RG 407, box 5907, National Archives, Washington, D.C..
256. Hall, "A Memoir of World War II," 22.
257. Blumenson, *Breakout and Pursuit*, 238–46 passim.
258. Ibid., 257.

259. Ibid.
260. Baumgartner, *16th Infantry, 1798–1946*, 128.
261. Knickerbocker, *Danger Forward*, 230–31.
262. Baumgartner, *16th Infantry, 1798–1946*, 130.
263. Ibid., 133.
264. Ibid., 140–43.
265. Ibid., 144–45.
266. Ibid., 146–48.
267. Blumenson, *Breakout and Pursuit*, 678–79.
268. Blumenson, *Breakout and Pursuit*, 682–83.
269. 1st Division World War II Combat Achievements Report, Chapter 29, "Battle of Mons," unpublished manuscript, Section 1988.31, box 177, MRC-FDM, 1-2.
270. Ibid., 3.
271. Ibid., 4-6.
272. Ibid., 2.
273. A patrol led by Staff Sergeant Warner W. Holzinger from the 5th Armored Division had actually been the first unit to enter Germany on the previous day, but it had returned to Belgium shortly afterwards.
274. Charles B. MacDonald, *The Siegfried Line Campaign,* The United States Army in World War II: The European Theater of Operations (Washington: GPO, 1963), 281.
275. Ibid., 68–70.
276. Ibid., 66–67.
277. Ibid., 72.
278. Ibid.
279. Ibid., 74–75.
280. Ibid., 77.
281. Ibid.
282. Ibid., 81, 87.
283. Madej, *German Army Order of Battle 1939-1945*, 2:24; MacDonald, *Siegfried Line Campaign*, 87.
284. Ibid., 88.
285. Baumgartner, *16th Infantry, 1798–1946*, 163–64.
286. MacDonald, *Siegfried Line Campaign*, 285.
287. Ibid., 284.
288. Ibid., 290.
289. Wilson, *D-Day Plus 18,262*, 24.
290. Dawson,Votaw interview, April 16, 1991, 34; MacDonald, *Siegfried Line Campaign*, 290–91.
291. Baumgartner, *16th Infantry, 1798–1946*, 167–71.
292. MacDonald, *Siegfried Line Campaign*, 292.
293. Ibid., 293.
294. Ibid.
295. Ibid.; Wilson, *D-Day Plus 18,262*, 24.
296. Charles Whiting, *Bloody Aachen* (New York: Stein and Day, 1976), 186.
297. Hall, "A Memoir of World War II," 24.
298. MacDonald, *Siegfried Line Campaign*, 411.
299. Hall, "A Memoir of World War II," 26.
300. White interview.
301. MacDonald, *Siegfried Line Campaign*, 416–17.
302. Transcript of an interview of Lieutenant Colonel Edmond F. Driscoll by Major Kenneth W. Hechler at Frant Lazne, Czechoslavkia, May 24, 1945, John B. Beach file, Military History Institute Archive, Carlisle Barracks, Pa., 2–3.
303. MacDonald, *Siegfried Line Campaign*, 418.
304. Driscoll interview, 4. As the one hundredth infantryman to win the Medal of Honor in World War II, Lindsey received the medal from President Harry S. Truman before a joint session of Congress in May 1945. There are some in the regiment who dispute that Lindsey actually performed the feats attributed to him that day, but rather, they claim, the actions, and therefore the medal, should rightfully be ascribed to Lieutenant Wood, Lindsey's platoon leader, who was captured not too long after the incident. Either way, the heroism displayed in that situation was indicative of the desperate fighting that day, and the story deserves an honored place in the history of the regiment.

305. MacDonald, *Siegfried Line Campaign*, 418.
306. Ibid., 477–78.
307. Ibid., 475.
308. Ibid., 480.
309. Ibid., 484.
310. Ibid.
311. Oswaldo Ramirez, *Breakout From Normandy*, 12–14, manuscript published by the 16th Infantry Regiment Association, 16th Infantry Regiment Association Archive, Fort Washington, Md.
312. MacDonald, *Siegfried Line Campaign*, 488.
313. Ibid., 489.
314. 1st Division World War II Combat Achievements Report, Chapter 28, "The Attack on Luchem," unpublished manuscript, section 1988.31, box 177, MRC-FDM.
315. Ibid., 4, 7.
316. Ibid., 9.
317. Ibid., 12.
318. MacDonald, *Siegfried Line Campaign*, 490.
319. "The Attack on Luchem," 12–13.
320. Ibid., 14.
321. Driscoll interview, 5–6.
322. Baumgartner, *16th Infantry, 1798–1946*, 184.
323. Letter from Mark Wendland to Colonel Gerald K. Griffin (Ret), July 20, 1998 in the possession of the author.
324. Oliver A. Carey, unpublished and untitled manuscript, Oliver A. Carey file, U. S. Army Military History Institute Archives, Carlisle Barracks, Pa.
325. Charles B. MacDonald, *A Time for Trumpets: The Untold Story of the Battle of the Bulge* (New York: Bantam Books, 1984, 1985), 403.
326. Baumgartner, *16th Infantry, 1798–1946*, 186
327. Ibid., 191.
328. Wendland letter.
329. Wolf, "The War Years of Karl E. Wolf," 11.
330. Ibid., 12.
331. 1st Division World War II Combat Achievements Report, chapter 4, "The Attack on Kreuzau, February 25, 1945, Company E, 16th Infantry," unpublished manuscript, Section 1988.31, box 177, MRC-FDM, 2–3.
332. Ibid., 6–13 passim.
333. Ibid., chapter 7, "The Attack on Vetweiss, February 27, 1945, Company I, 16th Infantry," 6–7.
334. Wolf, "The War Years of Karl E. Wolf," 14.
335. "The Attack on Vetweiss," 7–8.
336. 1st Division World War II Combat Achievements Report, Chapter 30, "The Attack on Bonn, March 8, 1945, Third Battalion, 16th Infantry," unpublished manuscript, section 1988.31, box 177, MRC-FDM, 5.
337. Wolf, "The War Years of Karl E. Wolf," 16; Baumgartner, *16th Infantry, 1798–1946*, 240.
338. Ibid., 241.
339. Ibid., 242.
340. Ibid., 235.
341. Hall, "A Memoir of World War II," 44.
342. Charles B. MacDonald, *The Last Offensive,* The United States Army in World War II: The European Theater of Operations (Washington: GPO, 1973), 345–46.
343. 16th Infantry, *Historical Report, April 1945*, May 1, 1945.
344. MacDonald, *The Last Offensive*, 380–81.
345. Ibid., 402.
346. Baumgartner, *16th Infantry, 1798–1946*, 259.
347. Ibid., 261.
348. Ibid.
349. 1st Division World War II Combat Achievements Report, chapter 3, "The Attack on Rübeland, April 18, 1945, Company C, 16th Infantry," 1.
350. Ibid., 3.
351. Ibid., chapter 2, "The Attack on Rübeland, April 18, 1945, Company B, 16th Infantry," 4.

352. Ibid., chapter 3, "The Attack on Rübeland, April 18, 1945, Company C, 16th Infantry," 4.
353. Ibid., chapter 2, "The Attack on Rübeland, April 18, 1945, Company B, 16th Infantry," 6.
354. Ibid., 7.
355. Ibid., 8.
356. Ibid.
357. Ibid., chapter 5, "Approaches to Eland and The Attack on Rothehütte," April 18, 1945, Company F, 16th Infantry," 1–7 passim.
358. Ibid., 7–8.
359. 16th Infantry, *Historical Report, April 1945*, May 1, 1945, 6.

Chapter 9—The Cold Warriors

1. Transcript of communications from the 1st Infantry Division G3 telephone log for May 9, 1945, Czechoslovakia file, 16th Infantry, MRC-FDM.
2. Ibid.
3. "German POW Riddle Solved," *Bridgehead Sentinel* (spring 1993): 12.
4. Headquarters, 16th Infantry, Report of Operations, May 8 to September 30, 1945, Reports of Operations, 16th Infantry, Records of the Adjutant General 1917–, RG 407, National Archives, College Park, Md., 2.
5. Hall, "A Memoir of World War II," 29.
6. 16th Infantry Report of Operations, May 8 to September 30, 1945, 1–2.
7. Ibid., 2–3.
8. Ibid., 3.
9. 16th Infantry Report of Operations, October 1 to December 31, 1945, 1–2.
10. 16th Infantry Report of Operations, January 1 to March 31, 1946, enclosure 2, "S-2 Activities," Weekly Counterintelligence Report, January 4, 1946, Reports of Operations, 16th Infantry, Records of the Adjutant General 1917–, RG 407, National Archives, Washington, D.C.
11. 16th Infantry Report of Operations, October 1 to December 31, 1945, enclosure 3 "S-2 Activities," 6.
12. Ibid., January 1 to March 31, 1946, Enclosure 1, "Strength and Operation Report," 3rd Battalion, March 26, 1946.
13. 16th Infantry Report of Operations, January 1 to March 31, 1946, enclosure 1, "Weekly Situation Reports, January 14, 1946, 2; February 18, 1946, 1.
14. 16th Infantry Report of Operations, October 1 to December 31, 1945, Daily Bulletin No. 123, November 24, 1945.
15. Ibid., January 1 to March 31, 1946, 2.
16. Ibid., enclosure 3, "Weekly Counterintelligence Reports," March 15, 1946, 2.
17. Ibid., April 1 to June 30, 1946, enclosure 3, "Weekly Counterintelligence Reports," May 17, 1946, 3–4.
18. Ibid., January 1 to March 31, 1946, enclosure 3, "Weekly Counterintelligence Reports," March 29, 1946, 3.
19. Ibid., April 1 to June 30, 1946, enclosure 5, "Extracts from the S3 Journal," 3–4.
20. Ibid., July 1 to September 30, 1946, "Troops Operational Activities," paragraphs 33–34.
21. James and Ronny Lipinski, interview by the author, December 14, 1998, 4523 North Pegram Street, Alexandria, Va.
22. 16th Infantry Report of Operations, October 1–31, 1946, chapter 8, "Army Welfare."
23. 1st Battalion, 16th Infantry Report of Operations, November 25, 1946, 1–2.
24. Ibid.
25. Ibid., S3 Journal extract, 2.
26. 5th Infantry Regiment, Operations Instructions No. 10, October 24, 1946.
27. 16th Infantry Report of Operations, October 1–31, 1946, chapter 8, "Army Welfare."
28. 3rd Battalion, 16th Infantry, Report of Operations, December 1–31, 1946, January 7, 1947, 3.

29. 1st Battalion, 16th Infantry, Report of Operations, July 1 to September 30, 1947, October 10, 1947, 2.
30. Ibid., 4.
31. Ibid., 1.
32. Ibid., 5.
33. 16th Infantry Report of Operations, March 1–31, 1947, 1–4.
34. 3rd Battalion, 16th Infantry, Report of Operations, June 1–30, 1947, July 2, 1947, 4.
35. Colonel William S. Hathaway (Ret.), taped memoir prepared by Col. Hathaway and provided to the author, Fayetteville, N.C., September 1, 1993. Tape held by the author.
36. Ibid., 3, 8.
37. 1st Battalion, 16th Infantry, Report of Operations, April 1 to June 30, 1948, 1.
38. 16th Infantry, Report of Operations, July 1 to September 30, 1948, 2.
39. Ibid., 3.
40. Ibid., 4.
41. Cullum, *Biographical Register*, 7: entry 7207, 8: entry 7207, 9: entry 7207.
42. 16th Infantry, Report of Operations, July 1 to September 30, 1948, 2, 4.
43. Hathaway interview.
44. Ibid., 4.
45. Headquarters, 16th Infantry Regiment, General Orders No. 3, October 8, 1948.
46. 16th Infantry, Report of Operations, July 1 to September 30, 1948, 5; Heavy Tank Company, Historical Narrative for Quarterly Period Ending December 31, 1948, January 3, 1949, 2; Donald Taylor, recorded interview by the author, July 24, 1998, Tropicana Hotel, Las Vegas, Nev.
47. 16th Infantry, Report of Operations, October 1 to December 30, 1948, 5, 7.
48. *Army Times*, December 30, 1948. The nickname "Rangers" has gone through several variations since its adoption. All of these variations were associated with the several battalions of the regiment formed under the Combat Arms Regimental System. Each variation is discussed in later chapters. In 1993, the author wrote to the Center of Military History in an attempt to get the nickname officially adopted, just as the 3rd Infantry is nicknamed "The Old Guard" and the 6th Infantry, "The Regulars." The reply stated that because the 75th Infantry was officially the "Ranger" regiment, the nickname could not also be officially designated for the 16th Infantry.
49. 16th Infantry, Report of Operations, October 1 to December 30, 1948, 7.
50. 3rd Battalion, 16th Infantry, Report of Operations, April 1–30, 1948, May 9, 1948, 2–4.
51. 3rd Battalion, 16th Infantry, History of Activities, September 1 to December 31, 1948, January 15, 1949, 2.
52. Ibid., 3, 5.
53. Headquarters, 16th Infantry Regiment, "Command and Unit Historical Report of the 16th Infantry Regiment for the Year of 1949," 3–12.
54. Ibid., 13.
55. Ibid.; *The Bridgehead Sentinel* 8, no. 2 (January 1950): 5.
56. Unit Historical Report 1949, 13.
57. Ibid., 15–16.
58. *The Bridgehead Sentinel* 8, no. 2 (January 1950): 6.
59. Unit Historical Report 1949, 17.
60. Ibid., 10, 16–17.
61. Pinder Barracks Chapel Historical Notes. When Pinder Barracks was closed down in 1991, Chaplain Stephen L. Hagler shipped these windows to the Cavalry Museum at Fort Riley, Kansas, which was then the home of the 1st Infantry Division. The author and Sergeant First Class Matthew McGinty were responsible for displaying one of these windows in the battalion headquarters of the 1st Battalion, 16th Infantry, where it can still been seen as of this writing. The 2nd Battalion, before its inactivation in 1994, also had one of the windows on display.

62. Unit Historical Report 1949, 26.
63. 3rd Battalion, 16th Infantry Regiment, "Yearly Narrative Historical Report 1949," 3–4.
64. Ibid.
65. Ibid., 5.
66. Ibid., 5–6.
67. Ibid., 5.
68. Headquarters, 16th Infantry Regiment, "Command and Unit Historical Report, 16th Infantry Regiment, 1950," 4–5.
69. Ibid., 23–24.
70. Ibid., 9–10.
71. Ibid., 12.
72. Ibid., 13–14.
73. "16th Inf Regiment Celebrates Organization Day," *The Nurnberg Post*, 3, no. 39 (October 6, 1950): 1, 3.
74. Cullum, *Biographical Register*, 7: entry 7498, 8: entry 7498, 9: entry 7498.
75. "Command and Unit Historical Report, 1950," 2–3.
76. Headquarters, 16th Infantry Regiment, "Command Report, of the 16th Infantry Regiment, January 1, 1951–January 31, 1951," 9.
77. Ibid., 35–41 passim.
78. Ibid., 27.
79. *Combat Forces Journal* 3, no. 1 (August 1952): 14–15.
80. Headquarters, European Command, Final Report, Exercise "Combine," 1951, 7–65 passim.
81. *The Bridgehead Sentinel* 10, no. 2 (January 1952): 24.
82. *The Bridgehead Sentinel* 10, no. 3 (April 52): 25.
83. Charles N. Branham, ed., *1967 Register of Graduates and Former Cadets* (West Point, N.Y.: West Point Alumni Foundation, 1967), 380, #7586.
84. Charles S. Silk, recorded interview by the author, July 24, 1998, Tropicana Hotel, Las Vegas, Nev.
85. Headquarters, 16th Infantry Regiment, "Command Report, of the 16th Infantry Regiment, January 1, 1952–December 31, 1952," 6.
86. Ibid., 18–19.
87. Ibid., 7.
88. Ibid., passim.
89. *The Bridgehead Sentinel* 10, no. 3 (April 1952): 30.
90. Daily Journal, 16th Infantry Regiment, file 228-08, Unit Historical Activities: 1955, 16th Infantry box, U.S. Cavalry Museum Archive, Fort Riley, Kans.
91. *The Bridgehead Sentinel* 14, no. 1 (October 1955): 1–3.
92. ROCID Evaluation Report, 1st Infantry Division, Fort Riley, Kans., August 1957, file 228-08, Unit Historical Activities: 1955, 16th Infantry box, U.S. Cavalry Museum Archive, Fort Riley, Kans.; *Army Times*, November 24, 1956, p. 2.
93. *Army Times*, December 1, 1956, p. 6.
94. Mahon and Danysh, *Infantry*, 91.
95. 1st Infantry Division Field SOP, July 1, 1957, file no. N-17439.1, Combined Arms Resource Library Archives, Fort Leavenworth, Kans.
96. "Rangers Receive Armor," *The American Traveler*, November 7, 1957, p. 8.
97. *The American Traveler*, June 12, 1957, p. 3; "Rangers Receive Recruits," *The American Traveler*, June 19, 1957, p. 3; *The American Traveler*, June 26, 1957, p. 3.
98. "Leading Hollywood Producer to Plan Movie on the 'Big Red One,' " *The American Traveler*, June 5, 1957, p. 1; "Hollywood Producer Always Plugs 'Red One,'" *The American Traveler*, July 3, 1957, p. 3.
99. "San Juan Flag Used in Charge Given Rangers," *The American Traveler*, October 17, 1957, p. 8.
100. "Ranger Historian Receives First World War Mementoes," *The American Traveler*, February 13, 1958, p. 7.
101. "Division Battle Groups Headed to Germany," *The American Traveler*, April 3, 1958, p. 1.
102. "16th Infantry Plans Air Operation," *The American Traveler*, June 5, 1958, p. 3; "Operation Ranger Strikes Fast, Hard," *The American Traveler*, June 12, 1958, p. 3.
103. "Great-Nephew Visits Grave of 16th Infantry Civil War Hero," *The American Traveler*, August 7, 1958, p. 7.
104. "Roughn's Ranger Crests Lasted a Lo-o-ong Time," *The American Traveler*, July 10, 1957, p. 8; "Paddy Roughn Leaves 16th Infantry," *The American Traveler*, February 26, 1959, p. 1.
105. "Former Ranger Medal of Honor Recipient Dies," *The American Traveler*, January 22, 1959, p. 1.
106. Movement Order Number 25, Headquarters 1st Infantry Division, Fort Riley, Kans., October 28, 1958, file 228-08, Unit Historical Activities: 1955, 16th Infantry box, U.S. Cavalry Museum Archive, Fort Riley, Kans.
107. In November 1998, Colonel Gerald Griffin (Ret.), Honorary Colonel of the Regiment of the 16th Infantry, and his wife, Pat, traveled to Fléville and met with the town mayor and other officials to present a plaque to the town on behalf of the regiment. During that visit, Colonel Griffin was able to confirm that the blue and white vair was indeed the basis of the Fléville coat of arms.
108. Letter of Commendation, February 20, 1961, from Lieutenant General Frederic J. Brown, commanding general of V Corps, to Colonel John K. Singlaub, commander, 1st Battle Group, 16th Infantry. Copy in the author's possession.
109. John J. Copeland, recorded interview by the author, July 24, 1998, Tropicana Hotel, Las Vegas, Nev.
110. Ibid.
111. Ibid.
112. "16th Infantry Unit History," unpublished article, 16th Infantry box, U.S. Cavalry Museum Archive, Fort Riley, Kans.
113. Copeland interview.
114. "Rangers Return Is Announced," *The Fort Riley Post*, February 7, 1964, p. 1; "Task Force 2-16 Arrives at Forbes After 6 Months in Germany," *The Fort Riley Post*, February 21, 1964, p. 1.
115. *The Fort Riley Post*, March 6, 1964, p. 1.
116. "16th Men Move to the Field for FTX," *The Fort Riley Post*, March 27, 1964, p. 9.
117. "Strike Command Chief Will Direct Missouri Exercise," *The Fort Riley Post*, October 16, 1964, pp. 1–2; *The Fort Riley Post*, October 30, 1964, p. 1; "Napier Awarded Joint Services Commendation Medal for GOLD FIRE I," *The Fort Riley Post*, June 25, 1965, p. 8.

Chapter 10—Cold War Interlude—Vietnam

1. Lieutenant Colonel Ed Coates (Ret.), recorded interview by the author, August 7, 1999, Galt House Hotel, Louisville, Ky.
2. Colonel Y. Y. Phillips (Ret.), recorded interview by the author, July 24, 1998, Tropicana Hotel, Las Vegas, Nev.
3. Matloff, *American Military History*, 622–39 passim.
4. Major Kenneth M. Alderson (Ret.), recorded interview by the author, August 6, 1999, Galt House Hotel, Louisville, Ky.
5. Ibid.
6. In an article written for *Army* magazine in September 1966, Lieutenant Colonel Y. Y. Phillips described these modifications to infantry battalions operating in Vietnam. In the article, Phillips called for formal establishment of a fourth line company and a fourth rifle platoon in the Vietnam-based infantry battalions. The U.S. Army adopted these modifications in 1967.
7. Medal of Honor citation for First Lieutenant Lloyd L. Burke, October 21, 1951.
8. Interview with Lieutenant Colonel Edward O. Yaugo, conducted by Lieutenant Colonel Michael E. Ekman, Senior Officers Oral History Program, Project 31-36, U.S. Army Military History Institute, Carlisle Barracks, Pa., 35–36.
9. "A Summary History of the 2nd Brigade, 1st Infantry Division," 2nd Brigade 1st Infantry Division Organizational History file, box 1, stack 270, row 29, compartment 21, shelf 1, Records of U.S. Forces in Southeast Asia, RG 472, National Archives, Washington, D.C. There is another version of Burke's wounding. Several members of the battalion have indicated that Burke was attempting to drop a grenade on the VC position, but the grenade went off either in, or just outside of, the chopper, wounding him and the others.

10. Phillips interview.
11. Operation Order #10 (Operation Caoutchouc), 071200 September 1965, 2nd Battalion, 16th Infantry, box 5, row 77, stack 270, Records of U.S. Forces in Southeast Asia, RG 472, National Archives, Washington, D.C; 2nd Battalion, 16th Infantry, Command Report for Quarterly Period Ending September 30, 1965, dated October 21, 1965, 16th Infantry file, U.S. Army Military History Institute, Carlisle Barracks, Pa., 7.
12. Letter from Colonel Y. Y. Phillips (Ret.) to the author, September 8, 1999.
13. Ibid.
14. "A Summary History of the 2nd Brigade," 6.
15. After Action Report, Bushmaster, 1st Battalion, 16th Infantry, November 24, 1965, box 6, row 77, stack 270, Records of U.S. Forces in Southeast Asia, RG 472, National Archives, Washington, D.C, 1.
16. Ibid., 3.
17. After Action Report, Bushmaster II and Bloodhound, 1st Battalion, 16th Infantry, December 13, 1965, box 2, row 77, stack 270, Records of U.S. Forces in Southeast Asia, RG 472, National Archives, Washington, D.C.
18. Ibid.
19. Phillips interview.
20. Colonel Gerald K. Griffin (Ret.), recorded interview by the author, May 31, 1999, 9317 Lancelot, Fort Washington, Md.
21. Press Release No. 4-1-66, 1st Infantry Division Information Office, January 2, 1966, 2nd Battalion, 16th Infantry News Information file, MRC-FDM; Press Release no. 3-1-66, January 1, 1966.
22. Phillips letter. There is some speculation that these men were not construction workers, but CIA operatives who had been identified and captured by VC counterintelligence agents. This incident initially received national publicity, but it was quickly toned down because of the sensitive nature of the prisoners' activities.
23. After Action Report, Operation Buckskin, 1st Battalion, 16th Infantry, February 5, 1966, box 6, row 77, stack 270, Records of U.S. Forces in Southeast Asia, RG 472, National Archives, Washington, D.C., 2.
24. Ibid., 1–7, passim.
25. Operation Order 5-66 (Operation Mallet), 2nd Battalion, 16th Infantry, January 27, 1966, box 5, row 77, stack 270, Records of U.S. Forces in Southeast Asia, RG 472, National Archives, Washington, D.C.
26. "Operational Report on Lessons Learned," 2nd Brigade, 1st Infantry Division, May 16, 1966, box 1, shelf 4, compartment 21, row 29, stack 270, Records of U.S. Forces in Southeast Asia, RG 472, National Archives, Washington, D.C., 5.
27. Operation Order 6-66 (Operation Mastiff), 2nd Battalion, 16th Infantry, February 18, 1966, box 5, row 77, stack 270, Records of U.S. Forces in Southeast Asia, RG 472, National Archives, Washington, D.C.; Matloff, *American Military History*, 645.
28. Operation Order 3-66 (Operation Mastiff), Headquarters, 1st Infantry Division, February 1966, file N-17439, Combined Arms Resource Library Archives, Fort Leavenworth, Kans.
29. Robert Hoenig, interview by the author, August 5, 1999, Galt House Hotel, Louisville, Ky.
30. After Action Report, Operation Mastiff, 1st Battalion, 16th Infantry, March 9, 1966, box 6, row 77, stack 270, Records of U.S. Forces in Southeast Asia, RG 472, National Archives, Washington, D.C., 2–5.
31. Hibbs earned the 1st Infantry Division's first Medal of Honor in Vietnam.
32. After Action Report, Operation Cocoa Beach, 1st Battalion, 16th Infantry, March 11, 1966, box 6, row 77, stack 270, Records of U.S. Forces in Southeast Asia, RG 472, National Archives, Washington, D.C., 1–3.
33. Combat After Action Report, 3rd Brigade, 1st Infantry Division, Operation Abilene, 1st Infantry Division After Action Report file, box 1, stack 270, row 29, compartment 18, shelf 3, Records of U.S. Forces in Southeast Asia, RG 472, National Archives, Washington, D.C., 7–10.

34. Colonel Gerald K. Griffin (Ret.), "No Road Back," unpublished manuscript in possession of the author, 117–18.
35. George C. Wilson, *Mud Soldiers: Life Inside the New American Army* (New York: Charles Scribner's Sons, 1989), 10.
36. Ibid., 11.
37. Ibid., 13.
38. Combat After Action Report, 2nd Brigade, 1st Infantry Division, Operation Abilene, 1st Infantry Division After Action Report file, box 1, stack 270, row 29, compartment 18, shelf 3, Records of U.S. Forces in Southeast Asia, RG 472, National Archives, Washington, D.C., 7–10.
39. Wilson, *Mud Soldiers*, 16–18.
40. Ibid., 19–20.
41. Ibid., 21–24.
42. *Danger Forward: The Magazine of the Big Red One*, Vietnam 1, pt. 1 (May 1967): 26. Interestingly, Robinson predicted his own fate. One day he had a conversation with Captains Nolan and Griffin in which he told them: "The first big battle I get into, I will be killed and win the Medal of Honor." He was right.
43. Wilson, *Mud Soldiers*, 27–29.
44. Ibid., 29–32.
45. Ibid., 35–36.
46. Ibid., 37–38; John Libs, interview by the author, August 6, 1999, Galt House Hotel, Louisville, Ky.
47. Combat After Action Report, 2nd Brigade, Operation Abilene, 19.
48. Combat After Action Report, 1st Infantry Division, Operation Birmingham, 1st Infantry Division After Action Report file, box 2, stack 270, row 29, compartment 18, shelf 3, Records of U.S. Forces in Southeast Asia, RG 472, National Archives, Washington, D.C., 13–15.
49. Griffin interview.
50. Ibid., 16; Combat After Action Report, 1st Brigade, 1st Infantry Division, Operation Birmingham, 1st Infantry Division After Action Report file, box 2, stack 270, row 29, compartment 18, shelf 3, Records of U.S. Forces in Southeast Asia, RG 472, National Archives, Washington, D.C., 2–3.
51. Combat After Action Report, 1st Infantry Division, Operation Birmingham, 17.
52. Combat After Action Report, 1st Battalion, 16th Infantry, May 24, 1966, Operation Birmingham, box 6, row 77, stack 270, Records of U.S. Forces in Southeast Asia, RG 472, National Archives, Washington, D.C., 5, 7.
53. *Pictorial History of the 2nd Brigade, 1st Infantry Division in Vietnam* (Tokyo, Japan: Dai Nippon Printing Co., 1967), 2:24.
54. Ibid., 2:28.
55. Ibid., 2:29; Annex H, Combat After Action Report, 1st Infantry Division, Operation El Paso II/III, 2nd Brigade, 1st Infantry Division After Action Report file, box 1, stack 270, row 29, compartment 21, shelf 5, Records of U.S. Forces in Southeast Asia, RG 472, National Archives, Washington, D.C., H1–2.
56. Press Release no. 305-7-66, 1st Infantry Division Information Office, undated, 1st Battalion, 16th Infantry News Information file, MRC-FDM.
57. Annex C, Combat After Action Report, 1st Infantry Division, Operation El Paso II/III, 2nd Brigade, 1st Infantry Division After Action Report file, box 1, stack 270, row 29, compartment 21, shelf 5, Records of U.S. Forces in Southeast Asia, RG 472, National Archives, Washington, D.C., C5–6.
58. *Pictorial History of the 2nd Brigade, 1st Infantry Division in Vietnam*, 2:44.
59. Ibid., 2:54, 2:68, and 2:76.
60. Combat After Action Report, 1st Battalion, 16th Infantry, Operation Danbury, After Action Report file, box 1, stack 270, row 77, compartment 3, shelf 2, Records of U.S. Forces in Southeast Asia, RG 472, National Archives, Washington, D.C., 1–5.
61. Press Release no. 989-9-66, "Gen. Deane Awards Badges," 1st Infantry Division Information Office, September 26, 1966, 2nd Battalion, 16th Infantry News Information file, MRC-FDM.

62. Combat After Action Report, 1st Infantry Division, Operation Tulsa, 1st Infantry Division After Action Report file, box 2, stack 270, row 29, compartment 18, shelf 3, Records of U.S. Forces in Southeast Asia, RG 472, National Archives, Washington, D.C., 2.

63. George L. MacGarrigle, *Combat Operations: Taking the Offensive, October 1966 to October 1967*, United States Army in Vietnam (Washington: GPO, 1998), 34–35.

64. Ibid., 36–38, 42.

65. Ibid., 45–47.

66. *2nd Brigade Pictorial History*, 2:70.

67. Ibid.

68. After Action Report, Operation Attleboro, 1st Infantry Division, April 6, 1967, Annex G, 2nd Brigade AAR, December 13, 1966, 16th Infantry Regiment Association Archive, 5–7.

69. Ibid., 6–10.

70. Operation Order 24-66 (Operation Fairfax), 2nd Battalion, 16th Infantry, November 30, 1966, box 5, row 77, stack 270, Records of U.S. Forces in Southeast Asia, RG 472, National Archives, Washington, D.C.

71. Press Release no. 1791-12-66, "Fairfax," 1st Infantry Division Information Office, December 18, 1966, 2nd Battalion, 16th Infantry News Information file, MRC-FDM.

72. After Action Report, Operation Healdsburg, 1st Battalion, 16th Infantry, December 26, 1966, box 6, row 77, stack 270, Records of U.S. Forces in Southeast Asia, RG 472, National Archives, Washington, D.C.

73. S. L. A. Marshall, *Ambush; The Battle of Dau Tieng, Also Called the Battle of Dong Minh Chau, War Zone C, Operation Attleboro, and Other Deadfalls in South Vietnam* (Nashville, TN: Battery Press, 1969), 131–55 passim.

74. Major Louis J. Murray Jr. (Ret.), interview by the author, August 7, 1999, Galt House Hotel, Louisville, Ky.

75. Lieutenant General Bernard W. Rogers, Vietnam Studies, *Cedar Falls–Junction City: A Turning Point* (Washington: GPO, 1974), 19–23.

76. Ibid., 20–23.

77. Battalion History, 1967, 1st Battalion, 16th Infantry, located in the 16th Infantry file, U.S. Army Military History Institute, Carlisle Barracks, Pa., 3. A "Rome plow" was a special bulldozer developed for jungle clearing operations by the Rome Manufacturing Co. of Rome, Georgia.

78. Press Release no. 2150-1-67, "ILL," 1st Infantry Division Information Office, January 26, 1967, 1st Battalion, 16th Infantry News Information file, MRC-FDM.

79. Murray interview.

80. MacGarrigle, *Taking the Offensive*, 111–12.

81. Rogers, *A Turning Point*, 83–85.

82. Murray interview.

83. Ibid., 113–15.

84. Medal of Honor citation for Platoon Sergeant Matthew Leonard, February 28, 1968.

85. Rogers, *A Turning Point*, 116.

86. Press Release no. 2614-4-67, "VC Rooted Out of Base Camp Area," 1st Infantry Division Information Office, April 16, 1967, 2nd Battalion, 16th Infantry, News Information file, MRC-FDM.

87. Press Release no. 2607-4-67, "HOT LZ," 1st Infantry Division Information Office, April 14,1967, 1st Battalion, 16th Infantry, News Information file, MRC-FDM.

88. Rogers, *A Turning Point*, 140–47.

89. Ibid., 150–51.

90. Press Release no. 3783, "SILVER STARS," 1st Infantry Division Information Office, September 23, 1967, 1st Battalion, 16th Infantry News Information file, MRC-FDM.

91. Combat After Action Report, 3rd Brigade, 1st Infantry Division, Operation Billings, 1st Infantry Division After Action Report file, box 2, stack 270, row 29, compartment 18, shelf 3, Records of U.S. Forces in Southeast Asia, RG 472, National Archives, Washington, D.C., 2–5.

92. James Mauchline, interview by the author, August 7, 1999, Galt House Hotel, Louisville, Ky.

93. Ibid.

94. MacGarrigle, *Taking the Offensive*, 342–43.

95. Murray interview.

96. Combat After Action Report, 3rd Brigade, 1st Infantry Division, Operation Billings, 2–5.

97. Combat After Action Report, 1st Brigade, 1st Infantry Division, Operation Billings, 1st Infantry Division After Action Report file, box 2, stack 270, row 29, compartment 18, shelf 3, Records of U.S. Forces in Southeast Asia, RG 472, National Archives, Washington, D.C., passim.

98. Combat After Action Report, 3rd Brigade, 1st Infantry Division, Operation Portland, 5 September 1967, 1st Infantry Division After Action Report file, box 3, stack 270, row 29, compartment 18, shelf 3, Records of U.S. Forces in Southeast Asia, RG 472, National Archives, Washington, D.C., 1–4.

99. Press Release, "New 'Ranger' Company," 1st Infantry Division Information Office, October 15, 1967, 2nd Battalion, 16th Infantry News Information file, MRC-FDM.

100. Combat After Action Report, 1st Infantry Division, Operation Shenandoah, 1st Infantry Division After Action Report file, box 3, stack 270, row 29, compartment 18, shelf 3, Records of U.S. Forces in Southeast Asia, RG 472, National Archives, Washington, D.C., 4–24.

101. After Action Report, 1st Infantry Division, Seal and Search of Ben Cui Hamlet, January 22, 1968, 1st Infantry Division After Action Report file, box 3, stack 270, row 29, compartment 18, shelf 3, Records of U.S. Forces in Southeast Asia, RG 472, National Archives, Washington, D.C., 1–5.

102. Battalion Supplement 1968, 1st Battalion, 16th Infantry, 16th Infantry file, Military History Institute, Carlisle Barracks, Pa.

103. "History of the 2nd Battalion, 16th Infantry, 'Rangers' for 1968" (hereinafter referred to as "History of 2-16 Infantry, 1968"), 16th Infantry file, U.S. Army Military History Institute, Carlisle Barracks, Pa.

104. Interview with Dennis Mozee at the home of Ival Lawhon, 1306 13th Street, St. Joseph, Mo., May 14, 1999.

105. "History of 2-16 Infantry, 1968"; *The First Infantry Division in Vietnam, 1965–1970* (Paducah, Ky.: Turner Publishing Co., 1993), 32.

106. After Action Report, 1st Battalion, 16th Infantry, Operation Ao Duty 3, June 13, 1968, stack 270, row 77, box 6, Records of U.S. Forces in Southeast Asia, RG 472, National Archives, Washington, D.C., 1-6.

107. Letter from Colonel Darrel L. Gooler (Ret.) to the author, August 22, 1999.

108. Battalion Supplement 1968, 1st Battalion, 16th Infantry; "History of 2-16 Infantry, 1968."

109. Ibid.

110. Robert B. Humphries, interview by the author, August 5, 1999, Galt House Hotel, Louisville, Ky.

111. Combat After Action Interview Report: Loc Ninh Operations September 11–15, 1968, 17th Military History Detachment, October 8, 1968, 1st Infantry Division After Action Report file, box 4, stack 270, row 29, compartment 18, shelf 3, Records of U.S. Forces in Southeast Asia, RG 472, National Archives, Washington, D.C., 7-1–7-3.

112. Ibid., 7-3.

113. Ibid., 7-4.

114. Ibid., 7-7.

115. "History of 2-16 Infantry, 1968."

116. Major General Willard Latham (Ret.), telephone interview with the author, August 21, 1999.

117. Battalion Supplement 1968, 1st Battalion, 16th Infantry. Latham's troops continued to wear their "Big Red One" shoulder patches long after they had been assigned to the 9th Division. Frequently, Ewell would hassle Latham about this practice, until finally, the troops were directly ordered to replace the 1st Division patch with that of the 9th Division. They immediately sewed their beloved "Big Red Ones" on their right shoulder as their preferred combat patch. Ewell, apparently, was still not pleased.

118. Operational Report of the 1st Infantry Division for the Period Ending January 31, 1969, February 19, 1969, 1st Infantry Division box, "Lessons Learned," U.S. Army Military History Institute, Carlisle Barracks, Pa., 10.

119. *First Infantry Division in Vietnam, 1965–1970*, 65.

120. 1969 Historical Supplement, 1st Battalion, 16th Infantry.

121. U.S. Army, "The First Infantry Division in Vietnam, 1969," 3:65.

122. Written notes from Colonel Kenneth G. Cassels (Ret.) to the author, August 24, 1999.

123. Ibid.

124. Combat After Action Report: The Battle of Binh Long Province, August 1969, 14th Military History Detachment, 1st Infantry Division After Action Report file, box 5, stack 270, row 29, compartment 18, shelf 3, Records of U.S. Forces in Southeast Asia, RG 472, National Archives, Washington, D.C., 48–51.

125. Memorandum from Major George J. Telenko to Commanding Officer, 11th Armored Cavalry Regiment, Subject: "Facts Surrounding 1st Bn, 16th Inf (Mech) Enemy Contact 011600 September 1969 Resulting in 2 US KIA and 54 US WIA," September 7, 1969, Command Reports, box 8, row 77, stack 270, Records of U.S. Forces in Southeast Asia, RG 472, National Archives, Washington, D.C..

126. 1969 Historical Supplement, 1st Battalion, 16th Infantry.

127. Press Release no. 00932, "Bandito's Ballad," 1st Infantry Division Information Office, September 25, 1969, 1st Battalion, 16th Infantry News Information file, MRC-FDM.

128. Letter from Colonel Kenneth G. Cassels to Major Wayne T. Boles, July 9, 1973, regarding the After Action Report on the Battle of Binh Long Province (Operation Kentucky Cougar), August 12, 1969, located in the Office of the Chief of Military History Collection, Vietnam War—Armor/Vietnam Folders, folder 14 (Mobile Defense), U.S. Army Military History Institute, Carlisle Barracks, Pa.

129. U.S. Army, "The First Infantry Division in Vietnam, 1969," 3:78.

130. Press Release, "Ben Cat Guerrillas," 1st Infantry Division Information Office, December 4, 1969, 2nd Battalion, 16th Infantry News Information file, MRC-FDM. The "Hoi Chanh" were VC defectors who were willing to provide the U.S. and ARVN units with information about their former comrades.

131. 1969 Historical Supplement, 1st Battalion, 16th Infantry, January-February 1970.

132. Annual Historical Supplement for 1966, 3rd Battalion, 16th Infantry, February 21, 1967, file of the 3rd Battalion, 16th Infantry, U.S. Army Military History Institute, Carlisle Barracks, Pa.

133. 1969 Historical Supplement, 1st Battalion, 16th Infantry.

Chapter 11—From the Heartland to Deutschland

1. The officer presenting the 1st Division flag to Linville was Lieutenant General Vernon P. Mock, Fifth Army commander, who had commanded the 16th Infantry in 1953–54. Also present for the ceremony was General James K. Woolnough, CONARC commander, who had served as the regimental executive officer in World War II.

2. Lieutenant General Ronald L. Watts (Ret.), recorded telephone interview by the author, December 22, 1999, Greensboro, Georgia.

3. Lieutenant Colonel Kevin Richards, recorded interview by the author, October 13, 1999, Fort Leavenworth, Kans.

4. History of the 1st IDF, April 1970–August 1991, 35–36. This is an unpublished manuscript in the possession of the author.

5. Ibid., 35.

6. Ibid., 48.

7. Ibid., 39.

8. Headquarters, 1st Battalion, 16th Infantry, Annual Historical Supplement [1975], February 17, 1976, 1.

9. History of the 1st IDF, 44.

10. Ibid., 46.

11. Ibid., 43.

12. Ibid., 19–20.

13. Ibid., 18–19, 23; Headquarters, 1st Battalion, 16th Infantry, Annual Historical Supplement [1976], February 25, 1977, 2.

14. History of the 1st IDF, 33.

15. Ibid., 47.

16. Ibid., 55.

17. When the author was assigned to the 2nd Brigade in September 1983, a few of the old timers from the 2nd Battalion, 9th Infantry, who still remained from the days in Korea, preferred to think of themselves as "Manchus." One could still see "Manchu" stencils on some unit equipment and markings on signs in the battalion billets at Camp Forsyth. With the battalion's move up to Custer Hill later that year, the markings finally disappeared.

18. Headquarters, 2nd Battalion, 16th Infantry, Annual Historical Supplement [1970], February 5, 1971, 3–4.

19. Headquarters, 2nd Battalion, 16th Infantry, Annual Historical Supplement [1972], March 30, 1973, enclosure 3, "The Arkansas River Trace."

20. Ibid.

21. Headquarters, 2nd Battalion, 16th Infantry, Annual Historical Supplement [1972], January 27, 1974, enclosure 3, "2-16th AIT Training Cycle."

22. Watts interview.

23. Ibid.

24. Ibid.

25. Headquarters, 2nd Battalion, 16th Infantry, Annual Historical Supplement [FY 1980], October 7, 1980, 1.

26. Headquarters, 2nd Battalion, 16th Infantry, Annual Historical Supplement [FY 1982], October 28, 1982.

27. Lieutenant Colonel Thomas M. Carroll, recorded interview by the author, December 10, 1999, Fort Leavenworth, Kans.

28. Ibid.

29. Richards interview.

30. Ibid.

31. *Fort Riley Post*, May 22, 1987, p. 1.

32. Ibid., p. 2

33. Ibid., March 24, 1989, p. 5.

34. Ibid., April 28, 1989, p. 4.

35. Ibid., May 26, 1989, p. 1.

36. Ibid., November 17, 1989, p. 9.

37. Ibid., November 22, 1989, pp. 1–2.

38. Ibid., July 13, 1990, p. 1.

39. 187th Infantry Brigade (Separate), *The Quarterly Report* 1, no. 3 (spring 1974): 4.

40. Ibid., 2, no. 1 (fall/winter 1975): 11.

41. Ibid.

42. Ibid.

43. *Courier Gazette* (Rockland, Maine), November 22, 1983.

44. *The Otis Notice* 3, no. 12 (March 1983): 1.

45. Ibid., 14–15.

46. History of the 1st IDF, 31.

47. Ibid., 31–32.

48. Ibid., 32.

49. Ibid., 34.

50. Headquarters, 4th Battalion, 16th Infantry, Annual Unit Historical Report [1985], June 10, 1986, 1.

51. History of the 1st IDF, 36–37.

52. Ibid., 42.

53. Ibid., 43.

54. Ibid., 53.

55. *Bridgehead Sentinel*, (January 1991): 7.

56. *Fort Riley Post*, June 16, 1989, p. 3.
57. History of the 1st IDF, 55.
58. Ibid., 56.
59. Headquarters, 5th Battalion, 16th Infantry, Annual Historical Feeder Report [FY 1983], December 28, 1983, 4.
60. *Fort Riley Post*, April 28, 1989. p. 1.
61. Colonel Sidney F. Baker (Ret.), recorded telephone interview by the author, January 2, 2000, Harker Heights, Tex.
62. Ibid.
63. *Fort Riley Post*, May 15, 1990, p. 1.
64. Anne W. Chapman, *The Origins and Development of the National Training Center, 1976–1984*, TRADOC Historical Monograph Series (Fort Monroe, Va.: U.S. Army Training and Doctrine Command, 1992), 3.

Chapter 12—Desert Duels

1. Jay C. Mumford, *Rangers in Iraq: Task Force Ranger, 2nd Battalion, 16th Infantry in the Persian Gulf War, 10 November 1990 to 12 May 1991*, unpublished manuscript printed at Fort Riley, Kans., 1991, 4.
2. Ibid.
3. History of the 1st IDF, 58.
4. Ibid., 59–60.
5. Ibid., 60.
6. Ibid.
7. Mumford, *Rangers in Iraq*, 7.
8. Ibid., 8.
9. Ibid. A "conex insert" is a cardboard box measuring about 4 feet x 4 feet x 8 feet. It is used to categorize and protect equipment during shipment. These conex inserts are, in turn, placed within a "Milvan," which is a shipping container measuring 10 feet x 10 feet x 30 feet that is designed to fit onto a trailer carriage for hauling by a tractor truck or for shipment by train or ship.
10. Baker interview.
11. Ibid.
12. Ibid.
13. Mumford, *Rangers in Iraq*, 11.
14. Ibid., 13.
15. Ibid.
16. Ibid., 16.
17. Ibid., 21.
18. Baker interview.
19. Major Brian Zahn, "5-16 Infantry 'Devil Rangers,'" chap. 7 in *1st Brigade Desert Shield/Desert Storm,* ed. Jim Stockmoe (Fort Riley, Kans.: 1st Infantry Division, U.S. Army, 1992), 55–56.
20. Ibid., 56–57.
21. Robert H. Scales Jr. *Certain Victory: United States Army in the Gulf War* (Washington, D.C.: GPO, 1993), 113–14.
22. Mumford, *Rangers in Iraq*, 27.
23. Ibid., 28–29.
24. Baker interview.
25. Scales, *Certain Victory*, 225.
26. Ibid., 225–26.
27. Baker interview.
28. Scales, *Certain Victory*, 226.
29. Stockmoe, *1st Brigade History*, 59.
30. Ibid., 59-60.
31. Mumford, *Rangers in Iraq*, 30.
32. Ibid.
33. Ibid., 31.
34. Ibid., 34.
35. Ibid.
36. Ibid., 35.
37. Ibid.
38. Stockmoe, *1st Brigade History*, 59.
39. Ibid., 60–61.
40. Ibid., 62.
41. Baker interview; Stockmoe, *1st Brigade History*, 63.
42. Ibid.

43. Ibid., 64.
44. Mumford, *Rangers in Iraq*, 39–40. Baker recalled that after the negotiations were complete, Generals Schwarzkopf and Yeosock exited the tent and were then asked by the platoon leader of one of the "Devil Ranger" guard platoons from C Company if the generals would mind having their picture taken with his platoon. Schwarzkopf and Yeosock readily agreed, and about thirty happy 16th Infantry soldiers got their pictures taken with the men who commanded the winning side.
45. Ibid., 40.
46. Lieutenant Colonel Daniel Fake to Colonel William S. Hathaway (Ret.), March 7, 1991, "Dagwood Dispatches," 2, no. 2, p. 6.
47. Lieutenant Colonel Sidney "Skip" Baker to Colonel William S. Hathaway (Ret.), March 5, 1991, "Dagwood Dispatches," 2, no. 2, p. 5.
48. Headquarters, 1st Infantry Division, Chronological Summary of Events, March 26, 1991, located in the 1st Infantry Division file, "Kuwait-Iraq," MRC-FDM.
49. "Exercise Challenges Soldiers," *Fort Riley Post*, July 26, 1991, p. 2; "Infantry Badge Tests Soldiers' Skills," *Fort Riley Post*, October 4, 1991, p. 1.
50. "Off-Post Training Scenario Realistic," *Fort Riley Post*, October 25, 1991, p. 1.
51. "Infantry Wins Awards," *Fort Riley Post*, September 25, 1992, p. 4.
52. Colonel William S. Knoebel, recorded interview by the author, October 5, 1999, Fort Leavenworth, Kans.
53. Ibid.
54. Ibid.
55. Ibid.
56. Ibid.
57. Ibid. This feat was particularly surprising, especially given the state of Captain Tim DeLass's D Company. DeLass's troops had performed yeoman work as the task force covering force for three nights straight. Most of his troops had received little, if any, sleep prior to this march; yet the entire company was present and accounted for the following morning.
58. Ibid.
59. Ibid.
60. The air assault force was composed of troops from the 82nd Airborne Division who had prepared diligently for this mission. It was actually a rather humorous sight to see these elite paratroopers getting off the helicopters with their helmets in their hands (the signal that a soldier was out of the fight) and walking dejectedly over to the assembly after having worked so hard for this mission. Upon reflection, it was also sobering to think about the actual results had it been real.
61. *Fort Riley Post*, August 1, 1991, p. 1.
62. *Fort Riley Post*, September 27, 1991, p. 1.
63. *Fort Riley Post*, October 2, 1992, p. 1.
64. *Fort Riley Post*, January 29, 1993, p. 2.
65. *Fort Riley Post*, June 25, 1993, p. 4.
66. Letter from Lieutenant Colonel Mark E. Hammond to Colonel William S. Hathaway (Ret.), Subj: Annual Update for the 3rd Battalion, 16th Infantry, August 26, 1992, copy in the author's possession.
67. Memorandum, Major General Roger W. Sandler to Commander, 3rd Battalion, 16th Infantry, Subj: FY 1992 Chief of Staff, Army Maintenance Excellence Award.
68. Knoebel interview.
69. *Bridgehead Sentinel*, (fall 1999): 5.

Select Bibliography

Select Bibliography

Primary Sources

Archival Documents

Combined Arms Research Library Archive, Fort Leavenworth, Kansas:
Coates, Colonel Charles H. Memorandum. Subject: Operations of the 16th Infantry on the Normandy Beachhead, D to D+2, July 21, 1944.

Division of the Philippines. "Roster of Troops Serving in the Philippines." Manila, P.I., 1905, 1906.

Field Order No. 1, Operation "Torch." HQ, 1st Infantry Division, October 10, 1942.

1st Division Field SOP, July 1, 1957.

Herman Göring Panzer Division in Sicily 1943, July 10–14, 1943. "Commentary."

Military Division of the Missouri. *Roster of Troops Serving in the Military Division of the Missouri*. Chicago: 1876.

The Military List, January 1, 1886. Washington, D.C.: J. H. Soulé and Co., 1886.

National Archives, College Park, Maryland:
Record Group 391: Regular Army Mobile Units 1821–1942.

16th Infantry. Correspondence. Headquarters, 16th Infantry, General Orders No. 18, December 16, 1917.

16th Infantry Histories. Regimental History for 1916.

———. War Diary of the 2nd Battalion, 16th Infantry.

Record Group 407: Records of the Adjutant General 1917–.

Citations. 16th Infantry. History Combat Team 16. Invasion of France. S3 Combat Report Covering Citation of the 16th Infantry Regiment for the Period, June 6, 1944.

Final Report-Army and Navy Joint Exercise Number 7. 1st Infantry Division Task Force. Memorandum. Subject: Constructive Information of 1st Division Task Force, February 3, 1941.

Oran Campaign. Combat Team 16. Intelligence Summary No. 2, HQ, Combat Team 16, October 24, 1942.

Plitt, Major Carl. "History of Combat Team 16, Battle of Coutances."

World War II Records of the 1st Infantry Division 1940–48. G3 Report of Operations, July 1–31, 1944.

Reports of Operations. 16th Infantry 1941–45. After Action Report, HQ, Combat Team 16, November 21, 1942.

Reports of Operations. 16th Infantry 1941–45. Memorandum. Lieutenant Colonel Charles J. Denholm to Commanding Officer, 16th Infantry, May 11, 1943. Subject: Assault on Hill 523.

———. Memorandum. Commanding Officer, 16th Infantry, to Commanding General, 1st Infantry Division, August 18, 1943. Subject: Reports After Action Against the Enemy.

———. Memorandum. HQ, 16th Infantry Regiment, to Commanding General, 1st Infantry Division, June 30, 1944. Subject: Comments and Criticisms of Operations Fox, Fabius I, and Neptune.

Reports of Operations. 16th Infantry 1941–45. 16th Infantry Historical Report for the Month of September 1943. October 3, 1943.

———. 16th Infantry Historical Report for the Month of October 1943. December 1, 1943.

———. 16th Infantry Historical Report for the Month of November 1943. December 4, 1943.

———. 16th Infantry Historical Report for the Month of December 1943. January 14, 1944.

———. 16th Infantry Historical Report for the Month of January 1944. February 7, 1944.

———. Infantry Historical Report for the Month of February 1944. March 4, 1944.

———. 16th Infantry Historical Report for the Month of April 1944. May 9, 1944.

———. 16th Infantry Historical Report for the Month of May 1944. Undated.

———. 16th Infantry Historical Report for the Month of April 1945. May 1, 1945.

———. Report of Operations, May 8 to September 30, 1945.

———. Report of Operations, October 1 to December 31, 1945.

———. Report of Operations, January 1 to March 31, 1946.

———. Report of Operations, April 1 to June 30, 1946.

———. Report of Operations, July 1 to September 30, 1946.

———. Report of Operations, October 1–31, 1946.

———. Report of Operations, March 1–31, 1947.

———. Report of Operations, July 1 to September 30, 1948.

———. Report of Operations, October 1 to December 31, 1948.

———. Command and Unit Historical Report of the 16th Infantry Regiment for the Years 1949, 1950, 1951, and 1952.

Reports of Operations. 1st Battalion, 16th Infantry. Report of Operations, November 25, 1946.

———. Report of Operations, July 1 to September 30, 1947. October 10, 1947.

———. Report of Operations, April 1 to June 30, 1948.

Reports of Operations. 3rd Battalion, 16th Infantry. Report of Operations, December 1–31, 1946. January 7, 1947.

———. Report of Operations, June 1–30, 1947. July 2, 1947.

———. Report of Operations, April 1–30, 1948. May 9, 1948.

———. History of Activities, September 1 to December 31, 1948. January 15, 1949.

———. Yearly Narrative Historical Report 1949.

Record Group 472: Records of U.S. Forces in Southeast Asia.

Combat After Action Report, 1st Infantry Division, Operation Birmingham. 1st Infantry Division After Action Report File.

———. Combat After Action Report, 1st Infantry Division, Operation El Paso II/III. 1st Infantry Division After Action Report File.

———. Combat After Action Report, 1st Infantry Division, Operation Tulsa. 1st Infantry Division After Action Report File.

———. Combat After Action Report, 1st Infantry Division, Operation Shenandoah.1st Infantry Division After Action Report File.

———. Combat After Action Report, 1st Infantry Division, Search and Seal of Ben Cui Hamlet, January 22, 1968. 1st Infantry Division After Action Report File.

———. Combat After Action Report, 1st Brigade, 1st Infantry Division, Operation Billings. 1st Infantry Division After Action Report File.

———. Combat After Action Report, 2nd Brigade, 1st Infantry Division. Operation Abilene, 1st Infantry Division After Action Report File.

———. Operational Lessons Learned, 2nd Brigade, 1st Infantry Division, May 16, 1966. 2nd Brigade, 1st Infantry Division Organizational History File.

———. A Summary History of the 2nd Brigade, 1st Infantry Division, 2nd Brigade, 1st Infantry Division Organizational History File.

———. Combat After Action Report, 3rd Brigade, 1st Infantry Division. Operation Abilene. 1st Infantry Division After Action Report File.

———. Combat After Action Report, 3rd Brigade, 1st Infantry Division. Operation Billings. 1st Infantry Division After Action Report File.

———. Combat After Action Report, 3rd Brigade, 1st Infantry Division. Operation Portland, September 5, 1967. 1st Infantry Division After Action Report File.

———. After Action Report, Operation Bushmaster, November 24, 1965. 1st Battalion, 16th Infantry.

———. After Action Report, Operations Bushmaster II and Bloodhound, December 13, 1965. 1st Battalion, 16th Infantry.

———. After Action Report, Operation Buckskin, February 5, 1966. 1st Battalion, 16th Infantry.

———. After Action Report, Operation Mastiff, March 9, 1966. 1st Battalion, 16th Infantry.

———. After Action Report, Operation Cocoa Beach, March 11, 1966. 1st Battalion, 16th Infantry.

———. After Action Report, Operation Birmingham, May 24, 1966. 1st Battalion, 16th Infantry.

———. After Action Report, Operation Danbury. 1st Battalion, 16th Infantry.

———. After Action Report, Operation Healdsburg, December 26, 1966. 1st Battalion, 16th Infantry.

———. After Action Report, Operation Ao Duty 3, June 13, 1968. 1st Battalion, 16th Infantry.

———. Operation Order #10, Operation Caoutchouc, 071200 September 1965. 2nd Battalion, 16th Infantry.

———. Operation Order 5-66, Operation Mallet, January 17, 1966. 2nd Battalion, 16th Infantry.

———. Operation Order 6-66, Operation Mastiff, February 18, 1966. 2nd Battalion, 16th Infantry.

———. Operation Order 24-66, Operation Fairfax, November 30, 1966. 2nd Battalion, 16th Infantry.

———. Combat After Action Interview Report: Loc Ninh Operations, September 11–15, 1968. 17th Military History Detachment, 1st Infantry Division After Action Report File.

———. Combat After Action Interview Report: The Battle of Binh Long Province, August 1969. 14th Military History Detachment, 1st Infantry Division After Action Report File.

McCormick Research Center, First Division Museum at Cantigny, Wheaton, Illinois:
Brugger, Roger L. Transcript of D-Day Experiences, June 6, 1944. D-Day Transcripts File.

1st Division World War II Combat Achievements Report.

G3 Telephone Log, 1st Infantry Division, May 9, 1945. Czechoslovakia, 16th Infantry File.

Goldberg, First Lieutenant Hubert. "History of the Medical Detachment, 16th Infantry, November 1940 to May 1945."

Headquarters, 1st Infantry Division. Chronological Summary of Events, March 26, 1991. 1st Infantry Division File, "Kuwait-Iraq."

Mason, Stanhope B. "Reminiscences and Anecdotes of World War II."

News Information File. 1st Battalion, 16th Infantry.

News Information File. 2nd Battalion, 16th Infantry.

Rooney, Andy. CBS Television Interview with Joseph Dawson, Charles T. Horner, and William R. Washington, April 29, 1984. Transcript. Dawson File.

Votaw, Dr. John F. Interview with Joseph Dawson, April 16, 1991. Transcript. Dawson File.

U.S. Army Center of Military History, Fort McNair, DC:
"History of Company G Sixteenth Infantry, Fort Crook, Nebraska." 16th Infantry File.

"Regimental Record, 16th Infantry." 16th Infantry File.

———. "Continuation of the Regimental Record, 1905, 1906, 1907, 1908, 1909, 1910, 1911, 1912, 1913, 1914." 16th Infantry File.

"16th Infantry." 16th Infantry File.

"A.G.O. Form 016, Unit Historical Data Cards for the 16th Infantry." 16th Infantry File.

U.S. Army Military History Institute Archive, Carlisle Barracks, Pennsylvania:
Annual Historical Feeder Report [1983], 5th Battalion, 16th Infantry. 16th Infantry File.

Annual Historical Supplement for 1966, 3rd Battalion, 16th Infantry. 3rd Battalion, 16th Infantry File.

Annual Historical Supplement [1970], 2nd Battalion, 16th Infantry. 16th Infantry File.

Annual Historical Supplement [1972], 2nd Battalion, 16th Infantry. 16th Infantry File.

Annual Historical Supplement [1975], 1st Battalion, 16th Infantry. 16th Infantry File.

Annual Historical Supplement [1976], 1st Battalion, 16th Infantry. 16th Infantry File.

Annual Historical Supplement [1980], 2nd Battalion, 16th Infantry. 16th Infantry File.

Annual Historical Supplement [1982], 2nd Battalion, 16th Infantry. 16th Infantry File.

Annual Unit Historical Report [1985], 4th Battalion, 16th Infantry. 16th Infantry File.

Battalion History 1967, 1st Battalion, 16th Infantry. 16th Infantry File.

Battalion Historical Supplement 1968, 1st Battalion, 16th Infantry. 16th Infantry File.

Battalion Historical Supplement 1969, 1st Battalion, 16th Infantry. 16th Infantry File.

Carey, Oliver A. Untitled and unpublished manuscript. Oliver A. Carey File.

Cassels, Colonel Kenneth G. to Major Wayne Boles Regarding the After Action Report on the Battle of Binh Long Province, August 12, 1969.

Ekman, Lieutenant Colonel Michael E. Interview with Lieutenant Colonel Edward O. Yaugo. Senior Officers Oral History Program, Project 31-36. Transcript.

Dillon, William T. "Pearl Harbor and Beyond." Unpublished manuscript.

Hechler, Kenneth W. Interview with Lieutanant Colonel Edmund Driscoll, Frant Lazne, Czechoslovakia, May 24, 1945. Transcript. John B. Beach File.

History of the 2nd Battalion, 16th Infantry, "Rangers" for 1968. 16th Infantry File.

Operational Report of the 1st Infantry Division for the Period Ending January 31, 1969. 1st Infantry Division Box, Lessons Learned.

Pogue, Master Sergeant Forrest C. and Staff Sergeant J. M. Topete. Interview with Lieutenant John Spalding, Herve Belgium, February 9, 1945. Transcript. 16th RCT File.

2nd Battalion, 16th Infantry. Command Report for Quarterly Period Ending September 30, 1965. 16th Infantry File.

U.S. Cavalry Museum Archive, Fort Riley, Kansas:
Buck, Beaumont B. "Epitome of the Military Service of Colonel Beaumont B. Buck, U.S. Army." Major General Beaumont B. Buck Collection.

Commander, Medical Company, 16th Infantry Regiment to Commander, 16th Infantry Regiment, January 5, 1949. Subject: History of the Unit, 1949. 16th Infantry Collection.

Coppock, Edward R. Diary. 16th Infantry Collection.

"Daily Journal, 16th Infantry Regiment." 16th Infantry Collection.

"Notes on the 16th United States Infantry from the National Archive." An unpublished manuscript of information collected from the regimental returns of the regiment at the National Archives by an unknown author. 16th Infantry Collection.

McGarry, Donald E. "Command and Unit Historical Report, 16th Infantry Regiment, 1950." 16th Infantry Collection.

"Movement Order Number 25, HQ, 1st Infantry Division, Fort Riley, Kans., October 28, 1958." 16th Infantry Collection.

Noble, Captain Charles H. to the Adjutant General, U.S. Army, December 1898. 16th Infantry Collection.

"ROCID Evaluation Report, 1st Infantry Division, Fort Riley, Kans., August 1957." 16th Infantry Collection.

"Roster of Commissioned and Non-Commissioned Officers of the Sixteenth U. S. Infantry." Fort Crook, Neb.: Regimental Press, 1909. Major General Beaumont B. Buck Collection.

16th Infantry Unit History. 16th Infantry Collection.

Streeman, Mrs. Charles to Warrant Officer Harry R. Bradley, July 31, 1934. 16th Infantry Collection.

Author's Collection:
Brown, Lieutenant General Frederic J. to Colonel John J. Singlaub. Letter of Commendation, February 20, 1961.

Hammond, Lieutenant Colonel Mark E. Letter to Colonel William S. Hathaway (Ret.), "Subject: Annual Update for the 3rd Battalion, 16th Infantry," August 26, 1992.

Training Circular No. 2, HQ, 1st Infantry Division. "Standing Operating Procedure, 1st Division," January 6, 1940.

Wendland, Mark. Letter to Colonel Gerald K. Griffin (Ret.), July 20, 1998.

Miscellaneous:
Daniel, Wayne. "The 16th Infantry at Fort Concho, 1881." Fort Concho Museum, San Angelo, Tex., 1982.

McNaught, John S. Diary of John S. McNaught. Special Collections, Perkins Library, Duke University, Durham, N.C.

Government Documents
U.S. War Department. Adjutant General's Office. *Official Army Register for 1863.* Washington, D.C.: Government Printing Office, 1863.

U.S. War Department. *World War Records of the First Division, A.E.F.* Vol. 16. "16th Infantry Regiment War Diary."

U.S. War Department. General Order No. 60, 1944, Distinguished Unit Citation, Cannon Company, 16th Infantry, Gela, Sicily, July 11–13, 1943. 16th Infantry Regiment Association Archive.

———. "Annual Report of the Secretary of War for the Years 1867, 1874, 1876, 1880–1889, 1892, 1893, 1894, 1896, 1897" in *War Department Annual Reports, 1867–1897.* Washington, D.C.: Government Printing Office, 1867–1897.

———. *War Department Annual Reports, 1900, 1904, 1908, 1909.* Washington, D.C.: Government Printing Office, 1900, 1904, 1908, 1909.

———. *Order of Battle of the United States Land Forces in the World War.* Vol. 3, *Zone of the Interior,* pt. 2, *Territorial Departments, Tactical Divisions Organized in 1918, Posts, Camps, and Stations.* Washington, D.C.: Government Printing Office, 1988.

———. *The War of the Rebellion: A Compilation of Official Records of the Union and Confederate Armies.* Washington, D.C.: Government Printing Office, 1880–1901.

Newspapers
American Traveler. June 5, 12, 19, and 26, 1957; July 3, 1957; July 10, 1957; October 17, 1957; November 7, 1957; February 13, 1958; April 3, 1958; June 12, 1958; August 7, 1958; January 22, 1959; February 26, 1959.

Army and Navy Journal. September 9, 1865; October 21, 1865; November 25, 1865; June 23, 1866; July 21, 1866; May 4, 1867; April 27, 1867; February 20, 1869; October 29, 1870; November 11 and 18, 1871; January 6 and 13, 1872; April 18, 1874; October 31, 1874; February 5 and 27, 1876; September 10, 1891; September 6 and 13, 1919; December 20, 1919; August 30, 1924; August 31, 1935; March 7, 1936; September 4, 1937; October 23, 1937; November 6 and 20, 1937.

Army-Navy Register. October 11, 1924; April 18, 1931; March 28, 1931

Army Times. December 30, 1948; November 24, 1956; December 1, 1956.

Courier Gazette. (Rockland, Maine). November 22, 1983.

Dallas Morning News. January 13 and 14, 1916.

Fort Riley Post. February 21, 1964; May 22, 1987; March 24, 1989; April 28, 1989; May 26, 1989; June 16, 1989; November 17, 1989; November 22, 1989; May 15, 1990; July 13, 1990; July 26, 1991; October 25, 1991; September 27, 1991; September 25, 1992; October 2, 1992; January 29, 1993; June 25, 1993.

Nashville Republican Banner. April 20, 1875.

New York Times. January 30, 1915; August 26, 1915; July 31, 1919; September 18 and 20, 1919; November 11, 1920; January 3 and 4, 1923; October 5, 1923; August 5, 1925; September 3 and 9, 1925; September 3, 1926; October 6, 1925; November 30, 1925; November 20, 1926; January 6, 1927; May 7, 1928; June 3, 6, 17, 20, and 24, 1928; July 16, 1928; August 12, 1928; June 7, 1929; October 24, 1931; May 1, 1932; March 18 and 19, 1933; April 4, 1933; May 19, 1934; June 30, 1934; March 18, 1935; July 7, 1935; March 27, 1936; September 29, 1936; June 18 and 19, 1937; April 22, 1938; May 29 and 30, 1938; September 27, 1938; June 11, 1939; October 31, 1939; April 19, 1940; June 5, 1940; October 16, 1940.

Nürnberg (Germany) Post. October 6, 1950.

Otis Notice (Otis Air Force Base, Mass.). March 1983.

Interviews, Notes, and Tapes
Alderson, Kenneth. Interview by the author, August 1999.

Baker, Arthur. Interview by the author, July 24, 1998.

Carroll, Lieutenant Colonel Thomas M. Interview by the author, December 10, 1999.

Ciessau, Larry. Interview by the author, July 24, 1998.

Coates, Edward. Interview by the author, August 1999.

Copeland, John J. Interview by the author, July 24, 1998.

Daley, Edmund. Interview by the author, August 1999.

Davis, Lieutenant Colonel Steven L. Interview by the author December 1999.

Griffin, Colonel (Ret.) Gerald K. Interview by the author May 31, 1999.

Hathaway, Colonel (Ret.) William S. Interview by the author, September 1, 1993.

Hosler, Lewis W. Interview by the author, August 1999.

Humphries, Robert. Interview by the author, August 1999.

Jackson, William (Bill). Interview by the author, July 24, 1998.

Knoebel, Colonel William S. Interview by author, October 5, 1999.

Latham, Major General (Ret.) Willard D. Telephone interview by the author, March 1999.

Lipinski, James. Interview by the author, June 3, 1998.

———. Personal notes provided to the author, April 16, 1999.

———. Telephone interview by the author, October 15, 1998.

———. and Ronny Lipinski. Interview by the author December 14, 1998.

Mauchline, Robert. Interview by the author, August 1999.

Mozee, Dennis. Interview by the author May 14, 1999.

Murray, Louis. Interview by the author, August 1999.

Orten, Henry S. Interview by the author, July 24, 1998.

Phillips, Colonel (Ret.) Y. Y. Interview by the author, July 24, 1998.

Reynolds, Harley. Videotape comments of his D-Day experiences.

Reichert, Russell. Interview by the author, July 25, 1998.

Richards, Lieutenant Colonel Kevin. Interview by the author, October 13, 1999.

Roughn, Martin P. Telephone interview by the author, March 15, 1998.

Roughn, Martin P. Telephone interview by the author, March 21, 1998.

Roughn, Martin P. Interview by the author, July 24, 1998.

Shrake, Donald. Interview by the author, July 24, 1998.

Silk, Charles E. Interview by the author, July 24, 1998.

Taylor, Don. Interview by the author, July 24, 1998.

Teegarden, Chief Warrant Officer 4 (Ret.) Jack. Interview by the author May 14, 1999.

Watts, Lieutenant General (Ret.) Ronald L. Telephone interview by the author, December 22, 1999.

White, Colonel (Ret.) Eston T. Interview by the author, July 24, 1998.

———. Taped commentary of his World War II experiences, September 1998.

———. Taped answers to questions about the 16th Infantry's World War II experiences, August 15, 1998.

Unpublished Manuscripts

"Daily Casualty Report, June 6, 1944 to June 8, 1944." Unpublished manuscript printed by the 16th Infantry Regiment Association.

Griffin, Colonel (Ret.) Gerald K. "No Road Back." Unpublished manuscript in the author's possession.

Hall, Fred W., Jr. "A Memoir of World War II." Unpublished manuscript printed by the 16th Infantry Regiment Association.

Ramirez, Oswaldo. "Breakout from Normandy." Unpublished manuscript printed by the 16th Infantry Regiment Association, 16th Infantry Regiment Association Archives, Fort. Washington, Md.

Wilson, Donald E. "D-Day Plus 18,262, 1944–1994." Unpublished manuscript printed by the 16th Infantry Regiment Association, 16th Infantry Regiment Association Archives, Fort. Washington, Md.

Wolf, Karl E. "The War Years of Karl E. Wolf." Unpublished manuscript in the author's possession.

Book and Periodical Sources

Books

Ambrose, Stephen E. *D-Day, June 6, 1944: The Climactic Battle of World War II*. New York: Simon and Schuster, 1994.

American Battle Monuments Commission. *1st Division Summary of Operations in the World War*. Washington, D.C.: Government Printing Office, 1944.

Baltz, Louis J., III. *The Battle of Cold Harbor, May 27–June 13, 1864*. Lynchburg, Va.: H. E. Howard, Inc., 1994.

Battles and Leaders of the Civil War. Vol. 2. New York: The Century Press, 1887–88.

Baumgartner, John W. et al. *The 16th Infantry, 1798–1946*. Bamberg, Germany: Sebaldus Verlag, 1946.

Blumenson, Martin. *Breakout and Pursuit*. United States Army in World War II, The European Theater of Operations. Washington, D.C.: Office of the Chief of Military History, Government Printing Office, 1961.

Branham, Charles N., ed. *1967 Register of Graduates and Former Cadets 1802–1967*. West Point, N.Y.: West Point Alumni Foundation, 1967.

Catton, Bruce. *The American Heritage Picture History of the Civil War*. New York: American Heritage Publishing Co., 1960.

———. *Grant Takes Command*. Boston: Little, Brown and Co., 1969.

Chapman, Anne W. *The Origins and Development of the National Training Center, 1976–1984*. Fort Monroe, Va.: Office of the Command Historian, U.S. Army Training and Doctrine Command, 1992.

Clendenen, Clarence C. *Blood on the Border: The United States Army and the Mexican Irregulars*. New York: Macmillan Co., 1969.

Coakley, Robert W. *The Role of Federal Military Forces in Domestic Disorders, 1789–1878*. Army Historical Series. Washington, D.C.: Center of Military History, Government Printing Office, 1988.

Cochran, Rexmond C. *Gas Warfare in World War I, Study No. 3*. U.S. Army Chemical Corps Historical Studies. Aberdeen Proving Grounds, Md.: U.S. Army Chemical Corps Historical Office, 1957.

Coffman, Edward M. *The Old Army: A Portrait of the American Army in Peacetime, 1784–1898*. New York: Oxford University Press, 1986.

———. *The War to End All Wars: The American Military Experience in World War I*. Madison, Wis.: University of Wisconsin Press, 1986.

Commager, Henry Steele. *The Blue and the Gray*. New York: Bobbs-Merrill Co., 1950.

The Congressional Medal of Honor: The Names, The Deeds. Forest Ranch, Calif.: Sharp & Dunnigan Publications, 1984.

Cosmas, Graham A. *An Army for Empire: The United States Army in the Spanish-American War*. Columbia, Mo.: University of Missouri Press, 1971.

Cullum, George W. *Biographical Register of the Officers and Graduates of the United States Military Academy*. Vol. 1, 1802–1868. New York: Van Nostrand, 1868.

———. *Biographical Register of the Officers and Graduates of the United States Military Academy*. Vol. 2, 1802–1868. New York: Van Nostrand, 1868.

———. *Biographical Register of the Officers and Graduates of the United States Military Academy*. Vol. 3, 1868–1890. Boston: Houghton Mifflin, 1891.

———. *Biographical Register of the Officers and Graduates of the United States Military Academy*. Edited by Edward S. Holden. Vol. 4, 1890–1900. Cambridge, Mass.: Riverside Press, 1901.

———. *Biographical Register of the Officers and Graduates of the United States Military Academy*. Edited by Charles Braden. Vol. 5, 1900–1910. Saginaw, Mich.: Seeman & Peters Printers, 1910.

———. *Biographical Register of the Officers and Graduates of the United States Military Academy*. Edited by Wirt Robinson. Vol. 6, 1910–1920. Saginaw, Mich.: Seeman & Peters Printers, 1920.

———. *Biographical Register of the Officers and Graduates of the United States Military Academy.* Edited by William H. Donaldson. Vol. 7, 1920–1930. Chicago: Lakeside Press, 1930.

———. *Biographical Register of the Officers and Graduates of the United States Military Academy.* Edited by E. E. Farman. Vol. 8, 1930–1940. Chicago: Lakeside Press, 1940.

———. *Biographical Register of the Officers and Graduates of the United States Military Academy.* Edited by Charles N. Branham. Vol. 9, 1940–1950. West Point, N.Y.: Association of Graduates, U.S. Military Academy, 1950.

Davenport, Alfred. *Camp and Field Life of the Fifth New York Volunteer Infantry.* New York: Dick and Fitzgerald. Reprint, Gaithersburg, Md.: Olde Soldier Books, 1995.

Dupuy, R. Ernest and William H. Baumer. *The Little Wars of the United States: A Compact History from 1798–1920.* New York: Hawthorn Books, 1968.

Dyer, Frederick H. *A Compendium of the War of the Rebellion.* 2 vols. New York: Sagamore Press, 1959. Reprint Morningside Press, Broadfoot Publishing Co., 1994.

Finke, Blythe Foote. *No Mission Too Difficult!: Old Buddies of the 1st Division Tell All About World War II.* Chicago: Contemporary Books, 1995.

The First Infantry Division in Vietnam, 1965–1970. Paducah, Ky.: Turner Publishing Company, 1993.

Gabel, Christopher R. *The U.S. Army GHQ Maneuvers of 1941.* Washington, D.C.: U.S. Army Center of Military History, Government Printing Office, 1991.

Garland, Albert N. and Howard M. Smyth. *Sicily and the Surrender of Italy.* United States Army in World War II, The Mediterranean Theater of Operations. Washington, D.C.: Office of the Chief of Military History, Government Printing Office, 1965.

Harding, Edwin F., ed. *Infantry in Battle.* Washington, D.C.: The Infantry Journal, 1939. Reprint, Washington, D.C.: Government Printing Office, 1991.

Harrison, Gordon A. *Cross-Channel Attack.* United States Army in World War II, The European Theater of Operations. Washington, D.C.: Office of the Chief of Military History, Government Printing Office, 1951.

Heitman, Francis B., ed. *Historical Register and Dictionary of the United States Army, from Its Organization, September 29, 1789, to March 2, 1903.* Washington, D.C.: Government Printing Office, 1903.

History of the 1st IDF, April 1970–August 1991. n.p., 1991.

Hoehling, Adolf A. *The Fierce Lambs.* Boston: Little, Brown & Co., 1960.

Howe, George F. *Northwest Africa: Seizing the Initiative in the West.* United States Army in World War II. The Mediterranean Theater of Operations. Washington, D.C.: Office of the Chief of Military History, Government Printing Office, 1957.

Hunt, Elvid. *History of Fort Leavenworth, 1827–1927.* Fort Leavenworth, Kans.: General Service Schools Press, 1926.

James, D. Clayton. *The Years of MacArthur.* Vol. 3, *1880–1941.* Boston: Houghton Mifflin Co., 1970.

Knickerbocker, H. R., et al. *Danger Forward: The Story of the First Division in World War II.* Atlanta, Ga.: Albert Love Enterprises, 1947. Reprint, Nashville, Tenn.: Battery Press, 1980.

Laurie, Clayton D. and Ronald H. Cole. *The Role of Federal Military Forces in Domestic Disorders, 1877–1945.* Army Historical Series. Washington, D.C.: Center of Military History, Government Printing Office, 1997.

MacDonald, Charles B. *The Last Offensive.* United States Army in World War II. The European Theater of Operations. Washington, D.C.: Office of the Chief of Military History, Government Printing Office, 1973.

———. *The Siegfried Line Campaign.* United States Army in World War II. European Theater of Operations. Washington, D.C.: Office of the Chief of Military History, Government Printing Office, 1963.

———. *A Time for Trumpets: The Untold Story of the Battle of the Bulge.* New York: Bantam Books, 1984, 1985.

MacGarrigle, George L. *Combat Operations: Taking the Offensive, October 1966–October 1967.* United States Army in Vietnam. Washington, D.C.: U.S. Army Center of Military History, 1998.

Madej, W. Victor, ed. *German Army Order of Battle 1939–1945.* Vol. 2. Allentown, Pa.: Game Marketing Co., 1981.

Mahon, John K., and Romana Danysh. *Infantry.* Vol. 1, *Regular Army.* Army Lineage Series. Washington, D.C.: U.S. Army Center of Military History, Government Printing Office, 1972.

Marshall, S. L. A. *Ambush: The Battle of Dau Tieng, also Called the Battle of Dong Minh Chau, War Zone C, Operation Attleboro, and Other Deadfalls in South Vietnam.* Nashville, Tenn.: Battery Press, 1969.

Mason, Herbert M., Jr. *The Great Pursuit.* New York: Random House, 1970.

Matloff, Maurice. *American Military History.* Washington, D.C.: Government Printing Office, 1969.

Matter, William D. *If It Takes All Summer: The Battle of Spotsylvania.* Chapel Hill, N.C.: University of North Carolina Press, 1988.

Metz, Leon C. *Desert Army: Fort Bliss on the Texas Border.* El Paso, TX: Mangan Books, 1988.

Miller, Michael J. *The North Anna Campaign: "Even to Hell Itself," May 21–26, 1864.* Lynchburg, Va.: H. E. Howard, 1988.

Millett, Allan R. *The General: Robert L. Bullard and Officership and the United States Army 1881–1925.* Westport, Conn.: Greenwood Press, 1975.

Mumford, Jay C. *Rangers in Iraq: Task Force Ranger, 2nd Battalion, 16th Infantry in the Persian Gulf War, 10 November 1990 to 12 May 1991.* Fort Riley, Kans.: n.p., 1991.

Nofi, Albert A. *The Gettysburg Campaign, June and July, 1863.* New York: Gallery Books, 1986.

Palmer, Bruce, Jr. *The Palmer Family and the 16th Infantry.* Fort Washington, Md.: 16th Infantry Association, 1987.

Parker, James. *The Old Army: Memories, 1872–1918.* Philadelphia, Pa.: Dorrance and Co., 1929.

Pettit, Ira S. *The Diary of a Dead Man: Letters and Diary of Private Ira S. Pettit, Wilson, Niagara County, New York,...* Compiled by Jean P. Ray. Waverly, Iowa: Ray, 1976. Reprint, New York: Eastern Acorn Press, 1981.

Pictorial History of the 2nd Brigade, 1st Infantry Division in Vietnam. Vol. 2. Tokyo: Dai Nippon, 1967.

Powell, William H. *The Fifth Army Corps (Army of the Potomac). A Record of Operations during the Civil War in the United States of America, 1861–1865*. London: G. P. Putnam's Sons,, 1896.

———. *List of Officers of the Army of the United States from 1779 to 1900*. New York: L. R. Hamersly & Co., 1900.

Pride, Woodbury F. *The History of Fort Riley*. Topeka, Kans.: Fort Riley Cavalry School, 1926.

Reese, Timothy J. *Sykes' Regular Infantry Division, 1861–1864*. Jefferson, N.C.: McFarland and Company, 1990.

Richards, William V. "Sixteenth Regiment of Infantry." In *The Army of the United States: Historical Sketches of Staff and Line with Portraits of Generals-in-Chief*, edited by Theophilus F Rodenbough and William L. Haskin, 629–33. New York: Maynard, Merrill, and Co., 1896.

Roberts, Robert B. *Encyclopedia of Historic Forts: The Military, Pioneer, and Trading Posts of the United States*. New York: Macmillan Publishing Co., 1988.

Robinson, Charles M., III. *Frontier Forts of Texas*. Houston, Tex.: Lone Star Books, 1986.

Rogers, Lieutenant General Bernard W. *Cedar Falls—Junction City: A Turning Point*. Vietnam Studies. Washington, D.C.: Department of the Army, Government Printing Office, 1974.

Scales, Robert H. *Certain Victory*. The U. S. Army in the Gulf War. Washington, D.C.: Office of the Chief of Staff, U.S. Army, Government Printing Office, 1993.

Sears, Stephen W. *Landscape Turned Red; The Battle of Antietam*. New Haven, Conn.: Ticknor and Fields, 1983.

Smythe, Donald. *Guerrilla Warrior: The Early Life of John J. Pershing*. New York: Charles Scribner's Sons, 1973.

———. *Pershing: General of the Armies*. Bloomington, Ind.: Indiana University Press, 1986.

Society of the First Division, A.E.F. *History of the First Division During the World War, 1917–1919*. Philadelphia, Pa.: John C. Winston, 1922.

———. *Memorial Album, Pictorial History of the 1st Division*. San Diego, Calif.: Society of the First Division, 1946.

Sommers, Richard J. *Richmond Redeemed: The Siege of Petersburg*. Garden City, N.Y.: Doubleday and Co., 1981.

Steffin, Randy. *The Horse Soldier, 1776–1943: The United States Cavalryman—His Uniforms, Arms, Accoutrements, and Equipments*. Vol. 2. Norman, Okla.: University of Oklahoma Press, 1978.

Stinger, Hary R. *Heroes All!: A Compendium of the Names and Official Citations of the Soldiers and Citizens of the United States and Her Allies Who Were Decorated by the American Government for Exceptional Heroism and Conspicuous Service Above and Beyond the Call of Duty in the War with Germany, 1917–1919*. Washington, D.C.: Fassett Publishing Co., 1919.

Stockmoe, Jim. *Desert Shield/Storm History*. Fort Riley, Kans.: 1st Infantry Division, 1992.

The Story of the Sixteenth Infantry in France by the Regimental Chaplain. Montabaur-Frankfurt, Germany: Martin Flock Printing, 1919.

Thian, Raphael P., comp. *Notes Illustrating the Military Geography of the United States, 1813–1880*. Washington, D.C.: Adjutant General's Office, 1881. Reprint, Austin, Tex.: University of Texas Press, 1979.

Tompkins, Frank. *Chasing Villa: The Story Behind the Story of Pershing's Expedition into Mexico*. Harrisburg, Pa.: Military Service Publishing Co., 1934.

Trask, David F. *The War With Spain in 1898*. New York: Macmillan, 1981.

U.S. Army Center of Military History. *Correspondence Relating to the War with Spain*. Washington, D.C.: Government Printing Office, 1993.

U.S. Military Academy. Department of Military Art and Engineering. *The West Point Atlas of American Wars*. 2 vols. Edited by Vincent J. Esposito. New York: Praeger, 1959.

Urwin, Gregory J. W. *The United States Infantry: An Illustrated History, 1775–1918*. New York: Sterling Publishing Co., 1991.

Utley, Robert M. *Frontier Regulars: The United States Army and the Indian, 1866–1891*. Lincoln, Neb.: University of Nebraska Press, 1973.

Vandiver, Frank E. *Black Jack: The Life and Times of John J. Pershing*. 2 vols. College Station, Tex.: Texas A&M University Press, 1977.

Walker, Fred L. *From Texas to Rome: A General's Journal*. Dallas: Taylor Publishing Co., 1969.

Warner, Ezra J. *General in Blue: Lives of the Union Commanders*. Baton Rouge, La.: Louisiana State University Press, 1964.

Webb, Alexander S. *The Peninsula—McClellan's Campaign of 1862*. New York: Charles Scribner's Sons, 1885.

Webster's Military Biographies. Springfield, Mass.: G & C Merriam Co., 1978.

Whiting, Charles. *Bloody Aachen*. New York: Stein and Day, 1976.

Wilson, George C. *Mud Soldiers: Life Inside the New American Army*. New York: Charles Scribner's Sons, 1989.

Who Was Who in American History: The Military. Chicago: Marquis Who's Who, 1975.

Periodicals

Ames, John W. "The Second Bull Run." *Overland Monthly* 8 (1872): 399–406.

Bridgehead Sentinel. January 1950; January 1952; April 1952; October 1955; January 1991; spring 1993; fall 1999.

Combat Forces Journal. August 1952.

Dagwood Dispatches. 16th Infantry Regiment Association. June 1991.

Danger Forward: The Magazine of the Big Red One, Vietnam. May 1967.

Denno, Bryce F. "Eightball Cannoneers." *Field Artillery Journal* 51, no. 1 (January-February 1983): 15.

Infantry Journal. January 1924; March 1924; December 1927; March 1929; April 1929; April 1930; May 1930; August 1930; September-October 1931; November-December 1932; August 1952.

Johnston, Harold W. "A History of the 16th Infantry Regiment During the Indian Wars Period, 1865–1891." *Fort Concho Report* 19, no. 4 (winter 1987–88): 4.

Kellet, John M. "The Action at Robaa." *Infantry Journal* 63, no. 3 (September 1948): 13.

Lewis, F. W. The Regular Infantry in the Gettysburg Campaign." *Journal of the Military Service Institute of the United States* 45 (1909): 39–50.

187th Infantry Brigade (Separate). *The Quarterly Report* 1, no. 3 (spring 1974) and 2, no. 1 (fall-winter 1975).

Our Army. December 1929; March 1930; November 1940.

Patterson, John H. and R. J. C. Irvine. "Eleventh Regiment of Infantry." *Journal of the Military Service Institute of the United States* 12 (1891), 371–380.

Robbins, Richard. "The Regular Troops at Gettysburg." *Philadelphia Weekly Times* (January 4, 1879).

Rodenbaugh, T[heophilus] F., ed. "The Army in Civil War: The Eleventh Infantry." *Journal of the Military Service Institute of the United States* 48 (1911): 241–42.

Tatum, John M. "A Spell on the Yukon." *Infantry Journal* 44, no. 1 (January–February 1937): 32.

U.S. Army Recruiting News, February 15, 1924; June 1, 1924; August 1, 1926; July 1, 1927; July 1, 1928; April 1, 1930; May 15, 1930; January 1, 1936; June 1, 1936; January 1939.

White, John C. "A Review of the Regular Army During the Civil War." *Journal of the Military Service Institute of the United States* 48 (1911): 241.

Zogbaum, Rufus F. "The Regular Army in the Civil War." *North American Review* 167 (1898): 24.

Index

Photo and Map Credits

All the photographs in this book are in the public domain unless otherwise specified. The author has copies of them on file for reference.

16th Infantry Regiment Association Archive: 400, bottom left, Nürnberg Trials, bottom right, Honor Platoon; 401 top right, Furth; 421, top, Gibb, Horner, Robertson, middle, Jeter, Wood, bottom, Evans, Royce, O'Conner; 422, middle, Gee

(Author's Collection): 381, top right, Fléville (Author's Collection); 382, bottom left, Fléville; 386, bottom, Baby Peggy; 395, bottom, Colleville; 424, bottom, Henry

CARL Archive (Combined Arms Research Library): 418, bottom, Smith; 420, middle, Truesdell

U.S. Army Signal Corps Photographs from the National Archives and Records Administration (NARA): 370, top left, Ft. Independence (also 2); 371, bottom right, Ft. Douglas; 372, bottom left, Ft. Sherman, bottom right, Ft. Spokane; 373, bottom right, San Juan Hill; 374, top, San Juan Hill, bottom left, blockhouse; 375, bottom right, chow; 376, top left, Mexico, top right, El Valle, bottom, Dimanche; 377, top, Paris, bottom, training; 378, top left, rest, top right, gambling, bottom, practice; 379, top left, KIA, top right, burial, Gypse Hill; 380, top right, review, bottom, Pleissy; 381, top left, Chaudon, bottom, Pershing; 382, top, Thelonne, bottom right, Thelonne; 383, top left, refugees, top right, Sedan, bottom, Coblenz; 384, top left, Lueterode, bottom, Victory Arch; top right, Pershing; 389, top, World's Fair, bottom left, Harmony Church; 392, bottom left, Kasserine, bottom right Tunis; 393, top left, Troina, top right, Troina; 395, top right, wounded; 396, top, wounded; 397, top left, La Ferte-Macè, top right, Hürtgen, bottom, Faymonville; 398, top left, half-track; top right, Bonn, bottom, Bonn; 399, top left, Weser, top right, St. Andreasburg, bottom, St. Andreasburg; 400, top, honor guard; 401, bottom, Camp Funston; 402, top left, Ontos, top right, Medina, 402, bottom, aggressors; 403, top, Rohrbach, bottom, reflagging; 406, top left, Camp Ranger, top right, mortar pit, bottom, order; 407, top, 2-16, bottom, MG team (also 268); 408, top, call for fire, bottom, Rome plows; 409, top, firefight, bottom, sweep; 410, top, McDonald, bottom, 5th ARVN; 411, top, departure, bottom, Martin; 412, top, Nürnberg (also 320); bottom, aggressor; 413, top, Arkansas River Trace, bottom left, APC, bottom right, TOW gunner; 416, top, Russell; 417, bottom, Theaker, Worth; 418, top Morton, middle, Bell, Bundy, Allaire; 419, top, McCammon, Lacey; middle, Ford; 420, top, McCammon, top, Marmon, bottom, Cheadle, Taylor; 421, middle, Salgado; 424, top, Pinder, Monteith; bottom, Lindsey, Robinson

U.S. Army Military History Institute: 370, bottom left, Brownell (New York AG Office), bottom right, Stouch; 371, top right, Ft. Concho (also 44), bottom left, K Co. (also 52); 372, top left, Ft. Duchesne, top right, trooper (Kurt Sieman Collection); 374, bottom right, mounted officer (Curtis Buda Collection); 375, top, G Co. (Otto W. Schroeder Collection, also 80), G Co. (Schroeder Collection), bottom left, Ft. Bliss; 380, top left, Ansauville (Karl Truesdell Collection); 385, top left, Ft. Jay, top right, Ft. Jay; 386, top left, NYC, top right, Ft. Jay (Richard S. Allen Collection); 388, top left, barracks, top right, bugler (Frank R. McCoy Collection), bottom, B Co. (McCoy Collection); 387, top left, monument (Truesdell Collection), top right, chapel; 390, top, Falmouth (H. V. Milne Collection); 393, bottom, Richmond (Hanson Collection); 401, top right, Leonard (Samuel E. Gee Collection); 416, top, Chipman (Roger D. Hunt Collection), Gordon (William W. Lang Jr. Collection); 416, middle, Cooley, Fletcher, Huston, bottom, Ketchum, Granger; 417, top, Pennypacker, middle, Blunt, Hawkins, Penrose; 418, top, Gardner (M. F. Steele Collection), middle, Hines (C. L. Bolte Collection); 419, middle, Croft (Allan W. Jones Collection), bottom, Fuqua (Jones Collection), Williams (McCoy Collection)

McCormick Research Center, First Division Museum at Cantigny: 373, top,Bloody Ford (William Dinwiddie Collection, also 66), bottom left, Schroeder; 389, bottom right, Ft. Devens (Danney Ratcliff Collection); 390, bottom, Higgins Boats; 391, top, New River (BRO Photo Lab), bottom, New River; 392, top, Dill (BRO Photo Lab); 396 bottom, awards (Dwight D. Eisenhower Library, NARA); 404, top left, APC (also 240), 404, top right, Champagne bottom, C Co. (both BRO Photo Lab); 405, top, troops, bottom, Merrill (all BRO Photo Lab); 414, top, Schwarzkopf (Allan Smith Collection, also 346), bottom, Bradleys (both Allan Smith Collection); 417, bottom, Hood; 424, top, Schroeder; bottom, Leonard

Miscellaneous Sources: 385, bottom, World's Fair (courtesy of Henry Orten, also 122); 394, top, D-Day (U.S. Coast Guard, also 148,); 422, top, Palmer (courtesy of Gen. Bruce Clark); 424, top, Patterson (National Park Service)

Report of the Association of Graduates, United States Military Academy: 416, top, Floyd-Jones; 417, top, Voast, Hough; 418, top, Kennedy, bottom, Wilcox; 419, middle, Gerhardt, bottom, Phillipson

U.S. Cavalry Museum, Fort Riley, KS: 371, top left, band; 387, bottom right, parade; 419, top, Coppock; 420, middle, Rice, Baade, bottom, Fechet; 422, bottom, Doran

All maps by Steven Clay with the exception of the following: Maps 8-9 (Omaha Beach, First Wave Landings, 6 June 1944), 8-10 (Omaha Beach, Later Assault Landings, 6 June 1944), 8-11 (Omaha Beach, St. Laurent-Colleville Area, 6 June 1944), 8-12 (Omaha Beach, Evening of D-Day, 6 June 1944), and 8-13 (Operation Cobra-Coutances, 21-29 July 1944) first appeared in *Cross-Channel Attack* by Gordon A. Harrison (1951) a publication of the U.S. Army Center of Military History. They are provided courtesy of the Center of Military History.

Photos page 394, bottom, and 395, top left, by Robert Capa. Reprinted with permission of Robert Capa/Magnum Photos, Inc.

Name Index

Page numbers in boldface type indicate photos.

Subject Index

Page numbers in boldface type indicate photos.